Nineteenth-Century Literature Criticism

Guide to Gale Literary Criticism Series

When you need to review criticism of literary works, these are the Gale series to use:

If the author's death date is:

You should turn to:

After Dec. 31, 1959
(or author is still living)

CONTEMPORARY LITERARY CRITICISM

for example: Jorge Luis Borges, Anthony Burgess,
William Faulkner, Mary Gordon,
Ernest Hemingway, Iris Murdoch

1900 through 1959

TWENTIETH-CENTURY LITERARY CRITICISM

for example: Willa Cather, F. Scott Fitzgerald,
Henry James, Mark Twain, Virginia Woolf

1800 through 1899

NINETEENTH-CENTURY LITERATURE CRITICISM

for example: Fedor Dostoevski, George Sand,
Gerard Manley Hopkins, Emily Dickinson

1400 through 1799

LITERATURE CRITICISM FROM 1400 TO 1800
(excluding Shakespeare)

for example: Anne Bradstreet, Pierre Corneille,
Daniel Defoe, Alexander Pope,
Jonathan Swift, Phillis Wheatley

SHAKESPEAREAN CRITICISM

Shakespeare's plays and poetry

Gale also publishes related criticism series:

CONTEMPORARY ISSUES CRITICISM

Presents criticism on contemporary authors writing
on current issues. Topics covered include the social
sciences, philosophy, economics, natural science, law,
and related areas.

CHILDREN'S LITERATURE REVIEW

Covers authors of all eras. Presents criticism on
authors and author/illustrators who write for the
preschool to junior-high audience.

ISSN 0732-1864

R

Volume 8

Nineteenth-Century Literature Criticism

Excerpts from Criticism of the
Works of Novelists, Poets, Playwrights,
Short Story Writers, and Other Creative Writers
Who Died between 1800 and 1900,
from the First Published Critical
Appraisals to Current Evaluations

Laurie Lanzen Harris
Emily B. Tennyson
Editors

Cherie D. Abbey
Associate Editor

Gale Research Inc. · DETROIT · LONDON

STAFF

Contents

Preface   7

Authors to Appear in Future Volumes   11

Preface

The nineteenth century was a time of tremendous growth in human endeavor: in science, in social history, and particularly in literature. The era saw the development of the novel, witnessed radical changes from classicism to romanticism to realism, and contained intellectual and artistic ideas that continue to inspire authors of our own century. The importance of the writers of the nineteenth century is twofold, for they provide insight into their own time as well as into the universal nature of human experience.

The literary criticism of an era can also give us insight into the moral and intellectual atmosphere of the past, for the criteria by which a work of art is judged reflect current philosophical and social attitudes. Literary criticism takes many forms: the traditional essay, the book or play review, even the parodic poem. Criticism can also be of several types: normative, descriptive, interpretive, textual, appreciative, generic. Collectively, the range of critical response helps us to understand a work of art, an author, an era.

The Scope of the Work

The success of Gale's two current literary series, *Contemporary Literary Criticism (CLC)* and *Twentieth-Century Literary Criticism (TCLC),* which excerpt criticism of creative writing from the twentieth century, suggested an equivalent need among students and teachers of literature of the nineteenth century. Moreover, since the critical analysis of this literature spans almost two hundred years, a vast amount of critical material confronts the student.

Nineteenth-Century Literature Criticism (NCLC) presents significant passages from published criticism on authors who died between 1800 and 1900. The author list for each volume of *NCLC* is carefully compiled to represent a variety of genres and nationalities and to cover authors who are currently regarded as the most important writers of this era as well as those whose contribution to literature and literary history is significant. The truly great writers are rare, and in the intervals between them lesser but genuine artists, as well as writers who enjoyed immense popularity in their own time and in their own countries, are important to the study of nineteenth-century literature. The length of each author's entry is intended to reflect the amount of critical attention the author has received from critics writing in English and from foreign critics in translation. Articles and books that have not been translated into English are excluded. Each author entry represents a historical overview of the critical response to the author's work: early criticism is presented to indicate initial responses, later selections represent any rise or decline in the author's literary reputation. We have also attempted to identify and include excerpts from the seminal essays on each author, and to include recent critical comment providing modern perspectives on the writer. Thus, *NCLC* is designed to serve as an introduction for the student of nineteenth-century literature to the authors of that period and to the most significant commentators on these authors.

NCLC entries are intended to be definitive overviews. In order to devote more attention to each writer, approximately twenty authors are included in each 600-page volume compared with about sixty authors in a *CLC* volume of similar size. Because of the great quantity of critical material available on many authors, and because of the resurgence of criticism generated by events such as an author's centennial or anniversary celebration, the republication of an author's works, or publication of a newly translated work or volume of letters, an author may appear more than once. One or two author entries in each volume of *NCLC* are devoted to single works by major authors who have appeared previously in the series. Only those individual works that have been the subject of extensive criticism and are widely studied in literature courses are selected for this in-depth treatment. Charlotte Brontë's *Jane Eyre* and Charles Dickens's *Bleak House* are the subjects of such entries in *NCLC,* Volume 8.

The Organization of the Book

An author section consists of the following elements: author heading, biographical and critical introduction, principal works, excerpts of criticism (each followed by a bibliographical citation), and an additional bibliography for further reading.

- The *author heading* consists of the author's full name, followed by birth and death dates. The unbracketed portion of the name denotes the form under which the author most commonly wrote. If an author wrote consistently under a pseudonym, the pseudonym will be listed in the author heading and the real name given in parentheses on the first line of the biographical and critical introduction. Also located at the beginning of the biographical and critical introduction are any name variations under which an author wrote, including transliterated forms for authors whose languages use nonroman alphabets. Uncertainty as to a birth or death date is indicated by a question mark.

- A *portrait* of the author is included when available. Many entries also feature illustrations, including manuscript pages, letters, book illustrations, and representations of important people, places, and events in an author's life.

- The *biographical and critical introduction* contains background information that elucidates the author's creative output. When applicable, biographical and critical introductions are followed by references to additional entries on the author in past volumes of *NCLC* and in other literary reference series published by Gale Research Company. These include *Dictionary of Literary Biography, Children's Literature Review,* and *Something about the Author.*

- The list of *principal works* is chronological by date of first book publication and identifies genres. In those instances where the first publication was in other than the English language, the title and date of the first English-language edition are given in brackets. Unless otherwise indicated, dramas are dated by the first performance, rather than first publication.

- *Criticism* is arranged chronologically in each author section to provide a perspective on any changes in critical evaluation over the years. In the text of each author entry, titles by the author are printed in boldface type. This allows the reader to ascertain without difficulty the works being discussed. For purposes of easier identification, the critic's name and the publication date of the essay are given at the beginning of each piece of criticism. Unsigned criticism is preceded by the title of the journal in which it appeared. For an anonymous essay later attributed to a critic, the critic's name appears in brackets at the beginning of the excerpt and in the bibliographical citation.

- Important critical essays are prefaced with *explanatory notes* as an additional aid to students using *NCLC*. The explanatory notes provide several types of useful information, including: the reputation of the critic, the importance of a work of criticism, the specific approach of the critic (biographical, psychoanalytic, structuralist, etc.), and the growth of critical controversy or changes in critical trends regarding an author's work. In many cases, these notes include cross-references to related criticism in the author's entry or in the additional bibliography.

- A complete *bibliographical citation* designed to facilitate the location of the original essay or book follows each piece of criticism. An asterisk (*) at the end of the citation indicates that the essay is on more than one author.

- The *additional bibliography* appearing at the end of each author section suggests further reading on the author. In some cases it includes essays for which the editors could not obtain reprint rights. An asterisk (*) at the end of a citation indicates that the essay is on more than one author.

An appendix lists the sources from which material in the volume is reprinted. It does not, however, list every book or periodical consulted for the volume.

Cumulative Indexes

Each volume of *NCLC* includes a cumulative index to authors listing all the authors who have appeared in *Contemporary Literary Criticism, Twentieth-Century Literary Criticism, Nineteenth-Century Literature Criticism,* and *Literature Criticism from 1400 to 1800,* along with cross-references to the Gale series *Children's Literature Review, Authors in the News, Contemporary Authors, Contemporary Authors Autobiography Series, Dictionary of Literary Biography, Something about the Author,* and *Yesterday's Authors of Books for Children.* Users will welcome this cumulated author index as a useful tool for locating an author within the various series. The index, which lists birth and death dates when available, will be particularly valuable for those authors who are identified with a certain period but whose death date causes them to be placed in another, or for those authors whose careers span two periods. For example, Fedor Dostoevski is found in *NCLC,* yet Leo Tolstoy, another major nineteenth-century Russian novelist, is found in *TCLC.*

NCLC also includes a cumulative nationality index to authors. Authors are listed alphabetically by nationality, followed by the volume numbers in which they appear.

A cumulative index to critics is another useful feature of *NCLC*. Under each critic's name are listed the authors on whom the critic has written and the volume and page where the criticism appears.

Acknowledgments

No work of this scope can be accomplished without the cooperation of many people. The editors especially wish to thank the copyright holders of the excerpts included in this volume, the permissions managers of the book and magazine publishing companies for assisting us in securing reprint rights, and the staffs of the Detroit Public Library, University of Michigan Library, and Wayne State University Library for making their resources available to us. We are also grateful to Jeri Yaryan for her assistance with copyright research.

Suggestions Are Welcome

The editors welcome the comments and suggestions of readers to expand the coverage and enhance the usefulness of the series.

Authors to Appear in Future Volumes

About, Edmond Francois 1828-1885
Aguilo I. Fuster, Maria 1825-1897
Ainsworth, William Harrison 1805-1882
Aksakov, Konstantin 1817-1860
Aleardi, Aleadro 1812-1878
Alecsandri, Vasile 1821-1890
Alencar, Jose 1829-1877
Alfieri, Vittorio 1749-1803
Allingham, William 1824-1889
Almquist, Carl Jonas Love 1793-1866
Alorne, Leonor de Almeida 1750-1839
Alsop, Richard 1761-1815
Altimirano, Ignacio Manuel 1834-1893
Alvarenga, Manuel Inacio da Silva 1749-1814
Alvares de Azevedo, Manuel Antonio 1831-1852
Anzengruber, Ludwig 1839-1889
Arany, Janos 1817-1882
Arene, Paul 1843-1893
Aribau, Bonaventura Carlos 1798-1862
Arjona de Cubas, Manuel Maria de 1771-1820
Arnault, Antoine Vincent 1766-1834
Arneth, Alfred von 1819-1897
Arnim, Bettina von 1785-1859
Arnold, Thomas 1795-1842
Arriaza y Superviela, Juan Bautista 1770-1837
Asbjornsen, Peter Christian 1812-1885
Ascasubi, Hilario 1807-1875
Atterbom, Per Daniel Amadeus 1790-1855
Aubanel, Theodore 1829-1886
Auerbach, Berthold 1812-1882
Augier, Guillaume V.E. 1820-1889
Azeglio, Massimo D' 1798-1866
Azevedo, Guilherme de 1839-1882
Bagehot, Walter 1826-1877
Bakin (pseud. of Takizawa Okikani) 1767-1848
Bakunin, Mikhail Aleksandrovich 1814-1876
Banville, Theodore de 1823-1891
Baratynski, Jewgenij Abramovich 1800-1844
Barnes, William 1801-1886
Batyushkov, Konstantin 1778-1855
Beattie, James 1735-1803
Beckford, William 1760-1844
Becquer, Gustavo Adolfo 1836-1870
Bentham, Jeremy 1748-1832
Beranger, Jean-Pierre de 1780-1857
Berchet, Giovanni 1783-1851
Berzsenyi, Daniel 1776-1836
Black, William 1841-1898
Blair, Hugh 1718-1800
Blake, William 1757-1827
Blicher, Steen Steensen 1782-1848

Bocage, Manuel Maria Barbosa du 1765-1805
Boratynsky, Yevgeny 1800-1844
Borel, Petrus 1809-1859
Boreman, Yokutiel 1825-1890
Borne, Ludwig 1786-1837
Borrow, George 1803-1881
Botev, Hristo 1778-1842
Bremer, Fredrika 1801-1865
Brinckman, John 1814-1870
Brontë, Emily 1812-1848
Brown, Charles Brockden 1777-1810
Browning, Robert 1812-1889
Buchner, Georg 1813-1837
Burney, Fanney 1752-1840
Campbell, James Edwin 1867-1895
Campbell, Thomas 1777-1844
Carlyle, Thomas 1795-1881
Castelo Branco, Camilo 1825-1890
Castro Alves, Antonio de 1847-1871
Channing, William Ellery 1780-1842
Chatterje, Bankin Chanda 1838-1894
Chivers, Thomas Holly 1807?-1858
Clare, John 1793-1864
Claudius, Matthais 1740-1815
Clough, Arthur Hugh 1819-1861
Cobbett, William 1762-1835
Colenso, John William 1814-1883
Coleridge, Hartley 1796-1849
Coleridge, Samuel T. 1772-1834
Collett, Camilla 1813-1895
Comte, Auguste 1798-1857
Conrad, Robert T. 1810-1858
Conscience, Hendrik 1812-1883
Cooke, Philip Pendleton 1816-1850
Corbiere, Edouard 1845-1875
Crabbe, George 1754-1832
Crawford, Isabella Valancy 1850-1886
Cruz E Sousa, Joao da 1861-1898
Desbordes-Valmore, Marceline 1786-1859
Deschamps, Emile 1791-1871
Deus, Joao de 1830-1896
Dickinson, Emily 1830-1886
Dinis, Julio 1839-1871
Dinsmoor, Robert 1757-1836
Dumas, Alexandre (pere) 1802-1870
Dumas, Alexandre (fils) 1824-1895
Du Maurier, George 1834-1896
Dwight, Timothy 1752-1817
Echeverria, Esteban 1805-1851
Eden, Emily 1797-1869
Eminescy, Mihai 1850-1889
Engels, Friedrich 1820-1895
Espronceda, Jose 1808-1842
Ettinger, Solomon 1799-1855
Euchel, Issac 1756-1804
Ferguson, Samuel 1810-1886
Fernandez de Lizardi, Jose Joaquin 1776-1827

Fernandez de Moratin, Leandro 1760-1828
Fet, Afanasy 1820-1892
Feuillet, Octave 1821-1890
Fitzgerald, Edward 1809-1883
Fontane, Theodor 1819-1898
Forster, John 1812-1876
Frederic, Harold 1856-1898
Freiligrath, Hermann Ferdinand 1810-1876
Freytag, Gustav 1816-1895
Gaboriau, Emile 1835-1873
Ganivet, Angel 1865-1898
Garrett, Almeida 1799-1854
Garshin, Vsevolod Mikhaylovich 1855-1888
Gezelle, Guido 1830-1899
Ghalib, Asadullah Khan 1797-1869
Godwin, William 1756-1836
Goldschmidt, Meir Aron 1819-1887
Goncalves Dias, Antonio 1823-1864
Griboyedov, Aleksander Sergeyevich 1795-1829
Grigor'yev, Appolon Aleksandrovich 1822-1864
Groth, Klaus 1819-1899
Grun, Anastasius (pseud. of Anton Alexander Graf von Auersperg) 1806-1876
Guerrazzi, Francesco Domenico 1804-1873
Gutierrez Najera, Manuel 1859-1895
Gutzkow, Karl Ferdinand 1811-1878
Ha-Kohen, Shalom 1772-1845
Halleck, Fitz-Greene 1790-1867
Harris, George Washington 1814-1869
Hayne, Paul Hamilton 1830-1886
Hazlitt, William 1778-1830
Hebbel, Christian Friedrich 1813-1863
Hebel, Johann Peter 1760-1826
Hegel, Georg Wilhelm Friedrich 1770-1831
Heiberg, Johann Ludvig 1813-1863
Herculano, Alexandre 1810-1866
Hernandez, Jose 1834-1886
Hertz, Henrik 1798-1870
Herwegh, Georg 1817-1875
Herzen, Alexander Ivanovich 1812-1870
Hoffman, Charles Fenno 1806-1884
Holderlin, Friedrich 1770-1843
Holmes, Oliver Wendell 1809-1894
Hood, Thomas 1799-1845
Hooper, Johnson Jones 1815-1863
Hopkins, Gerard Manley 1844-1889
Horton, George Moses 1798-1880
Howitt, William 1792-1879
Hughes, Thomas 1822-1896
Imlay, Gilbert 1754?-1828?
Irwin, Thomas Caulfield 1823-1892

Issacs, Jorge 1837-1895
Jacobsen, Jens Peter 1847-1885
Jippensha, Ikku 1765-1831
Kant, Immanuel 1724-1804
Karr, Jean Baptiste Alphonse 1808-1890
Keble, John 1792-1866
Khomyakov, Alexey S. 1804-1860
Kierkegaard, Soren 1813-1855
Kinglake, Alexander W. 1809-1891
Kingsley, Charles 1819-1875
Kivi, Alexis 1834-1872
Klopstock, Friedrich Gottlieb 1724-1803
Koltsov, Alexey Vasilyevich 1809-1842
Kotzebue, August von 1761-1819
Kraszewski, Josef Ignacy 1812-1887
Kreutzwald, Friedrich Reinhold
    1803-1882
Krochmal, Nahman 1785-1840
Krudener, Valeria Barbara Julia de
    Wietinghoff 1766-1824
Lamartine, Alphonse 1790-1869
Lamb, Charles 1775-1834
Lampman, Archibald 1861-1899
Landon, Letitia Elizabeth 1802-1838
Landor, Walter Savage 1775-1864
Larra y Sanchez de Castro, Mariano
    1809-1837
Lautreamont (pseud. of Isodore Ducasse)
    1846-1870
Lebensohn, Micah Joseph 1828-1852
Leconte de Lisle, Charles-Marie-Rene
    1818-1894
Le Fanu, Joseph Sheridan 1814-1873
Lenau, Nikolaus 1802-1850
Leontyev, Konstantin 1831-1891
Leopardi, Giacoma 1798-1837
Leskov, Nikolai 1831-1895
Lever, Charles James 1806-1872
Levisohn, Solomon 1789-1822
Lewes, George Henry 1817-1878
Lewis, Matthew Gregory 1775-1810
Leyden, John 1775-1811
Lobensohn, Micah Gregory 1775-1810
Longstreet, Augustus Baldwin 1790-1870
Lopez de Ayola y Herrera, Adelardo
    1819-1871
Lover, Samuel 1797-1868
Luzzato, Samuel David 1800-1865
Macedo, Joaquim Manuel de 1820-1882
Macha, Karel Hynek 1810-1836
Mackenzie, Henry 1745-1831
Malmon, Solomon 1754-1800
Mangan, James Clarence 1803-1849
Manzoni, Alessandro 1785-1873
Mapu, Abraham 1808-1868
Marii, Jose 1853-1895
Markovic, Svetozar 1846-1875
Martinez de la Rosa, Francisco
    1787-1862
Mathews, Cornelius 1817-1889

McCulloch, Thomas 1776-1843
Merriman, Brian 1747-1805
Meyer, Conrad Ferdinand 1825-1898
Montgomery, James 1771-1854
Moodie, Susanna 1803-1885
Morike, Eduard 1804-1875
Morton, Sarah Wentworth 1759-1846
Muller, Friedrich 1749-1825
Murger, Henri 1822-1861
Nekrasov, Nikolai 1821-1877
Neruda, Jan 1834-1891
Nestroy, Johann 1801-1862
Newman, John Henry 1801-1890
Niccolini, Giambattista 1782-1861
Nievo, Ippolito 1831-1861
Nodier, Charles 1780-1844
Novalis (pseud. of Friedrich von
    Hardenberg) 1772-1801
Obradovic, Dositej 1742-1811
Oehlenschlager, Adam 1779-1850
Oliphant, Margaret 1828-1897
O'Neddy, Philothee (pseud. of
    Theophile Dondey) 1811-1875
O'Shaughnessy, Arthur William
    Edgar 1844-1881
Ostrovsky, Alexander 1823-1886
Paine, Thomas 1737-1809
Parkman, Francis 1823-1893
Patmore, Coventry Kersey Dighton
    1823-1896
Peacock, Thomas Love 1785-1866
Perk, Jacques 1859-1881
Pisemsky, Alexey F. 1820-1881
Pompeia, Raul D'Avila 1863-1895
Popovic, Jovan Sterija 1806-1856
Praed, Winthrop Mackworth 1802-1839
Prati, Giovanni 1814-1884
Preseren, France 1800-1849
Pringle, Thomas 1789-1834
Procter, Adelaide Ann 1825-1864
Procter, Bryan Waller 1787-1874
Pye, Henry James 1745-1813
Quental, Antero Tarquinio de 1842-1891
Quinet, Edgar 1803-1875
Quintana, Manuel Jose 1772-1857
Radishchev, Aleksander 1749-1802
Raftery, Anthony 1784-1835
Raimund, Ferdinand 1790-1836
Reid, Mayne 1818-1883
Renan, Ernest 1823-1892
Reuter, Fritz 1810-1874
Rogers, Samuel 1763-1855
Ruckert, Friedrich 1788-1866
Runeberg, Johan 1804-1877
Rydberg, Viktor 1828-1895
Saavedra y Ramirez de Boquedano,
    Angel de 1791-1865
Sacher-Mosoch, Leopold von 1836-1895
Saltykov-Shchedrin, Mikhail 1826-1892
Satanov, Isaac 1732-1805

Schiller, Friedrich von 1759-1805
Schlegel, August 1767-1845
Schlegel, Karl 1772-1829
Scott, Sir Walter 1771-1832
Scribe, Augustin Eugene 1791-1861
Sedgwick, Catherine Maria 1789-1867
Senoa, August 1838-1881
Shelley, Mary W. 1797-1851
Shelley, Percy Bysshe 1792-1822
Shulman, Kalman 1819-1899
Sigourney, Lydia Howard Huntley
    1791-1856
Silva, Jose Asuncion 1865-1896
Slaveykov, Petko 1828-1895
Slowacki, Juliusz 1809-1848
Smith, Richard Penn 1799-1854
Smolenskin, Peretz 1842-1885
Stagnelius, Erik Johan 1793-1823
Staring, Antonie Christiaan
    Wynand 1767-1840
Stendhal (pseud. of Henri Beyle)
    1783-1842
Stifter, Adalbert 1805-1868
Stone, John Augustus 1801-1834
Taine, Hippolyte 1828-1893
Taunay, Alfredo d'Ecragnole 1843-1899
Taylor, Bayard 1825-1878
Tennyson, Alfred, Lord 1809-1892
Terry, Lucy (Lucy Terry Prince)
    1730-1821
Thompson, Daniel Pierce 1795-1868
Thompson, Samuel 1766-1816
Thomson, James 1834-1882
Tiedge, Christoph August 1752-1841
Timrod, Henry 1828-1867
Tommaseo, Nicolo 1802-1874
Tompa, Mihaly 1817-1888
Topelius, Zachris 1818-1898
Turgenev, Ivan 1818-1883
Tyutchev, Fedor I. 1803-1873
Uhland, Ludvig 1787-1862
Valaoritis, Aristotelis 1824-1879
Valles, Jules 1832-1885
Verde, Cesario 1855-1886
Very, Jones 1813-1880
Villaverde, Cirilio 1812-1894
Vinje, Aasmund Olavsson 1818-1870
Vorosmarty, Mihaly 1800-1855
Wagner, Richard 1813-1883
Warren, Mercy Otis 1728-1814
Weisse, Christian Felix 1726-1804
Welhaven, Johan S. 1807-1873
Werner, Zacharius 1768-1823
Wescott, Edward Noyes 1846-1898
Wessely, Nattali Herz 1725-1805
Whitman, Sarah Helen 1803-1878
Wieland, Christoph Martin 1733-1813
Woolson, Constance Fenimore
    1840-1894
Wordsworth, William 1770-1850
Zhukovsky, Vasily 1783-1852

Horatio Alger, Jr.

1832-1899

(Also wrote under the pseudonyms of Arthur Lee Putnam, Arthur Hamilton, and Julian Starr) American novelist, biographer, short story writer, poet, and essayist.

Alger was one of the most widely read authors of juvenile fiction in the United States during the late nineteenth and early twentieth centuries. He wrote over one hundred books, all based on the principle that honesty, perseverance, and industry are certain to be rewarded. Almost invariably, his novels describe a virtuous boy's rise from poverty to prosperity. In an era of rapid industrial growth when many Americans were accumulating vast personal fortunes, Alger captured the imaginations of millions of young readers and underscored the ideals and aspirations of a changing American society. Alger's works are scarcely read today, but his name has entered the American vocabulary to signify the ''rags to riches'' success myth. Although Alger's stories are generally considered devoid of literary merit, he is of historical interest to the student of American culture because, as the critic Rychard Fink expressed it, ''It is dangerous to ignore a man whose ideas hang on so stubbornly.''

Born in Revere, Massachusetts, Alger was the oldest child of a Unitarian preacher and his wife. When he was twelve, the family moved to Marlborough, Massachusetts, where he attended Gates Academy in preparation for admission to Harvard College. In 1853, after his graduation from Harvard, Alger entered Cambridge Divinity School but withdrew shortly afterwards in order to become an assistant editor for the *Boston Daily Advertiser*. He held this post until the spring of 1854, when he was hired to teach at a boarding school in East Greenwich, Rhode Island. After briefly serving as the principal of a boys' academy in Deerfield, Massachusetts, Alger reentered Cambridge Divinity School and was ordained a minister in 1861.

During several years of irregular employment, Alger contributed essays, poems, and short stories to a variety of magazines and newspapers. His earliest literary efforts were directed toward adults; it was not until 1864 that he published his first novel for juveniles, *Frank's Campaign; or, What Boys Can Do on the Farm for the Camp*. In 1866, encouraged by the favorable reception of *Frank's Campaign* and its sequel, *Paul Prescott's Charge,* Alger resigned from his ministerial position at the Unitarian Church in Brewster, Massachusetts and moved to New York City, where he devoted himself to writing. The following year, his most successful novel, *Ragged Dick; or, Street Life in New York with the Boot-Blacks,* was serialized in the children's magazine *Student and Schoolmate*. The hero of the story, Dick Hunter, is a New York City bootblack who, by a combination of luck, pluck, hard work, thrift, and piety, becomes a respected and influential member of society. Alger followed the pattern set in *Ragged Dick* with little variation in a steady succession of enormously popular novels, including the *Tattered Tom* and *Luck and Pluck* series, sales of which almost equalled those of the *Ragged Dick* books. In addition, Alger composed several biographies of self-made statesmen, among them *From Canal Boy to President; or, The Boyhood and Manhood of James A. Garfield* and *Abraham Lincoln, the*

Backwoods Boy; or, How a Young Rail-Splitter Became President. Most of his novels are set in New York City during the latter half of the nineteenth century, and critics praise his accurate descriptions of the city's streets, boardinghouses, hotels, and restaurants. Alger gathered much of the information for his stories from conversations with young boys who lived in the Newsboys Lodging House, a philanthropic institution in New York City with which he was closely connected until his death.

The facts of Alger's life are difficult to determine. Prior to 1961, his only biographer was Herbert R. Mayes, whose *Alger: A Biography without a Hero* was published in 1928. A fictitious account of Alger's life based on a diary and letters that never existed, Mayes's biography was accepted as authoritative by the majority of Alger's critics for nearly forty years and is quoted as a reliable source in most reference texts. Almost all of the criticism of Alger's works written since 1928 relies to some degree on this fabrication, which was made partly plausible by a thread of biographical fact and a detailed listing of Alger's works, some of which Mayes invented. Mayes portrayed Alger as the repressed child of a stern Unitarian preacher who insisted on training his son for the ministry almost from birth. After graduating from divinity school, Mayes wrote, Alger rebelled against his father by fleeing to Paris, where he engaged in a series of ill-fated romances. According to Mayes,

Alger returned to the United States to write a "great novel" for an adult audience but succeeded only in producing an endless stream of stories for juveniles. The irony of Alger's life, Mayes concluded, was that the creator of the "rags to riches" myth died a frustrated and impoverished man. The first major attempt to discredit Mayes's biography, Frank Gruber's *Horatio Alger, Jr.: A Biography and Bibliography,* was published in 1961. In 1964, Ralph D. Gardner published his *Horatio Alger, or the American Hero Era,* another study devoted to dispelling the misconceptions about Alger's life generated by Mayes. Yet, it was not until 1972 that Mayes first admitted that his biography "literally swarms . . . with countless absurdities." Since Mayes's admission, several critics, most notably Jack Bales and Gary Scharnhorst, have documented the hoax.

Mayes's biography of Alger inspired a number of Freudian interpretations of his works. According to Norman N. Holland, the typical Alger story is a "wish-fulfilling constellation" in which Alger attempted to supplant his own domineering father by providing his hero with a benevolent substitute father. Malcolm Cowley also commented on this aspect, and further suggested that Alger sought vengeance on his father by making many of his heroes orphans and by attributing Horatio Alger, Sr.'s most pernicious characteristics to his stories' villains.

Alger's novels reached the height of their popularity during the decade following his death. As economic opportunities in American cities narrowed during the 1920s and 1930s, the books began to lose their credibility and appeal. There was little scholarly interest in Alger's works until the publication in 1945 of *Struggling Upward, and Other Works,* a reprinting of *Ragged Dick, Phil, the Fiddler; or, The Story of a Young Street Musician, Jed, the Poorhouse Boy,* and *Struggling Upward; or, Luke Larkin's Luck.* Most commentators share Richard Wright's opinion that Alger "was, is and will forever be the most terribly bad of writers," and his stories are consistently denounced for their stock characterization, repetitious plots, and stilted dialogue. Alger's historical and cultural significance is still debated. In the 1940s and 1950s, he was generally viewed as an apologist for business success, a man who applied the Protestant ethic to the urban world of the Gilded Age. Van Wyck Brooks faulted him for vulgarizing Ralph Waldo Emerson's doctrine of self-reliance by writing about boys whose motive was self-advancement instead of self-improvement. Russel Crouse, Kenneth S. Lynn, and Wright emphasized the monetary value which Alger placed on the virtues of hard work, thrift, and obedience and interpreted his heroes as would-be captains of industry who exploit every opportunity to succeed financially. Since the 1960s, Alger's role as a propagandist of capitalism has been repeatedly challenged and it is frequently argued that his stories do not sustain the "rags to riches" myth with which his name has become synonymous. John G. Cawelti, Michael Zuckerman, and Frank Shuffelton maintain that Alger was not an exponent of entrepreneurial individualism, because his typical hero's success is largely due to a chance encounter with a benevolent patron. They also point out that Alger's heroes aspire to middle-class respectability rather than wealth. Scharnhorst contends that Alger was primarily a moralist who hoped to imitate on a juvenile level the novels of Charles Dickens, which helped expose social injustices in England. Critics often note, however, that *Phil, the Fiddler,* which called attention to the *padrone* system, by which young street musicians were brought to New York from Italy and kept as virtual slaves, was the only Alger novel that contributed to social reform.

Recent critics offer varying explanations for Alger's apparent transformation in the middle of the twentieth century from a minor writer of popular children's stories into a prophet of business enterprise. Some commentators argue that after the Depression, Alger made a convenient scapegoat for the evils of unrestrained capitalism. Others contend that Mayes, who stated in his biography of Alger that all of his heroes "started poor and ended up well-to-do," was instrumental in creating the Alger legend. While today it is generally agreed that the fictional Horatio Alger hero does not embody the myth that has been ascribed to him, Alger remains significant as a cultural and historical phenomenon because of his influence on American ideals.

*PRINCIPAL WORKS

Bertha's Christmas Vision (short stories and poetry) 1856
Frank's Campaign; or, What Boys Can Do on the Farm for the Camp (novel) 1864
Paul Prescott's Charge (novel) 1865
Fame and Fortune; or, The Progress of Richard Hunter (novel) 1868
Ragged Dick; or, Street Life in New York with the Boot-Blacks (novel) 1868
Luck and Pluck; or, John Oakley's Inheritance (novel) 1869
Mark, the Match Boy; or, Richard Hunter's Ward (novel) 1869
Rough and Ready; or, Life among the New York Newsboys (novel) 1869
Ben, the Luggage Boy; or, Among the Wharves (novel) 1870
Rufus and Rose; or, The Fortunes of Rough and Ready (novel) 1870
Sink or Swim; or, Harry Raymond's Resolve (novel) 1870
Paul the Peddler; or, The Adventures of a Young Street Merchant (novel) 1871
Strong and Steady; or, Paddle Your Own Canoe (novel) 1871
Tattered Tom; or, The Story of a Street Arab (novel) 1871
Phil, the Fiddler; or, The Story of a Young Street Musician (novel) 1872
Slow and Sure; or, From the Street to the Shop (novel) 1872
Strive and Succeed; or, The Progress of Walter Conrad (novel) 1872
Bound to Rise; or, Harry Walton's Motto (novel) 1873
Try and Trust; or, The Story of a Bound Boy (novel) 1873
Brave and Bold; or, The Fortunes of a Factory Boy (novel) 1874
Julius; or, The Street Boy Out West (novel) 1874
Risen from the Ranks; or, Harry Walton's Success (novel) 1874
Grand'ther Baldwin's Thanksgiving, with Other Ballads and Poems (ballads and poetry) 1875
Herbert Carter's Legacy; or, The Inventor's Son (novel) 1875
Sam's Chance; and How He Improved It (novel) 1876

Shifting for Himself; or, Gilbert Greyson's Fortunes
(novel) 1876

The Western Boy; or, The Road to Success (novel) 1878;
also published as *Tom, the Bootblack; or, The Road to
Success*, 1880

The Young Adventurer; or, Tom's Trip across the Plains
(novel) 1878

*From Canal Boy to President; or, The Boyhood and
Manhood of James A. Garfield* (biography) 1881

*Abraham Lincoln, the Backwoods Boy; or, How a Young
Rail-Splitter Became President* (biography) 1883;
also published as *The Backwoods Boy; or, The Boyhood
and Manhood of Abraham Lincoln*, 1883

Do and Dare; or, A Brave Boy's Fight for Fortune (novel)
1884

Hector's Inheritance; or, The Boys of Smith Institute
(novel) 1885

Bob Burton; or, The Young Ranchman of the Missouri
(novel) 1888

The Erie Train Boy (novel) 1890

Five Hundred Dollars; or, Jacob Marlowe's Secret (novel)
1890; also published as *The Five Hundred Dollar
Check*, 1891

Struggling Upward; or, Luke Larkin's Luck (novel) 1890

Facing the World; or, The Haps and Mishaps of Harry Vane
(novel) 1893

In a New World; or, Among the Gold-Fields of Australia
(novel) 1893

Victor Vane, the Young Secretary (novel) 1894

The Young Salesman (novel) 1896

Frank and Fearless; or, The Fortunes of Jasper Kent
(novel) 1897

Walter Sherwood's Probation (novel) 1897

The Young Bank Messenger (novel) 1898; also published
as *A Cousin's Conspiracy*, date unknown

Jed, the Poorhouse Boy (novel) 1899

*Adrift in New York; or, Tom and Florence Braving the
World* (novel) 1904

Struggling Upward, and Other Works (novels) 1945

Alger Street: The Poetry of Horatio Alger, Jr. (poetry)
1964

*Many of Alger's works were originally published in periodicals.

PUTNAM'S MAGAZINE (essay date 1868)

["**Ragged Dick**"] is a well-told story of street-life in New York,
that will, we should judge, be well received by the boy-readers,
for whom it is intended.

The hero is a boot-black, who, by sharpness, industry, and
honesty, makes his way in the world, and is, perhaps, somewhat more immaculate in character and manners than could
naturally have been expected from his origin and training.

We find in this, as in many books for boys, a certain monotony
in the inculcation of the principle that honesty is the best policy,
a proposition that, as far as mere temporal success is concerned,
we believe to be only partially true. However, the book is very
readable, and we should consider it a much more valuable
addition to the Sunday-school library than the tales of inebri-
ates, and treatises on the nature of sin, that so often find place
there.

A review of "Ragged Dick," in Putnam's Magazine,
Vol. II, No. 7, July, 1868, p. 120.

THE NATION (essay date 1869)

For a thousand years, we suppose, we shall have books like
Mr. Alger's "**Rough and Ready**," and, as they say in the
South, for our own part "we have no use for them." . . . [We]
confess to some dislike of master "**Rough and Ready;**" for,
clearly, he is going to deceive many who believe in him. He
is a most noble, generous, just newsboy—full as he can hold
of good thoughts and good works. But will Mr. Alger figure
to himself, now, some nice little boy, with a clean collar on,
and his hair neatly brushed, and with fists not quite so hard as
brass knuckles, and a face unmarked by war-paint, and a hat
somewhere near the size of his head? And now, next, will he
please figure this pride of his mamma undertaking a half-hour's
stay in Printing House Square when the young gentlemen who
sell extras are congregated there? Or the City Hall Park will
do, and the array of boot-blacks will answer the purpose as
well as their friends the newsboys; they are equal in attainments
and character. And, having obliged us so far, will Mr. Alger
maintain that either of them would not certainly, in a very brief
time, cause a temporarily complete and painful change in our
clean young wayfarer's views of life? So far as we have the
pleasure of his acquaintance, the newsboy indulges but very
few of the softer emotions. He smokes ends of cigars which
he picks up in the street; he much prefers lemonade from the
street stalls to the performance of good actions; he would far
rather see virtue defended up in the Bowery Theatre than rescue
little girls from cellars in which their stepmothers ill-use them;
it has been doubted, indeed, if he has ever conceived of virtue
without a basket-hilted sword and a white dress presenting
themselves to his imagination at the same time. That he ever
volunteered to wake up a drunken gentleman who had fallen
asleep in a ferry-boat, no one will believe who is in the habit
of crossing the North or East Rivers. In short, he is not pious,
and does not order his life well; and there is a certainty that
whoever bases his notions of the newsboy's character on a
belief in the truthfulness of Mr. Alger's romance will get false
notions of the character of the average newsboy, and most
probably will not get true notions of the character of any newsboy, average or otherwise, who has ever with free foot trod
the foot-stool. And, next, perhaps the real newsboy will reveal
himself to this deceived reader of "**Rough and Ready;**" and
from that day out we have in him an enemy of the Newsboy's
Home, and a man who peremptorily declines to contribute
anything towards giving the young gentlemen their Thanksgiving dinner. As it happens. Mr. Alger has no excuse that we
hear of for doing as he has done. The newsboy is not a Christian
of the first two centuries; but he has his good points, too; and
at any rate he is an interesting figure as he stands. . . . [There]
is no need of depicting him in any imaginary aspect to make
him both respectable and interesting. The newsboys who read
"**Rough and Ready**," however they may approve it as a work
of fiction, will say "my eye" when asked to lay it to heart
and make it a practical guide. So, them the author has not
benefited. And the layman will, as we have said, form false
notions of the being which it is intended to depict; and that is
never well. (pp. 587-88)

"The Last of the Children's Books." in The Nation,
*Vol. IX, No. 235. December 30, 1869, pp. 587-88.**

THE LITERARY WORLD   (essay date 1875)

"**Gran'ther Baldwin's Thanksgiving**" contains some very agreeable poems. That which gives the name to the book is a faithful and graceful picture of a scene that will soon belong only to the past. "**Barbara's Courtship**" is an old, old story, very well told. "**John Maynard**" fitly commemorates a noble deed. "**My Castle**" embodies a thought worth remembering, in pretty verses. Mr. Alger is not a professional poet, and his work is not faultless artistically; but he writes with genuine feeling, and often with felicity and force. "**The Song of the Croaker**" is a very clever piece of satire.

> *A review of "Gran'ther Baldwin's Thanksgiving," in* The Literary World, *Vol. VI, No. 7, December 1, 1875, p. 101.*

THE LITERARY WORLD   (essay date 1877)

Horatio Alger, Jr., has no superiors among our writers of fiction for the young. He keeps to the happy medium between dulness and sensationalism, and under the guise of entertaining stories imparts useful lessons. His latest story, "**Shifting for Himself, or Gilbert Greyson's Fortunes**," is full of interest. . . . The incidents of [the hero's] career are lifelike and naturally connected, and the story as a whole is impressive and wholesome.

> *A review of "Shifting for Himself, or Gilbert Greyson's Fortunes," in* The Literary World, *Vol. VII, January, 1877, p. 117.*

S. S. GREEN   (essay date 1879)

> [*Green, who was a librarian in Worcester, Massachusetts, terms the juvenile fiction of Alger and William T. Adams "sensational." Although he objects to their reliance on "startling and unnatural" incidents to attract readers, he contends that their works serve useful purposes and should be available in public libraries.*]

[The books of William T. Adams ("Oliver Optic") and Horatio Alger Jr.] depend for their power to interest the reader upon the presence in them of accounts of startling incidents and not upon a description of the processes by which interesting conjunctions in life grow out of character, or upon narration replete with fine imagination or delicate humor.

These books are not condemned, however, because they have an interesting plot, but because the incidents are startling and unnatural, and the sole reliance of the writer for attracting readers. They have little literary merit, and give us incorrect pictures of life.

This is a correct description of sensational novels and stories. They are poor books. Poor as they are, however, they have a work to do in the world. Many persons need them. They have been written by men who mean well. . . .

Such exciting stories as are found in the circulating departments of our libraries do good in two ways. They keep men and women and boys from worse reading. I heard a year or two ago of the formation of a club among some boys to buy dime novels, copies of the *Police Gazette*, and other books and periodicals, from a railroad stall or news-room. Now, I felt very sure that if these boys had not been considered too young to take books from the public library, but had been allowed to read the stories of Messrs. Alger and Adams, that they would have been contented with these books, and not have sought worse reading. (p. 348)

[Sensational] books in the circulating departments of our public libraries do good in another way. They give young persons a taste for reading. It is certainly better for certain classes of persons to read exciting stories than to be doing what they would be doing if not reading. It is better to repress idleness in persons, the lower part of whose nature is sure to be awakened if they are not pleasantly employed. It certainly is a benefit done to such persons to enable them to grow up with a love of reading, even although they will read only sensational books, and their taste does not improve in regard to the selection of books. But the taste of many persons does improve. You smile as I make this assertion. . . . There is truth in the statement, nevertheless. A boy begins by reading Alger's books. He goes to school. His mind matures. He outgrows the books that pleased him as a boy. If boys and girls grow up with a dislike of reading, or without feeling attracted towards this occupation, they will not read anything. But if a love of reading has been cultivated by giving them when young such books as they enjoy reading, then they will turn naturally to reading as an employment of their leisure, and will read such books as correspond to the grade of culture and the stage of intellectual development reached by them. They will thus be saved from idleness and vice.

I have no doubt that harm comes to some young persons from reading the books of Oliver Optic. . . . These books are likely to leave the impression upon the minds of the young that they can get along by themselves without the support and guidance of parents and friends. But I take it comparatively few persons are deceived by these books, while the great bulk of readers get from them merely the enjoyment of the story. Perhaps there is no book that the average Irish boy likes better than one of Mr. Alger's stories. Now such a boy is likely to learn that his powers are subject to limitations, and not be led by these books to feel an overweening self-reliance. (pp. 348-49)

> *S. S. Green, "Sensational Fiction in Public Libraries," in* Library Journal, *Vol. IV, No. 9, September-October, 1879, pp. 345-55.**

THE LITERARY WORLD   (essay date 1885)

We do not particularly admire Mr. Alger's style and spirit [in *Hector's Inheritance*]. Neither is very elevated; and while the book is not one to do any particular harm, we cannot see how it is likely to do any particular good.

> *A review of "Hector's Inheritance," in* The Literary World, *Vol. XVI, No. 23, November 14, 1885, p. 408.*

THE CRITIC, NEW YORK   (essay date 1891)

There is nothing new about the story '**The $500 Check**,' by Horatio Alger, Junior, except the cover and the paper and possibly the pictures. The classification of the rich and poor into the evil and the good is as old as the parable of Dives and Lazarus. It is such an obvious, worn-out, theme for a story, that we wonder any author with the instinct of literary self-preservation should employ it. . . . [At] no period of the story will the reader be surprised, disappointed, or puzzled.

> *A review of "The $500 Check," in* The Critic, *New York, Vol. XVI, No. 414, December 5, 1891, p. 317.*

THE LITERARY WORLD (essay date 1893)

One's patience fails long before reaching the end of *In a New World,* the latest volume from the too prolific pen of Horatio Alger, Jr. One feels indignant not only with the writer, who might do something better than pour forth this unceasing stream of sensational, impossible literature, but with the boys who persistently read, enjoy, and talk them over. . . . Perhaps it is only fair to say that the writer intends always to lay stress on the qualities of energy, truth, and manliness.

> *A review of "In a New World," in* The Literary World, *Vol. XXIV, No. 24, December 2, 1893, p. 422.*

THE CRITIC, NEW YORK (essay date 1895)

Horatio Alger, Jr. is always sure of a public, no matter how bad his rhetoric, how unreal his situations, or how crude his workmanship. His latest book, **"Victor Vane, the Young Secretary,"** tells, as usual, of the impossible virtues, triumphs and successes of a boy of seventeen, who becomes private secretary and confidential adviser and friend to a Western Congressman, and transacts a large amount of important business in the most experienced fashion. Such stories as this call for little comment. We must recognize the fact that they have taken possession of the mind of the ordinary unreflective boy with a strong hold, and, if possible, supplement this taste for tales of street life with a liking for those that are truly literary.

> *A review of "Victor Vane, the Young Secretary," in* The Critic, *New York, Vol. XXIII, No. 697, June 29, 1895. p. 476.*

HORATIO ALGER, JR. (essay date 1896)

[*Here, Alger defines his conception of successful juvenile fiction.*]

A writer for boys should have an abundant sympathy with them. He should be able to enter into their plans, hopes, and aspirations. He should learn to look upon life as they do. . . . Boys object to being written down to. Even [Jacob Abbott's] Rollo books, popular as they were in their time, do not suit the boys of to-day. A boy's heart opens to the man or writer who understands him. . . . Boys soon learn whether a writer understands and sympathizes with them. I have sometimes wondered whether there ever was a boy like Jonas in the Rollo books. If so, I think that while probably an instructive, he must have been a very unpleasant companion for a young boy like Rollo.

A writer for boys should remember his responsibility and exert a wholesome influence on his young readers. Honesty, industry, frugality, and a worthy ambition he can preach through the medium of a story much more effectively than a lecturer or a preacher. I have tried to make my heroes manly boys, bright, cheerful, hopeful, and plucky. Goody-goody boys never win life's prizes. Strong and yet gentle, ready to defend those that are weak, willing to work for their families if called upon to do so, ready to ease the burden that may have fallen upon a widowed mother, or dependent brothers and sisters, such boys are sure to succeed, and deserve success.

It should not be forgotten that boys like adventure. There is no objection to healthy excitement. Sensational stories, such as are found in the dime and half-dime libraries, do much harm, and are very objectionable. Many a boy has been tempted to crime by them. . . . Better that a boy's life should be humdrum than filled with such dangerous excitement. . . .

One thing more, and the last I shall mention—a story should be interesting. A young reader will not tolerate dullness. If there are dull passages which he is tempted to skip, he is likely to throw the book aside. The interest should never flag. If a writer finds his own interest in the story he is writing failing, he may be sure that the same effect will be produced on the mind of the reader. It seems to me that no writer should undertake to write for boys who does not feel that he has been called to that particular work. If he finds himself able to entertain and influence boys, he should realize that upon him rests a great responsibility. In the formation period of youth he is able to exert a powerful and salutary influence. The influence of no writer for adults can compare with his. If, as the years pass, he is permitted to see that he has helped even a few of his boy readers to grow into a worthy and noble manhood, he can ask no better reward. (p. 37)

> *Horatio Alger, Jr., "Writing Stories for Boys—IV," in* The Writer, *Vol. IX, No. 3, March, 1896, pp. 36-7.*

An early depiction of Ragged Dick.

MALCOLM DOUGLAS (poem date 1920)

[*The following sentimental verse attests to Alger's popularity.*]

Horatio Alger, Jr., you were once my greatest joy:
I revelled in your stories when a happy, care free boy;
There was William Makepeace Thackeray, a novelist of
  note;
There were Bulwer, Scott and Dickens, but they got my
  childish goat;
They didn't have the pep and zip, Horatio, that you did,
For you got underneath the vest of every blooming kid,
And a myriad young critics felt your fascinating punch,
So they crowned you king, Horatio, of the literary
  bunch!

Horatio Alger, Jr., all the types of boys you drew,
Poor urchins of the streets, revealed the gentle soul of
  you;
There were Ragged Dick and Tattered Tom, with others
  of their kind,
Who all bespoke an honest heart, a pure, unselfish
  mind;
Through trials and temptations they most perilously
  passed
Till virtue was triumphant, good Horatio, at the last;
And as their thorny paths through life your humble
  heroes trod
Each chapter was illumined by your simple faith in
  God!

Horatio Alger, Jr., long ago your busy pen
Was laid aside, but to the hearts of grizzled, gray
  haired men
Come visions of their idol, and your name they often
  bless,
For you helped them not a little in their measure of
  success;
You were loved by hosts, Horatio, and you filled an
  honored place;
The memory of all your good time never can efface;
And, if but a single blossom each old boy admirer
  gave,
What a mountain of sweet fragrance there would rise
  above your grave!

> *Malcolm Douglas, "Horatio Alger, Jr.," in* The New
> York Herald, *Section 2, December 12, 1920, p. 2.*

WARREN BECK (essay date 1928)

Descending into an age given over to impressionistic writing,
Horatio Alger, Jr., stands unique by reason of the painstaking
candor of his method. [In **"Do and Dare"** he] never suggests
when he can state. He makes all transitions with loud trum-
petings. "Before describing the appearance of Herbert and
George Melville upon the scene," he says, "I will go back a
few minutes and relate what happened at the farmhouse."
Sometimes he goes back a few years, but he always gives
written notice. He watches with a parent's care over his reader's
intelligence and doesn't let it do any heavy lifting. "The sheet
of stamps contained twenty-five three cent stamps, representing
in value seventy-five cents." What more than that, you may
ask, could any author do for his customers?

One phrase, of his, merits particular notice—the "representing
in value seventy-five cents." That is Algerian for "worth seventy-five cents." Alger writes a thick and clotted language.
"Our hero," does not eat his meals, he "partakes of" them.
A tramp does not steal the silver, he "possesses himself of
it." Herbert does not merely come, or even arrive; he "puts

in an appearance." You and I would ask the ticket agent, "How
much to Chicago?" but Eben is "heard to inquire, 'What do
you charge for a ticket to Chicago'"; and when Eben finds he
has enough money he says further, "You may give me one."
It is to be hoped that the agent gave him two, both hard ones.
Not that Eben is the worst sinner. He is merely the juvenile
villain of the piece; our hero is even more punctiliously prosy.

However, it is not this overstuffed style which first sickens the
young devotee of Alger; rather, it is the everlasting stacking
of the cards in favor of a happy fate for all those present.
Usually there is an irreclaimable villain who "gets his need-
ings," but the rest of the dramatis personae are frugally gathered in. All the sinners of venial sins are pardoned, washed
up, and given good jobs. As for our polite and virtuous hero,
he is more nearly invulnerable than Achilles, and more nearly
infallible than Lindbergh. The bullets always miss him, but he
never misses a promotion. For a time the boy reader likes it,
but at last it gets to be too much. Even a generation whose
philosophy has been shaped by motion pictures, wherein the
good old U.S. cavalry swoops down the valley precisely on
time, begins to find fault with Alger's stories. Even a sixth
grade boy begins to realize that in life there are inexplicable
hitches, or, as Benvenuto Cellini said that God "does not
always pay on Saturdays."

So the boys outgrow Alger, and forget him before they have
time to discern his most horrible example. For in a book like
"Do and Dare" there is something worse than bad style and
prepaid destinies. In the empty eventfulness of such a story
there is an almost immoral dullness of feeling, a lack of anything like a sincere report of a real mood. When the author
does attempt to record a feeling, he reaches the depth of his
fatuity. His characters simply gibber; their emotions do not
track. A vengeful redskin having got the drop on a sturdy
hunter, by way of last words the hunter says, "It's enough to
disgust any decent man!" A timely deliverer (standard model)
shoots the savage through the heart, and the savage falls, "his
face distorted with rage and *disappointment*"*!* That is the average emotional tone—being shot is an annoyance. Nor is this
the callousness of criminality. The closest our immaculate hero
comes to an authentic human quiver is in the mild elation that
recurs with each raise of salary. In the entire book there is no
hint of the joy of life or its impending doom, there is neither
genuine humor nor honest pathos; and the whole range of those
emotions which justify and glorify human existence—pity, zest,
fortitude, mirth, reverence, love—lies untouched. Not only
untouched, but apparently unsought and even undesired. The
book lacks any deep intuitions, all fine devotions; in a word,
it lacks imagination. (pp. 2-4)

> *Warren Beck, "'Huckleberry Finn' versus 'The Cash
> Boy'," in* Education, *Vol. XLIX, No. 1, September,
> 1928, pp. 1-13.**

THE NATION (essay date 1932)

[We must confess that our] melancholy as we contemplate . . .
the transitoriness of [Alger's] literary fame is purely sentimental, and that it does not spring from any faith in either the
aesthetic merits of the works themselves or in their capacity
to elevate the moral standards of their readers. We once read
all of them on which it was possible to lay our hands and we
read them with a passionate loyalty, but it is hard even to
remember what their charm was or why we did not simply read
the same one over again as often as the need to read anything

arose. The formula was invariable, and always involved, first, the rescue of the banker's daughter from a mad dog or a runaway horse, and then a false suspicion of theft which raised its ugly head against our hero. Alger is said to have been distressed all his life with the desire to do "serious work," but we know of no one who ever revealed less promise, and it is our considered belief that the literary value of his novels is about as near absolute zero as it is possible for anything composed in intelligible sentences to be. . . .

Putting aside the nice ethical questions involved in the effort to evaluate the exact degree of moral beauty to be discovered in the general injunction "Be good so you can get rich," it is to be observed that all Alger's insistence upon the duty of thrift did not prevent him from being extremely improvident or from dying poor, and we are inclined to believe that the effect of his work could be pretty accurately measured by its effect upon him. If detective novels and gangster movies do the youth of the land no more harm than the Alger books did their fathers good, then the youngest generation is safe.

> *"The Cynical Youngest Generation," in* The Nation, *Vol. CXXXIV, No. 3476, February 17, 1932, p. 186.*

FREDERICK LEWIS ALLEN (essay date 1938)

[*In the following excerpt, which originally appeared in the* Saturday Review *on September 17, 1938, Allen criticizes Alger's works for their clumsy construction, simple style, and shallow characterization. However, he offers Alger backhanded compliments by crediting him with a "talent for improvisation" and noting that his dialogue has "at least the merit of transparency." Like Richard Wright (1945), Allen suggests that Alger indoctrinated Americans of the Gilded Age with the belief that capital comes as a reward from God to those who work diligently.*]

[Alger's] books were, and are, generally regarded by the critical as trash—yet their sales mounted into the millions, he was one of the most popular of all American authors, if not of all authors of all time; and there can be little doubt that he had a far-reaching influence upon the economic and social thought of America—an influence all the greater, perhaps, because it was innocently and naïvely and undogmatically exerted. (p. 157)

The Alger style was incredibly simple, matter-of-fact, and unoriginal. Whenever Alger turned aside from plain literal fact for a bit of analysis or description, he became a fountain-head of eighth-grade clichés. Nothing whatever was left to the reader's imagination. The dialogue, though it had little relation to the confusing way in which people speak in real life, had at least the merit of transparency. (p. 161)

Nor did any subtleties of character-drawing prevent one from determining immediately who were the good characters and who were the bad ones. They were labeled plainly. When Andy Grant, the poor farmer's son, met Conrad Carter, the rich squire's son, and said to him, "That's a new bicycle, isn't it?" Conrad replied,

> "Yes; I got tired of the old one. This is a very expensive one. Wouldn't you like to own a bicycle?"
>
> "Yes."
>
> "Of course, you never will."

From that moment on, the reader could feel sure that Conrad would never say a decent word or do a decent thing; that Andy would out-distance Conrad in the boat race and Conrad would whine excuses for his defeat; that Conrad would try to burn up Andy's boat and burn his own by mistake; and that when Andy's hard work in New York at last enabled him to pay off Squire Carter's mortgage on the Grant farm, Conrad would go into a dreadful rage, as all thwarted villains do. Similarly, the good characters were always definitely noble and uttered splendid sentiments. And always virtue triumphed. Thus the reading of an Alger story was like watching a football game in which you knew the names and numbers of all the players, and the home team made all the touchdowns.

Any writer who in thirty-three years turned out well over a hundred such books and whose memory (especially as he got on in life) was often faulty, must have been expected to make mistakes. Alger made them. Frequently he got his characters mixed, to the dismay of his publishers, who had to rearrange the names. But he had talent for improvisation. When his hero was to be taken out for a ride on the savage horse Bucephalus—which the villain hoped would run away and kill him—it would suddenly be divulged that the boy had been taking riding lessons the preceding year and had won a reputation as a rider of surpassing skill. Nothing had been said in preceding pages about this course of instruction, but Alger didn't bother to go back and insert a reference on page 45; the accomplishment was sprung upon the delighted reader, Bucephalus was mastered, and the story roared right ahead, to the triumph of the young Jehu and the downfall of the villain.

When one considers that the period in which these books were the delight of millions of American boys was that very period when the economic expansion of the United States was going on full tilt, to the accompaniment of every sort of financial knavery and speculative excess; and when one realizes that to most of these millions of young readers the Alger books provided their first intelligible picture of economic life and the making of an individual fortune, one looks again, with an analytical eye, to see how the Alger hero's fortune was achieved. And one notes, not without amusement, that the boy never got rich from the direct fruits of his industrious labor. How could he, starting in at $5 a week, even with rapid increases in pay? No; he got his hands on capital.

Sometimes this capital was inherited: the supposed orphan, ragged though he was, proved to be the son of a man whose supposedly worthless mining stock was good for $100,000. Sometimes the capital was a gift: rich Mr. Vanderpool was so impressed with the boy's pluck that he made over to him the $50,000 that the boy had helped him to save from the robbers. Or the boy was out in Tacoma, buying lots as a real-estate agent (on his boss's inside information that the Northern Pacific was to be extended to the Coast), and in a Tacoma hotel he befriended an invalid gentleman, who out of gratitude gave him a part interest in some lots that promptly soared in value and put him on Easy Street. The method varied; but when the time came for our hero to get into the money, it was a transaction in capital which won the day for him.

Yet always he was so good, and husbanded so prudently the $175 in his savings account (though he was generous, too, to the poor washer-woman and to the other bootblacks), that to the casual reader the lesson of these stories was not that hard work brings in but a pittance, or that the way to succeed is to stand in with the men who have the capital, but something quite different. The lesson was that capital comes as a reward from heaven to him who labors mightily and uses his head all the time. Work, save, be a good boy, shun the fleshpots, and presently the mining stock will fall into your lap and all will be well.

Possibly this explains something about the Gilded Age—when Americans worked furiously, and opened up the West, and accomplished wonders in invention and manufacturing; when the average American of moderate means was hard-headed, diligent, and on the whole fairly scrupulous; but when the ethical level of the big operations in capital was often well-nigh barbaric. Once capital began to fall into a man's lap, he did not inquire unduly whence it came. He had labored meritoriously; merit was always rewarded—was it not?—and now his reward was at hand; obviously it must come from heaven. One remembers Rockefeller saying, "God gave me my money," and one knows that other men of millions felt as he did. Who knows but that to some of them—and to some of their successors in more recent times—this conviction grew, in part at least, out of early lessons in economics from *Andy Grant's Pluck* or *Tom the Bootblack. . . .* (pp. 161-63)

> Frederick Lewis Allen, "Horatio Alger, Jr.," in Perspectives, *edited by Leonard F. Dean, Harcourt, Brace and Company, 1954, pp. 157-64.*

RUSSEL CROUSE (essay date 1945)

[*In his sarcastic, disparaging introduction to* Struggling Upward, and Other Works, *Crouse chides himself for enjoying Alger's works as a youngster, but notes that he admires him nonetheless because "for many years, in many words on many pages—he got away with literary murder." According to Crouse, Alger's popularity derived from his unbridled enthusiasm for financial success. His opinion is echoed by Richard Wright (1945), Kenneth S. Lynn (1955), and Rychard Fink (1962), but disputed by John G. Cawelti (1965), Michael Zuckerman (1972), Frank Shuffelton (1976), and Gary Scharnhorst (1980).*]

I have searched my soul and I cannot . . . recall any of the virtues of the Alger heroes, whom I once swore to emulate my whole life through, that I now possess. Believe it or not, I have not dashed into a burning building, or leaped into a swiftly-rushing rapids to save the life of a child for several years now. And—worst offense of all—I am not rich.

However, I am still an Alger admirer. I came by that admiration as a youth. I have just reread the Alger novels that comprise [**"Struggling Upward and Other Works"**] and I find that admiration renewed. But for a slightly different reason. I admire him now because, for many years, in many words on many pages—he got away with literary murder. (p. vii)

[Horatio Alger's books] are completely devoid of literary style. They reflect truth no more accurately than a Coney Island mirror. They contain about as much humor as the Greek Orthodox funeral service. They have neither sound construction nor true characterization. The more I ponder them at this ripe old age, the more annoyed I am at the thought that I enjoyed them as a boy. . . .

[The Alger hero] is always the same young man. He is poor, he is honest, he is manly, he is cheerful, he is ambitious. He always starts at the bottom and ends at the top. But do these noble attributes with which he is always so carefully endowed by Mr. Alger play the vital part in his ultimate success? They do not.

Let us take Ragged Dick, for example. Ragged Dick is a bootblack. He has many adventures, practically none of which has anything to do with the story of his progress. He has many

virtues, the vast majority of which have nothing to do with his final victory. Dick's ambition is to throw away his bootblack's box and become a clerk. But does he achieve this goal by hard work and perseverance? No, indeed. In the last chapter he leaps from a ferryboat into the churning bay to rescue a child who has toppled off the deck. For which the father, who should have been paying attention to the child in the first place, rewards Dick by giving him a job. (p. viii)

I may be quibbling, but I submit that [this is not] highly inspirational. Do we want the young men of America riding around on ferryboats waiting for children to fall off—perhaps even pushing them off—so that they may stage startling rescues and get jobs? (p. ix)

It seems to me that Mr. Alger could have done much better by the work-and-win theory. Too many of his heroes resemble the gentleman who, when asked how he had become a millionaire, replied that it was the result of "hard work and the fact that my father left me $1,000,000."

Nor would I chafe to this extent if the Ragged Dicks . . . acquired their good qualities from life itself and the experiences thereof. Instead they are imparted, for the most part, by a series of characters who appear from time to time, without so much motivation as the dropping of a hat and promptly launch into long and boring sermons on morality.

A newsboy will be standing on a corner minding his own business when up will step a gentleman, who apparently devotes his life to a search for such opportunities, to tell his helpless victim such pithy facts as "honesty is the best policy" or "good deeds are better than kind words." I might be more kindly disposed toward these elderly windbags if their conversation resembled in any way that which usually takes place between human beings.

Indeed, the same may be said of all of Alger's characters. They talk a peculiarly stilted form of English not known today and I feel sure not known except on the printed page of Mr. Alger's own time. It just isn't true talk.

You may have gathered by this time that I do not think highly of Mr. Alger as a *litterateur*. You are right. But perhaps I am being unfair to him. There is no denying the earnestness of the man and there is no gainsaying the fact that he was accepted by his audience. (pp. ix-x)

What was the secret of [the novels'] appeal? It lay, I think, in the deep and abiding homage they paid to success. And here, at long last, I am able to toss a laurel to Mr. Alger. No altar-boy ever worshipped more devoutly at the shrine of personal achievement than he. You will find that simple adoration in everything he wrote.

To Mr. Alger, it seems to me, the real heroes of his novels were not the newsboys and the bootblacks and the luggage boys who were his leading characters. They were, instead, the merchant princes, the opulent bankers, the successful lawyers whose careers the heroes were taught to emulate. It wasn't difficult for a rich man to go through the eye of Mr. Alger's needle. Any sort of achievement appealed to Mr. Alger. He even admired city aldermen.

Now if you will recall the period in the development of our nation at which these books appeared you will realize that they may have served a peculiar purpose. It was an era in which America was just beginning to find its potentialities. The resources were there. They had to be developed—and in their development America became great. Many of the men who developed them may have found their inspiration in Horatio Alger—in his adoration of achievement.

If my theory is correct more than one youth, after reading these books, set out to be a richer man, if not a better man. That many of them succeeded, possibly in both fields, is a tribute to a man who needs one at this late date. For if I have given Horatio Alger's memory a bad evening, at least I have the grace to be somewhat conscience-stricken at this point. It is only fair to say for him that he made no pretense to literary genius. (p. x)

Only one of his books can, by any stretch of the imagination, be said to have had any sociological significance other than that of holding up success as the great golden apple. In the middle of the last century many young Italian boys were brought to this country by unscrupulous padrones who sent them out into the streets of New York as itinerant musicians, took their earnings away from them and kept them in virtual slavery. Social workers interested Alger in their plight and he wrote **"Phil, the Fiddler."** But his was not the skill of a Zola. He did call attention to an evil but it took others to fan the sparks, which he may have created, into the fire that destroyed the system. (p. xiii)

> *Russel Crouse, in an introduction to* Struggling Upward, and Other Works *by Horatio Alger, Jr., Crown Publishers, 1945, pp. vii-xiv.*

RICHARD WRIGHT (essay date 1945)

[*Wright was an American novelist, short story writer, and essayist who established his reputation as a leading spokesman for Black Americans with his first novel,* Native Son. *In his review of* Struggling Upward, and Other Works, *Wright terms Alger the "most terribly bad of writers" and shamefully admits that he enjoyed reading his "swamp" of rhetoric as a boy. Like Frederick Lewis Allen (1938), Wright argues that Alger's works fostered the conviction among Americans during the Gilded Age that material possessions were gifts from God. According to Wright, Alger was one of American capitalism's most effective propagandists. This view is also advanced by Russel Crouse (1945), Kenneth S. Lynn (1955), and Rychard Fink (1962), but later disputed by John G. Cawelti (1965), Michael Zuckerman (1972), Frank Shuffelton (1976), and Gary Scharnhorst (1980).*]

[Even] though the old-fashioned, morally uplifting tales of Horatio Alger, Jr., were a part of the dreams of my youth—and maybe of the dreams of millions upon millions of other youths—I failed to get a sense of rediscovery by wading through them again.

Indeed, I had to drive myself through the 570 dreary pages of [*Struggling Upward and Other Works*]. . . . I felt ashamed over the fact that I had been so naive as to derive enchantment out of prose clogged with such clichés as *sudden appearance, eager curiosity, mysterious stranger, veiled contempt, modest expenses, an insignificant-looking man, urgent invitation, strikingly handsome, a picture of perfect health* and so on and so on.

The late Mr. Horatio Alger, Jr., was, is and will forever be the most terribly bad of writers. Of that there can be no doubt. All of his sociology, psychology, politics and insights into human nature are just so many bald lies burdening his 135 volumes and his millions of stale words.

But my report is not all negative. As I neared the end of the fourth story, entitled *Jed the Poorhouse Boy,* a glimmer of light broke through the fog. I detected, in the swamp of Alger's rhetoric, a meaning of which, I am sure, he himself was unconscious.

He was an utterly American artist, completely claimed by his culture, and the truth of his books is the truth of the power of the wish. The warm, Sunday-school glow that bathes his heroes is the glow of the dream and its irrational logic. Perhaps no other American writer ever took so much at their face value the popular delusions and the pious moral frauds of his time.

In Alger the theories of Max Weber's *Capitalism and the Spirit of the Protestant Ethic* find their most simple function and fulfilment. If you really want to know why John D. Rockefeller, Sr., identified his material possessions as gifts straight from God, then read Horatio Alger, Jr.

Alger was perhaps American capitalism's greatest and most effective propagandist. I do not mean, of course, that he was hired by John D. Rockefeller, Sr., and surely the Executive Committee of the Capitalist Class of 1875 did not hold an Extraordinary Plenum Session and vote to commission him to write books upholding the virtues of the free enterprise system. . . .

No, Alger's word-spinning was a long labor of love. Incredible as it is, the man believed in what he was doing. And I would guess that he sent more than one boy straight up to the top, to Fame and Fortune.

I am willing to hold Horatio Alger, Jr., up as a model to the Communists, Socialists and Liberals and to labor leaders in general. Instinctively, he knew something that they never seem to learn: that the masses are won to a cause not through the voicing of fears and threats and the announcing of ever-recurring, dire crises, but through instilling in them the feeling that they can find the fulfilment of their lives by participating in a new movement.

And how well Alger knew this! It colored every line he wrote. It was his passion. The Algerian world teemed with kind-hearted capitalists who itched to pick up stray, starving boys (but they had to be honest and loyal where money matters were concerned!) and buy them suits, feed them, give them jobs and put their feet on the ladder leading to Success.

Effort was not needed. Thinking was not mandatory. Hard work, yes, but not too much. But it was absolutely necessary to have the knack of being handy when a rich man's daughter fell off a ferry. . . . You rescued her, and you were rewarded. Alger's tales abound in coincidences. Indeed, his tales move by the mechanism of happy accidents, the kind of accidents that make dreams move and be. In short, his stories are the waking dreams of young men hungry to get ahead.

Here are a few Algerian concepts (I blush to do this, but a job is a job.): The mere look of a man's face is sufficient to indicate if he is honest or not. If a man should rob you of your last penny, then, when you meet him again, do him a favor. People are mean and cruel simply because they *are* mean and cruel. Most all poor people are good. Villainy is inevitably punished. And material success will surely crown virtue and godliness.

Could 200,000,000 copies of 135 books carrying such slop ever have been sold in America? Yes, they could and were. And the next time you are puzzled over the low cultural level of our country, stop and reflect that we could be much worse off, that the mere mental digestion of 200,000,000 copies of Horatio Alger, Jr.'s drivel was more than enough to cripple the spirit of a nation tougher than America. We are lucky that today there is a mood of honesty and objectivity in some parts of our land.

Not many nations of the earth have had to bear such a cultural handicap!

> Richard Wright, "Alger Revisited, or My Stars! Did We Read That Stuff?" in PM Sunday, September 16, 1945, p. M13.

R. RICHARD WOHL (essay date 1953)

[*In the following excerpt, which originally appeared in* Class, Status and Power: A Reader in Social Stratification *in 1953, Wohl attempts to account for Alger's initial success, the decline in his popularity, and his resurgent fame.*]

[We may address ourselves] to the involved paradox of Alger's literary reputation: how to account for his great, initial success with an audience of millions, the subsequent disappearance of this audience, and the puzzling phenomenon of his resurgent fame after his books had disappeared from view.

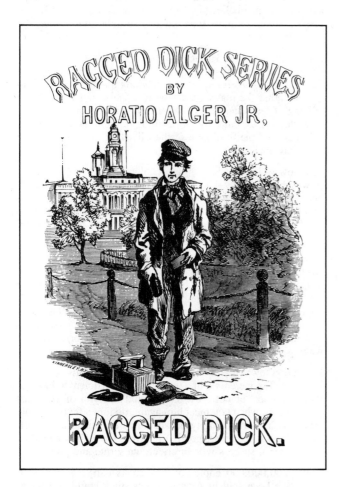

Title page of an early edition of Ragged Dick. *Courtesy of Prints and Photographs Division, Library of Congress.*

The period of Alger's greatest popularity coincided with the filling up of the nation's cities. Farm boys by the millions, seeking wider horizons and enlarged opportunity, left the farms on which they had been born to take up an urban existence. Alger became the apostle of this migration.

Alger helped define the aspirations of those boys—to make money, to get ahead, to make good—he described for them the experience which they were bracing themselves to undertake. His city (he mainly wrote about New York) was accurately described with a loving attention to authentic detail. It teems with people and traffic. It is a busy place, full of strange and various sights: colorful, noisy and knowing. His heroes may have always triumphed over the villains; but the tricksters, the criminals and confidence men, the drunkards, loafers and urchins were all truly and fully depicted. Their jargon was faithfully rendered; their follies and bad habits exactly catalogued.

His books, in addition, were full of practical and minute information about how one lived and worked in a city once one got there. One could learn from such a novel what kinds of boarding houses there were, and what was fair value in shelter; there were careful lists of the prevailing prices of food and clothing, utensils and amusement; an audience eager for just this kind of practical counsel snapped up these books as fast as they were printed.

Even if we did not know from other sources that Alger's books were addressed to youngsters in the hinterland, we might fairly infer it from an inquiry of what city life meant to the urban boy who actually lived in a slum because he was born there, had low status, and worked as a boot-black or match boy. Even in Alger's day there were too many such boys already in the cities for even that sanguine age to promise much opportunity or hope of advancement. These city boys—the unredeemed gamins in his novels—were systematically encouraged by benevolent urban philanthropists to forsake city life, to go West and try to set up as independent farmers! . . .

The city boy, wry, hardened and wise in the ways of the seamy side of slum life found no prophet at all in Alger. Had they been asked, they would have told Alger that his image of the city's life was already obsolete for many of those he was inspiring.

For Alger's audience at large, living away from the metropolis and not knowing the true state of affairs there, Alger's message was reinforced by some of the most potent and irreproachably respectable public opinion of the day. Protestant ministers had for decades addressed the fathers and mothers of the young people for whom Alger wrote and their message was identical with his. Sound morals in a sturdy character was the whole equipment for success in life, it was urged. The imputation of poverty or failure to social conditions, or prevailing institutions was a wicked falsehood, a positive evidence of evil. (p. 504)

The press, like the pulpit, echoed the same message that Alger sent out to his young folk. Popular novels, like pulpit oratory, reflecting metaphors which were fast growing obsolescent, preached the gospel of thrift, hard work, and endurance. In one such novel, representative of many, a young lady of unblemished character noted for her delicate sentiments finds occasion to say (and to be applauded for saying); "In the laboring class, property is a sign of good morals. In this country no one sinks to deep poverty except by vice, directly or indirectly." The ambiguities in the qualifying phrases for long escaped careful scrutiny.

Alger's original contribution to this tired controversy was to inject it into a new dimension. While the other great juvenile writers of his day—Oliver Optic, Edward Ellis and Henry Castlemon—were producing adventure tales full of pirates, cowboys and Indians, and war heroes Alger cut down this adult theme to fit the needs and understanding of children. In doing so, he had behind him the combined efforts not only of much articulate and expounded public opinion, but he geared his tales in with the very injunctions that many parents were giving their children to fit them for life as grown men and women.

His success was founded, too, in the solid example afforded by the many men who had started with nothing and built a fair fortune by their own exertions. (pp. 504-05)

Alger reported a common fact from the time of his own youth to an age already markedly different from the one in which he had grown up. For many opportunity was narrowing, industrialization and wage work offered a slim base for advancement for those employed in the shops and factories, although even then much room was left for the determined and the canny. It is revealing, however, that Alger dragged in luck rather than occupational strategy, not to explain success, but to explain how an aspirant got a foothold on the upward path. Alger's patrons interestingly enough are merchants not industrialists, another obsolete element in his outlook. His boys are not child laborers in factories but street-traders, messengers, shop-clerks.

As the cities filled, and a realistic picture of urban life became more general; as the face of industrialization was discerned in unfettered, uncontrolled growth, Alger's audience fell away in disbelief. By this time, millions of his books had been sold and read: the popular magazines had scattered his stories broadcast through the land. His name, his catchy titles, the skeleton of the plot he had endlessly repeated in his novels, remained behind in the memories of those to whom he had once been an inspiration. By word of mouth they carried his fame further than even his books could reach....

It is [Alger's] capacity to inspire and excite which has kept [his] name and fame alive even after his stories have collapsed under their simplicity—their uncritical, naive optimism. Their theme has universal appeal. In all ages, the disadvantaged hero struggling against odds, bearing witness to aspiration, but finally redeemed by success is a folk figure everywhere rejoiced in. It is not surprising, therefore, that a story cognate to this universal theme survives. All that was required for it to survive in association with Alger's name was that it be edited and revised to fit new conditions. In its modern version, the snug congruity between the altered legend and the changed circumstances is achieved. The new hero is a slum boy making his way in the modern world. As the stories which Alger had written disappeared there was no canon against which revision might be measured. Modification proceeded unchecked.

The society into which the new version fell was, in very many ways, much like the older world Alger knew. It believed in comfort, ample and conspicuous consumption; it believed, albeit a little differently, in the worth of work and the test of character in achieving a dream; it believed in earning privilege and its justification by meritorious achievement. In short, it believed in success: rich, juicy, and obvious. Alger's vastly publicized name and his slogans became detached from the rationale to which he had affixed them and were transferred, as something known and esteemed, to a new explanation, a new rhetoric of persuasion. (p. 505)

R. Richard Wohl, " 'The Rags to Riches Story': An Episode of Secular Idealism," in Class, Status, and Power: Social Stratification in Comparative Perspective, edited by Reinhard Bendix and Seymour Martin Lipset, second edition, The Free Press, 1966, pp. 501-06.

KENNETH S. LYNN (essay date 1955)

[*In his* The Dream of Success: A Study of the Modern American Imagination, *from which the following excerpt is drawn, Lynn traces the response of five American novelists, Theodore Dreiser, Jack London, David Graham Phillips, Frank Norris, and Robert Herrick, to the myth of success. Lynn begins his study with a discussion of Alger's works because, as he states below, "the Alger hero is the key to the meaning of the success mythology." His interpretation of Alger's stories is challenged by John G. Cawelti (1965).*]

While Alger was not the first American success writer, it is nevertheless true that the Alger hero is the key to the meaning of the success mythology. Alone, unaided, the ragged boy is plunged into the maelstrom of city life, but by his own pluck and luck he capitalizes on one of the myriad opportunities available to him and rises to the top of the economic heap. Here, in a nutshell, is the plot of every novel Alger ever wrote; here, too, is the quintessence of the myth. Like many simple formulations which nevertheless convey a heavy intellectual and emotional charge to vast numbers of people, the Alger hero represents a triumphant combination—and reduction to the lowest common denominator—of the most widely accepted concepts in nineteenth-century American society. The belief in the potential greatness of the common man, the glorification of individual effort and accomplishment, the equation of the pursuit of money with the pursuit of happiness and of business success with spiritual grace: simply to mention these concepts is to comprehend the brilliance of Alger's synthesis. (pp. 6-7)

The Alger hero often began life in places as rural as those frequented by Cooper's Natty Bumppo, but the significant action of his life took place on the sidewalks and in the counting rooms of New York, Cincinnati or Chicago. Alger made no bones about the existence of poverty. The city of the Alger myth was a glamorous, wonderful place, but it had its seamier side, its tenements and flophouses and sweatshops. Money was in the forefront of every Alger novel—how much the hero earned in his first job, how much he spent on food and rent, how much of a fortune he eventually compiled.... Alger's world was populated by Irish and Italians and Germans as well as by those whose ancestors were pioneers. The success myth, in the hands of its greatest expositor, was a grand and impossible dream, but part of its power derives from the fact that it was also a reflection of the contemporary world. (p. 8)

[Alger's] simple, but enormously compelling, vision of a fluid society which infallibly rewarded the plucky and lucky with fame and fortune had, in the opportunistic scramble after the Civil War, a solid basis in fact. But such was the rate of complication and diversification of American life that even within Alger's own lifetime his vision began to lose contact with the social situation it endeavored to describe.... In the complex multiverse which is the United States in the middle of the twentieth century, Alger's version of the success myth seems primitive and naïve, hopelessly inadequate to the task of ordering and interpreting our social experience to ourselves. Alger preached the gospel that hard work was the *sine qua non* of success, yet in contemporary America the "Protestant ethic" has given way to personality-selling as the classic means of rising in the world. The fact that men and women still do rise in the American world attests to the continued validity of Alger's belief in social mobility; but while the fact that American society is still fluid and open goes far toward explaining why Alger continues to exert a powerful pull on the American imagination, Alger's simplistic conception of mobility does no more than begin to comprehend the manifold processes which make for fluidity in modern American society. More obsolete than the Model T, Alger continues to be our mythmaker; until we show some of the same sort of ruthlessness about discarding outworn mythologies as we do about outdated motorcars, we shall never be able to get at the unprecedented meaning of American civilization today. (pp. 252-53)

> Kenneth S. Lynn, in his The Dream of Success: A Study of the Modern American Imagination, *Little, Brown and Company, 1955, 269 p.**

CLIFTON FADIMAN   (essay date 1957)

[*Fadiman became one of the most prominent American literary critics during the 1930s with his insightful and often caustic book reviews for the* Nation *and the* New Yorker *magazines. He also reached a sizeable audience as a radio talk-show host from 1938 to 1948. In the following excerpt, which originally appeared in an abbreviated form in* Holiday *in February, 1957, Fadiman credits Alger's works, which he nostalgically refers to as "algers," with a "certain feeble nobility." In addition, he favorably compares Alger's stories with modern comics and television programs for youngsters.*]

To make fun of algers is easy. But it is not hard to resist the temptation. They do not really make me laugh. In a wan, sickly way they make me sad. Trash? Yes, of course. Alger had no more writing talent than an Igorot. Yet the ostensible matter of his books, even though they carry no conviction, has a certain feeble nobility. Alger's heroes may be cutouts, but these cutouts make certain moral gestures that are at least pallid reflections of fine things: generosity, self-sacrifice, honor, manliness. It is true that these virtues do not win the jackpot for them. That is always the consequence of an accidental encounter with a passing philanthropist. But the philanthropist operates only when virtue presses his spring, never when villainy does. Goodness *does* pay off, if indirectly.

I have no wish to defend these books. Their qualities are few and dubious. Yet I cannot help wondering whether their moral world is so markedly inferior to that of our television shows for the young, in which a lust for violence and a passion for bad grammar struggle for domination. Is Tattered Tom half as much of a repulsive imbecile as Mr. Disney's Davy Crockett? Were the small fry of my childhood, innocently responding to Alger's bland Sunday school view of life, inferior except in point of sophistication to today's urchins so knowingly responding to the calculated sadisms of the comics?

I know that our higher-level juvenile literature is miles above Alger, more inventive, broader in scope, far better written. But it lacks something algers had. Though a foolish man, Alger is a *serious* man. For all his mandatory happy endings, he is not unaware that life is hard, even tragic. What writer of contemporary books for the young would think of including a scene like that in *Phil the Fiddler* in which poor little Giacomo dies of beatings and starvation? I am not demanding that misery be inserted into our bright juvenile literature. I merely wonder whether its doctrinal optimism is much more realistic than

Alger's Calvinistic creed of work, with its corollary acceptance of the notion that even the young have to endure and suffer. (pp. 42-3)

> Clifton Fadiman, "Horatio Alger, Fare Thee Well; or, The Road to Success," in his Any Number Can Play, *The World Publishing Company, 1957, pp. 37-54.*

NORMAN N. HOLLAND   (essay date 1959-60)

[*In a Freudian discussion of Alger's life and works predicated on Herbert R. Mayes's* Alger: A Biography without a Hero, *Holland portrays Alger as an "emotional cripple" whose mind was "happily matched to the minds of his young readers." He interprets Alger's novels as analogues of their author's emotional maladjustments and regards the typical Alger plot as a "wish-fulfilling constellation" in which Alger attempted to supplant his own domineering father by providing his hero with a kindly and benevolent substitute father figure. For an additional discussion of Alger's stories as wish-fulfillment fantasies, see Malcolm Cowley (1970).*]

[Alger] is probably the most popular author America has ever had, and one of the most popular the world has ever known. And one can only wonder why. Lamely written, shabby mixtures of the most rank distrust of human nature and the most fatuous idealism, what could thirty years of American children have seen in such gelded *gestes* [tales of adventure] as *From Canal Boy to President, or the Boyhood and Manhood of James A. Garfield, Walter Sherwood's Probation, or Cool Head and Warm Heart, Frank and Fearless, Risen from the Ranks, Hobart the Hired Boy,* and the rest. What made Alger so popular?

Alger's forte was hardly style. His lame sentences seem sired by *Roget's Thesaurus* out of a tourists' phrase-book. For example, "His eyes flashed, and his youthful form dilated with righteous indignation." " 'I believe you will,' said the officer, with a revulsion of sentiment in Tom's favor." Each novel seems one long freshman composition:

> Stretched out stiff and stark were two figures, cold in death. They were men of middle age, apparently. From each the scalp had been removed, thus betraying that the murderers were Indian.

Alger's real strength lies in good old-fashioned moral instruction, and his most helpful counsel for the budding Rockefeller seems to be, People are no damn good. In Alger's books, Our Hero must run a gauntlet of sneakthieves, pickpockets, armed robbers, and confidence men. He begins to be wise when he acquires a properly Calvinistic view of man:

> The young are by nature trustful. They are disposed to put confidence in those whom they meet, even for the first time. Unhappily, in a world where there is so much evil as there is in ours, such confidence is not justified. There are too many who make it a business to prey on their fellows, and select in preference the young and inexperienced.

This sludge of moral admonition through which the Alger plot limps seems hardly the sort of thing that would make boys rush out to read Alger's novels. Why then were they so popular?

The answer lies in the fact that Alger's own mind was so happily matched to the minds of his young readers. He himself remained a child all his life, an emotional cripple whose growth was twisted by the steady application of moral pressures in childhood. (pp. 549-50)

We use [the phrase "Horatio Alger Story"] to describe the career of a young man who works hard, lives cleanly, and makes a lot of money, but in so doing, we repress, as it were, the real content of the phrase. A true Alger hero works hard and lives cleanly for 150 pages, and then inherits $50,000. Like most popular literature from *True Romances* to Norman Vincent Peale the Horatio Alger story is a simple wish-fulfilling fantasy. In this respect, his works do not differ from other boys' books, [Burt L. Standish's] Frank Merriwell or [Edward Stratemeyer's] Tom Swift stories, for example. Alger's novels, however, sold many times the number of copies these others did, and his popularity suggests that Alger must somehow have tapped an especially rich psychological lode.

Certainly one wish Alger gratifies is the boy's desire to become a man. Alger's young readers identify with Our Hero and vicariously through him win "grit," "pluck," and other symbols of manliness and potency.... Money is another symbol for potency, as is the watch which some older man almost inevitably buys Our Hero.

Alger, however, does more than simply gratify a boy's wish to become a man. He provides a foil, the Other Boy. Half of an average Alger novel deals with Our Hero's opposite.... In Algerese, the Other Boy always looks "as though he has just stepped out of a bandbox." He takes trips to Europe and indulges expensive vices and sicknesses. He has, in short, all the things Our Hero seeks, but he gets them without effort. The Other Boy represents the infantile wish to get the symbols of adulthood without sacrificing the privileges of childhood. When Our Hero is rewarded at the end, when he inherits his fortune (thus, in a way, achieving adulthood without effort), it is the Other Boy who is punished, who atones for the guilt of success. Typically, in the simple pattern of the Alger novel, he is reduced to the boyish state Our Hero was in at the beginning.... (pp. 552-53)

The Alger mother also plays her part in the wish-fulfilling constellation. She is usually a weak, fretful woman, who dotes on Our Hero, even to the exclusion of the father. Thus, when in *Making his Way* Frank Courtney's mother dies, she ignores her husband, Frank's stepfather, to give Frank "one last glance of love." The Alger hero is also likely to be the Alger mother's chief economic prop. In *Brave and Bold,*

> Great was the dismay of Mrs. Rushton when she heard from Robert that he was discharged from the factory. She was a timid woman, and rather apt to take desponding views of the future.
>
> "Oh, Robert, what is going to become of us?" she exclaimed, nervously. "We have only ten dollars in the house, and you know how little I can earn by braiding straw."

Here again, money (potency) is critical. The hero usually leaves his mother to win success, but guides her destiny from afar by sending money home. Finally he returns unexpectedly to her adoring arms.... (pp. 553-54)

By far the most satisfying figure, however, is the Alger father, or, more properly, fathers, for there are typically three: the real father, the substitute father, and the wicked father. In most of Alger's books, the real father is dead. In many others the father is a father *manqué,* a man who seems strong and full of "grit," but somehow misses. (p. 554)

Not only could Alger's readers emotionally supplant their fathers—they didn't even have to feel guilty about it. Our Hero usually acquired a substitute father, another older man, by saving from peril either the older man himself or some woman attached to his family; the action, I suppose, must in many cases have stood for its opposite:

> Among the passengers was a stout, good-looking man, a New York merchant. . . .
>
> "It was providential, your seeing the rock," he said to the engineer. "We owe our lives to you."
>
> "You do me more than justice," replied the engineer. "It was not I who saved the train, but that boy."
>
> All eyes were turned upon Robert.

These substitute fathers are bountiful men who lavish praise and money on the heroes, take pleasure in relying on them, and encourage their efforts to become the man in the family. "Plucky young Bob Rushton" and Frank Courtney "with courage and self-reliance rarely found in one so young" are both befriended by wealthy New York merchants. In each case they are given important and responsible posts.... In each case these spirited young lads protect their patrons from other employees who are taking advantage of them, thus, in a sense, compensating for the advantage they themselves are taking of the real fathers. Herbert Carr in *Do and Dare* becomes companion to the invalid Mr. Melville and saves his life. Tom Nelson in *The Young Adventurer* is adopted by the other members of the wagon train, whom, in turn, he saves from Indians. Most of the substitute fathers buy the hero a watch, a recurring symbol in Alger for adulthood and potency. Like the real fathers, these substitute fathers are likely to be sick, old, or otherwise weakened.

The wicked fathers, on the other hand, are apt to be strong, powerful men, even if they are swindlers, misers, and bullies. Moreover, like Mr. Manning in *Making his Way* and Squire Hudson in *The Young Adventurer,* the evil fathers may be rivals for the love of Our Hero's mother. All these evil fathers either get unfairly or keep unfairly Alger's chief symbol of manliness, money, but in the end, they lose it. Alger's readers could thus project in this disguised and ostensibly just form the castration of their own stern nineteenth-century fathers. (pp. 555-56)

Writing books enabled Alger to surpass his father, yet avoid competing directly with him. Both in the pages themselves and in the fame they brought, he outdid his father, whom, in later life, he either squabbled with or ignored. Yet he could only write boys' books; at anything else he failed. He could write successfully only if his books compensated for his own rebellion against his father, that is, only if his books seemed to him to serve the high moral purpose of teaching the young to submit to their elders.

Actually, of course, the books showed the prospective merchant-prince replacing his father to become the sole support of an adoring mother—a delightful fantasy-version of the real nineteenth-century family situation. The Alger novel mirrors its social context in another way. As the nineteenth century progressed, opportunities for "poor boys" to make their way narrowed, yet the Calvinist belief that poverty was a sin lingered on. True virtue, potency, even divine grace, were shown by success in the things of this world: virtue brought its own reward, and other rewards too. At the same time, the Benevolent Employer without whom Our Hero could not succeed suggests the readers' and Alger's growing suspicion that virtue and industry unaided were no longer enough. The Benevolent Employer becomes a necessary supplement to Our Hero's merits, but also eases his conscience. That is, Our Hero, the budding merchant-prince, transfers his filial allegiance to another, distant, more benevolent Father who recognizes true merit and who economically rewards the good and punishes the bad. Money, "pluck," "grit," pocket-watches, and other symbols of potency are outward manifestations of this inward grace, this at-one-ness with a greater Father. At the same time, if a man fails, he must be guilty, he must have sinned against that all-knowing Father, as Alger himself had. (pp. 556-57)

Norman N. Holland, "Hobbling with Horatio, or the Uses of Literature," in The Hudson Review, *Vol. XII, No. 4, Winter, 1959-60, pp. 549-57.*

RYCHARD FINK   (essay date 1962)

[*Fink emphasizes Alger's significance as a cultural phenomenon, asserting that he affirmed the economic and social values of his age "with such conviction and energy that the big ideas he transmitted became even more credible." He joins Russel Crouse (1945), Richard Wright (1945), and Kenneth S. Lynn (1955) in stressing Alger's association with the American dream of success but adds that Alger's works are more than success manuals for aspiring boys because they express a "fascinating mixture of democratic equalitarianism and social criticism."*]

[A] student of American culture should give far more attention to the novels and ideas of Horatio Alger than is usually the case. There is no doubt that what he wrote was bilge, but it was inspired. His novels, it can be argued, wove a far firmer strand in the American character than the work of men with sounder intellectual credentials. (p. 6)

Horatio Alger's novels can be considered in two ways: as literature and as vehicles for the expression of social values. As literature, the less said of his books the better. A poet can command attention if he has written one good sonnet, but a novelist cannot be salvaged because of a few good lines.

Herbert R. Mayes, Alger's only biographer, argues rather briefly that Alger represents the beginnings of realism in American fiction. A. K. Loring, his publisher, insisted that Alger was the first to record accurately a large part of American city life in fiction. Such claims are hard to accept. True, there are hundreds of portraits and situations in Alger's novels that are accurate and realistic, but they are drops of water in an otherwise arid desert. One can also find caricature and irony, but neither are sustained enough to represent a clear literary posture. The best of Alger's jibes, for all the impact they undoubtedly had on the boys who read and chuckled over them, lapse into preachments or reflect the author's innocence. A good deal of Alger is funny, but only because we read him out of familiarity with a language whose meanings have shifted a good deal since his day. He is filled with unwitting double-

Illustration from the Ragged Dick *series. The Granger Collection, New York.*

meanings, as, for example, in this passage from **Ragged Dick:** the snob says to Dick, "'I've seen you before.' 'Oh, have you?' asks Dick wheeling around. 'Then p'r'aps you'd like to see me behind.'''

Alger is a monument to bad taste. He comes to us from the world of Victorian furniture and architecture. Like them, he is terrible; however, he is such a special instance of the terrible; however, he is such a special instance of the terrible that he exercises a fatal fascination. As long as any reader has the slightest touch of artistic masochism, an hour with an Alger novel will bring to life a bit of agonized fondness for him. Reading him, there will quite likely cross one's face what Mencken described as the expression of a physician contemplating an eczema. (pp. 15-16)

What were the obvious meanings in Alger's novels? His plot, which recurred with minor variations, depicted a poor boy eager for financial success who, through luck, pluck, and virtue, achieved his goal. Here is the idea of worldly success as it can come to the self-made common man.

None of this was invented by Alger. As a matter of fact, his social values do not derive from any creative thinking on his part. As George C. Homans, a brilliant contemporary social scientist, has remarked, one of the basic tasks of an age that is striving to understand itself is to raise the obvious to its highest level of generality. This is exactly what Alger did. He patterned a commitment to life that underscored the dominant myths, hopes, and prejudices of a majority of Americans. He echoed some of the most important ideas of the most complex revolution in modern social development—the movement in which ordinary men put themselves in the center of the universe. His books told American boys what they already half-believed and wanted to go on believing. Wish and faith fed upon themselves in Alger's novels, and it is doubtful that we will escape the consequences for some time to come. (pp. 17-18)

The arithmetic of success for [Alger's heroes] was pluck and luck plus the Protestant ethic. . . . [This] stemmed directly from [Benjamin Franklin's formula for success], but in Alger's calculations, the old printer-diplomat's deism was replaced by Alger's Unitarian faith. Not only was the Alger hero in the right place at the right time, but he was there with a wholesomeness of spirit. Emerson made the point well when he wrote, "There is always a reason, *in the man,* for his good or bad fortune, and so in making money." Such inwardness was many things, particularly an ability to recognize that material success was not a solitary and self-contained end. In the dialectic of living, it was also a beginning of social responsibility. (p. 25)

[It is not enough] to label Alger's novels as self-help books that preached success to aspiring boys. They carry other messages as well. If one looks closely at them, one sees that they also expressed a fascinating mixture of democratic equalitarianism and social criticism. Although no one has ever commented on it, Alger's influence on this level undoubtedly must have been great. There is no evidence that Alger intended this. Once again, all he did was express the obvious.

Alger did far more than push success upon his poor and honest heroes. He gave them dignity and planted it in their natures in such a way that it had the status of a natural right. He was far less kind to the sons of many of his rich villains. The self-seeking, dishonest, and conniving squires, businessmen, and lawyers he described spawned wretched little snobs. As Alger sketched them, they lacked all dignity and seldom picked up any along the way. (p. 27)

Kid gloves were the sign of depravity in all young Alger villains. They were always being put on, taken off, or waved in the faces of Alger heroes. The heart of the conflict between the two types was always the same: according to the villain, the Alger hero simply did not "know his place." **Brave and Bold** presents as good a sample of the problem as any of his novels. In this book, the hero, Robert Ruston, asks Hester Paine, the daughter of a rich lawyer, to walk home from a graduation exercise before the young villain, Halbert Davies ("smoothing his kid gloves"), could make the same request. Halbert is "mortified and angry" and swears that Robert will "be sorry for his impudence." The boys meet the next day (Halbert was "swinging his cane in his gloved hand"), and Robert is charged with "putting on airs for a factory boy."

> "You mustn't regard yourself as Miss Paine's equal because she condescended to walk with you," Halbert said. "You had better associate with those of your own class hereafter, and not push yourself in where your company is not agreeable."

> "Keep your advice to yourself, Halbert Davies," said Robert, hotly, for he felt the insult conveyed in these words. "If I am a factory boy I don't intend to submit to your impertinence; and I advise you to be careful what you say."

Using such scenes, Alger restated the case for democratic equalitarianism in the spirit of an unreconstructed Jacksonian. He underlined the American attitude that any common man, pauper or what have you, was the salt of the earth. The young villains always charged that the hero "puts on as many airs as if he were a prince instead of a beggar," or said, smugly, "Oh, you know, he is much below us in a social point of view." The Alger hero always defended his intrinsic worth as a freeborn American who was as good as any other man. He never would back away from any defense of wounded self-esteem. Robert Ruston tells Halbert Davies' father, "It will be a serious thing for me if I lose my place here, for my mother and I are poor, and my wages make the greatest part of our income. But I cannot make this apology you require. I will sooner lose my place." (pp. 28-9)

Alger was after more than fair treatment for his heroes. Little people of all kinds stood up for their rights in his pages: "You are very impertinent. You forget that you are nothing but a servant." "A servant has the right to be treated decently, Mr. Mark."

What was Alger after? On one side were many of the rich, mean and dishonest, willing to use power and position to hurt people. Their sons were not a bit better. On the other side were those on the way up, people with courage, good judgment, a feeling of responsibility—and the vote. The two forces must clash, and the victory must go to those whose strength is welded to virtue. Is this a morality tale? A fable? Or a proposition men must make come true?

There is evidence in over one hundred novels that Alger pleaded the case of the common man and doubted the morality of many of those who owned and managed society. Each novel, of course, had balance: some common men were thieves and jackals, and some rich men were honorable and wise. Yet

Alger's readers could learn a lesson whose meaning was not too [different] from the social criticism of people like Wendell Phillips. Perhaps some of the men who made the years after the Civil War an age of dissent learned part of their rebelliousness and doubt from Horatio Alger. In our own day, comic books were treated as juvenile nonsense until men like Frederic Wertham exposed the violence they preached. It is more than possible that the parents, teachers, and ministers who approved of Alger's preachments might also have missed part of his message.

The last big idea taught by Alger was the most obvious. He always included luck and good furtune in the pattern of success. Let Alger state the case: "His plan [was] a doubtful one, requiring for success not only pluck and persistency, but good health and luck. Not many boys can expect an uninterrupted course of prosperity when thrown upon their own exertions." Call it Providence or the breaks, Alger made it the real key to success.

His books had other messages. They supported the importance of education, deplored smoking and drinking, and insisted on truthfulness, cleanliness, and honesty. Alger joined McGuffey and the rest of the middle class in these matters. . . . (pp. 29-30)

Alger was a major pump station on the pipe line that carried the American dream. There was not an idea in anything he wrote that was not already in the thought and feelings of Americans. But Alger affirmed the obvious in his claptrap prose with such conviction and energy that the big ideas he transmitted became even more credible.

Today, Dale Carnegie and Norman Vincent Peale are his direct descendants. The Lloyd C. Douglas school of fiction follows his propositions. People live his plot and find it good and reasonable. He helped make success a quasi-religious moral idea that leaves people who fail (whether in spelling or in something bigger) with the conviction they are unloved. He stands for trying harder, wanting more, and contributing to the community chest. The people who want to distribute Sears, Roebuck catalogs to Russians to persuade them of America's superiority are his disciples, too.

Any person who wants to know his country should get acquainted with Horatio Alger. It is dangerous to ignore a man whose ideas hang on so stubbornly. (pp. 30-1)

> *Rychard Fink, in an introduction to* Ragged Dick and Mark, the Match Boy *by Horatio Alger, Jr., Collier Books, 1962, pp. 5-33.*

JOHN TEBBEL   (essay date 1963)

[From Rags to Riches: Horatio Alger, Jr., and The American Dream, *from which the following excerpt is taken, is a biographical and critical study in which Tebbel relies explicitly on Herbert R. Mayes's* Alger: A Biography Without a Hero. *Tebbel's study contains plot summaries of several of Alger's stories, including* Frank's Campaign, Ragged Dick, *and* Helen Ford, *as well as a bibliography of his works. Here, Tebbel assesses Alger's role as a reformer during the Gilded Age and discusses his conflicting attitudes toward the wealthy.*]

[Nearly all of Alger's books] are derived directly or indirectly from the author's involvement with the Newsboys' Lodging House, where he found an endless source of material and a psychological satisfaction which could well be the subject of psychoanalytic theorizing. Alger loved these boys, spent most of his later years with them, and through their confidences

learned in detail about the lives of street urchins, both before and after they came to New York. These facts, which he used freely in his fiction with little alteration, comprise a valuable social documentation which is often reminiscent of Dickens. Unfortunately, Alger had no compulsion to explore and probe, nor did he have the intellect to make his books the major reform novels they might have been. He could do no more than cast his stories into a single mold, and repeat the pattern endlessly because it was so wildly successful and the public clamored for more. (pp. 10-11)

Did growing boys in an expanding America love [Alger's] rags-to-riches formula because it excited their ambition and moved them to emulate it? That is the popular belief, but a closer reading and analysis of the Alger volumes leads to the suspicion that this was not the case. For beneath the stilted prose, the ponderous moralizing and the melodramatic plotting of Horatio Alger's books lurks the astonishing implication that the author himself did not believe in the American Dream and distrusted his own formula. He may have been selling something quite different to his young audience, whose members recognized it and whose elders were too obtuse to see beyond "Holy Horatio's" moral preachments.

Consider the stuff of which these books are made, and the kind of audience which was reading them so avidly. Fundamentally Alger's stories were about life in New York, except for those whose locales were California, Australia, the world of the traveling circus or some other equally strange and exciting environment. What could have been more fascinating to the millions of boys in the villages, towns and cities of America, earthbound by the lack of airplanes and automobiles? As late as the end of the first quarter of this century, there remained those millions in the small towns and on the farms who thought of New York City as their fathers and grandfathers had envisioned it—as the great, wicked metropolis, full of forbidden pleasures, the eyrie of the rich and powerful, the center of the universe. (p. 12)

For his eager provincial readers, Alger wrote about New York with something of the same wonder he had brought to the city from his native Massachusetts. . . . There was little of the real New York in Alger's books, but there was enough of it to titillate his young and unsophisticated readers. He gave them the sordid details as long as relations between men and women were not concerned; the prudery of his tales approaches the pathological. His descriptions of life in the city are parochial and almost wholly lacking in insight, with a few exceptions, but since his readers had nothing on which to base a comparison, they accepted uncritically and avidly what he *did* give them.

Against this background of myriad fascinations, Alger spun stories ideally suited to the fantasies of boys growing up in that time and place. How many millions of them must have dreamed of being in the Great City, poor but honest, hungry but talented, with the whole metropolitan oyster waiting to be opened. . . . [To] the Alger hero, [experience] meant getting ahead in the world and possibly amassing a fortune, in the authentic nineteenth-century manner. Cannily, Alger never carried the fantasy to the point of realization, except for a page or two of summary at the end. His young readers could understand and appreciate the agonies of the rise, because they were relatively poor and struggling upward themselves, wherever they might be in their commonplace environments, but they could no more comprehend the world of fulfillment than

Alger himself, who had not the slightest understanding of the rich and successful.

To his devoted readers, then, Alger gave a combination of exotic background and simple wish fulfillment related in terms anyone with no more than an eighth-grade education could understand. This was the real secret of his success. When he had exhausted New York, he turned to far places which boys would find as intriguing. Australia was as far away as the moon to most of them, and to read of it was like reading science fiction in another generation. As for California, it had been the place since 1849 where a man could go to seek his fortune. To "go West" was another boyhood dream on which Alger shrewdly capitalized. (pp. 13-14)

[If] money, material success, is the pinnacle of human accomplishment, as Alger and nineteenth-century society believed, the author's attitude toward those who have achieved it is difficult to understand. With the exception of those rich and successful men who befriend poor boys, exuding platitudes in an unctuous and sententious stream as they do so, the rich do not come off well in Alger's books. They are often shown as grasping and mean, conniving and not above any unscrupulous measure to acquire more wealth. Nor are their progeny much better. Rich boys in Alger novels are often cast as villains. Their idle ways and arrogance are contrasted with the straightforward, honest simplicity of the poor boys.

Alger frequently tries to find an excuse for such behavior. The sneering, ill-mannered rich boys are said to have been deprived of a mother's love at an early age, or they have been spoiled by an overindulgent father. Again, Alger draws a curious moral line between struggling for material success and simple greed. His good rich men go to church regularly and practice charity, albeit in rather small doses. The bad ones think about nothing except money, and how to get more of it.

As though this were not enough, Alger frequently deplores the idle life of the idle rich in their Fifth Avenue mansions, contrasting it with the misery all around them in New York. Here, one supposes, Alger was betrayed by the plain facts of life he saw about him every day. The rich were, for the most part, ostentatious, grasping, idle, unscrupulous and all the other things he said of them. In the absence of a large middle business and professional class, most other New Yorkers lived in circumstances ranging from grinding poverty to humble struggle. They were, in fact, no more virtuous than the rich, by and large, but Alger depicted them as living in an atmosphere of sweetness and light, content with their simple lives because their hearts were pure. Yet Alger implies that they would be happier with money. Whenever a hero is elevated to fortune, the epilogue discloses him as dispensing enough largesse to less fortunate relatives or friends so that they will be able to live in circumstances approximating his own.

These contradictions and others make it impossible to take Alger seriously, if anyone were tempted to do so. Andrew Carnegie was a far better prophet of the American Dream than Alger because he had traveled the distance from poverty to wealth, understood both worlds, and was able to write about them realistically. Moreover, his idealism was on a far higher plane that that of Alger, who talked vaguely about philanthropy in his books and gave his own money away with no sense of direction, or even of common providence. Carnegie believed in the American Dream—that a boy could rise, as he had, to wealth and position, but for him that was not the end of it. A

rich man, he said, at that point had an obligation to society to use his wealth for the betterment of mankind.

It is ironic that Alger lived in an era when there were enough real products of the American Dream to provide examples for any ambitious boy, yet he could only create the fantasy world of rags to riches, which nevertheless made him successful because it was also the fantasy of so many American boys. He might have written about the careers of such eminences as Peter A. B. Widener and Gustavus Franklin Swift, who rose from meat markets to wealth; or of Thomas Fortune Ryan, who began as an orphaned and penniless boy on a Virginia farm and in twenty years had a seat on the New York Stock Exchange; or John D. Rockefeller, a boy from an Ohio village who became one of the nation's first billionaires. These examples were everywhere in nineteenth-century America, yet Alger wrote about the street boys of New York and their melodramatic, implausible rises to fortune, which in fact actually occurred to a negligible number of them. (pp. 14-16)

> *John Tebbel, in his* From Rags to Riches: Horatio Alger, Jr., and The American Dream, *The Macmillan Company, 1963, 245 p.*

JOHN G. CAWELTI (essay date 1965)

[*One of the first commentators to argue that Alger's works belie the "rags to riches" myth with which his name has become synonymous, Cawelti challenges Kenneth S. Lynn's promotion of Alger as a spokesman for the American dream of success (see excerpt above, 1955). He dismisses the notion that Alger was an exponent of individualistic free enterprise and contends that his heroes aspire to middle-class respectability, a point that is repeated by Michael Zuckerman (1972), Frank Shuffelton (1976), and Gary Scharnhorst (1980). Rejecting the argument advanced by Frederick Lewis Allen (1938), Richard Wright (1945), and Lynn that Alger exalted the commercial practices of his age, Cawelti maintains that Alger reasserted the economic ideals of the eighteenth century, when American business was dominated by small mercantile establishments.*]

Alger's contemporary position as a symbol of individualistic free enterprise has obscured the actual characteristics of his stories. A number of misconceptions must be cleared away before we can get to the heart of the Alger version of what constitutes success. Here, for example, is a typical interpretation of the Alger hero [by Kenneth S. Lynn (see excerpt above, 1955)]:

> Alone, unaided, the ragged boy is plunged into the maelstrom of city life, but by his own pluck and luck he capitalizes on one of the myriad opportunities available to him and rises to the top of the economic heap. Here, in a nutshell, is the plot of every novel Alger ever wrote; here, too, is the quintessence of the myth. Like many simple formulations which nevertheless convey a heavy intellectual and emotional charge to vast numbers of people, the Alger hero represents a triumphant combination—and reduction to the lowest common denominator—of the most widely accepted concepts in nineteenth-century American society. The belief in the potential greatness of the common man, the glorification of individual effort and accomplishment, the equation of the pursuit of money with the pursuit of happiness and of business success with spiritual grace: simply to mention

Title page of the Luck and Pluck *series. Courtesy of Prints and Photographs Division, Library of Congress.*

> these concepts is to comprehend the brilliance
> of Alger's synthesis.

This passage illustrates several important misconceptions concerning Alger's books. In the first place, Alger's heroes are rarely "alone and unaided," and do not win their success entirely through individual effort and accomplishment. From the very beginning of his career, the Alger boy demonstrates an astounding propensity for chance encounters with benevolent and useful friends, and his success is largely due to their patronage and assistance. In the course of his duties Fred Fenton, the hero of *The Erie Train Boy,* meets a wealthy young girl named Isabel Archer—presumably named in homage to Alger's literary idol, Henry James—who gives him money to pay his mother's rent. In addition, he encounters an eccentric miner, who later helps him sell some land belonging to his late father, and the uncle of a wealthy broker, who gives young Fred his chance in business. Alger's heroes are well aware of their indebtedness to these patrons, and modestly make no pretense of success through their own efforts, although Alger assures his readers that they deserve their advancement. (pp. 108-09)

Nor did the Alger hero rise "to the top of the economic heap." . . . Usually the hero is established in a secure white-collar position, either as a clerk with the promise of a junior part-

nership or as a junior member of a successful mercantile establishment. None achieve anything resembling economic or political prominence. Moderate economic security would best summarize the pecuniary achievements of the typical Alger hero, in spite of such tantalizing titles as *Fame and Fortune, Striving for Fortune,* and *From Farm to Fortune.* For example, at the end of *Fame and Fortune,* the hero is in possession of a magnificent income of $1,400 a year, plus the interest on about $2,000 in savings. In Alger's mind, this was "fame and fortune."

We may admit that Alger's representation of economic reality was highly sentimentalized, but it is unfair to call him an uninhibited adulator of wealth who equated spiritual grace with business success. The true aim of the Alger hero is respectability, a happy state only partially defined by economic repute. Nor was Alger unaware that many men were successful as the result of questionable practices. He may have lacked knowledge of these practices, but Alger frequently reminded his readers that many wealthy and successful men were undeserving of their fortunes. One of his favorite villains is the wealthy, unscrupulous banker who accumulates wealth by cheating widows and orphans. On the whole, Alger's formula is more accurately stated as middle-class respectability equals spiritual grace.

Alger was no more an unrestrained advocate of the "potential greatness" of the common man than he was of the uninhibited pursuit of financial success. His heroes are ordinary boys only in the sense of their lowly origin. In ability and personal character they are far above average. Many boys in the Alger books are unable, in spite of their earnest efforts, to rise above a lowly position. Micky McGuire, a young slum boy who is a secondary character in the *Ragged Dick* series, is reformed at last through the efforts of Dick and his patron Mr. Rockwell. But the old maxim "No Irish Need Apply" still held for Alger.

> Micky has already turned out much better than
> was expected, but he is hardly likely to rise
> much higher than the subordinate position he
> now occupies. In capacity and education he is
> far inferior to his old associate, Richard Hunter,
> who is destined to rise much higher than at
> present.

Who, then, is the Alger hero, and what is the nature of the adventures in which he is involved? Alger has two types of heroes. The first, and probably the more popular, is the poor, uneducated street boy—sometimes an orphan, more frequently the son of a widowed mother—who rises to moderate affluence. The second is a well-born and well-educated middle-class youth whose father dies, leaving the son to fend for himself. In some cases a villainous squire or distant relative attempts to cheat the hero out of his rightful legacy, but, in the end, the hero is restored to his inheritance or succeeds in rising to his proper place.

Alger made desultory attempts to vary the character of his hero in each story, but such an achievement was beyond his skill, and the reader could be certain that, whatever the situation, and whether the hero smokes or uses slangy language, the same solid core of virtue is present. Alger's heroes, who range in age from around twelve to eighteen, are in the tradition of the didactic novels of self-improvement. One must give Alger some credit for making his young paragons a little less earnest and more lively than the placid prigs of T. S. Arthur. The Alger hero might begin as an intemperate spendthrift like Ragged

Dick, but soon he becomes a master of the traditional virtues of industry, economy, integrity, and piety. He is manly and self-reliant—two of Alger's favorite words—and, in addition, kind and generous. Never a genius, he is usually a boy of above-average intelligence, particularly in the area of mathematics, and is also a strenuous devotee of self-culture. The Alger hero is never snobbish or condescending; indeed, he is the veritable apotheosis of modesty. Thoroughly democratic in his tastes, he befriends other poor boys and is uniformly courteous to people of all classes. The Alger hero demonstrates to a high degree those traits that might be called the employee virtues: fidelity, punctuality, and courteous deference. It is upon these latter traits that Alger places the greatest stress.

Against his hero, Alger sets three types of boys who serve as foils to the hero's sterling qualities. One of these may be called the lesser hero. He is usually a slightly younger and less vigorous edition of the major figure. The lesser hero often has greater advantages than his friend, but he lacks the enterprise, the courage, and the self-reliance of the hero, and frequently depends on him for protection against the harsh urban world, enabling the hero to demonstrate his courage and generosity. Another boy who appears in almost all the Alger books is the snob. . . . The young snob shows the obverse of all the hero's virtues: he is lazy, ignorant, arrogant, and unwilling to work because he considers it beneath his station. He is overtly contemptuous and secretly envious of the hero's successes. Alger delights in foiling this little monster, usually by arranging for his father to fail in business, thereby forcing the snob to go to work at a salary lower than the hero's.

Another type appearing somewhat less frequently in the Alger books is the poor boy who lacks the intelligence and ability of the hero and is more susceptible to the corruption of his environment. Often he becomes involved in plots against the hero, but is usually won over when he recognizes his true manliness and forgiving character. Although sometimes reformed through the hero's efforts, the Micky McGuire type is doomed to remain in a subordinate but respectable position by his lack of intelligence and enterprise. Curiously enough, these dim-minded characters are Alger's most interesting and vivid creations, and foreshadow the "bad boy" heroes of later juvenile books. In addition, they frequently represent immigrant groups—Irish, Italians, Germans—who, not all bad, play a distinctly inferior role in Alger's version of America. (pp. 109-13)

The benevolent merchant, the villainous father-figure, and the gentle and appreciative mother are at the center of most Alger books. They are joined by a variety of minor figures, all of whom can be traced to the traditional stereotypes of the sentimental novel: the warm-hearted Irish woman, poor and crude, kind and generous, who helps the hero escape from the villain; the snobbish female with aristocratic pretensions; the "stage Yankee" who appears in an occasional novel as a friend of the hero; and a variety of minor villains, such as the miserly moneylender, the petty swindler, and, in the Western stories, the stagecoach robber.

From such material, together with carefully accumulated local color—the books are filled with detailed descriptions of New York City—Alger constructed his tales. . . . In generating the action, chance and luck play a dominant role. Alger was apparently aware that the unbelievable tissue of coincidences which ran through his stories put some strain on the tolerance of his youthful readers. In *Struggling Upward,* for example, Linton Tomkins, the lesser hero, chances upon practically every other character in the book in the course of a twenty-minute

promenade. Somewhat amazed at this feat, Alger can only remark that "Linton was destined to meet plenty of acquaintances." . . . However much the hero's good qualities may have been involved, and they often seem incidental, Alger is obsessed with luck. The chapter which contains the crucial turning point of the book is invariably entitled————'s Luck, and every accession to the hero's fortunes stems from a coincidence. . . . (pp. 114-15)

Alger's emphasis on luck resembles that found in the stories of T. S. Arthur and other apostles of the self-made man in the pre-Civil War era. Like them, he represents American society as an environment in which sudden and unaccountable prosperity frequently comes to the deserving like manna from heaven. To some extent, this reliance on luck or Providence is a literary short-coming. Both Alger and Arthur turned out books at a tremendous rate; sloppiness and inadequacies in plotting and motivation could be concealed in part by defending coincidence. Furthermore, accident, luck, and chance have always played a large role in folk and popular literature, for they allow for exciting plot manipulation and the maintenance of suspense. It is equally true that the form which the accidental takes in a given work is some indication of the beliefs of an author and his intended audience. (p. 116)

Alger ignores the religious implications of the accidental. In his stories, luck is seemingly independent of the divine, inhering in the particular social environment of America, with its absence of hereditary class distinctions and the freedom it allows. Because most of the great merchants had been poor boys themselves, they were always on the lookout for deserving young men to assist. If the hero has the daring and self-assurance to seize one of his many opportunities to come to the attention of a benevolent patron, and is also blessed with the virtues of industry, fidelity, and good manners, he is certain to get ahead.

Religion itself does not play a major role in the life of the Alger hero. His heroes pray and go to Sunday School willingly enough, but Alger places greater stress on their obligations to others—loyalty to family and employer, and personal assistance to the less fortunate. His books encourage humanitarianism in their emphasis on practical good works and frequent insistence that Americans extend opportunities for worldly success to the juvenile proletariat of the cities. Although, like most writers in the tradition of self-improvement, Alger attributes success and failure to qualities within the individual, he occasionally points out to his young readers that a stifling and corrupting environment can be a major cause of vice and failure. An important factor in the rise of his streetboy heroes is their removal from the streets, where, if they remain, moral decay and poverty are certain. Alger can hardly be granted a profound understanding of the contemporary scene, but sympathy for the underprivileged is strong in his books. Judging from the prominence of his themes, there is as much evidence that Alger was an important influence on future reformers as a popular model for incipient robber barons.

Luck is not the only element in the success of the Alger hero. He has to deserve his luck by manifesting certain important traits which show him to be a fit candidate for a higher place in society. He carries the full complement of middle-class virtues, but these are not solely industry, frugality, and piety. Far more important are those qualities of character and intellect which make the hero a good employee and a reputable member of middle-class society. To his hero's cultivation of these qualities Alger devotes much of his attention. The hero has to learn how to dress neatly and modestly, to eliminate slang and colloquialisms from his speech, and to develop a facility with the stilted and pretentious language that Alger took to be the proper medium of verbal intercourse among respectable Americans. In addition, he has to educate himself. Alger's conception of the liberally educated man is also closely tied to social respectability. It is particularly desirable for the hero to have a neat hand and mathematical ability, but it is also important that he show a smattering of traditional culture. A foreign language is usually the prescribed curriculum. Ragged Dick studies French, for example. Since a foreign language plays no part in the hero's economic life, it is apparently intended by Alger as a certificate of a certain kind of respectability. The ability to learn French or Latin, although he might never have an opportunity to use such a skill, shows that the hero has a respect for learning as an end in itself and is no mere materialist. Thus, the Alger hero is a pale reflection of the ideal of self-culture as well as a devotee of rising in society. (pp. 116-18)

Placed against Emerson and his philosophy of self-reliance, Alger is simply another exponent of the idealized version of the self-made man found in the novels of T. S. Arthur, Sylvester Judd, and other sentimentalists of the 1840's and 1850's. His understanding of social mobility is on the same level of abstracton and idealization. Emerson, in comparison, has a much more profound understanding of the implications of social mobility and the actual characteristics likely to lead to economic and social advancement, as well as a broader ideal of self-culture. It is as true of Alger as of Arthur that he presents the mobile society through the rose-colored glasses of the middle-class ethical tradition of industry, frugality, and integrity, and the sentimental Christian version of a benevolent Providence.

The great attainment of Alger's hero is to leave the ranks of the "working class" and become an owner or partner in a business of his own. Yet few of Alger's heroes have any connection with such enterprises as mining, manufacturing, or construction, the industries in which most of the large fortunes of the late nineteenth century were made. Alger's favorite reward is a junior partnership in a respectable mercantile house. This emphasis is a throwback to the economic life of an earlier period, when American business was still dominated by merchants whose economic behavior in retrospect seemed refined and benevolent in comparison to the devastating strategies of transcontinental railroad builders, iron and steel manufacturers, and other corporate giants. Alger's version of success is, in effect, a reassertion of the values of a bygone era in an age of dramatic change and expansion. (pp. 119-20)

Alger is a teacher of traditional manners and morals rather than an exponent of free enterprise. His fictions embody the values that middle-class Americans have been taught to revere: honesty, hard work, familial loyalty; good manners, cleanliness, and neatness of appearance; kindness and generosity to the less fortunate; loyalty and deference on the part of employees, and consideration and personal interest on the part of employers. These "bourgeois virtues" are strenuously displayed by the Alger hero and his benevolent patron, along with that strong respect for education and self-culture which is a considerable part of the middle-class heritage. On the other hand, the Alger villains represent those vices particularly reprehensible to many nineteenth-century Americans: they have aristocratic pretensions and try to adopt the airs of the leisure-class; they frequent theaters and gaming houses and are intemperate; they are disloyal to their families and often try to cheat their relatives; they

are avaricious, miserly, and usurious; and they lack integrity and are unscrupulous in business affairs. The conflict between middle-class virtues and vices is played out against a background of unlimited opportunities in which the virtues ultimately show themselves to be indispensable and the vices trip up their possessors.

At the time when Alger wrote, traditional commercial practices and ethics had been undermined by economic expansion. A lifetime of hard work often left a man worse off than when he began. The growing gulf between millionaire and employee and the increasing development of complex economic hierarchies were so circumscribing individual ownership and control that a clerk was better off working for others than attempting to found and operate his own business. Alger reasserts an older economic model, one that had begun to be out of date as early as 1830, but which still lingered in the minds of Americans as the ideal form of economic organization: a multiplicity of small individual businesses or partnerships. He certainly had little idea of the actuality of business enterprise in his day—nowhere in his novels do industrial corporations or the character types they produce appear—but he does have enough personal knowledge of New York City to give a certain plausibility and contemporaneity to his representation of American life. He is able to present the traditional pattern of middle-class economic ideals in late nineteenth-century dress and fill the bustling streets and thoroughfares of a nineteenth-century industrial metropolis with a nostalgic reincarnation of the ideal *eighteenth-century* merchant and his noble young apprentice. This moral and economic anachronism is an important source of Alger's popularity with adults. When, a generation or so later, the accumulation of social and economic change made it no longer tenable, even in fantasy, the books began to come down from the library shelves, classed as unrealistic and misleading, perhaps even dangerous, fairy tales.

Although parents encouraged their children to read Alger because he seemed to reassert the validity of hard work, economy, integrity, and family loyalty, this is probably not the source of his popularity with young boys. There were a great many reasons why children liked Alger. He writes of places that they were interested in. In these locales he places a set of characters whose activities have enough of the fantastic and unusual to be exciting, yet always retain enough connection with the ordinary activities of American boys to encourage an emotionally satisfying empathy. . . . Furthermore, Alger has a simple and unsophisticated sense of justice, which punishes the enemies of boyhood. The snobs, the bullies, the uncles and spinster aunts who do not like boys get their comeuppances in ways that must have appealed to a juvenile audience. Alger is hardly a master stylist, but his narrative and dialogue are simple, clear, and relatively fast-moving; and his diction, if formal and stilted, is not arcane or difficult.

These elements were undoubtedly important factors in Alger's popularity with his juvenile audience; and there was a further dimension to the Alger formula. Legion are the dangers of Freudian interpretation of literary works, but Alger cries out for this kind of treatment. . . . When we recall that the late nineteenth century was an era of relatively strict paternal discipline and control, it does not seem far-fetched to suggest that the Alger books may have been appreciated as phantasies of father-elimination. The rapid decline in the popularity of Alger books after World War I probably resulted in part from the changing character of familial relationships in the twenties and thirties. When new ideals of parent-child relationship became generally accepted, the Alger hero's victory over the villainous father-figure must have lost much of its bite. (pp. 121-23)

John G. Cawelti, "From Rags to Respectability: Horatio Alger," in his Apostles of the Self-Made Man, *The University of Chicago Press, 1965, pp. 101-23.*

MARCUS KLEIN (essay date 1967)

Alger's heroes do contain one complication of character, and it amounts to a thorough and constant irony. In it, it is to be suspected, is the attraction that drew [Alger's readers]. Alger's heroes speak the little capitalist pieties without cease. They are champions of neatness, punctuality, the fair exchange for an honest dollar. At the same time, however, either by origin or by some seeming mischief of chance, they are entirely disreputable. They are bootblacks or newsboys, only just not child beggars. In a favorite device, they are lost heirs who have been raised and educated by thieves. Or, what comes almost to the same thing, they are dispossessed heirs who are forced for a period to hit the streets.

If they say that they aspire to the middle classes and act appropriately, it is to be seen that they act deliberately, while it is the source of their energy and indeed the basis for their real virtue that they are not of the middle classes. They are not even lowly, but just out of things. They are prowlers in the city. Virtually by definition they are the unseen. When the Alger heroes are street boys by origin, which is to say when they are most pure, they speak a different language. Alger always apologizes for it, but he continuously exhibits it. The heroes do not lie, cheat, or steal, but they are in touch with those who do. Their surrogate fathers are likely to be burglars. Even when the heroes are dispossessed heirs, it is the whole function of Alger's story to put them into the nourishing tenement. And it is after all to the point that Alger's boys undergo no convincing moral development. Because they are not and do not become what they seem, they propose irreconcilable conflict.

Alger was blandly abstract about everything except for the racy, ratty, sheer existence of these boys, the amounts of money they make, and the usual locale of their action, New York. When Alger moves away from New York, he falls into his usual vagueness, but when he is on his scene the novels suddenly have street names and physical landmarks, and one of the few things Alger is able to prove dramatically is that his heroes know their way around New York. The fact implies something more than geography. They are city-wise. They are at home in the debris of the city—when we first see Ragged Dick, he is rising from his bed; he lives in Spruce Street in a wooden box. If Alger draws the specific conclusion merely that his heroes are rough and ready, it is anyway a part of the given case that they are something beyond that. They are potentially vicious. That is their glamor. They know the lower law.

And when these boys set out to make their way in the world—rehearsing the pieties at every step, encouraged by their endlessly homiletic author—they might well stir the imagination of a youngster by their very implication that they are cynical and subversive. They are sinister young con men, no matter what Horatio Alger said. (p. 54)

Marcus Klein, "The Homilies of Horatio," in The Reporter, *Vol. 37, No. 3, September 7, 1967, pp. 53-4.*

RICHARD WEISS (essay date 1968)

An examination of the Alger books belies the Alger myth. If his works reflect the spirit of a particular time, it was not the spirit of the gilded age.

Alger spoke very much as Ben Franklin had. He urged his readers not to smoke or drink, nor to stay up late, not to attend theaters or other places of entertainment. He preached frugality, hard work, and saving. He also told his readers to study and seek refinement and to be good to their mothers.

In one significant way, however, Alger departed from the traditional formulation of the Protestant notion of success. That was in his repeated emphasis on luck, an element that the Protestant ethic did not admit. His heroes all achieve wealth through a stroke of fortune.... They never make fortunes; they always find them. Alger himself admits that virtue does not always bring material rewards, though luck never comes to the wicked. Luck is always earned by those who have it, though it is not always had by those who have earned it. This resembles the Puritan notion of salvation. The saved are always virtuous, but the virtuous are not always saved. Alger's failures are not always wicked boys, either. Lack of ambition, energy, physical strength often retard the upward movement of his characters, who, while virtuous, will never "make it." (p. 308)

One receives the impression in reading his books that their inspirational quality springs more from a dread of despair than from a belief in opportunity. Confronted with the horrors of poverty, Alger attempted to give solace. Like other conscience-stricken members of his class, he was unable to view the consequences of industrialization with indifference. Most disturbing of these consequences was the plight of children. Youngsters surrounded by poverty and sickness needed something to sustain them in their early years. Deprived of virtually all material comforts, they must at least be given the hope of a better future. The popular tradition of mobility in American society provided a convenient means of doing so.

Both Alger's distaste for the results of industrialism and his assertion of the Protestant virtues are much more akin to the middle-class reform mentality of the period than to the naked acquisitiveness of the "man on the make." It is interesting to note that in terms of background, Alger fits the pattern of the genteel reformer rather well. He was born into a comfortable New England family, was educated at Harvard, and was the son of a Unitarian minister. He shared other characteristics of genteel reformers, among them a preference for Anglo-Saxons. Frequently, the ne'er-do-wells in his stories are "dark," as is Jasper in *Tom the Bootblack,* who is also "effeminate in appearance," "smooth, deceitful, and vain, running to dissipation, as far as he had opportunity." This is inconsistent with his attitude toward Italian street urchins in *Phil the Fiddler,* and it seems his bias sometimes conflicted with his humane inclination. For the most part, however, Alger's heroes are of rural American background, so the conflict is not often evident. Alger avoids dealing with the problem of the immigrants, who rarely appeared in his books.

Another facet of Alger's racial attitudes that appears in some of his works is the implicit belief in a kind of hereditary determinism.... Again, this seems inconsistent with Alger's notions of mobility.... One of the best examples of this hereditary determinism appears in *Jed, the Poorhouse Boy.* The hero, raised in a home for paupers and subject to all the degradations of such an upbringing, is a perfect gentleman. His manners would be the pride of any mother and his virtue in all things is beyond reproach. The mystery of a boy of such fine breeding, raised in such low circumstances, is finally dispelled by the revelation of his noble origins. . . . This belief in virtue transmitted through the blood provides one of the reasons for all of Alger's characters being orphaned. Poor boys are not likely to be the sons of good men who are alive. The absence of a father conveniently removes the problem of reconciling indigence with virtue.

Alger's settings are most often in the New York of the latter half of the nineteenth century, and his accurate descriptions of its streets, hotels, boardinghouses, and restaurants made his books valuable as guides to those unfamiliar with the city. But his attitude toward the city he described so well was one of hostility. While the city was a place of opportunity, it also was a place of unspeakable immorality. Virtue resided in the country. If the country boy could survive the city swindlers ready to prey on his innocence, his chances of success were greater than those of his city-bred equivalents. This was because he was usually stronger morally and had ''been brought up to work, and work more earnestly than the city boys.'' Country boys might come to the city to gain wealth, but city boys could well go to the country for moral regeneration. Alger also warned that ''of the tens of thousands who come from the country to seek clerkships, but a very small proportion rise above a small income.'' For the majority, it would be best to remain home. (pp. 309-11)

Alger's ideal differs in other important respects from the realities of the time. His heroes are never children of workers. They are generally impoverished through the death of their father, who was of the middle class. If their middle-class origins are not known, as in the case of Ragged Dick, their backgrounds are obscured altogether. (p. 312)

Alger's choice of benefactors reveals his nostalgia for the ''good old days.'' They are engaged in mercantile rather than industrial enterprises. The idealization of the benevolent merchant is hardly an accurate reflection of an age where industrial wealth predominated. It does, however, correspond to the widespread belief that the older form of enterprise honed finer character than the new.

None of Alger's heroes exhibits the aggressive acquisitiveness of the time. All are patient and virtuous, akin to the less grasping nature of the ideal man before the Civil War. The moderate fortunes his heroes accumulate are usually measured in five figures. Alger shared the distaste of the genteel middle class, which looked with disdain on the rise of the ''New Moguls,'' whose practice of ''Wall Street speculation'' was ''more dangerous even than extravagant habits of living.'' Alger never mentions the millionaire in his stories and never urges the accumulation of great wealth as a worthy ambition. (pp. 312-13)

[Some critics have] made Alger a symbol of the Gilded Age. Implicit in Alger's own work is a critique of the post-Civil War period—of industrialization, urbanization, mammoth fortunes, and the general decline of morals. His stories bespeak a belief in a society where men reaped the fruits of their labor according to their merit. Nothing could have been more alien to Alger than the extremes of wealth and poverty that were characteristic of this period. The social conflict generated by the new order also disturbed him. Alger's work reflects an attempt to recreate the more harmonious society in which he was raised. His heroes come from another time, another society, another reality. Rather than extol the dominant values of his day, he reacted against them. His books exalted a time

gone by, when the middle class had played the major role in American life. . . .

Straddling the worlds of the rural countryside and the urban metropolis, the Alger stories preserved the purity of the one while conveying the excitement of the other. In these stories, readers might find the reconciliation between different modes of life reality so harshly denied. People uprooted by the eddies of change found a kindred spirit in Alger, who, like them, was a stranger in a new society. (p. 313)

> Richard Weiss, ''Horatio Alger, Jr., and the Response to Industrialism,'' in The Age of Industrialism in America: Essays in Social Structure and Cultural Values, edited by Frederic Cople Jaher, The Free Press, 1968, pp. 304-16.

MALCOLM COWLEY (essay date 1970)

[*An American critic, editor, poet, translator, and historian, Cowley has made valuable contributions to contemporary letters with his editions of the works of such American authors as Nathaniel Hawthorne, Walt Whitman, and Ernest Hemingway, his writings as a literary critic for the* New Republic, *and his chronicles and criticism of modern American literature. His discussion of Alger's life and works is based on Herbert R. Mayes's* Alger: A Biography Without a Hero. *Like Norman N. Holland (1959-60), Cowley views the typical Alger story as a symbol of the author's lifelong attempt to supplant his own father. According to Cowley, Alger sought vengeance on his father by making many of his heroes orphans, attributing Horatio Alger, Sr.'s worst characteristics to his stories' villains, and providing his heroes with benevolent patrons to replace their fathers.*]

A very few of [Alger's] novels were written with a social purpose. Thus, ***Phil the Fiddler*** . . . is a memorial to the crusade that Alger led against the *padrone* system, by which hundreds of street musicians brought to New York from southern Italy were kept as virtual slaves. . . . The book helped to make the system illegal. ***Jed, the Poorhouse Boy*** . . . was intended to call attention to the plight of pauper children, and its early chapters bear a wraithlike resemblance to [Charles Dickens's novel] *Oliver Twist*. Jed himself is something of a scapegrace and has a sharper tongue than Alger's other heroes, besides an even greater talent for finding rich protectors. Skeptical readers might call the book *A Fagot's Progress*. But Phil and Jed are his boldest experiments in character, and most of his other heroes are stamped from the same metal with the same patented Alger die. (p. 80)

[Alger's books] can be read with some interest even today. . . . The style is formal to the point of burlesque, but correct except for a few Yankeeisms (''considerable'' as an adverb, for example) and absolutely clear; it shows the results of Alger's classical training. The chapters are short and consist chiefly of dialogue, which is sometimes so innocent that it acquires a double meaning. (''I want to show you some engravings,'' says the rich Miss Davenport to the hero of ***Tom Temple's Career***.) Still, the dialogue moves rapidly and is not without conscious humor of the sort one used to hear when boys were talking together outside a village store. Here is a fair sample from ***Ragged Dick***:

> One of the boys, a rather supercilious-looking young gentleman, genteelly dressed, and evidently having a very high opinion of his dress and himself, turned suddenly to Dick and remarked:

"SMASH YER BAGGAGE, MUM?"

Illustration from Ben, the Luggage Boy. *The Granger Collection, New York.*

"I've seen you before."

"Oh, have you?" said Dick, whirling around; "then p'r'aps you'd like to see me behind."

At this unexpected answer all the boys burst into a laugh with the exception of the questioner, who evidently considered that Dick had been disrespectful.

"I've seen you somewhere," he said in a surly tone, correcting himself.

"Most likely you have," said Dick. "That's where I generally keep myself."

Humor apart, the Alger books offer a curious picture of American culture after the Civil War. In the rather bleak world to which they introduce us, there is no art whatever, except that sometimes a young girl plays "Hearts and Flowers" on a square piano. There is no learning beyond the ability to read and cipher and, as all his heroes do, to write a flowing hand. There is no history: it is as if New York and the whole country from New England to the California diggings had been created overnight, with the excavations raw and the scaffolding still in place. Though Alger was an ordained clergyman, there is hardly a trace of religious feeling in his novels. Some of the heroes go to Sunday school, like Ragged Dick, but that is only because one of the teachers is a rich merchant who might help them to rise in the world. Here, from a book called **Hector's Inheritance,** is a sample of Alger's moral teaching:

"Have you any taste for any kind of liquor?"

"No, sir," answered Hector promptly.

"Even if you had, do you think you would have self-control enough to avoid entering saloons and gratifying your tastes?"

"Yes, sir."

"That is well. Do you play pool?"

"No sir," answered Hector, wondering whither all these questions tended.

"I ask because playing pool in public places paves the way for intemperance, as bars are generally connected with such establishments."

Playing pool is also a form of idleness, which leads to stealing, which sometimes leads to jail, but more often to poverty, the hell to which villains are assigned by his Yankee theology. His heaven is simply earning or being given a fortune (but always a modest one, for Alger himself had simple desires and a perfect ignorance of financial practices). Still, everything in his world has its cash value, and a boy who earns ten dollars a week rightly considers himself twice as good as a boy who earns five dollars a week. (pp. 81-3)

The world of [Alger's] novels is full of bullies, petty thieves, and confidence men. Even in the New England villages where most of his heroes are born, the leading citizen is likely to be a dishonest banker who steals the property of widows and orphans. Yet the same villages have their benevolent doctors, their self-sacrificing mothers; and the sturdy little hero, left homeless in the streets of New York, is certain to find a kind old merchant who buys him clothes and a watch. For all its bleakness, Alger's world is suffused with the optimism and faith in human nature of America in the Gilded Age. It is also suffused with a deep feeling of equality: family doesn't matter, trade or profession doesn't matter, national origin matters a little, but not a great deal; in the end nothing matters but money, and the honest newsboy has a better chance to earn it than a banker's idle son. (p. 83)

In [Alger's] novels the close personal relations are not sexual. They are sometimes fraternal—many of his heroes have beloved younger sisters—but more often they are parental and filial. The boldest approach to sexual passion is in the next-to-last chapter of *Sink or Swim*, which tells how Harry Raymond came back from the Australian gold fields with a fortune of $11,525—"which, for a boy of his age," Alger says, "was certainly a very comfortable capital." Little Maud Lindsay, "a bright, handsome girl of thirteen," was so glad to see him that she flung her arms around him. "Harry was rather embarrassed," Alger says, "at the unexpected warmth of his reception, but felt that it would be impolite not to kiss Maud in return, and accordingly did so." That is the only nonmaternal kiss in the twenty Alger books I have read and possibly in all the books he wrote (though not, I believe, in the posthumous books signed with his name). (p. 84)

Alger did not write down to boys. All the emotions in his novels are those proper to a preadolescent stage of development: rivalry with other boys, shame at wearing patched clothes, day dreams of running away (and of coming back to mother with a fortune), a possessive love for the mother, and rebellion against the wicked squire, who becomes a father symbol. Apparently these are Alger's emotions, obsessively relived instead of being merely remembered. The heroes are compensatory projections of the author, who dreamed of being as resolute as each of them, but who never disengaged himself from a painful family pattern—never, that is, except in the books he wrote for eternal boys like himself. (pp. 84-5)

Every popular novel is also, on one level, a myth or a fairy tale, and most often a very old one. The myth or tale is especially clear in the Alger novel (which is of course one book with seventy or more different titles). . . . Essentially it is the Greek myth of Telemachus, the supposed orphan who is forced to leave home and who sets out in search of a father. It is eventually the father's power, not his own, that restores him to his rightful place. (p. 85)

In Alger's version of the myth, the hero is always fatherless and is always a boy of noble principles. Though he plays the part of a bootblack, a newsboy, or a fiddler, his open and prepossessing features betray his princely nature. Usually he comes from a New England village that takes the place of rocky Ithaca, and his widowed mother is besieged by a wicked squire who assumes the joint role of Penelope's suitors. (p. 86)

Moralists used to complain at the turn of the century that the Alger hero did not earn his fortune by hard work, but had it drop into his lap. What they missed was the fairy-tale logic of the story. The hero is of course a prince in disguise, and he gains his little fortune by discovering the place and parentage that are his by right. Then he once again displays his princely character by rushing home to help his mother. Sometimes the adoptive father or uncle comes with him. "You need be under no anxiety about Luke and his prospects," the merchant says to the mother at the end of *Struggling Upward*. "I shall make over to him $10,000 at once, constituting myself his guardian, and will see that he is well started in business." Sometimes—for example, in *Sink or Swim*—the hero arrives on the very morning of the day when his mother is to be married to the wicked squire, but then he takes out a roll of greenbacks and Squire Turner slinks away. As for the end of Alger's story—

> My readers [he says] may like to know how James Turner turned out in life. [James is the squire's idle and malicious son.] A year since, he obtained the situation of teller in a bank, his father standing surety for him. He soon developed expensive tastes, and finally disappeared, carrying away thirty thousand dollars of the funds of the bank. This loss his father had to make good, and in consequence he has become a comparatively poor man, and a very sour, morose man at that. . . . So the wheel of fortune has turned and those who were once at the top are now at the bottom.

Virtue has been rewarded, vice punished, and the whole operation has been pecuniary. In that preoccupation with exact sums in dollars, and in that alone, the Alger fable resembles the typical American success story as enacted in fiction or life. There is, however, a difference even here. The robber barons loved money for its own sake and each was determined to have more of it than anyone else. "I'm bound to be rich! *Bound to be rich!*" John D. Rockefeller, Sr. once exclaimed. The Alger hero will never be truly rich, since he has a generous spirit that makes him incapable of clawing and gouging his way into a palace on Fifth Avenue. Money in the Alger novel is chiefly a symbol of other things: emotional security, for example, and affection (as of the adoptive father for his ward, or of the hero for his mother), and manly power. Money is the bow of Ulysses that slays the wicked suitor—though instead of being slain, in the Alger version, the suitor loses his money and hence his virility. The real theme of the Alger novel is not pecuniary but filial and paternal. Alger is revenging himself on his own father three times: first he kills him before the story opens by making the hero an orphan; then he gives Horatio Sr.'s worst traits to the wicked squire; and finally he provides the hero with a father-by-choice to love and understand him. (pp. 86-7)

The real message of the Alger books had a deeper appeal to preadolescent boys than the mere prospect of becoming a money baron. What I cannot understand is how the author of the message—that timid bohemian, that failure by his father's standards and double failure by his own, since he neither wrote a great novel nor amassed even a modest fortune—should come to be regarded as the prophet of business enterprise; nor why the family melodrama that he wrote and rewrote for boys like himself should be confused with the American dream of success. (p. 88)

Malcolm Cowley, "The Real Horatio Alger Story,"
in his A Many-Windowed House: Collected Essays

on American Writers and American Writing, *edited by Henry Dan Piper, Southern Illinois University Press, 1970, pp. 76-88.*

MICHAEL ZUCKERMAN   (essay date 1972)

[*In his review of the* Ragged Dick *series, Zuckerman argues that Alger's works do not sustain the "rags to riches" myth. He contends that beneath Alger's accounts of youthful success lies a less aggressive spirit of business enterprise than many of his critics have recognized. According to Zuckerman, Alger emphasized respectability, dependability, and charity rather than wealth, business acumen, and self-maximization, and he notes that "if Alger's world was a Carnegie world, it was surely not Andrew's but Dale's." Zuckerman also discusses Alger's interest in the "problem of proper parentage." Ultimately, he concludes, "Alger's every novel was a novel of nurturance, a novel whose dearest ideal was to be cared for and indulged, not to be self-sufficient and self-reliant."*]

We have imagined Alger our dreamer of success, our rhapsodist of rags-to-riches, our avatar of the self-made man—and it is true that Alger knew that tune and announced it unfailingly. He just never played it. In his tales success was but a subterfuge, and self-made men were nowhere to be found. Yet Alger was profoundly, even prophetically, American, and the deflected drive of his stories is essential to an understanding of the emergence of American industrial society. (p. 190)

[If the six novels in the Ragged Dick series, **Ragged Dick, Fame and Fortune, Mark, the Match Boy, Rough and Ready, Rufus and Rose,** and **Ben, the Luggage Boy**] seem overdependent on luck, patronage and the deus ex machina, it is because Alger was too. And if they do not emphasize free enterprise, it is because Alger did not do so either. Despite his homilies and preachments, he was simply not very interested in business, and he was certainly no exponent of entrepreneurial individualism. His heroes neither possess nor prosper by the virtues of self-seeking, and Alger never espoused them. To call him a social Darwinist, as so many have done, is an inconceivable canard. (pp. 192-93)

His comprehension of capitalistic individuals was no clearer than his conception of capitalist institutions.... Men make great fortunes and find that money alone buys no contentment. People of surpassing villainy "look out for number one" or mind only their own business, and in every volume it is the hero's enemy who is "intent only upon his own selfish gratifications."

Alger's favorites, on the contrary, are strangers to such strategies of self-maximization. For them "the best use of money" is in helping others. Dick never gets "so much satisfaction" as when he depletes his own savings to assist a fellow bootblack who has "supported his sick mother and sister for more'n a year," which Dick takes to be "more good than [he himself] ever did." Rufus puts his money where his morals are, buying a baseball bat from his own earnings to stave off a robbery of a man he does not even know. And all alike lavish charities on the needy whether worthy or unworthy.

In fact, profligacy prevails over parsimony at every turn. All six stories open on a note of heedless indulgence—for the theater, an apartment or food—and all six sustain that note thereafter. Boys who are fortunate splurge immediately and to the limit of their luck, sharing their strike with friends if they cannot spend it alone. Others who are down to their last pennies yet yield to "temptation" and buy apples and ice cream. And

few of the boys are any more frugal than Ben, who feels "very well satisfied" if he comes out "even at the end of the day." By and large they all place their bellies before their bank accounts and otherwise set gratification above accumulation. (pp. 193-94)

Unconcerned for the future, Alger's vagabonds could hardly pursue goals with the perseverance so celebrated in the success manuals of the 19th century. Alger did deliver an occasional descant on diligence, but in the tales themselves his heroes are hares, not tortoises. They work sporadically rather than steadily, and they work when they need money rather than for work's own sake. They are more nearly Galahads than Gradgrinds, giving up their own gainful opportunities on a moment's notice to protect the helpless or follow the action. And it is by just that temperamental disposition to knight-errantry rather than discipline or steady application that poor boys prosper. Dick is on the ferry to dive for Rockwell's son only because he takes "half holidays" to go on "excursions." Rufus finds economic security only as a consequence of quitting work early one day to wander around Battery Park.... (p. 195)

Only when the boys are ... beset by danger do they disclose concern for what they do. At their employment they evince no emotion at all, betraying not the slightest sign that they like or dislike their assigned tasks. Unlike Weber's Protestant capitalists, for whom the moral worth of work was so central, they find neither purpose nor personal fulfillment in their jobs. They just do what the work requires, gaining no intrinsic satisfaction from it, and they identify the good life with consumption and gratification far more than with production.

Disdaining the ascetic capitalist and the entrepreneurial self-seeker, Alger inevitably anathematized the social Darwinians. Against their assertions of the prerogatives of strength, he held the obligation of the powerful to protect the weak. Against Sumnerian standards of self-reliance, he suggested an endless round of charitable reciprocation. And against the Spencerian insistence on laissez-faire individualism, he urged that "we ought all to help each other." (p. 196)

Alger's heroes succeed, to the extent that their own attributes have anything to do with their success, because they are good, not because they have sharper fangs and longer claws than anyone else.... They are all, presumably, destined to develop like the successful stockbroker Alger so admired, who was

> a large-hearted man, inclined to think well of his fellow-men, and though in his business life he had seen a good deal that was mean and selfish in the conduct of others, he had never lost his confidence in human nature, and never would. It is better to have such a disposition, even if it does expose the possessor to being imposed upon at times, than to regard everybody with distrust and suspicion. At any rate it promotes happiness, and conciliates good will, and these will offset an occasional deception.

Such sentimental reliance on men's kindness made aggressive imposition unnecessary and even undesirable. It is only the Micky Maguires and the James Martins, the young toughs and the manipulators, and the counterfeitors, confidence-men and others of "few redeeming qualities," who use force and cunning for personal gain.... Alger never glorified strength or shrewdness in the struggle for success because he did not believe it was that sort of struggle.

The virtues Alger did exalt, revealingly enough, were the virtues of the employee, not the employer. Since his heroes do not succeed at the expense of others, it is not essential that they build better mousetraps, cut costs or innovate in any way. They have little enough initiative even in the streets and less in the shop. Indeed, when they enter upon their white-collar careers they promise their new bosses primarily to "try to make you as little trouble as possible." Dick will do "anything that is required" in the line of duty, but neither he nor any of the others ever re-think such duties. And no one ever asks them to. Employers themselves assure the boys that they "have only to continue steady and faithful" to be "sure to rise." None but the heroes' rivals—the preening pretenders to superiority by birth, such as Roswell Crawford—fail to content themselves with service in subordinate places, and the Roswell Crawfords come to bad ends.

As Alger would have it, then, success follows dependability and a desire to serve others. It attends those who obey orders cheerfully and serve others willingly. And it is available to all, for Alger posited no pinnacle of preeminence for which many compete and a few prove fit. The Alger stories were never about the fabulous few who rose from poverty to great riches: they were, at best, tales of a much more accessible ascent from rags to respectability. His nonpareils do not wax wealthy so much as they grow reputable, leaving the promiscuity of the streets for the propriety of a desk job. . . . There is not a robber baron in the bunch, nor even any remarkable fortune. The boys gain only "the fame of an honorable and enterprising man of business," which was all they ever aimed at anyway. "I'd like to be a office boy, and learn business, and grow up 'spectable," Dick confides at his first stirring of ambition; and even as he nears the end of his odyssey he sets his sights no higher. "Take my advice," he urges Mark, "and you'll grow up respectable and respected."

Such commitment to respectability implied also a commitment to others rather than to selfish aspiration. Respectability, in Alger's idea of it, could not come from within, but could only be conferred by others. Accordingly, his heroes require the good opinion of the herd for their own sense of success and for their very sense of self. And they seem to believe they can gain it by behaving the way the herd behaves or would want them to behave. Dick, for example, acquires clothes so modish as he moves out into "society" that Fosdick accuses him of dandyism: Dick answers that he wants "to look respectable. . . . When I visit Turkey I want to look as the turkeys do!" (pp. 197-99)

The Alger hero's very notion of his own nature depended, ineluctably, upon others. If Alger's world was a Carnegie world, it was surely not Andrew's but Dale's. Alger could not create self-impelled individuals because his stalwarts required a crowd for their sense of self. The quest for respectability imposed a communal derivation of identity, and a communal dedication of the self as well. Accordingly, when Alger offered examples outside fiction of the newsboy success story, he cited politicians, journalists, judges, a district attorney and a clergyman before arriving finally at "still others prosperous and even wealthy businessmen." Businessmen brought up the rear while public figures led because it was primarily the redemption of respectable citizens Alger sought. His aims were social and moral more than they were ever economic.

Alger's inability to conceive convincingly his heroes' inner resources made it quite impossible for him to maintain the traditional connection of character and success. He could—

and did, occasionally—claim it, but he could not bring it to life. His tales contradicted him at every such turn. The path to wealth was not, as it had been for Franklin, "as plain as the way to market." Instead there intervened always between constitution and conquest the sudden stroke of luck.

The typical Alger story, therefore, was one of casual contingency, not causal necessity. Bootblacks rise by diving for the drowning son of a rich man, newsboys by foiling attempted robbery, matchboys by the belated beneficence of a grandfather a thousand miles away. None ever attain eminence by diligent application; none are ever on a course of notable advancement before their big break. Alger knew the litany of industry and frugality as well as most men, but for him and his characters the failure of firm selfhood and the facts of late-19th century life kept getting in the way.

Primarily the problems were that these gamins of Gotham could not get the kind of work Alger wished for them and that, even if they could, they could not afford to take it. In the Algerine cosmos, nothing but a white-collar career would do, finally—protagonists had somehow to quit the street for a store—and in the Ragged Dick series not a single favorite ever secures a clerical position purely on personal initiative. Dick makes "several ineffectual applications" and surrenders for the season. His friend Fosdick solicits 50 appointments and suffers "as many failures." Ben gives up entirely after a few rebuffs; Rufus never even tries. And the reason is always the same: "it was generally desired that the boy wanted should reside with his parents" or "bring good references." Fosdick finds that to confess himself "a boy of the street" is usually "sufficient of itself to insure a refusal," and the others all share his discouragement in a system that supports no self-made men. They hustle on the streets precisely because they are alone and unaided and consequently can do no better, for they have no access to a countinghouse unless they can claim a place in a household. Unsponsored and unspoken for, their success can only be extra-systemic. In the very structure of the situation they can advance by no means but the lucky acquisition of a patron who will provide the profection they require. (pp. 200-02)

Luck, then, does not simply seal the success of those on the proper path. On the contrary, fortune's favor is indispensable to lift poor boys out of the ditch. Ragged Dick is not on his way before he saves Mr. Rockwell's son, for there is no way. Orphans of the city cannot afford an apprenticeship in respectability, since they have no parental subsidy to tide them over and can hardly survive on status alone. Only by benevolent patronage can they manage their entry upon a white-collar walk of life. Only from parental surrogates who set defiance of the market's determination of wages at "no consequence" can they extract salaries they cannot economically earn. Dick speaks for them all when he admits that he "was lucky" to have "found some good friends who helped [him] along."

So far from telling of a system so bountiful that any earnest lad could succeed if he tried, Alger's tales implied one that held the disprivileged down so securely that only by the unlikely advent of chance and championship could the impoverished even set foot on the social ladder. In the Alger novels of New York a steady undertone of desperation resonated beneath the scattered cries of lucky triumph. (pp. 202-03)

Not one of Alger's elect is ever self-employed at the end of a novel, nor do any of them ever really wish to be. Mark most obviously needs "some body to lean on," but even Dick admits that his deepest dreams involve "some rich man" who "would adopt me, and give me plenty to eat and drink and wear, without my havin' to look so sharp after it.'' It is not with his usual levity that he adds that he would ''like to have somebody to care for me,'' and later, when he wishes explicitly for a mother, there is the same ''tinge of sadness in his tone.''

Dick's fantasied confusion of men and mothers comes very close to the emotional core of the Alger stories, for though the boys all crave caretaking, they are quite particular about its provenance. Not any parent will do. Each of Alger's prodigies is seeking something very special, and it is no accident that in a nation still two-thirds rural and presumably patriarchal, every story in the series is conditioned on father-absence. Only one of the six tales even admits a flesh-and-blood father, and Ben runs away from him. In the others there are a few self-sacrificing mothers, an indulgent grandfather, a stern stepfather and a monstrous mother-substitute; and only those among them who abdicate their authority succeed in sustaining a relation with their wards. All who play the traditional masculine part— demanding and commanding—discover one day that their fledglings have flown the coop.

Over and over again in these stories. Alger returned to the problem of proper parentage. His fixation was overt in *Mark, the Match Boy* and *Ben the Luggage Boy,* more muffled in the others—the first two tell quite focally of falls from family and re-entry into its bosom, the rest dwell less on literal than on figurative kinships that are reclaimed as the protagonists find their patrons—but it pervaded the entire series. In every novel the hero experiences the unsettling sense that his own parents have failed him, that somewhere else his true parents are waiting to be found by accident and good luck. (pp. 204-05)

Ultimately, then, Alger's every novel was a novel of nurturance, a novel whose dearest ideal was to be cared for and indulged, not to be self-sufficient and self-reliant. Each of them begins with a boy alone and on his own, but each of them concludes with that boy safely sheltered in some secure niche where his future is assured because his protector will look after him forevermore. Alger allowed his every hero and half his supporting cast this movement from the streets to easy street, and it afforded him the essential drama and the irresistible consummation of all his narratives. (p. 207)

All the stories are . . . tales of a return to respectable estate. Their movement is not even from rags to respectability, for the subjects never really start in rags. They pass their formative years in the bosom of a family, and they are quite familiar with its comforts before they run away or are orphaned. In their success, they simply recover a condition that was originally theirs. (p. 208)

If Horatio Alger was the mentor of an emergent industrial society, then the Americans who grew up under his tutelage were surely schooled for service in the corporate bureaucracies which would in time transform the culture. For Alger never encouraged his audience to care so much for work as for the gratifications of income, and he never dared his readers to be as they might be so much as to do as their neighbors did. Beneath his explicit emphasis on striving upward ran a deeper desire for stability and security; beneath his paeans to manly vigor, a lust for effeminate indulgence; beneath his celebration of self-reliance, a craving to be taken care of and a yearning to surrender the terrible burden of independence. (p. 209)

Michael Zuckerman, ''The Nursery Tales of Horatio Alger,'' in *American Quarterly, Vol. XXIV, No. 2,* May, 1972, pp. 191-209.

FRANK SHUFFELTON   (essay date 1976)

[*Shuffelton's essay focuses on the lessons in morality, economics, and sociology Alger imparted to his juvenile audience. Like John G. Cawelti (1965), Michael Zuckerman (1972), and Gary Scharnhorst (1980), he argues that Alger was not, as many critics contend, an unrestrained adulator of wealth. ''The real winner'' at the end of each of Alger's novels, Shuffelton maintains, is ''middle class virtue seen as the essence of patriotism and morality.'' According to Shuffelton, Alger's heroes display democratic spirit in both school and business and their ''manifest destiny'' is the ''creation of an American society in which all social and cultural distinctions will be obviated.''*]

If Alger novels imparted lessons in which morality and economics inextricably entwined, they also provided sociological and psychological models of behavior. From school texts boys learned how the founding fathers revealed the American truth, but from the Alger novels they read on their own they learned, or thought they learned, what contemporary life in America was really like. Before they ever fled from the village, they discovered an imagined and imaginable version of the city in Alger's pages, and as they read about life in Alger's villages and boarding schools, they succumbed to a romanticized, almost mythically imagined view of their own hometowns. Alger's urban scenes are all the more compelling for his portrayal of the whole range of society in a city. He was in many ways

Cover of an early edition of From Farm to Fortune. *Courtesy of Prints and Photographs Division, Library of Congress.*

30 years ahead of his time in presenting life among the urban poor, and it is not until the advent of the so-called naturalists that we hear the speech and view the lives of bootblacks, newsboys, shop clerks, drunkards and gamblers in anything like the detail Alger gives us. If his views of the upper classes are hopelessly false and maudlin compared to the portrayal of a far more talented observer like Howells, he at least gives a comprehensive picture of a whole urban society, and in doing so, he encourages his readers to see the city as a possible field for their own endeavours. Whether he writes about the city or the country, Alger fits the variety of American life into a simple pattern, enabling readers to see the nation not as a bewildering range of diverse regions and localities but as a transcontinental repetition of the same temptations and opportunities. (pp. 53-4)

Just as Alger levels all distinctions of place into uniform versions of city or country, so he manipulates time to maintain an eternal present for his youthful readers. When Tom Nelson, the Young Adventurer, first sees the Kansas prairies on his way to the California gold fields, the narrator demythifies the landscape by observing, "At that early day the settlement of this now prosperous State had scarcely begun. Its rich soil was as yet unvexed by the plow and the spade." There will be no gropings after the sublime here; the prairies are fixed within the bounds of opportunity and industry which define Alger's America.

Only in the California gold fields or in Australia do real alternatives exist, and these are effectively removed from the reader by time in the first case and space in the other. In *The Young Miner* Tom Nelson almost intuitively realizes the historical transiency of the gold rush; he sells out his claim for a handsome profit, lifts the mortgage on the family farm in New Hampshire and reads for the law in San Francisco. Only as the West becomes like the East can an Alger hero settle into the "lucrative practice" fit for a mature man. Australia of course can never become sufficiently East for an Alger character; Harry Vane, the hero of *Facing the World* and *In a New World*, returns to New York with the $5,000 he earned in Australia, invests the money and takes a position with a shipping merchant. The marvellous landscapes and societies of the gold fields offer no real options to middle class life in a progressive American city, for they are merely geographical images of the providential incidents young men encounter in more conventionally set Algers. They are not end but initiation, just as saving wealthy men's daughters from runaway horses or betraying pickpockets to rich widows only start heroes on their way to success and do not reveal a pattern of experience that can be repeated. (pp. 54-5)

Alger's young men always pass up temporarily rewarding situations, gold mines, magic acts, etc., in favor of more solid careers offering less excitement and perhaps less potential for vast wealth but far more security and, more important, respect from society. Model characters end up reading for the law or taking a promising position in a mercantile establishment. Alger heroes opt for the middle way, and Alger is as interested in portraying the dangers of wealth as he is in portraying the threats of poverty. There are always two systems of villainy in an Alger novel, and the hero has as often need to defend himself from upper-class corruption as from blue collar crime. (p. 56)

The Alger hero unerringly moves toward the more successful ranks of the middle class by virtue of his superior gifts of adaptability in any unexpected situation. Like Emerson's self-reliant Yankee lad who "*teams it, farms it, peddles,* keeps a

school, preaches, edits a newspaper, goes to Congress, buys a township, and so forth," an Alger hero on the make is a veritable one-man chamber of commerce who can turn his hand to any honest job with equal facility. . . . But where Emerson can convince us that his Yankee boy is a model of Self-Reliance working out his true self through his experience, we come to suspect that the chameleon-like flexibility of Alger's heroes conceals a void at the heart.

If the apparent winner at the end of an Alger novel is the boy hero, the real winner is middle class virtue seen as the essence of patriotism and morality. Alger's heros triumph not only over poverty (or, in some cases, over wealth) but over all ethnic and cultural impediments to easy entry into the American bourgeoisie. Almost all Alger heroes have impeccably Anglo-Saxon names, often incredibly alliterative ones at that, but a few books describe the Americanization of immigrant boys who prove to be as apt for middle-class success as native born heroes. Andy Burke, the hero of *Only an Irish Boy,* enters the story as the out-of-work son of a widowed mother and ends as the proprietor of the village's general store. . . . In the book's last sentence Alger points the moral to his celebration of American receptiveness for all seekers of the middle-class dream: "He is not the first, nor will he be the last, to achieve prosperity and the respect of the community, though beginning life as 'only an Irish boy'." (pp. 58-9)

Intelligence and will power can overcome language and cultural barriers, but color is an almost insuperable bar to the kind of middle-class success Alger heroes find. Blacks and Chinese, portrayed in the broadest ethnic stereotypes (as are all of Alger's non-Anglo-Saxon characters, for that matter), are never accepted in the same way as . . . Andy Burke. Still, it is the hero's duty to encourage them to persevere in the ways of American bourgeois virtue. Luke Walton chides a Chicago street boy for heaving a brick through a Chinese laundryman's window: "A well-behaved heathen is better than a Christian such as you are." In *Frank's Campaign: or What Boys Can Do on the Farm for the Camp,* Frank Frost patiently teaches Pompey, the son of an escaped slave, to read and write and schools him in the behavior expected of an American citizen. But Pompey's social and economic possibilities are more seriously constricted than those of the typical Alger hero. "As soon as Pomp is old enough, Frank will employ him on the farm."

Similar to the way in which Frank Frost assumes the white man's burden, Horatio Alger becomes an evangelist for bourgeois virtue, the flame which keeps the melting pot working. He extolls all the institutions of society which help a man occupy a position at the center of his community. (p. 60)

Schools are less important to Alger for their curricula than they are as socializing institutions; they are a crucial democratizing force in American society. We often first meet his heroes in a schoolyard, a beleaguered Eden from which they are soon to fall through no fault of their own. Although the hero usually stands first in his class, more as a result of virtuous study habits than of sheer brilliance, the most important part of his character is his democratic instinct. We typically find the hero in the first paragraph engaged in conversation with a poor classmate whose father is "only" a shoemaker or small farmer, and we learn that the hero's snobbish rival disdains to associate with such students. The hero's fellow-students respect him because of his openness and his refusal to use his achievements as a basis for any self-assumed authority over them. The Alger hero is a friend of the common man and an enemy to social, moral

and economic tyrants who, like criminals, set themselves outside the body of working people and their families.

The school often turns out to be an almost ideal model of what
adult society ought to be; it clarifies the deceptions and hypocrisies of adult life by simplifying and enlarging them. The
would-be aristocrat's attempt to intrude the artificial class distinctions of the outside world reveals the viciousness of these
distinctions as he parades his wealth, acts out of petty jealousy
and collects a small circle of toadies. Also, like Alger's portrayal of adult life, school is apolitical; Alger understands democracy not as a political phenomenon, created by the citizen's
participation in the law making process, but as a sociological
fact, the attitudes concerning equality and the pursuit of happiness held by the great majority of virtuous Americans. Finally, school is a fit preparation for the world of commerce,
for in both realms of life the only relevant standards are those
of accomplishment and of morality.

Business, like school, is (or ought to be) democratic, and a
successful businessman is one who can recognize potential
managerial talent in any social milieu. Class distinctions are
meaningless in business, where the only criteria are honesty
and efficiency. But if a businessman's democratic spirit makes
him at once an economic success and a model American citizen,
his electing eligible young men to the benefits of his company
and his companionship makes him also a patriarchal figure of
authority. The hero is his equal as an American, yet at the
same time his subordinate within the frame of the business,
and it is the commercial context, along with that of the family,
which becomes most important for Alger. To live as a democratic American is for Alger a spiritual attainment, a function
of personality, whereas to be a dutiful son and honest employee
is a function of manners, realizable not in attitudes but only
in actions. The life of an Alger hero is a life of action—that
is a great part of his attraction for youthful readers—and it is
singularly devoid of spirituality or innerness. The hero, then,
is only nominally a democrat; more important are his dutiful-
ness and success in carrying out errands imposed by others.
His democracy is expressed as sympathy for all fellow Americans and not as the carrying out of independent, self-reliant
actions; he is other-directed, not inner-directed. (pp. 61-2)

Despite claims to the contrary . . . , Alger's novels are not
instruction manuals for would-be captains of industry but re-
cruiting pamphlets for the ranks of middle management. Alger
heroes give up their individuality—if they ever had any in the
first place—to join the ranks of junior executives. They are
untouched by art, by literature, by music beyond the mere level
of popular amusement. They are not strivers after the unknown,
after novelty, after the infinite, for their vision of the world is
limited. They are never fathers, only sons; years before Frederick Jackson Turner announced the closing of the frontier,
they recognized it and turned to the business of settling and
developing. Their manifest destiny is not potentially unlimited
expansion of the American imagination but the creation of an
American society in which all social and cultural distinctions
will be obviated. In them the spirit of mediation, of compromise, of the golden rule, triumphs, and rather than becoming
the heirs of Emerson, they are the ancestors of Babbitt. (p. 63)

Frank Shuffelton, ''Bound to Rise—But Not Too Far:
Horatio Alger and the Dream of Security,'' in Illinois
Quarterly, *Vol. 39, No. 1, Fall, 1976, pp. 51-64.*

GARY SCHARNHORST (essay date 1980)

[*In* Horatio Alger, Jr., *from which the following excerpt is drawn,*
Scharnhorst views Alger's works in relation to his Unitarian and
patrician background. His stated purpose is to "demythologize"
Alger by documenting his "genteel abhorrence" for the com-
mercial practices of the Gilded Age. Scharnhorst, who contends
that Alger was primarily a moralist and a reformer who had hoped
to imitate the social novels of Charles Dickens on a juvenile level,
discusses six themes in Alger's juvenile stories: beauty versus
money, rise to respectability, strength by adversity, country versus
city, old versus new world, and the search for identity. In addition,
he delineates Alger's sources and formal models and provides
one of the few studies of his adult fiction.]

An orthodox Unitarian, Alger would not have been pleased
with fiction that only praised wealth-gathering, and he certainly
would not have written such fiction himself. His crucial distinction between Beauty and Money, however, has usually been
ignored. A persistent critical interpretation of the standard Alger story holds that the hero rises, if not from rags to riches,
to at least a comfortable middle-class standard of living by
exploiting every available opportunity to succeed financially.
The hero's goal of wealth-in-abundance, according to this view,
colors all of his thoughts and actions. (p. 49)

A dissenting interpretation of the standard Alger story, however, holds that the hero is in fact a humanitarian rather than
a ruthless exploiter, and that he is rewarded in the denouement
of each initiation novel for his acts of charity. This interpretation, which suggests that the author was more concerned with
morality and beauty than with money, is supported by a reading
of Alger's adult fiction. To be sure, in the juveniles Alger did
describe the increase of the hero's bank account or detail the
steps taken in the acquisition of his birthright, but this mo-
neymaking was symbolic of his initiation into adulthood and
was a badge of his innate moral goodness, conferred by a
benevolent patron who, like God, recognized his worth and
rewarded him. Because most of the virtuous characters in Alger's adult fiction already have been initiated, the importance
of money to them is drastically reduced, as might be expected
on the basis of this interpretation. Because Alger in his adult
fiction labored under no requirement to elevate his characters'
stations as a sign of their election, as was prescribed by the
formula of his juveniles, the wage-earning and monetary reward of the juvenile hero is replaced in the parallel structure
of his adult fiction by courtship and marriage among the mature
characters. This correspondence between money in the juvenile
fiction and marriage in the adult fiction in turn suggests that
Alger conceived of personal happiness as the ultimate reward
for moral behavior. The moral climate of Alger's fictional
world remains constant in both his adult and juvenile works—
a factor that enabled him to rewrite some of his adult works,
such as *Timothy Crump's Ward* and **"Ralph Raymond's Heir,"**
for juvenile audiences. Indeed, the only apparent difference
between Alger's adult fiction and his juvenile fiction is the age
of the characters he depicts, not the values these characters
articulate and embody. In other words, Alger's adult fiction,
which develops the theme of "Beauty versus Money," informs
the myth he created in his juvenile books by correcting the
usual impression that he praised wealth-gathering alone or considered it a sufficient end unto itself. (p. 50)

[The] thematic contrast of Beauty and Money recurs in much
of Alger's . . . adult fiction. In his first twelve adult novelle,
written during a dozen years in the mid-nineteenth century,
Alger clearly favored the claims of Beauty over those of Money.
Sentimental and melodramatic, these works describe a world
in which the consequences of good and evil have been inexorably predetermined. The heroic characters strive not for fortune but for beatitudinal marital bliss. These works teach, as

Alger concludes his early novel *Helen Ford,* that "Happiness must be earned; it can never be bought. To those who, like Helen, consecrate their lives to the noblest objects, and study to promote the happiness of all around them, the blessing comes unsought." With no young heroes in transit struggling upward, the virtuous characters in these stories harbor few thoughts of money, and on those rare occasions when virtuous characters do think of money, they reveal their (and Alger's) low estimation of its worth relative to the value of Beauty. In *Helen Ford,* for example, a struggling artist complains to his friend and eventual lover Helen that "it is money that rules the world. Before its sway we must all bow, willing or unwilling. It is the want of money that drives me to abandon that which is the chief joy of my life. . . . [Painting] will gratify my aesthetic tastes; it will give me that which my soul craves; it will open to me a world of beauty in which I can revel; but, alas! it will not give me bread." In contrast, evil characters in these early stories covet filthy lucre and its perverse sexual correlate, seduction.

In the tradition of melodrama, the virtuous characters in these works inevitably are rewarded (by marriage, not necessarily by wealth) and the evil characters inevitably punished. For example, the hunchbacked, mercenary villain in Alger's early serial "Hugo, the Deformed" commits suicide rather than suffer arrest for kidnapping the chaste heroine, while the romantic hero and his betrothed at length "attain that peaceful and tranquil happiness which mutual love can alone bestow." In his novella *Ralph Raymond's Heir,* moreover, the two criminals who temporarily deprive an heir of his modest birthright and who hope to appropriate it for themselves die in a grisly murder-suicide similar to the violent end of "Hugo." . . . The sordid quest for personal profit is righteously condemned by Alger in every instance. Without exception, characters who are guilty of avarice are portrayed as miserable. For example, at the end of "Manson the Miser" Alger depicts old Peter Manson as he dies with "a few gold pieces firmly clutched in his grasp. He had received a sudden summons" while engaged Scrooge-like in counting his fortune. Justice is meted out in this fictional world not on a sliding scale of monetary gain or loss; rather, goodness is rewarded with happiness and evil is punished with spiritual and/or legal conviction or death. These works, in short, belie the interpretation of Algerism as unbridled capitalism, and suggests that Unitarian minister Alger believed, as he wrote in the preface to his juvenile novel *Sink or Swim* . . . , that "the consciousness of well-doing . . . itself is a rich reward." . . . (pp. 51-2)

The adult tales reveal by inference that Alger essentially wrote American morality fables, not business tracts or indiscreet celebrations of the American entrepreneur. The virtuous Alger protagonist invariably receives Good Fortune, but not necessarily wealth. His view thus must be contrasted with those of nineteenth-century clergymen who corrupted the traditional Protestant doctrine of the calling—which prescribed the stewardship duties of the man whom God had favored with worldly wealth—to sanctify mere wealth-getting and to justify the actions of the wealthy. . . . Alger dissented from this "theodicy of good fortune." "Sometimes the richest are the meanest," one of his juvenile heroes astutely observes [in *Bound to Rise*]. . . . Never an apologist for the robber barons of the Gilded Age, Alger set his fiction in an earlier, seemingly simpler, pre-industrial era, and always was more concerned with the moral uses of money than with money itself. In the Alger canon, money may be a means to attain success, but it never constitutes success by itself. Rather, the hero earns success and happiness

by his virtue, especially by his charity, and never by business acumen. A character who covets wealth or his neighbor's wife-to-be usually receives his just reward. Occasionally in his later novels, Alger described a world of more complex economic transactions in which the undeserving frustrate the Fates and gain wealth. "The wicked are sometimes prospered in this world," notes the wise guardian of [the Alger boy hero in *A Cousin's Conspiracy*]. Still, as he continues, "This world is not all." . . . Nearing the end of his life, seasoned by his knowledge that unethical business practices in a foreboding real world often reward the culprits, Alger appealed for an eschatological vindication of the moral principles that animate his fictional world. (p. 65)

[Alger's two most important formal models for his juvenile books] were Franklin's *Autobiography,* and the social novels of Dickens. Alger borrowed both his basic plot and symbols from the early pages of the *Autobiography,* to the point when young Ben returns to Boston from Philadelphia wearing a new suit and sporting a watch. . . . Just as Franklin described his apprenticeship in Philadelphia and triumphal return to Boston in the *Autobiography,* so did Alger typically allow his returned hero to deflate snobbish pretensions by walking the streets of his hometown wearing a new suit and displaying a watch. (p. 68)

Alger did not exhaust his interest in Franklin by recurrently depicting scenes from the *Autobiography* or employing a pair of symbols, however. Franklin's appeal during the Gilded Age was pervasive, as Louis B. Wright has explained, because "by a credible though partial perception" of Franklin's philosophy he became the "high priest of the religion of commercial success." By offering Franklin as a model worthy of emulation, Alger paradoxically served his eighteenth-century didactic purpose and remained topical in the late nineteenth century. It is not surprising, then, that five of his heroes and two of his patrons are named Ben, one patron claims to be descended from Franklin, and even the name "Ragged Dick" seems less Alger's invention than a rephrasing of "Poor Richard." Three of Alger's heroes deliberately model their lives after Franklin, and three others directly quote his adages. (p. 69)

Besides drawing on Franklin, Alger borrowed incidents, characters, and an authorial tone from Dickens. He ladled facts about the condition of the poor into his fiction because, as he observed [in *Tattered Tom*], it is difficult to sympathize with the social outcasts without a "knowledge of how the poorest classes lived." . . . Certainly Alger planned his fiction to be partly incisive social commentary. The following passage [from *Jed the Poor-house Boy*], for example, owes its tone to Dickens and its content to a more obvious factual source, Dorothea Dix, who at mid-century had pioneered the investigation of conditions in Massachusetts asylums: "Mrs. Fogson led the way into a large room where sat the paupers, a forlorn, unhappy-looking company. Two of the ladies were knitting; one young woman, who had lost her child, and with it her mind, was fondling a rag baby; two were braiding a rag carpet, and others were sitting with vacant faces, looking as if life had no attraction for them." . . . Alger apparently hoped to imitate Dickens's success in writing popular novels with a social purpose, though on the juvenile level. He often copied incidents and characters into his own fiction from four Dickens novels which feature a juvenile hero—*Great Expectations, David Copperfield, Nicholas Nickleby,* and *Oliver Twist.* For example, he introduced characters modeled after such Dickens characters as Wilkins Micawber in *The Young Outlaw* . . . , Sally Brass in *Hector's Inheritance* . . . , and Smike in *Grit*. . . . The Dickens work most often imitated by Alger, however, was *Oliver Twist*. . . . No fewer than fourteen Alger juveniles employ *Oliver* twists in the plot, usually the discovery of a locket containing pictures used to identify the hero, who had been kidnapped as a baby, and to reunite him with his prosperous family. Alger also modeled other incidents in his juvenile fiction after other parts of the novel, as in *Paul Prescott's Charge* . . . , in which his hungry hero asks the stern mistress of a boarding school "for more." . . . Similarly, in *Adrift in New York* . . . Alger transplanted the seedy Artful Dodger from the London slums to the New York slums, renamed him Tom Dodger, and converted him in the course of the novel from thief to respectable hero. And *The Young Explorer* . . . contains a "brutal villain" whom other characters compare with Bill Sykes. . . . In short, Dickens's works, especially *Oliver Twist,* provided a rich source of incidents and characters for Alger's juvenile fiction, and in addition offered a model authorial tone toward these materials which Alger sought to imitate.

Alger also derived incidents and characters from many other sources, and it is clear that he carefully selected his models in order both to reduce sensationalism and to inspire an interest in respectable literature among his readers. The plots of *Brave and Bold* . . . and *The Tin Box* . . . , for example, seem to be modernized versions of [Homer's] *The Odyssey* told from the point of view of Telemachus. Several Alger juveniles set at sea, among them *Facing the World* . . . and *In Search of Treasure* . . . , borrow incidents from [Daniel Defoe's] *Robinson Crusoe* and the sea tales of Richard Henry Dana and Herman Melville. Especially in his **"Pacific series"** of juvenile novels set in the Old West . . . and occasionally in other novels, Alger borrowed character and incident from James Fenimore Cooper's Leatherstocking tales, which he had read as a teenager. He also recast several of Mark Twain's novels for his juvenile audience, including *The Prince and the Pauper* in chapter XXVII of *Tom Brace* . . . and *Huck Finn* in *Bob Burton*. . . . Predictably, Unitarian minister Alger often used the parables of Jesus as literary models for incidents in his didactic fiction, especially those of the Good Samaritan, the Prodigal Son, and the Ten Talents. . . . In short, Alger was not only a formulaic writer, but an unoriginal one.

Alger's books are usually considered literary museum pieces at least partly because of his anachronistic style. To be blunt, Alger's prose is often laughable. Although he was not a craftsman, he did put flesh on the bones of his literary theory with a style that was distinctive. In addition to his basic symbols of new clothes and a watch, Alger used houses as status symbols and even gave an occasional villain yellow tusks as symbols of his venality. He effectively foreshadowed plot action by using devices such as fortune-tellers and playscripts. Still, his style may be best distinguished from the style of pulp juveniles written in "fiction factories" by the quality of his literary allusions.

A didactic writer in two senses—as a moralist and as an educator—Alger drew from a greater variety of literary sources than any other writer for boys. Many of his sources are predictable. He alluded to the Bible, for example, in about half of his novels, and he quoted or mentioned each of the Fireside poets at least twice, his Harvard teacher Longfellow most often. Surprisingly, perhaps, he alluded to Shakespeare in nearly half of his juvenile books, and quoted Milton in *Phil the Fiddler*. . . . A defender of classical learning, Alger quoted from Cicero in *Bernard Brooks' Adventures* . . . and Horace in *Walter Sher-*

wood's Probation . . . , and from several English neoclassical writers, including Joseph Addison in *Five Hundred Dollars* . . . , Oliver Goldsmith in *Dean Dunham* . . . , Thomas Gray in *Ralph Raymond's Heir* . . . , William Cowper in *The Young Musician* . . . , and Alexander Pope in *Andy Gordon*. . . . Alger also quoted from such diverse sources as Robert Burns in *Adventures of a Telegraph Boy* . . . and *Driven from Home* . . . , Thomas Paine in *Julius* . . . , and Tennyson in *Jack's Ward* . . . , and at various times alluded to Dante, Chaucer, Spenser, Dryden, Johnson, Watts, Wordsworth, Coleridge, Byron, Mill, Hugo, Voltaire, Goethe, and Schiller. Among his contemporaries he quoted Thomas Hood, Thomas Campbell, and the elder Henry James, and he referred to Carlyle, Emerson, Stowe, Howells, Stevenson, Edward Everett Hale, and Bayard Taylor. . . . By the diversity of his allusions, Alger, no mere hack writer, both revealed his erudition and enhanced the literary quality of his work.

Alger also treated a diversity of themes in his juvenile books, unlike his singular concern with "Beauty vs. Money" in his adult fiction. He developed six major themes in his juveniles, belying the critical commonplace that all of his books were alike. The first theme, the Rise to Respectability, was Alger's most important. . . . As John Cawelti has observed, "It is unfair to call [Alger] an uninhibited adulator of wealth who equated spiritual grace with business success. The true aim of the Alger hero is respectability, a happy state only partially defined by economic repute" [see excerpt above, 1965]. (pp. 71-5)

The recurrence in Alger's fiction of the theme of the Rise to Respectability underscores the inaccuracy of the widespread opinion that his heroes rise from rags to riches. Indeed, insofar as Alger's heroes prosper at all, they do so because they *deserve* prosperity, because they happily *earn* it with their virtue, however contrived the mechanism through which they obtain it. Daniel W. Howe explains [in *The Unitarian Conscience: Harvard Moral Philosophy, 1805-1861*] that the Harvard moralists believed "God had provided for the recompense of virtue; the righteous would prosper here on earth and receive a heavenly reward as well." As Alger restated the notion [in *Sink or Swim*], "The best way to strive for success is to deserve it." . . . Alger's heroes always merit their good fortune—an idea which, like respectability, is associated only tangentially to wealth.

A second major theme in Alger's juveniles is that characters can be Strengthened by Adversity. As Howe observes, the Unitarian theodicy taught "that suffering could be a useful device for character development. In consequence, there is a subordinate theme in praise of suffering which runs underneath the Unitarian chorus of joyful aspiration." Alger echoed this theme in many of his novels, especially those like *Strong and Steady* . . . and *Shifting for Himself* . . . in which a hero born to wealth is "unexpectedly reduced from affluence to poverty, and compelled to fight his own way in life." . . . Each of the eight volumes of the **"Luck and Pluck series,"** . . . thematically devoted "to the truth that a manly spirit is better than the gifts of fortune," . . . depicts a hero who is strengthened by adversity much as Alger hoped his readers would be. . . . Alger feigned no pity for those born into the working class, for with his faith in upward mobility he believed that early hardship would promote their eventual success, not impede it. . . . A poor boy should even consider his privation a blessing, Alger averred [in *Don the Newsboy*], for it may "give him that self-reliance of which the sons of rich men so often stand in need. . . . Let those boys who are now passing through the discipline of poverty and privation, take courage." . . .

Alger also adapted the theme of Beauty versus Money, which had been central to his adult fiction, to his juvenile novels. Generally, he developed the theme as he had in that apprenticeship work. Occasionally he affirmed the beauty of life over money, as in *Ralph Raymond's Heir* . . . : "Every day life is bartered for [money]; not always criminally, but sacrificed by overwork or undue risk, so insatiable is the hunger for gold, and so desperate are the efforts by which men seek to obtain it." . . . Usually, however, he used pairs of characters broadly representative of the ideas of beauty and money in order to contrast them. . . . In *The Erie Train Boy* . . . Alger reused the formula of his adult story "**Love**," which prescribed that a poor-but-beautiful woman be wooed and won despite the wiles practiced on her suitor by a rich-but-depraved woman. And in *Ben's Nugget* . . . he reused the basic plot of "**Farmer Hayden's Thanksgiving-Day**," in which a young woman resists the designs of a mercenary in order to marry her true love.

Alger also contrasted rural virtue and urban vice in his juvenile fiction. With this fourth theme, the Country versus the City, Alger adapted the nostalgic myth of the country boy as a moral exemplar to the modern notion of the city as sphere of economic opportunity. In his novel *Wait and Hope* . . . Alger offered a succinct summary of his standard contrast of country and city: "While a large city has more temptations than a small town, it also has more opportunities for improvement." . . . Though he modified the design of his stock hero as he groped for his métier, Alger retained this fundamental distinction, which was rooted in agrarian idealism, throughout his juvenile fiction. When the validity of the distinction was questioned in the 1920s by such figures as Sinclair Lewis and H. L. Mencken who announced an "escape from the village," the reputation of Alger and other celebrants of the country boy myth suffered accordingly. (pp. 76-8)

True to the traditional country boy mythology, Alger believed, as he wrote in *Chester Rand* . . . , that "it is country boys that make the most successful men." . . . Nevertheless, he discouraged the rural poor from migrating to the city. Ignorant of the social forces that herded the lower class from the country into cheap tenement districts, Alger seemed only to realize that the plight of these "cliff-dwellers" was complicated by their residence in the city. . . . Alger strongly discouraged his impressionable young readers, perhaps enticed by the modest success enjoyed by the heroes of his urban novels, from leaving their comfortable country homes for uncertain futures in the city. "There is many a hard-working clerk of middle age, living poorly, and with nothing laid by, in the city, who, had he remained in his native village, might have reached a modest independence," he once observed [in *Do and Dare*]. . . . He thus inferred that it is better to earn a modest competency in a village than risk a livelihood in the city—a conclusion that seriously undermines his reputation as an ideologue of success. Indeed, in some of his later novels about a socially and geographically mobile hero Alger even reversed the expected journey of the hero from country to city, instead transplanting a stunted street Arab into more fertile country soil. (p. 79)

Paralleling the contrast of country and city was a fifth theme in Alger's juveniles, the Old versus the New World. Just as he associated corruption with urban squalor and virtue with the rural village, Alger associated social rigidity with the Old World and mobility with the New. (p. 80)

The sixth major theme in Alger's juveniles may be labeled the Search for an Identity. Each of Alger's novels for boys, unlike his fiction for adults, is a story about a hero's initiation to

"self-reliance" or adult "independence" with the standard symbols of clothes, watch, and money merely denoting stages in his maturation. Frequently Alger adapted his version of the country boy myth to this imitation theme, as in *Ben the Luggage Boy* . . . in which the hero is transformed "from a country boy of ten, to a self-reliant and independent street boy of sixteen." . . . In all instances, the hero professes a desire to be free of dependence on a manipulative squire or stepmother. In *Luck and Pluck* . . . , for example, the hero protests that if his widowed stepmother "intends me to feel dependent, and breaks up all my plans, I will go to work for myself, and make my own way in the world." . . . In other words, money is the crucial key to the hero's initiation because it allows him to wield adult responsibility.

Moreover, Alger developed this Search for an Identity at a more literal level than symbolic initiation. As he wrote in [*Jed the Poorhouse Boy*], "Names are important," . . . and he illustrated this idea in two ways. First, with so many orphaned heroes populating his books, he often used names to mark their search for self-awareness. The evolution of Ragged Dick into Dick Hunter and finally into Richard Hunter, Esq., and the magical transformation of the poorhouse boy Jed into Sir Robert Fenwick, Bart., explicitly signal the success of their quests for self-discovery. Alger also depicted similar, though less obviously successful quests. In *Hector's Inheritance* . . . the hero must discover whether he deserves his classical Greek name: "Was he not Hector Roscoe after all? Had he been all his life under a mistake? If this story were true, who was he, who were his parents, what was his name?" . . . Secondly, Alger sometimes illustrated the importance of names by indicting the criminal use of an alias. "Generally, only criminals who are engaged in breaking the laws change their names," he explained [in *Andy Gordon*] . . . , and in *Paul the Peddler* . . . he lamented the self-deception practiced by a confidence man and wife who prey "upon the community in a variety of characters." . . . These characters exist as symbolic ciphers in Alger's world, deprived even of a name by which the author could refer to them. (pp. 81-2)

Although Alger did not systematically discuss in print his ideas about human nature, he did imply a theory through dozens of his juvenile books. Fundamentally, he believed—as did other Harvard Unitarians—that self-interest was both a universal human trait and, properly construed, a desirable one. . . . Rightly considered, self-interest could motivate acts of charity and other practical projects. When asked why he opens his home to the hero and his family, for example, the patron in *The Tin Box* . . . explains that "I'm a selfish old man, looking out for what will make my home happy." . . . The hero's father in *Helping Himself* . . . expresses his gratitude for "a son who, in helping himself, has been alive to help others." . . . With this theory of human nature, Alger could easily justify the political ambitions of the heroes of his biographies, as he did in Lincoln's case [in *The Backwoods Boy*]. "If it is said that Abraham Lincoln preferred Abraham Lincoln to any one else in the pursuit of his ambitions, and that, because of this, he was a selfish man, then I can see no objections to such an idea." . . . Had the Great Emancipator not been ambitious to rise in politics, so the argument goes, slavery might not have been abolished when it was. (p. 82)

Like other Unitarians, Alger rejected the Calvinist doctrine of innate depravity and accepted the Arminian beliefs in individual freedom and accountability. In his juvenile novel *In a New World* . . . the hero engages in a spirited debate with a villain who claims he was "fated to be" a highwayman; uneasy with this dogma, the hero proclaims that "I shouldn't like to believe as you do." . . . Although he accepted the Arminian faith in free will, Alger also believed in the inscrutable providence of God. . . . The hero of *In a New World,* though repelled by the doctrine of fate, places his "confidence and trust in an Over-ruling Power" and believes that "God had watched over him, and delivered him from danger and the schemes of wicked men." . . . The apparent contradiction in Alger's thought loses significance, however, in light of Howe's conclusion that the antebellum Harvard moralists who instructed Alger were content simply "to accept the freedom of the will as a datum of consciousness, that is, as a principle of common sense" instead of attempting to resolve the same contradiction in their own thought. "Nature was kind," Alger [commented in *Bernard Brooks' Adventures*], . . . and his faith in the benevolence of Nature led him to endorse doctrines of both free will and the providence of God, for each promised the eventual realization of greater human happiness on earth.

If Alger, with this elevated conception of human nature, seems to second Jefferson's claim in the Declaration of Independence that Nature has endowed all men with inalienable rights, it is because Alger also espoused a natural rights philosophy. . . . Chief among the natural rights defended by Alger and the other Harvard Unitarians was the right to hold property. The sanctity of private property is not questioned in Alger's fiction; indeed, several of his juveniles, including *Frank and Fearless* . . . , describe a hero's struggle to reclaim property his by birthright. Such a hero, according to Alger [in *Frank and Fearless*], is "not excessively fond of money" but simply will not allow himself "to be deprived of his rights." . . . The thematic thrust of these novels is not in the direction of the hero's wealth-getting, but his initiation to adult independence.

Similarly, in other books Alger acknowledged the natural right of revolution. While his heroes with their natural sense of justice always submit willingly to proper authority, they rebel against tyranny. (pp. 83-4)

Not only does the Alger hero vigorously defend his own rights, but he actively protects the rights of the weak and op-pressed. . . . Alger was neither a biological nor a social Dar-winist. . . . Against assertions of the prerogatives of strength, he held that it is the obligation of the powerful to protect the weak. . . . Nor did Alger accept the Sumnerian argument, a favorite one with such plutocrats as Rockefeller and Carnegie, that wealth accumulates in the hands of the wealthy because they have been naturally selected as the fittest. "It isn't the strongest men that earn the most," Alger confided to his readers [in *Slow and Sure* and *Tattered Tom*]. . . .

Although he did not interpret evolution in Darwinian terms, Alger did admit the inevitability of progress and supported his evolutionary optimism with a biological theory. Instead of ex-plaining improvements as a "survival of the fittest," however, he explained them in terms of Lamarck's theory that mental as well as physical characteristics could be inherited. Over several generations, according to this theory, the transmission of acquired characteristics would result in progressively greater intellectual powers and moral vigor. As Alger noted in *Jack's Ward* . . . , "it requires several generations of refined habits and exemption from the coarser burdens of life to produce" more perfect people. . . . Alger often traced both his hero's virtues and his snob's ugly traits to their respective parents. In *Frank and Fearless* . . . , for example, the hero's father ob-serves that "Jasper is an improvement on the parent stock. I

see in him more manliness and self-reliance than I possessed at his age." . . . The feckless snob in *Tom the Bootblack* . . . , on the other hand, "inherited his father's bad traits, his self-ishness and unscrupulousness, in addition to a spirit of de-ceitfulness and hypocrisy from his mother's nature." . . . Both heroes and snobs in Alger's stories, in short, inherit moral characteristics of their parents.

This biological theory influenced Alger's juvenile fiction in slightly different ways during three periods of his career. It enabled him in his early juvenile novels of reform to defend self-improvement, for he believed that the acquisition and transmission of virtue were steps vital to the elevation of the species. . . . Later, Lamarck's theory allowed Alger, especially in several books written during the 1880s and early 1890s, to stereotype racial and ethnic characters, despite his oft-repeated profession of racial and ethnic toleration. Believing that ac-quired characteristics could be genetically transmitted, Alger simply made the additional assumption during this period that behavior popularly attributed to some racial and ethnic groups had been so acquired. (pp. 86-7)

Finally, Lamarck's theory of development allowed Alger late in his life to flirt with a kind of hereditary determinism like that popular a few years later during the eugenics craze of the Progressive period. Although this seems incompatible with Al-ger's belief in upward mobility, it is an inconsistency analogous to his simultaneous endorsement of both free will and Provi-dence. Alger's heroes still *choose* to be good and deserve prosperity, even as Providence or hereditary determinism se-lects them to be good and prosperous. These heroes always are natural aristocrats, and in his later juvenile novels Alger simply provided them with parents and sometimes grandparents whose acquired virtue the heroes have inherited. The best ex-amples of this hereditary determinism appear in novels in which the hero, having been orphaned as a child and raised in a degrading environment, still displays "instinctive good breed-ing" in manners and appearance. (p. 87)

Of course, all of Alger's virtuous characters, even those formed from common clay, possess admirable instincts. Alger accepted the self-evident truth of the argument that, because Nature is benevolent, the instincts with which people are endowed by Nature are good. . . . But sound natural instincts also require cultivation to prosper into virtues. In other words, Alger be-lieved that virtue is not innate, although the individual with healthful instincts possesses an important incentive to virtue. (p. 92)

In his early juvenile reform novels, those written mainly before 1880, Alger was clearly an environmentalist, as is evinced by his faith in the refining influences of civilization and his appeals for the cultivation of natural instincts and training of the con-science. Occasionally he was even more explicit in discussing the influence of environment on the building of character. In *Slow and Sure* . . . he stated his rationale for benevolence: "Our destinies are decided more than we know by circumstances. If the street boys, brought up to a familiarity with poverty, and often with vice and crime, go astray, we should pity as well as condemn, and if we have it in our power to make the conditions of life more favorable for any, it is our duty, as the stewards of our common Father, to do what we can." . . . In short, in his early juveniles Alger suggested that right influ-ences *alone* were necessary to reform the poor. Only later [as in *From Canal Boy to President*] did he begin skeptically to admit that "It is not always easy to say what circumstances have most influence in shaping the destiny of a boy'' . . . and to qualify his earlier facile optimism. (pp. 98-9)

[Alger's] commitment to a social fiction with realistic dimensions seems apparent enough. His rationale for reform was best articulated by a patron in [*Do and Dare*]: ''Whatever talents we possess our Creator meant us to exercise for our benefit and the pleasure of the community.'' . . . This moral basis for reform led the mugwumpish Alger to endorse incidentally in his fiction such proposals as those for civil service, the liberalization of divorce laws, and female suffrage. Most of his interest in social reform, however, centered early around four major topics in addition to temperance: children's aid, other forms of charity and philanthropy, racial toleration, and education. (p. 105)

In the decades following his death, after his books were no longer published and popularly read, Alger acquired a reputation as an apologist for business success and a purblind defender of the faith of orthodox capitalism. To be sure, Alger did offer in his juvenile fiction his opinions regarding the proper conduct of business, but, in general, these opinions were simply his application to business of the same moral principles that animate the whole of his fictional world. These principles of political economy were the standard Unitarian views toward business and commerce, and, unfortunately, their significance in Alger's juvenile fiction has been grossly distorted. Alger himself believed only that he was translating the technical language of political economy into entertaining stories for his juvenile audience; as he wrote in *Herbert Carter's Legacy* . . . , ''Though political economy is generally studied in the junior or senior year at college, its principles, if familiarly illustrated, are not beyond the comprehension of a boy of fifteen.'' . . . In other words, Alger the moral teacher attempted only to describe the universal principles of political economy in less esoteric language for his less sophisticated audience, not to create a mythology of business success. (p. 117)

In his juvenile fiction Alger offered a broad critique of money as a measure of value and status. In the themes of the Rise to Respectability and Beauty versus Money . . . , Alger attributed relatively minor or secondary importance to money, compared to the greater claims of Respectability and Beauty. But these two themes, though they suggest the depth of Alger's critique of money and the business considerations it engenders, fail to indicate its breadth. Not only did Alger criticize the quest for business success from a variety of perspectives, he carefully qualified his description of his hero's quest in order to avoid sanctioning the accumulation of money through business dealings. Characteristically, Alger illustrated the contrasting opinions regarding the value of money in a debate between two characters [in *Strong and Steady*], an intemperate woman and the hero:

> ''It's a good thing to have money,'' said the woman, more to herself than to Walter.
>
> ''Yes,'' said Walter, ''it's very convenient to have money; but there are other things that are better.''
>
> ''Such as what?'' demanded the woman abruptly.
>
> ''Good health for one thing.''
>
> ''What else?''
>
> ''A good conscience.''

> She laughted scornfully. ''I'll tell you there's nothing so good as money. I've wanted it all my life, and never could get it. . . . Money is sure to do good, no matter how it comes,'' said the woman, fiercely. ''Think of what it will buy! A comfortable home, ease, luxury, respect. Some time before I die I hope to have as much as I want.''
>
> ''I hope you will,'' said Walter; ''but I don't think you will find it as powerful as you think.''
>
> (p. 131)

Alger profoundly distrusted any behavior that was motivated by the desire to accumulate money. As a Unitarian minister and writer of didactic fiction, he was fond of quoting the biblical verse ''the love of money is the root of all evil,'' to which he alluded in more than a dozen juvenile novels. . . . His strongest condemnation of a character was his declaration, as in *Chester Rand* . . . , that ''He has made money his god, and serves his chosen deity faithfully.'' . . . Alger often used three stock characters—the patron, the villain, and the hero—as vehicles for his condemnation of avarice and greed in business. The patron, usually wealthy and often a businessman, never covets greater wealth. . . . On the other hand, the villain, who acts as the patron's foil in the structure of the novel, invariably is portrayed as avaricious. Ironically, the villains are the only self-made men Alger depicted in his fiction, for he equated ''self-made'' with ''selfish.'' (p. 133)

Alger carefully qualified the rise of the third character, his hero, so that he would not appear to be sanctioning money-making alone. First, as a member of an organic community, the hero cannot be accurately characterized as ''self-made.'' Indeed, as Michael Zuckerman has noted, ''Not one of Alger's elect is ever self-employed at the end of a novel, nor do any of them really wish to be'' [see excerpt above, 1972]. Secondly, the hero, like his patron, is interested only in earning a competence or [as in *The Young Salesman*] a ''sufficiency of this world's goods,'' . . . not in accumulating a fortune. . . . Thirdly, Alger qualified his hero's quest for success by emphasizing his selfless motive. He wishes to rise not to satisfy a gnawing hunger for self-aggrandizement, but in order to be better equipped to help others, particularly his parents. Finally, Alger warned his readers that the hero's good fortune is exceptional, not typical. As he wrote in *Victor Vane* . . . , ''I do not wish my boy readers to look forward to the probability of equal good fortune. Let Victor's example stimulate them to equal fidelity and they are sure to attain a fair measure of success.'' . . . Not everyone will succeed, Alger averred, however happy his home and refined his habits.

In only one significant way was Alger influenced in the course of his long career by the popular image of the success enjoyed by the millionaire-industrialists like Carnegie and Rockefeller. As a result of his accommodation—not his contribution—to the success mythology of the Gilded Age, the rewards earned by his heroes are far greater in the novels he wrote after about 1889-90 than in the ones he wrote prior to that date. In his earliest novels the hero aspires to a respectable middle-class career as an accountant or salesman rather than to exorbitant wealth. . . . However, after about 1889-90, the hero acquires a stupendous fortune or, even more incredibly, a fiefdom. Alger continued to offer the four qualifications to the hero's quest—by noting his reliance on the help of others, his modest aspirations, his selfless motive, and the exceptional nature of his rise—but substantially increased the size of his reward. . . .

Alger apparently hoped after 1889-90 to increase sales by accommodating the stranger-than-fiction success stories of the Gilded Age millionaires. (pp. 134-36)

Whereas in the early Alger juveniles the hero must capitalize on his opportunities by rescuing a drowning child or returning a lost billfold, in the later books the hero enjoys Good Fortune as though he has been chosen by an inexorable fate to succeed. Ironically, these later novels with their fantastic endings did stem Alger's sales decline—albeit a generation too late—because they were probably the most popularly reprinted of his books during the period of his greatest sales early in the twentieth century. In other words, Alger may have acquired his modern reputation at least partly because an unrepresentative selection of his juvenile books became popular. (p. 136)

> Gary Scharnhorst, in his Horatio Alger, Jr., *Twayne Publishers, 1980, 170 p.*

ADDITIONAL BIBLIOGRAPHY

Alger, Horatio, Jr. "Advice from Horatio Alger, Jr." *The Writer* VI, No. I (January 1892): 16.
    A response to a letter from a young literary aspirant. Alger discusses how he became a successful author of juvenile stories.

———. "How I Came to Write 'John Maynard'." *The Writer* VIII, No. 12 (December 1895): 182-83.
    Personal reminiscence in which Alger briefly recalls the circumstances surrounding his composition of the popular ballad "John Maynard."

Bales, Jack. "The Truth about Alger." *Time* 104, No. 1 (1 July 1974): 6.
    A noteworthy letter to the editors. Bales faults the author of "Holy Horatio," an essay that appeared in *Time* on June 10, 1974 (see annotation below), for failing to mention that several of Alger's critics had questioned the authenticity of Herbert R. Mayes's *Alger: A Biography without a Hero* (see annotation below) prior to his confession that it was a fabrication. Bales is currently the editor of *Newsboy*, the Horatio Alger Society's publication.

———. "Herbert R. Mayes and Horatio Alger, Jr.; or the Story of a Unique Literary Hoax." *Journal of Popular Culture* VIII, No. 2 (Fall 1974): 317-19.
    Presents excerpts from Herbert R. Mayes's letters to William Henderson in 1972 in which Mayes first admitted that his *Alger: A Biography without a Hero* (see annotation below) "literally swarms . . . with countless absurdities."

Bennett, Bob. *Horatio Alger, Jr.: A Comprehensive Bibliography.* Mt. Pleasant, Mich.: Flying Eagle Publishing Co., 1980, 200 p.
    A bibliography of Alger's works "assembled primarily for the collector." Bennett provides a detailed description of all first editions of Alger's books, and he notes serializations of original titles and reprint title variations where applicable. Also included is a listing of poems, essays, and short stories written by Alger and the publications in which each has appeared.

Bowerman, Richard. "Horatio Alger, Jr.; or, Adrift in the Myth of Rags to Riches." *Journal of American Culture* 2, No. 1 (Spring 1979): 83-112.
    Rejects the notion that Alger was a popular spokesman for laissez-faire capitalism. According to Bowerman, "success" in Alger's works refers to the rehabilitation and relocation of street children rather than to the upward mobility of the poor.

Brooks, Van Wyck. "The Younger Generation of 1870." In his *New England: Indian Summer, 1865-1915,* pp. 184-203. New York: E. P. Dutton & Co., 1940.*

Faults Alger for vulgarizing Ralph Waldo Emerson's doctrine of self-reliance by writing for boys whose impetus was self-advancement rather than self-improvement.

Cawelti, John G. "Portrait of the Newsboy As a Young Man: Some Remarks on the Alger Stories." *Wisconsin Magazine of History* 45, No. 2 (Winter 1961-62): 79-83.
    A consideration of Alger's works within the context of late nineteenth-century children's literature. Cawelti attributes Alger's popularity to his "ability to express and resolve some of his juvenile audience's deepest ambivalences toward the adult world."

Coad, Bruce E. "The Alger Hero." In *Heroes of Popular Culture,* edited by Ray B. Browne, Marshall Fishwick, and Michael T. Marsden, pp. 42-51. Bowling Green, Ohio: Bowling Green University Popular Press, 1972.
    Assesses the motives of Alger's characters. Coad illustrates, through a close analysis of *Herbert Carter's Legacy; or, The Inventor's Son,* that "money, and little else, is what makes the Alger hero run."

Coyle, William. Introduction to *"Adrift in New York" and "The World before Him,"* by Horatio Alger, Jr., edited by William Coyle, pp. v-xvii. New York: Odyssey Press, 1966.
    Discusses the themes of success, individualism, social mobility, and urban life in Alger's works. In addition, Coyle identifies standard characters and episodes in Alger's stories.

Downs, Robert B. "Pluck and Luck: Horatio Alger, Jr.'s, *Ragged Dick,* 1868." In his *Famous American Books,* pp. 140-46. New York: McGraw-Hill Book Co., 1971.
    Describes the typical Alger plot and analyzes Alger's success formula.

Eaton, Anne Thaxter. "Widening Horizons, 1840-1890: The Field of Adventure in England and America, Frederick Marryat, George Henty, Robert Louis Stevenson, Oliver Optic, Richard H. Dana, Jules Verne." In *A Critical History of Children's Literature,* rev. ed., by Cornelia Meigs, Anne Thaxter Eaton, Elizabeth Nesbitt, and Ruth Hill Viguers, edited by Cornelia Meigs, pp. 214-24. London: Macmillan Co., 1969.*
    Briefly praises Alger for his humanitarianism.

Falk, Robert. "Notes on the 'Higher Criticism' of Horatio Alger, Jr." *The Arizona Quarterly* 19, No. 2 (Summer 1963): 151-67.
    A discussion of twentieth-century interpretations of Alger's life and writings that focuses on Herbert R. Mayes's *Alger: A Biography without a Hero* (see annotation below), Nathanael West's parody of the typical Alger novel, *A Cool Million; or, The Dismantling of Lemuel Pitkin* (see annotation below), and Norman N. Holland's analysis of Alger's works (see excerpt above, 1959-60). Falk argues that by concentrating on the monetary value which Alger appeared to place on the virtues of hard work, thrift, obedience, and patience, modern critics have failed to recognize that the stroke of luck the Alger hero invariably enjoys is the result of "divine providence."

Fiore, Jordan D. "Horatio Alger, Jr., As a Lincoln Biographer." *Illinois State Historical Society Journal* 46 (Autumn 1953): 247-53.
    Demonstrates that *Abraham Lincoln, the Backwoods Boy; or, How a Young Rail-Splitter Became President* follows the pattern of Alger's novels. While Fiore faults Alger's reliance on secondary sources, he concludes that Alger's biography of Lincoln "had value as a portrait for young people in the 1880s, when Horatio Alger, Jr., was perhaps more real to American boys than was Abraham Lincoln."

Gabriel, Gilbert W. "The Alger Complex." *The New Yorker* 1, No. 25 (8 August 1925): 6-7.
    Humorous description of Alger's idealism and its widespread acceptance by the American public.

Gardner, Ralph D. *Horatio Alger, or the American Hero Era.* Mendota, Ill.: Wayside Press, 1964, 505 p.
    Sympathetic treatment of Alger's life and writings by the foremost collector of his works and a self-proclaimed "Alger devotee." Gardner's expressed purpose is to provide readers with more ac-

curate biographical data than that presented in Herbert R. Mayes's *Alger: A Biography without a Hero* (see annotation below) which, Gardner states, contains "few facts, many errors and omissions, and must be considered as fiction." Gardner's study includes a bibliography of Alger's works that was reprinted under the title *Road to Success: The Bibliography of the Works of Horatio Alger* (see annotation below). In a review of a reprinted edition of Gardner's study, the later Alger biographer Gary Scharnhorst faulted the author for his reliance on Mayes's fabrication (see annotation below).

———. *Road to Success: The Bibliography of the Works of Horatio Alger*. Rev. ed. Mendota, Ill.: Wayside Press, 1971, 153 p.
    Updates Gardner's earlier bibliography of Alger's writings which was included in his *Horatio Alger, or the American Hero Era* (see annotation above). Compiled primarily for collectors of Alger's works, booksellers, librarians, and literary historians, Gardner's bibliography offers detailed descriptions of first editions and reprints of Alger's books and lists serializations and pseudonyms where applicable. In addition, Gardner assigns a monetary value to the various editions of each of Alger's books.

———. Introduction to *A Fancy of Hers. The Disagreeable Woman*, by Horatio Alger, pp. 1-19. New York: Van Nostrand Reinhold Co., 1981.
    Argues that accounts of Alger's homosexuality are based on inconclusive evidence. In addition, Gardner provides brief plot summaries and publication histories of *A Fancy of Hers* and *The Disagreeable Woman: A Social Mystery*.

Gruber, Frank. *Horatio Alger, Jr.: A Biography and Bibliography*. West Los Angeles: Grover Jones Press, 1961, 112 p.
    The first major attempt to discredit Herbert R. Mayes's *Alger: A Biography without a Hero* (see annotation below) which, Gruber writes, "is studded with . . . a vast number of factual errors and flights of the imagination." Protesting against Mayes's sensationalism, Gruber presents Alger as "an uninteresting figure" who "led a quiet life, a lonely life." In the bibliographic section of his work, Gruber provides the most accurate listing of Alger's books, short stories, and poems to have yet appeared.

Henderson, William. "A Few Words about Horatio Alger, Jr." *Publisher's Weekly* 203, No. 17 (23 April 1973): 32-3.
    Discusses the popular reception of Alger's novels during the nineteenth and twentieth centuries. Henderson also provides a brief extract from a letter he received from Herbert R. Mayes in July, 1972 in which Mayes first admitted that his *Alger: A Biography without a Hero* (see annotation below) was fictitious.

Holbrook, Stewart H. "Laissez Faire and Mr. Alger." In his *Lost Men of American History*, pp. 223-40. New York: Macmillan Co., 1946.*
    Argues that Alger, through the "Upward and Onward" theme of his stories, unwittingly brought the laissez-faire doctrine of the British philosopher Herbert Spencer to the American public during the last three decades of the nineteenth century. In addition, Holbrook summarizes Herbert R. Mayes's *Alger: A Biography Without a Hero* (see annotation below).

Hoyt, Edwin P. *Horatio's Boys: The Life and Works of Horatio Alger, Jr.* Radnor, Pa.: Chilton Book Co., 1974, 263 p.
    Biographical and critical study which emphasizes the evidence that Alger was homosexual. Hoyt's book is valuable primarily for its detailed plot summaries of several of Alger's stories, including *Paul Prescott's Charge, Ragged Dick, Mark, the Match Boy; or, Richard Hunter's Ward, Ben, the Luggage Boy; or, Among the Wharves*, and *Herbert Carter's Legacy; or, The Inventor's Son*. Although Hoyt, in the "Notes and Acknowledgements" section of his work, lists a number of primary sources, Alger bibliographers Gary Scharnhorst and Jack Bales (see annotation below) maintain that "apart from sensationalizing the evidence of Alger's homosexuality," Hoyt "merely summarizes" Ralph D. Gardner's *Horatio Alger, or The American Hero Era* (see annotation above).

Huber, Richard M. ". . . Religion Demands Success." In his *The American Idea of Success*, pp. 42-61. New York: McGraw-Hill Book Co., 1971.
    Demonstrates that Alger's works belie the "rags to riches" myth. Huber also discusses Herbert R. Mayes's *Alger: A Biography without a Hero* (see annotation below); noting that Mayes "would have uncovered a bigger story than any fantasy forged into a diary" had he "dug deeper into the sources," Huber quotes century-old records from the Unitarian Church in Brewster, Massachusetts which indicate that Alger was forced to resign his ministry in 1866 following charges that he was homosexual.

Kenner, Hugh. "The Promised Land." *The Bulletin of the Midwest Modern Language Association* 7, No. 2 (Fall 1974): 14-33.
    Compares Alger's prescription for success with that of F. Scott Fitzgerald in *The Great Gatsby*.

Lindberg-Seyersted, Brita. "Three Variations of the American Success Story: The Careers of Luke Larkin, Lemuel Barker, and Lemuel Pitkin." *English Studies* 53, No. 2 (April 1972): 125-41.
    Traces American response to the myth of success from the 1880s to the 1930s. Lindberg-Seyersted examines *Struggling Upward; or, Luke Larkin's Luck*, William Dean Howells's *The Minister's Charge; or, The Apprenticeship of Lemuel Barker*, and Nathanael West's *A Cool Million; or, The Dismantling of Lemuel Pitkin* (see annotation below) to display, respectively, "the full acceptance of the myth, a sincere questioning of it, and a total rejection."

Mayes, Herbert R. *Alger: A Biography without a Hero*. New York: Macy-Masius, 1928, 241 p.
    The first full-length biography of Alger. A fictitious account of Alger's life that was intended as a debunking of the anti-heroism vogue of the 1920s, Mayes's biography was accepted as authoritative by most of Alger's critics for nearly forty years and is quoted as a reliable source in most reference works.

Mott, Frank Luther. "For the Young in Heart." In his *Golden Multitudes: The Story of Best Sellers in the United States*, pp. 155-65. New York: Macmillan Co., 1947.
    Places total sales of Alger's works at 17,000,000, an estimate which many recent critics consider the most reliable.

Munsey, Frank A. "Two Veteran Authors." *Munsey's Magazine* 8, No. 1 (October 1892): 58-61.
    Biographical sketches of Alger and William T. Adams. Munsey's essay also includes a brief comparison of Alger's and Adams's fiction.

Nye, Russel. "Popular Fiction and Poetry: For It Was Indeed He, Books for the Young." In his *The Unembarrassed Muse: The Popular Arts in America*, pp. 60-87. New York: Dial Press, 1970.*
    Delineates Alger's most important cultural contributions to the late nineteenth century. Nye cites Alger's description of contemporary business practices, his emphasis on Puritan individualism, his recognition of the changing quality of urban life, and his affirmation of traditional middle-class values.

Scharnhorst, Gary. Review of *Alger: A Biography without a Hero*, by Herbert R. Mayes and *Horatio Alger, or the American Hero Era*, by Ralph D. Gardner. *American Literary Realism* XII, No. 2 (Autumn 1979): 355-58.*
    Compares Herbert R. Mayes's *Alger: A Biography without a Hero* (see annotation above) with Ralph D. Gardner's *Horatio Alger, or the American Hero Era* (see annotation above) upon the republication of both works. According to Scharnhorst, who concentrates on pointing out Gardner's "investigative shortcomings," Mayes "told a whopper which, to his credit, he never expected to be believed; and Gardner caught a carp which, in the telling, he pretends was a rainbow trout." Scharnhorst faults Gardner for omitting the evidence of Alger's homosexuality and identifies passages that he "borrowed" from Mayes's fabrication. In an introduction to *A Fancy of Hers. The Disagreeable Woman*, published in 1981, Gardner explains his failure to evaluate the evidence of Alger's homosexuality in his biography of the author (see annotation above).

————— and Bales, Jack. *Horatio Alger, Jr.: An Annotated Bibliography of Comment and Criticism.* The Scarecrow Author Bibliographies, no. 54. Metuchen, N.J.: Scarecrow Press, 1981, 179 p.

An indispensable annotated bibliography of commentary published from 1856 to 1980 on Alger's life and writings. Ironically, this bibliography, which is largely devoted to dispelling the misconceptions about Alger's life spawned by Herbert R. Mayes's *Alger: A Biography without a Hero* (see annotation above) and to tracing the spread of the Mayes myth, features an introduction by Mayes.

Schroeder, Fred. "America's First Literary Realist: Horatio Alger, Junior." *Western Humanities Review* XVII, No. 2 (Spring 1963): 129-37.

Praises Alger's early novels, particularly *Sam's Chance; and How He Improved It* and *The Young Outlaw; or, Adrift in the Streets,* as "concrete guidance" for homeless and worldly wise boys. Schroeder argues that Alger's early stories "stand alone in the history of children's literature in their stark honesty of urban realism." He further suggests that Alger's fiction influenced a number of later writers, including William Dean Howells, Mark Twain, Theodore Dreiser, and Stephen Crane.

Seelye, John. "Who Was Horatio? The Alger Myth and American Scholarship." *American Quarterly* XVII, No. 4 (Winter 1965): 749-56.

Discusses the impact of Herbert R. Mayes's *Alger: A Biography without a Hero* (see annotation above) on Alger scholarship.

Shepard, Douglas H. "Nathanael West Rewrites Horatio Alger, Jr." *Satire Newsletter* III, No. 1 (Fall 1965): 13-28.

Demonstrates, by comparing selected passages from *Andy Grant's Pluck* and Nathanael West's parody of the typical Alger story, *A Cool Million; or, The Dismantling of Lemuel Pitkin* (see annotation below), that West "'lifted'" portions of his novel directly from Alger's work.

Sisk, John P. "Rags to Riches." *The Commonweal* LXVII, No. 14 (3 January 1958): 352-54.

Maintains that American businessmen during the latter half of the nineteenth century were in "complete agreement" with Alger on the subject of character. According to Sisk, Alger's entrepreneur contemporaries believed that success in business could be achieved by practicing "Algerian self-denial."

Smith, Herbert F. "The Protestant Ethic." In his *The Popular American Novel: 1865-1920,* pp. 1-18. Boston: G. K. Hall & Co., Twayne Publishers, 1980.*

Maintains that Alger was a forerunner of the Realism movement in American literature.

"Holy Horatio!" *Time* 103, No. 23 (10 June 1974): 18.

Publicizes Herbert R. Mayes's admission that his *Alger: A Biography without a Hero* (see annotation above) was a fabrication. The critic suggests that Alger scholars were unaware of errors and contradictions in the biography prior to Mayes's confession, a suggestion that Jack Bales protested in a letter to the editors (see annotation above).

West, Nathanael. *A Cool Million; or, The Dismantling of Lemuel Pitkin.* In *The Complete Works of Nathanael West,* by Nathanael West, pp. 141-255. 1957. Reprint. New York: Farrar, Straus and Giroux, Octagon Books, 1978.

Satirizes the Alger success myth.

Wohl, R. Richard. "The 'Country Boy' Myth and Its Place in American Urban Culture: The Nineteenth-Century Contribution." In *Perspectives in American History,* Vol. III, edited by Donald Fleming and Bernard Bailyn, pp. 77-156. Cambridge: Charles Warren Center for Studies in American History, Harvard University, 1969.

Examines Alger's manipulation of the popular country boy legend in nineteenth-century children's literature. Unlike his predecessors who presented the country as "an imaginary Arcadia . . . free from all that was troubling and unsettled in the city," Wohl writes, Alger "glorified the city" and progressively eliminated the country, "except as a sort of ceremonial vestige," from his stories. By fusing the "mock-bucolic" country boy legend with a "novel, citified urbanity," Wohl contends, Alger transformed the legend "into an instrument to accommodate newly urban people to life in the city."

Charlotte Brontë

1816-1855

(Also wrote under pseudonym of Currer Bell) English novelist and poet.

The following entry presents criticism of Brontë's novel *Jane Eyre: An Autobiography*. For a complete discussion of Brontë's career, see *NCLC*, Vol. 3.

Jane Eyre (1847) is considered Charlotte Brontë's masterpiece and one of the most memorable novels in nineteenth-century literature. The plain yet confident, intelligent, and morally righteous Jane Eyre marked a departure from the typical heroine of nineteenth-century fiction, who was submissive, dependent, and beautiful, but ignorant. In the twentieth century, Charlotte Brontë is acclaimed as a precursor of feminist writings and an author whose talents, as evidenced in *Jane Eyre*, are far superior to those of many of her contemporaries.

The oldest surviving daughter in a family of six, Brontë helped raise her brother, Branwell, and two sisters, Emily and Anne. Their father, a strict clergyman, believed in self-education, and his family was forbidden to attend school or socialize with other children. Intellectual growth was encouraged by Mr. Brontë, however, and he introduced his family to the Bible and to the works of William Shakespeare, William Wordsworth, and Sir Walter Scott. Though the Bronte children were intellectually precocious, their cloistered upbringing created a sense of isolation that made social interaction outside the family difficult.

In 1824, Mr. Brontë sent Charlotte, Emily, Anne, and his two oldest daughters, Maria and Elizabeth, to Cowan Bridge, a school for the daughters of poor clergymen. Undoubtedly he selected the school for its low tuition, but the living conditions were intolerable and the discipline overly rigid. The "Lowood" section of *Jane Eyre* vividly conveys Charlotte's unhappy memories of her experience there. Within several months after their arrival, Maria and Elizabeth, weakened by poor diet and lack of rest, returned home where they died of malnutrition. Maria's death was especially traumatic for Charlotte and biographers believe that she was the inspiration for the character of Helen Burns, Jane's stoic friend at Lowood School.

After the deaths of their sisters, Charlotte, Emily, and Anne returned home. It was during this period that the sisters and their brother Branwell created the imaginary kingdom of Angria, which they chronicled in poems, stories, and plays. In these youthful writings, Angria provides the settings for wars, romance, and intrigue. Although the literary value of the Angrian chronicles is slight, they indicate the genesis of Charlotte's creative talents. During this period, Charlotte taught her sisters at home and worked briefly as a governess, an experience which she described in *Jane Eyre*. However, Brontë disliked her position and left in 1842 to study French in Belgium. There, she developed a passionate attachment to Constantin Héger, her married instructor. Héger provided Charlotte with a strong literary background and helped her develop the necessary confidence to write. Though their relationship was ill-fated, many scholars believe that Héger inspired the character of Jane Eyre's employer, Fairfax Rochester.

The Bettmann Archive, Inc.

Upon her return from Belgium, Charlotte discovered that Emily and Anne shared her interest in writing poetry, and the three published, at their own expense, *Poems by Currer, Ellis, and Acton Bell*. The sisters assumed male pseudonyms both to preserve secrecy and to avoid the patronizing treatment they believed critics accorded women. Nevertheless, the book received few reviews and sold only two copies. Undeterred by the lack of response, Charlotte continued to write. In 1847, she finished her first novel, *The Professor*, but could not sell it to a publisher. When one publishing house agreed instead to consider a lengthier, more exciting novel, Charlotte immediately completed *Jane Eyre*, which she had begun several months earlier. The novel, which Brontë presented as an autobiography edited by Currer Bell, met with immediate popular acclaim which has been sustained by succeeding generations of readers. Its appeal, both in the nineteenth century and the present, derives from Brontë's insightful depiction of a sensitive, intellectually aware woman who seeks love but is able to renounce her emotions for her moral convictions.

While *Jane Eyre* was immediately popular, initial critical reception of the novel varied. Several commentators admired the power and freshness of Brontë's prose; others, however, termed the novel superficial and vulgar. Perhaps the best known early review, by Elizabeth Rigby (see *NCLC*, Vol. 3), flatly condemned *Jane Eyre* as "an anti-Christian composition." Still other critics questioned the authorship of the novel. Some doubted that a woman was capable of writing such a work, while a critic in the *North American Review* contended that a man and a woman were coauthors. In another early assessment, George Eliot expressed her admiration for the novel but complained that Brontë's characters spoke like "the heroes and heroines of police reports."

Critical interpretations during the twentieth century have tended to be more specific in their approach. The characters of Jane, Rochester, and Bertha are the subjects of detailed analyses, and the nature and import of Rochester's disability is also debated. Critics frequently discuss the novel's structure, its symbolism, and its autobiographical elements. In the late twentieth century, *Jane Eyre* has inspired critical writing from a feminist perspective.

During the nineteenth century, critics often discussed the nature of Jane's character. Rigby had labeled Jane both immoral and anti-Christian as well as unlikeable, and George Saintsbury described her as "an underbred little hussy." By the turn of the century, however, critics tended toward Mary Ward's assessment of Jane as a character of courage and integrity. Cornelius Weygandt elaborated on Ward's interpretation, echoing William Makepeace Thackeray's depiction of Jane as "nobly planned." Another facet of Jane's character—her desire to be equal to her male counterparts—has also been discussed by a number of critics. G. Armour Craig contended that, in Jane's quest for maturity and personal freedom, she emerges as the superior individual in every relationship. In a similar vein, Martin S. Day and Maurianne Adams saw Jane as the mother in a parent/child relationship with Rochester. Conversely, Earl A. Knies and Adrienne Rich argued that in her marriage to Rochester Jane achieves a relationship of equality. Sandra M. Gilbert and Susan Gubar likened Jane's quest for parity to that of a pilgrim's struggle for freedom and prosperity.

Like Jane, the character of Rochester has inspired extensive critical controversy. Many early critics considered Rochester to be a monstrous creation. While nineteenth-century commentators discussed the nature of his personality, modern scholars have focused on his blinding and maiming following the fire at Thornfield. Richard Chase, Mark Schorer, and Craig proposed that Rochester's accident symbolized castration. On the other hand, Craik considered it a sacrificial reward, while Knies interpreted the injuries as an exorcism of Rochester's misdeeds. Such feminist interpreters as Nancy Pell argued that Rochester's crippling serves as a humbling experience; Maurianne Adams questioned whether his disability was meant to punish Rochester or rather to emphasize Jane's desire to feel needed by him.

Commentators are also divided in their interpretation of Bertha. Initially ignored by critics, Bertha was first analyzed by Chase as a symbol of the relationship between sex and intellect. In contrast to Chase, Craik called Bertha "the embodiment of ungoverned passion." Pell argued that she represented Rochester's desire to deny his past, but several later scholars noted that Bertha actually was a reflection of aspects of Jane's personality. To Adams, Bertha's imprisonment mirrored Jane's youthful confinement in the Red Room at the Reed home. In a similar vein, Gilbert and Gubar proposed that Bertha is a reflection of the angry side of Jane's personality; according to these critics, she is Jane's "dark double," symbolizing the rage Jane felt during her own isolation.

In the twentieth century, most critics have praised Brontë's narrative technique. Only Schorer disagreed, terming the struc-ture "nearly artless." Further, he argued that the story often borders on the absurd. Other critics, too, conceded that the plot is unrealistic, but pointed to other aspects which indicated Brontë's literary talent. Weygandt singled out specific passages that demonstrate the novel's powerful language. Kathleen Tillotson maintained that the novel's unity derives from the use of the heroine as narrator, and both Tillotson and Barbara Hardy agree that Jane's spiritual growth also unites the novel.

Symbolism, too, figures prominently in critical treatments of *Jane Eyre*. Lawrence E. Moser, Jane Millgate, and Adams all discuss the symbolic overtones of the paintings which Jane brings to Thornfield. To Moser, these works reveal both Jane and the author's personalities. In a similar vein, Millgate and Adams proposed that the paintings chart Jane's emotional maturation and also indicate various points of plot development. Tillotson discussed the recurrence of character in *Jane Eyre*. To her, the cruel Mr. Brocklehurst is reincarnated as St. John Rivers, and Jane's aunt, Mrs. Reed, reemerges as the snobbish Lady Ingram. Another symbolic interpretation was offered by Schorer, who traced the profusion of nature imagery underlying the drama of the novel.

While twentieth-century discussions of the novel's single theme still vary, most scholars agree that in *Jane Eyre* Brontë had wished to stress the possibility of equality in marriage. According to Chase, Brontë attempted to depict the neuroses of women in society. In another thematic interpretation, Hardy proposed that Brontë had intended to detail the power of human love while simultaneously indicating the role which Providence plays in the characters' lives. Similarly, Tillotson contended that the spiritual overtones of *Jane Eyre* present Brontë's message that a divine being governs our lives. More recently, both Craig and Pell maintained that Brontë sought to depict a woman's triumph over society's strictures.

While *Jane Eyre* undoubtedly reflects aspects of Brontë's own life, critics have disputed whether its merits result from autobiographical elements or from Brontë's creative vision. Saintsbury argued that Brontë relied too heavily on her own life for the plot and thus reduced the novel's dramatic impact. In an opposing view, Ward contended that Brontë's personality enhanced the emotional force of *Jane Eyre*. Weygandt concurred, stating that such immediacy of experience enriched the novel. Later, Tillotson maintained that Brontë was recording not so much her actual experiences as her youthful emotions. Perhaps the most concise assessment of Brontë's personal impact on the plot of *Jane Eyre* came from G. K. Chesterton, who termed the novel "the truest book that was ever written."

THE SPECTATOR (essay date 1847)

[*The following hostile review enraged Brontë because of its assessment of* Jane Eyre *as superficial.*]

Essentially, ***Jane Eyre, an Autobiography,*** has some resemblance to those sculptures of the middle ages in which considerable ability both mechanical and mental was often displayed upon subjects that had no existence in nature, and as far as delicacy was concerned were not pleasing in themselves. There is, indeed, none of their literal impossibilities or grotesqueness—we do not meet the faces of foxes or asses under clerical hoods; neither is there anything of physical grossness. But, with clear conceptions distinctly presented, a metaphysical consistency in the characters and their conduct, and considerable power in the execution, the whole is unnatural, and only critically interesting. There is one fault, too, in *Jane Eyre,* from which the artists of the middle ages were free—too much of artifice. Their mastery of their art was too great to induce them to resort to trick to tell their story. In the fiction edited by Currer Bell there is rather too much of this. Dialogues are carried on to tell the reader something he must know, or to infuse into him some explanations of the writer; persons act not as they would probably act in life, but to enable the author to do a ''bit o' writing''; everything is *made* to change just in the nick of time; and even the ''Returned Letter Office'' suspends its laws that Jane Eyre may carry on her tale with ''effect.''

The fiction belongs to that school where minute anatomy of the mind predominates over incidents; the last being made subordinate to description or the display of character. . . .

A story which contains nothing beyond itself is a very narrow representation of human life. *Jane Eyre* is this, if we admit it to be true; but its truth is not probable in the principal incidents, and still less in the manner in which the characters influence the incidents so as to produce conduct. There is a low tone of behaviour (rather than of morality) in the book; and, what is worse than all, neither the heroine nor hero attracts sympathy. The reader cannot see anything loveable in Mr. Rochester, nor why he should be so deeply in love with Jane Eyre; so that we have intense emotion without cause. The book, however, displays considerable skill in the plan, and great power, but rather shown in the writing than the matter; and this vigour sustains a species of interest to the last. (p. 1074)

> *A review of ''Jane Eyre,'' in* The Spectator, *Vol. 21, No. 1010, November 6, 1847, pp. 1074-75.*

THE ECONOMIST   (essay date 1847)

Of all the novels we have read for years [*Jane Eyre*] is the most striking, and, we may add, the most interesting. Its style as well as its characters are unhackneyed, perfectly fresh and lifelike, and the whole is as far removed from the namby pamby stuff of which fashionable novels are made, as from the cold, unnatural, and often disgusting productions of the French press. It is thoroughly English—even somewhat provincial—which latter leads, in some of the scenes, to a certain raciness decidedly agreeable. It must be said that the drawing in some cases approaches to coarseness, and that in others the art employed in the construction of the story is too evident; but these are venial faults, and worse than these may be forgiven an author who inspires his reader with such an interest in his heroes and heroines as we feel for Jane Eyre, Mr Rochester, her elderly lover, and in fact for all the characters introduced into the book.

> *A review of ''Jane Eyre: An Autobiography,'' in* The Economist, *Vol. V, No. 222, November 27, 1847, p. 1376.*

THE EXAMINER   (essay date 1847)

[*The critic praises* Jane Eyre *but doubts that a woman composed it. According to the critic,* Jane Eyre *is defective as a novel but forms an admirable autobiography.*]

There can be no question but that *Jane Eyre* is a very clever book. Indeed it is a book of decided power. The thoughts are

true, sound, and original; and the style, though rude and uncultivated here and there, is resolute, straightforward, and to the purpose. There are faults, which we may advert to presently; but there are also many beauties, and the object and moral of the work is excellent. Without being professedly didactic, the writer's intention (amongst other things) seems to be, to show how intellect and unswerving integrity may win their way, although oppressed by that predominating influence in society which is a mere consequence of the accidents of birth or fortune. There are, it is true, in this autobiography (which though relating to a woman, we do not believe to have been written by a woman), struggles, and throes, and misgivings, such as must necessarily occur in a contest where the advantages are all on one side; but in the end, the honesty, kindness of heart, and perseverance of the heroine, are seen triumphant over every obstacle. We confess that we like an author who throws himself into the front of the battle, as the champion of the weaker party; and when this is followed up by bold and skilful soldiership, we are compelled to yield him our respect.

Whatever faults may be urged against the book, no one can assert that it is weak or vapid. It is anything but a fashionable novel. . . . On the contrary, the heroine is cast amongst the thorns and brambles of life. . . . The hero, if so he may be called, is (or becomes) middle-aged, mutilated, blind, stern, and wilful. The sentences are of simple English; and the only fragrance that we encounter is that of the common garden flower, or the odour of Mr Rochester's cigar.

Taken as a novel or history of events, the book is obviously defective; but as an analysis of a single mind, as an elucidation of its progress from childhood to full age, it may claim comparison with any work of the same species. It is not a book to be examined, page by page, with the fictions of Sir Walter Scott or Sir Edward Lytton or Mr Dickens, from which (except in passages of character where the instant impression reminds us often of the power of the latter writer) it differs altogether. It should rather be placed by the side of the autobiographies of Godwin and his successors, and its comparative value may be then reckoned up, without fear or favour. . . .

The danger, in a book of this kind, is that the author, from an extreme love of his subject, and interest in the investigation of human motives, may pursue his analysis beyond what is consistent with the truth and vitality of his characters. In every book of fiction, the reader expects to meet with animated beings, complete in their structure, and active and mingling with the world; and he will accordingly reject a tale as spurious if he finds that the author, in his love of scientific research, has been merely putting together a metaphysical puzzle, when he should have been breathing into the nostrils of a living man.

The writer of *Jane Eyre* has in a great measure steered clear of this error (by no means altogether avoiding it), and the book is the better for it. (p. 756)

> *A review of ''Jane Eyre,'' in* The Examiner, *No. 2078, November 27, 1847, pp. 756-57.*

THE LITERARY WORLD   (essay date 1848)

[*Jane Eyre*], we will venture to say, will create a deeper interest and seize more strongly on the hearts of the reading public, than any work of fiction that has appeared since Miss Bremer's *Neighbors*. It is not a fiction, it is a transcript out of the real life of woman; it may be that some of the incidents are improbable or exaggerated, but the spirit of the book is truth itself. The machinery that carries on the story may have been invented, but the actual suffering, the sad experience, the sorrowing existence of the heroine, these are no cunning devices, and the story of these is the outpouring of the overcharged soul speaking in tones that find an echo in the reader's heart. The book is written with singular freshness; it is not "made up" in the usual "circulating library novel style," and filled with conventionalities and platitudes; it is vivid, real, and picturesque; the style is singular, but fascinating; the story is of singular interest, and rivets the attention to the last; the characters are drawn with a masterly hand, and individualized with singular power. Altogether, it is a work of great character and remarkable talent, and we feel assured that whoever commences it will not lay it down until the spell of enchantment is broken by the ending of the book.

> *A review of "Jane Eyre: An Autobiography," in* The Literary World, *Vol. II, No. 52, January 29, 1848, p. 633.*

GRAHAM'S MAGAZINE   (essay date 1848)

[*The critic indicates an admiration for* Jane Eyre *as a powerful and vivid novel, but faults the character of Rochester.*]

[That *Jane Eyre*] bears unmistakable marks of power and originality cannot be questioned, and in a limited range of characterization and description evinces sagacity and skill. The early portions of the novel are especially truthful and vivid. The description of the heroine's youthful life—the exact impression which is conveyed of the child's mind—the influences which went to modify her character—the scenes at the boarding-school—all have a distinctness of delineation which approaches reality itself. But when the authoress comes to deal with great passions, and represent morbid characters, we find that she is out of her element. The character of Rochester is the character of a mechanical monster. The authoress has no living idea of the kind of person she attempts to describe. She desires to represent a reckless man, made bad by circumstances, but retaining many marks of a noble character, and she fills his conversation with slang, makes him impudent and lustful, a rascal in every sense of the word, without the remotest idea of what true chivalric love for a woman means; and this mechanical automaton, whose every motion reveals that he moves not by vital powers but by springs and machinery, she makes her pure-minded heroine love and marry.

There has been a great deal of discussion about the morality of this part of the novel. The question resolves itself into a question of art, for we hold that truth of representation and morality of effect are identical. Immoral characters may be introduced into a book, and the effect be moral on the reader's mind, but a character which is both immoral and unnatural ever produces a pernicious effect. Now the authoress of *Jane Eyre* has drawn in Rochester an unnatural character, and she has done it from an ignorance of the inward condition of mind which immorality such as his either springs from or produces. The ruffian, with his fierce appetites and Satanic pride, his mistresses and his perjuries, his hard impudence and insulting sarcasms, she knows only verbally, so to speak. The words which describe such a character she interprets with her fancy, enlightened by a reminiscence of [Lord Byron's] *Childe Harold* and the *Corsair*. The result is a compound of vulgar rascalities and impotent Byronics. Every person who interprets her description by a knowledge of what profligacy is, cannot fail to see that she is absurdly connecting certain virtues, of which she knows a good deal, with certain vices, of which she knows nothing. The coarseness of portions of the novel, consisting not so much in the vulgarity of Rochester's conversation as the *naive* description of some of his acts—his conduct for three weeks before his intended marriage, for instance, is also to be laid partly to the ignorance of the authoress of what ruffianism is, and partly to her ignorance of what love is. No woman who had ever truly loved could have mistaken so completely the Rochester type, or could have made her heroine love a man of proud, selfish, ungovernable appetites, which no sophistry can lift out of lust. . . .

Byron's popularity, as distinguished from his fame, was mainly owing to the felicity with which he supplied the current demand for romantic wickedness. The authoress of *Jane Eyre* is not a Byron, but a talented woman, who, in her own sphere of thought and observation, is eminently trustworthy and true, but out of it hardly rises above the conceptions of a boarding-school Miss in her teens. She appears to us a kind of strong-minded old maid, but with her strong-mindedness greatly modified by the presumption as well as the sentimentality of romantic humbug.

> *A review of "Jane Eyre: An Autobiography," in* Graham's Magazine, *Vol. XXXII, No. 5, May, 1848, p. 299.*

GEORGE ELIOT [PSEUDONYM OF MARY ANN EVANS]   (letter date 1848)

[*Eliot is considered to be one of the foremost English novelists of the nineteenth century. Her novels, including* Middlemarch *and* The Mill on the Floss, *explore psychological and moral issues and provide intimate pictures of everyday life informed by a profound insight into human character.*]

I have read *Jane Eyre,* mon ami [my friend], and shall be glad to know what you admire in it. All self-sacrifice is good—but one would like it to be in a somewhat nobler cause than that of a diabolical law which chains a man soul and body to a putrefying carcase. However the book *is* interesting—only I wish the characters would talk a little less like the heroes and heroines of police reports. (p. 268)

> *George Eliot [pseudonym of Mary Ann Evans], in a letter to Charles Bray on June 11, 1848, in her* The George Eliot Letters: 1836-1851, *Vol. I, edited by Gordon S. Haight, Yale University Press, 1954, pp. 268-69.*

THE NORTH AMERICAN REVIEW   (essay date 1848)

[*The critic contends that* Jane Eyre *was written by both a man and a woman since Mr. Rochester appears to be the creation of a male imagination, yet other elements in the book are distinctly feminine. In addition, the critic states that the authors mar the work by their exaggerated treatment of human depravity.*]

[*Jane Eyre*] bears the marks of more than one mind and one sex, and has more variety than either of the novels which claim to have been written by Acton Bell [*Agnes Grey* and *The Tenant of Wildfell Hall*]. The family mind is strikingly peculiar, giving a strong impression of unity, but it is still male and female. From the masculine tone of *Jane Eyre,* it might pass altogether as the composition of a man, were it not for some unconscious feminine peculiarities, which the strongest-minded woman that ever aspired after manhood cannot suppress. These peculiarities refer not only to elaborate descriptions of dress, and the minutiae of the sick-chamber, but to various superficial refinements of feeling in regard to the external relations of the sex. It is true that the noblest and best representations of female character have been produced by men; but there are niceties of thought and emotion in a woman's mind which no man can delineate, but which often escape unawares from a female writer. There are numerous examples of these in *Jane Eyre*. The leading characteristic of the novel, however, and the secret of its charm, is the clear, distinct, decisive style of its representation of character, manners, and scenery; and this continually suggests a male mind. In the earlier chapters, there is little, perhaps, to break the impression that we are reading the autobiography of a powerful and peculiar female intellect; but when the admirable Mr. Rochester appears, and the profanity, brutality, and slang of the misanthropic profligate give their torpedo shocks to the nervous system,—and especially when we are favored with more than one scene given to the exhibition of mere animal appetite, and to courtship after the manner of kangaroos and the heroes of Dryden's plays,—we are gallant enough to detect the hand of a gentleman in the composition. (pp. 356-57)

The popularity of *Jane Eyre* was doubtless due in part to the freshness, raciness, and vigor of mind it evinced; but it was obtained not so much by these qualities as by frequent dealings in moral paradox, and by the hardihood of its assaults upon the prejudices of proper people. Nothing causes more delight, at least to one third of every community, than a successful attempt to wound the delicacy of their scrupulous neighbours, and a daring peep into regions which acknowledge the authority of no conventional rules. The authors of *Jane Eyre* have not accomplished this end without an occasional violation of probability and considerable confusion of plot and character, and they have made the capital mistake of supposing that an artistic representation of character and manners is a literal imitation of individual life. The consequence is, that in dealing with vicious personages they confound vulgarity with truth, and awaken too often a feeling of unmitigated disgust. The writer who colors too warmly the degrading scenes through which his immaculate hero passes is rightly held as an equivocal teacher of purity; it is not by the bold expression of blasphemy and ribaldry that a great novelist conveys the most truthful idea of the misanthropic and the dissolute. The truth is, that the whole firm of Bell & Co. seem to have a sense of the depravity of human nature peculiarly their own. It is the yahoo, not the demon, that they select for representation; their Pandemonium is of mud rather than fire. (p. 357)

A review of "Jane Eyre: An Autobiography," in The North American Review, *Vol. LXVII, No. CXLI, October, 1848, pp. 355-57.*

GEORGE SAINTSBURY   (essay date 1895)

[*Saintsbury was an English literary historian and critic of the late nineteenth and early twentieth centuries. A prolific writer, Saintsbury composed a number of histories of English and European literature as well as several critical works on individual authors, styles, and periods. In the following, first published in his* Corrected Impressions: Essays on Victorian Writers *in 1895, Saintsbury argues that while* Jane Eyre *is both original and forceful, it is "portrait painting" rather than "creative art," for it follows too closely the author's own experiences. Furthermore, he assesses Mr. Rochester as a "schoolgirl's or governess's hero" and Jane as somewhat unbred. Saintsbury's contention that Brontë's*

overly autobiographical aspects weaken Jane Eyre *is disputed by Mary Ward (1899-1900).*]

I do not think that with critical reading *Jane Eyre* improves, or even holds its ground very well. It has strength, or at any rate force; it has sufficient originality of manner; it has some direct observation of life within the due limits of art; and it has the piquancy of an unfashionable unconventionality at a very conventional time. These are good things, but they are not necessarily great; and it is to me a very suspicious point that quite the best parts of Charlotte Brontë's work are admittedly something like transcripts of her personal experience. It is very good to be able to record personal experience in this pointed and vivid way; and perhaps few great creators, if any, have been independent of personal experience. But they have for the most part transcribed it very far off; and they have intermixed the transcription with a far larger amount of direct observation of others, and of direct imagination or creation. Those who have not done so fall into the second or lower place, and do not often rise out of it. This is an experience for confirmation of which I can, I think, confidently appeal to all competent reviewers and most competent editors. A book appears, or an article is sent in, wherein this or that incident, mood, character, what not, is treated with distinct vigour and freshness. The reviewer praises, and looks with languid interest tempered by sad experience for the second book; the editor accepts, and looks with eagerness tempered by experience still more fatal for the second article. Both come, and lo! there is either a distinct falling off from, or a total absence of, the first fine rapture. I think Charlotte Brontë is the capital example of this familiar fact, in a person who has actually attained to literature.

Not that she never did anything good after *Jane Eyre*. I think better than most people seem to have done of *Shirley,* somewhat less well perhaps of *Villette* and *The Professor*. But in all, from *Jane Eyre* itself downward, there is that rather fatal note of the presence and apparent necessity of the personal experience. It is portrait painting or *genre,* not creative art of the unmistakable kind, and in the one case where there seems to be a certain projection of the ideal, the egregious Mr Rochester, even contemporary opinion—thankful as it was for a variation of type from the usual hero with the chiselled nose, the impeccable, or, if peccable, amiable character, and the general nullity—recognised at once that the ideal was rather a poor one. It was as much of a schoolgirl's or a governess's hero as any one of Scott's or Byron's. It is quite true that Rochester is not merely ugly and rude, but his ugliness and his rudeness are so much of him! And though Jane herself is much more than an underbred little hussy, I fear there is underbreeding and hussyness in her, where she is not a mere photograph. (pp. 277-79)

George Saintsbury, "Corrected Impressions: Three Mid-Century Novelists," in his The Collected Essays and Papers of George Saintsbury: 1875-1920, *Vol. II, E. P. Dutton & Co., 1923, pp. 276-82.**

MARY WARD   (essay date 1899-1900)

[*The following first appeared in 1899-1900 in Ward's preface to* Jane Eyre *in* The Life and Works of Charlotte Brontë and Her Sisters. *Ward identifies the novel's theme as Jane's confrontation with passion. Unlike George Saintsbury (1895), Ward stresses that it is the imposition of Charlotte's own personality on the sometimes inferior fictional material that insures the novel's greatness.*]

The true subject of *Jane Eyre* is the courage with which a friendless and loving girl confronts her own passion, and, in the interest of some strange social instinct which she knows as 'duty,' which she cannot explain and can only obey, tramples her love underfoot, and goes out miserable into the world. Beside this wrestle of the human will, everything else is trivial or vulgar. The various expedients—legacies, uncles, fires, and coincidences—by which Jane Eyre is ultimately brought to happiness, cheapen and degrade the book without convincing the reader. In fact ... *Jane Eyre* is on the one side a rather poor novel of incident, planned on the conventional pattern, and full of clumsy execution; on another side it is a picture of passion and of ideas, for which in truth the writer had no sufficient equipment; she moves imprisoned, to quote Mr Leslie Stephen, in 'a narrow circle of thoughts; if you press it, the psychology of the book is really childish; Rochester is absurd, Jane Eyre, in spite of the stir that she makes, only half-realized and half-conscious' [see *NCLC*, Vol. 3].

So far the objector; yet, in spite of it all, *Jane Eyre* persists, and Charlotte Brontë is with the immortals. What is it that a critic of this type forgets [?] ...

Simply, one might say, Charlotte Brontë herself. Literature, says Joubert, has been called the expression of society; and so no doubt it is, looked at as a whole. In the single writer, however, it appears rather as the expression of studies, or temper, or personality. And this last is the best. There are books so fine that literature in them is but the expression of those that write them. In other words, there are books where the writer seems to be everything, the material employed, the environment, almost nothing. The main secret of the charm that clings to Charlotte Brontë's books is, and will always be, the contact which they give us with her own fresh, indomitable, surprising personality—surprising, above all. In spite of its conventionalities of scheme, *Jane Eyre* has, in detail, in conversation, in the painting of character, that perpetual magic of the unexpected which overrides a thousand faults, and keeps the mood of the reader happy and alert ... The general plan may be commonplace, the ideas even of no great profundity; but the book is original. How often in the early scenes of childhood or school-life does one instinctively expect the conventional solution, the conventional softening, the conventional prettiness or quaintness ... And it never comes. Hammer-like, the blows of a passionate realism descend. Jane Eyre, the little helpless child, is never comforted; Mrs Reid, the cruel aunt, is never sorry for her cruelties; Bessie, the kind nurse, is not *very* kind ... she only just makes the story credible, the reader's assent possible. So, at Lowood, Helen Burns is not a suffering angel; there is nothing consciously pretty or touching in the wonderful picture of her: reality, with its discords, its infinite novelties, lends word and magic to the passion of Charlotte's memory of her dead sister, all is varied, living, poignant, full of the inexhaustible savour of truth, and warm with the fire of the heart.... (pp. 448-49)

> *Mary Ward, in an extract from* The Brontës: The Critical Heritage, *edited by Miriam Allott, Routledge & Kegan Paul, 1974, pp. 448-60.*

G. K. CHESTERTON   (essay date 1903)

[*Remembered primarily for his Father Brown detective stories, Chesterton was also an eminent biographer, essayist, novelist, poet, journalist, dramatist, and critic of the early twentieth century. His essays are characterized by their humor, frequent use of paradox, and rambling style. Chesterton praises Jane Eyre as*

"the truest book that was ever written".and maintains that it is Jane's very simplicity that allows her to experience fully the horrible forces of the world.]

Such a story as "**Jane Eyre**" is in itself so monstrous a fable that it ought to be excluded from a book of fairy tales. The characters do not do what they ought to do, nor what they would do, nor it might be said, such is the insanity of the atmosphere, not even what they intend to do. The conduct of Rochester is ... primevally and superhumanly caddish.... The scene in which Rochester dresses up as an old gipsy has something in it which is really not to be found in any other branch of art, except in the end of the pantomime, where the Emperor turns into a pantaloon. Yet, despite this vast nightmare of illusion and morbidity and ignorance of the world, "**Jane Eyre**" is perhaps the truest book that was ever written. Its essential truth to life sometimes makes one catch one's breath. For it is not true to manners, which are constantly false, or to facts, which are almost always false; it is true to the only existing thing which is true, emotion, the irreducible minimum, the indestructible germ. It would not matter a single straw if a Brontë story were a hundred times more moonstruck and improbable than "**Jane Eyre**." ... It would not matter if George Read stood on his head, and Mrs. Read rode on a dragon, if Fairfax Rochester had four eyes and St. John Rivers three legs, the story would still remain the truest story in the world. (pp. 6-8)

The shabby and inconspicuous governess of Charlotte Brontë, with the small outlook and the small creed, had more commerce with the awful and elemental forces which drive the world than a legion of lawless minor poets. She approached the universe with real simplicity, and, consequently, with real fear and delight. She was, so to speak, shy before the multitude of the stars, and in this she had possessed herself of the only force which can prevent enjoyment being as black and barren as routine. The faculty of being shy is the first and the most delicate of the powers of enjoyment. The fear of the Lord is the beginning of pleasure. (pp. 9-10)

Every one of us has had a day-dream of our own potential destiny not one atom more reasonable than "**Jane Eyre**." And the truth which the Brontës came to tell us is the truth that many waters cannot quench love, and that suburban respectability cannot touch or damp a secret enthusiasm. (p. 11)

> *G. K. Chesterton, "Charlotte Brontë," in his* Varied Types, *Dodd, Mead and Company, 1903, pp. 3-14.*

G. K. CHESTERTON   (essay date 1917)

[*Chesterton analyzes the coexistence of realism and romanticism in* Jane Eyre.]

The genius of Charlotte Brontë is unique in the only valuable sense in which the word can be applied; the only sense which separates the rarity of some gift in a poet from the rarity of some delusion in an asylum. However complex or even grotesque an artistic power may be, it must be as these qualities exist in a key, which is one of the most complex and grotesque of human objects, but which has for its object the opening of doors and the entrance into wider things. Charlotte Brontë's art was something more or less than complex: and it was not to be described as grotesque; except rarely—and unintentionally. But it was temperamental and, like all things depending on temperament, unequal: and it was so personal as to be perverse. It is in connection with power of this kind, however creative, that we have to discover and define what distinguishes it from the uncreative intensity of the insane. I cannot understand what it was that made the Philistines of a former generation regard *Jane Eyre* as morally unsound; probably it was its almost exaggerated morality. But if they had regarded it as mentally unsound, I could have understood their prejudice, while perceiving the nature of their error. *Jane Eyre* is, among other things, one of the finest detective stories in the world; and for any one artistically attuned to that rather electric atmosphere, the discovery of the mad wife of Rochester is, as that type of artistic sensation should always be, at once startling and suitable. But a stolid reader, trained in a tamer school of fiction, might be excused, I think, if he came to the conclusion that the wife was not very much madder than her husband, and that even the governess herself was a little queer. Such a critic, however, would be ill-taught, as people often are in tame schools; for the mildest school is anything but the most moral. The distinction between the liberating violence that belongs to virtue, as distinct from the merely burrowing and self-burying violence that belongs to vice, is something that can only be conveyed by metaphors; such as that I have used about the key. Some may feel disposed to say that the Brontë spirit was not so much a key as a battering-ram. She had indeed some command of both instruments, and could use the more domestic one quietly enough at times; but the vital point is that they opened the doors. Or it might be said that Jane Eyre and the mad woman lived in the same dark and rambling house of mystery, but for the maniac all doors opened continually inwards, while for the heroine all doors, one after the other, opened outwards towards the sun.

One of these universal values in the case of Charlotte Brontë is the light she throws on a very fashionable aesthetic fallacy: the over-iterated contrast between realism and romance. They are spoken of as if they were two alternative types of art, and sometimes even as if they were two antagonistic directions of spiritual obligation. But in truth they are things in two different categories; and, like all such things, can exist together, or apart, or in any degree of combination. Romance is a spirit; and as for realism, it is a convention. . . . [Romance] is an atmosphere, as distinct as a separate dimension, which co-exists with and penetrates the whole work of Charlotte Brontë; and is equally present in all her considerable triumphs of realism, and in her even greater triumphs of unreality.

Realism is a convention . . . : it is generally a matter of external artistic form, when it is not a matter of mere fashion or convenience, how far the details of life are given, or how far they are the details of the life we know best. . . . Works of the wildest fantasticality in form can be filled with a rationalistic and even a sober spirit: as are some of the works of Lucian, of Swift and of Voltaire. On the other hand, descriptions of the most humdrum environments, told with the most homely intimacy, can be shot through and through with the richest intensity, not only of the spirit of sentiment but of the spirit of adventure. Few will be impelled to call the household of Mr. Rochester a humdrum environment; but it is none the less true that Charlotte Brontë can fill the quietest rooms and corners with a psychological romance which is rather a matter of temperature than of time or place. After all, the sympathetic treatment of Mr. Rochester in *Jane Eyre* is not more intrinsically romantic and even exaggerative than the sympathetic treatment of Mr. Paul Emanuel in *Villette;* though the first may be superficially a sort of demon and the second more in the nature of an imp. To present Mr. Emanuel sympathetically at all was something of an arduous and chivalric adventure. And Charlotte Brontë was chivalric in this perfectly serious sense; per-

haps in too serious a sense, for she paid for the red-hot reality of her romance in a certain insufficiency of humour. She was adventurous, but in an intensely individualistic and therefore an intensely womanly way. It is the most feminine thing about her that we can think of her as a knight-errant, but hardly as one of an order or round table of knights-errant. Thackeray said that she reminded him of Joan of Arc. But it is one of the fascinating elements in the long romance of Christendom that figures like Joan of Arc have an existence in romance apart from, and even before, their existence in reality. This vision of the solitary virgin, adventurous and in arms, is very old in European literature and mythology; and the spirit of it went with the little governess along the roads to the dark mansion of madness as if to the castle of an ogre. The same tale had run like a silver thread through the purple tapestries of Ariosto; and we may willingly salute in our great country-woman, especially amid the greatest epic of our country, something of that nobility which is in the very name of Britomart. (pp. 49-54)

> G. K. Chesterton, "Charlotte Brontë As a Roman-
> tic," in Charlotte Brontë, 1816-1916: A Centenary
> Memorial, edited by Butler Wood, 1917. Reprint by
> E. P. Dutton and Company, 1918, pp. 49-54.

CORNELIUS WEYGANDT   (essay date 1925)

[Weygandt, in contrast to George Saintsbury (1895), argues that Brontë's power as a novelist stems from her personal experience. In addition, Weygandt provides a brief discussion of works which may have influenced the composition of Jane Eyre *and cites numerous passages as proof of the novel's powerful, evocative language.]*

The outstanding power of *Jane Eyre* and *Villette* alike is in their intensity and sincerity of self revelation. Both are written out of the experience as boarding-school pupil and governess and pupil-teacher of Charlotte Brontë. (p. 110)

There is a very great deal of diversity of opinion about the merits of the three books *Jane Eyre, Shirley,* and *Villette.* Perhaps just because there are only three of her stories that count a great many people have read all that is significant in Charlotte Brontë. Most of these have read [Emily Brontë's] *Wuthering Heights* too. In my experience there is another and very much larger group that has read only *Jane Eyre.* Does this mean that *Jane Eyre* has a universality of appeal denied to *Shirley* or *Villette,* or, for that matter, to *Wuthering Heights*? Or is it just chance that has won *Jane Eyre* such general recognition? It is, I think, that element of the mystery story in *Jane Eyre* that accounts for its popularity. If it were a mystery story and that only it would have passed as the stories of Lippard have passed with their passage on passage of passionate self-revelation; but its lyric joy in the beauty of the world, and the great portrait of Jane, of sombre tone quickened by wild light, have made it proof against the years. There is "flaming heart" in *Jane Eyre,* and "flaming heart" the world has never ignored in an artist. (p. 111)

[There] are many new points of view in Charlotte Brontë. Her presentation of life, too, is new, and the note she strikes is new, as new as the note of Poe. *Jane Eyre* is like no novel that preceded it. . . . Charlotte Brontë had not read Jane Austen when she began to write, and when she did read her she found nothing there to profit her own art of fiction. She had read Scott, and in her youth, had written: "All novels after his are worthless." There is something, perhaps, of Edgar Ravenswood in Mr. Rochester, but if there is, the debt is slight, and nowhere else in her, save in her description of landscape, is there any influence of Scott. Thackeray she came to admire only short of idolatry, but he was in no sense her master. From their mention in her writing we know that she had read [Jonathan Swift's *Gulliver's Travels,* Samuel Richardson's *Pamela,* and François Rabelais's *Rasselas*] but none of these books influenced her any more than the *Bewick's British Birds* (1804) she had likewise, as she would say, "perused." Her affiliations are with the poets rather than the novelists, and with the essayists who have risen to lyric prose. She harks back to *Ossian* and Carlyle; she foreshadows Meredith. Has not the famous description of Rachel, whom she called Vashti, the very accent of Meredith? "A great and new planet. . . . She rose at nine that December night: above the horizon I saw her come. She could shine yet with pale grandeur and steady might, but the star verged already on its judgment day. See near it was chaos— hollow, half-consumed—an orb perished or perishing—half lava, half glow." And does not the passage echo both Carlyle and MacPherson?

Yet most of Charlotte Brontë, ninety per cent of her, is of Haworth and her little experience of life and her native genius. (pp. 112-13)

There is much that is not fine in *Jane Eyre.* Thackeray was amused at the thrillingness to Jane of the fragrance of Mr. Rochester's cigar, "the trail of Havana incense," and he perplexed Miss Brontë with pleasantry on the subject. No doubt he smiled, too, at much else in this so palpably woman's man, as all men who have met Mr. Rochester since that day have smiled. Yet Mr. Rochester is not to be smiled away. Strip him of the feminine Byronics and you have a man there, a man of mettle and hard intent. There is much that is impossible in the story. Jane could not but have known there was a mad woman in the house. But these impossibilities . . . do not, somehow, matter much. And that mad woman's prowlings about the house furnish their share of drama to the story. As a child I was haunted by that scene of Jane's awakening in the night to see the maniac's face peering into her own; and forty years afterwards that scene scores with me as of old.

What delights me most now in *Jane Eyre* is the revelation of Jane, a woman not perfect, but "nobly planned," of that "passionate honor" Thackeray saw in Charlotte Brontë, and that Charlotte Brontë was able to transfer to Jane Eyre. What else most delights me now is the wealth of lyric passages in the story, capturings of mood, flashes of insight, descriptions of the countryside. This one moves me somewhat in the way the "Toys" of Coventry Patmore moves me:

> I covered my head and arms with the skirt of my frock, and went out to walk in a part of the plantation that was quite sequestered. . . . I leaned against a gate, and looked into an empty field in which no sheep were feeding, where the short grass was nipped and blanched. It was a very gray day; a most opaque sky 'onding on snaw,' canopied all; thence flakes fell at intervals, which settled on the hard path and on the hoary lea without melting. I stood, a wretched child enough, whispering to myself over and over again, "What shall I do?"—"What shall I do?"

There is more joy in Mr. Rochester's tribute to a gray day at Thornfield, though it ends, as so much in *Jane Eyre* ends, on a note of bitterness and aversion:

> I like this day; I like that sky of steel; I like the sternness and stillness of the world under frost. I like Thornfield; its antiquity; its retirement; its old crow-trees and thorn-trees; its gray façade, and lines of dark windows reflecting the metal welkin; and yet how long have I abhorred the very thought of it; shunned it like a great plague-house.

That "metal welkin," and the "hoary lea" of the former passage are rhetoric that one cannot explain away as symptomatic of the age. They persist in memory and hurt on every reading. Yet despite them how memorable are the passages! (pp. 114-15)

There is space, sweep, contours of half a continent, in this description of hard weather:

> The keen, still cold of the morning was succeeded, later in the day, by a sharp breathing from Russian wastes; the cold zone sighed over the temperate zone and froze it fast. A heavy firmament, dull and thick with snow sailed up from the north, and settled over expectant Europe.

Such passages as these do not arrest us on a first reading. They may even be skipped when our interest is the incident. When we read *Jane Eyre* the first time we are eager to find out how things are to go, as she grows up, with this passionate little girl, whose fortunes have so interested us from the moment of our meeting. The interest we have in her deepens with every change in her life. We are interested in her at Gateshead Hall; we are more interested in her at Lowood, though these school scenes are too long-drawn out; we are on tenter-hooks as to her fate at Thornfield. And when the marriage of Jane and Mr. Rochester is forbidden at the altar! Will it be "all for love and the world well lost"? Will Jane go with Mr. Rochester though she cannot be his wife? The old, old struggle between duty and desire is again presented, but we who know Jane have never a doubt. . . . Jane Eyre, like Charlotte Brontë, was a woman of "passionate honor." Yet the situation is dramatic, tense, almost agonizing. Her flight from Thornfield is finely told; the recital of her reduction to starvation a remarkable achievement for a writer who had no personal experiences of a like sort to serve as guide; and her return to Mr. Rochester, free but blind, at his call of need heard by her inward ear across the half of England, an admirably conceived short cut to a happy ending. (pp. 117-18)

*Cornelius Weygandt, "The Spectacle of the Brontës,"
in his* A Century of the English Novel, *The Century
Co., 1925, pp. 102-21.**

RICHARD CHASE (essay date 1947)

[*Chase acknowledges the feminist overtones of* Jane Eyre, *but asserts that the novel is far more than a tract encouraging equality of the sexes. He contends that the Brontës' heroines were "cultural heroines" as in mythology who transformed primeval society into orderly civilization. The author's universe, as perceived by Chase, is charged with sexual energy epitomized by Edward Rochester. His injury, according to Chase, is a symbolic castration. For a similar interpretation of Rochester's maiming, see the excerpts below by G. Armour Craig (1956) and Mark Schorer (1959).*]

Why do *Jane Eyre* and [Emily Brontë's] *Wuthering Heights* now seem the most exciting of Victorian novels? Because, I think, these novels translated the social customs of the time into the forms of mythical art, whereas many other Victorian novels were translated by the social customs into more or less tiresome canting. (p. 488)

In *Jane Eyre* and *Wuthering Heights* the universe is conceived as the embodiment of [sexual] energy or *élan*. In *Jane Eyre* the wondrous Helen Burns, as she is dying, places her faith in "the impalpable principle of life and thought, pure as when it left the Creator to inspire the creature: whence it came it will return; perhaps again to be communicated to some being higher than man—perhaps to pass through gradations of glory, from the pale human soul to brighten to the seraph! Surely it will never, on the contrary, be suffered to degenerate from man to fiend?" The "principle" of life and thought in the Brontë novels is sexual Energy; the universe is the stone and flesh which make the Energy palpable; it is a masculine universe. Art is the representation of the "principle" as the Brontë heroines perceived it embodied in nature, in man, in seraph, and in fiend. (p. 490)

In that somewhat fantastic Gothical-Byronic character Edward Rochester we have Charlotte Brontë's symbolic embodiment of the masculine *élan*. Jane Eyre's feelings toward Rochester are, as Freud would say, "ambivalent." He draws her to him with a strange fascination; yet she is repelled by his animalism and his demonism. She wishes to submit herself to him; yet she cannot. She is nearly enthralled by the "tenderness and passion in every lineament" of his "kindled" face; yet she shrinks from the flashing of his "falcon eye" and from the glamor of his self-proclaimed guilt and his many exploits among women of other countries (in France, Céline; in Italy, Giacinta; in Germany, Clara—"these poor girls" Jane calls them). She cannot permit the proffered intimacies of this man who keeps a mad wife locked up in his attic. And if her moral scruples would allow his embrace, still she could not endure the intensity of his passion. The noble, free companionship of man and woman does not present itself to her as a possibility. She sees only two possible modes of behavior: meek submission or a flirtatious, gently sadistic skirmishing designed to keep her lover at bay. Finally her sense of "duty" compels Jane to run away. The inevitable parting of the lovers had been forecast when the lightning, summoned from the sky by their first declaration of love, had split the garden chestnut tree asunder.

The splitting of the tree, however, symbolizes also two alternate images of Jane Eyre's soul, two possible extremes which, as she believes, her behavior may take. At one extreme is Bertha, Rochester's mad wife; at the other is St. John Rivers, the clergyman cousin whom Jane meets after she flees Rochester and who wants to marry her. Before the story can end, Jane must look into her Narcissus' mirror and purge these false images of herself. Bertha represents the woman who has given herself blindly and uncompromisingly to the principle of sex and intellect. . . . May not Bertha, Jane seems to ask herself, be a living example of what happens to a woman who gives herself to the Romantic Hero, who in her insane suffragettism tries herself to play the Hero, to be the fleshly vessel of the *élan*?

We may think that fear drives Jane away from Rochester; *she*, however, says that it is "duty." In St. John Rivers she meets duty incarnate. . . . Rivers has given up Rosamond Oliver, a charming and life-loving girl, and wants to marry Jane and take her to India, where he plans to devote himself to missionary work. Plainly, it would be a sexless marriage. Rivers wants a wife to "influence." He is cold, selfish, fanatical— a narrow bigot, who shakes Jane's confidence in "duty." She

cannot marry Rivers; she must purge her soul to the image of "duty" as she has of the image of Bertha.

How to resolve the plot? It must be done as Charlotte, the leader of her sisters in all practical matters, was accustomed to do things: by positive action. The universe conspiring against Jane Eyre, like the circumstances which so often conspired against the sisters, must be chastened by an assertion of will, catastrophic if necessary. And so she sends Rochester's house up in flames and makes him lose his eyesight and his left hand in a vain attempt to save Bertha. Rochester's injuries are, I should think, a symbolic castration. The faculty of vision, the analysts have shown, is often identified in the unconscious with the energy of sex. When Rochester had tried to make love to Jane, she had felt a "fiery hand grasp at her vitals;" the hand, then, must be cut off. The universe, not previously amenable to supernatural communication between the parted lovers, now allows them to hear each other though they are leagues apart. Jane Eyre now comes into her own. She returns to Rochester. (pp. 493-95)

[The] Brontë novels are concerned with the neuroses of women in a man's society. But surely this theme alone cannot account for the wonder and interest we feel in *Jane Eyre* and *Wuthering Heights*. The personalist theme involves a societal theme; the sexual involves the utopian. What is the large moral upshot of the relation between Jane and Cathy and their lovers? What is the ultimate significance of these heroines? Well, obviously *Jane Eyre* is a feminist tract, an argument for the social betterment of governesses and equal rights for women. But we have to see this propaganda and other explicit elements of the Brontë novels in comprehensive mythical images before we can begin to understand their full significance. . . . This poor orphan child with a mission in a hostile world is like Cinderella certainly. Also she is like Joan of Arc and, as Chesterton observes, the solitary virgin of the folktales who goes to the castle of the ogre [see excerpt above, 1917]. I suggest that to the Brontës this pilgrim virgin is a culture heroine. The culture heroes of mythology are those figures who, like Hercules, Prometheus, or the animal deities of the American Indians, slay the monsters or overcome natural or human obstacles or bring intelligence to men so that civilization can be born out of savagery and chaos—"transformers," the anthropologists call these culture heroes. It was the Victorian period which supposed that the primeval social order consisted of a murderous old man and his company of females and weaker males and which bequeathed the idea to Freud. . . . The purpose of the Brontë culture heroine as a mythical being is to transform primeval society into a humane and noble order of civilization. But this idea requires another excursus.

There are many methods of describing the transformation of primitive society into civilization. But the method most applicable to the problem as creative writers conceive it in novels and poems is that of A. J. Toynbee (*A Study of History*, 1933-38). Briefly, Toynbee's method is mythological: primitive society is a stasis presided over by a once creative Father-God, Whose perfection is also a stasis. God must be forced into the motion of further creativity by a wager flung to Him by the Devil. The human protagonist of the cultural tragedy (Toynbee follows the theme of Goethe's *Faust*) must perform a dynamic act, which will set God and the Devil at war. In the path of the culture hero there stands an Obstacle. The dynamic act of the hero hurls him against the Obstacle—if he is overcome by it, the Devil has won the wager and society fails to advance along the path of civilization; but if he overcomes it, God has won;

the Devil, who sought to perpetuate the death-like stasis, is routed; and God, the creative *Élan* or "the impalpable principle of life and thought," as Helen Burns calls Him, reasserts Himself in the soul of man. Our Brontë culture heroine . . . is the human protagonist of the cosmic drama. Rochester and Heathcliff are portrayed as being at once God-like and Satanic. In them the universal enemies may be set at war by a culture heroine who performs the decisive dynamic act. Then, if the Devil is overcome, a higher state of society will have been achieved. The tyrannical Father-God will have been displaced. The stasis will have been smashed by the creative *élan* of sex and intelligence. The Brontë heroines fail in their mission; they refuse to venture so much; they will not accept the challenge of the God-Devil, for fear the Devil should win. Yet when we understand these heroines in some such terms as the foregoing, they acquire a new significance: it had not occurred to us that the stakes were so great.

Charlotte Brontë, whose many practical predicaments . . . forced her to solve problems by forthright acts of will, made the plot of *Jane Eyre* proceed in a rhythm of stasis and activity. Thus we find Jane on a hillside near Rochester's estate after she has been hired as governess but before she has met Rochester. . . . As yet she has not found the driving force of the new life for which she hopes. The universe is frozen in the cold of winter; the world is silent, in "leafless repose." The pale moon presides over the scene. Then suddenly the stasis is shattered by a vigorous animal invasion; Rochester with horse and dog comes upon the scene. (pp. 496-99)

The aesthetic procedure of Charlotte Brontë makes her novel a series of set pieces, *tableaux*, or great scenes which periodically resolve themselves out of the interspersed areas of formless activity (like the charades staged by Rochester and Blanche Ingram for his aristocratic guests). . . . Charlotte constantly lays violent hands on the progress of her story. . . . And it is true that . . . [she does] not always seem to be fully aware of what is implied in . . . [her] own novels. In *Jane Eyre* this produces some remarkably naive and inapposite dialogue. (pp. 499-500)

The happy marriages at the end of *Jane Eyre* and *Wuthering Heights* represent the triumph of the moderate, secular, naturalistic, liberal, sentimental point of view over the mythical, religious, tragic point of view. The moral texture of these novels is woven whole cloth out of the social customs of the day. To the heroic marriage of free and God-like souls, to the futurist utopias of sexual society, the Brontës plainly preferred domesticity—and this despite the fact that no one knew better the readiness with which the Victorian family reverted to the primitive horde. They "rebelled" only in the sense that they transmuted the Victorian social situation into mythical and symbolic forms. And this reminds us that the fault of much of our criticism of 19th Century literature is to mistake art for rebellion. (pp. 505-06)

> *Richard Chase, "The Brontës: A Centennial Observance (Reconsiderations VIII)," in* The Kenyon Review, *Vol. IX, No. 4, Autumn, 1947, pp. 487-506.*

KATHLEEN TILLOTSON   (essay date 1954)

[*Tillotson praises the use of the first-person narrator in* Jane Eyre, *and considers it the key to the novel's unity. Jane's spiritual growth, according to Tillotson, adds to the novel's inclusiveness and forms the basis of Jane's development as a character. Barbara Hardy (1964) also emphasizes Jane's spiritual awareness.*]

'An Autobiography': the choice of this form is of vital importance to the structure of the novel [*Jane Eyre: An Autobiography*]. Not, however, because the author is ever transcribing experience. The criticism of the Brontë novels is so overlaid with biographical conjecture that it is well at the outset to recall Charlotte's explicit disclaimer;

> Jane Eyre was naturally and universally supposed to be Charlotte herself; but she always denied it, calmly, cheerfully, and with the obvious sincerity which characterised all she said.

The basis was no more than this: she determined to take, in defiance of convention, a heroine 'as small and as plain as [her]self' who should nevertheless be 'interesting'. . . . The crucially different circumstance—and to the common novel-reader's view, the 'interesting' one—is, of course, Jane Eyre's lack of family. The whole of Charlotte's life was conditioned by her duties as daughter and sister; Jane is free of all ties. She is also ignorant. To enter the being of Jane Eyre, the author deliberately discarded much of her own knowledge, quantitatively at least, of men: of father, brother, employers, curates, brothers of friends. Jane knows only three men, who indeed form the novel's pattern—Mr. Brocklehurst, Mr. Rochester, and St. John Rivers. What Charlotte Brontë used from her own experience was feeling, not fact; especially feeling drawn from its most detached and solitary phases—for example, the feeling of a young child at boarding-school, dumb sufferer and witness of harshness towards others; and of the governess at a family party. . . . (pp. 291-92)

For the peculiar unity of *Jane Eyre,* the use of the heroine as narrator is mainly responsible.

All is seen from the vantage-ground of the single experience of the central character, with which experience the author has imaginatively identified herself, and invited the engagement, again even to the point of imaginative identification, of every reader. For both author and reader the threads of actual common experience are unbreakable, if slender; and they lead into the realms not of daydream, but of art. Only ingenuousness or assured mastery would choose such a method; to charge its limitations with the utmost significance, to avoid all its pitfalls, is the fortunate achievement of very few. The single point of view may be easily held at the circumference of the narrative and the emotional interest; but Jane continually, quietly, triumphantly occupies the centre, never receding into the role of mere reflector or observer—as does David Copperfield [in Charles Dickens's novel of the same name] for several chapters at a time. Nor is she ever seen ironically, with the author hovering just visibly beyond her, hinting at her obtuseness and self-deception. . . . [The] reader of *Jane Eyre* at best keeps pace with the heroine, with her understanding of events (it would be a safe assumption that every reader shares her suspicions of Grace Poole) and of character, including her own. A special difficulty of presenting a central character in first-person narration (and one more incident to heroines, since custom allows women less latitude here) is that of combining enough self-description and self-analysis to define, with enough self-forgetfulness to attract. This difficulty also Charlotte Brontë circumvents; Jane is not tediously egotistical. . . . Jane is self-critical, but also self-respecting; her modesty attracts while never making the reader take her at her own initial valuation. We watch a personality discovering itself not by long introspection but by a habit of keeping pace with her own experience. It is from her own explicit record that we are convinced both of her plainness and her charm, her delicacy and her endurance, her humility and her pride. Contrivance is never obtrusive and on a first reading probably unnoticed as such; in the rapid current of the narrative the deliberate contribution of others' view of her is accepted unconsciously as part of our picture of Jane. . . . At Thornfield, Mr. Rochester's half-irritated speculations on Jane's appearance and nature build up a still clearer definition; but we are so much occupied in discovering his own still more mysterious character and attitude that we hardly notice *how* we are being helped to see Jane. (pp. 294-96)

Jane keeps no journal and writes no letters; she simply re-enters her experience, and even the vision of herself as retrospective recorder is rare and delicately timed. . . . (p. 297)

Rarely in self-analysis, though more often in description, are we aware of 'the quiet medium of time'; the tense of most of the novel is the just-after-present. . . . Truth to immediate experience extends to minutest detail; the description of Miss Temple is partly retrospective—'round curls, according to the fashion of those times . . . watches were not so common then as now . . .' but it ends with a quiet return to the child's view. . . . (p. 298)

The consistency and flexibility of the first person method is unusual, and its use in a narrative of childhood perhaps an absolute novelty in fiction. The novel would have lost incalculably had it started later in Jane's life—say, at her setting out for Thornfield. The early chapters are no mere prologue; they expound a situation, introduce and partly account for a character, and initiate the major themes of the whole novel. Presented as a child, she engages interest, sympathy, and admiration, which is yet kept clear . . . of a too generic compassion. . . . But, beyond all other examples in the novel, *Jane Eyre* arrests attention in its opening chapters by disclosing an individual character enmeshed in, yet independent of, unusual circumstances. And it is the opening of a poetic novel; season, scene, and character are interpenetrated. . . . (pp. 298-99)

An indoor scene on a winter's day; a child in disgrace, excluded from the family circle, reading a book in a curtained window-seat; a creature dependent, captive, yet with the liberty of adventure in imagination—a window to look out of, a book to read and pictures on which to build fancies. The double impression of constraint and freedom is burnt into the mind in those first few paragraphs; it is accompanied by the symbol (to become recurrent) of the window. From this retreat we see her dragged out, bullied, insulted; she is a terrified cornered animal—but one that fights back, with intellectual and imaginative resourcefulness. . . . John Reed's taunts skilfully conceal a piece of formal exposition, in which the outline of Jane's situation is conveyed to us—a child without status or adult protector. (pp. 300-01)

The deliberate dryness of tone and accompanying self-criticism make the early chapters less harrowing than they could have been. . . . (p. 302)

Figures in the pattern recur; Lady Ingram will remind Jane of Mrs. Reed, as a worldly cold-hearted mother of conventionally attractive daughters, who personifies the same threat to her happiness. The two sisters are indeed three times repeated, as the Brocklehursts, Ingrams, and Riverses. Most significantly, the image used for Mr. Brocklehurst is repeated for St. John Rivers—'at the fireside, . . . a cold cumbrous column, gloomy and out of place'. He gathers into himself the cousinship of John Reed, the formidable religious sanctions of Mr. Brocklehurst, and the desire for possession of Mr. Rochester: it takes

more than Jane's mature powers of resistance for her to fight back at this final enemy; supernatural aid is hers.

Above all, in these early chapters there is gradually disengaged from the generic impression of a child robbed of its birthright the individual figure of a heart hungering for affection. Save for a few unconsciously dropped crumbs from Bessie, at Gateshead her bread is stones; in the choric words of Bessie's song 'Men are hard-hearted', and the assurance that 'Kind angels only Watch o'er the steps of the poor orphan child' is as yet barren of comfort; there are no angels in Mr. Brocklehurst's religion. Lowood opens inauspiciously, with still harsher physical discomfort—not merely piercingly actual (the taste of the burnt porridge, the starved arms wrapped in pinafores) but symbolic of a loveless order of things. In Helen Burns and Miss Temple appear the first shadowings of hope; the warm fire and the cake from the cupboard in Miss Temple's room are assertions of individual loving-kindness, though also of its limited power; and Helen's comfort in injustice reaches her as from another world. . . . (pp. 303-05)

Part of the novel's inclusiveness and unity comes from Jane's spiritual growth: her individual religion [is] sharply distinguished from the loveless creeds of Mr. Brocklehurst, Eliza Reed, and St. John Rivers. . . . When therefore in her deepest despair 'One idea only still throbbed life-like within me—a remembrance of God' and 'begot an unuttered prayer' it is no merely rhetorical gesture. This is not to . . . [claim] *Jane Eyre* as a Christian novel; though it expresses, more directly than any other novel, the convictions of many creedless Christians in the eighteen-forties; the conviction that 'not a May-game is this man's life, but a battle and a march, a warfare with principalities and powers'. The master-influence of the decade is audible when Jane asserts to Rochester, 'We are born to strive and to endure'.

That the reader is aware of the 'other world', into whatever formulae he may choose to translate it, and that Jane's progress is one of spiritual growth as well as emotional adventure, is perhaps made most evident if one imagines the alternative issue. If Jane had yielded [to Rochester], the novel would still be 'serious'; a novel with a purpose indeed, striking a blow for insurgent feminism, the anarchy of passion, and the reform of the divorce laws. But it would have been smaller and narrower, and would have violated its own moral pattern.

It would also have lost had it ended with renunciation. The phase which ends with Jane's resistance and flight is in fact the third Act; there are ten chapters—nearly a third of the novel—before we reach harbour with, 'Reader, I married him'. They are the least appreciated part of the novel: but an essential part of its unity, knitted alike to the Thornfield and the Lowood chapters. For they show Jane becoming calm after suffering, again giving 'allegiance to duty and order', again studying, again teaching in a school, submitting to virtue in lovable form, as she had once submitted to Miss Temple. They also show her tempted by and withstanding the opposite temptation to Mr. Rochester's—that of duty and virtue which take no account of passion, personified in St. John Rivers, in appearance and manner Rochester's antithesis. . . . (pp. 308-10)

[The reconciliation of Jane and Rochester] is the most artful reconciliation possible—not only of Jane and Rochester, but of the different kinds of love threaded through the novel; and the appropriate assurance of future happiness to these so articulate lovers—after ten years' marriage she can still say, 'We talk, I believe, all day long'. The spiritual pattern is also resolved; not only by his new dependence on her, but by the disclosure that at the moment of the miraculous voice, he was calling to her, in penitence and prayer. 'I kept these things, then, and pondered them in my heart.' But the true climax, the justified superlative, is the last proposal:

> 'Jane suits me: do I suit her?'
> 'To the finest fibre of my nature, sir.'

with the typically practical consequence:

> 'The case being so, we have nothing in the world to wait for; we must be married instantly.'

The discovery and revelation of that fineness of fibre is this novel's triumph. There is no character in any novel of the eighteen-forties whom the reader knows as intimately as Jane Eyre: and it is an intimacy at all levels—alike with the fiery spirit and the shivering child. (pp. 312-13)

> *Kathleen Tillotson, "'Jane Eyre'," in her* Novels of the Eighteen-Forties, *Oxford at the Clarendon Press, 1954, pp. 257-313.*

G. ARMOUR CRAIG (essay date 1956)

[*Throughout the novel, Craig asserts, Jane ascends new "gradations of glory," for in every relationship or confrontation, Jane emerges as the superior individual. To Craig, inferiority in* Jane Eyre *is reflected as imprisonment, while superiority is synonymous with freedom. Craig also interprets* Jane Eyre *as the product of a single vision, and he does not discriminate between Jane and Charlotte; he contends that the powerful "I" of the novel is both the author and the heroine. This viewpoint is later disputed by Earl Knies (1969). Like Richard Chase (1947) and Mark Schorer (1959), Craig assesses Rochester's wounding as a form of castration.*]

[The] novels of the last century yield some surprising observations when we approach them through our interest in the outcome of private visions. They can show us how large the single consciousness must be when it achieves a sense of society, and they can show us the distinctions it must contain if the difference between the dreamer and the world is to be preserved. They can show us, in brief, just how much variety the mere social mind can support. No novel is more relevant to such an approach than *Jane Eyre*. The success of this work a literary historian must find too good to be true; it is the novel he must have invented if he had not found so many readers captured by it. For no heroine dreams more often or more successfully than the heroine of this strange romance.

After she has escaped from the "prison-ground" of Lowood to become governess at Thornfield, Jane's visions enlarge and become more frequent. Often, she tells us, she climbed to the attic of the big house and there "looked out afar over sequestered field and hill, and along dim sky-line," longing for "a power of vision which might overpass that limit." Whenever she was "restless" in the confines of her womanly duties she went to this high place and there, "safe in the silence and solitude," listened with her "inward ear" to "a tale that was never ended—a tale my imagination created, and narrated continuously; quickened with all of incident, life, fire, feeling, that I desired and had not in my actual existence." . . . The heroine of this vague inner narrative is of course Jane herself, but as the grammar of these fragments will have indicated, Jane Eyre is also the narrator of that larger history in which these recurring visions constitute an episode of indefinite length.

We begin to suspect that the outcome of this heroine's visions cannot but be in her favor, and our suspicions are soon justified.

Jane Eyre moves towards her unnamed goal beyond the skyline by a highly secular version of those "gradations of glory" . . . which Helen Burns believed in beyond this life. The first glorious gradation is of course Jane's elevation by her master's proposal of marriage. (pp. 31-2)

But Jane soon ascends another gradation. On her wedding day it is revealed that Rochester is already married. He grimly conducts the party back from the church to Thornfield, and there in the very attic where Jane was wont to dream—where indeed sometimes her dreams were interrupted by eerie laughter—shows them the secret of the manor: a grovelling madwoman whom he must keep locked up. It is clear that morally at least Jane has risen a little over her master: she has plotted no bigamy, she is no deceiver. (p. 32)

[With Jane's refusal, or at least her evasion, of St. John Rivers's marriage proposal,] Jane ascends the next gradation of glory. For St. John's proposal is made from the highest motives. He has judged Jane carefully and finds her sufficient for the duties he asks her to share. "A missionary's wife you must—shall be. . . . I claim you—not for my pleasure, but for my Sovereign's service." Of his own role he is certain: "I am the servant of an infallible master . . . my captain is the All-perfect." And he is certain of hers: "God and nature intended you for a missionary's wife." . . . The full, official, and authentic representative of religion, the embodiment of the power through which Jane has risen above the importuning of Mr. Rochester, has spoken. It is hardly conceivable that our heroine should rise above his claim.

But rise she does, when one midnight a little later St. John renews his suit. Jane is wavering: "Religion called—Angels beckoned—God commanded—life rolled together like a scroll. . . ." But in one of the great moments of Victorian literature her struggle suddenly ends. Her heart stands still "to an inexpressible feeling" which rouses her senses "as if their utmost activity hitherto had been but torpor." She hears her name called three times. . . . (pp. 33-4)

Two consequences of this unearthly conversation must be noticed. One is immediate. St. John, whose condition we can only imagine, is brushed aside. "It was *my* time to assume ascendancy. *My* powers were in play and in force." Jane orders him to leave and he obeys at once; he is in fact finished. The origin of the voice cannot be known, but it has demolished the claims of the servant of the All-perfect.

The second consequence is more startling. Leaving her cousins, Jane discovers Rochester living in a far-off manor in deep woods. She learns that Thornfield has been burned down, set on fire by the maniac in the attic, and that in trying to save her Rochester has been blinded and has lost his left hand. By Jane's return to him he is almost precisely as astonished as she had been by his proposal of marriage, and they seem at last equals by the reversals of their fortunes. . . . Moreover the moral equality Jane had claimed on the earlier occasion seems fully established now. Then, she had cried: "Do you think, because I am poor, obscure, plain, and little, I am soulless and heartless? I have as much soul as you—and full as much heart!" . . . We have seen her assert this fullness of heart in defiance of Rochester's wishes, but now, at their reunion, Rochester seems her equal in this respect also. For he tells her how he has begun "only of late" to see "the hand of God" in his doom. He has begun to experience "remorse, repentance," and has risen so far towards Jane's moral rank that he has even begun to pray. . . . He puts out his hand to be led, and we may imagine with what mighty crescendo of some heavenly Victorian Wurlitzer, is taken home by Jane, his "prop and guide."

But before they depart, Jane addresses a confidential observation to the only listener who can share it:

> Reader, it was on Monday night—near midnight—that I too had received the mysterious summons: . . . I listened to Mr. Rochester's narrative; but made no disclosure in return. The coincidence struck me as too awful and inexplicable to be communicated or discussed. . . .

But the reason she offers for her silence stands oddly beside Mr. Rochester's account of his repentance and conversion: "If I told anything," she says, "my tale would be such as must necessarily make a profound impression on the mind of my hearer; and that mind, yet from its suffering too prone to gloom, needed not the deeper shade of the supernatural." . . . The final gradation has been achieved; Jane stands alone in glory. Rochester may have risen to the moral level from which she once refused him, but she has overpassed even this peak.

To imagine a different consequence here is to see how impossible it is for Jane to be anyone's equal. We might rewrite the address to the reader as a confession to Rochester: "I too, O Edward, I too!" Such a disclosure in return ought to produce the happiest union of equals before God, though what kind of God is perhaps hard to say. But that Jane makes no such disclosure, despite the confusion of "gloom" and "shade" with Rochester's new religious state, is the most consistent stroke in the book. . . . [By] her dramatic overwhelming of St. John, Jane has overpassed the religious grounds on which Rochester now claims equality with her. Jane's own "heart," the private morality of her "soul," has carried her higher than the grounds of Rochester's conversion. The movement of her vision towards realization is so rapacious that no terms are left in which to account for it; certainly there were no terms beyond religion for a writer such as Charlotte Brontë. Her heroine has narrated herself into silence, and the novel must end.

In every relationship Jane rises from inferiority to superiority. Her inferiority is expressed again and again as imprisonment; her superiority appears as the narrative confirmation of her rightness in resisting imprisonment. . . . [Her] triumph over St. John makes her superior not only to the version of her nature that he insists on; it also makes her superior to the highest equality anyone can conceive of in this little world of gentlefolk, parsons, governesses, servants, teachers, and manufacturers—equality before the throne of God. The movement of this novel is literally transcendence with a vengeance.

It will long since have appeared that this recurring ascent is expressed symbolically, and few novels of the period are so thoroughly articulated in images. The sexual symbols are so frequent and crude that the novel might be subtitled The Red and The Black. The destruction of Rochester's strong hand and volcanic eyes, which has been called, no doubt rightly, a castration symbol, is monstrously prepared for in the paraphrase of a passage from the Sermon on the Mount with which Jane decides what she must do after learning that Rochester is married: "No; you shall tear yourself away, none shall help you: you shall, yourself, pluck out your right eye: yourself cut off your right hand: your heart shall be the victim; and you, the priest, to transfix it." . . . The subterranean sadism is all too rich, and the imagery is sometimes so gross that the reader

must laugh if he does not close his eyes and skip. Perhaps the grimmest joke in the book is the compliment offered to Jane by both St. John and Rochester: "You delight in sacrifice."

But these underground horrors are not the subject of *Jane Eyre,* inevitable though they may be as the vehicle, and relevant as they may be to all we know and infer about the life of its author. They are inevitable because there is no difference between the mind that knows the world of this novel and the mind that seeks to know it in terms of a private vision. In such a structure it becomes more and more difficult to distinguish between behavior and motive, and the narrative finally succumbs so completely to the motive that no irony is possible. But the horrors of its real subject are enough, for this novel like any other is about the mind and society, and the action of this novel is the triumph of one mind's version of society. When her story ends Jane has reduced not only the initially overpowering differences of rank; she has reduced to the shape of her own vision the power that, for Charlotte Brontë at least, supports all differences of rank. As he begins his last prayer to his "Redeemer," Rochester tells Jane that when she returned he feared she might not be "real" but might be "silence and annihilation." Perhaps Rochester is the prophet after all.

To eradicate the social difference between an orphan-governess and a gentleman might well involve the convulsion of a supra-Christian power. There can be no doubt, however, that the reduction of the world to the terms of a single vision, no matter how moral its content or how sanctified its motives, is attended by the most dreadful violence. The power of the "I" of this novel is secret, undisclosable, absolute. There are no terms to explain its dominance, because no terms can appear which are not under its dominance. The violence with which it simplifies the differences labeled "inferior," "poorer," "richer," "better," or "higher," the killing and maiming and blinding which are the consequences of its dialectic, tell us as clearly as fiction can that even fantasy must subdue a real world. Jane Eyre's vision masters her world, but the price of her mastery is absolute isolation. When she knows her world completely she is out of it by the most rigorous necessity. I know no other work that so effectively demonstrates the demon of the absolute. (pp. 35-41)

> *G. Armour Craig, "The Unpoetic Compromise: On the Relation between Private Vision and Social Order in Nineteenth-Century English Fiction," in* Society and Self in the Novel: English Institute Essays, 1955, *edited by Mark Schorer, 1956. Reprint by AMS Press Inc., 1965, pp. 26-50.**

MARK SCHORER   (essay date 1959)

[*This excerpt originally appeared as an introduction to* Jane Eyre *in 1959. Schorer finds the novel "compelling," although implausible. Its structure is "artless," akin to that of dramatic poetry rather than realistic fiction. Further, he discusses* Jane Eyre *as the culmination of the Angria tales that Brontë composed as a youth with her brother, Branwell. The character of Jane, according to Schorer, is dominated by passion; this argument runs counter to those of such earlier critics as Kathleen Tillotson (1954) and Barbara Hardy (1964), who considered Jane's spiritual development to be the key to her personality.*]

[*Jane Eyre*'s] weaknesses are obvious and have long been observed. The action is pitted with implausibities, indeed, absurdities. The account of the manners of an aristocratic life with which the author was unfamiliar is childish. The notion that a man can for years conceal a raging maniac in the attic of his house and keep even the servants ignorant of her presence there, especially since he is so unwise as to put her under the care of a gin-tippling attendant whose stupors permit her frequently to escape the attic and range cursing through the house, is truly ridiculous. To dress up one's hero in the skirts and shawls of an old gypsy fortuneteller and let him woo the heroine in that guise in his own house is to risk at least the loss of his Byronic austerity. To turn one's orphaned heroine out into the world alone, subject her to the most frightful physical and emotional ordeals, and then let her stumble up to a house one night only to discover that its inhabitants are cousins of whose existence she had not known, and then to let her inherit a fortune besides—this is to challenge the reader to throw the book aside as unworthy of serious attention. But the reader does not throw the book aside, not even when the whole plot turns on an act of mental telepathy that brings the protagonists to their bittersweet embrace at last. Nor does he do so through all the crudities of the characterization, which is sometimes as gross as that in the baldest melodrama: the unadulterated malignity of Mrs. Reed, the unadulterated goodness of Helen Burns, the unadulterated malice of Miss Ingram—these are only examples. He reads to the end, for somehow the whole of the novel is compelling and strong even though so much of it is composed of these silly, feeble parts.

Is it, one might ask, the total artistry of the structure, the whole organization so firm that it welds even the limpest materials together, holds even coincidence and miracle firmly in place? Hardly. The structure of *Jane Eyre* is nearly artless. It employs, to begin with, one of the oldest conventions in English fiction, a convention made famous by Defoe's *Moll Flanders* (in which Charlotte Brontë may have found her source for the telepathic episode)—the fiction that presents itself as fact, the memoir of a presumably real person. Charlotte Brontë called this not a novel but an autobiography; the "real" author was Jane Eyre herself, and Currer Bell was merely her editor. Like *Moll Flanders*, *Jane Eyre* is, within this convention, very loosely put together; in both, events are linked not causally but circumstantially. Things happen to happen, they do not *have* to happen. (pp. 87-8)

Jane Eyre does have certain organizing principles that give it the dramatic coherence of a novel, and one cannot say this of *Moll Flanders*. The action falls into four parts: the first ten chapters, which have to do with Jane's childhood and education, are introductory; the next seventeen chapters are concerned with her residence at Thornfield Hall, her developing love for its master, the collapse of their plans; the next eight chapters treat her flight, her life at Moor House and Morton, and the icy proposals of St. John Rivers; the final three chapters, returning her to Thornfield and a chastened Rochester, resolve the whole. The second and third sections are the heart of the book, and each of these is dominated by a male who symbolizes one of the two polar forces between which Jane's conflict is conducted. Rochester, licentious, remorseful, and handsomely ugly, is imperious physical passion; Rivers, chaste, self-righteous, and beautifully handsome, is equally imperious spiritual passion. Jane, who is independent will, refuses to accept either on his own terms: she will not be Rochester's mistress and she will not be Rivers's wife; Rochester cannot marry her and Rivers will not take her to India unless she marries him. The conflict is resolved when Jane returns to Thornfield and finds that it has been destroyed by a fire that killed Rochester's mad wife, who had been the legal barrier to marriage, and maimed Rochester himself in such a way as to suggest that it has subdued his rampant sexuality and thereby removed any ethical barrier. (pp. 88-9)

[Important] as it may be to know that the imagination that created Angria is likewise the imagination that created *Jane Eyre,* and interesting as it may be to see how nearly the situations and human types that struck the reverie of an adolescent girl are those that are still most prominent in the mind of the mature woman, one must yet recognize that we have transcended Angria. What in the early writings we must call fantasy we can here call vision. A number of things have happened to bring about the change.

Most important of these, perhaps, is the difference in characterization. If some of the minor characters are one-dimensional, the major characters are not. They are multi-faceted and of a certain complexity. Rochester is not only the Byronic *immoraliste;* he is also a landowner, a man with certain economic and social responsibilities, with humor to lighten his *Ich-schmerz* [self-weariness], and tenderness to soften his pride. St. John Rivers is likewise a complex conception: at once kindly and rigid, turbulent within and frigid without, in love and unyielding, he suffers from that spiritual pride that is the mark of the religious fanatic and that can lead as readily to martyrdom as to acts of inflexible cruelty. It is Jane Eyre herself, however, who represents Charlotte Brontë's triumph of characterization and who, in fact, brings a new kind of heroine into English fiction. If we think of her in relation to some of Jane Austen's heroines, for example, they may seem more engaging and desirable, but it is Jane Eyre who is motivated by desire itself. . . . [Passion] is the key to her character. It is above all a passionate sense of the right of her own integrity to *be*. It breaks out first when, as a little girl, she tells Mrs. Reed that she does not like her; it breaks out most remarkably when, just before Rochester's proposal of marriage, she insists on her equality with him. It is the passion of Jane Eyre that imbues the whole novel—since it is all told from her point of view—and that animates those elements that give the whole its visionary quality. Similarly, it is the complexity that passion arouses in all these characters that gives the central ethical conflict a certain depth that enables us to take it seriously as we cannot take seriously the conflicts in Angria.

Another and hardly less important change lies in the fact that Angrian conflicts have been moved from imaginary lands of cloud into a real world, a world of social classes and institutions, no less than of natural landscapes. The presentation of manners may be naïve, but the observations on the injustices of charity schools, the hypocrisy of much religion, the cruelty of outmoded divorce laws, the vicious snobbery of a class system, are all sound, and they enter into what we have already called the polemical bias of the book. So while the novel is chiefly concerned with subjective conflicts of a sometimes nearly hysterical order, these are substantially located in a social texture that is objective and mundane.

If society as here presented is in general at odds with the heroine's subjective ambitions for self-realization, the natural settings are, rather, reflective of their immediate state; as in most dramatic poetry, natural phenomena are the external representatives of psychological conditions. Natural setting, then, provides a kind of tenuous symbolic substructure to the novel, not only heightening but expressing thematic conflict. This technique, perhaps quite unconscious, is particularly observable in Charlotte Brontë's use of vegetation, especially the priapean tree—dormant, blasted, blossoming.

In that long wintry season that was Jane Eyre's youth, trees are bare; the second sentence makes the announcement: "We had been wandering . . . in the leafless shrubbery an hour in the morning." In her reveries, little Jane decides that no magic is left in England, that the elves "were all gone out of England to some savage country where the woods were wilder and thicker." (pp. 89-92)

Nearly every important scene in the development of the passion of Rochester and Jane Eyre takes place among trees—in an orchard, an arbor, a woods, a "leafy enclosure." When Jane returns from her visit to Gateshead, she finds Rochester seated among roses, beside "a tall briar, shooting leafy and flowery branches across the path," and shortly after, their first embrace and his proposal of marriage take place among "trees laden with ripening fruit," near a blossoming chestnut tree. (pp. 92-3)

When the marriage is halted, it is as if a "Christmas frost had come at midsummer . . . the woods which twelve hours since waved leafy and fragrant as groves between the tropics, now spread, waste, wild and white as pine-forests in wintry Norway. My hopes were all dead. . . ." (p. 94)

We have perhaps labored this documentation of a single but major strand of imagery in *Jane Eyre* to suggest that its basic organizing principle is like that of dramatic poetry rather than like that of conventionally realistic fiction. From this poetic strain comes its visionary quality and its sustained tone of agitation and excitement. In a realistic novel, much of the action would be intolerable, but in *Jane Eyre,* as it is written, the tone gives it all a visionary coherence and reality. (p. 95)

> *Mark Schorer, " 'Jane Eyre'," in his* The World We Imagine: Selected Essays, *Farrar, Straus and Giroux, 1968, pp. 80-96.*

DONALD W. CROMPTON   (essay date 1960)

[*Crompton praises the structural unity of* Jane Eyre *and comments on Brontë's use of symbolism. In particular, he points to the antithesis of surface and depth and its representation in the novel's characters.*]

[It] has always seemed to me that many books can be found to be better than they are by by-passing the main issues and concentrating on playing hunt-the-slipper with theme and symbol. Take, for instance, *Jane Eyre*. The more one goes into *Jane Eyre* the richer the structural unity of the book becomes. Leaving aside the more obvious technical devices—the supernatural signs, the dream omens, the weather symbolism which enacts the theme at every point—one still has left a character pattern, built up on a series of parallels and antitheses, which if it lacks the finesse of a Jane Austen, nevertheless is very effective in developing that 'concentration of the area of action' which Edwin Muir saw as the essence of the dramatic novel. At the lowest level it reveals itself as a physical separating out into the opposing camps of dark and light—where light represents conventional beauty of face and form and dark the reverse. Physically, Jane and Rochester (dark-haired, dark-eyed and plain) are opposed to the unsympathetic characters, (many of whom are 'given' fair hair and blue or gray eyes) Mrs. Reed, Georgiana, St. John Rivers, the Dowager Lady Ingram, Blanche Ingram, Mason, Bertha Rochester, and even John Reed (who, after a gross and unhealthy childhood, blossoms into a 'fine-looking young man'). This opposition is made explicit in Jane's remark about having a theoretical reverence for beauty but shunning anything 'bright but antipathetic'. The

reason for it is clear. Conventional beauty in *Jane Eyre* invariably connotes either the empty head or, more frequently, the hard, shrivelled heart incapable of feeling, and it is appropriate that the eyes (the windows of the soul) should be used symbolically to suggest it. Hence, we find that Mrs. Reed has a 'cold gray eye', the Dowager Lady Ingram a 'fierce and hard' one, Georgiana and Eliza eyes that give 'an indescribable hardness' to their countenances, Mason an eye 'large and well cut but the life looking out of it . . . tame and vacant', and St. John Rivers an eye which is 'a cold, bright, blue gem'. On the other hand, Rochester has 'very fine eyes with hidden depths' and Jane's eyes 'look soft and full of feeling'. This opposition is further reinforced in the general characterisation. On the one hand, it is 'right' that Louisa Eshton and Mary Ingram should think Mason a 'beautiful man', that Georgiana should think Rochester 'an ugly man', that Blanche Ingram should react to the 'black Bothwell' in Rochester rather than to the softness lying behind the eyes, that Eliza should be attracted by 'the Rubric' of the Common Prayer Book: on the other, it is equally 'right' (though Jane Austen would not have thought so) that Jane and Rochester should talk at length about going to the moon for a honeymoon.

At a deeper level, this antithesis between surface and depth is associated with a more fundamental contrasting of the Classical and the Romantic point of view. Throughout the novel this opposition also has been suggested in the description of the central characters. Blanche Ingram's beauty is 'Grecian' and *regular;* she has 'harmonious lineaments' and is 'moulded like a Diane', whereas Jane's features are '*irregular*' and 'grace and harmony' are 'quite wanting'. Similarly, St. John Rivers, with his 'Greek face', 'Classic nose' and 'Athenian mouth and chin' is the 'graceful Apollo' to Rochester's craggy, misshapen 'Vulcan'. A stream of images suggests the violence of the author's rejection of the Classic ideal which, to her, is synonymous with coldness, hardness and emptiness. 'Nothing bloomed spontaneously' in the 'soil' of Blanche's personality. St. John Rivers is a 'statue', 'ivory', a 'cold cumbrous column'; he is 'like chiselled marble', 'serene as glass', and Jane is brought under his 'freezing spell'. St. John's remark to Jane: 'I am cold: no fervour infects me' and her reply: 'Whereas I am hot, and fire dissolves ice' is more, in the wider context, than Jane exercising her gift for repartee. (pp. 360-62)

Even if this analysis is allowed, however, its value as an approach to *Jane Eyre* is relatively very slight. Perhaps it might be used to support the view that Charlotte . . . could manipulate the melodramatic framework in such a way that it corresponded with her own intense vision of life. Having made the point, however, one is still left with the fact (which cannot be argued here but is at least generally accepted) that . . . *Jane Eyre*—whatever its structure—is relatively immature in conception and execution and yields little more from sustained consideration than it does from a single reading. In some ways, of course, it is a remarkable novel, but one feels that the major qualities it has lie outside anything which might be described as the scheme of the novel. (p. 362)

> *Donald W. Crompton, "The New Criticism: A Caveat," in* Essays in Criticism, *Vol. X, No. 3, July, 1960, pp. 359-64.**

MARTIN S. DAY   (essay date 1960)

[*In his examination of marriage in* Jane Eyre, *Day points out that, as mates for Jane, St. John Rivers is compatible in all but love, while Rochester is suited only in love. Rochester becomes acceptable to Jane only after his disfigurement, when he has been symbolically reduced to a child and Jane becomes the parent. In addition, Day provides one of numerous interpretations of Bertha Mason.*]

Although created as opposites almost point by point, the two suitors of Jane have one significant quality in common. The Rochester from whom Jane flees and the Rivers she refuses are both domineering males. Both strive to overpower her will and to rule her.... In the battle of the sexes, Jane, though self-confessedly little, plain, and undistinguished in talents, will not accept the position of inferior. (pp. 498-99)

Jane Eyre dismisses the loveless but otherwise compatible Rivers for the loving but otherwise incompatible Rochester. What now is to be her marital relationship with her choice?

Perhaps the most melodramatic chapter in any romance of love is the twenty-sixth chapter of *Jane Eyre.* The tempestuous Rochester and the passionate governess are about to join in wedlock at the altar. As the clergyman asks if there is ''any impediment why ye may not lawfully be joined together in matrimony,'' an objection is startlingly raised by an onlooker. The whole company then sweeps up to the mysterious third floor of Thornfield to find the bestial madwoman, the living wife of Rochester. (p. 499)

Victorian readers could readily conclude that the madwoman was the symbol of Rochester's ill-spent youth. For his sins he had this horrible weight imposed upon him, and it remained as the visible bar to his union with Jane. Only when he had suffered for his sins by maiming and disfigurement, only when his sins had been burnt away and his nature had achieved a transforming wholesomeness, only then could he be united with his true love.

Such an interpretation is attractive and, to the usual Victorian, logical. Close examination of the text, however, does not substantiate this hypothesis. Before the lurid revelations of Chapter XXVI there are ample objections to the marriage of Jane and Rochester; however, the basis of these objections is not his sin but the lovers' mutual incompatibility.

The passages between the lovers' wooing and the thwarted marriage contain three types of opposition to the marriage of Jane and Rochester. The first objection comes from Mother Nature, who applauds and condemns in this novel in appropriately Wordsworthian fashion: The horse-chestnut tree beneath which the lovers lyrically romanced is sundered by a thunderbolt into two charred fragments. The second objection springs from persons other than the lovers. The madwoman invades the bedroom of Jane and rends the bridal veil. Mrs. Fairfax appears quite dubious about the marriage. The third objection lies in the doubts and worries of Jane herself. The actions of nature and the presence of the madwoman seem clearly to be symbolic, the stuff of romantic poetry, but the doubts of Mrs. Fairfax and of Jane herself belong to realistic fiction. (pp. 499-500)

Herein lies the genuine cause for the break-up between Jane and Rochester. She came to his mansion as an 18-year-old governess with little knowledge of life and none of men. In Rochester, twice her age and many times her experience, she had sought a father to love and to be loved by in return. In one of his earliest protracted conversations with Jane, Rochester points out, ''I am old enough to be your father'' . . . and his manner thereafter is rather patronizingly paternalistic. In referring to Jane he maintains a steady tattoo of ''Little girl,''

''Little friend,'' ''Child,'' ''Elf,'' ''Little darling,'' ''Childish and slender creature.'' . . . Rochester glories in his role as protector: ''Have I not found her friendless, and cold, and comfortless? Will I not guard, and cherish, and solace her?'' Lacking a real father, Jane at first was drawn to the brawny, confident figure of Rochester. He could offer what she had never before known: masculine wisdom of the world, masculine assurance, and masculine protection—in short, the father's role. If marriage should occur as originally planned, he would be the entirely dominant member, the pillar of wealth, strength, and ability, while Jane would be the protected and the ruled, the inferior member of the marriage in every respect; in short, she would be in a daughter's role.

This father-daughter relationship between Rochester and Jane is not satisfactory to her. (p. 502)

Probably every intelligent woman walking the long aisle to where the bridegroom waits will wonder about the marriage as she proceeds. Will it work out properly? Is theirs a reasonable and durable partnership? Those women who are not too sure of the answers may here query themselves: Will anyone object at the last moment? Should anyone object? For a girl with Jane's problem the question will almost certainly change to a prayer: ''Please, oh please, won't someone object? It's wrong, I tell you. Please object!'' In *Jane Eyre,* in the very midst of the wedding ritual, the objector astoundingly leaps forward and Jane is spared a union that she inwardly detests.

The chief reason, then, for the existence of the madwoman is to prevent Jane from entering into the wrong partnership with Rochester. Charlotte Brontë had to produce some excuse palatable to herself, to her class, and to her age; so Jane's flight from Rochester appears thoroughly justified when a living wife of Rochester is produced. At the same time the subhuman Bertha Mason makes us sympathize with the bedeviled Rochester.

Those who wish a more psychoanalytical approach (and the intense subjectivity of the novel makes it fair game) may suggest that the madwoman is a projection of Jane. Any sensible observer would be thunderstruck to see Rochester turned down by Jane on the eve of the wedding. An insignificant governess refusing the hand of Mr. Rochester, especially when she says she loves him! The girl must be mad! And the break-up is precisely because of madness, the madwoman embodying the apparent irrationality that permits Jane to escape from Rochester. (pp. 502-03)

She is called back to Rochester when she experiences religious ecstasy combined with passion. In the midst of this trance she telepathically hears her lover calling for her. We later learn that Rochester's cry to her across the many miles occurred when he was undergoing a like experience. Jane is impelled to return because she at last believes that he needs her more than she might need him. Their fortunes have been violently reversed, and she finds Rochester blind and maimed, his left hand amputated. Thornfield and the madwoman have been destroyed. Rochester is poor and friendless, a helpless inmate of unhealthy Ferndean. She now comes to him as an heiress, strong in her youth. Jane is the pillar of wealth, strength, and ability, while Rochester is the protected and the ruled, the inferior member of the marriage, which, in fact, she actually proposed. . . .

The roles have now been exactly switched. No longer is Rochester the parent and Jane the child. Now she is the parent and he is the child. (p. 504)

Martin S. Day, ''Central Concepts of 'Jane Eyre','' in The Personalist, Vol. XLI, No. 4, October, 1960, pp. 495-505.

BARBARA HARDY   (essay date 1964)

[This essay makes an analysis of dogmatic or ideological form, discussing Defoe, Charlotte Brontë and E. M. Forster. Hardy stresses the role of Providence throughout Jane Eyre and echoes Kathleen Tillotson's contention (see excerpt above, 1954) that Jane's spiritual development lends a moral unity to the work. However, Hardy argues that the accent on Providential guidance is a weakness. Since the novel is propelled by Jane's beliefs, Hardy argues, Jane Eyre does not always depict Jane's religious growth. Rather, according to Hardy, the novel's moral pattern is evidenced more in the character of Jane's classmate Helen Burns. Hardy also echoes Richard Chase's perception of the universe of Brontë's novels as ''coherent and consistent'' (see excerpt above, 1947).]

Defoe, Charlotte Brontë, Hardy, and E. M. Forster are all novelists who use their art to embody an ideology. Because of the very nature of the ideology, their art shapes character and action in a special way.

If we use the word dogmatic in its neutral sense we should probably say that most interesting novels have a dogmatic form, organizing their action and characters with a systematic moral significance. When Dickens classifies individuals and families and institutions according to their capacity for love and true charity, as he does in Bleak House, the novel has a dogmatic form. When George Eliot presents her characters in the recognizable categories of selfishness and unselfishness, as she does in all her novels, her form is dogmatic. (pp. 51-2)

In the case of the dogmatic forms which concern me here, there is a single and simplified belief which excludes much of the varied causality to be found in life, which is metaphysical in character and has precise moral consequences. In Robinson Crusoe and Jane Eyre the action and characters are shaped by the dogmatism of a special belief, the belief in Providence. In Jude the Obscure the action and characters are organized as illustrations of the opposite belief, in an absence of Providence which allows nature and society to frustrate the individual and create a pattern not significantly different from one which would illustrate a malignant God. E. M. Forster uses his characters and actions to illustrate more tentatively the possible sources of faith in meaningful existence. Just as James may on occasion make his selection from life restricted or implausible in order to make the novel dramatically shapely and concentrated, so these four novelists make their selected life conform, in similar restriction or implausibility, to their belief in the presence or absence of a powerful and practical Providence. Yet James usually succeeds in making his symmetry and economy express life without falsification, and Defoe and Charlotte Brontë and Hardy succeed, to a large extent, in reconciling dogma and realism. They write novels, not tracts. Their characters and actions are more than merely illustrative. (p. 53)

Defoe, both in Robinson Crusoe and other novels, uses Providence not as a convenient deus ex machina [an artificial device used to resolve dramatic conflicts] in a story of little religious interest, but as an informing principle. When we come to the nineteenth century the concept of Providence is plainly outworn and discredited, and we find Dickens, George Eliot, and Meredith defining the egocentric or mercenary character by evoking just that faith in a special Providence which is taken for granted in Defoe. Podsnap, Casaubon, and Harry Richmond are ex-

amples of faith in discredited Providence, and this devaluation has an interesting place in novels which explore the responsibility and conflict of individuals and social relations. But in one of the most interesting early Victorian novels, Jane Eyre, Providence is still very much alive. The dubious moral implication of egocentricity and material profit are gone but the formal implications remain much the same. Providence is not a dead word when used by Charlotte Brontë. . . . [Jane Eyre] is structurally very like Robinson Crusoe. There is the same rising intonation of optimistic faith, the same pattern of prayer and answer, and a very similar intercession of dreams, portents, and coincidences. Jane Eyre, however, is not a novel about religious conversion, and perhaps this is to be regretted.

Jane is like Crusoe in her disregard of Heaven. What he puts first is adventure, what she puts first is human love. Her early passionate sense of injustice is rebuked by Helen Burns, who refers her to the approval of conscience and the kingdom of spirits and warns her, 'You think too much of the love of human beings'. Although Jane's conversion to Helen's values is cursorily treated, and indeed taken for granted in her discovery of value and activity as pupil and teacher at Lowood, by the time she comes to leave we have reached the second stage of the action, where prayer is substituted for the demand for justice.

Like Robinson Crusoe, Jane finds that prayer always meets a practical response, and the relationship of prayer and answer is an important thread in the action. She prays first for liberty but feels the prayer 'scattered on the wind', so—testifying to the discipline she tells us she has acquired—she substitutes the prayer for 'a new servitude' and thinks hard about ways and means. (pp. 61-2)

The practical answers of Providence return in Jane's crisis. The vision recalls her painting of the Evening Star—moonlit, vapourish, glorious-browed, shining in the blue—and speaks to the spirit as the painted vision had been seen by the spirit, saying, 'My daughter, flee temptation'. Later, alone and hungry on the moor, re-enacting Bessie's hymn which is an important source for feeling, image, and situation, she asks again, 'Oh, Providence, sustain me a little longer! Aid—direct me!'. The 'false light' of the hymn has been left behind, and what now appears as an ignis fatuus [a deceptive goal] is in fact the light of her cousin's house. . . . St John speaks to Jane when she has reconciled herself to death and asserted her faith, 'Let me try to wait his will in silence'. Finally her appealing prayer receives a direct answer when she is tempted to accept her cousin's proposal and is saved by hearing Rochester's voice. This is the conversation of her prayer and Rochester's, for his cry to her has been the response to her prayer: 'Show me, show me the path!' and her response to him has answered his prayer, now that he has become capable of prayer like Crusoe, after punishment and repentance. (pp. 62-3)

It is only after Rochester too has been converted and has repented that Providence can join their prayers as human question and answer, and reconcile the human and the divine, reason, conscience, and passion. (p. 63)

[Kathleen Tillotson argues convincingly that] Jane's converse with the invisible world gives the novel its moral unity which makes us accept her decision as inevitable [see excerpt above, 1954]. This unity is not entirely an individual one, but is rather imposed from without, like the pattern of Robinson Crusoe. And the unity of theme is only one aspect of unity. This is not to deny that the novel is animated and individual: Jane's conflict between discipline and passion for instance, before the great choice comes up, is delicately and plausibly dramatized in her defensive teasing and sparring, as well as being individualized and generalized in her relations with her aunt and cousins, and with her second set of cousins. To say that the novel is defined by an external doctrine is not to deny its realism, and we have only to compare it with stereotyped religious novels . . . to see the superior subtlety of Charlotte Brontë's psychology and imagination. The moral pattern of the novel can be simply described, in terms of the conflict between human love and heavenly faith, passion and reason, rather as Mr Rochester's phrenological fortune-telling expresses it, as the conflict in which reason reins feeling, judgement overrules passions and desires, wind, earthquake and fire are succeeded by the still small voice of conscience. The psychological detail and personality of that conflict, within Jane and externalized in other characters, are not simply schematic. The Providential form allows for some free play of human relationships, both at their best, in Jane's own history and development, and at their weakest, in the traces of Angrian fantasy in Rochester's character and marriage and in the conclusion. There are places in the novel when this Providential form is a source not of unity but disintegration.

This weakness is by no means easy to pin-point, since it is a defect in belief rather than a straightforward literary lapse, though it is the literary consequences of belief which concern me most in this discussion. Both *Robinson Crusoe* and *Jane Eyre* are novels whose action relies on supernatural machinery and in each case it is not the artifice of fantasy but the fantasy of belief, which determines the movement and the motivation. (pp. 63-4)

In *Jane Eyre* the religious explanation determines motive and action in . . . [an] insistent and consistent fashion. And yet there is a gap in the novel which seems to be the result of its ideological pattern. This gap is one which may not be apparent to readers sharing Charlotte Brontë's beliefs, since they, like Charlotte Brontë, may be able to assume that faith is the product of growth and education. It is this assumption which allows the novelist to show two distinct stages in Jane's feelings and beliefs and leave the middle stage of transition undramatized. Yet it is a vital part of the novel's causality.

Jane is shown as passionate and intelligently rational. She begins with a need for love and self-respect and suffers aggression, rejection, and humiliation. Helen Burns puts her finger on Jane's 'excessive' need for human love and it is significant that Jane meets her friend's unquestioning faith with doubts and questions. When Helen confronts the sense of outrage with 'Love your enemies', Jane replies that this is impossible. When Helen on her death-bed affirms her faith and tells Jane, 'I am going to God', Jane asks, 'Where is God? What is God?' and, 'You are sure that there is such a place as heaven; and that our souls can get to it when we die?' She thinks to herself, 'Where is that region? Does it exist?'

We come to see that Jane achieves a rational discipline, and the tacit disappearance of her sense of outrage is acceptable enough as a consequence of maturity, especially since she has at Lowood found both affection and self-respect. We are not surprised when she forgives her aunt. This is an intelligible adult act of feeling which the child could not have achieved. What we do not come to see is exactly how Jane comes to accept Helen Burns's faith, even though such faith is at the root of her decision to leave Rochester. She has presumably moved away from her early doubts about Heaven by the time she comes to see her dying aunt, and her doubts are now of a different kind, about the actual destination of her aunt's spirit: 'Whither will that spirit—now struggling to quit its material tenement—flit when at length released?' There is an explicit reminder of Helen's death-bed, but our attention is not drawn to Jane's change in belief. She still speaks of *Helen's* beliefs. Her moment of affirmation comes with her moral crisis and test, not before it and she then affirms her need for dignity and self-respect, fully backed by the preceding action, and her faith that the 'invisible world' is impelling her towards the renunciation of Rochester. She has told us earlier that her love for Rochester 'stood between her and every thought of religion' but the actual growth of that religious feeling is the one thing the novel takes for granted and does not demonstrate. Every other detail in their courtship and conflict has roots which can be traced back to the beginnings. Her rejection of his extravagant gifts is entirely in keeping with her sense of dependence and memories of humiliation, and her hard-won independence and dignity comes out convincingly in her relations with the Ingrams, her wary pride as she keeps Rochester at a distance, and the characteristic flash, during her great moral conflict, when she remembers his cast-off mistresses and—prudently if unfairly—distrusts him. It is this pride and common sense which assert themselves at the time of choice. The religious argument is bound to be less convincing outside her faith just because Charlotte Brontë seems to have found it unnecessary to include religious development in the otherwise full and detailed account of Jane's growth. (pp. 65-7)

The question and answer of Jane's moral debate speaks in two voices, the voice of Christian law and the voice of personal prudence. Her love pleads for Rochester and indiscreetly flouts Jane's self-respect by asking, 'Who in the world cares for *you?* or who will be injured by what you do?' The answer is conventionally Christian in its content, but its tone is that of the child who complained so bitterly of injustice and humiliation, sharpened now by the experience of dignity and status, strengthened by rational detachment:

> Still indomitable was the reply—'*I* care for myself. The more solitary, the more friendless, the more unsustained I am, the more I will respect myself. I will keep the order given by God; sanctioned by man.' . . .

Yet this is far from being a novel where we can ignore the religious references and observe only the psychological development. After Jane discovers that Rochester is already married she longs to die and there is only one sign of life: 'One idea only still throbbed lifelike within me—a remembrance of God.' We feel, I suggest, less that this one lifelike idea is the inevitable strength of a demonstrated faith, less that she would be violating a law which we have seen her learn in the course of her struggles, than that she is saved by the intervention of God.

It is true, as Kathleen Tillotson argues, that if Jane did not resist Rochester and the strong plea of love, 'the moral pattern of the novel would be violated'. I do not think, however, that the moral pattern is one which fully informs the dramatic psychology of the novel. In places it is taken for granted and not given proper emphasis. . . . Jane acts and reasons from precepts which have been presented strongly in Helen Burns, and much less emphatically in Jane herself. We have not seen the process of her religious education and faith, and the divine law which she invokes in the crisis has not been associated with either her feelings or her reason. Her choice comes from grace rather than from a continuity of moral and spiritual habit. The distinction is indicated by Charlotte Brontë herself, when Helen Burns tells Jane not to rely on her 'feeble self, or . . . creatures feeble as you'. . . . Jane's *character* seems to demonstrate the strength of the individual and human relationships, but the *action* demonstrates the need for heavenly resources. (pp. 67-9)

[George Eliot rejected *Jane Eyre*] because she disapproved of the divorce laws, though she had not yet broken the commandment Jane keeps: 'All self-sacrifice is good—but one would like it to be in a somewhat nobler cause than that of a diabolical law which chains a man soul and body to a putrefying carcase' [see excerpt above, 1848]. . . . I do not think the weakness of the moral pattern lies in the nature of Jane's decision, or in Charlotte Brontë's silence on the subject of divorce law. Its weakness comes from imposing an ideology on to a realistic psychological pattern. The comparison with *Robinson Crusoe* should make it plain that I am using the word 'imposed' in a precise sense. Both novels show a belief in divine intercession and dramatize the workings of heavenly power and grace. I am not objecting to *Jane Eyre* because it expresses the belief that motivation is more than a personal and social matter but because it delineates faith in a rather muffled fashion. . . . Defoe and Charlotte Brontë make the Providential intervention crucial, both in action and conflict. *Robinson Crusoe* combines the hero's development with the ways of God in a way which has none of the strains of Charlotte Brontë's complex story, where the actual relations and conflict of Jane and Rochester could be seen quite independently of the Providential pattern, at least up to their parting. But the action depends largely on that pattern, in its coincidences and its final outcome. The framework of the novel is consistently Providential, but within the frame there are omissions and simplifications. I suggest that we should not hasten to condemn Charlotte Brontë for writing out of neurotic fantasy nor praise her for moral consistency and sound psychology without examining the ways in which the ideology informs the novel as a whole.

It is the ideological assumption which makes it possible for the fantasy to work, both in the destruction of Rochester and in the happy ending. Whether or not we agree with Richard Chase [see excerpt above, 1947] that the dominant pattern is that of domesticated myth—'the tempo and energy of the universe can be quelled, we see, by a patient, practical woman'— we should surely observe the importance of the Providential form. Chase observes that the universe is 'chastened by an assertion of will', and says that after the blinding of Rochester 'The universe, not previously amenable to supernatural communication between the parted lovers, now allows them to hear each other though they are leagues apart'. The universe is acting in a coherent and consistent manner, for it is Providence answering Rochester's prayer after confession and expiation. We may well observe that his actual conversion is even less elaborated than Jane's, and once again it is a pattern of action and change imposed from without, grace rather than organic process, which determines and completes the story. (pp. 69-70)

> *Barbara Hardy, "Dogmatic Form: Daniel Defoe, Charlotte Brontë, Thomas Hardy, and E. M. Forster," in her* The Appropriate Form: An Essay on the Novel, *The Athlone Press, 1964, pp. 51-82.**

LAWRENCE E. MOSER, S.J. (essay date 1965)

[*Moser provides an interpretation of the three paintings in* Jane Eyre *as surrealistic. According to Moser, they are "intimately linked with psychic human experience." Further, Moser contends that these pictures reveal both Jane and Brontë's personalities. The critic proposes that three meanings exist in each painting: the internal meaning to Jane herself, the symbolic relation to other aspects of the novel, and the actual significance to Brontë. Another interpretation of the paintings is provided by Jane Millgate (1968).*]

Charlotte Brontë, odd creature that she was in many respects, would certainly have shuddered had she thought that anyone would try to describe her work as a delimited instance of the surrealistic, yet there is ample evidence that this characteristic psychological tension consistently racked the creative life of the youngest of the Brontë sisters. There are only certain parts of this surrealistic canon into which *Jane Eyre* can be fitted; to these aspects we had best confine our attention. It is well to remember, however, that an equal number of well-founded arguments might be proposed that would exclude the novel from what could be called strict surrealism and that might exclude as well some points of my interpretation. My point is that, since the character "Jane Eyre" does in the novel produce three paintings of a decidedly surrealistic bent . . . , there is no lack of cogency at all in approaching them from this particularized point of view. On the contrary, such an angle of approach seems the only logical consequence of the author's deliberate and detailed focus on these paintings, a sure indication of their degree of functionally symbolic import.

Basically, the surrealistic is one form of tending toward absolute sincerity inasmuch as it recognizes that the most profound psychical structure of the person is most sincerely laid bare in involuntary and instinctive actions such as dreams; automatism is its keystone. From this it follows that surrealism is to be intimately linked with psychic human experience and has its roots in introspection as a way of life. The artifact produced can only emerge as a mirror of the artist's personality and, either consciously or unconsciously, as a constant "depiction of himself which is not a self-portrait." (pp. 275-76)

[When we come to] *Jane Eyre,* we are, of course, immediately struck by the over-all tone of the work; something beyond the real lurks here, something frantic and almost uncontrolled, yet something that is not just Gothic. . . . Certain central episodes of intense experience dominated with their peaks the jagged psychic life of Charlotte Brontë; she could scarce help transferring and transforming them into the views and attitudes of the fictional Jane Eyre, and expressing them in her character's paintings as much as in the narrative of the novel.

Mention of these paintings occurs at Thornfield Manor just after Mr. Rochester has subjected Jane, Adele's newly arrived governess, to a rather brusque and harsh inventory of her capabilities. At Rochester's request, and as an indication of her cultural qualifications, Jane produces from her portfolio some watercolors that she had done at Lowood, the boarding school that had taken such a toll of her in sorrow, loneliness, and suffering. (pp. 276-77)

[In] a passage of remarkable inventiveness and skill, the created character, Jane Eyre, re-expresses her own and her author's experiences in the form of quasi-surrealistic paintings which . . . reduce to symbol the real and fictional summits of their lives. If, therefore, we accept such a surrealistic explanation of the paintings, we may find in them a redefinition of the structure and central themes of the novel, as well as a new means of perceiving the coherence of the whole work. In proposing such an interpretation, I have no fear of the "biographical fallacy," since the paintings are to be viewed not as mere fictional creations, but as though they were independent works (which they are) in a form that lays its foundations upon self-revelation, in other words, surrealism.

Reversing this creative process, I should now like to attempt the transition from portrait to person: from the three paintings, to Jane Eyre, to Charlotte Brontë herself. This possible interpretation, I would again insist, is founded upon the surrealistic tenet that art of necessity mirrors the artist's personality and mentality, in this case both Jane's and Charlotte's, and tends violently toward a complete revelation of self.... [There] are at least three types of meaning in the paintings: what I have chosen to call the internal, the external, and the actual. The internal is the meaning they may have for Jane herself in her fictional situation, and consequently must refer to events prior to her departure from Lowood where the works were executed; the external is the symbolic meaning which the pictures may carry with relation to other subsequent events in the plot development of the novel itself; the actual meaning is, of course, the significance of the paintings in the real life of Charlotte Brontë herself.

On the internal level, the first picture in question is an image of Jane; she is the foam-flecked cormorant enisled in Matthew Arnold's "sea of life." The bracelet, the only truly bright object in the picture, is her own gentle, kind, and generous heart whose possession and purity she has retained despite the death and terror that surrounded her at Lowood and left such an indelible impression upon her personality. The female corpse is thus more exactly a symbol of Helen Burns, for it was through her in life and in death that Jane for the first time really gained a solid possession of her own heart. Externally, the work may foreshadow Bertha Mason Rochester, for it was only by her death that Jane would ultimately gain the response of love and kindness for which her soul craved. Again, all unwittingly perhaps, Charlotte Brontë may have here furnished us as well with a figure of the bitterness tormenting her own childhood; of Maria Brontë's early and heartbreaking death in 1825 just after leaving Cowan Bridge School, the archetype of Lowood; of her desperate clinging to the dreamlands of Angria and Gondal while immured on every side by the piercing loneliness and crumbling tombstones of Haworth Parsonage.

The vision of the "Evening Star" in the second painting again in some respect portrays Jane. She herself tells us that the likeness was portrayed "in tints as dusk and soft as I could combine," a representation in pigment of the tenderness of her nature and of the gnawing hunger of her emotions for kindness, companionship, and love. In this case also, the star, as the lone bright point of the painting, reveals the beauty and simplicity of her heart. Yet is there not a lack of control reflected in those "dark and wild" eyes, a sense of tension in the shadowy hair "torn by storm," indeed a succinct pictorial expression of Jane's starving for the love she needs and can not yet have. In the development of the plot, two critical junctures in Jane's career are suggested: her wild dismay as she finds herself forced to leave Rochester ..., and later to leave St. John Rivers ..., despite the overwhelmingly attractive ability of these men to fill in their own ways the abysmal emptiness of her heart. Yet throughout the whole runs once again the persistent theme of Charlotte's childhood in all its lovelessness, a note that recurs with variations as a dominant motif.

Upon first encountering the third painting of the "Kingly Crown," I could not immediately form any internal connection with Jane's previous life at Lowood School. Closer consideration, however, has led me to assume that the inspiration was most probably founded in Miss Temple's departure from

Lowood ..., an absence that drew a veil, so to speak, over the temporarily happy Jane. The crown, again the only point of light in the portrait, once more symbolizes her affectionate heart and its love. Yet now she finds herself in contact once again with the haunting specter of cold, hard loneliness and lovelessness, the iceberg; and, while she still retains possession of her own heart, on this occasion a mass of "black drapery" with all its mournful connotations severs Jane from actual contact with the consolations of love. Separation had previously entered Jane's life, to be sure, in the death of Helen Burns, but that separation ultimately fused more closely together those concerned and never really withdrew the presence of the beloved. Jane had certainly yielded her heart to Miss Temple, her earliest adult friend; now Miss Temple was taking part of it away with her. This theme of division of self is restated at a later date when Jane comes to her senses in the devastating realization that she has left her heart and her love with Rochester; only by cleaving to him can she in any true and meaningful sense rediscover herself. Jane did not soon forget this first true separation of her life, an isolation from a person whom she deeply and fervently loved; neither did Charlotte herself soon forget her separation from M. Constantin Héger, her tutor in Brussels.... (pp. 278-81)

Gilbert Highet has said that "we inhabit two worlds and ... we should let them interpenetrate to get the best out of them both." For Charlotte Brontë these two worlds did to some extent coincide in a literary unity which with a fair degree of probability may be perceived. Both worlds merge in the varied tones of life and literature; quasi-surrealistic art itself voices Jane's and Charlotte's desperate message of the primacy of love. (p. 281)

Lawrence E. Moser, S.J., "From Portrait to Person: A Note on the Surrealistic in 'Jane Eyre'," in Nineteenth-Century Fiction, Vol. 20, No. 3, December, 1965, pp. 275-81.

JANE MILLGATE (essay date 1968)

[*Millgate states that the three paintings in* Jane Eyre *chart Jane's emotional growth and reflect varying points in the story's development. Another interpretation of the pictures is provided by Lawrence E. Moser (1965).*]

One important way in which Jane's vision is given expression in the novel is through the description of her pictures. These, as outward manifestations of her emotional state at particular moments, obviously offer one means, among many, of charting her growth to maturity. It seems possible to argue, however, that they also assist us in distinguishing between the shifting narrative perspectives of the novel by providing an instrument for measuring the angle and coloration of the narrative at a given point. (pp. 315-16)

The first direct view we have of a ... personal form of expression is in the description of the three pictures which Rochester picks out from Jane's portfolio. As has often been remarked, these are highly Romantic in tone and subject matter, and play a premonitory role in the overall pattern of the novel. Although Jane insists that their subjects appeared before her 'spiritual eye' ..., and that each painting is a direct if 'pale portrait' ... of that vision, the sources of the principal images are quite clearly literary: this is most obviously true of the third picture, a strange mixture of Milton and Bewick, but all three contain features common to the magazines and 'keepsake' volumes of the early nineteenth century. Even though Rochester is impressed by their being 'for a school girl, peculiar' . . . , the reader finds their portentousness, lack of originality, and naivety somewhat embarrassing—and this cannot be dismissed simply as a modern reaction. (p. 316)

If biographical interpretation is relevant here, it is so in relation not to Charlotte Brontë but to the eighteen-year-old Jane Eyre: whereas the superintendent's picture indicated accomplishments with social and economic value, these pictures reveal Jane's emotional status. Clearly, she has made little progress here; the pictures speak all too plainly of the conditions of isolation in which they were produced and of that unhealthy fascination with the dismal which was both product and curse of Jane's affection-starved childhood. The experience of the lonely schoolgirl artist is still painfully narrow and she must go to literary sources for most of her images, so that she differs from the rejected child of the opening chapter only in being able to project images of her plight instead of merely absorbing them in passivity.

The central Thornfield episodes of the novel are presented largely in terms of the same vision which produced the pictures, and the latter thus provide an early clue by which the emotional coloration of those episodes—including the highly Romantic depiction of Rochester—can be discerned and properly evaluated. The way Jane's creative imagination goes to work on its materials is quite precisely revealed in the genesis of the pictures she actually completes while at Thornfield, those contrasting portraits of 'a Governess, disconnected, poor, and plain' and of 'Blanche, an accomplished lady of rank' . . . which she intends as medicine for a mind which love of Rochester has infected with wishful thinking. (pp. 316-17)

[Blanche] is a literary product even before she is re-interpreted by Jane. Her dress, speech, taste, all exhibit an excessive Byronism, and what we receive, in the narrative as in the pictures, is the blending of Jane's conception of Blanche with Blanche's image of herself. Precisely the same process is at work in the accounts of Rochester at this point in the novel; what makes him seem so melodramatic is that he is the product of two literary imaginations, his own and Jane's, both fully understood and controlled by the author. Rochester behaves, quite deliberately and self-consciously, like a Byronic hero, taking up dramatic poses, singing Corsair songs, acting arbitrarily and inscrutably; he talks of his past in *Childe Harold* terms; he delights in dressing up and playing exotic roles. When such a figure is presented through the still more naively Romantic imagination of the eighteen-year-old Jane Eyre the coloration becomes positively violent.

The validity of seeing a combined creative endeavour at work in this central portion of the novel is established by the next group of pictures, whose fairy-tale and Romantic elements have their origin equally in Jane's own wishful thinking and in Rochester's literary and fanciful version of their love. . . . Fairy-tale elements cluster round the relationship of Jane and Rochester from their first meeting, but in Jane's case they serve mainly to suggest her closeness to childhood, while her common sense is constantly asserting itself to brush aside old superstitions and to mock Rochester's persistent toying with images of Elf-land. The realistic side of Jane finds an ally in the sternly materialistic Adèle, who insists that Jane is no fairy, and calls Rochester 'un vrai menteur' [a real liar]. . . . Nevertheless, Rochester continues to play with images drawn from Arabian Nights tales, fairy stories and ballads, and with references to Jane as some kind of small bird, and no matter how much Jane may overtly resist this indulgence in fantasy, her

Gateshead vignettes reveal how completely her imagination has been ensnared.

The responsibility for the evasion inherent in the creation and continuation of this dream-world thus rests jointly with Jane and with Rochester, both of them burdened with pasts whose surviving effects they have not yet seriously confronted. Jane finds images for her day-dreams in Rochester's fantastic conversation, and her sense of everyday values is no match for her Romantic imagination and her inexperience, both of which impel her to respond positively to Rochester's Byronic pose. The thirty-year-old narrative voice emphasizes the moments of realism, but the struggle between common sense and Romantic sensibility finds immediate expression only in haunted dreams and in strained, self-conscious day-time behaviour which matches in its archness the artificiality of Rochester's desire to deck his bride in silks and jewels.

The flight from Thornfield following the interrupted marriage ceremony marks the turning-point for Jane, and she undergoes a trial on the moors which brings her face to face with the real meaning of the personal worth and independence to which she had somewhat prematurely laid claim. The newly-found humility of the schoolmistress of Morton shows itself in her next pictures, which are of ordinary subjects taken from life. . . . (pp. 317-19)

There is one further stage, and it is marked, significantly enough, by the total cessation of Jane's artistic activities. In the account of Jane's married life in the final chapter, all her imaginative activity and pictorial skill are devoted to the severely practical yet emotionally satisfying task of embodying in words, for the benefit of her blind husband, whatever passes immediately before her eyes. . . . Jane's powers of visual realization, far from being suppressed, now share in that exaltation and fulfilment which her whole being has found in the daily demands of an altruism from which the maturity of her love has shorn every hint of self-sacrifice.

Earlier in the novel Charlotte Brontë has exploited the considerable freedom afforded by the first-person convention to manipulate and vary the narrative distance in order to achieve her dual purpose of depicting both the story and the personal development of the story-teller; in so doing, as we have seen, she makes full use of Jane's paintings to mark clear points on the scale of narrative involvement. Now, in the last chapter, the closing up of the gap between the narrator and the events narrated is coincident with, and dependent upon, a final integration of all aspects of Jane's personality. If there is, at this stage, no further mention of painting or drawing, that is because measurements of narrative involvement are no longer required and, equally, because the aptitudes and impulses which Jane displayed in her pictures are now devoted not to compulsive self-expression, nor even to coolly objective portraiture, but to human communication of a peculiarly intense and passionate kind. To say that Jane Eyre, the heroine, merges at last with Jane Rochester, the narrator, is to make at one and the same time a statement about the novel's technique and about the novel's meaning. (p. 319)

Jane Millgate, "Narrative Distance in 'Jane Eyre': The Relevance of the Pictures," in The Modern Language Review, *Vol. 63, No. 2, April, 1968, pp. 315-19.*

W. A. CRAIK (essay date 1968)

[*Craik concurs with Kathleen Tillotson (1954) in her contention that the novel's unity derives partially from using the heroine as narrator. In her general study of structure and characters, Craik points out that character development becomes more clearly delineated as Jane matures. Unlike many earlier critics, including Richard Chase (1947) and G. Armour Craig (1956), who state that Rochester's wounding is a punishment for his depraved youth, Craik interprets the injury as a "paradoxical reward for virtue." In addition, Craik also analyzes a number of minor characters and discusses the symbolism of various settings.*]

The most obvious things in **Jane Eyre** are the simple single story and the personality of its narrator Jane herself, with Mr Rochester coming a very close third. Everything that is done bears directly on these three. This is partly the result of having a narrator who is also the hero, but the concentration shows it is more than a natural consequence.... Like [Emily Brontë's] *Wuthering Heights*, **Jane Eyre** might be called a love story. This would be true in one way, since it shows that the marriage at the end is the moral and artistic culmination of the whole—not merely a convenient rounding-off of a whole collection of different kinds of material.... In another way it is considerably less than the truth, since by the time this marriage is reached it has come to represent the resolution of moral and emotional conflicts, and the growth of moral and emotional grasp of life as a whole; for all of which the word 'love-story' is a very inadequate counter. The story really examines that period of life in which its heroine (and in secondary place its hero also) makes the most influential decisions of her life; the period which arouses the most extreme emotions of which her nature is capable, and brings out and tests the strength of the moral principles which rule her.

The reader's emotional and moral sympathy with Jane Eyre is vital, and no one questions Charlotte Brontë's power of obtaining and keeping it. But complete emotional sympathy generally suggests complete identification, the reader feeling that he actually becomes the character throughout, or for long portions of the action. **Jane Eyre** obviously approaches this state at points, but this is not really the whole truth, and Charlotte Brontë never meant the story to produce so total an immersion.... Jane, who cares passionately for Mr Rochester, preserves her detachment from him; and Charlotte Brontë takes care that the reader, who comes rapidly to care passionately about Jane, shall preserve his degree of detachment as well. The reader is quite often addressed, and so forced to think of himself and his own personality as very much a thing apart from the narrator's, and the demands that he shall do so grow more frequent as the story goes on. They increase in direct proportion to the emotional and moral complexity of the material. (pp. 71-3)

There are two obvious narrative stances available: the story can either be seen and revealed by Jane at the age at which she experiences it, or it can be interpreted by the Jane who is supposedly looking back at her youth from the age of about thirty—the age she claims to be in the last chapter, where she says she has been married ten years. Charlotte Brontë uses both stances frequently. But as the action develops, other points of view are taken up within this main framework. The eighteen-year-old Jane at Thornfield has the opportunity to revisit the scene of her first sufferings and her first defiance, Gateshead, and to reassess both herself and those who hurt her; and there are many other equally vital but even smaller time-lapses and retrospects: Jane at Lowood looks back and tells her sufferings at Gateshead to Miss Temple; at Morton, she contrasts herself as schoolteacher with what she would have been as Mr Rochester's mistress; and the whole of the section at Thornfield is punctuated by pauses for Jane to review, analyse or assess what

has gone before. These degrees of involvement make it easy to suppose that when we have reached the most detached narrator, we have reached the author. It is easy to feel that Jane Eyre at her wisest and most omniscient is Charlotte Brontë herself, and probably the majority of readers do so, consciously or not, at some time during their acquaintance with the work. It is the measure of Charlotte Brontë's triumph. It is natural to like Jane, and when we know that many of the things that happen to her, and many of the places she goes to, belong equally to Charlotte Brontë, it is both natural and inviting to think that Jane and Charlotte may be equated. It is a temptation that must be resisted if one intends to get the most possible out of the novel.

These degrees of detachment are never automatic or systematized; they are always determined by the emotion and the attitude to it that is necessary both in Jane and in the reader. At the beginning of the story the method is created and established. It would be all too easy here to assume complete identification with the ten-year-old Jane, see all through her eyes, and make her sufferings quite unnaturally painful, and her adult tormentors monstrous or merely ridiculous.... In Charlotte Brontë's closest contemporary, Dickens, the Murdstones are as terrible to the young David Copperfield [in the novel of the same name] as the Reeds to Jane, while the pathos is probably even more painful to the reader, since David cannot rise against them as Jane does, and since he has to watch them torture his mother too; yet to the reader the Murdstones are mere grotesques, on whom he is never asked to spend a serious thought. The superiority of Charlotte Brontë's method is proved in the novel as a whole, since the Reeds return eight years later, and while they impress Jane the independent young woman very differently, they are still—especially Mrs Reed—very recognizably themselves. (pp. 75-9)

[It] would seem natural on the whole for the narrative detachment to decrease and simplify, as it does in *David Copperfield*. In fact the tendency is the opposite, and the more the emotional pressure increases, the more Jane's understanding of herself and ours of her is clarified by the way the narrator reveals them. The closest-knit section of the book in all ways is that at Thornfield, from Mr Rochester's first appearance on the icy causeway to his last in despair when Jane leaves him. This section consists of a series of emotional surges forward, with pauses or even withdrawals between them, like the waves of a rising tide. At every pause the reader is made to stand away from the emotional experience, and assess it in relation to others, to moral standards, or simply to ordinary common life. This is achieved by a shift in the narrator's view, and Jane herself stands away from events.... Jane's assessments are usually—when Blanche Ingram has appeared—repressions, but they show the same uncompromising and rational fairness.... (pp. 80-1)

It is clear that on the question of attitude to material alone, the first-person narrator is being used with great subtlety and with a sure hand. Jane is a great advance on Crimsworth in this respect. Even though *Wuthering Heights* and [Anne Brontë's] *Agnes Grey* both precede **Jane Eyre,** Charlotte Brontë has not borrowed from them, since neither uses its narrator in this way. But the use does show that Charlotte Brontë shared with Emily this desire to make her novel a complete vision of life, where one event does more than merely follow another, and events are constantly seen in the light of the significant events which precede and come after them, even though Charlotte's methods are on the surface less revolutionary than Emily's. This constant reference of past to present action may account for another resemblance between *Jane Eyre* and *Wuthering Heights:* there is no real attempt at anything approaching a sub-plot. (p. 84)

As a mere love story, the Thornfield and Ferndean sections seem to be the only vital ones, and the others—the two Gateshead ones, Lowood and Moor House—become extraneous padding or biographical self-indulgence. This very elementary carping is easily done away with. No reader denies the power of Jane's story of her childhood, and few would fail to see that the qualities of the adult Jane are present or developed or foreshadowed in the ten-year-old cousin at Gateshead, and the passionate friend of Helen Burns. But Charlotte Brontë has undoubtedly taken great risks with her plot; no writer could use it as a model and expect coherence in his own work; the Gateshead section is a complete plot in itself, the story of an oppressed child who rises against her tyrants and succeeds in escaping them; so is the Lowood story, that of a lonely girl, who, through Helen Burns, experiences suffering and death and the value of friendship; even more striking is the apparently completely separate Moor House story, where Jane begins a new life as a village schoolmistress, acquires three new cousins, comes into a fortune, and is sought in marriage by St John Rivers. What is more, all these plots are more realistic, more obviously likely, than the central one—of a man of property, with an insane wife concealed in the house he actually uses, who courts the governess of his illegitimate daughter, attempts to commit bigamy, and when that has failed, loses his sight and his hand in attempting to save the life of his wife, before being reunited (through a supranormal event) with the woman he has injured. But their common purpose unifies them: and great care is taken on the practical level to make sure that no detail is inaccurate. A sound structural basis is provided, and while the effect is frequently an emotional one, there are no practical inconsistencies. (p. 85)

The characters other than Jane and Rochester are of widely different types, and are presented in very different styles. While there have been many to disparage the presentation of the gentry, at the house-party, there have been few to praise the many successes who are necessarily less obtrusive: Mrs Fairfax, or Bessie, or St John Rivers. Again the problem is one of recognizing the novel's purpose. None of these characters can exist and stand alone as characters can when the narrator is the author. They exist as Jane sees them, not as Charlotte Brontë might have done. . . . The range from which characters are drawn corresponds to the society in which Jane moves. The degree to which they are congenial indicates their worth, and by implication the moral worth of their kind and class. This moral worth is always an element in their presentation, a matter on which the reader is never left in any doubt, the only possible exceptions to the generalization being Mr Rochester and St John Rivers. . . . Lynn, Colonel and Mrs Dent, to the magistrate Mr Eshton; and at the lowest are the family servants Bessie and Robert Leaven at Gateshead, Hannah at Moor House, Leah and Grace Poole at Thornfield, John and Mary at Ferndean. At intervals between these range the Reed family, the Rivers family, Mrs Fairfax, Adèle, Bertha Mason and her brother, the Lowood characters Miss Temple, Helen Burns and Mr Brocklehurst, and a few vividly-realized incidental persons such as the few people Jane meets at Morton, and the proprietor of the inn, who tells her where to find Mr Rochester. The characters group themselves obviously according to the place and episode in which they appear, but there are resemblances and parallels between them and their relation to Jane, which appear as the story progresses. Generally speak-

ing, characters are simple in the opening sections, and grow more subtle the further the story progresses, as Jane's capacity for subtle appreciation increases, and as the moral growth requires elaborate personalities to reveal it. (pp. 87-8)

The Reed family are a demonstration of Jane's power to overcome her circumstances, and link with and balance the Riverses—another family of two sisters and a brother, whose relations with Jane are another, more searching, test of her powers of resistance. Eliza and Georgiana Reed have only the personality necessary to show in contrasting forms the absence of human sympathy Jane suffers: Eliza 'would have sold the hair off her head if she could have made a handsome profit thereby' . . . , while Georgiana's curls are essential to her; they are her virtues, and claims to affection. The simplicity of the representations make them forceful, and emphasize the pain they cause the child Jane, yet the simple attributes can be taken and made to work morally when they reappear as grown-up young women. Both are credible recreations, since the basis of character is the same. (p. 88)

Mr Brocklehurst is one of the links between Gateshead and Lowood. He is unlike the Reeds in the attitude we adopt towards him, and an example of one of the attributes Charlotte Brontë is often denied—humour. He is a comic grotesque. (pp. 90-1)

The teachers Miss Miller, Miss Scatcherd, and Mlle Pierrot are of the stock types that [Charlotte Brontë] used in *The Professor,* and uses again in *Villette;* they serve their purpose and are unobtrusive, allowing us to concentrate on the more vital Miss Temple and Helen Burns. These two both have the literary virtue of being interesting though noble characters. There is tact in stressing Helen's slovenliness before revealing her fortitude, and in deliberately underplaying her learning . . . ; and tact also in keeping Miss Temple at a distance: we never see her relations with Jane as she grows older and more intimate with her. . . . Both Helen and Miss Temple demonstrate Jane's need simply for human affection, and her power to inspire it, before she meets Mr Rochester and the force of love is added. They prove also that Jane chooses the highest when she sees it. (p. 92)

At Thornfield there is another change in the type and the presentation of characters. As governess, Jane now has a social as well as a personal position, and the people she meets are consequently seen in their place in society as well as in their individual selves. Social position is to be at odds with personal worth and personal relationships at Thornfield: it is the essence of these society characters that their rank is wholly disproportionate to their personal worth; and the culmination is Mr Rochester's social contract to his mad wife. (pp. 92-3)

The house-party displays a different type of minor character, with less relevance outside the incidents where they actually appear and a great deal less realism—or, as Charlotte Brontë might have said, 'more real than true'. They resemble Mr Brocklehurst in distressing Jane and being comic and grotesque at the same time. Once one recognizes the comedy, the obvious improbabilities become much less offensive, and one reads Blanche and her corsair-song, and the resplendent dowagers Lady Lynn and Lady Ingram, not so much as one reads Thackeray's satiric portraits, but Fielding's.

There is a gusto in Charlotte Brontë's language which prevents any suspicion that Jane is envious of these people, and suggests that she may know very well that she is exaggerating details of dress and modes of speech. (pp. 94-5)

Bertha Mason (whom it is offensive even to think of as Bertha Rochester) is the incubus of Thornfield, who has no 'character' until Mr Rochester reveals her history . . . , and whose character when it is finally exposed is no real surprise, though her existence is a shock. She is the embodiment of ungoverned passion, contrasting with Blanche, who has none (but who yet looks like her . . .), and demonstrates both the power and the failing of Mr Rochester, who will not send her to Ferndean because it is unhealthy, but insists on his right to act as if she does not exist. She develops from the vague to the explicit, from the unseen possessor of the laugh, who starts a mysterious fire in the night, to the violent attacker of Mason which seems the climax to her activities but is not so, since her worst offence is simply to exist as Mr Rochester's wife. She is the purveyor of horror. . . .

A character more important to the novel as a whole than her part in the action would suggest is Adèle Varens. Seemingly only the pretext for Jane's presence at Thornfield, Adèle is structurally invaluable. She is clearly a touchstone of character. . . . (p. 97)

In sharp contrast to anyone at Thornfield are the characters at Morton: St John, Diana and Mary Rivers, Hannah, Rosamond Oliver and the few villagers and farmers. Charlotte Brontë's touch with the rustics is sure: when Jane is starving, their equally unsentimental and unmalevolent treatment gives vivid conviction to her sufferings. (p. 98)

Mary never appears without Diana, and is really a shadow of her, and both are overshadowed by their brother. They are the first women friends Jane has had since she left Lowood and Miss Temple, and represent the pleasures of the intellect, which Jane has not had, or missed. Despite their beauty, they are not at all young-lady-like and nor are their conversations with Jane. St John is a finely-observed study of a man who turns egotism and ambition to the service of religion. He is the most important single character in the book after Mr Rochester, and is obviously his antithesis, religious, idealistic, handsome, cold-blooded. . . . His treatment, solemn, using Biblical allusion, and constantly described in terms of marble, and even as a pillar, all recalls that other columnar clergyman, Mr Brocklehurst. It is surprising that he can generate enough power to become the danger he is to Jane at the end of the episode, and that the reader shares her unwilling admiration for one who tempts her to do violence to her own nature, in antithesis to Mr Rochester, who tempted her to violate her moral standards. (pp. 99-100)

There remain only the two people at the heart of the book— Mr Rochester and Jane. Mr Rochester has been seen by many as the idealized, even the impossible, hero. . . . But he does not completely fill the romantic bill, and we are pulled up smartly if we try to make him. . . . As usual, the attempt to identify the character with an actual person does not get us very far. . . . The other more respectable impulse, to explain historically, and analyse Mr Rochester's undoubted debt to Byronism, does not go far either, since the great interest of Mr Rochester is in what Charlotte Brontë creates out of her materials, rather than the nature of the materials themselves. Proof of this is that although in his place in the novel he convinces us completely, he cannot be taken out of his context: he exists as part of Jane's consciousness, and for his relation to her. But within this context we have no reservations about him other than those Charlotte Brontë specifically intends, and the impulse to think of him as isolable, as if 'real', is a measure of the success she has achieved by her autobiographical method.

To describe a hero only by what the heroine sees, when the former must reveal more of himself to the reader than the other can observe, and when that other must be hampered by youth, inexperience, and passion, is a great achievement.

Mr Rochester is both the remote hero and the man whom Jane understands because she is 'akin' to him; he is a man whose moral nature is like Jane's, who is yet the one who tempts her to evil; he is a good man who suffers a dreadful punishment for his sin. Here for the first (and perhaps the only) time we have the romantic hero who becomes not less but more exciting as he becomes familiar, for whom marriage is the triumph, not merely the convenient and correct end to the adventures of courtship, who does not 'dwindle into a husband'. . . . (pp. 101-02)

The essence of Mr Rochester is to be unpredictable, to shock with the unconventional and the unexpected; but it is essential that the reasons for his behaviour shall be clearly and unambiguously discernible, in retrospect if not at the time. (p. 102)

[We] are constantly being called upon as the action progresses to try to judge Mr Rochester at the same time as we come with Jane under his spell, by standards which he himself is not aware of and will not admit. (p. 103)

The whole of his association with Jane is a series of surprises, of shocks to which Jane responds and draws back for periods of assessment, before the next shock impinges. By this means, he, like St John Rivers, develops a kind and degree of power we should not suspect from his beginnings, natural though it seems when we reach the end. These delays Mr Rochester introduces into the courtship have many uses, besides the obvious ones of producing suspense and excitement. They allow Jane to classify and come to terms with her experience; they show Mr Rochester's self-control and consciousness of his feelings and so make him worthy of Jane, since he is not acting merely on passion and impulse; at the same time there can be no doubt that he is morally at fault in committing a calculated legal crime, and violating Jane's known nature. He clearly enjoys the invidious relationships of this long courtship (as in a way Jane clearly does also), deliberately building up the excitement: almost all his speeches to Jane after Blanche arrives are ambiguous declarations or invitations. (p. 104)

Mr Rochester at Thornfield is coherent enough, but many readers have wondered whether he is the same man whom Jane meets and marries at Ferndean. . . . He is certainly changed, just as Mrs Reed changed between Chapters I and 2I; but Charlotte Brontë has no doubts about him: what is emphasized is that he is still essentially the man he was, vigorous and in the prime of life. He is reintroduced by his full name, his relationship with Jane is instantly re-established, he speaks with the same voice in the same terms, using the pet-name Janet, and seeing her as 'a fairy', making the same brisk leaps from the impassioned to the practical. . . . The main differences are that he is blind and maimed, and that he hesitates to ask her to marry him. Again it is over-sentimental to over-estimate the disaster, and Charlotte Brontë never does so. Mr Rochester blind is still a romantic figure, to be seen as a falcon or as Vulcan (as he could not be with one leg for instance). . . . He is realistically allowed to recover a good deal of his sight. . . . It is right, too, that Mr Rochester's injuries are not his moral punishment for the suffering he caused Jane (his mental tortures are that). He is injured as a paradoxical reward for virtue: if he had not tried to save Bertha he would not have been hurt. This is not at all poetic justice, but there is a real psychological rightness about it, just as there was when he would not shut Bertha away at Ferndean because it was too unhealthy . . . and she might die.

There remains very little to be said about Jane Eyre herself, because more than most eponymous heroines she is the whole of the novel in which she appears. Sympathy with her is essential, and there can be few characters in fiction to whom it has been so readily given. She calls up emotions every reader must recognize and probably have experienced, and at the times and ages that most people felt them, though in the novel they are intensified: Jane in terror of a bullying boy cousin, hating a powerful aunt, cringing from public exposure at school, giving her heart to a school-friend and a kind teacher, all readily find echoes in the reader's past; and when Jane's circumstances become stranger, we continue to respond as she does, and feel the truth of the response. With her passions Jane combines qualities more rational, equally sympathetic, which every reader's vanity flatters him he possesses too: sound common sense, the power to see herself as others see her, a robust sense of humour, the power to act right under the most powerful of temptations, and survive the most testing physical conditions. (pp. 105-08)

The shape of the novel is very much represented by the places where the action occurs, which Charlotte Brontë makes an essential part of the structure, as well as the atmosphere, of her stories. Places have indeed as much character as people, and serve many of the same purposes, a use which *Jane Eyre* shares with *Wuthering Heights,* or, to name a later novelist, Hardy. They operate by accurately and vividly selected detail, and often on more than one level. Just as a single person is felt and judged in different ways at the same time, so places may arouse a variety of conflicting feelings, and the tensions, beginning fairly simply with the child's view of Gateshead, increase in complexity through Lowood, Thornfield, Morton, and Ferndean. Gateshead is plainly a place of torment, the house of the Reeds, where all the rooms are places of cold and dread. . . . (p. 109)

Lowood is physically hard and aesthetically repulsive. A reader's immediate recollections of it are of burnt porridge, 'a strong steam redolent of rancid fat', 'a keen north-east wind, whistling through crevices of our bedroom windows all night long, [that] had made us shiver in our beds, and turned the contents of the ewers to ice' . . . , girls 'in brown stuff frocks of quaint fashion, and long holland pinafores' . . . , whose hair is not allowed to curl, even naturally. But the pleasures are more mature and more extensive. Sensuous pleasure remains; in food for the famished such as Miss Temple's supper ('How fragrant was the steam of the beverage, and the scent of the toast', and that ever memorable 'good-sized seed-cake' . . . ; and in the scenery ('prospects of noble summits girdling a great hill-hollow, rich in verdure and shadow; a bright beck, full of dark stones and sparkling eddies' . . .). (pp. 110-11)

Such simple combinations of good and bad prepare for the much more subtle use of Thornfield. The place has several aspects: freedom and happiness are embodied in some parts of the house, in its gardens, and in the surrounding landscape; while the sinister and evil are embodied in the upper storeys (especially at night); the grand world of society, heartless and tasteless, belongs in the drawing-room. These are all directly related to Jane's association with Mr Rochester, and help us to feel the moral weight of what happens. Jane first meets Mr Rochester outside, in Hay Lane; he tells her about Céline in the cold wintry garden, standing outside the house as he is

standing, mentally, outside his own experiences and coldly assessing them; after Mason has been attacked and departed, Mr Rochester sits in the garden in summer sunrise with Jane, reviewing in the dawn of his new emotions the painful and violent ones of his youth, which link so closely with what has just happened inside the house; he proposes to Jane in the garden, in the orchard on Midsummer-eve, where all is 'Eden-like' and as he said before 'all is real, sweet and pure'. . . . The proposal is unlawful, but its spirit is not, and the setting of it cannot fail to make us feel so. By contrast what happens indoors is ambiguous or evil. . . . Thornfield is precious because Jane has 'lived in it a full and delightful life' . . . ; but it is insubstantial and doomed to perish, representing the falsity that must be burned away by suffering before Jane and Mr Rochester can come together, and that Jane's dreams of it as a crumbling ruin foreshadow. . . . (pp. 111-12)

Moor House is in many ways its antithesis: the building is a symbol of security and family unity, a place Jane can 'care for' in the most practical sense, as the 'cleaning down' process with Hannah proves. . . . It provides Jane with a family and a function, but subjects her to more anxiety than Thornfield ever did, when St John's [*sic*] calls her to submit to a soulless and self-destroying marriage of duty. To read about Moor House reproduces Jane's experiences there: it is both less absorbing than Thornfield, and a great deal more trying. On the other hand, Moor House and Jane's life there gain dignity, power and health from the surrounding hill-country. (p. 112)

[The] various sections of the story have a moral and artistic relevance to the main action and to each other which helps to prevent any feeling that the book has a broken back. The story is unified also in ways more obviously structural. Innumerable threads of association and construction link section to section and incident to incident; and Charlotte Brontë creates proportioned emphasis, subtle parallels, and a sense of layers of simultaneous action to her basically linear story. The mere proportion of space occupied plays a large part in suggesting relative importance to the reader: four chapters for Gateshead, six for Lowood, fifteen for Thornfield (interrupted by a single very long chapter when Jane returns to Gateshead); one long chapter for her suffering and starvation, seven for Morton, and three for Ferndean. Within the Thornfield period there is only one chapter before Mr Rochester appears, twelve chapters for the courtship (more than is spent on anything else in the novel), but also two very long ones which cover the span between the wedding and Jane's flight. It can clearly be seen that the narrative movement runs against the natural passage of time, but nevertheless time and the hour run through the roughest day. References to season and weather, and even dates and days of the week, are frequent and exact as well as atmospheric: the intervals of time between Jane's arrival at Thornfield in October and Mr Rochester's proposal on Midsummer Eve are carefully noted, and equally accurate are those between her midsummer agony on the moors, St John's news of her fortune brought on a snowy November the fifth, and her return to Ferndean on a wet Thursday summer evening (the third of June). Jane does not live wholly in the present (as fictional characters so often do) but is always aware of her own past and possible future—she imagines with frightening truth what marriage to St John would entail—and she recognizes death as an accepted fact for others and herself. . . . (pp. 113-14)

The most obvious and mechanical reason why Jane returns [to Gateshead] is to hear Mrs Reed's deathbed confession telling her of the uncle to whom she will owe both the breaking off of her wedding and also her fortune. It is much more organically a culmination of what has gone before, and an anticipation of what is to come. The culmination is necessary because Jane is to return to Thornfield to face the two greatest emotional experiences of her life: Mr Rochester's and her own mutual declarations, and her renunciation of him. For these to have their full power we must see Jane as a whole being, a part of all that she has met, moulded to this experience by all that has happened to her hitherto. (p. 115)

Within the larger individual sections of the action, the movement varies, but Charlotte Brontë tends always to work in terms of the big scene, completely realized and dramatically presented. She likes to use the effect of shock on her reader, but she never loses her emotional continuity; she therefore moves from one big scene to the next, by a variety of methods: the smaller (but significant) intermediate scene, the pause for Jane's reflection and analysis of what has passed, and, very rarely, the juxtaposition of sharply contrasting important scenes. She is also careful to provide proper preparation where shock is unsuitable; and the prefatory material, though of various kinds, is always concerned with building up the right associations, or recalling the necessary personalities. The result is a wave-like movement, with a drawing-back between each surge of an incoming tide. Attention to continuity descends even to the nice placing of chapter divisions. The most interesting place to examine her structural methods is where they are at their finest and most sustained, that is, during the fifteen chapters chronicling the events at Thornfield. These move by a series of exciting, even sensational, events, seen in entirety. The sense of shock is as much in the material as the presentation, and Charlotte Brontë never cheats by cutting a scene off short to get her excitement. (p. 116)

Since Charlotte Brontë's method is in many ways a dramatic one, she uses a good deal of dialogue. *Jane Eyre* has the advantage over *Villette* and *The Professor* that its characters (all except Adèle and Sophie) are English-speaking. Charlotte Brontë has a fine ear for characteristic idioms of class and age, which the deliberate and obvious artificiality of the house-party dialogues tends to obscure. She moves in a narrow compass, making little use of dialect, having no character to compare with Emily Brontë's Joseph; Hannah, the only really broad speaker, is generally reported, and her direct speech gets its flavour from idiom rather than pronunciation. . . . (p. 120)

Charlotte Brontë's style is like no one else's. This is generally agreed and immediately obvious. Being odd, it has often been called bad, by those who have preconceived notions of what a novelist's style should be, and in particular a Victorian lady novelist's. But as Mr Rochester says in another context, 'unheard-of combinations of circumstances demand unheard-of rules'. . . . Both Charlotte Brontë and Emily found this to be so in their writing; both solved their own problem in their own way, and while Charlotte occasionally allows herself to copy other novelists (the voice heard most frequently besides her own is that of Thackeray, whom she greatly admired), her best effects are always her most individual ones. Again the distinction must be made between Charlotte Brontë and her creation Jane Eyre. While Jane has many of Charlotte Brontë's characteristics, it is clear that what she says is almost always 'in character'. . . . (p. 121)

With *Jane Eyre* Charlotte Brontë establishes what the novel is to be and do in her hands, and has found her course between what she herself summarized as the 'real' and the 'true'. . . . (p. 122)

W. A. Craik, "'Jane Eyre'," in her The Brontë Novels, *Methuen & Co. Ltd.*, 1968, 266 p.

EARL A. KNIES   (essay date 1969)

[*Knies, like Kathleen Tillotson (1954), expresses admiration for the first-person narrative in* Jane Eyre *and adds that the character of Jane is the novel's triumph. Disagreeing with G. Armour Craig (1956), Knies finds a disparity between Jane and her creator. Knies contends that Jane is equal to Rochester, rather than his superior, as Craig argues. He also states that Rochester's mutilation from the fire is a symbolic exorcism of the evil in his nature, in opposition to the opinions of Craig, Richard Chase (1947), and W. A. Craik (1968). Knies's arguments are supported by Nancy Pell (1977).*]

When we search for the evidences of Charlotte's struggle to get the situation of the story [of *Jane Eyre*] before us, we have difficulty finding them. Weaknesses there are, but they are not the result of an inadequate method. On the other hand, most of the strengths clearly *are* the result of the method. The opening chapter does a masterful job of getting the story going, giving us enough of the basic situation to make the action meaningful but at the same time avoiding extensive exposition. At the end of the chapter we are forcibly drawn into the story as those four sets of hands are laid on Jane—and us, for we have already been compelled to make an emotional commitment. *The Professor* had begun with the awkward letter device and then proceeded in a reasonably strict chronological order from that point onward. *Jane Eyre* plunges immediately into the action of the story without any preliminary flourishes, and, although its development is also chronological, necessary information about events preceding the time of the story is periodically being presented in a thoroughly natural way, for we learn about these events at the same time that Jane does. Thus, although the chronological arrangement keeps the story line perfectly clear and easy to follow, *Jane Eyre* is really a mosaic of bits of the past and the present.

The skill with which these expository passages are blended into the forward motion of the narration is apparent in the following examples. While Jane is lying ill after her terrifying experience in the Red Room, she overhears Bessie and Abbot, the maids, talking about her parents, and she learns "for the first time" the conditions under which she had become an orphan. The revelation does not seem unnatural, however, for it is worked smoothly into the maids' conversation. . . . Further information about Jane's background is revealed by Mrs. Reed on her deathbed. She tells how her husband had taken Jane at the death of her parents and how Mrs. Reed had hated her from the first. This bit of exposition is functional in the scene, since it emphasizes the intensity of a hatred that Mrs. Reed is unable to overcome even when death is imminent. (pp. 105-06)

The finest piece of exposition is that which occurs when Jane returns to Thornfield after hearing Rochester's call. She discovers the Hall in ruins, and to learn what happened she goes to the local inn, where the host is perfectly happy to answer her questions but is at the same time unaware of her identity. He therefore replies to her questions with a true innkeeper's expansiveness, telling her not only what she wants to know but also a great deal about herself. (p. 107)

The examples of exposition discussed above illustrate the skill with which Charlotte Brontë conducted her first-person narrative. That skill is even more apparent when we consider some of the other difficulties traditionally attributed to first-person narration. . . . There simply are no details of plot which do not have an immediate bearing on Jane; the only things that *are* important are the things she knows. She must learn some important things at second hand, but the manner of their presentation is perfectly natural. Because she presents exposition dramatically—through scene rather than through summary—we are present when Rochester tells about his past, when the innkeeper tells about the burning of Thornfield—and so everything seems to be happening within Jane's consciousness even though the events took place when Jane was not actually present. (pp. 108-09)

The real triumph of *Jane Eyre* . . . is, of course, the character of Jane. . . . [Yet critics comment on the inability of first-person narration] to make a deep study of the central character. . . . (p. 109)

[Within] the conventions of first-person narration it is possible to present an admirable character without obvious self-glorification or pretentious humility. Charlotte Brontë's heroines have a particular advantage because they are characters not liked by everyone they meet and because they are plain. The frankness with which these facts are accepted by Jane and Lucy makes us more willing to accept the good things they must tell us about themselves. Moreover, even though a first-person narrator cannot write essays on himself, he can see himself as others see him if he is the kind of person who invites frank comments from other people. Every person in the book helps, to some extent, to characterize Jane, either by direct comment about her or by her reaction to them. Much of her characterization comes through Rochester, who constantly amazes Jane with his ability to read her thoughts. (p. 110)

The interaction among the personages of the novel, then, carries much of the burden of characterization. Even though Jane enlists our sympathy in such a way that we feel about the various characters much as she does, still, we are not forced to accept her feelings simply because they are hers; her friends and foes are presented dramatically, in such a way that we can accept or reject them on the basis of their actions. We do not, for example, dislike Mrs. Reed or Brocklehurst or Blanche Ingram merely because Jane does, but we do dislike them for the same reason that she does: we are repelled by their meanness, their hypocrisy, their pettiness. . . .

Of course, Jane does characterize herself through the things she says and does, and her frankness, both in talking to characters within the novel and in talking to us, convinces us of her reliability. We never get the feeling that she is trying to varnish the truth. (p. 111)

This complete honesty, this perfect candor, then, provides a structure upon which the reliability of the narrative is built. Once we believe in Jane, we are willing to suspend our disbelief about incidents in the novel which seem improbable. Jane's belief in dreams and the supernatural provides a setting in which the call from Rochester can take place. The supernatural imagery running through the novel sets a tone and creates an atmosphere within which supernatural occurrences do not seem improbable. (pp. 112-13)

The world of *Jane Eyre* is one in which dreams come true—literally.

But point of view is more than a way of getting the events of the story before the reader, more than a method of characterization. It is also a way of looking at the material which provides definite effects which no other point of view could. . . .

[In *Jane Eyre*,] Jane seems to be trying to dispense with time completely, and in exciting or particularly memorable moments it does disappear; Jane is there again, living the experience for the first time with no later knowledge. (p. 114)

When Jane turns her head, everything outside the range of her vision passes out of existence. Any novelist focuses his attention and excludes irrelevant details, of course, but very few novelists do so in such an obvious way. There is no life going on around the fringes of this narrative: nothing exists except those things which Jane perceives. But they exist with an intensity seldom equaled, for Jane does not merely tell about an event; she *re*creates it. Thus *Jane Eyre* is almost as "dramatic" (in a critical sense) as a novel can be. Jane the narrator does not come between us and the narrative but rather becomes part of it. Because she seldom analyzes her experience from the vantage point of time, narration and narrator become one. The implications of this technique in interpreting the novel become important. G. Armour Craig finds the single vision a decided limitation [see excerpt above, 1956]. (p. 116)

Jane can dominate, or at least comprehend, her world because it is a personal one, a . . . limited one. . . . Even though *Jane Eyre* raises some social problems, they are carefully limited to her own situations. There is no need for a second narrator to examine them in a broader context. Second—and more important—Craig fails to distinguish between Charlotte Brontë and Jane Eyre. Jane herself does not create Mrs. Reed, or Lowood, or Rochester's past, or St. John Rivers and his sisters; she perceives and reacts to them, but she does not dominate them. It is Charlotte Brontë who shows that Jane's decisions are the right ones through the patterns of the novel. It is Charlotte Brontë's dialectic that makes mutilation and blinding necessary, just as Dickens' dialectic makes the death of Esther's mother, Lady Dedlock, necessary. The "I" of *Jane Eyre* is absolute only in the sense that it is reliable, that we need not suspect that Jane is lying to us, and in that it creates a fictional reality, a framework within which potentially absurd situations seem credible. We may dislike Charlotte Brontë's morality as evidenced in the novel, but we need not criticize her art for that reason. Jane *does* carry most readers along with her in her judgments, but that can hardly be called a weakness.

In other words, although *Jane Eyre* is a subjective novel, it is not wholly so. Most of the characters and situations might be said to have an objective reality in addition to the subjective interpretation that Jane superimposes upon them. If we do not accept the convention that Jane reproduces conversations with accuracy, for example, it becomes impossible for us to make anything at all of the novel. Unless there is something objective for us to balance against her subjectivity, we can have no idea of its quality. Almost all important personages in the novel characterize themselves to some extent through their speech and actions. . . . Once we accept the framework of the novel— Jane and her perceptions—as valid, then what goes on within that framework can hardly be considered mere subjective distortion. No one is characterized as fully as Jane is, of course. . . . (pp. 117-19)

The story of the novel is the story of Jane's development, and in the process of the novel various conflicts are resolved.

The dominant theme of the novel is, of course, love, and the progress of the novel is a search for it. But a satisfactory relationship involves more than mutual attraction, no matter how intense it may be; love, in Charlotte Brontë's terms, must be based upon moral and individual integrity. No relationship between a man and woman can be complete unless each retains his uniqueness as an individual, and that in turn requires a firm religious orientation. (p. 120)

[The breakup of Jane and Rochester's wedding] does more than save Jane from marrying a bigamist. The quality of the love that each felt for the other, fervent though it may be, is unsatisfactory. When Jane finally comes to a full awareness of what has happened, her thoughts return to God, who had previously been obscured by Rochester: "One idea only still throbbed life-like within me—a remembrance of God: it begot an unuttered prayer" . . .—not articulated, however, in time to save her from the whole consciousness of her "life lorn," her "love lost," her "hope quenched," her "faith death-struck." But the returning awareness of God ultimately gives her the strength she needs to resist Rochester's pleadings and her own temptation to become his mistress. Rochester tells her of his own past as well as the course of his growing love for her, his belief that she could save him from his own mistakes and his family's deceit. . . . She comes perilously close to yielding when he puts his argument into yet another context: "Is it better to drive a fellow-creature to despair than to transgress a mere human law—no man being injured by the breach? for you have neither relatives nor acquaintances whom you need fear to offend by living with me." . . . (pp. 131-32)

And therein lies the terrible loneliness and the extreme complexity of Jane's decision. . . . (p. 132)

[Nevertheless,] she flees Thornfield, finally and miraculously stumbling half-dead onto the doorstep of her only living relations. Nowhere in the novel is credibility strained further. Part of Jane's longings are satisfied at Moor House when she discovers that she does have relatives; and the fortune left her by her Uncle John raises her social status. Both of these occurrences have more thematic than realistic justification and seem largely gratuitous. But we soon forget coincidence once the relationship between Jane and St. John is established. For this episode is functional and part of the careful balance of the plot, not just a diversion to pass time between the flight and the call from Rochester. This man driven by duty to renounce all earthly pleasures is a clear contrast to Rochester and a representative of one side of Jane's personality. . . . He offers her purpose in life, and to one who has had an unfortunate love affair, the appeal of the convent—or its equivalent—is always strong. (p. 133)

St. John's proposition is even more outrageous in its way than Rochester's, for it involves a spiritual prostitution instead of a physical one. St. John wants marriage without love, Rochester love without marriage. Neither alternative offers a satisfactory solution to the problem of personality.

The mysterious call from Rochester—the voice which seems to Jane to be in *her*, not in the external world—comes just in time. Regaining her composure, Jane breaks from St. John and returns to Thornfield to find it in ruins. She discovers Rochester maimed and blinded from his unsuccessful attempt to rescue his mad wife from the fire she had started. . . . Equality, not superiority, is the keynote, and the end brings a marriage of true minds, not a triumph for either side. When we consider Rochester's final arguments before Jane left we can see clearly that his sin was not so much sexual as religious. . . . [His mutilation is] an involuntary fulfillment of the Biblical injunction: "And if thy right eye offend thee pluck it out, and cast *it* from thee. . . . And if thy right hand offend thee, cut it off, and cast *it* from thee; for it is profitable for thee that one

of thy members should perish, and not *that* thy whole body should be cast into hell." It is Rochester's attempt to set aside God's law and decide his own course of action that is his sin. (pp. 134-35)

Once Jane finishes teasing Rochester about St. John in a scene that is reminiscent of his use of Blanche Ingram to tease her, once she makes it clear that she wants to marry him, Rochester again shows his old colors. "Jane suits me: do I suit her?" he asks. . . . The main difference between this marriage and the one that might have been is that it is based upon mutual respect and understanding, that the sins of the past have been expiated. . . . They come together as equals, not as victor and vanquished in the battle of the sexes; but the intensity of their love has not diminished. . . . In their marriage all the conflicts of the novel are resolved. Jane is at peace with God and man, and especially with herself. (pp. 135-36)

It becomes apparent, then, that the construction of *Jane Eyre* is not in the least haphazard. The structure of the novel is symphonic, based upon an elaborate pattern of repetition of the major themes with variations. In the Gateshead portion of the novel, the major themes—love, religion, and independence—are introduced. In the Lowood portion they are put into new perspective largely through Jane's contact with Helen Burns, who is in direct contrast with Mrs. Reed, the dominant personality of the first section. The Thornfield and Moor House sections provide further contrasts: Rochester's stormy, impetuous love is followed by St. John's cold and practical proposal. In rejecting both—or, more accurately, in achieving a synthesis of the two—Jane qualifies herself for the ideal union she achieves at the end—a union of equals "at God's feet."

Parallel scenes and statements further bind the various sections of the novel. The Jane who would be willing to be kicked by a horse rather than live without love is finally able to reject a love which she expects never again to find the equal of. Bertha's attempt to burn Rochester in bed is repeated on a larger scale near the end of the book. Foreshadowing is so extensive that when something happens we have a vague feeling of having encountered it before. The novel is full of echoes. (p. 137)

And because everything in the novel revolves around Jane and comes to bear on her, first-person point of view is not merely a device for getting the story told; it is part of the story itself. There is no other way to tell it, for from no other point of view would it be the same story. (pp. 137-38)

> *Earl A. Knies, in his* The Art of Charlotte Brontë, *Ohio University Press, 1969, 234 p.*

ADRIENNE RICH (essay date 1973)

[*Rich, a noted American poet, provides one of the first feminist interpretations of* Jane Eyre. *She indicates that Jane dislikes Rochester's method of courting, since he treats her as an object. When Jane finally marries, Rich contends, it is not because Rochester is symbolically castrated but rather because she does not have to sacrifice her own identity. Rich also acknowledges the strong roles women play in* Jane Eyre; *the figures of Helen Burns and Miss Temple are seen as examples of women who support and encourage each other. Ultimately, Rich assesses* Jane Eyre *as a novel that provides alternatives for women. This essay originally appeared in* Ms., *October, 1973.*]

Like Thackeray's daughters, I read *Jane Eyre* in childhood, carried away "as by a whirlwind." . . . I have never lost the sense that it contains, through and beyond the force of its creator's imagination, some nourishment I needed then and still need today. Other novels often ranked greater, such as *Persuasion, Middlemarch, Jude the Obscure, Madame Bovary, Anna Karenina, The Portrait of a Lady* [novels by, respectively, Jane Austen, George Eliot, Thomas Hardy, Gustave Flaubert, Leo Tolstoy, and Henry James]—all offered their contradictory and compelling versions of what it meant to be born a woman. But *Jane Eyre* has for us now a special force and survival value. . . . (p. 89)

Jane Eyre is different from *Wuthering Heights,* and not because Charlotte Brontë lodged her people in a world of governesses and employers, of the love between men and women. *Jane Eyre* is not a novel in the Tolstoyan, the Flaubertian, even the Hardyesque sense. *Jane Eyre* is a tale.

The concern of the tale is not with social mores, though social mores may occur among the risks and challenges encountered by the protagonist. Neither is it an anatomy of the psyche, the fated chemistry of cosmic forces. It takes its place between the two: between the realm of the given, that which is changeable by human activity, and the realm of the fated, that which lies outside human control: between realism and poetry. The world of the tale is above all a "vale of soul-making," and when a novelist finds herself writing a tale, it is likely to be because she is moved by that vibration of experience which underlies the social and political, though it constantly feeds into both of these. . . . (p. 90)

Charlotte Brontë is writing—not a *Bildungsroman* [apprenticeship novel]—but the life story of a woman who is *incapable* of saying *I am Heathcliff* (as the heroine of Emily's novel does) because she feels so unalterably herself. Jane Eyre, motherless and economically powerless, undergoes certain traditional female temptations, and finds that each temptation presents itself along with an alternative—the image of a nurturing or principled or spirited woman on whom she can model herself, or to whom she can look for support. (p. 91)

Jane Eyre is *not* "always a governess." She addresses us first as a literally motherless, and also fatherless child, under the guardianship of her aunt, Mrs. Reed, who despises and oppresses her. The tale opens with images of coldness, bleakness, banishment. . . .

Moments after the novel begins, John Reed provokes Jane's childish rage by striking her in the face and taunting her with her poverty and dependency. Thus, immediately, the political/social circumstances of Jane's life are established: as a female she is exposed to male physical brutality and whim; as an economically helpless person she is vulnerable in a highly class-conscious society. Her response to John's gratuitous cruelty is to "fly at him" and threat to be dragged off and locked into the "Red Room," where her uncle had died and which is rumored to be a haunted chamber.

Here begins the ordeal which represents Jane's first temptation. For a powerless little girl in a hostile household, where both psychic and physical violence are used against her, used indeed to punish her very spiritedness and individuality, the temptation of victimization is never far away. To see herself as the sacrificial lamb or scapegoat of this household, and act out that role, or conversely to explode into violent and self-destructive hysterics which can only bring on more punishment and victimization, are alternatives all too ready at hand.

In the Red Room, Jane experiences the bitter isolation of the outsider, the powerlessness of the scapegoat to please, the abjectness of the victim. But above all, she experiences her situation as unnatural:

> Unjust!—unjust! said my reason, forced by the agonizing stimulus into precocious though transitory power; and Resolve, equally wrought up, instigated some strange expedient to achieve escape from insupportable oppression—as running away, or if that could not be effected, never eating or drinking more, and letting myself die.

I want to recall to you that the person who is going through this illumination—for "dark" and "turbid" as her feelings are, they are illuminating—is a girl of ten, without material means or any known recourse in the outer world, dependent on the household she lives in for physical support and whatever strands of human warmth she can cling to. She is, even so, conscious that it could be otherwise; she imagines alternatives, though desperate ones. It is at this moment that the germ of the person we are finally to know as Jane Eyre is born: a person determined to live, and to choose her life with dignity, integrity, and pride.

Jane's passion in the Red Room comes to its climax; she hallucinates, screams, is thrust back into the dreaded death-chamber, and blacks out. Her ensuing illness, like much female illness, is an acting-out of her powerlessness and need for affection, and a psychic crisis induced by these conditions. (pp. 91-3)

Lowood is a charity school for the poor or orphaned genteel female destined to become a governess. It is a school for the poor controlled by the rich, an all-female world presided over by the hollow, Pharisaical male figure of Mr. Brocklehurst. He is the embodiment of class and sexual double-standards and of the hypocrisy of the powerful, using religion, charity, and morality to keep the poor in their place and to repress and humiliate the young women over whom he is set in charge. He is absolute ruler of this little world. However, within it, and in spite of his sadistic public humiliation of her, Jane finds two women unlike any she has ever met: the superintendent Miss Temple, and the older student Helen Burns.

Miss Temple has no power in the world at large, or against Mr. Brocklehurst's edicts; but she has great personal attractiveness, mental and spiritual charm and strength. Unlike the Reeds, she is of gentle birth yet not a snob; unlike Bessie she is not merely sympathetic but admirable. She cannot change the institution she is hired to administer but she does quietly try to make life more bearable for its inmates. (p. 94)

Helen Burns is strong of will, awkward and blundering in the practical world yet intellectually and spiritually mature beyond her years. Severe, mystical, convinced of the transitory and insignificant nature of earthly life, she still responds to Jane's hunger for contact with a humane and sisterly concern. She is consumptive, soon to die, burning with an other-worldly intensity. . . . (pp. 94-5)

Both Miss Temple's self-respect and sympathy, and Helen's transcendent philosophical detachment, are needed by Jane after her earthly humiliation by Mr. Brocklehurst. For if at Gateshead Hall Jane's temptations were victimization and hysteria, at Lowood, after her public ordeal, they are self-hatred and self-immolation.

Jane is acutely conscious of her need for love: she expresses it passionately to Helen Burns.

"... to gain some real affection from you, or Miss Temple, or any other whom I truly love, I would willingly submit to have the bone of my arm broken, or to let a bull toss me, or to stand behind a kicking horse, and let it dash its hoof at my chest—"

Her need for love is compounded with a female sense that love must be purchased through suffering and self-sacrifice; the images that come to her are images of willing submission to violence, of masochism. Helen calms her, tells her she thinks "too much of the love of human beings," calls on her to think beyond this life to the reward God has prepared for the innocent beyond the grave.... (p. 95)

The discipline of Lowood and the moral and intellectual force of Helen and Miss Temple combine to give the young Jane a sense of her own worth and of ethical choice. Helen dies of consumption with Jane in her arms held like "a little child"; Miss Temple later marries an "excellent clergyman" and leaves Lowood. Thus Jane loses her first real mothers. Yet her separation from these two women enables Jane to move forward into a wider realm of experience....

One of the impressive qualities of Charlotte Brontë's heroines, the quality which makes them more valuable to the woman reader than Anna Karenina, Emma Bovary, and Catherine Earnshaw combined, is their determined refusal of the romantic. They are not immune to it; in fact, they are far more tempted by it than are the cooler-headed heroines of Jane Austen; there is far more in their circumstances of orphaned wandering and intellectual eroticism to heat their imaginations—they *have,* in fact, more imagination. Jane Eyre is a passionate girl and woman; but she displays early an inner clarity which helps her to distinguish between intense feelings which can lead to greater fulfillment, and those which can only lead to self-destructiveness. The thrill of masochism is not for her, though it is one of her temptations as we have seen; having tasted a drop of it, she rejects it. In the central episode of the novel, her meeting with Mr. Rochester at Thornfield, Jane, young, inexperienced, and hungry for experience, has to confront the central temptation of the female condition—the temptation of romantic love and surrender.

It is interesting that the Thornfield episode is often recalled or referred to as if it *were* the novel **Jane Eyre.** (pp. 95-6)

If the Thornfield episode is central, it is because in it Jane comes to womanhood and to certain definitive choices about what it means to her to be a woman. There are three aspects of this episode: the house, Thornfield itself; Mr. Rochester, the Man; and the madwoman, Jane's alter ego.

Charlotte Brontë gives us an extremely detailed and poetically convincing vision of Thornfield. Jane reaches its door by darkness, after a long journey; she scarcely knows what the house is like till the next day when Mrs. Fairfax, the housekeeper, takes her through it on a tour which ends in the upper regions, on the rooftop. The reader's sense of its luxury, its isolation, and its mysteries is precisely Jane's, seen with the eyes of a young woman just come from the dormitory of a charity school— a young woman of strong sensuality. But it is the upper regions of the house which are of crucial importance—the part of the house Jane lives in least, yet which most affects her life. Here she first hears that laugh—"distinct, formal, mirthless"—which is ascribed to the servant Grace Poole and which she will later hear outside her own bedroom door. Here, too, standing on the roof, or walking up and down in the corridor, close to the very door behind which the madwoman is kept hidden, she gives silent vent to those feelings which are introduced by the telling phrase: "Anybody may blame me who likes...." (p. 97)

We see little of Bertha Rochester; she is heard and sensed rather than seen. Her presence is revealed by three acts when she escapes into the inhabited part of the house. Two of these are acts of violence against men—the attempted burning of Mr. Rochester in his bedchamber, and the stabbing of her brother when he visits Thornfield. The third act is the visit to Jane's bedroom on the night before her wedding and the tearing of the wedding veil, the symbol of matrimony. (She does not, interestingly enough, attack Jane.) Only after Bertha's existence is publicly revealed is Jane taken into the madwoman's chamber and sees again, waking, "that purple face—those bloated features." (p. 99)

In his long account of the circumstances of his marriage to Bertha—a marriage arranged for financial reasons by his father, but which he undertook for Bertha's dark sensual beauty— Rochester makes no pretense that he was not acting out of lust. Yet he repeatedly asserts *her* coarseness, "at once intemperate and unchaste," as the central fact of his loathing for her. Once she is pronounced mad, he has her locked up, and goes forth on a life of sexual adventures, one result of which has been the child Adèle, daughter of his French mistress. Rochester's story is part Byronic romance, but it is based on a social and psychological reality: the 19th-century loose woman might have sexual feelings, but the 19th-century *wife* did not and must not; Rochester's loathing of Bertha is described repeatedly in terms of her physical strength and her violent will—both unacceptable qualities in the 19th-century female, raised to the nth degree and embodied in a monster.

Mr. Rochester is often seen as the romantic Man of Fate, Byronic, brooding, sexual. But his role in the book is more interesting: he is certainly that which culture sees as Jane's fate, but he is not the fate she has been seeking. When she leaves Lowood for Thornfield, when she stands on the roof of Thornfield or walks across its fields longing for a wider, more expansive life, she is not longing for a man. We do not know what she longs for, she herself does not know; she uses terms like liberty, a new servitude, action. Yet the man appears, romantically and mysteriously, in the dusk, riding his horse— and slips and falls on the ice, so that Jane's first contact with him is with someone in need of help; he has to lean on her to regain his seat on horseback. Again at the novel's end it is she who must lead him, blinded by fire. There is something more working here than the introduction of a stock romantic hero.

Mr. Rochester offers Jane wider horizons than any she has known; travel, riches, brilliant society. Throughout the courtship there is a tension between her growing passion for him and her dislike of and uneasiness with the *style* of his lovemaking. It is not Rochester's sensuality that brings her up short, but his tendency to make her his object, his creature, to want to dress her up, lavish jewels on her, remake her in another image. (pp. 99-100)

Jane's parting interview with Mr. Rochester is agonizing; he plays on every chord of her love, her pity and sympathy, her vulnerability. On going to bed, she has a dream. Carried back to the Red Room, the scene of her first temptation, her first ordeal, in the dream, Jane is reminded of the "syncope," or swoon, she underwent there, which became a turning point for her; she is then visited by the moon, symbol of the matriarchal spirit. . . . (p. 101)

> I watched her come—watched with the strangest anticipation; as though some word of doom were to be written on her disc. She broke forth as moon never yet burst from cloud: a hand first penetrated the sable folds and waved them away; then, not a moon, but a white human form shone in the azure, inclining a glorious brow earthward. It gazed and gazed on me. It spoke to my spirit: immeasurably distant was the tone, yet so near, it whispered in my heart—
>
> "My daughter, flee temptation."
>
> "Mother, I will."

Her dream is profoundly, imperiously, archetypal. She is in danger, as she was in the Red Room; but her own spiritual consciousness is stronger in womanhood than it was in childhood; she is in touch with the matriarchal aspect of her psyche which now warns and protects her against that which threatens her integrity. Bessie, Miss Temple, Helen Burns, even at moments the gentle housekeeper Mrs. Fairfax, have acted as mediators for her along the way she has come thus far; even, it may be said, the terrible figure of Bertha has come between Jane and a marriage which was not yet ripe, which would have made her simply the dependent adjunct of Mr. Rochester instead of his equal. Individual women have helped Jane Eyre to the point of her severest trial; at that point she is in relation to the Great Mother herself. On waking from this dream, she leaves Thornfield, with a few pieces of clothing and twenty shillings in her purse, to set forth on foot to an unknown destination.

Jane's rebellion against Rochester's arrogance—for in pleading with her to stay with him against the laws of her own integrity, he is still arrogant—forces her to act on her own behalf even if it causes him intense suffering, even though she still loves him. Like many women in similar circumstances, she feels that such an act of self-preservation requires her to pay dearly. She goes out into the world without a future, without money, without plans—a "poor, obscure, plain, and little" figure of a woman, risking exposure to the elements, ostracism, starvation. By an act which one can read as a final unconscious sacrificial gesture, she forgets her purse with its few shillings in the stagecoach, and thus is absolutely destitute, forced to beg for the leftovers a farmer's wife is about to feed to her pig. In this whole portion of the novel, in which Jane moves through the landscape utterly alone, there is a strong counterpull between female self-immolation—the temptation of passive suicide—and the will and courage which are her survival tools. (pp. 102-03)

"Reader, I married him." These words open the final chapter of *Jane Eyre.* The question is, how and why is this a happy ending? Jane returns to Thornfield to find it "a blackened ruin"; she discovers Rochester, his left hand amputated and his eyes blinded by the fire in which he vainly attempted to save the life of his mad wife. Rochester has paid his dues; a Freudian critic would say he has been symbolically castrated. Discarding this phallic-patriarchal notion of his ordeal, we can then ask, what kind of marriage is possible for a woman like Jane Eyre?

Certainly not marriage with a castrate, psychic or physical. (St. John repels Jane in part because he is *emotionally* cas-

trated.) The wind that blows through this novel is the wind of sexual equality—spiritual and practical. The passion that Jane feels as a girl of twenty or as a wife of thirty is the same passion—that of a strong spirit demanding its counterpart in another. . . . (pp. 104-05)

Coming to her husband in economic independence and by her free choice, Jane can become a wife without sacrificing a grain of her Jane Eyre-ity. Charlotte Brontë sets up the possibility of this relationship in the early passages of the Thornfield episode, the verbal sparring of this couple who so robustly refuse to act out the paradigms of romantic, Gothic fiction. We believe in the erotic and intellectual sympathy of this marriage because it has been prepared by the woman's refusal to accept it under circumstances which were mythic, romantic, or sexually oppressive. . . . (p. 105)

In telling the tale of Jane Eyre, Charlotte Brontë was quite conscious, as she informed her publisher, that she was not telling a moral tale. Jane is not bound by orthodoxy, though superficially she is a creature of her time and place. As a child, she rejects the sacredness of adult authority; as a woman, she insists on regulating her conduct by the pulse of her own integrity. She will not live with Rochester as his dependent mistress because she knows that relationship would become destructive to her; she would live unmarried with St. John as an independent co-worker; it is he who insists this would be immoral. The beauty and depth of the novel lie in part in its depiction of alternatives—to convention and traditional piety, yes, but also to social and cultural reflexes internalized within the female psyche. In *Jane Eyre,* moreover, we find an alternative to the stereotypical rivalry of women; we see women in real and supportive relationship to each other, not simply as points on a triangle or as temporary substitutes for men. (p. 106)

> *Adrienne Rich, "'Jane Eyre': The Temptations of a Motherless Woman," in her* On Lies, Secrets, and Silence: Selected Prose, 1966-1978, *W. W. Norton & Company, 1979, pp. 89-106.*

NANCY PELL   (essay date 1977)

[*Pell discusses* Jane Eyre *from a feminist perspective. She views the novel as Brontë's critique of the social and economic strictures of her time. Like Earl Knies (1969) and Adrienne Rich (1973), Pell contends that the marriage of Jane and Rochester is one of equality. To Pell, Bertha symbolizes Rochester's repressed awareness of his social situation. Other interpretations of Bertha include those by Richard Chase (1947), W. A. Craik (1968), Maurianne Adams (1977), and Susan Gubar and Sandra M. Gilbert (1979).*]

In *Jane Eyre* Charlotte Brontë's romantic individualism and rebellion of feeling are controlled and structured by an underlying social and economic critique of bourgeois patriarchal authority. Although this does not describe the entire scope of the novel, which includes countercurrents and qualifications as well, the formal and dramatic elements of a social critique are manifest in Jane's resistance to the illegitimate power of John Reed, Mr. Brocklehurst, and St. John Rivers; allusions to actual historical incidents involving regicide and rebellion; and, finally, the dynamics of Rochester's two marriages—both his marriage to Jane and his earlier marriage to Bertha Mason.

The dramatic presentation of Jane Eyre's struggles at Gateshead Hall involves the reader not only in the child's awareness of her oppression but also in the analysis of its source. She describes her habitual mood as "humiliation, self-doubt, forlorn depression"; accustomed as she is "to a life of ceaseless reprimand and thankless fagging,'' there are especially terrible moments of "unutterable wretchedness of mind" which reduce her to silent tears. (pp. 399-400)

Further dimensions of Jane's conflict are revealed by the narrator's interjections, the voice of the adult woman writing at a distance of some twenty years. She tells us that Jane was opposed to her aunt and cousins in temperament, capacity, and propensities and was therefore "a useless thing, incapable of serving their interest, or adding to their pleasure." . . . (p. 401)

Obviously, the shaping consciousness is always Jane's; the novel is subtitled "an autobiography" and is narrated as such. The device of an adult woman presenting the drama of her childhood, however, has more than one consistent effect. When the adult voice is overtly obtrusive, as in the first example—"a useless thing, incapable of serving their interests"—it sounds like an ironic gesture toward fairness that deliberately fails to convince. The reader has just been led, moment by moment, through the vivid drama of Jane's violent and tyrannical mistreatment, which takes up again immediately after the "mature" voice stops. Elsewhere this mature voice has a more indirect and validating function. When Mrs. Reed shuts Jane up in the red room she tells the child, "This violence is all most repulsive. . . . It is only on condition of perfect submission and stillness that I shall liberate you." We receive her words not as immediately transcribed by the child, but as the experience remembered, selected, and redramatized by the adult woman. The older narrator seems to be endorsing the child's experience. . . . The conditions on which the adults in Jane's world would have approved of her are drawn in terms of such extravagant prejudices or demands for subjection that the author leads us to give our sympathy and encouragement to the child who resists and defies them.

The Reverend Robert Brocklehurst, the "straight, narrow, sable-clad" minister . . . , personifies the religious aspect of self-suppression and constraint that Jane will meet again in Helen Burns and St. John Rivers. Charlotte Brontë's picture of established spiritual authority in *Jane Eyre* is devastating, as the reviewer Elizabeth Rigby discerned [see *NCLC*, Vol. 3]. Brontë goes beyond obvious anticlericalism to articulate an alternate religious system; she replaces the "mighty universal parent," the father God whom Helen Burns trusts and St. John presumes to represent, with "the universal mother, Nature" . . . , symbolized most often by the moon and its light. (pp. 401-02)

In the first interview with Brocklehurst we see Jane moving beyond her largely instinctive responses to John Reed toward a more developed intellectual resistance to the threat the minister represents. . . .

Jane's healthy impulses lead her to refuse to deny herself the good things that are presently available to her. When Dr. Lloyd asks if she would like to go to live with some relatives on her father's side of the family who, though poor, might be kind to her, Jane says no: "I could not see how poor people had the means of being kind." She knows that the Reed's servants literally cannot afford to be kind, and they are the only poor people whom she has known at first hand. Young Jane's sense of poverty is concrete rather than abstract. . . . (p. 403)

That same admirably concrete vision is turned to more affirmative account when Jane describes her satisfaction with her increasingly active life at Lowood. . . . Her comforting fantasies have changed from food to creative cultural achievement. The same spirit that motivates Jane's refusal to embrace the supposed love of her poor relatives animates her healthy and

vigorous ability to draw sustenance—without subscribing to Helen Burns's asceticism—from the plainness and rigor of Lowood school. (pp. 403-04)

Jane's commitment to life is so strong that we are likely to forget how thoroughly this novel is pervaded by death. . . . It is against the background of the very real possibility of death, emphasized by both the novel's plot and its imagery, that we see Jane's strategies for life being worked out.

Refusal to accept her death at the hands of others is Jane's chief motive for resisting St. John's commanding proposals of marriage. (p. 404)

St. John's resemblance to John Reed is impressive; their names alone reflect a similarity between them. St. John is the only person besides young Reed who causes Jane to fear for her life. . . . [Both men] die as suicides of a sort; John Reed is rumored to have killed himself over gambling debts, and St. John Rivers, as he expected, succumbs to the climate of India in the service of his Sovereign.

Two allusions in the novel to actual rebellions in English history suggest Charlotte Brontë's awareness that Jane's struggle for a wider life has significant historical implications. First, after a lesson at Lowood school on tonnage and poundage in the early reign of Charles I, Helen Burns confesses her admiration for the Stuart king. . . . Jane criticizes Helen, both for her visionary passivity and for her royalist sympathies. "If people were always kind and obedient to those who are cruel and unjust," Jane objects, "the wicked people would have it all their own way: they would never feel afraid, and so they would never alter, but would grow worse and worse". . . . Her resistance to the abuse of power, even the Stuart prerogatives, here clearly places Jane among the regicides. . . . Eventually Jane comes to comprehend the value of self-restraint through the example of Miss Temple, director of Lowood, whose quiet resistance to Mr. Brocklehurst's policies of deprivation has nothing to do with axiomatic stoicism. (pp. 405-06)

The second reference to historical revolutionary antecedents is both more subtle and more powerful in its implications. Early in the novel the servant Abbot suspects that young Jane is "a sort of infantine Guy Fawkes"; the passage is echoed later on when Jane has become a school mistress in the village of Morton. She receives a visit from St. John on the occasion of a holiday from her duties on the fifth of November. Although the day is not named, it is the traditional British Guy Fawkes Day. The date is not without ambiguities however. In addition to marking the discovery of the Catholic plot to blow up the Houses of Parliament in 1605, it is also the anniversary of the landing of William and Mary at Torbay in the "Glorious Revolution" of 1688. Thus both violent and bloodless rebellions are juxtaposed on the occasion of Jane's passing from the dispossessed to the possessing class. For during his brief visit, St. John—who knows Jane only as Jane Elliott—looks at a sketch that she has drawn and discovers her true name, Jane Eyre, written on the portrait cover. This disclosure leads to the rediscovery of lost connections between Jane and the Rivers family and establishes her possession of the legacy of twenty thousand pounds from her uncle John Eyre. The repeated image of Guy Fawkes and the ambiguous historical allusions to the Fifth of November thus accompany the moment that unites Jane's past and her future.

Throughout *Jane Eyre* Charlotte Brontë presents marriage in the context of equality between the partners. "Equality," for Jane, always has an active social definition which is first made explicit, apart from marriage, when she meets Alice Fairfax on her arrival at Thornfield Hall. Jane has expected to be treated with coldness and stiffness, in short, like a governess. She is greatly surprised by the friendly conversation of her supposed employer and superior. . . . The presence of Mrs. Fairfax serves as a continuing reminder of the social inequality of Jane and Rochester. The housekeeper is astonished when she learns that they are to be married, not because she thinks it impossible that Rochester could sincerely love Jane, but because she has known the family for many years and is convinced that "gentlemen in his station are not accustomed to marry their governesses." . . . (pp. 406-07)

Jane's clarity about equality and inequality between herself and Rochester has several aspects. In their first meetings, on the icy Millcote road and later in the library at Thornfield, they recognize each other's physical and psychological similarities; neither is conventionally attractive or socially graceful. Rochester claims advantage over Jane, however, on the basis of his wider experience of the world; Jane disagrees, reminding him primly that "your claim to superiority depends on the use you have made of your time and experience." . . . Although Jane does not realize it, her remark touches the heart of the matter—Rochester's acquiescence in the marriage that his father and elder brother arranged for him in order to secure Bertha Mason's dowry of thirty thousand pounds. His ten years of searching on the continent for a woman who would restore his lost innocence parallels Jane's ten years at Lowood, where she has grown from the child who flew at John Reed in furious rages to a young woman who competently supports herself in a society about which she has few illusions. (p. 408)

In spite of Jane's sensitivity to being Rochester's employee, she is perfectly aware that she has grown to love him and rejects the Pamela-role [inspired by Samuel Richardson's novel, *Pamela,*] of fleeing from him whenever he approaches her. Their most famous encounter takes place at the foot of Thornfield's ancient chestnut tree. Rochester tells Jane that he is soon to be married to Blanche Ingram and that he will help Jane to secure a new position in Ireland. The ocean suddenly seems very wide to Jane, but wider still the ocean of wealth, caste, and custom which separates her from Rochester. . . . The revelation that Rochester already has a wife living, however, changes Jane's prospects, although not her love itself, and reminds her of the power that social position exerts over even the most passionate devotion. (pp. 408-09)

Few critics have paid much attention to Rochester's wife, Bertha Mason; the rest politely avert their eyes, tactfully disregarding a lapse of good taste, an unfortunate Gothic regression. (p. 410)

There is indeed a grim justice in the fact that Rochester's only instance of open, public involvement with Bertha comes at the moment of his physical crippling. Their secret has all along crippled his life socially and psychologically. He has been determined to deny this throughout the past fifteen years; his marriage and all that has followed from it are his experiences-of-the-world on which he claimed superiority to Jane. Jane challenges this claim during their first conversation in the library, and it seems to me that Bertha is the psychological symbol, not of Charlotte Brontë's repressed hostility against the male universe, but of Edward Rochester's repressed awareness of his true social situation.

Jane is not repelled by the truth about Rochester; ultimately she has great sympathy for his situation. . . . [While] Rochester acknowledges that he was plotted against and cheated into his marriage by his "avaricious and grasping" father, he refuses to acknowledge that he, like Jane, is a social victim. He continues to play the role of master not only with his household servants but toward all men and women. (pp. 411-12)

Rochester's bitterness against society is thus personally cynical rather than socially perceptive like Jane's. . . . He indulges in the luxury of scorn for Blanche Ingram. He has no sympathy for one who, like himself in his youth, is compromised in her choice of a mate by an elder brother's precedence in the family economy and who is, in addition, excluded because of her sex from ever inheriting entailed family land. . . .

Rather than his father or elder brother, however, the primary object of Rochester's rage is Bertha, who is actually his fellow victim in their arranged marriage. Jane is critical of this, saying that he is "inexorable for that unfortunate lady: you speak of her with hate—with vindictive antipathy. It is cruel—she cannot help being mad." . . . Bertha Mason has become such a monster to Rochester because she receives a doubly displaced resentment, more correctly directed against the economics of primogeniture and Rochester's own compromised self. . . . He says that he continues to care for Bertha because he is disinclined "to indirect assassination, even of what I most hate." . . . How much more complex than this his involvement with her is, in fact, appears when twice in the novel Rochester deliberately identifies himself with symbolic Berthas—women who are social outcasts and yet possess peculiar powers over other people. First, he speaks to Jane about "arranging a point with [his] destiny":

> "She stood there, by that beech-trunk—a hag like one of those who appeared to Macbeth on the heath of Forres. 'You like Thornfield?' she said, lifting her finger; and then she wrote in the air a memento, which ran in lurid hieroglyphics all along the house-front, between the upper and lower row of windows. 'Like it if you can! Like it if you dare!'" . . .

Like Macbeth, Rochester suffers his destiny appearing to him in the form of witches; like Macbeth, he has a wife who went mad. The second incident is dramatic rather than metaphoric: during the house party Rochester successfully disguises himself—even from Jane at first—as an old gypsy woman come to the great house "to tell the gentry their fortunes." . . . Rochester's inability to acknowledge his past seems to compel him to fantasies of the future under the control of Bertha's image. (pp. 412-14)

The legacy that Jane receives from her uncle in Madeira makes possible her reunion with Rochester and also significantly redefines her relationship to patriarchal structures. "An independent woman now," Jane proceeds to redefine the term. Previously she has rejected the independence exemplified in Helen and St. John, who despise the natural and human realms of life. She has refused as well the mockery of independence found in Eliza Reed's advice to her sister Georgiana. (p. 415)

Rochester has not simply been humbled by divine retribution; he no longer acts the role of master exclusively because he has learned something about the limits of his own power. Jane likens him to "Nebuchadnezzar in the fields" . . . , referring to the biblical account . . . of a king's loss of both power and sanity. His injuries also recall Jacob's wrestling with the angel . . . , an additional biblical precedent that associates crippling with understanding. . . . Since all along Bertha has represented

Rochester's attempt to deny his origins, it seems appropriate that even in her death the persistence of denial remains with him in the form of bodily injury. Rochester says that his injuries are punishments for his intended sexual aggression toward Jane—''I would have sullied my innocent flower.'' But the association of these injuries with Bertha, rather than Jane, points to the circumstances of his first marriage—and its aggression against both Bertha *and* Rochester—as the ''crime'' of which the diminishing of his power is the outward and visible sign. Social and psychological suffering denied have become physically inescapable, and, recognized as such, neither proves as unbearable nor as isolating as before.

Jane's affirmation of interdependence rather than of autonomy helps to explain the genuineness of her acceptance of Rochester, but it also points to the problem of their reabsorption into the system of inheritance and primogeniture that has made their earlier lives so difficult. Jane's division of her legacy among her cousins to secure each a competency is an important gesture, as I have indicated, but the larger society remains unaltered. Both Rochester and Jane have acquired their wealth in untimely or arbitrary ways through the deaths of their predecessors in the line of inheritance. (pp. 417-18)

Even though it is rooted in economic realities and social relationships, the practical and the real, Jane Eyre's resistance and rebellion are a private struggle. (p. 418)

Yet the struggle is not utterly isolated. In the central feminist assertion of the novel Jane looks out from the rooftop of Thornfield Hall and confesses to feeling discontented and restless. At this moment her strivings are more than simply the effort for individual survival; there is a sense of comradeship with other women of her class.

> Millions are condemned to a stiller doom than mine, and millions are in silent revolt against their lot. Nobody knows how many rebellions besides political rebellions ferment in the masses of life which people earth. Women are supposed to be very calm generally: but women feel just as men feel; they need exercise for their faculties, and a field for their efforts as much as their brothers do; they suffer from too rigid a restraint, too absolute a stagnation, precisely as men would suffer. . . . It is thoughtless to condemn them, or laugh at them, if they seek to do more or learn more than custom has pronounced necessary for their sex.

Here at the center of a novel about one woman's struggle for independence and love is a woman who is utterly restrained and considered socially dead, who, nevertheless, breaks through her restraints and occasionally wreaks havoc in the house of which she is the hidden, titular mistress: burning her husband in his bed; tearing Jane's wedding veil; and finally burning Thornfield to the ground. Woman under too rigid a restraint—a woman offered as an object in a marriage settlement—displays in perverse ways the power that she is continually denied. (p. 419)

> *Nancy Pell, ''Resistance, Rebellion, and Marriage: The Economics of 'Jane Eyre','' in* Nineteenth-Century Fiction, *Vol. 31, No. 4, March, 1977, pp. 397-420.*

MAURIANNE ADAMS (essay date 1977)

[*Adams notes two major themes in* Jane Eyre: *the need to be loved and the need to be a significant individual, and she points out the work's symbols and their correlation to Jane's emotions. Adams, like Adrienne Rich (1973) and Susan Gubar and Sandra M. Gilbert (1979), stresses that* Jane Eyre *is a feminist novel, but adds that Jane is initially not comfortable with her feminist awareness. Adams assesses various motifs as a means of interpreting Jane's development. Like Jane Millgate (1968) and Lawrence E. Moser (1965), Adams examines the significance of Jane's paintings but interprets them as the ambivalence of Jane's expectations. Adams considers Jane's dreams of central importance, terming them ''the dark underside of her rational self-control.'' Finally, Adams analyzes the relationship of Jane and Rochester; she points out the significance of Jane's time at Moor House, which she considers a focal point in her development.*]

Jane Eyre's childhood and her efforts to achieve adult womanhood are characterized by two needs, at times in competition with one another: the one to love and be loved, and the other to be somebody in her own right, a woman of achievement and integrity, with an outlet in the world for her passions and her energies.

The major theme is, I believe, the first of these two, the romantic theme, and the novel concludes in romantic terms, although I might note the forested-in, stagnant and physically oppressive atmosphere at Ferndean. (It was too unhealthy to send Bertha there!) I think that the hemmed-in and darkened visual quality of Ferndean indicates the price exacted by domestic romance, the impossibility of reconciling Jane's desperate need to be loved, to be useful, with her less urgent venturesomeness and independent curiosity.

Necessarily, these two major themes have further complications in Jane's narrative, just as they do often enough for women in real life. The first of these, the romantic theme, has interlocking elements I have commented on already—(1) Jane's need to *be* loved (this, I believe, is a more clearly and urgently articulated force in the novel than her direct experience of loving) as it competes with fears of a life without love and is fed by childhood starvation for love; (2) her causal linking of lovelessness and rejection with the continued experience of economic, social, and personal dependence; (3) her alienation from the social and domestic world around her (Reeds, Brocklehursts, Ingrams, and Eshtons) and her fears that they constitute the *only* world, that she will remain alienated by her lack of beauty and unfeminine traits; (4) her uncontrollable outbursts of mutiny and rage which might afford momentary relief to her integrity and sense of outraged justice but which scarcely endear her to the social superiors whose love and approval she craves; and (5) her explicit differentiation of her ''real'' family (Reeds are all she knows, until her fortuitous encounter with the Rivers) from her ''spiritual'' kin (first Helen Burns, later Edward Rochester), a split perpetuated until the happy Moor House resolution of the familial elements—blood, spiritual affinity, economic inheritance and interdependence, even religious persuasion and social status.

The second theme, the desire to *be* somebody, complicates integrity with a drive toward upward mobility. This second theme as it emerges in the novel is uneven and inconsistent, characterized by the sporadic outbursts of mutiny and rage mentioned above, but in every instance undermined by regret, loneliness, and an over-eagerness to serve others as a means of earning their approval and love.

Jane Eyre, like other novels about women, traces the competing and possibly irreconcilable needs for perpetual love and perpetual autonomy. Jane's brief stint as a teacher at Morton constitutes her single experiment in autonomy and independence, but even it is marred by loneliness, and by a sense of personal waste in the rural countryside. Clearly, *Jane Eyre* is a developmental novel, a female *Bildungsroman* as it were, and necessarily the interactions of personal and social roles and dilemmas differ from those of a male developmental novel, as they differ in life experience. *Jane Eyre* presents a girl emerging into womanhood, and it does so in essentially domestic contexts, contexts which nonetheless make severe demands upon Jane's person, integrity, status, family, and financial position.

Rereading *Jane Eyre* I am led inevitably to feminist issues, by which I mean the status and economics of female dependence in marriage, the limited options available to Jane as an outlet for her education and energies, her need to love and to be loved, to be of service and to be needed. These aspirations, the ambivalence expressed by the narrator toward them, and the conflicts among them, are all issues raised by the novel itself and not superimposed upon it by an ideological or doctrinaire reader. . . . We begin, then, with a nine-year-old child at Gateshead. She sits withdrawn into a window-seat, cut off by a red moreen curtain from the Reed family clustered around the drawing-room hearth. The curtain is a barrier which serves to protect Jane, to isolate her, and to reinforce her identification both with interior space (she daydreams over her book) and with the barren landscape on the other side of the uncurtained windowpane. (pp. 139-41)

Jane's continuing dependence, as a child, a poor relation, a charity schoolgirl, and a governess, is primary and it is explicit: "My first recollections of existence included . . . this reproach of dependence". . . . Her alternatives are retreat and rage. Symptomatically, Jane's outburst of mutinous fury in the opening pages of the book is triggered by John Reed's violation of her sole remaining sanctuary. Jane's protective withdrawal thus is not to be confused with total acquiescence. (p. 141)

It does not require great psychological insight to understand Jane's coping devices and their image-equivalents in the inner and outer landscapes of Jane's fantasy and social worlds. Jane's estrangement from social and familial life is imaged by her protective isolation from domestic interiors, while her spirit is constantly vigilant to search out spiritual affiliation in the outer landscape—she meets both Helen Burns and Edward Rochester outdoors. Both interior and exterior landscapes afford important interpretive clues, and the psychic demarcation of the Gateshead drawing room (where Jane is unwelcome) from the fantasy/natural icy landscapes (with which Jane feels at one) is repeated with careful attention to nuance and detail at Thornfield, where Jane meets with Rochester as kin and equal, beyond the orchard wall, screened in by beech trees and sunken fences. This sequestered world, equivalent in some ways to the earlier window-seat retreat, is now mutually shared. . . .

The recurrent clues afforded by domestic interiors and external landscapes as to Jane's estrangement or her affinities, serve a further visual purpose. They image in the world of society a retreat and alienation from the adults from whose hands Jane must take her daily bread; this, in personal and psychological terms, has consequences for a far more profound and dangerous dissociation of spirit from flesh. This split is revealed in the recurrent references to Jane as a caged bird, an image by which Jane is seen as simultaneously fettered (to her flesh and to her social position) and free (to her inward fantasy and spiritual space). It is in connection with this dissociation or alienation of Jane's psyche from her position in social space that plain Jane, and symbolic Eyre have special interpretive value. (p. 142)

The images suggest that Jane's interaction with Rochester in the initial Thornfield phase of their relationship is in spirit only, dissociated from the alternative examples of social womanhood that surround her, those large and fleshly creatures, her Aunt Reed, Rochester's wife, and his presumptive bride-to-be, Blanche Ingram.

It is significant for later developments in the novel to understand the psychogenesis of the ethereal Jane by tracing it back to her early trauma of extreme ostracism, her incarceration in the Red Room, an episode in which her outburst against John Reed's taunts is followed by solitary confinement and an even more extreme psychic withdrawal. It is as if the sole protective retreat available is her inner and non-corporeal self. The terror haunting the Red Room is not the ghost of her dead uncle, nor the shadows in the garden outside, but the image of Jane's self etherealized in the darkened mirror. . . . (p. 143)

There is an important psychological process implicit in [the] mirror image, which is related to the relative absence of overt and explicit sexuality in Jane's relationship with Rochester. Jane has pulled inward, and withdrawn from a physical self occupying social and familial space at Gateshead, into a "placeless" or status and space-free spiritual and moral identity, occupying thin air. Jane withdraws into her imagination and her spiritual integrity, a process by which ego is reduced to its irreducible and invulnerable inner core. Withdrawal, however, is not to be understood as simply negative. Although the elfin and visionary mirror image also presents to Jane an image of terrifying supernaturalism, this effect is the pagan antecedent for Helen Burns's mystic and Christian anticipation of that happy day when the spirit would be freed from the fetters of the flesh. Under the influence of Helen's "doctrine of equality of disembodied souls" . . . , Jane's terrifying vision of herself is eventually transmuted by the coeval claims of Christian supernaturalism and human justice. Jane can in the same utterance deny both flesh and the social world defined by the flesh, and thus claim Rochester as her equal, as if she were spirit addressing spirit. . . . If the early vision of herself in the Red Room mirror prepares for a spiritualized or elfin Jane born of the cast-off Jane, it also produces a Jane capable of "charming" Rochester beyond the capacities of a mere Blanche Ingram. (pp. 143-44)

In the "both/and" manner Jane's narrative has of pursuing a personal and economic dilemma simultaneously, using the psychic mode of fantasy interchangeably with the social mode of realism, Rochester had indeed fortuitously emerged as a spirit-being intimately associated with Jane's most traumatic childhood experience of psychological withdrawal. He is thus Jane's spirit-mate in the sense that Jane appears supernatural to him. The mutual identification and recognition of each in the other suggests a modality of love as fusion.

But the spiritual kinship which is an important dimension of Jane's and Rochester's love—and indeed, an affiliation leading directly to their reunion at the end of the novel, brought together by that otherwise inexplicable spiritual call—is balanced by Rochester's solidity for Jane as a social presence in the outside world. Rochester is introduced into Thornfield mere paragraphs after we read of Jane restlessly pacing the Thornfield battlements, wearied by her passive life, aching for a wider field of activity and for more various experience. This is an important occasion in the novel, for it defines the single moment of understanding that might be called feminist ("women feel just as men feel; they need exercise for their faculties and a field for their efforts as much as their brothers do"). . . . (pp. 144-45)

Although her outrage at injustice becomes more explicit as she grows older, only on one occasion are the upheavals of Jane's passionate integrity identified with an overt feminist understanding. What seems to me most significant about her extended psychic explosion on Thornfield's battlements is not so much the fact of its existence within a novel that takes autonomy and action in the real world as at least one of its themes, but rather the various subterfuges by which it is quickly undermined. The recurrent apologies that attend it suggest Jane's uneasiness with her feminist awareness. Further, the passage is actually the second occasion upon which Jane wishes to be up and out in the active world of towns, and to burst through the constraints of domestic service in other people's households. (p. 145)

Bertha's role in undercutting Jane's feminist outrage is not without purpose in that Bertha characterizes the dangers of ungoverned passion and rage, forced into demonic intensity. She is like Jane in the Red Room, a hidden and ostracized figure, locked into solitary confinement and thereby presenting a monstrous equivalent to Jane's "deep ire and desperate revolt." Jane calls our attention to the anxiety that attends her awareness of her own fluctuations between repression and rage. But she does not note what the pattern of her narrative implies, that the rage, indignation and rebelliousness characteristic of Jane the child finds a feminist voice in Jane the woman. . . . (p. 146)

Jane's aspirations are also displaced in their pure form to the other major male character in her narrative. St. John is the male embodiment of Jane's ambitions. (pp. 147-48)

The nature and limits upon Jane's capacity for exploration and autonomy are tested at Morton, where she is economically independent, engaged in worthwhile and serviceable work, but bereft of emotional sustenance. Jane's refusal of a loveless marriage, even though it would allow her to fulfill the aspiring and ambitious side of her nature through missionary work, is a further test of her venturesomeness. Although the alleged social impossibility of her accompanying St. John as a coworker but not wife is an impediment obviously not of her making, it does appear that Jane's feminism is ambivalent at best, and her drive toward autonomy and an independent working life is undermined by her need for a sustaining and nurturing love. Sides of her nature are presented as polar opposites, without an alternative posed by which they might be fused. Jane's life is posed in terms of contrasting locales, opposing imageries, irreconcilable life choices.

But Jane's integrity is quite another matter. She consistently bridles at efforts to exploit her dependent status, whether the motives be sadistic (John Reed), possessive (Rochester), or egocentric (St. John). She will not marry St. John because she is afraid to lose her independence. (p. 148)

Even the relation with Rochester is characterized by a pervasive word-play on "master" and "governess" in what appears to be, in part at least, Jane's struggle for self-mastery and self-governance at Thornfield. The more unrelenting and competitive struggle between two strong wills and similar temperaments in Jane's parallel conflict with St. John, is expressed with far stronger reference to the "fetters" and "ascendancy" of the male and the "thralldom" of the female, perceptions which carry the reader back to the petty tyrannies of John Reed (whose name and intials St. John Rivers echoes). . . . (pp. 148-49)

The plot of *Jane Eyre* follows psychic necessity in a way we have come to expect of dream-work. One characteristic of

Jane's narrative is her inordinate attentiveness to the details of her dream life. Similarly, the plot, understood as the manipulation of the world to conform to desire and inner necessity, is complicated by the censorship exercised by Jane's reason, even while her dreams and fantasies serve as psychological and interpretive clues to the reader. Jane's imagination is constantly at work creating a tale independent of any source other than its own creative and compensatory power. . . . Jane's triptych, painted at Lowood but displayed at Thornfield, images the ambivalence that accompanies her great expectations in a series of psychological landscapes which repeat the elemental language of the novel (air and water, in one case iced over), with much of the scene submerged below the waterline or horizon in a suggestion of the relationship of Jane's conscious and unconscious life. The first of the series shows a swollen sea claiming all but a partially submerged mast, a golden bracelet, and the arm from which the bracelet has been washed or torn. This symbolic association with Blanche Ingram's jewels and Rochester's lavish wedding gifts prefigures and reinforces the submerged fears expressed in Jane's dream of buoyant but unquiet seas. . . . The second painting images a female form which Rochester interprets as evening star and wind, an etherealized cluster that anticipates the moon, not moon "but a white human form" prefigurative of the white apparition that warns Jane to flee Thornfield, as well as the wind on which Jane's initial supplications for liberty are lost, but which subsequently carry Rochester's entreaties to her at Moor House at the moment of their greatest crisis and triumph. The third panel depicts the ice-bound landscape of Jane's despair. The triptych's symbolic relevance to Jane's emotional and religious crises at Thornfield and later, suggests a technique of illuminating through pictorial and dream montage many of the implicit personal themes.

Jane's compulsively active dreamlife is further characterized by recurrent, anxiety-ridden, and regressive nightmares, with images of barriers, closed doors and phantom-children. The Thornfield nightmares focus upon the psychic as well as the social obstacles to Jane's imminent marriage, through a recapitulation of Jane's obsessive anxiety over her humiliating childhood and perpetual homelessness. Jane's dreamlife is the dark underside of her rational self-control. (pp. 149-50)

Jane's anxiety dreams on the eve of the wedding express her premonitions of rebirth as a deformed adult. Jane's nightmares find symbolic reinforcement in a landscape of separation and division, represented by a chestnut-tree riven to its roots, apples divided (the ripe from the unripe), drawing-room curtain pulled down, moon eclipsed by curtains of dense clouds. The dream motifs are mutually reinforcing: a consciousness of some barrier dividing her from her husband-to-be; the burdensome child; the strain to overtake Rochester, despite fettered movements; then a second dream of Thornfield in ruin, the child still in Jane's arms, impeding her progress, nearly strangling her in its terror while Rochester disappears like a speck on a white track. Two nightmares dramatize a single although complex perception. Associating the adult woman Jane Rochester with the abandoned and alien child Jane Eyre of her earliest memories, they identify the abandoned child with the anticipated yet feared prospect of awakening a "young Mrs. Rochester—Fairfax Rochester's girl bride." (p. 151)

It is clear that marriage at this point in the novel is not a smooth developmental transition so much as a rupture, raising a host of questions which the work, to its credit, does address. There is the question of identity: Who, and what, is a "Mrs. Rochester''? There is the question of continuity: Can one imagine an equal and independent adulthood as female and wife, given the background of one's daily humiliations as someone else's dependent throughout childhood and adolescence? And there is the question of integrity and power: Is there an imaginable mutuality that does not perpetuate the master/subordinate economics of Jane's status at Thornfield?

Jane reaches the threshold of marriage three times in the novel. She cannot cross it until she can meet her "master" as his partner and equal, his equal by virtue of her inheritance and family solidarity, his partner by virtue of their interdependence. Before she leaves Thornfield, Jane's visions of herself as an adult are simultaneously regressive and parental. Her blighted hopes leave "Jane Eyre, who had been an ardent expectant woman—almost a bride . . . a cold, solitary girl again". . . . Now, the hope of mature love, a feeling "which was my master's—which he had created" is thwarted. Jane's articulation of her disappointment points to an aspect of her dependence on Rochester not noted earlier—*he makes of her a woman;* she is not a woman in her own right. Without him, she is once again a child, with all the terrors of her situation as a child reactivated. . . . Subsequently, in what cannot be ignored as role reversal, Jane's nurturing custodianship of the blinded and maimed Rochester is again parental rather than sexual. The sole distinguishing feature of the child born of their marriage (the dailiness of marital life is scarcely commented on at the end of the novel) is that he is a child-Rochester, his father in miniature. (pp. 152-53)

[Family] harmony, a sense of belonging somewhere and to someone, is identified by Jane with her own psychic "kind" or kindred, and with sympathetic understanding and shared feelings and tastes. . . . [On] Rochester's side, the cord of "natural sympathy" which he admits binds him to her, also has subtle umbilical nuances. . . . (p. 153)

We all know, having read **Jane Eyre** many times over, that in the end she seems to have it both ways, or indeed, *all* the ways that the novel presents as worth having. Jane regains her lover, stumbles upon her real family, discovers her status and is showered by an inheritance that gives her far more money than she can possibly use, thus turning her into the protector and head-of-household at Moor House that Rochester had been at Thornfield. All this, with no loss of integrity, and only a slight softening around the edges of her north-of-England orneryness. The "happy" ending, which resolves some issues but sweeps others under the carpet, is presented, as suggested early on in this discussion, in the Cinderella mode, although with important differences. The bare outlines of the plot suggest that Jane *is* Cinderella, supplanting bad foster-parents and sisters with good (from Reeds to Rochester/Rivers) and winning a chastened Prince Charming as well. . . . [We] have in Jane a Cinderella reimagined, unsubmissive and unrelenting on the issues of paying her own way and of being loved for her better moral and personal qualities. No passive capitulation into the arms of Prince Charming for her, but continued governess pay at thirty pounds *per annum,* even after the ringing of the wedding bells. For this impoverished young woman, once again, the social and economic dilemmas of status cannot be severed from the marital and sexual dilemmas of role. Perpetual degradation in poverty keeps Jane from her spiritual kin and kind, while the degradation of a dependent marriage to a social superior would alienate Jane from her better self.

The Cinderella paradigm will carry us a long way in understanding the interaction of personal and social motifs in both Jane's romantic and worldly aspirations. The significance of the Moor House episode rests in the fact that the Cinderella dilemmas are resolved within the family structure in which they initially occur. They are resolved, that is, through the discovery of a nurturant and self-supporting sisterhood. Prince Rochester does *not* lift Cinderjane out of her misery. Looked at in this way, and focussing upon the characterizing domestic and interior housecapes that are the major "landscape" of this novel, cruel stepsisters crop up like the recurrent bad dreams they in fact embody, the perpetual reinforcers of Jane's dispossession at Gateshead, Lowood, and Thornfield. And as if to insist upon this Cinderella equation, the cruel stepsisters turn up wealthy and favored by nature, with a cruel mama in tow, evil female mother/daughter triads of Reeds, Brocklehursts and Ingrams, fortune's darlings, all of them marriageable and promising in the accepted terms of the day and of the novel. But these figures are exorcized by the Rivers sisters, whose fostering sisterhood is anticipated in the earlier triads of Maria Temple, Helen Burns, and Jane Eyre. And as if to further the emerging equation of sisterhood with spiritual kinship, and of sisterhood and kinship with equivalent social status, there is the fact that both pairs of "good" foster-sisters are themselves impoverished governesses, earning their keep while trying to maintain their integrity.

From this analysis, it follows that Jane's transition from poor orphan into secure woman could not possibly be achieved through marriage to Rochester at Thornfield. Instead, at Moor House she reenacts an emotional and psychic equivalent to the experiences of infancy and childhood, moves quickly through the maturational process—becoming a younger, then an older sister, and, finally, an heiress, the cause of her family's reunification, independence, and status in the larger world. As in the way of folktale and fantasy, the evil stepmother is exposed and punished, and the stepsisters who had lorded it over the orphan are cast down; accordingly, the Reeds are destroyed one by one and the Brocklehursts and Ingrams evaporate from the scene, their psychic function now complete.

Despite the careful paralleling of psychic and status motifs in the presentation of Jane's situation, there is a clear primacy established of the personal over the social/economic issue, however much the second might prove a necessary precondition for independence in the first. Jane's inheritance, when it finally comes to her, seems at first only another painful reminder of her isolation. Far more satisfying is the discovery that she is indeed part of a family, a family whom she might now assist. (pp. 154-56)

One can imagine alternative endings to the one offered by this novel. The themes traced out in the Rochester-romance, an aspect of Jane's narrative that receives more than its fair share of critical attention, are in fact resolved at Moor House in a familial scene that provides warmth, kinship, status and shared wealth. A twentieth-century novel might well have ended on this note, with cousins marrying or not as they wish, and with Jane continuing at Morton or finding some larger arena for her energies, her commitments, her education and skill. Some women's lives have always pursued this course, likely enough with similar sacrifice, in Brontë's time and earlier; Charlotte Brontë is herself an instance, in her life, if not in her fiction.

There are, however, determinant characteristics of this novel that make a non-romantic resolution of the personal and social themes out of the question. First, there is considerable ambivalence expressed toward the aspiration to be truly free, to live out as fully as possible one's ambitions and aspirations. Second, Jane's energies are transformed into a form more socially acceptable for a woman, in her desire to serve and be of use. . . .

But finally, and I think most importantly, questions of estate and position, status, integrity and equality are resolved in the romantic mode, in what is undeniably a romantic novel, which is to say one characterized by fortuitous interventions which enable events and the world to conform to the shape of wish and desire. *Jane Eyre* is marked by the fantasy that love is a fusion of souls, a conception of love out of which it is difficult to imagine an ongoing, humdrum daily adult life. (p. 157)

At the risk of seeming heartless, it seems important to say that Rochester is not so central to Jane's own story as an easy reading might suggest, and as the neglect of the Moor House episodes in the interpretive and critical literature on this novel appears to confirm. Clearly Rochester's possessive mastery is purged (literal fire putting out symbolic fire) at the same point in the narrative chronology at which Jane is exorcizing the icy wastelands of her moral conscience. Similarly, the decline in Rochester's status is a precondition of their marriage, but it is difficult to determine whether his physical maiming is to be read as the harsh biblical punishment for adultery and pride, or whether its very harshness draws our attention to Jane's extreme, perhaps excessive, need to be needed, as yet another requisite for their married interdependence. The gap between them during the early days at Thornfield loomed very large indeed; thus the measures necessarily taken to close that gap might seem excessive to twentieth-century eyes.

What does seem clear is that to marry prior to Moor House would mean an exchange of childhood for adult dependence, bound this time by diamond fetters. Jane's suspicion, that as his wife she would be his mistress, and as his mistress his slave, is given substance by the unexpected Gothic twist to the plot. What is important is not Jane's moral scruple, but the certain inference that psychic kinship and spiritual equality cannot transcend the social degradation of a dependent relationship. (p. 158)

> *Maurianne Adams, "'Jane Eyre': Woman's Estate," in* The Authority of Experience: Essays in Feminist Criticism, *edited by Arlyn Diamond and Lee R. Edwards, The University of Massachusetts Press, 1977, pp. 137-59.*

SANDRA M. GILBERT AND SUSAN GUBAR (essay date 1979)

[*Gubar and Gilbert provide the most extensive feminist study of* Jane Eyre. *Like Mark Schorer (1959), the critics assess* Jane Eyre *as a completion of Brontë's earlier Angrian chronicles, tracing the heroine's development. The primary conflict in the novel, according to Gubar and Gilbert, is the confrontation between Bertha Mason and Jane. The critics argue that since Bertha is Jane's double, the encounter between the two represents Jane's struggle against the difficulties her life has presented. For Gubar and Gilbert, Jane's life is a pilgrimage, like that depicted in John Bunyan's* Pilgrim's Progress. *The culmination of Jane's voyage, the critics maintain, is Jane's "marriage of true minds" at Ferndean. This argument is presaged by Richard Chase (1947). For other feminist interpretations, see Adrienne Rich (1973), Nancy Pell (1977), and Maurianne Adams (1979).*]

Jane Eyre is a work permeated by angry, *Angrian* fantasies of escape-into-wholeness. Borrowing the mythic quest-plot—but not the devout substance—of Bunyan's male *Pilgrim's Progress*, the young novelist seems here definitively to have opened her eyes to female realities within her and around her: confinement, orphanhood, starvation, rage even to madness. (p. 336)

We tend today to think of *Jane Eyre* as moral gothic . . . , the archetypal scenario for all those mildly thrilling romantic encounters between a scowling Byronic hero (who owns a gloomy mansion) and a trembling heroine (who can't quite figure out the mansion's floor plan). Of, if we're more sophisticated, we give Charlotte Brontë her due, concede her strategic as well as her mythic abilities, study the patterns of her imagery, and count the number of times she addresses the reader. . . . ''Well, obviously *Jane Eyre* is a feminist tract, an argument for the social betterment of governesses and equal rights for women,'' Richard Chase somewhat grudgingly admitted [see excerpt above, 1947]. . . . But like most other modern critics, he believed that the novel's power arose from its mythologizing of Jane's confrontation with masculine sexuality.

Yet, curiously enough, it seems not to have been primarily the coarseness and sexuality of *Jane Eyre* which shocked Victorian reviewers (though they disliked those elements in the book), but, as we have seen, its ''anti-Christian'' refusal to accept the forms, customs, and standards of society—in short, its rebellious feminism. They were disturbed not so much by the proud Byronic sexual energy of Rochester as by the Byronic pride and passion of Jane herself, not so much by the asocial sexual vibrations between hero and heroine as by the heroine's refusal to submit to her social destiny. . . . [What] horrified the Victorians was Jane's anger. And perhaps they, rather than more recent critics, were correct in their response to the book. For while the mythologizing of repressed rage may parallel the mythologizing of repressed sexuality, it is far more dangerous to the order of society. The occasional woman who has a weakness for black-browed Byronic heroes can be accommodated in novels and even in some drawing rooms; the woman who yearns to escape entirely from drawing rooms and patriarchal mansions obviously cannot. (pp. 337-38)

Her story, providing a pattern for countless others, is . . . a story of enclosure and escape, a distinctively female *Bildungsroman* in which the problems encountered by the protagonist as she struggles from the imprisonment of her childhood toward an almost unthinkable goal of mature freedom are symptomatic of difficulties Everywoman in a patriarchal society must meet and overcome: oppression (at Gateshead), starvation (at Lowood), madness (at Thornfield), and coldness (at Marsh End). Most important, her confrontation, not with Rochester but with Rochester's mad wife Bertha, is the book's central confrontation, an encounter . . . not with her own sexuality but with her own imprisoned ''hunger, rebellion, and rage,'' a secret dialogue of self and soul on whose outcome, as we shall see, the novel's plot, Rochester's fate, and Jane's coming-of-age all depend.

Unlike many Victorian novels, which begin with elaborate expository paragraphs, *Jane Eyre* begins with a casual, curiously enigmatic remark: ''There was no possibility of taking a walk that day.'' Both the occasion (''that day'') and the excursion (or the impossibility of one) are significant: the first is the real beginning of Jane's pilgrim's progress toward maturity; the second is a metaphor for the problems she must solve in order to attain maturity. . . . [While] the world outside Gateshead is almost unbearably wintry, the world within is claustrophobic, fiery, like ten-year-old Jane's own mind. Excluded from the Reed family group in the drawing room because *she* is not a ''contented, happy, little child''—excluded, that is, from ''normal'' society—Jane takes refuge in a scarlet-draped window seat where she alternately stares out at the ''drear November day'' and reads of polar regions in Bewick's *History of British Birds.* The "death-white realms" of the Arctic fascinate her; she broods upon "the multiplied rigors of extreme cold" as if brooding upon her own dilemma: whether to stay in, behind the oppressively scarlet curtain, or to go out into the cold of a loveless world.

Her decision is made for her. She is found by John Reed, the tyrannical son of the family, who reminds her of her anomalous position in the household, hurls the heavy volume of Bewick at her, and arouses her passionate rage. Like a "rat," a "bad animal," a "mad cat," she compares him to "Nero, Caligula, etc." and is borne away to the red-room, to be imprisoned literally as well as figuratively. (pp. 338-40)

But if Jane was "out of" herself in her struggle against John Reed, her experience in the red-room, probably the most metaphorically vibrant of all her early experiences, forces her deeply into herself. For the red-room, stately, chilly, swathed in rich crimson, with a great white bed and an easy chair "like a pale throne" looming out of the scarlet darkness, perfectly represents her vision of the society in which she is trapped, an uneasy and elfin dependent. . . . It is, in other words, a kind of patriarchal death chamber, and here Mrs. Reed still keeps "divers parchments, her jewel-casket, and a miniature of her dead husband" in a secret drawer in the wardrobe. . . . Is the room haunted, the child wonders. At least, the narrator implies, it is realistically if not gothically haunting. . . . For the spirit of a society in which Jane has no clear place sharpens the angles of the furniture, enlarges the shadows, strengthens the locks on the door. And the deathbed of a father who was not really her father emphasizes her isolation and vulnerability. (p. 340)

[The] little drama enacted on "that day" which opens *Jane Eyre* is in itself a paradigm of the larger drama that occupies the entire book: Jane's anomalous, orphaned position in society, her enclosure in stultifying roles and houses, and her attempts to escape through flight, starvation, and—in a sense which will be explained—madness. And that Charlotte Brontë quite consciously intended the incident of the red-room to serve as a paradigm for the larger plot of her novel is clear not only from its position in the narrative but also from Jane's own recollection of the experience at crucial moments throughout the book: when she is humiliated by Mr. Brocklehurst at Lowood, for instance, and on the night when she decides to leave Thornfield. In between these moments, moreover, Jane's pilgrimage consists of a series of experiences which are, in one way or another, variations on the central, red-room motif of enclosure and escape. (p. 341)

[The] allusion to pilgriming is deliberate, for like the protagonist of Bunyan's book, Jane Eyre makes a life-journey which is a kind of mythical progress from one significantly named place to another. Her story begins, quite naturally, at *Gateshead,* a starting point where she encounters the uncomfortable givens of her career: a family which not her real family, a selfish older "brother" who tyrannizes over the household like a substitute patriarch, a foolish and wicked "stepmother," and two unpleasant, selfish "stepsisters." The smallest, weakest, and plainest child in the house, she embarks on her pilgrim's progress as a sullen Cinderella, an angry Ugly Duckling, immorally rebellious against the hierarchy that oppresses her. . . . (p. 342)

A hopeless pilgrimage, Jane's seems, like the sad journey of Wordsworth's Lucy Gray, seen this time from the inside, by the child herself rather than by the sagacious poet to whom

years have given a philosophic mind. Though she will later watch the maternal moon rise to guide her, now she imagines herself wandering in a moonless twilight that foreshadows her desperate flight across the moors after leaving Thornfield. And the only hope her friend Bessie can offer is, ironically, an image that recalls the patriarchal terrors of the red-room and hints at patriarchal terrors to come—Lowood, Brocklehurst, St. John Rivers:

> Ev'n should I fall o'er the broken bridge passing,
>   Or stray in the marshes, by false lights beguiled,
> Still will my Father, with promise and blessing
>   Take to His bosom the poor orphan child.

It is no wonder that, confronting such prospects, young Jane finds herself "whispering to myself, over and over again" the words of Bunyan's Christian: "What shall I do?—What shall I do?". . . . (pp. 342-43)

What she does do, in desperation, is burst her bonds again and again to tell Mrs. Reed what she thinks of her, an extraordinarily self-assertive act of which neither a Victorian child nor a Cinderella was ever supposed to be capable. Interestingly, her first such explosion is intended to remind Mrs. Reed that she, too, is surrounded by patriarchal limits: "What would Uncle Reed say to you if he were alive?" Jane demands. . . . (p. 343)

Significantly, the event that inspires little Jane's final fiery words to Mrs. Reed is her first encounter with that merciless and hypocritical patriarch Mr. Brocklehurst, who appears now to conduct her on the next stage of her pilgrimage. As many readers have noticed, this personification of the Victorian superego is—like St. John Rivers, his counterpart in the last third of the book—consistently described in phallic terms: he is "a black pillar" with a "grim face at the top . . . like a carved mask," almost as if he were a funereal and oddly Freudian piece of furniture. . . . But he is also rather like the wolf in "Little Red Riding Hood." (pp. 343-44)

Simultaneously, then, a pillar of society and a large bad wolf, Mr. Brocklehurst has come with news of hell to remove Jane to *Lowood,* the aptly named school of life where orphan girls are starved and frozen into proper Christian submission. Where else would a beast take a child but into a wood? Where else would a column of frozen spirituality take a homeless orphan but to a sanctuary where there is neither food nor warmth? Yet "with all its privations" Lowood offers Jane a valley of refuge from "the ridge of lighted heath," a chance to learn to govern her anger while learning to become a governess in the company of a few women she admires.

Foremost among those Jane admires are the noble Miss Temple and the pathetic Helen Burns. And again, their names are significant. Angelic Miss Temple, for instance, with her marble pallor, is a shrine of ladylike virtues: magnanimity, cultivation, courtesy—and repression. (p. 344)

Yet it is clear enough that [Miss Temple] has repressed her own share of madness and rage, that there is a potential monster beneath her angelic exterior, a "sewer" of fury beneath this temple. Though she is, for instance, plainly angered by Mr. Brocklehurst's sanctimonious stinginess, she listens to his sermonizing in lady like silence. (p. 345)

Perhaps for this reason, repressed as she is, she is closer to a fairy godmother than anyone else Jane has met, closer even to a true mother. By the fire in her pretty room, she feeds her starving pupils tea and emblematic seedcake, nourishing body and soul together despite Mr. Brocklehurst's puritanical dicta. . . .

Rather awful as well as very awesome, Miss Temple is not just an angel-in-the-house; to the extent that her name defines her, she is even more house than angel, a beautiful set of marble columns designed to balance that bad pillar Mr. Brocklehurst. And dispossessed Jane, who is not only poor, plain, and little, but also fiery and ferocious, correctly guesses that she can no more become such a woman than Cinderella can become her own fairy godmother.

Helen Burns, Miss Temple's other disciple, presents a different but equally impossible ideal to Jane: the ideal . . . of self-renunciation, of all-consuming (and consumptive) spirituality. . . . One's duty, Helen declares, is to submit to the injustices of this life, in expectation of the ultimate justice of the next. . . . (pp. 345-46)

Helen herself, however, does no more than *bear* her fate. "I make no effort [to be good, in Lowood's terms]," she confesses. "I follow as inclination guides me". . . . Labeled a "slattern" for failing to keep her drawers in ladylike order, she meditates on Charles I, as if commenting on all inadequate fathers ("what a pity . . . he could see no farther than the prerogatives of the crown") and studies *Rasselas*, perhaps comparing Dr. Johnson's Happy Valley to the unhappy one in which she herself is immured. "One strong proof of my wretchedly defective nature," she explains to the admiring Jane, "is that even [Miss Temple's] expostulations . . . have no influence to cure me of my faults." Despite her contemplative purity, there is evidently a "sewer" of concealed resentment in Helen Burns, just as there is in Miss Temple. And, like Miss Temple's, her name is significant. Burning with spiritual passion, she also burns with anger, leaves her things "in shameful disorder," and dreams of freedom in eternity. . . . (p. 346)

This is not to say that Miss Temple and Helen Burns do nothing to help Jane come to terms with her fate. Both are in some sense mothers for Jane, as Adrienne Rich has pointed out [see excerpt above, 1973], comforting her, counseling her, feeding her, embracing her. And from Miss Temple, in particular, the girl learns to achieve "more harmonious thoughts: what seemed better regulated feelings had become the inmates of my mind. I had given in allegiance to duty and order. I appeared a disciplined and subdued character". . . . Yet because Jane is an Angrian Cinderella, a Byronic heroine, the "inmates" of her mind can no more be regulated by conventional Christian wisdom than Manfred's or Childe Harold's thoughts. . . . Her way of confronting the world is still the Promethean way of fiery rebellion, not Miss Temple's way of ladylike repression, not Helen Burns's way of saintly renunciation. What she has learned from her two mothers is, at least superficially, to compromise. If pure liberty is impossible, she exclaims, "then . . . grant me at least a new servitude". . . . (pp. 346-47)

It is, of course, her eagerness for a new servitude that brings Jane to the painful experience that is at the center of her pilgrimage, the experience of *Thornfield,* where, biblically, she is to be crowned with thorns, she is to be cast out into a desolate field, and most important, she is to confront the demon of rage who has haunted her since her afternoon in the red-room. Before the appearance of Rochester, however, and the intrusion of Bertha, Jane—and her readers—must explore Thornfield itself. This gloomy mansion is often seen as just another gothic trapping introduced by Charlotte Brontë to make her novel

saleable. Yet not only is Thornfield more realistically drawn than, say, Otranto or Udolpho, it is more metaphorically radiant than most gothic mansions: it is the house of Jane's life, its floors and walls the architecture of her experience. (p. 347)

The third story is the most obviously emblematic quarter of Thornfield. Here, amid the furniture of the past, down a narrow passage with "two rows of small black doors, all shut, like a corridor in some Bluebeard's castle" . . . , Jane first hears the "distinct formal mirthless laugh" of mad Bertha, Rochester's secret wife and in a sense her own secret self. And just above this sinister corridor, leaning against the picturesque battlements and looking out over the world like Bluebeard's bride's sister Anne, Jane is to long again for freedom, for "all of incident, life, fire, feeling that I . . . had not in my actual existence". . . . These upper regions, in other words, symbolically miniaturize one crucial aspect of the world in which she finds herself. Heavily enigmatic, ancestral relics wall her in; inexplicable locked rooms guard a secret which may have something to do with *her;* distant vistas promise an inaccessible but enviable life. (p. 348)

Many of Jane's problems, particularly those which find symbolic expression in her experiences in the third story, can be traced to her ambiguous status as a governess at Thornfield. . . . But Jane's difficulties arise also . . . from her constitutional *ire;* interestingly, none of the women she meets at Thornfield has anything like that last problem, though all suffer from equivalent ambiguities of status. Aside from Mrs. Fairfax, the three most important of these women are little Adèle Varens, Blanche Ingram, and Grace Poole. All are important negative "role-models" for Jane, and all suggest problems she must overcome before she can reach the independent maturity which is the goal of her pilgrimage.

The first, Adèle, though hardly a woman, is already a "little woman," cunning and doll-like, a sort of sketch for Amy March in Louisa May Alcott's novel. Ostensibly a poor orphan child, like Jane herself, Adèle is evidently the natural daughter of Edward Rochester's dissipated youth. Accordingly, she longs for fashionable gowns rather than for love or freedom, and, the way her mother Céline did, sings and dances for her supper as if she were a clockwork temptress invented by E. T. A. Hoffman. Where Miss Temple's was the way of the lady and Helen's that of the saint, hers and her mother's are the ways of Vanity Fair, ways which have troubled Jane since her days at Gateshead. For how is a poor, plain governess to contend with a society that rewards beauty and style? May not Adèle, the daughter of a "fallen woman," be a model female in a world of prostitutes?

Blanche Ingram, also a denizen of Vanity Fair, presents Jane with a slightly different female image. Tall, handsome, and well-born, she is worldly but, unlike Adèle and Céline, has a respectable place in the world: she is the daughter of "Baroness Ingram of Ingram Park," and—along with Georgiana and Eliza Reed—Jane's classically wicked stepsister. But while Georgiana and Eliza are dismissed to stereotypical fates, Blanche's history teaches Jane ominous lessons. First, the charade of "Bridewell" in which she and Rochester participate relays a secret message: conventional marriage is not only, as the attic implies, a "well" of mystery, it is a Bridewell, a prison, like the Bluebeard's corridor of the third story. Second, the charade of courtship in which Rochester engages her suggests a grim question: is not the game of the marriage "market" a game even scheming women are doomed to lose?

Finally, Grace Poole, the most enigmatic of the women Jane meets at Thornfield—"that mystery of mysteries, as I considered her"—is obviously associated with Bertha, almost as if, with her pint of porter, her "staid and taciturn" demeanor, she were the madwoman's public representative.... And that Grace is as companionless as Bertha or Jane herself is undeniably true. Women in Jane's world, acting as agents for men, may be the keepers of other women. But both keepers and prisoners are bound by the same chains. In a sense, then, the mystery of mysteries which Grace Poole suggests to Jane is the mystery of her own life, so that to question Grace's position at Thornfield is to question her own.

Interestingly, in trying to puzzle out the secret of Grace Poole, Jane at one point speculates that Mr. Rochester may once have entertained "tender feelings" for the woman, and when thoughts of Grace's "uncomeliness" seem to refute this possibility, she cements her bond with Bertha's keeper by reminding herself that, after all, "*You* are not beautiful either, and perhaps Mr. Rochester approves you".... Can appearances be trusted? Who is the slave, the master or the servant, the prince or Cinderella? What, in other words, are the real relationships between the master of Thornfield and all these women whose lives revolve around his? (pp. 349-51)

Jane's first meeting with Rochester is a fairytale meeting. Charlotte Brontë deliberately stresses mythic elements: an icy twilight setting out of Coleridge or Fuseli, a rising moon, a great "lion-like" dog gliding through the shadows like "a North-of-England spirit, called a 'Gytrash' which . . . haunted solitary ways, and sometimes came upon belated travellers," followed by "a tall steed, and on its back a rider." Certainly the Romanticized images seem to suggest [a] universe of male sexuality.... Yet what are we to think of the fact that the prince's first action is to fall on the ice, together with his horse, and exclaim prosaically "What the deuce is to do now?" Clearly the master's mastery is not universal. Jane offers help, and Rochester, leaning on her shoulder, admits that "necessity compels me to make you useful." Later, remembering the scene, he confesses that he too had seen the meeting as a mythic one, though from a perspective entirely other than Jane's. "When you came on me in Hay Lane last night, I . . . had half a mind to demand whether you had bewitched my horse".... Significantly, his playful remark acknowledges *her* powers just as much as (if not more than) her vision of the Gytrash acknowledged *his*. Thus, though in one sense Jane and Rochester begin their relationship as master and servant, prince and Cinderella, . . . in another they begin as spiritual equals. (pp. 351-52)

His need for her strength and parity is made clearer soon enough—on, for instance, the occasion when she rescues him from his burning bed (an almost fatally symbolic plight), and later on the occasion when she helps him rescue Richard Mason from the wounds inflicted by "Grace Poole." And that these rescues are facilitated by Jane's and Rochester's mutual sense of equality is made clearest of all in the scene in which only Jane of all the "young ladies" at Thornfield fails to be deceived by Rochester in his gypsy costume: "With the ladies you must have managed well," she comments, but "You did not act the character of a gypsy with me".... The implication is that he did not—or could not—because he respects "the resolute, wild, free thing looking out of" Jane's eyes as much as she herself does, and understands that just as he can see beyond her everyday disguise as plain Jane the governess, she can see beyond his temporary disguise as a gypsy fortune-teller—or his daily disguise as Rochester the master of Thornfield. (p. 353)

But of course, as we know, there is an impediment, and that impediment, paradoxically, pre-exists in both Rochester and Jane, despite their avowals of equality. Though Rochester, for instance, appears in both the gypsy sequence and the betrothal scene to have cast away the disguises that gave him his mastery, it is obviously of some importance that those disguises were necessary in the first place. Why, Jane herself wonders, does Rochester have to trick people, especially women? What secrets are concealed behind the charades he enacts? One answer is surely that he himself senses his trickery is a source of power, and therefore, in Jane's case at least, an evasion of that equality in which he claims to believe. Beyond this, however, it is clear that the secrets Rochester is concealing or disguising throughout much of the book are themselves in Jane's—and Charlotte Brontë's—view secrets of inequality.

The first of these is suggested both by his name, apparently an allusion to the dissolute Earl of Rochester, and by Jane's own reference to the Bluebeard's corridor of the third story: it is the secret of masculine potency, the secret of male sexual guilt. For, like those pre-Byron Byronic heroes the real Restoration Rochester and the mythic Bluebeard (indeed, in relation to Jane, like any experienced adult male), Rochester has specific and "guilty" sexual knowledge which makes him in some sense her "superior." . . . Rochester's apparently improper recounting of his sexual adventures *is* a kind of acknowledgment of Jane's equality with him. His possession of the hidden details of sexuality, however—his knowledge, that is, of the *secret* of sex, symbolized both by his doll-like daughter Adèle and by the locked doors of the third story behind which mad Bertha crouches like an animal—qualifies and undermines that equality. (pp. 354-55)

That both Jane and Rochester are in some part of themselves conscious of the barrier which Rochester's sexual knowledge poses to their equality is further indicated by the tensions that develop in their relationship after their betrothal. Rochester, having secured Jane's love, almost reflexively begins to treat her as an inferior, a plaything, a virginal possession—for she has now become his initiate, his "mustard-seed," his "little sunny-faced . . . girl-bride." (p. 355)

Finally, Rochester's ultimate secret, the secret that is revealed together with the existence of Bertha, the literal impediment to his marriage with Jane, is another and perhaps most surprising secret of inequality: but this time the hidden facts suggest the master's inferiority rather than his superiority. Rochester, Jane learns, after the aborted wedding ceremony, had married Bertha Mason for status, for sex, for money, for everything but love and equality.... In a sense, then, the most serious crime Rochester has to expiate is not even the crime of exploiting others but the sin of self-exploitation, the sin of Céline and Blanche, to which he, at least, had seemed completely immune.

That Rochester's character and life pose in themselves such substantial impediments to his marriage with Jane does not mean, however, that Jane herself generates none. For one thing, "akin" as she is to Rochester, she suspects him of harboring all the secrets we know he does harbor, and raises defenses against them, manipulating her "master" so as to keep him "in reasonable check." In a larger way, moreover, all the charades and masquerades—the secret messages—of patriarchy have had their effect upon her. Though she loves Rochester the man, Jane has doubts about Rochester the husband even before she learns about Bertha. In her world, she senses, even the equality of love between true minds leads to the inequalities and minor despotisms of marriage. (pp. 355-56)

Jane's whole life-pilgrimage has, of course, prepared her to be angry . . . at Rochester's, and society's, concept of marriage. Rochester's loving tyranny recalls John Reed's unloving despotism, and the erratic nature of Rochester's favors ("in my secret soul I knew that his great kindness to me was balanced by unjust severity to many others" . . .) recalls Brocklehurst's hypocrisy. But even the dreamlike paintings that Jane produced early in her stay at Thornfield—art works which brought her as close to her "master" as Helen Graham (in *The Tenant of Wildfell Hall*) was to hers—functioned ambiguously, like Helen's, to predict strains in this relationship even while they seemed to be conventional Romantic fantasies. The first represented a drowned female corpse; the second a sort of avenging mother goddess rising (like Bertha Mason Rochester) . . . in "electric travail" . . . ; and the third a terrible paternal specter carefully designed to recall Milton's sinister image of Death. (p. 357)

Given such shadowings and foreshadowings, then, it is no wonder that as Jane's anger and fear about her marriage intensify, she begins to be symbolically drawn back into her own past, and specifically to reexperience the dangerous sense of doubleness that had begun in the red-room. The first sign that this is happening is the powerfully depicted, recurrent dream of a child she begins to have as she drifts into a romance with her master. . . . Even more significantly, the phantom-child reappears in two dramatic dreams Jane has on the night before her wedding eve, during which she experiences "a strange regretful consciousness of some barrier dividing" her from Rochester. (pp. 357-58)

What are we to make of these strange dreams, or—as Jane would call them—these "presentiments"? To begin with, it seems clear that the wailing child who appears in all of them corresponds to "the poor orphan child" of Bessie's song at Gateshead, and therefore to the child Jane herself, the wailing Cinderella whose pilgrimage began in anger and despair. . . . [Until] she reaches the goal of her pilgrimage—maturity, independence, true equality with Rochester (and therefore in a sense with the rest of the world)—she is doomed to carry her orphaned alter ego everywhere. The burden of the past cannot be sloughed off so easily—not, for instance, by glamorous lovemaking, silk dresses, jewelry, a new name. Jane's "strange regretful consciousness of a barrier" dividing her from Rochester is, thus, a keen though disguised intuition of a problem she herself will pose.

Almost more interesting than the nature of the child image, however, is the *predictive* aspect of the last of the child dreams, the one about the ruin of Thornfield. As Jane correctly foresees, Thornfield *will* within a year become "a dreary ruin, the retreat of bats and owls." Have her own subtle and not-so-subtle hostilities to its master any connection with the catastrophe that is to befall the house? Is her clairvoyant dream in some sense a vision of wishfulfilment? And why, specifically, is she freed from the burden of the wailing child at the moment *she* falls from Thornfield's ruined wall?

The answer to all these questions is closely related to events which follow upon the child dream. For the apparition of a child in these crucial weeks preceding her marriage is only one symptom of a dissolution of personality Jane seems to be experiencing at this time, a fragmentation of the self comparable to her "syncope" in the red-room. Another symptom appears

early in the chapter that begins, anxiously, "there was no putting off the day that advanced—the bridal day". . . . It is her witty but nervous speculation about the nature of "one Jane Rochester, a person whom as yet I knew not." . . . Again, a third symptom appears on the morning of her wedding: she turns toward the mirror and sees "a robed and veiled figure, so unlike my usual self that it seemed almost the image of a stranger" . . . , reminding us of the moment in the red-room when all had "seemed colder and darker in that visionary hollow" of the looking glass "than in reality." In view of this frightening series of separations within the self—Jane Eyre splitting off from Jane Rochester, the child Jane splitting off from the adult Jane, and the image of Jane weirdly separating from the body of Jane—it is not surprising that another and most mysterious specter, a sort of "vampyre," should appear in the middle of the night to rend and trample the wedding veil of that unknown person, Jane Rochester.

Literally, of course, the nighttime specter is none other than Bertha Mason Rochester. But on a figurative and psychological level it seems suspiciously clear that the specter of Bertha is still another—indeed the most threatening—avatar of Jane. What Bertha now *does,* for instance, is what Jane wants to do. Disliking the "vapoury veil" of Jane Rochester, Jane Eyre secretly wants to tear the garments up. . . . Bertha, in other words, is Jane's truest and darkest double: she is the angry aspect of the orphan child, the ferocious secret self Jane has been trying to repress ever since her days at Gateshead. (pp. 358-60)

It is only fitting, then, that the existence of this criminal self imprisoned in Thornfield's attic is the ultimate legal impediment to Jane's and Rochester's marriage, and that its existence is, paradoxically, an impediment raised by Jane as well as by Rochester. For it now begins to appear, if it did not earlier, that Bertha has functioned as Jane's dark double *throughout* the governess's stay at Thornfield. Specifically, every one of Bertha's appearances—or, more accurately, her manifestations—has been associated with an experience (or repression) of anger on Jane's part. (p. 360)

These parallels between Jane and Bertha may at first seem somewhat strained. Jane, after all, is poor, plain, little, pale, neat, and quiet, while Bertha is rich, large, florid, sensual, and extravagant. . . . Is she not, then, . . . a monitory image rather than a double for Jane? . . . And of course, in one sense, the relationship between Jane and Bertha is a monitory one: while acting out Jane's secret fantasies, Bertha does (to say the least) provide the governess with an example of how not to act, teaching her a lesson more salutary than any Miss Temple ever taught.

Nevertheless, it is disturbingly clear from recurrent images in the novel that Bertha not only acts *for* Jane, she also acts *like* Jane. The imprisoned Bertha, running "backwards and forwards" on all fours in the attic, for instance, recalls not only Jane the governess, whose only relief from mental pain was to pace "backwards and forwards" in the third story, but also that "bad animal" who was ten-year-old Jane, imprisoned in the red-room, howling and mad. . . . Bertha's incendiary tendencies recall Jane's early flaming rages, at Lowood and at Gateshead, as well as that "ridge of lighted heath" which she herself saw as emblematic of her mind in its rebellion against society. It is only fitting, therefore, that, as if to balance the child Jane's terrifying vision of herself as an alien figure in the "visionary hollow" of the red-room looking glass, the adult Jane first clearly perceives her terrible double when Bertha puts on the wedding veil intended for the second Mrs. Rochester, and turns to the mirror. (pp. 360-62)

For despite all the habits of harmony she gained in her years at Lowood, we must finally recognize, with Jane herself, that on her arrival at Thornfield she only "*appeared* a disciplined and subdued character" [ital. ours]. Crowned with thorns, finding that she is, in Emily Dickinson's words, "The Wife—without the Sign," she represses her rage behind a subdued facade, but her soul's impulse to dance "like a Bomb, abroad," to quote Dickinson again, has not been exorcised and will not be exorcised until the literal and symbolic death of Bertha frees her from the furies that torment her and makes possible a marriage of equality—makes possible, that is, wholeness within herself. At that point, significantly, when the Bertha in Jane falls from the ruined wall of Thornfield and is destroyed, the orphan child too, as her dream predicts, will roll from her knee—the burden of her past will be lifted—and she will wake. (p. 362)

That the pilgrimage of this "savage, beautiful creature" must now necessarily lead her away from Thornfield is signalled, like many other events in the novel, by the rising of the moon, which accompanies a reminiscent dream of the red-room. Unjustly imprisoned now, as she was then, in one of the traps a patriarchal society provides for outcast Cinderellas, Jane realizes that this time she must escape through deliberation rather than through madness. (p. 363)

[Jane's wanderings on the road] are a symbolic summary of those wanderings of the poor orphan child which constitute her entire life's pilgrimage. . . . Far and lonely indeed Jane wanders, starving, freezing, stumbling, abandoning her few possessions, her name, and even her self-respect in her search for a new home. . . . Yet because Jane . . . has an inner strength which her pilgrimage seeks to develop, "kind angels" finally do bring her to what is in a sense her true home, the house significantly called *Marsh End* (or Moor House) which is to represent the end of her march toward selfhood. Here she encounters Diana, Mary, and St. John Rivers, the "good" relatives who will help free her from her angry memories of that wicked stepfamily the Reeds. And that the Rivers prove to be literally her relatives is not, in psychological terms, the strained coincidence some readers have suggested. For having left Rochester, having torn off the crown of thorns he offered and repudiated the unequal charade of marriage he proposed, Jane has now gained the strength to begin to discover her real place in the world. (pp. 363-64)

The qualifying word *seems* is, however, a necessary one. For though in one sense Jane's discovery of her family at Marsh End does represent the end of her pilgrimage, her progress toward selfhood will not be complete until she learns that "principle and law" in the abstract do not always coincide with the deepest principles and laws of her own being. Her early sense that Miss Temple's teachings had merely been superimposed on her native vitality had already begun to suggest this to her. But it is through her encounter with St. John Rivers that she assimilates this lesson most thoroughly. . . . [St. John] has an almost blatantly patriarchal name, one which recalls both the masculine abstraction of the gospel according to St. John ("in the beginning was the *Word*") and the disguised misogyny of St. John the Baptist, whose patristic and evangelical contempt for the flesh manifested itself most powerfully in a profound contempt for the *female*. Like Salome, whose rebellion against such misogyny Oscar Wilde was later also to associate with the rising moon of female power, Jane must symbolically, if not literally, behead the abstract principles of this man before she can finally achieve her true independence.

At first, however, it seems that St. John is offering Jane a viable alternative to the way of life proposed by Rochester. For where Rochester, like his dissolute namesake, ended up appearing to offer a life of pleasure, a path of roses (albeit with concealed thorns), and a marriage of passion, St. John seems to propose a life of principle, a path of thorns (with no concealed roses), and a marriage of spirituality. His self-abnegating rejection of the worldly beauty Rosamund Oliver—another character with a strikingly resonant name—is disconcerting to the passionate and Byronic part of Jane, but at least it shows that, unlike hypocritical Brocklehurst, he practices what he preaches. And what he preaches is the Carlylean sermon of self-actualization through work. . . . (pp. 364-65)

Jane's early repudiation of the spiritual harmonies offered by Helen Burns and Miss Temple is the first hint that, while St. John's way will tempt her, she must resist it. That, like Rochester, he is "akin" to her is clear. But where Rochester represents the fire of her nature, her cousin represents the ice. And while for some women ice may "suffice," for Jane, who has struggled all her life, like a sane version of Bertha, against the polar cold of a loveless world, it clearly will not. (p. 366)

Though in many ways St. John's attempt to "imprison" Jane may seem the most irresistible of all, coming as it does at a time when she is congratulating herself on just that adherence to "principle and law" which he recommends, she escapes from his fetters more easily than she had escaped from either Brocklehurst or Rochester. Figuratively speaking, this is a measure of how far she has traveled in her pilgrimage toward maturity. Literally, however, her escape is facilitated by two events. First, having found what is, despite all its ambiguities, her true family, Jane has at last come into her inheritance. Jane Eyre is now the heir of that uncle in Madeira whose first intervention in her life had been, appropriately, to define the legal impediment to her marriage with Rochester, now literally as well as figuratively an independent woman, free to go her own way and follow her own will. But her freedom is also signaled by a second event: the death of Bertha. (pp. 366-67)

Jane's return to Thornfield, her discovery of Bertha's death and of the ruin her dream had predicted, her reunion at Ferndean with the maimed and blinded Rochester, and their subsequent marriage form an essential epilogue to that pilgrimage toward selfhood which had in other ways concluded at Marsh End, with Jane's realization that she could not marry St. John. At that moment, "the wondrous shock of feeling had come like the earthquake which shook the foundations of Paul and Silas' prison; it had opened the doors of the soul's cell, and loosed its bands—it had wakened it out of its sleep." . . . For at that moment she had been irrevocably freed from the burden of her past, freed both from the raging specter of Bertha (which had already fallen in fact from the ruined wall of Thornfield) and from the self-pitying specter of the orphan child (which had symbolically, as in her dream, rolled from her knee). And at that moment, again as in her dream, she had *wakened* to her own self, her own needs. Similarly, Rochester, "caged eagle" that he seems . . . , has been freed from what was for him the burden of Thornfield, though at the same time he appears to have been fettered by the injuries he received in attempting to rescue Jane's mad double from the flames devouring his house. That his "fetters" pose no impediment to a new marriage, that he and Jane are now, in reality, equals, is the thesis of the Ferndean section. (pp. 367-68)

It has not been her goal . . . to quell "the tempo and energy of the universe," but simply to strengthen herself, to make herself an equal of the world Rochester represents. And surely another important symbolic point is implied by the lovers' reunion at Ferndean: when both were physically whole they could not, in a sense, *see* each. other because of the social disguises—master/servant, prince/Cinderella—blinding them, but now that those disguises have been shed, now that they are equals, they can (though one is blind) see and speak even beyond the medium of the flesh. . . . And now, being equals, he and Jane can afford to depend upon each other with no fear of one exploiting the other.

Nevertheless, despite the optimistic portrait of an egalitarian relationship that Brontë seems to be drawing here, there is "a quiet autumnal quality" about the scenes at Ferndean. . . . The house itself, set deep in a dark forest, is old and decaying: Rochester had not even thought it suitable for the loathsome Bertha, and its valley-of-the-shadow quality makes it seem rather like a Lowood, a school of life where Rochester must learn those lessons Jane herself absorbed so early. As a dramatic setting, moreover, Ferndean is notably stripped and asocial, so that the physical isolation of the lovers suggests their spiritual isolation in a world where such egalitarian marriages as theirs are rare, if not impossible. True minds, Charlotte Brontë seems to be saying, must withdraw into a remote forest, a wilderness even, in order to circumvent the strictures of a hierarchal society.

Does Brontë's rebellious feminism—that "irreligious" dissatisfaction with the social order noted by . . . *Jane Eyre*'s Victorian critics—compromise itself in this withdrawal? Has Jane exorcised the rage of orphanhood only to retreat from the responsibilities her own principles implied? . . . In all her books, writing . . . in a sort of trance, she was able to act out that passionate drive toward freedom which offended agents of the status quo, but in none was she able consciously to define the full meaning of achieved freedom—perhaps because no one of her contemporaries, not even a Wollstonecraft or a Mill, could adequately describe a society so drastically altered that the matured Jane and Rochester could really live in it.

What Brontë could not logically define, however, she could embody in tenuous but suggestive imagery. . . . Nature in the largest sense seems now to be on the side of Jane and Rochester. *Ferndean,* as its name implies, is without artifice—"no flowers, no garden-beds"—but it is green as Jane tells Rochester he will be, green and ferny and fertilized by soft rains. . . . For not the Celestial City but a natural paradise, the country of Beulah "upon the borders of heaven," where "the contract between bride and bridegroom [is] renewed," has all along been, we now realize, the goal of Jane's pilgrimage.

As for the Celestial City itself, Charlotte Brontë implies here (though she will later have second thoughts) that such a goal is the dream of those who accept inequities on earth, one of the many tools used by patriarchal society to keep, say, governesses in their "place." Because she believes this so deeply, she quite consciously concludes *Jane Eyre* with an allusion to *Pilgrim's Progress* and with a half-ironic apostrophe to that apostle of celestial transcendence, that shadow of "the warrior Greatheart," St. John Rivers. "His," she tells us, "is the exaction of the apostle, who speaks but for Christ when he says—'Whosoever will come after me, let him deny himself and take up his cross and follow me'". . . . For it was, finally, to repudiate such a crucifying denial of the self that Brontë's "hunger, rebellion, and rage" led her to write *Jane Eyre* in

the first place and to make it an "irreligious" redefinition, almost a parody, of John Bunyan's vision. And the astounding progress toward equality of plain Jane Eyre . . . , answers by its outcome the bitter question Emily Dickinson was to ask fifteen years later: "'My husband'—women say— / Stroking the Melody— / Is *this*—the way?'" No, Jane declares in her flight from Thornfield, *that* is not the way. *This,* she says—this marriage of true minds at Ferndean—this is the way. (pp. 368-71)

> *Sandra M. Gilbert and Susan Gubar, "A Dialogue of Self and Soul: Plain Jane's Progress," in their* The Madwoman in the Attic: The Woman Writer and the Nineteenth-Century Literary Imagination, *Yale University Press, 1979, pp. 336-71.*

ADDITIONAL BIBLIOGRAPHY

Allen, Walter. "The Early Victorians." In his *The English Novel: A Short Critical History,* pp. 133-207. London: Phoenix House, 1963.*
> A brief assessment of *Jane Eyre.* To Allen, Jane is the dominant force in the novel because she is "wholly real," while Rochester is only "a most powerful symbol of virility."

Blom, M. A. "*Jane Eyre*: Mind As Law unto Itself." *Criticism* XV, No. 4 (Fall 1973): 350-64.
> Examines Brontë's attitudes and ideals and their influence on the characters, incidents, and scenery of *Jane Eyre.*

Burns, Wayne. "Critical Relevance of Freudianism." *The Western Review* 20, No. 4 (Summer 1956): 301-14.*
> Attempts to define Brontë's methods of symbolizing emotional expression and repression in *Jane Eyre.*

Ewbank, Inga-Stina. "Charlotte Brontë: The Woman Writer As an Author Only." In her *Their Proper Sphere: A Study of the Brontë Sisters As Early-Victorian Female Novelists,* pp. 156-204. Cambridge: Harvard University Press, 1966.
> Analyzes *Jane Eyre* in terms of Brontë's own principle of artistic truth. Ewbank details how Brontë imaginatively recreated her personal experiences within the frame of a novel.

Hagan, John. "Enemies of Freedom in *Jane Eyre.*" *Criticism* 13 (Winter 1971): 351-76.
> Discusses the obstacles Brontë faced in her personal life and their representation in *Jane Eyre.*

Hardy, Barbara. *"Jane Eyre" (Charlotte Brontë).* Notes on English Literature, edited by John Harvey. Oxford: Basil Blackwell, 1964, 95 p.
> A detailed classroom guide to *Jane Eyre.* Hardy includes a list of questions designed to aid the student at the end of each chapter.

Langford, Thomas. "The Three Pictures in *Jane Eyre.*" *The Victorian Newsletter,* No. 31 (Spring 1967): 47-8.
> A discussion of the three pictures that Jane shows Rochester. These paintings represent, according to Langford, the three stages of development in Jane's life: childhood and adolescence, womanhood, and emotional maturity through marriage.

Leavis, Q. D. "Dating *Jane Eyre.*" *The Times Literary Supplement,* No. 3300 (27 May 1965): 436.
> An attempt to ascertain the correct time period for the setting of *Jane Eyre.* Leavis states that it is impossible to determine because of the conflicting evidence provided in the novel.

Martin, Robert Bernard. *"Jane Eyre."* In his *The Accents of Persuasion: Charlotte Brontë's Novels,* pp. 57-108. London: Faber & Faber, 1966.
> An interpretation of *Jane Eyre* as a novel which seeks a balance between reason and passion.

Miyoshi, Masao. "The Colloquy of the Self: 1850." In his *The Divided Self: A Perspective on the Literature of the Victorians*, pp. 159-226. New York: New York University Press; London: University of London Press, 1969.*

Considers *Jane Eyre* to be a fusion of Charlotte's own life and elements of Gothic fantasy.

Muir, Edwin. "The Dramatic Novel." In his *The Structure of the Novel*, pp. 41-61. New York: Harcourt, Brace and Co., 1929.*

Criticizes the killing of Bertha Mason as a literary "falsehood" that hindered both Jane's emotional development and her progression as a character.

O'Neill, Judith, ed. *Critics on Charlotte and Emily Brontë*. Readings in Literary Criticism, edited by Judith O'Neill, no. 2. London: George Allen and Unwin, 1968, 115 p.

Includes a collection of early critical response to *Jane Eyre*.

Passel, Anne. *Charlotte and Emily Brontë: An Annotated Bibliography*. New York: Garland Publishing, 1979, 359 p.*

Includes a twenty-two page section of bibliographical listings for criticism on *Jane Eyre*. Passel has added brief annotations to each entry.

Prescott, Joseph. "*Jane Eyre*: A Romantic Exemplum with a Difference." In *Twelve Original Essays on Great English Novels*, edited by Charles Shapiro, pp. 87-102. Detroit: Wayne State University Press, 1960.

A discussion of the use of romantic conventions in *Jane Eyre*, including Biblical allusions, didacticism, and characterization.

Sadoff, Dianne F. "Charlotte Brontë: Masters and Mastery." In her *Monsters of Affection: Dickens, Eliot & Brontë on Fatherhood*, pp. 119-69. Baltimore: Johns Hopkins University Press, 1982.

An interpretation of paternal imagery in Charlotte Brontë's work, with a section devoted to *Jane Eyre*. Sadoff contends that Jane, like the rest of Brontë's heroines, desired the men in her life to be father figures capable of mastering her.

Shannon, Edgar F., Jr. "The Present Tense in *Jane Eyre*." *Nineteenth-Century Fiction* 10, No. 2 (September 1955): 141-45.

An analysis of the use of the present tense in *Jane Eyre*. Shannon argues that Brontë's occasional use of the present tense "not only heightens the immediacy of certain scenes but also marks and foreshadows the structural divisions of the novel."

Wagner, Geoffrey. "*Jane Eyre*, with a Commencement on Catherine Earnshaw: Beyond Biology." In his *Five for Freedom: A Study of Feminism in Fiction*, pp. 103-37. London: George Allen & Unwin, 1972.

Assesses the sadistic aspects of *Jane Eyre*. Wagner indicates that most of the relationships in the novel contain elements of sadism.

West, Katharine. "Early Victorian." In her *Chapter of Governesses: A Study of the Governess in English Fiction, 1800-1949*, pp. 54-86. London: Cohen & West, 1949.*

An assessment of Brontë's treatment of Jane as a governess in relation to similar subjects in other early Victorian novels.

Yuen, Maria. "Two Crises of Decision in *Jane Eyre*." *English Studies* 57, No. 3 (June 1976): 215-26.

A discussion of Jane's two major decisions and how they helped to reinforce her independence. According to Yuen, the first important decision occurs when Jane leaves Thornfield, and the second pivotal moment takes place when she refuses to marry St. John Rivers.

William Cowper

1731-1800

English poet, satirist, letter writer, hymn writer, essayist, and translator.

Considered one of the forerunners of Romanticism in England, Cowper was one of the most popular poets of the eighteenth century: his comic ballad "The Journey of John Gilpin" established his literary reputation, his *Olney Hymns* were incorporated into Evangelical liturgy, and his satires enjoyed widespread popularity. He is remembered today for the spontaneity and simplicity of his nature lyrics, the earnest, personal tone of his religious poetry, and the wit embodied in his satires and letters.

Cowper was born in Great Berkhamsted, England, into a distinguished aristocratic family. His father's ancestors were prominent public servants in government and the law, and his mother was a descendant of the seventeenth-century English poet John Donne. Mrs. Cowper's death in childbirth in 1737 remained one of the poet's most traumatic experiences, and many biographers attribute Cowper's mental instability and habitual melancholy to his early loss. The next year, Cowper attended Dr. Pitman's school at Markyate. There, he was mercilessly bullied by older boys, an ordeal which appeared to haunt Cowper throughout his life. As a result, he developed what is believed to have been a psychosomatic eye ailment. Following his recuperation, he attended the Westminster school from 1741 to 1748, and then lived in London's Middle Temple, a law court, until 1763, first as a law student and later as Commissioner of Bankrupts. While at the Middle Temple, Cowper befriended other young intellectuals, experimented with writing, and avidly studied classical literature. In 1756, Cowper fell deeply in love with his cousin Theodora, but the romance ended tragically when their parents refused to permit them to marry. This experience marked the onset of Cowper's emotional decline. Already physically and mentally frail, he suffered a nervous breakdown following a suicide attempt in 1763 and was hospitalized at St. Albans for two years. His recuperation was thought to stem partly from his conversion to Evangelicalism; when he left the hospital, he lived in Huntington with the Unwins, an Evangelical minister and his family. After the death of the Reverend Unwin in 1767, Cowper and the rest of the household moved to Olney, where Cowper pursued a literary career. Here he completed his best work and enjoyed a period of unprecedented happiness. Though an invalid for most of his life, Cowper apparently experienced a great sense of well-being from his Evangelical beliefs and the orderly rural life in Olney. However, in 1773 he again succumbed to mental illness. Biographers speculate that his illness derived from anxiety over his announced engagement to Mary Unwin, the widow of the Evangelical minister, and the religious gloom brought on by the association with his fanatical pastor, John Newton. He and Mrs. Unwin never married, but moved together to Weston where Cowper suffered two more breakdowns in 1786 and 1794. In 1795, Cowper witnessed the long illness and death of his devoted companion. Despite his personal difficulties, Cowper was considered one of his generation's greatest poets, and shortly before his death he was

rewarded with the tribute of a royal pension arranged by his friend, the noted author William Hayley.

Cowper's first major publication was the *Olney Hymns*. The collection of Evangelical hymns was a collaborative effort between Cowper and his spiritual mentor John Newton, who contributed the greater number of the pieces. Several of Cowper's hymns, especially "There is a Fountain Filled with Blood," "God Moves in a Mysterious Way," and "Oh for a Closer Walk with God," became popular over the years and have now passed into Evangelical tradition. Commentators on the hymns praise their personal tone, vivid Biblical imagery, and the recurrent theme of humanity's need for salvation. Yet the hymns have also been criticized for their doctrinal inaccuracy and fanatic narrative voice. His next important work was *Poems,* which includes the long poem "Table Talk," four satires on philosophical subjects, and shorter lyrics such as "Boadicea" and "Verses Supposed to be Written by Alexander Selkirk." These works are characterized by his natural diction, spontaneity, and fresh emotional response to nature. Many of the poems demonstrate his didactic tendency: Cowper repeatedly explored the proper moral relationship of human beings with nature, with society, and with God. Cowper's next volume, *The Task,* won for him critical as well as popular esteem. A poem in six books, *The Task* treats Cowper's usual themes, but its witty, satirical manner differs from the meditative and didactic tone of his earlier poetry. Because of its excellent descriptive detail and easy, conversational handling of blank verse, *The Task* met with immediate success. Critics also credit Cowper in *The Task* with introducing new themes into English poetry, including such subjects as the love of animals and domestic life. Cowper included in the same volume "The Journey of John Gilpin," a ballad ostensibly about the adventures of a tailor, but in reality a raucous parody of poetic conventions. The poem was so well received by the public that it became an artifact of popular culture. Conversely, Cowper's translation of *Homer's Iliad and Odyssey* received mixed reviews, including the charge that it was too bland and unmusical. The *Poems* of 1798 includes "On the Receipt of My Mother's Picture," "The Castaway," and "Yardley Oak." Among these are found Cowper's most elegiac and ecstatic poems as well as his darkest and most despairing. Many critics contend that these poems, especially "Yardley Oak," foreshadow the descriptive and meditative poetic style of Romanticism. Cowper's *Memoir of the Early Life of William Cowper, Esq.*, published posthumously, recounts his first attack of mental illness, his subsequent treatment, and his religious rebirth. Critics praise the work's candor and analytical detachment, yet it is his letters, published in *The Life and Works of William Cowper*, that have most sustained his reputation in the twentieth century. His letters are unanimously admired for their humor, precise observation, and ability to make everyday subjects interesting. In addition, critics note that Cowper's correspondence vividly depicts his love of nature and genuine humanitarianism.

Cowper's position as a transitional figure between the Neoclassic and Romantic periods in English literature has inspired critical interest in his life and works. Many critics, including Walter Bagehot and George Saintsbury, argue that Cowper's satiric and didactic tendencies place him closer to the eighteenth-century moralists than the early Romantics. But other critics point out that the structure of Cowper's satires is overly diffuse and uneven and his narrative stance is too timid to be likened to that of such eighteenth-century poets as Alexander Pope. These critics contend that Cowper's use of blank verse, his interest in nature, his focus on everyday life, and his emotional response to the world around him link him to Romantic poets like George Crabbe, Robert Burns, and William Wordsworth. Nevertheless, early reviewers considered his blank verse unpoetical; William Hazlitt criticized Cowper's weakness in depicting nature, and Alfred Austin and J. C. Bailey wrote that Cowper's interest in common themes trivializes his poetry. Yet others have praised his shrewd social commentary and self-analysis, and they find that Cowper's poetry, like his life, encompasses both the high emotionalism of the Romantic era and the structure and rationalism of the Neoclassical era.

Of Cowper's poetry, *The Task* has inspired the most critical commentary. Many critics, beginning with an anonymous reviewer in the *Monthly Review* in 1786, have censured the structure of *The Task* for its apparent lack of unity and plan. More recently, Morris Golden disputed this charge by citing Cowper's interweaving of themes and counterthemes; he described the poem as "a unified recording and communication of an intense emotional perception of reality." Despite ongoing interest in *The Task*, the majority of recent critical activity concerning Cowper's works has been generated by his *Memoir* and correspondence. Discussions of the *Memoir* have largely focused on the characteristics of Cowper's narrative persona, and critics generally follow Barrett John Mandel in terming Cowper an unreliable narrator. John N. Morris, pursuing a

different thread in the *Memoir*, has sought out the connections between Cowper's mental illness and his search for a personal style. Critics have also debated whether Cowper's genius lies in his poetic or his letter writing ability. Robert Lynd and Norman Nicholson have argued for the latter, but other critics have faulted various aspects of Cowper's letters. Lytton Strachey felt that Cowper's letters were elegantly written but that "they lack the juices of life"; Saintsbury thought them interesting but "small-beerish." Mark Van Doren, however, praised Cowper's spontaneity and the mixture of joy and despair in his letters, and William Henry Irving contended that Cowper's style is "probably unparalleled in the history of the familiar letter." His editor, the English poet and essayist Robert Southey, also declared Cowper the best letter writer in the English language.

Cowper was a transitional figure in English literature, and his works embody both eighteenth and nineteenth-century styles and concerns. Because of the influence of his style on William Wordsworth and other Romantic poets, he remains an important precursor of Romanticism in England. For modern scholars, his works shed significant light on an era of evolution in English letters.

PRINCIPAL WORKS

Olney Hymns [with John Newton]   (hymns) 1779
Poems (poetry) 1782
*The Task (poetry) 1785
Homer's Iliad and Odyssey [translator]   (poetry) 1791
Poems (poetry) 1798
**Memoir of the Early Life of William Cowper, Esq.
   (memoir) 1816
The Life and Works of William Cowper. 15 vols.   (letters,
   poetry, hymns, and essays) 1835-37
The Correspondence of William Cowper. 4 vols.   (letters)
   1904

*This work includes the ballad "The Journey of John Gilpin," which was originally published in the *Public Advertiser* in 1782.

**This work was written in 1766.

THE CRITICAL REVIEW (essay date 1785)

[William Cowper's *The Task*,] though not free from defects, for originality of thought, strength of argument, and poignancy of satire, we speak in general, is superior to any that has lately fallen into our hands. We here meet with no affected prettiness of style, no glaring epithets, which modern writers so industriously accumulate; and reversing Homer's exhibition of his hero in rags, convey the image of a beggar, clothed in 'purple and fine linen.' . . . [Cowper] proceeds to describe an ambulatory excursion. The reflections he makes in it naturally arise from the objects which present themselves to his view; and the scenery is depictured in chaste and exact colouring. We meet with no meretricious ornaments; no superfluity of epithets and crouded figures, which often throw an indistinct glare over modern poetic landscapes, instead of representing their objects in a clear and proper light. His vindication of the long colonnade of correspondent trees against the encroachments of the present taste, and wish to

> reprieve
> The obsolete prolixity of shade,

will doubtless be reprobated by the votaries of Brown, and modern improvement. We, however, question whether they do not impress the mind with more sublime and awful ideas, than they could effect by any other mode of arrangement. (pp. 251-52)

The subject-matter is sometimes serious, and sometimes comic. The transitions are in many places happily contrived: in others, too abrupt and desultory. . . . Our follies and vices are sufficiently numerous, but those of our forefathers, if we judge from the writers of their days, were little or nothing inferior. We are censured for wearing

> habits costlier than Lucullus wore.

Our mutability in fashions is justly ridiculed; but our modes of dress are not, in general, remarkably costly. Our ancestors flowing wigs, in the reign of good queen Anne, was probably a more expensive and absurd fashion than any in modern days. . . . We consider this reflection on our military gentlemen as too pointed, if not unjust; particularly if he means to intimate that our public misfortunes are owing to their misconduct. . . . [But if] some few of Mr. Cowper's satiric observations are trite and threadbare, the generality are no less justly conceived than forcibly expressed. (pp. 253-54)

Our author's excellency, in faithfully delineating the scenes of nature, has been already mentioned. A striking instance of it is to be found in his description of a winter's morning. The objects are brought immediately before our view: and the village cur, with which we shall close our extract, is peculiarly excellent, and painted from the life. . . . It is but justice . . . to observe, before we conclude our review of this poem, that the religious and moral reflections with which it abounds, though sometimes the diction is not sufficiently elevated, in general possess the acuteness and depth of Young, and are often expressed with the energy of Shakspeare. (pp. 255-56)

> *"Cowper's 'Task', a Poem," in* The Critical Review, *Vol. LX, October, 1785, pp. 251-56.*

THE MONTHLY REVIEW (essay date 1786)

Amidst the multitude of dull, or flimsy, or insipid things that issue from the press under the name of poems, we are now and then relieved by a production of real genius; though it is very seldom that we are furnished with an entertainment that mingles delight and improvement in so perfect a degree as [William Cowper's **The Task**]. . . . The Author is always moral, yet never dull: and though he often expands an image, yet he never weakens its force. If the same thought occurs, he gives it a new form; and is copious, without being tiresome. He frequently entertains by his comic humour; and still oftener awakens more serious and more tender sentiments, by useful and by pathetic representations;—by descriptions that soothe and melt the heart, and by reflections which carry their alarm to the conscience, and rouse and terrify guilt in its closest retreats.

The poet writes under the strong impression of Christian and moral truths, and we *feel* him to be in earnest when he pleads their cause, and deplores the neglect that is shewn them by some and the insults that are offered them by others. Conviction gives force to imagination; and the poet dips his pen in the stream that religion hath opened in his own bosom.

Mr. Cowper possesses strong powers of ridicule; and Nature formed him for a satirist of the first order. He sees folly under every disguise; and knows how to raise a laugh at her expence, either by grave humour or more sportive raillery. He is alive to every feeling of compassion, and spares none that violate the laws of humanity. His benevolence is as extensive as the creation; and though the *particular* impressions which religion hath made on his mind, and the general corruption of the times, have thrown a *shade of melancholy* (it will be called *spleen* by some persons) over his writings, yet we always behold an amiable and generous principle shining through the cloud, and struggling to overcome the evils which it deplores.

The great defect of the present poem is a want of unity of design. It is composed of reflections that seem independent of one another; and there is no *particular* subject either discussed or aimed at. (pp. 416-17)

An imagination like Mr. Cowper's is not to be controuled and confined within the bounds that criticism prescribes. We cannot, however, avoid remarking, that his muse sometimes passes too suddenly from grave and serious remonstrance to irony and ridicule. The heart that is *harrowed* and alarmed in one line, is not prepared to smile in the next. Instances of this improper association need not be pointed out: they too frequently occur; and the severe and ludicrous destroy one another. We were most displeased with what the Poet says at the close of his very striking picture of the ill effects of drunkenness:

> Drink, and be mad then: 'tis your country bids;
> Gloriously drunk, obey the important call,
> Her cause demands the assistance of your throats,
> Yet all can swallow, and she asks no more.

The satire is strongly expressed; but is not the irony ill-timed and misplaced? Are we allowed to indulge a sportive vein, when public disgrace and private calamity is the object?

But Mr. Cowper's wit is too vigorous and too copious to be repressed or restrained within the limits that circumscribe more wary and correct poets; though no one feels more serious abhorrence of vice, or more tender compassion for the distressed. (pp. 417-18)

If the Poet meant his satire for the *atheist,* he hath not said enough; but if for the *philosopher,* he hath said too much. We readily give up your *Spinosas* and your *Mirabeaus* . . . as fit subjects for his ridicule. But let him not throw his shafts of wit at random, lest they should fall on better men, and wiser philosophers; on those who, like himself, were the friends of human kind, and the warm advocates of virtue and religion.

But the defects of this poem bear a very small proportion to its beauties:—and its beauties are of no common account. They are happily conceived, and forcibly expressed. His language is the natural and unforced result of his conceptions: and though it is sometimes careless and prosaic, and seldom rich or ornamented, yet it is vigorous and animated, and carries the thought home to the heart with irresistible energy. (pp. 418-19)

The **Epistle to Mr. Hill** is sprightly and pleasant;—the tribute of affection and esteem to the merits of an honest friend.

The *Tirocinium, or Review of Schools,* contains some severe strictures (we will not say how just) on the general mode and effect of public education, as it hath been long conducted in this country; and contrasts it with private tuition, in order to shew the great superiority of the latter, particularly in respect of its moral tendency.

The *History of John Gilpin* is a ballad of mixed humour, and shews the strong tendency of the Author to ridicule; but it is too well known, and its merits have been too publicly decided on to need applause, or to be affected by censure. (p. 425)

"Cowper's 'Poems,' Vol. II," in The Monthly Review, *London, Vol. LXXIV, June, 1786, pp. 416-25.*

ALEXANDER KNOX   (essay date 1796)

[*This essay originally appeared in the* Flapper *on May 14, 1796.*]

[Cowper,] perhaps in as high a degree as any man who ever lived, is the poet of nature; led by his excursive muse through many a mazy path, he returns to the scenes which nature herself has formed with ever new delight; from these he takes the darling subjects of his poetic pencil; and though in his hands they seem to display new beauties and appear more interesting, they lose nothing of their familiarity. His descriptions strike every mind which is endued with the common powers of discernment; his thoughts meet something in unison with themselves in every heart that is human.

I believe I need not scruple to assert that in the power of giving universal gratification Cowper very much exceeds even Thomson himself. Thomson undoubtedly describes what every man may see, and what indeed almost every man has seen at one time or other; but Cowper describes what every man *must* see; he takes his materials from the everyday walks of life; he seizes on those little domestic circumstances which perhaps no poet before him ever thought of making use of, and he forms from them pictures which astonish no less than they please. We wonder at the interest we now for the first time take in what we have so often seen without any pleasurable sensation, and we wonder still more that such an effect should be so easily produced; we observe no labor, no search for ornament, but on the contrary, an execution as artless as the conception is vigorous. In this, perhaps, also Cowper has a material advantage over Thomson; the latter leaves no circumstance unexpressed, no grace neglected, no aid of coloring omitted—all is beautiful, but all is elaborate. Cowper, on the contrary, looks out for nothing; he takes just so much as has made an impression on his own mind, and which will of course produce the effect on the mind of his reader, and having completed his design with a few masterly strokes, he hurries on to some new subject. The descriptions of Thomson are like the most highly finished paintings of the Flemish school; those of Cowper are little more than sketches, but they are the sketches of a Raphael.

Let it not be thought that I wish to depreciate by an invidious comparison [Thomson,] the admirable author of the *Seasons.* His pure gold could not be tarnished by the breath of malevolence, nor has it anything to apprehend from the assay of candid criticism. But the excellence of Cowper has no need of being illustrated by contrast—to know him is to admire him. In particular, it is impossible to look into his invaluable *Task* (the work in which he has given the most unbounded license to his fancy) without being charmed even to transport at the wildly beautiful varieties of vivid description and glowing thought, of images the gravest and the gayest, the most hu-

morous and the most pathetic, the most obvious in substance, and in manner the most novel, which, following each other in rapid succession, would almost bespeak a magic creation like that of the airy phantoms in the cave of Prospero. (pp. 1105-06)

The discerning reader will easily perceive that simplicity is a prevailing character in the poetry of Cowper, and that his thoughts appear to retain on paper the very order and shape which they assumed at first in his mind. One consequence of this certainly is that his verses are unequal and that many of his lines, if they stood alone, or were fraught with less noble matter, could not be considered as more than prose which had fallen by accident into a metrical form. In such cases Cowper seems never once to have thought of stopping to correct or improve. He was too powerfully attracted by the objects that lay before him; perhaps also he considered the occasional occurrence of verses comparatively flat as advantageous on the whole, and that the remark of Horace,

Operi longo fas est obrepere somnum,

[When a work is long, a drowsy mood
may well creep over it,]

implied a precept as well as a permission.

Another consequence of Cowper's writing precisely as he thought is a total dereliction of all method. This might seem at first sight to be the very thing which he intended; but on a closer view he appears frequently to have formed some previous plan from which the fervidness of his mind carries him away, and he wanders on through a wilderness indeed, but like that of Eden "a wilderness of sweets," over which the fancy of his reader delights to follow him. He describes this versatile turn in his own happy manner. . . . (pp. 1108-09)

Alexander Knox, "Cowper, I," in Eighteenth-Century Critical Essays, *Vol. II, edited by Scott Elledge, Cornell University Press, 1961, pp. 1104-09.*

ALEXANDER KNOX   (essay date 1796)

[*This essay originally appeared in the* Flapper *on May 28, 1796.*]

In the remarks which I gave lately on the poetry of Cowper [see excerpt above] I observed that in his descriptions he avoids all unnecessary minuteness of detail and confines himself to those striking features which are most likely to make a forcible impression on the mind. Though in this particular he seems merely to have followed the instinctive bent of his genius, he has perhaps attained one of the most desirable ends of poetic skill and labor. A poet who describes justly and beautifully will necessarily give pleasure, even though he should say all that can be said and anticipate every conceivable idea. But he will afford a much more exalted delight when he impregnates the mind with the seeds of new conceptions, and instead of thinking exclusively for his reader, inspires him with a power of thinking for himself. (p. 1110)

[Although] Cowper shuns minuteness of description, he very frequently . . . describes minute or trivial matters—and it is certain that on these a master of the imitative arts can display his excellence no less than on the most dignified subjects. For example, there is nothing very remarkable or striking in a lighted candle—we see it without a thought—but a lighted candle may be so painted as to excite both pleasure and surprise and perhaps to arrest the attention of a common observer more powerfully than the best executed landscape or history piece. In like manner it would hardly be imagined that there could be anything very interesting in the appearance of a boor going from his cottage at peep of day to hew timber in a neighboring wood. And yet from this familiar circumstance Cowper has formed a poetic sketch [in *The Task*] which it is scarcely possible to read without being delighted.... (pp. 1111-12)

[The] descriptive powers of Cowper appear to me to be invaluable. By the happiest choice of subjects and the most lively representation of them he perpetually allures the wandering fancy to the sources of harmless satisfaction, and even his most trifling pictures are so many new proofs that to a well-formed and uncorrupted mind the means of innocent amusement are inexhaustible. (p. 1113)

There is scarcely anything which more contributes to make Cowper's poetry popular than the power which he possesses of enlivening his descriptions with strokes of the most genuine humor, and it frequently heightens the effect that we find this where we least expect it. (p. 1114)

His verse might no doubt frequently admit of improvement—his expressions scarcely ever. His fancy, softly ductile and strongly tenacious, receives and keeps the vivid impress of each object, and the cast from so fair a mould must of course present every feature and lineament with the ease of nature and the accuracy of truth. I would beg leave to recommend this observation in particular to the examination of my critical readers, and I dare to believe many of them will join me in the opinion that in choice of expression (if choice it can be called where there is no mark of forethought) Cowper yields to no poet in the English language. (pp. 1114-15)

> *Alexander Knox, "Cowper, II," in* Eighteenth-Century Critical Essays, Vol. II, *edited by Scott Elledge, Cornell University Press, 1961, pp. 1110-15.*

ALEXANDER KNOX   (essay date 1796)

[*This essay originally appeared in the* Flapper *on June 11, 1796.*]

Amongst the advantages which Cowper has possessed from his moral dispositions I cannot overlook those which he has enjoyed from his piety. In him humanity has been sublimed by religion, and his imagination as well as his language evidently appears to be heightened by his deep acquaintance with the Holy Scriptures. (p. 1119)

After enlarging so much on the beauties of Cowper it may be expected that I should take some notice of his blemishes. I scarcely lament that by the narrowness of my limits I am obliged on this particular to be very brief. I have already hinted at the frequent occurrence of passages in which nothing of poetry is to be found but the form of the line. In this instance I conceive Cowper to have sacrificed the dignity of his verse to his earnestness to do good, as on every such occasion he pursues, perhaps beyond those bounds which his general plan prescribed, some subject so merely moral as not to be susceptible of poetic imagery; and let it be remembered that the merely theological parts of *Paradise Lost* have subjected even Milton to somewhat of a similar charge. A severe critic might also accuse Cowper of dwelling in a few instances on subjects scarcely worthy of his pen, and I own I myself could wish that his love for gardening had permitted him to be less exact in describing the apparatus for a hotbed. I fear too that his piety (a matter of infinitely more importance than all the rest) may

" 'John Gilpin's spouse said to her dear,
'Though wedded we have been
These twice ten tedious years, yet we
No holiday have seen.' "

An illustration from the first edition of "The Journey of John Gilpin."

be less attractive from being marked by some peculiarity of opinion and perhaps tinged by that morbid melancholy under which Mr. Cowper is known to have long struggled. But still it is sincere, it is ardent, it is venerable, and on the whole his praise is (and what more valuable can there be) that what Johnson has said of Watts may be said with no less justice of Cowper. "He is one of those few poets with whom youth and ignorance may be safely pleased, and happy will that reader be whose mind is disposed by his verses to copy his benevolence to man, and his reverence to God." (pp. 1120-21)

> *Alexander Knox, "Cowper, III," in* Eighteenth-Century Critical Essays, Vol. II, *edited by Scott Elledge, Cornell University Press, 1961, pp. 1115-21.*

[FRANCIS JEFFREY]   (essay date 1803)

[*Jeffrey was a founder and editor (1803-1829) of the* Edinburgh Review, *one of the most influential magazines in early nineteenth-century England. A liberal Whig and a politician, Jeffrey often allowed his political beliefs to color his critical opinions. His literary criticism, perhaps the most characteristic example of "impressionistic" critical thought dominant during the first half of the nineteenth century, stressed a personal approach to literature. Jeffrey felt that literature should be judged by his own conception of beauty (a beautiful work being that which inspires sensations of tenderness or pity in the reader), rather than by such Neoclassical criteria as restraint, clarity, order, balance, and proportion. Seeking a universal standard of beauty and taste, Jeffrey exhorted artists to "employ only such subjects as are the natural signs, or the inseparable concomitants of emotions, of which the greater part of mankind are susceptible." In addition, Jeffrey wanted literature to be realistic and to observe standards of propriety. Though he became famous for his harsh criticism of the Lake poets (Samuel Taylor Coleridge, William Wordsworth, and Robert Southey), Jeffrey was an exponent of moderate Romanticism, and praised the work of John Keats, Lord Byron, and Walter Scott. Jeffrey was widely influential throughout his lifetime and helped to raise the status of periodical reviewing in nineteenth-century England.]*

[Cowper's great merit] appears to us to consist in the boldness and originality of his composition, and in the fortunate audacity with which he has carried the dominion of poetry into regions that had been considered as inaccessible to her ambition. The gradual refinement of taste had, for nearly a century, been weakening the figure of original genius. Our poets had become timid and fastidious, and circumscribed themselves both in the choice and the management of their subjects, by the observance of a limited number of models, who were thought to have exhausted all the legitimate resources of the art. Cowper was one of the first who crossed this enchanted circle, who regained the natural liberty of invention, and walked abroad in the open field of observation as freely as those by whom it was originally trodden; he passed from the imitation of poets, to the imitation of nature, and ventured boldly upon the representation of objects that had not been sanctified by the description of any of his predecessors. In the ordinary occupations and duties of domestic life, and the consequences of modern manners, in the common scenery of a rustic situation, and the obvious contemplation of our public institutions, he has found a multitude of subjects for ridicule and reflection, for pathetic and picturesque description, for moral declamation, and devotional rapture, that would have been looked upon with disdain, or with despair, by most of our poetical adventurers. He took as wide a range in language, too, as in matter; and, shaking off the tawdry incumbrance of that poetical diction which had nearly reduced the art to the skilful collocation of a set of appropriated phrases, he made no scruple to set down in verse every expression that would have been admitted in prose, and to take advantage of all the varieties with which our language could supply him.

But while, by the use of this double licence, he extended the sphere of poetical composition, and communicated a singular character of freedom, force, and originality, to his own performances, it must not be dissembled, that the presumption which belongs to most innovators, has betrayed him into many defects. In disdaining to follow the footsteps of others, he has frequently mistaken the way, and has been exasperated, by their blunders, to rush into an opposite extreme. In his contempt for their scrupulous selection of topics, he has introduced some that are unquestionably low and uninteresting; and in his zeal to strip off the tinsel and embroidery of their language, he has torn it . . . into terrible rents and beggarly tatters. He is a great master of English, and evidently values himself upon his skill and facility in the application of its rich and diversified idioms: but he has indulged himself in this exercise a little too fondly, and has degraded some grave and animated passages by the unlucky introduction of expressions unquestionably too colloquial and familiar. His impatience of controul, and his desire

to have a great scope and variety in his compositions, have led him not only to disregard all order and method so entirely in their construction, as to have made each of his larger poems professedly a complete miscellany, but also to introduce into them a number of subjects that prove not to be very susceptible of poetical discussion. There are specimens of argument, and dialogue, and declamation, in his works, that partake very little of the poetical character, and make rather an awkward appearance in a metrical production, though they might have had a lively and brilliant effect in an essay or a sermon. The structure of his sentences, in like manner, has frequently much more of the copiousness and looseness of oratory, than the brilliant compactness of poetry; and he heaps up phrases and circumstances upon each other, with a profusion that is frequently dazzling, but which reminds us as often of the exuberance of a practised speaker, as of the holy inspiration of a poet. (pp. 81-2)

[It] does not appear to us, either that [satire] was the style in which he was qualified to excel, or that he has made a judicious selection of subjects upon which to exercise it. There is something too keen and vehement in his invective, and an excess of austerity in his doctrine, that is not atoned for by the truth or the beauty of his descriptions. Foppery and affectation are not such hateful and gigantic vices, as to deserve all the anathemas that are bestowed upon them; nor can we believe that soldiership, or Sunday music, have produced all the terrible effects which he ascribes to them. There is something very undignified, too, to say no worse of them, in the protracted parodies and mock-heroic passages with which he seeks to enliven some of his gravest productions. . . . All his serious pieces contain some fine devotional passages: but they are not without a taint of that enthusiastic intolerance which religious zeal seems so often to produce. In a few places, there are symptoms of superstition, also, that do not produce even a good poetical effect. (pp. 82-3)

It is impossible to say any thing of the defects of Cowper's writings, without taking notice of the occasional harshness and inelegance of his versification. From his correspondence, however, it appears that this was not with him the effect of negligence merely, but that he really imagined that a rough and incorrect line now and then had a very agreeable effect in a composition of any length. (p. 83)

Though it be impossible, therefore, to read the productions of Cowper, without being delighted with his force, his brilliancy, and his variety; and although the enchantment of his moral enthusiasm frequently carries us insensibly through all the mazes of his digressions, it is equally true, that we can scarcely read a single page with attention, without being offended at some coarseness or lowness of expression, or disappointed by some 'most lame and impotent conclusion.' The dignity of his rhetorical periods is often violated by the intrusion of some vulgar and colloquial idiom, and the full and transparent stream of his diction is broken upon some obstreperous verse, or lost in the dull stagnation of a piece of absolute prose. The effect of his ridicule is sometimes impaired by the acrimony with which it is attended; and the exquisite beauty of his moral painting and religious views is injured in no small degree by the darkness of the shades which his enthusiasm and austerity have occasionally thrown upon the canvas. With all these defects, however, Cowper will probably very long retain his popularity with the readers of English poetry. The great variety and truth of his descriptions; the minute and correct painting of those home-scenes, and private feelings with which every one is internally familiar; the sterling weight and sense of most of his observations, and, above all, the great appearance of facility with which every thing is executed, and the happy use he has so often made of the most common and ordinary language; all concur to stamp upon his poems the character of original genius, and remind us of the merits that have secured immortality to Shakespeare. (p. 84)

[That Cowper's translation of Homer] is a great deal more close and literal, than any that had previously been attempted in English verse, probably will not be disputed by those who are the least disposed to admire it; that the style into which it is translated is a true English style, though not perhaps a very elegant or poetical one, may also be assumed; but we are not sure that a rigid and candid criticism will go farther in its commendation. The language is often very tame, and even vulgar; and there is by far too great a profusion of antiquated and colloquial forms of expression. In the dialogue part, the idiomatical and familiar turn of the language has often an animated and happy effect; but in orations of dignity, this dramatical licence is frequently abused, and the translation approaches to a parody. (p. 85)

In Cowper's elaborate version [of *The Iliad*], there are certainly some striking and vigorous passages, and the closeness of the translation continually recals the original to the memory of a classical reader; but he will look in vain for the melodious and elevated language of Homer in the unpolished verses and colloquial phraseology of his translator. (p. 86)

> [*Francis Jeffrey*], *"Hayley's 'Life of Cowper'," in*
> The Edinburgh Review, *Vol. II, No. III, April, 1803,*
> *pp. 64-86.*

[FRANCIS JEFFREY]   (essay date 1804)

[*Jeffrey, who earlier reviewed Cowper's poems (1803), found Cowper's letters more to his liking. He especially praises their "profusion of witty and humorous passages" and Cowper's "great ease and familiarity" of expression.*]

[Of Cowper's letters] we may safely assert, that we have rarely met with any similar collection, of superior interest or beauty. Though the incidents to which they relate be of no public magnitude or moment, and the remarks which they contain be not uniformly profound or original, yet there is something in the sweetness and facility of the diction, and more perhaps in the glimpses they afford of a pure and benevolent mind, that diffuses a charm over the whole collection, and communicates an interest that cannot always be commanded by performances of greater dignity and pretension. This interest was promoted and assisted, no doubt, in a considerable degree, by that curiosity which always seeks to penetrate into the privacy of celebrated men, and which had been almost entirely frustrated in the instance of Cowper, tilt the appearance of this publication. Though his writings had long been extremely popular, the author was scarcely known to the public; and having lived in a state of entire seclusion from the world, there were no anecdotes of his conversation, his habits or opinions, in circulation among his admirers. The publication of his correspondence has a great measure supplied this deficiency; and we now know almost as much of Cowper as we do of those authors who have spent their days in the centre and glare of literary or fashionable notoriety. These letters, however, will continue to be read, long after the curiosity is gratified to which perhaps they owed their first celebrity: for the character with which they make us acquainted, will always attract by its rarity,

and engage by its elegance. The feminine delicacy and purity of Cowper's manners and disposition, the romantic and unbroken retirement in which his life was passed, and the singular gentleness and modesty of his whole character, disarm him of those terrors that so often shed an atmosphere of repulsion around the persons of celebrated writers, and make us more indulgent to his weaknesses, and more delighted with his excellences, than if he had been the centre of a circle of wits, or the oracle of a literary confederacy. The interest of this picture is still further heightened by the recollection of that tremendous malady, to the visitations of which he was subject, and by the spectacle of that perpetual conflict which was maintained, through the greater part of his life, between the depression of those constitutional horrors, and the gayety that resulted from a playful imagination, and a heart animated by the mildest affections.

In the letters now before us, Cowper displays a great deal of all those peculiarities by which his character was adorned or distinguished; he is frequently the subject of his own observations, and often delineates the finer features of his understanding with all the industry and impartiality of a stranger. But the most interesting traits are those which are unintentionally discovered, and which the reader collects from expressions that were employed for very different purposes. Among the most obvious, perhaps, as well as the most important of these, is that extraordinary combination of shyness and ambition, to which we are probably indebted for the very existence of his poetry. Being disqualified, by the former, from vindicating his proper place in the ordinary scenes either of business or of society, he was excited, by the latter, to attempt the only other avenue to reputation that appeared to be open, and to assert the real dignity of the talents with which he felt that he was gifted. If Cowper had acquired courage enough to read the journals of the House of Lords, or been able to get over the diffidence which fettered his utterance in general society, his genius would probably have evaporated in conversation, or been contented with the humbler glory of contributing to the Rolliad or the Connoisseur. (pp. 273-75)

One of the most remarkable things in [Cowper's letters], is the great profusion of witty and humorous passages which it contains, though they are usually so short, and stand so much connected with more indifferent matter, that it is not easy to give any tolerable notion of them by an extract. His style of narrative is particularly gay and pleasing, though the incidents are generally too trifling to bear a separation from the whole tissue of the correspondence. (p. 276)

Cowper's religious impressions occupied too great a portion of his thoughts, and exercised too great an influence on his character, not to make a distinguished figure in his correspondence. They form the subject of many eloquent and glowing passages: and have sometimes suggested sentiments and expressions that cannot be perused without compassion and regret. (p. 280)

[The chief merit of Cowper's letters] consists in the great ease and familiarity with which every thing is expressed, and in the simplicity and sincerity in which every thing appears to be conceived. [Their] chief fault, perhaps, is the too frequent recurrence of these apologies for dull letters, and complaints of the want of subjects, that seem occasionally to bring it down to the level of an ordinary correspondence, and to represent Cowper as one of those who make every letter its own subject, and correspond with their friends by talking about their correspondence. (p. 282)

[The fragment **"Yardley Oak"**] is addressed to a very ancient and decayed oak in the vicinity of Weston. We do not think quite so highly of this production as the editor appears to do; at the same time that we confess it to be impressed with all the marks of Cowper's most vigorous hand: we do not know any of his compositions, indeed, that affords a more striking exemplification of most of the excellences and defects of his peculiar style, or might be more fairly quoted as a specimen of his *manner*. It is full of the conceptions of a vigorous and poetical fancy, expressed in nervous and familiar language; but it is rendered harsh by unnecessary inversions, and debased in several places by the use of antiquated and vulgar phrases. (p. 283)

> [*Francis Jeffrey*], *"Hayley's 'Life of Cowper, Vol. III'," in* The Edinburgh Review, *Vol. IV, No. VIII, July, 1804, pp. 273-84.*

THE NORTH AMERICAN REVIEW   (essay date 1816)

As philosophers, we may smile at the portents, prodigies, and divine interpositions which occur so frequently in the works of Cowper, and which, according to his letters, he often observed and experienced. Practical, sensible men, who are satisfied with the world and its inhabitants, as it has pleased God to make them, would not do the solitary and desponding bard justice, were they to form their opinion of him from the many passages written in the spirit of the following extract [from *The Task*]:

> I see that all are wanderers, gone astray,
> Each in his own delusions; they are lost
> In chase of fancied happiness, still woo'd
> And never won. Dream after dream ensues;
> And still they dream that they shall still succeed,
> And still are disappointed. Rings the world
> With the vain stir? I sum up half mankind,
> And add two-thirds of the remaining half,
> And find the total of their hopes and fears,
> Dreams, empty dreams.
>
> (pp. 235-36)

Men of extensive and profound views of human life, and such as think that there are not so great fluctuations of happiness, and virtue and vice, as there are in the notions entertained concerning them, do not condole with Cowper in his lamentations over the follies and enormities of the present times, and do not very sorrowfully mourn at the reported 'sickness and death of the hoary sage Discipline.' In reading such things, they consider who the writer is, and what sort of people they generally are, by whom he expects to be read. Cowper requires of us very liberal allowances on account of his character, situation, and habits of thinking. It is not surprising that such a satirist as he, should not choose proper objects, or aim his shafts with skill. His religious prejudices and views of life, have a tendency to make the man who adopts them, ridiculous, useless, and unhappy. But we do not read poetry to learn the rules of living and judging; we commonly regard it as an instrument to excite a delicate and refined pleasure, and the means of chastening and softening our sensibilities. In this respect Cowper is a poet. Can any one read him, and not be animated by the glow of benevolence which is diffused through his writings? It must be a hard heart that is not touched by the tenderness of his sentiments, and a dull sensibility, that is not moved by his lively and accurate representations of nature. Those who relish social and domestick enjoyments, find in Cowper the best finished descriptions of the scenes of their happiness. His style is pure, not unfrequently elegant, and always easy. He has little fire, brilliancy, or sublimity; he frequently delights, but never astonishes. (p. 236)

> *"Cowper's Poems," in* The North American Review, *Vol. II, No. V, January, 1816, pp. 233-41.*

THE QUARTERLY REVIEW   (essay date 1816)

Much cannot be said for Cowper's Latin poetry. It wants ease and harmony, and classical perfection; nor is the absence of these qualities compensated by any extraordinary force of style or beauty of idea. Indeed, there is a certain degree of artifice requisite in writing modern Latin poetry; and artifice of a kind alien to Cowper's genius. The merit of this sort of composition consists more in choice of expression, embellishment of common thoughts, and well-wrought imitation of three or four standard writers, and less in vivid description or the sublimities of action and passion, than that of English poetry. (p. 117)

[The first verses in **Poems, by William Cowper, of the Inner Temple, Esq.**], display at the age of seventeen that exuberant humour which attended our author in after-life. The *Epistle to Lloyd* is full of liveliness, and that to Lady Austen unites innocent gaiety with just and dignified reflection. (p. 118)

The fragment on the Four Ages might have been the introduction to a second *Task:* that on the Yardley Oak is, perhaps, the most characteristic specimen of Cowper; with his usual alloy of homeliness, and want of selection, it exhibits a copiousness of thought and expression, worthy of Dryden or Cowley. (pp. 118-19)

At the time when our poetry began to emerge from the bondage of formality and pomp, Cowper appeared to advance the cause of nature and true taste. With an opinion sufficiently high of Pope and his contemporaries, modest and unenterprizing, alive to censure, and seemingly scarcely conscious that he was an innovator, he yet helped essentially to restore the elder vigour and simplicity, by presenting to us the primitive Muse of England in her own undisguised features, her flexibility of deportment, her smiles and tears, her general animation and frequent rusticity. From the effects which this exhibition produced on the public, satiated with classical imitation and antithesis, he may be reckoned among the patriarchs of the present school of poetry.

Cowper's qualities are, copiousness of idea, often without sufficient choice; keenness of observation, descending occasionally to wearisomeness or disgust; an addiction to elevated thought and generous feeling; and a pliable manner, passing easily from the tender to the sublime, and again to the humorous. In the very throng and press of his observations on the most serious subjects, it is not unusual to encounter an effusion of wit, or a familiar remark. This may seem a strange anomaly in a writer of Cowper's turn; yet it is to be accounted for. The subjects in question were the constant themes of his meditation, the fountains of his actions, his hopes, his duties; they were inwoven with his mind, and he spoke of them with that familiarity, perfectly distinct from lightness, with which men naturally speak of what is habitual to them, though connected with their happiness, and involving many hopes and fears. It must be confessed, however, that he sometimes uses expressions, which, in a person of different principles, would be interpreted as the language of levity.

His great work, the *Task,* was welcomed on its appearance with general acclamation. It has ever since continued to rank with the most popular poems. This performance, so singular in its nature and original, has a sufficient admixture of faults: some passages are tedious, others uninteresting, and others even revolting. The language is often tinged with meanness, and pathos and beauty are sometimes interrupted by witticism. The charm of the work consists in its tender, generous and pious sentiments; in the frankness and warmth of its manner, its sketches of nature, eulogies of country retirement, interesting allusions to himself and those he loves; the refreshing transitions from subject to subject, and the elasticity with which he varies his tone, though the change is not always without offence; and the glow, which when a poet feels, he is sure to impart to others. We share his walks, or his fire-side, and hear him comment on the newspaper or the last new book of travels; converse with him as a kind familiar friend, or hearken to the counsels of an affectionate monitor. We attend him among the beauties and repose of nature, or the mild dignity of private life; sympathize with his elevations, smile with him at folly, and share his indignation at oppression and vice—and if he sometimes detains us too long in the hot-house, or tires us with political discussion, we love him too well to wish ourselves rid of him on that account. He is most at home on nature and country retirement—friendship—domestic life—the rights and duties of men—and, above all, the comforts and excellencies of religion: his physical dejection never overcasts his doctrines; and his devout passages are, to us, the finest of his poem. There is not in Milton or Akenside such a continuation of sublime thoughts as in the latter parts of the fifth and sixth books. The peroration is remarkably graceful and solemn. (pp. 119-20)

Table Talk is a distinct production, a kind of *Task* in Miniature. . . . It abounds with passages of wit, energy and beauty, and is replete with good sense. . . . The seven succeeding poems are mostly sets of precepts and remarks, characters and descriptions, delivered in a poetical manner. Here, as elsewhere, his wit, always powerful, is often clumsy, and sometimes, from being more intent on the sentiment than the expression, his language deviates into prose. There is, besides, a want of system in the subjects of each piece, which in some injures the continuity of interest. Still there is so much unsophisticated description, and sentiment, and humour—the richness of the poet's heart and mind are so diffused over the whole, that they will always be read with delight. He who would behold the full beauty of Christianity, might be referred to these poems—especially the last four.

Cowper's light pieces are characterized by vigour, playfulness, and invention; debased sometimes by inelegance, and even by conceits. His *Tales* are excellent. The verses for the *Bills of Mortality* are poetical and impressive; and the *Epistle to Hill* is quite Horatian. His lines on his mother's picture display remarkably his powers of pathos. Such a strain of mellowed and manly sorrow, such affectionate reminiscences of childhood unmixed with trifling, such an union of regret with piety, is seldom to be found in any language.

His translation of Homer retains much of the old poet's simplicity, without enough of his fire. Cowper has removed the gilded cloud which Pope had cast over him; and his version, though very imperfect, is the more faithful portrait of the two.

In the *Task,* the author has introduced a new species of blank verse; a medium between the majestic sweep and continuous variety of Milton and Akenside, and the monotony of Young and Thomson. It is suited to his subject, smooth and easy, yet sufficiently varied in its structure to give the ear its proper entertainment. Sometimes, as in the description of the Sicilian earthquake, and the Millennium, he seems to aspire higher. He affects much the pause on the third and seventh syllables, the latter of which combines dignity with animation more than any other. It must be confessed, however, that he has not avoided flatness and uniformity. His rhyme has the freedom and energy of Dryden's, without its variety. His diction resembles his versification; forcible, but often uncouth. It is the language of conversation, elevated by metaphors, Miltonic constructions, and antiquated expressions, above the level of prose.

His letters are full of the man—of his mildness, philanthropy, and domestic temper; his pensiveness and devotion, his over-strained timidity, and his liveliness of imagination. . . . [The] letters, like the anecdotes in Boswell's *Johnson,* compensate for the scantiness or ordinary quality of the narrative with which they are interwoven. We think them equal to any that we have met with. There is a delightful playfulness pervading them, which is perhaps the most attractive quality of an epistle. (pp. 120-22)

His opinions on various subjects, expressed in these letters, flow less from any expansion of intellect or depth of penetration, than from plain sense, a cultivated understanding, and that clear-headedness which attends on virtue, and which enables it to discern many things which superior faculties, blinded by a bad heart or vicious habits, fail of discerning.

In the morality of his poems, Cowper is honourably distinguished from most of his brethren. Our poets have too often deviated into an incorrect system of morals, coldly delivered; a smooth, polished, filed-down Christianity; a medium system, between the religion of the Gospel and the heathen philosophy, and intended apparently to accommodate the two. There is nothing to comfort or guide us, no satisfying centre on which to fix our desires; no line is drawn between good and evil; we wander on amid a waste of feelings sublimated to effeminacy, desires raised beyond the possibility of gratification, and passions indulged till their indulgence seems almost a necessary of life. We rise with heated minds, and feel that something still is wanting. In Cowper, on the contrary, all is reality; there is no doubt, no vagueness of opinion; the only satisfactory object on which our affections can be fixed, is distinctly and fully pointed out; the afflicted are consoled, the ignorant enlightened. A perfect line is drawn between truth and error. The heart is enlisted on the side of religion; every precept is just, every motive efficacious. Sensible that every vice is connected with the rest; that the voluptuous will become hard-hearted, and the unthinking licentious; he aims his shafts at all: and as Gospel truth is the base of morality, it is the groundwork of his precepts. (p. 122)

"Cowper's 'Poems and Life'," in The Quarterly Review, *Vol. XVI, No. XXXI, October, 1816, pp. 116-29.*

THE CHRISTIAN OBSERVER (essay date 1818)

[The captivating accuracy of Cowper's] descriptions, the lively playfulness of his wit, his just delineations of character, his delicate poignancy of satire, and, above all, the affecting and majestic simplicity of those passages in which he touches on religion, the subject nearest his heart, constitute the charms which endear his poetry even to those who dissent from his opinions or would criticize his numbers.

Investigating the cause of this general popularity, we may trace it, in the first place, to the simplicity of his language, which makes him intelligible even to the poor and unlearned; whom also he naturally delights by the accuracy with which he describes the scenes they daily behold. Even a peasant may be charmed with his description of a farm-yard on a snowy day . . . and a very short walk in any cultivated part of England is sufficient to recal to our minds numberless passages from his poems, by making us feel the accuracy with which he has described the face of nature, and the instincts and habits of its wild inhabitants. If we ascend through all the gradations of intellectual or fashionable society, we shall still find Cowper admired. The former are pleased with his expressive diction, or beguiled by his playful humour; and many a female mind, whom fashionable gaiety and dissipation have detained from improving study, delights to recal, by a perusal of *The Task,* those recollections of early days and simple pleasures which are associated with the lines of this favourite bard. But it is Cowper's higher praise, that his just and scriptural views of true religion have procured him readers of a class who are in general but little conversant with poetry, and have rendered him preeminently the poet of the religious world. (p. 301)

This writer vindicates his claim to the character of a poet by uniting pleasure with instruction; thus accomplishing what the Sabine bard held to be the legitimate object of poetry. He pleases, or he would not be popular with one class of readers: he instructs, or he would be rejected by another: both agree in their opinion of his merits, and have conferred upon him a rank among the writers of our country, from which he is not likely to be deposed, while a taste for genuine simplicity or for unfeigned piety continues to distinguish the British nation. (p. 302)

Cowper has been deemed an enemy to innocent mirth; and this supposed austerity has been attributed to the influence of his religious opinions. . . . Cowper's own enjoyments were those to which religion both lent a sanction, and imparted a zest; and he has portrayed so forcibly the sensations they excited, that the reader feels convinced that the passage, "the innocent are gay," was prompted by his own sensations, when free from the pressure of constitutional malady. That he had not a particle of the cynic in his disposition, is evinced by the constant inclination he felt to associate every object presented to him with something belonging to man; his joys, his sorrows, his hopes, or his fears. (p. 304)

> *"Essays on Cowper's Poem of the 'Task': No. I,"* in The Christian Observer, *Vol. XVII, No. 5, May, 1818, pp. 300-04.*

THE CHRISTIAN OBSERVER   (essay date 1819)

In a poem so excursive as *The Task,* it is always a difficult matter to manage the transitions from one subject to another; a difficulty for which a poet rarely obtains due credit when he surmounts it, although he will certainly be censured when he fails. For a harsh and abrupt transition forces itself on our notice, while the mind passes imperceptibly from one object to another, where each is properly introduced, and follows the preceding in a natural order; and as it is not immediately sensible of the distance between the first topic and the last, none but an attentive reader will observe the minute and well-adjusted concatenation of the whole, by which the mutual dependency of all its parts is preserved. Cowper was in danger of bewildering himself and his reader in the exuberance of

subjects which a winter's morning walk presented to his view. This, however, he has avoided: and, by a most judicious selection of topics, he has opened this book with a description of a winter's morning, the beauty of which must be appreciated, not less by those who refuse to be pleased except in accordance to critical rules, than by those who are contented to admire, without analyzing the sources of their gratification. (p. 87)

> *"Essays on Cowper's Poem of the 'Task': No. IV,"* in The Christian Observer, *Vol. XVIII, No. 2, February, 1819, pp. 87-91.*

WILLIAM HAZLITT   (essay date 1819)

[One of the most important commentators of the Romantic age, Hazlitt was an English critic and journalist. He is best known for his descriptive criticism in which he stressed that no motives beyond judgment and analysis are necessary on the part of the critic. A critic must start with a strong opinion, Hazlitt asserted, but he must also keep in mind that evaluation is the starting point— not the object—of criticism. The following essay was first published in Hazlitt's Lectures on the English Poets *in 1819.]*

[Cowper] lived at a considerable distance of time after Thomson; and had some advantages over him, particularly in simplicity of style, in a certain precision and minuteness of graphical description, and in a more careful and leisurely choice of such topics only as his genius and peculiar habits of mind prompted him to treat of. *The Task* has fewer blemishes than [Thomson's] *The Seasons;* but it has not the same capital excellence, the 'unbought grace' of poetry, the power of moving and infusing the warmth of the author's mind into that of the reader. If Cowper had a more polished taste, Thomson had, beyond comparison, a more fertile genius, more impulsive force, a more entire forgetfulness of himself in his subject. If in Thomson you are sometimes offended with the slovenliness of the author by profession, determined to get through his task at all events; in Cowper you are no less dissatisfied with the finicalness of the private gentleman, who does not care whether he completes his work or not; and in whatever he does, is evidently more solicitous to please himself than the public. There is an effeminacy about him, which shrinks from and repels common and hearty sympathy. With all his boasted simplicity and love of the country, he seldom launches out into general descriptions of nature: he looks at her over his clipped hedges, and from his well-swept garden-walks; or if he makes a bolder experiment now and then, it is with an air of precaution, as if he were afraid of being caught in a shower of rain, or of not being able, in case of any untoward accident, to make good his retreat home. He shakes hands with nature with a pair of fashionable gloves on, and leads 'his Vashti' forth to public view with a look of consciousness and attention to etiquette, as a fine gentleman hands a lady out to dance a minuet. He is delicate to fastidiousness, and glad to get back, after a romantic adventure with crazy Kate, a party of gypsies or a little child on a common, to the drawing room and the ladies again, to the sofa and the tea-kettle—No, I beg his pardon, not to the singing, well-scoured tea-kettle, but to the polished and loud-hissing urn. . . . He has some of the sickly sensibility and pampered refinements of Pope; but then Pope prided himself in them: whereas, Cowper affects to be all simplicity and plainness. He had neither Thomson's love of the unadorned beauties of nature, nor Pope's exquisite sense of the elegances of art. He was, in fact, a nervous man, afraid of trusting himself to the seductions of the one, and ashamed of putting forward his pretensions to an intimacy with the other: but to be a coward, is not the way to succeed either in poetry, in war, or in love! Still he is a genuine poet, and deserves all his reputation. His worst vices are amiable weaknesses, elegant trifling. Though there is a frequent dryness, timidity, and jejuneness in his manner, he has left a number of pictures of domestic comfort and social refinement, as well as of natural imagery and feeling, which can hardly be forgotten but with the language itself. Such, among others [in *The Task*], are his memorable description of the post coming in, that of the preparations for tea in a winter's evening in the country, of the unexpected fall of snow, of the frosty morning (with the fine satirical transition to the Empress of Russia's palace of ice), and most of all, the winter's walk at noon. Every one of these may be considered as distinct studies, or highly finished cabinet-pieces, arranged without order or coherence. . . . His satire is also excellent. It is pointed and forcible, with the polished manners of the gentleman, and the honest indignation of the virtuous man. His religious poetry, except where it takes a tincture of controversial heat, wants elevation and fire. His Muse had not a seraph's wing. I might refer, in illustration of this opinion, to the laboured anticipation of the Millennium at the end of the sixth book. He could describe a piece of shell-work as well as any modern poet: but he could not describe the New Jerusalem so well as John Bunyan;—nor are his verses on Alexander Selkirk so good as Robinson Crusoe. The one is not so much like a vision, nor is the other so much like the reality.

The first volume of Cowper's poems has, however, been less read than it deserved. The comparison in these poems of the proud and humble believer to the peacock and the pheasant, and the parallel between Voltaire and the poor cottager, are exquisite pieces of eloquence and poetry, particularly the last. (pp. 91-4)

His character of Whitfield, in the poem on *Hope*, is one of his most spirited and striking things. It is written *con amore*. . . . Cowper's verses on his mother's picture, and his lines to Mary, are some of the most pathetic that ever were written. His stanzas on the loss of the Royal George have a masculine strength and feeling beyond what was usual with him. The story of *John Gilpin* has perhaps given as much pleasure to as many people as any thing of the same length that ever was written. (pp. 94-5)

> *William Hazlitt, "On Thomson and Cowper," in his* The Collected Works of William Hazlitt: Lectures on the English Poets and on the Dramatic Literature of the Age of Elizabeth Etc., *Vol. 5, edited by A. R. Waller and Arnold Glover, McClure, Phillips & Co., 1902, pp. 85-104.**

THE NORTH AMERICAN REVIEW   (essay date 1824)

[*The Correspondence of William Cowper, Esq. with several of his most intimate Friends*] will be found full of the same exquisite ease and unrivalled playfulness, which gave [previous collections of his letters] so great a charm. Those to Mrs King especially possess an unequalled fascination, and are of themselves sufficient to ensure a hearty welcome to the book, and to confirm the author's claim to the first place in the catalogue of epistolary writers.

The letters to Mr Newton, sometimes quite as sportive and humorous, are generally more grave, sometimes melancholy, always free and frank, letting us more intimately into the recesses of his feelings, and introducing us to the real state of his soul. These letters are frequent in the deepest and most touching pathos; and more instructive to the student of human

nature and human character than all the others; painful from the disclosures they make of the miserable servitude and tremendous terrors in which his spirit dwelt, harassed by the most appalling doubts, which sometimes drove him to despair, and kept him always covered in a dismal darkness, from the midst of which his pleasantry and wit break forth in perpetual flashes, that startle you from a sense of their incongruity with his situation, while yet they charm you from their nature and truth; delighting you with the loveliness and frankness they exhibit, while you weep that so fair and beautiful a soul should be so enveloped in wretchedness. (p. 466)

There is probably now no man of letters, not even excepting Dr Johnson, whose history and character are more intimately and minutely known than those of Cowper. Johnson has been portrayed to the world in all his dimensions of greatness and littleness, in his own familiar conversation reported by his 'faithful chronicler' Boswell. Cowper has been no less faithfully made known by his own letters, which open to us, with the most obvious and unsuspecting frankness, his opinions, his feelings, his whims, his history, and his whole heart. All his writings indeed speak of their author. He is identified with them. They disclose his features on every page. The poet and the man are one, and are seen to be one. This is one cause of the interest with which his works are read, as if they were a collection of anecdotes respecting the man's feelings and the operation of his mind, a sort of autobiography. This imparts to his verse the charm of truth and personality, which belongs to his letters, and again throws over his letters the fascinating beauty of poetry. They are but different modes of expressing the same soul; and while the language lasts they will be read with similar interest and delight, as twin productions of the same mind. (pp. 466-67)

> *"Cowper's Correspondence," in* The North American Review, *Vol. XIX, No. XLV, October, 1824, pp. 465-67.*

[W.B.O. PEABODY]   (essay date 1834)

As a poet, Cowper was a man of great genius, and . . . enjoyed a popularity almost unexampled. The strain of his writing was familiar even to homeliness. He drew from his own resources only; throwing off all affectation and reserve, he made his reader acquainted with all his sentiments and feelings, and did not disguise his weaknesses and sorrows. There is always something attractive in this personal strain where it does not amount to egotism, and he thus gained many admirers, who never would have been interested by poetry alone. The religious character of his writings was also a recommendation to many, beside those who favored views of that subject similar to his own. There were those who felt, like Burns, that 'bating some scraps of Calvinistic divinity, *The Task* was a noble poem.' There was a wide sympathy, a generous regard for all the human race expressed in it, which gave his readers a respect for his heart. Then, too, his views of nature were drawn from personal observation; all his readers could remember or at any time see those which precisely resembled the subjects of his description. He associated no unusual trains of thought, no feelings of peculiar refinement, with the grand and beautiful of nature, while at the same time the strain of his sentiment was pure, manly and exalted. By addressing himself to the heart universal, and using language such as could be understood by the humble as well as the high, he influenced a wider circle than any poet who went before him; and by inspiring a feeling of intimacy, a kind of domestic confidence in his readers, he made his works 'household words,' and all who shared his feelings became interested in his fame. (pp. 26-7)

[Among Cowper's early poems,] *Expostulation,* which treats the sins of his country in a solemn tone of remonstrance and warning, is an admirable poem; it breathes a spirit resembling that of one of the ancient prophets,—grave, dignified and stern. Its sound is that of a trumpet blown to warn the people,—a sound, which wakes no angry passion, but before which the heart stands still and listens with a shuddering chill of dread. *Conversation* is next in excellence; it is written in a fine strain of humor, not with the 'droll sobriety' of Swift, nor the grave irony of Fielding, but with a wit peculiarly his own, such as makes his letters the best English specimen of that kind of writing, and at times affords a singular contrast with his gloom. (p. 28)

The Task is a work of more pretension than his other writings, we mean in its form: for it has no singleness of subject, and is in fact a collection of poems, in each of which the topic which affords the name serves only as a text, to which the images and sentiments of the writer are attached by the most capricious and accidental associations. One advantage of this freedom is, that it affords an agreeable variety; it excludes nothing above or beneath the moon; it requires no unity of thought, or manner, and permits the poet to pass from the serious to the playful, at his pleasure, without formal apology or preparation. Cowper certainly availed himself of the privilege, and made his readers acquainted with all his feelings, circumstances, and opinions, affording a curious example of a man, reserved to excess in social life, and almost erring on the side of frankness in his writings, if we can possibly call that frankness excessive, which simply tells what all the world was burning to know. . . . The effect of [*The Task*] was greater than can now be imagined: it conducted many to the pure fountains of happiness which are found by those who commune with nature, and many to those sources of religious peace, which keep on flowing when all earthly springs are dry. It tended to make man feel an interest in man, and opened the eyes of thousands to those traditional abuses, which are detested as soon as the attention of the world is directed full upon them: and in a literary point of view, it gladdened the hearts of all who felt an interest in English poetry, by reviving its old glories at the moment when the last beam of inspiration seemed to have faded from the sky.

Those who take their impression of Cowper's translation of Homer from tradition, may perhaps think it an entire failure. A failure the critical world has pronounced it: but it may be well to inquire, whether it would be possible to satisfy the public expectation; and whether any one could possibly have succeeded better? We think it evident that the failure arose from the nature of the undertaking: it was an attempt to convey an idea to English readers of writings which are called inimitable, and therefore untranslatable. . . . We recommend to our readers, who feel an interest in the reputation of Cowper, and lament his failure in this great undertaking, to consider what they may reasonably look for, and having thus given some distinctness to their views, to read the work. This will be doing justice to the translator, and, if we may trust our own experience, they will find their candor amply repaid. At the same time, we do not think Cowper's versification remarkably happy. It was wrought with infinite pains, and corrected and revised, till the music satisfied his ear: but in *The Task,* and in the Translation, he pleases more by expressive and eloquent language, than by any peculiar sweetness in the sound. (pp. 29-30)

Many of Cowper's smaller pieces, in which he followed the suggestions of his own feelings without waiting for others to prescribe his subject, and urge him to write, are among the most beautiful exhibitions of his power. The lines addressed to Mary, his faithful and devoted friend, who made so generous a sacrifice of all other enjoyments to the single one of securing his comfort, of guarding him against the assaults of disease, and sustaining him when the blow had fallen, are one of the most affecting tributes which genius ever paid to virtue. And the lines addressed to his mother, on receiving her picture from a friend, are equally touching and sweet. . . .

[Cowper] claims our notice, as a man remarkable both for his intellectual history and power, the former being extraordinary almost without example, and the latter such as is not often exceeded. (p. 31)

> [*W.B.O. Peabody*], *"Life of Cowper,"* in The North American Review, Vol. XXXVIII, No. LXXXII, January, 1834, pp. 1-32.

ANNE BRONTË   (poem date 1842)

[*Anne, the youngest of the famous Brontë sisters, was a nineteenth-century English poet, novelist, and hymn writer. Her tribute "To Cowper" was written on November 10, 1842.*]

> Sweet are thy strains, Celestial Bard,
>   And oft in childhood's years
> I've read them o'er and o'er again
>   With floods of silent tears.
>
> The language of my inmost heart
>   I traced in every line—
> *My* sins, *my* sorrows, hopes and fears
>   Were there, and only mine.
>
> All for myself the sigh would swell,
>   The tear of anguish start;
> I little knew what wilder woe
>   Had filled the poet's heart.
>
> I did not know the nights of gloom,
>   The days of misery,
> The long long years of dark despair
>   That crushed and tortured thee.
>
> But they are gone, and now from earth
>   Thy gentle soul is passed.
> And in the bosom of its God
>   Has found its Home at last.
>
> It must be so if God is love
>   And answers fervent prayer;
> Then surely thou shalt dwell on high,
>   And I may meet thee there.
>
> Is He the source of every good,
>   The spring of purity?
> Then in thine hours of deepest woe
>   Thy God was still with thee.
>
> How else when every hope was fled
>   Couldst thou so fondly cling
> To holy things and holy men
>   And how so sweetly sing—

Of things that God alone could teach?
   And whence that purity;
That hatred of all sinful ways,
   That gentle charity?

Are these the symptoms of a heart
   Of Heavenly grace bereft,
For ever banished from its God,
   To Satan's fury left?

Yet should thy darkest fears be true,
   If Heaven be so severe
That such a soul as thine is lost,
   O! how shall I appear?

(pp. 84-5)

Anne Brontë, "To Cowper," in her The Poems of
Anne Brontë: A New Text and Commentary, *edited
by Edward Chitham, The Macmillan Press Ltd., 1979,
pp. 84-5.*

REV. GEORGE GILFILLAN (essay date 1854)

[Cowper's] poetry proceeded on the three postulates, "Nature around me, God above me, my own Soul within me;" and for the time all things else were forgotten. He stood up to illustrate the beauties of that nature which he loved with a passion, to proclaim the supremacy of the gospel of that God whom he adored, although it was with trembling and without hope, and to relieve the burden of personal conviction and prophetic impulse which lay on his own soul. Hence the fresh forcefulness of his poetry. Here was a man venturing to look at nature with his own eyes; dashing away the coloured spectacles of the past; solicitous for no words but the words of truth and soberness, and for no effects but such as simplicity and natural power were able to produce, and had before, although at rare intervals, produced, in poetry. His sayings are often distinguished by a daring commonplace. He utters what might seem to others mere truisms, with such a blunt directness, with such an *empressement* of manner, that they assume the air of, and are in a degree originalities. How differently are the words "Good morning!" pronounced by men of different temperaments and dispositions; how much character may be discovered in the very mode in which they are uttered; and how much more they tell when proceeding from a deep chest, and spoken in fresh, cheerful, ringing tones! And it is precisely the same with what are called commonplaces. In the mouth of a commonplace man they are trite and dull to the last degree; in the mouth of a Cowper they are deeply interesting. . . . This simplicity is by no means a bare and bald, still less a weak or infantine simplicity. There are babyisms and puerilities in Wordsworth, and, worst of all, they are perpetrated consciously, and on system; but there are none in Cowper. Homeric simplicity is in him always combined with Homeric strength, and nowhere does he discover his masterdom more than in those little copies of verses, such as his mortuary lines, some of his Olney hymns, his fables, and smaller lyrics. In these, his genius may be said merely to *stir*, not to move; and yet what power these stirrings discover, and what profound effects they produce! In *occasional* poetry, Cowper has no superior; and only, we think, in this country, two rivals, namely, Burns and Campbell, who both knew as well as he what poems of small compass can effect, if written with vehement sincerity, bold simplicity, and thorough unity of feeling. **"Boadicea,"** indeed, may be considered the germ of all the fine battle odes of Campbell. It comes out as "from a mould." Every word in it is simple as water, and the whole

is strong as the waterfall. It is not a composition, but a gush. The **"Lines attributed to Alexander Selkirk"** are equally fine, in a different style. We find the same simplicity in all his natural descriptions. He seldom seeks to picture what he has never beheld; he has never seen hills, nor expects to see them, poor fellow! "unless he sees them in Heaven." (pp. viii-ix)

Cowper's poetry is distinguished by its variety, and the combination of powers it exhibits. We find in it strong sense, united with the true inspiration of the poet, as well as with wit, humour, and sharp stern sarcasm. Next to Shakspeare and Burns, Cowper is perhaps the most thoroughly sensible of all our poets. Except when he is trifling on purpose, there is scarcely a line of nonsense to be found in all his writings. . . . His sense is not so exquisitely sharpened on its edges as Pope's, but is much broader and stronger; and if its points are not so polished and glittering, its momentum and weight are far stronger. But besides this, he has no small degree of the "vision and the faculty divine." He has the insight, the eyesight, the enthusiasm, the swift combinations, and the abandonment of the true bard. This mood he, however, seldom if at all reaches, except under the influence of righteous indignation. He is never fully a poet till he is stung into being one. (pp. x-xi)

Fresh, fearless, and strong, are always the thought and the imagery of Cowper. You can hardly open his poetic works without encountering one of those marked and memorable sentences, which look up from the page like eyes, and which you know have long since become proverbs. Such sentences strike you the more, because they are not cast into the artificial form of aphorism or antithesis. They are just bold, blunt truths, uttered in words as few as forcible. (p. xiv)

Cowper's principal defect is, perhaps, that of music. He has, indeed, written many melodious verses, but his verse, on the whole, wants that springy elastic motion, those finely-managed sinkings and swellings of sound, which distinguish the musical masters of the lyre. . . . His model for blank verse is Milton; but though he keenly appreciated, he has failed to reproduce the merits of Milton's verse, its artistic use of accents, and selection of words; its adaptation of sound to sense, and those great choral harmonies which surge on, like indivisible waves of music. He succeeds best in the regular "ding dong" of the ballad and the smaller lyric.

We may also charge Cowper's poetry with want of artistic finish and epic completeness. He is not so much an artist as he is a prophet. He has so much to say, that he is comparatively indifferent as to how he says it. A spirit from the dead needs not to wear superb draperies, or to be anxious about the arrangement of his shadowy attire. Cowper has a message from the Eternal to utter, and if he does not always remember to deliver it in accordance with the rules of art and the requirements of regular composition, let him be forgiven on account of the intensity of his purpose. He did indulge sometimes in careless combinations of language—in rugged rhythm—in blunt and coarse images; and there is often an impatience in his mode of hurrying from theme to theme, instead of the grand calm which should distinguish the series of events or thoughts characterizing a complete poem. But he aspired to be a didactic lyrist; and this class of poets are, more than any other, entitled to certain immunities, especially if their lyre be crossed at times by the fiery fingers of a Supernal Hand, and if their melodies rise to the blended influences of genius and of God. (pp. xx-xxi)

His minor poems are remarkable for their number, their shortness, their simplicity, and the fine edge which he often unexpectedly, and by a single word, gives to what seemed an obvious thought. Like his own Vinny Bourne, he seems to have the key into the soul of beasts and insects, and to be able, like that Carpathian shepherd in Johnson's splendid fable of "The Vultures," to understand the language of the birds of prey. His **"Castaway,"** and many more, are just the wringings of his miserable heart. Best of all are his **"John Gilpin"** and his **"Lines on the Receipt of a Mother's Picture"**—two productions, the one of which has excited more laughter, and the other started more tears, than, perhaps, any two poems of the same compass in the world, and which alone might have established his name as one of the truest and greatest of British Poets. (p. xxiii)

> *Rev. George Gilfillan, "The Poetry of William Cowper," in* The Poetical Works of William Cowper, Vol. II *by William Cowper, edited by Rev. George Gilfillan, James Nichol, 1854, pp. v-xxiii.*

WALTER BAGEHOT   (essay date 1855)

[*Bagehot was a prominent nineteenth-century English economist, journalist, and critic. In this essay, originally published in the* National Review *in 1855, he agrees with William Hazlitt's estimation (1819) that to Cowper "nature is simply a background" for meditation.*]

There is no writer more exclusively English [than William Cowper]. There is no one—or hardly one perhaps—whose excellences are more natural to our soil, and seem so little able to bear transplantation. (p. 229)

As a poet, Cowper belongs, though with some differences, to the school of Pope. (p. 256)

What Pope is to our fashionable and town life, Cowper is to our domestic and rural life. This is perhaps the reason why he is so national. It has been said no foreigner can live in the country. We doubt whether any people, who felt their whole heart, and entire exclusive breath of their existence to be concentrated in a great capital, could or would appreciate such intensely provincial pictures as are the entire scope of Cowper's delineation. A good many imaginative persons are really plagued with him. Everything is so comfortable; the tea-urn hisses so plainly, the toast is so warm, the breakfast so neat, the food so edible, that one turns away, in excitable moments, a little angrily from anything so quiet, tame, and sober. (pp. 258-59)

It is these in-door scenes, this common world, this gentle round of 'calm delights,' the trivial course of slowly-moving pleasures, the petty detail of quiet relaxation, that Cowper excels in. The post-boy, the winter's evening, the newspaper, the knitting needles, the stockings, the waggon—these are his subjects. His sure popularity arises from his having held up to the English people exact delineations of what they really prefer. Perhaps one person in four hundred understands Wordsworth, about one in eight thousand may appreciate Shelley, but there is no expressing the small fraction who do not love dulness, who do not enter into

> Homeborn happiness,
> Fireside enjoyments, intimate delights,
> And all the comforts that the lowly roof
> Of undisturbed retirement, and the hours
> Of long uninterrupted evening know.
>
> (pp. 259-60)

The subject of these pictures, in point of interest, may be what we choose to think it, but there is no denying great merit to the execution. The sketches have the highest merit—suitableness of style. It would be absurd to describe a postboy as sonneteers their mistress—to cover his plain face with fine similes—to put forward the 'brow of Egypt'—to stick metaphors upon him, as the Americans upon General Washington. The only merit such topics have room for is an easy and dextrous plainness—a sober suit of well-fitting expressions—a free, working, flowing, picturesque garb of words adapted to the solid conduct of a sound and serious world, and this merit Cowper's style has. On the other hand, it entirely wants the higher and rarer excellences of poetical expression. There is none of the choice art which has studiously selected the words of one class of great poets, or the rare, untaught, unteachable felicity which has vivified those of others. No one, in reading Cowper, stops as if to draw his breath more deeply over expressions which do not so much express or clothe poetical expressions, as seem to intertwine, coalesce, and be blended with the very essence of poetry itself.

Of course a poet could not deal in any measure with such subjects as Cowper dealt with, and not become inevitably, to a certain extent, satirical. The ludicrous is in some sort the imagination of common life. . . . It is in this contrast that humour and satire have their place—pointing out the intense unspeakable incongruity of the groups and juxtapositions of our world. To all of these which fell under his own eye, Cowper was alive. A gentle sense of propriety and consistency in daily things was evidently characteristic of him; and if he fail of the highest success in this species of art, it is not from an imperfect treatment of the scenes and conceptions which he touched, but from the fact that the follies with which he deals are not the greatest follies—that there are deeper absurdities in human life than **'John Gilpin'** touches upon—that the superficial occurrences of ludicrous life do not exhaust or even deeply test the mirthful resources of our minds and fortunes.

As a scold, we think Cowper failed. He had a great idea of the use of railing, and there are many pages of laudable invective against various vices which we feel no call whatever to defend. But a great vituperator had need to be a great hater; and of any real rage, any such gall and bitterness as great and irritable satirists have in other ages let loose upon men, of any thorough, brooding, burning, abiding, detestation, he was as incapable as a tame hare. His vituperation reads like the mild man's whose wife ate up his dinner, 'Really, Sir, I feel quite *angry!*' Nor has his language any of the sharp intrusive acumen which divides in sunder both soul and spirit, that is necessary for fierce and unforgettable reviling.

Some people may be surprised, notwithstanding our lengthy explanation, at hearing Cowper treated as of the school of Pope. It has been customary, at least with some critics, to speak of him as one of those who recoiled from the artificiality of that great writer, and at least commenced a return to a simple delineation of outward nature. And of course there is considerable truth in this idea. The poetry (if such it is) of Pope would be just as true if all the trees were yellow and all the grass flesh-colour. He did not care for 'snowy scalps,' or 'rolling streams,' or 'icy halls,' or 'precipice's gloom.' Nor for that matter did Cowper either. He, as Hazlitt most justly said [see excerpt above, 1818], was as much afraid of a shower of rain as any man that ever lived. At the same time, the fashionable life described by Pope has no reference whatever to the beauties of the material universe. . . . But the rural life of Cowper's poetry has a constant and necessary reference to the country, is identified with its features, cannot be separated from it even in fancy. Green fields and a slow river seem all the material of beauty Cowper had given him. But what is more to the purpose, his attention was well concentrated upon them. As he himself said, he did not go more than thirteen miles from home for twenty years, and very seldom as far. He was, therefore, well able to find out all that was charming in Olney and its neighbourhood, and as it presented nothing which is not to be found in any of the fresh country parts of England, what he has left us is really a delicate description and appreciative delineation of the simple essential English country.

However, it is to be remarked that the description of nature in Cowper differs altogether from the peculiar delineation of the same subject, which has been so influential in more recent times, and which bears, after its greatest master, the name Wordsworthian. To Cowper nature is simply a background, a beautiful background no doubt, but still essentially a *locus in quo*—a space in which the work and mirth of life pass and are performed. . . . After a very few lines [of nature description] he returns within doors to the occupation of man and woman—to human tasks and human pastimes. To Wordsworth, on the contrary, nature is a religion. . . . Of this haunting, supernatural, mystical view of nature Cowper never heard. Like the strong old lady who said, '*She* was born before nerves were invented,' he may be said to have lived before the awakening of the detective sensibility which reveals this deep and obscure doctrine.

In another point of view, also, Cowper is curiously contrasted with Wordsworth, as a delineator of nature. The delineation of Cowper is a simple delineation. He makes a sketch of the object before him, and there he leaves it. Wordsworth, on the contrary, is not satisfied unless he describes not only the bare inanimate outward object which others see, but likewise the reflected high-wrought feelings which that object excites in a brooding self-conscious mind. His subject was not so much nature, as nature reflected by Wordsworth. Years of deep musing and long introspection had made him familiar with every shade and shadow in the many-coloured impression which the universe makes on meditative genius and observant sensibility. Now these feelings Cowper did not describe, because, to all appearance, he did not perceive them. He had a great pleasure in watching the common changes and common aspects of outward things, but he was not invincibly prone to brood and pore over their reflex effects upon his own mind.

> A primrose by the river's brim,
> A yellow primrose was to him,
> And it was nothing more.

According to the account which Cowper at first gave of his literary occupations, his entire design was to communicate the religious views to which he was then a convert. He fancied that the vehicle of verse might bring many to listen to truths which they would be disinclined to have stated to them in simple prose. And however tedious the recurrence of these theological tenets may be to the common reader, it is certain that a considerable portion of Cowper's peculiar popularity may be traced to their expression. He is the one poet of a class which has no poets. In that once large and still considerable portion of the English world, which regards the exercise of the fancy and the imagination as dangerous—snares, as they speak—distracting the soul from an intense consideration of abstract doctrine, Cowper's strenuous inculcation of those doctrines has obtained for him a certain toleration. Of course all verse is perilous. The use of single words is harmless, but the employment of two, in such a manner as to form a rhyme—the

regularities of interval and studied recurrence of the same sound, evince an attention to time, and a partiality to things of sense. Most poets must be prohibited; the exercise of the fancy requires watching. But Cowper is a ticket-of-leave man. He has the chaplain's certificate. He has expressed himself 'with the utmost propriety.' The other imaginative criminals must be left to the fates, but he may be admitted to the sacred drawing-room, though with constant care and scrupulous *surveillance*. Perhaps, however, taken in connection with his diseased and peculiar melancholy, these tenets really add to the artistic effect of Cowper's writings. The free discussion of daily matters, the delicate delineation of domestic detail, the passing narrative of fugitive occurrences, would seem light and transitory, if it were not broken by the interruption of a terrible earnestness, and relieved by the dark background of deep and foreboding sadness. It is scarcely artistic to describe 'the painted veil which those who live call life,' and leave wholly out of view and undescribed 'the chasm sightless and drear,' which lies always beneath and around it.

It is of the '**Task**' more than of Cowper's earlier volume of poems that a critic of his poetry must more peculiarly be understood to speak. All the best qualities of his genius are there concentrated, and the alloy is less than elsewhere. . . . [Cowper's poetry] always has a thread of argument on which he is hanging his illustrations, and yet he has not the exclusive interest or the undeviating energetic downrightness of mind which would ensure his going through it without idling or turning aside; consequently the thoughts which the rhyme suggests are constantly breaking in upon the main matter, destroying the emphatic unity which is essential to rhythmical delineation. His blank verse of course is exempt from this defect, and there is moreover something in the nature of the metre which fits it for the expression of studious and quiet reflection. (pp. 260-66)

[In Cowper's letters, detail] was his forte and quietness his element. Accordingly, his delicate humour plays over perhaps a million letters, mostly descriptive of events which no one else would have thought worth narrating, and yet which, when narrated, show to us, and will show to persons to whom it will be yet more strange, the familiar, placid, easy, ruminating, provincial existence of our great grandfathers. Slow, Olney might be,—indescribable, it certainly was not. We seem to have lived there ourselves. (pp. 270-71)

His genius was domestic, and tranquil, and calm. He had no sympathy, or little sympathy, even with the common, half-asleep activities of a refined society; an evening party was too much for him; a day's hunt a preposterous excitement. It is absurd to expect a man like this to sympathise [in his translation of Homer] with the stern stimulants of a barbaric age, with a race who fought because they liked it, and a poet who sang of fighting because he thought their taste judicious. As if to make matters worse, Cowper selected a metre in which it would be scarcely possible for any one, however gifted, to translate Homer. The two kinds of metrical composition most essentially opposed to one another are ballad poetry and blank verse. The very nature of the former requires a marked pause and striking rhythm. Every line should have a distinct end and a clear beginning. . . . And this is the tone of Homer. The grandest of human tongues marches forward with its proudest steps: the clearest tones call forward—the most marked of metres carries him on:—

> Like a reappearing star,
> Like a glory from afar—

he ever heads, and will head, 'the flock of war.' Now blank verse is the exact opposite of all this. . . . And if the true object of translation were to save the labour and dictionaries of construing schoolboys, there is no question but [Cowper's] slavish adherence to the original would be the most likely to gain the approbation of those diminutive but sure judges. But if the object is to convey an idea of the general tone, scope, and artistic effect of the original, the mechanical copying of the details is as likely to end in a good result as a careful cast from a dead man's features to produce a living and speaking being. On the whole, therefore, the condemnation remains, that Homer is not dull, and Cowper is. (pp. 271-73)

Walter Bagehot, "William Cowper," in his Literary Studies, *Vol. 1, E. P. Dutton & Co., 1911, pp. 227-74.*

[ALFRED AUSTIN]   (essay date 1872)

[*In one of the first detailed studies of* The Task, *Austin considers Cowper primarily a satirist, "whatever he himself may have thought." Austin criticizes Cowper's limited perspective and the "tiresome" and "garrulous" quality of his blank verse.*]

It is quite startling, after being told that Cowper was essentially the lover of nature, the man who brought back a misled people to the due worship of the beautiful, to turn to the passages in which he attempts to render in language the shifting and numerous aspects of the earth, the sky, the seasons. He certainly claims to be all that certain critics have declared him to be; and perhaps his own assertions have misled them. (p. 462)

But when we follow Cowper into the country, into his rural delights, what does he offer us? Are we to be contented with such bald trite stuff as the following?

> I saw the woods and fields at close of day:
> A variegated show; the meadows green,
> Though faded; and the lands where lately waved
> The golden harvest, of a mellow brown,
> Upturned so lately by the forceful share.
> I saw far off the weedy fallows smile
> With verdure not unprofitable, grazed
> By flocks, fast feeding, and selecting each
> His favourite herb; while all the leafless groves
> That skirt the horizon wore a sable hue,
> Scarce noticed in the kindred dusk of eve.
> To-morrow brings a change, a total change!

Surely this is terrible. This is what Tom, Dick, and Harry see; and pretty much what Tom, Dick, and Harry say, or perhaps would not think it worth while to say. And this is the poetry which was an improvement upon Pope! (p. 463)

We shall probably seem to have been exclusively occupied with the depreciation of Cowper, though we certainly sat down to extol him; and we have no wish here to reverse the celebrated part once played by Balaam. We are distinctly of opinion that Cowper is rather underrated than overrated in these days, at least in the sphere of letters. (p. 464)

For he was a satirist before all things, whatever he himself may have thought. No doubt he was an enthusiast; but satire is only the seamy side of enthusiasm. The author of 'Table-Talk,' 'Truth,' 'Expostulation,' and 'The Progress of Error,' is the same writer as the author of 'The Task,' but which his literary genius finding a more natural outlet in the former than in the latter. His range of observation in either case is, unfortunately, limited; but he displays a real and thorough-going

zest when he is exposing the vices with which he is but imperfectly acquainted, that is by no means so perceptible in his raptures concerning external nature which he certainly should have known so intimately. How admirable is his description of the "ancient prude," in 'Truth'!

> Conscious of age, she recollects her youth,
> And tells, not always with an eye to truth,
> Who spanned her waist, and who, where'er he came,
> Scrawled upon glass Miss Bridget's lovely name,
> Who stole her slipper, filled it with Tokay,
> And drank the little bumper every day;
> Laughs at the reputations she has torn,
> And holds them dangling at arm's length in scorn.

It is only lack of fit subjects that prevents Cowper's satiric muse from putting forth its full force. He knew of the follies and vices of mankind only in books and by imagination, and the consequence is that his satire is, as a rule, too general and sweeping. Yet it is full of power. . . . How exquisitely too does Cowper tread upon that dainty borderland which lies between invective and eulogium, in which poetry seeks for its choicest contrasts. After an indignant burst against "the demigod Voltaire," how dexterously he shifts the note in the following touching passage!

> You cottager, who weaves at her own door
> Pillow and bobbins, all her little store;
> Content though mean, and cheerful if not gay,
> Shuffling her threads about the livelong day,
> Just earns a scanty pittance, and at night
> Lies down secure, her heart and pocket light;
> She, for her humble sphere by nature fit,
> Has little understanding and no wit;
> Just knows, and knows no more, her Bible true—
> A truth the brilliant Frenchman never knew;
> And in that charter reads, with sparkling eyes,
> Her title to a treasure in the skies.

Nor is it only in pathetic moments that Cowper proves himself to be at once the satirist and the poet. Seldom, it is true, but occasionally, he waxes inflamed by really fancy-bred indignation, and pours out his soul in such lines as these:

> 'Twas thus, till Luxury seduced the mind
> To joys less innocent, as less refined.
> Then Genius danced a bacchanal; he crowned
> The brimming goblet, seized the thyrsus, bound
> His brows with ivy, rushed into the field
> Of wild imagination, and there reeled
> The victim of his own lascivious fires,
> And, dizzy with delight, profaned the sacred wires.

That Cowper's talents were mainly of the satiric order is to be seen, however, with conclusiveness in 'The Task.' Doubtless he intended, from the outset, to be more or less didactic; and such was the intention too of Lady Austen, who suggested to him the subject. But the original design was in the main descriptive, and for a certain time Cowper adhered to the idea with which he started. He was to be descriptive and playful; and description and playfulness chiefly mark Book I., which is occupied with 'The Sofa.' (pp. 465-67)

Still, in this first book he on the whole sticks to his design. He amply atones, however, for his self-denial, in the second, which is called 'The Time-Piece'—why, it would be difficult to say. Here he bursts forth a satirist full-fledged. (p. 467)

The third book opens with a confession that he has been sadly wandering from his theme. Could anything more be urged to prove our point? He intended to sing **'The Sofa,' 'The Garden,'** and **'The Time-Piece;'** but he has, he says, got entangled in thickets and brakes, and has lost his "devious course uncertain." In other words, he purported to be a pleasant writer and trifler in verse, and he finds to his horror that he has become a satirist, a thunderer against Mammon. . . . (p. 469)

The fourth book of **'The Task'** is the best known and most popular of all, for it portrays the delights of a winter evening, and Cowper here sticks to his theme with more fidelity than usual. Yet even here he has a fling at public-houses, at fashionable entertainments, at the loss of country manners, at the transformation of the fair shepherdess of old romance into a person adorned with lappets, and indebted to the smart wig-weaver, with elbows ruffled, and French heels, and causing the spectator to wonder that she has not a footboy behind her—at the neglect displayed by magistrates and the mischief wrought by the militia! He is just as incapable out-of-doors as when housed in a cosy drawing-room of keeping his eye upon external objects. When he takes his winter morning walk, he manages for a time to be interested by the foddering of cattle, by woodmen and their dogs, by the sun and the icicles; but these suggest to him the Empress of Russia's palace of ice, and then he flies off at a tangent to discuss the tastes of monarchs. . . .

Let him make what resolutions he will, or select for himself what themes he may, he inevitably falls back upon invective. That is why we are so strongly disposed to regret that his exclusively country life, his secure and placid existence among charming and cultivated female companions, was not broken by some less melancholy and more inspiring vicissitudes than fits of madness, and religious hypochondria. It is to be feared that we have thus lost a really great satirist. For Cowper had all the natural gifts of the rhyming satirists; all that he wanted was, first, experience, and then prompting opportunity. We believe that, had he been left to his own devices, and had he had to fight out his own path in life, he would have equalled any of our English satirists in form and have surpassed them all in earnestness. But in that case he would not have chosen blank verse for his medium. He would have stuck to the rhymed heroics, which he managed with considerable skill in his earlier works—to

> the line that ploughs its stately course,
> Like a proud swan conquering the stream by force.
>
> (p. 470)

But Cowper has the defects of his virtues: he writes blank verse so easily and so well, that he piles on his words without measure. In the drama, the author feels that each particular character has something to say, and he is limited by that something; but when the author is himself the speaker he is bound neither by the necessity of the situation nor by any inherent difficulty in his metre from being intolerably garrulous. Hence most writers of blank verse are tiresome, and Cowper is ineffably so. Rhymed heroics would have necessarily curtailed his lengthy disquisitions, and he would often have had to compress into two lines what in **'The Task'** he spreads over a dozen. Satire especially in blank verse lacks point, and satire without point is nothing. (p. 471)

The fine **'Ode on Boadicea,'** and the **'Lines on the Loss of the Royal George,'** are perhaps Cowper's best claims to be regarded as a poet; but his love verses to his cousin, whom he

was not allowed to marry, lead us almost conclusively to think that for poetry—poetic poetry—he had little inclination or genius. Could he but have lived in the world, and retained his moral earnestness, he would doubtless have been our English Juvenal. (p. 472)

[*Alfred Austin*], *"Cowper As a Satirist," in* Temple Bar, *Vol. XXXVI, November, 1872, pp. 457-72.*

STOPFORD A. BROOKE   (lecture date 1872)

[*Brooke was an Irish minister and critic. In this lecture, delivered in 1872, he commends the "wide range" and "personal passion" in Cowper's poetry and remarks that Cowper was the first English poet to attempt to "cover the whole range of Man, to think of Man as one people."*]

[With Cowper, for the first time in England] an attempt is made in poetry to cover the whole range of Man, to think of Man as one people; to spread poetical interest over all who wear a human face. And it was done, as is commonly the case when the impulse is received from an idea which has not yet taken any political form, quite unconsciously. Cowper talked as naturally of *all men* as Pope did of one of two classes of men: he asks how he and any man that lives could be strangers to each other; he conceives of his poetic work as for the service of mankind; and such an aim was now for the first time possible. A universal idea of Man had passed from political philosophers to the people, and the undefined emotion it stirred in the people was felt and thrown into form by the poets.

But the revolutionary idea of the unity of Man was in Cowper's mind grounded on a theological one, on God as the common Maker of Man. He speaks of "the link of brotherhood, by which one common Maker bound him to the Kind." And his work for men was to make them out of sin and death into life with God, for they are

> Bone of my bone, and kindred souls to mind.

To this religious element of a universal brotherhood in God is to be traced the large range of his human view. He looked abroad and saw all men related to God, it mattered not of what nation, caste, or colour. As such they had equal rights and equal duties in a spiritual country of which all were citizens; for, as he writes, the limiting power of his doctrinal theology departs and the individual theology of the poet who sympathises with all men, takes the upper hand. East, west, north, and south, his interest flew. In his satires he touches, not with savage bitterness, but with a gentleness which healed while it lashed, on nearly every phase of human life in England; on the universities and the schools, the hospitals and the prisons; on cities and villages; on the statesman, the clergyman, the lawyer, the soldier, the man of science, the critic, the writer for the press, the pleasure-seeker, the hunter, the musician, the epicure, the card-player, the ploughman; the cottager, and fifty others. Their good side, their follies, their vices, are sketched and ridiculed and praised. The range of his interest was as wide as human life, and as he sketched, he saw as the one ideal and the one remedy for all—the Cross of Christ. Whatever we may think of his religion or the manner of it, there is no doubt but that it indefinitely extended his poetic sympathy, and that in this extension of sympathy we find ourselves in another world altogether than that of Dryden, Pope, or Gray. It is no longer intellectual interest in man, or sentimental interest; it is vivid, personal, passionate.

It went beyond classes of men, it was an interest in his nation; but he derived his patriotism and drew the passion with which he informed it from the connection of his country with God. It was God who was the King of England, and was educating the nation; and this conception bound all citizens together into mutual love of one another and the whole. On this ground he made his impassioned appeal to his countrymen to throw off their vices and follies and to be worthy of their high vocation; would they not, he asked, be true to Him who had wrought so gloriously among them? This is the note of many a passage in the *Task,* of the whole of his poem of *Expostulation;* and it is not a note of merely lyric interest in England's glory on the seas, like Thomson's *Rule Britannia,* nor one of intellectual passion . . .—it is a note that thrills with emotion for England as God's nation, and having a work to do for Man. We already breathe the air of the patriotic poetry of Wordsworth.

Nor does this interest in Man remain fixed in England. God had children, bone of the poet's bone, and flesh of his flesh, in other lands. From the banks of the Ouse his heart carried him to Greenland, to Italy, to France, to the islands of the Pacific, to the shores of Africa and South America. In these distant lands were his brothers, and he transferred the inalienable rights of Man from the free and civilised European to the slave and the savage; there was no man, he thought, who ought not to feel himself allied to all the race.

The noblest right of Man was liberty, and this in Cowper's thought was the gift of God to Man. Whoever took it away did the most accursed of all sins. His poetical theology saw God as the deliverer and avenger of the oppressed. He traces the ruin of Spain to the wrath of God for its crimes against its subject races. He places the cause of the slave in the hands of God.

In Cowper the poetry of human wrong begins, that long, long cry against oppression and evil done by man to man, against the political, moral, or priestly tyrant, which rings louder and louder through Burns, Coleridge, Wordsworth, Shelley, and Byron, ever impassioned, ever longing, ever prophetic—never, in the darkest time, quite despairing.

The wide range given to it by Cowper, the personal passion in it, the glance it took forward to a brighter time, its theological element of God as the source of freedom and the avenger of tyranny, are all elements distinctly new to our poetry, above all new in their tremendous power of awakening and maintaining the humane emotions which must create a human poetry. (pp. 42-4)

In connection with the poetry of Man as seen from the personal point of view, no English poet has ever excelled Cowper when he writes of the daily human affections. In him, one might almost say, began in English poetry that direct, close, impassioned representation, in the least sensational manner, of such common relations as motherhood, filial piety, friendship, married love, the relation of man to animals—and in him they are made religious. There is nothing more pathetic yet more simple in English poetry than the lines on his mother's picture, or the sonnet and lines addressed to Mary Unwin. In the lines on the picture and in the sonnet, the natural piety of the relations of a son to a mother, and of a friend to a friend, are bound up with religion; and the infinite pitifulness of both are somewhat relieved by hope in God. In the later lines to Mrs. Unwin, when she was nearly as insane as he, there is no religion. It is "passionless despair, but the despair which loves to the last." (p. 48)

He was partly saved from [the morbidness of religious gloom] by his humour—humour which is the guard of intellectual and moral sanity. But however saved, Cowper's treatment of all moral subjects is distinguished from his treatment of his personal religion by an essential manliness of tone. Nowhere in our poetry is there heard a finer scorn of vanity, ambition, meanness; nowhere is truth more nobly exalted, or justice more sternly glorified. And his tenderness for the weak and poor and wronged is as sweet as his hatred of oppression is strong. We breathe throughout an invigorating air. (p. 49)

Some of his finest work was done when his soul trembled with the horror of coming hell, and it is possible here and there, in the midst of poems which breathe peace and simple gladness, to catch far off the note of that terror and pity which gives to the sequestered life of this lawyer's clerk the interest and power of tragedy. No pity is more touching than that he bestows on suffering, none more childlike and pathetic than that which he lavishes upon himself. He speaks of his fate as if it belonged to another man, caressing, as the case is with many of the insane, his own misery with the gentlest words . . . : ·

> I was a stricken deer that left the herd
> Long since; with many an arrow deep infixed
> My panting side was charged, when I withdrew
> To seek a tranquil death in distant shades.
> There was I found by one who had Himself
> Been hurt by the archers. In His side he bore,
> And in His hands and feet, the cruel scars.

What an infinite, long-continued self-compassion in the words! The note heard in them is low and sorrowful, and does not rise into passion; but the whole passage is exalted not into, but towards the region of great poetry, partly by its pictorial quality, but chiefly by the sudden yet natural introduction of Christ coming through the woods to heal him, and the association of his fate with that of the Saviour. In the *Lines on receipt of my Mother's Picture,* where he uses one of his favourite sea similes, the same self-pity takes to itself the element of passion, but it does not touch its deepest depth, for a shadow of hope remains.

> But me scarce hoping to attain that rest,
> Always from port withheld, always distressed—
> Me howling blasts drive devious, tempest tost,
> Sails ripped, seams opening wide, and compass lost,
> And day by day some current's thwarting force
> Sets me more distant from a prosperous course.
> Yet oh! the thought that thou art safe—and he!
> That thought is joy, arrive what may to me.

One sees that most of the intensity in that arises from the conviction that there is an irreversible fate against him. Continually, by hard striving, bringing himself near to port, continually driven away by a superior power; contending, weak as he was, with destiny till the last, yet knowing the contest to be in vain; he has unconsciously put himself into the position in which Greek Tragedy placed its heroes, but in the midst of an unheroic time and scenery, and with a heart not fitted to wage the battle of Oedipus; so that, though the mental position is tragic, the poetry wants the sublimity and the force of tragedy. Still there is profound passion in it, working especially in the complete transference of himself into the soul of the tormented ship, and in the splendid use of the word "devious" in the third line. Unpretentious as the verses are, the stamp of passion is far deeper set upon them than in similar lines in Byron, where even his colossal power could not overcome the unreality of his self-pity.

But it is in the last poem which Cowper wrote, in the midst of the three last years of his madness and his life, that this self-compassion does reach the centre of intensity. In the *Castaway,* a poem in its sphere of the very highest class, where simplicity of pitiful narration is set in melodious verse by an art which had now become Nature—Cowper mingles up his fate with that of the drowned sailor of Anson's ship. He cannot help beginning in the first person; realising the terrible night and the swift ruin as his own. He makes himself the sailor:—

> Obscurest night involved the sky,
>   The Atlantic billows roared,
> When such a destined wretch as I,
>   Washed headlong from on board,
> Of friends, of hope, of all bereft,
> His floating home for ever left.

He changes then to description in the third person, but we feel as we read of the long struggle of the swimmer, "supported by despair of life;" as he describes the pitiless blast which forbade his friends to rescue him, the useless succour of the cask and cord which served only to prolong his agony, the bitter thought that they were right to leave him—that we are looking into the heart of Cowper's life. With what exquisite simplicity of words, and yet with what a grasp of misery, is the next verse conceived—

> He long survives, who lives an hour
>   In Ocean, self-upheld;
> And so long he, with unspent power,
>   His destiny repelled;
> And ever as the minutes flew
> Entreated help, or cried Adieu.

We are now relieved by a change from the doom of the sailor to the grief of Anson for his fate, and then, in a sudden rushing of misery, in which the impassioned imagination rises almost into a wild cry, and the verse in the last two lines becomes abrupt, and the voice choked, he again dashes himself into the fate of the sailor, and both perish in the seas:—

> No voice divine the storm allayed,
>   No light propitious shone,
> When, snatched from all effectual aid,
>   We perished, each alone;
> But I beneath a rougher sea,
> And whelmed in deeper gulfs than he.

                                                  (pp. 50-2)

Stopford A. Brooke, "Cowper," in his Theology in the English Poets: Cowper, Coleridge, Wordsworth & Burns, *E. P. Dutton & Co., 1910, pp. 40-54.*

DAVID SIME (essay date 1880)

If originality be one of the main tests of genius, then Cowper is perhaps one of the most undoubted geniuses of the whole of the last century. (p. 365)

Nothing is more striking than the difference between Cowper's satire and that of the period—it is a difference altogether of kind; and nothing could indicate more clearly, not only the originality of Cowper's poetry, but the advent of a noble inspiration. The satire of the period was at best but little better than polished and incisive slander; its personal element was its keenest, but it was also its only sting. There was neither mercy nor pity blended with its blame. It aroused no true remorse, it excited no genuine joy, no hearty laughter. Above all, it re-

claimed no heart, it swept away no vice, and it led the way to no reform whatever. Cowper's satire, on the other hand, is as impersonal and as unselfish as his love of virtue, for it is based on a high faith in humanity. It is as impersonal as it is constructive, and altogether arose from his fine nature being as sensitive to the absence as to the presence of high influences.

The striking originality of his poetry was from the very outset manifested not only in his pronounced religious tone, but even in the very subject of his verse.

It was something startlingly new to find a poet deliberately choosing such bold commonplace themes as Table Talk, Conversation, Retirement, and such like. If it indicated nothing else, however, it indicated the possibility of an altogether new departure from the beaten and hackneyed path of poetry. This in itself was no small matter. But the world was not prepared for such originality. It rejected the small book of verse, and accepted the verdict of the dullest of its many obscure scribes, "that it was no better than a dull sermon." So it has ever been, for it needs a genius to detect a genius. This first reception was all the more extraordinary, because his very next work took the whole world by storm. All at once, the world was enchanted, and discovered that there was a true poet in the land, a very Jaques of the Forest of Arden. Yet the one work was a true forerunner of the other, the only essential difference between them being the introduction of a most fascinating and a most exalted egotism. This, after all, was but the flowering of the same delightful genius. The sincerity, the earnestness, the love of pensive solitude, with its accompanying love of nature, mankind, and God, are the same in both works. And it was precisely this charming sincerity and this high moral tone that were so very new. Even in the most moral of **"The Moral Satires"** [in Cowper's *Poems* of 1782], there is not the slightest trace of affectation. Everywhere the author is easy, graceful, and, while very pious, delightfully natural. As he tells us himself, "his raptures are not conjured up to serve occasions of poetic pomp, but genuine." His genuineness of emotion, his love of pure and exquisite spontaneity—even to the extent of a complete carelessness of method and plan— apart altogether from his lofty moral tone and delicious musings in retirement, not only strike new chords of poetry in the literature of the day, but reveal the fact that it is quite a new order of poet who is striking the chords. He will write of nothing of which his whole soul is not full, yet his genius will only concern itself with what most concerns him in his grandest and most silent moods. . . . Affectation, insincerity, even poetic exaggeration he loathes as falsehood. Much as he loves and much as he was influenced by Milton, he has not a trace of his splendid pedantry. To take up such a poem, even now-a-days, as **"The Task,"** or even **"Retirement,"** is like taking a peaceful stroll in the woods on a summer evening. Although a hundred years have passed away, we still feel, with his contemporaries, that we are in a fresh and an altogether delightful atmosphere; and all the more so because we are in the company of a poet who reflects the fresh beauty, the peacefulness, the loveliness, and the solitary grandeur of nature as wonderfully and as sweetly as a tranquil lake among the mountains reflects the glory of the midnight sky. Cowper's poetry is a protest and a reaction against the shallow affectation and the insincerity of his fellow poets. (pp. 366-68)

There is absolutely nothing of the dramatic quality in his genius. He is not an artist, any more than he is a scientific savan. This is apparent even in his charming little pictures and vignettes of rural life. No descriptions could be more finished and more elegant. They are made to be carried about. So far, he is a genuine painter—one of the Little Masters; but only so far, for he not only carefully and studiously paints in the minutest details of his scenes and characters, leaving nothing for the reader's imagination, but unconsciously, although very forcibly, he also paints himself as an integral part of them all. . . . [Cowper's imagination] was introspective and prospective, and herein lay the whole of the originality of his poetry. In his retirement from the outer world his imagination was full, not of men, but of man,—not of man as he was, but as he might be. This glorious ideal vision was with him by day and by night, and imparted to his verse a lofty moral tone that came upon the world like an inspiration. This solitary singer is neither an artist, nor a philosopher, nor a scientific savan—being utterly incapable of explaining any mystery under the sun—but he is a seer of such visions, and a dreamer of such dreams, that

> His ear is pained,
> His soul is sick with every day's report
> Of wrong and outrage with which earth is filled.

Nothing could show this ideal tendency of his genius more thoroughly than the wonderful lines to his mother's picture. This noble hymn to a beautiful memory—for his mother passed away from him when he was but a wondering child—is the passionate utterance of a soul that has yearned all his days for ideal purity and love. The picture is but a symbol of the far away dreams. No mediaeval devotee's adoration of the Madonna could be sweeter or purer. (pp. 369-71)

It may be said, and with justice, that Cowper's standpoint was after all but the standpoint of the Puritan. So far as the Puritan was fired by the belief of individual worth and the native dignity of the individual soul, this is true. But Cowper's standpoint was on a higher, a sublimer ground. Cowper valued the individual soul because he valued and passionately loved the whole race. Puritanism also loved humanity, but it loved Puritan humanity more. Puritanism had little of the beauty, the tenderness, the sympathy, and the wonder of Cowper's imagination. It was single-eyed in its aim, pre-eminently practical. One of its best features was its patriotism—it was strongly, passionately patriotic,—not more so, however, than Cowper; and with this remarkable difference, that Cowper's patriotism implied the very widest cosmopolitanism. He loved his own country—not only because it was his native land, but because of all others it most loved the world. And Cowper's cosmopolitanism even possesses something more than the defiant revolutionary thrill which found its best and noblest utterance in such a song as "A man's a man for a' that," for he represents the world as not only made for the benefit of every individual man, but, grander still, every man as specially made for the benefit of the world. (p. 372)

There were many courageous, many fearless, and many brilliant minds in the eighteenth century. In his retirement, however, and in his high musings, Cowper is not the least striking figure of them all. He stands absolutely alone. But his solitude is the splendid solitude of a prophet, whose voice will reach through the ages. (p. 373)

> David Sime, "The Originality of Cowper's Poetry,"
> in The Catholic Presbyterian, Vol. IV, No. XXIII,
> November, 1880, pp. 365-73.

JAMES RUSSELL LOWELL   (essay date 1890)

[*Lowell was a celebrated nineteenth-century American poet, critic, essayist, and editor. He is noted today for his satirical and critical*

An illustration from the first edition of "The Journey of John Gilpin."

writings, including A Fable for Critics, *a book-length poem featuring witty critical portraits of his contemporaries. Often awkwardly phrased, and occasionally vicious, the* Fable *is distinguished by the enduring value of its literary assessments.*]

I find in Cowper the first recognition of a general amiability in Winter. The gentleness of his temper, and the wide charity of his sympathies, made it natural for him to find good in everything except the human heart. A dreadful creed distilled from the darkest moments of dyspeptic solitaries compelled him against his will to see in *that* the one evil thing made by a God whose goodness is over all his works. Cowper's two walks in the morning and noon of a winter's day are delightful, so long as he contrives to let himself be happy in the graciousness of the landscape. Your muscles grow springy, and your lungs dilate with the crisp air as you walk along with him. You laugh with him at the grotesque shadow of your legs lengthened across the snow by the just-risen sun. I know nothing that gives a purer feeling of out-door exhilaration than the easy verses of this escaped hypochrondriac. But Cowper also preferred his sheltered gardenwalk to those robuster joys, and bitterly acknowledged the depressing influence of the darkened year. . . . Perhaps his poetry bears truer witness to his habitual feeling, for it is only there that poets disenthral themselves of their reserve and become fully possessed of their greatest charm,—the power of being franker than other men. In the Third Book of *The Task* he boldly affirms his preference of the country to the city even in winter:—

> But are not wholesome airs, though unperfumed
> By roses, and clear suns, though scarcely felt,
> And groves, if inharmonious, yet secure
> From clamor, and whose very silence charms,

To be preferred to smoke? . . .
They would be, were not madness in the head
And folly in the heart; were England now
What England was, plain, hospitable kind,
And undebauched.

The conclusion shows, however, that he was thinking mainly
of fireside delights, not of the blusterous companionship of
nature. (pp. 268-69)

[I call *The Task* a] good *human* bit of writing, imaginative,
too,—not so flushed, not so . . . highfaluting (let me dare the
odious word!) as the modern style since poets have got hold
of a theory that imagination is common-sense turned inside
out, and not common-sense sublimed,—but wholesome, masculine, and strong in the simplicity of a mind wholly occupied
with its theme. To me Cowper is still the best of our descriptive
poets for every-day wear. And what unobtrusive skill he has!
How he heightens, for example, your sense of winter-evening
seclusion, by the twanging horn of the postman on the bridge!
(p. 270)

> *James Russell Lowell, ''A Good Word for Winter,''*
> *in his* Literary Essays, *Vol. III, Houghton, Mifflin*
> *and Company, 1890, pp. 255-90.**

EDWARD DOWDEN   (essay date 1897)

[*Dowden was an important nineteenth-century Irish critic who is
best known for his Shakespearean criticism. His comments on
Cowper's ''revolutionary feeling in favor of simplification'' are
later contested by Leslie Stephen (1909).*]

Cowper feared that the whole course of human things was
tending from good to ill and from ill to worse. Human nature
left to itself appeared to Rousseau essentially beautiful and
pure; Cowper held a different creed, and he was no sharer in
the optimism of the Revolution. The Second Book of **''The
Task''** was named **''The Time-Piece,''** because it was intended,
as the author informed Newton, to strike the hour that gives
notice of approaching judgment.

Thus, although he was far from being a spirit of Revolution,
Cowper mourns in Revolutionary fashion over the growth of
luxury and the evils of a spurious civilization; thus he pleads
for a return to simplicity of manners. (pp. 37-8)

But though Cowper gives expression to the Revolutionary feeling in favor of simplification and to the passion of human
brotherhood, no one can imagine the poet of Olney, masculine
as his spirit was, flinging himself with fury against the thrones
of kings or the palaces of prelates. In political matters he
desired not revolution but temperate reform. And with Cowper
the circumference which rounded all subjects of thought and
feeling, and towards which his mind constantly expanded, was
the idea of God. If he reverenced truth, it was not in the spirit
of those proud forerunners of the Revolution who did homage
to human reason; he bowed the head and bowed the knee before
what he deemed to be divine truth. If he spoke of equality, it
was of the equality of all souls before the Supreme. The fraternity which he regarded as most perfect is the fraternity of those
who are brethren in Christ. He invokes charity as the first and
fairest of virtues, but he maintains that genuine charity is the
offspring of divine instruction; we become sensible of our own
poverty, our frailty, our deep disease, and so we learn pity for
our fellows. He chooses Hope for his theme; but he has no
vision of a terrestrial paradise to be realized by scientific progress or the overthrow of earthly tyrannies. It is from the very

vanity of this world that our highest hope is born; the whole
creation groans and travails. But hope that is seen is not hope;
and the fulfilment shall be only when the Lord of earth shall
descend, ''propitious in his chariot paved with love.'' Cowper
pleads for simplicity, for a return to nature; but he adds that
Nature of herself cannot restore to man the glories he has lost;
to effect this, grace must come to the aid of Nature.

Thus the gospel of Rousseau is translated by Cowper into the
gospel according to St. Paul. The combination is a curious and
interesting one for literary study, of the sentiment of the Revolution with the faith and fervor of the Evangelical revival.
(pp. 39-41)

> *Edward Dowden, ''Precursors of Revolution,'' in his*
> The French Revolution and English Literature, *1897.*
> *Reprint by Kennikat Press, Inc., 1967, pp. 3-46.**

ALFRED AINGER   (lecture date 1898)

[*This essay was originally delivered as a lecture in 1898.*]

Cowper is indeed under some very obvious obligations to Pope.
His little sketches of character, interspersed among matter purely
didactic, his ''Miss Bridgets,'' and ''Voltaires''; his types of
the Bore, and the Military Braggart; and the Squire's Son sent
on his travels, only to show how the ''dunce'' when

> Sent to roam
> Excels the dunce that has been kept at home,

are clearly modelled on the ''Chloes,'' and ''Narcissas,'' and
''Sir Balaams'' of Pope. But then how different—just because
the writers themselves were so different! The essence of Cowper, in such moods, is his *playfulness*, and playfulness had no
part in the genius of Pope. There is a smile on the lip, and a
twinkle in the eye, in Cowper's satire, as well as a recognition,
all the while, of the ''still, sad music of humanity''—a sense
of the ''pity of it all''—a spiritual quality, in short, which has
no counterpart in the equipment of the author of the *Dunciad*.
Not that Cowper is incapable of scorn—it is indeed one of his
strongest points—but then it is only for those who are as yet
trifling with the graver aspects of religious truth and issues of
human conduct. For the ordinary man of the world's attitude
towards the faith which was all in all to *him*, he has no pity,
or rather no patience. Take the wonderfully graphic (almost
dramatic) picture of the amateur theologians—the *Bon-vivant*,
the Colonel, the Ensign, and the young Chaplain—over their
wine; discussing one of the cardinal doctrines of the newly
revived religion, *Faith* as against *Works*. It is in the section of
the satire called **''Hope.''**

The inevitable influence of Pope is apparent in particular lines;
but then, as I have said, being so *dramatic*, that circumstance
alone breaks up and relieves the eternal recurrence of the epigrammatic couplet. It loses the Popian *finish*, but it gains in
human reality. (pp. 282-83)

Cowper is not one of those poets who have directly founded
or influenced a school of poets. He stands, from this point of
view, rather aside, in a back-water. His obvious and close
association with a certain school of theology in great part accounts for this. But poets are not without their influence on
the subsequent progress of poetry merely because they have
not inspired or guided any particular disciple. There is such a
thing as influencing the general atmosphere in which the poetic
heart and spirit of man alone can thrive; and I think Cowper
did this for his generation and those that followed. He greatly

widened the range and scope of subjects in which it was supposed poetry had any right to intervene. For though Cowper lived in the country, and made his friendships largely among ladies . . .—it is quite a wrong idea of him to imagine that the subjects which interested him were all or chiefly of the same sort. He was a thorough Englishman. (pp. 296-97)

Alfred Ainger, "Some Leaders in the Poetic Revival of 1760-1820—Cowper," in his Lectures and Essays, *Vol. I, The Macmillan Company, 1905, pp. 273-99.*

J. C. BAILEY (essay date 1905)

[Cowper] lives by the power with which he reveals the strength, the tenderness, the poetry that may be found in the commonest relations of life's every day, by the loving insight which discovered and so affectionately chronicled the charms that make the plainest English landscape a feast of beauty to those who see as he saw. His poetry is a kind of Divine accident. None of the obvious calls that make other men poets operated on him—no inspiration of surroundings, no spur of ambition, no inner sense of a poetic mission. In his early life, verse-writing was only an occasional amusement: in his later years it was only a partner with his spade, his walking-stick, and his box of tools, in the task of keeping the most terrible of diseases at bay. Yet even so, by simple effluence of the poet in him, what he wrote became the greatest poetry of that generation. He made no choice of subject, formed no poetic scheme or plan: one may often wish he had; but that was not the spirit in which he set to work. He made his poetry as he made his incomparable letters, out of anything and nothing, out of just what came into his head: and, happily for us, what came into his head includes, with much that we could wish away, the **"Royal George,"** the sonnet and lines **"To Mary,"** and the great passages of the **"Task."** He is, all through, an accidental, occasional, only half-conscious poet. (p. xi)

[Cowper's short pieces are] simple, tender, spontaneous. Probably no poet, in all the history of the art, did so little casting about for a subject. He just took what came. That is the secret of his rare sincerity; it is also, no doubt, the cause of his too frequent triviality. If he could have added something more of artistic seriousness to his spontaneity, he would have known that, though the highest poetry finds its origin in these suggestions from within that arise we know not how and seem to be a part of ourselves, yet not all such suggestions have poetic value; and many, which have, require very deliberate and conscious development before their value can be realized. But his was, all through, a talent that understood neither its limitations nor its possibilities.

Of the only other verse written by Cowper before the time of his first volume, little need be said. Hymns have rarely been literature, and Cowper's religious convictions were too definite and too narrow to allow him to handle his subject with the necessary freedom of an artist. . . . But it is not their literary merit that has kept them alive. They live by the evident, almost breathing, sincerity of their every word: by their visible character of actual personal feeling and experiences. . . . The truth is that his hymns have the strength and the weakness of a very simple nature. Only such a nature, that of the "little child" of the Gospels, can feel the love of Christ, His almost visible and sensible companionship, as Cowper does; but only a larger nature, a mind of greater breadth and culture, can utter the mystery of faith. For Cowper there is no mystery; the scheme of this world and the next, of God and man, and God's dealings

with man, is quite plain: except on the side of character, he does not feel anything of the temper which said, "God is in heaven; and thou upon earth: therefore let thy words be few." The fine note of such hymns as **"O Strength and Stay, upholding all creation,"** or **"God of the living,"** where the rare quality consists as much in the consciousness of the darkness that surrounds us as in the living faith that lights it up, enough of it at least for life and hope, that is altogether beyond Cowper. At the same time, it must be said that he never falls into the opposite note, the besetting sin of the religious verse of his school. He never addresses his Master with the familiarity which shocks and pains all reverent feeling in some hymns which have been only too well known. From that, no doubt, his education saved him: it was not for nothing that he had been born in an English rectory and brought up at Westminster School. But his narrowness of creed, and indeed of mind, allows him to define on these high themes with the confident and prosaic precision of a lawyer. And even in the hymns, perhaps, it is no strictly religious subject that brings him out best as a poet; but rather his own special theme, the praise of Retirement. (pp. xxxiii-xxxiv)

Will not every one feel at once that the simpler sort of natural beauty has rarely been more admirably touched [than in Cowper's **"The Task"**]? Here is, at last, the real and full Cowper, and he preaches all the better for forgetting to preach. Nothing quite like these descriptive passages existed before in our own, or, so far as I know, in any other language. They are, as Cowper claims, absolutely sincere; he has himself, with his own eye, seen everything he describes: it is a great deal more than other men see; and he has found a great deal more in it. And not only his observation but his feelings are entirely his own; the whole is what the French call *vécu:* the personal note is everywhere, though linked, as it must be in all art that is to count, with the note of the universal. The feeling to which the poet gives utterance is his own, but not all or only his own: it is representative as well as personal; he speaks not as an isolated individual, but as the spokesman of the human race. Of its feeling, only, of course, not of its thought: no one must look to Cowper for anything like profound thought; he is too far away from all intellectual influences for that, too content behind the narrow walls of his self-chosen cloister. His function is the interpretation of some of our best and purest feelings; as we read him we are conscious that we, too, have experienced such feelings as his, though less in degree and of less fine quality; he expresses for us what we cannot express for ourselves: that is his first work; and the second is to lead us on and up to new and higher emotions of the same order, of which his poetry brings us our first revelation. Many poets have failed in the second task because they have ignored or disdained the first. In Cowper we begin with the familiar, with what belongs to us all, and are carried, almost without knowing it, into the world that was his only, and not ours,—the poetic world of his own creation and consecration. (pp. xliv-xlv)

"Yardley Oak" is a fragment; but Cowper has left nothing in which his imagination rises higher. It would be curious to know if he had been reading Shakespeare at the time he wrote it. Certainly it stands alone among his works in being rather akin to Shakespeare than to Milton, both in the particular vein of reflection and in the movement of the blank verse. (p. lvi)

No truer poet than William Cowper ever wrote [in] the English language. He did greater things than he knew, and if he had known their greatness might have done greater still. It is possible to look at Nature through many different sorts of glasses.

The Elizabethans looked at her chiefly through a glass of rather far-fetched fancy; Milton chiefly through a richly coloured glass of universal scholarship; Thomson through one of rhetoric, abstraction, and Deism. Cowper's way is quite unlike any of them. Neither fancy, nor learning, nor philosophy came between him and his object. His creed does occasionally; his sympathetic tenderness always. Otherwise it is the thing itself, river, tree, or hill, that he gives us in naked simplicity. That simplicity was the central element in his character, and it is the secret both of what he confessed and of what he discovered. The perfectly simple can ask questions and reveal facts which no one else can reveal or ask. So it was with Cowper. He takes up his pen to amuse himself, to describe his walks, his friends, and his garden, and his pets, and in the result finds himself, as it were by accident, a great poet, and a poet of a new order. He, more than any one else, discovered that a man may be himself, and may tell the plain truth, and yet be a poet. It is a discovery which has since been pushed too far; but in his day it was real and important. Previous poets had used their own experiences and feelings often enough, but as a rule they had dressed them up for appearance on the printed page. That is a perfectly legitimate thing to do. But Cowper did not do it, and that he did not is both his strength and his weakness. It is his weakness, because by confining himself to a plain confession of his own feelings and doings, and those of his little circle of friends, he could not attempt to deal with human life in its variety and complexity, as his contemporary Crabbe did both before and after him with such vigour and truth, and because not only human life as a whole, but also Nature as a whole, was, by these restrictions, out of his reach. The large philosophy of Wordsworth was as impossible for him as the universal portrait gallery of Crabbe. But this limitation was also Cowper's strength. For it may have been only on condition of renouncing loftier ambitions that he succeeded in placing himself, his own heart, and his little world, on the page of his verse, with such admirable ease, intimacy, and truth. And to have done that is to be immortal, for, in poetry, immortality lies just there—in the felicitous marriage of what is beautiful and what is true. (pp. lvii-lviii)

J. C. Bailey, in an introduction to The Poems of William Cowper *by William Cowper, edited by J. C. Bailey, Methuen & Co., 1905, pp. ix-lviii.*

LYTTON STRACHEY (essay date 1905)

[*Strachey is best known as a biographer whose iconoclastic reexaminations of historical figures revolutionized the course of modern biographical writing. In this essay, written in 1905, Strachey disparagingly appraises Cowper's letters, concluding that they are "stricken with sterility."*]

The letters of Cowper, though they rank high in English literature, do not require much comment. As far as they go, they are perfect, but they hardly go anywhere at all. Their gold is absolutely pure; but it is beaten out into the thinnest leaf conceivable. They are like soap-bubbles—exquisite films surrounding emptiness, and almost too wonderful to be touched.

Cowper had nothing to say, and he said it beautifully; yet it is difficult not to wish that he had had something more to say, even at the expense of expressing it a little less well. His letters are stricken with sterility; they are dried up; they lack the juices of life. In them, the vast and palpitating eighteenth century seems suddenly to dwindle into a quiet and well-appointed grave. The wheel had come full circle: the flute of Addison was echoed at last by the flute of Cowper; perfection had returned upon itself. (p. 48)

Lytton Strachey, "Gray and Cowper," in his Characters and Commentaries, *edited by James Strachey, Harcourt, Brace and Company, 1933, pp. 43-9.**

LESLIE STEPHEN (essay date 1909)

[*Stephen is considered to be one of the most important literary critics of his age. In his moral criticism, Stephen argues that all literature is nothing more than an imaginative rendering, in concrete terms, of a writer's philosophy or beliefs. It is the role of criticism, he contends, to translate into intellectual terms what the writer has told the reader through character, symbol, and plot. Stephen's analyses often include biographical judgments of the writer as well as the work. As Stephen once observed: "The whole art of criticism consists in learning to know the human being who is partially revealed to us in his spoken or his written words." Like Edward Dowden (1897), Stephen discusses Cowper's attitude toward revolutionary poetry. However, Stephen implicitly disagrees with Dowden in concluding that although Cowper "felt the incapacity of the old order to satisfy the emotional needs of mankind," he sought no "radical remedy" for it.*]

[Cowper's] most ludicrous verses have been written in his saddest mood. It would be, he adds, "but a shocking vagary" if the sailors on a ship in danger relieved themselves "by fiddling and dancing; yet sometimes much such a part act I." His love of country sights and pleasures is so intense because it is the most effectual relief. "Oh!" he exclaims, "I could spend whole days and nights in gazing upon a loving prospect! My eyes drink the rivers as they flow." And he adds, in his characteristic vein of thought, "if every human being upon earth could feel as I have done for many years, there might perhaps be many miserable men among them, but not an unawakened one could be found from the Arctic to the Antarctic circle." The earth and the sun itself are, he says, but "baubles;" but they are the baubles which alone can distract his attention from more awful prospects. His little garden and greenhouse are playthings lent to him for a time, and soon to be left. He "never framed a wish or formed a plan," as he says in the "**Task**," of which the scene was not laid in the country; and when the gloomiest forebodings unhinged his mind, his love became a passion. He is like his own prisoner in the Bastille playing with spiders. All other avenues of delight are closed to him; he believes, whenever his dark hour of serious thought returns, that he is soon to be carried off to unspeakable torments; all ordinary methods of human pleasure seem to be tainted with some corrupting influence; but whilst playing with his spaniel, or watching his cucumbers, or walking with Mrs. Unwin in the fields, he can for a moment distract his mind with purely innocent pleasures. The awful background of his visions, never quite absent, though often, we may hope, far removed from actual consciousness, throws out these hours of delight into more prominent relief. The sternest of his monitors, John Newton himself, could hardly grudge this cup of cold water presented, as it were, to the lips of a man in a self-made purgatory.

This is the peculiar turn which gives so characteristic a tone to Cowper's loving portraits of scenery. He is like the Judas seen by St. Brandan on the iceberg; he is enjoying a momentary relaxation between the past of misery and the future of anticipated torment. Such a sentiment must, fortunately, be in some sense exceptional and idiosyncratic. And yet, once more, it fell in with the prevailing current of thought. Cowper agrees with Rousseau in finding that the contemplation of scenery, unpolluted by human passion, and the enjoyment of a calm domestic life, is the best anodyne for a spirit wearied with the perpetual disorders of a corrupt social order. He differs from him, as we have seen, in the conviction that a deeper remedy is wanting than any mere political change; in a more profound sense of human wickedness, and, on the other hand, in a narrower estimate of the conditions of human life. His definition of Nature, to put it logically, would exclude that natural man in whose potential existence Rousseau more or less believed. The passionate love of scenery was enough to distinguish him from the poets of the preceding school, whose supposed hatred of Nature meant simply that they were thoroughly immersed in the pleasures of a society then first developed in its modern form, and not yet undermined by the approach of a new revolution. The men of Pope and Addison's time looked upon country squires as bores incapable of intellectual pleasure, and, therefore, upon country life as a topic for gentle ridicule, or more frequently as an unmitigated nuisance. Probably their estimate was a very sound one. When a true poet like Thomson really enjoyed the fresh air, his taste did not become a passion, and the scenery appeared to him as a pleasant background to his Castle of Indolence. Cowper's peculiar religious views prevented him again from anticipating the wider and more philosophical sentiment of Wordsworth. Like Pope and Wordsworth, indeed, he occasionally uses language which has a pantheistic sound. He expresses his belief that

> There lives and works
> A soul in all things, and that soul is God.

But when Pope uses a similar phrase, it is the expression of a decaying philosophy which never had much vitality, or passed from the sphere of intellectual speculation to affect the imagination and the emotions. It is a dogma which he holds sincerely, it may be, but not firmly enough to colour his habitual sentiments. With Wordsworth, whatever its precise meaning, it is an expression of an habitual and abiding sentiment, which rises naturally to his lips whenever he abandons himself to his spontaneous impulses. With Cowper, as is the case with all Cowper's utterances, it is absolutely sincere for the time; but it is a doctrine not very easily adapted to his habitual creed, and which drops out of his mind whenever he passes from external nature to himself or his fellows. The indwelling divinity whom he recognises in every "freckle, streak, or stain" on his favourite flowers, seems to be hopelessly removed from his own personal interests. An awful and mysterious decree has separated him for ever from the sole source of consolation.

This is not the place to hint at any judgment upon Cowper's theology, or to inquire how far a love of nature, in his sense of the words, can be logically combined with a system based upon the fundamental dogma of the corruption of man. Certainly a similar anticipation of the poetical pantheism of Wordsworth may be found in that most logical of Calvinists, Jonathan Edwards. Cowper, too, could be at no loss for scriptural precedents when recognising the immediate voice of God in thunder and earthquakes, or in the calmer voices of the waterbrooks and the meadows. His love of nature, at any rate, is at once of a narrower and sincerer kind than that which Rousseau first made fashionable. He has no tendency to the misanthropic or cynical view which induces men of morbid or affected minds to profess a love of savage scenery simply because it is savage. Neither does he rise to the more philosophical view which sees in the seas and the mountains the most striking symbols of the great forces of the universe to which we must accommodate

ourselves, and which might therefore rightfully be associated by a Wordsworth with the deepest emotions of reverential awe. Nature is to him but a collection of "baubles," soon to be taken away, and he seeks in its contemplation a temporary relief from anguish, not a permanent object of worship. He would dread that sentiment as a deistical form of idolatry; and he is equally far from thinking that the natural man, wherever that vague person might be found, could possibly be a desirable object of imitation. His love of nature, in short, keen as it might be, was not the reflection of any philosophical, religious, or political theory. But it was genuine enough to charm many who might regard his theological sentiments as a mere recrudescence of an obsolete form of belief. . . . Cowper said, substantially, Leave the world, as Rousseau said, Upset the world. The reformer, to say nothing of his greater intellectual power, naturally interested the world which he threatened more than the recluse whom it frightened. Limited within a narrower circle of ideas, and living in a society where the great issues of the time were not presented in so naked a form, Cowper's influence ran in a more confined channel. He felt the incapacity of the old order to satisfy the emotional wants of mankind, but was content to revive the old forms of belief instead of seeking a more radical remedy in some subversive or reconstructive system of thought. But the depth and sincerity of feeling which explains his marvellous intensity of pathos is sometimes a pleasant relief to the sentimentalism of his greater predecessor. Nor is it hard to understand why his passages of sweet and melancholy musing by the quiet Ouse should have come like a breath of fresh air to the jaded generation waiting for the fall of the Bastille—and of other things. (pp. 218-22)

> *Leslie Stephen, "Cowper and Rousseau," in his* Hours
> in a Library, Vol. II, *revised edition, Smith, Elder
> & Co., 1909, pp. 193-222.**

OLIVER ELTON   (essay date 1912)

[Elton echoes the comments of Edward Dowden (1897) regarding the rebellious, innovative quality of Cowper's poetic views. In addition, he admires "the easy finesse of the transitions" in The Task, *but judges Cowper's translations of Homer's poetry unlively and unpoetical.]*

Cowper's *task,* though he did not know it and refused to be called 'one of the *literati,*' was the revival of poetical taste, and in a measure of poetry itself.

His value as a craftsman and inventor is high. He struck out and used beautifully more than one of the styles, which were presently to be taken over into the stock of the poets and elaborated. *The Wreck of the Royal George* lies close behind the heroic songs of Campbell and Tennyson; *Yardley Oak,* and the landscapes of *The Task,* forerun some of the ruminations in [Wordsworth's] *The Prelude* and *The Excursion;* and if the pictures of the postman, the wagoner, and the gipsies have not been followed, it is because they cannot be improved. So Cowper's humorous and domestic verses carry on a tone which is heard again, with a difference, in Locker-Lampson and Austin Dobson long afterwards. And the newness of his work was seen at once; he was not too far beyond his public for recognition. *The Task* and *John Gilpin* were read by every one, and if Cowper's popularity has faded, and his retiring figure is easily hidden behind his successors, still Time has spared much of his verse, and has sifted it with far more kindness than that of the loud, demonstrative Youngs and Churchills. Of Cowper's prose the life is assured; and if he rises to higher and stranger things in his verse, his prose is more safely charmed against uncertainty of style. But his prose, unlike his verse, does not initiate; it carries on one of the best traditions already in existence, and its pedigree down from Addison is of the purest. Both in prose and verse it is his instinct to be confidential, and this strain of confessional writing, in which so much of the matter is sad and unhappy, while much is blithe— the strain that we hear in *The Task* and *The Castaway,* and the poem on the hares, and the correspondence, is one that Cowper acclimatised in English letters, just as Rousseau had acclimatised it in European letters. (pp. 76-7)

The range of [Cowper's] letters and the qualities by which they attract are not hard to describe. The *lyra heroica* [heroic strain], and the high Wordsworthian strain, are not there; but otherwise the whole of the natural man, and the whole of Cowper's inward struggle, are represented in them. It is hard to say anything about their form, except that it is always right. Any limitations in the letters are not due to inexpressiveness or bad writing, but to Cowper's character. For this reason they do not enter into competition with Swift's letters, or Carlyle's, or with those of Keats or Coleridge; the mental horizon and the whole colouring are different. But though the stage is smaller, the scene has plenty of variety and motion. Cowper reviews it, moved less by any strong current of the blood than by a happy little excitement of the nerves. . . . Perhaps Chaucer and Cowper, however dissimilar, have the same central quality—vivacity. Chaucer would have delighted in the interview with the gentleman, Mr. Cox, who came to get out of Cowper the *Stanzas subjoined to the yearly Bill of Mortality of the parish of All Saints, Northampton;* and he, too, would have consented.

> A plain, decent, elderly figure made its appearance, and being desired to sit, spoke as follows . . . [Cowper replies] 'Mr. Cox, you have several men of genius in your town, why have you not applied to some of them? There is a namesake of yours in particular, Cox the statuary, who, everybody knows, is a first-rate maker of verses. He surely is the man of all the world for your purpose.' 'Alas, sir, I have heretofore borrowed much help of him, but he is a gentleman of so much reading that the people of our town cannot understand him.'

We can see how such writing is a form of the author's conversation. He tells of domestic nothings, sends light intimate confidences about his tea-parties, his digestion, or his money matters. Everything is gently alive, and we have to read on. It is the record of the week-day man. In a truly English and eighteenth-century tone he exclaims: 'Pulpits for preaching, and the parlour, the garden, and the walk for friendly and agreeable conversation.' It is the tone of many a country house to-day; equable, well-mannered, cheerful—no vulgarity, little passion, good or bad, and not too much thinking, even on Sundays. Time goes quickly in such places: even when, as with Cowper, there is both thinking and passion; and at the age of forty-nine he writes:

> My days steal away silently and march on (as poor mad King Lear would have made his soldiers march) as if they were shod with felt; not so silently but that I can hear them.

But for the illness within, such a life might have been without events. It is the chequering of soft lights with heavy shadows

that gives these letters their distinction, and makes them the picture of a soul. (pp. 78-9)

In his views of poetry Cowper is a rebel, and his 'gentleness' need not be exaggerated. Even in his moral poems of 1782 he is seen escaping from the current style, though he uses the traditional couplet. In *The Task* and *Yardley Oak* he finds his own style. And he tells us what the tyranny with which he broke, and where he sought for inspiration. He broke with Pope, and Johnson, and artifice. He was inspired by the love of Milton and the love of simplicity, and his real feat is to have found a poetic language that reconciled these two affections. (p. 85)

[But following Milton,] he follows him amiss, as in the rhetorical wastes of the *Winter Morning's Walk,* it is more from a wrong choice of subject than from failure of ear or style. The *Homer* must be called a painful instance of failing ear, though it aims at Milton's dignity. But Cowper shows his mastery of the epic style in his original pieces; not so much in the startling passages where he rises to its full pitch, as in the level, simple, descriptive parts, where he carries it delicately down to the rendering of domestic things; a kind of verse that approaches prose, but is decisively severed from prose by the poetry that hangs in the air like the minute sparkles of dust that he describes as rising from the threshing-floor. Indeed, for his quieter pencillings Cowper may well have caught a hint from those of [Milton's] *Paradise Regained,* or from the lines that describe the man who comes out from the reeking town to enjoy the smell of 'tedded grass'; a text that would be much to Cowper's mind, and may also interpret our own feeling when we open *The Task* after closing [Pope's] *The Dunciad.* This subdued method he often uses:

> Yes, thou mayst eat thy bread, and lick the hand
> That feeds thee; thou mayst frolic on the floor
> At evening, and at night retire secure
> To thy straw couch, and slumber unalarmed.

There is Milton in this, but there is also simplicity, and simplicity is Cowper's other star. He desires it, and often reaches it. He does not study any author in order to do so; it comes to him by nature. In his verse he sometimes swerves from it, either towards the noble elaboration that Milton taught him, or towards a false elaboration; but in prose he has it always. He has it in his expression not only of simple and winning things, but of elusive and painful things. . . . The virtue of [Cowper's] style is that we do not look at it, but look through it, and the result is a classic.

As a light poet Cowper derives from the school of Prior, but substitutes country grace and neatness for town finish. The verse of affectionate and happy compliment addressed to women, such as *The Rose* and *Catharina,* is peculiarly his. He also loves a fable, with a little perfunctory moral attached, the story of which is drawn from experience; sometimes we find it told again in his letters. *The Dog and the Water-Lily* and *The Retired Cat* are of this order. . . . *The Diverting History of John Gilpin* (which might be credited to the shade of Goldsmith, did we not know its authorship) is the most cheerful and vociferous thing that Cowper wrote, and yet has all his neatness and finish too; qualities to which the slyly-inserted, loose-hanging ballad tags contribute not a little. A favourite metre for quite other effects is the 'rocking-horse' or anapaestic quatrain; of this Cowper was born a master, and in his hands it escapes those dangers of cloggedness on the one side, and of mawkishness on the other, to which it has often fallen. Well do some of

Cowper's youthful lines compare with the popular and famous effects, in the same measure, of Moore and Byron:

> Bid adieu, my sad heart, bid adieu to thy peace;
> Thy pleasure is past, and thy sorrows increase;

One stanza of this lyric is worthy—and no more could be said in the matter of lyrical melody—of Edgar Allan Poe, whose insuperable line

> And the fever called living is conquered at last,

is as true a mirror of his own temper as these are of Cowper's:

> Already deprived of its splendour and heat,
> I feel thee more slowly, more heavily beat;
> Perhaps overstrained with the quick pulse of pleasure,
> Thou art glad of this respite to beat at thy leisure;
> But the sigh of distress shall now weary thee more
> Than the flutter and tumult of passion before.

'The poplars are felled' is better known; it has the 'same whispering sound,' which rose in the former piece, one of Cowper's few love-poems, to a light wail, and in this one sinks to something just above silence. Of the two heroic lyrics, written in another tune, as though to the 'harp the Cambro-Britons used,' *Boadicea* is the more conventional, in the pattern of Gray, and is better in rhythm than in phrase. There is no such flaw in *The Loss of the Royal George.* It is not in any pattern at all, it has no precedent nearer than Drayton, it is freer of blemish than anything of the sort in Campbell; and we can the better feel the perfection of its almost hard simplicity, by imagining in how opposite a mode of excellence, in what symphonies of undulating prose, the same 'vision of sudden death' might have been treated by De Quincey. Here Cowper quits himself and his usual manner; while in the lines *To the Nightingale,* which point as nobly and as plainly forward to the best of the same kind in Wordsworth, as it excels Logan's (or Michael Bruce's) verses *To the Cuckoo,* printed only eleven years earlier, he is back again with himself and his troubles; and wins us thereby perhaps more thoroughly than Wordsworth himself, who always refuses or does not desire to complain. But it is one of Cowper's many herald poems, and is dated 1792.

By the side of verse like this, the bulky moral satires that Cowper had produced ten years before seem of a past generation. To do them justice, they must be compared with the school from which they are seen emerging. The first of them is called *Table Talk,* but the title of another, *Expostulation,* better expresses their temper, and as a whole they are the medium of the author's opinions rather than of his genius. The influence of Churchill, Cowper's schoolfellow, whom he portrays with a generous touch, has been suggested; and some of the invectives might be those of a shriller Churchill. Cowper writes better than that ferocious improviser, whom he admired too much; but he knows the world less well. He beats the air when he rates society at large. In attacking slavery and inhumanity it is not enough to be on the right side. But anything that really comes within the sharpened ken of the recluse, he touches vividly at once. He excels in the formal rhymed character, as in that of the fashionable preacher, or of the

> fine puss-gentleman that's all perfume,

or of the elderly prude whom he saw in Hogarth's drawing. (pp. 88-91)

The Task is neither a formal garden nor a woodland; it is more like a park cunningly and irregularly laid out, where we do not see too much at once and are for ever recrossing our own steps unexpectedly. There are grass, and water, and arbours; it is a pity that, do what we will, we should so often, round sudden corners, come on the same uncomely preaching-box amid the greenery. Still Cowper achieves his wish to secure 'much variety and no confusion' in this lively offshoot of the dull old local and didactic poem. Such literary origins betray themselves in the dull unreadable stretches of the book. Much of the style is simply that of Cowper's earlier satires, like *Truth and Hope,* with the rhymes gone. The poet is here his own judge:

> Since pulpits fail, and sounding-boards reflect
> Most part an empty ineffectual sound,
> What chance that I, to fame so little known,
> Nor conversant with men or manners much,
> Should speak to purpose, or with better hope
> Crack the satiric thong?

All the same, we can admire the easy finesse of the transitions in *The Task,* and the impression of art which is left amidst the absence of plan. Cowper is himself the *subject,* in the philosophical sense, of the poem; he is present in all he describes, and takes us along with him. It is his own shadow that he watches in the winter morning's walk, and the word *we*—meaning himself, and the reader his friend and companion—is always recurring:

> Hence, ankle-deep in moss and flowery thyme,
> We mount again, and feel at every step
> Our foot half sunk in hillocks green and soft
> Raised by the mole.

It is this introduction of himself that makes Cowper a neighbour of the romantic poets. He has not the magic carpet of Coleridge, he is tied to the valley of Ouse; but he confides in his reader, he *signs* every landscape and 'interior,' as a place that has become part of his inner vision. It is true that the passages, which show that a new painter of natural things has appeared, are sometimes stiffened out with a poetic diction that would be pedantic were it not really half-playful; the 'fleecy tenants' of the sheepfold, the 'leaning pile deciduous' of the haystack. . . . In *Yardley Oak* this dissolving stage of the high epical or didactic style is again evident.

The simplest and best of these scenes occur in *The Sofa,* the first of the six books, and in the beginning of the fourth, *The Winter Evening;* but they are seldom far off. Much is gained by the feeling that the artist is not making a set picture, but is himself moving from point to point of what he describes, fearful of being tired or tiresome. He denotes the different colours of the leaves, with no attempt to carry the fancy beyond them, with no mystery, just as they come, and as if no one had seen them before, but rather as if he were sorting out green tints for a pleasant embroidery-pattern. (pp. 91-3)

[Cowper's] style, which is sensitive to . . . changes of theme, is a new thing in our poetry, and its varieties invite discrimination. They may, despite their different levels and intensities, be regarded as modifications of the same pattern, and not as patches of pied materials carefully sewn in. This pattern, as suggested already, is the epic language of Milton transposed for Cowper's purposes. . . . Encouraged by . . . finding his powers, Cowper tries, towards the close of his long poem, and at intervals throughout it, to raise his language to a climax for the utterance of his religious and social faith. But this lofty, reflective sort of writing, while it shows the piety and beauty of his spirit, is not often successful; and he hardly accomplishes it very well, except in the unfinished *Yardley Oak,* one of his last original compositions in verse. . . . (pp. 93-4)

The birth and glory, the decay and mutations of a noble tree are themes that might easily drop into prose or platitude. It might, on the other hand, awaken a high imagination; we can surmise what Wordsworth, in happy hour, might have done with it. Cowper's is a poem midway between these opposites; it is a poem of the fancy, with a current of didactics; and it has a relieving element of play, rising to imaginative power; and it is wrought with such extreme study as almost to burden itself with refinements. It is of a different tribe to the ruminations of Blair, Young, and their company, on the mutability of things. The versification, however, has several of the marks of the school, such as those epithet-guarded nouns, as in 'excoriate forks deform,' and prominent 'wens globose,' which go back to Milton, but which are here half-playful; and also the awkward final monosyllable (a blemish of Milton's followers), which jerks the line to its knees at the end of a paragraph:

> And all thine embryo vastness, at a gulp.

Still, the metre is a worthy outgrowth and adaptation of the slow-moving Miltonic one, with a great frequency and rich variety of pause, and many single verses of high nobility:

> Thought cannot spend itself, comparing still
> The great and little of thy lot, thy growth
> From almost nullity into a state
> Of matchless grandeur, and declension thence,
> Slow, into such magnificent decay.

Cowper failed to make an ending; after finishing with the oak, he starts on a curious analysis, which proves too hard to carry further, of the mind of Milton's Adam; and so, with a large image, he breaks off:

> History, not wanted yet,
> Leaned on her elbow, watching Time, whose course,
> Eventful, should supply her with a theme.

The translations of [Homer's] *Iliad* and *Odyssey,* which distracted for Cowper 'so many thousand hours,' were also part of his campaign on behalf of simplicity against rhetoric. In the Prefaces to his first and to his revised editions of the *Iliad* we have his full mind. He rejected rhyme and chose blank verse, he tells us, because a rhymed version cannot be faithful, and can only be an imitation or paraphrase. . . . He does not touch on the difficulties of his metre, such as the inequality of the English decasyllable, in its length and contents, to the hexameter; but is satisfied with saying, that the example of Milton shows it can be used with energy and harmony—a harmony enhanced by occasional roughness—for a long translated poem. That this is true, the fragments of the *Iliad* translated by Tennyson will show; but Cowper could not give either the energy or the harmony. He seems to lose the command of those qualities, that he shows in his original verse; and the reason is less any failure of power, than his principle of fidelity, and the fetters of the diction he has chosen. And it is chosen in order that it may not resemble Pope's, and may resemble Homer's. The result is, that he loses also the speed and sonority which Pope attains.

Cowper found that Homer ends his periods with the end of a line, and does the same. He varies his pauses within the line very studiously, though more by effort than with a true instinct; but his closes are nearly always bad in his *Homer,* as they often are in his own blank verse. In this he failed to escape from the grand fault of the eighteenth-century poets. (pp. 95-7)

Cowper's plain diction, which he defends, is a step in the right path; but his fault is, that unlike Homer he does not make it poetical. . . . In his revisions, in deference to critics, he smoothed out some of the rough rhythms and made many other changes, but this did not mend matters. The importance of his version is therefore chiefly historical; in that he wrought faithfully at the meaning, and said farewell to rhetoric, and used, though he did not master, the greatest of metrical instruments. (pp. 97-8)

[Cowper's translations of Milton's Latin poems] are full of sympathy, but, being put into a form (although a supple one) of the eighteenth-century couplet, and 'tagged with rhyme,' they fail to give the impression of the original or its intensity and curious ruggedness. (p. 98)

> *Oliver Elton, "William Cowper," in his* A Survey of English Literature: 1780-1830, *Vol. I,* Edward Arnold (Publishers) Ltd., *1912, pp. 72-99.*

GEORGE SAINTSBURY (essay date 1916)

[*Saintsbury was an English literary historian and critic of the late nineteenth and early twentieth centuries. A prolific writer, Saintsbury composed a number of histories of English and European literature as well as several critical works on individual authors, styles, and periods. Asserting that "you cannot dislike anything in Cowper," Saintsbury characterizes Cowper's epistolary style as neither overly exciting nor overly cloying. Saintsbury also singles out "Yardley Oak" and "The Castaway" as Cowper's two best poems.*]

[If Cowper's range of subject in his letters] is somewhat small-beerish it is the freshest and most refreshing, the most delicately tasted, and the most enlivening if not stimulating small beer that ever came from honest malt and hops and pure water. You cannot dislike anything in Cowper, and it must, again, be a very peculiar and unenviable person who despises anything in him. There is—how there comes to be may be discussed presently—extraordinary variety, monotonous as a mere abstract of his life may seem. All attractions, or all except the—

> Grand, epic, homicidal, six-feet-high

dignities, and the half or wholly illicit allurements of the letter kind are there. He has neither history nor scandal, neither passion nor deliberate fun-making; but he has almost everything else.

But for those who can look deeper, or at any rate further than "the subject," there is far more reason why Cowper deserves perhaps the highest place among English letter-writers—certainly a place equal to the highest. It is simply that he had the art of letter-writing—the secret of epistolary presentment—as hardly anybody else has had it. His epistles delight because there is in them an infinite virtue of delectation—a formula in respect of which Molière, of all people, was least likely to be blind to the valid as well as the ludicrous side of it. . . . [This art is of course present in all letter writers], but nowhere is it in such quintessence as in Cowper. All of them, even Gray, are laboured sometimes, or if laboured is too strong a word for him, slightly self-conscious. Cowper never is, while on the other hand he never even approaches that most offensive of attitudes—over-innocence, super-simplicity,—in its various forms of trifling, gush, and other objectionable things. To some extent this may have been a result of the very limited society in which he passed the later part of his life. . . . The detestable habit of reading aloud in which he is known to have indulged, and which was so common in the eighteenth century as to be one of its worst blemishes, is of course murderous to talk. But the gift of familiar expression was probably in the family. And Cowper, debarred by choice or circumstance from free oral use of it, turned the stream on to paper, writing as nobody else, except Madame de Sévigné, has ever written. The femininity in him is of course undeniable, and he showed it sometimes rather unfortunately. But he made the very best use of it here. Something, as part cause of his supremacy, may be perhaps also allowed to his double character of poet and letter-writer, a conjunction which has proved fertile and fortunate in later times. (pp. 249-51)

How glad one is to be free or almost free in the letters (it appears there but seldom) from the windy and ignorant rhetoric of the satires and didactic pieces! Much of *The Task* is itself charming stuff, which might have been also charming in letter form, but it admits treatment which, quite welcome in verse, might in prose have approached that ''fine writing'' which is very rarely in place anywhere, and which the style of the century did not suit.

On the other hand Cowper, who was not in the least a professional poet, never, good as he was at occasional verse, dreamt of manufacturing it to order out of the ordinary details of his life; and so had all or most of these, except when the occasion called for verse-celebration (as in the various cat-anecdotes, the tributes for fish, and others), for material of the letters themselves, which were sometimes half in verse.

With what astounding art he made these materials up has already been observed. . . . It may almost be said that he can make a letter out of nothing at all but his own wits, without any of the antics of those who have written elaborately on Nothing with a capital N. As he never excites, so he never cloys. He ''trifles'' (in the good sense which is now almost obsolete) with most if not all things; he never trifles with any in the bad. He can deal with serious matters quite seriously, though not in the least dully. . . . He can be extremely interesting—more so, to speak frankly, than he is in the works themselves—in writing about his translations. No one has hit off such a scene as the visit of a canvassing parliamentary candidate better, while no one has more poignantly expressed the difficulties of a bachelor (permanent or ''grass'' it does not matter) in catering for himself. (pp. 251-53)

When he talks nonsense it is generally, of course not quite always, in verse; and, whether in verse or prose, it generally comes from some actual ignorance of facts, or from some distortion of prejudice which his withdrawal from books and persons has prevented from being dispelled. Of the century's most precious possession, Common Sense, Cowper, once more, has an ample share; if ever he seems to lack it we may be sure, once more also, that the special conditions which have prevented him from bringing it to bear are precedent. (p. 254)

What Cowper might have been as a poet is perhaps only shown in *Yardley Oak* and *The Castaway*. The rest—even *John Gilpin*, even the best passages in *The Task* and the prettiest of the smaller poems—is second-rate of various degrees, from the very ''best second'' to something much above the average. These two are first-rate, though they differ remarkably in individual quality. The last, as is often the case with last words, has more of the older fashion in it—the first that of the time which was to come. In the magnificent and terrible *Castaway* there is nothing outside the eighteenth century except a certain

concentration and intensity which are rarely found there, and which rather sublimate and transform the usual phenomena than add anything to them. It is all quite quiet; the diction, while not offensively ''poetic,'' is ordinary, and to some extent conventional; it has a concrete subject, a story of the time which you could illustrate easily in the charming fashion of that time. A vignette heading of the ship with bursting canvas, and a tailpiece of ''the cask, the coop, the floating cord'' almost impose themselves. (pp. 339-40)

It is rather the fashion, I believe, just now to belittle *Yardley Oak*, at any rate to deny that it, to any considerable extent, anticipates Wordsworth. This last point need not be argued at any length here, for it is in a way out of our bounds. But the value of the poem itself is not. There is a combination of massiveness and ''atmosphere'' about the piece which I at least do not know where to match earlier in the actual century, and which, out of Spenser and Shakespeare, I cannot remember having been reached by any other earlier English poet, for Milton could hardly have taken the point of view. And as we read it, besides enjoying its poetical excellence, we have to remember how many of the minor influences coming on the century it embodies or at least suggests—the historic sense, hitherto unknown, the imaginative envisagement of everything, the half-pantheistic feeling of the community of man and nature and God. The poem, as has been hinted before, perhaps outruns the eighteenth century proper a little; but it may be claimed by that century as its own, not merely in sheer chronology, not merely in virtue of the diction, which could be spared, but in virtue also of a certain *justesse* [precision] and moderation of thought and phrase which are essentially Augustan. (pp. 341-42)

George Saintsbury, ''Letters, Diaries, and the Like,'' and ''The Setting of the Augustan Sun,'' in his The Peace of the Augustans: A Survey of Eighteenth Century Literature As a Place of Rest and Refreshment, *G. Bell and Sons, Ltd., 1916, pp. 213-57, 329-73.**

ROBERT LYND (essay date 1920)

['**The Progress of Error**'] is not a book that can be read with unmixed, or even with much, delight. It seldom rises above a good man's rhetoric. Cowper, instead of writing about himself and his pets, and his cucumber frames, wrote of the wicked world from which he had retired, and the vices of which he could not attack with that particularity that makes satire interesting. The satires are not exactly dull, but they are lacking in force, either of wit or of passion. They are hardly more than an expression of sentiment and opinion. The sentiments are usually sound,—for Cowper was an honest lover of liberty and goodness,—but even the cause of liberty is not likely to gain much from such a couplet as

> Man made for kings! those optics are but dim
> That tell you so—say, rather, they for him.

Nor will the manners of the clergy benefit much as the result of such an attack on the 'pleasant-Sunday-afternoon' kind of pastor as is contained in the lines:

> If apostolic gravity be free
> To play the fool on Sundays, why not we?
> If he the tinkling harpsichord regards
> As inoffensive, what offense in cards?

These, it must in fairness be said, are not examples of the best in the moral satires; but the latter is worth quoting as evidence of the way in which Cowper tried to use verse as the pulpit of a rather narrow creed. The satires are hardly more than denominational in their interest. They belong to the religious fashion of their time and are interesting to us now only as the old clothes of eighteenth-century evangelicalism. The subject-matter is secular as well as religious, but the atmosphere almost always remains evangelical. (p. 39)

Cowper, to say truth, had the genius, not of a poet but of a letter-writer. The interest of his verse is chiefly historical. He was a poet of the transition to Wordsworth and the revolutionists, and was a mouthpiece of his time. But he has left only a tiny quantity of memorable verse. . . . There is little in **The Task** to make it worth reading to-day, except to the student of literary history. Like the Olney Hymns and the moral satires it was a poem written to order. . . .

It was the publication of **The Task** and **John Gilpin** that made Cowper famous. It is not **The Task** that keeps him famous to-day. There is, it seems to me, more of the divine fire in any half-dozen of his good letters than there is in the entire six books of **The Task**. One has only to read the argument at the top of the third book, called **'The Garden'** in order to see in what a dreary didactic spirit it is written. (p. 40)

The writing of blank verse puts the poet to the severest test, and Cowper does not survive the test. Had **The Task** been written in couplets, he might have been forced to sharpen his wit by the necessity of rhyme. As it is, he is merely ponderous—a snail of imagination labouring under a heavy shell of eloquence. In the fragment called **'Yardley Oak'** he undoubtedly achieved something worthier of a distant disciple of Milton. But I do not think he was ever sufficiently preoccupied with poetry to be a good poet. (p. 41)

As a letter-writer he does not, I think, stand in the same rank as Horace Walpole and Charles Lamb. He has less wit and humor, and he mirrors less of the world. His letters, however, have an extraordinarily soothing charm. Cowper's occupations amuse one, while his nature delights one. His letters, like Lamb's, have a soul of goodness, and we know from his biography that in life he endured the severest test to which a good nature can be subjected. . . .

[Cowper's letters] have an eighteenth-century restraint, and freedom from emotionalism and gush. But behind their chronicle of trifles, their small fancies, their little vanities, one is aware of an intensely loving and lovable personality. Cowper's poem, **'To Mary,'** written to Mrs. Unwin in the days of her feebleness, is, to my mind, made commonplace by the odious reiteration of 'my Mary!' at the end of every verse. Leave the 'my Marys' out, however, and see how beautiful, as well as moving, a poem it becomes. (p. 42)

His quiet prose gave him a vehicle for that intimacy of the heart and fancy which was the deepest need of his nature. He made a full confession of himself only to his friends. In one of his letters he compares himself, as he rises in the morning, to 'an infernal frog out of Acheron, covered with the ooze and mud of melancholy.' In his most ambitious verse he is a frog trying to blow himself out into a bull. It is the frog in him, not the intended bull, that makes friends with us to-day. (p. 45)

Robert Lynd, "William Cowper," in The Living Age, *Vol. CCCVI, No. 3965, July 3, 1920, pp. 36-45.*

W. P. KER (lecture date 1923?)

[*This essay was originally delivered as a lecture, but the date of address is unknown. W. P. Ker died in 1923.*]

There is no poet who trusts himself as fully as Cowper does to association of ideas, who lets his mind wander so freely. All his long poems are discourses, *sermones* (using a Latin name that included all kinds of essay in verse).

Cowper's form of blank verse is original. It is a form of verse resembling his rhyming couplets in not putting the diction or phrase, the style of the author, emphatically and oppressively before the mind of the reader. It is a form of verse that escapes notice in order to bring out the meaning of the thought which it is a medium for conveying. Cowper's problem was partly the same as Wordsworth's: to find a poetic interpretation of reality that should bring ideas drawn from reality into the mind of the reader without any rhetorical interruption that might distract the reader's thoughts from the sense to the style of the poet.

Landscape was, on the whole, better understood in the eighteenth century than it was after the appearance of the 'romantic' authors, because the 'romantic' authors took the mind away from pure landscape to other allied interests, such as the interests of historical association.

Cowper, like Wordsworth, is misjudged when thought of as a pure landscape poet. Both Cowper and Wordsworth tried to render life. Usually it is life from which the natural landscape is inseparable, life in which landscape has a large share; but what they are interested in is not the scene by itself, not the people by themselves, but the scene as animated by the people, the whole life in which the different elements are inextricable. (p. 231)

W. P. Ker, "Lecture-Talk: The English Poets," in On Modern Literature: Lectures and Addresses, *edited by Terence Spencer and James Sutherland, 1955. Reprint by Scholarly Press, Inc., 1971, pp. 211-38.**

E. M. FORSTER (essay date 1932)

[*Forster was a prominent English novelist, critic, and essayist whose works reflect his liberal humanism. Forster comments that Cowper's bicentenary was appropriately uneventful because, he asserts, Cowper "belongs to the unadvertised, the unorganized, the unscheduled" and has therefore been forgotten.*]

The bicentenary of Cowper's birth was celebrated last November with befitting mildness. . . . And even if the men of letters had piped up, the public at large would have declined to listen. For who reads Cowper to-day? This is surely his last appearance upon the general stage. Wordsworth (to mention a spiritual kinsman) still keeps his place; in the great holocaust of literature that is approaching he will survive for a little. Cowper perishes. His magic is too flimsy to preserve him, and his knowledge of human nature is too much overshadowed by fears of personal damnation to radiate far down the centuries:

> Those twinkling tiny lustres of the land
> Drop one by one from Fame's neglecting hand,

he wrote, "on observing some names of little note recorded in the *Biographia Britannica,*" and the epitaph might be his own. . . .

It is not an unsuitable moment for him to perish, for England is perishing, and he was English. He was not British or enlightened or far-sighted or adaptable. He was English, and most so when he forgot his nationality and took a country walk. . . .

Of course he was an invalid, and his attachment to local scenes can be discounted on that account. He had not enough vitality to seek new experiences, and never felt safe until habits had formed their cocoon round his sensitive mind. But inside the cocoon his life is genuine. He might dread the unknown, but he also loved what he knew; he felt steadily about familiar objects, and they have in his work something of the permanence they get in a sitting-room or in the kitchen garden. He does not greet them with surprise nor with any felicitous phrase. It is rather the instinctive acceptance which is part of rural life. Consequently, to read him is really to be in England, and the very triteness of his moralizing keeps us planted there. Brilliant descriptions and profound thoughts entail disadvantages when they are applied to scenery; they act too much as spot lights; they break the landscape up; they drill through it and come out at the antipodes; they focus too much upon what lies exactly in front. Cowper never does this. He knows that the country doesn't lie in front of us but all around. . . .

The country Cowper loved is precisely what is going to disappear. The grander scenery of England will probably be saved, owing to its importance in the tourist industry, but it will pay no one to preserve a stray elm, puddles full of ranunculus, or mole hills covered with thyme; and they, not the grandeur, are England. They will be swept aside by pylons and arterial roads, just as Cowper himself is being trodden underfoot by the gangs of modern writers who have been produced by universal education. Excellent writers, many of them. Writers of genius, some of them. But they leave no room for poor Cowper. He has no further part in our destinies. He belongs to the unadvertised, the unorganized, the unscheduled. He has no part in the enormous structure of steel girders and trade upon which Great Britain, like all other Powers, will have to base her culture in the future. That is why his bicentenary fell flat.

E. M. Forster, "William Cowper, an Englishman," in The Spectator, *Vol. 148, No. 5403, January 16, 1932, p. 75.*

Cowper's house at Olney.

KENNETH MacLEAN (essay date 1949)

[MacLean was one of the first critics to discuss Cowper's Memoir *as a record of mental illness and psychological terror. He praises the "sincerity and simple truth" in Cowper's poems and letters.]*

Cowper's **Memoir** is a document in neurotic terror, and the terror it directly describes is, we feel, central to all his writings. True, he expresses many feelings that seem conventionally and pleasantly romantic—a love of the country, a liking for simplicity, a sentimental taste for tear-stained faces. But such sentiments cannot be understood in reference to a romantic movement: they can be seen properly only in reference to the Cowper whose nerves needed the isolation of Olney, whose neurotic rigor asked for a severe puritan plainness in speech, whose instability expected tears. Neurosis and not the romantic movement was responsible for everything that he was as a writer—the very need itself to write and enshrine the dying life, the tone of sincerity which cannot still tell quite all the truth, the limited symbolism from the garden of Orchardside. Needless to say, Cowper interests our times greatly, hardly less than Byron whom he so much resembles in their common sense of injury and damnation.

> The world and I fortuitously met;
> I ow'd a trifle, and have paid the debt;
> She did me wrong, I recompens'd the deed . . .

We wonder particularly about his devastating modern nihilism which allowed for daily walks and daily letters and a daily number of verses but left the whole great course of things to a ruining providence. (p. 258)

The basic imagery of the Olney hymns is, I believe, the country village. We hear indeed as so frequently in Protestant religious writings the language of landholding and property. To speak of the religious experience in the language of the village was to speak closely to the parishes of England, and of New England as well, where the spirit of Cowper, its healthier part so largely exploited by Emerson, has been particularly at home. In these country hymns we feel little of that sense of innocence which Blake is shortly to associate with the village symbol. The Olney hymns are poems in religious, in primitive fear, and emotions of fear, let us remember, were little considered by poets in Cowper's time. Part of the fear stems from a feeling of hatred for God, imaged in materials we think of especially as Emily Dickinson's, steel and stone. The art of these hymns in all ways suggests this New England poet, who perhaps did not overlook one title, "The Narrow Way." Cowper has her same restricting wit which will call the Lord's Supper a "treat." He has too some of her expanding imaginative phrasing. And in both poets agony is lyrical. These careful hymns are reassuring to anyone anxious about Cowper's art. He was not above allowing his publisher to emend his poems. Nonetheless, he knew the business of poet. (p. 260)

In time Cowper discovered that the poetic creation of language was very helpful in drowning out inner voices of despair.

> There is a pleasure in poetic pains
> Which only poets know.

And as he wrote to save his own soul, he developed with his longer poems an aesthetic which had something to do with the saving of the soul of poetry in his day. Before Wordsworth he was spokesman for a prose-like speech in poetry, and though there is much of the homely elegance of a Hitchcock chair in his verse, he sometimes achieved Wordsworthian naturalness, in the blank verse of **"The Task"** most frequently. He also practiced and preached in his longer poems that free-running, digressive manner which Wordsworth, Keats, and Byron were to exploit in a poetry of association. The winged fancy, the runaway horse, the grasshopper—these varied symbols preside over Cowper's new achievement in free form. (p. 261)

The poems of 1782 set some of the themes for **"The Task,"** an important national poem. But **"The Task"** is more than just a social poem. Its chief theme is surely nature and the soul. Of all things in nature, air and wind seemed to have interested Cowper most.... Cowper's attention to air is reflected in his interest in flowers and flowering shrubbery. He loved the air of flowers—in the garden, carnation, mignonette, canary lavender—by the summerhouse, pinks and roses—in the Wilderness, honeysuckle and lilac. No one was more sensitive than this poet to the fragrance of England's disappearing commons. It was perhaps Cowper's interest in air which drew him to the Throckmortons' lawn many a time to see a balloon go up in the year after Montgolfier's experiment. Cowper the correspondent always assured his confiding friends that he was "hermetically sealed." But it was the wind moving through the air that the poet was most conscious of, the wind that in the first splendid descriptions in **"The Task"** sweeps the skirts of the woods, making the sound of waves on a shore. It was Cowper's Leibnizian notion that nature, the dancing girl, is never at rest; and he supposed that the wind was the primary element at the center of this motion. These thoughts are expressed in a passage in the excellent first book of **"The Task,"** beginning "By ceaseless action all that is subsists." But there is no Leibnizian harmony for Cowper, for like Hopkins he felt God beating in the wind, the God of his own damnation—"He who has commanded me to wither,"—He by whose will "the flow'rs of Eden felt the blast,"—He by whose pleasure still the fiend of famine "blows mildew from between his shrivel'd lips." This presence makes the final experience of nature a fearful one. And so, while there are many rhythmical moments in **"The Task,"** its essential mood is fear. Aren't we always retreating from the fresh open scene where Wordsworth keeps us into weather-houses, greenhouses, alcoves, colonnades? Aren't we clinging beside garden walls? Isn't the huge Russian ice palace pictured in the opening of the fifth book simply the greatest and biggest shelter of all? Aren't we shutting shutters on winter evenings, giving ourselves occupational therapy with our hooks, our weaving of nets for fruit, our twining of silken threads on ivory reels? Peeping at the world through the "loop-holes of retreat"—the newspapers! The stricken deer is hiding in the shade.

But comedy always stands closely beside fear in Cowper's pages. Shy in any company, Cowper found relief for his embarrassment in watching people's motions and gestures. Sterne would call this "translating." Imprisoned in his Olney house, he was devoted to the street window. Obviously a peace treaty had been signed: "Every man's posture bespoke a pacific turn

of mind." He saw the surface of human life, and this surface is essentially comic. His delightful poem, **"Conversation,"** is full of the comedy lying before an eye which would see a person conversing with his face too close to the other person's. In his very first poem we are amused simply in watching the walk of a peasant who is missing one heel. **"The Task"** is rich in comic observation. Indeed, it begins with all the comedy that can slide, twitch, sprawl, or doze on the seat of a chair. Cowper especially loved the comedy that lies in shadows. (pp. 262-64)

Poetry had something of a period in his life, but not the letter which he always wrote. He was an authority on the letter, who knew among other things that the "epistolary race" is "always won by him that comes in last." His letters have often been called the finest in English. One claim surely might well be made for them—that they contain as much of the myth of England as any piece of English literature. Here is the English character fully represented in the writings of one whom we should think incapacitated to the point of being unable to represent anything. This may be a commentary at once upon psychological disturbance and upon the suitability of English culture to a human soul. The Cowper of the letters is the complete Englishman—liking a well-cocked hat—taking his exercise—medicating shamelessly—very timid about bathing machines—feminine in his humor—liking privacy—defending the home against polygamous relations—relishing "fine" food, even as much as Hazlitt—like Lamb, deaf to music—gentlemanly but not lordly—charitable—patriotic—independent—bold enough to be ready to thresh Dr. Johnson's old jacket till the pension jingled in his pocket! These letters are an intimate picture of an Englishman. And since they are letters they particularly exhibit an English trait without which there would be no letters—a deep sense of friendship, not unlike a Prospero's.

So much health combined with such weakness, the very health growing out of the disease—this essential but much forgotten irony lies in Cowper's letters.... We sense terror as well as melancholy in these letters when Cowper takes us inside his mind where thoughts stand in sober livery, the tallest and loudest among them calling, "It is all over with thee; thou hast perished." We partly see the dreams of this mind, and we hear Cowper express his disturbing and very modern opinion that dreams are true.

The tone of despondency and terror is just as it should be in the letters. Cowper has subdued the direct statement into quiet phrases and sentences. Some of these we shall never forget: "On this very day twenty-two years ago left I London." "Yesterday was one of my terrible seasons ..." "Nature revives again; but a soul once slain lives no more." "There is a mystery in my destruction ..." One sentence we shall remember because it puzzles: "Mine is merely a case of relaxation." The sense of terror is restrained in the letters. It is also, we note, most skillfully transferred into the symbols of those excellent poems frequently enclosed in a letter. In some of these Cowper has drawn upon his beloved sea imagery as in **"The Castaway,"** his last poem and an ultimate image in lonely terror.... Most of these poems, which are surely Cowper's greatest achievement, draw their imagery from the garden at Orchardside and near by. And this is what we see about this garden. We see the head of a rose snapped off as one is shaking raindrops from it. We see kittens hypnotized by a snake's forked tongue, and we see a large man killing the small snake. We see a pet rabbit going to his last long home. Tiney had been safe in the garden walls from the pursuit of greyhounds. He had known the security of russet apple peels and Turkey carpets. But the protected life had no security from death. (pp. 264-66)

Cowper's poems and letters are a record of a terror which must interest the modern reader. What is particularly remarkable about this record is its mark, often painful, of sincerity and simple truth. Nothing has been faked. This is human terror. This is terror in a garden. (p. 267)

> *Kenneth MacLean, "The Poets: William Cowper,"*
> *in* The Age of Johnson: Essays Presented to Chauncey Brewster Tinker, *Yale University Press, 1949,*
> *pp. 257-67.*

MARK VAN DOREN (essay date 1951)

[*Van Doren, the younger brother of the editor and author Carl Van Doren, was one of America's most prolific and diverse twentieth-century writers. Van Doren's criticism is aimed at the general reader, rather than the scholar or specialist, and is noted for its lively perception and wide interest. He here states that Cowper's main concern in life was neither his letters nor his poetry, but rather "his immortal soul." He adds that if there is an art of being spontaneous, "Cowper is its master."*]

The chief business of William Cowper's life was not to write letters, though the letters he wrote are one of the two reasons he is remembered now. The other reason is his poems. But they were not his chief business either. What really occupied him was his immortal soul, concerning which he was entirely serious—some say, insanely serious, and it is a fact that he went insane four times between his twenty-first and his fifty-sixth year, and that his seventh decade passed for the most part in lamentable eclipse. Or, if insanity is not the word, he was four times depressed, or melancholy, or in despair, beyond the power of any friend or doctor to effect a cure. And it is true that one cannot separate his liability to derangement from his dedication to certain religious views, so that one is tempted to say he went mad with thinking of his soul. In any case that soul was his principal concern, and any letters he wrote, or any poems he composed, took second place for him along with the animals he petted, the landscapes he looked at, and even the friendships he cultivated. (p. 1)

A dark streak runs through those letters, and enough has been said of that. What is the character of their light? For they are brilliant with light, and as long as anybody exists to read them they will be capable of giving joy.

Strangely enough, or perhaps not strangely, this desperate man was capable of pure joy. It showed in the way he loved the objects and animals about him, but above all it showed in the way he loved his friends. He loved them so much that he knew they wanted to hear him talk about himself. The letter which merely answers another letter is no letter at all; or one that answers it too soon; or one that waits too long. He had a delicate sense of the mean in these matters, and observed it punctiliously. He never forgot that his friends wanted to hear of him, not from him. So it was of himself he talked—where he had walked this morning, what he was wearing, and how he felt and thought. Nor were his thoughts about such things as the American War and the revolution in France the thoughts they would be most eager to hear. As a patriot and a Whig he was scarcely unique; as William Cowper he was unique, and he knew exactly what this meant. The letters of William Cowper could have been written by no other man.

He freely told people that he loved them, and they were never embarrassed, for there was a saving wit in every one of his sentences. This wit cannot be defined. Its essence is in no single phrase, it is captured in no single letter; it simply is everywhere, and grows imperceptibly on us as we read. It is the wit of a genius in conversation who understood with what emphasis any given thing should be said, or with what lack of emphasis. (pp. 15-16)

His letters, he liked to say, were talk. One of his didactic poems is called **"Conversation,"** and in it we can discover how well he comprehended the subtleties of the art. Arguments, long stories, discussions of one's health, assertions of one's unworthiness to be talking at all, and points of religion—one had to be careful how one handled these. And then of course one had to be spontaneous. Doubtless there is no art of being spontaneous, but if there be one, Cowper is its master. (p. 16)

His letters are informal, as befits the fact that they often forget to say what they were written to say, so that the "important" topic is but a scribble at the close. Yet they have their own natural form, molded by the subjects that take over as his pen races across the paper. . . . He had a method. After a beginning by way of salutation, he soon found himself warming to a theme he had not supposed would engage him; this he went on with as long as he pleased, and here perhaps will be the heart of the document; but he almost never forgot to trail off in messages to others, in thanks for gifts, in postscripts about little or nothing, or in tantalizing references to matters that might have been made the principal burden of the epistle, yet were not. The whole is a complete thing, proper in each of its parts.

This obscure, half-mad stranger in an undistinguished village could have degenerated in his environment and remained unknown. Instead he grew wiser and richer every year, even if unhappier; and ended by expressing civilization as few men have expressed it. The wonder of the fact is scarcely to be explained. It is clearly to be seen, however, in every page of the letters he wrote without any thought that they would escape the flames. (pp. 17-18)

> *Mark Van Doren, in an introduction to* The Selected Letters of William Cowper *by William Cowper, Farrar, Straus and Young, Inc., 1951, pp. 1-18.*

NORMAN NICHOLSON (essay date 1951)

[*Nicholson, a noted Cowper scholar, here suggests that although many of Cowper's hymns are mediocre, they occupy "a period of great importance in Cowper's development as a poet." Nicholson praises Cowper's imaginative use of Old Testament imagery and his ability to probe "deeply to the inner meaning of his symbols."*]

[The majority of Cowper's] hymns are lukewarm—full of platitudes and borrowed piety, though they never fall into the religiosity of the worst nineteenth-century hymns ('Day is dying in the west'). The reason for Cowper's comparative failure as a hymn writer may be that he was not really a hymn *singer*. Even in his most fervent moods he was never enthusiastic about public worship on a larger scale than that of family prayers, so that he had little experience of hymn singing as a great corporate act, which carries away the individual in the sweep and flood of a common ritual and a common purpose. Nevertheless, in a handful of his hymns when the draught blows through the dying clinkers of faith to make them blaze with intense light and longing, he was able to write verses which a congregation could take to its heart instantly and wholly. (p. 61)

Of all Cowper's hymns, the two or three which are most strikingly his own belong, oddly enough, more to the manner of Wesley than that of Watts, though they do not show much direct influence. Cowper had little of Wesley's superb technical virtuosity and nothing at all of his uninhibited fervour. He was shy and diffident, and even when he joined in what one might call the mass enthusiasms of the Evangelicals, he never quite merged his emotions with those of the others. Yet, like Wesley, he was able to bridge the gap between the devotional poem (the personal expression of a personal feeling) and the hymn. He did this, as Wesley did, by expressing the emotion so that it could be shared by the congregation, each one of whom associated himself with the 'I' of the hymn. This is all the more remarkable since he did not deal with the stock emotions of the Revival. His verses have none of the crudity and violence of the popular preacher, and they rarely reinforce their appeal by reference to the better-known passages of Scripture. They tell, in fact, of spiritual experience which might often have been beyond the range of many of the singers, yet they are able to evoke an immediate response. Each one feels that here is an experience which, at least, he *might* have had, an experience he can understand and accept. Wesley identifies himself with the singer; Cowper calls on his sympathy. (pp. 71-2)

['**Oh! for a closer walk with God**'] surely is first and foremost a devotional poem, a *personal* poem. The second and the third stanzas, for instance, have clear reference to Cowper's own life-story, and both have a delicacy of perception and sentiment which could hardly be shared by the average rough-and-tumble Methodist of the time. The very first stanza, with its mellow light, so different from the fierce glare of the mission-room, shows an appreciation of the contemplative life and a longing for calm, which you might not expect to attract the many who looked to the Revival for spiritual excitement. This road, you feel sure, will not see much traffic. Yet the hymn is quite astonishingly good for congregational singing. The imagery is so simple, so clear and glowing, that everyone recognises its truth. Those who turn to hymns with throats hot with passion, thirsting for the brandy of the Saved, find suddenly that these cool verses have a real meaning for them. The response is often rather wistful, no doubt, often rather sentimental, but it is often genuine too. Man's nostalgia for innocence, his longing for Eden or the womb, are here expressed in a backward look at Huntingdon, and the days with the Unwins.

This hymn is a very pure product of the particular branch of the Revival to which Cowper belonged, and what it lacks in grandeur and mystery is made up in tenderness and sincerity. Even its very music has the subdued note of those Anglicans who are still not quite used to singing out loud in church. It is a hymn which can stand very well by itself, without a tune—indeed, it is one of the most musical in our language. It has a murmured undertone, a soft organ pedal, due, for the most part, to the frequent use of assonance instead of rhyme. Cowper probably did not use assonance as a first preference—he thought of it as an imperfect form of rhyme which, by custom, was permissible in a hymn, but to us today it gives a soft and sidling sound to the verses, much more attractive than hard rhyme.

'**Hark, my soul! it is the Lord,**' is another personal poem which nevertheless succeeds as a hymn, but in some others of this type the verses fail to be more than devotional poems. (pp. 72-3)

We come now to another aspect of Cowper's hymns, perhaps the most important of all. It has been noticed how both Watts and Wesley packed their verses with Biblical references. (p. 74)

Cowper, too, felt the myth [of the Bible] flame through his imagination like fire through dry gorse. Like 'Israel in ancient days' he had:

> a view
> Of Sinai in a blaze.

It was fierce and bright, but it was also short-lived. His Biblical references, after this period, are mostly as dry and legalistic as the theological controversies of his sect, though occasionally he catches something of an Old Testament eloquence.

Yet, I believe that this period is of great importance in Cowper's development as a poet. It was then for the first time that his imagination came to life; it was then that his ears heard the tidal roar of the psalms and the sou'westerly gales of the prophets; it was then that his eyes saw the coloured chronicles, banners emblazoned with heraldic beasts—ram, eagle, serpent, pentecostal dove and paschal lamb. The brightness was not to last long, and, indeed, it was not the sort of light which Cowper, as a poet, was equipped to transcribe into verse—the homely '**Apocalypse**' at the end of *The Task* is truer to him than all the lightning of *Isaiah*. (p. 77)

The myth left its direct mark on many of the Olney Hymns, and can be seen in some of those which we have already quoted. It comes to its fullest glow and glory in the splendid sacramental hymn, '**There is a fountain.**' Let us admit that of all Cowper's hymns this is the one which has been the most criticised and even ridiculed. . . . If this hymn is in bad taste, then Christianity itself is in bad taste. One has only to compare it with a piece of Victorian sentimentalism like 'There is a green hill,' to realise that in the latter there is a loss not only in literary power, but in understanding of the mystery—a weakening and watering-down not only of style but of dogma.

Cowper's mind was less Miltonic than that of Watts—his effects are rarely grand and never sonorous. Even in this hymn, which combines sacramental and anatomical imagery with a boldness equal to that of Donne, there is the same *emotional* reticence, the same ruminative tenderness which we find in '**Oh! for a closer walk with God.**' But while Cowper cannot equal Watts in his scenic effects, he is able, being the greater poet, to penetrate much more deeply to the inner meaning of his symbols. In this poem we are aware, not only of the rituals of the Old Testament, but of sub-strata of significance which cannot be explained by rational exegesis. There are hints and quiverings of meaning and of experience which go far beyond the conventional religious life of eighteenth-century Anglicanism. It may be true that Cowper's poetry on the whole is lacking in unconscious content; that his images too rarely become symbols; but here, at least, this is not so. For my own part, there are few poems in the English language which evoke such a response in the lower layers of consciousness: it seems to set root-tips moving and searching in my mind, drawing on the hidden stories of unrememberable memory. It may make the agnostic groan and the humanist shudder, but ['**There is a Fountain**'] remains a superb hymn and a remarkable expression of Evangelical piety at its purest. . . . (pp. 78-9)

Norman Nicholson, in his William Cowper, *John Lehmann, 1951, 167 p.*

WILLIAM HENRY IRVING (essay date 1955)

The uncanny, almost disconcerting clarity with which [Cowper] brings to life . . . the "me to thee" relationship is astonishing and probably unparalleled in the history of the familiar letter. He has the shy willingness to talk about his own quirks and quiddities—not all of them by any means pleasant, as he well knew—and, as he develops the picture of himself in our minds, along with it he manages to make clearer and more clear the diverse characters of the men and women to whom he wrote. They may have thought themselves safe and superior in his hands—he is nearly always kindly—but they probably underestimated his power to see them in the round complete, though there is little danger that we should fail to realize them after a leisurely reading through [*The Correspondence of William Cowper*]. In the letters both Cowper and his friends arise and walk.

The tragedy in the background of Cowper's personal story is by no means conspicuous in the letters, except at the very end. He refers from time to time to his various breakdowns, but always in sensible fashion with no hint of melodrama and little of self-pity. With some few of his correspondents he uses the customary phraseology of evangelical piety, and occasionally tensions of a religious sort become apparent, especially in correspondence with men like the curious schoolmaster prophet Sam Teedon. Morbidity does appear, but it is not at all frequent. (pp. 346-47)

In his letters he was himself. Nobody was making impossible demands of him, and if anyone had made an attempt to set him up as a letter writer, to this at least he would have had the correct and unarguable reply: letters are not for wit unless the wit is spontaneous; strain nullifies all quality in them. Of this he had no doubt. For him there could be no models whose excellence he would try to equal. For him there could be no rules that must be followed. For him there could be no elegance of style in one mode or another. He must write what came into his head to the friends he loved and write it without thinking much about the manner of expression. For this reason he offers very little on the art of letter writing. The whole phrase would probably have seemed a contradiction in terms to him, since sincerity of feeling was, as we say, the heart of the matter. . . . He always plays down craftsmanship in letters, that is, following certain patterns and merely imitative skill in handling phrases. Spontaneity is everything. He knows that simplicity in style and the correct and effortless use of the King's English is the necessary base for the whole business, that this simplicity is not a matter for rules, and indeed can hardly be acquired by trying. (pp. 350-53)

One gets the impression that Cowper feels that there is something almost occult about the process of composition. Get the pen firmly in hand, you restless, postponing soul! Great Nature awaits your willing passivity in this as in all other creative acts, he seems to say. The ploughing and sowing and fertilizing must be done, and that even the critics can talk about. The energizing force eludes our analysis. Perhaps with his deeply religious temperament Cowper may have found it easier to think in some such way about the problem. In his practice of the art he lets us assume that something outside himself is taking over. Enthusiasm is the word for it, especially as we remember its Greek antecedents. (pp. 353-54)

His attitude to metaphors is rather curious. He likes them short for one thing and feels that the long-winded variety will surely halt at the latter end of their progress. Like Swift here also, he would have no dealings with metaphors that were stuck on the outside of the sentence structure. They must be ground into the substance of thought, like the gold streaks in Venetian glass ornaments. He preferred to suggest a kind of dramatic parallelism when he used this figure, as when he tells about the caller with the raucous voice and the way the robins immediately undertook to rival him.

Always the laboured style offends him. . . . The thing that needs to be emphasized is not his attitude towards style, but his feeling for the special mental attitude needed in the letter writer. The letter is not an essay on a particular subject and one cannot prepare to write it. It may have no subject at all to begin with. And it will not always come off. (pp. 355-56)

Cowper was not very good at answering special queries or at retailing the village gossip. The qualities that lead one back to the reading of his letters are far different from his thank-you notes for fish and oysters that recur so frequently. We go back to them because they provide not facts but life. In effect they do for us what good poetry does; they renew or enlarge our experience of living. . . . (p. 357)

William Henry Irving, "Walpole and Cowper," in his The Providence of Wit in the English Letter Writers, *Duke University Press, 1955, pp. 328-59.**

MORRIS GOLDEN (essay date 1960)

[Unlike many modern critics, Golden contends that The Task *is a unified work, and he examines its themes and structure to support his view.]*

I think it is demonstrable that, considered from many viewpoints, [Cowper's *The Task*] *is* unified. Most conspicuously, it presents a central theme to which everything is connected and upon which everything reflects—the theme of seeking the ideal of stability, harmony, order. In **"The Sofa"** this theme is delicately explored in various ways, with the sofa itself acting as a symbol of the edge of excess, with rural nature seen as the best earthly balance between wildness and savagery on the one hand and the city's profligacy on the other. In **"The Time-Piece,"** the latter is developed, in both its causes and its consequences, and is balanced by the manifestations of the former in natural disturbances which are reflections of God's wrath. **"The Garden"** shows the precariousness of this natural balance on earth—to achieve an ordered life, the retreater must occupy himself with minute discriminations (such as those essential to raising cucumbers or maintaining a hothouse) in a small, enclosed domestic group; he derives from the garden only a diluted, corrupted remnant of man's lost paradisal innocence and must work hard to retain it. **"The Garden"** ends with an awareness of London, an earthly hell existing in opposition to any earthly version of paradise. In **"The Winter Evening"** the fallibility of this earthly retreat is first suggested and then demonstrated. (Indeed, the fact that there is such a thing as winter, as is shown in the last book, is a refutation of the idea that paradise is possible on earth before Judgment Day, and in this way the last half of the poem is something of a balance to the first half.) God's storms and man's corruption disturb, each in its way, the unstable simulacrum of stability that man can build up in the country. Book V, in the sharp clarity of the cold morning, shows primarily the awareness of how delusive appearances of earthly stability may be, using as example what is presumably the highest power available on earth, that of absolute monarchs. It argues that their authority is based on futile and barren excess which causes distortion in both the kings and their subjects. The only escape from the chaos of arbitrary human activities is conversion, through which comes an internal order ("freedom") for one with grace. In the last book, which appropriately begins with a recollection of innocent childhood and a stern but kindly father, we see a vision in Judgment Day of primal innocence and the primal Father. (As in the poem on his mother's picture, Cowper's imagination yearns back to the days remembered as those of unified innocence, before he was sent off to school.) In the Judgment Day scene, all the narrative and thematic "rays of information," as Cowper called them in another context, meet—God, both stern and kind, destroys and creates, in a vision of ultimate harmony and balance.

In other elements, the poem is still organized around this theme. Books II and V, for example, concentrate more than the others on man's blind delusions and their violent consequences; Books III and IV are a unit, developing both the best possible activity and the best possible situation on earth and showing how even these are cankered by man's viciousness and God's imminent wrath. Books I and VI, too, have the connection of dealing with nature, and its significance, generalized away from the more specific time schemes and even environments of the other books.

Other themes, and smaller elements of structure, are also joined in what seems to me a satisfactorily unified way. That of illusion and delusion, so effectively humanized in the first book in the actions of the drowned sailor and Crazy Kate, works its way toward the clarity and truth of the Judgment Day passage, by way of, among other significant parts, all of **"The Time-Piece"** and **"The Winter Morning Walk."** The ambivalence of God's position in relation to Cowper, beginning with Cowper's apology in **"The Sofa"** for not being conspicuously active, runs through the various descriptions of God's power and wrath in the other books and comes, again in the Judgment Day vision, to God's combination of merciless destruction of evil and glowing reward of good; after this vision, Cowper returns to the **"Sofa"** self-justification, but this time his passive, contemplative good has come to be the most that a virtuous man can do in this world. The issue of stultification as against acute living, begun with the symbol of the sofa, is settled in the freedom by conversion in the fifth book and the active ecstasy of Judgment Day in the sixth. Again, the relaxation at the very end is more actively virtuous than even the earlier walking, since we now know that the relaxer is full of balanced inward vitality.

Still smaller elements echo the singleness of conception of this. . . . The freed prisoner, who early has savored only earthly nature, in the fifth book is brought to a full realization of grace, and his realization is presented to us in the sixth. The deluded sailor, who early jumps to his death, is reincarnated as a traveler who sees himself approaching the shore of heaven. Those who are already wise in their forsaking of worldly society and in their discovery of nature . . . move on to become those who are fully blessed in discovering nature's significance. The earthly city, the low-lying final goal of all the world's filth in the first book, becomes in the last the Salem, the new Jerusalem, toward which flow all the saved spirits. The vicious hunters who have despoiled the country, the depraved who have corrupted it, the deluded and mad who have forced the stricken deer into a distorted near-solitude, have been destroyed, and all those hosts remaining form a heavenly society. On an even smaller, though more evocative scale, all the sounds that pervade *The Task,* the jarring village noises, hideous city din, soothing country music (which on earth includes, as Cowper is careful to point

out, inharmonious bird noises) are purified to a universal harmony on Judgment Day; and the poem ends with the poet's prayer that his earthly song will be pure enough in sound, as it is in motivation, to please God.

Similarly, *The Task* fulfills the final test for unity—break it where we will, its contents are discoverably arranged in their characteristic triple form: brutalism-balance-decadence (which, in view of Cowper's mental preoccupations, could also be written: God's power-harmonious and static balance—man's intolerable chaos). From the stool, elbow-chair, sofa triad at the very beginning to the heaven, Judgment Day, earth triad in the end, everywhere Cowper's theme appears, whether in major symbolic structures such as the quiet country between the wilderness and the city or in lesser ones such as the decent, virtuous poor between the brutalized wagon-driver and the drunken thief.

"A regular plan," in the sense that Goldwin Smith [the author of *The Life of Cowper*] used the words, *The Task* may not have, and the transitions may not at first seem inevitable. But it is a question worth considering, whether any good poetry has ever depended for its organization exclusively, or even primarily, on this sort of surface regularity. Is it necessary that in older poetry the interstices between the emotionally valid segments of the poem be prosaically filled in? and is current poetic practice, on the program set forth by T. S. Eliot and followed by our contemporaries, a radical departure from the truth of the past? Or is poetry primarily a unified recording and communication of an intense emotional perception of reality, with or without passive connectives? If the latter, then, despite occasional garrulity, *The Task* is a unified and a good poem. (pp. 151-55)

> *Morris Golden, in his* In Search of Stability: The Poetry of William Cowper, *Bookman Associates, 1960, 189 p.*

JOHN N. MORRIS (essay date 1964-65)

[*In this essay, originally published in the* American Scholar *in 1964-65, Morris designates Cowper's* Memoir *as "the debut of the literary person as an introspective autobiographer." Morris asserts that Cowper succeeded in his attempt "to wrest meaning from the experience of guilt" and that "the madhouse was the place of his 'second nativity'."*]

If Cowper's *Memoir* does not mark the debut of introspective autobiography as literature, it constitutes the debut of the literary person as an introspective autobiographer. (p. 144)

William Cowper was the first of what was to become the numerous class of intellectuals who recognized private experience to be a source of "wisdom" and [his autobiography] . . . is evidence that he and those who came after him may owe this recognition in large part, both to certain heroes of religion and to a number of obscure, nearly anonymous, and markedly unintellectual persons.

The private experience in which Cowper deals is extreme experience—the experience of conversion, but conversion preceded and in fact determined by madness. More explicitly than his predecessors, he recognizes his mental crisis for what it was, a decline into absolute insanity. And, by both recognizing it and (in a complicated way) approving it, Cowper helps to begin the modern project of making available to serious attention abnormal states of mind, a project that for better or worse has vastly enlarged the scope of our moral and imaginative concerns.

One virtue of Cowper's book is its sharpness of focus. . . . [He] leaves out of account nearly everything that does not bear directly on the main matter of his story: his passage through madness and despair to faith and relative (and temporary) serenity. The work is "a history of my heart, so far as religion has been its object," he says in the first paragraph . . . , and he is almost perfectly loyal to the formal principle here enunciated. He tells us little of his childhood—we wish that he told us more, for we suspect it to be more relevant than he imagined—but what he does record seems much to the point. One characteristic of Cowper implicated in his collapse was his extreme shyness, a dauntedness of spirit that prevented his appearing before any board of examiners or any body that could be conceived of as a court of judgment. An early expression of this timidity occurred when he was at school. There he became the favorite victim of a bully a few years older than he. So strongly did this boy's cruelty impress "dread of his figure" on Cowper's mind "that I well remember being afraid to lift up my eyes upon him higher than his knees". . . . It may be that Cowper's later terror in the face of authority, a terror expressed in his frenzy at the prospect of examination before the House of Lords and in his recurrent conviction that he was mysteriously, irretrievably damned, had something to do with this early acquaintance with cruel and whimsical power. And the reader notices the economy and force with which Cowper renders his old fear: "I knew him by his shoe-buckles better than any other part of his dress," he writes . . . , a sentence that in the manner of a novelist enacts the emotion, rather than merely giving it a name. (pp. 144-45)

Cowper searchingly confronts his recollections. His descriptions appear to issue from a desire to be rigorously exact, as though his report were subject to verification. Possibly there is something self-protective about this; by treating one's feelings like objects, one separates oneself from them a little. In any event, the record is remarkably and movingly clear. (p. 163)

Control of the sort that Cowper exercises in his autobiography—control in the sense both of the formal coherence of the whole and of the deliberate clarity of particular formulations—is . . . not merely an aesthetic but a moral concern. . . . [He] focuses sharply on "the history of my heart, so far as religion has been its object." And, further, . . . he insists on understanding his experience. Cowper . . . was terrified of judgment—but the judgment of others, not himself. Or, rather, in his sanity, he understands his fear of judgment to be the mark of madness. That understanding is a result of his willingness to enter at last into judgment on himself, to recognize . . . that his hopelessness of grace was itself the sin to which it seemed to be a response. And . . . Cowper insisted that the world make sense. Even in his madness he did this. His greediness of conscience, seeking in his past something to convict himself of, expresses several things, no doubt; but one of them is a horror at the apparent senselessness of his sufferings. The notion that he was irrevocably damned, painful though it was, was preferable; it permitted justice, of however harsh a sort, and, with justice, God to exist. (pp. 164-65)

Or so we may read his story. This much is certain: . . . Cowper's autobiography may be described as an account of the attempt to wrest meaning from the experience of guilt. The passage from madness to sanity, from damnation to blessedness, is the passage from a wrong opinion to a right one about what that meaning is. These books make clear how mortally

dangerous a journey it is. And hence these books declare their subjects to be heroes—heroes in a sense of the term easier for us to understand than for their contemporaries and themselves.

These chronicles of suffering are not chronicles of weakness. They detail crisis and collapse; but they end in victory, of however compromised, limited, and ambiguous a sort. Surely it is testimony to the essential strength of the self of a Cowper . . . that it insists on exploring the regions outside the fold of salvation, refusing the comforts (which at the same time it values and longs for) of faith which it fears will somehow annihilate it. This adventure in insanity is sin; but it is perhaps not a sin easy for us altogether to condemn. As Cowper testifies, it is a sin like Satan's, in which, from Cowper's lifetime to the present, many men have found everything to admire. (pp. 165-66)

What I am suggesting here is that the strength of the adventurous, Satanic self, the strength that I have been praising, is not only the strength to make the journey but to *survive* it, to carry it through to some purpose. And that purpose is a man's daylight dealings with reality. The voyages out and back are one. And the return, one hopes, is not to the same condition from which one started, but to earned control, a new health. . . . The power to conceive, to plan, to work, and to bring a work to a conclusion is not the desire of the artist alone, but of every man. That power, that health, is what . . . Cowper achieved—achieved by surviving. It was incomplete power, to be sure. Cowper's journey had to be made again. . . . [The] madhouse was the place of his "second nativity". . . . (pp. 167-68)

John N. Morris, "Religious Lives: William Cowper and the Uses of Madness," in his Versions of the Self, *Basic Books, 1966, pp. 143-68.*

PATRICIA MEYER SPACKS (essay date 1967)

[*In her discussion of the hymns and the poetry, Spacks focuses on Cowper's use of imagery. Of the hymns, she notes that "their strength derives almost entirely from the quality of their psychological insight," rather than from powerful imagery. Cowper's imagistic patterns portray "a world in which the human need for perceptual order is dominant," and his satisfaction, Spacks argues, comes from his role as an observer. Spacks attributes the later success of* The Task *to Cowper's ability to suggest inner states through imagery of the external world.*]

What is particularly striking about Cowper's hymns as compared with his other work is their essentially slight dependence on imagery: their strength derives almost entirely from the quality of their psychological insight, and their attempts to translate that insight into images are rarely and incompletely successful. Key images identified by critics include the worm, the thorn, the tempest, the fig tree, and fetters. To this we may add imagery of light, of battle, and of streams or fountains. All are commonplaces of Evangelical discourse; most are common to religious language in general. And, upon examination, few seem truly essential to Cowper's record of religious agony occasionally modified by the faint hope of salvation. (pp. 165-66)

[Hymn number IX, **"The Contrite Heart,"**] is almost bare of figurative language; the only clear metaphor is "Insensible as steel"—the broken heart of the final stanza seems not metaphorical but literal. The hymn's power derives largely from its very bareness, and from the conviction with which the poet describes and analyzes his own emotional tension. Conflict is the essence of the poem. Initially, there seems to be a clash between the conventional—the automatic, easy assurance of the first two lines—and the personal: the bewilderment expressed in the succeeding two lines, underlined by the fact that they address a conventionally "gracious" God. Then Cowper redefines the opposition between conventional and personal as one between the expected (the speaker should "hear" the word of God) and the actual (he hears in vain). He is literally "of two minds": one weakly "inclin'd" toward God; the other, more forceful, "Averse to all that's good." Willing to go through the prescribed motions, the sufferer is constantly brought up short by awareness of his own feelings: he *thinks* himself inclined to love God, but *feels* averse to good; he cries, conventionally, "My strength renew," only to *feel* his own weakness; he *knows* that "saints" love church, does what they do, but *feels* the lack of resultant comfort.

The Donnean appeal of the final stanza is fully justified by the exposition that precedes it. It is an appeal that emotion resolve conflict—not knowledge or even faith: God can "decide" the speaker's doubt only by making him *feel* intensely and unambiguously. The extreme economy of the final two lines helps to make them climactically moving. The poet's heart is unavoidably passive: it either is or is not broken; the stress on passive verb forms (increased by the use of *be* as the final rhyme word) emphasizes the human helplessness which is so often Cowper's theme. In contrast, only God is capable of meaningful action: He can "break" (the strong physical connotations of the word increase its power, suggesting the possibility that the will of God could shatter the whole personality) or "heal" all breaks, all human maladies; and breaking as well as healing may be a mode of salvation—through the restoration of feeling.

This evocation of God as all-powerful, but apparently strangely unwilling to use His power, and of man as forced by his own divided state into a condition of helpless passivity, is central to Cowper's thought. The same ideas emerge frequently in his other hymns, but rarely with as much energy and conviction as in **"The Contrite Heart."** . . . [The theme of hymn number XI, **"Jehovah Our Righteousness,"**] is the nature and destructiveness of the divided human spirit. This time Cowper concentrates on how good impulses can turn into their opposites: prayer into sin, praise into "self-applause," "Divine desire" into impatience; the heart, traditionally the repository of gentle feelings, is actually "a fountain of vile thoughts." Yet the final stanza somewhat smugly asserts the poet's superiority to others because he recognizes his own inability to achieve virtue and therefore relies solely on the goodness of God.

This conclusion is logical enough: the rational content of the poem consists of an elaboration of the opening two lines, and the concluding stanza defines an attitude toward the facts the poem has described. But that attitude, although logically plausible, contradicts the emotional emphasis of the stanzas that precede its statement. One may object to the imagery of serpent and fountain, but its emotional purport is clear: it insists upon self-disgust as the necessary consequence of man's awareness of his sinful nature. To deny that self-disgust in the conclusion exemplifies the very weakness pointed to in the second stanza: "I cannot make thy mercies known / But self-applause creeps in." Although self-awareness is the subject of the hymn, there is none in the resolution. The disdain for less knowledgeable "others" implied by *gaudy*, the easy assurance of the pronouncement, "The Lord for ever mine"—these are far from the sense of doubt and questioning earlier conveyed.

The most moving stanzas are the second and third, most specifically concerned with the nature of inward contradiction,

most direct in their statement of the problem. Their paucity of imagery also distinguishes them: "that holy flame" is the only clear metaphor. ("Creeps in," in the preceding stanza, has undeveloped metaphoric implications.) This rather commonplace image exists in dramatic conjunction with expression of a very different sort: the holy flame of divine desire reveals itself to be simply impatience, and one perceives the relative pretentiousness of the metaphor when the quality it refers to receives a different "name." The problem of using language properly is implicit in all but the final stanzas of this hymn: the sinner's self-examination is largely examination of the difficulty of expressing in words any inner integrity he may have. Sin contaminates the words of prayer; the effort to "speak" God's praises turns to self-applause; the name of divine desire becomes the name *impatience*.

Partly because the poem's concerns are mental (or spiritual) and verbal problems, the concreteness of sin conceived as serpent is disturbing: twining and sliding are motions too physical for the context. On the other hand, when Cowper treats sin simply as spiritual fact, in the second stanza, its force is considerably greater. The heart as "fountain of vile thoughts" is momentarily impressive, but as the image is elaborated its details become so concrete and specific as to remove stress from the main point. We may even find ourselves lost in contemplation of how and why the "self" manages to float on the surface of its own heart. The image is vivid, but its meaning becomes shadowy; the relation between the self and the heart is both obscure and grotesque.

The danger of grotesquerie is often imminent for Cowper because of his singular lack of tact in converting his ideas to images. . . . Cowper's frequent references to the blood of Christ make it clear that he conceives it not as an image but as a symbol: what it stands for is of course immeasurably more important than what it *is.* Yet since the poet insists on reminding us in some detail of what precisely it *is,* readers less tradition-steeped than he are likely to have difficulty making the transition from image to meaning. "Comfortable thoughts arise / From the bleeding sacrifice," observes another hymn (number VIII, **"O Lord, I Will Praise Thee"**); it is difficult to imagine anyone but Cowper composing such a couplet. The adjective *bleeding* presumably reminds him of the symbolic import of Christ's sacrifice; for the reader, it turns a relatively abstract noun into a sharp and perhaps unpleasant image. The attempt to evoke a Christian paradox by speaking of *comfortable* thoughts fails; the paradox is too easy to be convincing.

The most vivid single example of Cowper's lack of control of his images is the final hymn of his Olney series, which systematically turns the natural world into a series of emblems for Christ. . . . The grotesque conjunction of "the blushes of the skies" and "his bleeding beauties" is the most startling element in [this hymn], but . . . , the padding of its opening lines, the anticlimax of its conclusion, are also characteristic of Cowper the hymn-writer at his worst. Although the implied personification of this stanza is thematically appropriate, in the second stanza the personification emphasizes the awkwardness of the emblematic treatment, and in the final stanza it is simply irrelevant: how does evening conceived as a person "point to an eternal rest" in any way importantly different from that of evening as a physical phenomenon? . . . Cowper's images, in his hymns, frequently seen to have a sort of fatality, to call one's attention inexorably to the "original" rather than the "secondary sense." And his imagery is often "metaphysical" in two ways: its references, although they may purport to deal with the realm of concrete actuality, really concern only the realm beyond the physical; and the images often embody "the most heterogeneous ideas . . . yoked by violence together." Unfortunately Cowper at his most "metaphysical" resembles John Cleveland ("my pen's the spout / Where the rain-water of mine eyes runs out") more than John Donne; his extravagances, traditional though they often are, are imperfectly controlled, and likely to alienate rather than to attract the reader.

Yet the imagery of these hymns, when it is less extreme, is strangely revealing. Most deeply-felt of Cowper's images of the sinner's state seem to be those of storm and of battle. God may be a pilot in the storm (Hymn XXXVIII), or He may actually calm the storm (Hymn XLI); He may control the course of battle and supply the weapons (IV, V), or guard the city against besiegers (XIV), or brighten the Christian's armor in answer to prayer (XXIX); when the satanic "foe" takes the guise of bird of prey, God becomes a sheltering bird, protecting His children beneath His wings (XXIV). Only in the last of these functions, though, does God seem vividly present to the poet's imagination. Cowper's reiterated imagery of light (his favorite emblem of God) and of streams and fountains is more convincing. His most typical positive adjectives and nouns (*calm, pleasant, cheerful, peace, comfort*) suggest the state of restored innocence for which he, as a Christian, yearns, a state emblemized by the calm cheer of light, the steady flow of the fountain.

The conjunction of these facts is suggestive; two stanzas from Hymn LVIII, **"The New Convert,"** hint their significance:

> No fears he feels, he sees no foes,
> No conflict yet his faith employs,
> Nor has he learnt to whom he owes
> The strength and peace his soul enjoys.
>
> But sin soon darts its cruel sting,
> And, comforts sinking day by day,
> What seem'd his own, a self-fed spring,
> Proves but a brook that glides away.

The polarities of Cowper's universe are here suggested and partly described. On the one side is the realm of "conflict." The new convert may postpone awareness of it, but he cannot avoid its actuality; he will ultimately be forced to "see" the foes which have existed all along; his comforts will "sink" as inevitably as the brook glides away. Conflict implies depletion of human resources; it involves a falling away from the state of "strength and peace," of enjoyment, calm, cheer, which is Cowper's most potent vision. He dreams, too, of a never-exhausted fountain of grace, as he dreams of, and believes in, a divine source of spiritual light. But faith and perception seem, in this hymn at least, fundamentally opposed: faith temporarily protects a man from "seeing" what is to be seen; as the power of sin counteracts that of faith, he comes to realize that the inexhaustible spring is only a transient brook. In some of the most convincing hymns Cowper's perceptions of nature support him in his non-rational conviction of the essential hostility of the universe he inhabits. Yet his fundamental effort in all his poetry was to justify, and thus to retain, his dream of idyllic peace, in which he might return to the child-like state of the new convert.

In the hymns, by their very nature, Cowper's religious conviction dominates his poetic gifts. (pp. 166-73)

[In **The Task,** the] observer is more important than the phenomena he perceives. (p. 179)

The reduction of nature to an object of aesthetic perception implies the possibility of a close relation between nature and art; this relation is a significant part of Cowper's subject, although his concern with it sometimes emerges only through his choice of metaphors. His description of rural scenes frequently insists, explicitly or implicitly, on the fact that nature provides "works of art" for contemplation. Like many eighteenth-century poets, Cowper often perceives landscapes as spatially organized like paintings, but he seems more aware than most of what he is doing. A typical passage is full of indications of spatial relationships: *there, here, there, far beyond.* But it also expresses the perceiver's conscious—or almost conscious—pleasure in having discovered a point of view from which nature and people in the natural world can be considered as purely aesthetic phenomena. (pp. 179-80)

The scenes Cowper describes frequently have this sort of neatness, orderliness—frequently, but by no means always. The first book [of **The Task**], however, describes the natural universe almost entirely from the point of view of the connoisseur of·art, whose eye orders even the relative confusion of the forest.

> Nor less attractive is the woodland scene,
> Diversified with trees of ev'ry growth,
> Alike, yet various. Here the gray smooth trunks
> Of ash, or lime, or beech, distinctly shine,
> Within the twilight of their distant shades;
> There, lost behind a rising ground. . . .

Once more we have the *here-there* organization; Cowper asserts confidently, "No tree in all the grove but has its charms" . . . , and then specifies with sharp visual detail the individual attractions of each, providing a brilliant objectification of that Augustan ideal of "order in variety" hinted by the opening lines of the passage. He can perceive the panorama of hill and valley between wood and water as "a spacious map" . . . with no implied deprecation of its beauty: the fact that it is describable in terms of human achievement suggests its praiseworthy orderliness. The effect of this reference to nature as a map is at the opposite pole from that of Smart's "All scenes of painting crowd the map / Of nature," which dramatizes the poet's impression of an overflowingly rich universe, in which the distinction between the works of God and those of man becomes finally irrelevant. Cowper's metaphor describes a world in which the human need for perceptual order is dominant. (pp. 180-81)

The greatest pleasure for Cowper is unquestionably aesthetic contemplation, contemplation as an observer. Actual participation in life is dangerous and debilitating; life can become "A peddler's pack, that bows the bearer down" . . . ; men cling to it although it is essentially meaningless, long for society through mere dread of solitude. Cowper's images of all but peasant life are characteristically images of deprivation and desperation. To the horrors of the urban life which, through its very gaiety, "fills the bones with pain, / The mouth with blasphemy, the heart with woe" . . . , the poet opposes, once more, his vision of nature as essentially designed for human contemplation:

> The earth was made so various, that the mind
> Of desultory man, studious of change,
> And pleas'd with novelty, might be indulg'd. . . .

The principle of change and contrast in nature seems now to exist to fulfill man's aesthetic needs: man may become bored with individual "prospects," but other prospects always exist;

he may contemplate landscapes interrupted by hedges which provide visual variety; the shapeless gorse offers "ornaments of gold" . . . made more pleasing because opposed to the "deform'd" . . . bush itself. (pp. 182-83)

The essence of spiritual liberty is its permanence, in comparison with which nature itself seems transient. In His visible works, God,

> finding an interminable space
> Unoccupied, has fill'd the void so well,
> And made so sparkling what was dark before.
> But these are not his glory. . . .

On aesthetic grounds, man supposes that "so fair a scene" . . . must be eternal—as he supposes the permanence of the ice palace on the basis of visual evidence (the adjective *sparkling*, like *glitter* in the lines quoted below, may remind one of the connection between the two phenomena). Yet nature, considered in terms of the divine plan, is merely another sort of artifice, the product of an "artificer divine" . . . who has Himself "pronounc'd it transient, glorious as it is" . . . because He values spiritual, not physical, permanence. Cowper's values are similar; he elaborates for almost two hundred lines on the value, the essentiality, of spiritual liberty. Yet the resolution of the discussion of spiritual freedom accepts once more the profound aesthetic value of nature, and makes the ability to perceive this value a touchstone of one's spiritual state. . . . The beauty of the world is God's special gift to man; visual "possession" of "delightful scenery" is more valuable than wealth. . . . If God is the source of proper perception, He is also the *end* of perception: this is the final word of Book V [of *The Task*]. The hired faculties which liberty creates lead man ultimately to God, healing the potential and sometimes actual split felt between God and nature as objects of contemplation. . . . The ability to appreciate the "scenes" which nature provides becomes thus virtually a test of one's spiritual condition; the belief in the aesthetic superiority of nature to art is not a matter merely of personal response, but a product of the realization that nature has intrinsic significance which no work of art can achieve. Elsewhere in *The Task,* some of the most compelling passages of natural description attempt to define and delineate this significance. The substructure which justifies such attempts is probably most apparent in Book V, itself comparatively bare of description.

For Cowper, then, the act of visual perception, which had provided subject matter and metaphors for poets throughout the eighteenth-century development of the poetry of image rather than action, finally takes on metaphysical importance. . . . For Cowper the seeing itself implied the transcendental truth; the physical power of vision became a spiritual reality. (pp. 192-94)

One striking fact about the relatively weak moralistic sections of *The Task* is that they are so radically different in technique from the worst of Cowper's hymns. If the special talent manifested in the hymns is the ability to turn the perceptive faculty inward, to define and render directly certain sorts of psychic activity and psychic stasis without significant recourse to visual metaphor, the talent which created *The Task* seems adept at rending inner states by suggestion, through reference to and reliance on imagery of the external world. Conversely, the hymns at their worst depend most heavily on metaphor; *The Task,* whose central subject is concrete reality in its spiritual context, is at its worst often almost bare of imagery, lapsing into concern only with abstractions. There is a kind of metaphor

(although a weak and sketchy one) in "ghostly counsel" dropping, a "disregarded thing"; aside from that, and the vague metaphoric possibilities of *touch* . . . , *empty school* . . . , the only metaphor in the two passages is "The brightest truth that man has ever seen," a reference characteristic of Cowper's conventional interest in light as an emblem of spiritual reality, but hardly more than a reference.

But if these passages manifest little distinct visual awareness, they also demonstrate little psychic awareness. What "perception" they display seems theoretical ("philosophical," Cowper might say) rather than direct, the product of what the poet has been told, not what he has himself "seen." Cut off from his deepest sources of feeling, he produces impoverished language; the more barren sections of *The Task,* which by implication deny the validity of that very perception that the poem at its best strongly affirms, are boring. (pp. 202-03)

The greatest achievement of *The Task* . . . [is the fusion of religious, aesthetic, and emotional meaning]. In the hymns, Cowper conveyed his fear that man must move inevitably from an infantile state of pure dependence and complete comfort to an anguished awareness of conflict and the loss of peace, comfort. Elsewhere in *The Task,* he reminds us that the eye is "guiltless": no blame can attach to aesthetic contemplation; passivity is associated with lack of vice. In the flower passage, contemplation is not merely guiltless; it becomes essentially an act of worship, of such total worship that it involves the poet's entire sensibility—his desire for peace, for beauty, for piety; his emotional and religious yearnings, his intellectual convictions. The act of visual perception has finally become fully inclusive as it leads Cowper back to his ideal state of faith and ease. (p. 206)

> *Patricia Meyer Spacks, "William Cowper: The Heightened Perception," in her* The Poetry of Vision: Five Eighteenth-Century Poets, *Cambridge, Mass.: Harvard University Press, 1967, pp. 165-206.*

BARRETT JOHN MANDEL (essay date 1970)

[*Like Kenneth MacLean (1949) and John N. Morris (1964-65), Mandel interprets the* Memoir *as a psychological record. He explores the discrepancy between the rational narrative persona which Cowper intended to project and the disturbed personality which actually comes across to the reader.*]

It is clearly very difficult to read William Cowper's *Memoir* without recognizing a significant difference between the self-portrait Cowper wishes to convey and the one that actually exists in the pages of his autobiography. From beginning to end, the *Memoir* is characterized by a split between what Cowper intended (his abortive attempts to fashion a verbal construct as controlled as **"John Gilpin"** or **"The Castaway"**) and what his inner compulsions forced him, in fact, to produce. The Aristotelian critic whose task it is to examine the formal structure of the *Memoir*—the way in which its elements achieve organicism within a form—would have to judge the autobiography as seriously flawed art. But the psychological critic, interested in knowledge of Cowper as a man, would find the *Memoir* a compelling, even important, document. Both critics would be correct. If the nineteenth- and twentieth-century critics see Cowper as mentally unhealthy when the author sees himself as perfectly sound, it is because the artifact Cowper has modeled as his "life" is somehow flawed. It does not achieve its purpose.

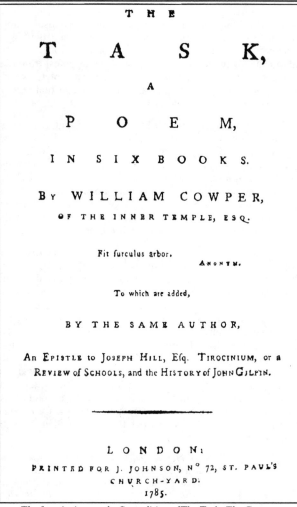

The frontispiece to the first edition of The Task. *The Granger Collection, New York.*

as to overlook opportunities of nurturing them. Both motifs are essential to his overall self-view.

Cowper chose the convenient Puritan and evangelical conversion pattern: preconversion, conversion, and postconversion experiences. For Cowper, life took on meaning because he had been converted. Salvation justified his miserable existence. The conversion was destined to give a definite structure both to his memories and to an autobiography whose purpose was to trace the growth of his religious sensibility. The combination of his artistic purpose and his shaping of experience made it inevitable for Cowper to create a narrator (for the postconversion period) who would serve the norms of the autobiography by speaking in the *persona* of a converted and healthy religious enthusiast.

Cowper writes to convey his belief that God engineered the whole conversion. . . . It is Cowper's artistic obligation, given his organizing principle and "conversion" form, to make God's controlling role manifestly clear. And, though ultimately he fails, when he does succeed in various sections of the work, he is very convincing indeed. (pp. 433-34)

Nowhere has Cowper's real psychological state damaged the governing design of the autobiography as much as in his treatment of his mental derangement. Because of his firm belief that his insanity represented the major torment of his preconversion days—the punishment of a wrathful God—Cowper had no choice but to include in the *Memoir* his descent, step by dizzying step, into the nether world of madness. Psychiatrists may find Cowper a manic depressive and suggest that his mental derangement generated his belief in a brutal evangelical God, but as an autobiographer Cowper was obliged to write what he saw, and what he "saw," as he turned over the memories of his mental collapse, was that the hideous episode in his life was merely one part, albeit one of the most significant parts, of the more important conversion experience. Cowper's plan was to demonstrate that God made use of madness (by allowing Satan to torment the sinner) as an instrument of punishment. The artistic demands on Cowper's *Memoir,* if the autobiography is to reflect his deep-rooted belief and his emergence into mental health, require him to subordinate the mental instability to the larger concerns of his spiritual conversion. But instead this subordinate element in his life story gets so disastrously out of hand that Cowper, without realizing it, magnifies it to the point that it seems to subsume the conversion experience itself, almost as if the conversion were a product of the mental instability (the last thing Cowper would have wanted to suggest). Such "misrepresentation" arises from the mental problems' seeming to have a life of their own, often utterly out of the narrator's control. The narrating "religious zealot" is dedicated to showing how and when God permitted Satan to afflict the protagonist with the fateful blow. The real "moment" of insanity—the one Cowper is consciously presenting—comes in the period of religious frenzy after an attempted suicide. (pp. 434-35)

What he fails to recognize is that the electric language he uses to describe his professed moment of insanity is indistinguishable from language used to describe his emotional reactions as early as the clerkship episode. "In this situation such a fit of passion . . . seized me when alone in my chambers that I have cried out aloud and cursed the hour of my birth, lifting up my eyes to heaven . . . in the hellish spirit of rancorous reproach and blasphemy against my maker". . . . In the *Memoir* signs of mental instability that appear *before* Cowper has said that God used madness as a punishment are bound to work against the art of the piece. (p. 436)

Cowper's conscious intention presents no difficulties. The principle underlying his choice of particular memories, their arrangement, emphasis, and stylistic treatment clearly reflects his wish, stated in the first paragraph of the *Memoir,* to provide "a history of my heart so far as religion has been its object." (pp. 432-33)

Cowper attempts to unify his self-study by treating all his experiences as important only insofar as they will lend themselves to religious interpretation. Having decided that the *essence* of his life has been the discovery of God's grace, the major principle of selection becomes simple: does this event in my life, he asks himself, help to illuminate the progress I have made toward God? Such a governing purpose limits Cowper to rather sketchy treatment of certain periods of his life. For example, he describes only those episodes from his first school which throw light on the "history of my heart so far as religion has been its object." By the same token, he mentions his second school, not because he is enamoured with his school days, but because at Westminster "occurred the second instance of serious [religious] consideration"—he learns that he is mortal. . . . Cowper does not care to digress on the rich and imaginative life of a schoolboy; he is organizing the exceedingly selective events of his boyhood to show that the seeds of religion were in him at an early age and that he was so sinful

One continues to discover in the *Memoir* secular causal connections that would fully account for Cowper's experience of insanity if God were never mentioned. The governing design of the work exerts virtually no control over what would appear to be "natural" causality.... The form of the autobiography demonstrates Cowper's belief that his personality had undergone basic changes. The narrator assures the reader that a new normalcy was a result of the New Birth. But even after his conversion Cowper betrays signs of abnormality. He has not undergone any great *emotional* changes, at least none that show up in his *Memoir* as appreciably different from earlier emotional states. He merely finds a direction for his mental extremism. (p. 438)

The religious convert who narrates the tale believes that he is speaking about a pawn swept along by God into and through a traumatic insanity to the providential asylum and recovery. The figure he actually shows, however, is more uniformly disturbed, less prone to revolutionary changes in character. For the author of the *Memoir,* the conversion was an experience qualitatively different from all previous experiences. But the intensity of diction, the bizarre setting, and the failure of the narration to serve the artistic form of the work give the conversion itself the appearance of another manifestation of the mental disorder. (pp. 438-39)

Cowper's *Memoir* is an invaluable document to the student of autobiography, for its failures as much as for its successes. Cowper uses all the artistic tools of the autobiographer—narrative, interpretation, selection, order, scale, dialogue, imagery—as he attempts to model a "William Cowper" acceptable to himself. But while he labors to create a protagonist who will meet the demands of his authorial imagination, the reader becomes increasingly aware and fascinated by the "second" Cowper rising, at first obscure as a swamp bogey, from the autobiographer's unconscious mind. As one reads through the tormented pages of the *Memoir,* this second image of William Cowper becomes increasingly convincing; like the picture of Dorian Gray [in Oscar Wilde's *The Picture of Dorian Gray*], it is an image "truer" than the model who sits for the picture. By the end of the *Memoir,* the reader realizes that he is closing the book on two William Cowpers: the one who has emerged from the shadows and has become the "truth" of the autobiography behind the author's back, as it were, and the paler one, the one consciously created by the author to stand as his testimony to the first three decades of his life.

Sir Leslie Stephen has written, revealingly, "It may be reckoned . . . as a special felicity that an autobiography, alone of all books, may be more valuable in proportion to the amount of misrepresentation which it contains." Autobiography does indeed often become more interesting in relation to the information one can infer about the author from the material he has presented. William Cowper's *Memoir* is an interesting human document because of the vast insight it unintentionally affords into the poet's immense power of rationalization and his utter self-deception. One's interest in the *Memoir* lies in watching an intelligent artist produce a fascinating literary work that reveals his inability to understand himself. (pp. 441-42)

Barrett John Mandel, "Artistry and Psychology in William Cowper's 'Memoir'," in Texas Studies in Literature and Language, *Vol. XII, No. 3, Fall, 1970, pp. 431-42.*

VINCENT NEWEY (essay date 1982)

[In **'On the Receipt of My Mother's Picture'**] we are struck as much by Cowper's controlling artistry as by his extraordinary daring and intimacy in laying open the secret recesses of the heart:

> Oh that those lips had language! Life has pass'd
> With me but roughly since I heard thee last.
> Those lips are thine—thy own sweet smiles I see,
> The same that oft in childhood solaced me;
> Voice only fails, else, how distinct they say,
> 'Grieve not, my child, chase all thy fears away!'
> The meek intelligence of those dear eyes
> (Blest be the art that can immortalize,
> The art that baffles time's tyrannic claim
> To quench it) here shines on me still the same. . . .

This is an 'excess' both natural and perfected. The whispering assonance, the liquid 'l's and soft 's's that gently accuse the silence of the picture, the fluent yet formal rhythms, the unforced but regular emphasis of the rhymes—all give shape and discipline to the feelings they simultaneously, and so faithfully, express. Cowper is pushing more than ever at limits, but his care and his evident sincerity win our assent for what would otherwise be an embarrassing moment of self-exposure. The audacity of the revelation is of course part of the appeal of **'On the Receipt of My Mother's Picture'**—its peculiar fascination. Yet considering the difficulty of the theme—a man's love for his mother and the commonly repressed wish for the security of infantile dependence—it is also amazing how readable the poem is, how fit for an intelligent audience.

But there is much more to the work than that. Cowper's sudden reaction to the unexpected 'gift . . . out of Norfolk' is the starting point of a mental journey leading to a discovery of the restorative power of recollection and 'fancy'. Already in the opening passage he has made inward gains from the act of remembering and imagining: the first couplet is a cry of longing and absence but we soon recognize in the mountings and levellings of the verse a spirit both quickened and calmed, as the mind brings the picture 'to life' according to its needs, supplying a reassuring voice where there is none, renewing the benign influences and 'guiding light' of the past ('. . . here shines on me still the same'). By the end of the poem he becomes clearly conscious of what he has achieved:

> By contemplation's help, not sought in vain,
> I seem t'have liv'd my childhood o'er again;
> To have renew'd the joys that once were mine,
> Without the sin of violating thine:
> And while the wings of fancy still are free,
> And I can view this mimic shew of thee,
> Time has but half succeeded in his theft—
> Thyself remov'd, thy power to soothe me left. . . .

At first it had been the portrait that had been seen as 'baffling' time; now Cowper understands his own strength, acting on and through that lifeless 'mimic shew' to recover 'lost' joys in and for the present. There is nothing sentimental about these lines: the impression is of a mind ready to accept the confinements of Time, Change, and Loss but confident in the knowledge, guaranteed by all that has gone before in the poem, that they may be transcended by 'contemplation's help' and on 'the wings of fancy'. Cowper values his wishes and his freedom to satisfy them but respects the limits and limitations of reality. And this, as we shall see, was no easy balance; the process of **'On the Receipt of My Mother's Picture'** includes uncertainty too, an effort to reconcile desire and acceptance, surmise and rational 'knowing', poetry as therapeutic fiction and poetry as wide-awake self-abnegation.

'On the Receipt of My Mother's Picture', then, is not only a poem of emotion. It is a contemplative poem and a poem about the uses of contemplation. It is also, thirdly, an elegiac tribute. . . . (pp. 245-47)

In **'On the Receipt of My Mother's Picture'**, . . . the 'heart' does dictate every 'flowing' line. Emotional process and the process of writing the poem are one process—even when Cowper is following the most commonplace conventions. The elegist's claim to sincerity, for example, which appears in Thomson or Tickell as overt statement and a generic requirement, emerges in the middle of Cowper's poem as part of an intimate display of feeling that is itself demanded by, and evolves out of, recollections of early childhood:

> All this still legible in mem'ry's page,
> And still to be so, to my latest age,
> Adds joy to duty, makes me glad to pay
> Such honours to thee as my numbers may;
> Perhaps a frail memorial, but sincere,
> Not scorn'd in heav'n, though little notic'd here. . . .

Or, similarly, the 'consolation' of the subject's heavenly repose is charged with, and complicated by, the poet's own deep longing for peace:

> But was it such?—It was.—Where thou art gone
> Adieus and farewells are a sound unknown.
> May I but meet thee on that peaceful shore,
> The parting sound shall pass my lips no more! . . .

The uncertain hope of 'May I but . . .'; the sense of heaven as rest as much as reward; the generality of 'The parting sound . . . no more', which evokes a whole life of dereliction akin to that of separation without dissipating the pressure of a specific memory of pain and a specific desire to renew the innocence to which he had bidden a premature farewell when he 'wept a last adieu' behind his mother's hearse: all points a particular personality, not only behind the poem but forming itself in the course of the poem. The ingredients of a public rhetoric have become the integral features of a drama of mind.

Clearly, then, Cowper carries the 'sincerity' and 'naturalness' of 'personal elegy' to fresh limits. . . . In Cowper, . . . the change from deliberate rhetorical construction to quasi-natural organism is complete. We are aware always of continuum and progression, of a unity developing from within: developing, that is, simultaneously from within the mind of the poet and from within the poem, since the poem *is* a flowing of the consciousness. Each point is a growing-point contributing to a larger unintentioned structure. (pp. 251-52)

Although there is from the beginning [of **'On the Receipt of My Mother's Picture'**] a conscious artistry, the poem is in essence a spontaneous psychological event so fundamentally private and instinctive that to read it we must, by a willing trespass, involve ourselves in its momentum, must make it an out-growth of our own minds as well. But the spontaneous, the psychological, the instinctive, is not necessarily the patternless or purposeless. 'Life has pass'd / With me but roughly since I heard thee last': as we saw earlier, Cowper's habitual sense of aloneness steers and determines the act of contemplation, sensitizing his perceptions of the past so that they burgeon into present consolations. This might be called a logic of recoil: sad thoughts prompt their own dissolution in countervailing moments of release; the conviction that life has been one long, continuous process of suffering leads on to, and is

answered by, the forging of a very different continuity in a happy recovery of childhood happiness.

Now, the structure of **'On the Receipt of My Mother's Picture'** consists very largely in this opposition between dark and bright continuities. Cowper does not immediately pursue the implications of the recognition that 'Fancy shall weave a charm for my relief— / Shall steep me in Elysian reverie'. That opportunity for escape is stored up for the future, and he returns squarely to the sense of self as a prisoner of time and circumstance, perceiving in his early loss of his mother the start of a destiny of unaccountable deprivation. (pp. 253-54)

[There] are two journeys in **'On the Receipt of My Mother's Picture'**: life as journey and poem as journey. And the latter is even at this point by no means entirely an unprosperous course. It is true that Cowper is driven dangerously inwards to a solipsistic view of his being-in-the-world, completing his vision of a perverse 'unity' linking past, present, and future, and all the space between, in a chain of unbroken adversity, where the child who was 'disappointed still' and 'still deceiv'd' is father of the adult-victim, 'day by day', of some 'current's thwarting force', the man dispossessed of the heavenly paradise that is the mirror-image at the opposite end of life's ocean of the infant paradise which he prematurely lost. At the same time, however, the self as *me*—victim and object—is balanced by the self as *I*, the active 'I' who comes face to face with and embraces the shadow within, richly poetizing his 'fate', making of it something spectacular. Cowper's triumph in this poem is in part a triumph of tragic insight and tragic acceptance—a triumph signalized not only by the act of courageous self-confrontation and the 'realization' of self through exact metaphoric amplification of a felt predicament but also by the aspect with which he emerges on the other side of this precarious moment. For he 'breaks out' with:

> But oh the thought, that thou art safe, and he!
> That thought is joy, arrive what may to me.
> My boast is not that I deduce my birth
> From loins enthron'd, and rulers of the earth;
> But higher far my proud pretensions rise—
> The son of parents pass'd into the skies. . . .

There is no great liberation of spirit in this, but there is a firm effort of will and a genuine release. In the joy and pride he takes from the thought of his parents' possession of the haven from which, on all the evidence, he is excluded, in the selflessness of this recognition, and in the openness to an unknown and unpromising future of the cry 'arrive what may to me', we perceive not simply a capacity for making the best of things but also the 'stiffening', salutary, cathartic effect of the climactic vision of personal insecurity, exposure, and extreme distress.

It is, however, the other victory, of contemplative solace, that means most to Cowper in the final analysis:

> And now, farewell—time, unrevok'd, has run
> His wonted course, yet what I wish'd is done.
> By contemplation's help, not sought in vain,
> I seem t'have liv'd my childhood o'er again;
> To have renew'd the joys that once were mine. . . .

Thus the poetic journey ends in calm, all passion spent, and with a fresh insight into that journey itself. The *poem* becomes at last an object of contemplation and source of soothing thoughts—a 'memory's page' in its own right, in which, with a quiet satisfaction and philosophic mind, Cowper can read his success in renewing the joys of his 'innocent sweet simple years'. He draws as it were a secondary delight from the previous recollections, which have acquired the status themselves of a significant 'moment', a 'spot of time'. There is, moreover, a further advance in perception, as Cowper realizes that the Elysian reveries and momentary dreams that circumvent the laws and pressures of 'what here we call our life' will continue to be available to him. (pp. 262-64)

['The Castaway' stands apart in] the completeness with which Cowper penetrates the theme of darkness and destiny. Much of his poetry had rung the changes on this theme—quietly in **'On the Receipt of my Mother's Picture'**, obliquely in poems such as *John Gilpin*, forcibly in **'Lines written during a Period of Insanity'**, which foreshadows **'The Castaway'** in its determined self-command and self-assertiveness, though not the frenzy that is thereby just held in check:

> *Him* [Abiram] the vindictive rod of angry justice
> Sent quick and howling to the centre headlong;
> *I*, fed with judgment, in a fleshly tomb, am
>   Buried above ground. . . .

Like many of Cowper's 'works of affliction', these are the lines of a resourceful and articulate poet—witness above all the final climactic extension of the idea of 'living death' first introduced by the play on 'quick' (which is of course both adverb and epithet, *alive*). The sapphic metre places the experience as far as possible from the representative and shared, but it is impossible all the same to consign it to the realms of case-history, or be in any other way comfortably detached, when a subjective condition is so powerfully objectified and generalized as in that trailing image of mental torment as physical torture, where food becomes an instrument of punishment, the flesh a burial-cell, and life an agony of confinement.

This poem is the perfect example of how potentially overwhelming affliction prompted Cowper to creative achievement. (pp. 279-80)

[The first thing we notice in **'The Castaway'**] is perhaps the stanza-form itself, consisting of the familiar 'common metre' of eights and sixes—a favourite with both Cowper and Watts—but extended by a final octosyllabic couplet. We have seen already how the simple rhythmic and rhyme pattern of the form allows individual words and phrases to be given concentrated force. Here, however, there is a further important effect. The relentless but hesitant pulse of the four-line unit constitutes what might be termed the rhythm of 'stressful continuity', while the momentarily climactic (or suspensive) emphasis of the couplets suggests, at the close of each stanza, the constant possibility of sudden ending. The 'music' of the poetry enacts both the described event and the poet's psychological involvement in it.

By 'described event' I do not mean just the repeated rise and fall of the sea and the mariner's body, though this is always present either in the background or, as the instant of drowning approaches, in the fore:

> He long survives, who lives an hour
>   In ocean, self-upheld;
> And so long he, with unspent pow'r,
>   His destiny repell'd;
> And ever, as the minutes flew,
>   Entreated help, or cried—Adieu! . . .

In the split lines and recurrent 'up and down' of the iambic measure the motions of wave and victim inextricably merge.

But physical phenomena are the least of what we witness. The shape and movement of the verses also enforce a sense of the mariner's shockingly basic situation and responses. The dominant, unstoppable rhythms of the poem are the rhythms of an irresistible force, the energies of Nature and of Fate; their partial and temporary arrestment at 'self-upheld' (where the preceding comma breaks up the flow of the verse) mirrors the castaway's fundamental helplessness in the face of his destiny. On another, more conspicuous level, however, they are the rhythms of his own doings, sufferings, and reactions—above all of a battle to sustain life, which at this point fades into desperate entreaties for help and cries of farewell. All the flow and ebb of slowly failing strength and hope is caught in the see-saw balance of that last line: 'Entreated help, or cried—Adieu!'. The verse endings often depict life in a symbolic attitude, usually with the same mixture of pathos and respect for the nobility of man: the mariner's romantic gesture of farewell—Adieu—is in keeping with the heroism of his long fight against destiny, and with the heroism of mind which allows him to understand his ship-mates' haste to save themselves even though . . . bitter felt it still to die / Deserted, and his friends so nigh'.

Yet our immediate concern is not with this representational force and concentration but with the fact that each ending could so easily be the last—is momentarily felt as terminus. It is not simply that the protagonist could go under at any point. So could the poet himself; for all his control, his mind and creation are always at risk. In the 'stressful continuity' and potential termini, the haltings and the willed forwards-thrust, of **'The Castaway'** we witness Cowper's own endeavour as he propels himself among images of his life and death, his past and present destiny, any one of which might 'sink' him. The insecurity of his 'floating home', the hostility of fate, the 'lasting strife' of solitary struggle against despair and spiritual death, the ineffectual aid of friends, the certainty of doom—Cowper re-views his whole sad existence in a brief span, breasting the dangerous surges of gloomy self-centred vision. (pp. 304-06)

It is not only that Cowper keeps faith with the castaway's defence of life, but that he finds within himself the capacity to embrace all that is darkest in the darker side of existence. Stature in adversity is not just an attribute of the mariner-castaway, nor of a past self whose resilience Cowper unashamedly values; it belongs also to the poet-castaway of the continuous present whose vision of self and of life subdues all the pressure of negation, whether of despair, or self-pity, or the denial of hope, into its own positive, tersely rich perspectives.

So the poem continues to its climax, balancing pathos with celebration, recognition of man's imprisoned state with a tough respect for those qualities of mind and instinct by which his condition may be opposed though never escaped; and always the sober logicality and generalizing properties of the style turn the particular into the universal, to the point where we forget that we are witnessing what is after all an extreme and selective version of reality. (pp. 308-09)

Developing and coming face to face with the habitual 'truth' of his own dark imagination, the poet of **'The Castaway'** found a last home within its confines. In solitary struggle and a solitary death he discovered not only horror but privilege; from the archetypal figure of the 'much-afflicted' and 'much enduring' hero-sufferer he took for himself a last positive identity.

An ageless identity, moreover. The dead 'immortalized' by **'The Castaway'** is above all the poet himself. Cowper's fate is far from the kind Odysseus fears in a moment of despondency during the storm—to be 'un-noted, and for ever dead'. By a familiar paradox, in recording how he perished he gives himself an enduring voice and presence. . . . Never more than in **'The Castaway'** does his poetry justify his destiny, affliction and all. By a superb irony, he achieved through art what he long felt was denied him by God—a life of value and a life after death. (p. 313)

> Vincent Newey, in his *Cowper's Poetry: A Critical Study and Reassessment,* Barnes & Noble Books, 1982, 358 p.

MARTIN PRIESTMAN (essay date 1983)

[A] key to much that is characteristic in Cowper can be found in a certain kind of mental geography; or perhaps, given Cowper's armchair interest in travel, topography. It remains to establish the features of this topography more precisely.

The characteristics of the 'up/down' vertical dimension are perhaps the easiest to establish, as being the most traditional: 'up' is heaven, elevation, salvation; 'down' is hell, dejection, damnation. But there is often a paradoxical tension between the two: as God can treasure up his bright designs deep in unfathomable mines, so man can find himself buried above ground. The relationship is not always one of such frozen absurdity: there is sometimes a connection in time: one can lead to the other. Thus in another hymn the speaker, once 'a grovelling creature' finds himself raised by joy and love to the top of Mount Pisgah, where he surveys the promised land. But at this moment there is necessarily another recognition:

> How glorious is my privilege!
>   To thee for help I call;
> I stand upon a mountain edge,
>   Oh save me lest I fall! . . .

It is traditional that pride comes before a fall; nonetheless the apparent inevitability with which a top becomes an 'edge' is particularly Cowperesque. To avert such crises it is sometimes prudent to descend of one's own volition, as at the beginning of *The Task* the poet escapes with pain from the 'advent'rous flight' of religious poetry to 'repose' on the sofa. (pp. 31-2)

Such an attitude to the vertical dimension is perhaps most easily understood within the context of Cowper's cyclic manic-depression. We are not concerned with the precise nature of his mental state here, but it is undeniable that his depressions, at least, were cyclical; and he was sufficiently conscious of his mental rhythms to distrust elevation at the same time as naturally seeking it. This is repeatedly connected, in his autobiographical writings, to an imagery of clifftops and precipices. (p. 32)

The spatial symbolism of the vertical dimension is not, of course, peculiar to Cowper. It is inherent in our language and fundamental in our patterns of thought; more especially within a Christian cosmography. But what is characteristically Cowperian is the playing on this symbolism to produce tension and paradox. Equally characteristic is the consistency with which the symbolic system merges into actual physical experience as he registers it. The experience at Southampton is as much a creation of Cowper's as are the lines to Newton, and so are his later reactions to it: the self-consistency of his mental topography enables him imaginatively to connect the metaphysical paradoxes of Calvinism with the real, physical landscape of land, sea, hills and sky.

Cowper's handling of non-vertical space is more complicated. Tradition, after all, has an iron grip on the vertical, whereas the qualities of the horizontal are less clearly defined. Traditionally, indeed, in the great scale of being, the horizontal can be seen more or less as a temporary accident. Cowper, however, compelled to abandon the vertigoes of height and depth, explores the horizontal exhaustively. (pp. 33-4)

[The] sea is an important locus of Cowper's preoccupation with expanse. The sea is almost, however, a dimension of its own for him; and this is because its appearance as the most perfect of horizontals conceals the terrors (and just occasionally the blessings) of the vertical. Its surface is itself a paradox: a delusive line between tempests above and depths below. Images of sea-storms and drowning are so omnipresent in Cowper's work that the point needs no further stressing. Apart from its active terrors, the sea also functions as a medium of separation, in a recurrent imagery of isolated sea-shore figures gazing out across it. (p. 34)

Land for Cowper is the locus of safety and reliability, but also of imprisonment and monotony. Its paradoxes are complex but elusive, because in reading we take land for granted. Yet its contours are so intimately mental that Cowper does not stop being symbolic when he becomes 'loco-descriptive'. (pp. 36-7)

Prospects are generally either seen from above, with exultation; or along the level, with weariness or lassitude. The prospect seen from above is related to ownership and the Pisgah-sight of the promised land, and is thus used sparingly; but with the right mental attunement, or in the context of a well-regulated walk and close attention to the physical lie of the land, as in the landscape descriptions of the first book of *The Task,* it can be used with a fully positive value. The sparingness is important, however; in the fifth book of *The Task* it is made clear that only the redeemed are really entitled to such prospects. The 'prospect' in its other sense—of the view taken along the level of the land that lies ahead—reveals one of its essential qualities in **'The Shrubbery'**, where 'prospects waste' admonish Cowper 'not to roam' because of 'sorrows yet to come'; and elsewhere the prospect in this sense is associated with weariness and labour. These negative kinds of prospect are paradoxically contrasted with the positive kind in Cowper's retrospect on his life in the sixth book of *The Task,* where his spirit takes effortless and 'comprehensive views' back over a life that has been a 'prospect oft so dreary and forlorn'. . . . The power to take such 'comprehensive views' at all is seen as belonging to a specially 'composed' frame of mind; a frame of mind, in fact, in which mental experience can be comprehended 'as in a map'.

These alternative types of prospect are often, as in the last example, closely interrelated in terms of the 'ups' and 'downs' of both mental and physical landscapes; and where the contours flow reasonably smoothly into each other, as in much of *The Task,* the typical threats of both can be used to neutralize each other so as to yield an overall impression of pleasurable variety. (pp. 38-9)

[Landscape] tends to be measured in terms of movement across it—the effortless movement of the eye or the prospectively laborious movement of the body. A prospect, however, consists chiefly in taking stock from a fixed point; it remains to explore the actual physical and mental experience of journeying from *A* to *B*, with no prospect specifically in sight. Here the appropriate language is often not visual but tactile. The emphasis is on the physical conditions of the terrain and the nature of the traveller's exposure to it. (p. 39)

Martin Priestman, in his Cowper's "Task": Structure and Influence, *Cambridge University Press, 1983, 217 p.*

BILL HUTCHINGS (essay date 1983)

[*Though such earlier critics as J. C. Bailey (1905), Oliver Elton (1912), and George Saintsbury (1916) have noted that Cowper's "Yardley Oak" is one of his best and most important works, Hutchings's study is one of the first extensive critical treatments of the poem.*]

[With **Yardley Oak**] we reach Cowper's most extreme experiment in the writing of nature poetry. Instead of the defining couplets of **Retirement** and **Heroism,** or the stanzaic control of some of the shorter poems (even where, as in **The Poplar-Field,** neatness has started to give way to a freer prolixity), Cowper here writes in marvellously supple blank verse. The success of the couplet poems is to enforce objective stability on material potentially disruptive, hence giving the pleasures of both certainty and incipient tension; while the stanzaic poems explore greater relativity in a more tensely-controlled form, thus making the exploration more pressing and forceful, but necessarily less prolonged and thoughtful—even the freer form of **The Poplar-Field** can only rish a short span before becoming repetitive. **Yardley Oak**'s blank verse allows of a greater length, and so gives the movement of the poet's mind greater scope. This is crucial to the poem, for the interplay of poet and nature takes place against an extended view of time, in which a sense of poetic contemplation is helpful in rendering the subject as well as the poet's thought-processes.

The poem may be seen as the expression of the necessary futility of attempts to rediscover a stability. As with **The Poplar-Field,** the central image seems to invite a stable view: what more assured than a solid oak tree? Such, indeed, could have been the case. (pp. 180-81)

[But] the relationship between poet and object is established as more important than the tree itself. At the poet's birth, itself long ago as man measures time (a fact neatly implied by "winters" standing for "years"), the tree was already a veteran. This is not a straightforward metaphor in the mode of Cowper calling himself "a withered tree" in a letter, but he tempts us towards interpretation of this kind: remove the parenthesis after "past" (as reading aloud inclines one to do) and the shattered veteran becomes nicely ambivalent between tree and aged poet; while the language goes on to allow human reference with the trunk and the hint of "poor bare forked animal". But anthropomorphism in fact becomes increasingly ridiculous as the lines move on: "hollow-trunk'd" is absurd enough, while "excoriate forks deform", in its deliberately excessive Latinate orotundity . . . , exposes "forks" in jokingly spare simplicity. The language, indeed, shifts a great deal: "Survivor sole", with its grandiose inversion, gives way to the apologetic "hardly such".

This refusal to commit the poem to the assured seriousness of a single tone is a recurrent and key feature. When the tree was just an acorn, a thievish jay might have swallowed

> Thy yet close-folded latitude of boughs
> And all thy embryo vastness, at a gulp. . . .

The mock-heroic self-consciousness of the grandiose style is beautifully exposed by the concluding phrase, an amused rendering of the speed with which the small bird can swallow the potentially vast tree. The inversion of size, the huge oak suddenly seen as vulnerable, is both serious and comic. Similarly, an account of the growth of the acorn to the state of what Cowper later, tongue-in-cheek, calls "treeship" is heroic in tone, employing such Latinate constructions as "vegetative force instinct" and "Fost'ring propitious" and referring to a mythological analogue, only to end up with the assertion "thou becam'st a twig", a splendidly monosyllabic Anglo-Saxon anticlimax. There are many other examples of this procedure in **Yardley Oak.** This is not Cowper's own "uncertainty of stance", but a deliberate effect, combining the humorous with the disturbing. The shifts in language, the shift in our expectation of what the poem is to be, are designed to make *us* feel uncertain of our position, to unsettle *our* stable assumptions. Cowper is in control of his verse; but that verse is expressing the problems of controlling the implications of the wide-ranging subject.

In one sense, Cowper is equating aged poet with aged tree; but he is also contrasting them. Above all, the poet's mind is observed in the act of playing with the possibilities, so that the language wants to suggest both serious commitment and playfulness. The intricacy of this contrapuntal figuring is amazing:

> Time made thee what thou wast—King of the woods;
> And Time hath made thee what thou art—a cave
> For owls to roost in. . . .

The curve of the verse is from nobility to pathos, from time as creator to time as destroyer, the pattern of growth and decay. So the language moves from the abstract "Time", through the proud "King of the woods" to the wry conclusion. The lines seem to sum up a view of time, to express the poet's final view of the tree (and of age, or whatever). But forty lines later the poet returns obsessively to the same subject:

> Time was, when, settling on thy leaf, a fly
> Could shake thee to the root—and time has been
> When tempests could not. . . .

The pattern here obviously recalls that of the earlier lines, but the same structure bears an opposite tonal movement, from the trivial and small to the grand and noble. We read the two half-lines in opposite ways: "For owls to roost in" keeps to a regular iambic beat, while the "not" insists on emphasis. Thus the very rhythm of the poetry is reversed. At a number of points, indeed, Cowper subtly breaks up our expectations of the rhythm. Here the poet imagines the tree's growth to a state

> Of matchless grandeur, and declension thence
> Slow into such magnificent decay. . . .

The regularity of the first line misleads us to expect the conventional movement from greatness to fading, for in the second line "decay" is awarded the grandeur and pride of "magnificent". The placing of "Slow" acts as a rhythmic analogy to the thematic interruption.

There can be no stable tone in **Yardley Oak** because awareness of time, which is at the centre of the poem and dominates Cowper's characterization of both tree and poet, demands relativity of view. The tree was old when the poet was young; the tree is old when the poet is old; the poet can imagine the genesis of what is older than he is. . . .

Our view of time is totally dependent on the means by which it is measured. The tree is record of a vast period and symbol of its reduction to miniature proportions. The poet's years, which seem many to us, are but few when measured on the tree. But few, too, would the tree's many years seem if it could measure as the poet is doing. (pp. 183-86)

Yardley Oak reveals how the poet's mind is tasked with problems (with a wry in-joke at the title of Cowper's greatest poem). History has been supplied with a theme, which is time itself. As a fallen man, the poet, as he enters the fabric of his poems, is obliged to render his own inadequacy by a radical uncertainty: his quill is now "thought-tracing", not assertive, as the subject has been re-defined from the days of *Retirement*. Nature has changed from a means of expressing the stability of an assured viewpoint to a means of expressing the complex task of a man burdened with the need to think and to write in verse which reflects that task. (pp. 186-87)

Cowper's progress as a writer of original verse is marked by the relationship he forges between poetic control and the capacity of his subject-matter to be so controlled. With the *Olney Hymns,* external disciplines—the material is biblical or derived from evangelical tradition, the forms are established, the audience is fixed—mean that rigorous control is essential for complete success. Cowper's choice of the couplet form for his moral satires derives from well-established eighteenth-century tradition, while his method—involving the playing off of negative against positive and the use of characteristical satire—is at the same time conventional and appropriate to the form. Similarly, the fable manner of some of his earlier short poems is traditional and allows for straightforward presentation of moral aphorisms. In all these kinds, we find Cowper skilfully applying to his own beliefs familiar forms: with complete ease he adapts past manner to present needs.

His real originality, however, lies for the most part in his later work. Crucial here is his ability to achieve writing of a conversational flexibility, with a freedom of expression controlled by a particular tone of voice. Such flexibility is required in order to deal with experiences, ideas and feelings which do not so easily fit established forms. To write about the relativity of time, the fragility of life, the fact of death or the complexities which underlie the most seemingly trivial of incidents involves Cowper in a reconsideration of the relationship between poet and material. As the controlled nature of the material yields to matter of relative instability, Cowper's command over his technique remains remarkably constant, even as that command has to adjust. Artistic control may be there to heighten tension, to highlight the poet's isolation when confronted with man's lack of control over his environment, over time, over himself. (pp. 233-34)

> *Bill Hutchings, in his* The Poetry of William Cowper, *Croom Helm, 1983, 246 p.*

ADDITIONAL BIBLIOGRAPHY

Boyd, David. "Satire and Pastoral in *The Task.*" *Papers on Language & Literature* 10, No. 4 (Fall 1974): 363-77.
      Discusses the interplay between the satiric and the pastoral modes in *The Task* and concludes that Cowper employed both for didactic purposes. According to Boyd, Cowper was unsuccessful in satisfying the demands of the two modes and, at the end of *The Task,* he retreated "into a winter-world of safe sterility."

Brown, Wallace Cable. "Young and Cowper: The Neo-Classicist 'Malgre Lui'," pp. 120-41. In his *The Triumph of Form: A Study of the Later Masters of the Heroic Couplet.* Chapel Hill: The University of North Carolina Press, 1948.*
      A study of Cowper's handling of the heroic couplet form. Brown concludes that, though Cowper's couplets are within the Neo-classic tradition, they anticipate the Romantic poetic style.

Cecil, David. *The Stricken Deer; or, The Life of William Cowper.* Indianapolis: Bobbs-Merrill Co., 1930, 341 p.
      Presents the facts of Cowper's life "in the most intimate detail." Cecil's biography, though influential, is considered overly sentimental by many critics.

Davie, Donald A. "The Critical Principles of William Cowper." *The Cambridge Journal* VII, No. 3 (December 1953): 182-88.
      A reevaluation of Cowper's critical opinions. Davie asserts that it is a mistake to designate Cowper a pre-Romantic, for he was "very consciously and deliberately a neo-classical poet" who valued taste, judgment, decorum, and purity of language.

Fairchild, Hoxie Neale. "Early Romanticism." In his *The Noble Savage: A Study in Romantic Naturalism*, pp. 57-96. New York: Russell & Russell, 1961.*
      A brief study of Cowper's relationship to Romantic naturalism. Fairchild argues that although Cowper felt that man was becoming "too neglectful of nature's gifts," he did not view the concept of the Noble Savage as ideal.

Fausset, Hugh I'Anson. *William Cowper.* New York: Harcourt, Brace & Co., 1928, 319 p.
      A biography. Fausset depicts Cowper as a victim of the qualities that made him "a precursor of the Romantic movement." In particular, Fausset blames the pernicious influence of "a fatalistic religion" for Cowper's melancholia. Praising his poetry in general, Fausset argues that Cowper's style was his most distinctive characteristic.

Feingold, Richard. "William Cowper: State, Society, and Countryside" and "Art Divorced from Nature: *The Task* and Bucolic Tradition." In his *Nature and Society: Later Eighteenth-Century Uses of the Pastoral and Georgic,* pp. 121-53, pp. 155-92. New Brunswick, N.J.: Rutgers University Press, 1978.
      An examination of *The Task* as "a public poem" that focuses on Cowper's attitude toward the social world and his pastoral art. *The Task,* Feingold claims, reflects Cowper's desire to discover and praise "public virtue." Feingold concludes that *The Task* is a resolution of the conflict between Cowper's poetic instincts toward harmony and his observations as a critic of society.

Gilbert, Dorothy Lloyd, and Pope, Russell. "The Cowper Translation of Mme Guyon's Poems." *PMLA* LIV, No. 4 (December 1939): 1077-98.*
      Discusses the spiritual and literary affinities between Cowper and the French religious poet Jeanne Marie Bouvier de la Mothe-Guyon. Gilbert and Pope stress that in his translation of Guyon's poems, Cowper "avoids over-emphasis and effusion." His translation, according to Gilbert and Pope, respects the tone of the original and incorporates subtle changes which help to "reset the original in its proper light."

Hartley, Lodwick C. *William Cowper: Humanitarian.* Chapel Hill: University of North Carolina Press, 1938, 277 p.
      An exploration of Cowper's humanitarian instincts and their origin in the eighteenth-century concept of benevolence. Hartley argues that "the basis for Cowper's humanitarian sympathy is his own suffering", which led to an empathetic appreciation of the suffering of others. He stresses that Cowper's ideals—the "doctrine of work" and social betterment through religion—are quite practical. Extracting his social views from his poetry and letters, Hartley proposes that Cowper was a "staunch friend of truth and a fearless foe of oppression." Hartley is considered one of the most prominent Cowper scholars of the twentieth century.

———. "'The Stricken Deer' and His Contemporary Reputation." *Studies in Philology* XXXVI, No. 4 (October 1939): 637-50.
      An overview of contemporary Cowper criticism. Hartley reminds readers that, despite the "Poor Cowper" image which has per-

sisted since the nineteenth century, "good sense" and "sound judgment" were the qualities most frequently mentioned by Cowper's contemporaries.

———. *William Cowper: The Continuing Revaluation, an Essay and a Bibliography of Cowperian Studies from 1895 to 1960.* Chapel Hill: University of North Carolina Press, 1960, 159 p.

A bibliography of Cowperian studies from 1895 to 1960. Hartley also includes chapters on Cowper's literary reputation and work.

Hearn, Lafcadio. "Notes on Cowper." In his *Interpretations of Literature, Vol. I,* pp. 37-50. New York: Dodd, Mead and Co., 1929.

A general appraisal of Cowper as a poet. Hearn denies that Cowper's religiosity adversely affected his poetry and praises his emotion-filled descriptions of nature.

Huang, Roderick. *William Cowper: Nature Poet.* London: Oxford University Press, 1957, 150 p.

A discussion of Cowper as a critic, poet, and lover of nature. Praising his natural descriptions, Huang stresses that what sets Cowper apart from other English nature poets is his "deep and unaffected interest in, and an almost instinctive understanding of, the inner life and significance of the nature of God's creation."

Kroitor, Harry P. "Cowper, Deism, and the Divinization of Nature." *Journal of the History of Ideas* XXI, No. 4 (October-December 1960): 511-26.

Contends that Cowper's attitude toward nature was influenced by the changing relationship between science, natural theology, and deism in the eighteenth century. Kroitor states that Cowper condemned the deists and the "speculatists" and believed that God is revealed through the study of nature.

Martin, Bernard. *John Newton: A Biography.* London: William Heinemann, 1950, 372 p.*

A biography of John Newton, Cowper's spiritual advisor, his confidant, and his collaborator on the *Olney Hymns.* Interspersed throughout the narrative are references to Cowper's life and works.

Martin, L. C. "Vaughan and Cowper." *The Modern Language Review* XXII, No. 1 (January 1927): 79-84.*

Traces the influence of the metaphysical poet Henry Vaughan's *Silex Scintillans* on Cowper's "Retirement." The two works, Martin suggests, provide similar treatments of the theme of finding pleasure in nature.

Neve, John. *A Concordance to the Poetical Works of William Cowper.* 1887. Reprint. New York: Burt Franklin, 1969, 504 p.

Covers Cowper's major poems, but excludes the translations and most of the minor poems.

Nicholson, Norman. *William Cowper.* Bibliographical Series of Supplements to "British Book News" on Writers and Their Work, edited by Bonamy Dobrée, no. 121. London: Longmans, Green & Co., 1960, 40 p.

A brief general introduction to Cowper's life and works. Nicholson considers Cowper to be "the forerunner of the Romantics" and praises the mock-heroic style of *The Task,* terming it "a parlour parody of Milton."

Quinlan, Maurice J. *William Cowper: A Critical Life.* Minneapolis: University of Minnesota Press, 1953, 251 p.

A biography that treats Cowper's life in relation to his works. Quinlan deems Cowper "one of the most pathetic and puzzling figures in English biography" and considers him an important transitional figure between the Neoclassical and Romantic periods in English literature. One of Cowper's most important qualities, according to Quinlan, is his ability to establish an understanding with his readers.

Reynolds, Myra. "Indications of a New Attitude toward Nature in the Poetry of the Eighteenth Century." In her *The Treatment of Nature in English Poetry between Pope and Wordsworth,* pp. 58-202. 1909. Reprint. New York: Gordian Press, 1966.*

Argues that Cowper "was the preacher of the new religion of Nature" in English poetry and that his descriptions of nature stem from his personal and theoretical convictions.

Russell, Norma. *A Bibliography of William Cowper to 1837.* Oxford Bibliographical Society Publications, n.s. vol. XII. Oxford: Oxford Bibliographical Society, 1963, 339 p.

Includes listings of all editions of Cowper's works, as well as reviews by Cowper and works edited or revised by Cowper. In addition, Russell provides information on biographies and criticism of Cowper, Cowperiana, and many illustrations and portraits.

Ryskamp, Charles. *William Cowper of the Inner Temple, Esq.: A Study of His Life and Works to the Year 1768.* Cambridge: Cambridge at the University Press, 1959, 274 p.

A critical biography that describes Cowper's "life, connections, and literary activities" while a student and commissioner at the Middle Temple. Ryskamp also presents several poems, letters, essays, and reviews here reprinted for the first time.

Sainte-Beuve, C.-A. "William Cowper; ou, De la poésie domestique (4 décembre 1854)." In his *Causeries du lundi, Vol. XI,* pp. 449-65. Paris: Garnier Frères, Libraires, 1856.

An influential essay in which Sainte-Beuve discusses Cowper as "the poet of home life." This essay is not available in English translation.

Spacks, Patricia Meyer. "The Soul's Imaginings: Daniel Defoe, William Cowper." *PMLA* 91, No. 3 (May 1976): 420-35.*

Suggests that Cowper's *Memoir* is an example of "naïve" autobiography and that his narrative persona is unreliable "because of the necessary discrepancy between willed submissiveness to God and the elements of personality not contained by that submissiveness." Spacks supports her arguments by emphasizing the differences between the serenity of the *Memoir* and the despairing tone of "The Castaway."

Stephen, Sir Leslie. "Characteristics: The Literary Reaction, Cowper." In his *History of English Thought in the Eighteenth Century, Vol. II,* pp. 452-53. 1876. Reprint. London: John Murray, 1927.*

Discusses Cowper as a transitional and didactic poet. Stephen praises Cowper's nature poetry as well as his satires, which differ from those of Alexander Pope because they focus on the individual rather than on society as a whole.

Stock, R. D. "Religious Love and Fear in Late-Century Poetry: Smart, Wesley, Cowper, Blake." In his *The Holy and the Daemonic from Sir Thomas Browne to William Blake,* pp. 314-73. Princeton: Princeton University Press, 1982.*

Contends that, among eighteenth-century religious poets, "Cowper is the great portraitist of a daemonic god." Stock discusses terror in the *Memoir* and the poetry and concludes that Cowper's "convoluted and morbid Christianity gave him insight as well as torment."

Thomas, Gilbert. *William Cowper and the Eighteenth Century.* London: Ivor Nicholson and Watson, 1935, 395 p.

A biography that focuses on Cowper in relation to eighteenth-century literature and philosophy. Thomas expounds on his idea that "Cowper was temperamentally not a creator, but a commentator."

Wright, Thomas. *The Life of William Cowper.* 2d ed. London: C. J. Farncombe & Sons, 1921, 368 p.

A biography containing a bibliography of criticism about Cowper to 1921, a genealogical table of the Cowper family, and a list of letters not found in Wright's 1904 edition of Cowper's correspondence.

David (Davy) Crockett

1786-1836

American autobiographer.

Crockett is best known for the frontier exploits, both fictitious and real, that made him a folk hero to both his contemporaries and to modern Americans. Although the Crockett legend was initially cultivated by a series of books that were falsely attributed to him, most critics now agree that Crockett wrote only *A Narrative of the Life of David Crockett of the State of Tennessee,* an autobiography that is considered a classic of early American humor. This work, which Crockett composed with the help of Thomas Chilton, is often praised for its lively style, colorful backwoods language, and exaggerated, tall-tale humor.

Crockett was born on the eastern Tennessee frontier. Forced to work during his youth to help pay off the family debts, he received little formal education. From 1813 to 1815, he volunteered as an army scout in the Creek Wars. He began his political career as a justice of the peace in 1817, and the following year he was elected Lawrenceburg town commissioner and lieutenant colonel in the local militia. His campaigns for a seat in the Tennessee legislature in 1821 and 1823 set the tone for his political career. Recognizing that his hardworking constituents were hungry for entertainment rather than rhetoric, Crockett filled his short speeches with common sense, humorous anecdotes, and tall tales, and then invited his audience to join him at the liquor stand. Yet he also defended the rights of his constituents who were, like him, poor uneducated frontiersmen. In the state legislature and in the United States Congress, to which he was elected in 1827, 1829, and 1833, Crockett fought for debtor relief, equitable land laws, and reform of the state banking system.

Originally a Jacksonian Democrat, as a congressman, Crockett increasingly found his views in opposition with President Andrew Jackson. Many critics observe that Crockett was manipulated as a political pawn in the controversies between the Jacksonian Democrats and the Whigs and that both parties used the press to capitalize on Crockett's carefully cultivated backwoods image throughout his political career. He was first elected to Congress as a Tennessee "coonskin" politician like the president. Jackson's supporters in Washington, who considered themselves representatives of Western frontiersmen, encouraged Crockett's depiction as an uneducated but heroic and capable backwoodsman who supported the president. During this period the Whig newspapers ridiculed the congressman as an example of the illiterate, uncouth common man who had elected Jackson. Yet when Crockett broke with the president in 1828 by supporting the Tennessee Vacant Land Bill, and again in 1830, by opposing his Indian Removal Bill, the Democrats and Whigs reversed their opinions of him. The Whigs then used him as an effective symbol to counter the appeal of Jackson's frontier image. Crockett lost his bid for reelection in 1831 and barely won in 1833. In 1835, when he learned that he had lost again, he told the Tennessee voters, "you can go to hell; I'm going to Texas." He died the following year while defending the Alamo.

Five books have been attributed to Crockett, and despite critical dissension over his part in each, most modern scholars agree

From *Dictionary of American Portraits,* Dover Publications, Inc., 1967

that he contributed only to the *Narrative* and *The Life and Adventures of Colonel David Crockett of West Tennessee,* which also appeared as *Sketches and Eccentricities of Col. David Crockett of West Tennessee. The Life and Adventures* was published anonymously in 1833, and modern critics claim that it was written either by Mathew St. Clair Clarke or James Strange French. In his preface to the *Narrative,* published the following year, Crockett denied knowing the author, yet the similarity in content of these two works has led critics to conclude that Crockett provided the author of *The Life and Adventures* with biographical information and humorous anecdotes. Critics now believe that the other three works attributed to Crockett—*The Life of Martin Van Buren, An Account of Col. Crockett's Tour to the North and Down East,* and *Col. Crockett's Exploits and Adventures in Texas*—were written as Whig propaganda designed to exploit his appeal and blunt Jackson's popularity with frontiersmen. *The Life of Martin Van Buren,* published in 1835 and probably written by Augustin Smith Clayton, is a satiric attack on Jackson's hand-picked successor. *An Account of Col. Crockett's Tour to the North and Down East,* also published in 1835, was probably written by William Clark and is based primarily on newspaper accounts of Crockett's speeches during his successful tour of Whig strongholds in the East. Critics agree that the final work, *Col. Crockett's Exploits and Adventures in Texas,* was probably written by Richard Penn Smith.

Published in 1836 soon after Crockett's death, this work took advantage of his popularity following his heroic defense of the Alamo. Its claim to authenticity is based on Smith's contention that it contained Crockett's diary from his final year in Texas, but modern critics have proved that most of the book was fabricated after Crockett's death.

Crockett wrote his *Narrative* with the assistance of Thomas Chilton, a legislator from Kentucky, whose contribution is still disputed. In his preface, Crockett indicated that he asked a friend to review the *Narrative*'s spelling and grammar. Although some recent critics believe this was the extent of Chilton's role, others contend that he influenced its language and style. Still others maintain that Crockett merely provided the subject matter while Chilton actually wrote the *Narrative*. However, most modern critics agree that Crockett was primarily responsible for its style, content, and format and that it is the only work of all those attributed to him that Crockett wrote.

The *Narrative* is the account of the experiences of a backwoodsman who unintentionally stumbles into politics, written in his own words for his friends back home. Critics agree that the *Narrative* was influenced by the works of Benjamin Franklin and Seba Smith, an early nineteenth-century American political satirist. Like Benjamin Franklin's *Autobiography,* the *Narrative* is marked by candor and common sense, while its comic rustic speech and mockery of Jacksonian politics recalls Smith's "Major Jack Downing" letters. The *Narrative* also demonstrates Crockett's skill as a storyteller. He used first-person narration to present himself as a modest common man speaking in a familiar tone to an audience that was presumed to share his experiences and values. His praise of common sense over book learning coupled with his colloquial style encouraged his readers' interest and identification with him and made the work popular. Critics praise the directness and simplicity of the *Narrative*'s language and its accurate rendition of the backwoods vernacular, and they credit it with introducing a new style of realistic writing into American literature. In addition, the *Narrative* is considered an early example of the Literary Southern humor that flourished during the nineteenth century and whose key elements include regional dialect, invented words, colorful phrases, and exaggeration. For example, hyberbole is also an important feature of the work's presentation of biographical fact. Throughout the *Narrative,* Crockett magnified his ignorance and hunting prowess and downplayed his accomplishments as a soldier, community leader, and legislator. While modern critics consider the *Narrative* the only source of accurate information about Crockett's life, they acknowledge that the account is often embellished, and many critics question its veracity and accuracy as a historical document. There is also general agreement over its faults, as effectively summarized by Joseph J. Arpad. He contended that the *Narrative* suffered from the intrusion of invective against Jackson, from the unselective use of material, including dull and tedious events, and from the lack of a literary structure.

The *Narrative,* though central to Crockett's literary reputation, represents only a part of his legacy; he is best remembered as Davy Crockett, the frontiersman of legend. Though initially created in the works falsely attributed to him, the Crockett legend flourished as a result of a series of almanacs published from 1835 to 1856. These almanacs contain information about weather and farming as well as stories about Crockett's frontier exploits that portray him as a heroic figure capable of superhuman feats, an eccentric "b'ar hunter" and Indian fighter who rode lightning bolts and tamed wild beasts. By defying nature, the legendary figure conquered the worst fears of frontier society. This persona gained credence with his depiction in several nineteenth-century literary works, including James Kirke Paulding's popular play, *The Lion of the West.* Renewed interest in Crockett in the twentieth century was inspired by Walt Disney, who, in the 1950s, produced a movie version of his life that, along with a popular television series, rekindled enthusiasm for the mythical Crockett.

Today, cultural historians view the legendary representation of Crockett, the bold, brash trail blazer, as the embodiment of the spirit of his era. His position as an American hero has been thoroughly studied, with particular emphasis on the role of humor in the development of his heroic stature. Since the mid-twentieth century, critics have devoted attention to the authorship controversy surrounding the various works attributed to Crockett and have attempted to separate fact from fiction in the story of his life. James Atkins Shackford's scholarly biography, published in 1956, represents a significant departure in Crockett criticism: it helped to dispel the pervasive belief that the historical Crockett was unknowable because the legend had obscured the man. While interest in the Crockett legend continues unabated, a few scholars have recently begun examining the *Narrative* with the same degree of critical attention, concentrating primarily on such literary qualities as its style, structure, narrative technique, and literary models. The enduring appeal of the mythical frontiersman of the Crockett legend, coupled with the colloquial style and tall-tale humor of the *Narrative,* assure Crockett's place in American literature and culture.

(See also *Dictionary of Literary Biography,* Vol. 3: *Antebellum Writers in New York and the South* and Vol. 11: *American Humorists, 1800-1950.*)

PRINCIPAL WORKS

A Narrative of the Life of David Crockett of the State of Tennessee [with Thomas Chilton]   (autobiography) 1834

DAVID CROCKETT   (essay date 1834)

[*In the preface to his* Narrative, *Crockett explained his decision to write an autobiography. He repudiated* The Life and Adventures of Col. David Crockett of West Tennessee, *calling it false, and claiming ignorance of its author, and offering the* Narrative *as his vindication. Critics agree that Crockett's dismissal of style, spelling, and grammar, which is included in the following excerpt from the preface, won the respect of his audience, who were often unschooled workers who believed, like Crockett, that "big men have more important matters to attend to than crossing their* t's—, *and dotting their* i's—, *and such like small things." The reference to "Doctor Jackson, L.L.D." is a satirical allusion to Andrew Jackson, who had recently received an honorary law degree, and a "heel tap," mentioned in the last paragraph, is a drop of whiskey left in a glass after one has finished drinking.*]

In the following pages I have endeavoured to give the reader a plain, honest, homespun account of my state in life, and some few of the difficulties which have attended me along its journey, down to this time. I am perfectly aware, that I have related many small and, as I fear, uninteresting circumstances;

A watercolor portrait of Crockett by Anthony Lewis DeRose inscribed with Crockett's motto.

but if so, my apology is, that it was rendered necessary by a desire to link the different periods of my life together, as they have passed, from my childhood onward, and thereby to enable the reader to select such parts of it as he may relish most, if, indeed, there is any thing in it which may suit his palate.

I have also been operated on by another consideration. It is this:—I know, that obscure as I am, my name is making considerable deal of fuss in the world. I can't tell why it is, nor in what it is to end. Go where I will, everybody seems anxious to get a peep at me. . . . There must therefore be something in me, or about me, that attracts attention, which is even mysterious to myself. I can't understand it, and I therefore put all the facts down, leaving the reader free to take his choice of them.

On the subject of my style, it is bad enough, in all conscience, to please critics, if that is what they are after. They are a sort of vermin, though, that I sha'n't even so much as stop to brush off. If they want to work on my book, just let them go ahead; and after they are done, they had better blot out all their criticisms, than to know what opinion I would express of *them,* and by what sort of a curious name I would call *them,* if I was standing near them, and looking over their shoulders. They will, at most, have only their trouble for their pay. But I rather expect I shall have them on my side.

But I don't know of any thing in my book to be criticised on by honourable men. Is it on my spelling?—that's not my trade. Is it on my grammar?—I hadn't time to learn it, and make no pretensions to it. Is it on the order and arrangement of my book?—I never wrote one before, and never read very many; and, of course, know mighty little about that. Will it be on the authorship of the book?—this I claim, and I'll hang on to it, like a wax plaster. The whole book is my own, and every sentiment and sentence in it. I would not be such a fool, or

knave either, as to deny that I have had it hastily run over by a friend or so, and that some little alterations have been made in the spelling and grammar; and I am not so sure that it is not the worse of even that, for I despise this way of spelling contrary to nature. And as for grammar, it's pretty much a thing of nothing at last, after all the fuss that's made about it. In some places, I wouldn't suffer either the spelling, or grammar, or any thing else to be touch'd; and therefore it will be found in my own way.

But if any body complains that I have had it looked over, I can only say to him, her, them—as the case may be—that while critics were learning grammar, and learning to spell, I, and "Doctor Jackson, L.L.D." were fighting in the wars; and if our books, and messages, and proclamations, and cabinet writings, and so forth, and so on, should need a little looking over, and a little correcting of the spelling and the grammar to make them fit for use, its just nobody's business. Big men have more important matters to attend to than crossing their *t*'s—, and dotting their *i*'s—, and such like small things. (pp. 6-10)

But just read for yourself, and my ears for a heel tap, if before you get through you don't say, with many a good-natured smile and hearty laugh, "This is truly the very thing itself—the exact image of its Author,

DAVID CROCKETT."
(pp. 10-11)

David Crockett, in a preface to his A Narrative of the Life of David Crockett of the State of Tennessee, *E. L. Carey and A. Hart, 1834, pp. 3-11.*

BUFFALO BILL [PSEUDONYM OF WILLIAM F. CODY] (essay date 1888)

[*Buffalo Bill was a nineteenth-century American famed for his exploits as a buffalo hunter and as an Army scout in campaigns against the Indians. His popular "Wild West" exhibition introduced elements of Western life throughout the eastern United States and Europe. In the following excerpt from his autobiography, he identifies the qualities that made Crockett a good storyteller and pioneer.*]

[If] I were asked to name the most singular, and in many respects the most remarkable, man in the history of pioneer settlement in the great west I should, without a moment's consideration of others, say: "Davy Crockett." He possessed a rare combination of astonishing traits of character that marked him for a prominent place among western men. . . . Few men could tell a story better, and none had a more abundant supply of motherwit at his fingers' ends, than Davy Crockett. He could play the fiddle too, dance a jig, and shoot with the best riflemen of the times. These were accomplishments that went very far in recommending him to public favor, but they were the least of his powers of attraction. He possessed those bolder traits and faculties of pride and ambition, a heart that was absolutely fearless as it was honest, open, generous and sympathetic. Bravery and generosity had a perpetual home in his bosom, and he may be said to have carried his character on his sleeve, so easy was it to read and understand. (pp. 157-58)

Crockett was full of self-complacency and pushed himself forward, though never in a vainglorious or offensive manner. But he knew how to measure his own merit, and has done the public a service, while gratifying an excusable pride, by leaving us an autobiography [*A Narrative of the Life of David Crockett*] that has carried delight into thousands of homes. (p. 158)

In summing up the character of Davy Crockett I may, without exaggeration, pronounce him a prototype of all that is noble, courageous, honest and unselfish devotion to principle. Had he been at Troy at the historic siege Homer would have immortalized him in his heroic verse. (p. 306)

> *Buffalo Bill [pseudonym of William F. Cody], "Life of Davy Crockett," in his* Story of the Wild West and Camp-Fire Chats, *R. S. Peale & Co., 1888, pp. 157-306.*

HAMLIN GARLAND   (essay date 1923)

[*Garland contends that while the* Narrative *accurately reflects Crockett's life story, it was most likely not written entirely by him. Unlike later critics, Garland was unimpressed by the style of the* Narrative, *calling it at best inadequate and at worst commonplace.*]

The most characteristic figure of the New World for the first two centuries was the man of the "trace" or trail: the settler who, carrying a rifle and an axe, adventured into the wilderness and there hewed out a clearing, built a cabin, and planted corn. . . . Europe colonized in clans or tribes; American immigration was individual. Men like Boone and Crockett moved alone, hunted alone, planted alone, and harvested alone. . . . (pp. 3-4)

In Crockett's autobiography the reader will find the picture of such a man, a blunt, bold, prosaic account of a life, epic in

A portrait of Crockett and his hunting dogs painted by John Gadsby Chapman in 1834, shortly after Crockett's tour of the East. This is considered the best likeness of Crockett. The Bettmann Archive, Inc.

its sweep. That he wrote it as it stands is doubtful, but that he talked it is unquestionable. The internal evidence is unmistakably genuine. Other so-called lives of Crockett are spurious, but the *Narrative of the Life of David Crockett, of the State of Tennessee . . .* bears every evidence of being substantially his own expression. No one else could have permitted such a singular mixture of naïve boasting and homely humor. "The whole book is my own," he declares, "every sentiment and sentence" [see excerpt above, 1834]; and this is the fact, although, as he admits, some little change was made here and there in the spelling and grammar. No hack-writer would use such expressions as "lick me up," "get me some decent clothes," and "the balance of my money." The homely details of his life as wagon boy, his senseless wanderings as a youth, are all in this authentic narrative; so, too, is his boastful reference to the fact that at the age of fifteen he did not know a single letter of the alphabet. . . . The inconsistencies of Davy's spelling are accounted for also by the statement that it was touched up a little here and there. He talked so much better than he could write that his book is but the limited expression of a man who could tell a story easily, racily, and with individual humor. His writing does him an injustice. At his best he wrote with sad inadequacy; at his worst he is commonplace.

The history of his experience in the Creek war is singularly lacking in interest. It comes to nothing, or next to nothing. He tells of eight "carting trips" which are filled with tests of endurance, but which have little effect on the campaign; and yet he succeeds in expressing the ferocious temper of the white soldiers, a score of whom shot a Creek woman "full of holes" because she had bravely fired a bow and arrow into their advancing ranks. . . . This part of his story is not pretty, but it is essential to the self-revelation. The skill and bravery of the woman defending her house counted for nothing with the twenty men who shot her, and the cynical humor of Crockett's description of the burning of the house in which her warriors had taken refuge is highly enlightening. The vengeful spirit of the white settler is there expressed in all its barbaric pitilessness. (pp. 4-5)

[Crockett] embodied the spirit of the West. His whimsical humor and his elemental dignity, combined with a frank confession of his ignorance concerning cities, books, and parlors, gave him so great a renown that some one, perhaps facetiously, suggested him for the Presidency—a fact which he took mightily to heart. . . .

That he was "whimsical" is undoubted. He was in a crude sort the direct progenitor of Lincoln and Mark Twain. He was always ready with a story and he had the authentic note of American humor, the element of exaggeration. At his highest, he was picturesque, vivid, and true to his locality. At his lowest, he reflected the tricks of the professional "Sam Slick" and "Sut Lovengood" humorists of his time. That he was sometimes coarse and that his stories are often without point is evident from the records we have of him, but the reader must also remember that the reporters of that day were not skilled in reproducing characteristic utterances and that David could not write himself down for the very "amusing cuss" he must have been. (p. 6)

[Crockett's] fame, like that of Daniel Boone, is securely woven into [history] . . . , and with all his faults he will remain an almost perfect embodiment of the American trail-maker. (p. 10)

> *Hamlin Garland, in an introduction to* The Autobiography of David Crockett *by David Crockett, Charles Scribner's Sons, 1923, pp. 3-10.*

LUCY LOCKWOOD HAZARD (essay date 1927)

If John Smith suggests the England of Shakespeare, and William Byrd the England of Steele, Crockett foreshadows the America of D. W. Griffith. His heroisms are all of the cinema variety; his strutting center stage is as different from the grandiose self-glorifications of Smith as it is from the large-minded native dignity of William Byrd. If *The Narrative of the Life of David Crockett of the State of Tennessee* were less obtuse in its self-esteem it would be intolerable; but the imperturbable aplomb of Crockett's swagger is so superbly sustained that it outbrazens criticism. (p. 63)

> Lucy Lockwood Hazard, "The Southern Frontier: A Study in Romanticism," in her The Frontier in American Literature, Thomas Y. Crowell Company, 1927, pp. 46-93.*

VERNON LOUIS PARRINGTON (essay date 1927)

[*An American historian, biographer, and critic, Parrington is best known for his unfinished literary history of the United States,* Main Currents in American Thought. *Though modern scholars now disagree with many of his conclusions, they view Parrington's work as a significant early attempt at fashioning an intellectual history of America based on a broad interpretive thesis. Written from the point of view of a Jeffersonian liberal,* Main Currents in American Thought *has proven a widely influential work in American criticism. In the following, Parrington analyzes the* Narrative *as a literary work, traces the evolution of the Crockett legend, and discusses Crockett in relation to the era in which he lived. Parrington strongly praises the* Narrative *as a classic of the American frontier whose homespun materials and authentic vernacular contribute to a realistic portrait of backwoods life. The Crockett legend, according to Parrington, was a "deliberate fabrication" created by Whig politicians who used an unwitting Crockett as a weapon to fight Jackson's popularity. Yet Parrington's portrait is not altogether sympathetic. Like Charles A. Beard and Mary R. Beard (see Additional Bibliography), he discredits the common belief that Crockett was a hero. Instead, Parrington views him as a member of the new "coonskin democracy," uneducated frontiersmen who came to power with Jackson, and describes him as a "sloven" and a "true frontier wastrel."*]

[A] *Narrative of the Life of David Crockett of the State of Tennessee* was woven from the same stuff that Longstreet made use of, but the fabric is of far better texture. It is the great classic of the southern frontier, far more significant than [Longstreet's] *Georgia Scenes*, far more human and vital. Realistic in method, it is romantic in spirit. In its backwoods vernacular it purveys the authentic atmosphere of the cabin and the canebrake; it exhibits the honesty, the wit, the resourcefulness, the manly independence of a coonskin hero; it reveals, in short, under the rough exterior of a shiftless squatter and bear-hunter, qualities that are sterling in every society where manhood is held in repute. It is an extraordinary document, done so skillfully from life that homespun becomes a noble fabric and the crudest materials achieve the dignity of an epic.

The thing had long been waiting to be done. The literary romantics had tried their hand at the frontier materials and had failed, and then came a realist of the Georgia school who used the stuff as he found it and created a lasting document. A practiced writer collaborated with a picturesque talker, and the fame of the Tennessee Congressman was made. Romantic America found a new hero and Davy Crockett reaped a surprising reward. He had the good fortune to preempt the romance of the backwoods, to file on an unsurveyed tract of western life, and when the lines were run it was found that his claim

embraced all that was native and picturesque along the Mississippi frontier. Popular imagination seized upon him and endowed the mighty hunter of the canebrakes with the fugitive romance that had been gathering for years. He was erected into a mythical figure that drew to itself the unappropriated picturesque that sprang spontaneously from the crude western life. How this astonishing result came about, how good fortune came to single out Davy Crockett for her smiles, offers a somewhat amusing commentary on the ways of an unsophisticated generation.

That in its later development, if not in the beginning, the Davy Crockett myth was a deliberate fabrication scarcely admits of doubt, nor that its immediate purpose was frankly partisan. It did not spring from the soil of the Tennessee canebrakes; it was created at Washington. It was not the spontaneous product of popular imagination; it was the clever work of politicians. The successive stages through which it passed in its triumphant progress can be traced fairly accurately with the aid of a little historical imagination. Roughly they were three; the exploitation of Davy's canebrake waggery, the exploitation of his anti-Jackson spleen, and the exploitation of his dramatic death at the Alamo. The first phase is embodied in the *Sketches and Eccentricities of Col. David Crockett, of West Tennessee . . .* ; the second, in *An Account of Col. Crockett's Tour to the North and Down East . . .* , and *The Life of Martin Van Buren . . .* ; and the last, in *Col. Crockett's Exploits and Adventures in Texas. . . .* Midway between the first and second stages stands *A Narrative of the Life of David Crockett, of the State of Tennessee . . .* , which may be accepted in the main as authentic autobiography. None of the five was written by Crockett. He probably had a hand in the first in spite of his repudiation of the work, for most of the important facts of his life and the language of many of the picturesque episodes were taken from its pages to be reproduced in the *Narrative*. The *Tour* and *Martin Van Buren* were claimed by him and were certainly done under his eye and with his help, but the *Exploits* is quite as certainly sheer fabrication, done by a hack writer after Davy's death. It was the politicians who contributed most to the success of the myth. They exploited Davy as a convenient weapon against Jackson, saw their work prosper beyond all expectation, get out of their hands, enlarge itself to a cento of backwoods romance and pass into folklore. It was an unforeseen outcome that must have been vastly amusing to those who set the thing going. (pp. 165-66)

[The creation of the Crockett legend began] with the publication of the *Sketches and Eccentricities of Col. David Crockett*, that came from the clever pen of some journalist with a liking for the new vein of backwoods humor. A Whig bias runs through the pages, but the book is more a character sketch than a political document. The first embroiderings laid upon the original homespun are seen in an extravagance of picturesque language—an extravagance quite lacking in the more realistic *Narrative*. (p. 168)

The touching up of the picturesque in the *Sketches* seems to have been a little too much for Davy, who resented the note of clownishness; but he was not the man to permit undue modesty to blight so agreeable a myth in its tender stage. He loved to swagger in the public eye too much for that, and he joined heartily with his new political friends to clothe it in more dignified dress. His incredible egotism was aroused and he swallowed the Whig bait, hook, line and sinker. He began to take himself seriously and set about the business of propagating the myth. . . . The autobiography was quickly followed by the *Tour,* and this by the *Life of Martin Van Buren,* each more obvious propaganda than the last, and frankly designed to undermine the popularity of the President and his advisers with the coonskin democracy.... In the *Life of Martin Van Buren* the mask is dropped and all the malicious gossip of the Congressional lobby is poured out on "little Van," the "heir-apparent to the 'government.'" The backwoods character is retained only in an occasional coarseness or deliberate lapse of grammar inserted in a text that is written with vigor and skill.... Davy is pretty much lost out of its pages and its contribution to the myth was probably slight.

It is in the *Tour* ... that the myth expands more genially. A clever and amusing campaign document, it is a masterpiece of Whig strategy to gull the simple. The loquacious Davy joined heartily with his managers to cash in on his reputation. His egotism was played upon at every turn and he was quite unconscious that he had become a mere cat's-paw to pull Whig chestnuts out of the coals. (pp. 168-69)

Yet from this crude romanticism, this picturesque propaganda of coonskin days, one solid contribution remains—the autobiography [*A Narrative of the Life of David Crockett of the State of Tennessee*]. It is a striking bit of realism, done after the manner of the Longstreet school. There is politics in it, of course. Written just after Davy had gone through a bitter campaign from which he had emerged triumphant, it is a bold pronouncement that he wears no collar marked "My dog—Andrew Jackson." ... But it is much more than a political tract; it is a vital frontier document. The main facts of his biography, as set down there, may be accepted as true, and the general picture of backwoods existence in Tennessee; but the humor has been elaborated and the effect of the picturesque heightened by his collaborator. Such added touches were only natural. The real Davy was very far from romantic. An honest picture of the Tennessee democracy in its native habitat would reveal few idyllic features. It was a slovenly world and Davy was pretty much of a sloven. Crude and unlovely in its familiar details, with its primitive courtships and shiftless removals, its brutal Indian campaign and fierce hunting sprees, its rough equality, its unscrupulous politics, its elections carried by sheer impudence and whisky, the autobiography reveals the backwoods Anglo-Irishman as an uncivilized animal, responding to simple stimuli, yet with a certain rough vigor of character. Wastefulness was in the frontier blood, and Davy was a true frontier wastrel.... Willing to endure almost incredible hardships to obtain a keg of gunpowder to celebrate Christmas, risking his skin to kill a bear with a butcher knife, he was never much given to mending fences or enlarging his plow lands. He was a hunter rather than a farmer, and the lust of killing was in his blood. With his pack of hounds he slaughtered with amazing efficiency.... Davy was but one of thousands who were wasting the resources of the Inland Empire, destroying forests, skinning the land, slaughtering the deer and bear, the swarms of pigeons and turkey, the vast buffalo herds. Davy the politician is a huge western joke, but Davy the wastrel was a hard, unlovely fact.

Strip away the shoddy romance that has covered up the real man and the figure that emerges is one familiar to every backwoods gathering, an assertive, opinionated, likable fellow, ready to fight, drink, dance, shoot or brag, the biggest frog in a very small puddle, first among the Smart Alecks of the canebrakes. Davy was a good deal of a wag, and the best joke he ever played he played upon posterity that has swallowed the myth whole and persists in setting a romantic halo on his coonskin

cap. Yet in spite of the romantic machinery the play turns out to be broad farce. (pp. 171-72)

> *Vernon Louis Parrington, "The Frontier in Letters: Romance and the Inland Empire," in his* Main Currents in American Thought, an Interpretation of American Literature from the Beginnings to 1920: The Romantic Revolution in America, 1800-1860, *Vol. 2, Harcourt Brace Jovanovich, Inc., 1927, pp. 153-72.**

HOWARD MUMFORD JONES   (essay date 1939)

[*A distinguished twentieth-century American critic, humanist, and literary scholar, Jones is noted for his illuminating commentary on the development of American culture and literature. In his foreword to Richard M. Dorson's volume of tales about Crockett collected from the almanacs, Jones notes the gradual transformation of Crockett into a figure of epic proportions.*]

If, seventy-five years ago, anyone had suggested that Davy Crockett was somebody you had to look up in a book, he would have been looked upon as insane and un-American. Davy Crockett was a living reality like George Washington, Napo-

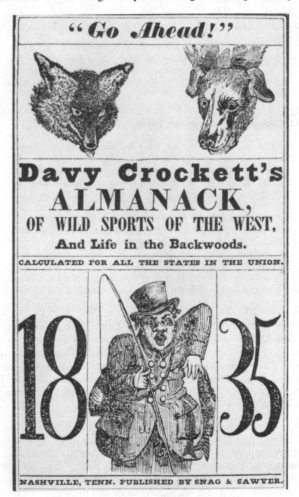

The front cover of the first Davy Crockett's Almanack. *This series contains humorous stories that depict the adventures of Crockett and other frontier heroes. Comic almanacs like this one were immensely popular in the United States before the Civil War.*

leon, and Satan. He was an immortal part of the national mythology, secure of a place in the American pantheon. (p. xi)

Wasteful of our literary inheritance as we have been of our
natural resources, we have forgotten Crockett and what he
stood for. But if he has passed from the memory of the populace, there is no reason why oblivion should wholly overcome
him. If we cannot have him orally around a campfire, let us
at least have him typographically in [the Crockett almanacs].
(pp. xii-xiii)

The Crockett of the almanacs is, of course, not the Crockett
of the autobiography, and neither is quite the Crockett of history. It is instructive to watch the literary transformation which
Crockett undergoes. In his final, or epic, incarnation he is the
creation of wild, poetic energy. The impression of lawless
lyricism is, I think, the most lasting impression I carry away
from this material. I do not refer to physical exuberance only,
or to the mere extravagance of linguistic humor, but to the
invention of words and phrases of almost lyric charm. The
metaphoric language of the almanacs, when it is at its best,
has all the freshness of dawn. . . . To parallel these extraordinary inventions we have to hunt in other literatures—for
example, the wonderful conceptions which are found in Welsh
and Irish tales. The language of mythology is, by convention,
more beautifully molded, but the lyric exuberance is much the
same. (pp. xiii-xiv)

> *Howard Mumford Jones, in a foreword to* Davy
> Crockett: American Comic Legend, *edited by Rich-
> ard M. Dorson, Rockland Editions, 1939, pp. xi-xiv.*

WALTER BLAIR (essay date 1940)

[*In his discussion of Crockett, Blair presents two distinct critical
concepts. First, he reviews the Crockett legend to determine the
incidence of "gumption," "mother wit," and "horse sense"—
qualities that were greatly admired by Crockett's contemporaries
and helped assure his fame. Then, Blair postulates that there are
six versions of Davy Crockett. The first is a real person, "the
flesh and blood being." The second through the fifth versions are
myths that were created by the pro-Jackson and anti-Jackson
newspapers, both before and after Crockett's ideological split
with Jackson. Only "Crockett the Sixth," the legendary being
discussed in the excerpt below, is still known today. Blair's essay
is indicative of the twentieth-century critical trend that emphasizes
the mythical rather than the historical Crockett.*]

One who studies what historians say about David Crockett . . . ,
hunter in the Tennessee canebrakes, Congressman, and hero
of the Alamo, will find many contradictions in their interpretations. Some call him a rascal, some call him a hero, and
some claim that—in alternate periods—he was each. Outside
the history books, a great deal has been written about a mythical
Davy Crockett, a legendary giant who still lives and accomplishes superhuman feats. (p. 443)

The basic fact that emerges from such a study is that one source
of information about a man active in politics in the 1830's—
the newspapers—in this instance may easily confuse the scholar.
The reason, probably, is that in journals of the day Crockett
was unmercifully exploited for political purposes. Journalists
used him thus, I think, because he happened to offer very good
material for a type of political argument which was being discovered in his heyday—the argument based on the great respect
in America for mother wit. Most of what was written about
the man, in other words, was definitely shaped to appeal to
the national love for gumption.

The image the name of Crockett conjures up today is, it appears, anything but that of a person tied up with a virtue so
unimaginative as horse sense. The Tennessean, as he is now
recalled, is a backwoods demigod, a fabulous hunter and fighter
wafted to immortality in the rifle smoke of the Alamo. And
the frontier yarnspinners created an even more fantastic figure
than people now recall. (pp. 443-44)

Such a preposterous biography [as that presented in the al-
manacs] would seem to be very remote from common sense.
It seems, one would say, to be a creation of the West which
passed hours by campfires genially manhandling facts until
those facts vanished in woodsmoke from the workaday world
and, greatly changed, turned up in fantastic fairylands inhabited
by the Big Bear of Arkansaw and other creatures as imaginary.
If the tall tales of wilderness yarnspinners gave the only clue
to the character of Crockett, one might decide that he had
nothing to do with homespun philosophy.

But there was a quirk of Crockett's character, in real life, which
made frontier folk elect him and re-elect him to the state legislature and to the United States House of Representatives.
That he was poor, that he was uneducated, made no difference
to them: they thought he could get along because they guessed
he had good horse sense. This fact suggests the paradox of
Crockett's renown. He won fame and office because he had
horse sense; he remained famous because of the nonsense associated with his memory. (p. 445)

Crockett the Sixth [was] the mythical demigod whose fantastic
life history was unfolded in the almanacs.

This Crockett had little or no political value, and the happenings
in his comic career leaped from the green earth into a backwoods fairyland. Is it possible to think of this rider of thunderbolts as a natural product of a section worshipful of gumption? I believe that this hero of frontier fantasy is such a product,
in two ways:

First, these yarns originated by fireside tale-tellers, or written
down to be enjoyed by fireside readers, are escape literature
of a kind likely to be peculiarly charming to farmers and woods-
men. Their demigod hero, in one aspect, is less notable for
his tremendous abilities than he is for his limitations. Another
demigod might have used his superhuman powers to create a
great symphony, a great work of art, or a great epic; he might
have set up a perfect system of government under which all
men were free and happy; he might have conquered new realms
of knowledge—but not Davy. The nonsense about Davy showed
him conquering with ridiculous ease the stubborn physical world
which frontier folk had to battle with the aid of common sense.
Sickness, rocky farm land, cold, Indians and varmints—the
pests of the common sense world—were the effortless conquests of this campfire creation. Even the fantasies of frontier
folk, in other words, were given practical chores to perform.

In the second place, this picture of Crockett the Sixth was a
sort of horse sense "rationalization." The one interesting aspect of characterization which persisted in all the newspaper
Crocketts—the one element of consistency—was the mythical
element. The boasts of Davy the Second and Third, "whiskey
can't make me drunk; I can wade the Mississippi, leap the
Ohio, ride upon a streak of lightning," and so forth, were talk
fitting for a superhuman being. Crockett the Fourth displayed
his clownishness partly by making similar boasts. Even the
Narrative, official autobiography of Crockett the Fifth, used
expressions which were appropriate to a fantastic creature rather
than a common man. . . . (pp. 460-61)

What myth-makers did, then, was make Davy's boasts come true—put him in an imaginary world consistent with the kind of beasts and people his tall talk described. Temporary things such as changing political alignments vanished, but the one abiding element—strangeness—remained. As early as 1832, the legend-makers had begun to develop this abiding version of their hero: the apotheosis was suggested in a news story, widely reprinted, which read:

> APPOINTMENT BY THE PRESIDENT. David Crockett, of Tennessee, to stand on the Allegheny Mountains and catch the Comet, on its approach to the earth, and wring off its tail, to keep it from burning up the world!

The *Narrative* was written not only as a protest against political misrepresentation but also as an antidote to the legendary picture already being sketched. Ironically, it stimulated legends: the women, for example, whom Davy had sketched in a few phrases in the book, were given complete life histories in the almanac tales. There, they were fit companions of Demigod David: they wore hornets' nests garnished with eagle feathers for Sunday bonnets; they could wade the Mississippi without wetting their shifts; they could outscream a catamount or jump over their own shadows.

The folk mind, in short, refusing to be misled by the political propaganda associated with Crockett the First, the Second, the Third, the Fourth and the Fifth, in time made known the People's Choice for immortality—the only consistent character it could find in a mess of contradictory portraits, Crockett the Sixth. And today, if you get far enough away from paved roads and roadside pop stands in Tennessee and Kentucky and sit by the fire with backwoods yarnspinners, you will learn that this Crockett, somewhere or other, is still carrying out his boasts in superhuman ways. (pp. 461-62)

> Walter Blair, ''Six Davy Crocketts. . .,'' in Southwest Review, *Vol. XXV, No. 4, July, 1940, pp. 443-62.*

DANIEL G. HOFFMAN (essay date 1961)

[According to Hoffman, Crockett was popular during three distinct periods. During the first, Crockett was known as a politician whose appeal Hoffman characterizes as ''dangerous and demagogic.'' In the second phase, which began shortly before Crockett's death, he was celebrated as the heroic frontiersman of the almanacs. His most recent renown occurred during the 1950s, when he became a popular hero for the juvenile audience. While most critics praise the vivid and engaging style of the Narrative, *Hoffman describes the work as ''one of the most pedestrian and circumstantial of American biographies'' and contends that Crockett was not the actual author.]*

[Crockett had two early] careers as a figure of the popular imagination. The first corresponds more or less to the events of his own lifetime, as these are recounted in his supposed autobiography. . . . The popular appeal of this Crockett is easy to assess, even though the book to which a friend more literate than he signed his name is one of the most pedestrian and circumstantial of American biographies. Crockett's amanuensis, the author of ***A Narrative of the Life of David Crockett, of the State of Tennessee*** . . . , was not an able writer. . . . Despite the opportunities many of Crockett's Indian fights and bearhunts afforded him to draw the long bow, only in the accounts of the Colonel's electioneering does his style approach the vividness of a well-told yarn. Nowhere in Crockett's bear-slaughtering is there the slightest imaginative transfiguration

A wood-cut from Davy Crockett's Almanack, *1837, that depicts Crockett in the garb of Colonel Nimrod Wildfire, the hero of James Kirke Paulding's contemporary popular play* The Lion of the West.

of reality or sense of terror to be overcome which characterizes the best oral narratives of hunting, or such early literary adaptations of these as T. B. Thorpe's famous story, ''The Big Bear of Arkansas.''

Despite its flatness, however, this life of Crockett had popular appeal because the career it presented confirmed a stereotyped pattern of American life already valid in the popular imagination. It tells ''how I worked along to rise from a canebrake to my present station in life,'' and gives jocular intimations that a seat in Congress is only a way-station on the road to the White House. This is not merely a success story, a rags-to-riches fable; it is an incarnation of the democratic dogma at its lowest level. Crockett appears as the commonest of the common, one who rises above the high and mighty by virtue of his mother-wit, which only the common can share.

In this first phase of his popularity, Crockett seems to offer a paradigm of the triumph in a democratic culture of mere familiarity as a principle of policy. . . . [What made him a success during his lifetime was] his ability to feel out the meanest level of approach in dealing with his constituents, to conceal from them his ignorance of the matters on which he will have to deliberate, and to undercut his opponents in stumping the district. The appeal of Crockett as politician is dangerous and demagogic. (pp. 6-7)

But Crockett as politician fades from the popular memory even during his own lifetime, and the outlines of the second phase of his renown begin to emerge. Now, in *Colonel Crockett's*

Exploits and Adventures in Texas . . . , the magnetism of Crockett the Frontiersman already attracts incident and anecdote from free-floating comic traditions, both oral and journalistic, and his adventures verge on the fabulous. The climax, of course, is the apocryphal account of his heroic death at the Alamo. Thereafter, as Constance Rourke observes in her biography of Crockett [see Additional Bibliography], the popular imagination took license to make of him what it would.

The best indication of what his second image became is found in the anecdotes from the Crockett almanacs. These antebellum publications—crude, comic, slapdash—defined a folk hero with far more accuracy than they predicted the weather. . . . Here is a genre of popular literature—the yarn—scarcely removed from oral tradition. The most accomplished of these almanac stories derive their rhetorical structure, their vividly animistic imagery, and their compelling combination of the humorous, the grotesque, the heroic, and the horrible from the art of the folk raconteur. (pp. 7-8)

When Crockett appears as a virtual demigod he . . . [represents] communal values colored by folk fantasy. He symbolizes man's uneasy relation to nature on the frontier. His aggressions against bears and his command of lightning and waterspouts are surely imaginative reactions to real perils. If this second Crockett is mythical, the myth is that man can easily conquer Nature and control it. In the most Promethean of his exploits—his rescuing the world from icy darkness by freeing the earth and sun from the frozen machinery of the universe—his reward is not the vulture and the rock, but this:

> The sun walked up beautiful, salutin' me with sich a wind o' gratitude that it made me sneeze. I lit my pipe by the light o' his top-knot, shouldered my bear, an' walked home, introducin' people to the fresh daylight with a piece of sunlight in my pocket.

There is not even the recognition of tragic possibility, much less of tragic fate, in these ebullient assertions of man's superhuman powers. The frontiersman knew tragedy enough in the life he lived and the deaths he died, but his folktales and popular writings transformed the materials of tragic fate into either melodrama or farce. (pp. 8-9)

[The] third Crockett is an artifact of neither folklore nor historical record, but of contemporary popular culture. There was no oral tradition of extant folktales to be tapped by the authors of television programs, radio scripts, motion pictures, comic strips, juvenile storybooks, jingles, songs, and advertisements. Both the historical Crockett and the almanac folk hero had been so long dead that the revived Crockett [was made] . . . completely anew, to fit contemporary needs and to dramatize contemporary concepts of character. (p. 9)

> *Daniel G. Hoffman, "The Deaths and Three Resurrections of Davy Crockett," in* The Antioch Review, *Vol. XXI, No. 1, Spring, 1961, pp. 5-13.*

JOHN G. CAWELTI   (essay date 1965)

Despite some exaggerations and a rather large dose of anti-Jacksonian polemic, Crockett's own version of his life is a remarkably realistic document for the time. Davy makes little attempt to gloss over his repeated failures to make a living before entering politics, and though he occasionally drops into the pose of the natural man, he lays no claim to genius, outstanding virtue, or any other intellectual abilities or distinc-

tions. Indeed, he appears remarkably like what he must have been: a crude, uneducated, but shrewd frontier politician with a keen eye for the main chance. He himself recognized that the sources of his political success lay in his personality and in his ability to turn off any serious political discussion with a joke or a tall tale. Like Jack Downing, he presents himself as a man of ordinary common sense and patriotism, honest, self-seeking, with a willingness to learn, a solid nerve, and a self-reliance embodied in his famous motto "GO AHEAD." . . . [Crockett's] narrative of his career provides Americans with one of the first realistic treatments of a man of few intellectual or cultural gifts whose vigor, nerve, and ability to advertise himself made him rise from the canebrake to considerable political prominence, and ultimately to something of a national myth. (pp. 68-9)

> *John G. Cawelti, "The Age of the Self-Made Man," in his* Apostles of the Self-Made Man, *The University of Chicago Press, 1965, pp. 39-76.**

JOSEPH J. ARPAD   (essay date 1972)

[*Arpad differs with the views presented by many modern critics, including James Atkins Shackford (see Additional Bibliography), Walter Blair (1940), and Shackford and Stanley J. Folmsbee (1973), who consider the* Narrative *the only reliable source of*

A title page from one of the Crockett Almanacs. *The Granger Collection, New York.*

information about Crockett's life. Arpad contends that Crockett exaggerated certain personal traits and events while omitting others in order "to satisfy America's desire for a romantic frontier hero." Thus, according to Arpad, the Narrative *should be read as a literary work, not as a historical document. In his assessment of the* Narrative *as literature, Arpad notes its affinities with the works of Benjamin Franklin, Seba Smith, and Mark Twain. Arpad then discusses some of the* Narrative's *supposed literary faults, including its lack of structure and its intrusive, eccentric narrator, and demonstrates how these qualities contribute to its "spontaneity and authenticity."*]

[*A Narrative of the Life of David Crockett*] may appear credible and real, exhibiting the kind of authenticity that the author promises in his preface [see excerpt above, 1834]. . . . But the reader should beware. Although the autobiography is unquestionably related to reality, it is, nevertheless, something of a hoax, an imaginative story told by Crockett to satisfy America's desire for a romantic frontier hero. The fabulous nature of the account may be seen by noting the inaccuracies and the errors of omission and emphasis, which appear too consistent and with apparent purpose to pass for mere failures of the author's memory. It may be seen, too, by investigating the sources, analogues, and influences that impinged upon the composition of the work. When such evidence is considered in conjunction with what is known about the actual character of the man, it indicates that *A Narrative of the Life of David Crockett* should be read less as biographical history and more as literature, as a classic in the native tradition of American humor. (p. 7)

[At] least two literary models helped Crockett shape his autobiography. The first, Benjamin Franklin's *Autobiography* . . . , provided the archetype of "poor boy makes good" upon which Crockett modeled his phenomenal "rise" from backwoods obscurity to national prominence. . . . [Crockett's] autobiography not only mirrors the pattern of Franklin's success, it also echoes the aphoristic sayings and crackerbox philosophy of Poor Richard: "Be always sure you're right—then GO AHEAD," "I determined to stand up to my lick-log, salt or no salt," and "This reminded me of the old saying—'A fool for luck, and a poor man for children.'"

The second literary model [was] the "Major Jack Downing" letters of Seba Smith. . . . As Smith later described the intent of his creation:

> The author of these papers, wishing . . . to give increased interest and popularity to his little daily paper, bethought himself of the plan to bring a green, unsophisticated lad from the country into town with a load of axe-handles, hoop poles, and other notions, for sale, and while waiting the movements of a dull market, let him blunder into the halls of the legislature, and after witnessing for some days their strange doings, sit down and write an account of them to his friends at home in his own plain language.

Crockett's autobiography reveals this same innocent mentality and viewpoint: a green, unsophisticated backwoodsman who accidentally blunders into the complex world of politics and who then writes an account of his experiences "to his friends at home in his own plain language." . . . [Like] Downing's correspondence, [Crockett's autobiography] is a letter written from Washington to his friends back home, even to the point of concluding the work with his characteristic manner of closing a letter. It further reflects the Downing persona in its irregularities of spelling, oddities of punctuation, and loose grammar—all of which Crockett insisted be retained.

But undoubtedly the greatest influence on the composition of the autobiography was the author's own abilities as an oral storyteller. One need only read his marvelous bear stories aloud to recognize that Crockett conceived the story of his life in terms of oral presentation. His successful retention of its oral nature in print indicates he subordinated, rather than was mastered by, these advisory influences and literary models during the composition of his autobiography. (pp. 29-31)

Today, few would question that Crockett's [*Narrative*] deserves attention as a seminal work in the native tradition of American literature. But beyond its significance as literary history, the autobiography has a literary merit all its own, which has earned it a place as a popular favorite among generations of Americans.

The work does have defects. Crockett's invective against Jackson frequently becomes an annoying intrusion upon the narrative, especially since he fails to give adequate motivation for his animosity. At times, the events he narrates appear dull, tedious, or irrelevant, making one wish that the author had shown more discretion in selecting his materials, rather than following the method (announced in the preface) of putting "all the facts down, leaving the reader free to take his choice of them." And the ending is inadequate, even as autobiography. Without any plot or theme to structure the narrative, Crockett has nothing to resolve at the end, and hence the reader is left hanging, vaguely unsatisfied and expecting further word from the narrator about his exploits and adventures.

These faults, however, may be considered virtues. The intruding eccentricities of the narrator, the lack of apparent selection, and the lack of imposed literary structure lend a sense of reality to the work, a spontaneity and authenticity that come from observing the conventions of everyday life rather than the conventions of literature. One thinks of Mark Twain's "How to Tell a Story" and his *Adventures of Huckleberry Finn* when reading the autobiography. The art of storytelling, as Twain rightly explained, lies not in the content of the story but in the manner in which the story is told. The narrator's presence must always be felt, his personality informing every episode. Crockett's autobiography exemplifies this kind of narration, the colloquial style of expression. Like Huck Finn's storytelling, Crockett's narration permits a vigorous revelation of sentiment and humor, not possible in either genteel diction or artful structures. In his use of earthy metaphors and similes, he exploits the "local color" of life in the Mississippi River country and gives the reader a sense of time and place peculiar to the region. These techniques, performed with such apparent ease by Crockett, became the studied hallmark of a later realistic movement in American literature. (pp. 35-6)

Joseph J. Arpad, in an introduction to A Narrative of the Life of David Crockett of the State of Tennessee *by David Crockett, edited by Joseph J. Arpad, College & University Press Publishers, 1972, pp. 7-37.*

JAMES A. SHACKFORD AND STANLEY J. FOLMSBEE (essay date 1973)

[*Shackford and Folmsbee first discuss the* Narrative's *place in American literary tradition and culture and then examine the work as a historical document containing the roots of the real Crockett. After considering the works falsely attributed to Crockett to de-*

termine their influence on his political career and the development of the Crockett myth, Shackford and Folmsbee conclude that these spurious works have distorted the view of Crockett's life and that the Narrative *is the only authentic Crockett work.*]

A Narrative of the Life of David Crockett is an important document in three major areas of American culture. As a literary work, it is one of the earliest autobiographies to be published, only a decade and a half after the virtually complete version of the first of all, Benjamin Franklin's. Another American success story, it belongs in the long series of autobiographies telling similar stories, from Franklin to Malcolm X. It is also a very early extended example of American humor, the first of the Southwest variety.... It is, furthermore, a document of importance in the history of American English, being replete with dialectal usages, proverbial expressions, and spellings representing non-standard pronunciations. Crockett is credited, in fact, with being the first to use in print some half a dozen such locutions. His **Narrative** is, finally, a historical document. (p. ix)

Behind the myth represented by the popularized Davy Crockett stands an authentic folk hero, a man not as ''supernatural'' or extravagant as his mythical counterpart but nonetheless a fascinating figure. Here in the **Narrative** may be discovered the factual roots of the real David Crockett, the frontier humorist and teller of tall tales, the naïve yet wily mountaineer who feigned more ignorance than could be found in his makeup, the politician, the Indian fighter, and the rough-and-ready hero....

[The **Narrative**], when unadorned by explication, is confusing and often misleading to the contemporary reader. Written for Crockett rather than by his own hand, it was politically inspired, leading to several intentional deviations from the truth (although the historical facts are generally quite accurate), as well as a number of unintentional errors, chiefly in the dating of events; additionally, the work is filled with historical allusions, which are quite difficult to appreciate unless the historical background and the political motivation are understood. Thus, by the time the largely fictitious [*Col. Crockett's Exploits and Adventures in Texas*] and the equally unreliable [*An Account of Col. Crockett's Tour to the North and Down East*] had been added to the **Narrative**, the real David Crockett and the myth were hopelessly intertwined. A succession of reprints, each including at least one of the spurious additions, continued to obscure the historical Crockett from scholars and the general public alike. (p. x)

The **Narrative**, as clearly shown by Crockett's letters ..., was ghost-written by Thomas Chilton.... (p. xv)

Although the language of the **Narrative** is largely Chilton's, the information was supplied by Crockett.... In addition, considerable use was made of *Life and Adventures*, for which Crockett had presumably supplied most of the information similarly to [Mathew St. Clair] Clarke (the author of that work), despite his assertions to the contrary. A very careful comparison of the authentic records about Crockett with the autobiographical account of them reveals only two forms of discrepancies: first, a few additions and several seemingly deliberate alterations that may be attributed to Crockett's intention of having the **Narrative** serve partially as campaign literature for him; and second, errors not in stating fact but in supplying dates. The rest of the **Narrative**, however, is so meticulously accurate, as established by surviving records, that it proves conclusively that, in context, the work is all Crockett's—as he claimed it was. Thus, the guiding spirit, the realism, the hu-

morous adventure, the historical fact, the rude but real heroism—these are largely Crockett's. Despite various expressions which seem to have emanated from Chilton, the general style, too, is Crockett's. (p. xvi)

[The fictitious account] in the *Tour of the North* plus the famous *Life and Adventures* distort the historic picture of Crockett's life and the story of the Alamo. The only reliable source available for ascertaining the truth about David Crockett remains the **Narrative** itself.... The **Narrative**, in our opinion, is a classic in American history as well as in American literature and in the American variety of English. (p. xx)

> *James A. Shackford and Stanley J. Folmsbee, in an introduction to* A Narrative of the Life of David Crockett of the State of Tennessee *by David Crockett, The University of Tennessee Press, Knoxville, 1973, pp. ix-xx.*

RICHARD SLOTKIN   (essay date 1973)

[*In this excerpt from his thorough study of violence in the American frontier myth, Slotkin focuses on Crockett's legendary hunting skills and concludes that this ability made him an American hero.*]

The sources of the Crockett myth are difficult to unravel. In one sense he is a product of the eastern stereotype of the frontiersman as lowbrow and clown. In another he is clearly a product of western popular literature—a clown whose apparent simplicity masks a cleverness that is superior to city wit and a human sensitivity more profound than the effusive sentimentality of the city, for all its being concealed under a bantering, ironic manner. Crockett (or his ghost writer) portrays the colonel's eccentricities and pursuits as examples of the highest heroic virtues and, at the same time, emphasizes that Crockett is the representative man of his section.

Crockett's life, as he presents it in **A Narrative of the Life of Col. David Crockett** ..., is a sequence of exploits in which he gradually grows from poor frontier farmer to war hero to successful politician to successful speculator to successful hunter. His failures are also exploits—chances for him to demonstrate his resilience, his ability to resist the hard knocks and scramble back to his feet. His vocations of hunter, politician, and speculator blend into one another until they seem different phases of the same quest, the same picaresque movement from the bottom to the top of the social heap. After a successful trapping season, he comes to town to sell his peltry, passes a few words with some local politicians, and is immediately drafted for the legislature. Between political campaigns he engages in a successful lumber speculation and, without pause for breath, embarks on an epic bear hunt. It is in the bear hunt that he is most himself. Politics and business do not involve as much of his passion or his talent, since they do not provide the same opportunity for concrete engagement with an antagonist. In the bear hunt the forces opposing him, keeping him from his desires, become tangible. They can be met in direct, open combat and vanquished. The triumph is more satisfying because the struggle is physical rather than cerebral, and the slain bear is more tangible and permanent evidence of his prowess than any set of paper profits or votes on a tally sheet. The source of Crockett's satisfaction with politics lies in his association of vote-getting and hunting, as when he belabors the metaphor of the canvass as a bear or ''coon'' hunt.

Crockett dwells with great pleasure on the act of killing itself, the moment in which he has most clearly asserted his power

A depiction of Crockett speaking before his constituents. Courtesy of Prints and Photographs Division, Library of Congress.

over the beasts of the forest. . . . Sheer quantity comes to delight the colonel, for once the repeated killing is done, he has only the bears' bodies as testimony to his deeds. The "105 bears" [that Crockett claimed to have killed in one season] are neither more nor less to him than the profits he realizes (or attempts to realize) on his lumber and other business speculations, or the votes he garners as he "stalks" the hustings. They are quantifiable indicators of the degree of his prowess, symbols of great deeds of skill. Women—those Puritan symbols of Christian values and civilization—play no ameliorating role in Crockett's universe. His wives . . . do not figure prominently in his narrative; they appear chiefly as conquests of a hunt, as do bearskins, votes, and a powerful reputation in the community. (pp. 414-15)

Two mythic associations made the Crockett figure acceptable as a symbol of American values—his association with the image of the self-restrained, professional hunter Boone through the invocation of hunting as his characteristic activity; and his association with the values of civilization, represented by the white woman and her male associate, the farmer, who together bring civilized value and progress into the wilderness. As Parrington says [see excerpt above, 1927], Crockett is no farmer, no cultivator or improver of the soil; yet that is certainly what he pretends to be, and the pretense is supported by the mythic linkage of the hunter and the farmer as joint redeemers of the wilderness. But it is the *hunter* quality that sets the hero apart from the yeomanic herd and makes him the hero. Not the cultivator, but the *conquistadore* is the American Aeneas. (p. 555)

Richard Slotkin, "The Fragmented Image: The Boone Myth and Sectional Cultures (1820-1850)" and "A

Pyramid of Skulls," in his Regeneration through Violence: The Mythology of the American Frontier, 1600-1860, *Wesleyan University Press, 1973, pp. 394-465, 517-68.**

RICHARD BOYD HAUCK   (essay date 1982)

[*The diversity of Hauck's study makes it unique in Crockett criticism. The first section contains a factual account of Crockett's life as well as the following discussion of the* Narrative *as a "valuable work of comic art." The second part is a biography of the Davy Crockett of legend. In the conclusion, Hauck reprints portions of Crockett's writings to demonstrate "his humor and his command of backwoods idiom."*]

In producing the *Narrative,* Crockett enjoyed the collaboration of a skilled writer, Thomas Chilton, a congressman from Kentucky. The text itself stands as the evidence of Chilton and Crockett's distinctive achievement, and it shows that [Chilton] shared the Tennessean's way of talking and understood his storytelling style. Stanley Folmsbee . . . believed that the book was essentially Crockett's in terms of its content and Chilton's in terms of its language [(see excerpt above, 1973). However, its] . . . language is artistically true to the style of both Crockett and his public image, the legendary Davy. Chilton and Crockett exercised just enough artifice to make their portrayal of Crockett's hyperbolic talk and lively storytelling convincing. Being from contiguous states within a single geographical region, they knew the same backwoods usages and figures of speech, and they worked them into the book judiciously, selecting those most likely to be widely perceived as authentic. A more ac-

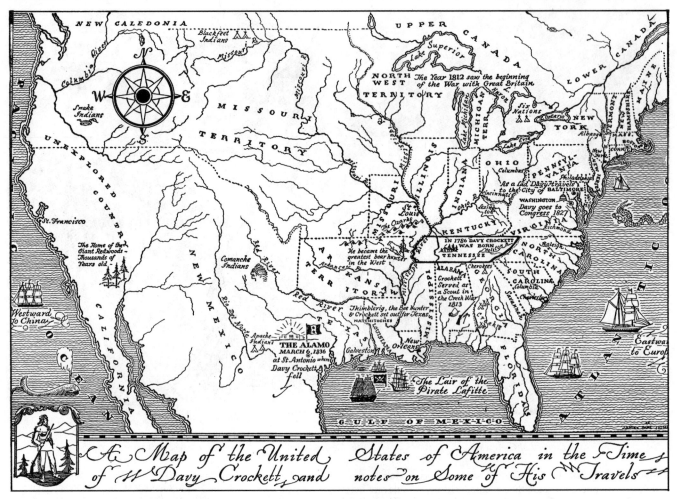

A map of the United States in Crockett's day. From Davy Crockett, *by Constance M. Rourke. Illustrated by James Mac Donald. Copyright 1934 by Harcourt Brace Jovanovich, Inc. Copyright renewed 1962 by Alice D. Fore. Reprinted by permission of the publisher.*

curate assessment than Folmsbee's would assign the technical details of writing to Chilton, the stories to Crockett, and the book's credible language to the partnership.

The special backwoods idioms are embedded in a first-person narration addressed in a familiar tone to an implied reader who is assumed to be an honest, practical, and open-minded fellow. As the narrator, Crockett is posed as a friendly, modest, straight-shooting common man. He speaks in perfect confidence, as if he knew the reader to be a sympathetic listener. . . . The narrator's language is a fully developed model, or artificial representation, of the backwoods or rural vernacular. It is consistent in its deviations from standard English, and its idioms are authentic, which is readily demonstrated by pointing out that most of them have survived in vernacular American speech.

Crockett's pronunciations and rhythms are suggested rather than literally duplicated in every detail. The art which makes the language credible is not forced by excessive misspelling, strained metaphor, or esoteric diction. These last three devices are the sure indicators of an inept or inexperienced writer who implicitly asks his reader to remain aloof from his dialect-speaking persona. The storytelling style and content of the *Narrative* are thus distinctly Crockett's. The subtler techniques by which it achieves an illusion of authenticity, the most im-

portant of which would have been restraint, are probably the effect of Chilton's good judgment. The reader who is not a dialect specialist is more likely to identify the book's style as being generally representative of American backwoods tall talk and less likely to associate it with a definite region or even a specific class of folks.

It is the book's finely managed art which invites comparison with Benjamin Franklin's *Autobiography*. . . . Like Franklin's, Crockett's autobiography stresses the facts most useful to an idea of the man's whole attitude toward life, rather than pretending to display all the facts of his life. Each author omits mentioning his serious faults, like Franklin's callous treatment of his wife or Crockett's bad habit of missing congressional roll calls, but each happily recalls a few harmless mistakes in order to illustrate how much he has learned from sad experience.

Both Franklin and Crockett declare their moral purposes, insisting that they have an obligation to instruct their readers in the fundamental public values—honest political behavior, common sense, hard work, and pursuit of the common good. . . . Both life stories are presented as paradigms illustrating the American ideals of individualism and self-reliance. Both narrators cultivate aphorisms and anecdotes, and neither takes himself too seriously.

Indeed, the form of both autobiographies is so clearly invented and their details so carefully reconstructed that either might be thought of as a humorous didactic novel. The episodes are derived from each author's history, but they are enlarged and made significant by his talent for truthful fiction. In both, the narrator is a cheerful, brilliant eccentric who unselfconsciously promotes inventiveness, independence, and optimism. This is why the two autobiographies tell us so much about each man's comic imagination, even though they give us only some of the historical details and omit anything that would badly damage the image being created before the reader's very eyes.

There is, however, a large and telling difference between the two autobiographies. Franklin knew his life served as a great example, so he selected a few incidents which would illustrate his many accomplishments and wove these into a rhetorical design showing that he had used his freedom very well. He encourages young Americans to do likewise. Franklin was quite literally a self-made man, and his autobiography is a deliberate re-creation of that original self-creation. . . . Crockett's autobiography, on the other hand, contains nearly all of the historically important events of his life up through his last term in Congress, and ends with January 1834, only two years and two months before his death at the Alamo. Much art went into the language of Crockett's recollections and the rhetoric embellishing his image, but it must not have been difficult to decide which successes to include and which failures to exclude. Crockett's *Narrative* is distinguished by its style, not its historical content. (pp. 4-7)

Crockett was painfully aware of how easily his folksy, unlettered manner could be parodied. He was always surprised and overly pleased by admiration and support, and other politicians could take advantage of his naiveté by flattering him or arranging some public honor. He was so seldom rewarded with political success that any measure of adulation tended to distort his judgment. It seems natural for him to have played up his image: he was a born showman, a yarn spinner, an actor. At the end of the preface, he tells us that another of his motives for writing an autobiography is to clarify his public role [see excerpt above, 1834]. . . . (p. 7)

Crockett's contemporary reader would have entered the *Narrative* in much the same way he prepared to see a strolling actor, watch a stage comedian, hear a political orator, or participate in a joke and story session: on guard, willing to play the game, and with disbelief suspended for the moment. In spite of his painful awareness of his naiveté, Crockett often managed to transform his supposed limitations into advantages by using his backwoods style in a productive mockery of itself. . . . [In] his preface, he says that he has no "pretension" to grammar and dismisses spelling by declaring that it is "not my trade." These gestures are designed to engage the sympathies of a large audience of workers, farmers, and settlers. The backwoods style of self-deprecation deflates the pretensions of educated opponents and defuses the volatile self-consciousness of unlettered folks. Implicitly, Crockett invites them to take his side in the game of common sense against book learning. He can safely expect his reader to know that whenever he modestly says he is surprised that an ordinary man like himself has been mentioned as a candidate, he is really saying he considers himself a prime candidate. Crockett's genius is displayed throughout his *Narrative* as a clear understanding of how best to evoke his audience's sense of values. Besides all this, the book is humorous and entertaining in its own right— a valuable work of comic art and an exemplary artifact of popular culture. (p. 8)

Richard Boyd Hauck, in his Crockett: A Bio-Bibliography, *Greenwood Press, 1982, 169 p.*

ADDITIONAL BIBLIOGRAPHY

Albanese, Catherine L. "Citizen Crockett: Myth, History, and Nature Religion." *Soundings* LXI, No. 1 (Spring 1978): 87-104.
Asserts that the Crockett of legend represents Americans' hopes and dreams.

———. "King Crockett: Nature and Civility on the American Frontier." *Proceedings of the American Antiquarian Society* 88, Part 2 (1979): 225-49.
Examines how some of the exploits attributed to Crockett in the almanacs and the *Narrative* contributed to the development of the Crockett myth. Albanese states that these works, though exaggerated, are representative of contemporary American values and beliefs.

———. "Savage, Sinner, and Saved: Davy Crockett, Camp Meetings, and the Wild Frontier." *American Quarterly, Special Issue: American Culture and the American Frontier* 33, No. 5 (Winter 1981): 482-501.
Uses excerpts from the Crockett almanacs to examine the myth of the American frontier. Albanese finds a connection between the absence of civilizing forces on the frontier and "an answering wildness in the American spirit."

Beard, Charles A., and Beard, Mary R. "New Agricultural States." In their *The Rise of American Civilization, Vol. I*, rev. ed., pp. 507-41. New York: Macmillan Co., 1946.*
A historical survey. Like Vernon Louis Parrington (see excerpt above, 1927), the critics depict Crockett as one of the illiterate Westerners who, along with Andrew Jackson, pushed their way into national politics.

Blair, Walter. "David versus Davy," "Davy versus Captain Fear of Hell's Gulch," and "Davy II, Davy III, and Mose." In *America's Humor: From Poor Richard to Doonesbury*, by Walter Blair and Hamlin Hill, pp. 122-32, pp. 133-42, pp. 143-51. New York: Oxford University Press, 1978.*
A survey of American comic writing that compares various interpretations of Crockett: the historical figure, the legendary hero, and the Crockett depicted in dramas, movies, and television.

Blankenship, Russell. "The West." In his *American Literature As an Expression of the National Mind*, rev. ed., pp. 220-30. New York: Cooper Square Publishers, 1973.*
A survey of American intellectual history, in the tradition of Vernon Louis Parrington (see excerpt above, 1927) and Charles A. Beard and Mary R. Beard (see annotation above), that briefly discusses Crockett. Blankenship describes Crockett as ignorant, illiterate, and shiftless and comments that "if he had possessed a few ideas, he would have been a dangerous demagogue, but without them he was thoroughly harmless." This essay was first published in 1931.

Boorstin, Daniel J. "Heroes or Clowns? Comic Supermen from a Subliterature." In his *The Americans: The National Experience*, pp. 327-37. New York: Random House, 1966.*
Examines Crockett as a candidate for national hero worship and identifies the elements of his appeal.

Dorson, Richard M. "Davy Crockett and the Heroic Age." *Southern Folklore Quarterly* VI, No. 2 (June 1942): 95-102.
Outlines the similarities between the Crockett legends and heroic literature.

———, ed. *Davy Crockett: American Comic Legend*. New York: Rockland Editions, 1939, 171 p.
A collection of stories and woodcuts from the Crockett almanacs. Dorson's introductory essay provides an overview of frontier hu-

mor and legend, and his selections demonstrate the themes typical to the almanacs that created the Crockett legend.

Heale, M.J. "The Role of the Frontier in Jacksonian Politics: David Crockett and the Myth of the Self-Made Man." *The Western Historical Quarterly* IV, No. 4 (October 1973): 405-23.
  Contends that during the early nineteenth century life on the frontier came to symbolize American values and that Crockett, with the aid of contemporary politicians, promoted his image as a self-made man to capitalize on American esteem for the frontiersman.

Hofstadter, Richard. "The Decline of the Gentleman." In his *Anti-Intellectualism in American Life*, pp. 145-71. New York: Alfred A. Knopf, 1963.*
  Discusses Crockett as a symbol of anti-intellectualism.

Hubbell, Jay B. "The Road to Disunion, 1830-1865: David Crockett." In his *The South in American Literature: 1607-1900*, pp. 662-66. Durham, N.C.: Duke University Press, 1954.
  Assesses Crockett's contribution to the American tradition of tall tales.

Kilgore, Dan. *How Did Davy Die?* College Station: Texas A & M University Press, 1978, 48 p.
  A comprehensive review of historical sources that concludes that Crockett was captured alive at the Alamo and executed by Santa Anna's troops.

Lofaro, Michael A. "From Boone to Crockett: The Beginnings of Frontier Humor." *Mississippi Folklore Register* XIV, No. 2 (Fall 1980): 57-74.*
  Identifies the roles of Crockett and Daniel Boone in the growth of frontier humor.

Miles, Guy S. "David Crockett Evolves, 1821-1824." *American Quarterly* VIII, No. I (Spring 1956): 53-60.
  Rebuts charges that Crockett was ignorant of legislative matters.

Murdock, Frank. *"Davy Crockett; or, Be Sure You're Right, Then Go Ahead."* In *"Davy Crockett" & Other Plays*, by Leonard Grover, Frank Murdock, Lester Wallack, G. H. Jessop, and J. J. McCloskey, edited by Isaac Goldberg and Hubert Heffner, pp. 115-48. Princeton: Princeton University Press, 1940.
  A dramatic popularization of the Crockett legend, first produced in 1872.

Null, Marion Michael. *The Forgotten Pioneer: The Life of Davy Crockett*. New York: Vantage Press, 1954, 183 p.
  An anecdotal biography. Null unabashedly admires Crockett, calling him "one of America's greatest pioneers."

Paulding, James Kirke. *The Lion of the West*. Rev. ed. Edited by James N. Tidwell. Stanford, Calif.: Stanford University Press, 1954, 64 p.
  A widely successful 1830 comic drama about the adventures of an American frontiersman. Despite Paulding's denials, contemporaries believed that the hero, Colonel Nimrod Wildfire, was modeled after Crockett.

Rourke, Constance. *Davy Crockett*. New York: Harcourt, Brace and Co., 1934, 276 p.

A fictional biography that describes Crockett's life and historical era in great detail. Rourke considers the *Narrative* "a classic in our literature because it was one of the first to use the American language with fullness and assurance, and because it reveals a way of life in a distinctive style." Many modern critics agree that Rourke's work contributed to the twentieth-century resurgence of interest in Crockett.

Seelye, John. "A Well-Wrought Crockett: Or, How the Fakelorists Passed Through the Credibility Gap and Discovered Kentucky." In *Toward a New American Literary History: Essays in Honor of Arlin Turner*, edited by Louis J. Budd, Edwin H. Cady, and Carl L. Anderson, pp. 91-110. Durham, N.C.: Duke University Press, 1980.
  Traces the development of the Crockett legend in the almanacs.

Shackford, James Atkins. "The Author of David Crockett's Autobiography." *The Boston Public Library Quarterly* 3, No. 4 (October 1951): 294-304.
  Examines previously unpublished letters to prove that the *Narrative* was written jointly by Crockett and Thomas Chilton. Shackford, whose opinion is widely respected on this matter, concludes that Chilton was responsible for its form while Crockett provided the content.

———. *David Crockett: The Man and the Legend*. Edited by John B. Shackford. Chapel Hill: University of North Carolina Press, 1956, 338 p.
  The definitive biography. Unlike earlier writers who glorified the Crockett legend, Shackford concentrates on the "real" Crockett. Modern critics consider this a well-researched, historically accurate work, and they generally accept Shackford's conclusions about the authorship of the works attributed to Crockett.

Shapiro, Irwin. *Yankee Thunder: The Legendary Life of Davy Crockett*. New York: Julian Messner, 1944, 205 p.
  A fictional biography. In his preface, Shapiro notes the difficulty in differentiating between Crockett's many identities. His work focuses on "the mythical Crockett, the Crockett of legend and folksay, of the tall tales and fireside yarns and almanac stories."

Smith-Rosenberg, Carroll. "Davey Crockett as Trickster: Pornography, Liminality and Symbolic Inversion in Victorian America." *Journal of Contemporary History* 17, No. 2 (April 1982): 325-50.
  Analyzes the Crockett myth as evidence of the effect of social change on nineteenth-century attitudes toward the family and sexuality.

Stone, Irving. "Four Loves Had Davy Crockett." In his *The Irving Stone Reader*, pp. 753-65. Garden City, N.Y.: Doubleday & Co., 1963.
  A sentimental biographical sketch that discussess Crockett's life and loves.

Zanger, Jules. "The Frontiersman in Popular Fiction, 1820-60." In *The Frontier Re-examined*, edited by John Francis McDermott, pp. 141-53. Urbana: University of Illinois Press, 1967.*
  Examines three popular images of the frontiersman in fiction: Crockett, a comic character, vulgar yet heroic; Daniel Boone, an elusive, solitary, mythic figure; and the successive versions of Natty Bumppo in James Fenimore Cooper's "Leatherstocking Tales."

Charles Dickens

1812-1870

(Also wrote under the pseudonym of Boz) English novelist, short story writer, dramatist, poet, and essayist.

The following entry presents criticism of Dickens's novel *Bleak House* (1853). For a complete discussion of Dickens's career see *NCLC*, Vol. 3.

Critics view *Bleak House* as the apex of Dickens's intellectual and artistic development and one of the most important novels produced in nineteenth-century England. In *Bleak House* Dickens explores the themes of social and personal responsibility through a piercing, pessimistic satire of Chancery Court. Commentators on the novel praise Dickens's realistic depiction of society, his masterful handling of structure, his ability to create vivid characters, and his evocative use of imagery. Dickens employs the fictional case of Jarndyce vs. Jarndyce to scrutinize the role of institutions in society, to chart the intertwining of individuals' lives, and to expose the deterioration of social systems in general. In the novel, the case, initiated by two Jarndyce heirs feuding over the family inheritance, has dragged on for so long that no one even remembers who the original plaintiffs were. Dickens depicts Chancery Court as the focal symbol of societal disorder and oppression of the powerless. After *Bleak House,* he continued to focus on one specific institution in each novel to expose the moral and physical decay of society.

The son of a minor government official who was consistently in debt, Dickens came to know the miseries of poverty and the vagaries of the English legal system early in life. When Dickens was ten years old, his father was sent to debtors' prison, and the boy was forced to work for low wages in a blacking warehouse until his father's release five years later. His first-hand knowledge of the life of the London poor served Dickens well in his career, and critics have consistently commended his sympathetic treatment of their plight. Dickens also worked as a law clerk and court stenographer and became well acquainted with proceedings in the London courts. *Bleak House* displays his familiarity with the world of the law through his authentic description of the course and ramifications of Jarndyce vs. Jarndyce.

Dickens enjoyed unparalleled success as a novelist and maintained popularity with the public throughout all phases of his career. His early novels, written between 1836 and 1841, included *Sketches by Boz, Posthumous Papers of the Pickwick Club, Oliver Twist, The Life and Adventures of Nicholas Nickelby,* and *The Old Curiosity Shop* and were renowned for their sentimentality, good-natured humor, and colorful characters. Critics noticed an increased interest in social issues and the role of money as a corrupting force in the novels of Dickens's middle phase from 1843 to 1850, which includes *Dealings with the Firm of Dombey and Son* and *The Personal History of David Copperfield.* With *Bleak House* Dickens entered what is known as his "late period," characterized by a sense of deep pessimism and alienation. Other novels in this group are *Hard Times, Little Dorrit, Our Mutual Friend,* and *Great Expectations.* Like *Bleak House,* they are also distinguished by a more unified tone, careful plotting of structure, and sustained

use of imagery. The mood in these later novels has been described as dark and foreboding, aided by such pervasive symbols as fog, disease, garbage, and impersonal institutions.

Esther Summerson, the central character of *Bleak House,* functions as the novel's focal point, but the story involves many other characters whose lives intersect with hers. The narrative is related alternately by Esther and by an anonymous omniscient narrator. An orphan raised by an aunt, Esther goes to live at Bleak House as the ward of John Jarndyce. All the denizens of Bleak House are waiting for the Chancery Court's decision about the inheritance suit of Jarndyce vs. Jarndyce. A prominent theme of the novel is Esther's voyage of self-discovery and her progression towards maturity and acceptance. At the conclusion of the novel, Esther is happily married to Allan Woodcourt, a young doctor. The claimants in the Jarndyce suit learn that, though the case is finally settled, the entire inheritance has been absorbed by court costs—a final ironic note on the futility of the court system.

Bleak House was first published serially, from March 1852 to September 1853, in twenty monthly installments. While it enjoyed great popularity with the reading public, the novel was poorly received by contemporary reviewers. Many severely criticized Dickens's fondness for sensational plot elements, melodrama, and characterization which verged on caricature.

John Stuart Mill pointed out that Dickens's treatment of female characters and women's rights was "vulgar," and G. H. Lewes condemned the description of Krook's death by spontaneous combustion as a scientific impossibility. Reviewing *Bleak House* in *The Spectator,* George Brimley cited "an absolute want of construction" as its major flaw. In fact, most early commentators missed the experimental implications of Dickens's handling of structure in the novel, terming *Bleak House* a disorganized and confusing compilation of subplots. Only a few, such as Henry Fothergill Chorley, acknowledged that in its construction the novel exhibited "an important advance" on Dickens's previous works. Some reviewers were offended by the boldness of Dickens's social criticism; others, like John Ruskin, considered the novel to be an accurate recreation of modern urban life.

One frequently debated topic among twentieth-century critics is the success or failure of Dickens's structural and narrative technique. Characterization, particularly that of Esther, continues to interest commentators on *Bleak House.* Critics also often discuss the role of symbolism, social commentary, and satire in the novel.

Opinions varied widely on the question of Dickens's handling of structure in *Bleak House.* While Brimley failed to discern any pattern in the construction of the novel, Chorley praised the cohesiveness of its plot elements, and John Forster was the first to indicate admiration for Dickens's "studied and elaborate care" in structural development. Most twentieth-century critics agree that Dickens's structural experiment in *Bleak House* is ultimately successful. Algernon Charles Swinburne, G. K. Chesterton, Edmund Wilson, and Lionel Stevenson all praised the unity of the various subplots in *Bleak House;* Vladimir Nabokov, in his discussion of the interrelatedness of characters and events in the novel, pointed to Dickens's technical control over all the elements of this story as "an obvious sign of greatness." Some critics, including Edgar Johnson, Morton Dauwen Zabel, and J. Hillis Miller, noticed that the structure of *Bleak House* mirrors its major themes. Though most critics believe that the double narrative both functions smoothly and contributes depth and resonance to the themes of *Bleak House,* a few commentators disagree. Taylor Stoehr contended that the split narrative effect camouflaged "the basic emotional contents" of the novel and destroyed the overall unity. In addition, Robert Alan Donovan argued that the structure of *Bleak House* is successfully based upon the pattern of mystery and discovery typical of the detective story narrative. Wilson, Stevenson, and Zabel also considered *Bleak House* a detective story.

Characterization in *Bleak House* has also been the subject of much debate. Although Chorley admired the portrayal of the waifs and strays, he and other early reviewers of the novel criticized Dickens's exaggerated character types; however, Chesterton wrote that the characters in *Bleak House* were more "delicately" and "faintly" drawn than usual for Dickens. Critics have acclaimed Dickens's satiric portrayals of the evangelist Mrs. Jellyby and the self-righteous Smallweed· family, and some also speculated that Dickens used the English poet and critic Leigh Hunt as his model for the conniving dilettante Harold Skimpole. Monroe Engel has suggested that Jo, the crossing-sweeper, be considered the central character in *Bleak House;* his argument echoes the sentiments of Chorley who maintained that Dickens "has never produced anything more rueful, more pitiable, more complete than poor Jo."

Most critics agree that Esther is the central character in *Bleak House,* and they devote more attention to her than to any other character in the novel. Early reviewers indicated that they considered Esther perhaps too idealized to be realistic. They were also troubled by her naïveté, which they perceived as diminishing her credibility as a narrator. Later commentators on the novel also assessed Esther as unsatisfactory, labelling her virtues and efficiency "tiresome" and "revolting" and criticizing her lack of imagination and understanding. Conversely, critics such as Q. D. Leavis argued for Esther's central importance, noting that her character embodies an "interesting psychological consistency," and that she functions well as the "registering consciousness" in *Bleak House.*

Analyses of Dickens's use of symbolism also figure prominently in studies of *Bleak House.* Johnson, Engel, Murray Krieger, Trevor Blount, and Donovan, among others, discussed the implications of the Chancery Court in *Bleak House.* Johnson wrote that Chancery is a crucial symbol which exposes the abuses of the English legal system, and that the novel reveals "the whole dark muddle of organized society." To Blount, Chancery represents "a touchstone of moral reality," whereas Krieger interpreted it as the "suprahistorical curse" upon the human condition. Many critics also focus on the fog as the novel's pervasive symbol. While Wilson and Zabel stated that the fog represents Chancery Court, A.O.J. Cockshut contended that it is also a symbol of general uncertainty. To Johnson, the fog stands for the "forces that suffocate the creative energies of mankind." Like the omnipresent fog, disease also functions as a symbol which links the lives of individuals in the novel; Engel, Stoehr, and John Lucas point to Dickens's message that evil, like disease, spreads throughout all elements of society. Such modern critics as Johnson, Stoehr, and Blount discussed the episode of spontaneous combustion as a symbol of the inevitable self-destruction of evil. All these interpretations point to Dickens's dark vision of society in *Bleak House.*

Most critics agree that in the novels of his "late period," Dickens's scorn for social injustice becomes increasingly explicit. Though interpretations of its themes vary, scholars generally find in *Bleak House* evidence of Dickens's concern with social and individual responsibility. Twentieth-century commentators praise Dickens's artful combination of structure, characterization, symbolism, and satire employed to launch a powerful attack on "The System" which, in his view, perpetuated human suffering. Johnson proposed that, with *Bleak House,* Dickens "created the novel of the social group, used as an instrument of social criticism." Through satire of the Chancery Court, Dickens indicted what Wilson termed "the indifference and egoism of the middle class;" similarly, Zabel perceives *Bleak House* as a condemnation of "the implacable materialism and hypocrisy of a new age." Such recent critics as Blount and John Lucas asserted that the key to Dickens's success as a social critic lies in his realistic depiction of characters and situations in *Bleak House.* However, to Stefan Zweig and George Gissing, both earlier critics, Dickens's prose lacks realism: Zweig remarked that Dickens too often lapses into sentimentality, and Gissing criticized his "almost total disregard for probability." All these exemplify disagreements over the realism issue which has continued since the book's publication. Perhaps one of the most balanced views is that of Zabel, who argues that Dickens was indeed reacting to real conditions in England and Europe, and that he did so in *Bleak House* through "a supreme tour de force of dramatic artifice and contrivance."

(See also *Something about the Author*, Vol. 15, and *Dictionary of Literary Biography*, Vol. 21: *Victorian Novelists Before 1885.*)

G. H. LEWES   (letter date 1853)

[*Lewes was one of the most versatile men of letters of the Victorian era. A prominent English journalist, he founded and edited the radical periodical* The Leader *with Thornton Leigh Hunt; from 1865-66, he served as the first editor of* The Fortnightly Review, *which he had also helped to establish. Much absorbed by questions of science and philosophy, Lewes made original contributions in the fields of physiology and psychology, and he was instrumental in introducing to England the philosophical doctrines of Auguste Comte. His life of Goethe is regarded as a biographical masterpiece. Critics often cite Lewes's influence on the novelist George Eliot, to whom he was companion and mentor, as his principal contribution to English letters, but they also credit him with critical acumen in his literary commentary, most notably in his dramatic criticism. Both publicly and in his extensive private correspondence with Dickens, Lewes asserted that "Spontaneous Combustion is an* impossibility." *The role of spontaneous combustion in* Bleak House *is later discussed by Jack Lindsay (1950), Edgar Johnson (1952), A.O.J. Cockshut (1962), Trevor Blount (1970), and Morton Dauwen Zabel (see Additional Bibliography).*]

My Dear Dickens,—What you write is read wherever the English language is read. This magnificent popularity carries with it a serious responsibility. A vulgar error countenanced by you becomes, thereby, formidable. Therefore am I, in common with many of your admirers, grieved to see that an error exploded from science, but one peculiarly adapted to the avid credulity of unscientific minds, has been seriously taken up by you, and sent all over the world with your imprimatur—an act which will tend to perpetuate the error in spite of the labours of a thousand philosophers. . . .

My object in [this letter] will be to show, that the highest scientific authorities of the day distinctly disavow the notion of Spontaneous Combustion; that the evidence in favour of the notion is worthless; that the theories in explanation are absurd; and that, according to all known chemical and physiological laws, Spontaneous Combustion is an *impossibility*. . . .

It is due to you that I should declare a large majority on your side. Works on medical jurisprudence, Dictionaries, and Encyclopaedias, lend the theory their authority. Medical men frequently adopt it. So that you, not specially engaged in any subjects of this nature, may well be excused for having adopted it.

On the other hand, it is necessary I should declare that these authorities are insignificant, beside the authorities ranged against them. What are medical dictionaries and works on jurisprudence compared with authorities of such commanding eminence as LIEBIG, BISCHOFF, REGNAULT, GRAHAM, HOFMANN, and OWEN? I only name those whom I *know* to have pronounced unequivocally on this point, but I believe you will find no one eminent organic chemist of our day who credits Spontaneous Combustion. (p. 137)

Man, the hungry logophagist, swallowed the phrase Spontaneous Combustion as soon as it was thrown out to explain certain unexplained deaths; and semi-science built up theories to accredit it. Science, when grown older and wiser, saw through it; and eliminated the testimony to certain facts from the additions unconsciously furnished by imagination.

I utterly reject the evidence, partly because it is bad evidence for anything, but mainly because it testifies to a physical impossibility.

Let us not deceive ourselves respecting the value of reported cases. You, Dickens, would not believe a whole neighbourhood of respectable witnesses who should declare that the lamp-post had been converted, by a flash of lightning, into an elm tree. No, not if they swore to having *seen* it. Why? Simply because you would rather believe these witnesses in error than disbelieve the millions of testimonies *implied* in the establishment of those scientific truths which contradict such a transmutation. Although the notion of Spontaneous Combustion may not be so *obviously* impossible as the change from a lamp-post into an elm tree, yet I believe it is *really* so; and if the testimony of reported cases be allowed to shake our faith in the simple laws of organic chemistry, hereafter to be adduced, on the same ground respectable testimony may shake our faith in the impossibility of a lamp-post becoming an elm. (p. 138)

> *G. H. Lewes, in a letter to Charles Dickens, in* The Leader, *Vol. IV, No. 150, February 5, 1853, pp. 137-38.*

[HENRY FOTHERGILL CHORLEY]   (essay date 1853)

[*While he praises Dickens's technical progress in* Bleak House, *Chorley is critical of his "resolution to startle," evidenced by exaggerated characterization and plot elements. In commenting that Esther strikes him as "over-perfect," Chorley early isolates a point to be much debated in later criticism of the novel.*]

There is progress in art to be praised in [**'Bleak House'**]—and there is progress in exaggeration to be deprecated. At its commencement the impression made is strange. Were its opening pages in anywise accepted as representing the world we live in, the reader might be excused for feeling as though he belonged to some orb where eccentrics, Bedlamites, ill-directed and disproportioned people were the only inhabitants. Esther Summerson, the narrator, is, in her surpassingly sweet way, little less like ordinary persons than are Krook and Skimpole. Her own story was of itself sadly romantic enough—the provident beneficence of Mr. Jarndyce to her was sufficiently unlike Fortune's usual dealings with those born as she was—to have sufficed for the marvels of one number. But on her mysterious summons to town to join the delightful wards in Chancery with whom she makes an instant and cordial friendship, she is thrown, on the very moment of arrival, into company with a sharp-witted and coxcombical limb of the law, in Guppy,—with an overweening philanthropist, who lets everything at home go to rack and ruin for the sake of her foreign mission, in Mrs. Jellyby,—with an infuriated madman who has a mysterious lodger and a demoniacal cat, in Krook,—and with a ruefully fantastic Chancery victim in poor little Miss Flite. Nay, when she gets to the house of her guardian, he, too, must needs be marked out as a curiosity by his whimsical manner of wreaking his vexation at sin, sorrow and meanness, on the weather,—while his guest happens to be none other than such a rare specimen of the man of imagination as Mr. Harold Skimpole.—Here is "the apple-pie made of quinces" with a vengeance, if there ever was such a thing!—Granting the simple heroine of Mr. Dickens to possess the immediate power of the daguerreotype in noting at once the minutest singularities of so many

The frontispiece to the first edition of Bleak House.

exceptional people—granting her, further, in its fullest extent, the instantaneous influence for good in word and in deed which she exercises over every person with whom she is brought into contact,—it surely befalls few such angels of experience, simplicity and overflowing kindness to enter Life through the gate of usefulness down a highway lined with figures so strange as the above. The excuse of Esther's creator, we suppose, lies in the supposed necessity of catching his public at the outset, by exhibiting a rare set of figures in readiness for the coming harlequinade. But in **'Bleak House'** they stand in one another's way. . . .

This resolution to startle, besides being bad in itself, leads the novelist, even though he have of the richest *cornucopia* of humours at his disposal, into two faults,—both of which may be seriously objected against **'Bleak House.'** First, from noticing mere peculiarities, he is beguiled into a cruel consideration of physical defects,—from the unnatural workings of the mind, the step to the painful agonies of the body is a short one. The hideous palsy of Grandfather Smallweed, and the chattering idiocy of his wife, belong to the coarse devices which are losing their hold on the popular taste even at the minor theatres.—The death of Krook—attacked as an impossible catastrophe, and defended by our novelist on medical testimony—would be false and repugnant in point of Art, even if it were scientifically true. We would not willingly look into fiction for the phenomena of *elephantiasis*, or for the hopeless writhings of those who suffer and perish annually in the slow sharp pains of cancer. Again,—in his determination to exhibit snub minds and pimpled tempers, principles that squint, and motives that

walk on club-feet (analogous to the mis-shapen figures which ought not to come too frequently even from the professed caricaturist's pencil)—it is difficult, perhaps, for the novelist to avoid touching on another forbidden ground, to abstain from that sharpness of individual portraiture which shall make certain of his *dramatis personae* recognizable as reproductions of living people. . . .

[We] now turn to the admirable things which this last tale by Mr. Dickens contains.—And first, though he has been thereby led away from his great Chancery case further than may have been his original intention, we must signalize the whole machinery by which Lady Dedlock's private history is gradually brought to day—as admirable in point of fictitious construction,—an important advance on anything that we recollect in our author's previous works. Not a point is missed,—not a person left without part or share in the gradual disclosure—not a pin dropped that is not to be picked up for help or for harm to somebody. The great catastrophe is, after all, determined as much by the distant jealousy of Mrs. Snagsby, the fretful law-stationer's wife, as by the more intimate vengeance of the discarded lady's maid. Capital, too,—of an excellence which no contemporary could reach,—is the manner in which Mr. Bucket the detective officer is worked into the very centre and core of the mystery, until we become almost agreed with Sir Leicester Dedlock in looking on him as a superior being in right of his cool resource and wondrous knowledge. Nor has Mr. Dickens wrought up any scene more highly and less melo-dramatically than those of the night-ride into the country in which the over-perfect Esther is included—and of the despairing affectionate, hopeless expectation of the deserted husband in the town-house. It is curious, however, to observe how completely our novelist's power has failed him on the threshold of the dank grave-yard, where the proud and desperate lady lies down to die of remorse and shame,—how despotically he has chosen to forget that such a catastrophe could not really have been hushed up in the manner hinted at in his closing chapters. We are not sorry to be spared a second inquest over the body of the faithless woman, having assisted at like rites over the corpse of the outcast lover of her youth,—we can dispense with the excitement of the trial of Mademoiselle Hortense, the murderess, and the horrors of her execution,—but such events there must have been;—and to have overlooked them so completely as Mr. Dickens has done in winding up his story, is an arbitrary exercise of his art, made all the more striking by the minute painting with which other parts of the narrative are wrought.

In his own particular walk—apart from the exaggerations complained of, and the personalities against which many have protested—Mr. Dickens has rarely, if ever, been happier than in **'Bleak House.'** Poor miserable Mr. Jellyby, with all hope, life, and energy washed out of him by the flow of his wife's incessant zeal—the dancing-school in which the African missionary's daughter finds her mission—the cousins who cluster round Sir Leicester Dedlock, giving an air of habitation to the great house, by filling up its empty corners,—could have been hit off by no one else so well. Then, with all his inanity, pomposity, and prejudice in favour of his order, the Lincolnshire baronet is a true gentleman:—we are not only told this, we are made to feel it. His wife is a comparative failure: a second edition of *Mrs. Dombey,*—with somewhat of real stateliness superadded. Trooper George is new:—and here, again, Mr. Dickens is masterly, in preserving (though with some exaggeration) the simplicity, sentimentality, and credulity of the original nature which made the man a roamer,—and which have a strong and real life in many a barrack and in many a ship of war. Mr. Snagsby "puts too fine a point" on his intimations concerning the spectre that destroys his home peace, somewhat too ceaselessly. The queerest catch-word may be used too mercilessly, even for a farce,—much more for a novel.— Perhaps among all the waifs and strays, the beggars and the outcasts, in behalf of whose humanity our author has again and again appealed to a world too apt to forget their existence, he has never produced anything more rueful, more pitiable, more complete than poor Jo. The dying scene, with its terrible morals and impetuous protest, Mr. Dickens has nowhere in all his works excelled. The book would live on the strength alone of that one sketch from the swarming life around us. Mr. Bucket is a jewel among detectives:—and the mixture of professional enjoyment and manly, delicate consideration in his great scene with Sir Leicester Dedlock, is marked and carried through with a master's hand. Esther is, as we have hinted, too precociously good, too perpetually self-present, and too helpful to every one around her to carry a sense of reality:—nor are her virtues made more probable by the fact that she is the chronicler of her own perfection,—though with disclaimers manifold. (p. 1087)

> [*Henry Fothergill Chorley*], *in a review of "Bleak House," in* The Athenaeum, *Vol. 2, No. 1351, September 17, 1853, pp. 1087-88.*

[GEORGE BRIMLEY]   (essay date 1853)

> [*Unlike Henry Fothergill Chorley (1853), Brimley cites an "absolute want of construction" as the greatest fault of* Bleak House. *Like Chorley, he objects to Dickens's "love of strong effect," his tendency to turn characters into caricatures, and his "utterly untrue and inconsistent" portrait of Esther.*]

Bleak House is, even more than any of its predecessors, chargeable with not simply faults, but absolute want of construction. A novelist may invent an extravagant or an uninteresting plot— may fail to balance his masses, to distribute his light and shade— may prevent his story from marching, by episode and discursion: but Mr. Dickens discards plot, while he persists in adopting a form for his thoughts to which plot is essential, and where the absence of a coherent story is fatal to continuous interest. In *Bleak House,* the series of incidents which form the outward life of the actors and talkers has no close and necessary connexion; nor have they that higher interest that attaches to circumstances which powerfully aid in modifying and developing the original elements of human character. The great Chancery suit of Jarndyce and Jarndyce, which serves to introduce a crowd of persons as suitors, lawyers, law-writers, law-stationers, and general spectators of Chancery business, has positively not the smallest influence on the character of any one person concerned; nor has it any interest of itself. Mr. Richard Carstone is not made reckless and unsteady by his interest in the great suit, but simply expends his recklessness and unsteadiness on it, as he would on something else if it were non-existent. This great suit is lugged in by the head and shoulders, and kept prominently before the reader, solely to give Mr. Dickens the opportunity of indulging in stale and commonplace satire upon the length and expense of Chancery proceedings, and exercises absolutely no influence on the characters and destinies of any one person concerned in it. The centre of the arch has nothing to do in keeping the arch together. The series of incidents which answers to what in an ordinary novel is called plot, is that connected with the relationship of the heroine (again analogically speaking) to her mother. . . . [Not only is

the story both meagre and melodramatic,] but it is so unskilfully managed that the daughter is in no way influenced either in character or destiny by her mother's history; and the mother, her husband, the prying solicitor, the French maid, and the whole Dedlock set, might be eliminated from the book without damage to the great Chancery suit, or perceptible effect upon the remaining characters. We should then have less crowd, and no story; and the book might be called "Bleak House, or the Odd Folks that have to do with a long Chancery Suit." This would give an exact notion of the contents of a collection of portraits embracing suitors, solicitors, law-writers, law-stationers, money-lenders, law-clerks, articled and not-articled, with their chance friends and visitors, and various members of their respective families. Even then, a comprehensive etcetera would be needed for supernumeraries. So crowded is the canvass which Mr. Dickens has stretched, and so casual the connexion that gives to his composition whatever unity it has, that a daguerreotype of Fleet Street at noon-day would be the aptest symbol to be found for it; though the daguerreotype would have the advantage in accuracy of representation. In addition to all other faults of construction, the heroine is made to tell her adventures in an autobiographic narrative; and as this would not suffice, under the conditions of a mortal existence limited to one spot in space at a time, for the endless array of persons who have to talk and be funny and interesting, the writer interealates chapters in his own person,—a mixture which has the awkwardest effect, and is left in its natural awkwardness with no appliances of literary skill to help it out.

The result of all this is, that *Bleak House* would be a heavy book to read through at once, as a properly-constructed novel ought to be read. But we must plead guilty to having found it dull and wearisome as a serial, though certainly not from its want of cleverness or point. On the contrary, almost everybody in the book is excessively funny, that is not very wicked, or very miserable. . . . Mr. Dickens selects in his portraiture exactly what a farce-writer of equal ability and invention would select,—that which is coarsely marked and apprehended at first sight; that which is purely outward and no way significant of the man, an oddity of feature, a trick of gesture or of phrase, something which an actor can adequately present and in his presentation exhaust the conception. And this tendency to a theatrical method shows itself again in the exaggerated form which his satire assumes, and which even when the satire is well directed robs it of its wholesome effect. (pp. 923-24)

The love of strong effect, and the habit of seizing peculiarities and presenting them instead of characters, pervade Mr. Dickens's gravest and most amiable portraits, as well as those expressly intended to be ridiculous and grotesque. His heroine in *Bleak House* is a model of unconscious goodness; sowing love and reaping it wherever she goes, diffusing round her an atmosphere of happiness and a sweet perfume of a pure and kindly nature. Her unconsciousness and sweet humility of disposition are so profound that scarcely a page of her autobiography is free from a record of these admirable qualities. With delightful naïveté she writes down the praises that are showered upon her on all hands; and it is impossible to doubt the simplicity of her nature, because she never omits to assert it with emphasis. This is not only coarse portraiture, but utterly untrue and inconsistent. Such a girl would not write her own memoirs, and certainly would not bore one with her goodness till a wicked wish arises that she would either do something very "spicy," or confine herself to superintending the jam-pots at Bleak House. Old Jarndyce himself, too, is . . . dreadfully amiable and supernaturally benevolent. . . . This gentleman is one of the most original and happiest conceptions of the book, a humourist study of the highest merit. Mr. Tulkinghorn, the Dedlock confidential solicitor, is an admirable study of mere outward characteristics of a class; but his motives and character are quite incomprehensible, and we strongly suspect that Mr. Dickens had him shot out of the way as the only possible method of avoiding an enigma of his own setting which he could not solve. Tulkinghorn's fate excites precisely the same emotion as the death of a noxious brute. He is a capital instance of an old trick of Mr. Dickens, by which the supposed tendencies and influences of a trade or profession are made incarnate in a man, and not only is ''the dyer's hand subdued to what it works in,'' but the dyer is altogether eliminated, and his powers of motion, his shape, speech, and bodily functions, are translated into the dye-tub. This gives the effect of what some critics call marvellous individuality. It gives distinctness at any rate, and is telling; though it may be questionable whether it is not a more fatal mistake in art than the careless and unobservant habit which many writers have of omitting to mark the effect of occupations upon the development and exhibition of the universal passions and affections. Conversation Kenge and Vholes, solicitors in the great Jarndyce case, have each their little characteristic set of phrases, and are well marked specimens of the genus lawyer; but as they only appear in their professional capacity, we are not entitled to question them as to their qualities as men.

The allied families of Jellyby and Turveydrop are in Dickens's happiest vein, though Mrs. Jellyby is a coarse exaggeration of an existing folly. They may, we think, stand beside the Micawbers. Mrs. Jellyby's daughter Caddy is the only female in the book we thoroughly relish: there is a blending of pathos and fun in the description of her under the tyranny of Borrioboola Gha, that is irresistible; and her rapid transformation from a sulky, morose, overgrown child, to a graceful and amiable young woman, under the genial influence of Esther Summerson, is quite Cinderella-like, and as charming as any fairy tale. . . . Poor Joe, the street-sweeping urchin, is drawn with a skill that is never more effectively exercised than when the outcasts of humanity are its subjects; a skill which seems to depart in proportion as the author rises in the scale of society depicted. Dickens has never yet succeeded in catching a tolerable likeness of man or woman whose lot is cast among the high-born and wealthy. Whether it is that the lives of such present less that is outwardly funny or grotesque, less that strikes the eye of a man on the lookout for oddity and point, or that he knows nothing of their lives, certain it is that his people of station are the vilest daubs; and Sir Leicester Dedlock, Baronet, with his wife and family circle, are no exceptions. (p. 924)

[Mr. Dickens] must be content with the praise of amusing the idle hours of the greatest number of readers; not, we may hope, without improvement to their hearts, but certainly without profoundly affecting their intellects or deeply stirring their emotions. Clever he undoubtedly is: many of his portraits excite pity, and suggest the existence of crying social sins; but of almost all we are obliged to say that they border on and frequently reach caricature, of which the essence is to catch a striking likeness by exclusively selecting and exaggerating a peculiarity that marks the man but does not represent him. (pp. 924-25)

[*George Brimley*], ''Dickens's 'Bleak House','' in *The Spectator*, *Vol. 26, No. 1317, September 24, 1853, pp. 923-25.*

[JOHN FORSTER] (essay date 1853)

[*Forster was an English historian, editor, and one of Dickens's earliest biographers. In his review of* Bleak House, *he praises Dickens's realistic characterization, satire, and delineation of structure, though he acknowledges an ''artificial tone'' in certain parts of Esther's narrative.*]

[That new groups of people as familiar and real as any that in life they may have known; that it overflows with immitable grace and tenderness; that it is stored with the most subtle wit, and with a humour, hearty and true, that sets always instinctively at work our pleasantest and kindliest emotions; that mirth and pathos abound in it, that its satire is always just and manly, and that it is full of generous indignation against social usages that create wrong and perpetuate suffering among us,—is simply in other words to say that it is a book written by Mr Dickens. That it has also faults is to say that it is not quite a miracle, even though written by him. Many faults truly may be found with it, and such as properly accompany great qualities. (p. 643)

The first remark we are disposed to make on *Bleak House* has relation to its plot. The conduct of the story appears to us singularly skilful. Not without justice has it been objected that the habit of writing a story in monthly parts is apt to lead to a greater concern for the part than for the whole, and to interfere with the steady and continuous working of every event up to the final issue. But let us in the present instance with no less justice remark, that the habit of reading a story in parts is equally apt to prevent many readers from noticing how thoroughly a work so presented to them is calculated for perusal as a whole. The studied and elaborate care bestowed upon the construction of *Bleak House* is very manifest. Event leads to event; and chance words, or the deeds of chance people, that seem perfectly irrelevant, are seen everywhere, precisely as in real life, exerting a direct and powerful bearing on the course taken by a train of incidents whereof the issue is one of life or death, of happiness or misery, to men and women perfectly unknown to them. Taking the mere surface view of such treatment, it would of course be easy to exhibit its apparent want of connection and design, and to display in the attempt only our own very real want of sagacity. This subtle linking together of the deeds and interests of many people, so far as they bear on the progress of one given set of incidents, is in fact truer to nature, infinitely truer, than the common plan of representing half a dozen men and women acting and re-acting on each other exclusively, as if they were fenced out from the surrounding world. Its drawback is that it compels the use of a large number of characters which come and go during the progress of the story; and, as their purpose in the narrative is not always evident until the reader can look back from the journey's end over the ground he has traversed, they may now and then cause some confusion in the reader's mind, and produce an effect like that of an over-crowded picture. But the art rather than the artist is there in fault.

Be this as it may, never in any former work has Mr Dickens made use of a plot so evidently planned beforehand with minute consideration, or throughout so elaborately studied. Even the fits of the little law-stationer's servant aid directly in the chain of little things that lead indirectly to the catastrophe of Lady Dedlock's death. So dexterously indeed are the many little incidents of this kind leading to great results managed throughout *Bleak House,* that we can hardly feel surprise if the results should by not very careful readers be received as substantive and independent facts, and the small precedent details held altogether separable from them, as a mere cloud of isolated incidents. A novel may have its too superficial readers, as life has its too hasty observers.

At the close of his preface Mr Dickens marks incidentally the general character of the tale by the intimation that in it he has purposely dwelt upon the romantic side of familiar things. Marvellous is the skill with which, towards this intention, the great Chancery suit on which the plot hinges, and on incidents connected with which, important or trivial, all the passion and suffering turns, is worked into every part of the book. Whenever the occasion arises, or the art of the story-teller requires, the thick atmosphere of law that rises out of Jarndyce v. Jarndyce is made to cling like a fog about the people in the story. . . .

Taking the story piecemeal, as a mere gallery of pictures and persons, we are disposed to think that there are particular groups in *Bleak House* finer than anything that even Mr Dickens has yet produced in the same way. Exquisitely true and tender as are his descriptions of the suffering classes in former writings, we can remember none by which we have been touched so deeply, or that has been graced by so much of the very finest writing, as the entire tale of the street-wandering Joe as it may be gathered from the pages of the book before us. In the trooper George, the Bagnets, and their humble household, we have another of those fine, broad, hearty exemplifications of humour in which Mr Dickens delights, in which all the ludicrous features of every object or incident are intensely enjoyed and made prominent, yet with a most genuine and charming sentiment at the same time underlying it all. Nothing is repulsive; everything is large, laughable, and true; and the most homely and ungainly figures become radiant with the spirit of goodness. The character of Esther Summerson has been much elaborated, and the early portions of her narrative are as charming as anything Mr Dickens has ever written—indeed some of the best things in the book may be found throughout it, full as it is of noble fancies, and delicate and graceful thoughts; but we suspect that Mr Dickens undertook more than man could accomplish when he resolved to make her the *naïve* revealer of her own good qualities. We cannot help detecting in some passages an artificial tone, which, if not self-consciousness, is at any rate not such a tone as would be used in her narrative by a person of the character depicted. Yet the graces and virtues of Esther have won so many hearts that we do not care to dwell on our objection to his method of displaying them; and as to the one or two other characters of the book which we might have wished away, these are quite lost in that crowd of fresh and ever real creations that will live while the language continues. Mrs Jellyby and her despondent husband, her daughter Caddy and the Turveydrops, the trooper George and his man Phil, the brickmakers' wives and the dead infant, the law-stationer and his little woman, Boythorn and Skimpole, Mr Chadband and the Coavinses, the mother of Mr Guppy, the inscrutable and impassable Tulkinghorn, to say nothing of poor Miss Flite or the immortal Bucket, and a dozen others, have been added here to the long list of ideal people with whom Mr Dickens has made his countrymen intimately and permanently acquainted. (p. 644)

[*John Forster*], in a review of "Bleak House," in The Examiner, No. 2384, October 8, 1853, pp. 643-45.

PUTNAM'S MONTHLY   (essay date 1853)

[*In one of the few contemporary American assessments of* Bleak House, *the anonymous reviewer for* Putnam's Monthly *magazine* *compliments Dickens on the convincing characterization in the novel. The reviewer's major criticism is that the plot does not conclude in a significant catastrophe, and the reviewer speculates that Dickens may "take up the broken thread of the narrative again."*]

In *Bleak House,* Dickens exhibits his greatest defects, and his greatest excellencies, as a novelist; in none of his works are the characters more strongly marked, or the plot more loosely and inartistically constructed. One-half of the personages might be ruled out without their loss being perceived, for, although they are all introduced with a flourish, as though they had an important part to perform, yet there would be no halt in the story if they were dropped by the way, as some of them are— Mr. Boythorn and his canary, for instance—without our being able to discover for what purpose they were brought out. Yet, who would wish not to have known Mr. Boythorn? (p. 559)

The chief personage of *Bleak House* is Esther Summerson, a gentle, loving, true-hearted and womanly creation; she possesses all the good points of the feminine character; and it was no wonder that Mr. Guppy should, at last, entertain so strong an affection for her. It was a redeeming trait in that gentleman's character, and we like him for it. But nothing can be more palpable than the strange contrast between the character of this estimable lady, and the manner in which she narrates it herself, confessing that she never was good for any thing, that she is awkward and so on, and then going deliberately to work to draw her own portrait in the most flattering manner, all the time perfectly conscious, too, that she was doing it. Esther is a perfect character, and naturally developed, with the sole exception that her picture of herself is an unnatural contrivance. (p. 561)

[The characters in *Bleak House*] are not mere names, nor lay figures, but distinct and striking individuals, who are remembered and alluded to as real personages who have impressed themselves upon us by their characteristics of mind and manner. . . .

The ostensible motive in *Bleak House* was to expose the evils of the Court of Chancery, and we are continually reminded by hints and pointed remarks through the earlier parts of the work that the dire catastrophe of the history of Jarndyce and Jarndyce, the culminating point of the narrative, is to result from the termination of that great suit. Yet, after all, nothing comes of it, and our horror of the iniquities of that institution are not in the slightest degree raised, or our feelings excited by the death of Richard Carstone, of a fever, which, under any circumstances, must have terminated his worthless life. There is not, in fact, any catastrophe at all, at the close; the climaxes keep occurring all the way through; our overwrought expectations, which the great writers of fiction never disappoint, are at last dashed, not by an inadequate revelation, but by a most provoking break in the midst of a sentence. Perhaps the author meant by this to hint that he intended to take up the broken thread of the narration again, and give it a proper winding up. We hope he did. (p. 562)

"Characters in 'Bleak House'," in Putnam's Monthly, Vol. II, No. XI, November, 1853, pp. 558-62.

JOHN STUART MILL   (letter date 1854)

[*An English essayist and critic, Mill is regarded as one of the greatest philosophers and political economists of the nineteenth century. At an early age, Mill was recognized as a leading advocate of the utilitarian philosophy of Jeremy Bentham, and he was a principal contributor to the* Westminster Review, *an English periodical founded by Bentham that later merged with the* London Review. *During the 1830s, after reading the works of William Wordsworth, Samuel Taylor Coleridge, and Auguste Comte, he gradually diverged from Bentham's utilitarianism. He acknowledged the importance of intuition and feelings and attempted to reconcile them with his rational philosophy. As part owner of the* London and Westminster Review *from 1835 to 1840, Mill was instrumental in modifying the periodical's utilitarian stance. He is considered a key figure in the transition from the rationalism of the Enlightenment to the renewed emphasis on mysticism and the emotions of the Romantic era. Mill was an early advocate of women's rights and in this excerpt from a letter of 1854 he chastises Dickens for his "vulgar impudence" in ridiculing the rights of women in* Bleak House. *The position of women in the novel is also analyzed by Belle Moses (1911) and Ellen Moers (1973).*]

That creature Dickens, whose last story, *Bleak House,* I found accidentally at the London Library the other day and took home and read, much the worst of his things, and the only one of them I altogether dislike, has the vulgar impudence in this thing to riducule rights of women. It is done too in the very vulgarest way, just the style in which vulgar men used to ridicule 'learned ladies' as neglecting their children and household.

> *John Stuart Mill, in an extract from a letter to Mrs. Richard Watson in March, 1854, in* Charles Dickens: A Critical Anthology, *edited by Stephen Wall, Penguin Books, 1970, p. 95.*

JOHN RUSKIN   (essay date 1880)

[*Ruskin, one of the leading English theorists and critics of the nineteenth century, had three major areas of accomplishment. He was a renowned art critic, and near the end of his life he devoted himself to political and economic issues. He also wrote literary criticism, which is informed by these concerns as well as by his broad knowledge of the Bible and Classical and contemporary literature. Ruskin's critical theory combines several key elements. Foremost to Ruskin was the connection between art and morality: "Poetry is the suggestion, by the imagination, of noble grounds for the noble emotions." To Ruskin, literature should include that which is just, true, honest, and pure; beauty exists only where art demonstrates a moral truth. His aesthetic theory focuses on nature and is permeated with a religious spirit. According to Peter Quennell, Ruskin was "a poetic visionary with a passionate, instinctive love of life, deeply enamored of the beauty of the visible world and capable of translating that passion into superbly expressive and melodious language." Ruskin comments on the profusion of deaths in* Bleak House; *he claims that they support "the modern theology that the appointed destiny of a large average of our population is to die like rats in a drain." This essay was originally published in the* Nineteenth Century *in June, 1880.*]

The monotony of life in the central streets of any great modern city, but especially in those of London, where every emotion intended to be derived by men from the sight of nature, or the sense of art, is forbidden for ever, leaves the craving of the heart for a sincere, yet changeful, interest, to be fed from one source only. Under natural conditions the degree of mental excitement necessary to bodily health is provided by the course of the seasons, and the various skill and fortune of agriculture. (p. 211)

[Under] these laws of inanition, the craving of the human heart for some kind of excitement could be supplied from *one* source only. It might have been thought by any other than a sternly tentative philosopher, that the denial of their natural food to

human feelings would have provoked a reactionary desire for it; and that the dreariness of the street would have been gilded by dreams of pastoral felicity. Experience has shown the fact to be otherwise; the thoroughly trained Londoner can enjoy no more excitement than that to which he has been accustomed, but asks for *that* in continually more ardent or more virulent concentration; and the ultimate power of fiction to entertain him is by varying to his fancy the modes, and defining for his dullness the horrors, of Death. In the single novel of *Bleak House* there are nine deaths (or left for deaths, in the drop scene) carefully wrought out or led up to, either by way of pleasing surprise, as the baby's at the brickmaker's, or finished in their threatenings and sufferings, with as much enjoyment as can be contrived in the anticipation, and as much pathology as can be concentrated in the description. Under the following varieties of method:

One by assassination	Mr. Tulkinghorn
One by starvation, with phthisis	Joe
One by chagrin	Richard
One by spontaneous combustion	Mr. Krook
One by sorrow	Lady Dedlock's lover
One by remorse	Lady Dedlock
One by insanity	Miss Flite
One by paralysis	Sir Leicester

Besides the baby, by fever, and a lively young French woman left to be hanged.

And all this, observe, not in a tragic, adventurous or military story, but merely as the further enlivenment of a narrative intended to be amusing; and as a properly representative average of the statistics of civilian mortality in the centre of London.

Observe further, and chiefly. It is not the mere number of deaths . . . that marks the peculiar tone of the modern novel. It is the fact that all these deaths, but one, are of inoffensive, or at least in the world's estimate, respectable persons; and that they are all grotesquely either violent or miserable, purporting thus to illustrate the modern theology that the appointed destiny of a large average of our population is to die like rats in a drain, either by trap or poison. Not, indeed, that a lawyer in full practice can be usually supposed as faultless in the eye of Heaven as a dove or a woodcock; but it is not, in former divinities, thought the will of Providence that he should be dropped by a shot from a client behind his fire-screen, and retrieved in the morning by his housemaid under the chandelier. Neither is Lady Dedlock less reprehensible in her conduct than many women of fashion have been and will be: but it would not therefore have been thought poetically just, in old-fashioned morality, that she should be found by her daughter lying dead with her face in the mud of a St. Giles's churchyard. (pp. 212-13)

> *John Ruskin, in an extract from* Charles Dickens: A Critical Anthology, *edited by Stephen Wall, Penguin Books, 1970, pp. 211-15.*

G. K. CHESTERTON   (essay date 1907)

[*Remembered primarily for his detective stories, Chesterton was also an eminent biographer, essayist, novelist, poet, journalist, dramatist, and critic of the early twentieth century. His essays are characterized by their humor, frequent use of paradox, and rambling style. His* The Victorian Age in Literature *is considered a standard source. Chesterton observes that* Bleak House *"rep-*

resents the highest point of [Dickens's] intellectual maturity,'' particularly because the novel is so artfully organized around ''a cycle of incidents.'' Praising Dickens's handling of imagery and symbolism in Bleak House, *Chesterton posits that Rick Carstone and Caddy Jellyby are the two most successfully drawn characters in the novel. Chesterton's evaluation of the structure of* Bleak House *antedates later positive appraisals by Lionel Stevenson (1943), Edgar Johnson (1952), Robert Alan Donovan (1966), and Morton Dauwen Zabel (see Additional Bibliography).]*

Bleak House is not certainly Dickens's best book; but perhaps it is his best novel. Such a distinction is not a mere verbal fancy; it has to be remembered rather constantly in connection with his work. This particular story represents the highest point of his intellectual maturity. Maturity does not necessarily mean perfection. . . . We can say more or less when a human being has come to his full mental growth, even if we go so far as to wish that he had never come to it. Children are very much nicer than grown-up people; but there is such a thing as growing up. When Dickens wrote **Bleak House** he had grown up.

Like Napoleon, he had made his army on the march. He had walked in front of his mob of aggressive characters as Napoleon did in front of the half-baked battalions of the Revolution. And, like Napoleon, he won battle after battle before he knew his own plan of campaign; like Napoleon, he put the enemies' forces to rout before he had put his own force into order. Like Napoleon, he had a victorious army almost before he had an army. After his decisive victories Napoleon began to put his house in order; after his decisive victories Dickens also began to put his house in order. The house, when he had put it in order, was 'Bleak House.'

It is important to remember this preliminary point, because it is this that in some way separates **Bleak House** from all the previous works of its author. Apart from what there was to arrange in it, it is the best arranged. Apart from whether it was worth constructing, it is the best constructed. . . . [Dickens's] earlier novels] were all rambling tales, for the very simple reason that they were all about rambling people. They were novels of adventure; they were even diaries of travel. Since the hero strayed from place to place, it did not seem unreasonable that the story should stray from subject to subject. This is true of the bulk of the novels up to and including **David Copperfield,** up to the very brink or threshold of **Bleak House.** (pp. v-vi)

When we come to **Bleak House,** we come to a vital change in artistic structure. The thing is no longer a string of incidents; it is a cycle of incidents. It returns upon itself; it has recurrent melody and poetic justice; it has artistic constancy and artistic revenge. It preserves the unities; even to some extent it preserves the unities of time and place. The story circles round two or three symbolic places; it does not go straggling irregularly all over England like one of Mr. Pickwick's coaches. People go from one place to another place; but not from one place to another place on the road to everywhere else. Mr Jarndyce goes from Bleak House to visit Mr Boythorn; but he comes back to Bleak House. Miss Clare and Miss Summerson go from Bleak House to visit Mr and Mrs Bayham Badger; but they come back to Bleak House. The whole story strays from Bleak House and plunges into the foul fogs of Chancery and the autumn mists of Chesney Wold; but the whole story comes back to Bleak House. There is in it this sense of something pivotal and permanent; it is one of the few books of the world of which the name is really appropriate.

The whole point could be quite sufficiently proved from the admirable first chapter; even from the first few paragraphs of the first chapter. Dickens's openings are almost always good; but the opening of **Bleak House** is good in a quite new and striking sense. (p. vii)

The description of the fog in the first chapter of **Bleak House** is good in itself; but it is not merely good in itself, like the description of the wind in the opening of **Martin Chuzzlewit;** it is also good in the sense that Maeterlinck is good; it is what the modern people call an atmosphere. Dickens begins in the Chancery fog because he means to end in the Chancery fog. He did not begin in the 'Chuzzlewit' wind because he meant to end in it; he began in it because it was a good beginning. This is perhaps the least short way of stating the peculiarity of the position of **Bleak House;** of course it is a symbolic form, but that is only because it is short; if brevity is the soul of wit, symbolism is the soul of brevity. In this **Bleak House** beginning we have the feeling that it is not only a beginning; we have the feeling that the author sees the conclusion and the whole. The beginning is alpha and omega: the beginning and the end. He means that all the characters and all the events shall be read through the smoky colours of that sinister and unnatural vapour.

The same is true throughout the whole tale; the whole tale is symbolic and crowded with symbols. Miss Flite is a funny character, like Miss La Creevy; but Miss La Creevy means only Miss La Creevy. Miss Flite means Chancery. The rag-and-bone man, Krook, is a powerful grotesque; so is Quilp; but in the story Quilp only means Quilp; Krook means Chancery. Rick Carstone is a kind and tragic figure, like Sidney Carton; but Sidney Carton only means the tragedy of human nature; Rick Carstone means the tragedy of Chancery. Little Jo dies pathetically like Little Paul; but for the death of Little Paul we can only blame Dickens; for the death of Little Jo we blame Chancery. Thus the artistic unity of the book, compared to all the author's earlier novels, is satisfying, almost suffocating. There is the motif, and again the motif. Almost everything is calculated to assert and re-assert the savage morality of Dickens's protest against a particular social evil. The whole theme is that which an Englishman as jovial as Dickens defined shortly and finally as the law's delay. The fog of the first chapter never lifts.

In this twilight he traced wonderful shapes. . . . Let any one who thinks that Dickens could not describe the semitones and the abrupt instincts of ordinary human nature simply take the trouble to read the stretch of chapters which detail the way in which Carstone's mind grew gradually morbid about his chances in Chancery. Let him note the manner in which the mere masculinity of Carstone is caught; how as he grows more mad he grows more logical, nay, more rational. Good women who love him come to him, and point out the fact that Jarndyce is a good man, a fact to them solid like an object of the senses. In answer he asks them to understand his position. He does not say this; he does not say that. He only urges that Jarndyce may have become cynical in the affair in the same sense that he himself may have become cynical in the affair. He is always a man; that is to say, he is always unanswerable, always wrong. The passionate certainty of the woman beats itself like battering waves against the thin smooth wall of his insane consistency. I repeat: let any one who thinks that Dickens was a gross and indelicate artist read that part of the book. If Dickens had been the clumsy journalist that such people represent, he never could have written such an episode at all. A clumsy journalist would

have made Rick Carstone in his mad career cast off Esther and
Ada and the others; the great artist knew better; he knew that
even if all the good in a man is dying, the last sense that dies
is the sense that knows a good woman from a bad; it is like
the scent of a noble hound.

The clumsy journalist would have made Rick Carstone turn on
John Jarndyce with an explosion of hatred, as of one who had
made an exposure—who had found out what low people call
'a false friend' in what they call 'his true colours.' The great
artist knew better; he knew that a good man going wrong tries
to salve his soul to the last with the sense of generosity and
intellectual justice. He will try to love his enemy if only out
of mere love of himself. As the wolf dies fighting, the good
man gone wrong dies arguing. This is what constitutes the true
and real tragedy of Richard Carstone. It is strictly the one and
only great tragedy that Dickens wrote. It is like the tragedy of
Hamlet. The others are not tragedies because they deal almost
with dead men. The tragedy of old Dorrit is merely the sad
spectacle of a dotard dragged about Europe in his last childhood. The tragedy of Steerforth is only that of one who dies
suddenly; the tragedy of old Dombey only that of one who was
dead all the time. But Rick is a real tragedy, for he is still
alive when the quicksand sucks him down.

It is impossible to avoid putting in the first place this pall of
smoke which Dickens has deliberately spread over the story.
It is quite true that the country underneath is clear enough to
contain any number of unconscious comedians or of merry
monsters such as he was in the custom of introducing into the
carnival of his tales. But he meant us to take the smoky atmosphere seriously. Charles Dickens, who was, like all men
who are really funny about funny things, horribly serious about
serious things, certainly meant us to read this story in terms
of his protest and his insurrection against the emptiness and
arrogance of law, against the folly and the pride of judges.
Everything else that there is in this story entered into it through
the unconscious or accidental energy of his genius, which broke
in at every gap. But it was the tragedy of Richard Carstone
that he meant, not the comedy of Harold Skimpole. He could
not help being amusing; but he meant to be depressing.

Another case might be taken as testing the greater seriousness
of this tale. The passages about Mrs Jellyby and her philanthropic schemes show Dickens at his best in his old and more
familiar satiric manner. But in the midst of the Jellyby pandemonium, which is in itself described with the same abandon
and irrelevance as the boarding-house of Mrs Todgers or the
travelling theatre of Mr Crummles, the elder Dickens introduced another piece of pure truth and even tenderness. I mean
the account of Caddy Jellyby. If Carstone is a truly masculine
study of how a man goes wrong, Caddy is a perfectly feminine
study of how a girl goes right. Nowhere else perhaps in fiction,
and certainly nowhere else in Dickens, is the mere female
paradox so well epitomized, the unjust use of words covering
so much capacity for a justice of ultimate estimate; the seeming
irresponsibility in language concealing such a fixed and pitiless
sense of responsibility about things; the air of being always at
daggers drawn with her own kindred, yet the confession of
incurable kinship implied in pride and shame; and, above all,
that thirst for order and beauty as for something physical; that
strange female power of hating ugliness and waste as good
men can only hate sin and bad men virtue. Every touch in her
is true from her first bewildering outbursts of hating people
because she likes them down to the sudden quietude and good
sense which announces that she has slipped into her natural

place as a woman. Miss Clare is a figurehead, Miss Summerson
in some ways a failure; but Miss Caddy Jellyby is by far the
greatest, the most human, and the most really dignified of all
the heroines of Dickens.

With one or two exceptions, all the effects in this story are of
this somewhat quieter kind, though none of them are so subtly
successful as Rick Carstone and Caddy. Harold Skimple begins
as a sketch drawn with a pencil almost as airy and fanciful as
his own. The humour of the earlier scenes is delightful—the
scenes in which Skimpole looks on at other people paying his
debts with the air of a kindly outsider, and suggests in formless
legal phraseology that they might 'sign something' or 'make
over something,' or the scene in which he tries to explain the
advantages of accepting everything to the apoplectic Mr Boythorn. But it was one of the defects of Dickens as a novelist
that his characters always became coarser and clumsier as they
passed through the practical events of a story, and this would
necessarily be so with Skimpole, whose position was conceivable even to himself only on the assumption that he was a mere
spectator of life. Poor Skimpole only asked to be kept out of
the business of this world, and Dickens ought to have kept him
out of the business of *Bleak House*. By the end of the tale he
has brought Skimpole to doing acts of mere low villainy. This
altogether spoils the ironical daintiness of the original notion.
Skimpole was meant to end with a note of interrogation. As
it is, he ends with a big, black, unmistakable blot. Speaking
purely artistically, we may say that this is as great a collapse
or vulgarization as if Richard Carstone had turned into a common blackguard and wife-beater, or Caddy Jellyby into a comic
and illiterate landlady. Upon the whole it may, I think, be said
that the character of Skimpole is rather a piece of brilliant
moralizing than of pure observation or creation. Dickens had
a singularly just mind. He was wild in his caricatures, but very
sane in his impressions. Many of his books were devoted, and
this book is partly devoted, to a denunciation of aristocracy—
of the idle class that lives easily upon the toil of nations. But
he was fairer than many modern revolutionists, and he insisted
on satirizing also those who prey on society not in the name
of rank or law, but in the name of intellect and beauty. Sir
Leicester Dedlock and Mr Harold Skimpole are alike in accepting with a royal unconsciousness the anomaly and evil of
their position. But the idleness and insolence of the aristocrat
is human and humble compared to the idleness and insolence
of the artist.

With the exception of a few fine freaks, such as Turveydrop
and Chadband, all the figures in this book are touched more
delicately, even more faintly, than is common with Dickens.
But if the figures are touched more faintly, it is partly because
they are figures in a fog—the fog of Chancery. Dickens meant
that twilight to be oppressive; for it was the symbol of oppression. Deliberately he did not dispel the darkness at the end of
this book, as he does dispel it at the end of most of his books.
Pickwick gets out of the Debtor's Prison; Carstone never gets
out of Chancery except by death. This tyranny, Dickens said,
shall not be lifted by the light subterfuge of a fiction. This
tyranny shall never be lifted till all Englishmen lift it together.
(pp. viii-xii)

> *G. K. Chesterton, in an introduction to* Bleak House
> *by Charles Dickens, 1907. Reprint by Dutton, 1972,*
> *pp. v-xii.*

BELLE MOSES   (essay date 1911)

*[In one of the first studies devoted solely to women in the novels
of Dickens, Moses centers on the varied types of "girl heroines"*

The title page to the first edition of Bleak House.

in Bleak House. *To Moses, the novel is primarily "a sweet story of home." In addition, she claims that Dickens's portrayal of such female characters as Esther was memorable despite the limited range of types known to him. For a fuller treatment of female characters in* Bleak House, *see the excerpt below by Ellen Moers (1973).]*

The chief attraction which **"Bleak House"** would naturally possess for any girl reader would be the very youthful element running through the story, the very delightful home center which *Bleak House* became, and, above all, the dear little housekeeper with her basket of jingling keys, who flitted through the quaint old-fashioned place. "Dear Dame Durden" her Guardian called her, though her real name was *Esther Summerson,* and on the happy morning of her arrival at *Bleak House* she received the household keys in the inevitable little basket, and became the gentle, ministering spirit in the rambling, irregular, delightful *Bleak House,* of which *Mr. Jarndyce* (a descendant of the famous *Jarndyce vs. Jarndyce*) was the genial elderly master. (pp. 252-53)

It is a sweet story of home—this **"Bleak House,"** and the evil doings of Chancery Court seem very far away from the peaceful seclusion of the quaint mansion. Here *Esther* lived contented year after year, while the tangled meshes of the intricate plot drew her at last into the shadow—but only for a while, for she emerged into the light again, a proud and happy woman.

In **"Bleak House"** we have many glimpses of home life, not always so charming as the life at *Mr. Jarndyce's,* but interesting because of the contrast and the unspoken sermons that haunted the four walls.

Take the *Jellybys* for instance, where *Esther* and *Ada Clare* stopped during the Court session, before they went to *Bleak House. Mrs. Jellyby* was a great philanthropist, and all her thoughts were centered on the Africans and how to help them, and all her time was taken up in corresponding with public bodies and private individuals, while the *Jellyby* household went to rack and ruin. (pp. 255-56)

Dickens was a wonderful artist, and, though he rarely painted a landscape, his interiors were always exceptionally good, and this picture of bad housekeeping was surely enough to make one shudder. He often showed us poor housekeeping, where the small housekeeper made the most of her meager surroundings, but *Mrs. Jellyby,* or more properly poor *Caddy,* could have made a happy home for the little *Jellybys,* if her wishes had been granted and Africa had been blotted from the map.

There was another little housekeeper in this same book; her name was *Charlotte Neckett,* familiarly known as *Charley,* and she lived up "three-pair back" in a room that hugged the roof, and she was only thirteen—and she went out washing by the day—and she took care of a tiny brother and sister, for they were orphans.

The room was poor and bare, and the food was often scarce, but *Charley* had just that knack which Dickens loved so in his girls; her capable hands were never idle, and there was an air of home even in the poor garret, with its one chair and its big uncomfortable bed. And how she cared for the two children! It was beautiful to see her, for Dickens made these poor little hard-working girls of flesh and blood, and beside them his other girls looked like shadowy little creatures.

But we must not forget that, in writing of girls, Dickens had only a few types from which to choose. With him, it was either the good little angel—too good almost—or the little slavey, or the pretty, plump, middle-class little maid, who happened to have a perfect genius for housekeeping. The little narrow-chested girls of his period had no tennis to broaden them, no rowing, no basket-ball, no golf. They were simply little home bodies, whose mission it was to make happiness, to find a suitable mate, to marry, and to have a family.

In rapid succession throughout his other books Dickens has introduced us to innumerable girls, whose charm has endured all these years—even to this day, when the athletic, vigorous, brainy young girl puts the quiet home-mouse to shame. There is an atmosphere of sweet lavender about these little heroines of long ago, while the jingle of their key-basket is a sound we like to hear. (pp. 258-60)

> *Belle Moses, in her* Charles Dickens and His Girl Heroines, *D. Appleton and Company, 1911, 331 p.*

ALGERNON CHARLES SWINBURNE (essay date 1913)

[Swinburne was an English poet, dramatist, and critic. He was renowned during his lifetime for his lyric poetry whose explicitly sensual themes shocked his contemporaries, and he is remembered today for his rejection of the mores of the Victorian age. Here, Swinburne praises the double point of view in Bleak House *and notes the "wealth and variety of character" in the novel. For other assessments of narrative technique in* Bleak House *see the excerpts by William Axton (1965), Albert J. Guerard (1969), Q.*

D. Leavis (1970), Joan D. Winslow (1976), Morton Dauwen Zabel (see Additional Bibliography), and Taylor Stoehr (see Additional Bibliography).]

[In] **'Bleak House'** the daring experiment of combination or alternation which divides a story between narrative in the third person and narrative in the first is justified and vindicated by its singular and fascinating success. 'Esther's narrative' is as good as her creator's; and no enthusiasm of praise could overrate the excellence of them both. For wealth and variety of character none of the master's works can be said to surpass and few can be said to equal it. When all necessary allowance has been made for occasional unlikeliness in detail or questionable methods of exposition, the sustained interest and the terrible pathos of Lady Dedlock's tragedy will remain unaffected and unimpaired. Any reader can object that a lady visiting a slum in the disguise of a servant would not have kept jewelled rings on her fingers for the inspection of a crossing-sweeper, or that a less decorous and plausible way of acquainting her with the fact that a scandalous episode in her early life was no longer a secret for the family lawyer could hardly have been imagined than the public narrative of her story in her own drawing-room by way of an evening's entertainment for her husband and their guests. To these objections, which any Helot of culture whose brain may have been affected by habitual indulgence in the academic delirium of self-complacent superiority may advance or may suggest with the most exquisite infinity of impertinence, it may be impossible to retort an equally obvious and inconsiderable objection.

But to a far more serious charge, which even now appears to survive the confutation of all serious evidence, it is incomprehensible and inexplicable that Dickens should have returned no better an answer than he did. Harold Skimpole was said to be Leigh Hunt; a rascal after the order of Wainewright, without the poisoner's comparatively and diabolically admirable audacity of frank and fiendish self-esteem, was assumed to be meant for a portrait or a caricature of an honest man and a man of unquestionable genius. To this most serious and most disgraceful charge Dickens merely replied that he never anticipated the identification of the rascal Skimple with the fascinating Harold—the attribution of imaginary villainy to the original model who suggested or supplied a likeness for the externally amiable and ineffectually accomplished lounger and shuffler through life. The simple and final reply should have been that indolence was the essential quality of the character and conduct and philosophy of Skimpole—'a perfectly idle man: a mere amateur,' as he describes himself to the sympathetic and approving Sir Leicester; that Leigh Hunt was one of the hardest and steadiest workers on record, throughout a long and chequered life, at the toilsome trade of letters; and therefore that to represent him as a heartless and shameless idler would have been about as rational an enterprise, as lifelike a design after the life, as it would have been to represent Shelley as a gluttonous and canting hypocrite or Byron as a loyal and unselfish friend. And no one as yet, I believe, has pretended to recognise in Mr. Jarndyce a study from Byron, in Mr. Chadband a libel on Shelley. (pp. 35-9)

> *Algernon Charles Swinburne, in his* Charles Dickens, *edited by T. W-D., Chatto & Windus, 1913, 84 p.*

STEFAN ZWEIG (essay date 1919)

[*Zweig asserts that Dickens's novels belong to the genre of sentimental melodrama; he argues that they fail to exert a powerful*

emotional influence "because the great moments in them are forced." His view contrasts with that of John Lucas (1970). This essay was originally published in Zweig's Drei Meister: Balzac, Dickens, Dostojewski *in 1919.]*

I have described Dickens as "content," yet in a sense he was never satisfied with his work. He was famous—but he had not won his fame as a writer of tragedy. With ever-renewed spirit he sought to rise to tragic levels, and time after time he merely attained to melodrama. The frontier line of his powers was clearly drawn. His attempts to cross it were invariably lamentable. English readers may find *A Tale of Two Cities* and **Bleak House** works of high creative power; for us Germans they are damned, because the great moments in them are forced. And yet the author's endeavour to be genuinely tragical is commendable: he heaps plot upon plot; he overwhelms his heroes with catastrophes as crushing as rock-falls; he calls the terrors of rainy nights to his aid; he brings in mob riots and revolution, lets loose all the furies of horror and disaster. But the reader experiences no more than a slight shiver down the back; a purely physical reflex, not the shudder of the soul. We are never profoundly shaken while reading his books; their storms do not wreak havoc in our souls so that from sheer agony of tension the heart yearns for the lightning to flash forth and in the crash of thunder to find release. Dickens confronts us with peril after peril; yet we are in no way alarmed. . . . [True, in Dickens], we meet with abysses. He fills them with gloom, he depicts their dangers—and yet the shudder does not come; one does not get the thrill of that plunge into fathomless depths, that feeling which is perhaps the climax of artistic enjoyment. We are always safe with Dickens, as if we were holding a banister, for we know beforehand that he will not let us fall; we know that the hero will not come to grief in the end; the twin angels, compassion and justice, who are never absent from the skies of this English author, will see to it that he comes scatheless through all his troubles. Dickens does not possess the brutality essential to give a writer courage to tackle the really great tragedies of life. He is not heroic, but sentimental. Tragedy is a will to defiance; sentimentality is a longing for tears. Dickens was never able to reach the shores where dwell the tearless, wordless, ultimate powers of despairing pain. (pp. 81-2)

The philosophy underlying his works, the philosophy which is built into their very foundations and upon which their entire architectural strength depends, is not the philosophy of a free artist but that of an Anglican citizen. Dickens claps a censorship on to the emotions, instead of allowing them free vent; he does not, as does Balzac, permit them to overflow their banks, but guides them through locks and channels and dykes where they turn the mills of the bourgeois moral code. Parsons, preachers, common-sense philosophers, schoolmasters, and the like, seem to be looking over his shoulder as he composes; each has a finger in the pie; they prevail upon him to make his novel an example and a warning to the young people of his day, instead of letting him develop his ideas along the lines of an unfettered reality. (p. 83)

> *Stefan Zweig, "Dickens As Melodramatist and Moralist," in his* Master Builders, an Attempt at the Typology of the Spirit: Three Masters, Balzac, Dickens, Dostoeffsky, Vol. 1, *translated by Eden Paul and Cedar Paul, The Viking Press, 1930, pp. 81-5.*

GEORGE GISSING (essay date 1925)

[*Gissing, an English novelist, critic, and essayist, is best known for his* Charles Dickens: A Critical Study, *one of the earliest and most comprehensive studies of Dickens's work. Profoundly influenced by Dickens's novels, Gissing was admired for the naturalistic and compassionate treatment of poverty in his works. Though he chastises Dickens for relying on coincidence in* Bleak House, *Gissing also credits him with deft handling of satire and picturesque characterization and description. Satiric elements in* Bleak House *are also studied in the excerpt by Ellen Moers (1973) and in works by Louis Crompton, Sylvia Bank Manning, and H. P. Sucksmith (see Additional Bibliography).*]

In the fable of **Bleak House** there is much ingenuity, but an almost total disregard of probability; the fitting of incidents suggests a mechanical puzzle rather than the complications of human life; arbitrary coincidence takes the place of well-contrived motive, and at times the motive suggested is glaringly inadequate. Briefly, the plot is not a good plot; infinite labour was wasted in a mistaken direction; and here, as in so many of Dickens's novels, we have to enjoy the book in spite of its framework.

To make matters worse, the scheme is not homogeneous; intermingled with this weft of elaborate pattern are patches of a totally different order of work, the chapters of autobiography supposed to be written by Esther Summerson. In *Copperfield*, the first-person narrative was a great success, for it was indeed Dickens himself who spoke throughout, with all his qualities of humour and observation, vigour and pathos, allowed free play; one understands that the memory of his delight in achieving that masterpiece tempted him to a repetition of the same method. The result was most unfortunate. Of Esther Summerson as a woman we are liable to form no conception whatever, and we utterly refuse to believe that any hand save one penned the chapters bearing her signature. An attempt is made to write "in character," but it is speedily abandoned, and I imagine it would be an easy thing, by the changing of a very few words on each page, to incorporate these Esther portions with the rest of the narrative. The object, presumably, of writing a book in this way is to obtain the effect of varied points of view regarding characters and events; but it is of necessity a mistake in art. (pp. 223-25)

So much for technicalities. To come to the root of the matter, **Bleak House** is a brilliant, admirable, and most righteous satire upon the monstrous iniquity of "old Father Antic the Law," with incidental mockery of allied abuses which, now as then, hold too large a place in the life of the English people.

Needless nowadays to revive the controversies which the book excited; we know that the Court of Chancery disgraced a country pretending to civilization; we know that, not long after the publication of **Bleak House,** it submitted to certain reforms; yet it is interesting to remember that legal luminaries scoffed at Dickens's indignation and declared his picture utterly unlike the truth.... [In] the end, the laugh was on his side, and with a laugh he triumphed. Not a little remarkable, when one comes to think of it, this immunity of the great writer. Humour, and humour alone, could have ensured it to him. It is all very well to talk of right prevailing, of the popular instinct for justice, and so on; these phrases mean very little. Dickens held his own because he amused. The noblest orator ever born, raising his voice in divine wrath against Chancery and all its vileness would not have touched the "great heart of the People" as did these pages which make gloriously ridiculous the whole legal world from His Lordship in his High Court down to Mr. Guppy on his high stool.

The satire is of very wide application; it involves that whole system of pompous precedent which in Dickens's day was responsible for so much cruelty and hypocrisy, for such waste of life in filth and gloom and wretchedness. With the glaring injustice of the Law, rotting society down to such places as Tom-all-Alone's, is associated the subtler evils of an aristocracy sunk to harmful impotence. With absurd precedent goes foolish pride, and self-righteousness, and every form of idle egoism; hence we have a group of admirable studies in selfish conceit—Harold Skimpole, Mr. Turveydrop, Mr. Chadband, Mrs. Jellyby. Impossible to vary the central theme more adroitly, more brilliantly. In **Bleak House** London is seen as a mere dependance of the Court of Chancery, a great gloomy city, webbed and meshed, as it were, by the spinnings of a huge poisonous spider sitting in the region of Chancery Lane; its inhabitants are the blighted, stunted and prematurely old offspring of a town which knows not fresh air. Perfect, all this, for the purpose of the satirist. In this sense, at all events, **Bleak House** is an excellently constructed book.

There is no leading character. In Richard Carstone, about whom the story may be said to circle, Dickens tried to carry out a purpose he had once entertained with regard to Walter Gay in **Dombey and Son.** That of showing a good lad at the mercy of temptations and circumstances which little by little wreck his life; but Richard has very little life to lose, and we form only a shadowy conception of his amiably futile personality. Still less convincing is his betrothed, Ada, whose very name one finds it difficult to remember. Nothing harder, to be sure, than to make a living picture of one whose part in the story is passive, and in **Bleak House** passivity is the characteristic of all the foremost figures; their business is to submit to the irresistible. Yet two of these personages seem to me successful studies of a kind in which Dickens was not often successful; I cannot but think that both Sir Leicester Dedlock and John Jarndyce is, each in his way, an excellent piece of work, making exactly the impression at which the author aimed.... [Jarndyce belongs to] the world of eccentric benevolence; he is the kind of man Dickens delighted to portray; but Mr. Jarndyce is far more recognizably a fellow-mortal than his gay predecessors; in truth, he may claim the style of gentleman, and perhaps may stand for the most soberly agreeable portrait of a gentleman to be found in all Dickens's novels. Sir Leicester, though he shows in the full light of satiric intention, being a figurehead on the crazy old ship of aristocratic privilege, is a human being akin to John Jarndyce; he speaks with undue solemnity, but behaves at all times as *noblesse oblige,* and, when sinking beneath his unmerited calamities, makes no little claim upon our sympathetic admiration. (pp. 225-31)

That the Dedlock tragedy is the least impressive portion of the book results partly from Dickens's inability to represent any kind of woman save the eccentric, the imbecile, and the shrew (there are at most one or two small exceptions), and partly from the melodramatic strain in him, which so often misled his genius. Educated readers of to-day see little difference between these chapters of **Bleak House** and the treatment of any like "mystery" in a penny novelette. There is no need to insist on these weaknesses of the master; we admit them as a matter of critical duty, and at the same time point out the characteristics, moral and intellectual, of Victorian England, which account for so many of Dickens's limitations. Had he not been restrained by an insensate prudishness from dealing honestly with Lady Dedlock's story, Lady Dedlock herself might have been far more human. Where the national conscience refuses to recognize certain phases of life, it is not wonderful that national authors should exhibit timidity and ineptitude whenever they glance in the forbidden direction.

Instead of a picture, we get a cloudy veil suggestive of nameless horrors; it is the sort of exaggeration which necessarily results in feebleness.

Dickens was very fond of the effect produced by bringing into close contact representatives of social extremes; the typical instance is Lady Dedlock's relations with crossing-sweeper Jo. Contemporary readers saw in Jo a figure of supreme pathos; they wept over his death-bed, as by those of Paul Dombey and of Little Nell. . . . Does there, I wonder, exist in all literature, a scene less correspondent with any possibility of life than that description of Jo's last moments? Dickens believed in it—there is the odd thing. Not a line, not a word, is insincere. He had a twofold mission in life, and, from our standpoint, in an age which has outgrown so many conditions of fifty years ago, we can only mark with regret how the philanthropist in him so often overcame the artist.

His true pathos comes when he does not particularly try for it and is invariably an aspect of his humour. The two chief instances in this book are the picture of Coavinses' children after their father's death, and the figure of Guster, Mrs. Snagsby's slave-of-all-work. Nothing more touching, more natural, more simple, than that scene in Chapter XV where Esther and her companions find the little Coavinses locked up for safety in their cold garret, whilst the elder child, Charley, is away at washing to earn food for them all. (pp. 232-36)

The wonderful thing about such work as this is Dickens's subdual of his indignation to the humorous note. It is when indignation gets the upper hand, and humour is lost sight of, that he falls into peril of unconsciously false sentiment.

Among the characters of this book there is not one belonging to the foremost groups of Dickens's creations, no one standing together with Mr. Micawber and Mr. Pecksniff; yet what novel by any other writer presents such a multitude of strongly-featured individuals, their names and their persons familiar to everyone who has but once read *Bleak House*? . . . [Most] of them illustrate the main theme of the story, exhibiting in various forms the vice of a fixed idea which sacrifices everything and everybody to its own selfish demands. The shrewdly ingenious Skimpole . . . , the lordly Turveydrop, the devoted Mrs. Jellyby, the unctuously eloquent Mr. Chadband, all are following in their own little way the example of the High Court of Chancery—victimizing all about them on pretence of the most disinterested motives. The legal figures—always so admirable in Dickens—of course strike this key-note with peculiar emphasis; we are in no doubt as to the impulses ruling Mr. Kenge or Mr. Vholes, and their spirit is potent for evil down to the very dregs of society, in Grandfather Smallweed and in Mr. Krook. The victims themselves are a ragged regiment after Dickens's own heart; crazy Chancery suitors, Mr. Jellyby and his hapless offspring, fever-stricken dwellers in Chancery's slums, all shown with infinite picturesqueness—which indeed is the prime artistic quality of the book. For mirth extracted from sordid material no example can surpass Mr. Guppy, who is chicane incarnate; his withdrawal from the tender suit to Miss Summerson, excellent farce, makes as good comment as ever was written upon the law-office frame of mind. That we have little if any frank gaiety is but natural and right; it would be out of keeping with the tone of a world overshadowed by the Law. (pp. 237-40)

In his Preface [Dickens] tells us that he had "purposely dwelt on the romantic side of familiar things." But the word romantic does not seem to be very accurately applied. In using it, Dick-

ens no doubt was thinking of the Dedlock mystery, the involvement of a crossing-sweeper in aristocratic tragedies, and so on; all which would be better called melodrama than romance. What he did achieve was to make the common and the unclean most forcibly picturesque. From the fog at the opening of the story to Lady Dedlock's miserable death at the end, we are held by a powerful picture of murky, swarming, rotting London, a marvellous rendering of the impression received by any imaginative person who in low spirits has had occasion to wander about London's streets. Nowhere is Dickens stronger in lurid effects; for a fine horror he never went beyond Chapter XXXII—where it would, of course, be wide of the mark to begin discussing the possibility of spontaneous combustion. Masterly descriptions abound; the Court in Chapter I, the regions of the Law during vacation in Chapter XIX, Mr. Vholes's office in Chapter XXXIX, are among the best. The inquest at the Sol's Arms shows all Dickens's peculiar power of giving typical value to the commonplace; scene and actors are unforgettable; the gruesome, the vile, and the ludicrous combine in unique effects, in the richest suggestiveness. And for the impressive in another kind—still shadowed by the evil genius of the book, but escaped from the city's stifling atmosphere—what could be better than Chapter LVII, Esther's posting through the night with Inspector Bucket. This is very vigorous narrative. We, of course, forget that an amiable young lady is supposed to be penning it, and are reminded of those chapters of earlier books where Dickens revels in the joy of the road.

As a reminder that even in *Bleak House* the master did not altogether lose his wonted cheeriness by humble firesides, one may recall the Bagnet household, dwelling at a happy distance from Chancery Lane. Compare the dinner presided over by the Old Girl beside her shining hearth with that partaken of by Mr. Guppy, Mr. Jobling and Mr. Smallweed at their familiar chop-house. Each is perfect in its kind, and each a whole world in little. (pp. 240-43)

> *George Gissing, in his* The Immortal Dickens, *1925. Reprint by Kraus Reprint Co., 1969, 243 p.*

EDMUND WILSON   (essay date 1941)

[Wilson is considered America's foremost man of letters in the twentieth century. A prolific reviewer, creative writer, and social and literary critic endowed with formidable intellectual powers, he exercised his greatest literary influence as the author of Axel's Castle (1931), a seminal study of literary symbolism, and as the author of widely read reviews and essays in which he introduced the best works of modern literature to the reading public. Wilson's criticism displays a fundamental concern for the historical and psychological implications of literary works. Alert to literature's significance as "an attempt to give meaning to our experience" and its value for the improvement of humanity, he also believed that "the real elements . . . of any work of fiction are the elements of the author's personality: his imagination embodies . . . the fundamental conflicts of his nature." Related to this is Wilson's theory, formulated in The Wound and the Bow (1941), that artistic ability is a compensation for a psychological wound. Although he is often criticized for holding to the latter theory, most commentators agree with Alfred Kazin, who stated "Wilson is not like other critics; some critics are boring even when they are original; he fascinates even when he is wrong." Wilson ascribes to Dickens the creation of a new literary genre, "the detective story which is also a social fable." In addition, he explores the function of fog symbolism in Bleak House, commenting that it "obscures and impedes" every action in the novel. Other critics who investigate detective story elements in the novel include Lionel Stevenson (1943), Robert Alan Donovan (1966), and Morton Dau-

An illustration of Tom-all-alone's from the first edition of Bleak House.

wen Zabel (see Additional Bibliography). Fog imagery is also traced in excerpts by Edgar Johnson (1952), A.O.J. Cockshut (1962), and Morton Dauwen Zabel (see Additional Bibliography).]

In **Bleak House,** the masterpiece of [his] middle period, Dickens discovers a new use of plot, which makes possible a tighter organization. (And we must remember that he is always working against the difficulties, of which he often complains, of writing for monthly instalments, where everything has to be planned beforehand and it is impossible, as he says, to 'try back' and change anything, once it has been printed.) He creates the detective story which is also a social fable. It is a *genre* which has lapsed since Dickens. The detective story—though Dickens' friend Wilkie Collins preserved a certain amount of social satire—has dropped out the Dickensian social content; and the continuators of the social novel have dropped the detective story. These continuators—Shaw, Galsworthy, Wells—have of course gone further than Dickens in the realistic presentation of emotion; but from the point of view of dramatizing social issues, they have hardly improved upon **Bleak House.** In Shaw's case, the Marxist analysis, with which Dickens was not equipped, has helped him to the tighter organization which Dickens got from his complex plot. But in the meantime it is one of Dickens' victories in his rapid development as an artist that he should succeed in transforming his melodramatic in-

trigues of stolen inheritances, lost heirs and ruined maidens—with their denunciatory confrontations that always evoke the sound of fiddling in the orchestra—into devices of artistic dignity. Henceforth the solution of the mystery is to be also the moral of the story and the last word of Dickens' social 'message.'

Bleak House begins in the London fog, and the whole book is permeated with fog and rain. In **Dombey** the railway locomotive—first when Mr. Dombey takes his trip to Leamington, and later when it pulls into the station just at the moment of Dombey's arrival and runs over the fugitive Carker as he steps back to avoid his master—figures as a symbol of that progress of commerce which Dombey himself represents; in **Hard Times** the uncovered coal-pit into which Stephen Blackpool falls is a symbol for the abyss of the industrial system, which swallows up lives in its darkness. In **Bleak House** the fog stands for Chancery, and Chancery stands for the whole web of clotted antiquated institutions in which England stifles and decays. All the principal elements in the story—the young people, the proud Lady Dedlock, the philanthropic gentleman John Jarndyce, and Tom-all-Alone's, the rotting London slum—are involved in the exasperating Chancery suit, which, with the fogbank of precedent looming behind it like the Great Boyg in *Peer Gynt,* obscures and impedes at every point the attempts of men and women to live natural lives. Old Krook, with his legal junkshop, is Dickens' symbol for the Lord Chancellor himself; the cat that sits on his shoulder watches like the Chancery lawyers the caged birds in Miss Flite's lodging; Krook's death by spontaneous combustion is Dickens' prophecy of the fate of Chancery and all that it represents.

I go over the old ground of the symbolism, up to this point perfectly obvious, of a book which must be still, by the general public, one of the most read of Dickens' novels, because the people who like to talk about the symbols of Kafka and Mann and Joyce have been discouraged from looking for anything of the kind in Dickens, and usually have not read him, at least with mature minds. But even when we think we do know Dickens, we may be surprised to return to him and find in him a symbolism of a more complicated reference and a deeper implication than these metaphors that hang as emblems over the door. The Russians themselves, in this respect, appear to have learned from Dickens.

Thus it is not at first that we recognize all the meaning of the people that thrive or survive in the dense atmosphere of **Bleak House**—an atmosphere so opaque that the somnolent ease at the top cannot see down to the filth at the bottom. And it is an atmosphere where nobody sees clearly what kind of race of beings is flourishing between the bottom and the top. Among the middle ranks of this society we find persons who appear with the pretension of representing Law or Art, Social Elegance, Philanthropy, or Religion—Mr. Kenge and Mr. Vholes, Harold Skimpole, Mr. Turveydrop, Mrs. Pardiggle and Mrs. Jellyby, and Mr. and Mrs. Chadband—side by side with such a sordid nest of goblins as the family of the moneylender Smallweed. But presently we see that all these people are as single-mindedly intent on selfish interests as Grandfather Smallweed himself. This gallery is one of the best things in Dickens. The Smallweeds themselves are artistically an improvement on the similar characters in the early Dickens: they represent, not a theatrical convention, but a real study of the stunted and degraded products of the underworld of commercial London. And the two opposite types of philanthropist: the moony Mrs. Jellyby, who miserably neglects her children in order to dream of doing good in Africa, and Mrs. Pardiggle, who bullies both her children and the poor in order to give herself a feeling of power; Harold Skimpole, with the graceful fancy and the talk about music and art that ripples a shimmering veil over his systematic sponging; and Turveydrop, the Master of Deportment, that parody of the magnificence of the Regency, behind his rouge and his padded coat and his gallantry as cold and as inconsiderate as the Chadbands behind their gaseous preachments. Friedrich Engels, visiting London in the early forties, had written of the people in the streets that they seemed to 'crowd by one another as if they had nothing in common, nothing to do with one another, and as if their only agreement were the tacit one that each shall keep to his own side of the pavement, in order not to delay the opposing streams of the crowd, while it never occurs to anyone to honor his fellow with so much as a glance. The brutal indifference, the unfeeling isolation of each in his private interest, becomes the more repellent the more these individuals are herded together within a limited space.' This is the world that Dickens is describing.

Here he makes but one important exception: Mr. Rouncewell, the ironmaster. Mr. Rouncewell is an ambitious son of the housekeeper at Chesney Wold, Sir Leicester Dedlock's country house, who has made himself a place in the world which Sir Leicester regards as beyond his station. One of the remarkable scenes of the novel is that in which Rouncewell comes back, quietly compels Sir Leicester to receive him like a gentleman and asks him to release one of the maids from his service so that she may marry Rouncewell's son, a young man whom he has christened Watt. When Lady Dedlock refuses to release the maid, Rouncewell respectfully abandons the project, but goes away and has the insolence to run against Sir Leicester's candidate in the next parliamentary election. (This theme of the intervention of the industrial revolution in the relations between master and servant has already appeared in *Dombey and Son* in the admirable interview between Dombey and Polly Toodles, whom he is employing as a wetnurse for his motherless child. Polly's husband, who is present, is a locomotive stoker and already represents something anomalous in the hierarchy of British society. When the Dombeys, who cannot accept her real name, suggest calling Polly 'Richards,' she replies that if she is to be called out of her name, she ought to be paid extra. Later, when Dombey makes his railway journey, he runs into Polly's husband, who is working on the engine. Toodles speaks to him and engages him in conversation, and Dombey resents this, feeling that Toodles is somehow intruding outside his own class.)

But in general the magnanimous, the simple of heart, the amiable, the loving and the honest are frustrated, subdued, or destroyed. At the bottom of the whole gloomy edifice is the body of Lady Dedlock's lover and Esther Summerson's father, Captain Hawdon, the reckless soldier, adored by his men, beloved by women, the image of the old life-loving England, whose epitaph Dickens is now writing. Captain Hawdon has failed in that world, has perished as a friendless and penniless man, and has been buried in the pauper's graveyard in one of the foulest quarters of London, but the loyalties felt for him by the living will endure and prove so strong after his death that they will pull that world apart. Esther Summerson has been frightened and made submissive by being treated as the respectable middle class thought it proper to treat an illegitimate child, by one of those Puritanical females whom Dickens so roundly detests. Richard Carstone has been demoralized and ruined; Miss Flite has been driven insane. George Rouncewell,

the brother of the ironmaster, who has escaped from Sir Leicester's service to become a soldier instead of a manufacturer and who is treated by Dickens with the sympathy which he usually feels for his military and nautical characters, the men who are doing the hard work of the Empire, is helpless in the hands of moneylenders and lawyers. Caddy Jellyby and her husband, young Turveydrop, who have struggled for a decent life in a poverty partly imposed by the necessity of keeping up old Turveydrop's pretenses, can only produce, in that society where nature is so mutilated and thwarted, a sickly defective child. Mr. Jarndyce himself, the wise and generous, who plays in *Bleak House* a rôle very similar to that of Captain Shotover in Bernard Shaw's *Heartbreak House* (which evidently owes a good deal to *Bleak House*), is an eccentric at odds with his environment, who, in his efforts to help the unfortunate, falls a prey to the harpies of philanthropy.

With this indifference and egoism of the middle class, the social structure must buckle in the end. The infection from the poverty of Tom-all-Alone's will ravage the mansions of country gentlemen. Lady Dedlock will inevitably be dragged down from her niche of aristocratic idleness to the graveyard in the slum where her lover lies. The idea that the highest and the lowest in that English society of shocking contrasts are inextricably tied together has already appeared in the early Dickens—in Ralph Nickleby and Smike, for example, and in Sir John Chester and Hugh—as a sort of submerged motif which is never given its full expression. Here it has been chosen deliberately and is handled with immense skill so as to provide the main moral of the fable. And bound up with it is another motif which has already emerged sharply in Dickens. Dickens had evidently in the course of his astonishing rise, found himself up against the blank and chilling loftiness—what the French call *la morgue anglaise* [English haughtiness]—of the English upper classes: as we shall see, he developed a pride of his own, with which he fought it to his dying day. Pride was to have been the theme of *Dombey:* the pride of Edith Dombey outdoes the pride of Dombey and levels him to the ground. But in *Bleak House,* the pride of Lady Dedlock, who has married Sir Leicester Dedlock for position, ultimately rebounds on herself. Her behavior toward the French maid Hortense is the cause of her own debasement. For where it is a question of pride, a high-tempered maid from the South of France can outplay Lady Dedlock: Hortense will not stop at the murder which is the logical upshot of the course of action dictated by her wounded feelings. Dickens is criticizing here one of the most unassailable moral props of the English hierarchical system. (pp. 30-6)

Edmund Wilson, "Dickens: The Two Scrooges," in his The Wound and the Bow: Seven Studies in Literature, *1941. Reprint by Farrar, Straus and Giroux, 1978, pp. 3-85.*

LIONEL STEVENSON   (essay date 1943)

[*In deeming* Bleak House *"a marvel of structural unity," Stevenson echoes G. K Chesterton (1907) and anticipates the arguments of Edgar Johnson (1952), Robert Alan Donovan (1966), and Morton Dauwen Zabel (see Additional Bibliography). Stevenson also regards* Bleak House *as a detective novel, as do Edmund Wilson (1941), Robert Alan Donovan (1966), and Morton Dauwen Zabel (see Additional Bibliography).*]

[*Bleak House*] is a marvel of structural unity. The central topic—the demoralizing injustice of the court of chancery—does not merely provide an atmospheric milieu for the whole story, but links the vast array of characters in one intricate pattern. The plot uses suspense, mystery, and detection so skilfully that the book is still regarded as the first full-length detective story. Its narrative method is yet more remarkable. Having discovered in *David Copperfield* the advantages of the first-personal presentation in enhancing the sense of reality, [Dickens] now undertook the more hazardous task of making the narrator a woman—and a modest, guileless young woman, at that. At once, difficulties supervened: the monotony of her artless diction, the artificiality of her innocent self-revelations, above all the fact that she could not possibly be cognizant of all the vast web of events that made the story. Accordingly, Dickens tried the unprecedented experiment of alternating first-personal chapters with others from the customary "omniscient" point of view. The effort of plausibly impersonating a naïve girl was therefore immeasurably complicated by the constant shifting of angle in the reader's mind.

Why, then, did Dickens attempt to look out through the eyes of Esther Summerson? By the time one has read a chapter, one is impressed by the resemblance to [Charlotte Brontë's] *Jane Eyre.* Esther's character, her style, her environment, are all straight out of Charlotte Brontë's novels. Dickens is thus undertaking a more serious and subtle psychological study. As Esther is only one strand of his web, he does not develop her emotional complexities as fully as Charlotte Brontë would have done, but there are some remarkable implications nonetheless. Although Dickens was never greatly addicted to love stories, he usually provided a hero and heroine of the stock pattern. With this heroine, however, he was radically unconventional. A handsome admirer was introduced, to be sure, but was immediately shipped off to the Orient for the duration of the story, and Esther's emotions were directed in two other channels— her intense (almost Lesbian) affection for the pretty doll-like Ada Clare, and the equally profound devotion between her and her elderly self-elected guardian.

With this strand in *Bleak House,* then, Dickens was meeting the competition of Charlotte Brontë. With another equally conspicuous strand he was challenging Thackeray. Sir Leicester and Lady Dedlock, their vast household and sycophantic associates, and all the glimpses of muddle-headed political intrigue that they provide, are delineated with mannered sarcasm straight out of *Vanity Fair.* The recognizable portraits of Leigh Hunt and Landor, which caused so much ill feeling, follow the lead of Thackeray's caricatures of John Wilson Croker and Theodore Hook.

The third competitive force—the proletarian novels of Kingsley and Mrs. Gaskell—bulks less largely but is equally significant. Mr. Wilson comments on the particularly effective little scenes in which Sir Leicester Dedlock's privileges are challenged by the self-made ironmaster, Rouncewell [see excerpt above, 1941]. But Mr. Wilson does not add the further point that this ironmaster's mother, the stately old housekeeper of the Dedlocks, is certainly a portrait of Dickens's own grandmother, housekeeper to Lord Crewe; and that here for the first time Dickens by implication admitted his own antecedents of domestic servitude. Even though the Rouncewell family plays a minor rôle in the story, they are depicted with a special sympathy that reveals the author's sense of identification with them. (pp. 403-05)

Lionel Stevenson, "Dickens's Dark Novels, 1851-1857," in The Sewanee Review, *Vol. LI, No. 3, Summer, 1943, pp. 398-409.*

VLADIMIR NABOKOV   (lecture date 1948)

[*A Russian-born American man of letters, Nabokov was a prolific contributor to many literary fields, producing works in both Rus-*

sian and English and distinguishing himself in particular with his novels Lolita *(1955) and* Pale Fire *(1962). Nabokov was fascinated with all aspects of the creative life: in his works he explored the origins of creativity, the relationships of artists to their work, and the nature of invented reality. Here he praises Dickens's vivid characterization, skilled narration, and concern for moral issues. However, Nabokov adds, Dickens fails to make adequate connections between characters throughout the* Bleak House *narrative. The following was originally delivered as a lecture at Cornell University in 1948.*]

A writer might be a good storyteller or a good moralist, but unless he be an enchanter, an artist, he is not a great writer. Dickens is a good moralist, a good storyteller, and a superb enchanter, but as a storyteller he lags somewhat behind his other virtues. In other words, he is supremely good at picturing his characters and their habitats in any given situation, but there are flaws in his work when he tries to establish various links between these characters in a pattern of action.

What is the joint impression that a great work of art produces upon us? (By us, I mean the good reader.) The Precision of Poetry and the Excitement of Science. And this is the impact of *Bleak House* at its best. At his best Dickens the enchanter, Dickens the artist, comes to the fore. At his second best, in *Bleak House* the moralist teacher is much in evidence, often not without art. At its worst, *Bleak House* reveals the storyteller stumbling now and then, although the general structure still remains excellent.

Despite certain faults in the telling of his story, Dickens remains, nevertheless, a great writer. Control over a considerable constellation of characters and themes, the technique of holding people and events bunched together, or of evoking absent characters through dialogue—in other words, the art of not only creating people but keeping created people alive within the reader's mind throughout a long novel—this, of course, is the obvious sign of greatness. When Grandfather Smallweed is carried in his chair into George's shooting gallery in an endeavor to get a sample of Captain Hawdon's handwriting, the driver of the cab and another person act as bearers. "'This person,' [the other bearer, he says] 'we engaged in the street outside for a pint of beer. Which is twopence.... Judy, my child [he goes on, to his daughter], give the person his twopence. It's a great deal for what he has done.'

"The person, who is one of those extraordinary specimens of human fungus that spring up spontaneously in the western streets of London, ready dressed in an old red jacket, with a 'Mission' for holding horses and calling coaches, receives his twopence with anything but transport, tosses the money into the air, catches it over-handed, and retires." This gesture, this one gesture, with its epithet "over-handed"—a trifle—but the man is alive forever in a good reader's mind.

A great writer's world is indeed a magic democracy where even some very minor character, even the most incidental character like the person who tosses the twopence, has the right to live and breed. (pp. 123-24)

Vladimir Nabokov, "Charles Dickens: 'Bleak House'," in his Lectures on Literature, *edited by Fredson Bowers, Harcourt Brace Jovanovich, 1980, pp. 63-124.*

JACK LINDSAY   (essay date 1950)

[*Through his exposition of the Dedlock plot in* Bleak House, *Lindsay argues, Dickens illustrates the theme of "the new in-*

dustrialist against the feudal landowner." Lindsay represents Dickens as a social reformer, and suggests that Krook's death by spontaneous combustion "is a symbolic statement of revolution." For other viewpoints on the role of spontaneous combustion in Bleak House, *see the excerpts by Edgar Johnson (1952), A.O.J. Cockshut (1962), Trevor Blount (1970), and Morton Dauwen Zabel (see Additional Bibliography).]*

[*Bleak House*] depends largely on the romantic themes of lost heritages and mysterious births. The interest centres round Lady Dedlock; but though ostensibly it derives from romantic concepts of guilt and persecution, the moral and intellectual force of the artistic symbols transforms Lady Dedlock's story into the main expression of a revolt against ruling values. A guilty society pillories her for love and its misfortunes, and finally drives her to destruction. Thus she is set against the legal mechanism, the State, as the suffering individual on whom the burden of guilt descends socially and psychologically. With her guilt that a false code of social ethics creates, there is bound up the real guilt of her submission, her fear, her failure to cleave to lover and child; and her tormented pride, torn by this double pressure, makes her tragic death an inevitable aspect of the break in secrecies and hates which the revelation of the truth implies. (p. 303)

Lady Dedlock's fate thus raises the full human dilemma posited by the existence of the law or State. The obvious conflicts precipitated by the law have relevance to the issue; but they would be incomplete without this revelation of the full complexity of the problems of guilt, nemesis, purification, recognition. Dickens in his allegorical way indicates this point with the woman's name. Her husband may represent the obstructive feudal forces, which desire deadlock in social conflict; she herself concentrates the main psychological issues implicit in the human condition under these circumstances, the spiritual deadlock.

On the political side Dickens brings one issue right out into the open: that of the new industrialist against the feudal landowner. He gives Sir Leicester all possible credit; he is a good feudal landlord and preserves decency and dignity under the most trying domestic circumstances. But he is drawn unmistakably as the representative of decadent social forces, and against him is set the hardy northern industrialist who stands for a totally different set of social values. Dickens puts Sir Leicester in the best possible light, but with his limitations made evident; while the ironmaster, member of a rising class, has his own native sense of dignity to oppose to the feudal concepts. He in no way represents the money-forces, the Dombeys or the Merdles; rather he represents a phase of industrialism when the hard-working entrepreneur (often a worker with specially inventive vein) has little dependence yet on banks or capital outside his own small reserves. The type does not recur in Dickens's work; for the phase was already, after 1850, nearing its end, doomed by the vast extension of the credit-mechanism and of world commerce. (pp. 303-04)

There is yet one more point of symbolism which has been missed by commentators, though it stands boldly at the core of the story: the "spontaneous combustion" of Krook, the so-called Lord Chancellor, the unpleasant rag-and-bones merchant with his many underhand dealings. Krook is a deliberate doubling of the part of the Chancellor, meant to represent the filth and darkness which is the other side of the law's respected dignitaries and deeds. His blowing up is a symbolic statement of revolution.

The importance of the symbolism to Dickens is shown by his determined effort to vindicate the physical possibility of such a blowing up. His preface attempts to give evidence and cite authorities in support of the fantastic event. He never wrote better than in the passages where he piles up the suspense and sense of evil round the greasy death of Krook; and he finishes off the account with words which leave beyond any doubt the import of the symbolism for him.

> Help, help, help! come into this house for Heaven's sake!
>
> Plenty will come in, but none can help. The Lord Chancellor of that Court, true to his title in his last act, has died the death of all Lord Chancellors in all Courts, and of all authorities in all places under all names soever, where false pretences are made, and where injustice is done. Call the death by any name Your Highness will, attribute it to whom you will, or say it might have been prevented how you will, it is the same death eternally—inborn, inbred, engendered in the corrupted humours of the vicious body itself, and that only—Spontaneous Corruption, and none other of all the deaths that can be died.

By using basic romantic themes and by projecting characters of great dynamic force, Dickens had shown his power, from *The Old Curiosity Shop* onwards, of making the crisis of his story seem the crisis of all men, of a whole society. But now he goes deeper and finds symbols to express basic moments of change, revolution, world collapse and renewal. Krook stands for the "rotten rags" of a doomed society; and his destruction is an essential part of the whole scheme of human renovation.

It is worth while noting also the way in which the central duality of Krook-Chancellor and the symbolic explosion of inner corruptions are reinforced by the theme of the fog with which the book opens. The material fact of the fog is used to communicate the sense of a spiritual darkness, a socially pervasive veil of untruth. This ubiquitous darkness, with the spider's web of the law operating at its core, is linked with the horrible night of decay and foulness when Krook explodes, and with the ceaseless drip of pitting rain that rots the home of the Dedlocks. (pp. 304-05)

> *Jack Lindsay, in his* Charles Dickens: A Biographical and Critical Study, *Andrew Dakers Ltd., 1950, 459 p.*

EDGAR JOHNSON   (essay date 1952)

[*Like Edmund Wilson (1941), A.O.J. Cockshut (1962), and Morton Dauwen Zabel (see Additional Bibliography), Johnson considers the fog a significant motif in the symbolic pattern of* Bleak House. *Johnson's emphasis on the importance of Chancery in the novel antedates the similar views of Monroe Engel (1959), Murray Krieger (1960), Trevor Blount (1965), and Robert Alan Donovan (1966). Johnson remarks that Esther "is almost cloyingly unselfish" and that Krook's death heralds "the complete annihilation" of a corrupt society. Jack Lindsay (1950), A.O.J. Cockshut (1962), Trevor Blount (1970), and Morton Dauwen Zabel (see Additional Bibliography) also discuss the social implications of the spontaneous combustion episode in* Bleak House.]

The key institution of *Bleak House* is the Court of Chancery, its key image the fog choking the opening scenes in its dense, brown obscurity and pervading the atmosphere of the entire story with an oppressive heaviness. But both law and fog are

Mr. Smallweed breaks the pipe of peace.

An illustration from the first edition of Bleak House.

fundamentally symbols of all the ponderous and murky forces that suffocate the creative energies of mankind. They prefigure in darkness visible the entanglements of vested interests and institutions and archaic traditions protecting greed, fettering generous action, obstructing men's movements, and beclouding their vision. Surviving out of the miasmal swamps and ferocities of the past, these evils, like prehistoric monsters, unwieldy, voracious, and dreadfully destructive to human welfare, move stumbling and wallowing through quagmires of precedent. *Bleak House* is thus an indictment, not merely of the law, but of the whole dark muddle of organized society. It regards legal injustice not as accidental but as organically related to the very structure of that society.

Though the fog-enshrouded court is only a symbol for this more sweeping arraignment, it is nevertheless the central symbol of the book. (p. 73)

[From the opening chapter of *Bleak House*] the story sweeps relentlessly on, showing how the glacial processes of the court wreck the lives of countless victims. The protracted struggle destroys Gridley, the angry man from Shropshire, "who can by no means be made to understand that the Chancellor is legally ignorance of his existence, having made it desolate for half a century." Prolonged waiting overthrows the sanity of poor little Miss Flite, the tiny spinster dwelling with her birds in her starved tenement, and saying "I was a ward myself. I

was not mad at that time. I had youth and hope. I believe, beauty. It matters very little now. Neither of the three served, or saved me." She and Gridley bathe the long perspective of waste in flames of molten indignation and pathos.

The great lawsuit of the book is the classic case of Jarndyce and Jarndyce. In it, "every difficulty, every contingency, every masterly fiction, every form of procedure known in that court, is represented over and over again," and in it the court costs have already amounted to between sixty and seventy thousand pounds. "It is a cause," one of the lawyers says with unconscious irony, "that could not exist, out of this free and great country." And in it, in one way or another, almost every character of the story is involved. (pp. 74-5)

What Dickens has done here, in fact, has been to create the novel of the social group, used as an instrument of social criticism. Though to a certain extent, in *Vanity Fair*, Thackeray had anticipated him, Thackery used his story more in the spirit of *Everyman* or *Pilgrim's Progress*, as a moral commentary upon human nature, hardly more than suggesting that people's lives were shaped and twisted by social institutions. But from the beginning of his career Dickens had been deeply concerned with institutions, although at first he was able to do no more than sandwich his attacks on them between episodes of melodrama and comedy or relate them to his story only by implication. With *Dombey and Son* he had attempted a more integral suffusion of social criticism and narrative, but for all its successes *Dombey* achieves neither the scope nor the depth of *Bleak House*. (pp. 75-6)

From one point of view this is a gain in "realism," but from another it is an artistic loss. For if there is a danger of Dickens's intricate structures seeming contrived and overmelodramatic, with their missing documents and hidden sins rising up out of the past, there is also a strength in tightness and intensity of development. This advantage Dickens potently exploits by creating a sense of taut inevitability that deepens immeasurably the emotional impact. The movement of *Bleak House* becomes a centripetal one like a whirlpool, at first slow and almost imperceptible, but fatefully drawing in successive groups of characters, circling faster and faster, and ultimately sucking them into the dark funnel whence none will escape uninjured and where many will be crushed and destroyed. In pure emotional power *Bleak House* ranks among Dickens's greatest books.

Lady Dedlock, like Edith Dombey, is one of those defiant spirits who have got into a false position and who therefore despise themselves and revenge their own self-contempt by treating the world with arrogant scorn. Ambitious for aristocratic rank, she had not married Captain Hawdon and had been deceived into believing that their baby daughter Esther had died at birth. Later, as Sir Leicester's wife and a leader of fashionable society, she has found her triumph dead-sea fruit. Having denied the forces of love and life, she can find no sound basis for rebellion. Mingled with the false guilt imposed by a conventional code of ethics is the real guilt of her submission to its standards, her hidden cowardice, her failure to be faithful to her lover and child. The fictitious conception of honor dictated by the morality of society has involved her in a tragic emotional dilemma, of which her very name, Honoria Dedlock, is symbolic.

Esther Summerson, the daughter of whose survival she has been kept in ignorance, is almost cloyingly unselfish, noble, and devoted, and rather tiresome in her domestic efficiency. The reader wearies of her jingling her keys as the little housekeeper of Mr. Jarndyce's home, and of her being called Dame Durden, Dame Trot, and Little Old Woman, and other nicknames, of everyone affectionately confiding in her and seeking her advice, and of her so invariably resigning her own desires, repressing her griefs, and telling herself that she is very fortunate.

Few of the other main characters are as richly or deeply realized as those in either *Dombey and Son* or *David Copperfield*. Ada Clare, one of the wards in chancery under Mr. Jarndyce's protection, is a reversion to the colorlessness of Madeline Bray and Mary Graham. Richard Carstone, the other ward, is a spirited sketch—but only a sketch—of psychological and moral deterioration. Mr. Jarndyce probably makes amends to the nobler aspects of Dickens's father for the good-humoredly derisive caricature of Micawber: even the name John Jarndyce is a softened echo of John Dickens. Like Mr. Pickwick, a lovable old fool who rescues all the victims of oppression (just as John Dickens had brought his son out of the despair of the blacking warehouse), John Jarndyce is a noble-hearted eccentric who protects every sufferer from misfortune and saves those who will let themselves be saved. Unlike Mr. Pickwick, however, he is gently purged of all trace of absurdity. But though his harmless oddities help to humanize his goodness, he does not escape a certain sentimentality of delineation.

Surrounding these central characters crowd a host of others who stand for all the forces or classes of society—philanthropy, art, manners, religion, trade, industry, the poor, the aristocracy, law, government, politics. And, aside from those altogether broken or brutalized by misery, like the crossing sweeper Jo and the colony of brickmakers near St. Albans, almost all these figures are revealed as corrupted by a predatory and selfish pursuit of their own interests. Those who come off best are the small tradesman and the industrialist, Mr. Snagsby the law stationer and Mr. Rouncewell the ironmaster. But even Mr. Snagsby is portrayed as afraid of and subservient to Mr. Tulkinghorn and unable to prevent his wife from exploiting the poor workhouse slavey Guster, who comes cheap because she is subject to fits. And Mr. Rouncewell is one of those craftsman-entrepreneurs who have made their way by invention and hard work; he has contributed to the welfare of society and is not a financial spider preying on its prosperity like Mr. Bounderby, the banker-industrialist of *Hard Times*.

What a gallery are all the rest! There is Mrs. Jellyby, dreaming moonily of helping the African natives on the banks of Borioboola-Gha while she ignores the horrors of the London slums and neglects her own family. There is Mrs. Pardiggle, who browbeats the poor and bullies her children to enhance her own sense of power. There is Harold Skimpole, with his iridescent chatter about art and music and his whimsical paradoxes disguising his parasitic idleness. There is Mr. Turveydrop, that bloated parody of the Prince Regent, in his stays and rouge and padding, using his elegant deportment to batten on his devoted son and deluded daughter-in-law. There are the oily Chadband and the bitter Mrs. Chadband, he with his flatulent pseudoreligious magniloquence and she with her gloomy ironbound harshness satirizing the emptiness and the cruelty of the evangelical creeds.

In such a society, where religion degenerates into perversions of its inspiration, culture into the cheating and cadging of Skimpole, and courtesy into the coldhearted parental cannibalism of Turveydrop, mere self-preservation also sinks at its lowest into the hideous rapacity of Grandfather Smallweed. (pp. 76-9)

Cumulatively, these characters make *Bleak House* both an anatomy of society and a fable in which its major influences and institutions are portrayed by means of sharply individualized figures. Dickens's method is at the same time realistic and figurative. Mrs. Jellyby, never seeing anything nearer than Africa, Mrs. Pardiggle, forcing her children to contribute their allowances to the Tockahoopo Indians, are themselves; but they are also the types of a philanthropy that will do nothing to diminish the profitable exploitation of England's poor. Mrs. Pardiggle will hand out patronizing little booklets to debased brickmakers who are unable to read; she will not work to obtain them a living wage or decent homes with sanitary facilities. Neither she nor Mrs. Jellyby will do a thing to abolish a pestilent slum like Tom-all-Alone's or to help an orphan vagrant like Jo. (p. 79)

Even more marked, however, in *Bleak House* is the use of poetic imagery and symbolism to underline and parallel the meaning of its patterns. The fog of the opening chapter is both literal and allegorical. It is the sooty London fog, but it covers all England, and it is the fog of obstructive procedures and outmoded institutions and selfish interests and obscured thinking as well. Miss Flite's caged birds symbolize the victims of Chancery, and the very names she has given them in her insanity are significant: "Hope, Joy, Youth, Peace, Rest, Life, Dust, Ashes, Waste, Want, Ruin, Despair, Madness, Death, Cunning, Folly, Words, Wigs, Rags, Sheepskin, Plunder,

Precedent, Jargon, Gammon, and Spinach.'' Later, Miss Flite adds two more birds to the collection, calling them ''the Wards in Jarndyce.'' And always outside the cage lurks the cat Lady Jane, waiting, like the lawyers, to seize and tear any that might get free. Lady Jane is sometimes seen as a tiger and sometimes as the wolf that cannot be kept from prowling at the door. Mr. Vholes, skinning his tight, black gloves off his hands as if he were flaying a victim, is constantly described, as are the other lawyers, in metaphors drawn from beasts of prey. And there is a further imagery of spiders spinning their traps, entangling flies within strand upon strand of sticky and imprisoning filaments, hanging their meshes everywhere in gray and dusty clotted webs. (pp. 79-80)

But the law is only the archetype of those vested interests that plunder society under the guise of being society, that strangle the general welfare, that grow fat on the miseries of the poor. It is one of the instruments that give ''monied might the means abundantly of wearying out the right,'' the visible symbol behind which lurk the forces of greed and privilege spinning their labyrinthine webs of corruption. Spread out over the fair English landscape are Chesney Wold, with its noble dignity, its green garden terraces and stately drawing rooms, Bleak House, with its orderly comfort and generous master, Rouncewell's with its productive and self-respecting industry. But Rouncewell's is no more than part of the whole—a part, too, that will reveal its own dark evils under the deeper analysis of *Hard Times*. Bleak House, at its best and for all its warm intentions, is itself helplessly enmeshed and can make only frustrated gestures to reach out a helping hand. And Chesney Wold has its corollary and consequence in Tom-all-Alone's and the wretched hovels of the brickmakers: its dignity is built on their degradation.

Chesney Wold and Tom-all-Alone's are thus also symbols in the symbolic structure. For Dickens does not mean that Sir Leicester Dedlock, or even the aristocracy as a class, is personally responsible for social evil, any more than are the Lord Chancellor or Carboy and Kenge or Inspector Bucket. Individually they may all be amiable enough, but they are instruments of a system in which the stately mansion and the rotting slum represent the opposite extremes. Inspector Bucket, officially the bloodhound of the law, is personally a bluff and kindhearted fellow, Conversation Kenge merely a florid rhetorician, the Lord Chancellor a harmless old gentleman. And to Sir Leicester, who epitomizes the system, Dickens is chivalrously magnanimous.

Sir Leicester is a good feudal landlord, a kind and generous master to his servants, loyal to his family, devoted to his wife. (pp. 81-2)

But, for all his private virtues, he has no hesitation about trying to bully or buy a victory in parliamentary elections, although he bitterly resents the corrupt opposition to his own purposes that makes this expensive course necessary. The ''hundreds of thousands of pounds'' required to bring about the triumph of his own party, he blames on the ''implacable description'' of the opposition and the ''bad spirit'' of the people. (p. 82)

The ''implacable'' opposition is, of course, merely a rival faction contending for the spoils of office, and, no matter which party wins, the country is still dominated by wealth and privilege manipulating all the puppetry of political juntas. This is true even when the candidates of Mr. Rouncewell, the ironmaster, capture a few seats, and will continue to be true when they fill the House, despite Sir Leicester's gasping conviction

that ''the floodgates of society are burst open, and the waters have—a—obliterated the landmarks of the framework of the cohesion by which things are held together!'' All that the rising power of the industrialists really means is that they too will force their way into the coalition of exploitation formed by their predecessors, the landed aristocracy, the lawyers and politicians, the merchants and the bankers. (p. 83)

All this structure of venality rises upon a foundation of exploitation, destitution, and misery. We are shown the wretched hovels of the brickmakers at St. Albans, ''with pigsties close to the broken windows,'' old tubs ''put to catch the droppings of rainwater from a roof, or . . . banked up with mud into a little pond like a large dirt-pie.'' (pp. 84-5)

Worse still is the urban slum of Tom-all-Alone's, a black, dilapidated street of crazy houses tumbling down and reeking with foul stains and loathsome smells dripping with dirty rain, and sheltering within its ruined walls a human vermin that crawls and coils itself to sleep in maggot numbers on the rotting boards of its floors among fetid rags. . . . There dwells Jo, with his body exuding a stench so horrible that Lady Dedlock cannot bear to have him come close to her; and thence comes Jo, munching his bit of dirty bread, and admiring the structure that houses the Society for the Propagation of the Gospel in Foreign Parts. ''He has no idea, poor wretch, of the spiritual destitution of a coral reef in the Pacific, or what it costs to look up the precious souls among the cocoa-nuts and bread-fruits.'' And when Jo lies dying of neglect, malnutrition, and disease, the narrative swells into an organ-toned and accusing dirge: ''Dead, your Majesty. Dead, my lords and gentlemen. Dead, Right Reverends and Wrong Reverends of every order. Dead, men and women, born with Heavenly compassion in your hearts. And dying thus around us every day.''

Counterpointed with the death of Jo is that of Richard Carstone, for high-spirited and generous youth, with every advantage, is no less prey to the infection of an acquisitive society than helpless ignorance and misery. All Richard's buoyancy and courage, his gentleness and frankness, his quick and brilliant abilities, are not enough to save him. Gradually he becomes entangled in the fatal hope of getting something for nothing, stakes everything on the favorable outcome of the chancery suit, neglects his capacities, fosters his careless shortcomings, dissipates the little money he has, feverishly drifts into suspicion and distrust of his honorable guardian, argues that Mr. Jarndyce's appearance of disinterestedness may be a blind to further his own advantage in the case. How, Richard asks, can he settle down to anything? ''If you were living in an unfinished house, liable to have the roof put on or taken off—to be from top to bottom pulled own or built up—tomorrow, next day, next week, next month, next year,—you would find it hard to rest or settle.'' By early manhood his expression is already so worn by weariness and anxiety that his look is ''like ungrown despair.''

Richard Carstone and poor Jo, Miss Flite driven insane, Gridley dying broken on the floor of George's shooting gallery and George in the toils of the moneylenders, Mr. Tulkinghorn shot through the heart in his Lincoln's Inn Fields chambers beneath the pointing finger of allegory, Sir Leicester humbled, heartbroken, and paralyzed, Lady Dedlock dead, disgraced, and mud-stained outside the slimy walls of the pauper graveyard where her lover lies buried—all are swept on to frustration or defeat in the titanic intensity of this dark storm of story. Everywhere the honest, the generous, the helpless, the simple, and the loving are thwarted and crippled. John Jarndyce, the violently good master of Bleak House, can rescue only a distressingly small number of those he sets out to save. In a life of poverty and struggle imposed by a society where nature itself is deformed and tainted, poor Caddy Jellyby and her husband Prince Turveydrop can give birth only to an enfeebled deaf-and-dumb child. For *Bleak House* (like Shaw's *Heartbreak House,* of which it is a somber forerunner) is in its very core symbolic: *Bleak House* is modern England, it is the world of an acquisitive society, a monetary culture, and its heavy gloom is implied by the very adjective that is a part of its title.

But the mood of *Bleak House* is not one of resignation or despairing sorrow; it is that of indignation and grim, fire-eyed defiance. Dickens is no longer, as Shaw points out, merely the liberal reformer who takes it for granted that "the existing social order" is "the permanent and natural order of human society, needing reforms now and then and here and there, but essentially good and sane and right and respectable and proper and everlasting." He has become instead a revolutionist, to whom "it is transitory, mistaken, dishonest, unhappy, pathological: a social disease to be cured, not endured." It is this that troubles numbers of readers in Dickens's later books, which are his greatest ones, and makes those readers prefer the earlier stories. It is now the very root-assumptions of that social order that Dickens is attacking and insisting must be destroyed.

One of the forms taken by the discomfort of such readers is the repeated criticism that Dickens could not portray a gentleman. At the time of Sir Mulberry Hawk and Lord Frederick Verisopht this might have been true; by the time of Sir Leicester Dedlock it was so no longer. It should be observed that Thackeray, who was never accused of a failure to understand gentlemen, paints them far more savagely than Dickens does; he makes Sir Pitt Crawley mean, dirty, illiterate, and brutal, and almost the entire aristocracy profligate, sycophantic, ill-bred. But Thackeray took the stability of society for granted, whereas Dickens was by now demanding a radical reconstruction of society. So Thackeray may be smiled upon as a genteel satirist who merely exposed the flaws of the polite world, and Dickens must be thrown out of court as one who had no understanding of the upper classes. "It would be nearer the mark," Shaw says drily, "to say that Dickens knew all that really mattered in the world about Sir Leicester Dedlock," and that Thackeray "knew nothing that really mattered about him. . . . Thackeray could see Chesney Wold; but Dickens could see through it."

He could see through Lombard Street and Threadneedle Street and the City, too; and, as he was soon to prove, he could see through Birmingham, Manchester, Leeds, and Preston. He sees the world about him as a conflict between the forces of love and life and those of acquisition, retention, and greed, with pride and cruelty everywhere inflicting the most frightful mutilations upon helplessness. But not without having recoil back upon themselves the inevitable consequences of the system that embodies their working nor without evils being engendered that spread almost at random everywhere. Sir Leicester cannot protect the woman he loves and honors; the Lord Chancellor himself cannot speed the slow movement of chancery or prevent it from grinding its victims, of whatever class they may be. Esther Summerson's face cannot be saved from having its beauty ruined as long as there are waifs like Jo and plague spots like Tom-all-Alone's.

In this society of shocking extremes the highest and the lowest are inextricably linked to each other. Dickens had shown this before, in *Barnaby Rudge* with Sir John Chester and Hugh, in *Dombey and Son* with Edith Dombey and Alice Marwood, but

in *Bleak House* it becomes central to the very structure and meaning of the plot. Tom-all-Alone's, Dickens shows us, has his revenge. (pp. 85-8)

And just as Tom-all-Alone's sends out its noxious vapors poisoning society, its waifs bearing pollution and infection, its criminals returning evil for the evil that has formed them; just as Tom-all-Alone's slowly and piecemeal crumbles into ruins from the rottenness of its old beams and reeking plaster, now one and now another house crashing down into dust and rubbish: so the internal rottenness of the social structure that not merely tolerates but perpetuates Tom-all-Alone's must inevitably destroy itself in the end, die of its own self-engendered diseases, annihilate itself by its own corruption. Such is the symbol of Krook's death by Spontaneous Combustion. . . . (pp. 88-9)

It is Dickens speaking with the voice of prophecy. For the sham Lord Chancellor and his shop clearly symbolize not only the real Court of Chancery and all the corruptions of all law, but "all authorities in all places under all names soever"—all the injustices of an unjust society. And they are no longer subjects for local cure or even amputation. Nothing will do short of the complete annihilation that they will ultimately provide by bursting into flames through their own corruption. (p. 89)

> *Edgar Johnson, "'Bleak House': The Anatomy of Society," in* Nineteenth-Century Fiction, *Vol. VII, No. 2, September, 1952, pp. 73-89.*

MONROE ENGEL   (essay date 1959)

[*Engel contends that in* Bleak House *Dickens confronts authority in its many guises and probes the question of individual and social responsibility. Depicting Chancery as a symbol of irresponsibility and unreality, Dickens, according to Engel, settles on death as a "touchstone of reality." For other discussions of the role of Chancery in* Bleak House, *see the excerpts by Edgar Johnson (1952), Murray Krieger (1960), Trevor Blount (1965), and Robert Alan Donovan (1966).*]

In *Bleak House,* as in *Dombey and Son,* death functions as a touchstone of reality. It is a measure of the wretchedness of man's earthly sojourn, awful and profound, but—and this is much to the point—more kindly than the torments imposed by society. (p. 117)

Jo is an extreme example of a recurrent type in Dickens' novels: the child already old with knowledge of the ways and miseries of the world. Guppy and Smallweed are repellent examples of the same type. But Jo, a far more extreme version, though repellent too, also stirs our compassion. Among many other things, Jo knows about dying. When Charley tells him he shouldn't sleep at the brick kiln, because people die there, he says: "They dies everywheres. . . . They dies more than they lives, according to what *I* see." And when it comes Jo's time to die, the fears he has are not of death. His only fear is of being taken back to Tom-All-Alone's. He thinks of death as being "moved on as fur as ever I could go and couldn't be moved no furdur." (pp. 118-19)

Jo is a central character in *Bleak House.* He might, in fact, be called *the* central character. In his notes for Chapter XXIX, Dickens wrote: "Then connect Esther and Jo." And by one means or another, Jo is "connected" with virtually all the characters of importance in *Bleak House.* This is not accident, nor even the storymaker's simple and inevitable extension of

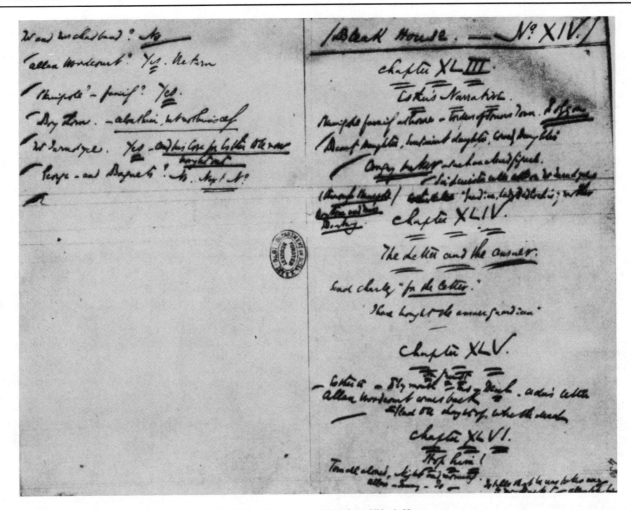

From Dickens's outline of the plot of Bleak House.

coincidence to tie his story together. The notes to **Bleak House** begin with several lists of possible titles for the novel. Every list but the final and deciding one starts with the title "Tom-All-Alone's." (p. 119)

Dickens is vehement against that moneyed world of fashion which is "wrapped up in too much jeweller's cotton and fine wool, and cannot hear the rushing of the larger worlds, and cannot see them as they circle round the sun." He insists that this ignorance does not just befall the well-to-do but that it is actually willed by them, that part of the *status quo* they wish to preserve is the *status quo* of their own ignorance, the peculiar ignorance of "ladies and gentlemen . . . who have agreed to put a smooth glaze on the world, and to keep down all its realities. . . . Who have found out the perpetual stoppage."

Such a "perpetual stoppage" is, of course, as impossible as Dombey's "double door of gold" to "shut out all the world." Truth has terrible ways to assert itself, and not even wealth, though it has many protections, is a barrier to infection. Tom-All-Alone's will have its revenge. "Even the winds are his messengers, and they serve him in these hours of darkness. There is not a drop of Tom's corrupted blood but propagates infection and contagion somewhere. It shall pollute, this very night, the choice stream . . . of a Norman house, and his Grace shall not be able to say Nay to the infamous alliance. There is not an atom of Tom's slime, not a cubic inch of any pes-

tilential gas in which he lives, not one obscenity or degradation about him, not an ignorance, not a wickedness, not a brutality of his committing, but shall work its retribution, through every order of society, up to the proudest of the proud, and to the highest of the high. Verily, what with tainting, plundering, and spoiling, Tom has his revenge." Jo carries his fever about with him as he is hounded around the country. Charley catches it from him, and Esther Summerson catches it from Charley. They have been kind to Jo, but the realist Dickens knows that the fruits of social injustice are not distributed in any strict accordance with deserving. And at Jo's bedside, when he is dying, both Mr. Jarndyce and Allan Woodcourt think "how strangely Fate has entangled this rough outcast in the web of very different lives."

Epidemic is nature's counterpart for revolution. In Dickens' mind, disease and oppression were closely linked. . . . The misery that makes people long for death also and similarly breeds violence. By this time in the fifties, revolution seemed a dreadful and present possibility to Dickens. It is surely the possibility that lurks in the fog and mire of **Bleak House**. (pp. 120-21)

A kind of inevitable dissolution is the hope, but how much is invested in this hope? Will the Dedlocks (surely the name is symbolic: dead-lock) break up or must they be broken up? Toward the end of **Bleak House** it is the suit of Jarndyce and

Jarndyce that "lapses and melts away," but not Chancery, and it is clear that Dickens has grave doubts that enough will happen by peaceful process. When Esther and Ada visit the bricklayers' house with Mrs. Pardiggle, they both feel "painfully sensible that between us and these people there [is] an iron barrier." Miss Flite, who in her own flighty way is a social realist too, expects a judgment on the Day of Judgment when she will release or give flight to those birds, Hope, Joy, etc., which symbolize all that is frustrate and imprisoned in the hell of the world. Mr. Boythorn says that the only possible way to reform Chancery is to blow it to atoms "with ten thousand hundredweight of gunpowder," and in the next instant he calls Sir Leicester Dedlock "the most stiff-necked, arrogant, imbecile, pigheaded numskull, ever, by some inexplicable mistake of Nature, born in any station of life but a walking-stick's."

It is the obduracy of the old bad system that makes the hope for gradual or peaceful improvement seem so small to Dickens—this obduracy, and terrible ignorance too, for the fog and mire of *Bleak House* are the fog and mire of ignorance. The willful ignorance of the upper classes is based on a limited concept of self-interest; but middle-class ignorance is something else. Mr. Turveydrop—in whose name the dropping that is a bow or curtsey and the dropping that is animal excrement become inextricably combined—is a genteelly impoverished and hypocritical worshipper of the upper classes, a gentlemen's gentleman, part of that middle class that Dickens describes as no class at all, but only a fringe on the mantle of the upper class. Mr. Bayham Badger, another member of this no-class, prides himself ridiculously on the gentility of his wife's former husbands.

This pretentious ignorance, amounting to a failure of self-interest, is specially galling to Dickens, for he feels that there is nothing to hope from a man who fails to recognize even his own needs and reasonable claims, whose pretensions cause him to be ignorance of his own interests. In this cataloguing of kinds of ignorance, there is the self-deluding ignorance too of the Mrs. Jellybys and Mrs. Pardiggles, who find it easier to do good deeds at a distance than to do their duty close by. And there is Krook, who has his own brand of ignorance—the stubborn, self-destroying, and vicious but still comic ignorance of craft—and won't ask anyone to teach him to read because they might teach him wrong.

The most dangerous ignorance of all, though, is the ignorance of those too down-trodden in the world to know or care. A couple of years later, Dickens was to tell a friend that "the alienation of the people from their own public affairs" was "extremely like the general mind of France before the breaking out of the first Revolution." To every question addressed to him, Jo says "*I* don't know nothink [no-think?]." Dickens compares Jo to a vagabond dog, and says: "Turn that dog's descendants wild . . . and in a very few years they will so degenerate that they will lose even their bark—but not their bite." The logic of the drama scarcely requires Dickens' explanation.

Bleak House confronts authority—the authority of office, and of money, and of family—with the misery of the world. Mr. Gridley asks who is responsible, and Esther tells Mr. Skimpole that she fears "everybody is obliged to be" responsible. Responsibility is part of Esther Summerson's great and revolting virtue. Most of the other impossible young women in Dickens' novels spring from the usual source for perfect young women in fiction, the area of erotic wish-fulfillment. But Esther stirs no chord of desire, and it is more likely that Dickens has created her as some kind of *alter ego* for himself, deprived of his aggressive force and talent but made kind and lovable instead. Lovable, too, for herself—not for her beauty, which for a time she loses, not for her wealth and influence, which she never has. She starts as an unloved child, as Dickens at least fancied that he was himself, and there are certain aspects of her childhood that remind us of Pip and David Copperfield, the only other first-person narrators in Dickens' novels, and each in some sense a self-portrait. But Dickens had to take back all that he thought the world owed him for his lost childhood, and more, by the force of his own hand, whereas everything comes back to Esther Summerson through love. Yet it requires none of this speculation to see that Esther has a schematic place in the novel by being responsible: as John Jarndyce is, as Charley is, as Mrs. Bagnet is, as Allan Woodcourt is, as Bucket is, as the Rouncewell family are; and as Skimpole, and Mrs. Jellyby, and Mrs. Pardiggle, and Mr. Chadband are not. As Sir Leicester Dedlock is only by his own insufficient lights.

The attack on Chancery, and on the law and legal process, is an attack on irresponsibility. The law, we are told, takes no responsibility for anything but itself. Its first principle is "to make business for itself." It makes hypocritical claims, of course, to much more: Mr. Tulkinghorn talks of his devotion to Sir Leicester Dedlock, and Vholes talks always of putting his shoulder to the wheel, and of his responsibility to his growing daughters, and to his old father in the Vale of Taunton. But all this is mere sham, and what the legal gentlemen really intend is to enrich and dignify themselves. There are, too, many kinds of responsibility. Attractive responsibilities are easy, but it is the unattractive ones that are the real test. The poor, Dickens knows and shows, are unattractive, like Jo:

> Dirty, ugly, disagreeable to all the senses, in body a common creature of the common streets . . . Homely filth begrimes him, homely parasites devour him, homely sores are in him, homely rags are on him: native ignorance, the growth of English soil and climate, sinks his immortal nature lower than the beasts that perish. Stand forth, Jo, in uncompromising colours! From the sole of thy foot to the crown of thy head, there is nothing interesting about thee.

It is easy to be responsible for pretty Rosa, or rosy Mrs. Rouncewell. But who will be responsible for Jo, or for Nemo, the wretched nobody that Captain Hawdon becomes after he has failed in responsibility. For Esther's illegitimacy too is regarded in the light of responsibility, not of sexual morality, and both her father and her mother are made to pay a final price for their irresponsibility toward her.

The very point being made, and that helps substantiate this novel's realism, is that responsibility is difficult, indirect, often very obscure, but that the price of irresponsibility must be paid nonetheless. This is conveyed obviously by the fog-law analogy; less obviously but perhaps more tellingly by the indirect exactions made by disease, epidemic. Only when we have paid the price for our irresponsibilities—secret or unclear as they may be—can be "begin the world." Chancery is the set theme of this novel, death is the reality against which the foggy irresponsibility of legal process is assessed, and epidemic—moving by terrible indirection—symbolizes all too realistically the disaster that continued irresponsibility will bring. (pp. 122-26)

Monroe Engel, in his The Maturity of Dickens, *Cambridge, Mass.: Harvard University Press, 1959, 202 p.*

MURRAY KRIEGER   (essay date 1960)

[Krieger explores Dickens's technique for depicting simulta-neously the realms of "social-economic reality" and "nightmar-ish fantasy." He concludes that, in the case of Chancery, Dickens is unsuccessful since the court cannot be both an institution and "an inevitable intrusion upon the human condition." Other critics who debate Dickens's portrayal of Chancery include Edgar John-son (1952), Monroe Engel (1959), Trevor Blount (1965), and Robert Alan Donovan (1966).]

[In Dickens's *Bleak House*,] the legal court and the absurd court merge in the impossible actuality of Chancery. The world of social-economic reality and of nightmarish fantasy, the po-litical and metaphysical levels have a single narrative source full enough to sustain both at once. We feel the symbol of Chancery as Dickens creates it supports an equal sense of cogency on either level. (p. 138)

But this rooting of the symbolic level in the bedrock of a detailed social reality comes at a cost. For Rick Carstone, Chancery is more than just an oppressive social institution capable of reform; it is rather an unshakeable and suprahis-torical curse upon the human condition. Totally irrational, bathed in the accretion of fogs of many generations, run by an enor-mous machinery of dehumanized creatures who justify what they cannot control, this monstrous collection of debris asserts itself upon the suitor before the court—born into the case or thrust into it—with the promise of a total resolution that it cannot help but frustrate and a bright future that it cannot help but blight. Its monumental absurdity that promises the clarity of order attracts irresistibly, feeds slowly and long, destroys utterly. It functions as this more than social evil, as this sphinx, for Rick, for Miss Flite, for Gridley, and for countless others, even as such symbols of the court as Krook and Mr. Tulk-inghorn considerably exceed mere human dimensions. Yet there is in *Bleak House* another possible attitude toward the court, that of John Jarndyce, which can ensure freedom from it. Though a part of that great memorial of Chancery practice, Jarndyce and Jarndyce, by birth, "he has resolutely kept himself outside the circle." . . . Unlike the others, he simply stays away from court and takes no interest. And it works, for he remains un-affected.

But is one free, once so totally involved, merely to wash his hands? Rick, once dragged in, insists that Chancery "taints everybody" . . . with no possibility of exemption. To be born into an unsettled case is to be thrust into a senseless world that one must struggle to straighten out before the leisure of living can begin. And if the nature of the court precludes the chance of anything ever being settled, then the struggle is a desperate and ill-fated one but cannot be abandoned on that account. For one is not free to abandon it. Thus Chancery grows into a metaphysical entity reflecting the nature of existence as much as the legal tangles and abuses of Victorian England. But then along comes John Jarndyce to short-circuit this significance. Through the force of his virtuous will, though continually chal-lenged he does stay outside successfully and does well to do so. All who follow him, like Esther and George Rouncewell, don his coat of invulnerability, finally manage what K. thought of as "a mode of living completely outside the jurisdiction of the Court," and with it manage a happy ending. A happier ending for all will come, presumably, when the court system is reformed.

Is the court an inevitable intrusion upon the human condition, then, or is it just an actual court and no more, one that can simply be ignored by the wise and changed by the well-mean-

ing? It cannot be both as Dickens seems to make it. His dif-ficulty may arise in large part from his rooting the court in reality. This raises the always delicate problem of creating symbolic levels without threatening the literal believability of the actuality from which they spring. . . . Of course, one must admit that these imperfections in *Bleak House* may not mean that Dickens could not resolve his technical problem so much as that he wanted to appease the tastes of Victorian readers and so inserted the sentimental story of Esther Summerson to compensate for the gloom and the terror of Rick's tragic in-volvement. Unfortunately, the serenely happy ending of the one totally reduced the immense capacities for vision in the other. (pp. 139-40)

Murray Krieger, "The World of Law As Pasteboard Mask," in his The Tragic Vision: Variations on a Theme in Literary Interpretation, *1960. Reprint by The University of Chicago Press, 1966, pp. 114-53.**

A.O.J. COCKSHUT   (essay date 1962)

[Like Murray Krieger (1960), Cockshut examines Dickens's blending of realistic and symbolic description in Bleak House, *remarking that the fog which pervades the novel "is at once the most actual and the most symbolical of all fogs." In addition, he concludes that in his characterization Dickens "came near to . . . being fair." For the first time, according to Cockshut, he exposes both individual and social evils.]*

Bleak House begins, as everyone knows, in a fog. And probably most readers have felt that this was important. There is an obvious and explicit connection between this fog and the mental fog of the law courts. But there is also something more. The world of **Bleak House** is a world in which no problem is really faced, in which nothing is understood, in which the meaning of words has decayed. Hints of this come early: "Another ruined suitor, who periodically appears from Shropshire, and breaks out into efforts to address the Chancellor at the close of the day's business, and who can by no means be made to understand that the Chancellor is legally ignorant of his exis-tence after making it desolate for a quarter of a century. . . ."

They are all in the same boat. Normal distinctions of judgment, intelligence, even of sanity, break down. The Lord Chancellor does not understand. Jo, the crossing sweeper, does not un-derstand. The mad Miss Flite doesn't understand. Even the excellent Jarndyce completely mistakes the character of Harold Skimpole.

It is this universal threat of uncertainty, of course, that sur-rounds with an aura of horror the people who are generally agreed to be crazy. Miss Flite, with her "judgment on the Day of Judgment," Krook, with his insane parody of the Lord Chancellor, are, in a sense, right. They estimate the probable working of the legal system more accurately than do the sen-sible men. Their madness can be seen as a window upon a strange world of sanity. Yet it is madness all the same. We are reminded of the mad characters in Jacobean plays. There is hardly a parallel in the Victorian period.

Yet all this was achieved without any sacrifice of that mar-vellous vividness in the presentation of physical objects and of peculiarities of behaviour, which Dickens had possessed from the first. The fog is at once the most actual and the most symbolical of all fogs.

By making some of the bitterest opponents of the legal system crazy, Dickens extended the range of his social criticism. He was very prone to fits of impotent irritation and superficial reforming zeal. Temperamentally, he may have been inclined to condemn all the abuses and anomalies of law in a lump as manifestly absurd. But in *Bleak House* he has passed beyond this point. In a world of such uncertainty even law courts may be suspected of having some positive value. However, this is revealed only gradually.

The point at which Dickens most obviously emerges from his habit of condemning authority and order without reservation is in the character of Skimpole. Skimpole is the answer to the question, which the younger Dickens would never have thought of asking: "What would Pickwick be like if he had no money?" Skimpole is portrayed with all the bitterness of personal disillusionment. Skimpole had, as it were, taken in Dickens himself, for he was peculiarly susceptible to the cant of a false generosity, as are most men, who, like him, are avaricious and ashamed of being avaricious. So Skimpole's talk has that peculiar note of being just too convincing to be true. (pp. 127-28)

[Chapter 8, "Covering a Multitude of Sins,"] is a packed and fascinating chapter, containing Mr. Jarndyce's attack on Wiglomeration and a study of the slow, self-righteous workings of official charity. The chapter achieves an extraordinary balance. It contains in miniature the forces which prevent the book as a whole from being just a cheap attack on the legal system. It is as if truth lay undetected in the midst of three kinds of error— official justice, official charity, and the bogus, informal good will of Skimpole, which can appear to the unwary eye so very like a viable alternative to the other horrors.

Skimpole's "good nature" is a kind of mirror-image of Jarndyce's. And it is significant that Jarndyce cannot see through him, while Esther easily does so. Skimpole stands as a monument to the hard-won fairness of mind of a man naturally prejudiced, the creation of a natural individualist unwillingly convinced of the need for routine, order and restraint. And this conviction came to its full development just when he was attacking the most absurd of all embodiments of these venerable ideas, the Court of Chancery. And on the opposite side, there is a moving, though much less noticeable monument to the same new feelings—the figure of Neckett, the bailiff, whom Skimpole named Coavins. (pp. 129-30)

Neckett represents routine, law and order in their basest, but still genuine form, just as the Jarndyce case itself shows them at their most pompous and absurd. (p. 130)

Neckett gives a hint of an important moment in Dickens's development. Even in *Oliver Twist* and in the early chapters of *David Copperfield* written not long before, evil had remained mainly an external threat. The lost solitary fugitive, hemmed in by dark powers, is (along with his fantastic humour) Dickens's main contribution to the mythology of literature. By this I mean the ideas which an author's name suggests to people who have hardly read him. But in *Bleak House* we get something new, only faintly foreshadowed in a few scenes of *The Old Curiosity Shop* and *Barnaby Rudge*. The evil without does not only threaten and pursue; it now calls out to the evil within, and sometimes finds a ready answer. Consequently, a new value is seen to reside in the "undickensian" ideas of order, restraint, convention of which Neckett is the lowest and dullest, and therefore the most impressive representative. (pp. 130-31)

[The correspondence of outer and inner evil] occurs more strikingly in Chapter 14, where incurable delusion is placed squarely beside monstrous oppression. On one side are Miss Flite's birds, with their terrifying list of names, representing the practices and victims of Chancery—"Hope, Joy, Youth, Peace, Rest, Life, Dust, Ashes, Waste, Want, Ruin, Despair, Madness, Death, Cunning, Folly, Words, Wigs, Rags, Sheepskin, Plunder, Precedent, Jargon, Gammon and Spinach." (This has some claim to be called the best list in literature.) But in the same chapter and in the same house is Krook, the sham Chancellor, who won't allow himself to be taught to read, because someone might teach him wrong and "I'd rather trust my own self than another." Dickens had always been aware of obsessions, but usually in the past he has been concerned with their superficial humorous side. If we compare Mr. Dick's obsession with Krook's, the difference will be obvious. The satirical attack on the legal system is strengthened rather than weakened by this new balance, and new respect for order. (p. 131)

Now we turn to a part of the novel which no one, I suppose, regards as wholly satisfactory—the Dedlock story. Dickens was trying here to incorporate a well-worn literary tradition into a new type of art. The traditional melodramatic plot with guilty secrets and long-lost heirs, like all popular and traditional stories, embodies some deep human feelings—notably a sense of the unexpectedness of life, and the fortuitous character of advantages of wealth and education. . . . Dickens tried something which is always very difficult—to give new life to a dying tradition. (pp. 133-34)

But the fact remains that despite the unconvincing nature of Lady Dedlock's guilty secret, and her husband's comic opera obstinacy, something important was being attempted in the Dedlock story. It was a way of conveying something easy to state, and very difficult to grasp imaginatively, the corporate nature of society. The melodramatic plot is designed to reveal the interconnection between the wretches of Tom-all-alone's, and the ladies who furnish material for the fashionable intelligence. It is attempting in terms of plot and character to give what is conveyed by the key images of the spontaneous combustion of the body of the pseudo-Lord Chancellor, and the pollution of the atmosphere by the filthy dwellings of the poor. It is a strange experience to find these three things together— one a development of an antiquated theatrical tradition, one a naïve piece of Victorian pseudo-science, reminiscent of Zola's *Dr. Pascal,* and the third, air pollution, a grim fact which most novelists would have found utterly intractable for art. Taken together, they might be called a picture in miniature of the strangeness of Dickens's achievement.

Dickens was wise to choose simultaneously a number of different ways of presenting his view of corporate society, so difficult as it is to apprehend imaginatively. It is an idea we need to be shown, not told. Of course, beyond the three methods of presentation just mentioned, there were others, more obvious. Take, for instance, the case of Krook, the imitation Lord Chancellor. Without the support offered by the Dedlock story and the germ-dirt image, Krook might be taken as a fantasy, merely ornamental. But once the idea is established that society is a seamless fabric, Krook can take his full part as a grotesque illustration of a sober truth. Dickens was very cunning. For he divested himself of responsibility for the fantasy. Krook in his madness is deliberately aping the real Lord Chancellor; so that the obvious absurdity of the comparison between them appears as a strange foible of human nature, objectively reported. . . . Once this element of deliberate burlesque by Krook is established, we are free to notice something else—Krook's profound inner conformity, deeper than anything he is aware of, to the spirit of the constitution. "Read," says Tony to Mr. Guppy. "He'll never read. He can make all the letters separately, and he knows most of them separately when he sees them; he has got on that much under me; but he can't put them together," and, "But his whole stock from beginning to end, may easily be the waste paper he bought it as, for anything I can say. It's a monomania with him, to think he is possessed of documents." Here Krook is unconscious of the part he is playing, that of the legal system, burdened with precedents, unable to see life for disjointed facts. The combination of deliberate parody and this pervasive unguessed likeness is impressive. And if the incident of the spontaneous combustion is, on the whole, a failure, it is largely redeemed by what immediately follows, the inquest. Never has the power of law to discover facts and miss realities been better conveyed. Yet even here balance is maintained. If Skimpole prevents us sneering too easily at respectable routine, Chadband is there to give us pause when we laugh at legal verbiage. Chadband, like Skimpole, is not an attack on the vices of other people, but on a corrupt form of one of the author's own qualities. Chadband shows us what happens when sentimental goodwill congeals into an icy rigidity. And this leads to my last and most important point. In *Bleak House,* while retaining to the full his wonderful and violent energy, and swarming invention, he came near to that great and perhaps unattainable target of being fair. No one, reading *Nicholas Nickleby* would have believed it possible. (pp. 134-36)

> A.O.J. Cockshut, in his The Imagination of Charles Dickens, *New York University Press, 1962, 192 p.*

TREVOR BLOUNT (essay date 1965)

[*Arguing that Chancery "functions in the novel as a touchstone of moral reality," Blount maintains that Esther, unlike John Jarndyce, is able to come to terms with reality in* Bleak House. *For other viewpoints on the role of Chancery in* Bleak House, *see the excerpts by Edgar Johnson (1952), Monroe Engel (1959), Murray Krieger (1960), and Robert Alan Donovan (1966).*]

[In the general context of *Bleak House,*] Chancery must not be regarded as a danger to be shunned by pretending it does not exist, but a challenge to be faced up to and overcome. Dickens obviously deplores the abuses that existed and *Bleak House* is in part intended as specific propaganda against such iniquities. Nevertheless Dickens, as a successful man of the world, recognized them as part of the more or less inevitable consequence of the selfishness and sinfulness that will never be eradicated, however mordant the satire or persuasive or terrifying the sermon. *Bleak House* accepts this pragmatic attitude but goes beyond it. Part of the strength of the novel lies in the fact that it does not fall into the weaknesses that Dickens ridicules in Mrs. Pardiggle, Mrs. Jellyby and Mr. Chadband: an inability to face up to reality and to see plainly what their various forms of distorted vision obscures from them. Regarded in this light, Chancery—though it is often deplorable, and though one must strive to remedy its malfunctioning—embodies an unavoidable part of the human condition, a part which challenges pessimism and which must not be shirked. It is evil; but it is rather like the evil of the Weird Sisters in *Macbeth.* Macbeth succumbs to an inner moral weakness; he is not an unqualified victim of hostile circumstance. To be sucked into Chancery is to be victimized if, as in the case of Gridley, it happens through no fault of the person concerned. But to go voluntarily into Chancery in the hope of easy success, as Richard Carstone does, is to make a wrong moral choice. . . . In his charm and evident good intentions Richard is a more ingratiating Skimpole, for Skimpole's specious fancies are in-

tended (within the economy of the novel) to be attractively witty—as we can judge from their effect on Esther Summerson and others. Moreover, fancy (emblematized, for example, by Esther's little gifts to Peepy Jellyby) is one of the desiderata in the novel's scale of values. But by itself fancy is not enough; various elements must combine to make a socially integrated person, and Skimpole's selfishness eventually alienates Esther. One of the strengths of *Bleak House* is its moral realism in this respect. Thus Richard is found lacking, although in so many ways he is a hero-figure. In consequence, Chancery will grind him to powder, and "easy" money will provide a will o' the wisp luring him on to the marshes where the symbolic mud of chapter I will trap him. The choice is his. He disregards John Jarndyce's good advice, suspecting him—a further variation of the theme of "blindness" and misprison—of self-interest; and he fails to take warning from the fate of Miss Flite. He is once rescued from the foils of usury; but he is not to be rescued from the meshes of Chancery, for Dickens's earlier belief in providential Brownlows has given way in this novel to a realistic presentation of what happens to innocents who court danger once too often. (pp. 116-18)

Chancery also provides a test by which to estimate John Jarndyce and Esther Summerson. Jarndyce is in so many ways the ideal presented by the novel that is remarkably honest and subtle of Dickens to modify him in this way. In some respects he stands for the early Dickensian answers—rather like Pickwick or the cheerybles or Scrooge and the turkey—and we first meet him in chapter III offering "the best plum-cake" and "a little pie" to the infant Esther. These, Dickens now implies, are an inadequate solution to human need. Esther refuses them, showing that of itself such charity cannot establish the desired contact. . . . At best, such charity merely solves the externals of the problem, treats the symptoms but not the root cause. The benevolent impulse in Jarndyce is held up for our admiration; it is out-going, and shares much of the goodness fully embodied in Esther. But his answer, put so simply, is insufficient. The remedy required is not the altruistic gesture of the rich philanthropist but a social impulse of fellow-feeling in which everyone must play a part. As an individual Jarndyce himself feels the injustices that others suffer, and feels them keenly: this is the principal significance of the East Wind that afflicts him at every instance of selfishness and acquisitiveness. (It is also significant that he should be characterized by a euphemism: a linguistic shunning of reality.) But despite his sensitive compassion, John Jarndyce's answer is, taken in isolation, the wrong answer. He cocoons himself . . . against the cold wind of truth. . . . It is not enough to insulate himself in a "quantity of wrappings". True: he does not succumb like Richard to the false blandishments of Chancery. But what he does is almost as regrettable: he runs away, ignores it, pretends it does not exist. But in that the scandals of Chancery symbolise evil, it is not to be ignored so casually. A fully integrated person, the moral structure of the novel seems to imply, must confront evil, grapple with it, and emerge victorious.

Esther, the heroine of the novel, who embodies the positive values underlying Dickens's satiric attacks, does in fact come to terms with evil in this way. She comes to realize her illegitimacy, and to realize what in terms of social disability and shame such an outcast state involves. To some extent she realizes that she, like Jo, is a social outsider. The inner stain will be emblematized in the marks on her ravaged face. But the beauty of her soul, her radiant humility, her denial of self in the way she lives (as it were) through others—in this respect a complete contrast to Mrs. Pardiggle and the way she treats her children—will shine through the scars and Allan Woodcourt will testify: "don't you know that you are prettier than you ever were?" . . . True beauty will be valued above superficialities.

On the level of moral fable this is reason enough why Esther will not marry John Jarndyce. Unlike him, she has come to terms with reality: suffered the worst it can do (despite her innocence), and yet succeeded triumphantly. . . . John Jarndyce is limited by his insulation from reality: not so patrician an aloofness as Sir Leicester Dedlock's family pride; not so myopic as the "blindness" of the professional philanthropists; not so self-seeking as that of the usurers and lawyers. But nevertheless John Jarndyce has his shortcomings. Seen in this light, Chancery—with its obstructive ritual, callous unconcern, and poisonous degeneracy—is not only iniquitous in itself; it functions in the novel as a touchstone of moral reality. (pp. 118-20)

> *Trevor Blount, "Chancery As Evil and Challenge in 'Bleak House'," in* Dickens Studies, *Vol. I, No. 3, September, 1965, pp. 112-20.*

WILLIAM AXTON   (essay date 1965)

[*Axton explains Esther's inconsistencies by proposing that Dickens depicted her as "a character divided against herself." In conclusion, Axton praises Dickens for his challenging narrative technique. Other critics who interpret Esther's characterization in the novel include Albert J. Guerard (1969), Q. D. Leavis*

(1970), Joan D. Winslow (1976), and Taylor Stoehr (see Additional Bibliography).]

Although Charles Dickens clearly intended Esther Summerson for the heroine of ***Bleak House,*** many readers have found her character ambiguous, if not repugnant. Esther's portion of the narrative has to them a disingenuous ring. The picture she paints of herself is too good to be true, or at least too good to be credible. Professing her small worth, Esther contrives to allude to her virtues at every turn; insisting on her plainness, she is preoccupied with the question of her good looks to the very last words of the novel. Avowedly reluctant to speak ill of anyone, Esther is a master of ironic commentary; she damns with faint praise, employs paraphrase with devastating effect, and claims to be perplexed by those whose conduct she condemns. For these and other reasons, many readers find in Esther a dreadful parody of the ideal Victorian woman.

Readers critical of Esther have in consequence questioned Dickens' characterization and conduct of narrative. Specifically, is Esther another female paragon to whom Dickens felt so committed that he lost critical control over her presentation? Or did the novelist intend for Esther to play some deeply ironic role in the narrative? The answer, I believe, is neither. Rather, Esther's personal inconsistencies comprise an objective study of a character divided against herself by contending forces clearly discernible in her personal history; and her portion of the narrative illustrates this inner conflict. (pp. 545-46)

A map of London at the time of Bleak House.

Dickens designed the inconsistencies in Esther's character to illustrate an inner conflict between her sense of an inherited moral taint and personal worthlessness, prompted by the circumstance of her illegitimate birth, and a contrary awareness that she is a free moral agent, responsible for her quality and identity through her own acts. When the reader first meets Esther as a child, he finds her quailing before her aunt's imputation of a stain inherited from her parents' sin. The girl, her aunt says, has been "orphaned and degraded from the first" by the "sins of others," which may be "visited upon [her] head, according to what is written." She was not born in "common sinfulness and wrath," but "set apart." . . . Esther's reaction to this accusation, however, is ambiguous. She resolves to try,

> as hard as ever I could, to repair the fault I had been born with (*of which I confessedly felt guilty and yet innocent*), and . . . strive as I grew up to be industrious, contented, and kind-hearted, and to do some good to some one, and win some love to myself if I could. . . .

From the beginning of the novel, then, Esther's character is defined by an inner struggle between a sense of inherited guilt, which urges her toward self-abnegating expiation in service to others, and a contrary sense of personal innocence, which expresses itself in a desire for self-realization and fulfilled identity in love.

This struggle in Esther centers on the choice between lovers that forms the climax of the girl's personal career in the novel. Shall she, prompted by the fear of having inherited a disfiguring moral taint at her birth, sacrifice the chance of achieving a fully satisfying love relationship with Allan Woodcourt in order to marry her elderly guardian, Mr. Jarndyce, to whom she is drawn by gratitude? Or is she to find self-realization in marriage to the handsome young doctor, and truly "win some love" to herself? And deeply involved in this choice are the related questions of her physical beauty and moral worth.

These ambiguities in Esther's character find direct expression in the girl's narrative style. It is no profoundly original insight of Dickens to make such a sensitive, guilt-ridden, and inhibited person as Esther, when she serves as a narrator, alternatively stress and depreciate those admirable qualities others find in her, or judge others in a tentative, self-effacing, and oblique manner, even when she is confronted by manifest wrongdoing. The victim of a morbid self-consciousness, Esther stands condemned before the tribunal of her own conscience while at the same time she is pleading her case. Thus the girl cannot employ Mr. Jarndyce's pleasant crochet of the "east wind" in the face of evil or pain. Instead, she must rely on her repertory of indirect evaluation and commentary, which necessarily exposes such a character to charges of hypocrisy, "mock-modesty," "revolting virtue," and "tedious goodness."

Esther's opening words set the tone of her narrative, with their faintly embarrassing mixture of self-depreciation, oblique self-congratulation, and indirect commentary. . . . Although, as we soon learn, the girl has the most acute insight of anyone in *Bleak House,* the dominant note here is an emphatically repeated denial of her cleverness. But she goes on to indicate, first, where her intellectual strength lies—in her perceptiveness; second, the reason for this condition—an emotional starvation, moral degradation, and spiritual constraint so profound that even now, a mature and happy woman, she cannot look back on those days without tears; and, third, the agent of her

persecution—her aunt and guardian, Miss Barbary. The settled conviction of her small worth contends in Esther with a sense of persecution. Successfully stripped of its identity, the cowed spirit rebels in self-affirmation and oblique criticism of its persecutor: in praise that blames, as in Esther's circumspect depiction fo Miss Barbary's pathologically inhumane righteousness; and in blame that praises, as in Esther's self-deprecation, so exaggerated—"I had always rather a noticing way— not a quick way, O no!"—that it becomes an indirect assertion of self and condemnation of those who made her as she is. Indeed, that "O no!" borders on unconscious irony. Finally, these lines suggest two other aspects of Esther's character which later pages are to develop in detail: first, the fact that, given proper emotional conditions, the girl's perceptions quicken and sharpen; and second, her habit of analytical reflection from the alien position of an emotional innocent, which puts her outside of, but makes her curious about, conventional experience. Later, of course, this desire to understand what is going on about her becomes an important means of ironic evaluation.

In sum, Esther's narrative style was designed to depict what we would now call a morbid personality existing behind a superficially busy and cheerful mask—a function of Esther's resolve, given the circumstances of her birth, "to be industrious, contented, and kind-hearted, and to do some good to some one." Of Dickens' intuitive grasp of the mechanism of Esther's illness there can be little doubt, however imperfect may be his understanding of its subtle details as viewed from the perspective of modern psychology; for throughout the novel, Esther continues to employ the tropes and figures introduced in her opening words to describe herself and to view those around her. With this necessary limitation: as a narrator, Esther must also be more than a character; she must be as well a device of the author to establish a coherent system of values consonant with those of Dickens' portion of the narrative. And what is more, she must, though writing from the point of view in time of a mature and happily married woman, maintain a due regard for the perspective of the young and inexperienced girl she was when the events that she describes took place.

Even the smallest details of narrative may allude to Esther's personal dilemma when she is telling us about herself. For example, in the first conference with her guardian following her arrival at Bleak House, Esther voices the fear that she will be unequal to the duties imposed upon her as mistress of the establishment. Mr. Jarndyce assures her of his entire confidence. . . . (pp. 546-50)

Esther's response to the nicknames bestowed upon her by her friends at Bleak House is as ambiguous and indirect as her attitude toward her aunt, though less intensely expressed. In so far as they express affectionate approval of her desire to be "industrious, contented, and kindhearted," these pet names are gratefully received; but in so far as they obscure or ignore her given names, they tacitly deprive Esther of a measure of identity and reduce her to the relative anonymity of a housekeeper. The reasoning behind Esther's ambivalent attitude toward her nicknames becomes clear when we examine their associations, for they all refer to the witches, hags, spinsters, widows, and comic old dames of folklore and nursery rhyme. They combine to suggest to Esther that, being tainted by the circumstances of her birth, she is so repugnant to others that she will never "win some love" to herself, that she is doomed to live out her life as a dame, an old maid, a housekeeper.

The theme of love appears in the novel when Allan Woodcourt enters Esther's life; but the course of true love is blocked by a number of circumstances: the girl's sense of being unworthy, her disfigurement by smallpox, Mr. Jarndyce's proposal, and old Mrs. Woodcourt's opposition to the match. This last matter occasions a typical example of Esther's narrative reticence. Near the middle of the novel, on the eve of Caddy Jellyby's marriage to Prince Turveydrop, Mrs. Woodcourt pays a second and extended visit to Bleak House, where she renews her earlier insinuations about Esther's birth and engages in pointed recitals of her son's distinguished Welsh lineage. Her intention is, of course, to convince Esther of her unworthiness to be the young doctor's wife. . . . [It is clear from such situations] that Esther's reticence is not confined merely to the relations between herself and the reader and between herself and the other characters: it is a fundamental part of her character, in which there are psychological sores, disfigurements, and tender places that she cannot bring herself to look at or touch directly, although she wishes truthfully to indicate their presence. Of these sensitive areas, the possibility of winning Allan Woodcourt's love to herself alone, in spite of her illegitimate birth, is the most prominent; but it is so sensitive a subject that she cannot bring herself consciously to admit to its existence. For this reason Esther cannot define precisely why Mrs. Woodcourt's genealogical talk makes her "uncomfortable"; and her attitude is further complicated by her reluctance to condemn others.

The narrative context in which Mrs. Woodcourt's visit occurs further deepens the ironies of Esther's situation and the ambiguities of her feelings. She is experiencing a growing but as yet unadmitted realization that Mr. Jarndyce loves her with a love greater than that of a guardian, and her gratitude will allow her neither to ignore nor dismiss this fact. The courtship of Richard Carstone and Ada Clare and the approaching nuptials of Caddy Jellyby and Prince Turveydrop place Esther's love-plight in high relief. Under the pressure of these circumstances, therefore, it would be difficult indeed for a reserved and guilt-ridden twenty-one-year-old to confront directly the personalities, events, and inner feelings in which she finds herself enmeshed. She can do little more than proceed as she does—by indirection, half statement, implication, and perplexity.

It is in the light of these internal pressures that one must read the central episodes of Esther's career in the novel: her disfigurement by smallpox, her discovery that Lady Dedlock is her mother, Mr. Jarndyce's proposal and her acceptance, and the final recognition scene with Allan Woodcourt, in which, too late, he declares his love. Esther's choice of lovers has been determined by her contradictory feelngs of guilt and innocence; but these feelings focus on the intermediate matter of her physical beauty. If her illegitimacy is a disfigurement, her attractiveness comes into question; and Esther's fear of being thought morally tainted issues in her neurotic suspicion that she is plain-looking if not ugly, and hence debarred from winning any love to herself. Moreover, this moral and psychological disfigurement is objectified in her actual physical disfigurement from smallpox. Hard upon this comes Mr. Jarndyce's proposal. Her acceptance is couched in familiar terms:

> he did not hint to me, that when I had been better-looking, he had had this same proceeding in his thoughts, and had refrained from it. That when my old face was gone from me, and I had no attractions, he could love me just as well as in my fairer days. That the discovery of my birth gave him no shock. That his generosity rose above my disfigurement, and my inheritance of shame. . . .

> Still I cried very much; not only in the fulness of my heart after reading the letter, not only in the strangeness of the prospect . . . but as if something for which there was no name or distinct idea were indefinitely lost to me. I was very happy, very thankful, very hopeful; but I cried very much. . . .

Esther defines her conscious thoughts as they were at that time; but her unconscious thoughts, which motivate a portion of her actions, remain unexamined for reasons of narrative decorum. The reader is allowed to see only their consequences—here in Esther's contradictory tears and in her sense of something lost. Presumably, this sort of tact as a narrator is prompted by her desire to give an accurate picture of herself as she then was, with all the limitations of a very young woman in the midst of overwhelming and still uncompleted actions.

Similar considerations validate Esther's depiction of other characters and events which do not directly involve her, for she is called upon to describe and assess people in a wholly unfamiliar milieu, from a position at once demanding and anomalous. Hence her indirections. Possessed of the shrewdest insights and finest discriminations of anyone in the novel, but temperamentally incapable of overt condemnation, Esther is torn between the desire to evaluate and the contrary impulse to judge not, lest she be judged. Characteristically, she chooses a middle course: her assessments are communicated, but only in the oblique terms of unconscious irony. (pp. 550-53)

This latter technique of oblique commentary, exploited to the fullest by Esther when dealing with other characters, is premised on Esther's initial assessment of herself—that she has not a quick understanding except where her sympathies or affections are aroused. When, therefore, she meets with insensitivity, cruelty, or irresponsibility, as in the case of Mrs. Woodcourt, she responds with perplexity or confusion. . . . [Early] in the novel, Mrs. Jellyby's concern for remote charitable projects, coupled with her neglect of her home and family, elicits this quiet condemnation: "'It quite confuses me. I want to understand it, and I can't understand it at all. . . . It *must* be very good of Mrs. Jellyby to take such pains about a scheme for the benefit of Natives—and yet—Peepy and the housekeeping!'" . . . Harold Skimpole, the novel's paradigm of the irresponsible adult, prompts a similar perplexity in Esther:

> If I felt at all confused at that early time, in endeavouring to reconcile anything he said with anything I had thought about the duties and accountabilities of life (which I am far from sure of), I was confused by not exactly understanding why he was free of them. That he *was* free of them, I scarcely doubted; he was so very clear about it himself. . . .

Here, ringed round with qualifications, demurrers, and understatements, lack of "cleverness" and "quick understanding," combined with a "noticing way," lead Esther to ask a simple and pointed question about Skimpole's irresponsibility that puts him in a very damaging light with the reader. A few pages later Mrs. Pardiggle occasions a similar "confusion" in Esther . . . , and throughout the novel instances of false charity and irresponsibility are firmly placed in the scale of values by Esther's consistent perplexity.

Esther's studied incomprehension need not be employed only in ironic ways, however, for often, as in the case of Richard Carstone's growing irresponsibility arising out of his hopes in the Jarndyce case, it is used to express anxiety concerning someone she loves. In such cases this device resembles Esther's use of discreet reticence in reference to herself. Quite early in the novel, for example, the girl indicates the source of that weakness in Rick's character which will eventually destroy him: "With a buoyancy and hopefulness and a gaiety that hardly ever flagged, Richard had a carelessness in his character that quite perplexed me—principally because he mistook it, in such a very odd way, for prudence." . . . There follows a brief anecdote to illustrate this foible in the young man, before the narrative turns to other matters. But in this, as in other instances of a similar kind, Esther's perplexity is closely allied to that discomfort she feels when her sensibilities have been touched at some sensitive place. An unpleasant topic is introduced, but Esther refrains from handling it directly.

At other times, Esther employs with damaging effect the clear-sighted vision of one who occupies the vantage ground of the innocent, the detached observer who sees with devastating precision. Such a technique is essentially more Dickens', who employs it constantly when writing as an omniscient narrator, than Esther's; but its use is validated in the girl's case by the alienation her childhood experiences have bred in her, by the anomalous social position she occupies, and by her "silent, noticing ways." (pp. 554-55)

Finally, Esther is no less effective when she employs paraphrase as a mode of tacit critical commentary. Like her clear vision, Esther's sharp ear for the false note allows her to present unsympathetic characters so that they condemn themselves in their own words. By this device, again, Esther is freed from the onus of direct judgment. There are many instances of this technique employed against Esther's favorite targets—Mrs. Jellyby, Mr. Turveydrop, Mrs. Pardiggle, even Richard Carstone—but Harold Skimpole provides perhaps the most dramatic example. When Esther is recuperating at Lawrence Boythorn's house in Lincolnshire from the effects of her demoralizing disfigurement by smallpox, she is visited by Richard Carstone, Vholes, and Skimpole. The latter addresses her, she tells us, in this manner:

> He was charmed to see me; said he had been shedding delicious tears of joy and sympathy, at intervals for six weeks, on my account; had never been so happy as in hearing of my progress; began to understand the mixture of good and evil in the world now; felt that he appreciated health the more, when somebody else was ill; didn't know but what it might be in the scheme of things that A should squint to make B happier in looking straight; or that C should carry a wooden leg, to make D better satisfied with his flesh and blood in a silk stocking. . . .

Coming at a time when the reader's sympathies for the girl are most fully aroused, Skimpole's words fall with appalling insensitivity. And this effect is heightened by Esther's omission of subjects and change of tense, so that his remarks take on the quality of a dreary catalogue of empty sentiments, as if it were an automatic reiteration or recital like a worn-out record.

In all these examples one can perceive how the ambiguities of Esther's narrative express the ambiguities of her character and of her position as a narrator. Her troubled consciousness of a guilty inheritance inhibits performance of her narrative functions; but her keen moral insight encourages her to make value judgments on every hand. Similar motives account for her

reticence, or even silence, about sensitive areas of her own character; and this tendency is heightened by Esther's wish to give a clear picture of herself as she then was from a point of view in time several years after the events of the novel take place. Esther's solution is to steer a middle course: her moral evaluations are communicated, but only in an oblique and indirect way. In trying thus to free Esther to judge, and yet not to be judged, Dickens chose to follow a difficult narrative course which has exposed him to the charge of having made his heroine a hypocrite. But if the thesis advanced in this essay is accepted, the novelist may be exonerated. (pp. 556-57)

William Axton, "The Trouble with Esther," in Modern Language Quarterly, *Vol. XXVI, No. 4, December, 1965, pp. 545-47.*

ROBERT GARIS   (essay date 1965)

[*Garis suggests that the main thrust of* Bleak House *is Dickens's attack on the System, which he carries out as a "theatrical performance rendered by a theatrical artist . . . proving a case." However, Garis contends that Dickens's insistence on social protest rather than drama seriously undermines his ability to achieve dramatic complexity in the novel.*]

Dickens's attack on System consists for the most part of a gallery of exhibits of human behaviour. He constructs this gallery by a remarkable capitalization on his early methods of characterization. In the Dickens theatre we are always an audience for the people, the landscapes, the houses, we meet; in *Bleak House* Dickens has made us into a special kind of audience, one that instantly tried to see what relationship each new person, each new house, each new landscape, has to the great case against System. And no one has any trouble seeing these relationships. Mrs. Jellyby, for instance, is the overlord of a tiny system of organized benevolence, whom Mr. Jarndyce sent Esther, Ada, and Richard to visit 'on purpose'—he says so explicitly. . . . What did they learn, and how did they learn it? Not a moment is lost in answering these questions: not a detail connected with the name Jellyby but serves as a piece of evidence for Dickens's, and in this case also Mr. Jarndyce's, attack on System. The Jellybys live 'in a narrow street of high houses, like on oblong cistern to hold the fog. There was a confused little crowd of people, principally children, gathered about the house at which we stopped, which had a tarnished brass plate on the door, with the inscription, JELLYBY.' . . . Every detail here is a judgement, and the judgement is emphatic and simple. The narrowness of the street speaks instantly of a lack of freedom, and attacks that condition. A street should not be a cistern to hold the fog, and if Mrs. Jellyby chooses to live on this street it means that she likes fog. In the first chapter we saw the Lord High Chancellor sitting at the centre of the fog; Mrs. Jellyby is then like him. Crowds of people should not be confused, children should not be in crowds, a brass plate should not be tarnished. Because we are in the Dickens theatre, listening to Dickens's attack on System, we translate every detail into a judgement with a rapidity which makes the judgements very simple ones. (p. 109)

But there is one significant difference between Dickens's methods in *Bleak House* and his methods earlier. Since every detail about Mrs. Jellyby is now meaningful in moral, judgemental terms, very characterization is offered to us for immediate judgement and condemnation, and therefore her lack of inner life, her inability to change, her inability to engage in any action is also offered to us for condemnation. When Caddy Jellyby tells her that she is going to be married, Mrs. Jellyby is offered an opportunity to engage in a human action; the fact that she does not take the opportunity is the final confirmation of her systematized existence, her inability to meet experience, and this inability is very firmly brought to our attention and condemned.

The majority of the characters in *Bleak House,* who make up the majority of the exhibits in the great case against System, are, like Mrs. Jellyby, systematized. Whether they are rulers or victims, Dickens makes us see that they never change, that they are not truly alive, that they are subordinated entirely to routine. Dickens views these systematized people with varying degrees of condemnation, with horror in some cases, with amused tolerance in others. Taken together, they very richly embody a powerful demonstration and denunciation of the world of System.

This world, the 'world of *Bleak House*', is not a world we live in—more accurately, not a world we have the illusion of living in as we have the illusion of living in the world of novels as diverse in method and tone as *Emma* or *The Trial* or *Resurrection* or *The Sound and the Fury.* The world of *Bleak House* is a theatrical performance rendered by a theatrical artist who is proving a case. Accordingly, the standards by which we judge it are those by which we judge an argument: we do not ask, then, 'Is it real'? but 'Is it convincing'? (p. 113)

Dickens's image of the world of System depends on this basic talent of his theatrical art not only for its argumentative success but for its moral beauty and value.... Dickens's overt purposes in *Bleak House* [are] argumentative, ... very loudly and insistently so. The question arises, and not only for the oversensitive modern mind, whether there is not something rather unlovely in the contrived rhetoric of this loud, insistent, vehement voice which is so eager to denounce what it hates and to convince us by this denunciation. If we sense purposeful contrivances and manipulations on every page of *Bleak House,* what prevents us from getting an overpowering, overriding impression of the human will in action? Why do these loud points and purposes not come to seem an imposition on us, a tyranny over us which is at least as oppressive as the tyranny of Chancery? (pp. 116-17)

[The] central and wonderful truth about Dickens, which silences our criticism, is that he can perform his own plan with a spontaneous energy of invention which entirely burns away the atmosphere of mechancially insensitive wilfulness. The planning remains perfectly obvious, but there is new life available to the artist at every moment as he performs his plans. Dickens's theatrical impersonation of the world of System is as alive as its subject is dead. And, in the Dickens theatre, this means that we believe he is telling the truth.

What the world of System lacks, of course, is the complexity that goes with drama. It is as flat as its inhabitants, and this is inevitable and right. A mechanical being cannot embody any very complex meaning and cannot be the vehicle for any very complex judgement. Mrs. Jellyby, Mr. Snagsby, and the rest of the mechanized characters are assessed with accuracy and often with subtlety, and with a great range of feeling and tone. Dickens has clearly demonstrated why we cannot take these characters seriously as morally active human beings with inner lives. But this means that the moral judgements embodied by these characters and their world are not complex moral judgements. Dickens's attitude towards this world is a serious one, in the sense that it is impassioned and urgent and compelling. But his judgement is that it cannot for a moment be accepted

as a possible way of life for human beings. It is a mistake from first to last for human beings to enter into System, for System is absolutely hostile to everything that makes them human. System, then, is not *criticized* as a complex moral phenomenon, but single-mindedly denounced and rejected. (p. 117)

Bleak House is interested in denunciation, not drama, and the unique energy and resourcefulness of Dickens's rhetoric, the generosity of his invention, the 'act of life' in that wonderful voice itself—these not only ratify Dickens's case against System but establish and make valid the remarkable simplicity of the case. The experienced audience in the Dickens theatre will be fully aware of that simplicity, and will therefore be insured against any important confusion or dissatisfaction at Dickens's failure to achieve dramatic complexity when the opportunity might seem to have presented itself. All this, of course, is not to say that failure is anything but failure. (p. 143)

> *Robert Garis, in his* The Dickens Theatre: A Reassessment of the Novels, *Oxford at the Clarendon Press, Oxford, 1965, 259 p.*

ROBERT ALAN DONOVAN   (essay date 1966)

[*Echoing G. K. Chesterton's comments on* Bleak House *(1907), Donovan explores the integration of subject and technique in the novel. In particular, Donovan discusses Dickens's symbolic use of Chancery, "the mundane equivalent of hell," to carry out his theme of responsibility and its corollary, dependency. For further interpretations of the role of Chancery in* Bleak House *see the excerpts by Edgar Johnson (1952), Monroe Engel (1959), Murray Krieger (1960), and Trevor Blount (1965). Donovan remarks that* Bleak House *is "a novel without a center," for its structure is based on the concept of discovery, "the typical pattern of the detective story." Other critics who discuss detective story elements in* Bleak House *include Edmund Wilson (1941), Lionel Stevenson (1943), and Morton Dauwen Zabel (see Additional Bibliography).*]

The main theme of *Bleak House* is responsibility. The content of the book may most succinctly be described as a series of studies in society's exercise (more often the evasion or abuse) of responsibility for its dependents. In his earlier novels Dickens characteristically locates the source of evil in specific human beings, the villains in his typically melodramatic plots. Sometimes he makes evil grow out of sheer malignity (Quilp), but even when the evil represented is of a predominantly social character it is generally personified, in the acquisitiveness of a Ralph Nickleby, for example, or the officious cruelty of a Bumble. But *Bleak House* has no villain. It offers a jungle without predators, only scavengers. Evil is as impersonal as the fog which is its main symbol. The Court of Chancery, the main focus of evil in the novel and the mundane equivalent of hell, harbors no devil, only a rather mild and benevolent gentleman who is sincerely desirous of doing the best he can for the people who require his aid. (p. 209)

Dickens found in the Court of Chancery specifically, and in the law generally, the true embodiment of everything that was pernicious. The law touched Dickens often enough in his private life, and the actual cases of victims of legal proceedings always roused his indignation even when he was not personally involved. The result was a vein of legal satire beginning with the Bardell-Pickwick trial and running throughout the novels, but it is not Dickens's private grievance against the law that I am here concerned with. The law was to become for him a means by which as an artist he could most faithfully and effectively image a world gone wrong. Like Jeremy Bentham,

Dickens was apalled by the chaos of the British law; its random accumulation of statute law, common law, and precedents in equity; its overlapping and conflicting jurisdictions; its antiquated and mysterious rituals and procedures. But Bentham was only appalled by the lack of intelligible system, not by the law itself, and he accordingly set out to put things right. Dickens, on the other hand, who shared with such other Victorian writers as Browning, Trollope, and W. S. Gilbert a profound misunderstanding and distrust of the legal mind, was as much disturbed by legal system as the lack thereof. It is perhaps suggestive that Dickens's satire does not merely attack abuses of the law, it attacks the fundamental postulates of the British legal system. Dodson and Fogg are contemptible less because they are lawyers than because they are grasping, mean, and hypocritical human beings. Dickens aims a subtler shaft at Perker, Mr. Pickwick's solicitor, an amiable and seemingly harmless man who cannot restrain his admiration for the acuity of Dodson and Fogg, and it is Perker, not his opponents, who is the prototype of the lawyers of *Bleak House:* Tulkinghorn, Vholes, and Conversation Kenge. None of these proves to be guilty of anything approaching sharp practice; on the contrary, they are all offered as examples of capable and conscientious legal practitioners, and the evil they give rise to is not a consequence of their abusing their functions but of their performing them as well as they do. (pp. 209-11)

The law, especially British law, is an instrument of justice which often seems to the layman to put a higher value on consistency and orderly procedure than on justice itself. That in any given instance the law is capable of doing manifest injustice, no one would deny, but that the elaborate body of procedures, fictions, and precedents is the safest guarantee against capricious or arbitrary judgment, and in the long run, in the majority of cases, the most efficient mechanism of seeing justice done is the common ground for the defense of systems of jurisprudence. Justice becomes a by-product of law, and the law itself, by a kind of natural descent from the primitive trial by combat, assumes the character of an intellectual contest in which attack and counterattack, the play of knowledge, ingenuity, and skill, are of transcendent interest, even when the result is a matter of indifference. It amounts to no parodox, then, to say that the lawyer cares nothing for justice; he cares only for the law. Of the justice, that is to say, of the social utility, of his professional activity he is presumably convinced antecedently to his engaging in it, but he goes about his business secure in the knowledge that justice will best be served by his shrewdness in outwitting his adversary. To the lawyer the law is intellectual, abstract, and beautiful, like a game of chess, and it is just here that the fundamental ground of Dickens's quarrel with him lies. Justice for Dickens was generally open and palpable. He couldn't understand why man's natural emotional response to injustice wasn't a sufficient impetus to lead him to correct it if he could. With the abstract and intellectual approach to the evils of life Dickens had no sympathy and no patience at all, and the law, therefore, became for him a comprehensive symbol of an attitude toward life that seemed to him perverse and wrong. Dickens's anti-intellectualism is concentrated and brought to bear in his satire on the law.

But there is special point and relevance to the attack on Chancery in *Bleak House.* In the first place, Chancery exemplifies more perfectly than the law courts properly so-called the characteristically slow and circuitous processes of British jurisprudence. Its ritual was more intricate, its fictions more remote from actualities, its precedents more opaque, than those of the Queen's Bench, or the Exchequer, or the Court of Common

Pleas. And of course the slowness of Chancery proceedings was legendary. . . . [The High Court of Chancery] provided a microcosm of the legal world of nineteenth-century England, magnifying the law's essential features and reducing its flaws to absurdity. In the second place, Chancery is specially appropriate as an image of the kind of responsibility that *Bleak House* is really about. The Lord Chancellor's legal responsibility is of a curious and distinctive character. The law courts, with their various ramifications and subdivisions, civil, criminal, and ecclesiastical, exist to provide a bar where anyone who believes himself injured according to the common or statute law may plead his case. But the law has many loopholes, and it is desirable that some provision be made to redress wrongs which are not covered by any exisitng law. Moreover a considerable body of potential litigants—chiefly widows and orphans—being unable to plead in their own behalf, must be protected against injustice. The Lord Chancellor's Court was devised for just such a purpose, to provide relief where the ordinary channels of legal procedure offered none. (pp. 211-13)

At one end of the scale is the Lord Chancellor in Lincoln's Inn Hall, at the other is Jo, society's outcast, with no proper place of his own, "moving on" through the atrocious slum of Tom-All-Alone's, itself a "monument of Chancery practice," for its dismal and neglected appearance proclaims its connection with Chancery. Who will take responsibility for Jo? Not government, engaged in an endless wrangle over the proper emolument for the party faithful; not religion, in the person of Mr. Chadband sermonizing over Jo's invincible ignorance; not law, concerned only with Jo's "moving on"; not organized charity, which finds the natives of Borrioboola-Gha or the Tockahoopo Indians a great deal more interesting than the dirty home-grown heathen. Jo subsists entirely on the spasmodic generosity of Snagsby, who relieves his own feelings by compulsively feeding half-crowns to Jo, or on the more selfless generosity of Nemo, who supplies Jo's only experience of human companionship until Esther and George and Allan Woodcourt come to his aid. Jo's function as an instrument of Dickens's social protest is clear. In his life and in his death he is a shattering rebuke to all those agencies of church and state which are charged with the care of the weak and the helpless and the poor, from the Lord Chancellor's court down to the Society for the Propagation of the Gospel in Foreign Parts. And Jo's experience throws a strong glare on the causes of their inadequacy; they fail conspicuously and utterly because they are nothing more than machines, because they are illuminated from the head, never from the heart, because, ultimately, they fail to acknowledge Dickens's most important moral and social maxim, that human beings can live together only on terms of mutual trust and love.

Between the Lord Chancellor and Jo, Dickens illustrates every relation of dependency which is possible in civilized society, in every one of which, as we have seen, the Lord Chancellor himself participates by a species of legal fiction. Consider, for example, the condition of parenthood. Every child begets a responsibility in his parents; in *Bleak House* Dickens examines a wide range of cases in order to trace the extent to which that responsibility is successfully discharged. Only a very few parents in the sick society of this novel manage to maintain a healthy and normal relation with their children; one must contrive to get as far from the shadow of Chancery as Elephant and Castle, to find a domestic happiness like the Bagnets'. The virtuous mean of parental devotion is the exception; more often we have the excess, like Mrs. Pardiggle's ferocious bullying of her children, or still oftener the deficiency, instanced by

Mrs. Jellyby's total neglect of her family, or Harold Skimpole's similar behavior toward his. But the real symptom of disease is the frequency with which we find the normal relation between parent and child inverted. Skimpole is, as he frequently avers, a child, but the engaging qualities which this pose brings to the surface are quickly submerged again in his reckless self-indulgence, and his avocations, harmless or even commendable in themselves, the pursuit of art and beauty, become like the flush of fever, a sign of decay when we recognize that they are indulged at the expense of his responsibilities as the head of a family, and that his existence is so thoroughly parasitical. But just as there are parents who turn into children, a few children turn into parents. Charley Neckett, for example, at the death of her father is rudely thrust into maturity at the age of thirteen with a brother of five or six and a sister of eighteen months to care for. . . . Even Esther herself exhibits a kind of reversal of roles. Like Charley (and a good many other characters in the story) she is an orphan, and her relations with the other inmates of Bleak House are curiously ambiguous and ill-defined. She is ostensibly the companion of Ada Clare and the ward of Mr. Jarndyce, both of which offices confer upon her a dependent status, yet in this household she assumes the moral leadership, a leadership which is explicitly recognized by the others' use of such nicknames as Little Old Woman, Mrs. Shipton, Mother Hubbard, and Dame Durden. (pp. 214-16)

[*Bleak House*] is an intricate, if not always very systematic, study of the bonds which link human beings together. The very shape of his imaginative vision is perhaps given by the invariability with which people are seen as demonstrating potential or actual relations of responsibility or dependency toward one another. Here are masters and servants, landlords and tenants, employers and employees, professional men and clients, officers and men, all enforcing the inescapable truth that men and women share a common destiny. . . . [The] breadth and the closeness of Dickens's analysis of society imply both his conviction that man cannot evade the consequences of his brotherhood with every other man, and his belief that human brotherhood can never be adequately affirmed or practiced through agencies which are the product of the intellect alone. (pp. 219-20)

It is virtually impossible to put all the events of *Bleak House* into a single causal sequence, or even into several, as long as we understand by "events" what that word normally signifies, that is, births, deaths, betrothals, marriages, whatever, in short, is likely to be entered in the family Bible, and perhaps also such other occurrences (of a less public and ceremonial nature) as quarreling, making love, eating, drinking, working, etc., which may have an interest of their own. *Bleak House* is full enough of "events" in this sense; I count nine deaths, four marriages, and four births. The difficulty is in assigning their causes or their consequences. What are we to make of the death of Krook for example? The question is not one of physiology; I don't propose to reopen the question of spontaneous combustion. The question is properly one of psychology: how is Krook's death related to the play of human motives and purposes? The answer, of course, is that it is not so related at all; it is a simple *deus ex machina* whose only artistic justification is to be sought at the level of symbolism. Rick Carstone's death, by contrast, is integrated with plot, for though its physiological causes may be as obscure as those of Krook's death, its psychological causes are palpable and satisfying. . . . Events have a way of taking us by surprise, for even though Dickens is careful to create an appropriate atmosphere whenever he is

about to take someone off, the time and manner of death are generally unpredictable.

The artistic center of the novel is generally taken to be Chancery, but if so it seems to me that Chancery functions as a symbol, not as a device of plot. We are permitted glimpses from time to time of what "happens" in Chancery, but Jarndyce and Jarndyce obviously follows no intelligible law of development, and so it is meaningless to talk about a Chancery plot or subplot. Furthermore, though Chancery affects the lives of many, perhaps all, of the characters in *Bleak House,* it does not do so in the sense that significant events take place there. The only event in the Court of Chancery that proves to have significant consequences for the people outside is the cessation of Jarndyce and Jarndyce when the whole property in dispute has been consumed in legal costs. But this is itself a conclusion reached by the stern requirements of economics rather than by the arcane logic of the law. Chancery affects men's lives the way God does, not by direct intervention in human affairs, but by commanding belief or disbelief.

In a few instances events align themselves in something approaching a genuine causal sequence. The story of Rick Carstone, for example, who undergoes a slow moral deterioration because he is gradually seduced into believing in Chancery, provides an example of a meaningful pattern of events. But Rick's story is neither central, nor altogether satisfying, principally, I believe, because it is observed only at intervals, and from without. It remains true that it is all but impossible to describe what happens in *Bleak House* by constructing a causal sequence of events.

The difficulty largely disappears, however, when we stop trying to discover a more or less systematic pattern of events, and try instead to define the organization of the book in terms of discovery, the Aristotelian anagnorisis. The plot, in this case, is still woven of "events," but the word now signifies some determinate stage in the growth of awareness of truths which are in existence, potentially knowable, before the novel opens. Events, in the original sense of that term, become important chiefly as the instrumentalities of discovery. Krook's death, for example, leads to the unearthing of an important document in Jarndyce and Jarndyce, and incidentally to the disclosure of a complex web of relations involving the Smallweed, Snagsby, and Chadband families. The murder of Tulkinghorn and the arrest of Trooper George are red herrings, designed to confuse the issue, but ultimately they make possible the complete unveiling of the pattern of human relations that it is the chief business of the novel to disclose. The progressive discovery of that pattern is, then, the "plot" of the novel, and it constitutes a causal sequence, not in that each discovery brings about the next, but in that each discovery presupposes the one before. We need to know that Lady Dedlock harbors a secret which she regards as shameful before we can discover the existence of some former connection between her and Nemo, and we need to be aware of that connection before we can add to it the more important discovery that Esther is the daughter of Nemo and Lady Dedlock. And so on, until the whole complicated web stands clearly revealed.

This kind of structure is, as everyone knows, the typical pattern of the detective story. Such fundamentally human concerns as crime and punishment lie outside the scope of detective fiction, in which the murder may take place before the story begins, and the retribution may finally catch up with the murderer after it ends. The plot of the detective story consists simply in the discovery—withheld, of course, as long as possible—of the one hypothesis which will account for all the disparate facts or "events" that make up the story. The interest is centered, in classical specimens of the genre, not in the events, but in the process by which the events are rendered meaningful, ordinarily in the activity of the detective as he proceeds toward a solution. *Bleak House,* of course, has many detectives. Not counting the unforgettable Inspector Bucket "of the Detective," a great many characters are at work throughout the novel at unraveling some private and vexing problem of their own: Mr. Tulkinghorn, stalking Lady Dedlock's secret with fearful persistency, or Mr. Guppy, approaching the same mystery from Esther's side, or Mrs. Snagsby, endeavoring to surprise her husband's guilty connections, or even Esther herself, troubled by the riddle of her own mysterious origin and still more mysterious participation in the guilt of her unknown mother. But the presence or activity of a detective is incidental to the main scheme of such fiction, from *Oedipus Tyrannus* onward, to present a mystery and then solve it. The beginning, middle, and end of such an action can be described only in terms of the reader's awareness; the beginning consists of the exposition in which the reader is made aware of the mystery, that is of the facts that require explanation; the end consists of his reaching a full understanding of the mystery which confronted him, for when all is known the story must come to an end. The middle, then, is comprised of his successive states of partial or incorrect knowledge.

The mystery presents itself, in the typical detective novel, with crystalline purity. Someone has been murdered; the problem is to discover, in the graphic but ungrammatical language of the usual cognomen, Who done it? In *Bleak House* the problem is somewhat different. It is true that there is a murder, and that the murderer must subsequently be picked out of three likely suspects, but the main mystery, the one that sustains the motion of the whole book and gives it a unity of plot, is not a question of determining the agent of some past action (though the mystery may be formulated in these terms) so much as it is a question of establishing the identity of all the characters involved, and in the world of *Bleak House* one's identity is defined according to his relations to other people. . . . Esther's identity is secure when she discovers who her parents are, and this is certainly the heart of *Bleak House*'s mystery, but that discovery comes shortly after the middle of the book, when Lady Dedlock discloses herself to Esther. The novel is not complete until all the relations of its various characters are recognized and established (or re-established) on some stable footing. Sir Leicester Dedlock must adjust his whole view of the world to conform to the discovery he makes about his wife; harmony must be restored between Mr. Jarndyce and Rick; Esther must discover her true relation to Mr. Jarndyce—and to Alan Woodcourt. Even the minor characters must be accounted for: Trooper George must become once again the son of Sir Leicester's housekeeper and the brother of the ironmaster; Mr. and Mrs. Snagsby must be reconciled as man and wife; all misunderstandings, in short, must be cleared away.

One of the most curious features of *Bleak House,* one of the attributes which is most likely to obtrude itself and bring down the charge of staginess is Dickens's careful husbandry of characters. That he disposes of so many may perhaps be worthy of remark, but still more remarkable is the fact that he makes them all, even the most obscure, serve double and triple functions. . . . That the novel thus smacks of theatrical artifice constitutes a threat to the "bleakness" of *Bleak House,* for we are never confronted, in this world, by the blank and featureless face of total strangers, the heart-rending indifference of the

nameless mob; all the evils of this world are the work of men whose names and domestic habits we know, and for that reason, it would appear, are deprived of most of their terrors.

Perhaps the most serious charge that can be brought against the artistry of *Bleak House* grows out of some of the characteristic features which I have been discussing. How can the discerning reader avoid being offended, it will be argued, by a novel which obviously wants to say something serious and important about society, but at the same time contrives to say it in the most elaborately artificial way possible? How can we be serious about social criticisms which come to us through the medium of the most sensational literary genre, and are obscured by every artifice of melodrama? The objection seems to be a damaging one, but I wonder if Dickens's employment of the techniques of the detective story and of melodrama may not enforce, rather than weaken, his rhetorical strategy. The plot, as I conceive it, consists of the progressive and relentless revelation of an intricate web of relations uniting all the characters of the novel, by ties of blood or feeling or contract. (pp. 221-27)

The bleakness of *Bleak House* is the sense of hopelessness inspired by the knowledge that men and women, subjected to the common shocks of mortality, will nevertheless consistently repudiate the claims which other people have on them. The sense of hopelessness is intensified and made ironic by the closeness, figuratively speaking, of their relations to other people (sometimes, of course, the closeness is literal, as in the hermetic little community of Cook's Court, Cursitor Street). It is appropriate that the novel should be shaped by discoveries rather than by events, for the sense of hopelessness, or bleakness, can hardly be sustained in a world that can be shaped to human ends by human will. The events of this novel are accidental in a double sense; most of them are unplanned and unpredictable, and they are moreover nonessential to the view of human experience that Dickens is concerned to present. Human relations, the ones that are important, are not constituted by events (though they may be revealed by events— Esther's smallpox, for example), because events just happen, they follow no intelligible law either of God or man. Human relations are inherent in the nature of society, and the duty of man is therefore not something arbitrary and intrinsically meaningless which can be prescribed and handed down to him by some external authority (like law); it is discoverable in, and inferable from, his social condition and only needs to be seen to command allegiance. The tragedy of *Bleak House* is that awareness of human responsibility invariably comes too late for it to be of any use. Nemo's, or Coavinses's, or Jo's membership in the human race is discovered only after his death, and Sir Leicester Dedlock awakens to recognition of the true nature of the marriage bond only when his wife has gone forth to die. Still, it is important to have that awareness, and the most effective way to produce it, surely, is to make its slow growth the animating principle of the novel. (pp. 227-28)

Bleak House is a novel without a center. There is no single character to whom the events of the story happen, or with reference to whom those events are significant. It is not even possible . . . to understand the novel as a unified system of coordinate plots or of plot and subplots. Except for this want of a center the novel might be compared to a spider web in which each intersection represents a character, connected by almost invisible but nonetheless tenacious filaments to a circle of characters immediately surrounding him and ultimately, of course, to all the other characters. But the spider web has a center (and a villain), so a more appropriate comparison might be made to a continuous section of netting, or better still, to the system of galaxies which make up the universe. It appears to a terrestrial observer that all the other galaxies are receding from him at an unthinkable rate of speed, implying that his own post of observation constitutes the center of things. Yet the centrality of his own position is merely a function of his special point of view. So with **Bleak House.** Esther is, in this special sense, the "center" of the novel, not because she so regards herself, but because she supplies the central observation point, because relations are measured according to their nearness or farness from her just as astronomical distances are measured in parsecs—heliocentric parallax (in seconds of arc) as recorded for a terrestrial observer. To pass, for example, from Esther to Nemo (or some other intermediate character) to George to Matthew Bagnet is to move, so to speak, from the center outward. But Esther is not really the center of the novel. To think of her as such is to destroy or at least to do serious violence to Dickens's view of the world and transform his indictment of society into a sentimental fable. To deprive the novel of its specious center, to provide it with a new perspective which, like stereoscopic vision, adds depth, is an important function of the omniscient point of view. (pp. 230-31)

[The secret of Dickens's success in **Bleak House**] is partly in that instinctive and unfathomable resourcefulness of the artist, which enables him to convert his liabilities into assets, to make, for example, out of such an unpromising figure as Esther Summerson, just the right point of view character for the first-person portion of the novel. But the real greatness of **Bleak House** lies in the happy accident of Dickens's hitting upon a structural form (the mystery story) and a system of symbols (Chancery) which could hold, for once, the richness of the Dickensian matter without allowing characters and incidents to distract the reader from the total design. The mysterious and sensational elements of the plot are not superimposed on the social fable; they are part of its substance. The slow but relentless disclosure of the web of human relations which constitutes the novel's inner form makes a superb mystery, but what makes it a monumental artistic achievement is that it is also and simultaneously one of the most powerful indictments of a heartless and irresponsible society ever written. **Bleak House** is the greatest of Dickens's novels because it represents the most fertile, as well as the most perfectly annealed, union of subject and technique he was ever to achieve. (p. 237)

> *Robert Alan Donovan, "Structure and Idea in 'Bleak House'," in his* The Shaping Vision: Imagination in the English Novel from Defoe to Dickens, *Cornell University Press, 1966, pp. 206-37.*

ALBERT J. GUERARD (essay date 1969)

[*Characterizing* Bleak House *as "a truly audacious experiment" in narrative technique and controlled point of view, Guerard assesses Dickens's style in the context of the development of the modern impressionist novel. Like Algernon Charles Swinburne (1913), Morton Dauwen Zabel (see Additional Bibliography), William Axton (1965), Q. D. Leavis (1970), and Joan D. Winslow (1976), Guerard concludes that Esther's portion of the narrative in* Bleak House *succeeds as a stylistic experiment.*]

[**Bleak House** was,] more than is usual with Dickens, a controlled and even innovative experiment in novelistic form. The interlocking of the narratives, the complicated impressionist game of anticipations and recurrences and delays, especially

the experiments in point-of-view and narrative voice—these technical and rhetorical issues, though often mentioned, deserve to be more fully explored.

We necessarily bring certain predispositions and expectations to **Bleak House.** We know that Dickens is not writing two separate or distantly related novels, as Faulkner would in *Wild Palms.* We assume from the first that there will be connections between them. Moreover, we know that much of any Dickens novel is simply entertainment for its own sake. A great deal of irrelevance will turn out to be truly irrelevant. Yet we also know that any event, any chance scrap of conversation, any suddenly appearing buffoon or miserable stray, may prove to be important.

Reading, then, we experience life as unorganized often incoherent flow, rich in digression, yet all the while we remain alert for open or secret connections. And of course we know, at a second reading, that there are two halves of the novel. In the first several hundred pages we begin to explore a mystery and watch the gradual creation of a world. We come to know several secrets. The second half, much more direct and dramatic, deals with the tragic impact of knowledge.

The structure of **Bleak House** offers, of course, an example of expressive form. The confusions of the "police-tale" plot—its irrelevances and monstrous delays, its real incoherence at times, its incidents that fail to connect or connect in absurd ways—reflect the novel's overall vision of society as incoherent, muddled, drifting. But even the counterpoint of the two narratives is in a way expressive. Esther's narrative conveys a struggle to create or preserve a quiet, decent, orderly world, and a family circle sheltered from environing chaos. Esther long continues to see the fog of Chancery from a distance. But Bucket draws her into nightmare, into an appalling and violent pursuit she scarcely understands at all. So there is Esther's story of struggle for connection and love. "Only connect." Against it is juxtaposed the roving conductor's present tense narrative of lost or broken human connections and buried causality. His is a narrative of people probing the darkness around them or leading meaningless lives of compulsive repetition. The structure of **Bleak House,** even at its most exasperating, reflects its fictional world.

But the novel's movement is also, and more importantly, rhetorical: engaged in manipulating the reader's sympathies, moral attitudes, hopes, fears. It not merely provides a variety of themes and interests and entertainments, but interweaves them in such a way as to achieve peculiar and even grotesque effects. (pp. 333-34)

On the whole Dickens succeeded remarkably well in reconciling discontinuous part publication with the demands of overall vision and structure. The threads of plot are tightly held from the start, and characters remain true to what they have been, remarkably so in terms of dialogue. Once Dickens had caught and created an individualizing manner of speaking, he almost never lost it. Moreover, certain peculiarities of structure would have much the same effect on the reader of the completed volume and the reader of monthly parts: the almost *terza rima* alternation, at times, of the two narratives. The recurrence of dramatic scenes or theatrical effects every few chapters would create anticipation in the reader of the monthly parts as well as moments of excitement. But these anticipations and excitements exist to a degree also for us. They should displease only the Jamesian purist, or the reader who insists on seeing **Bleak**

House as social comment or philosophical vision only. (pp. 334-35)

Where does **Bleak House** stand in the history of impressionist fiction? There is an obvious sense in which the atmosphere of the novel, and especially of its opening, may suggest impressionist painting.... (p. 337)

In **Bleak House** the paucity of the early hints and the multiplication of interests, as well as the interlocking of narratives, point to later impressionist works. But the Hawdon-George-Tulkinghorn plot certainly furnishes the most striking, if most tiresome, example of impressionist confusion and delay. The great difference, of course ... is that the mystifying seems to exist for its own sake. Granted an overall seriousness of theme as well as an attempt to reflect life's disorder directly, **Bleak House** does not have the intense awareness of psycho-moral ambiguity that we find in [Conrad's] *Lord Jim* or, for instance, [Melville's] *Benito Cereno*. In Chapters 19-34 the issue is not primarily psychological. Hence our impatience may be comparable to our impatience with Conrad when, in the Patusan military chapters, he continues to use the disgressive impressionist method.

Much has been made of the novel's grand symbolic insistences and controlled play of imageries, as well as of its intricately manipulated plot. In novelistic terms, however, the technical triumph is one of point-of-view and narrative voice. Esther's narrative is told in a plausible voice, and one that modulates effortlessly from her quiet plain unprofessional opening to pleasing Dickensian rhythms and to a spoken style that yet maintains a slight formality. Some critics have complained that she is allowed to write too well, as though a different hand had stepped in to take over the narrative. But Dickens quickly and wisely establishes this privilege, while always preserving the sense that a person (and not a very complex person) is speaking or thinking aloud. Ultimately Esther must have the power to write the pages of sensitive Proustian intuition, or to narrate with swift and dramatic force the discovery of her mother at the gate of the burial ground. Already by the end of her second chapter (while remaining her ''simple'' self) she is authorized to use such a word as ''purblind,'' and to achieve a striking ending of a chapter: ''The purblind day was feebly struggling with the fog when I opened my eyes to encounter those of a dirty-faced little spectre fixed upon me. Peepy had scaled his crib, and crept down in his bed-gown and cap, and was so cold that his teeth were chattering as if he had cut them all.''

The important distinction is that Esther is simple but not artless, though her art is well concealed. A very little more insistence on her lack of cleverness would have been damaging, or any discussion of her ''authority'' to report this or that. In fact she moves effortlessly in her very first chapter from panoramic summary to fully remembered scene; she assumes a total power to recall action, place, dialogue. Should we even say ''recall''? Most of her narrative (nominally written eight years later) creates for us a normal fictional present. In only one respect does her narrative regularly or repeatedly fail, and that is in presenting Krook and Miss Flite, and perhaps even Skimpole. There is too great a discrepancy between her calm consciousness and quiet voice and the eccentricities she has to report. The result is that the eccentricities themselves seem to have been imposed on her narrative from without, forced authorial conceptions rather than pure autonomous creations. On the other hand, Esther reports vividly the comic scenes of Guppy's proposals. Nothing is more difficult for a retrospective narrator

than to bring himself, herself dramatically onto the scene. In the first proposal ... a very few fine strokes—Guppy's curious scrutinizing glances and her movement behind the protective table—enable us to see both Guppy and Esther, as well as listen to his desperate chatter. We are there.

So I suspect it is Esther's sickening goodness, rather than any deficiency in her narrative, that has led a number of critics to look for technical flaws.... Nevertheless, perhaps the main reason for the seeming weakness of Esther's narrative manner is that the manner of the ''roving conductor,'' speaking in the present tense, is so extraordinarily successful. This second narration is an example of fully conscious and sophisticated *expertise*. Moreover it released (and this does not always accompany *expertise*) a very pleasing voice capable of several successful variations or styles. The nominal limitations it put upon itself—that the narrator was *not* exactly the author, and as a rule could *not* go into the consciousness of the characters—prevented Dickens from indulging his worst rhetorical temptations. The point-of-view kept him at a distance. (pp. 339-41)

By the end of the second chapter we are very close to Lady Dedlock, not within her but watching her, as she reacts with surprise to the copyist's handwriting. The roving conductor no more knows the future, at this moment, than she does.

He may take us, ''as the crow flies'' ..., from one place to another, from the Court of Chancery to Chesney Wold. He is not at all an embodied person (named or unnamed) but rather a personalized, often suave and ironic watching consciousness. He watches and responds humanly (and sometimes with shock as well as curiosity) *to what is happening now*. The great opening chapter establishes a theme, a setting, a fictional world; but also establishes the wide powers of this watching consciousness. We know from the magisterial surview of this fog-bound world that our conductor can take us anywhere, even into the cabin of a ''wrathful skipper'' or onto the deck where his apprentice boy is shivering. But also (as we learn by the sixth and seventh paragraphs of the novel) he can in some sense participate in the public or group consciousness, and can ask the kind of question a moderately informed person might ask: ''Who happen to be in the Lord Chancellor's court this murky afternoon besides the Lord Chancellor, the counsel in the cause, two or three counsel who are never in any cause, and the well of solicitors before mentioned?'' Our roving conductor can do almost anything in terms of narration. But not everything. Often he is simply a recording presence. If necessary, however, he can summarize a conversation, or telescope a scene, or give a quick summary of the past. Telescoping, which would seem a function of memory, can occur within this immediate present. (pp. 341-42)

The normal mode of impressionist narration is memory, the free wandering memory of Marlow [in Conrad's *Heart of Darkness*] or of Faulkner's Miss Rosa [in *Absalom, Absalom!*]: memory which can do anything, and need not trouble itself about transitions. Dickens' roving conductor, nominally imprisoned in the present, achieves some of this impressionist freedom. Repeatedly he seems to present an unselective flow of life, brute life in all its digressiveness.... (p. 343)

But the roving conductor, like Esther, knows when to efface himself in the great dramatic moments, or when to confine himself to stage directions. Thus the confrontation of Guppy and Lady Dedlock. Similarly, in the major scene of Bucket's revelations ..., the conductor frequently does no more than record the superb dialogue and give very brief stage directions.

But here too he occasionally intervenes, with comment or conjecture, to distance us briefly from the action and so intensify strain. And he can choose to give us a rapid and playful summary of Mrs. Snagsby's incoherent and irrelevant speech, rather than let it interrupt too long the essential drama.

Why does this watching presence, and narration in the present tense, give such a peculiar effect of people as puppets acting roles determined by their characters and destinies? It is something more than that sense of a web of inescapable connection, or the general vision of destinies controlled by secret actions of the past. The characters seem literally helpless as they move about a room or from one place to another. On the one hand, they are extraordinarily real, and extraordinarily free from *authorial* control: real beings, whom the conductor watches. Yet our sense remains that they are not free, that they are stuck on a platform that has moved out of the past and is moving into the future. The events are happening now, and the characters cannot stop them from happening. Moreover, they are largely unaware of the connections which, we know, will affect them.

The reasons for this helplessness seem to be technical (or fictional) not philosophical. For one thing, we see things happen, people move and speak, without having been exposed to the memories, reflections, and physical sensations which contribute to choice; we see people act without experiencing, directly, their inner lives. Moreover, they cannot, as we watch them, throw themselves into the past or project themselves into the future. In the world of fiction too they are, only, here. Also (and this is very important) they are being watched by that ghostly roving conductor but are unaware that they are being watched. This is an experience everyone has from time to time. If we watch a solitary person move about a room, silently, he seems to us to be a puppet bereft of freedom. He recovers it when he looks up to see the watcher.

If the roving conductor achieves these very particular effects, he also provided Dickens with a congenial method: one that stimulated or released a pleasing voice. . . . The point of view, with all its limitations as well as freedoms, stimulated certain qualities of language. With brooding aloof tones the speaker or watcher of these mysteries seems also to be responding to a mysteriousness inherent in life itself.

Esther's narrative purports to be a written document, but often gives an impression of quiet speech and undramatic remembering. The longer sentences accumulate items as they would occur to a mildly relaxed mind; the syntax may become looser and the rhythms more slack. But there are many occasions when Esther's prose seems truly self-effacing: the plainest possible medium for communication of an event or scene. The roving conductor does not pretend to be writing, though his prose at times is composed and literary. . . . We have indeed the sense of a man thinking aloud or speaking aloud, but to no particular audience; or, again, the effect (in Graham Greene's phrase for *Great Expectations*) of "quiet interior speech." The openings of chapters and especially of monthly parts tend to be phrased with studied delicacy and care, and there are a few set pieces which are in a wholly written not spoken prose—that long set piece and highly composed paragraph on stillness, for instance, immediately prior to the death of Tulkinghorn. (pp. 344-46)

Possibly the most distinctive quality of the roving conductor's voice is its unhurried pace: a sense that it is moving wholly at its ease, even in rather long and elaborate sentences. This is a matter of rhythm but also of syntax. The sentences may be complicated but are seldom periodic, and the surprises—the sudden turns the syntax may take—seem to be natural turns of mind rather than literary flourishes. (pp. 346-47)

Present tense narration necessarily implies an interior or a speaking voice. What else can it naturally be, unless it is only a camera unable to comment? But the concept of a personal voice in writing involves especially the way the mind moves. Does the way a particular style moves—through hesitation, digression, backtracking, etc.—seem to imply a personality, a voice speaking rather than machine writing? With the roving conductor, pleasing unpretentious rhythms sometimes counterbalance highly compressed or highly organized analogical observation. So too colloquial asides may support and justify striking analogy. . . . (p. 347)

We must remember, finally, that these calm and unexcited voices—Esther's and the roving conductor's—are instruments of control in rendering a disorderly, chaotic and at times hysterical world. The reunion and separation of Esther and Lady Dedlock . . . might have led, in another Dickens novel, to a dreadful exordium in blank verse; but here to these calm, plain and moving statements of almost Biblical directness: "We held one another for a little space yet, but she was so firm that she took my hands away, and put them back against my breast, and with a last kiss as she held them there, released them, and went from me into the wood." The roving conductor becomes, of course, more excited than this at certain moments of high drama, or of public indignation. And there is the death of Jo . . . , in which Dickens' own voice breaks through: the cart all shaken to pieces, the groping in the dark, the learning of the Lord's Prayer, the "Dead, my lords and gentlemen"—to vie, in its shameless and doubtless successful appeal to the emotions, with any of the other deaths in Dickens' fiction. But such outbursts are rare. All in all, the roving conductor was exceptionally successful in engaging the author's best dramatic and stylistic impulses, while suppressing or limiting the worst.

Such, from the vantage of the technique and rhetoric of fiction, *Bleak House* appears to be: a certainly flawed, very uneven, at times tiresome narrative, and one that doubtless attempted too much, but with its moments of high reward. Clearly the exercise in impressionist digression and delay failed to become as meaningful as that of, say, *Lord Jim;* nor does the drama of perception take on the psychological seriousness of *Absalom, Absalom!* Dickens was not Conrad nor Faulkner nor Henry James in conscious experimentation with the art of fiction. And doubtless criticism will always return to *Bleak House* rather for its creation of life and its dark yet comic vision of the human lot; or even, it may be, for [its] philosophical insights. . . . My intention has been only to redress slightly the balance, and to say that the strength of *Bleak House* derives not alone from these larger meanings, or from its big obvious symbolisms. There was also a truly audacious experiment in structure and point-of-view and narrative voice, and an expertness both instinctive and calculated.

Without *Bleak House* and *Our Mutual Friend,* in any event, the modern impressionist novel would not have been the same. (pp. 348-49)

Albert J. Guerard, "'Bleak House': Structure and Style," in The Southern Review, *Vol. V, No. 2, April, 1969, pp. 332-49.*

Q. D. LEAVIS (essay date 1970)

[*An influential English critic, Leavis edited the quarterly review* Scrutiny *with her husband, F. R. Leavis. In her writings, Leavis*

*promoted a conservative approach to literature, one that would
uphold the tradition of such stylists as George Eliot, Henry James,
and Joseph Conrad. According to Leavis, ''literary criticism is
not a mystic rapture but a process of the intelligence." Positing
that Esther's characterization has traditionally been underrated
by critics of* Bleak House, *Leavis remarks that Esther is, in fact,
''Dickens's first successful attempt at creating a girl from the
inside." Further, she praises Esther's ''interesting psychological
consistency'' and strong character. Leavis's view offers a contrast
to that of Taylor Stoehr (see Additional Bibliography).]*

[Esther] is fully human and framed to be a very carefully
complete study of what a sensitive child is made into in such
circumstances as are posited for her. Her aunt is a very moderate version of a Murdstone; Esther understood her to be 'a
good, good woman' and that it was Esther's own fault that she
was illegitimate. On her aunt's death she feels obliged to bury
her doll, her only friend, with tears—in a grave in the garden;
it is left to us to deduce, since Esther doesn't understand her
action herself, that she was showing herself obedient to the
rule laid down for her of 'submission, self-denial, diligent
work'. Esther, like Little Dorrit the child with the stigma of
prison birth, accepts her lot without complaint or self-pity and
is even excessively docile, though Esther nonetheless suffers
from the 'wound' she knew she had received in childhood,
'the fault I had been born with (of which I confessedly felt
guilty and yet innocent)'—the child's confusion between what
it is told it should feel, and what it feels instinctively, could
hardly be better put. She undertakes to atone by being useful
and trying to win love. Thus is explained her constantly noting
down compliments paid her and marks of affection shown her,
which are to her necessary proofs that she has won the right
to be alive. Yet, ignoring the care and the wonderful imaginative insight it has taken to build up and maintain Esther's
case, criticism habitually complains of her for showing the
traits that are proof of Dickens's indignant and compassionate
understanding of an aspect of the life of his time that only a
great novelist could demonstrate. Esther can hardly believe
people when they tell her how useful, pretty and lovable she
is and writes it all down to be able to. Esther has never been
Pet or Baby to anyone and even in Mr. Jarndyce's circle her
excessive maturity is recognized by nicknames like 'Dame
Durden' and 'Little Old Woman'.

Esther has an interesting psychological consistency, and is the
more remarkable for being Dickens's first successful attempt
at creating a girl from the inside—Florence Dombey is convincing only in childhood and Agnes never at any time. Esther
is even a young lady too, so that to have established her through
autobiography is a real triumph for such a thoroughly masculine
writer. We know more about Esther than any other young
woman in Dickens's novels and she has more reality than any
except Bella Wilfer (before Bella's marriage). Esther is always
true to her own peculiarities but they are not mannerisms; her
individual sensibility is shown in her unusual sensitiveness to
her surroundings anywhere and her quite personal descriptions
of natural scenery. Chapter III, Esther's first, is as a chapter
one of the very best Dickens ever wrote in a mode not committed to satire (as the remarkable first chapter of *Dombey* is).
Her submissiveness makes her blame herself whenever as a
child she is unsuccessful in winning the affection she craves,
but she never criticizes the others, so that her submissiveness
becomes painful to us, as it was meant to. The psychology of
an illegitimate child of her time can never have been caught
with greater fidelity. She is intelligent through the intensity of
her sensibility but, unlike Pip, not morally timid or weak. On
the contrary, she demands respect by her strength of character

and resourcefulness, which comes out in all her contacts with
Mr. Guppy, in her sympathy with Miss Flite, Caddy, Jenny,
Jo and any other unfortunates she meets, and in her very natural
self-compensation in instinctively mothering younger girls like
Charley, Caddy and Ada. It is in keeping too that she doesn't
allow herself to entertain the idea that Allan Woodcourt is
attracted by herself or that she is entitled to love and marry
him, and that she should persuade herself it is her duty to refuse
him in order to marry her guardian out of gratitude—this looks
like Dickens reconsidering the idea of the Strong marriage and
admitting his mistake there, for Jarndyce himself sees such a
marriage would be wrong and resigns Esther to a more appropriate husband. Esther has forced herself to burn the treasured
posy Woodcourt had left for her exactly as she had buried the
beloved doll in her younger phase. [One is constantly surprised
by Dickens's persistence in 'filling in' Esther when he has so
much else on his hands in this demanding novel.] What is even
more remarkable is Dickens's imaginative insight into her reactions to exceptional situations, as when, her looks having
been ruined by the smallpox, she cannot bear to meet Ada in
case she sees signs in Ada's face of being shocked or repelled;
after steeling herself to the meeting she hides behind the door
at the last minute. When she learns from her mother the secret
of her birth her second reaction—the first having been to re-
assure and comfort her mother—is to relapse into the feelings
of her childhood and wish she had never been born. While it
is Dickens who had treasured the anecdote of the village girl
who, though literate, follows her illiterate bridegroom in making a cross instead of signing the marriage register, in order
not to 'shame him', it is appropriate that the novelist should
give it to Esther to tell and comfort herself with because it
represents the delicacy of feeling which she desires to find in
others at this point, to support her in her distress, against her
fear of being shamed by those she loves. All this and much
more in Esther's history is proof that Dickens had the true
creative artist's power of feeling himself into and sustaining a
character who is as far as possible from being himself. But
there is even more striking testimony, in demonstrating that
Dickens also understood that such a nature under such strains
must develop signs of psychic stress, and though Esther is not
driven to the borders of mania like Miss Wade, Dickens gives
remarkably convincing glimpses of her difficulties. . . . [Es-
ther's] last dream is the one that is representative of the theme
of the novel, a nightmare version of what Ada and Richard
had debated at the beginning of the novel when they had been
inducted into the Chancery world where there is no freewill
except in moral decisions. Esther can pray 'to be taken off'
and not to be a 'part of the dreadful thing' but it is only by
her love and sympathy that she can get off. We are in *Bleak
House* well on the way to the prison world of *Little Dorrit*
where each is locked into his own appointed or self-made cell,
and to the still worse state of Pip in *Great Expectations* who,
wholly passive, has not even moral choice until his world falls
into ruins around him and he sees that he is tied hand and foot
to the Newgate society by a contract he never knowingly entered into. Esther's sensibility is unique in Dickens's novels
not only in being essentially feminine but in being different
from the sensitiveness shown by other unhappy Dickens children, even Little Dorrit, who is a working-girl and not a lady
and whose experience is limited to the society of the poor, and
her possibilities of action very circumscribed. And Esther is
mature, not innocent with David Copperfield's disabilities, her
early experiences having given her a precocious understanding
of the painfulness of life and the cruelty of circumstance which
enables her to understand John Jarndyce's kind of innocent

goodness and appreciate it and *yet* see that it was as to Skimpole self-indulgent and that Skimpoles need firm treatment (which she can and does provide). Yet she has womanly tact and, like the Ibsen of *The Wild Duck,* she sees that in some circumstances it is better to let well alone, in accordance with which she hopes that Caddy and Prince will never see through Mr. Turveydrop but go on believing in him happily since they will have to put up with him anyway. Esther is not sentimentalized and as a good angel is altogether more acceptable than Agnes, showing an advance on that part of the previous novel. For Dickens is also prepared to show us Esther's limitations—her shrinking from criticism of mothers (psychologically this is right, from her), as in her attempt to stop Caddy from judging her mother to have failed in her duty—Dickens is clearly on Caddy's side here—and her own effort to deny her dislike of Mrs. Woodcourt who is anxious her son should not be recognized by Esther as a suitor.

It is necessary to insist on the success Esther represents for the novelist since she is so important to the novel as the registering consciousness and has been consistently under-rated by critics; it is she through whom we apprehend the truth about Mr. Vholes who is thus brought into the mode of the book as not merely a legal shark, like Conversation Kenge and Guppy, but a thematic presence. We might not rejoice in Esther's society ourselves but she is impressive as a similar character, Fanny Price, is in *Mansfield Park* (another link with that novel, and there is something incipiently Victorian about both Fanny herself and Jane Austen's attitude to her). Through Esther, as through Fanny, we get a just apprehension of the other performers in her world. (pp. 155-60)

> Q. D. Leavis, "'Bleak House': A Chancery World,"
> in Dickens the Novelist by F. R. Leavis and Q. D.
> Leavis, 1970. Reprint by Pantheon Books, 1971,
> pp. 118-86.

TREVOR BLOUNT (essay date 1970)

[Blount presents Krook as the unified embodiment of "the themes of self-deception, blindness, and hypocrisy" and his death as the self-destructiveness of evil. For other perspectives on Krook's significance in the novel see the excerpts by Jack Lindsay (1950), Edgar Johnson (1952), A.O.J. Cockshut (1962), and Morton Dauwen Zabel (see Additional Bibliography).]

Krook—gin-sodden, sordid, grasping, mean, petty, enclosed, squalidly evil—is not important in himself [in **Bleak House**]. His death is the death of one of Dickens' eccentric recluses: a male Miss Havisham [from **Great Expectations**]. But he is the simulacrum of his brother Chancellor, and the Rag and Bottle Emporium is a travesty of that other graveyard of wasted usefulness, that other storehouse of wasteful papers and documentation, the Court of Chancery itself. But the symbolism extends even beyond the specific Chancery satire. Dickens is prophesying self-destruction to "all authorities in all places under all names soever, where false pretences are made, and where injustice is done." The sweep of Dickens' castigation derives its force and validity from the vividness of character and incident—the dramatic impact of Krook as a personage, the filth of his Marine Stores (the dirt conflicting with the "sea" reference), and the weirdness of his death—of which the whole novel is composed. But each element supports and quickens the meaning of every other component. Dickens talks of "false pretences," and we see how the themes of self-deception, blindness, and hypocrisy (all related together as a form of moral myopia) interfuse and intermingle. He talks of

"injustice," and it is Jo, Guster, Charley, Caddy, Prince, Richard, and Miss Flite, and even the infant Esther, whom we link together. The novel is organized in parallels and welded together with unmistakable correspondences. The death of Krook is important in itself in terms of plot and mystery; yet it is even more important when combined with its affiliated threads of significance. It "is the same death eternally—inborn, inbred, engendered in the corrupted humours of the vicious body itself." Evil will end by poisoning itself: this is the positive moral standard underlying the specific satire in the novel. (p. 191)

Krook is a sinister parody of the Lord Chancellor, and his emporium is a comment on Chancery muddle. Krook as allegorical figure is a stronger element in the novel than Krook just as Krook, and as we read we regard him on this double level simultaneously. Dickens moves with such dexterity and rapidity from scene to scene, each caught with incisive accuracy, that we do not ask for an inner life for Krook. He is important for what his projection makes him and for what he represents, not for what he feels. We accept him as an outline of a man, boldly drawn, yet having no inward experience. We do not enquire why, on the simply psychological level, he has a liking for dust and must, or why he is impelled to buy and not to sell. He *is* useless acquisitiveness; and the inner emptiness almost represents the pointlessness of what he does. But he is just one manifestation of the vice, and he forms part of the intricate system of parallels and cross-references that distinguish the force, truth, and method of Dickens' maturer novels, with their acute social analysis, from the high-spirited picaresque of his earlier career. The system of cross-references achieves variety of impact through plot manipulation, vivid visual portraiture, and an economical double-tiered frame of allusion. Dickens' scenes are, as regards meaning, rather reminiscent of a mediaeval "pageant," with one level of meaning a comic Heroding on the ground; on the cart, another level of serious satire; and up above, a third level of generalized moral relevance. Thus Krook's shop is an absurd flight of imagination—an exercise in the macabre. But it also equates with pernicious muddle, heartache and waste: the sins of Chancery. Beyond this again, moreover, is the implied attack on all obstructive systems, the true function of which is lost in formalities that have degenerated into senseless ends-in-themselves, whereas once they might have been means-to-an-end. (pp. 197-98)

[What is extraordinary about Dickens's use of spontaneous combustion] is the way he has taken the salient points from the learned accounts he consulted and incorporated them so smoothly into his scenes and episodes. But they are made multifunctional: story material in themselves, at once startling and vivid, and yet splendidly appropriate to the thematic concerns of the novel as a whole. . . . There is the "heap of ashes"; the "greasy and stinking moisture"; the "moist ash-coloured soot"; the probing nature of the sootflakes that "penetrated the drawers" and "even got into a neighbouring kitchen," so that "in the room above the said soot flew about"; the "greasy, loathsome, yellowish liquor"; "the unusual stink." Dickens' account even parallels the mention . . . of the liquor trickling down the "lower part of the windows," and the "gluish moisture" spread over the room where the combustion itself took place. But what he has borrowed, he has improved on. The gradual hinting of what is happening—the stench, the soot, the grease, the state of the actual room—is made by turns darkly comic and startlingly horrific. By humor, by plot-matter, and by touching-in the normal life of the neighborhood, Dickens "places" and controls the sensationalism. The associated details—the white ash and the black log—of the charred remains, hark back to the original description of Krook, with his froth of white stubble and his gnarled skin. The alcoholism that must ''cause'' his combustion is made functional, too, that is, made part of the recurrent theme of isolation and insulation, and the related theme of escape. The gin-bottles are made part of the idea of Krook's trade in rags and bottles, while, at times, Krook is thought of as a bundle of rags. So, in running imagery, thematic parallels, ''externalized'' characterization, and suspenseful narrative, the materials of ''science'' are transmuted into multifunctional, artistic elements. Beyond even this, however, it is necessary for us to suspend our disbelief temporarily and to try to imagine that the phenomenon of spontaneous combustion can actually occur. . . . Even more important, however, is the weight and force that the symbol acquires if we do, in fact, make the necessary imaginative leap. Dickens makes the connection quite plain. It is an instance to add to his use of topical materials like the burial ground scandals, Chancery abuses, and the Ministerial Crisis involving Lord John Russell. For Dickens, his metaphors and symbols had to work on the level of pure, firm-based fact if their wider metaphorical and symbolic significance was to be truly valid. If we make the leap of imagination in the case of spontaneous combustion, therefore, and not only admire Dickens' art but ''believe'' in his ''science,'' the power of the Krook simulacrum as a parody of the High Court of Chancery derives added force. What Dickens dramatized in the case of Krook he means to apply equally to Chancery itself—and even, by implication, to all the parallels with Chancery (such as Parliament, child-farms, benevolent societies, and missionary organizations) which are focused in *Bleak House* as a whole. The Krook travesty has a generalized relevance, therefore, and it represents in its extreme form the moral affirmation the novel makes in the face of evil. Thus the assertion that the self-engendered poisons of evil will eventually work their own destruction is given positive, yea-saying authority. Such a positive commitment on the part of Dickens is necessary to balance and qualify the objective realism—for which Dickens still lacks his due—that clearly records, though with tender compassion, the death of a romantic idealist like Richard Carstone and of a victim of neglect like Jo, in a world where acquisitiveness prospers and petty treachery secures a ''fypunnote.'' (pp. 210-11)

> Trevor Blount, ''Dickens and Mr. Krook's Spontaneous Combustion,'' in Dickens Studies Annual, Vol. I, edited by Robert B. Partlow, Jr., Southern Illinois University Press, 1970, pp. 183-211.

JOHN LUCAS (essay date 1970)

[*Lucas maintains that* Bleak House ''*composes a visionary judgement about a whole society*'' *through Dickens's effective contrasting of disease and death imagery with* ''*positive images of the moral life.*'' *His assertion that the realism of the novel contributes to its* ''*power to disturb*'' *contradicts the commentary of Stefan Zweig (1919).*]

[Dickens's *Bleak House*] seems to me by far the most upsetting of all his works. Such a statement may lead me into difficult territory. I realize that the affective fallacy could be wheeled up to dispossess me of the critical relevance that I find in *Bleak House*'s power to disturb. Still, I see no way round accepting that Dickens wanted to upset his readers and that he succeeded. . . . Again and again, *Bleak House* destroys our comfortable notion of art as a refuge, an enclosed world answering to its own laws and prescriptions; it turns outward to the real

Photograph of Dickens taken in 1859. The Bettmann Archive, Inc.

world and in so doing banishes for ever the idyllic world of the *Pickwick Papers*.

The art that consoles a rotten society has no worthy purpose. Hence Dickens's hatred of Skimpole. Sir Leicester Dedlock approves of Skimpole as an artist, and he is even more approving when Skimpole calls himself 'a perfectly idle man. A mere amateur'. . . . And Dickens has a wonderfully witty contempt for Sir Leicester 'condescendingly perusing the backs of his books, or honouring the fine arts with a glance of approbation'. (p. 204)

And yet though Dickens is . . . quite certain what the purpose of art must be, he is far from dreaming that it is capable of breaking open the frozen seas within all men. He knows only too well that the artist must accept the misappropriation of his purpose. In a brilliant and vicious scene, Skimpole recommends turning Jo out, and then sings a ballad about a peasant boy 'Thrown on the wide world, doom'd to wander and roam, / Bereft of his parents, bereft of a home', a song 'that always made him cry, he told us'. . . . There is a vibrancy and power about Dickens's hatred of Skimpole that seems to me to mark something new in the novels, an absolute determination to reject any notion that art is sufficient unto itself. The point may be difficult to grasp in the abstract, but *Bleak House* everywhere affirms it. (p. 205)

In forcing his readers to recognize that the fictional world of *Bleak House* turns out to be about the real one, Dickens forces them to the acknowledgement of a world they wish to deny. . . . [In] large part *Bleak House* is upsetting precisely because of its use of actualities. For the novel is about England as a society which is failing of mutuality, and it brings out the absence of 'the loving union of multitudes of human lives in generous feeling and noble purpose.' . . . And as Dickens's audience is repeatedly offered what look to be fictions that turn out to be facts, so the characters in the novel themselves mime their readers' efforts to escape reality only to find it thrust at them. For many of the characters practise escape-routes that lead them inexorably back to face what they wish to escape from; the novel is unremitting in its methods of denying the denials of brotherhood.

Carlyle's statements about brotherhood are meant to be definitive of mid-Victorian England. *Bleak House* is no less definitive. Its scale is dizzying. For it is about England, no less, and it composes a visionary judgement about a whole society seen—or so it feels—in all its randomness, a mighty maze utterly without a plan. One of the most brilliant tricks of a novel which is surely the most brilliant in the language is to set the omniscient narrative in the continuous present, so that we have a sense of events being recorded as they happen rather than as they have been assimilated and understood (nobody could take seriously Dickens's casual pretence that the novel is set in the late 1830s). And the fact that in the end the multiple narratives form a pattern, gives a final authority to the concept of brotherhood; we are brought to accept the inevitability of what had appeared to be only contingent. Esther's narrative complements this trick, since it has to do with what seem to be entirely different matters and yet all the while is moving closer to the other narrative, until there is a total fusion of the two in the girl's reunion with the mother who has denied her. To put it rather differently, the novel realizes a moral pattern whilst miming the collapse of a social framework. (pp. 207-08)

We can begin conveniently enough with a remark of Sir Leicester Dedlock's. '"The floodgates of society are burst open, and the waters have—a—obliterated the landmarks of the framework of the cohesion by which things are held together."' . . . Sir Leicester is haunted by his apocalyptic imagination, and although his fears are comically treated, the novel as a whole takes seriously the collapse which he envisages. (p. 209)

Throughout the novel, Sir Leicester is treated with this courteous ruthlessness; and the narrator's poised and comprehensive knowledge give him an authority we do not feel ourselves in a position to challenge. By being even more civilized than Sir Leicester, he defeats him at his own game.

Sir Leicester's game is, of course, assuming that he embodies the natural right of government. . . . Once we grasp this fact we shall see that Dickens's satire against Sir Leicester's concern for the country is no trivial matter; it confronts some of the most deeply held convictions of the age. And as a whole the novel demonstrates that England's 'governors' have barely the glimmering of an idea about what England actually is. Dickens's pointing to this is more than his making a Disraelian formulation of two nations; for *Bleak House* demonstrates that there are multitudes of people living in profound ignorance of each other, so that the dream of government can be no more than a solipsistic game. . . . (pp. 211-12)

As a prestigious institution which destroys people's lives, Chancery is an apt instance of the mindless futility of law in all its aspects. For law has become a letter; justice means a blind adherence to formulae. . . . [The scene in which Jo is moved] offers us a glimpse of a world about which the Doodles, Coodles and Dedlocks are in as profound ignorance as Jo is of them. But that is not its main purpose nor what makes for

its real strength. Its greatness and centrality lie in how much it typifies about the society that Dickens explores in *Bleak House*. Casual though it may seem, it has the sort of relevance and justness that I have suggested Dickens repeatedly manages to find for all his best work. It is intensely dramatic in its rendering of the novel's central issues. It also has about it something of the reporter's desire to make his readers acknowledge the unfamiliar; but beyond that it characterizes law as a dreadful madness. Coming across this scene we remember the Dodger's contemptuous remark that 'This ain't the shop for justice'. But the matter is more profound now; the policeman's passionless impartiality is a revealing parody of the prized impartiality of the law. It simply has no reference to the human beings it is supposed to serve. The policeman does not feel any personal dislike for Jo; he is merely doing his duty. But doing your duty in this society is an offence against decency and men's interests. And . . . much of the horror of the social situation that Dickens presents in *Bleak House* is caused by people doing their duty. (pp. 213-14)

Law, religion, education. They do not create and minister to the just society. On the contrary, they are products of an unjust society. Responsibility is in the hands of individuals and therefore futile; Jarndyce's powerlessness is in sharp contrast to the efficacy of the Cheerybles, because the very comprehensiveness of *Bleak House* requires a social mimesis that automatically rules out benevolence as a factor conditioning what society is. At best, Jarndyce is a recommendation. He is certainly different from those parodies of individual responsibility, Mrs. Jellyby and Mrs. Pardiggle.

The unjust society creates the hell of Tom-all-Alone's, of Jo, Krook, Nemo, the brickmakers, of all those untouchables who are denied identity and can be known only to the narrator. (p. 221)

In the great scene where Lady Dedlock makes Jo lead her to her lover's grave we are witness to one of the many denials of shared humanity which the novel presents. He is not to touch her, not to come near her, not to speak to her. The scene has a naked strength that both makes it immediately powerful and also serves a wider purpose of emblematizing a general condition that Dickens wants to shock us into an awareness of. Lady Dedlock cannot deny Jo. They are linked not just through her lover who is Jo's friend, but because she has to come to his world, as she finally returns to it in order to die. Her effort to escape, to keep clear, is metaphoric of a general condition which produces such perversions of the human as to make further attempts to keep clear all too understandable. Even the humane physician finds it difficult to acknowledge Jo. Woodcourt has to make 'a strong effort to overcome his repugnance' before he can go near the boy, and he 'constrains himself to touch him'. (pp. 223-24)

Jo *is* repulsive, the fact cannot and must not be ignored or softened, or it will demean the shock that comes from realizing that he is the inevitable product of a diseased society. Jo is a brutal and irreducible fact, as Dickens's audience had to know, and his infection is part of a general disease. The famous visionary passage about Tom-all-Alone's revenge—'It shall pollute this very night, the choice stream (in which chemists on analysis would find the genuine nobility) of a Norman house, and his Grace shall not be able to say Nay to the infamous alliance'—does not merely substitute typhoid for Blake's syphilis as emblem of retributive justice; it points up the fact that what is rotten in the state cannot be avoided by any amount of travel or denial or ignorance. For the innocent suffer, as

Esther's pock-marked face makes plain, and what may at first seem a randomness of suffering yields on closer inspection to the awareness of a formidable disease that takes root at all levels. Hence the echoic pattern of *Bleak House,* far grander and more comprehensive than *Dombey and Son.* And it is worth noting here how far Dickens has moved from *Oliver Twist.* In the early novel Fagin's black underground world made ominous but infrequent irruptions into the daylight world of the good, respectable society. Now, the corruption is everywhere.

Among children, for example. It is impossible to miss the number of diseased or maimed children in *Bleak House.* Quite apart from Jo, we have the Snagsby's epileptic maid Guster, Jenny's baby who dies and joins the 'five dirty and unwholesome children . . . all dead infants' of the brickmaker's family, Caddy's deaf and dumb child, the Smallweed family, which gives birth to men and women rather than children, and who 'bear a likeness to old monkeys with something depressing on their minds'; . . . and of course Esther herself, born into the knowledge which her godmother gives her, that her life has a shadow on it and that she is set apart. We may add to the list the childlessness of Sir Leicester Dedlock, whose sterility provides one version of the diseases that threaten the future health of England. And we shall see the pattern beginning to thicken still more if we consider the number of unnatural parent-child relationships in the novel. It is hardly necessary to list all these, they are so many and so obvious; it is enough to suggest how they add to the picture of a radical corruption of human values.

Underlying all the corruptions are, I think, the desire and often the need for money, and considerations of class; and on one or both of these motives most of the characters in the novel base their conduct. (pp. 224-25)

[Many characters in *Bleak House*] are trapped in the web of a corrupt system, and if they can be accused of complicity in it they can also be defended on the grounds that they do what they have to do out of economic necessity or duty to others. This is what the system does to individuals. And at its worst it enforces loyalty even on those whom it most obviously destroys; Jo after all does his duty in sweeping the crossing, day in, day out. Even he is a victim of a concept which so frequently turns into the cant of Mrs Jelleby, for whom 'public duties' are her 'favourite child'.

And yet the alternative is worse. The dream of breaking out of bondage to the system depends on an escapist notion of great expectations, a purely economic dream of freedom which destroys Gridley, Miss Flite, Rick, Lady Dedlock, and comes near to destroying George. All of them try to escape, none can; and I think myself that this is not intrusive moralizing on Dickens's part. He is not saying that freedom cannot be bought. Lady Dedlock buys it. But the cost in human terms is too high. . . . In the presentation of Lady Dedlock we have a relentless yet compassionate study of a person who damages herself terribly in trying to find freedom, for the search inevitably requires an attempt to escape from human commitment and produces an impoverishment of life. There is nothing shrill or pietistic about this; in his exploration of the society in which people find themselves, Dickens makes us aware of the pressures that can cause individuals to seek freedom. But he is no less aware of the cost; and Rick, Gridley and Miss Flite are all images of human beings for whom relationships have become unreal or warped as a result of their pursuit of that dream of freedom which feeds so destructively on them. George too is tainted by it. He runs away to enlist '"Making believe that

I cared for nobody, no not I, and that nobody cared for me"'. . . . But for all that he is committed to others, and it saves him.

And this brings us back once more to Dickens's study of the nature of duty. . . . *Bleak House* by and large offers convincing images of the moral life. And I think that they convince just because Dickens is so acutely aware of the problems and dilemmas of duty, to say nothing of the terrible pressures that it can exert. . . . The scene where we break in on that unexpected world of the children for whom [Charley] cares is without doubt immensely moving, but in its presentation of the girl's marvellous goodness it is also immensely exhilarating. Without fuss or special pleading, Dickens offers us an example of the moral life as an enriching and deeply humanizing process.

I realize that in using such terms I sound morally strident, but then Dickens, in common with all the greatest artists, has the ability to uncover those central truths about life for which there are only the obvious words. (pp. 235-36)

There are other such images in *Bleak House.* Phil Squod, the Bagnets, Woodcourt, Snagsby, Caddy and young Turveydrop are all examples of the moral life. They all manage to 'survive under . . . discouragement', as Esther says of Caddy. And the very fact that they do so is sufficient to act as refutation against any idea that Dickens's view of mid-Victorian society is one of unrelieved gloom or pessimism. These people are opposed to Mrs Jelleby who sweeps 'the horizon in search of duties' rather than performing 'her own natural duties and obligations'. (p. 237)

I think that in *Bleak House,* Dickens's awareness of the nature of change is extremely complex, so that even the rape of the countryside has to be balanced against our final vision of Chesney Wold:

> a vast blank of over-grown house looking out
> upon trees, sighing, wringing their hands, bow-
> ing their heads, and casting their tears upon the
> window-panes in monotonous depression. . . .

It is a deeply ambiguous image. Nature mourns the passing of the Dedlocks, of what might therefore seem to be the death of a natural order. Yet nature itself is dispossessed of all vitality. It is as though Dickens feels it necessary to provide this image as a corrective against the suggestions of health and life released in his other pastoral images.

Dickens's complex use of nature is crucial to his rendering of social change. So, too, is his use of the young. Many of them carry in their bones inherited ills. The destruction of youth and beauty of which we hear so much in *Bleak House* does not merely belong to the novel's rhetoric, it is fundamental to the imaging of the difficult and often disastrous process of change, of the corruptions of the past which linger into the present and condition the future. Yet for all the horror implicit in Caddy's mute child and the deaths of Jo and Rick, Dickens's vision is not one of total gloom. For against disease and death are the positive images of the moral life which can make themselves out of such horror. And it is part of the complex greatness of *Bleak House* that it should allow us to understand that change comes about through or is potential in such people as Charley, Phil and Snagsby, frail though they may seem in comparison with the forces set against them. The novel does not have to intrude a message or an ideal. On the contrary, in spite of Esther's way out—and even she carries the mark of society's ills—*Bleak House* denies the possibility of freedom, either from history, society or the self. But in forcing us to accept this,

Dickens also forces us to accept the truth that human beings are not inevitably crushed by the social forces they encounter and that despair is therefore ill-judged or an improper and Dedlock-like declaration of preferences. (pp. 242-43)

John Lucas, in his The Melancholy Man: A Study of Dickens's Novels, *Methuen & Co. Ltd., 1970, 353 p.*

J. HILLIS MILLER (essay date 1971)

[*Miller defines* Bleak House *as "a document about the interpretation of documents." The reader's task, Miller argues, is to interpret the meaning of the novel, just as the characters in the novel struggle to make sense of the circumstances influencing their lives. Miller's discussion of detective story elements echoes the earlier studies by Edmund Wilson (1941), Lionel Stevenson (1943), Robert Alan Donovan (1966), and Morton Dauwen Zabel (see Additional Bibliography).*]

Bleak House is a document about the interpretation of documents. Like many great works of literature it raises questions about its own status as a text. The novel doubles back on itself or turns itself inside out. The situation of characters within the novel corresponds to the situation of its reader or author.

In writing *Bleak House* Dickens constructed a model in little of English society in his time. In no other of his novels is the canvas broader, the sweep more inclusive, the linguistic and dramatic texture richer, the gallery of comic grotesques more extraordinary. As other critics have shown . . . the novel accurately reflects the social reality of Dickens's day, in part of the time of publication in 1851-3, in part of the time of Dickens's youth, in the late twenties, when he was a reporter in the Lord Chancellor's court. The scandal of the Court of Chancery, sanitary reform, slum clearance, orphans' schools, the recently formed detective branch of the Metropolitan Police Force, Puseyite philanthropists, the Niger expedition, female emancipation, the self-perpetuating procrastinations of Parliament and Government—each is represented in some character or scene. Every detail of topography or custom has its journalistic correspondence to the reality of Dickens's time. Everything mirrors some fact—from the exact references to street names and localities—mostly, it has been noted, within half a mile of Chancery Lane—to the 'copying' of Leigh Hunt and Walter Savage Landor in Skimpole and Boythorn, to such out-of-the-way details as the descriptions of a shooting gallery, a law stationer's shop, or the profession of 'follower'. Like Dickens's first book, *Sketches by Boz, Bleak House* is an imitation in words of the culture of a city.

The means of this mimesis is synecdoche. In *Bleak House* each character, scene, or situation stands for innumerable other examples of a given type. Mrs Pardiggle is the model of a Puseyite philanthropist; Mrs Jellyby of another sort of irresponsible do-gooder; Mr Vholes of the respectable solicitor battening on victims of Chancery; Tulkinghorn of the lawyer to great families; Gridley, Miss Flite, Ada and Richard of different sorts of Chancery suitors; Mr Chadband of the hypocritical Evangelical clergyman mouthing distorted Biblical language; Bucket of the detective policeman, one of the first great examples in literature; Jo of the homeless poor; Tom-all-Alone's of urban slums in general; Sir Leicester Dedlock of the conservative aristocracy; Chesney Wold of the country homes of such men. Nor is the reader left to identify the representative quality of these personages for himself. The narrator constantly calls the reader's attention to their ecumenical role. For each Chadband,

Mrs Pardiggle, Jo, Chesney Wold or Gridley there are many more similar cases. Each example has its idiosyncrasies (who but Chadband could be just like Chadband?), but the essence of the type remains the same.

Bleak House is a model of English society in yet another way. The network of relations among the various characters is a miniature version of the interconnectedness of people in all levels of society. From Jo the crossing-sweeper to Sir Leicester Dedlock in his country estate, all Englishmen, in Dickens's view, are members of one family. The Dedlock mystery and the case of Jarndyce and Jarndyce bring all the characters together in unforeseen ways. This bringing together creates a web of connection from which no character is free. The narrator formulates the law of this interdependence in two questions, the first in reference to this particular story and the second in reference to all the stories of which this story is representative. . . . (pp. 11-12)

In the emblematic quality of the characters and of their 'connexions' *Bleak House* is an interpretation of Victorian society. This is so in more than one sense. As a blueprint is an image in another form of the building for which it is the plan, so *Bleak House* transfers England into another realm, the realm of fictional language. This procedure of synecdochic transference, naming one thing in terms of another, is undertaken as a means of investigation. Dickens wants to define England exactly and to identify exactly the causes of its present state. As everyone knows, he finds England in a bad way. It is in a state dangerously close to ultimate disorder or decay. The energy which gave the social system its initial impetus seems about to run down. Entropy approaches a maximum. Emblems of this perilous condition abound in *Bleak House*—the fog and mud of its admirable opening, the constant rain at Chesney Wold, the spontaneous combustion of Krook, the ultimate consumption in costs of the Jarndyce estate, the deaths of so many characters in the course of the novel (I count nine).

With description goes explanation. Dickens wants to tell how things got as they are, to indict someone for the crime. Surely it cannot be, in the phrase he considered as a title for *Little Dorrit,* 'Nobody's Fault'. Someone must be to blame. There must be steps to take to save England before it blows up, like the springing of a mine, or catches fire, like Krook, or falls in fragments, like the houses in Tom-all-Alone's, or resolves into dust, which awaits all men and all social systems. It is not easy, however, to formulate briefly the results of Dickens's interpretative act. His two spokesmen, the narrators, are engaged in a search. This search brings a revelation of secrets and leads the reader to expect an explanation of their meaning. The novel as a whole is the narrators' reports on what they have seen, but these can only be understood by means of a further interpretation—the reader's.

Bleak House does not easily yield its meaning. Its significance is by no means transparent. Both narrators hide as much as they reveal. The habitual method of the novel is to present persons and scenes which are conspicuously enigmatic. The reader is invited in various ways to read the signs, to decipher the mystery. This invitation is made openly by the anonymous, present-tense narrator through rhetorical questions and other devices of language. The invitation to interpret is performed more covertly by Esther Summerson in her past-tense narrative. Her pretence not to understand the dishonesty, hypocrisy or self-deception of the people she encounters, though she gives the reader the information necessary to understand them, is such an invitation, as is her coy withholding of information which she has at the time she writes, but did not have at the time she has reached in her story: 'I did not understand it. Not for many and many a day'. . . . (pp. 13-14)

Moreover, the narrators offer here and there examples of the proper way to read the book. They encourage the reader to consider the names, gestures and appearances of the characters as indications of some hidden truth about them. Esther, for example, in spite of her reluctance to read signs, says that Prince Turveydrop's 'little innocent, feminine manner' 'made this singular effect upon me: that I received the impression that he was like his mother, and that his mother had not been much considered or well used'. . . . The anonymous narrator can tell from George Rouncewell's way of sitting, walking, and brushing his palm across his upper lip, as if there were a great moustache there, that he must 'have been a trooper once upon a time'. . . . (p. 14)

The reader of *Bleak House* is confronted with a document which he must piece together, scrutinize, interrogate at every turn—in short, interpret—in order to understand. Perhaps the most obvious way in which he is led to do this is the presentation, at the beginning of the novel, of a series of disconnected places and personages—the Court of Chancery, Chesney Wold, Esther Summerson as a child, the Jellyby household and so on. Though the relations among these are withheld from the reader, he assumes that they will turn out to be connected. He makes this assumption according to his acceptance of a figure close to synecdoche, metonymy. Metonymy presupposes a similarity or causality between things presented as contiguous and thereby makes storytelling possible. The reader is encouraged to consider these contiguous items to be in one way or another analogous and to interrogate them for such analogies. Metaphor and metonymy together make up the deep grammatical armature by which the reader of *Bleak House* is led to make a whole out of discontinuous parts. At the beginning of the second chapter, for example, when the narrator shifts 'as the crow flies' from the Court of Chancery to Chesney Wold, he observes that both are alike in being 'things of precedent and usage', and the similarity between Krook and the Lord Chancellor is affirmed in detail by Krook himself. . . . (pp. 14-15)

Such passages give the reader hints as to the right way to read *Bleak House*. The novel must be understood according to correspondences within the text between one character and another, one scene and another, one figurative expression and another. If Krook is like the Lord Chancellor, the various Chancery suitors—Miss Flite, Gridley, Tom Jarndyce and Richard Carstone—are all alike; there are similarities between Tulkinghorn, Conversation Kenge and Vholes; Tom-all-Alone's and Bleak House were both in Chancery; Esther's doll is duplicated with a difference by the brickmaker's baby, by the keeper's child at Chesney Wold and by Esther herself. Once the reader has been alerted to look for such relationships he discovers that the novel is a complex fabric of recurrences. Characters, scenes, themes and metaphors return in proliferating resemblances. Each character serves as an emblem of other similar characters. Each is to be understood in terms of his reference to others like him. The reader is invited to perform a constant interpretative dance or lateral movement of cross-reference as he makes his way through the text. Each scene or character shimmers before his eyes as he makes these connections. Think, for example, how many orphans or neglected children there are in *Bleak House,* and how many bad parents. The Lord Chancellor himself may be included, figuratively, among the latter, since his court was charged in part to ad-

minister equity to widows and orphans, those especially unable to take care of themselves. The Chancellor stands *in loco parentis* [in the place of parents] to Ada and Richard, the 'Wards in Chancery'.

In this system of reference and counter-reference the differences are, it is important to see, as essential as the similarities. Each lawyer in the novel is different from all the others. Esther did not die, like the brickmaker's baby, though her mother was told that she was dead. The relation between George Rouncewell and his mother is an inverse variant of the theme of bad parents and neglected children. Krook is not the Lord Chancellor. He is only a sign for him. The man himself is kindly enough, though certainly a bit eccentric. The Lord Chancellor is a kindly man too, as he shows in his private interview with Ada and Richard. They are sinister only in their representative capacities, Krook as a symbol of the disorder, avarice and waste of Chancery, the Lord Chancellor as the sign of the authority of his court. An emblem is always to some extent incompatible with its referent. A sign with ominous or deadly meaning may be an innocent enough old weather-beaten board with marks on it when it is seen close up, or it may be the absurd painting of 'one impossible Roman upside down', as in the case of the 'pointing Allegory' on Mr. Tulkinghorn's ceiling. . . . The power of a sign lies not in itself but in what it indicates. *Bleak House* is made up of a multitude of such indications. (pp. 15-16)

> *J. Hillis Miller, in an introduction to* Bleak House *by Charles Dickens, edited by Norman Page, Penguin Books, 1971, pp. 11-34.*

ELLEN MOERS   (essay date 1973)

> [*Moers inquires into Dickens's treatment of female characters in* Bleak House, *"the single 'woman question' novel in the Dickens canon." She asserts that, while most women characters are handled satirically by Dickens, Esther's function in* Bleak House *"is to try to repair the social damage." For earlier views on the role of women in* Bleak House *see the excerpts by John Stuart Mill (1854) and Belle Moses (1911).*]

[I would like to propose *Bleak House*] as the single 'woman question' novel in the Dickens canon. Like Chancery injustice, public ill-health, Parliamentary misgovernment and the rest, the women's issue seems here to be treated by Dickens as a major social theme, rather than as a diversion. And the twenty women characters of the novel can be seen to stand together as women. . . . The women of *Bleak House* look different, as a group, from the other women of Dickens: more forceful, more independent, more capable. Why this should be true is a complex question to which I can offer, in conclusion, only brief speculations. My main purpose is to argue that in this novel of 1853 Dickens conveyed his own response, a deeper and wider one than has been recognised, to the fact of female energies unleashed at the mid-century.

Mrs Jellyby and Mrs Pardiggle, those memorably acid caricatures of the Woman with a Mission, are the novel's most prominent signpost to Dickens's concern with the current question of woman's proper place. They show, of course, that his immediate, surface reaction to mid-century feminism was clear hostility—so clear that *Bleak House* seemed to such a reader as John Stuart Mill 'much the worst' of Dickens's novels, 'and the only one of them I altogether dislike' [see excerpt above, 1854]. Signposts of a different order are the two women characters to whom Dickens assigned unusual roles (unusual in

Dickens's fiction, that is): the person who tells the story in half the chapters, his heroine; and the person who commits the crime, the mystery figure at the end of the chase, his murderess. Worth remarking is the linkage of three 'tonal' areas of **Bleak House**—satirical comedy, moral sentiment, and melodramatic mystery—through the fact of femaleness.

For example, Esther Summerson, the heroine-narrator, is linked to the anti-feminist satire via the interesting, minor female figure of Caddy Jellyby. Exploited and neglected daughter of a mother with a Mission, Caddy serves to dramatise Dickens's initial point: that the misdirection of female energies to social causes, at the cost of domestic responsibilities, brings havoc to marriage, home, family, indeed all society. (pp. 13-14)

Esther's function here is to try to repair the social damage. It is Esther who teaches Caddy the wifely arts, helps her with her trousseau, and manages her wedding, an event ignored by Mrs Jellyby. It is Esther who nurses like Peepy Jellyby, and who pacifies the other neglected children of that barbarous household by telling them fairy tales—the rightest of all right educational procedures, in Dickens's well-known view. (p. 14)

For Dickens seems to have worked with a pattern for the heroine of **Bleak House:** she was to represent Right Woman in direct opposition to what he conceived as the Wrong kind. How far he meant to go in proposing Esther as an ideal of wide social consequences is shown by the tribute he pays her, in the words of Inspector Bucket, when she comes through the final chase scenes with flying, even royal colours. 'My dear,' says Bucket, 'when a young lady is as mild as she's game, and as game as she's mild, that's all I ask, and more than I expect. She then becomes a Queen, and that's about what you are yourself'. . . . Esther's mildness is an essential part of Dickens's ideal of womanhood. As his journalism shows, Dickens was repelled aesthetically and physically by the sheer bulk and noise of the 'agitating' feminist of his day. The woman who, 'calmly and quietly', does right for its own sake, as he wrote in *Household Words* shortly before **Bleak House**, 'sets a righteous example which never can in the nature of things be lost and thrown away.'

Esther's quietness, however, is not quietism; it is remarkable how much of an opportunity Dickens gives her to set an example and make her influence felt. She speaks up and speaks out, often and firmly. . . . The pivot of the novel, Esther's disfiguring illness, is the result of the epidemic spread by the pauper boy she brings home to be nursed at Bleak House.

Esther is in fact game, as well as mild: an intelligent, enterprising, wide-ranging force in the novel. Complex yet psychologically consistent, . . . Dickens's characterization of his single autobiographical heroine is that of a strong woman. And she does not stand alone: **Bleak House** is full of strong women. Every woman in the novel, whatever her moral or social role, appears to be in one sense or another a figure of force. This is in part what makes **Bleak House** unusual, and what subtly but pervasively alters the love relationships, tilts the emotional centre, and shifts the masculine point of view in the novel. (pp. 14-16)

Women work in **Bleak House;** significantly, married women work. The trooper's wife, Mrs Bagnet, is an interesting example, because Dickens intends her to be a wholly admirable, as well as a domineering woman. She dominates her home, her children, and every man in sight, starting with her grateful husband. A first-rate housekeeper, Mrs Bagnet is however also a female entrepreneur, who has begun a thriving business with

(as her husband puts it) 'two penn'orth of white lime—a penn'orth of fuller's earth—a ha'porth of sand—and the rest of the change out of sixpence, in money. That's what the old girl started on. In the present business'. . . . The business, incidentally, is a musical instruments shop, nothing to do with women's ordinary work—unlike, for example, Mrs Micawber's school project (doomed to failure) or Jenny Wren's doll-dressmaking.

The same can be said of the work of Mrs Bucket, the wife brought on surprisingly at the end of the novel to take over a share of her husband's duties as a detective. ('And,' says Bucket, 'she has acted up to it glorious!' . . . The same can be said also of Caddy Jellyby's enterprise, the dancing school: man's work at the time, as old Beau Turveydrop reminds us. Caddy marries into the Turveydrop family not only to be wife and mother, but also to help run a complicated and demanding business, and a good job she makes of it. The last view Dickens gives of Caddy in the novel is the one of financial success (she rides around in her own carriage) as well as female independence: her husband has gone lame and Caddy now runs the dancing-school business of her own. . . . (p. 17)

Thus the theme of woman's work outside the domestic sphere affects much more in **Bleak House** than Dickens's satire of the Woman with a Mission. It may penetrate even into his treatment here of female madness. Elsewhere in Dickens the mad women are ordinarily sexually warped, but there is nothing sexual about Mrs Smallweed, the senile grandmother of that Satanic clan, whose parrot shrieks reveal her obsession with high finance. Money is, of course, the obsession of all the Smallweeds, male or female, but Dickens may also want us to see his portrait of Mrs Smallweed as that of a woman gone mad *because* she has only money on the brain—a subject normally excluded from woman's sphere. (pp. 17-18)

There is an unusual amount of talk about divorce in **Bleak House,** perhaps because in the milieu of the Dedlocks it is a real possibility. But the idea of the broken marriage is raised also in connection with the Snagsbys, a couple whose marital difficulties possibly reflect some of the strains in Dickens's own home. (p. 18)

The decisive episode in the making of Esther's marriage to the man she loves seems to be not so much Jarndyce's final act of generosity as Esther's own symbolic pursuit: that odd, independent journey she makes to the port of Deal, which gives her the opprotunity to be 'among the first to welcome [Allan Woodcourt] home to England'. . . . Chance may provide the opportunity, but Esther seizes it, and on her own motion arranges a private interview with the young doctor—when, in a significant gesture, she raises her veil to him. Her ostensible motive is to show him the ruins of her beauty, destroyed by illness. But the effect of Esther's action is to renew rather than terminate the love affair that culminates in her happy marriage.

Deal is not the only place Esther goes to more or less on her own. She visits the Inns of Court and the back streets of London, covers the countryside with Inspector Bucket, inspects the habitations of rural poverty and landed aristocracy. Her freedom of motion, far from the confines of Bleak House, is of course a precondition of her role as narrator of a wide-ranging tale. But Esther's independent and often sudden and impulsive journeyings are not unique in **Bleak House:** there is a good deal of free-wheeling motion on the part of the women of the novel. Lady Dedlock goes off in careening flight, while Sir Leicester stays at home, immobilised by a stroke; Caddy Jellyby gets about in style, while Turveydrop goes lame. Jenny tramps off to the city, and Mrs Bagnet, in a moment of crisis, abandons her household to the care of her husband and, old trooper that she is, tucks up her skirts and marches off alone to the country. . . .

Separated off by themselves in this fashion, the strong women of *Bleak House* seem to present a travesty of the novel familiar to us all. For *Bleak House* is of course Dickens's imagining of a world run down, of weakness and confusion, of futility and paralysis. From Richard Carstone to Skimpole, the refrain is 'no Won't—simply Can't': waste of energy, the drying up of the will at its personal source is Dickens's point about the human consequences of such an institution as Chancery. What do all these active, pushy women have to do with the inanition of the Boodle-Coodle-Doodle system of government, of an Establishment in Dedlock? What does Esther's clearsightedness have to do with the blindness of social Fog? What does all the female motion in *Bleak House* have to do with a world Dickens shows to be in a state of Perpetual Stoppage—where poor Jo is ironically told to Move On! by representatives of a social order that has itself stopped moving?

There appears in fact to be an incongruity between the man's world and the woman's world of the novel, which may be Dickens's point: that the masculine world of *Bleak House* has fatally slowed down, while the feminine world is alarmingly speeding up. Neither development caused Dickens at mid-century, and at the outset of his final phase, to regard the future as anything but bleak. (It was a future which included such as Mrs Jellyby, last glimpsed going in for 'the rights of women to sit in Parliament' . . .—the very height of folly.) But there is more than mockery to Dickens's response to feminist agitation; there is in *Bleak House* a sense of anxiety that approaches respect, and an imaginative concern with the movement of women.

I have left until this point in my argument the most mysterious female figure in the novel: the murderess. Mademoiselle Hortense, Lady Dedlock's discharged maid, is an enigmatic character except for one point: Dickens insists on her as a woman of passion, dangerous passion. Her motive for killing lawyer Tulkinghorn is neither mercenary nor sexual, but seems to be mainly for revenge upon Lady Dedlock, on whom Hortense tries to throw suspicion of the crime. (pp. 20-1)

Why does Hortense do this, asks Esther? In what sense is her oddly self-destructive gesture, performed out of sight of Lady Dedlock, a 'retaliation'? What does Dickens mean to imply with his image of a woman in perilous motion, to which he returns for emphasis at the end of the scene? Contrasts at least were in his mind. The last line of Chapter 18 is: 'Still, very steadfastly and quietly walking . . . , a peaceful figure too in the landscape, went Mademoiselle Hortense, shoeless, through the wet grass.' 'Moving On' is the title of the following chapter, Dickens's evocation of a dead Chancery world, one *without* motion. Here Jo is berated by the constable for his obstinate immobility: 'He WON'T move on.'

Reckless, indepedent motion out of doors is a persistent metaphor of feminism or female heroism in our literature, where to rebel against the confinement of 'woman's place' is often, most dramatically, simply to go, to move, to walk. (pp. 21-2)

Ellen Moers, " 'Bleak House': The Agitating Women," in The Dickensian, *Vol. LXIX, No. 369, January, 1973, pp. 13-24.*

JOAN D. WINSLOW   (essay date 1976)

[*Winslow contends that by denying "the imaginative reality which so distinguishes the third person narrator," Esther markedly limits her ability to understand herself and her world. She suggests that the division within Esther's character indicates "a larger division found within Dickens's fictional world" between morality and imagination. For another detailed analysis of Esther's characterization see the excerpt by Q. D. Leavis (1970).*]

Esther Summerson has long been a problem, even an embarrassment, for admirers of *Bleak House*. It seems certain that Dickens intended her to be a positive moral force in the novel, the ideal of the responsible, loving, ordering human being that the unhappily chaotic world of *Bleak House* so desperately needs. Yet many readers confess a distaste for her. . . .

A number of critics have attempted to explain [the] combination of inhibition and ambivalent modesty in terms of Esther's psychology, and their general consensus is that her behavior is quite appropriate for such a repressed character, handicapped by a sense of worthlessness and guilt instilled during childhood. (p. 1)

Esther's inhibition of another one of her mental powers, her imagination, causes a profound inadequacy in her way of understanding herself and her world, an inadequacy that can be revealed most effectively through a combined character-narrator. Although highly valuing Esther's moral goodness, Dickens makes it plain that her tendency to reject her imagination, and her corresponding preference for certainty, clarity, fact, and reasonableness, lead her to crucial failures in understanding, which cripple her ability to deal with important personal crises.

This attitude toward her imagination is most easily seen when Esther's way of understanding and reporting her world is compared with that of the omniscient narrator in *Bleak House*. The unusual alternating-narrator structure of the novel draws attention to the contrast between the two. Esther is straightforward, responsible, involved, while the third-person narrator is an extravagantly fantastical yet aloof spectator. Each narrates thirteen sections, and it is at the beginnings of these sections that we are most conscious of the change in narrative manner. It is to be expected that Dickens would in these beginnings distinguish most sharply between his narrators. An examination of the first few paragraphs of each new narrative section yields an important finding. Almost every one of these beginnings is concerned to an unusual extent with the mental realm of imagination, knowledge, and certainty. The two narrators contrast sharply with respect to their mental attitudes, much more so than with respect to their moral attitudes. It is not, however, solely through the contrast between the two narrators that Dickens points out the inadequacy of Esther's mode of apprehension; if we look at only the series of beginnings of Esther's sections, we see revealed a remarkable drama in which Dickens first establishes her clear, rational mode of apprehension and then shows it to be inadequate in very important ways, ways which greatly affect the course of the story. (p. 2)

The most striking distinction of the beginnings of his sections, though, is their emphasis on the imagination—both as a topic of the narration and as an attribute of the narrator. It is a powerful transforming imagination that is described here: the mastiff at rainy, deserted Chesney Wold dreams of sunny weather and the house full of company "until he is undecided about the present, and comes forth to see how it is" . . . ; Snagsby, calling up the image of a brook that once ran near his shop, and meadows that were nearby, is so refreshed by this vision of the country that he "never wants to go there." ... But it is the narrator himself who possesses the most powerful imagination, in chapter nineteen transforming Chancery in summer into a sleepy harbor, and in chapter one accomplishing the brilliant metamorphosis of London into a primeval land of mud and fog. Such an imagination easily becomes animistic and magical; Bucket's magical forefinger ..., Mr. Vholes's stubborn and belligerent office ..., and vengeful "Tom," the personification of the slum Tom-all-Alone's ..., are all given life by the imagination of the narrator.

Esther Summerson is a very different kind of narrator, one who strives for certainty, who prefers the factual to the figurative, and who tries to understand and give order to her story. Her very first words call attention to her mentality; she tells us that she finds it difficult to begin because she is not "clever." ... In the next paragraph she characterizes her mental powers more specifically: having "a noticing way" is her aptitude, and— unlike the third-person narrator—understanding is her goal. We learn more about Esther's way of thinking, though, from the unconscious revelations she makes. In each of her first three paragraphs, she briefly entertains an imaginative fancy or an exaggeration and quickly rejects it, forcing herself to be literal and factual. (p. 3)

[Dickens is concerned] at the beginning with characterizing Esther's mode of thinking; he is establishing Esther as one who has a responsibility toward the truth and on whom we can rely. What is significant is that this characterization is done primarily through negatives, through calling our attention to what Esther's mind is *not*: not clever, not quick, not animistic, not exaggerative, not metaphoric. Here is the first suggestion that Esther's way of understanding the world is somehow deficient, a suggestion that will gradually be developed into a definite statement. But to be more accurate, it is not that Esther lacks these powers, for she does imagine and exaggerate and transform, however briefly. Rather, she refuses these powers; she denies the imaginative reality which so distinguishes the third-person narrator. (p. 4)

[His] choice of imagery to define Esther's mode of perception evidences the superb correspondence Dickens has established between narrative method and theme. Darkness, fog and sunshine are important symbols in the novel. The fog and darkness symbolize the condition of the fictional world; confusion, obfuscation and dreariness characterize Chancery, Chesney Wold, and all of the places of the novel where characters fail to perform their human responsibilities and thus allow the slide toward disintegration and chaos to gain impetus. Much of this failure is linked to a refusal to see—to look clearly and responsibly at the world; the Lord High Chancellor, who in chapter one manages to avoid recognizing the complaints of the man from Shropshire by remaining "legally ignorant" of him, is the first of many such examples. The uncertainty, lack of involvement, and preference for imagination over fact, which characterize the methods of the third-person narrator, perfectly match the world he describes.

Esther Summerson, as her name indicates, is the "summer sun" that can drive away the fog and darkness. Thematically, then, Esther, with her orderly, responsible, loving attitude toward those around her, is opposed to the forces of fog and darkness; the contradictory effects of Esther and Mrs. Jellyby on Caddy illustrate this opposition. Thus Esther's thematic significance is paralleled by her clear, orderly, controlled narrative method. (pp. 4-5)

In his criticism of Esther's tendency to reject imaginative and emotional truths, Dickens makes Esther's temporary blindness during her illness play a central role. He makes her physically blind in order to call our attention to her imaginative and emotional blindness. The blindness itself is not necessary to the novel's social themes; Esther's illness alone would be sufficient to link protected Bleak House with the evils of the slum Tom-all-Alone's, forcing the recognition of the connection of responsibility among all classes. It would be possible to read Esther's blindness as symbolic of society's, but such a reading seems inappropriate, for she is one of the few characters in the novel who is not morally blind. That the wrongs of the slum so demand attention that the "fairness" of Tom's revenge is irrelevant is a valid point made by the illnesses of Charley and Esther. Esther's blindness, however, seems to have other import. That Dickens intended a connection between the blindness and Esther's mental attitude is indicated by the attention given to her perception at the beginning of this seventh section.

In describing the effects of her illness, Esther tells us of an altered perception, an initiation into the irrational powers of the mind, and her rejection of this lesson. The description of the effects of her illness focuses on her mental state—or to be more precise, the alterations in her normal mental perceptions that take place during her illness. (pp. 6-7)

Although the physical blindness ends, Esther's mental blindness, her over-reliance on the rational and factual, continues. Dickens uses a second effect of Esther's illness to demonstrate her mistaken attitude; it has left its physical marks on Esther's face, marks which Esther interprets, because of their physical certainty, as more real than the love between herself and Woodcourt, which she must only feel, imagine and trust. She is unable to understand that her invisible qualities of character can be more apparent to one who loves her than her scarred face. This failure of vision on Esther's part leads her to betray her emotions by giving up her love for Allan and deceiving herself into believing that she is happy in accepting Jarndyce's proposal of marriage. It also permits her to be easily deceived by Jarndyce when he later plots to bring about a marriage between her and Allan. Although Dickens means Esther's way of approaching the world to be admired for its opposition to disorder and irresponsibility, he sees it as inadequate in its failure to recognize the reality of non-literal imaginative and emotional truths.

Dickens exposes Esther's self-deception at the beginning of her twelfth section, which opens with the preparations for the wedding between Esther and Jarndyce. We see her refusing to face her reluctance to marry him, drawn to making quiet preparations, which happen to permit her to keep her plans from Ada, and giving various excuses for this secrecy.... The purpose of Esther's maneuvering here is quite obvious. Such an effort of repression prevents her from recognizing the various clues to Jarndyce's real plans to provide a happy future for her. While we recognize something suspicious in Jarndyce's behavior, Esther does not.

The second line of action in which Esther refuses to allow her emotions and imagination to serve her involves Lady Dedlock. By the beginning of her eighth section she knows that Lady Dedlock is her mother. This knowledge arouses powerful emotions in Esther, which her own tendency toward repression, strengthened by the need for secrecy, causes her to react against severely. She refrains from mentioning her mother's name, tries to avoid conversations in which she might hear it, and when mention of Lady Dedlock does occur in her presence, she quickly escapes or mentally counts or repeats something in order to block out the conversation. These methods of repression and avoidance fail, of course; Esther cannot stop thinking of Lady Dedlock.

Esther's difficulty in handling this new relationship is imaginative as well as emotional. The fact that Lady Dedlock has two identities apparently the proud and distant lady and secretly the unhappy, guilty mother—is difficult for Esther to understand. (pp. 7-9)

The culmination of this line of action is the pursuit of Lady Dedlock by Esther and Mr. Bucket, and it is here that Esther's mental attitude does its greatest harm. For it is her failure to imagine her mother's emotional life—in particular, her failure ever to wonder about her mother's feelings toward her father—that is responsible for the tragic end of the pursuit. . . . Had Esther been able to imagine Lady Dedlock's feelings, and suggest that in such distress, her Dedlock life shattered, her mother might have sought this man from her earlier life, then perhaps Bucket's considerable knowledge and investigative powers would have enabled him to guess her destination sooner.

Perhaps Esther represses the thought of her father for another reason. The parallel between herself and her mother is too dangerous: each life has a younger man, loved and given up, and an older man chosen, for reasons other than love, to marry. Thus Hawdon is linked to Allan, and the thought of Allan is one Esther is trying to repress. For whatever complex reasons, Esther, rather than freeing her feelings and imagination to help her speculate about her mother's state of mind, directs her "every effort" toward subduing the emotions Bucket's arrival has aroused and toward attempting "fully to recover [her] right mind." (p. 9)

This failure to penetrate imaginatively beyond the surfaces of things remains Esther's chief weakness. At the end of her narrative Dickens again raises the telling question of her attractiveness. When Allan, able to see in Esther more than her mirror reflects, asks, "Don't you know that you are prettier than you ever were?", Esther records her answer: "I did not know that; I am not certain that I know it now." . . . Significantly, though, the novel leaves her on the brink of a more imaginative vision; she is entertaining an attitude of "supposing" that she does have beauty, and the novel ends without moving as usual to her rejection of that fancy.

Although this ending may indicate that Esther is moving toward a greater trust in the immaterial at the end of the novel, she has not matured imaginatively during the course of it. . . . She comes to recognize Allan's love and Lady Dedlock's tragedy by being confronted with them, not through any growth in herself or any change in her way of thinking, and these confrontations have no effect on that way of thinking. There is no evidence, in fact, that Esther ever recognizes that the betrayal of her imaginative powers served her so badly in these two personal crises. Thus a changed, matured perspective is not available to help place her limitations into a context of greater awareness. Instead, Dickens has the ironic light come from the contrast with the very different mental attitude of the third-person narrator. (pp. 10-11)

This division within the person of Esther Summerson reflects a larger division found within Dickens' fictional world. Despite his own use of his great power of imagination for moral ends, Dickens often seems to find goodness incompatible with imagination and intelligence. His most morally admirable characters tend to be weakly imagined and themselves dull and unima-

ginative while his villains and rogues are frequently the characters most vividly imagined as well as those with the greatest powers of imagination and intelligence. . . . It is not surprising, then, that this division shows up most obviously in *Bleak House*, where the ideally good character is also a narrator, and one whose clear, orderly, responsible narrative technique is symbolically related to the moral force in the novel. Bucket himself discovers this division in Esther: he learns of the inadequacy of her imaginative understanding as they pause before the entrance to the graveyard and he tries in vain to make her understand that the woman lying there is her mother, yet that same night he remarks that Esther has conducted herself so well during the difficult pursuit that she is a "pattern" of behavior. Neither assessment need be judged wrong, for Dickens himself has distinguished between her exemplary moral behavior and her inhibited imagination. (p. 11)

> *Joan D. Winslow, "Esther Summerson: The Betrayal of the Imagination," in* The Journal of Narrative Technique, *Vol. 6, No. 1, Winter, 1976, pp. 1-13.*

ADDITIONAL BIBLIOGRAPHY

Axton, William F. "Religious and Scientific Imagery in *Bleak House*." *Nineteenth-Century Fiction* XXII, No. 4 (March 1968): 349-59.
> Discusses the ways in which Dickens's use of apocalyptic imagery in *Bleak House* reflects some of the intellectual concerns of his time. Axton stresses Dickens's interest in evolution, providence, and biology.

Barnard, Robert. *Imagery and Theme in the Novels of Dickens.* Norwegian Studies in English, no. 17. Bergen, Norway: Universitetsforlaget; New York: Humanities Press, 1974, 164 p.
> A study of Dickens's search for form and technique as reflected in his major novels. Barnard characterizes *Bleak House* as the "most fully realized" of Dickens's novels and praises its organization, unity, and imagery.

Blount, Trevor. "Poor Jo, Education, and the Problem of Juvenile Delinquency in Dickens' *Bleak House*." *Modern Philology* LXII, No. 4 (May 1965): 325-39.
> Suggests that Dickens's portrayal of Jo in *Bleak House* is based on his knowledge of actual cases involving "destitute juveniles" in and around London.

———. "Dickens's Slum Satire in *Bleak House*." *The Modern Language Review* LX, No. 3 (July 1965): 340-51.
> Asserts that Dickens's concern for bringing about social change in England "is nowhere put more plainly" than in *Bleak House*. Comparing scenes from *Bleak House* with contemporaneous newspaper articles, Blount praises Dickens's ability to combine indignation with compassion in the novel.

———. "The Importance of Place in *Bleak House*." *The Dickensian* LXI, Part III, No. 347 (September 1965): 140-49.
> Examines Dickens's use of both real and imaginary landscape in *Bleak House*. Blount proposes that Dickens manipulated setting to enhance the characterization and atmosphere of the novel.

Burke, Alan R. "The Strategy and Theme of Urban Observation in *Bleak House*." *Studies in English Literature, 1500-1900* IX, No. 1 (Winter 1969): 659-76.
> Maintains that *Bleak House* is Dickens's "first mature use of the city" where the author explores the motif of observation by and of city dwellers.

Butt, John. "*Bleak House* Once More." *The Critical Quarterly* 1, No. 4 (Winter 1959): 302-07.
> Argues that Dickens modeled Miss Flite in *Bleak House* on a Miss R——, a plaintiff in the Court of Chancery in the 1830s. Citing

the successful transformation from real person to symbolic character, Butt praises Dickens for "reconciling social criticism with the art of fiction."

——, and Tillotson, Kathleen. *Dickens at Work*. London: Methuen & Co., 1957, 238 p.
    A general survey of Dickens's novelistic technique which documents the contemporary issues and news items reflected in *Bleak House*. By treating such topics as law reform, Bloomerism, and slum renovation, Butt and Tillotson demonstrate the topicality of *Bleak House*.

Chesterton, G. K. *Charles Dickens*. London: Methuen & Co., 1960, 224 p.
    An overview of Dickens's life and career. Chesterton places *Bleak House* in Dickens's third phase of development as a novelist because it exhibits "every characteristic of his new realistic culture."

Cohan, Steven. "'They Are All Secret': The Fantasy Content of *Bleak House*." *Literature and Psychology* XXVI, No. 2 (1976): 76-91.
    Argues that characters in *Bleak House* generally suffer from "some kind of psychic trauma" and that their actions are dictated by the logic of fantasy. Guilt, one of the main themes Cohan identifies in the novel, stems from social irresponsibility and sexual corruption.

Collins, Philip. *Dickens and Crime*. 2d ed. Cambridge Studies in Criminology, edited by L. Radzinowicz, vol. xvii. London: Macmillan & Co., 1964, 371 p.
    Relates Dickens's writings about crime to the rest of his work and to the social and historical characteristics of his age.

Crompton, Louis. "Satire and Symbolism in *Bleak House*." *Nineteenth-Century Fiction* 12, No. 4 (March 1958): 284-303.
    Analyzes Dickens's use of satire in *Bleak House* as it is expressed through imagery, symbolism, and the conflict between the real and the ideal. Crompton contends that Dickens's depiction of society in the novel is "unmatched in English fiction."

Dabney, Ross H. *Love and Property in the Novels of Dickens*. Berkeley and Los Angeles: University of California Press, 1967, 175 p.
    An inquiry into the treatment of love and finances in Dickens's novels. In his chapter on *Bleak House*, Dabney stresses Dickens's depiction of the tension between accepted social values and "the standards which really count."

Davis, Earle. *The Flint and the Flame: The Artistry of Charles Dickens*. Columbia: University of Missouri Press, 1963, 333 p.
    An examination of Dickens's novelistic technique. Davis places *Bleak House* in Dickens's dark period and further argues that it is "completely suffused with a social microcosmic pattern."

Deen, Leonard W. "Style and Unity in *Bleak House*." *Criticism* III, No. 3 (Summer 1961): 206-18.
    Assesses thematic and stylistic unity in *Bleak House*. Though he finds serious disunity in both its plot and point of view, Deen concludes that the novel is finally unified by Dickens's style.

Delespinasse, Doris Stringham. "The Significance of Dual Point of View in *Bleak House*." *Nineteenth-Century Fiction* 23 (December 1968): 253-64.
    Explores the interplay between the two narrative voices in *Bleak House*. Delespinasse describes the characteristics of each and contends that both narrators are necessary for the clarification of the novel's ultimate point of view.

Dyson, A. E., ed. *Dickens: "Bleak House," a Casebook*. Casebook Series, edited by A. E. Dyson. Nashville: Aurora Publishers, 1970, 284 p.
    A collection of essays on *Bleak House* which includes contemporary reviews, early studies, more recent commentary, and articles on the social background of nineteenth-century London.

Eliot, T. S. "Wilkie Collins and Dickens." In his *Selected Essays*, pp. 409-18. New York: Harcourt, Brace and Co., 1950.*

Compares Dickens's technique in *Bleak House* with that of Wilkie Collins in his mystery novels. Eliot proclaims *Bleak House* "Dickens's finest piece of construction."

Ford, George H. "Self-Help and the Helpless in *Bleak House*." In *From Jane Austen to Joseph Conrad: Essays Collected in Memory of James T. Hillhouse*, edited by Robert C. Rathburn and Martin Steinmann, Jr., pp. 92-105. Minneapolis: University of Minnesota Press, 1958.
    Appraises Dickens's attitude toward different social groups in *Bleak House*. Ford proposes that Dickens favors the helpless in society and that he often portrays those with the ability to help themselves, like the Smallweeds, as selfish.

Fradin, Joseph I. "Will and Society in *Bleak House*." *PMLA* LXXXI, No. 1 (March 1966): 95-109.
    Contends that *Bleak House* is a novel about that which "transcends social criticism." Dickens placed his faith in personal salvation, Fradin claims, not in the reform of public institutions but in the individual "act of private vision."

Friedman, Norman. "The Shadow and the Sun: Notes toward a Reading of *Bleak House*." *Boston University Studies in English* 3, No. 1 (Spring 1957): 147-66.
    An exploration of the theme of personal responsibility in *Bleak House*. Focusing on the character of Esther, Friedman details Dickens's use of imagery and symbolism to develop the main themes in the novel.

Hardy, Barbara. *The Moral Art of Dickens*. New York: Oxford University Press, 1970, 155 p.
    A survey of Dickens's handling of the interaction between society and the individual in his novels. Hardy argues that in *Bleak House* Dickens's "art is more strongly divided" than in his other novels, even though his version of society here is "clearest and most complex."

Harvey, W. J. *Character and the Novel*. London: Chatto & Windus, 1965, 222 p.*
    Addresses Dickens's technique for developing individual plots while keeping the unity of the novel as a whole intact in *Bleak House*. One key element in Dickens's success in this area, Harvey contends, is his use of Esther as a "moral touchstone" in *Bleak House*.

Holdsworth, William S. *Charles Dickens As a Legal Historian*. The Storrs Lectures. New Haven: Yale University Press, 1928, 157 p.
    Describes actual court procedures and problems in English law and assesses their use in *Bleak House*.

House, Humphry. *The Dickens World*. 2d ed. London: Oxford University Press, 1971, 231 p.
    Provides background information on the history, economics, religion, politics, and sociology of Dickens's era. House also contrasts Dickens's portrayal of certain contemporary events with historical accounts.

Jackson, T. A. *Charles Dickens: The Progress of a Radical*. New York: International Publishers, 1938, 302 p.
    Explores the relation between Dickens's work and his historical period. Jackson maintains that the final mood of *Bleak House* is one of defeatism and that Dickens's radicalism "might easily have emerged as positive Socialism or Communism."

Manning, Sylvia Bank. *Dickens As Satirist*. Yale Studies in English, edited by Richard S. Sylvester, vol. 176. New Haven: Yale University Press, 1971, 256 p.
    A comprehensive study of Dickens's satiric purpose and technique. Manning traces the "incoherent, crumbling" outlines of the world of *Bleak House* and proposes that Dickens's only solution for the chaos of society lies in "individual escape."

Monod, Sylvère. *Dickens the Novelist*. Norman: University of Oklahoma Press, 1968, 512 p.
    An inquiry into Dickens's life and career. Monod comments that *Bleak House* embodies Dickens's "most energetic criticism" of

social problems, but he also notes the intrusiveness of Dickens's didacticism in his later period.

Ousby, Ian. "The Broken Glass: Vision and Comprehension in *Bleak House*." *Nineteenth-Century Fiction* 29, No. 4 (March 1975): 381-92.

Traces the way in which characters in *Bleak House* interpret their world. Ousby demonstrates that many of them tend to focus on unrelated details and therefore jeopardize their understanding of "a continuous and ordered whole."

Ragussis, Michael. "The Ghostly Signs of *Bleak House*." *Nineteenth-Century Fiction* 34, No. 3 (December 1979): 253-80.

A detailed examination of the motif of nomenclature in *Bleak House*. Ragussis demonstrates that the novel leads the reader to believe that clarity is impossible because "it is in the nature of language to present a mystery."

Serlen, Ellen. "The Two Worlds of *Bleak House*." *ELH* XLIII, No. 4 (Winter 1976): 551-66.

Contrasts the world view of the omniscient narrator with that of Esther in *Bleak House* and finds them mutually exclusive. Serlen argues that the moral outcome of *Bleak House* is pessimistic since the only road to salvation, as in the case of Esther, involves the refusal to acknowledge unpleasant realities.

Smith, Grahame. *Charles Dickens: "Bleak House."* Studies in English Literature, edited by David Daiches, no. 54. London: Edward Arnold, 1974, 61 p.

A brief, informative introduction to the point of view, characterization, structure, and language of *Bleak House*.

Stoehr, Taylor. *Dickens: The Dreamer's Stance*. Ithaca, N.Y.: Cornell University Press, 1965, 299 p.

A study of dream-like elements in the novels of Dickens. Stoehr interprets Dickens's use of a split narrative technique in *Bleak House* as his "major means of camouflaging the basic emotional contents" of the novel. The unity of *Bleak House* suffers, Stoehr alleges, because "there seems to be no controlling narrative stance."

Sucksmith, H. P. "Dickens at Work on *Bleak House:* A Critical Examination of His Memoranda and Number Plans." *Renaissance and Modern Studies* IX (1965): 47-85.

An account of Dickens's number plans and other materials used in writing *Bleak House*. Sucksmith traces Dickens's methodology, maintaining that *Bleak House* is indeed a carefully crafted novel.

Wilkinson, Ann Y. "*Bleak House:* From Faraday to Judgment Day." *ELH* XXXIV, No. 2 (June 1967): 225-47.

An insightful study of the various ways in which the physical world of *Bleak House* reflects Dickens's moral concerns. Wilkinson suggests that Dickens skillfully intertwines science and fiction to achieve thematic complexity in the novel.

Zabel, Morton Dauwen. "The Terms of the Appeal, Nineteenth to Twentieth Century: Dickens, the Undivided Imagination." In his *Craft and Character: Texts, Method, and Vocation in Modern Fiction*, pp. 15-49. New York: Viking Press, 1957.

Discusses narrative structure, symbolism, and detective novel elements in *Bleak House*. Zabel categorizes Dickens as "a dramatist of history and of moral life" and suggests that by employing dual narrators in the novel, Dickens achieved "a depth of focus" and "a moral resonance."

Zwerdling, Alex. "Esther Summerson Rehabilitated." *PMLA* LXXXVIII, No. 3 (May 1973): 429-39.

Disputes the popular view that Esther's characterization is unsuccessful. Dickens's aim, according to Zwerdling, was to study through Esther "the effect of a certain kind of adult violence on the mind of a child."

Joseph Freiherr von Eichendorff

1788-1857

German poet, novelist, dramatist, essayist, critic, translator, and novella and fairy tale writer.

Primarily because of the exquisite sensitivity with which he evoked the German landscape in poetry and prose, Eichendorff has been described as Germany's greatest lyric poet and the most lyrical of the German Romantic novella writers. Some of his best-known poems are included in the novella *Aus dem Leben eines Taugenichts (Memoirs of a Good-for-Nothing)*. This work, which is renowned throughout Germany for the beauty of its nature descriptions and the infectious optimism of its wandering hero, has been interpreted as both a parody and the quintessence of German Romanticism, establishing Eichendorff as a somewhat equivocal figure in relation to the movement as a whole. Critics generally agree, however, that whether he satirized or epitomized Romanticism in *Memoirs of a Good-for-Nothing,* Eichendorff added depth and purity to the literature of the late Romantic era. Drawing on a highly developed moral sense, he eschewed some of the sentimental and imaginative excesses of the later Romantics in his fiction, and he is universally acclaimed for recapturing the mystical simplicity of the German folk song in his nature poems.

Eichendorff was born in Castle Lubowitz, which was part of his family's ancestral estate located near the town of Ratibor in the Prussian province of Silesia. Privately educated under strict Catholic guidelines as a young boy, he was enrolled at the Catholic *gymnasium* at Breslau in 1801. In 1805, he and his elder brother Wilhelm began the study of law at Halle University. Eichendorff was particularly impressed by the lectures of Henrik Steffens, a member of the Jena Romantic circle, but his most significant early contact with the leaders of the Romantic movement came in 1807, when he and his brother continued their studies at Heidelberg University. There Eichendorff associated closely with the Romantic writers Clemens Brentano and Achim von Arnim, whose collection of German folktales and lyrics, *Des Knaben Wunderhorn,* encouraged his own interest in the folk songs of Silesia. The critic Glyn Tegai Hughes also identifies Joseph Görres as an important influence during this period, crediting the writer with helping Eichendorff to reconcile his perception of the supernatural qualities of nature with his conservative religious views. Subsequently, Eichendorff composed an account of his student life, "Halle und Heidelberg," which appeared in a posthumous collection of essays entitled *Aus dem literarischen Nachlasse.*

Eichendorff's first poems were published in the periodical *Zeitschrift für Wissenschaft und Kunst* in 1808, the year in which he and Wilhelm left the university. A trip to Berlin, where the brothers were introduced to major figures of the German Romantic national movement—Heinrich von Kleist, Johann Gottlieb Fichte, and Adam Müller—followed in 1809. In 1810, the failing financial condition of the Eichendorff estate forced Joseph and Wilhelm to abandon their plans to assist their father at Lubowitz. Seeking employment in Vienna with the Austrian civil service, they became close associates of one of the initiators of European Romanticism, Friedrich Schlegel, and his wife, Dorothea. Eichendorff's first major work, the Romantic *Bildungsroman,* or apprenticeship novel, *Ahnung und Gegen-*

wart, belongs to this period. Eichendorff returned to Silesia in 1813 to serve in the Prussian War of Liberation against Napoleon; several years after leaving the military service in 1816, he faced the sale of his family's estate, which had been ruined by the war and his father's extravagance. Many commentators suggest that the loss of Lubowitz deeply affected Eichendorff, accounting for the nostalgic tone that critics detect in his descriptions of the unspoiled German countryside. In practical terms, his family's financial collapse forced Eichendorff to follow a career as a civil servant: from 1816 to 1844, he published some of his most important creative works as he administered Catholic affairs in the Prussian ministry of culture. Eichendorff's post retirement years were largely devoted to translating the religious plays of the Spanish poet and dramatist Pedro Calderón de la Barca and to writing such literary histories as *Über die ethische und religiöse Bedeutung der neueren romantischen Poesie in Deutschland* and *Geschichte der poetischen Literatur Deutschlands.* In these works, Eichendorff expressed his belief that closeness to God is the source of all true art, and he criticized the German Romantics and other writers for subverting the religious and ethical foundations of literature. He died in his daughter's home in the Silesian town of Niesse.

Eichendorff's poems exhibit many of the characteristics of German folk song. In particular, he followed the folk tradition of combining simple diction with emotional distancing in his nature descriptions to suggest the mystical qualities of the physical world. One of Eichendorff's favorite techniques in achieving this effect was to employ loose syntactical constructions and heavily connotative verbs, investing his humble subject matter with larger, often supernatural, symbolic values. Egon Schwarz underscored this quality of Eichendorff's verse when he remarked that Eichendorff had indirectly expressed "something of a cosmology" in the twelve-line lyric "Mondnacht." Literary scholars note that Eichendorff's cosmology represents a significant departure from the prototypal Romantic attitude toward nature. While Johann Wolfgang von Goethe and other Romantic writers tended to stress the pantheistic unity of God, humanity, and nature, Eichendorff emphasized the demonic as well as the divine potential of the physical world. Nature in his work partakes of the divine only when one recognizes it as the province of the Creator; to consider it an extension of the self or to approach it solely as a source of self-gratification is to subvert the moral order of the universe and to separate oneself from God.

Eichendorff's religious orientation is also regarded as a primary thematic constituent of his novels and novellas. According to Oskar Seidlin and other critics, a definite theology of existence lies beneath the weltering Romantic surface of wandering heroes, enchanted gardens, and love intrigues in Eichendorff's fiction. As Seidlin has observed, Eichendorff frequently conveyed his message by using symbolic landscapes and metaphoric plots to reflect the spiritual condition of his protagonists. *Ahnung und Gegenwart* and the novella *Das Marmorbild* (*The Marble Statue*) are often used to illustrate Eichendorff's "hieroglyphic" technique, for both works feature the attempted seduction of an artist-hero by a Venus figure whose paralyzing influence is mirrored in the surrounding enchanted landscape. Eichendorff has also been interpreted as a satiric artist who employed symbolism to express his dissatisfaction with contemporary literature and society. In Thomas A. Riley's opinion, for example, *Ahnung und Gegenwart* is primarily an allegorical tale satirizing the anti-religious aspects of the German Romantic movement. *Memoirs of a Good-for-Nothing* has been similarly interpreted, but not without engendering controversy. While modern critics generally agree that the novella contains parodic elements, they sometimes identify Eichendorff's satire as a relatively benign, nostalgic form of Romantic self-irony. Thus, in the criticism of Ralph Tymms, *Memoirs of a Good-for-Nothing* is characterized as a "half-affectionate, half-satirical epilogue to the romantic dream," an equivocal tribute to the waning Romantic spirit.

Tymms's perspective underscores the emergence of a distinct trend toward sophistication in Eichendorff criticism. Before the post-World War II era, critics were generally content to admire the surface qualities of Eichendorff's writing, praising his lyric genius and lauding *Memoirs of a Good-for-Nothing* for its straightforward appeal to traditional German values. This attitude was expressed most clearly in the commentary of Thomas Mann and E. K. Bennett; while Bennett focused on Eichendorff's lyricism, denying that his characters and landscapes had significance beyond their ability to create atmosphere, Mann emphasized Eichendorff's unpretentiousness, citing *Memoirs of a Good-for-Nothing* as evidence of the noncritical, "humane-romantic" nature of the German people. Later-day critics such as Seidlin and Riley continue to praise Eichendorff's lyrical manner, but they insist on a complex reading of the matter which it clothes. The changing critical perspective on *Memoirs of a Good-for-Nothing* epitomizes this development: long regarded as the "pearl of the Romantic novella," it has recently been interpreted as both a mockery of Romantic conventions and as the German counterpart of John Bunyan's *Pilgrim's Progress*.

The intensity of the debate inspired by Eichendorff's works surely augurs well for his continuing critical reputation as a significant and interesting figure in German literature. More importantly, perhaps, his writings have become an established part of the German cultural tradition and are likely to thrive in the imagination and affections of the German people.

PRINCIPAL WORKS

Ahnung und Gegenwart (novel) 1815
Das Marmorbild (novella) 1819; published in
    Frauentaschenbuch
  [*The Marble Statue* published in *Fiction and Fantasy of*
    German Romance: Selections from the German
    Romantic Authors, 1790-1830, 1927]
Krieg den Philistern [first publication] (drama) 1824
Aus dem Leben eines Taugenichts (novella) 1826;
    published in *Aus dem Leben eines Taugenichts und Das*
    Marmorbild
  [*Memoirs of a Good-for-Nothing*, 1866; also published as
    The Happy-Go-Lucky; or, Leaves from the Life of a
    Good-for-Nothing, 1906]
Die Freier [first publication] (drama) 1833
Dichter und ihre Gesellen (novel) 1834
Gedichte (poetry) 1837
Das Schloss Dürande (novella) 1837; published in
    Urania
Geistliche Schauspiele von Calderon [translator; from the
    dramas of Pedro Calderón de la Barca] (dramas)
    1846-53
Über die ethische und religiöse Bedeutung der neueren
    romantischen Poesie in Deutschland (criticism) 1847
Erlebtes (autobiography) 1857
Geschichte der poetischen Literatur Deutschlands
    (criticism) 1857
Aus dem literarischen Nachlasse (essays) 1866
Sämtliche Werke des Freiherrn Joseph von Eichendorff
    (novel, poetry, dramas, essays, journal, and letters)
    1908-
The Happy Wanderer (poetry) 1925
Joseph von Eichendorff: Neue Gesamtausgabe der Werke
    und Schriften. 5 vols. (poetry, novellas, novels,
    dramas, fairy tales, journals, translations, and
    autobiography) 1957-60

Selections from Eichendorff's poetry in English translation have appeared in *An Anthology of German Poetry from Hölderlin to Rilke in English*.

THE ATLANTIC MONTHLY (essay date 1866)

[*In reviewing Charles Godfrey Leland's 1866 translation of* Memoirs of a Good-for-Nothing, *the critic describes Eichendorff's works as feeble and incoherent and dismisses the novella as "mere fantasticality." Thomas Mann (1918) discerns an underlying cultural significance in the Good-for-Nothing's fantastic adventures.*]

[*Memoirs of a Good-for-Nothing*] is an extravaganza, in marked contrast to all the other romances of Eichendorff, in so far as it is purposely farcical, and they are serious; but we imagine it does not differ from them greatly in its leading qualities of fanciful incoherency and unbridled feebleness. . . . A young student of the German language, struggling through the dusty paths of the dictionary to a comprehension of the tale, would perhaps think it a wonderful romance, when once he had achieved its meaning; but being translated into our pitiless English, its poverty of wit and feeling and imagination is apparent; and one is soon weary of its mere fantasticality.

> *A review of "Memoirs of a Good-for-Nothing," in*
> The Atlantic Monthly, *Vol. XVIII, No. CVI, August,*
> *1866, p. 256.*

THOMAS MANN   (essay date 1918)

[*Mann, a German writer who is considered one of the greatest novelists of the twentieth century, epitomizes the tendency of early commentators to emphasize the surface qualities of Eichendorff's art. In Mann's case, this emphasis was integrally related to his objection to the cultural repercussions of World War I. Perceiving the democratic politicization of Europe to be hostile to Germany and anathema to the German national character, he published a lengthy disquisition in German on the nonpolitical nature of the German people and their art entitled* Betrachtungen eines Unpolitischen (Reflections of a Nonpolitical Man) *in 1918.* Memoirs of a Good-for-Nothing *was one of the works that Mann selected to illustrate his views on the nonpolitical nature of the German ethos. Accordingly, he depicts the novella as a work devoid of all social, political, and literary pretensions, emphasizing the simple folk characteristics of the Good-for-Nothing and hailing him as the symbol of the "affable humane-romantic" German human being. For a discussion of the relationship between* Memoirs of a Good-for-Nothing *and German cultural nationalism, see excerpt below by Ronald Taylor (1966).*]

From the Life of a Good-for-Nothing. Does one remember? And would one not like to refresh the charming memory right now, and defiantly to read the floating, resonant story again, which, when we read it before, was perhaps in the form of a dog-eared pulp edition, and in the meantime has taken on the most elegant book form: of imposing format, printed in clear and large Gothic letters on beautiful, strong paper, even decorated with drawings by an ingenious little gentleman who seems curiously anachronistic and who has the romantic-prepolitical name of Preetorius? This, you see, is the way it recently reappeared, in the midst of the war, and this, too, this bibliophilic honor that has come to the *Good-for-Nothing* just now is perhaps a sign of the times that a writing such as the one in hand has reason to take note of in some detail. (pp. 273-74)

To call [the story] unpretentious would already be saying too much. It is pure ironic playfulness, and the author himself makes fun of it when toward the end he has someone say: "Well, then, in conclusion, as is self-evident and fitting for a well-bred novel: disclosure, repentance, reconciliation, and we are all happily together again, and the wedding is the day after tomorrow!" But the novel is anything but well-bred; it lacks every solid center of gravity, all psychological ambition, all social-critical will, and all intellectual discipline; it is nothing but dream, music, letting go, the floating sound of a post horn, wanderlust, homesickness, luminous balls of fireworks falling in a park at night, foolish blissfulness, so that one's ears ring and one's head buzzes with poetic enchantment and confusion. But it is also a folk dance in Sunday best and travelling organ-grinders, an artist's Italy seen in a German-romantic way, a happy boat trip down a beautiful river while the evening sun gilds the woods and valleys and the shores re-echo with the sounds of a French horn, the singing of wandering students who "swing their hats in the morning glow," health, vigor, simplicity, courting, humor, drollery, ardent lust for life and a continual readiness for song, for the purest, most refreshing, wonderfully beautiful singing. Yes, the melodies that resound there, that are strewn in everywhere as if it were quite natural to do so—they are not ones that we merely take for granted, they are jewels of German lyric, highly praised, old and dear to our ears and hearts; but here they are in their proper places, still without any patina of fame, not yet in the song treasury of youth and of the people, fresh, original, and brand new: things like **"Wherever I go and look,"** or **"Whoever wants to wander to foreign lands,"** with the final cry, "I greet you, Germany, from the bottom of my heart!" or **"The faithful mountains stand guard,"** and then the magical stanza that a woman disguised as a wandering painter sings to the zither on the balcony into the warm summer night, a stanza that like all of the songs is prepared musically in a way that is still prosaic— "From far away in the vineyards one still heard at times a vine-grower singing; in between there was often lightning in the distance, and the whole area trembled and rustled in the light of the moon"—and which, to be sure, is no longer in keeping with the national tradition, but a *non plus ultra*, a bewitching essence of romanticism—

> Loud revels of the people rest:
> Earth now rustles as in dreaming
> With all trees in wonder streaming,
> What the heart has scarcely guessed,
> Olden times, their gentle weeping,
> And soft feelings, awesome, sweeping
> Summer lightning through one's breast.

(pp. 274-75)

Here is the good-for-nothing's character. His needs fluctuate between such complete idleness that his bones crack from laziness, and a vagabond longing full of vague expectation for distant places that makes him see highways as bridges—bridges that swing out over the shining country far over mountains and valleys. He is not only useless himself, he also wishes to see the world as useless, and when he has a garden to take care of, he throws out the potatoes and other vegetables that he finds in it and plants it all, to the astonishment of the people, with selected flowers that he wishes, admittedly, to give to his high lady, and that therefore do have a purpose, if only an impractical-sentimental one. He is from the family of youngest sons and simple Simons of fairy tales from whom no one expects anything and who then nevertheless solve the problem and marry the princess. In other words, he is a child of God who receives the Lord's gifts in sleep, and he knows it, too; for when he goes out into the world, he is not guided by his father's words about earning his bread, but exclaims lightly that he is going to seek his fortune. . . . And yet, even though from his grateful soul he loves and ardently listens to the beautiful world of his travels, the vigorous crowing of the roosters over the lightly waving wheat fields, the larks flying between the morning clouds high in the sky, the serious noonday and the whispering night, he is still not at home in the world, and usually does not take part in the happiness of those who feel at home in it. . . . He compares himself to a rolled-up hedgehog, to a night owl that squats in a dilapidated house, to a bittern in the reeds of a lonely pond. And then he takes his violin from the wall and says to it: "Come here, you loyal instrument!

Our kingdom is not of this world!'' He is an artist and a genius—something that is not his own claim nor the author's, but that is proven most beautifully by his songs. Nevertheless, his character does not have the slightest trait of eccentricity. Its nature is not problematic, demoniacal or morbid. Nothing is more characteristic of him than his ''horror'' at the wildly beautiful, overexcited speeches of the painter in the Roman garden, a bohemian of decorative manner who blusters with grotesque gaiety about genius and eternity, about ''thrills, wine drinking and the pangs of hunger,'' and who in the process looks quite as pale as a corpse in the moonlight with his hair tangled from dancing and drinking. The good-for-nothing slips away. Although he is a vagabond, a musician, and in love, the bohemian life is not in his nature at all—for the bohemian life is an extremely literary form of romanticism that is alien to nature, and he is completely unliterary. He is of the people, his melancholy is that of the folksong, and his joy in life is of the same spirit. He is healthy, but in no way vulgar, and he cannot put up with crazy things. He ''commends himself to God's guidance, takes out his violin, and plays through all his most beloved pieces so that the lonely forest resounds quite cheerfully.'' This romanticism, then, is neither hysterical nor phthisic nor lascivious nor Catholic nor fantastic nor intellectual. This romanticism is completely nondegenerate and on track; it is human, and its basic tone is melancholy-humoristic. Wherever this tone becomes droll, it is noticeably reminiscent of that of a very great contemporary Germanic humorist who is also of the people and a passionate vagabond: of Knut Hamsun. *''Parlez-vous français''* [Do you speak French?] I finally said fearfully to him. ''He shook his head and I was very glad, for of course I could not speak French, either.'' The good-for-nothing also reveals himself to be a humorist in matters of love. His love is not ''pale as a corpse.'' It, too, is human, that is, melancholy, passionate and humorous. He would never, as the Latin student who takes him for a girl does, fall at anyone's feet with *Iddio* [My God] and *cuore* [heart] and *amore* [love] and *furore* [madness]. When ''everything, everything, is fine,'' and he can have his grand lady, since she is, praise the Lord, only a doorman's niece, he is ''so completely satisfied in his soul,'' and from his pocket he takes a handful of unshelled almonds that he still has with him from Italy. ''She took some of them, too, and we cracked and stared contentedly into the quiet countryside.'' This is so spontaneously humorous that no unwanted comicality can arise, and one remembers that the simple Simons of fairy tales do not conduct themselves more exaltedly, either, when they win the princess. The good-for-nothing is innocent to the point of clumsiness in sexual matters, and gets, untouched and unaware, out of very tricky situations that he falls into because of the intrigue. It is a great poetic accomplishment that his purity does not have the effect of stupidity. It is the purity of the folksong and of the fairy tale, and therefore healthy and not eccentric. He has a naiveté and a free human nature in common with figures such as Wagner's forest youth, the hero of [Rudyard Kipling's] *Jungle Books,* and Kaspar Hauser. But he has neither Siegfried's muscular hypertrophy nor Parzival's saintliness, nor Mowgli's half-animal nature, nor Hauser's psychological cellar color. These would all be eccentricities; the good-for-nothing, however, is in no way extreme. He is a human being, so much so that he cannot and does not want to be anything else at all: this is exactly why he is a good-for-nothing. For obviously one is a good-for-nothing when one claims to be nothing else than precisely a human being. Also, his human nature is hardly differentiated, it has something abstract, it is really only defined in the national sense—but this, to be sure, very strongly; it is

convincingly and exemplarily German, and although its format is so modest, one would like to cry out: this is truly the German character!

Preetorius understood and rendered this figure wonderfully.... The illustrator does not make his hero ''beautiful,'' although the book says of him: *''Come è bello''* [How handsome he is]! But the good-for-nothing's beauty is certainly nothing more than the shining through of his divinely childlike nature, and the illustrator acted correctly in following the drift of his humoristic talent and in not showing an ideal youth but rather a clumsy Simple Simon. His good-for-nothing—and now one will probably always have to see him this way—is a fellow in a brown swallow-tailed coat and awkward trousers, with stand-up collars, a comical, unruly growth of hair and a sharp-nosed, endlessly naive, simple and good face. The artist gave very much with very sparing, but exact and ingeniously appropriate means: with the writer's formula in mind, he produced a symbol of pure humanity that is touching and cheerful in its unpretentiousness, of affable humane-romantic humanity, once again, then: of the German human being. (pp. 275-78)

> *Thomas Mann, ''On Virtue,'' in his* Reflections of a Nonpolitical Man, *translated by Walter D. Morris, Frederick Ungar Publishing Co., 1983, pp. 273-314.**

CHESTER NATHAN GOULD   (essay date 1934)

[*In contrast to Thomas Mann (1918), who recognizes no critical intent in* Memoirs of a Good-for-Nothing, *Gould argues that the work constitutes a parodic satire of Romanticism. According to his interpretation, Romantic primitivism—particularly as it manifested itself in enthusiasm for purposeless wandering, folk song, and peasant life—is the chief object of Eichendorff's satire. For further commentary on parody in* Memoirs of a Good-for-Nothing, *see excerpt below by Ralph Tymms (1955).*]

Historians of German literature have lauded Eichendorff's tale, *Aus dem Leben eines Taugenichts,* as the pearl of the romantic *Novella*. It is my thesis that these criics are mistaken and that *Taugenichts* is from beginning to end very much a satire on certain phases of German romanticism. (p. 167)

Taugenichts has hardly a plot. The greater part is a series of scenes, each of which starts out sweetly romantic and ends with romanticism made ridiculous. In one scene after another the hobby-horses of later romanticism, particularly of primitivism, are trotted out and made to lose the race.

Purposelessness [*Zwecklosigkeit*] is the primitivistic hobby-horse with which Eichendorff amused himself most. The entire action of the *Novelle* exemplifies it; Taugenichts takes one step after another without any good reason, he would just like to do so, and that is all. He tires of one employment after another and moves on to something else, chance takes him this way and that, and he gets back to his starting place, no better or wiser, but happy, and the greatest good fortune, love, is put into his hands, though he has done nothing to deserve it.

The author especially amused himself with one phase of *Zwecklosigkeit*, i.e., yielding to the impulse of the moment, notably the impulse to sleep.... When Taugenichts goes to sleep on the *Wagentritt* [coach-step] of the carriage while the wind whistles through his hat, or on the box of a carriage that bumps him a yard high and lets him fall to the right and left and down backwards over the box and jounces his head so hard that his hat flies off, or in Rome under a tree or on a sidewalk, or on a lawn, or anywhere, then the gentle reader who believes that

Taugenichts represents only lovely romanticism would do well to re-examine the grounds of his belief.

In the first chapter, folk-song, a hobby-horse beloved of primitivism, is led out to lose the race. Taugenichts is rowing a picnic party across a pond, and a fat lady—there is nothing more pathetic than a romantic fat lady—asks him to sing. . . . Taugenichts sings his song and most of the young people cast curious or jesting glances at him, but not so [an] honest-to-goodness lover of folk-song; as man to man he grasps Taugenichts by the hand and says something—that Taugenichts can not remember. The author is amused, not only by the artificial interest in folk-song, but by the upper-class man who pays unnecessary attention to the lower-class man. It would be interesting to know at whom Eichendorff was here aiming his shaft. (pp. 171-72)

We shall follow Taugenichts to see how the author is playing with him, and with romanticism. Taugenichts is able to change his position as gardener, with which he was pleased except for the work, to that of toll-collector, which pleased him much better, for here he had nothing to do except to sit still and smoke—*Zwecklosigkeit* again. He loves a fair and dainty lady, who, he is certain, is the count's daughter, but every time he is near her he makes a fool of himself. After disgracing himself thus he leaves early one Sunday morning for Italy. There is no reason for his going to Italy and he does not know the way and no real events happen to him there, though it is a pleasant journey—*Zwecklosigkeit* still. On this same Sunday morning he meets a peasant in costume going to church, as all romantic peasants should do. Taugenichts politely asks the way to Italy. Of course this was a surprising question and the peasant would have no idea where Italy was, but he might have been polite. Instead he was impudent and gave Taugenichts no information of any sort. Taugenichts sees a fair orchard and climbs over the fence and goes to sleep under a tree and dreams beautiful dreams, but awakes to hear this same peasant abusing him violently for trespassing on the grass and not going to church. Taugenichts wisely takes to his heels. The peasant is short, stubby, with bowlegs, popeyes, and a nose that has been side-tracked. But he, his dress, behavior, and appearance play no rôle in the story. Why was he described in such detail? Eichendorff is jesting with the romanticists who picture the humble as the possessors of real virtue, and showing us that the underclass are not nature's noblemen, but that they are at the bottom of the ladder because they are inferior. (pp. 172-73)

[Taugenichts] continues his demonstration of *Zwecklosigkeit* by wandering until he finds a lazy person who directs him to a village. And now a treat for the responsive romantic heart that thrills at the folk: folk-music, folk-dance 'neath the linden, the sturdy Germanic folk conducting itself with folk-virtue! Taugenichts enters the village playing dance tunes on his violin, and the village youths and maids dance to his music beneath the village linden. Shades of Jakob Grimm! But youth is not unspoiled; a village lad pompously offers Taugenichts a small coin, which he refuses. A sweet-lipped village maid bears him a mug of wine, a suitable reward for a wandering minstrel! But she turns out to be a scheming flirt, and we suspect that she is no better than she should be. The session of the village elders in the inn ends with a fight and a drunkard is thrown out. At sight of him the girl runs away in fear and we are left to guess what claims he has on her. In this village at least, the romanticism of lowly life is down and out.

Taugenichts wanders on; night comes, and the moon. He hears hoof-beats and climbs a tree. A horseman comes into contact with Taugenichts' pendant legs, grabs them and asks, "Who is here?" "Nobody," yells Taugenichts in terror. The horseman draws a pistol and orders him to lead them to the town of B——. Taugenichts leads, though he has no idea where B—— is—*Zwecklosigkeit!* (p. 173)

After a night in [an] inn Taugenichts wakes up to find his companions gone.

They are really an eloping couple, the lady dressed as a man, and have been overtaken by a spy, a terribly romantic spy, whom they elude thus. But the carriage and four proceed with Taugenichts, who is now in Italy and can not find out where he is going, for he can not speak Italian; a triumph of *Zwecklosigkeit*. He is taken off the main road to an old castle in the mountains, where a lady in male garb is evidently awaited. Taugenichts is taken for this person, which complicates things with the chambermaid. (pp. 173-74)

Now a woman in man's clothing was a frequent thing in romantic literature, and in romantic life, . . . but a man in man's clothing taken for a woman is a super-quip. . . .

[His keepers] become aware of his desire to leave, and in the night they lock his door and furnish him all the shivers that a night in the ghostly halls of an ancient castle should by rights afford a romanticist; a little lantern, cloaked figures, muffled steps, whispers, profound silence—Taugenichts falls over a chair and makes a frightful noise, still deadlier silence, the key creaks in the lock, it is turned three times, the steps shuffle away. All this plays no rôle in the story. Eichendorff . . . is amusing himself by parodying the cheap romance of hoary castles and ghostly chambers. (p. 174)

[Eichendorff takes] pains to make every member of the lower class either stupid or mean or incapable of refinement. Taugenichts is given an amusing name, at every step he betrays himself, he is crude and ill-mannered, he makes noises when he should be quiet, at dinner with the priest he leans over the table and stretches out his arms on it, and at the end when he has attained the fair lady of his dreams and should be ecstatically happy he sits with her on a bench and the two munch the almonds he has brought in his pockets from Italy. No pains are spared to show where he belongs socially. The beautiful gracious lady whom he worshipped from afar turns out to be like himself, of the lower class. She was an orphan who had been brought up in the castle by the countess; there she learned many things, good behavior and the like, but it made no difference in her nature and she was still under-class, crude, and perfectly happy to sit on a bench with Taugenichts, munching almonds. And the final blessing to the new couple by Herr Leonhardt, the nobleman, "Liebt euch wie die Kaninchen und seid glücklich" [live like the rabbit and be happy], by its reference to the animal which is everywhere the symbol of fecundity, shows clearly his attitude of kindly contempt.

The only person of humble origin who rises is the priest, who has become a gentleman by the grace of God. The theological students, of humble origin, are still crude, but they may look forward with comfort, for ordination will make them into persons of refinement, fit associates for the gentry. It was the aristocrat in Eichendorff that made him oppose primitivism, the Catholic in him that permitted this exception.

Occasionally the heavens open, and we see in the glorified background Eichendorff's own class, the nobility, who, with serene assurance, he endows with property, breeding, and grace.

He who reads the story carefully will find far more than I have indicated. *Aus dem Leben eines Taugenichts* is not the pearl of the romantic *Novelle*. In it an artist who had almost sublimated the anger of his soul found relief in a merry jest that expressed his diasagreement with and amusement at certain romanticists. (pp. 176-77)

> Chester Nathan Gould, "Literary Satire in Eichendorff's 'Aus dem Leben eines Taugenichts'," *in* The Journal of English and Germanic Philology, *Vol. XXXIII, No. 2, April, 1934, pp. 167-77.*

E. K. BENNETT   (essay date 1934)

[*Bennett, an English novelist, short story writer, and essayist of the early twentieth century, is credited with bringing techniques of European realism to the English novel. He is best known as the author of* The Old Wives' Tale *and the* Clayhanger *trilogy, realistic novels depicting life in an English manufacturing town. Bennett identifies lyricism as the distinguishing characteristic of Eichendorff's novellas, maintaining that his characters and landscapes chiefly serve as vehicles for creating "lyrical moods." Such later critics as Oskar Seidlin (1957) and Lawrence Radner (1970), who emphasize the symbolic nature of Eichendorff's art, take exception to Bennett's point of view.*]

Eichendorff is, with Tieck and Hoffmann, the most original and individual of the Romantic writers of Novellen. He excels in the presentation of lyrical moods. Yet he never achieves the same intensity and sinister effects as those which were at Tieck's command. Though he may conjure up malevolent forces their power is not unassailable, and the heroes of his stories who have withstood their magic return to the serene light of day after the night magic has faded. But, apart from these darker aspects of nature mysticism, his presentation of the various moods of nature is more subtly perceived, more exquisitely rendered than anything Tieck can achieve. He has not Hoffmann's power of drawing characters, above all eccentric and grotesque figures, nor the same quality of ironic criticism. None of the characters who pass through the action of his stories is sharply realized and presented as an individual. None, with the possible exception of the Taugenichts, who withholds his name but reveals so much of his feelings, remains in the memory as a recognizable personality. The persons of his stories are themselves lay figures, bearers of lyrical moods; just as his landscapes are lyrical moods and not descriptions. Irony with him has divested itself of its more trenchant qualities and has become no more than a playful touch which corrects at once any tendency to sentimentality.

'Ein Roman nach der lyrischen Seite gebildet' [a novel with the lyrical aspects developed] was Schelling's definition of the Novelle, and Friedrich Schlegel had stressed the lyrical quality inherent in the genre as such. With Eichendorff this aspect of the Novelle is exploited to the full. No further development along this line is possible or the characteristic outline of the Novelle must inevitably be lost in the mist of lyricism. The creation of Stimmung [atmosphere] . . . becomes with Eichendorff the predominant feature of the Novelle and, by its very predominance, cries a halt to this line of development. (pp. 74-5)

> E. K. Bennett, "The Romantic Novelle," *in his* A History of the German "Novelle": From Goethe to Thomas Mann, *Cambridge at the University Press, 1934, pp. 47-76.**

S. S. PRAWER   (essay date 1952)

[*Prawer challenges Eichendorff's reputation as serene nature poet by contrasting his sensitivity to the demonic potential of nature with Johann Wolfgang von Goethe's perception of nature's divinity. For additional discussion of Eichendorff's treatment of nature, see excerpts below by Oskar Seidlin (1957), Gillian Rodger (1961), Lawrence Radner (1970), Egon Schwarz (1972), and Glyn Tegai Hughes (1979).*]

[It] is of course as a nature poet that Eichendorff is known above all: as one who loved the woods and hills and streams of his native landscape and saw in them, like his 'froher Wandersmann' [happy wanderer] a reflection of the goodness of God. . . . But it has often been noticed how consistently Eichendorff refused to look closely at nature. The landscape of his poems lies in the past (*Jugendsehnen*) or in darkness or twilight (*Nachts, Im Walde*); it is dimly seen in the distance or glimpsed in passing (*Wanderschaft, Wandernder Dichter*). Eichendorff never affords his readers that close view of the natural scene or that sense of the unity of Nature and man, to which Goethe has accustomed us. He is pre-eminently the poet of twilight, the gloaming in which the noise and bustle of the world abates so that isolated sounds (ein Posthorn im stillen Land [a mail-coach horn in the quiet countryside]) may be heard all the more clearly. (p. 132)

Where Goethe's organ was the eye, Eichendorff's is the ear. . . . [In them, we witness] the contrast between plastic poetry, appealing through the eye to the intellect and emotions . . . and musical poetry, appealing through the ear to the emotions, to the virtual exclusion of intellect. And where the 'Augenmensch' [visual man] Goethe sees dusk as the coming of a different kind of light. . . . Eichendorff conceives it as the coming of darkness and terror, as the coming (to use his own poetically ambiguous term) of 'Graun' [grayness]. Nature to Goethe is divine, partakes with man of the essence of God: there is therefore an indissoluble unity between man and the world he perceives. For Eichendorff, the Fall of Man had transformed a Nature originally beautiful and good into something no less demonic than those undercurrents of the human mind which E.T.A. Hoffmann so terrifyingly presented. Unity is lost. Man must *beware* of a Nature grown mysterious and dangerous. Man can no longer feel at home in his twilight world. (p. 136)

> S. S. Prawer, "The Romantics," *in his* German Lyric Poetry: A Critical Analysis of Selected Poems from Klopstock to Rilke, *1952. Reprint by Barnes & Noble, Inc., 1965, pp. 112-37.**

RALPH TYMMS   (essay date 1955)

[*Tymms assesses Eichendorff's relationship to the Romantic movement by examining his use of Romantic conventions in Ahnung und Gegenwart and* Memoirs of a Good-for-Nothing. *Essentially, he depicts the relationship as dynamic, opining that Eichendorff imitated Romantic conventions in* Ahnung und Gegenwart *but later mocked them with affectionate detachment in* Memoirs of a Good-for-Nothing. *Tymms claims that the "half-affectionate, half-satirical" nature of* Memoirs of a Good-for-Nothing, *combined with the Good-for-Nothing's realization of the "'impossible' romantic dream" of requited love, presages the denouement of the Romantic movement in Germany. For additional discussion of Eichendorff's relationship to the Romantic movement, see excerpts below by Thomas A. Riley (1959), Gillian Rodger (1961), Ronald Taylor (1966), and Martin Swales (1976).*]

[Eichendorff's novel *Ahnung und Gegenwart*] follows the romantic convention, stretching back through Tieck's *Magelone* to [Goethe's] *Wilhelm Meister,* of interpolating lyrics: and though they include his best there does seem to be too many of them: the narrative has rather the air of an operatic libretto when characters burst into song as often as they do here, for (including ballads) the poems inserted in this way must number little short of fifty. Inappropriately enough, as it would seem, the novel which is crammed to this extent with lyrics is predominantly a *Zeitroman* [novel of the times], concerned with conditions and problems of the author's own time and milieu: it follows closely in the tracks of Arnim's *Gräfin Dolores* . . . , and there are echoes, though they are fainter ones, of the *Künstlerroman* [artist's novel]: [Tieck's] *Sternbald* and the hybrid *Godwi* [by Brentano], for Eichendorff clearly shared at any rate the romantic receptiveness, and even imitativeness. The most obvious provenance is no doubt *Wilhelm Meister* for a number of the—by this time—practically stereotyped characters and situations: Count Friedrich, the hero (who has also a great deal in common with Count Karl, the priggish hero of *Gräfin Dolores,* condemned to love a frivolous, worldly woman), Leontin (the 'romantic' or romance name is very Goethean!), Erwin, (the disguised girl, who acts as Friedrich's servant) and the little cocotte Marie have respectively a strong family resemblance to Wilhelm Meister, Lothario, Mignon and Philine. Countess Rosa, loved by Friedrich, is easily recognizable as Dolores herself, in Arnim's novel, and the beautiful, sultry, Italian countess Romana reintroduces passionate female characters from *Godwi*—especially the aristocratic hetaera Lady Hodefield, and the Countess (Violetta's mother), who shares Romana's liking for dressing up as a man. That is not to say that Eichendorff has merely devised a romantic pastiche: but it is of significance that as great a writer as he should be content with characterization, or typification of character, which had become part of the *Wilhelm Meister*-romantic convention, or myth, and was almost as impersonal by this time as, say, the conventions of the folk-song—the allegorical formulations of millwheels and broken rings, and all the rest of it. And it is the same with the situations in the novel: Eichendorff writes with freshness and vigour, and poetic sensibility, but the incidents he describes in this superlative, well-knit style are in many cases the common coin of romantic fiction—one need enumerate only the dreams and premonitions, the interpolated topical literary satire (directed against August Lafontaine, an ephemeral contemporary novelist), the phantom of a deceived sweetheart, the *Doppelgänger* (Rudolf is Leontin's double), the picturesque and awful medieval castles, the Tieckian décor—gruesome and uncanny glades, horrific Alpine crags, and robbers' dens, which set off Eichendorff's habitual scenes of smiling, sunlit plains and other gentle aspects of nature. Yet even these conventional romantic motifs are fitted with great virtuosity into the total design, a conception of great variety and richness of theme, and one which—unlike many other romantic projects—is complete: it is an impressive achievement, especially when one recalls that it is the work of a young man of twenty-three or -four. (pp. 331-32)

The relationship to romanticism is a deeper one in Eichendorff's *Novelle: Aus dem Leben eines Taugenichts (From the Life of a Ne'er-do-Well),* written at the end of the romantic age—in 1826: but it is a relationship which is doubtless based on mockery, and essential detachment from the mannerisms and conventions of romantic fiction. The ne'er-do-well hero is best understood as a parody of the aimless, artistic, hypersensitive type of romantic hero—borne along on wings of song, impulse, mood and vague longing, incapable of settling down

for long within the confines of ordinary society, and the denizen instead of a purposeless world of indeterminate aspiration for its own sake. Eichendorff's hero has all the youthful gaiety, good looks and charm in the world: he is much more understandably irresistible than the meek, drab scholar in Brentano's *Chronika,* winning hearts as he roams the world: and Eichendorff allows himself the joke of grafting this traditional characterization of the hero of the *Künstlerroman* on to the happy-go-lucky *Hans im Glück* of the Fortunatus-legend in the chapbooks: for the *Taugenichts* never comes to harm, he is a ne'er-do-well who does do well for himself after all, though he flouts all the laws of merit and the rules of application and industry as the Enlightenment had formulated them. (It is as if Eichendorff, at the end of the romantic age, wishes to show by this caricature of romantic fecklessness, how far the movement has wandered away from its original insistence, in the *Athenäum* days, on the artist's ethical and semi-magian responsibility.) Yet the *Taugenichts,* for all his apparent aimlessness, is like the poets, or even the intermediate class of semi-poets (as Novalis describes them mysteriously in *Die Lehrlinge zu Sais*), who intuitively go straight to the heart of the mystery of nature, while their drudging fellows are shut out from the paradise of revelation. . . . And if he does not care for hard work and regular hours, he is none the less (or all the more!) good-natured, unaffected and harmless. In the tradition of Tieck and Brentano, lyrical interpolations give a musical touch to the atmosphere: but it is an atmosphere of Eichendorff's own nature-piety, projected most explicitly in the wonderful poem—untarnished by romantic self-pity and self-torture, as fresh and spontaneous as anything in the 'old-romantic' lyrics of the *Wunderhorn,* and yet with a modern awareness of its own simplicity and of unquestioning faith in an ordered pattern of divine creation: 'Wem Gott will rechte Gunst erweisen, / Den schickt er in die weite Welt, / Dem will er seine Wunder weisen / In Berg und Wald und Strom und Feld.' [Whom God would show his highest favor, he sends into the wide world; He reveals to them the wonder of mountain and forest and stream and field.]

The first pages in particular have something of the magic of the opening chapter of [Novalis's novel] *Heinrich von Ofterdingen,* but it is the late-romantic, inherently sophisticated counterpart which is presented here to the strange and wonderful book with which the romantic movement made its poetic début in Germany: here are no premonitions of a wondrous aesthetic mission, no symbolism—merely a vague yearning to wander out into the world of nature in search, not of a miraculous Blue Flower, whose very significance is swathed in ambiguity, but of fortune (so long as it involves no effort or hard work), and this vague yearning to subside effortlessly into a life of graceful vagabondage is brought to a head by the aspirant-vagabond's father, who turns him out, as a useless idler. This is how the story opens:

> The wheel in my father's mill was rumbling and splashing again merrily, the snow dripped down busily from the roof, the sparrows twittered and fluttered about; I sat on the door-step and wiped the sleep from my eyes; I was enjoying the warm sunshine. Out came my father from the house; he had been banging about in the mill since daybreak and his nightcap was on crooked: he said to me: "You good-for-nothing! There you are sunning yourself again, stretching yourself until your bones ache, and letting me do all the work by myself. I cannot

feed you here any longer. Spring is almost here, off you go into the world and earn your own bread.'' ''Very well,'' I said, ''if I am a good-for-nothing that is what I will do: I will go out into the world and make my fortune!''

Yet does the rest of the tale live up to this beginning—in which all the youthfulness, artlessness and unsophistication of romanticism finds its magical (if slightly ironical) expression? Sure enough, the *Taugenichts* wanders off into the world, he idles when he can, and stretches his limbs luxuriously, he sleeps, his main activity is his childlike self-surrender to mood (he weeps when the fulfilment of his love seems unlikely, but when fortune smiles on him again he prances about for dear life, like a child, or a fool), but it all seems an extension of this first *mise en scène*: he exists, as a wonderful romantic invention, a projection of the romantic capacity for self-mockery, but what he does—or, rather, what happens to him—is of secondary consideration, an artificial concoction of episodes which constantly arouses the reader's admiration for the artifice, but never lets one forget the inherent artificiality. The *Wanderlust*-motif is Eichendorff's distinctive contribution from the start, and one expects the Ne'er-do-well's ways to lie in the midst of unspoiled natural scenery: instead he is caught up in the convolutions of a popular romantic novelette, rushed in carriages from place to place, set down at intervals in elaborate pleasure-gardens and the grounds of deserted Italian mansions, involved in the intrigues of the fashionable world: and this kaleidoscopic play of fortune he accepts in an uncomprehending way that recalls the intersection of social spheres in Brentano's *Kasperl und Annerl;* it all happens to the intermittent accompaniment of Tieckian hunting- and post-horns. The ending is practically a parody in itself of Wilhelm Meister's marriage, or rather the imbroglio of consanguinity preceding it, at the end of the *Lehrjahre:* it is also a reversal of the conventional romantic cult of unfulfillable longing, since the beautiful 'countess' who has haunted the *Taugenicht*'s dreams when he was a poor vagabond, then gardener's boy and tollhouse-keeper, proves not to be a countess at all, but a foster-child of the noble family: and therefore he is eligible to achieve the object of his longing by marrying this hitherto almost mythically remote figure from another world of grandeur. In other respects, too, the tale is a pastiche of romantic motifs, strung together with the series of anecdotal events which make the whole thing a deliciously lively and entertaining invention, but not in any sense a depiction—still less an interpretation—of real life, or of the problems of human relationship (even to the extent to which truly romantic novels often propound an allegorical interpretation). The device of the simple boy wandering through the world of fashion and its elaborate love-intrigues is a romantic exaggeration of episodes in *Wilhelm Meister,* and there are constant echoes of the later chapters of *Franz Sternbald* and of *Godwi:* one might even credit Eichendorff with sufficient 'distance' from his own work to suppose that he implies a parody of *Ahnung und Gegenwart* itself, with its imbroglios and disguises. It is all very charming and ingenious—and senseless!—and as a parody it is romanticism's summing-up of its own insincerity, as well as of several of its own most attractive features: that includes the simple fun, for the *Taugenichts* is always doing and saying the wrong thing, in his boyish simplicity of heart—tripping up and falling headlong, physically and metaphorically, in the most comical but engaging fashion (Sternbald was unsophisticated too, in the eyes of worldlings, and Hoffmann's heroes are frequently artless fellows, unversed in the ways of the world, though they may be initiated into the mysteries of the higher, poetic, magical world).

The final justification of the *Taugenichts,* and his marriage to the fabulous 'countess', represent the fulfilment of the 'impossible' romantic dream; and with fulfilment romantic longing lost its purpose, its reason for existence: Eichendorff's *Novelle* is a half-affectionate, half-satirical epilogue to the romantic dream; little more remained to be said on the subject or in the idiom, of romanticism in German literature. (pp. 335-39)

> *Ralph Tymms, ''Middle and Later Phases of Romanticism: Fouqué, Chamisso, Eichendorff, Uhland, Kerner,'' in his* German Romantic Literature, *Methuen & Co., Ltd., 1955, pp. 325-46.**

OSKAR SEIDLIN   (essay date 1957)

[*Seidlin's highly regarded explication of Eichendorff's symbolic landscapes represents a significant departure from such earlier commentators as Thomas Mann (1918) and E. K. Bennett (1934), who emphasize the surface qualities of Eichendorff's art. The thesis of his essay, that Eichendorff's landscapes function as visible theology, is indicated in his insistence that ''Eichendorff's landscapes are not self-contained pictures, vehicles for the transmission of subjective emotions; . . . they express the ontology of man's fate and existence.'' Like S. S. Prawer (1952), Seidlin notes that Eichendorff rejects the Romantics' pantheistic view of nature; however, he attributes Eichendorff's attitude to a respectful awareness of the separateness of the Creator from creation and extends Prawer's discussion by remarking that Eichendorff's landscapes reflect human redemption as well as damnation. For further commentary on Eichendorff's landscapes, see excerpts below by Gillian Rodger (1961), Lawrence Radner (1970), Egon Schwarz (1972), and Glyn Tegai Hughes (1979).*]

[For] Eichendorff and in Eichendorff's work nature and landscape are a system of symbols; not, as has been so readily and generally assumed, an evocation of moods, a hypnotic stimulant of feeling, but a cryptogram which has to be deciphered, a pictorial sign language which . . . is often referred to as a mass of hieroglyphs. In his first great work, in *Ahnung und Gegenwart,* we read: ''How true it is that each landscape has by nature an idea of its own which tries to become articulate, as if by stammering words, in its brooks, trees and mountains.'' . . . And in his late short novel, *Eine Meerfahrt,* the hieroglyph is no longer used simply as a simile for nature, but actually becomes one and the same with her: ''All around them the rising morning gilded over the initials of a wondrous, unknown writing.'' . . .

Thus forewarned we ought not to yield unquestioningly to the sensuous magic of Eichendorff's landscapes, to the lure of their atmospheric spell; we shall have to ''read'' them faithfully, all the more faithfully the more plainly and truly they seem to speak. So it may be appropriate to begin with the plainest and truest of Eichendorff's works, with *Aus dem Leben eines Taugenichts,* and further with the plainest and truest scene of the whole book. By ''plain and true'' I mean that here for the first and only time in the little story a locality is clearly identified and geographically fixed: the immediate surroundings of Rome, and finally the city itself. Yet what does our little hero see when he approaches the goal of his long and circuitous roamings? Still quite some distance away, at the mere mention of the name, there rises from his memory a fantastic landscape. As a boy, still in his childhood home, he saw mirrored on the sky among the moving clouds a city with strange mountains and precipices on the blue sea, with golden gates and shimmering towers upon which angels are singing in golden gowns— a fairy tale dream, we must say, hardly a description of the city of Rome. But then, after all, he is still some distance away, just imagining things in anticipation. Yet now he comes closer; the city, so he tells us, is actually spreading underneath his feet. But what does he see now? A long wisp of fog hovering above a sleeping lion, over whom mountains stand guard like dark giants. At that point we are thoroughly in doubt whether the landscape which Eichendorff conjures up before us has anything to do with Rome and its environs. Our doubts become certainty when, reading on, we hear that before finally reaching the city gates the little Good-for-nothing has to cross a big lonely heath, bleak and still as the grave, covered with ruins and withered, twisted shrubbery. But that isn't enough. Suddenly the underworld opens up before us: there buried below the gloomy heath is an old city from which the heathens often rise to the surface to lead the lonely wanderers astray. No less than three times does the word "grave" appear in this short description of the bleak plain, and three times as well, the word "heath" plus its derivation "heathen"—a derivation which, we are convinced now, we must not take as an etymological pun, but as a metaphysical signpost. Those ghosts from the underworld have no power over our little hero; he strides on without looking to right or left. For now the city rises before him, and lo and behold! it *is* the city he had seen in his childhood dreams, with gates and towers shimmering in golden light as if angels were standing on every pinnacle. Do we still have to ask what this Roman landscape means? Is it not clear that we are treated here not to a scenic description but to a theo-, logical vision: the celestial city, beginning and end of man's roaming, primordial image and distant lure of salvation, reachable only by crossing, undaunted, the heathenish heath, dry, lightless, and full of subterranean temptations? Only if we faithfully read the "word" which transmits the hope for redemption and terror of damnation as it is inscribed in this Roman landscape, only then shall we discover the little Good-for-nothing in his full stature. He is the brave Christian knight on the road: his childish naïveté is the seal of innocence, his stubborn love for the lady fair is the shield and weapon of faith, his wanderlust is the quest for man's true homestead, his moments of dejection are the fear and trembling which seize us at the realization that we do not belong, do not rest secure in God's hand, his merry singing and fiddling are a grateful paean in praise of the Creator.

Landscape as visible theology, serving as the key with which deeper perspectives of the unfolding story are opened up—this is a feature occurring again and again in Eichendorff's writings. Sometimes the scenic picture carries within itself its own commentary, or at least a clue to its meaning. In *Ahnung und Gegenwart* Friedrich, the protagonist, has a dream in which

> he saw an unlimited horizon, sea, rivers and countries, immense wrecked cities with broken gigantic columns, the old manor house of his childhood strangely in ruins. Some ships floated in the background toward the sea; upon one of them stood his deceased father as he had often seen him in portraits, looking unusually serious. Yet everything was as if wrested from the twilight, vague and unrecognizable as a huge blurred picture; for a dark storm swept over the whole view, as if the world were burnt, and the immense smoke settling down over the devastation. . . .

Here there is no doubt for a moment that we are observing the eschatological vision of the apocalypse and not simply an uncanny Romantic landscape. In the foreground of the picture is a child of "wonderful dignity and beauty" who points with a rosy finger at the wild scenery and, at the end of the description, emerges again, this time leaning against a huge cross, and talking to the sleeper: "If you love me truly, go down with me; as a sun you will rise again, and the world will be free." The whole Christian doctrine of salvation, including the passion, the day of judgment, and the resurrection has here become tangible in a land- and seascape.

It will not do to dismiss the almost allegorical character of this scene and scenery by pointing out that we are, after all, dealing with a dream vision. The very greatness of Eichendorff's work and world consists just in the fact that vision and description of so-called reality are inseparable, that for him vision is really that which can be seen. It can almost be stated as a rule that the more clearly a description is related to a specific locality, the more visionary it turns out to be. We noticed it in the Rome episode of *Aus dem Leben eines Taugenichts;* we find it anew in the opening scene of *Ahnung und Gegenwart*. Again, it is the only instance in the whole voluminous novel where a concrete locality is pictured.

> Whoever has traveled up river on the Danube from Regensburg knows the magnificent spot which is called "the whirl." Steep mountain gorges surround the strange place. In the middle of the stream rises a curiously shaped rock, from which a tall cross looks down, consoling and peaceable, into the chute and collision of the raging waves. No human being is to be seen here, no bird sings; there is only the continuous, century-old roaring of the woods on the slopes, and of the terrible vortex which draws all life into its unfathomable abyss. The mouth of the vortex opens from time to time, with a glimmer dark as the eye of death. . . .

For all we know that may be the description of a specific scene near Regensburg, but undeniably it is the vision of life's stream, rushing madly and in circular motion into the dark mouth of death but for the unshakable rock upon which the sign and voucher of salvation was erected. Clearly, then, Eichendorff's landscapes are not self-contained pictures, vehicles for the transmission of subjective emotions, but they express the ontology of man's fate and existence. (pp. 646-49)

To realize the degree of complexity and completeness with which the emblematic landscape foreshadows the existential condition, it may be worth looking more closely at one of the scenic designs [in the novella *Das Marmorbild*]. When Florio for the first time strays into the orbit of the dangerous enchantress, her garden is described as follows:

> High galleries formed by arched beech trees received him there with their solemn shadows, among which golden birds fluttered like blown-off blossoms while tall, strange flowers, the like of which Florio had never seen, dreamily moved to and fro in the soft wind with their yellow and red chalices. In the great loneliness there splashed monotonously innumerable fountains, playing with gilded spheres. . . . Florio looked in surprise at the trees, fountains, and flowers, for it seemed to him as if all this had become submerged long ago, as if the stream of days were flowing above him with light, bright ripples, and the garden were lying down

there enchanted and in bondage, dreaming of
life gone by. . . .

Let us try to decipher the hieroglyph which this strange garden
represents. It is a space sealed off by the vaulted tree branches
against the sky, the heavenly light, filled with shadows, uncanny shadows indeed. For if, as we are told, the birds are
fluttering among them, we cannot conceive of them as simply
shadows on the ground thrown by the beech trees, but willy-
nilly they assume a third dimension, and with that the lightless,
shadowy world of the tree gallery changes imperceptibly into
the ominous world of shadows. The birds which populate this
world move like blown-off blossoms, not propelled by their
own will, but drifting passively, helplessly gliding downwards,
animals without anima. In this world vegetative life, telluric
life, the flowers, grow tall, they are bound to the earth, caught
within themselves—dreaming—glowing proudly in their fiery
colors—red and yellow—burning with their own light since
we know that the light from above, from the genuine source
of all light, cannot filter through to them. And the fountains
complete the picture of vacuity and futility: a monotonous
perpetuum mobile [perpetual motion], a motion continuously
sinking back into itself, a senseless playing with shimmering
toys, up and down, rising and falling, incessantly. Do we still
need Florio's observation that this garden is submerged, cut
off from the stream of days which, in bright ripples, passes
over it? The shadowiness which the day cannot penetrate, the
emasculated will, the captivity in one's own self, the burning
color which needs no outside source of light, the automatic
motion spending and replenishing itself by inane circling—this
is the garden of sin, sin as a garden; and if we were called
upon to give it a name, sloth, the deadliest of the seven deadly
sins, might do better than any other. This garden, as scenery,
evokes precisely the horror which a little later, when Florio
enters the castle of the enchantress, will be produced in a scene.
The spell which the garden prefigured will then become actuality, with all the familiar elements present: the shadows,
the paralysis of the will, the deadly introversion and repetition,
magnificently expressed by the fact that in all the female pictures on the tapestries Florio seems to recognize the sorceress'
countenance, in all the male likenesses his own features. Yet
Florio will be saved. While the temptation is closing in on
him, he hears from the outside an old pious song, and at the
moment of highest danger he prays "from the deepest depth
of his soul: God, my Lord, do not let me get lost in the world!"
. . . The break-through has come: grace, waiting and offered,
has been accepted by man's prayer; sloth has been vanquished.
The spell is broken. When Florio emerges, he finds another
garden, tiny and modest, shimmering in the bright light of
morning, with vines growing sturdily around a little farmhouse
on whose roof there strut, merrily cooing, the turtle-doves, the
birds of sweet and faithful love. (pp. 649-51)

[Eichendorff] has often been blamed for his narrow range, his
almost monomaniac fixation on the same basic settings—garden, forest, meadow, river, mountain gorges, heath—and for
the primitive simplicity of the colors which he has on his
palette, and which are lacking in variety, shades, and transitions. Yet if we realize that his landscapes actually enact the
basic situations of religious existence, quest and home-coming,
threat of temptation and hope for salvation, nearness to and
distance from God, then it will not surprise us to see the same
panorama over and over again. What mattered to him was to
bring into sharp focus, through the hieroglyph of the landscape,
the essential truth he had to convey, and for this reason the
scenic view had to be revelatory, but not richly impressionistic

or realistically individualized. The two gardens in *Eine Meerfahrt,* one barren and shadowed by rocks, the other neat, green,
and nestling under a cross, picture not just real estate, but the
real state of souls, some dried up, the others fertile because
they have been moistened by the waters of eternal life. Any
attempt at being more explicit about the two gardens would
have made their meaning less explicit. (pp. 651-52)

[Eichendorff's landscapes have] a definitely structural function
and serve as the joints and hinges on which the whole work
moves and swings. The scenic views are like landmarks on a
net of coordinates which, if properly connected, represent the
curve, the rise, turning point, and fall of the outer and inner
action. (p. 653)

A glance at *Ahnung und Gegenwart* . . . [reveals] the structural
function of Eichendorff's landscapes. . . . At the beginning of
the twentieth chapter we read that Friedrich suddenly recognizes the landscape around him as the one where his journey
had started at the beginning of the book. Quite literally the
story has returned to its origin, Friedrich is again at his starting
point. But starting point means home, and man's home is at
the same time his destination. Advancing, if it is real advancing
and not just running in circles, consists in tracing one's steps
back to the origin. And this is exactly what the novel does
from this point on: while it advances it traces its steps back,
and it is through the reappearance of the landscapes that this
movement is achieved and organized. The story moves ahead
toward its end, the many loose threads of action are now being
gathered up and woven into the final pattern and resolution,
but the scenery, familiar to us from the beginning, proclaims
at every point: we are back again, returning to the origin,
approaching home. There is the mill in the dark glade where
Friedrich had his first encounter with a hostile world, and now
it has reappeared, cleansed of danger and threat; what at his
start into the world was a deceptive and treacherous refuge, is
now a true and friendly shelter. The landscape of his childhood
years, which he conjured up at the beginning of the book in
his confessions to Rosa, is present again, really spreading out
before him: "Suddenly Friedrich remembered: 'This is my
home,' he called out. 'What I see here and all around, everything reminds me like a magic mirror of the place where I
grew up as a child. The same forests, the same paths, only the
beautiful ancient castle I find no more on the mountain.'" . . .
While the line of the story and action declines and falls toward
its end, the scene and scenery rise higher and higher until
Friedrich will finally reach the top of the mountain, and on it
the cross, home and destination, point of origin and terminal
in one. It is the landscape that makes the design apparent,
design in its double meaning: purpose and aim as well as
structure and composition of the narrative. (p. 654)

It has been often and duly noted that [Eichendorff's] favorite
view of the land is from a point above, a total panorama seen
from great height. The same situation repeats itself in his works
over and over: a horseback ride or a walk through the mountains
and forests, a sudden clearing in the woods, and there, far
below the observer, stretches the green valley with fields, gardens, and villages, and in the distance, but still quite distinct,
the shimmering band of a river. Without exaggeration we might
call it *the* Eichendorff perspective. But why is this specific
view so persistent? It is clear that Eichendorff insists on distance; nature and landscape are experienced as objects, distinctly removed from the organ through which they are perceived. "Man is," so we read in Eichendorff's *Geschichte des
Romans,* "so to speak the eye of nature"; while being part of

it he sees it as the thing opposite him, he is at every moment actor and spectator in one. Yet this means that his view is in perspective, that he rejects the blissful claim of identity of man and nature which has always been considered the hallmark of romanticism. . . . Against Faust's exclamation "Feeling is all" [in Johann Wolfgang von Goethe's drama *Faust*], the superman's empathic dissolution into the great Oneness, Eichendorff would pit a "Seeing is all," watching a spectacle offered to our eyes. Indeed, "What a spectacle!" yet Eichendorff would never continue with Faust's exasperated and morose complaint "but oh, naught but a spectacle!"

All this is, of course, nothing but a corollary to Eichendorff's more basic insistence upon the separation of nature, the created world, and God, the Creator. Ever since the days of the dawning Renaissance God had been drawn into the creation, until finally in the pantheistic creed of identity nature became the direct revelation of the absolute spirit. German romanticism was a high point in this development; here the complete fusion of the material and the spiritual was proclaimed—God had immersed himself totally into the world. . . . For Eichendorff, the devout Catholic, such a divinization of nature amounted to paganism; and I think it is for this reason that his work does not contain the infinite, all-enveloping landscape in which the romanticists reveled, the fusion of the real and the ideal, the temporal and the eternal. This explains the great clarity of Eichendorff's scenic views no matter how wide the vista that is being offered. Even the river in the far distance is still distinct; it does not merge with the sky above. It has been often noted that one of his favorite landscape features, the garden, has a definite eighteenth-century rococo tinge. But I would take exception to the common explanation that the form and pattern of his gardens were determined by the park of Lubowitz manor, the estate where he was born and grew up. He needed the rococo garden because its clear arrangement, its distinct form and design point to a gardener in the background, a creator, a supreme maker who has drawn, sketched, and shaped this plot of land. (pp. 655-57)

[One] of the most fascinating features of [Eichendorff's] art is the mysterious correspondence between and coincidence of landscape and time. . . . [Everyone] even slightly familiar with Eichendorff will recall how consistently at the climactic point of his stories the image of home, the castle with its gardens and forests, appears, this almost stereotyped landscape which points to youth, origin, to the whole cluster of metaphysical concepts and associations which Eichendorff connects with "origin." Landscape and nature envelop time, keep it dormant and enchanted, preserve the past for the future, ready to be reactivated, waiting to be called forth from its hiding place. The numerous ruins, covered with creepers and grass, are not scattered about as picturesque props, but they symbolize lived time which is being kept slumbering or imprisoned by nature. In *Ahnung und Gegenwart* we read: "When they [Friedrich and Leontin] emerged from the woods and stepped upon a projecting rock, they suddenly saw coming from the miraculous far away distance, from old fortresses and eternal forests the stream of ages past . . . the royal river Rhine." . . . The river Rhine is here the "stream of ages past"; it not only conveys and alludes to, but actually is history. And the swim which the two friends take in the river clearly indicates that scenic view stands here for historic event, for the leap into the Rhine takes place in our novel just before the two friends enter upon their soldierly careers and exploits by which Eichendorff anticipated the war of liberation against Napoleon. This dive into the Rhine, the stream of ages past, is actually the hero's com-

mitment to and leap into German history. What is presented here as a scenic view is in reality history, past, present, and future. Through the medium of landscape Eichendorff articulates again and again the perspective of time, its pastness and future encompassed in the present. . . . (pp. 657-58)

Yet this perspective of time which opens up in the landscape, this intermingling, crossing, and blending of past, present, and future as revealed in scenic images, point symptomatically to Eichendorff's basic conviction that nature herself stands within the process and under the dictate of history and time, of *that* history and time of which all actual history and time is only a preliminary reflection: namely, the history of salvation. Nature, being creature, lives the same cycle, the same possibilities of innocence, sin, resurrection, and redemption as does her fellow creature, man. The life of nature as Eichendorff sees and renders it is not primarily the biological rhythm of birth, growth, decay, and death, but the religious tension between distance from God and closeness to grace. In this connection it seems interesting to me that death of and in the scenic surroundings is not rendered by Eichendorff through the common metaphor of winter, which does represent the low point of bios, but through the sultry midday landscape, cornfields and woods in their full biological growth, yet oppressed by the heavy, stifling air in which no breath, no anima stirs. . . . There are the innumerable enchanted gardens . . . the green meadow which turns into a crystalline castle in the ballad **"Der Gefangene"** . . .—the spellbound forests, the paralyzed fields smoldering in the heat of noon. This is nature unredeemed, caught in its earth-bound origin, cut off from the light above—again and again the idea appears that these places are submerged, have sunk below the surface, motionless, lifeless. The concept of the enchanted landscape which appears in Eichendorff's work with such persistence is anything but the ubiquitous stock-in-trade used to titillate our nerves and to give us esthetically pleasant goose flesh. "Spellbound" is here to be taken as literally as possible: the state of hypnotic fixation on one's own self, the sinking back into the inside, the dreamy imprisonment in brooding and introspection, in short, a state of life arrested within its own magic circle, and incapable of breaking through its own shell. (pp. 658-59)

What this landscape needs to return to life is a shock, a sudden act of awakening, a quick tearing away of the heavy shroud. And this is exactly what it gets again and again in Eichendorff's work. Here we may find the answer to the question why Eichendorff so persistently prefers one specific mode of daybreak. It is literally a break, stressing the suddenness, the almost explosive quality, the momentous act of awakening. There is no lingering in the twilight zone, no slow seeping through of the light; Eichendorff's morning comes not with a whimper but with a bang. It seems to me much more than an idiosyncratic formula when we read over and over in his works: the sun was *just* rising, *at this very moment* the sun rose, always the emphasis on the shock, on the active and activating moment of day's arrival. For Eichendorff it is the first ray that matters, the ray into which the lark throws herself, rising higher and higher, almost drunk with the feeling of being awake. This is more than just morning; this is the moment of resurrection when the first ray of grace suddenly touches the dark, sleeping landscape.

Thus Eichendorff's landscapes are not simply props, not simply background against which a play is being enacted; they are, as much as man himself, dramatis personae, the drama being the miracle play of God and his creation. (pp. 659-60)

Oskar Seidlin, "Eichendorff's Symbolic Landscape," in PMLA, 82, Vol. LXXXII, No. 4, September, 1957, pp. 645-61.

THOMAS A. RILEY   (essay date 1959)

[*Riley explicates* Ahnung und Gegenwart *as an allegory concerning religion and its relation to the literature of the Romantic
movement. For a broader discussion of the role of metaphoric
literary commentary in Eichendorff's works, see excerpt below
by Lawrence Radner (1970); Egon Schwarz (1972) provides additional discussion of* Ahnung und Gegenwart.]

[*Ahnung und Gegenwart*] stands today as a mysterious yet
fascinating piece of literature, apparently read by many. Its
popularity is evidenced by its appearance since the Second
World War in at least six new editions in Germany, Austria,
and Switzerland. The beauty and interest of individual episodes, the charm of world-famous poems set like jewels in a
rich prose, its musical, lyrical treatment of moods, emotions,
colours, and characters, the apparently deeply felt and in parts
easily understood religiosity in a puzzled world seeking solutions to great problems, attract readers who do not ask for
explanations of the book as a whole.

The mysteries of the book come to a large extent from its
characters, many of them strange and unrealistic to an extreme.
They have sometimes been explained away as the work of a
sensitive poet who found it difficult to think logically but easy
to produce irrational moods in the reader by means of his gifts
as a lyric poet. . . .

It is possible, however, that much of this lack of firm outline
in the characters comes from the fact that Eichendorff is offering in *Ahnung und Gegenwart* a rationalistic, well-thought-
out web of literary allegories concerned mostly with religion
and its relation to the literature of the Romantic movement in
the years around 1811. (p. 204)

Eichendorff wishes to tell us through *Ahnung und Gegenwart*
that without a healthy religious life a nation cannot have a
healthy literature, a healthy art, or any happy political existence. The novel thus takes on great similarity to Novalis's
Die Christenheit oder Europa. In Wilhelm Meister's development [in Johann Wolfgang von Goethe's novel *William Meis-
ters Lehrjahre*] the greatest, most influential factor is life itself;
in Heinrich von Ofterdingen's it is poetry; in *Ahnung und
Gegenwart*, the most important single factor is religion. The
novel represents thus a break with earlier Romantic tradition
and development and deserves careful study as a milestone in
the onward march of the Romantic movement. (p. 205)

The plot of *Ahnung und Gegenwart* retold as literary criticism
in poetic form, as I see the novel, runs thus: Friedrich, the
religiously inclined poet, a Catholic and representative of the
new and best trends among Romantic poets in 1811, very
suggestive in person and personality of Achim von Arnim,
meets and becomes a friend of Leontin, the imaginative poet
(suggestive of Brentano), and falls in love with Leontin's sister,
Rosa, an allegorical figure representing the worldly, superficially Catholic poetry of 1811 (Tieck?). She might be called
False Romantic Poetry. That love is a mistake on Friedrich's
part, leading him into false paths and suffering, for he, like
Parzival, needs maturing, especially in his judgements of life.
With Friedrich as his doting servant goes the beautiful but
confused 'gypsy' girl, Erwin-Erwine, possibly the false *Sehnsucht* [yearning] of Novalis, Tieck, Goethe . . . , and their
imitators, a kind of pagan wood sprite, who sings a bewitching

song left from pre-Christian days. Dressed in a blue costume
with golden ornamentation, she could be 'die Sehnsucht' in
person, the blue flower of Romanticism . . . , representing a
false attitude towards religion and nature. Friedrich must learn
to disregard weak, merely poetic, emotional reactions such as
'die Sehnsucht' or 'mystiche Überschwenglichkeit' [mystical
exaltation],as Eichendorff called it in his *Literatur Deutschlands*. . . . (p. 210)

Long before awakening to the hidden evil in those two beauties,
Friedrich goes adventuring with Leontin, somewhat like Parzival and Gawaine. They come to the heart of Germany, the
best and most typical people of which are represented by Herr
von A., a simple country gentleman, possessed of much land,
but in his half-peasant way of life symbolic of the best qualities
in the populace of Germany. Herr von A.'s daughter, Julie, a
contrast to the shallow Rosa and the sick Erwine, represents
the new Romantic school of poetry, the healthy folk tone set
by *Des Knaben Wunderhorn*. She could be called allegorically
Die Naturwahrheit [truth of Nature]; Herr von A.'s housekeeper is Enlightenment or 'Tante Aufklärung' [Aunt Enlight-
enment]. . . . On this country estate a third poet joins the two,
Viktor, representative of the grotesque humour which, Eichendorff feels, is and should be important in Romantic literature. He could be regarded as 'Der Humor' [Humor] in
person. There are suggestions in Viktor of *Bogs, der Uhr-
macher* [the clockmaker.] In the foreground when Friedrich and
Leontin arrive on this estate . . . is the most popular literary
genre of the day, 'Die Ritterdichtung' [Knight poem], represented by 'Der Ritter von der traurigen Gestalt' [the Knight of
the sorrowful countenance], possibly a caricature of Fouqué
himself, the Don Quixote of Romanticism.

Here in the midst of sunlight, bird songs, and the healthy
reactions of an unsophisticated circle of country people (Herr
von A., Viktor, and Julie), Friedrich and Leontin experience
a premonition of what literature, properly viewed, can mean.
The imaginative poet Leontin falls in love with Julie (*Naturwahrheit* [truth of nature]), but since he has much of the old
Romantic wildness, sensuality, and immorality in his character,
he fears her clean simplicity and runs away. He must purify
himself before he can come to see the need of the sacrament
of marriage. Friedrich's love, False Romantic Poetry, has already deserted country life for the city, whither Friedrich follows. 'Ahnung' [premonition] a feeling for the beauty and
happiness possible in literature and life when the right attitudes
are there, gives place to the sinister 'Gegenwart' [present], a
depiction of the evil existent in the literary, intellectual, and
religious life of Eichendorff's present, the year 1811.

In Book II, the Prince and the Minister might represent in such
an interpretation the charming but vicious character of the established literature of the day, the great names, especially
Goethe's, before whom all Germany is bowing. The Prince
has the key to Marie's door, and thus has access to the girl
who represents 'Die Sinnlichkeit' [sensuality]. As Friedrich
comes to see the sensuality of such men (as Eichendorff pictures
them), the gap between their writings and their living horrifies
him, and he awakens to the need of fleeing from their false
poetry and religion. . . . After refusing to succumb to the beautiful, fascinating seductress Romana (the False Religious tendencies of Romanticism), and after overcoming his love for
Rosa (the False Romanticism of such writers as Tieck and
Wackenroder), he abandons the evil atmosphere of the high
nobility of literature and flees back to the world of nature, to
the mountains.

In Book III he takes part in an uprising of the healthy mountain people against atheism and enlightenment, negative movements from a foreign country which are supported by renegades from his own circle. He is wounded in an heroic period of warfare, finds a brief happiness in having fought for his religion, and comes to see the proper relationship between religion, art, and nature. By putting into action his high ideals he has come far on his way to unity and perfection of character. (pp. 210-12)

But still other tests are waiting. He first watches the terrible end of his most evil temptress, Romana (False Religion), reviews his former life by revisiting the scenes of his youth that have meant much to him but which, because he has matured, now have little meaning, and passes on to 'höhere Prüfungen' [higher trials], to the tests that Protestant philosophy and other intellectuality impose on the religious character. With Leontin as his companion, Friedrich walks unharmed and with considerable amusement through the labyrinth of the intellectual life of the Protestant Germany of 1811. . . . The symbolism of the labyrinth and its surroundings might be interpreted approximately thus:

The 'forest' toward which Friedrich and Leontin are heading is in symbol the 'jungle' of contemporary life, the land of bad taste. The reader thinks of the heroes of medieval epics, Gawaine, Iwein, or Eree, who move from one scene of horrid enchantment to another. But each of Eichendorff's scenes of chapter XXI, when studied, turns out to be a disguised reference to life in the years around 1810-12. The two men come first to a garden, which is nothing but a burlesqued and caricatured park of Eichendorff's time. It is an incredible confusion of styles; silly labyrinths, Greek temples, Chinese pagodas, and artificial Gothic ruins compete for space in a garden that should be devoted to the simplicity of nature. There they find in ruins Friedrich's family castle, symbol perhaps for medieval Catholic Germany destroyed by the Reformation and the following Protestant years. . . . The three most characteristic literary forms of 1812 then catch their attention, caricatures and parodies, first, of the sickly pastoral novel (Loeben, Schütz), then the foolish imitations of Novalis (Loeben), and finally the superficial chivalric romance (Fouqué).

The park and its surroundings belong to and reflect the unhappy, confused character of Friedrich's rationalistic brother Rudolf, a philosopher and former artist, whom Protestant intellectual attitudes have spoiled. He, in contrast to the naïve, unphilosophical, Catholic Friedrich, represents Protestantism at its worst. He resembles especially Tieck's hero-villain William Lovell, but he also could represent an expression of mockery and dislike for Tieck's very Protestant *Franz Sternbald* and Dorothea Schlegel's anti-Catholic *Florentin*. There are elements in the sinister Rudolf of both Sternbald and Florentin. (p. 212)

Long divided into two parts (satire on the distraught literary characters of Tieck, Kleist, and Jean Paul) because of his ironic Fichtean concept of existence, Rudolf has already killed his other self and is now living as the intellectual centre of a group of literary fools (satire on Fouqué, Loeben, Heinse, and others, among them possibly even Novalis and Tieck). . . . As a caricature of Protestantism he might be called allegorically by a phrase especially favoured by Eichendorff when scolding Protestant literature in the *Literatur Deutschlands:* 'Die Emanzipation des Subjekts' [the emancipation of subjects].

Having stood the test of contact with this unhappy world of the intellect of the year 1811, Friedrich climbs to a higher peak, where a group of monks headed by a wise servant of God take him into their midst. Just as Parzival became the King and the Guardian of the Grail, Friedrich has found salvation by renouncing poetry and finding the road to God. Leontin, now married to true Romantic poetry, cannot follow to such heights, but abandons 'enlightened' Europe to live in another part of the world where genuine poets are free to develop in healthy surroundings. Faber, the symbol of insincerity in Romanticism (*Der Dicher von Profession*) [the professional poet], stays in Europe where he is happy and financially successful. (p. 213)

Thomas A. Riley, ''An Allegorical Interpretation of Eichendorff's 'Ahnung und Gegenwart','' in The Modern Language Review, *Vol. LIV, No. 2, April, 1959, pp. 204-13.*

G[ILLIAN] RODGER   (essay date 1961)

[*Rodger explores Eichendorff's individuality as a Romantic writer, attributing his uniqueness to his ability to resolve the Romantic conflict between reality and ideality. According to Rodger, Eichendorff's idealism, particularly as it is reflected in his presentation of nature, was founded on actual experiences and intrinsic values, thus investing his work with an authenticity and realism not found in other Romantic writers. Rodger notes with approval, however, that, despite his realism, Eichendorff ''stood consciously aloof from the prosaic* Biedermeier,'' *a reference to a broadly conceived class of German literature frequently associated with the mediocrity of middle-class values.*]

At first sight Eichendorff reveals little that would allow his investigator to distinguish him usefully from his contemporaries. The very facts of his life seem to reflect Romanticism in its uneasy ambivalence. The circumstances of his youth—his birth on 10 March 1788 into an ancient, aristocratic, Catholic family, his idyllic childhood in the beloved castle of Lubowitz, near Ratibor in Upper Silesia, his carefree years as a student in Halle and Heidelberg—contrast both with the troubled state of contemporary Europe and with the pattern of his later life—his unsatisfying military service, his bitter surrender of the family estates, his prosaic years as a married man, the anxieties of his career as a civil servant and his death in retirement at Niesse on 26 November 1857. Thus the course of Eichendorff's life itself suggests the essential Romantic conflict of real and ideal, and indeed he seems, again at first sight, to have resolved this conflict in characteristic Romantic manner, by shunning the harshness of reality and fleeing to an ideal world created by his poetic talent. (p. 62)

Yet, if we look more closely at the superficially conventional features of Eichendorff's life and poetic activity we become aware of their distinctive character and of the individuality of his Romanticism. Can we, for example, use the familiar, if misleading, words ''Romantic escapist'' to describe a man who was passionately interested in contemporary events and projects, such as the rebuilding of the castle of Marienburg or the completion of Cologne Cathedral? Dare we gloss over the section of Eichendorff's work which, far from offering him an escape from reality, reflects his consciousness of the world, its troubles and preoccupations? His historical essays, his political treatises (for example, *Preußen und die Konstitutionen* or *Über Garantien*), his works of contemporary literary criticism (the section on Romanticism in *Geschichte der Poetischen Literatur Deutschlands,* for instance) are too often ignored and, together with his autobiographical study *Erlebtes,* testify to his awareness of reality and his willingness to consider its problems.

On the evidence of such interests and works, it is thus impossible to dismiss Eichendorff as "weltfremd" [unworldly]. On the other hand, by far the greater part of his activity was imaginative, linking him with more obviously Romantic traditions, and it is in the imaginative section of his writing that the essential nature of his achievement may be revealed. His sense of reality, illuminated at this stage, should, however, serve as a helpful clue to subsequent discovery. (pp. 62-3)

In outline, Eichendorff's imaginative works . . . confirm his allegiance to the irrational traditions of Romantic literature and fail to differentiate him significantly from his fellow Romantics. The detail of these works, however, offers clear evidence of his unique Romantic attitude and talent.

In their geographical and historical settings, for example, his imaginative works are strikingly inconsistent with Romantic fashion. For the most part, the themes of the novels and lyrics are set in the roughly contemporary world of the French Revolution, in contemporary Italy or Germany, or in the unchanging world of nature. They therefore offer Eichendorff no opportunity for escape from his immediate surroundings by flight either into a pseudomediaeval world or into exotically remote lands. (pp. 65-6)

The characters which he situates in these settings are also, despite their appearance, distinct from Romantic traditions of unreality. Students of all types, noble, and right-thinking (Friedrich, for example), carefree and improvident (like Fortunat), excessively sentimental or sober and prosaic, jostle each other through the novels, reminiscing about their University days, singing popular songs, tramping the countryside, playing their guitars and fiddles. These are personalities of Romanticism no doubt, but they are personalities clearly founded on the fact of Eichendorff's own experience and acquaintance. The man who is mirrored in Friedrich and Fortunat, the man who describes so evocatively the pursuits, tastes and nostalgias of students, is manifestly the same man who writes in *Erlebtes* of his life in Halle and Heidelberg and who recalls his own experiences in lyrical confession. And not only the students, but also the eccentric, actors, soldiers, aristocrats, innkeepers, hermits who people the landscapes of his novels have a basis of contemporary reality, frequently admitting of autobiographical or of allegorical interpretation. Furthermore, the situations in which these characters find themselves—meetings, reunions, journeys, celebrations, impromptu friendships, adventurous escapades, mistakes of identity, revelations of relationship—are situations natural to the flowing, involved novel of Romanticism (and indicative of the influence of *Wilhelm Meister*); they are, however, equally reflective of Eichendorff's own youthful experience of travel, social intercourse and carefree exploits and are equally linked by allegorical significance to the contemporary world of literature, society and religion. (p. 66)

[Eichendorff's] heroes are young, linked by common ideals and high-born; or, if not high-born in the social sense (as in the case of the *Taugenichts*), they belong to a moral aristocracy subscribing to the same ideals. All of Eichendorff's heroes delight in music-making, poetry, nature, travel in "the wide world" and thus contrast with his many minor stay-at-home characters of a *Biedermeier* cast. And here surely is evidence that Eichendorff's characters, situations and themes are built on a foundation not only of external autobiographical reality, not only of allegorical reality—the basis, after all, of much

Romantic writing—but also of inner moral reality. His fictitious characters share his own personal delights and ideals, and the themes underlying the complex episodic structure of his novels coincide less with the wild, irrational themes of Romanticism than with the mild and practical preoccupations which he himself expresses directly in his lyrics: the search for perfect existence, friendship, ideal love, the enjoyment of nature, hunting, travelling and above all the awareness of God.

Eichendorff's choice of setting, character, situation and theme suggests, therefore, that the essence of his Romanticism must lie in his creative attitude to real experience. This impression is corroborated and clarified when we examine more closely his handling of certain significant themes. The theme of nature, for example, is particularly enlightening in this respect. Again and again his characters and situations are related to nature and to a recognizable natural location, visualized, clearly and completely, from above. . . . [But] if his landscapes seem restricted in variety, it is not because of any lack of creative imagination on his part, but rather because one particular landscape filled his mind's eye at all times. That was the landscape of Upper Silesia, the Oder and Lubowitz, his home. The coincidence of this real location and Eichendorff's ideal landscape is proved by those lyrics in which he writes descriptively and explicitly of Lubowitz and its surroundings. *Die Heimat,* for example, addressed "An meinen Bruder" [To my brother], opens thus:

> Denkst du des Schlosses noch auf stiller Höh,?
> Das Horn lockt nächtlich dort, als ob's dich riefe,
> Am Abgrund grast das Reh,
> Es rauscht der Wald verwirrend aus der Tiefe.
>
> [Do you still remember the castle on the quiet
> hill? There, at night, the horn sounds entic-
> ingly, as if it were calling you; the deer grazes
> by the ravine; the forest murmur rises disturb-
> ingly from the depths.]

On reading these and many similar lines, one realizes that the stock landscape of his novels and poems, far from being the product of a limited imagination, is in fact a vividly remembered reality, transformed into an ideal world, topographically inaccurate, but symbolic and poetic.

Since it involves thus the transmutation of precise reality into significant poetry, there is in Eichendorff's presentation of nature none of the unreal fantasy and hazy outline which characterize most Romantic scenes. And in similar terms one may account for the distinction to be drawn between the themes of love and religion as presented by Eichendorff and as presented by his fellow Romantics, by Novalis or Brentano, for example. Love, in Eichendorff's works, does not necessarily mean eroticism, nor yet does it have heavy mystical implications. As a theme it runs for the most part (except for isolated moments of sensuality) mildly, nostalgically and symbolically through his novels and lyrics. On the other hand, domestic bliss and its mirror-image, the responsibility and restriction of family ties, are conspicuously lacking in his poetic representation of love—a feature which, if it differentiates his conceptions from those of *Biedermeier,* also suggests his escapist attitude to at least one aspect of his life.

The two themes of nature and love Eichendorff constantly translates into the more profound terms of religion. The translation is frequently effected by symbolism but is always easy and natural, for his delight in nature and his intimations of love lead directly to his recognition of divine power and providence. His conception of the close relationship of God and nature is, however, neither mystical nor obscure. On the contrary, it is childlike and profoundly sincere and is of course matched and enhanced, particularly in his lyrics, by the translucent style in which he expresses it. His attitude of mind, clearly not that of a religious fanatic, distinguishes him from, for example, Brentano. Eichendorff, one must remember, was a Catholic born and bred and his religion had never needed to undergo the crisis of conversion which inflamed Brentano's mind; his faith was one of deep, broad-minded and undemonstrative conviction and was taken for granted as an essential part of his life. . . . As a result, Eichendorff does not dramatize his religious themes self-consciously; he does not even point an obvious moral, or, indeed, glorify moral subjects. He allows himself, rather, through his heroic characters or in his own voice in the lyrics, to express simply and modestly his profound and constant conviction of God's providence. This conviction notably affects his presentation of the theme of death, for he regularly ignores its unpleasant aspects of horror, decay and finality and suggests rather his belief in its positive significance as release or escape, symbolizing it repeatedly as a homecoming. Thus the theme of religion, which so often in Romantic literature implies affectation and pseudo-mediaevalism, springs for Eichendorff, like his other themes, from the reality of his own experience, and of all these themes it is the most profound, intimate and expressive. (pp. 67-9)

Just as Eichendorff's religious feelings were awakened by nature, so also was his awareness of magic heightened by it; its phenomena seemed to him to possess a mysterious live quality, explicable only in supernatural terms. Inevitably, his supernatural world, as presented mainly in his ballads, is situated, invisibly, in the heart of the forest. The recurrent fairy characters of this world, however, have their origin not in Eichendorff's imagination but in the sagas of Silesia (as told to him in childhood by his nurse), and the magical forests are the factual forests surrounding Lubowitz. In other words, although in his novels he usually explains away supernatural happenings in a rational and unromantic manner, in his ballads he presents them with simple belief. This belief had its roots, like his religion, deep in his childhood's experience and, far from conflicting with his religion, it exteriorized for him the fascination of God's realm of nature in a microcosm of magical sound, vision and scent. It is not surprising that Eichendorff's supernatural world of the forest is a world of entrancing enchantment, independent of the contemporary horror cult and contrasting in its subtlety with the extravagantly fantastic magic of Tieck and Hoffmann. (p. 69):

Synaesthesia was, of course, a notion dear to the hearts of the Romantics, but in Eichendorff's works it is so far from being hackneyed as to create the more vivid effects: "Draußen aber", he writes characteristically in *Dichter und ihre Gesellen*, "war unterdes der Abend verklungen und verblüht." [Outside, however, the evening had meanwhile died softly away and had withered]. This method of creating atmosphere can easily be overworked and can lead to an unhappy excess in description of vague and subjective emotionalism; indeed, Eichendorff's ever-recurring phrase "wie im Traum" [as in a dream] is in this way unhelpful and uncommunicative. In the main, however, his description is saved from this danger not only by his sparing use of synaesthetic effects, but also by the flashes of imagery which lighten again and again his potentially turgid and sentimental conceptions. Eichendorff, as his ballads testify, was capable of inventing his own magic and frequently, by magical suggestions, he communicates atmospheric impressions directly and vividly to his reader's imagination. In this

way, for instance, he conveys the colour, mystery and tranquillity of an old garden: "Es war, als hätte ein wunderbarer Zauberer über Nacht seine bunten Signaturen über das Grün gezogen und säße nun selber eingeschlummert in dem Labyrinth beim Rauschen der Wasserkünste und träumte von der alten Zeit, die er in seine stillen Kreise gebannt." [It was as if a wondrous wizard had, overnight, signed his name in gay colours on the greensward and now was himself sitting fast asleep in the labyrinth by the splashing fountains and dreaming of the old days which he kept spellbound in the breathless circles of his magic.] Often, too, Eichendorff's imagery involves not the irrational terms of the supernatural but precise observation of real phenomena: the first pink streaks of dawn over the clear night sky, for example, are likened to the cloud of breath on a mirror. For this reason Friedrich Schlegel was unable to decide whether Eichendorff's works were art or nature, and indeed his descriptive style has been called realistic, "realistisch-impressionistisch" [realistic impressionism] and compared to Constable's vivid communication of reality. Furthermore, from time to time, Eichendorff's predominantly imaginative description is punctuated and enhanced by a stroke of pure realism. "Das Mädchen war arg durchnäßt," we read in *Dichter und ihre Gesellen*, "mit dem dünnen, vom Regen knapp anliegenden Kleide, mit den lang herabhängenden, tröpfelnden Locken sah sie wie ein Nixchen aus, das eben den Wellen entstiegen" [The girl was soaked through; with her thin dress clinging, wet with rain, to her body and with her long hair dripping, she looked like a little water-sprite that had just risen from the waves]—a sentence which demonstrates his effective combination of the two extremes of evocative description, the realistic and the imaginative.

Clearly, judged by contemporary standards, Eichendorff's manner of narration is unusually precise and vivid. He himself felt that to strip his style of its realism would be to rub and blur the fresh colours of a painting, and just for this reason he did not fall into the Romantic errors of excessive subjectivity, vagueness and emotional turgidity. (pp. 70-1)

And also from a purely stylistic point of view Eichendorff was saved by the nature of his talent from exaggerated emotionalism. His prose style, distinguished of course by its lyricism, is lucid at all times and serves well his complex plots and episodes. His lyric style, based as it is on the vocabulary, constructions and rhythms of the folk-song, is a model of transparent simplicity and seeming artlessness and testifies to his profound love of music. Formally too Eichendorff keeps a firm hold on the fluid subject-matter of novel, *Novelle* or poem and steers a confident course among the obstacles which his abundantly inventive imagination provides. The conclusions of his most complex novels, *Ahnung und Gegenwart* and *Dichter und ihre Gesellen,* are reached with comparative ease and, if the multiple thematic threads are rarely all tied up, their confusion is resolved in an impression of dense unity. The action of his novels, one may feel, is impeded by the many interpolated songs, but otherwise when he uses the characteristic devices of Romantic prose-writing he does so to solve, rather than to complicate, his formal problems. Episodic confusion is frequently clarified by his recourse, for example, to the tale-within-a-tale structure favoured by Tieck; *Ahnung und Gegenwart* is presented in a significant cyclic form; audience and narrator are frequently differentiated; *Die Glücksritter* and *Das Schloss Dürande* are controlled by the sections in which they are cast. In fact, formally, Eichendorff subscribed to Romanticism, but handled the techniques characteristic of the movement in such a way as to avoid its common pitfall of rhapsodic diffusion.

In this way, as can be seen, serious examination of Eichendorff's achievement gives promise of interesting conclusions. In the first place, of course, it reveals him as an undoubted Romantic, linked by a common attitude to Tieck and the Schlegels, Brentano and Hoffmann. He was a Romantic in his love of music, in his preoccupation with spiritual values and dislike of philistines, in his fondness for supernatural invention, his delight in the folk-song, his attitude to formal problems and his predilection for certain literary genres. Yet Eichendorff's Romanticism was clearly his own and is distinguished from that of his contemporaries above all by its realistic qualities. (p. 72)

Even his *Sehnsucht* [yearning]—that most Romantic of attitudes, with its two-fold direction towards past and future—is tinged by the reflection of reality. He yearned, not for a past of Romantic pseudomediaeval artificiality, but for an actual place, real people, actual situations and an actual stage in his own life. His *Sehnsucht* was not a vague imagining of the unattainable, but the remembering and idealising of the already experienced:

> Nicht Träume sind's und leere Wahngesichte,
>   Was von dem Volk den Dichter unterscheidet.
>   Was er inbrünstig bildet, liebt und leidet,
> Es ist des Lebens wahrhafte Geschichte.

> [It is not dreams and vain chimeras that distinguish ordinary people from the poet. What he ardently creates, loves and suffers is the true story of life.]

Eichendorff's memory, as well as his imagination, was the vehicle of his yearning and together they created an ideal world which was neither unreal nor fantastic. In this world he perceived certain symbols of the ideal, significant symbols in that they too had played their part in his actual experience. In his poems old age, winter, autumn, fallen leaves, the symbols of decay, are more than balanced by the many symbolic presentations of ideal existence. Youth, "das gelobte Land der Jugend" [the promised land of youth]; spring, the season of youth; music, its expression; the forest, enchanted by spring; the carefree *Spielmann* [musician] who wanders, singing, through it—these symbols of the ideal coalesce in the general symbol, Eichendorff's old home, Lubowitz. And through the symbol of Lubowitz Eichendorff received deep intimations of his ideal world in its ultimate form and the future goal of his yearning, the Kingdom of God. If he yearned back, in his own recurrent word "wälderwärts" [in the direction of the forest], to the lost past of Lubowitz, so also he yearned forward to a future of ideal existence, a future promising not the vague illusions of a *Fata Morgana* [mirage] but the recovery of happiness and the certain fulfilment of faith. (p. 73)

It remains now to be seen whether any real value attaches to Eichendorff's individual kind of realistic Romanticism. Clearly, it differentiates him from his fellow Romantics in a number of significant ways. Unlike Tieck, for example, Eichendorff avoided the pitfall of artificiality; unlike Novalis, he never lost contact with the real world in flights of religious or erotic imagination; his knowledge of reality was first-hand and not, as was Arnim's, indirectly and academically acquired. Eichendorff indulged neither in the extravagances of Brentano, nor in the fantasy of Hoffmann; his subjectivity was never embarrassing (indeed his unwillingness to bare his soul is demonstrated by

his unusually detached diary-writing). He avoided the worst excesses of *Schundromantik,* with its sentimental and self-conscious themes and its false and emotional style, and on the other hand he stood consciously aloof from the prosaic *Biedermeier.* His *Vaterlandsliebe* [patriotism] could not be confused with *Deutschtümelei* [sentimental German nationalism]; on the contrary, he wrote in disapproval of "die . . . moderne Vaterländerei; ein imaginäres Deutschland, das weder recht vernünftig, noch recht historisch war" [the modern patriotic cult; an imaginary Germany which was neither properly sensible, nor properly historical]. (pp. 73-4)

In this way, one may perceive the negative value of Eichendorff's realistic Romanticism in his spontaneous and conscious avoidance of emotional falsity, exotic exaggeration or bizarre unreality. But what of its positive values? It has been said that Romanticism's distinctive feature was "the surrender to unbounded and uninhibited imagination"; Eichendorff, however, did not surrender unconditionally and his imagination was held in check, invigorated and strengthened by his awareness of the threefold reality of past, present and future. His art is romanticised reality, real-life presented in the irrational terms which memory and imagination impose. And for this reason his works are healthier, sturdier and, with their richness of allegory and above all of symbolic meaning, infinitely more significant and sincere than most Romantic writing. This is why the conception of Eichendorff as a naive and superficial nature-poet is so far from the truth. This is why he can be described not only, glibly, as Germany's greatest lyric poet or the creator of the Romantic *Lied* [song] but also, more accurately, as . . . a penetrating commentator on contemporary social, literary and ethical problems and as a bold champion of timeless spiritual values. There were, of course, other realistic Romantics—one thinks of the tragic Kleist, of Arnim and his merciless detail, of the academic pedantry of Uhland, of Hoffmann with his bizarre observation or of the bitterly ironic Heine—but their very inability to reconcile the real and the ideal illuminates, by contrast, the rare and happy balance of Eichendorff's Romanticism, implying, as it does, not disharmony and conflict, but the close, peaceful and fruitful interaction of imagination and reality. (pp. 74-5)

One must remember, however, that the Romantic formula was relevant not only to the problems of artistic creation but also to the problems of living. . . . And from this point of view too, Eichendorff may be regarded as an unusually successful exponent of Romanticism, since he resolved the striking dichotomy of his life, with its two sharply distinguished and disharmonious phases, in terms of Romantic ideals. By his art he transformed the second prosaic and troubled phase into a continuation, on an imaginative level, of his idyllic youth. In his latter years he stilled the pain of grief, loss and anxiety, so modestly revealed in his letters, by his faith in the reality of God's providence, but also by his poetic contemplation of past happiness. . . . [By] his poetic activity, as well as by his religious faith, he created for himself a life of unity and inner harmony, a life which contrasts with Kleist's or Heine's and yet which is in a sense more Romantic than theirs. For the dominant aim of Romanticism was the fusion of life and art, the bridging of the gulf between ideal and real, the dream-world and the world of reality. It is this Romantic task which Eichendorff was uniquely successful in performing and he thus emerges from investigation as the most significant example not only of the Romantic poet but also of the Romantic man. (pp. 75-6)

G[illian] Rodger, *"Joseph von Eichendorff,"* in German Men of Letters: Twelve Literary Essays, *edited by Alex Natan, Oswald Wolff (Publishers) Limited, 1961, pp. 61-76.*

RONALD TAYLOR   (essay date 1966)

[*Taylor places* Memoirs of a Good-for-Nothing *within the mainstream of the Romantic movement and traces its popularity to the appeal of Romanticism to nineteenth-century German cultural nationalism. His remarks on the cultural significance of the novella supplement the commentary of Thomas Mann (1918), who hails the Good-for-Nothing as the quintessence of "the German human being."*]

Few are the works that have claimed such artless and unwavering affection in their native country as Eichendorff's *Aus dem Leben eines Taugenichts* (*Memoirs of a Good-for-Nothing*). And equally few are the writers that have been so readily and so completely identified with the fortunes of a single work as its author. To be sure, he wrote other stories, as well as dramas, verse epics and literary essays, and his lyric poetry is among the sincerest and most touching in the whole of German literature. Yet none of his other extended works has ever been taken by the German people to their hearts, while some of his best-known, most charming lyrics are in fact to be found set like jewels in the lyrical narrative of the *Taugenichts*. Posterity, indeed, has not judged wrongly, for the tale that the Good-for-nothing tells is a fragment of the spiritual autobiography of his creator, a presentation of the values with which the Romantics of the nineteenth century sought, in their diverse ways, to infuse their lives and their art. (p. 7)

The reasons for the popularity of *Aus dem Leben eines Taugenichts* are not far to seek. Its lyrical charm, its directness, its accessibility, its closeness to nature, its cheerful optimism—these are some of its more obvious endearing qualities. Of deeper and broader significance, however, are those characteristics which merge under the shadow of two vague, but none the less real, collective concepts which dominate the literature of nineteenth-century Germany: the concept of Romanticism, and the concept of German cultural nationalism.

However elusive a comprehensive definition of the term 'Romantic' may be, no one would question its applicability to this story, or deny the peculiarly German character of the 'Romanticism'. Its praise of the joys of nature; its illumination of an ideal life governed by the power of love and the flight of fancy; its portrayal of a world in which goodness and happiness are one; the utter unrealism and anti-utilitarianism of its philosophy; its enthronement of Art as the God-given mediator between the ephemeral 'facts' of material existence and the eternal realities of the spirit; its anti-intellectualism and its faith in the heuristic power of dreams: such are the 'Romantic' values, clothed in an idyllic, and sometimes embarrassingly banal, whimsicality of style, which the story of Eichendorff's anti-hero transmits.

In the context of nineteenth-century Germany these qualities could not but assume the role of national characteristics. Love of nature became praise of the Fatherland; the supremacy of the spirit called for a Utopian vision of national character and historical destiny; and the release of spiritual energy was to reveal in unconditional terms, through the intercession of the holy trinity of Nature, Love and Art, the true personality of the German people, the cultural ethos of *Deutschtum* [German nationalism]. In his aimless and often ill-starred wanderings, his naïve, improbable exploits in the name of his love for a woman whom he takes for a countess, and his unfailing re-

course to poetry and song in his moods of ecstasy, the Good-for-nothing leads—if so active a term can be used—his life in response to the dictates of this trinity. (pp. 8-10)

Above all, above the life of this gay, sunny creature, to whom every day is a Sunday and every moment a time for rejoicing, there presides a benevolent deity, a deity concerned that the blissful serenity of the Good-for-nothing shall become the lot of all mankind, and desirous of being worshipped in this image. It is the direct, uncomplicated faith of 'God's in His Heaven, all's right with the world'. And embodied in this very directness—for the Good-for-nothing himself, for Eichendorff, and for the Germany of the nineteenth century—lie both its claim to universal validity and its power of ultimate persuasion. (p. 10)

Ronald Taylor, in an introduction to Memoirs of a Good-for-Nothing *by Joseph von Eichendorff, translated by Ronald Taylor, Calder and Boyars, 1966, pp. 7-10.*

LAWRENCE RADNER   (essay date 1970)

[*Radner expounds on the didactic nature of Eichendorff's art, arguing that his imaginative works essentially constitute metaphoric commentaries on "what 'Poesie' (poetry) was and what it should be." Radner's argument, which is founded on an allegorical interpretation of the love relationships of Eichendorff's poet-heroes, parallels key elements in the criticism of Oskar Seidlin (1957) and Thomas A. Riley (1959).*]

It is difficult for scholars to realize that Eichendorff is not the Romanticist we think him to be. Eichendorff is basically a critic; he judges and condemns not only his own early efforts as a poet, but the society in which he lives. There is in this man a surprising and even painful hardness. He himself says the poet is "das Herz der Welt" [the heart of the world]. But Eichendorff became even more than that. He is the conscience of the nineteenth and the twentieth century. And we still ignore him, because man does not like to be reminded of what he should not be. (pp. 3-4)

Preconceived notions concerning criticism, creative talent, and didactic poetry have blinded us to the possibility that great poetry, even lyric poetry, may be primarily didactic and critical. Eichendorff is keenly analytical, his lyricism is highly rational, his romanticism is classical. He combines the contradictory and the paradoxical, and that is a good definition of early German Romanticism at its best. No later than 1807 Eichendorff became a critic, first of his own earlier poetry and then, very quickly, of the Romantic movement. However, he was a constructive critic. What "Poesie" [poetry] was and what it should be constitute the content, the subject matter, of his own creative works. . . .

Unfortunately, and because scholars have not examined Eichendorff's use of words, it is not clearly known how poetry is represented in his creative works. "Poesie" is a woman. Her name may be Rosa, Romana, Bianca, Venus, Annidi, Juana, "die gnädige Frau" [the gracious woman], to cite just a few. Eichendorff insists that the poet dare not deal in abstractions but must give the idea in flesh and blood. The relationship between the poet-hero and the "woman" is a precise definition of that poetry which holds the hero enthralled. The fact that this is always presented as a love affair points to another dimension which scholarship has missed. Creativity is the manifestation of love, and the poet's words and his use of imagery are carefully designed to suggest the movement of love. (p. 4)

Eichendorff tells us there are two laws in man's spiritual world. He calls them centripetal and centrifugal force. The former is divine love and draws man upward or in toward what he calls the center of all being. The other is also love, but a love which denies obedience to the first love and thus moves the creature down or away from the center. Upon these two laws or loves is based the entire noetic structure in our poet's works....

All of Eichendorff's poetry involves movement, because love is both a seeking and a doing; therefore our poet has his characters drawn, as it were, by centripetal or centrifugal force. Depending upon which love draws the poet-hero, he moves toward an ever more restricting finiteness or seemingly infinite expansion. This is the secret of Eichendorff's use of "Raum" [space]. Whenever the poet-hero allows himself to be drawn by divine love, the nature imagery suggests expansion; if the poet's song speaks only of his own love, then that same imagery is used to imply limitation or restriction. The process continues to the point of "Erstarrung" [rigidity]. But, and this is the theme of deception which is always present in such a development, the poet-hero may feel that his own love draws him toward an infinitely expanded existence. Eichendorff would show us that man's own love deceives him.... [The] entire **"Marmorbild"** story is based upon one question: "Ist's Liebe, ist's Andacht, / Was so dich beglückt" [Is it love or is it devotion which makes you so happy]? This novella is also the clearest but not the only example of inversion; the poet-hero thinks he rises when he is actually sinking, he thinks his song expresses "Andacht" and it is only "Liebe." (p. 5)

[It] is highly probable that Eichendorff's imagery can be reduced to air, fire, earth, and water, the ancient insight concerning creation.... If one now combines this reduction of imagery with the principles of two laws or loves in Eichendorff's works, the mystery suddenly deepens. The reference to two laws or loves means that Eichendorff is concerned with two realities, both of which he describes with the same imagery. That is why deception is such a significant factor in his works.... [It is the fundamental experience of the poet heroes] Friedrich, Raimund, Florio, Otto, Lotario, [and] the "Taugenichts." For each, the beloved is "Poesie" who becomes flesh and blood; but because "Poesie" is their own love become visible, they are deceived by themselves, by their own song.... But this is not all. Eichendorff's imagery is metamorphic. By this I mean that air becomes song which becomes light which becomes a stream; or stream ("Fluss") becomes light which becomes song. The process is reversible. All of Eichendorff's nature symbolism is drawn into his reduction process.... Criticism has always suggested that Eichendorff is limited in his range of themes. I suggest we consider the law of commutations and permutations. Given a small number of items, let us say ten, the number of possible combinations becomes astounding. This is the secret of Eichendorff's variations upon a theme. The delicate shading and subtlety which this man achieves is truly amazing. (pp. 5-6)

The two loves which form the basis for all that Eichendorff would say to us are not opposite poles, as we usually understand them in magnetism. It is true that he clearly describes the relationship between them as "feindlich" [hostile]. Centripetal and centrifugal forces move in opposite directions. And yet man's love, which in and of itself tends to deny God, is man's only key to the first love. And that is what Eichendorff would teach us. Out of denial acceptance is born, and rebellion becomes obedience. Only a Saul could become a Paul. But this is also the ground of man's helplessness.... [This] new man

is not man's work. "Was wahr in dir wird sich gestalten" [Your inner truth is still to be shaped.] That is why Eichendorff throughout his life and in all of his works is the implacable enemy of those religions, for which he has a host of names, which imply that man makes the new man. In his own words, man would save himself and be his own god. But this new man is always a variation of the old man. That is why in Eichendorff's works the poet-hero always is confronted with his own image. "Poesie," because it is but the movement of his own love, cannot be a Beatrice. For this we need another woman, and another "Bild" must be present in the heart of the poet. (pp. 6-7)

Eichendorff insists that in the poet's mind and heart must be a vision of Truth and Beauty which is one with his religion. Combine this with the points discussed above and we have what is tantamount to an equation: religion = Truth and Beauty = "Bild" [image] = "Poesie" [poetry] = woman. But "Dichten und Glauben" [thought and belief], although they have a common root, are different in function. The poet tells us that faith enters the depths and is concerned with "Anschauung der Wahrheit" [contemplation of truth], while "Dichten" seeks to embellish what faith has seen. That is why they are one, yet basically different. Now look at our equation and keep in mind the definitions just given. Then "Dichten" becomes a seeing and embellishing of Truth and Beauty, of "das Bild" of woman, of religion. Then what is a "Marmorbild"? It is religion-Truth-Beauty-"Poesie"-woman who has turned to stone. It is the image in Florio's heart, and she is reborn in the springtime of his love and is given life by his song.... Florio's "Bild" is his word (song) become flesh. As she takes more and more life from him, he loses his. The entire novella reeks of death; its fragrance trembles in the air disguised as the essence of flowers, and the "woman" is a flower, standing for his song, his poetry, the movement of his love. [But the image of the "Taugenichts"] remains in his heart. The woman does not become flesh. Once, he makes a mistake; he tries to see his love. For this he pays a price. And that is why, if scholars would seek to understand these two novellas, they must learn to view them as opposite sides of the same coin. "Das Bild," a woman who is "Poesie," plays a dominant role in both stories, and her name is Venus. Each is a goddess of love and queen of the garden. The earthly Venus must learn her songs from the poet; she has none of her own because her grave is silent. The heavenly Venus teaches him her song, the song from on high which bursts into man's heart in a crescendo of light. It is the Magnificat, the "Grundmelodie" [underlying melody] asleep in nature and in the depths of man's heart. (pp. 7-8)

It seems a reasonable assumption that one could select perhaps ten to fifteen emblematic terms [found in Eichendorff's works], show how each is used in significant contexts, and thus arrive at an Eichendorff definition of the word.... [In actuality,] one enigmatic term could not be given a full definition without bringing in other terms. For example, spring becomes a song, which becomes a flower, which becomes a woman, who is a star; and the entire constellation is part of a certain "Morgenrot" [aurora of dawn] which is the symbol for a love. This is why we have called Eichendorff's imagery metamorphic; one term flows into another and the whole has a unity. It is as though the poet consciously brought to bear his superb artistry to show that all things are reduced to one. I have become convinced that this amazing unity suggested by his imagery was not only deliberate but necessary. He insists that all revolutions are basically religious in nature. This means that he judges the value of whatever is new by the relationship with God effected by the innovation. If it brings man closer to God, it is good; if it effects denial, he rejects it. This same statement applies to his poetry; it is, after all, nothing more than a restatement of centripetal and centrifugal force, of what I have called the movement of love. And these words suggest that particular oneness or unity which I see reflected in everything the poet wrote. (pp. 8-9)

Let us see how Eichendorff metamorphoses his imagery and imparts a sense of mystery and deception [in **Ahnung und Gegenwart**].

In Rosa's eyes Friedrich seems to see nature. But when she is described as a painted spring, then we must conclude that she is, somehow, artificial. As a consequence, the nature "seen" in her eyes is as *false* as the spring which she represents. And then we come to a spring which is an image of Venus, a marble statue. Even nature is mysteriously suspect because a pond has been changed into an entire region. If we examine all of Eichendorff's words which concern water, such terms as "Fluss, Strom, Meer, Quelle" [river, current, sea, spring], then we slowly realize . . . that the water symbolism is designed to suggest the poet's song. With this in mind we recall that Venus arises from the pond. Clearly, the pond must be related to the song which "contains" Venus. Thus guided, we are not surprised to read that a certain song courses like blood through Venus' body, giving her life. Therefore the pond is the deep within the poet from which arises "Das Bild," his version of Truth and Beauty, which is his religion and which he embellishes with song; his flowers. But the pond also becomes "eine unermessliche Landschaft" [an immeasurable landscape]! It must follow that this nature is not nature as critics have, with remarkable obstinacy, continued to describe it. The pond is a veritable world in which a certain song is sung, and in that world nature is not nature because the trees are not trees, the birds are not birds, the flowers not flowers, and the fountains are not fountains. It is a world which exists within Florio, and it is exactly what Raimund in **"Die Zauberei im Herbste"** calls "ein wunderbares, dunkles Reich der Gedanken" [a wonderful, mysterious realm of thoughts]. . . . (p. 10)

[Whatever] the artist makes can never be that for which he searches. Eichendorff repeatedly asserts this truth. Nature, he tells us, is both mute and blind; man is the eye and most powerful voice in the hierarchy of created things. Consequently, he informs us that nature cannot speak to man of God unless He is already within man. This means that nature is to man what he is to himself. This means, furthermore, that the song asleep in all things will not be released until the poet sings the same song. And that song is a hymn of praise to the Lord God on high. Nature, which obeys the Law, knows no other song. And this same song is produced by the sunbeam as it touches the string of the violin which is the love of the "Taugenichts." That is why their kingdom is not of this world. The "Taugenichts" is the minstrel of our Lady; he sings her song, the Magnificat. It is written that man is to love God above all and his neighbor as himself. Man disobeys. He does not seek the will of the Lord, nor work to get it done. That is why Christ tells Friedrich in a dream: Love me and the world will be free. Free of what? Free of man's love which is a seeking of his own will. Love, not intelligence, is man's most precious gift. It is also the most dangerous. I accept, as the most workable definition of man, that he is the one creature on earth filled with a consuming desire to be more than he is. Power for this expansion is provided by love, a seeking of his

own will. That is precisely why the poet says it leads down to "Absonderung, zur Zerstörung und zum Hasse" [isolation, to devastation, and to hatred]. . . . (p. 11)

Lawrence Radner, in his Eichendorff: The Spiritual Geometer, *Purdue University Studies, 1970, 372 p.*

EGON SCHWARZ (essay date 1972)

[*Focusing on Eichendorff's literary craftsmanship, Schwarz provides a close, technical analysis of* Ahnung und Gegenwart *and the poem "Mondnacht." His commentary is especially noteworthy for its discussion of the role of women in Eichendorff's fiction, the stylized quality of his landscapes, and the connotative power of his poetry. Schwarz's remarks are taken from his* Joseph von Eichendorff, *a study designed to introduce Eichendorff to English-speaking readers.*]

[**Ahnung und Gegenwart**] is by no means Eichendorff's greatest artistic accomplishment. But it is the great novel of his youth which contains the fullest statement of his concerns and in which one can find the seeds of almost all his later works. . . . [Here] the author's poetic devices, not yet manipulated with the synthetic skill of future years, are most easily recognizable. (p. 24)

[**Ahnung und Gegenwart**] differs markedly from the realistic novels of the nineteenth century and their successors in the twentieth, to which most modern readers are accustomed. There is no firmly delineated action, the characters are psychologically undeveloped, and though the author attempts . . . to create some sort of suspense, it is not of the kind generally encountered in present-day fiction. (p. 25)

In the ordinary sense, **Ahnung und Gegenwart** does not have much of an action. The main characters are always on the move, but hardly do anything that would reveal personality or narrative purpose. (p. 26)

One night they will spend in a humble village inn, the next in an elaborate castle, the third in a haystack, and a fourth in a remote mill which is really a hiding-place for robbers. Their activities, so far as they cannot simply be subsumed under the heading of *Wanderschaft* [journeying], consist of hunting, singing, writing poetry, attending parties, and engaging in lengthy conversations. (p. 27)

Eichendorff succeeded in imposing order and continuity upon this seeming chaos by two means: subdivision and suspense. The term subdivision refers to the chapters and the three main parts or sections, called "books." The chapters are generally very short . . . and skillfully modeled. Usually a new chapter starts with a change of scenery or a shift in perspective. It is either devoted to a new character or written in a different key. The chapter endings are also incisive: sometimes they coincide with the termination of a day, at other times they are punctuated by a lyrical poem or a carefully composed cadence. All this assists in varying and structuring the monotony of the comings and goings provided by the plot. . . .

[The three "books" into which the novel is divided] present a three-phased movement which does a great deal to enhance the intellectual and artistic dignity of the novel. It might be possible to designate the three steps corresponding to the three books as the personal, the social, and the philosophical, each of which constitutes a significant dimension of the entire work. Furthermore, each book performs a function in the unfolding of the narrative which we may call exposition, complication, and solution (or introduction, expansion, and explication). In this manner, each book, though based on its predecessor, represents a step into a higher conceptual sphere and is, at the same time, accompanied by a widening of the narrative horizon. That the three phases also correspond to Eichendorff's three theological categories, origin, alienation, and return, is their principal artistic merit. This is no mean achievement for an incipient prose writer and goes a long way toward counteracting the lack of a firm line of action. (p. 30)

The first book introduces the main characters: Friedrich, Leontin, Rosa, Faber, Erwin, Marie, Viktor, Julie and her family. But they are all treated as individuals. Whenever the individual is transcended and relationships are delineated, it is always a question of the relationship between two characters. This is a book of the most uninhibited and unmotivated traveling. Toward its end, however, the action converges at the country estate of Herr von A. Here the reader gets a glimpse of the landed gentry, their family life, pleasures, worries, and ideals. This is an appropriate preparation for the next book, which mainly deals with problems of society. The predominant themes of discussion in the first book show a similar progression from the individual to the social. At first the conversations almost exclusively center around poetry and the creative process, but gradually they are replaced by subjects dealing with training and education.

The second book is set almost completely in the capital or "Residenz".... In the tradition of Antonio de Guevara's *Libro de Menosprecio dela corte y albança dela aldea* (*Book of Scorn for the Court and Praise for the Country,* 1539), and indeed of the classical authors of pastorals and idylls, the city and the court are for him repositories of evil and corruption. Therefore, the second could also be called the satirical book. Sexual mores, politics, the corrupt nobility, affected literature, and the literary *salons* come in for severe and sometimes amusing criticism.

It must be said at the outset that this criticism is much too vague and devoid of precise observation to be entirely successful, but there is no doubt that it represents Eichendorff's settling of accounts with his times which he accuses of being superficial, mendacious, lacking in courage, and oblivious of true religion. From the point of view of structure, this book constitutes an expansion of the first. A few new characters are introduced (the Prince, the Minister, the literary crowd and, most importantly, the allegorical figure of Romana is fully developed). The major characters of the first book, Leontin and Faber, are carried over but play a marginal role. However, the relationship of Friedrich and Rosa, the main love interest of the novel, is moved into the center and resolved. But here, too, the crucial aspect consists of the supra-individual factors working upon and destroying this love affair between two people seemingly predestined for each other. What separates them is precisely what constitutes the main issue of *Ahnung und Gegenwart,* the conflict between the old and the new.

Technically speaking, the third book brings the denouement, the fulfillment of all individual destinies; philosophically speaking, it offers the solution of all the riddles and the answer to all the problems that have been raised. The third book can thus be said to be one extended *anagnorisis* [recognition scene]. Characteristically, the dialogue, as far as it is not intended to clear up the obscure past, revolves around life and religion. The conclusion is dedicated to the question of how the gifted individual should respond to his degenerate times. Eichendorff's answer is devastating: Friedrich turns his back on the community by becoming a monk, and Leontin by emigrating to America. It should be clear to the reader that in this context America is not a part of Western civilization but a kind of Rousseauistic Utopia, an image of the primitive, unspoiled good life.

From this analysis it ought to be clear that Eichendorff has succeeded in imprinting, by the skillful use of subdivisions, a powerful rhythm on his novel and in bringing it to an impressive climax.

Eichendorff's other ordering device is the technique of suspense. With its aid he attempts to energize a plot which is more lyrical than dramatic. By constantly hinting at mysteries, by gradually revealing hidden elements in the backgrounds of his characters, by setting up riddles which are solved only piecemeal, and by staging recognitions between separated friends and lost relatives, he tries to tie together distant parts of his story, thus showing an awareness that novels require a denser fabric than a plot mainly based on *wanderlust* can provide. But since the characters are insufficiently developed (or rather, since the function of character is not primarily psychological), all the reader experiences is the *desire* to create suspense, not the suspense itself. (pp. 30-2)

Early in the novel, a suspicion is aroused that the boy Erwin is a girl in disguise and that his abnegated devotion to Friedrich is love transmuted into subservience. Throughout the book, this idea is nourished by reports of Erwin's strange behavior which would be comprehensible only if recognized as female jealousy. It is not until the third book that Erwin is identified as the miller's girl, who so bravely assisted Friedrich against the murderous robbers. And only at the very end of the novel is it revealed that she also happens to be Friedrich's niece, the daughter of his brother Rudolf and the girl Angelina who played such an important role in Friedrich's childhood. The suggestion of incestuous love, which this revelation contains, has been, through the ages, a literary cipher to illustrate the insurrection of the senses and the unconscious against morality which, in turn, explains the necessity to have Erwin or Erwine end in insanity and premature death. In this sense, the Erwin complex is tied up with one of the central concerns of *Ahnung und Gegenwart.* But since Erwine is never brought to life as a believable character, since her existence is, as it were, merely asserted and not proven, it remains a mere strand of color in the kaleidoscope of the novel and therefore, no matter how mysterious, fails to stir more than the mildest curiosity in the reader. (pp. 32-3)

[Mystifications such as this] may be failures as exciting secrets which the reader is burning to see solved. But they are eminently successful in giving the impression that human existence is incomplete and confused if lived without a clear religious consciousness, and that a deeper truth lurks behind the surface appearances. It is precisely this tormented quest for clarification of the enigma that impels the main figures toward their self-fulfillment; and the great revelations at the end which meticulously bind together the fragments of the novel are perfect objective correlatives for the philosophical clarification and decision making that is taking place simultaneously.... [Eichendorff's] achievement as a writer consists in fusing an element of tradition (Romantic mystification) with an element of narrative technique (suspense), and in giving to both the symbolic force of representing his feeling of life....

Sociologically speaking, the characters of *Ahnung und Gegenwart* belong, with very few exceptions, to the aristocracy. (pp. 34-5)

Obviously, this focus on the aristocracy is biographically motivated. Eichendorff was profoundly aware of the French Revolution, but its consequences interested him only insofar as they affected his own social class. While *Ahnung und Gegenwart* has many overtones of the political period novel, the historical moment is analyzed mainly as to its meaning for the nobility and, particularly, for its best representatives. (p. 36)

[Men] and women in this novel are given, perhaps unconsciously to the author, very different treatment. If one regards *Ahnung und Gegenwart* as a novel of salvation, a search for the right and just life—and it is imperative to regard it thus—one perceives that most of the male characters achieve an honorable way out of their own predicaments and those of their times, while the author does not tire of inventing ever new forms of degradation, shipwreck, and tragic death for his feminine characters.... The only exception is Julie, who is allowed to share her husband Leontin's heroic American exile, unimpaired in mind and body, but not before she has pledged, in a poetic but nonetheless serious vow, to remain, even in those remote parts, a faithful, self-sacrificing Teutonic maiden. She sings her romance "Of the German Virgin" in response to a question by Leontin which would be utterly tactless from a newly-wed husband if it were not so characteristic of Eichendorff's suspicious attitude toward women: "Will you be wholly a woman and, as Shakespeare says, submit to the unbridled drives that seize and tear you this way and that, or will you always have enough courage to subordinate your life to a higher ideal?"

The men, on the other hand, fare much better. Unwilling to compromise with their degenerate contemporaries, Friedrich and Leontin achieve dignity by haughtily withdrawing from the scene, while Faber remains unperturbed and keeps on doing exactly what he has always done. The only shipwrecked male character is Robert. After fulfilling his function as chief explicator of mysteries, he rejects Friedrich's exhortation to seek his solace in religion. It must be presumed that he remains forever disgruntled. Whether marrying Rosa is meant as a punishment for the prince's many sins and hypocrisies must be left for the individual reader to decide. But whatever his verdict, he will agree that none of the heroes is as badly off as most of the heroines. The reason for this blatant inequality is simple enough. Its origin is the Christian, romantic-medieval mythology, from which Eichendorff derives his values. In this system, women are held to be closer to original sin than men. They are basically sensual creatures who have difficulty controlling their evil drives and consequently end in the abyss. They are beautiful but treacherous beings from whom sweet temptations emanate. But unless one makes a lucky find—that is the lesson to be learned from this novel—it is safer to stay away from them. (pp. 36-7)

What are Eichendorff's characters? Compared to the flesh-and-bone variety populating realistic fiction, they remain a shadowy lot. Each appears in a typical situation and is given a name, which is enough for his identification. Let us take Marie, the young forester's girl, as an example. She is first perceived through Friedrich's eyes, sitting on a dead deer and singing a duet with a young hunter in which hunting is likened to the love play between the sexes, the quarry being identified as the female part. Marie and her situation form a picture which may be called an erotic emblem or pattern. From now on, whenever she appears, she is engaged in some sort of erotic activity, expecting or chased by a man, eluding a pursuer, mistaking one masked lover for another, defending the body of a dead

lover, sometimes in tears and close to the recognition of her tragic plight, but mostly in gay, lighthearted abandonment to her function. This is precisely what she is: a function in a larger scheme with hardly a personality of her own. (pp. 37-8)

All of this is connected with the nature of Eichendorff's plot as it has been described. Since the action does not flow from the will power of the individuals but is a stereotyped pattern superimposed upon them from without for the benefit of a greater plan, the characters cannot possibly exhibit that three-dimensional quality which we associate with spontaneous, self-sufficient life. It is quite evident that Eichendorff did not employ any of the many methods with which such an effect is achieved. There is no analysis of emotions or thoughts, there are hardly any inner conflicts and none of the little inconsistencies and subtle contradictions that make a fictional construct spring to life. In short, there is not a trace of psychology. Also lacking are the various devices for expressing, mirroring, and faceting the personality in the exterior world which are so eagerly adopted by writers more intent upon character creation than Eichendorff—devices that show a figure as the author sees him, as he sees himself, as he is seen by fellow characters, or as he expresses himself in actions, conversation, dreams, diaries, and letters, in sudden crises, and especially in conflict with other figures or the world. Of this vast arsenal of techniques Eichendorff makes very modest use. We learn about the main characters only the preciously few things which the author tells us in his own voice or in their conversations, where a personalized tone is rarely attempted. One means of self-expression is, of course, the numerous poems and *Lieder* [songs] that are attributed to practically every character in great abundance.... But while these poems are largely adapted, in thought and mood, to the occasions out of which they arise, they are but an uncertain guide to an understanding of character. (pp. 39-40)

It is quite obvious that ulterior meanings are attached to many of the poems which Eichendorff has inserted into his narrative; to some of the interpolated tales such as that of Ida, the bride of the water ghost; to certain localities, like Rudolf's castle at the end of the novel with its curious inhabitants who, just like their host, are torn between the ethos of ancient times and the moral dearth of their own; and even to the descriptions of certain landscapes and personalities. (p. 42)

The very beginning of *Ahnung und Gegenwart* offers an excellent example. The first sentence of the novel, which reports the rise of the sun and the progress of a ship down the Danube, is not likely to arouse suspicions. But near the end of the first paragraph, when the narrator dramatically abandons his role as a seemingly objective observer and adds his own undisguised commentary, one realizes that the mood of careless frivolity and youthful mischief is not there for its own sake alone but as a contrast to a more serious attitude toward life soon to be introduced. The words "Und so fahre denn, frische Jugend! Glaube es nicht, dass es einmal anders wird auf Erden" (Travel on, unspoiled youth! Never mind that things will change someday on earth) establish an enormous distance between the author and this scene, reducing it to a vignette which he intends to manipulate in order to bring out some abstract truth.

After the individualized statements of the first paragraph, the generalizing opening of the second one strikes a well-calculated mood of solemn significance, and it is now that the allegory central to the entire novel is unfolded....

> Whoever has traveled down the Danube from
> Regensburg, knows the magnificent place called

the Whirlpool. Steep forest ravines surround
the wonderful site. In the middle of the river
stands a strangely shaped rock from which a
tall cross looks down, full of solace and peace,
into the surge and strife of the mutinous waves.
Not a person is to be seen here, not a bird is
singing, only the forest covering the mountains
and the dreadful circle which pulls all life down
into its unfathomable gullet, have been rustling
here monotonously for centuries. From time to
time the mouth of the vortex opens up, gazing
darkly, like the eye of death. All at once man
feels lost in the power of the hostile, unknown
element, and the cross on the cliff emerges in
its greatest and most sacred significance.

No one accustomed to read a novel on a level only slightly
deeper than that of mere plot, will fail to understand the momentous meaning of this passage. . . . [A] variety of signals
contrives to extend the purport of the sentences beyond their
surface meaning. For one thing, there is the abrupt change of
key which precedes the allegorical passage and at the same
time serves as a hint as significant things to come. The choice
of adjectives is a further means to create contrast. The place
is called "magnificent" in the introductory sentence and again,
in apparent synonymy, "wonderful." Yet in German "wun-
derbar" also means miraculous, a connotation reinforced by
the presence of the cross. When the author says that it "looks
down full of solace and peace" into the river, he goes beyond
the requirements of pure description. Certainly, solace and
peace are traditional attributes of religious faith and inject a
spiritual element into the scene. (pp. 42-4)

By proclaiming the peace and solace emanating from the cross,
Eichendorff emphasizes its symbolic and non-natural character,
lifting it, as it were, out of its immediate setting into a different
sphere of the imagination. This logic and the skillful manipulation of attributes compels the reader to regard the waves,
too, as only a symbol of some sort of higher reality, just as
the cross stands for Christ and the Church. What element,
contrasted with the solace and peace of religion, is found in
such turmoil, he unwittingly asks; and the following details of
description, carefully chosen for their emotional and connotative properties, gradually suggest an answer. The eddy is a
"dreadful circle which pulls all life down into its unfathomable
gullet." Is it Nature or Life that is embodied in this elemental
phenomenon? Such, at least, are the abstractions that forcibly
come to mind. The horror is accentuated by the sudden desolation of a scene which was teeming with life and gay with
noises only a short while ago: "Not a person is to be seen
here, not a bird is singing." Man's impotence in the face of
a devouring threat (suggested by nouns such as "mouth" and
"gullet") is further emphasized by the reference to lapses of
time which vastly exceed the limited span of his life ("have
been rustling here monotonously for centuries"). Thus one can
add Time, which inexorably engulfs us, to the abstractions that
have been hovering over the passage. (p. 44)

As if afraid that the symbolic significance of all this might be
missed, Eichendorff now abandons, for a moment, the realm
of objects in which he has pretended to be moving, and enters
into the sphere of ideas, frankly interpreting his panorama:
"All at once, man feels lost in the power of the hostile, unknown element, and the cross on the cliff emerges in its greatest
and most sacred significance." He still has not said—and could
not say without destroying the passage artistically—what the

"unknown element" exactly is. But he has been utilizing an
age-old system of metaphors which is well understood by all
those who are even vaguely acquainted with the traditions of
religious writing. Man's ship of existence is traversing the
treacherous and often turbulent waters of life threatening to
engulf the heedless voyager who is intent only upon the pursuit
of his pleasures. If, however, he chooses to navigate by the
cross of Christ, erected on the rock of the Church, he will
avoid shipwreck and reach the harbor safely. Eichendorff's
merit as a a narrator is to have woven the various threads of
this allegorical tradition into the fabric of his own work, and
to have endowed a boat trip on the Danube with the philosophical meaning characteristic of his entire novel. (p. 45)

Objects of sense perception become strangely transparent in
Eichendorff's hands. The entire physical world in which man's
terrestrial life is bound to take place, and which can be juicily
robust and self-sufficient in other writers, becomes, in his
workshop, a flimsy, diaphanous veil through which the great
spiritual meanings shine powerfully at all times. These are often
so pervasive that they rob the surface phenomena, delightful
as they are, of much of their solid material impenetrability.
(pp. 54-5)

Very unlike the Romantic writers, Eichendorff never uses his
landscapes for the reflection or projection of feelings, whether
his or those of his characters. What is created by them is space,
not feelings—the peculiar space of Eichendorff's world in which
even the most conventional happenings are transformed into
something poetic or at least into something very much the
author's own.

But there is something else about this space to which not enough
attention has been paid, but which harbors a strange contradiction. In spite of its great expanses . . . , Eichendorff's space
is circumscribed in a fashion that the empirical space of our
everyday life is not. In so many instances that to speak of
"concidence" is impossible, the entire world of the protagonist
is most implausibly placed within one and the same landscape.
Take, for example, the end of **Ahnung und Gegenwart** which,
because of its preferred position at the conclusion, cannot be
taken lightly. . . .

> Friedrich had not noticed any of it. Calmed and
> blissfully happy, he had stepped out into the
> quiet garden of the monastery. There he still
> saw on one side Faber journey out between
> rivers, vineyards, and blossoming gardens into
> the flashing, colorfully agitated life; from the
> other side he saw Leontin's ship with its white
> sail disappear at the most distant elevation of
> the ocean between heaven and water. The sun
> was just rising magnificently. . . .

[In] spite of its enormous scope, reaching from horizon to
horizon, [this landscape] holds only the elements necessary for
the occasion and no more. This fact makes it shrink spiritually
at the very moment when it has achieved an amazing physical
extension. The reason is not difficult to find for this is not an
ordinary landscape, a part of the world that imposes itself on
the view with all its richness and unpredictable detail, but a
scene *created by the glance of the viewer* and containing just
those phenomena which the author needs for the occasion.
Eichendorff's landscape is a stylized, symbolic, metaphysical
landscape. Perhaps the most revealing word in the passage is
"life." It would not be there were this not the concluding
cadence of the novel. Faber, ostensibly taking another of his

horseback trips, does not traverse a concrete, well-defined region of this earth, but is going back into *Life*. Leontin, on the other hand, is still adventurous and active and braves the ocean to find his salvation in faraway lands. So perilous, in fact, is his undertaking and so radical his quest that there is nothing between the treacherous element and the heavens but he himself. The puny ship with a single sail is a symbolic translation of the enormity of his enterprise.

Friedrich, as the central figure, supplies the perspective. As every human being must, he occupies the center of his horizon while his friends are on either side. We know what it is that he has ceased to notice: Rosa's, his former beloved's, fainting and departure. For the first time in his career, he is becalmed. Again he steps out from an interior into the open, into freedom. His foreground is the convent garden. All the trouble and turmoil is over, and all mysteries are explained. The sun can rise and illuminate the scene once and for all. (pp. 62-4)

Eichendorff's world is extensive and full of delightful detail, but not infinite or representative of independent empirical space. Eichendorff's "what is" comprises a total "reality," and not only our world of sense data. The dense carpet of our sense perceptions is in his fiction but a transparent film spread over an ultimate truth. He does not bother to account for its individual traits too closely. Many of them seem identical with the ones of which our own world is composed. But our deception lasts only for a moment. For Eichendorff combines them in an arbitrary fashion—not duplicated in the normal world—to form beautiful patterns for his own purpose. And even this must not be regarded as his final aim. What he really wants to accomplish with his veil is, by making it as delicate as possible, to let shine through what is underneath it. What Eichendorff is after is not beauty but truth. (p. 65)

The poem **"Mondnacht"** (**Moon Night**) is generally classed with Eichendorff's sacred poetry, but basically it has no more religious ingredients than most of his nature poems.

> Es war, als hätt' der Himmel
> Die Erde still geküsst,
> Dass sie im Blütenschimmer
> Von ihm nun träumen müsst'.
>
> Die Luft ging durch die Felder
> Die Ähren wogten sacht,
> Es rauschten leis die Wälder,
> So sternklar war die Nacht.
>
> Und meine Seele spannte
> Weit ihre Flügel aus,
> Flog durch die stillen Lande,
> Als flöge sie nach Haus.
>
> It was as if the heaven
> Had gently kissed the earth,
> And now in blossoms' shimmer
> She had to dream of him.
>
> The air went through the fields,
> Smoothly waving grain,
> And softly rustling woods,
> So star-clear was the night.
>
> And my soul spread
> Wide its wings,
> Flew through the quiet lands
> As if for home.

Here we are almost exclusively dealing with pure sound. Even someone without command of German would be moved by this rhythmic and symphonic intensity. The progression of the vowel rows in the four first lines, *a ä i, e i ü, i ü i, i äu ü,* has something captivating about it that cannot be specified. And so it goes with all the stanzas. The poem is all of one casting. In addition, it has such an overwhelming simplicity of expression that one could call it cunningly constructed if it weren't so unintentional and completely unpretentious. "Die Luft ging durch die Felder": can there be anything simpler than that? But even this inconspicuous little sentence is artfully constructed. The verb of motion "went" is somehow so childish and so primitive that immediately the idea of magic in nature as conceived by childish individuals or primitive peoples comes to the fore.

On the level of meaning, this "going" transforms the air into a divine messenger who establishes a connection between heaven and earth. This, in turn, beautifully fits the air of creaturely piety breathed by the entire poem. Of course, this only becomes clear when seen together with other details that are similarly employed. The rhyme "Himmel-Schimmer" also has this childish-primitive quality. Actually it is no real rhyme and, singled out, seems the product of a childish soul so stirred by religious feeling that he has failed to find the rhyming words. Now we notice that whenever is the relationship between above and below, heaven and earth referred to, a similar slight discrepancy appears (cf. the rhyme in the last stanza "spannte-Lande" . . .) to signify that the correspondence can never be complete. (pp. 98-9)

How unlikely that something approaching a cosmology is concealed behind this pure simplicity, and yet this is the case. One is almost tempted to ignore the meaning of the words and just absorb the sound. But the stanzas contain a message. Nature's capacity to enchant is not just presented as a fact but as resulting from a mythological cause. The divine origin is reverently cloaked in impenetrability by the use of the subjunctive construction of the first line, thus presented as the object of faith. It signifies that we cannot assert it with certainty; but it seems that the unspeakable fascination emanating from even the simplest of phenomena in nature is of divine origin, and mans' love for them is nothing but the reflection of this erotic, procreating union, most delicately expressed in the verb "geküsst" (kissed). The second stanza details these phenomena: night, summer, springtime—the "Wogen der Ähren" (smoothly waving grain) being an attribute of summer, the "Blütenschimmer" (blossoms' shimmer) one of spring. They are not just grouped together in the passage but, as in the first pages of **Taugenichts,** occur together. This serves to reinforce the mythical character of the seasons. Spring is not a *phase* but a *potency* of the earth.

As in the Bible, this procreation progresses in hierarchic steps, rising from the tellurian phenomena to the height of creation, the human being. The cosmic kiss of heaven impels man, or rather his esoteric side, to wander. In the last stanza, the circle of creation is completed. The beauty of earth culminates in the human soul, which lifts itself in flight to heaven. How movingly its return to the heavenly homeland is conveyed, again finding expression in the conjectural subjunctive and the imperfect rhyme. Simultaneously, however, the hard-sounding "spannte" finds its mild and hope-bearing resolution in the softness of the assonance "Lande."

In this unsurpassable composition, Eichendorff's quiet lyrical poetry, its inseparable blend of simplicity and refinement, celebrates its mythical climax. (pp. 100-01)

[Eichendorff] had his limitations. His motives were few, the range of his interests was limited, and his intellect was not of the first order. His poetic world was small, but amazingly coherent and endowed with vibrating intensity, a goodness of the heart, and a vital joy rare in serious literature. Its lack of breadth is compensated for by depth—not the abstruse and oracular profundity that often passes for greatness in Germany and elsewhere, but the diaphanous depth of feeling coupled with serenity. Eichendorff is an unpretentious, healthy, and lovable author. In his prose writings he created not only a distinctive style and intriguing conditions of time and space, but also unforgettable situations and characters. In poetry he excelled because of his delicate sense of language and a musicality that inspired some of the best German composers. He was a past master of the short *Lied*-like poem, a genre which, in turn, is Germany's finest contribution to the world's lyrical heritage. From a broad international point of view, taking into account his shortcomings as well as his merits and accomplishments, Joseph von Eichendorff can be characterized as a great minor poet worthy of a prominent place in world literature. (pp. 164-65)

Egon Schwarz, in his Joseph von Eichendorff, *Twayne Publishers, Inc., 1972, 184 p.*

MARTIN SWALES (essay date 1976)

[Swales contends that Eichendorff poses and resolves valid psychological conflicts in Memoirs of a Good-for-Nothing, *thus countering Thomas Mann (1918) and other critics who depict the novella as an unproblematic fairy tale. While Swales defends the "realism" of the work, he also admits that it has a paradisal quality, explaining that Eichendorff achieves this effect by exploiting the possibilities of the Good-for-Nothing's first person narration. According to Swales, the Good-for-Nothing's ability to look back on his problematic past with ironic yet affectionate nostalgia makes the work "both a living tribute to, and a critique of, Romanticism."]*

By any standards, Eichendorff's *Aus dem Leben eines Taugenichts* is a conciliatory work. The one tension which informs the story is, as many commentators have noted, that of 'Heimat' [home] and 'Ferne' [distance]. These two concepts imply the seemingly contradictory experiential demands of stability, continuity, home, on the one hand, and of novelty, adventure, wandering, on the other. The work is, of course, conciliatory because the story told embodies not simply the living out of this tension, but also its resolution. We note, for example, that the plot is circular, that the Taugenichts leaves his home in Austria and wanders to Italy, but only to return along the Danube to his home at the end of the story. Moreover, in the scene with which the work closes, the Taugenichts is finally able to marry his beloved. He has thought of her as some distant, unattainable figure . . . , but she turns out to be the niece of the porter, to be of his familiar world. The promise of happiness, intense perhaps because of its very unattainability, finds its true fulfilment by partaking even of the homely world of the porter. The resolution of the story involves a sythesizing of the two warring directions—and not the obliteration of one in favour of the other. The Taugenichts may return 'home' at the end, but this does not mean that he has to go back to his father's mill. He is anything but a disillusioned pragmatist reluctantly abandoning his dreams in order to embrace the prosaic reality of hard work. He marries at the castle of the 'Graf' [count], and he and his wife are to be given part of the estate . . . as their future home. Furthermore, the Tauge-

nichts proposes: 'Gleich nach der Trauung reisen wir fort nach Italien, nach Rom, da gehen die schönen Wasserkünste, und nehmen die Prager Studenten mit und den Portier'. . . . What he suggests here is a way of life which reconciles the demands of 'Heimat' and 'Ferne' in that it allows him to wander in search of new experience while at the same time guaranteeing the basic security and human companionship of a 'mobile home'. . . . In view of the sheer rightness of the solution, I find it hard to concur with Hughes when he speaks of 'the blank impossibility of envisaging a middle-aged Taugenichts' [see Additional Bibliography]. The ending of the story surely suggests that the middle-aged Taugenichts will differ from the young Taugenichts only in so far as he is able to hold in serene balance those forces which were at war in the young man. One must, after all, remember that the youthful Taugenichts, as depicted in the story, is prey not only to 'Wanderlust', but also to the seductions of a sedentary existence. His joy in being 'Zolleinnehmer' [toll-collector], his love for the dressing gown and 'Schlafmütze' [nightcap]—those ciphers for the 'pipe-and-slippers' pleasures of social well-being—expresses precisely the desire for security, for 'Heimat', which makes him the markedly unstrenuous wanderer that he is. The triumphant conclusion to the story allows him to have his cake and eat it. (pp. 36-7)

[Present-day readers may feel] that *Aus dem Leben eines Taugenichts* is simply too serene, too sunny a work to recommend itself to modern literary tastes. The tension between 'Heimat' and 'Ferne' is very much the hero's problem and his alone: the world does not resist such solutions as he may find. Indeed, the world will do its level best to give him a beneficent prod in the right direction when necessary. Hence, the actual events depicted lack any real bite; when they suggest obstacles or difficulty, they do not imply the intractable resistance of reality, but rather the confusions which are bound to beset anyone who has, like our hero, the unfortunate ability to jump to conclusions—or to fall over his feet at the most inopportune of moments. As objectors to the story quite rightly point out, many of the Taugenichts' discomfitures are so inherently—and innocently—humorous that they never present a significant threat to his untried optimism.

But what of the moments in the story when the hero does seem to lapse into real despair, when his tears flow with unselfconscious abandon? Do not these represent a real threat? It is surely not enough to say that the Taugenichts is mistaken in his moments of despair, that he has misunderstood the true nature of the situation in which he finds himself. Of course, he may have misunderstood, he may have failed to recognize the world for the infinitely generous guardian angel that it is. This still would not, of itself, prove that the Taugenichts is not threatened. He is prone to violent fluctuations of mood, to an oscillation between despair and elation that allows of no middle ground. In psychological terms, the tension between 'Heimat' and 'Ferne' as experienced by the Taugenichts would seem to be real enough. Is he not threatened by his own lability, by his own inveterate incapacity for any kind of emotional stability?

Why is he not a Werther-figure? Why does he not belong in that large company of doomed wanderers that inhabit the pages of Tieck's and Jean Paul's novels?

We could, of course, say that the ending gives us the answer. But it still fails to explain why we know, long before we have reached the end of the story, that this is a conciliatory work, that everything wll turn out well. Obviously, if the answer lies anywhere, it must be in the *way* the story is told—and not in *what* is told. (pp. 37-8)

A brief analysis of one passage.can help to make the central point.

In chapter II, the Taugenichts has been asked to bring some flowers to the garden of the residence for the 'schöne gnädige Frau' [beautiful, gracious lady], flowers which she needs as part of her costume for the masked ball which she is to attend that evening. The Taugenichts waits impatiently for her arrival—and then, as the emotional pressure becomes too great, he, characteristically, climbs a tree. From this vantage point he witnesses the arrival of the maid and her mistress. But when the latter removes her mask, he discovers 'es war wahrhaftig die andere ältere gnädige Frau' [it was actually the other, older gracious lady]! . . . Then he sees his beloved appear on the balcony of the residence, in the company of a good-looking officer. Both receive the cheers of the guests. The Taugenichts concludes that she must be married, and that he has been cherishing vain hopes. Then follows this paragraph:

> Alles das versenkte mich recht in einen Abgrund von Nachsinnen. Ich wickelte mich, gleich einem Igel, in die Stacheln meiner eigenen Gedanken zusammen: vom Schlosse schallte die Tanzmusik nur noch seltener herüber, die Wolken wanderten einsam über den dunkeln Garten weg. Und so saß ich auf dem Baume droben wie die Nachteule in den Ruinen meines Glückes die ganze Nacht hindurch. . . .
>
> (p. 38)

The first sentence appears to convey suffering of genuine— and disturbing—proportions. Yet immediately, a corrective is implied. 'Ich wickelte mich, gleich einem Igel, in die Stacheln meiner eigenen Gedanken zusammen' [I wrapped myself up, like a hedgehog, in my prickly thoughts], we read. The simile has a puncturing effect. Despair, we feel, cannot be intimated as unrelieved if the protagonist is seen to resemble a hedgehog. And the undercutting is strengthened in the very next sentence: 'Und so saß ich auf dem Baume droben wie die Nachteule' [and so I sat above in the tree, like an owl]. Once again, we have an image from the natural world. Here the image is potentially more flattering than that of the hedgehog. Owls may be presumed to have dignity, repose, wisdom: there are all manner of useful metaphorical possibilities which can be brought into play. The problem is that the metaphorical resonances never really take hold—because the literalness of the situation—'auf dem Baume'—is too strong. The Taugenichts really *is* up a tree. He is 'droben'—up there—and we look at him with much sympathy, but surely with not a little affectionately ironic detachment. And we do so because the narrator makes us adopt this stance. It is the narrator's perspective as onlooker which makes possible the images of the hedgehog and the owl, which relativizes the intensity of the Taugenichts' despair. The narrative blends intimacy and detachment, blends closeness to the hero with a measure of implicitly incredulous distance from him. (pp. 38-9)

I have commented on the use of certain images which imply a degree of comic detachment. These appear frequently—both with reference to the Taugenichts and to the other characters in the story. . . . Such images imply a somewhat unhinged human world—but not a threatened one. They supply a register of conciliatory comedy which is sustained throughout the story

and which guarantees its happy outcome—long before that outcome becomes a fact.

It follows from all this that Eichendorff is using here a certain possibility within first-person narration—the constant interplay of the experiencing 'I' and the narrating 'I'. In one sense, this constellation is always implicit, because any first-person narration must imply a narrative act after the event. But frequently little is made of this: indeed, we as readers can be made to suspend disbelief and to enter the story as though it were written by the experiencing self. Eichendorff has, however, capitalized on the artistic possibility of the two selves which coexist in the act of narration.

There are two references at the beginning of the story which make clear the temporal separation of the two selves. When the Taugenichts is employed at the castle, the gardener sees fit to give him many words of useful advice: 'Es waren noch mehr sehr hübsche, gutgesetzte, nützliche Lehren, ich habe nur seitdem fast alles wieder vergessen' [And there were many more such lovely, well-put, useful teachings, except that I've since forgotten almost everything]. And, shortly afterwards, when the Taugenichts recalls his life at the castle, he exclaims— 'ach, das alles ist schon lange her' [ah, it's been a long time]! . . . Such remarks clearly suggest that the story is told by the older, more mature self who is able to look back on adolescence with the wisdom of hindsight.

It is, however, significant that these references to the gulf in time between experiencing self and narrating self never recur. We lose all precise sense of the two selves being separated by many years—because the narrating self does not choose to write from a position of overt knowingness or of scrupulously maintained temporal detachment. Rather, he is content to enter the experiential framework of the acting self, to share the perceptions, aberrations, confusions—but without losing himself in them. He retains enough detachment to be able to highlight the comedy of what happened. The two selves are fused in a narrative act which blends intimacy and detachment, blends warmth with conciliatory and affectionate irony.

My remarks on the narrative perspective of Eichendorff's story would seem to have given powerful ammunition to those of its detractors who object that it is such an unproblematic work that it can only be read as an escapist fairy-tale masquerading as reality.

Obviously, nothing can remove the paradisal quality from the story. But, in my view, the use of the narrative perspective intimates to us, the readers, a psychological possibility which validates the serenity of the story as a whole. The question we must ask ourselves is not: is the world like this (to which the answer clearly is 'no'), but: do we ever feel that we can be 'narrators' to our own experience in the way that happens in this story (to which the answer must be 'yes'). In the human capacity for conciliatory nostalgia—and for the narrative act to which it can give rise—is to be found the deepest and most persuasive truth of *Aus dem Leben eines Taugenichts*. For we are all surely able to recount past experiences with that carefully sustained mixture of empathy and distance which is the hallmark of Eichendorff's story. Indeed, it is precisely this interplay which produces narrative liveliness, for the act of narration minimizes the separation of the two selves. 'Past' and 'present' lose their precise temporal force and become part of that immediate fictive constellation which allows the 'Ich' [I] to be both up a tree—and to be his own onlooker. The distance between past and present becomes transmuted into the spatial detachment of the adverb 'droben' [overhead]. It is this on-looker's perspective as an all-pervasive presence which sustains the narrative act of Eichendorff's story. And the good-humour inherent in this perspective tells us that all will end well—long before we reach the conclusion to the story. The good-humour is sufficient intimation: we do not need any explicit indication of the lessons which our immature hero has to learn. We do not need sententious comments which would imply the wisdom of hindsight. The attitude of the onlooker tells all: it is the narrative expression of a nostalgia so conciliatory that overt judgment is unnecessary. Indeed, one is tempted to say that, if the story is concerned with the hero's progression to the point where 'Heimat' and 'Ferne' as psychological possibilities can be united in harmonious coexistence, the narrative tone of the work is the enactment of that psychological harmony as consistently intimated perspective. For the narration itself persuades us that we can achieve a coherent, sustaining relationship towards human affairs which values both immediacy and detachment, both security and disorientation, both 'Heimat' and 'Ferne'.

Many critics have, quite rightly, insisted on the importance of locating Eichendorff's tale in its literary-historical context. It was published in 1826, and has been seen as a transitional work, standing between Romanticism on the one hand and 'Biedermeier' on the other. However much literary-historical generalizations are viewed with scepticism nowadays, the argument seems to me to have much force. There are many references in the story—both explicit and implicit—to Romantic writings, to certain recurrent themes and figures. What, in my view, must be stressed is the fact that the presence of Romanticism as a theme is subordinate to, and a function of, the narrative and psychological implications which I have discussed above. It is that combination of empathy and detachment, that deeply affectionate, ironically tinged nostalgia which makes the work both a loving tribute to, and a critique of, Romanticism. The psychological conciliations allow for literary-historical conciliations. (pp. 39-41)

> *Martin Swales, "Nostalgia As Conciliation: A Note on Eichendorff's 'Aus dem Leben eines Taugenichts' and Heine's 'Der Doppelgänger,'" in* German Life & Letters, *n.s. Vol. XXX, No. 1, October, 1976, pp. 36-45.**

GLYN TEGAI HUGHES (essay date 1979)

[*In his essay "Natural and Supernatural: Eichendorff, with Görres," excerpted below, Hughes emphasizes the complexity and depth of Eichendorff's sense of the past, discerning in his nature poetry a primitivistic appreciation of the supernatural mysteries of the physical world. According to Hughes, this appreciation, balanced by Eichendorff's portrayal of nature within the context of Christian redemption, added purity and depth to outworn Romantic poetic conventions.*]

[In Eichendorff's poems, the old motifs of Romanticism are] given new vitality by context, by being related to a profound sense of the fragility of the phenomenal world and by a tension between the magic of the senses and the threat of the dark, between eternity and history. The very familiarity of these newly charged motifs is reminiscent of the folksong. In his *Geschichte der poetischen Literatur Deutschlands* Eichendorff distinguishes the folksong from the art lyric: the former presents experience directly and in an apparently disconnected way; it is a hieroglyphic picture language. In the Naturlied (and, in this context, the reference is to a poem actually about nature)

we are frequently surprised, as we are in children, by a warmly intimate understanding of external nature and its symbolism, and by the profound insight into the mysterious spirit-world of animals. Forest, springs, clouds respond to human emotions, the nightingale sings the inexpressible; everything is as fairy-tale-like as in dreams. . . . (p. 110)

Eichendorff equally appears to respond intuitively to the natural world and certainly to relate mood to landscape. His style, too, seems at first to be very close to folksong or, at any rate, to *Des Knaben Wunderhorn*. The diction is relatively simple, though the vocabulary is naturally somewhat more extensive than that of the folksinger. The stanzaic forms are generally unadventurous and, although rhythmic patterns are sometimes used to provide speed or tension, there is little experimentation with form. The general impression is one of fluidity, and improvisation; but how much should we trust our first impressions? Would simplicity and improvisation have borne such powerful echoes into our own day? Did Schumann and Hugo Wolf, Mendelssohn, Brahms and Richard Strauss find no more in him?

There have been recent attempts . . . based on the later poems, to prove that his handling of language is highly conscious and subtle, deforming accepted syntactical patterns and creating abnormal semantic relationships in order to point the hieroglyphic character of his motifs. This is partly convincing but, even without going so far, we may see looseness of grammatical forms, the impersonal use of verbs, devices to deprive nouns of their concreteness, synaesthetic connexions, carefully judged acoustic correspondences, that all belie the simple, unreflecting poet.

Wordsworth, in the 'Immortality' ode, took up the myth of pre-existence to idealize the child's state of grace, its total harmony with the universe. Eichendorff's point of reference is personal: the happy days at Lubowitz. But both are archetypal; we are dealing with the common childhood of humanity. Fortunato's song in *Das Marmorbild* is one 'that, like memories and echoes from some other world that is our homeland, comes to us through the little paradise garden of childhood.' . . .

The garden of childhood had its thunderclouds, paradise is invaded by history; but the childhood vision, the 'freshness of a dream', is also the poet's re-creative power. On the level of simple theology, Eichendorff reintroduced the beauty of the world (as in the 1837 poem **'O Welt, du schöne Welt, du'**) into the scheme of grace. In socio-economic terms, he idealized the claims of preindustrialized life and paved the way for generations of innocents, and others, longing for the simple life. He held a remarkable balance between certainty and unease, sensuality and spirituality, Christian redemption and the darkness of the collective imagination, natural and supernatural.

What excites about Eichendorff is that, behind the apparent quiet conventionality, there combine in unusual strength the claims of sensuous natural beauty and of the transcendental. The aesthetic daemon is there all right, but under firm control. (pp. 110-11)

> *Glyn Tegai Hughes, "Natural and Supernatural: Eichendorff, with Görres," in his* Romantic German Literature, *Holmes and Meier Publishers, Inc., 1979, pp. 98-111.**

ADDITIONAL BIBLIOGRAPHY

Brown, Marshall. "Eichendorff's Times of Day." *The German Quarterly* L, No. 4 (November 1977): 485-503.
  Examines the distinctive rhetorical qualities of Eichendorff's "Der Abend" and its companion poems.

Farquharson, R. H. "Poets, Poetry, and Life in Eichendorff's *Ahnung und Gegenwart.*" *Seminar* XVII, No. 1 (February 1981): 17-34.
  Maintains that Eichendorff offers significant commentary on "the reality of life in general and poetry in particular" in *Ahnung und Gegenwart.*

Fuerst, Norbert. "The Age of Grillparzer (1820-1850): The Age of Heine?, Heine and Eichendorff." In his *The Victorian Age of German Literature: Eight Essays,* pp. 80-4. University Park: Pennsylvania State University Press, 1966.*
  An incisive comparison of Eichendorff's and Heinrich Heine's verse.

Hesse, W. G. "The Equivocal Taugenichts." In *Festschrift for Ralph Farrell,* edited by Anthony Stephens, H. L. Rogers, and Brian Coghlan, pp. 81-95. Australisch-Neuseeländische Studien zur deutschen Sprache und Literatur, edited by Gerhard Schulz and John A. Asher, vol. 7. Bern: Peter Lang, 1977.
  Underscores the Good-for-Nothing's ambiguous response to man, love, nature, and religion, thus challenging those who interpret *Memoirs of a Good-for-Nothing* as a Romantic idyll as well as those who regard it as an ironic commentary on Romantic values.

Hubbs, Valentine C. "Metamorphosis and Rebirth in Eichendorff's *Marmorbild.*" *The Germanic Review* LII, No. 4 (November 1977): 243-59.
  A psychological interpretation of *The Marble Statue* based on Carl Jung's concept of individuation.

Hughes, G. T. *Eichendorff: "Aus dem Leben eines Taugenichts."* Studies in German Literature, edited by L.W. Forster and B. A. Rowley, no. 5. Great Neck, N.Y.: Barron's Educational Series, 1961, 64 p.
  A critical analysis of *Memoirs of a Good-for-Nothing* suggesting that neither Germanicism nor Romanticism served as Eichendorff's inspiration in writing the novella. According to Hughes, *Memoirs of a Good-for-Nothing* is best understood as the "German Pilgrim's progress," for the Good-for-Nothing represents "man stripped to his essentials—disinterested, unencumbered, 'good-for-nothing' except to be God's creature."

McGlashan, L. "A Goethe Reminiscence in Eichendorff." *Monatshefte* LI, No. 4 (April-May 1959): 177-82.*
  Discusses the significance of thematic parallels in the first lyric in *The Marble Statue* ("Was klingt mir so heiter") and Johann Wolgang von Goethe's poem "Ganymed."

Nygaard, Loisa. "Eichendorff's *Aus dem Leben eines Taugenichts:* 'Eine leise Persiflage' der Romantik." *Studies in Romanticism* 19, No. 2 (Summer 1980): 193-216.
  Explicates *Memoirs of a Good-for-Nothing* as a self-conscious, ironic reflection of the Romantic failure to recover its lost sense of immediacy and wholeness of being.

Pickar, Gertrud Bauer. "Spatial Perspectives in Eichendorff's *Aus dem Leben eines Taugenichts.*" In *Studies in Nineteenth Century and Early Twentieth Century German Literature: Essays in Honor of Paul K. Whitaker,* edited by Norman H. Binger and A. Wayne Wonderley, pp. 131-37. Germanistische Forschungsketten, no. 3. Lexington, Ky.: APRA Press, 1974.

An examination of the narrator's spatial perspective in *Memoirs of a Good-for-Nothing* which emphasizes the simplicity and naiveté of his world view.

Radner, Lawrence R. "Eichendorff's *Marmorbild*: 'Götterdämmerung' and Deception." *Monatshefte* LII, No. 3 (March 1960): 183-88.
  Interprets the poem "Götterdämmerung" as an expression of the theme of deception in *The Marble Statue,* the novella in which the poem appears.

——. "The Garden Symbol in *Ahnung und Gegenwart.*" *Modern Language Quarterly* XXI, No. 3 (September 1960): 253-60.
  Identifies the garden as a symbol for the soul in *Ahnung und Gegenwart.*

——. "The Instrument, the Musician, the Song: An Introduction to Eichendorff's Symbolism." *Monatshefte* LVI, No. 4 (April-May 1964): 236-48.
  A detailed examination of the music motif in Eichendorff's works.

Riley, Thomas A. "Eichendorff and Schiller: The Interpretation of a Paragraph in *Ahnung und Gegenwart.*" *Monatshefte* L, No. 3 (March 1958): 119-28.*
  Interprets a passage in *Ahnung und Gegenwart* as a satire on the German dramatist Friedrich Schiller and his imitators.

Schumann, Detlev W. "Eichendorff's *Taugenichts* and Romanticism." *The German Quarterly* IX, No. 4 (November 1936): 141-53.
  Challenges Chester Nathan Gould's interpretation of *Memoirs of a Good-for-Nothing* (see excerpt above, 1934) and elucidates the "profoundly romantic nature" of Eichendorff's novella.

——. "Some Scenic Motifs in Eichendorff's *Ahnung und Gegenwart.*" *The Journal of English and Germanic Philology* LVI (1957): 550-69.
  Discusses Eichendorff's symbolic use of landscape and light in *Ahnung und Gegenwart.*

Sims-Gunzenhauser, William D. "The Treacherous Forest of Symbols: Duality and Anti-self-consciousness in Eichendorff and Baudelaire." *Comparative Literature Studies* XVII, No. 3 (September 1980): 305-15.*
  Predicates an affinity between Eichendorff and the French poet Charles Baudelaire based on their mutual sense of temporal and existential dualism.

Wolff, J. "Romantic Variations of Pygmalion Motifs by Hoffmann, Eichendorff and Edgar Allan Poe." *German Life and Letters* n.s. XXXIII, No. 1 (October 1979): 53-60.*
  Relates Eichendorff's treatment of the Pygmalion motif in *The Marble Statue* to the views on life after death, sex, religion, and art characteristic of Romanticism.

Workman, J. D. "The Significance of the *Taugenichts* for Eichendorff." *Monatshefte* XXXIII, No. 2 (February 1941): 64-76.
  Attempts to identify Eichendorff's purpose in writing *Memoirs of a Good-for-Nothing* and to place the novella in the evolution of Eichendorff's thought. Workman concludes that *Memoirs of a Good-for-Nothing* represents a "glorification of the ideals of Eichendorff's youth, a challenge hurled in the face of a generation too much concerned with the things of this world," and he detects in the work "a gradual reconciliation with the limitations of bourgeois existence, a first step in the direction of literary *Biedermeier.*"

Zernin, Vladimir. "The Abyss in Eichendorff: A Contribution to a Study of the Poet's Symbolism." *The German Quarterly* XXXV, No. 3 (May 1962): 280-91.
  Discusses the "progressive evolution" of the symbolism of the abyss in Eichendorff's works.

Susan (Edmonstone) Ferrier

1782-1854

Scottish novelist.

Ferrier is noted for her contribution to the regional Scottish novel and to the English novel of manners. Critics concur that her reputation rests primarily on her ability to humorously depict the manners and morals of nineteenth-century Scottish society. Following in the tradition established by such authors as Samuel Richardson and Frances Burney, Ferrier, with her contemporaries Jane Austen and Maria Edgeworth, popularized the novel of manners. While less insightful and acute than Austen's, Ferrier's bold satire is considered one of her greatest attributes. Because she believed the novel should instruct as well as amuse, moralizing abounds in her three novels: *Marriage, The Inheritance,* and *Destiny; or, The Chief's Daughter.* However, many critics find Ferrier's didacticism obtrusive and concur that it is the greatest shortcoming of her works.

Ferrier's father was an Edinburgh lawyer who was the legal agent and intimate friend of the Duke of Argyll and who became Principle Clerk of Session, where he met and befriended Walter Scott. Ferrier associated with many of the distinguished writers of her day, including Scott, Francis Jeffrey, John Wilson, Robert Burns, and Joanna Baillie. The Duke of Argyll often invited Ferrier and her family to his castle at Inverary, where Ferrier became friends with the Duke's niece Charlotte Clavering. At Clavering's suggestion, Ferrier began her first novel. The two originally planned to collaborate on the work; however, because their temperaments and goals differed radically, they eventually abandoned the idea of coauthorship, although the work included one chapter by Clavering. When *Marriage* was published by William Blackwood, it was an immediate success. However, Ferrier did not complete her next novel, *The Inheritance,* for eight years. Solely responsible for the care of her father from 1818 until his death, she was often too involved in domestic and social activities to devote much time to writing. Ferrier completed her final novel, *Destiny,* in 1831 but declined to write more, stating that she could no longer compose anything that pleased her.

Critical assessment of Ferrier has not varied substantially since her initial reception. While critics acknowledge that Ferrier's style was influenced by the clear prose of the eighteenth-century moralist Jean de la Bruyere, they also note that her works reflect the traits of the popular novel: simplistic plots, abundant quotations and misquotations, and stilted dialogue. Commentators further contend that Ferrier sometimes created implausible incidents in her plots for the sake of advancing a moral, and that characters, plots, and subplots often do not form a unified whole. Ferrier's works include a large number of eccentric characters. While critics largely consider Lady MacLaughlin and the three aunts of *Marriage* to be particularly memorable and cite them with Miss Pratt of *The Inheritance* as examples of Ferrier's keen powers of observation and talent for humorous character portrayal, several have argued that these minor characters undermine the structure of her novels. Because of the similarity of their subject and approach, Ferrier is often compared to Austen, and just as often criticized for lacking the insight and satirical acumen of her fellow novelist.

All of Ferrier's novels were generally popular successes, but most critics agree that *The Inheritance* is her best work. They contend that in addition to incorporating the humorous elements of *Marriage, The Inheritance* surpasses her other novels in structure and characterization. While Ferrier continued in this book to promote the virtues of Christian piety and the humble Scottish life, many scholars note that the didacticism of *The Inheritance* is less obtrusive than that found in *Marriage.* Critics disagree as to the quality of *Destiny.* While a number of commentators have expressed admiration for its structural unity and treatment of the theme of idolatry, others maintain that it lacks the elegance and spontaneity of her previous novels. However, critics agree that the best features of *Destiny,* like those of her two earlier novels, are its descriptive passages and colorful characterizations. As the author of humorous and vivid representations of Scottish society, Ferrier continues to attract the attention of literary historians.

PRINCIPAL WORKS

Marriage [with Charlotte Clavering]   (novel)   1818
The Inheritance   (novel)   1824
Destiny; or, The Chief's Daughter   (novel)   1831

Memoir and Correspondence of Susan Ferrier, 1782-1854
   (letters)   1898
The Works of Susan Ferrier. 4 vols.   (novels and letters)
   1929

BLACKWOOD'S EDINBURGH MAGAZINE   (essay date 1818)

Marriage, is at once discovered to be the work of a female hand, both by the minute accuracy of its ordinary details, and by the exquisite originality and instinctive fidelity of its female portraits. . . . [The author possesses] all those talents which lend eminent dangerousness to the character of a spy. She is, in the first place, both as acute and as extensive an observer, as Miss Edgeworth herself; like her, she pourtrays, with equal facility and accuracy, every gradation of social life, from the highest tone of the cool and indifferent metropolis, where every body's maxim is ''nil admirari'' [equanimity], down to the enthusiastic ignorance of a poor Highland laird's ''purple'' daughters, and the tawdry blue-stockingship of a young lady from the manufacturing district of the Lowlands. But our author knows and feels many things of which no trace is to be discovered in the witty pages of the Irish spinster. She has, in short, been in love in her time, and that has given her a mighty advantage over her calm and satirical rival. She thus unites some of the best qualities of Edgeworth and Burney; and has composed a novel, which, although very defective, both in the design and the conduct of its fable, and marked, besides, with many failings characteristic of an unpractised writer, contains in it almost as much of nature, humour, good sense, and amusement, as are to be found in any one of their most admired productions.

The plot is by no means excellent. One whole third of the book is over before we hear a word of the personage in whom its principal interest is designed to centre. But the truth is, that the heroine of *Marriage,* like the heroes of [Walter Scott's novels] *Waverley* and *Guy Mannering,* is among the most uninteresting members of the whole fabulae personae. The work consists of a series of scenes and portraits, most of them excellent in themselves, but few of them deriving much advantage from the general arrangement and purposes of the gallery in which they are inserted and displayed. We dare say, the author, after she had written her book, and considered with herself whether there were no one among her personages by whose name it should be called; and finding, with her usual discernment, that there was in reality no such individual, she christened it *Marriage;* and thus very prudently divided the compliment among some half-score of her heroes and heroines, whom, towards the conclusion of the work, she had conducted, pair by pair, to that blessed consummation. (pp. 286-87)

> *A review of ''Marriage,'' in* Blackwood's Edinburgh
> Magazine, *Vol. III, No. XV, June, 1818, pp. 286-94.*

THE BRITISH CRITIC   (essay date 1818)

We know not to whom we are indebted for this very entertaining novel [*Marriage*]; judging from the particular nature of the talent which it displays, we should feel little hesitation in ascribing it to a female pen; and had the authoress of ''Pride and Prejudice'' been alive, and a native of Scotland, our conjectures would certainly have fastened upon her as the authoress. The

humour contained in the novel before us, is considerably broader than that in which Miss Austin [*sic*] indulged, and the characters are not generally to be found in common life, as was usually the case with those which she pourtrayed; nor are they drawn with the same minuteness of touch. Miss Austin was a miniature painter; the author of *Marriage* paints in oil and upon canvass: the picture of life and manners which is exhibited, is bold and highly coloured; sometimes it even offends, from the too great heaviness of the touch. But though working with different materials, and with a correspondent difference of manner, the same sort of *mind* seems to pervade the production before us, as used to afford us so much pleasure in the writings of Miss Austin; and it is moreover projected upon the same principles of novel writing. The story is made to be altogether of subordinate importance; instead of forming a whole, or presenting the mind, when finished, with the recollection, as it were, of one large picture, it more resembles a port folio of sketches. When we have laid the book down, our memory is full of my aunt Grizzy and Lady Maclaughlan and Lady Emily; but of the hero and heroine of the tale, what they did and how they suffered, we remember comparatively nothing.

It is always to be presumed that the best and most virtuous young lady, in a novel, is the heroine, and the bravest and handsomest and politest gentleman, the hero. This is the only clue which is afforded us, for distinguishing the hero and heroine of the novel before us. It commences with a runaway match, on the part of a young lady, whose want of perfection manifestly excludes her from any right to occupy the character of a heroine; it is not till the end of the first volume, that the true heroine, the fruits of this run-away match, is born, and not till the middle of the second, that she comes fairly upon the scene; at the end of the third volume this young lady marries a gentleman, to whom the reader is scarcely introduced, and the story then dies a natural death.

Such is the outline of the tale, and the parts are filled up with no other incidents, than such as might have taken place in any ill-regulated family. The interest excited is entirely ascribable to the characters who pass to and fro upon the scene; and in delineating these, the writer displays inimitable skill and humour. (pp. 100-01)

> *A review of ''Marriage, a Novel,'' in* The British
> Critic, *n.s. Vol. X, July, 1818, pp. 100-04.*

BLACKWOOD'S EDINBURGH MAGAZINE   (essay date 1824)

The author of these works [*Marriage* and *The Inheritance*] is evidently a *female*—and as evidently one that has had abundant opportunities of observing society in a great *variety* of its walks. Add to this a keen relish for the ridiculous—a profound veneration for the virtuous—a taste in composition extremely chaste, simple, and unaffected—and perhaps the literary character of this lady has been sufficiently outlined. She has much in common with the other great authoresses of her time—but she has also much to distinguish her from them. She unites the perfect purity and moral elevation of mind visible in all Mrs Baillie's delightful works with much of the same caustic vigour of satire that has made Miss Edgeworth's pen almost as fearful as fascinating. Without displaying anything like the lofty poetic imagination of the former of these sisters in renown, or having anything like that most poetical power of pathos which relieves and embellishes the keen piquancy of the other's humorous vein—she exhibits so much quickness of perception, so much facility of thought and style, such an admirable equilibrium of mind, such a fine charity woven into the very web of sarcasm,—and withal, the views she has taken of life and manners are so very extensive, as well as true—that it is impossible for us to deny her a place considerably above any other female who has come before the British public in these days, as a writer of works of imagination. She has *all* that Miss Austin [*sic*] had—but she is not merely a Scotch Miss Austin. Her mind is naturally one of a more firm, vigorous, and so to speak, masculine tone; . . . [this lady] can paint the inmates of the cottage, the farm-house, the manse, the mansion-house, and the castle; aye, and most difficult, or at least most rare of all, my lady's saloon [*sic*] too—all with equal truth, ease, and effect. In this particular respect she is far above not only Miss Austin, but Miss Burney, and confesses equality with no female author our country has as yet produced, except only the great novelist of Ireland [Maria Edgeworth]. (p. 659)

[In *The Inheritance* the reader] will find many more characters than *Marriage* contained; he will find among these some copies, to be sure;—but he will also find not a few originals, at least as excellent as any of those in *Marriage;* and, what is best of all, he will no longer be put in mind of a gallery of portraits. The characters of *The Inheritance* are brought out in a very well conceived, and carefully and skilfully executed, fable,—they do not appear merely, but act; and, in short, the whole conception and execution of the work attest clearly and indubitably to the striking progress which the authoress has made in almost every branch of her art since the period of her debut. Nothing can be better than some things in *Marriage;* but *The Inheritance* is not only rich in things as good as those were, but has all the additional merits of felicitous design, and judicious concoction. In one word, *Marriage* was a very clever book, but this is an admirable novel.

The story, though, in *essentialibus,* no great story, is wonderfully well managed—so well, that the interest neither flags nor halts for one moment, until we are within a score or two of pages of the third volume. (p. 674)

> *A review of "The Inheritance," in* Blackwood's Edinburgh Magazine, *Vol. XV, No. LXXXIX, June, 1824, pp. 659-74.*

THE PORT FOLIO   (essay date 1825)

"The Inheritance" is attributed to a lady; but as she has not thought proper to throw up her veil, the English critics have not presumed to hazard any further conjecture, as to the source to which we are indebted for a novel which assuredly deserves to be ranked among the best of the present day. Her story is contrived with more ingenuity than those [by Sir Walter Scott] of the Waverley class, and greater attention is paid to the style, which is always easy, perspicuous, and correct. Her sentiments are such as belong to her sex. We are never offended by profanity or revolting coarseness. The dialogue is sprightly and unaffected. It does not appear to be the aim of the writer to develop individual character; her object is rather to pourtray general manners: how far she has succeeded, we dare not decide, because we can only judge . . . by the report of men and books. It is enough for us to pronounce, that she has produced two very delightful volumes, in which there is much to delight the fancy, and something to purify the heart. (p. 129)

> *A review of "The Inheritance," in* The Port Folio, *Vol. XIX, No. 274, February, 1825, pp. 129-32.*

J. BAILLIE   (letter date 1831)

[*A minor Scottish poet and dramatist, Baillie was a friend of Ferrier.*]

I received your very kind present of your [novel *Destiny*] about three weeks ago, and am very grateful for the pleasure I have had in reading it, and for being thus remembered by you. . . . The first volume struck me as extremely clever, the description of the different characters, their dialogues, and the writer's own remarks, excellent. There is a spur both with the writer and the reader on the opening of a work which naturally gives the beginning of a story many advantages, but I must confess that your characters never forget their outset, but are well supported to the very end. Your Molly Macaulay is a delightful creature, and the footing she is on with Glenroy very naturally represented, to say nothing of the rising of her character at the end, when the weight of contempt is removed from her, which is very good and true to nature. Your minister, M'Dow, hateful as he is, is very amusing, and a true representative of a few of the Scotch clergy, and with different language and manners of a great many of the English clergy—worldly, mean men, who boldly make their way into every great and wealthy family for the sake of preferment and good cheer. Your Lady Elizabeth, too, with all her selfishness and excess of absurdity, is true to herself throughout, and makes a very characteristic ending of it in her third marriage. But why should I tease you by going through the different characters? Suffice it to say that I thank you very heartily, and congratulate you on again having added a work of so much merit to our stock of national novels. (pp. 227-28)

> *J. Baillie, in a letter to Susan Ferrier in May, 1831, in* Memoir and Correspondence of Susan Ferrier: 1782-1854, *edited by John Ferrier and John A. Doyle, Eveleigh Nash & Grayson Limited, 1929, pp. 227-28.*

[JOHN WILSON]   (essay date 1831)

[*A Scottish critic, essayist, novelist, poet, and short story writer, Wilson is best known as Christopher North, the name he assumed when writing for* Blackwood's Edinburgh Magazine, *a Tory periodical to which he was a principal contributor for over twenty-five years. He is chiefly famous for his* Noctes Ambrosianae, *a series of witty dialogues between characters such as the Ettrick Shepherd and Timothy Tickler originally published in* Blackwood's *between 1822 and 1835, in which contemporary issues and personalities are treated at once with levity, gravity, and pungent satire. In the following discussion between North and Tickler, taken from the* Noctes Ambrosianae, *Wilson acknowledges the weaknesses of Ferrier's novels, including poor plots, disproportionate episodes, and use of caricatures instead of characters; yet, he praises Ferrier's depiction of Scottish society and lauds her works for their "specimens of sagacity," "flashes of genuine satire," "sterling good sense," and "mature and perfect knowledge of the world."*]

Tickler.—. . . [Miss Susan Ferrier's] novels, no doubt, have many defects, their plots are poor, their episodes disproportionate, and the characters too often caricatures; but they are all thickset with such specimens of sagacity, such happy traits of nature, such flashes of genuine satire, such easy humour, sterling good sense, and, above all—God only knows where she picked it up—mature and perfect knowledge of the world, that I think we may safely anticipate for them a different fate from what awaits even the cleverest of juvenile novels.

North.—They are the works of a very clever woman, sir, and they have one feature of true and melancholy interest quite peculiar to themselves. It is in them alone that the ultimate breaking-down and debasement of the Highland character has been depicted. Sir Walter Scott had fixed the enamel of genius over the last fitful gleams of their half-savage chivalry, but a humbler and sadder scene—the age of lucre-banished clans— of chieftains dwindled into imitation squires, and of chiefs content to barter the recollections of a thousand years for a few gaudy seasons of Almacks and Crockfords, the euthanasia of kilted aldermen and steamboat pibrochs was reserved for Miss Ferrier.

Tickler.—She in general fails almost as egregiously as Hooke does in the pathetic, but in her last piece ['**Destiny; or, The Chief's Daughter**'] there is one scene of this description worthy of either Sterne or Goldsmith. I mean where the young man [Ronald Malcolm]—supposed to have been lost at sea revisits, after a lapse of time, the precincts of his own home, watching unseen in the twilight the occupations and bearings of the different members of the family, and resolving, under the influence of a most generous feeling, to keep the secret of his preservation.

North.—I remember it well, and you might bestow the same kind of praise on the whole character of Molly Macaulay. It is a picture of humble, kind-hearted, thorough-going devotion and long-suffering, indefatigable gentleness, of which, perhaps, no sinner of our gender could have adequately filled up the outline. Miss Ferrier appears habitually in the light of a hard satirist, but there is always a fund of romance at the bottom of every true woman's heart who has tried to stifle and suppress that element more carefully and pertinaciously, and yet who has drawn, in spite of herself, more genuine tears than the authoress of 'Simple Susan.' (p. 533)

> [*John Wilson*], " '*Noctes Ambrosianae*': *No. LVIII*,"
> in *Blackwood's Edinburgh Magazine, Vol. CLXXXV,*
> *No. XXX, September, 1831, pp. 531-63.*

WALTER SCOTT   (letter date 1831)

[*Scott was a Scottish novelist, poet, historian, biographer, and critic of the Romantic period who is best known for his historical novels, which were a great popular success.*]

If I had a spark of gratitude in me I ought to have written you well nigh a month ago to thank you in no common fashion for '**Destiny**,' which by the few, and at the same time the probability, of its incidents, your writings are those of the first person of genius who has disarmed the little pedantry of the Court of Cupid and of gods and men, and allowed youths and maidens to propose other alliances than those an early choice had pointed out to them. (p. 247)

> *Walter Scott, in a letter to Susan Ferrier in 1831, in*
> Memoir and Correspondence of Susan Ferrier: 1782-
> 1854, *edited by John Ferrier and John A. Doyle,*
> *Eveleigh Nash & Grayson Limited, 1929, pp. 247-48.*

[JOHN FERRIER]   (essay date 1842)

[*John Ferrier, Ferrier's grandnephew, compiled and edited the* Memoir and Correspondence of Susan Ferrier. *In the following excerpt from an anonymously published essay he appraises the structure and characters of her works. While he finds her plots weak and many characters ludicrous, he extols Ferrier's moral principles and "rare gift of genuine humor."*]

[We] should regret on our own account, if another opportunity should be suffered to pass, without recording our feelings of gratitude and esteem for one who has added so much to our picture gallery of original character, and enlarged the boundaries of innocent enjoyment, without admitting an image or a sentiment which even a Christian moralist could disapprove.... [Yet Miss Ferrier's '**Marriage**,' '**The Inheritance**,' and '**Destiny; or the Chief's Daughter**'] are truly Novels, not 'dramatic sermons'.... [They] are pervaded not so much by the form as by the spirit of religion;—not paraded in the conventional language of a sect, but appearing as a natural spring of action in the characters—a source of consolation, endurance, or improvement.

These novels made their appearance while the public mind was fascinated by the brilliant fictions of Scott—succeeding each other with a rapidity which suggested the idea rather of creation than of composition—combining more of those higher qualities of mind which are seldom found in unison, and appealing to a more varied class of feelings than any works of fiction since the days of Shakspeare. To find patient audience, even after a well-graced actor leaves the stage, is proverbially not an easy task; but to tread the scene along with him, and divide some portion of the public attention with one who can scarcely be said to have ever left the stage vacant for any other actor ... unequivocally showed that this authoress possessed independent and original powers of mind. True, her fictions were not stimulating or highly imaginative: ['**Marriage**'], at least, had no pretensions to rouse curiosity by a dexterously-constructed plot. They dealt, in the outset, far more with the absurdities and the weaknesses of human life, than with scenes of tenderness or passion; and yet they were at once felt to possess peculiar and sterling merits of their own, though of a more sober and homely order—a sagacity and power of observation with regard to the peculiarities of character, and of dexterous combination of these into a consistent whole; the rare gift of genuine humour as opposed to mere wit and smartness; and, latterly, also a command over the resources of the pathetic, which could scarcely have been anticipated from the shrewd and somewhat dry and caustic tone of '**Marriage**,' the earliest production of the authoress. These qualities secured to the writings of Miss Ferrier, even during the ascendency of Scott, not indeed a noisy popularity, but yet an enviable place in the opinion of those whose opinion in such a question was most valuable; and now that the fascination produced by his genius has settled into a more sober, though not less deep feeling of admiration, and that the world has grown somewhat weary of the pomp and circumstance of chivalrous and historical pageants ..., the solid but unobtrusive excellences of her novels will appear more and more conspicuous, as the stars come out with an independent lustre when the sun retires.

It was fortunate for the authoress that the tastes and qualities of her mind were so essentially different from those of the great novelist with whom she was brought in contact [Scott], as probably to exclude the wish as well as the power of imitation. A mind so thoroughly cultivated as hers—so instinct with fine and excellent feeling—so alive both to natural and moral beauty—could never, of course, be destitute of poetical susceptibilities:—and indeed a love of poetry, and a delicate appreciation of its beauties, appear in many a brief allusion in the course of these volumes; but still the turn of her mind, as indicated in her works, appears the very reverse of *romantic*. Though not without a sympathy with the poetical character of the past, it is not there that she finds her home. She does not willingly enter on such a region of shadows, which the light of a stronger genius than hers is required to illuminate, but draws her materials from the present, and leans willingly on the support of realities.

The characters she paints, the objects she has in view, the incidents which she describes, are in general plain and practical, and of ordinary occurrence. Thus if, on the one hand, she subjects herself to this severe test—that we can all judge of the truth of her portraits; on the other, she never can experience, in real life, a want of individuals fitted to sit for their pictures, and whose tempting lineaments, impressed with the stamp of oddity or peculiarities of humour, appear to court the pencil. (pp. 498-500)

Yet this power of literal delineation is not without its dangers. It is apt to fix the eye too much upon mere weaknesses and peculiarities of character. The tiresome, the vulgar, the selfish, and disagreeable, are found, in fact, to be more susceptible of delineation, by distinctive traits which insure recognition, than the possessors of good feeling and good sense; just as all distortion is sure to be more easily copied than the flowing outline of perfect grace; and hence there is often a tendency in such fictions to 'people the 'isle with Calibans' [a character from William Shakespeare's 'The Tempest'], and to make the personages in general mere bores, oddities, and exceptional characters, to the exclusion of those cast in a better and healthier mould—upon whose feelings and movements, after all, the interest of every well constructed story must depend. With this tendency to the grotesque . . . , Miss Ferrier, in her first novel, was justly chargeable. It seemed as if with a reluctance, not unnatural in a female, to the display of those deeper sensibilities of which her later works have given undoubted proof, she thought it safer to approach the public from behind the comic mask of sarcastic and humorous delineation; to expose silliness, cunning, and selfishness, rather than to paint generous impulses, or strong passions—to postpone feeling to humour, and to rest the chief interest, or at least novelty and characteristic force of her work, on the creation of a group of anomalies and eccentricities, arrayed in strong contrast to each other. That these indicated close observation of nature, and that many of the characters were drawn with a wonderful coherency and look of life, was indisputable. The sketches of the old aunts at Glenfern, Jacky, Nicky, and Grizzy—particularly the latter;—of Mrs Macshake . . . and, above all, that of the epicurean physician, Dr Redgill . . . , are equal to any that could be produced from the best of our English novel readers. But bores in real life must be bores also in fiction; we are at first amused by the odd company into which we have got; but when we have 'made perusal of their faces,' become acquainted with their peculiar tricks, and watched for a little how the master-feeling or master-weakness influences their conduct, till we have got the key to their character, we become weary of such an association—refuse to be shut up any longer in such 'a ship of fools,' and long, as we could do in real life, for the relief afforded by a return to good sense and right-mindedness. Add to this, that even where the individual delineations are not in themselves exposed to the objection of caricature, they are apt to produce the effect of caricature by their combination. Possibly within a range of some hundred miles in Scotland, such a trio of maiden aunts—a laird—a Sir Sampson, and Lady Maclauchlan, might be found; but the imagination refuses to believe that so strange a set of originals could ever be congregated in one Highland parlour, at Glenfern. But in truth, in the two creations last named, Miss Ferrier appears to us to have deviated into the regions of actual caricature; as well as in her exaggeration of the earlier miseries which the London

fine-lady, and her lap-dogs, encounter in their desolate Highland residence; which remind us too forcibly of those accumulations of petty annoyances, and ridiculous *contretemps* [inopportune and embarrassing occurrences], out of which the authoress of 'Cecilia' [Frances Burney] was too much disposed to compound the staple of her novels.

In truth, it must be admitted, that in **'Marriage'** the incidents generally were little conducive to the interest of the novel. Of story, it had as little as the knife-grinder. The tale wandered up and down without advancing—passed from one generation to another—moved from Scotland to England, and back again, with no other principle of progress or development, but that of giving the widest scope for the exhibition and opposition of the strange beings to which it had lent a temporary existence. As a mere tale it excited, in truth, no interest whatever. . . . [The] desultory movement of the story, and the want of any strong interest in the individual scenes themselves, enabled the reader to resign or resume it, without risk of breach of engagement, or oblivion of the dinner bell. On re-perusing it recently, the sketches of London fashionable life seem to us to wear a superficial air. Even the love scenes—generally the stronghold of female composition—seem drawn with a certain reserve and timidity. Altogether, it may be doubted whether the appearance, for it was little more, of a connected narrative, did not rather impair than set off the effect of the characters; and whether an avowed gallery of Scottish originals *à la Bruyère* [in the style of the seventeenth century French moralist Jean de La Bruyère], without such an accompaniment, would not have impressed the public with a higher notion of the powers of the writer.

But in spite of the crudity of the tale in point of plot, and the predominance of scenes and personages calculated on the whole rather to weary than to please, it was not difficult to detect, in the vivacity and consistency of the sketches, the shrewdness and point of the dialogue, and even in some glimpses of more tender feeling which were allowed as if by stealth to appear—powers which a greater degree of self-reliance, and a more careful study of the arts of composition, could not fail to cultivate into excellence. (pp. 500-02)

[In] Miss Ferrier's next novel, **'The Inheritance,'** the advance made in artistic skill and dexterity was remarkable. She had learned . . . to feel her own strength, and to confide in her command over the higher passions and more tender emotions, as well as over the ludicrous and the grotesque. In this novel, an interesting story unrolls itself before us on an ample canvass; not, indeed, altogether without something of a theatrical development—for the visits of the intrusive American stranger, do a little remind the reader of the movements of those mysterious personages who hover, wrapped in cloaks, in the background of the stage, in the last act of melodramas—but still on the whole artfully arranged; exciting, and at last satisfying, the curiosity of the reader, by a striking, if not perfectly probable denouement. We are raised above the petty miseries and *tracasseries* [worries] of **'Marriage,'** into a sphere where higher passions are felt to be at work for higher objects. Scenes of strong pathos, and stirring interest, alternate with the mere common places and conventionalities of Lord Rossville's drawing-room; and the reader forgets the impertinences of Miss Pratt, and the *niaiseries* [foolish talk] of Mrs Major Waddell, in the intense curiosity with which he watches the plots of the selfish Delmour maturing before his eyes . . . , and the many touching and beautiful traits which occur in the masterly portrait of old uncle Adam. This is a character which is obviously a favourite with Miss Ferrier, and which she has, in substance, repeated in the Inch Orran of **'Destiny.'** At first he looks utterly repulsive and hopelessly heartless—a petrifaction as bleak and hard as the spot on which he seems to have become rooted for life. But as the barest spot, when looked into, is found to be not without some patches of verdure in its bosom, and springs that well forth to fertilize the apparently sterile soil, so in uncle Adam the cherished recollection of a boyish passion which has clung to him through life, infuses a vein of sympathetic feeling into his stern breast, and opens for him, through all the frosts of age and disappointment, a source of natural tears. Nothing can be better than the idea of supposing uncle Adam in his turret at Rossville so fascinated with 'Guy Mannering,' on which he has accidentally laid his hands—that he delays and at last postpones his departure indefinitely, that he may have the pleasure of seeing poetical justice done on Glossin. The tinge of romance which lingers in his character, gives an air of probability to the incident, and renders it at once a characteristic trait and a delicate compliment.

The family of the Blacks—the Major—his lady constantly asserting the privilege and dignity of the new-married woman—the pompous inanity of the Peer—the bustling impertinence of the impassive Miss Pratt—are sketched with equal skill and care. But the authoress has really abused her power over the reader, by the unrelenting manner in which she has linked this tiresome busy-body with the whole course of the tale, and the most interesting of its scenes of passion and suspense—so that the reader is constantly wishing that the Hearse which brought her to Lord Rossville's might be permitted to take her back. The omnipresence of this tormentor, and the scenes with the American, Lewiston, we think the chief drawbacks of the tale. The idea of the American borrowing the name of his cousin, and passing himself off as the real father of the heroine, appears not a very likely one; and the success of the scheme with Mrs St Clair, who had seen the true Lewiston, less probable still.

The last of Miss Ferrier's novels, **'Destiny, or the Chief's Daughter,'** appeared in 1831; and though few novelists can be expected to proceed in a regular course of improvement, such we think was in this instance the case. Its framework seems more compact and well ordered than even that of **'Inheritance;'** it has equal simplicity with more variety; the story works itself out in natural progression, without the aid of mysterious Americans and nocturnal *rencontres* [meetings], while over all is cast a hue of gentleness and tenderness. . . . [In **'Destiny'** there] is abundance of cheerfulness—here, too, there is a sprinkling of the comic. The same power of inventing creatures at once extravagant and natural which had shadowed out the Macshakes, Redgills, Pratts, Uncle Adams, of **'Marriage'** and **'Inheritance'**—reappears; though fortunately more in snatches and passing glimpses, in the cockney Ribbles and the moderate minister M'Dow. But, as we have said, these eccentricities hang more loosely on the story, and interrupt but slightly its strong, natural, and pathetic interest. The whole picture of the establishments at Glenroy and Loch Dhu; the growth of the contrasted characters of the children of the Laird and his cousin; the blank produced in the mind of the old chief by the sudden death of his son—are conceived and executed with a skill which no female writer of the present day has surpassed. There are some passages in the description of the desolate father's distress, when the heir of his Halls and hopes is taken from him . . . which it is difficult to peruse without tears. The hero, Ronald Malcolm, too, pleases us better than those of **'Marriage'** or **'Inheritance'**—Douglas, or Lyndsay. His mixture of high spirit, impetuosity, rashness, and generosity, are more

interesting than the uniform self-possession and Grandisonlike propriety of his predecessors. But surely it was a mistake to make the whole course of the tale hinge on so ultra-romantic and sentimental a proceeding, as the voluntary disappearance of the hero from his family and his country. A shipwrecked youth returning to his home, some years after his supposed loss at sea, stands gazing through the window of his paternal mansion at his father, mother, brother, and sisters, assembled in the room where he had played when a boy; he sees his mother again looking cheerful; a lover hanging over the chair of his favourite sister, and preparations on foot for a dance among the younger children. The twilight walk to Inch Orran—the scene itself as witnessed from the window, is touchingly painted. But when Ronald is described as so deeply mortified and surprised to find his loss forgotten at the distance of years, that he flies from the spot in despair—binds himself by 'a rash vow' never to return, till he can bestow on his parents the estate of which his return would have deprived them—and for nine years afterwards disappears entirely from the eyes of the reader—we pause and ask ourselves whether we have not accidentally exchanged a novel of Miss Ferrier's for some production of the Minerva press. (pp. 502-05)

On the whole, our admiration for [Miss Ferrier's] talents is only equalled by the respect we feel for the high principles which she has always advocated. Her novels, we believe, have taken their place in public opinion among the classical productions of their class—on a level with those of Miss Austen, and, unless we are much deceived, considerably above those of Miss Burney. (p. 505)

> [*John Ferrier*], *"Miss Ferrier's Novels," in* The Edinburgh Review, *Vol. LXXIV, No. CL, January, 1842, pp. 498-505.*

THE SATURDAY REVIEW, LONDON   (essay date 1882)

[As a novelist Miss Ferrier] is certainly only second to Miss Austen, and may fairly be put on a par with Miss Edgeworth, who may be said to have done for Irish what Miss Ferrier did for Scotch character, in giving to the world the results of an experience and observation which were minute without being narrow. There is of course this difference, that Miss Edgeworth's novels were mostly written with a more obvious purpose of pointing out abuses and suggesting remedies than is found in Miss Ferrier, although in this respect the influence of Miss Edgeworth, as in other respects the influence of Miss Austen, may be traced in *Marriage*. . . . (p. 86)

[It is in Miss Ferrier's] exceptionally fine appreciation and rendering of certain types of character, rather than in any interest afforded by the story as a story, that the great attractiveness of *Marriage* is to be found. The characters who move round the chief personages of the plot are more interesting than the chief personages themselves. . . . As in many of Scott's novels, it is the Scotch characters who give the book its tone and life. The picture of life at Glenfern, the characters of the laird and his sisters, Miss Jacky, Miss Grizzy, and Miss Nicky, of Sir Sampson, and notably of Lady MacLaughlan—these are the things which . . . will prevent [*Marriage*] from ever falling into the list of forgotten novels. It has also a value as a record of English manners of the time preserved by a keen observer who always wrote like a lady; but its most enduring charm will lie in the delineations of Scotch life and characters. As a work of art it is in various ways inferior to the two novels which followed it; . . . but it has, besides the attractions upon which we have dwelt, the special interest belonging to the first work of an author whom it at once made famous, and who followed it up with other works to which she devoted more skill and patience than are to be found in the vast majority of modern novels all heaped together. (pp. 86-7)

"Miss Ferrier's Novels," in The Saturday Review, *London, Vol. 53, No. 1369, January 21, 1882, pp. 86-7.*

THE SPECTATOR (essay date 1882)

[*The following excerpt begins with a letter from Ferrier to Charlotte Clavering, with whom she had intended to collaborate on* Marriage. *In this letter, Ferrier offers a criticism of Clavering's work and expounds her own "ethics of fiction."*]

Part of your plot I like much, some not quite so well,—for example, it wants a moral—your principal characters are good and interesting, and they are tormented, and persecuted, and punished, from no fault of their own, and for no possible purpose. Now, I don't think, like all penny-book manufacturers, that 'tis absolutely necessary that the good boys and girls should be rewarded and the naughty ones punished. Yet I think, where there is much tribulation, 'tis fitter it should be the *consequence* rather than the *cause* of misconduct or frailty. You'll say that rule is absurd, inasmuch as it is not observed in human life; that I allow, but we know the inflictions of Providence are for wise purposes, therefore our reason willingly submits to them. But as the only good purpose of a book is to inculcate morality and convey some lesson of instruction, as well as delight, I do not see that what is called a *good moral* can be dispensed with, in a work of fiction.

Miss Ferrier lived before the proclamation of the "Art for Art" gospel, and her phraseology is certainly out of date; but there is a core of strong common-sense in her view of the ethics of fiction, and her practice shows that she did not carry her conviction of the necessity for a "good moral" to any inartistic extreme. Fiction is a reflection of life, but of life as it presents itself to the eye which sees it steadily and sees it whole; and thus seen, it is enduringly ethical. In detail, it may appear unmoral, or even immoral; but when surveyed in the mass, the confusion falls into order, just as features which are separately plain and wanting in relation to each other, gain harmony, and even beauty, from a commandingly attractive expression; and the only defect of Miss Ferrier's view, or rather of her way of putting it, is that she seems to regard "the moral" as a thing to be attained by a skilful manipulation of the facts of life, rather than by an honest and fearless representation of them. (p. 158)

A number of edifying lessons may be drawn from *Marriage,* but anything like a set "moral" is nowhere to be found. We are introduced to several married couples, well and ill matched, principally the latter; but it cannot be said that Miss Ferrier has any teaching more definite than that happiness in marriage depends largely or altogether on congeniality of character and temperament, and this truth, though doubtless important, is not specially novel or illuminating. In matters of detail, we are inclined to think that Miss Ferrier is confusing, rather than helpful, to the diligent seeker after wise words. Lady Juliana

marries for love, and makes a mess of it; Adelaide Douglas marries without love, and makes a still greater mess of it. On the other hand, Alicia Malcolm also marries without love, at any rate without the highest love she is capable of feeling, and yet lives happily ever afterwards; so that the balance of evidence would seem to be in favour of the astounding "moral" that love in marriage is a mistake, were it not that the union which is, of course, the most important in the book, that of the hero and heroine, is a love-match which perfectly realises the approved ideal. As an instructive manual for presentation to "persons about to marry," Miss Ferrier's story must be pronounced a failure; but, happily, instructive manuals for all sorts and conditions of men, women, and children are tolerably numerous, while novels as lively and amusing as *Marriage* are intolerably rare; so, perhaps the emotion which, in the circumstances, has the best claim to be considered well regulated is one of gratitude for the presence of the amusement, rather than of regret for the absence of the moral.

Sir Walter Scott hit upon what is, perhaps, the most descriptive single epithet that could be applied to *Marriage,* when he described it as a "lively work." We cannot but derive from it the impression that, during its production, the author's high spirits never failed her, but that every sentence was the outcome, of genuine healthy enjoyment; and as this is just the one impression which we fail to derive from most of the imaginative literature of our own day, the man or woman who now makes its acquaintance for the first time will probably get from it a keener, because a less familiar, pleasure than that enjoyed by its earliest readers. Miss Ferrier was too much of a caricaturist to be a great humourist, and she fails in pathos as no great humourist has ever failed; but her humour was of a high, though not of the highest order. Even in mentioning caricature as a characteristic of her method, injustice would be done if the mention were not accompanied by a statement of the limits within which the criticism is applicable. In the humour with which she delineates personages whom she has studied from life, there is nothing of what can be fairly called caricature,— nothing but that slight sharpening of the angles of personality which is essential to vivid portraiture. The three aunts, Miss Jacky, Miss Grizzy, and Miss Nicky, are as far from being caricatures as are the Dodson sisters in [George Eliot's novel] the *Mill on the Floss,* whom we cannot help thinking of in connection with them. Another portrait, drawn with strictly restrained veracity, is that of Lady Maclaughlan, . . . who, curiously enough, reminds us of another of George Eliot's personages, Mrs. Cadwallader, in *Middlemarch.* Lady Maclaughlan is the most enjoyable character, in a book where enjoyable characters are far from rare. The scenes at Glenfern Castle . . . in which her ladyship makes her first appearance, are irresistibly amusing; and her reception, in her laboratory, of the coach-load of visitors who unexpectedly appear on Tuesday instead of on Thursday, the day named in the invitation, is an even finer triumph. Few writers have shown greater skill than Miss Ferrier in combining the abandon of burlesque with the restraint of realism; in approaching so near to the region of farce as to catch the inspiration of its riot-inspiring atmosphere, and yet never overstepping the boundaries of legitimate comedy. Perhaps her most farcically-conceived personage is Dr. Redgill, the *gourmand* physician, and her most farcical scene that in Mrs. Bluemits' drawing-room, where the assembled literary ladies indulge in copious quotations, interspersed with elegant remarks; but in the delineation of the character and the description of the intellectual assembly, she is a caricaturist rather than a pure humourist. She is strongest when she is most Scotch, and weakest when she is most English; it is only when she is on her native heath that we see her at her best, but when we do thus see her, the sight is delightfully memorable. Her nature, like that of many of her countrymen and countrywomen, was essentially critical, and when she attempts to draw an ideal character, such as Mrs. Douglas or Colonel Lennox, she sinks to a dead-level of unimpressive common-place. These lapses are, however, rare; the general impression left by her work is one of joyous mastery; and people who like to read a novel which they can not only admire, but really luxuriate in, will thank the publishers for this reprint of a story which is far too amusing to deserve the fate of remaining unknown to all but the few superior persons who know everything. (p. 159)

> *"Miss Ferrier's First Novel," in* The Spectator,
> *Vol. 55, No. 2797, February 4, 1882, pp. 158-59.*

THE SATURDAY REVIEW, LONDON   (essay date 1882)

[Miss Ferrier's novel *The Inheritance* is] more complete as a work of art than *Marriage,* and also, we are inclined to think, than *Destiny,* in which the plot is more strained than in *The Inheritance,* and which is to some extent overburdened by moral disquisitions. There are scenes and characters in *Destiny* which are as good as they can be; Mr. M'Dow, for instance, is worthy to stand side by side with Mr. Collins in Miss Austen's *Pride and Prejudice;* and old Inch Orran is a complete study, of which one only wishes there were more, of shrewd selfishness and caustic humour. But the heroine is, as in *Marriage,* a trifle too good, so that one is not disposed to disagree with the scheming Mme. Latour when she suggests that Edith is insipid; and there is a certain want of reality about the loves of Reginald and Florinda, while the actual conclusion, or perhaps we should say want of conclusion, of the novel is somewhat unsatisfactory. *The Inheritance* is, to our thinking, more free from faults, if not more full of merits, than either of the other two novels. (p. 214)

> *"Miss Ferrier's 'Inheritance'," in* The Saturday Review, *London, Vol. 53, No. 1373, February 18, 1882, pp. 214-15.*

GEORGE SAINTSBURY   (essay date 1882)

[*Saintsbury was an English literary historian and critic of the late nineteenth and early twentieth centuries. A prolific writer, Saintsbury composed a number of histories of English and European literature as well as several critical works on individual authors, styles, and periods. In the following appreciative review, Saintsbury finds that "of the four requisites of the novelist, plot, character, description, and dialogue, she is only weak in the first."*]

[Miss Ferrier's] books contain some excellent sentiments on the vanity of rank and fashion, but somehow they leave on the reader's mind an impression that . . . it was more comfortable to her to walk down her literary St. James's Street on the arm of an earl than on that of a simple commoner who would have been puzzled to tell the name and status of his grandfather. However this may be, her sketches were at least taken from the life, and she did not, like certain writers of our own day, talk familiarly of the Honourable Jem and the Honourable Jemima on the strength of seeing the one at a respectful distance in a club smoking-room, and the other across some yards of gravel and the railings of Rotten Row. (pp. 315-16)

[The idea of *Marriage*] is the introduction of a spoilt child of English fashionable life to a rough Highland home abounding

with characters. Miss Ferrier's way of working out this conception was to a certain extent conventional—it is doubtful whether, with all her power, she ever got quite as clear of convention as did her admirable contemporary, Jane Austen— but it brings about many very comical and delightful situations. (p. 316)

Lady Maclaughlan [is] one of the strongest and most original characters who had yet found a home in English fiction. Her defects are two only, that she is admitted to be very nearly a photograph from the life, and that, like too many of the characters of *Marriage,* she has but very little to do with the story. (p. 318)

[There] is a lively episode in which Mary Douglas is taken to see an ancient great-aunt in Edinburgh, whose account of the "improvements" of modern days is not a little amusing. Mrs. MacShake, indeed, is one of those originals, evidently studies from the life, whom Miss Ferrier could draw with a somewhat malicious but an admirably graphic pen. Similar characters of a redeeming kind in the second part of the book are Dr. Redgill, Lord Courtland's house physician, a parasite of a bygone but extremely amusing type, and Lady Emily, Lord Courtland's daughter, who is one of a class of young women whom for some incomprehensible reason no novelist before Miss Austen dared to make a heroine of. Mary herself, who is the heroine, is a great trial to the modern reader. (p. 321)

[It] can hardly be said that there is any story in *Marriage.* It is a collection of exceedingly clever caricatures, some of which deserve a higher title, and the best of which will rank with the best originals in English fiction. . . .

The individual studies and characters of *The Inheritance* are as good as those of *Marriage,* while the novel, as a novel, is infinitely better. In her first work the author had been content to string together amusing caricatures or portraits without any but a rudimentary attempt at central interest. *The Inheritance,* if its plot is of no great intricacy (Miss Ferrier was never famous for plots), is at any rate decently *charpenté* [well-constructed] and the excellent studies of character, which make it delightful to read, are bound together with a very respectable cement of narrative. (p. 322)

The Inheritance is a book which really deserves a great deal of praise. Almost the only exceptions to be taken to it are the rather violent alternations of [recognition and adventure], which lead to the conclusion and the mismanagement of the figure of Lewiston. This ruffian is represented as a Yankee, but he is not in the least like either the American of history or the conventional Yankee of fiction and the stage. He is clearly a character for whom the author had no type ready in her memory or experience, and whom she consequently invented partly out of her own head and partly from such rather inappropriate stock models of villains as she happened to be acquainted with. He is not probable in himself, nor are his actions probable, for a business-like scoundrel such as he is represented to be would have known perfectly well that forcing himself into Rossville Castle, and behaving as if it were his own property, was an almost certain method of killing the goose that laid the golden eggs. But these faults are not of the first importance, and the general merits of the book are very great. Gertrude herself is a consistent, lifelike, and agreeable character, neither too sentimental nor too humoursome, but perfectly human; all the other characters group well round her, and as for the merely satirical passages and personages they are wholly admirable. (p. 326)

[*Destiny*] is an advance even upon *The Inheritance,* and much more upon *Marriage,* in unity and completeness of plot, and it contains two or three of Miss Ferrier's most elaborate and finished pictures of oddities. But, as it seems to me, there is a considerable falling off in *verve* and spontaneity. (pp. 326-27)

Miss Ferrier's characteristics as a novelist are well marked and not likely to escape any reader. But nothing brings them out so clearly as the inevitable comparison with her great contemporary, Miss Austen. Of the many divisions which may be made between different classes of fiction writers, there is one which is perhaps as clearly visible, though it is perhaps not so frequently drawn, as any. There is one set of novelists (Le Sage, Fielding, Thackeray, Miss Austen, are among its most illustrious names) whose work always seems like a section of actual life, with only the necessary differentia of artistic treatment. There is another, with Balzac and Dickens for its most popular exponents, and Balzac alone for its greatest practitioner, whose work, if not false, is always more or less abnormal. In the one case the scenes on the stage are the home, the forum, the streets which all know or might have known if they had lived at the time and place of the story. These writers have each in his or her own degree something of the universality and truth of Shakespeare. No special knowledge is needed to appreciate them; no one is likely in reading them to stop himself to ask—Is this possible or probable? In the other case the spectator is led through a series of museums, many if not most of the objects in which are extraordinary specimens, "sports," monstrosities. . . . Of these two schools, Miss Ferrier belongs to the last, though she is not by any means an extreme practitioner in it. A moment's thought will show that the system of relying for the most part on thumb-nail sketches which she avowedly practised leads to this result. Not only is the observer prompted to take the most strongly marked and eccentric specimens in his or her range of observation, but in copying them the invariable result of imitation, the deepening of the strokes, and the hardening of the lines, leads to further departure from the common form. These eccentricities, too, whether copied or imagined, fit but awkwardly into any regular plot. The novelist is as much tempted to let her story take care of itself while she is emphasising her "humours" as another kind of novelist is tempted to let it take care of itself while he is discoursing to his readers about his characters, or about things in general. Hence the sort of writing which was Miss Ferrier's particular *forte* leads to two inconveniences—the neglect of a congruous and sufficient central interest, and the paying of disproportionate attention to minor characters. The contrast, therefore, even of *The Inheritance* with, let us say, [Miss Austen's] *Pride and Prejudice* is a curious one, and no reader can miss the want in the later book of the wonderful perspective and proportion, the classical avoidance of exaggeration, which mark Miss Austen's masterpiece. On the other hand, it is interesting enough to let the imagination attempt to conceive what Miss Ferrier would have made of Lady Catherine, of Mr. Collins, of the Meryton vulgarities. The satire would be as sharp, but it would be rougher, the instrument would be rather a saw than a razor, and the executioner would linger over her task with a certain affectional forgetfulness that she had other things to do than to vivisect.

Notwithstanding this drawback, notwithstanding her admitted inability to manage pathos (which in her hands becomes mere *sensibilité* [sensitivity] of an obviously unreal kind), and lastly, notwithstanding her occasional didactic passages which are simply a bore, Miss Ferrier is an admirable novelist, especially for those who can enjoy unsparing social satire and a masterly

faculty of caricature. She writes, as far as mere writing goes, well, and not unfrequently exceedingly well. It is obvious . . . from the general tone of her work that she was thoroughly well read. There are comparatively few Scotticisms in her, and she has a knack of dry sarcasm which continues the best traditions of the eighteenth century in its freedom from mere quaintness and grotesque. The character of Glenroy at the beginning of *Destiny* is nearly as well written as St. Evremond himself could have done it. . . . (pp. 329-30)

[Ferrier's main claim] to be read is unquestionably in her gallery of originals, or (as it has been, with the dispassionateness of a critic who does not want to make his goose too much of a swan, called) her museum of abnormalities. They may or may not have places assigned to them rather too prominent for the general harmony of the picture. They may or may not be exaggerated. There may or may not be a certain likeness to the fiendish conduct of the ancestor of the author's friend, Lord Cassillis, in the manner in which she carefully oils them, and as carefully disposes them on the gridiron for roasting. But they are excellent company. The three aunts, Lady Maclaughlan, Mrs. MacShake, Dr. Redgill, and in a minor degree the Bath *Précieuses* [excessively refined literary women] in *Marriage,* Lord Rossville, Miss Pratt, Adam Ramsay, and above all "Mrs. Major" in *The Inheritance,* Molly Macaulay, Mr. McDow, and the Ribleys, in *Destiny,* are persons with whom the reader is delighted to meet, sorry to part, and (if he have any affection for good novels) certain to meet again. When it is added that though she does not often indulge it, Miss Ferrier possesses a remarkable talent for description, it will be seen that she has no mean claims. Indeed, of the four requisites of the novelist, plot, character, description, and dialogue, she is only weak in the first. The lapse of an entire half-century and a complete change of manners have put her books to the hardest test they are ever likely to have to endure, and they come through it triumphantly. (p. 331)

George Saintsbury, "Miss Ferrier's Novels," in The Fortnightly Review, *Vol. XXXI, No. CLXXXIII, March 1, 1882, pp. 314-31.*

SIR GEORGE DOUGLAS   (essay date 1897)

[Miss Ferrier's *Marriage*] was disfigured by direct and unsparing portraiture of living persons among her acquaintance. Now no doubt this kind of writing may be productive of extreme mirth to persons qualified to read between the lines, and it must be acknowledged that Miss Ferrier's talent has made the mirth outlast its immediate occasion. Still, judged as art, this kind of thing is neither great nor gracious, and to her credit be it said that the authoress of *Marriage* lived to see that this was so, and to amend her style accordingly. (p. 112)

[Lady Maclaughlan in *Marriage*] is certainly one of the most memorable figures in all fiction. And among the most laughable scenes in all fiction must certainly be counted those in which in high dudgeon she cuts short her visit to Glenfern Castle, and—still better, and indeed unsurpassable—in which the ill-starred spinsters, mistaking the day, arrive to visit her when they are not expected.

Nor must it for a moment be supposed that such creations as this and the Aunts are mere masterpieces of the caricaturist. In Miss Ferrier's best characters it may almost be said to be a rule that caricature enters only into the details, and is never allowed to interfere with the main outline. An accusation far more justly to be brought against the authoress of this book is that of hard-heartedness, or a defect of sympathy and even of toleration for her own creations. Susan Ferrier was an uncompromisingly candid woman, as her interesting account of the visits paid by her to Sir Walter Scott are enough to show. That her heart was a kind one we know; but when she took pen in hand it was not her way to extenuate anything. Neither was she given to view persons or occurrences through any softening light of imagination or feeling. 'What a cruel thing is a farce to those engaged in it!' wrote another Scottish author. But she, having devised a farcically cruel situation, squares her shoulders and regards its development with a ruthlessness more proper perhaps to science than to art. Not a touch of compunction has she for her heroine—who, intolerably selfish and heartless as she is, is yet but a child and the victim of the harshest circumstance; not a touch of pity for the pathos and repression of such lives as those of the Aunts. In a word, tolerance is not her strong point. And, admirable as it is, her art yet suffers by the limitation of her sympathies. For one pines for the hundred little humanising touches by virtue of which the same characters—living though they be—might have lived with a fuller and more gracious life. It is stated that Miss Ferrier's favourite author was La Bruyère, and in such studies as those of Lady Placid and Mrs Wiseacre he is obviously the model followed. And, though her best creations surpass those of her master as a living character will always surpass an abstract type, yet in this, her earliest effort, she still retains a good deal too much of the frigid intellectual method of the Frenchman.

What will, perhaps, more generally be considered a legitimate ground for the unpleasant task of fault-finding is, however, the extremely inartistic construction of the book. As we approach the middle, we are surprised to find the interest shifted to an almost entirely new set of characters, who belong to a new generation. Thus at a time when Lady Juliana cannot be much more than eighteen years of age, she ceases to be prominent in the story, and after the briefest interval we are called on to follow the fortunes of her twin daughters, who are now nearing that age. The bridegroom, Douglas, and two of the Aunts disappear altogether from the book; and this is the more to be regretted because there are few readers but will infinitely prefer the racy humours of the elder generation to the insipid long-drawn-out love-affairs of the contrasted sisters, even when these are more or less successfully enlivened by the sallies of the shrewd Lady Emily, by the caricature figure of Dr Redgill . . ., and by the absurdities of the literary *précieuses* [excessively refined women] of Bath. (pp. 118-20)

In the endeavour to improve upon her first achievement, Miss Ferrier was triumphantly successful. 'The new book [*The Inheritance*],' wrote one of Mr Blackwood's correspondents at the time of its publication, 'is a hundred miles above *Marriage*.' Nor does this assertion overshoot the mark; for if the one is at most a bit of brilliant promise, the other is a superb performance. Foremost among its advantages must be counted, in place of the slip-slop of *Marriage*, an interesting and admirably-compacted plot, and a vigorous literary style—the latter marked indeed, yet not marred, by a mannerism of literary quotation. What was shapeless and redundant in *Marriage* is here moulded and restrained by exigencies of the story, with the result that characters well-defined, and skilfully contrasted and relieved, confront the reader standing bodily and firmly on their feet. (p. 121)

[The plot of *The Inheritance*] is a model of its kind, whilst from first to last the conduct of the narrative is perfect. Indeed

the *form* of the story could not be improved—a rare merit even in a masterpiece of British fiction; and though the book is a long one, it contains not a superfluous page. Among the numerous authors quoted in the course of it are Shakespeare and the Greek dramatists, and perhaps, without stretching probability too far, we may assume that the authoress had studied the latter as well as the former. In any case *The Inheritance* in its own degree unites principal characteristics of the Greek and the Shakespearian drama, for the web of circumstance inexorably woven about the innocent and unconscious heroine is entirely in the manner of the first, whilst the indifferent, life-like alternation of tragic and ludicrous incident in the narrative is of a piece with Shakespeare's irony. (pp. 124-25)

But if the book is remarkable for its admirable story, certainly not less remarkable is it for the extraordinary wealth of character which it portrays. Probably few 'novels of plot' are so rich in character, few 'novels of character' so strong in plot. It may be that some carping critic of the ungentle sex will be found to object to Lyndsay and to Delmour, the contrasted lovers of the heroine, as to 'a woman's men'—to urge that their demeanour is too consistently emotional, too demonstrative, to be founded upon any very solid base of character or of disposition. But supposing (which I am far from granting) that there were some truth in this, here at any rate all ground even for hypercriticism must end. (p. 125)

Miss Ferrier had reached middle life when she wrote *The Inheritance*, and perhaps the laughter which it provokes is less boisterous than that aroused by the first essays of her youth. But for a scene of high comedy—to select one from many—the first conversation of Miss Pratt and Uncle Adam would certainly be difficult to surpass. Finally, we have abundant evidence that in all that she wrote our authoress was actuated by a genuine desire for the moral and religious welfare of her reader; but in comparison to that of *Marriage*, her *tone* in this book is as is the influence of a well-guided life to a sententious homily delivered from a pulpit. In one word, there is no single point in her art in which she has not risen from what is crude and tentative to what is finished and masterly. (p. 127)

As *The Inheritance* represents the meridian of the writer's powers, so *Destiny* represents their decline—not because there are not some as good things, or very nearly as good things, in the latter as in the former, but because the whole is very much less good. The construction of *Destiny* is loose and inartificial, and almost from the outset the want of a strong frame-work which shall hold the contents together and keep them in place makes itself felt. Properly speaking, there are two stories in the story,—namely, that which centres in the disposal of the Inch Orran property and the adventures of Ronald Malcolm, and that which concerns itself with the development of the relations between Edith and her recalcitrant lover. In itself of course this would be no defect, but instead of being interwoven, or subordinated one to the other, the two stories are allowed to run parallel and distinct until near the end of the book. Thus their interest is dissipated—an effect which diffuseness of treatment materially increases. Idle pages and straggling incidents abound, and in fact the sense of form which was so conspicuous in *The Inheritance* is in *Destiny* conspicuous only by absence.

If we judge it as an essay in character-painting, rather than as a story, no doubt the novel comes off better. Again, as in *The Inheritance*, we have a gallery of masterly portraits—though this time the collection is smaller, and the paintings less highly-finished; and again we feel that these portraits are drawn, not from some conventional limbo of the novelist's, but from observation of life itself, backed up by true imagination. Among the group, the Reverend Duncan M'Dow bears off the palm from all competitors. This insufferable person . . . is a piece of life itself, and the description of his luncheon-party is as good as anything accomplished by the authoress. The incarnation of fashionable selfishness and frivolity in the person of Lady Elizabeth Malcolm runs him close; but she is probably a less entirely original creation than the Minister—not that she is in any sense a copy, but that the same sort of model has been oftener studied. If we seek for something pleasanter to contemplate, the simple warm-hearted Molly Macauley, the dreamer of dreams, and the devoted adherent of the Chief who snubs her, is an endearing figure. The Chief himself . . . is a conspicuous example of materialisation and degeneracy, though the dotage of his 'debilitated mind and despotic temper' becomes almost as tiresome to the reader as it became to Edith and Sir Reginald. The key to the character of Benbowie, Glenroy's echo, is not quite apparent. . . . The vignettes of Inch Orran, the 'particular man,' and his wife, also stand out in the memory, as does that of the odious Madame Latour. And from this it will be seen that, with one or two exceptions, the more disagreeable personages of the book remain the most in evidence, for the Conways and the family of Captain Malcolm fade into insignificance beside those whose names are enumerated above. And, though the crux is an old one, where the high purpose of the writer is so much insisted on, perhaps it may not be unfair to enquire how far exactly she can be held to succeed in her aims, when even the regenerate reader is ill at ease in the company of her good characters and enjoys himself among her awful examples. The artificiality of some of its dialogues and the triteness of some of its reflections are further symptoms of the enervation which has begun to invade the book. (pp. 128-30)

[If] Miss Ferrier's work lacks the sweetness and delicacy of Miss Austin's [*sic*], it has at its best a strength to which her English sister's makes no pretension. The portraits of the former are *bitten in* with a powerful acid unknown in the chemistry of the latter. But if she was sometimes *downright* to the verge of cruelty, Miss Ferrier's view of life was a sound one. She strikes unsparingly at the rawness and self-sufficiency which are characteristic defects of such large numbers of our countrymen; yet she remains without rival as a painter of Scottish society, and one at least of her novels deserves to rank with the masterpieces of British fiction. (pp. 132-33)

> *Sir George Douglas, "Miss Ferrier," in his* The Blackwood Group, *Oliphant Anderson & Ferrier, 1897, pp. 110-33.*

AUGUSTINE BIRRELL (essay date 1898)

[*This essay was written in 1898.*]

["**Memoirs and Correspondence of Susan Ferrier**"] is a dour book, not a little reminiscent of the wind-swept streets, stony, brass-plated houses of the "gray metropolis of the North" [Edinburgh], where, though be it remembered in the "old town," Miss Ferrier was born in 1782. (p. 30)

[As for Miss Ferrier's] three novels, it is perhaps enough to say that they delighted some of the best judges of Scotch tales that ever lived. . . . I was brought up to regard them with favour, and some of the strongest motives that prompt mankind still urge me to extol them as of the first order. Devoutly as I hope that they are indeed classics, I cannot conceal from myself that I notice stealing over them what looks suspiciously like

the hues of old age, decay, and death. A great deal of them is written in a style which does not obviously defy time—there are long, dreary bits in all three novels, and altogether I tremble. Miss Ferrier must be compared with Miss Burney and Miss Edgeworth—to pit her against Miss Austen is as absurd as to couple anybody with Shakespeare. Miss Ferrier is quite as good as Miss Burney, and has some advantages over Miss Edgeworth. (pp. 32-3)

Miss Ferrier took naturally to writing:

> For know that I am descended from a race of scribes. I was born amidst briefs and deeds. I was nurtured upon ink—my pap-spoon was the stump of an old pen, my christening robe was a reclaiming petition, and my cradle a paper-poke!

This early familiarity gave her writing from the first an assurance and grasp which, had her literary traditions only been a little sounder, might have secured her a longevity hardly likely to be hers. Still, however that may be, and it is perhaps idle to predict, Miss Ferrier was and must ever remain a considerable writer.

I cannot say that ["**Memoirs and Correspondence of Susan Ferrier**"], apart from many lively letters of Miss Ferrier's own, is very interesting. In fact, I have found it a little depressing. None the less, it is a true book. (p. 35)

> *Augustine Birrell, "Miss Ferrier," in his* More Obiter Dicta, *William Heinemann Ltd., 1924, pp. 30-5.*

THE ATHENAEUM (essay date 1899)

['**Memoir of Susan Ferrier**'] mainly consists of letters, and Susan Ferrier was not at all a good letter-writer. . . . [More] than seventy pages are taken up with . . . correspondence over '**Marriage**,' mainly Susan Ferrier to Miss Clavering. . . . Meant to be witty, these twenty or thirty letters are the most depressing that we have ever read, stupider even than the Swan of Lichfield's, flatter than would be champagne poured out eighty years ago. (p. 106)

> *A review of "Memoir of Susan Ferrier," in* The Athenaeum, *No. 3718, January 28, 1899, pp. 106-07.*

STEPHEN GWYNN (essay date 1899)

It is more than eighty years since *Marriage* was published, and you can buy it to-day in any book-shop for fourpence halfpenny. That shows at least a singularly robust power of survival, and immortality is freely claimed for authors who have very much less to show for it than a lady who has amused four generations of readers. If she had been content to do that, her fame might rest secure; but unhappily she was possessed with the desire to convey moral instruction, and that has overlaid her humour and her genuine faculty of creation with a dead weight of platitudes under which they must inevitably sink. (p. 419)

[*Marriage*] was a work full of extremely amusing studies taken direct from life; Lady MacLaughlan is in her way a true creation, and, fantastic as she is, she plainly belongs to the generation which produced Lady Hester Stanhope, a person as "man-minded" and eccentric (though stately even in her eccentricity) as Sir Sampson's directress. Even Lady Juliana, wild caricature though she may be, bears the same relation to the life of those days as a drawing by Gilray, and remains interesting to the student of the history of affectations. (p. 424)

Upon the whole *The Inheritance* is to be preferred to [*Marriage*]. Miss Pratt is beyond praise; she belongs to the same sisterhood as Lady MacLaughlan and the Misses, but Miss Ferrier had the power of keeping the individual character absolutely distinct while she stamps upon it the common characteristics of a particular society. Lord Rossville, the pompous nobleman for whose special confusion Miss Pratt is created, really rises above caricature, and the scenes between the pair are often excellently diverting; and one cannot too highly praise the art by which Miss Pratt, while remaining the same person, is made to present an entirely different side of her character to Uncle Adam. The story itself is of course a poor example of a superannuated fashion; we have to swallow it or skip it. . . . Indeed Miss Ferrier's whole work belongs properly speaking to the drama rather than to the novel; and it is surprising that, with her gift for strong and effective drawing of comic character and her perfect willingness to accept any convention in the way of plot, she did not furnish materials for at least a temporary success on the boards. (pp. 424-25)

It is hardly necessary to criticise *Destiny,* which presents the faults of the other novels in an exaggerated form and gives a singularly false and unreal view of life. Glenroy, the unreasonable Highland chief, compares very ill with King Corny in Miss Edgeworth's *Ormond* but there is an undeniable pathos in the portrait of this imperious old man, struck down with paralysis, more than ever imperious and unreasonable, yet absolutely dependent upon those whose convenience he had never for a moment considered. His henchman, Benbowie, not a servant, but a companion attached to him by a tie of unreasoning habit stronger than any devotion, is excellently rendered; he is not wanted to point a moral, and thus Miss Ferrier is content to make him live and he does live. Molly Macaulay, his pendant in the picture, remains almost the only likeable person in the sisterhood which began with the Misses. It is a sad pity that such powers of characterisation were practically nullified by a defective theory of art. The moralisings of the characters whom Miss Ferrier selects for admiration are in this book quite intolerable; and the minister, Mr. McDow, is a caricature so ugly as to be positively offensive, though drawn with a coarse strength. (p. 425)

> *Stephen Gwynn, "Miss Ferrier," in Macmillan's Magazine, Vol. LXXIX, No. 474, April, 1899, pp. 419-27.*

ROSE M. BRADLEY (essay date 1922)

Among the once popular novelists of the early nineteenth century Miss Susan Ferrier is practically forgotten. And yet at much the same time that Jane Austen was enjoying herself and delighting her own and future generations at the expense of provincial society in England, this Scottish lady was throwing a no less remorseless searchlight over those aristocratic circles north of the Tweed in which it was her privilege to move. The neglect into which her books have fallen is accountable, but not altogether merited. She was not a great artist, chiefly because she lacked the perfect balance of her famous contemporary. On the one hand her satire had a tendency to degenerate into caricature, and on the other her sensibility too often outweighed her sense. She was, moreover, caught in the shackles of that evangelical spirit of her time which obliged her in her merriest moments to provide a moral, and the 'Methodism' of

their virtuous friends, at which her exalted characters jeered, was her own unconscious stumbling-block. And yet her humour was irrepressible and her powers of observation scarcely less fine than those of the inimitable 'Jane.' Her wit, as keen as it was often kindly, fell alike upon the just and the unjust, and she knew how to tell a story filled with incident and co-incident, and hold the attention of her readers because her own interest would never weary in the tale that she was telling. She was the social historian of the Highland lairds and their castles of great and lesser degree, and of the people who frequented these castles. Her heart was essentially in the Highlands, for, though she transported each of her heroines temporarily to England, she had little of the English aristocracy or the middle classes that was good to say, and, according to her testimony, English society of that day regarded Scotland as a barbarous and semi-civilised country. (pp. 241-42)

[When, in Miss Ferrier's novel *Marriage*, Lady Juliana is] relieved of her Scottish husband and his ancestral surroundings, and restored through misfortune to much of her former splendour in the house of her brother, Lord Courtland, the moral in this case was not unduly enforced. But a moral she would have, and her heroines as a rule went sadly burdened with it, and in consequence have little of the spirit and audacity of so many of the lesser characters. Mary Douglas, Lady Juliana's discarded daughter, is the most reasonable of Miss Ferrier's heroines, and manages to retain a certain intelligence of her own in spite of an overweening sensibility, and the fact that she is removed from the care of a devoted aunt in Scotland to the Cinderella-like existence at Bath, to which her fashionable mother and twin sister do their best to condemn her. (p. 244)

Miss Ferrier's value as a social historian has not been sufficiently recognised. She wrote in the days when the lairds kept open house, of which the neighbouring parson, a favourite butt of the author's wit, and all the lesser members of the clan, took full advantage. . . . Ladies were still 'handed in' to dinner by their partners, were invited to take a glass of wine by the gentlemen, and the conversation of Dr. Redgill leaves nothing to the imagination of the plenty which was set before them. These were the days when the heroines of fiction could only show real emotion if they swooned upon all occasions and 'wept without control.' Miss Ferrier's ladies carried this sensibility to excess. It is said that Macaulay tried to count the number of swoons in *Inheritance,* but that his perseverance broke down before the task was accomplished. It is the more curious that Miss Ferrier should have over-weighted her heroines with so much sensibility, for neither she herself nor her friend Miss Clavering seems to have been unduly troubled with this weakness. The spirited Lady Emily, who defends her cousin from Lady Juliana's tyranny, seems to us to belong very much more to the author's own type, with her ironical humour, her good sense and vivacious intelligence. (pp. 246-47)

[*Marriage*] is the best known of Miss Ferrier's three novels, but *Inheritance* has quite as much to recommend it. The old-fashioned demand for incident in a novel is here amply satisfied, for the plot to impose a false heiress upon Lord Rossville is extremely elaborate and packed with sensation. (p. 247)

The author is certainly at her liveliest in the opening chapters [of *Destiny*], . . . but the plot itself is saturated with false sentiment. . . .

[There] is one character in the book which in its pure unselfishness and sweet reasonableness goes far to redeem much that is sentimental and commonplace. Molly Macaulay, Edith's devoted governess . . . is, as Miss Joanna Baillie truly says, 'a delightful creature' [see excerpt above, 1831]. She is, moreover, a rather unique type of the author's creation, for, in her, goodness can be allied with common sense and not swamped in the evangelical spirit of self-conscious piety. (p. 249)

> Rose M. Bradley, "Susan Ferrier: A Forgotten Satirist," in The Nineteenth Century and After, Vol. XCII, No. 546, August, 1922, pp. 241-50.

MURIEL MASEFIELD (essay date 1934)

The glory of Susan Ferrier's books is the character-drawing, in which lively satire is just sufficiently mitigated by touches of tenderness: she knew a variety of Scottish types, and a great number of individuals whose idiosyncrasies, fostered by the comparative remoteness of the Highlands and the proud faith of the Chief's family in their own tradition and standing as part of the immutable order of things, made them tempting and delightful material for a novelist. Unfortunately these gems of character are set in plots which abound in the paralysing tendencies of the minor novelists of the period: they are written to illustrate inexorable moral purposes, and there is frequent recourse in them to premature deaths, mysteries of birth and unexpected inheritances, in order to provide trials of virtue and apportion rewards and punishments with a lavish and confident hand. In *Marriage* the heroine, Mary Douglas, is too good to be altogether lovable, and she is rewarded by the totally unforeseen accession of her lover to the very Highland castle in the shadow of which she has been brought up by her dear adopted mother. . . . In *The Inheritance* Edward Lyndsay outrivals even Mary Douglas in conscious perfection of character, and no less than three Earls of Rossville die unexpectedly or prematurely in order that the hearts of the chief characters may be thoroughly searched out and the moral inexorably pointed. In *Destiny* an early death and a supposed loss in a ship-wreck serve the same moral and dramatic ends, and there are tedious conversations on such subjects as Sabbath keeping and the superiority of reading John Howard's Journal to amusing oneself with Pepys. Another trying habit of Susan Ferrier's is to make her characters burst into long quotations of verse. . . . (pp. 83-4)

Discounting these faults as chiefly due to the influence of period, which only genius can over-ride, we can still agree with the verdict of "Timothy Tickler," whose criticism was influential in his own day, that, in spite of defects, these novels are "all thick-set" with "sagacity, happy traits of nature, flashes of genuine satire, humour, sterling good sense and mature knowledge of the world" [see excerpt above by John Wilson, 1831]. (p. 84)

[The plot of *Destiny*] hinges on melodramatic circumstances, and the morality is obtrusive, but the character-drawing is excellent. The old Earl and his sister are convincing from the outset. Miss Pratt is a perfect example of the perennial visitor who contrives to spend the greater part of her life in other people's houses. (p. 87)

Destiny has less lively satire than the two earlier novels, but it is impregnated with Scottish scenery and Scottish air from start to finish: the brief episodes in England only serve to make the Highlands even more present to the mind. (p. 88)

It is a great pity that so much tedious matter is combined with the satirical humour, good feeling and insight which Susan Ferrier certainly possessed: but those who have acquired the judicious art of "skipping" will reap a pleasant harvest in these three novels, and lovers of Scotland should find more to be grateful for than to excuse. (p. 89)

> Muriel Masefield, "Susan Ferrier and Her Novels (Scottish Life)," in her Women Novelists from Fanny Burney to George Eliot, 1934. Reprint by Books for Libraries Press, Inc., 1967, pp. 82-9.

FRANK GENT (essay date 1945)

[Miss Ferrier's] clever, satirical, and most amusing novels of the Scottish upper and middle class of a hundred years ago fall into a category next to the very highest, and her work has been most undeservedly neglected. The great majority of those who read Fanny Burney, Thomas Love Peacock, and even Maria Edgeworth have never heard of Susan Ferrier. Jane Austen, that supreme artist, stands, of course, beyond comparison, but it can be confidently asserted that anyone who reads one of Miss Ferrier's novels will agree that it approaches nearer to Miss Austen's standard than do any of the writers just mentioned. Aunt Grizzy, for example, in Miss Ferrier's **'Marriage'** is as truly drawn and as entertaining as Miss Bates [from Miss Austen's novel 'Emma']. (p. 82)

Susan Ferrier indeed did more than give us bright and witty sketches of Scottish society. She presented us with a gallery of vivacious portraits of an age, more picturesque than ours, which was passing even as she wrote. . . .

No novelist has ever realised more fully than Susan Ferrier that the purpose of a novel is to interest and entertain. She was a born comedienne, a keen observer of character and incident, a piquant recorder, and she wrote with an enjoyment which carries the reader along. No books are more difficult to put down unfinished, and if this be a test of a good novel Miss Ferrier passes the test with flying colours. (p. 83)

['**Marriage**'] fills to the full the old definition of a novel as "a merry companion to shorten the tedious toil of weary ways." The story never flags, except for a few brief passages when the writer becomes a little sententious and points the moral. But that never lasts long, and after paying tribute to conventional sentiment the "merry companion" is on the road again.

Good as '**Marriage**' was, there were better things to follow. It is generally agreed that Miss Ferrier's second novel, '**The Inheritance,**' represents an advance on her first. The plot is more compact and better contrived, and the many excellent character studies are more closely woven into the pattern of the story. . . .

[The characters] are numerous, and most striking creations. Miss Ferrier was not so successful with the lovers, Colonel Delmour and Lyndsay, but she brings out well the tragedy of Mrs St Clair, whose schemes in the end go wrong. (p. 89)

[In '**Destiny**'], as in the other novels, we are presented with a rich gallery of portraits. The gem of the collection is the Reverend Duncan M'Dow, whom [Francis] Jeffrey called "an entire and perfect chrysolite." . . .

Of the other characters mention must be made of the Laird of Benbowie, with his fearful and wonderful waistcoats; the parsimonious Laird of Inch Orran; the Ribleys, amusing but conventional; and not least the simple but warm-hearted and endearing Molly Macauley.

Miss Ferrier is obviously more interested in and more successful with characters who are picturesque, amusing, and even odd. This is true of all her novels, and she has sometimes been accused of exaggeration and caricature. . . . (p. 90)

[Yet her] characters are not creatures of her comic fantasy, but men and women who lived, and who were in some cases perhaps too like their living originals for Miss Ferrier's complete peace of mind.

Many attempts have been made to compare Jane Austen and Susan Ferrier, but it would be more appropriate to speak of their contrasts; for they had little in common beyond their powers of observing and their urge to write. Miss Austen was incomparably the greater artist. She worked on her "two inches of ivory" with consummate skill and exquisite irony. Susan Ferrier worked on a larger, rougher canvas, with bolder and more sketchy strokes, but, to quote Sir George Douglas [see excerpt above, 1897] . . . , "if Miss Ferrier's work lacks the sweetness and delicacy of Miss Austen, it has at its best a strength to which her English sister makes no pretensions. The portraits of the former are bitten in with a powerful acid unknown in the chemistry of the latter," and it may perhaps be added that Miss Ferrier has on occasion touched deeper emotions and shown herself capable of dealing more adequately with a tragic situation. (p. 91)

> *Frank Gent, "Susan Ferrier, a Neglected Genius," in* Blackwood's Magazine, *Vol. 258, No. 1558, August, 1945, pp. 82-92.*

W. M. PARKER (essay date 1965)

[*Marriage*] suffers from an excess of characters. Susan Ferrier deals with human absurdities. She attacks the tiresome, the vulgar, the selfish. Her barbs are often inflicted unsparingly. Although she possesses masculine sagacity and shrewd observation, her real distinction is in comic exaggeration. (p. 12)

When we come to consider her second novel, *The Inheritance*, we recall the claim made that Susan Ferrier was doing for Scotland what Jane Austen and Maria Edgeworth had done respectively for England and Ireland, namely, producing characters that live in the hearts and minds of readers. A further claim, that she is the Scottish Jane Austen, cannot be readily accepted. If she never indulged in Maria's extreme didacticism she was equally incapable of Jane's delicate irony. Susan Ferrier's satire is robust and hardhitting in comparison. (p. 13)

[When] Susan Ferrier began *The Inheritance* we may guess that Jane Austen was at the back of her mind. Moreover, emulation of Miss Austen's expression seems to occur in one instance at least. We find this in the first sentence of the novel which corresponds, almost word for word, with the opening sentence of *Pride and Prejudice*. Susan Ferrier begins: 'It is a truth universally acknowledged that there is no passion so deeply rooted in human nature as that of pride.' Jane Austen opens with 'It is a truth universally acknowledged that a single man in possession of a good fortune must be in want of a wife.' These two sentences with the same initial six words appear to be a remarkable coincidence.

Again, it might be argued that Susan Ferrier was indebted to Jane Austen for the comic Miss Pratt whose endless stream of gossip bears a marked resemblance to that of the garrulous Miss Bates in *Emma*. (p. 14)

Commenting on *The Inheritance* in January, 1842, . . . [John Ferrier (see excerpt above)] noted that Susan Ferrier 'had learned . . . to feel her own strength, and to confide in her command over the higher passions and more tender emotions as well as over the ludicrous and the grotesque'. But she had not sufficient control over her exaggerations. Even in this more moderate novel they thrust themselves in, permeate here and there. (pp. 17-18)

[In *Destiny*] a lively sense of the ridiculous is still maintained and the satire continues to be hard. . . . Again we meet the usual quaint characters, hit off in customary style, and we come upon almost Trollopian descriptions of everyday occurrences. The caustic presentation of Mrs. Malcolm, one of the redeeming passages in the book, anticipates descriptive touches in Dickens. . . . (p. 19)

Occasionally Susan Ferrier gives way to affected diction. Such an artificial expression as 'when the overflowings of a generous heart are confined within the narrow limits of its own bosom, and the offerings of love are rudely rejected by the hand most dear to us' is scarcely forgivable.

The portrait of McDow is worthy of a place in the gallery of clerics in English fiction. . . . We feel that had Susan Ferrier written a Disruption novel she would have found ample material in the social problems of ministers and their wives who quitted the manse and a secure social position for uncertain prospects in the wilderness of 'vulgar, unendowed dissent'. (p. 20)

[John Ferrier] rated *Destiny* too highly when [he] declared that the presentations of the establishments at Glenroy and Loch Dhu 'are conceived and executed with a skill which no female writer of the present day has surpassed', and, reviewing Susan Ferrier's three novels in the same article, . . . placed them 'on a level with those of Miss Austen', and, indeed, 'considerably above those of Miss Burney'. Such praise was surpassed some thirty years later by William Forsyth, Q.C. and man of letters, who considered that Susan's three novels, '*Marriage, Inheritance,* and *Destiny,* especially the two former, are among the best in the English language'. While we may not agree with these extravagant eulogies nevertheless the novelist who could create Lady MacLaughlan, Uncle Adam, Miss Pratt, and the Rev. McDow was certainly not devoid of the gift of successful characterisation. (pp. 20-1)

> *W. M. Parker, "Susan Ferrier," in his* Susan Ferrier and John Galt, *Longmans, Green & Co., 1965, pp. 8-23.*

NELSON S. BUSHNELL (essay date 1968)

One of the concerns implicit in [*Marriage*] is with the manners of two contrasted cultures, English and Scottish. Both are presented by the narrator and illustrated through the activities of the fictitious characters, but the tone of the presentation is colored by the device of showing the impact of each culture upon a representative of the other. The English representative, Lady Juliana, being an unsympathetic character, the reader tends to reject her adverse criticisms, while he is likely to share the admirable Mary's distaste for aristocratic English social behavior. It should be noted, however, that Mary's own point of view is not as representatively Scottish as, say, that of the Glenfern aunts, for Mary herself is half-English by blood and through her upbringing by the half-English Mrs. Alicia Douglas.

As would be expected from a Susan Ferrier, the picture of Scottish manners is much more inclusive than that of the English. Her Scottish material is derived on the whole from personal familiarity, and covers a variety of classes and local cultures, predominantly Highland but not excluding Lowland and metropolitan (Edinburgh). The novel reveals to us a social structure that is relatively homogeneous, with an easy, frank intercourse between town and country, between lairds and their subordinates. The prevailing social tone, forthright and practical to the verge of coarseness, allows single-sided "humors" characters to flourish. (p. 218)

The treatment of English manners is consistently unsympathetic and satirical, and nowhere more forcefully than in the exhibition of the hobbies and preoccupations of fine ladies: the quest for clothes of conspicuous style, for livery and upholstery of newest fashion and uncommon elegance, and for footmen of exalted physique.... (p. 223)

Miss Ferrier virtually ignores English manners outside the aristocracy—except for Mary's idyllic glimpse of church-bound villagers (in a second-hand "literary" manner), and Lady Emily's contemptuous allusion to elopement as a popular fad.... (p. 224)

The structure, such as it is, of *Marriage* is not so much strengthened as it is determined by the manners material. The bipartite design presents in the first volume the Highland scene under the impact of Lady Juliana's intrusion, and in the remaining two volumes, after a lapse of some seventeen years, Mary's gentler but no less antipathetic contact with the Courtlands and their circle near Bath. Volume III is distinguished from Volume II by the added attention to the Lennox family at Rose Hall, introduced late in Volume II.

Within these major divisions the structure is episodic, the successive episodes being arranged to provide contrast, or to display examples of manners unrelated to the central story. The first major episode, Lady Juliana's sojourn at Glenfern, is prolonged to exploit the clash of cultures within it; then the scene shifts to a very different sort of Highland life, at Lochmarlie Cottage; and after the birth of twin girls Lady Juliana is restored to England, in preparation for an entirely new set of interests in Volumes II and III. Volume II opens with alternate scenes in Scotland and England, to bridge the lapse of time; then Mary's journey to join her mother and sister permits the introduction of Lowland and Edinburgh manners. The remainder of Volume II deals with Mary's life at the Courtlands' Beech Park, and introduces brief visits to Rose Hall (parallel to the Glenfern-Lochmarlie Cottage contrasts in I), in preparation for Volume III. The final volume moves back and forth between the Courtland and Lennox menages, with periodic side-trips to exhibit other varieties of manners: the condolence call; Aunt Jacky's letter; Aunt Grizzy's letter, and arrival at Bath; lunch with Mrs. Pullens (domestic economy in the upper middle class); and tea with Mrs. Bluemits (the Blue-stockings); Adelaide as duchess in London and at Norwood Abbey; with a return to the Highlands at the very end.

The author seems to have sensed a casualness of design in this story and has made a few half-hearted attempts at coherence, introducing the Scottish volume with an English scene, returning to England in the interpolated history of Mrs. Alicia Douglas ..., and interlarding the English volumes with news from Scotland. Furthermore, Volume I introduces a prophecy that Glenfern will some day support Loch Marlie (realized though not recalled in the denouement); and at least one of the

interpolated episodes, the condolence call, relates itself to the central story by introducing two characters, Mrs. Downe Wright and the Duke of Altamont, who will complicate Mary's progress toward matrimony. On the other hand, the final complication, the Lennox-MacLaughlan feud, by the tardiness of its introduction calls attention to a wasted opportunity to enhance coherence.

A more powerful and basic coherence is achieved by the persistence of certain types of character: Glenfern's in Sir Sampson; the old Earl of Courtland's in Frederick and the younger Lindore; Juliana's and Alicia's in Adelaide and Mary respectively; the Duke of L.'s in Altamont. A related use of character is the juxtaposition of the complementary Lady Emily and Mary; their mutual affection engages the reader's, and he is tempted to conjecture that together they approximate a projection of the author's own contradictory nature. It is in this field of characterization that the manners become powerfully functional in *Marriage,* and we are faced at the outset with the anomalous situation that the manners of the period not only permitted but even encouraged the development of individual, one-faceted originals; in Scotland, the eccentric is the typical. Glenfern, his sisters, his daughters, Sir Sampson, Lady MacLaughlan, each is a peculiar product of the older Highland manners lingering at the turn of the century, each has his own special involvement in the pressing concerns of everyday life. Correspondingly, the languid nonchalance cultivated by the English aristocracy not only produces representative types like the Courtland men, like the Dukes of L. and Altamont, like Juliana and Adelaide, but also permits the burgeoning of its own eccentrics: the sycophantic gourmand Dr. Redgill, the suggested guests for the ball, and the naturalized Englishwomen Mrs. Pullens, and Mrs. Bluemits with her entourage. (pp. 225-26)

[The very title of] *Marriage* suggests a focus of moral interest. Critics have been tempted (not without color of justification) to compare Susan Ferrier with Jane Austen, but a common characteristic (common likewise among their contemporaries) of announcing at the outset a general or abstract concept central to the ensuing novel in fact highlights a basic contrast in their interests. Jane Austen's stated themes: pride, sensibility, persuasion, are all psychological qualities; marriage on the other hand is a social institution, and in a book on marriage, manners must be an end in themselves, and not merely the begetters, or the outward signs, of traits of personality. In exploring the theme and the institution of marriage through some fifteen or sixteen examples, as well as in frequent discussions of the topic ..., the author appears to suggest that love-matches (unsupported by common sense and self-restraint), such as Juliana's with Harry Douglas, and marriages of convenience (unleavened by love, or at least respect), such as Adelaide's with Altamont, are equally doomed to disaster. Only such a marriage as serves a rational purpose and is founded upon mutual love or respect can truly succeed.... (p. 227)

An examination of the novel *Marriage* leaves the final impression that the chief impetus which it reflects is a delight in comically extravagant characters; it is likely that the challenge of identifying their originals in Scottish society was partly responsible for the initial popularity of the book. Further sources of delight were the affectionate amusement generated by archaic Highland manners, and the comic contempt aroused by English aristocratic behavior. As these manners contribute to the flowering of ridiculous characters, and to their active concerns and mutual pressures, the function of manners in the novel extends itself. The need of carrying its load of manners helps to determine the structure of the narrative. And finally, manners are central to the exploration of the theme. Quite clearly, then, Susan Ferrier's first novel confirms and augments a current in the development of prose fiction, a current released by her predecessor Fanny Burney, and reaching maximum depth and force in the novel of manners as it issued from the contemporary pens of Maria Edgeworth, Walter Scott, and Jane Austen. (pp. 227-28)

> *Nelson S. Bushnell, "Susan Ferrier's 'Marriage' As Novel of Manners," in* Studies in Scottish Literature, *Vol. V, No. 4, April, 1968, pp. 216-28.*

HERBERT FOLTINEK   (essay date 1971)

While *Marriage* is quite patently devoted to a documentation of social and cultural conditions, the author's indebtedness to the late eighteenth-century school of novel-writing cannot be overlooked. Its didactic lesson, involving a suitable punishment for the 'victims of self-indulgence' and rich rewards for the well-tutored child, is in accordance with the convention of the educational novel. Conversely, the numerous and extensive character sketches, often featuring figures whose bearing on the plot is slight, would place the author firmly among the followers of the character-painting of Fielding and Smollett. But such traditional elements are always observed rather than imitated by Ferrier and never mar the narrative texture of which they form a part. While the organization and tone of the character drawings would seem to derive from earlier examples there is little doubt that their material was assembled from personal impressions, and as the action progresses the well-rounded figures and vividly conceived scenes assume more weight than the educational point they serve to illustrate. (p. xi)

While most assessments of Susan Ferrier's narrative art assign her to the regional school of Maria Edgeworth, Scott, and Galt, her importance for the less reputable 'fashionable novels' is usually overlooked. The 'fashionable' tale, which attained such prominence in the twenties and thirties, hardly ever introduces a main figure who is as immune to the follies of high life as the heroine of *Marriage;* but the cold-hearted beauty and her passionate paramour who enact the sub-plot in the third volume of the novel might well be regarded as prototypes of the amorous entanglements so typical of the genre, and Lady Juliana's craving for refined amusements and exclusive luxury in fact anticipates one of its main themes. Susan Ferrier herself would probably have taken little account of such convenient pigeon-holes. She endeavoured to portray 'every gradation of social life' whether her object was the Scottish peasantry, of whom there appear unfortunately far too few in her works, or the family of an English lord. And though the social scene is by no means complete, its characters and situations are so arranged as to assume the significance of a survey of human conduct in general. (pp. xii-xiii)

[Though] we may fail to be persuaded by the moral lesson of *Marriage,* its important function within the narrative structure can hardly be denied. The plot of the novel is largely directed by didactic impulses. Slight as it may seem, it serves to combine the various character portrayals, dialogue passages, and descriptions, which Susan Ferrier's lively imagination suggested to her, into an organized narrative account.

Susan Ferrier's contemporaries were inclined to set her second novel, *The Inheritance,* above her first work; some even gave preference to *Destiny,* her third attempt, in which a growing

tendency to comprehend human behaviour in black and white colours becomes apparent. These, after all, were novels with a 'compact and well ordered' framework that could not fail to hold the ordinary reader's interest during its perusal. A more detached view of the works will reveal that the author had sought to control her material by freely employing the devices of melodrama. . . . The chief merit of *The Inheritance* is undoubtedly found in a series of lively scenes involving Scottish middle-class characters that have hardly a function in the artful plot as such. *Destiny* is decidedly weaker than that. Here the uneasy machinations of the story are ill combined with an increasing amount of moralizing, and the paleness that infects very nearly all the figures and incidents of the book betrays them as second impressions of her earlier and more vigorous inventions. Though an occasional telling scene, a quick exchange of dialogue, still show her mastery, the overall flagging of energy is unmistakable. (pp. xvii-xviii)

[Though Ferrier's] characters, situations, and episodes never grow into a tissue of manifold relationships and various conceived connections as they do in the hands of greater artists, she was well able to compound them into an organic whole. *Marriage* needed the element of moral fable to become a tale, but the didactic scheme is in fact only the most tangible aspect of the structural unity of the novel.

There is hardly a figure that could be omitted without leaving a noticeable gap in the progress of the plot. Few readers will wish to miss the epicurean Dr. Redgill, whose unabashed adherence to his master passion provides much of the amusement. Of equal importance, however, is his function in the narrative proper; upon Mary's arrival at Beech Park he soon takes sides with the ingenuous visitor from the land of vigorous appetites, only to oppose the heroine at a later instance when this will help to throw her now well-established personality into better relief. (p. xix)

A definite weakness arises from the author's neglect to take account of the passing of time between volumes I and II. More than fifteen years have intervened when the narrative is fully resumed, and Lady Juliana's twins have ripened into young ladies; but no visible change appears among the members of the Glenfern circle. They all recover their former station as if awakened from a charmed sleep. . . . In this respect Susan Ferrier stands convicted of a flagrant offence against the intended truthfulness of her account. But this lapse cannot be held too severely against her; it closely approximates to a traditional practice, of keeping the minor figures static while the main characters are allowed to develop.

Susan Ferrier may have lacked the all-comprehending energy of the great authors, but she was well able to employ the structural principles of contrast and analogy and could make the novel a meaningful system of attitude, incident, and comment. Her use of setting offers a final and striking example of her artistic perception and skill: one of the most pervasive structural antitheses in the narrative is the emphasized contrast between the harsh North and the pleasant but variable South; a fundamental polarity which even the extensive sphere of conduct and observation cannot entirely contain. The Scottish Highlands appear bleak and forbidding as a background to the 'unfortunate association of manners and characters' described in the introductory chapters, and the shallow Juliana is indeed unable to reconcile contrary modes of life and thought. To Mary, who becomes the heroine in the second part of the novel, the Highlands seem a sheltering refuge and source of strength to help her bear her predicament in the alien atmosphere of

Beech Park. *Marriage* contains seminally much that is developed and brought to perfection in the great Victorian novel. (pp. xx-xxi)

Herbert Foltinek, in an introduction to Marriage: A Novel *by Susan Ferrier, edited by Herbert Foltinek, Oxford University Press, London, 1971, pp. vii-xxi.*

WENDY CRAIK (lecture date 1971)

[*In Craik's consideration of Ferrier's comic methods, the critic suggests that Ferrier's novels, despite their didacticism, restricted subject matter, and conventional plots, clearly demonstrate her ability to "invent and handle all kinds of comic social situations, and to render farcical and grotesque ones credible." The following was originally presented as a lecture at a conference held at the University of Edinburgh on August 15-21, 1971.*]

[It] would have been much to Miss Ferrier's advantage if Sir Walter Scott had stuck to poetry and never turned his mind to novel-writing. It would also be to her advantage if no critic of her had ever heard of Jane Austen. Being Scots—and an Edinburgh Scot at that—she is inevitably compared with the former; and being a woman who writes novels of manners, she is unavoidably likened to the latter. She is not really like either of them. She is not, let me admit from the start, playing in their league. Though not among the great novelists of the world, she *is* among the good ones, and among those of the good ones who offer lasting and undating enjoyment. Her general claims, not only to fame, but to being read a century and a half after she wrote, rest upon the very little historical sense needed to relish her, because she writes best about characters—and eccentric ones at that—and because she is at her best in the comic sides of a novelist's business. Although . . . she has far from infinite variety, her merits are of the kind that age cannot stale nor custom wither. What is more, they are very much her own merits, unlike those of other novelists before or after. Her Scottish characters—that is, all her best characters—are different from Sir Walter's, Galt's or Smollett's, not only in kind, but in the uses to which she puts them and the means by which she presents them. They are also, of course, unlike Jane Austen's. But the temptation to look at her as if she were a Scottish Jane Austen is equally a disservice, because her intentions and her means are unlike Miss Austen's, and the quality of the entertainment she provides is even more dissimilar. (p. 322)

Susan Ferrier's greatest power is that of provoking the kind of amusement that vents itself in mirth, and she has that rare power of prodding even the silent solitary student into outright laughter. She has no rigid or limited formula for comedy, but, rather, a wide variety of methods. Before coming on to them, though, in the interests of fairness, I must point out her limitations. . . . (p. 323)

Miss Ferrier has the deficiencies as well as the virtues of the minor and the amateur writer. She wrote three novels. . . . She was wise to do so. Reading them, one doesn't regret her small output. Plainly she had only material enough for three, if that. *Marriage* has by far the most gusto; and if *The Inheritance* has more polish, it has also more *longueurs* [tedious passages]; by the time she writes *Destiny* the sands of inspiration are running out. Illness and domestic circumstances may account partly for the tiredness of the writing, the lifeless morality and trite sentiment, but there is no doubt that she suffered from restricted subject matter. She admitted to drawing from life, from using real acquaintances as starting-points, if not models; and even in Regency Edinburgh, and in the castles and estates of the West Coast and Highlands, the supply of memorable and outrageous eccentrics of a kind she could use was not inexhaustible. The kind she could use is drawn from the gentry . . . , the landed and professional range, from the clergy to the titled—never the poor nor the very rich (indeed, there is a striking lack of ready cash throughout her novels). Her range of characters is limited also by her talents. She never tackles the coarse or the brutal, or gets her fun from cruelty, as Smollett could; nor is she in any real sense a satirist. The ridiculous arouses her delight; folly, providing it is ludicrous, her mirth. She exposes and exploits them. She does not make them serve any moral end. The reader is heartily thankful that she does not. By nature she is seriously and conventionally moral and high-principled, in the Evangelical way. She feels herself obliged to be a moral writer, not only by personal conviction, but also by the conventions of the novel of manners. But her didacticism flourishes quite apart from her humour; it exercises itself upon her young heroines, and upon her serious portraits—which are undeniably and regrettably dull. Fortunately it doesn't seem to occur to her that caricature may be personally cruel, that these kinds of foibles, and grotesqueries of behaviour, or the ridiculous manifestations of stupidity, may yet exist alongside honest good nature. She is not, in fact, an intelligent or a self-conscious writer. Her thinking is hardly worth the name, her standards are sound eighteenth-century ones, but naïve. (pp. 323-24)

Just as the spirit of the age and the models before her thus oblige her to write at times what does not suit her, they oblige her also to have a story; and so, after *Marriage,* she chooses incidents and hangs them on to plots that could have been, and were, done by any lady novelist from Fanny Burney and Maria Edgeworth onwards: clichés as plots, they can be summarized in clichés: separated twins, long-lost relatives, heiresses who, through being changed over at birth, are not heiresses at all; charming but unprincipled wastrel suitors, long-lost kinsfolk and heirs, the honest country girl caught up in the heartless and frivolous society of profligate London, villainous blackmail and mysterious secrets. She has to write novels of the customary length, and so digresses and discourses like Fielding on an off day; she pads with quotations from the standard poets, from *Elegant Extracts,* and from pious tracts like a conscientious schoolgirl; and she introduces passages of instructive and stilted sentimental dialogue like the worst parts of [Samuel Richardson's] *Sir Charles Grandison.* When she tries, as in *Destiny,* to write a more serious work, her evangelical principles, honest though they are, drag her down. When she attempts, as in *The Inheritance,* to write a coherently-plotted one, any reader can see from a third of the way through, that the charming suitor is no good, and that the virtuous one will win in the end, that the heiress is not who she thinks she is, and that the villainous American, though he may be able to deprive her of her title, will never succeed in establishing himself as her parent. Though the reader may not know whose *daughter* she is, he knows whose *grand-daughter,* and he knows that, in the atmosphere of this novel, nobody of refinement is a bastard, and that no young man of impeccable virtue who marries a heroine is ever doomed to have a drunken, swearing father-in-law. If one cannot actually guess the outcome of the plot . . . , one can guess more than one is really interested to know. Even in character-drawing she can sometimes flag. There are times when, realizing that she is temporarily stale, she abruptly and deliberately thrusts a fresh character before the reader to refresh him, herself, and her story. An instance in *The Inheritance* is Miss Becky Duguid, the poor spinster whom all her relations impose on and exploit. When she appears, not only does the story halt, but the technique falters. The account of Miss Duguid is static, like the analyses of personages found in Goldsmith's history and (ultimately) in Clarendon; the letters sent to her by those who make a convenience of the poor willing spinster are both improbably grotesque, and far too long. (pp. 324-25)

One might perhaps call [Miss Ferrier] a 'primitive', because she invents new means, and embarks on new material, without seeming to realize her originality. She began *Marriage* some time before Scott produced *Waverley,* although it was published five years after. Although she may have read Smollett and the other Scots writers, she makes no sign in her manner of writing of being aware of others who *are* near her in her good things, Smollett and John Galt immediately, and Fanny Burney further off, none of whom she much resembles in effect, although like Smollett and Galt she draws on Scottish types and dialect speakers. Her great powers are to invent and handle all kinds of comic social situations, and to render farcical and grotesque ones credible; to invent and to delineate from life all kinds of comic characters, from the eccentric to the outright grotesque, both men and women, and to handle these characters both individually and in groups; and to present her incidents and characters with a remarkably wide range of techniques: all the usual ones of description and idiosyncratic speech, and many much less predictable ones of racy idiom, reported thought, literary allusion and quotation, unexpected interaction, wit, deflation, anti-climax, prolific and marvellously chosen detail, and even manipulation in the reader of some of the emotions most difficult to handle, like embarrassment. (p. 325)

While the plot [of *The Inheritance*] plods its weary way, with Gertrude spending her fortune, suffering at the hands of her feckless, selfish betrothed and of her mother's mysterious blackmailer, a rich succession of continuous comic situations absorbs and entertains us, alongside and inter-related. Mr. Ramsay provides much of the fun, along with the chatterbox and busy-body Miss Pratt. Her garrulity is a delight, and Miss Ferrier's inspiration magnificently employs Miss Pratt's talents: for mis-hearing and getting things wrong, for loving to be right and know what others don't, and for money. So she and Mr. Ramsay have a bet on the identity of whom Gertrude really admires, and their respective suspenses, about this and the respective five guineas that they have staked, gives true comic coherence to the action. Mr. Ramsay provides another kind of coherence. He is held captive at Gertrude's house, not by her pleas, or by social decorum, but by a copy of [Walter Scott's] *Guy Mannering.* The stresses of serious existence at the house are registered, on a comic level, by the strength of Mr. Ramsay's fascination with his reading, opposed to his wish to get home away from it all.

Over the shorter interval, too, Susan Ferrier has a wholly original method of rendering drama by farce. A superb, rightly well-known instance is the death of Gertrude's uncle, Lord Rossville. Since he must die to leave Gertrude as heiress, his death must be dealt with. Since he is himself another of Miss Ferrier's fine range of comic bores, he plainly cannot die tragically or even melodramatically. Miss Pratt's personality gives Susan Ferrier means for introducing the perfect machinery. In a blinding snowstorm in the middle of winter the splendid sequence of incidents begins: when Miss Pratt, to Lord Rossville's utter horror, consternation and outrage, arrives in a hearse, with all the trappings. Miss Ferrier's invention, once on the wing, soars higher and higher. When Miss Pratt has made her entry,

> 'There's eight horses and four men,' said Lady Betty, who had been pleasing her fancy by counting them. 'Whose burial is it?'
>
> 'It's Mr M'Vitae's, the great distiller. I'm sure I'm much obliged to him—for if it hadn't been for him, poor man! I might have been stiff and stark by this time.'

The outrage perpetrated on the Earl's sense of his own dignity by the arrival of a hearse at his front door, is worsened by its being a *distiller's* hearse, and receives a worse blow when, the snow being impassable, he has to give lodging to horses and men for the night:

> There was something in having a hearse, and the hearse of Mr. M'Vitae, the radical distiller, thus forced within his walls, he could not away with. Death, even in its most dignified attitude, with all its proudest trophies, would still have been an appalling spectacle to Lord Rossville; but in its present vulgar and burlesque form, it was altogether insupportable. Death is indeed an awful thing, whatever aspect it assumes. The King of Terrors gives to other attributes the power of terrifying: the thunder's roar—the lightning's flash—the billow's roar—the earthquake's shock—all derive their dread sublimity from Death. All are but instruments of his resistless sway. . . .

The regulation of tone is superb. The mixture of idioms—the tritely rhetorical and the homely—serves to make us acknowledge the serious aspects of death, and prepare us for it as an actual event, while the very rhetoric, in its emptiness, preserves the comic spirit. The arrival of the hearse is such a fine grotesque event in itself, and Miss Pratt's emergence from it so hilarious an anticlimax, that the idea of death, thus introduced, enters the reader's mind almost without his noticing it, with all the atmosphere of comedy that Miss Ferrier requires to subdue the Earl's death, when it happens, to her comic design, and to make it, though not at all callous, superbly funny.

It is this kind of narrative art that constitutes Susan Ferrier's claim to be a novelist, and not, as so many accounts of her would suggest, merely a creator of a gallery of superb characters. Her most famous characters are of course well known and much praised: Lady Maclaughlan in *Marriage,* Mr. Ramsay and Miss Pratt (already mentioned) in *The Inheritance,* the Rev. Duncan McDow in *Destiny.* But she has a nice and original skill (which later novelists such as Dickens were to use, though perhaps never to better effect): the group portrait. Take the bunch of nieces in *Marriage:* Bella, Becky, Betty, Baby and Beeny, 'five awkward purple girls' indistinguishable in name and virtually so in personality.

> They had . . . exchanged their thick morning dresses for their muslin gowns, made, by a mantua-maker of the neighbourhood, in the extreme of a two-year-old fashion, when waists *were not.*
>
> But as dame nature had been particularly lavish in the length of theirs, and the stay-maker had, according to their aunt's direction, given them *full measure* of their new dark stays, there existed a visible breach between the waists of their gowns and the bands of their petticoats, which

> they had vainly sought to adjust by a meeting.
> Their hair had been curled, but not combed,
> and dark gloves had been hastily drawn on to
> hide red arms.
>
> (pp. 327-29)

[One] of Miss Ferrier's most memorable of all creations [is] Miss Pratt's nephew, Anthony Whyte, who achieves immortality by never appearing at all. Earlier by nearly forty years than Mrs. Gamp's Mrs. Harris, he is perhaps even finer than her because there is, indubitably, 'sich a person', though such as what remains a hilarious mystery: it is inconceivable that he should be as Miss Pratt represents him, because she never interprets aright anyone whom we do meet. He is even more of a literary mystery than the nature of Hamlet.

There is plainly more to Miss Ferrier's humour than merely describing characters, or even endowing them with personal idioms like Miss Bell Black's reiterated appeal to 'the eyes of the world' or 'a woman in her position': she contrives never to pay visits anywhere, you remember, in her position as successively betrothed, bride, wife, and mother. These excellences are obvious to any responsive reader, as is her sure hand with bores, whom, in *Marriage* and *Inheritance* at least, she represents by a fine shorthand of their own boring qualities, or even better, by having bores mutually cut each other out by all sorts of ingenious interruption. Miss Ferrier has learned the great truth that no one is as soon wearied of a bore as another different kind of bore.

She herself, as narrator, provides much of her own comedy, and is almost another character from what she is in her serious, reflective, or sentimental moods. Both her relations with her reader and her idiom are engaging and disarming. After one of her most successful comic letters from a comic character she remarks:

> The perusal of this letter was a severe tax on
> Gertrude's patience, as it has doubtless been
> upon all who have read it.

and later, she describes the scene which her unhappy heroine is listlessly watching, which contains an 'old gentlewoman knitting a large thick-shaped white lamb's-wool stocking':

> Much might be said upon this subject [of her
> dexterity]; but, doubtless, my readers love a
> well knit story as much as a well knit stocking;
> and it would be like letting down a stitch to
> enter upon a long digression at present.

The digression she has already supplied has in fact been a most useful one, since it re-creates for the reader the sense of nothing happening, of time standing still or only drearily proceeding, which has afflicted the heroine. The mood of a homely Scottish Mariana in a moated Grange has been beautifully caught.

Others of [Miss Ferrier's] talents associated with creating mood cannot be so easily instanced, because they depend on the length with which they are told. A nice instance occurs, in chapter iv of *The Inheritance,* of real comedy springing from manipulated embarrassment when Gertrude tries to offer help to an invalid cottar and his loquacious wife. The cottar is, if not bed-ridden, chair-ridden, and hag-ridden. His wife never lets him speak, and rejects for him Gertrude's proffered soup, milk, coat, carpet and chair, and asks instead for money to buy grave-clothes.

If Miss Ferrier is not a literary writer, she has the amateur's power to put her reading to effective and very unselfconscious use. Shakespeare is clearly in her blood and breath. Quotations, misquotations, echoes, and paraphrases abound, used with wonderful freedom and ingenuity. How brilliantly Lord Rossville exposes his own self-complacent rhetoric in this ghastly paraphrase:

> 'It was a maxim of Julius Caesar's, unques-
> tionably the greatest conqueror that ever lived,
> that his wife must not only be spotless in her-
> self, but that she must not even be suspected
> by others.'

His own quality as a bore is thus put quite *beyond* suspicion. (pp. 329-30)

I should like to offer a word of praise, not the less genuine and fervent for being both negative and positive, and to remark, not only how little she uses phonetic transcript of Scottish speech, but how well she suggests it, and how pointedly she contrasts it with her formal, if rather lifeless, English. Her ear for the Scottish tongue—her own tongue—is so sensitive that she uses idiom to suggest accent, and only for her broader speakers resorts to unorthodox spelling. I must however quote one of these. Bell Waddell and her Major, having just produced their first-born, a girl, suggest names to the crusty Mr. Ramsay:

> 'I think Andromache is such a beautiful name,
> and so off the common—'

> 'Andrew Mackaye's a very gude name for her,
> to be sure,' said Uncle Adam, gravely.

(p. 331)

Wendy Craik, ''Susan Ferrier,'' in Scott Bicentenary Essays, *edited by Alan Bell, Scottish Academic Press, Ltd., 1973, pp. 322-31.*

VINETA COLBY (essay date 1974)

[Miss Ferrier was] much in tune with her times. If occasionally she became surfeited with heavy moralizing, she was equally suspicious of the frenzies and passions of romances. Byron, Mrs. Radcliffe, Maturin, and Mackenzie were her secret favorites, to be confessed laughingly and somewhat guiltily in letters to her intimate friends. But in her more rational and sober moments, of which there seem to have been a considerable number, she scorned the melodramatic and sensational and opted for the conventional course. . . . (p. 99)

[*Marriage*] proved enormously popular, successful enough to rank Miss Ferrier with Jane Austen and Maria Edgeworth as writers who, in Sir Walter Scott's words, ''have all given portraits of real society far superior to any thing man, vain man, has produced of the like nature.'' What these ladies had in common, however, was less the fashionable novel of society than the novel of education. For Susan Ferrier, professing impatience with the moralizing and didacticism of much of the fiction of her day yet compelled by her training and disposition to defend the moral purposes of fiction, the education novel was an ideal solution and compromise. On the one hand it offered the appealing romantic ingredients of youthful characters involved in trials and problems deriving from their innocence, their ignorance or their inexperience. . . . On the other hand, by showing the rewards of virtue, patience, and prudence, the education novel served its moral purpose. Furthermore, it drew realistically but also poetically upon the physical and social scene in which the characters grow up and develop morally. While not a regionalist in the manner of Sir Walter Scott, Susan Ferrier made capital of the landscape and local color of Scotland and of the peculiar national characteristics of the Scots. She delighted her nineteenth-century readers with eighteenth-century humours types—eccentrics and "originals" like cranky but lovable Uncle Adam Ramsay and rattle-brained spinster Miss Pratt of *The Inheritance*. . . . (pp. 99-100)

Like Maria Edgeworth, Susan Ferrier is today read mainly for her "local color." But in their day, as we noted in Scott's tribute, these novelists were appreciated for more than mere regionalism. Scotland and Ireland were educational laboratories offering scenes and social situations that tested and marked the developing natures of the leading characters. . . . In all three of Susan Ferrier's novels, characters show their real natures— and the quality of their early education—by the way in which they respond to the Scottish landscape. (p. 100)

Susan Ferrier was less successful than either Maria Edgeworth or Jane Austen in balancing her hardcore social realism with her sentimentality and didacticism. Miss Edgeworth really did not try to achieve a balance. Miss Austen had the art to conceal her efforts. But in Miss Ferrier there are only great lumps of moralizing thinly disguised as part of the hero's or heroine's adventures in growing to maturity. Her first novel *Marriage* might more accurately have been titled "Education," for its theme is the effect of childhood conditioning and training upon character. (p. 102)

[In *The Inheritance*], the heroine's education gets relatively less attention since she comes fully grown upon the scene and her background must be obscured for the purposes of the mystery-plot. (p. 103)

[The] links among the three leading women novelists [Austen, Edgeworth, and Ferrier] of this first quarter of the nineteenth century were more solid than graceful compliments and imitation, more even than the strikingly similar circumstances of their personal lives—all three spinsters of upper-class families, devoted to their parents (Susan and Maria to their fathers, Jane to her ailing mother) and nephews and nieces. They were also women of rare wit and intelligence, responding with sensitivity to the changing ideas of their time, to new concepts of the purpose of life itself, to a recognition of the importance and inevitability of social change and personal growth. They were keenly aware of new approaches to teaching and learning, new knowledge of how man (and woman) learns, how he adapts himself to the realities of daily existence even while he strives to transcend reality and achieve spiritual fulfillment.

These women were gifted too with common sense and the kind of redeeming humor that spared them the pretentiousness and solemnity of many of their sister- and brother-novelists. At heart probably as sensitive, introspective, and romantic as any creative artist, they found the richest source of expression in the circumstances of life both as they literally knew it and as they hopefully envisioned its possibilities. Education—the cultivation of the mind and the heart—was the instrument of social reform and of personal self-government that was most accessible to them. (pp. 104-05)

The education of the heart comes from within, but all these novelist-educators knew that it must be carefully nurtured and directed by sympathetic teachers—ideally mothers or mother-figures. When these are lacking, others are supplied—helpful older sisters . . . , friendly older women (Mrs. Douglas and Mrs. Malcolm in Susan Ferrier's novels), . . . even sympathetic

male friends who sometimes evolve into lovers. . . . A few young heroines [like Susan Ferrier's Gertrude] are their own teachers, learning instinctively, thanks to the fundamental soundness of their hearts. . . . (p. 107)

> *Vineta Colby, "The Education of the Heart: Maria Edgeworth and Some Sister-Teachers," in her* Yesterday's Woman: Domestic Realism in the English Novel, *Princeton University Press, 1974, pp. 86-144.**

FRANCIS RUSSELL HART   (essay date 1978)

[*Hart classifies Ferrier's works as didactic satires designed to educate. In addition to discussing her use of caricature, the critic focuses on the novels' common theme of idolatry.*]

[The chief female humor of *Marriage* is the] local sybil, Lady MacLaughlan. The wife of a grotesque old baronet, Lady MacLaughlan is a rural bluestocking with a laboratory atop her house, with absolute intellectual self-assurance, a conviction that most other people in her world are fools (in this she is correct), and no manners whatsoever. She is a provincial termagant with no apparent compassion and yet humane wisdom. Her marvelous remedies are rural—fruits of the natural sagacity underlying the bluestocking humor—but they have no local significance. Her generic importance is strictly social and intellectual, not cultural.

The novel is about marriage, of course, and is formed around that thematic problem, more or less as an Austen or Burney novel would be formed. Marriage is a problem in social identity and maturity, and it rewards the successful completion of a social education. But Mary's social education is as distinguishable from Evelina's [in Burney's novel *Evelina*] as from Emma Woodhouse's [in Austen's novel *Emma*]. Its lessons are the satiric-pastoral themes of the novel: natural goodness and stupid vulgarity are not limited to locality or class; place offers universal options of urbanity and provinciality, simplicity and luxury; a longing for one's childhood scenes is natural, and local attachments and pieties are good. Time is not, as in Galt, an ambiguous cultural improvement, but a Thackerayan mutability. In time, some become wiser—that is, less vulgarly attached to worldly things; some act impiously as though time did not touch them, like the vain ones of [Austen's] *Persuasion* and [Thackeray's] *Henry Esmond*. (pp. 58-9)

Critics commonly speak of Ferrier as a caricaturist, without indicating how caricature is to be identified or judged. We can apply to *Marriage* D. W. Harding's astute perception of Jane Austen: the shifting limits of caricature are part of her fictional method. In the social context of *Marriage,* caricature is the representation of character too foolish or vulgar to grasp the norms of enlightened intelligence. The novel is arranged in "gradations of intellect," of taste and humanity. Dr. Redgill is a humorist-monomaniac, who cares only about eating. Lady Juliana seems incredibly selfish and naive, Lady MacLaughlan incredibly despotic and intolerant. Mrs. Douglas, the norm of enlightened piety, seems exaggeratedly compassionate and contented. But we become acclimatized to these extremes, and they are analyzed into believability by the narrator. Always, too, the narrator reminds us that the severest judgment must be tempered by a faith in providence: "Neither are the trifling and insignificant of either sex to be treated with contempt, or looked upon as useless by those whom God has gifted with higher powers." . . . We should be forewarned, then, to weigh our satiric responses to caricature in Mary's London experience. The last word on the matter is Lady MacLaughlan's:

fools are fools; God in his wisdom has sent them; true folly and vulgarity are to be judged by a divine wisdom and not by a worldly mind.

The humorous older woman in *The Inheritance* is unlike Lady MacLaughlan; and the differences call attention to basic differences between the novels, as well as suggesting the direction of Susan Ferrier's development. Miss Pratt has been compared in her bustling garrulity with Austen's Miss Bates [in her novel *Emma*]. In some respects she may be classed with Miss Ferrier's caricatures, of which this novel is full: vulgar petty bourgeois nabobs, mothers who are nothing but mothers, aunts who represent "auntimony" and have an entire chapter devoted to them—caricatures because Ferrier focuses so emphatically on their humorously generic qualities. But Miss Pratt's role is important and individual enough to lift her above her generic level. (pp. 60-1)

Because Miss Pratt is the gossipy heart of the shire and the parish, her activity and talk impart particular reality—in this she resembles Miss Bates—to a provincial world that otherwise remains somewhat abstract. Like Lady MacLaughlan's, her style has no cultural individuality. . . . It is characterized simply by its dashes and breathless runs, its gossipy energy. Its constant is reference to her young kinsman Anthony Whyte, who never appears and yet becomes one of the novel's most particular persons. Everything is personality to Miss Pratt, and Anthony Whyte comically attests to this fact, as well as to her essential unselfishness.

To the pompous Lord Rossville she becomes something more grotesque. Her most extraordinary arrival is in the middle of a snowstorm in a plumed hearse, commandeered from the mourners of M'Vitae the distiller. . . . Lord Rossville retires, unable to free himself from the train of ideas excited by the spectacle; in the morning he is found dead. The garrulous county busybody in a comedy of provincial manners has become a memento mori. Yet the intrusion is wholly fitting, for the comedy has a grim, medieval piety to inform its satire of vanity and vulgarity. Susan Ferrier is a forerunner of Muriel Spark. There is therefore no point in lamenting the submergence of Ferrier the satirist in Ferrier the Christian moralist: they are inseparable.

The combination is complicated further by a mixture associated with Dickens: that is, the transformation of satiric survey into romance of inheritance. Ferrier's title, *The Inheritance,* signals a similarity to Galt's *Entail,* for here too are contrasted true and false kinds of inheritance—worldly pomp and pride contrasted with natural and Christian piety. The romance that develops this distinction gradually replaces satire. The narrative becomes so preoccupied with the heroine's suffering, with the chastening of an idolatrous worldling in order that she may come into her true inheritance, that humorous figures such as Lord Rossville and Miss Pratt must be withdrawn. Even Uncle Adam, having served humorously as a "Scots type well observed," must change from cultural humor into a moral touchstone (not unlike Touchwood in Scott's *St. Ronan's Well*) in his unmannered simplicity. (pp. 61-2)

[Gertrude] can have no Austenite counterpart. Initially, emphasis is placed on her naturalness as contrasted with the artificiality of her supposed mother; and she remains essentially open, loving, and conscientious even during her temporary fall into distracted dissipation in London. She is almost Richardsonian in distraught moral sensibility. The lies of the great world chain her; her inheritance destroys her natural freedom,

and her pained subjection to fraud and mockery confirms the narrator's characteristic comment, "Man is not born to be free . . . Tis to the Christian alone that such freedom belongs." . . . She must be severely chastened, lose everything, become nameless and homeless and humble, before the freedom of her true inheritance can be attained.

The ordeal suits her nature. She anticipates some of the women of George Eliot in her imaginative ardor, a trait repeatedly stressed. She lives in and by her imagination. She is capable of "agony of spirit" because "her ardent and enthusiastic nature" makes her "susceptible." Her "nature [is] lofty, and her disposition generous; but her virtue [is] impulse—her generosity profusion." . . . The spiritual danger of this nature is idolatry, and idolatry is the growing imaginative preoccupation of Susan Ferrier.

Gertrude is duped and infatuated in her love for Colonel Delmour. . . . He is false, selfish, supercilious. But the key to her suffering is not in his villainy but in her idolatry. She is warned early and repeatedly. She cannot believe the warnings "because all the affections of a warm, generous, confiding heart, were lavished on this idol of her imagination, which she had decked in all the attributes of perfection." . . . She is blinded. . . . Delmour boasts to Gertrude of the idolatry of his love, scornfully contrasting Lyndsay's "cold-blooded, methodistical" or "puritannical" way. She sees the error: "I am afraid tis in your imagination alone I stand any chance for being deified." . . . Yet in London she loves being the "idol of the day." It is only when her entire world has become unreal, her very name gone, that she can name her sin: "I had power and I misused it—I had wealth and I squandered it—I had an idol, oh! my God!—and thou wast forgot!" . . . (pp. 62-3)

Social satire and presbyterian piety join, then, in Gertrude's experience. The heroine who loves idolatrously and is chastened through infatuation and disinheritance is also satirically revolted by the vulgarities of petty worldliness. Indeed, worldliness and vulgarity, the objects of satire, are also idolatries; grotesque mutability and death are constant reminders of the vanity of human idols. Like Evelina, Gertrude must suffer association with her mother's kin. But she must learn the lesson of *Marriage* and Lady Emily, the lesson taught by Lady MacLaughlan. It is her true lover Edward Lyndsay who teaches her the enlightened taste and Christian piety that Susan Ferrier promulgates in her novels of manners. (pp. 63-4)

The lesson includes a new acceptance of the humble Scottish life that surrounds her. It is fitting that her real inheritance, Uncle Adam's estate, is the one house with ancestral identity in a specific Scottish locale. It is a house bound to a legendary peasant past, associated with Adam's lost love, the peasant girl Lizzie Lundie, who turns out to have been Gertrude's grandmother. Thus, her ultimate inheritance combines the presbyterian piety her suffering has taught her with the ancestral peasant tradition in which she finds her name, her security, and her peace at last.

Destiny is Susan Ferrier's only novel of manners in the regional mode. Most commentators find it disappointingly evangelical or pietistic. In fact, the religious didacticism has not increased; rather, the satiric caricature such commentators relish in the earlier novels is virtually gone. To say that penetration of character is gone with it, however, is to overlook the changed nature and function of character in *Destiny.* We see the change if we look at the humorous older woman and also at the male figure—the idolatrous and humorous estate landlord—who replaces the grotesque Glenfern of *Marriage* and the ludicrous Lord Rossville of *The Inheritance*.

The novel opens directly on a local Highland group, the decadent chief of Glenroy, his kinsman-hanger-on Benbowie (ancestors, both of Compton Mackenzie comedy), and his loyal kinswoman and housekeeper Mrs. Macauley. The group is Susan Ferrier's finest humorous creation, and it is also her fullest characterization of cultural locality. The closest approximation to satiric caricature is M'Dow, the Highland minister from Glasgow. M'Dow is Ferrier's Mr. Collins [from Austen's novel *Pride and Prejudice*], yet he is primarily a ridiculous example of the worldly Scottish minister, from a vulgar Glasgow background, whose worldliness functions like Miss Pratt's gossip. He is equally garrulous and his visits are as frequent and unexpected. His worldliness allows him to describe local manse life in exhaustive detail: he thinks only of his "augmentation," his improvements to the manse, and his food. M'Dow, however, is the only figure in the Highland section to be classed as satiric.

Glenroy himself is culturally typical in humor, totally different in kind from Lord Rossville of *The Inheritance*. Rossville combined the smallness and rigidity of mind, the pompous garrulity, of other Ferrier provincials. Milieu makes little difference in his characterization. The "petty foibles of his mind" are denoted as universals of provincial character; he is simply "a sort of petty benevolent tyrant," with a mind filled to capacity with "little thoughts, little plans, little notions, little prejudices, little whims." Glenroy, too, is provincial; but he explicitly typifies a late phase in the decadence of Highland aristocracy. His infatuated efforts to alter history make him, in idolatry and pathos, a Highland counterpart to Galt's Claude Walkinshaw. And while he remains true to type, the fluctuation of mood and the mental confusion in his development as bereaved father give him the high degree of dramatic individuality that Walkinshaw also achieves. Ferrier's preoccupation with idolatry, in short, has been made local and historical. The "destiny" of the title is more a historic problem than the "inheritance" of the earlier novel. "Idolatry" is now centered on parents and their hopes for their heirs. Glenroy's hopes center idolatrously on his son, and when his son dies, they pass over his devoted daughter (like those of Dickens's Dombey) and center with a growing desperation on his adopted heir, Reginald. Even Captain Malcolm's pious wife, longing for her "lost" son (in an Enoch Arden subplot), is susceptible, and saved only by her sober faith. Ironically, Glenroy's adoptive heir, Reginald, is himself damned as an idolater in love; and the suffering that Glenroy's daughter undergoes in loving him derives from her idolatry.

Edith's mild character should not conceal her kinship to Gertrude. And her education parallels those of the earlier heroines. At her father's death she is left disinherited to become a dependent in exile, the sad last of her line, cast among vulgar relatives in London to discover the Ferrier lesson that meanness, smallness, and idolatry can be found in the most cosmopolitan of worlds. The city bourgeoisie and her high-life relatives are equally mean. She also learns compassion for such smallness.... (pp. 64-6)

In identifying the spiritual ill for which Edith must suffer exile and disinheritance, the narrator uses terms almost Johnsonian: "Edith had religious feeling, but she had not religious principle; and thus, what might have been the medicine to check and mitigate the fever of her heart, had served rather as the ailment to feed and pamper its sickly sensibilities." ... She

has known and forgotten that true love cannot be idolatrous—hence, in true love "there can be no illusion." (p. 66)

Destiny can be seen as a Scottish analogue to *Persuasion*—a romantic analogue, to be sure, and a Christian one. The vain Sir Walter has become a Highland chief, his heir is his infatuation, his daughter is as sadly neglected as poor Anne ever was. The need for time to mature judgment and affection is part of Edith's experience, too. There is no natural process of maturing; rather, Edith's is the Pauline death-rebirth cycle of Christian romance. Suitably, the true lover that was Austen's Wentworth is Ferrier's Captain Malcolm, reported dead at sea, dead to his family by choice for thirteen years (the Enoch Arden motif). Recovered from her idolatry, Edith turns unknowingly to her childhood friend Malcolm, meeting him again in the presence of the goodnatured admiral and his wife, who resemble Austen's Crofts. Her "second spring" of affection is, unlike Anne's, a religious renewal; her second love is free of the illusion of idolatry. (pp. 66-7)

Edith's faith, rooted in childhood, has been with her throughout, in the shape of the novel's humorous older woman, Mrs. Macauley. Mrs. Macauley, unlike her antecedents Lady MacLaughlan and Miss Pratt, is a local type, a Highland widow devoted to her chief, who speaks in a soft Highland accent, reflects a distinctively simple and provincial outlook, yet in her simplicity represents Christian piety and a providential view of time. She travels to London with Edith and preserves her charity, good humor, and fidelity in exile. She speaks for providence in modest defiance of her chief, and is called a fool and a dangerous predestinarian. And true to her Gaelic tradition, she has the book's final word, suitably on man's blindness, God's providence, and the destiny alloted to time and place.... Through Mrs. Macauley's loyalty, there is an affirmation of local affection not found in Susan Ferrier's earlier novels. The final return of Edith and her devoted retainer to the Highlands is not just Gertrude's generalized return to local piety and pastoral tranquillity. The return in time and place is specific, and at the same time romantic. It is notable that as Scottish fiction becomes, like Susan Ferrier's novels, increasingly focused on and evocative of particular time and place, it also moves away from novel to romance. (pp. 67-8)

> *Francis Russell Hart, "The Other Blackwoodians: Moir, Ferrier, Lockhart, Wilson," in his The Scottish Novel: From Smollett to Spark, Cambridge, Mass.: Harvard University Press, 1978, pp. 53-86.*

ADDITIONAL BIBLIOGRAPHY

Copeland, Charles Townsend. "Miss Austen and Miss Ferrier: Contrast and Comparison." *The Atlantic Monthly* LXXI, No. CCCCXXVIII (June 1893): 836-46.*

> Compares and contrasts the works of Ferrier and Jane Austen. Copeland focuses on their subject matter, characterization, and style.

Grant, Aldine. *Susan Ferrier of Edinburgh.* Denver: Alan Swallow, 1957, 174 p.

> The only biography of Ferrier. Aldine provides a sympathetic portrait of Ferrier's character and personality.

Gwynn, Stephen. "The Decay of Sensibility." *The Living Age* CCXXII, No. 2875 (12 August 1899): 419-28.*

> Humorously examines the propensity of nineteenth-century fictional heroines to faint at times of stress or excitement. Gwynn employs examples from the novels of Ferrier and Jane Austen.

''Miss Ferrier's Novels.'' *The Nation* XXXVII, No. 950 (13 September 1883): 230-32.

    An appreciative overview of Ferrier's novels that includes laudatory letters to Ferrier from Sir Walter Scott, William Blackwood, and Joanna Baillie.

Rosa, Matthew Whiting. ''From Susan Ferrier to T. H. Lister.'' In his *The Silver-Fork School: Novels of Fashion Preceding ''Vanity Fair,''* pp. 55-73. New York: Columbia University Press, 1936.*

    Places *Marriage* within the tradition of the fashionable novel.

''Miss Ferrier's Novels.'' *Temple Bar* LIV (November 1878): 308-28.

    Describes the superior sophistication of Victorian literary society compared with that of Ferrier's day. The critic uses Ferrier's *Marriage* and *Inheritance* to illustrate the literary naïveté of her era.

''Susan Edmonstone Ferrier, 1782-1854: Critical Essay.'' In *The World's Best Literature,* edited by John W. Cunliffe and Ashley H. Thorndike, pp. 5649-51. The Warner Library, Vol. 9. New York: Warner Library Co., 1917.

    A brief biographical and critical introduction.

Ugo Foscolo

1778-1827

(Born Niccolò Foscolo; also wrote under the pseudonym of Didimo Chierico) Italian poet, novelist, essayist, translator, and dramatist.

Foscolo is regarded as one of the greatest Italian lyric poets since Petrarch. In his best-known works, the poem *I sepolcri (The Sepulchres)* and the novel *Ultime lettere di Jacopo Ortis (Letters of Ortis)*, Foscolo joined his love of country and of literature to call for freedom and to honor the immortal writers of the past. These works helped to unify Italians during a divisive period. Because he successfully incorporated both ancient and modern material in these and other works, Foscolo is now considered a transitional figure between classicism and romanticism.

Foscolo was born to a Venetian father and Greek mother on the Greek island of Zante. His father, a doctor, died in 1788, leaving the family in poverty. They moved to Venice, where Foscolo studied philosophy and literature and began to write poetry. Soon, he attracted the interest of the influential Countess Isabella Teotochi Albrizzi who welcomed him into her literary circle, which included the poets Ippolito Pindemonte and Melchiorre Cesarotti. Foscolo's first extensive literary recognition came in 1797 with his tragedy *Tieste,* which prompted the celebrated Italian dramatist and poet Vittorio Alfieri to predict, "if the author is only nineteen he will surpass me."

Foscolo combined literary and political pursuits throughout much of his life. As a young man with revolutionary ideals, he supported Napoleon Bonaparte, and his ode *Bonaparte liberatore* celebrates the French invasion of Italy which Foscolo believed would lead to Venetian independence. Foscolo became disillusioned, however, when the French signed the Treaty of Campoformio and allowed the Austrians to assume control of Venice. To avoid persecution for his beliefs, Foscolo left Venice for Milan. There, in 1798, he fell in love with Teresa Monti, for whom he wrote the first version of *Letters of Ortis.* After serving in the National Guard of Bologna and Genoa, he moved to Florence and revised and published his novel, now inspired by his latest love, Isabella Roncioni. *Letters of Ortis,* which critics often refer to as *Last Letters of Jacopo Ortis,* recounts the experiences of its protagonist, Jacopo. Jacopo's letters reveal his sense of betrayal and despair following the signing of the Treaty of Campoformio and his desperate love for Teresa, engaged to marry another man. *Letters of Ortis* was hailed throughout Italy, and with the neoclassical odes and sonnets published in *Poesie,* also written during this period, solidified his growing reputation.

From 1804 to 1806, Foscolo served as a soldier in Napoleon's expeditionary force in Northern France, where his romantic involvement with an Englishwoman, Sophia Hamilton, bore a daughter, Floriana, who cared for him in later years. In 1806, he returned to Italy and began work on *The Sepulchres.* This 295-line, blank verse poem records Foscolo's reaction to the French Edict of Saint Cloud, which forbade all distinguishing features on graves. Citing the church of Santa Croce in Florence, where many great Italians are buried, Foscolo maintained that tombs inspire the living and provide a bridge to the past.

He then called forth historical and mythological figures to demonstrate the richness of history.

With the success of *The Sepulchres,* Foscolo was awarded the position of Professor of Italian Eloquence at the University of Pavia in 1808. In his famous inaugural lecture *Dell'origine e dell'ufficio della letteratura,* he simultaneously traced the origin of literature and the development of civilization. These historical studies support his view that the writer's role is that of a mediator between a despotic government and a disorderly populace and that the writer's duty is to direct public opinion. His contemporaries believed that the inflammatory, anti-tyrannical rhetoric in Foscolo's lectures contributed to Napoleon's decision to abolish the chair of eloquence at all Italian universities. Foscolo then moved to Milan where he wrote *Aiace,* a drama that also drew the wrath of the authorities because many viewed it as a veiled attack on Napoleon, the pope, and other contemporary leaders. Subsequently, Foscolo moved to Florence to escape his critics, where he resumed writing *Le grazie, carme.* Although he first developed the idea for this poem in 1802 and worked on it sporadically for twenty years, he never completed it. The poem consists of three hymns: the first, to Venus, is set in prehistoric Greece and records the birth of the Graces and of civilization; the second, to Vesta, occurs in contemporary Italy and glorifies the crafts of daily life, while the third, to Pallas, takes place outside time and space in a divine, metaphysical realm and celebrates the imagination and creation.

In 1814, as the Napoleonic Empire crumbled, the Austrians resumed control of much of Italy. Unwilling to take the Austrian oath of allegiance, Foscolo instead chose exile in Switzerland, where he lived until moving to London in 1816. His first years in England were very rewarding. He established contact with his daughter Floriana, was greeted hospitably in literary and social circles, and submitted articles to leading London periodicals. During his exile, Foscolo concentrated almost exclusively on composing essays; his critical writings on Dante, Tasso, Boccaccio, and Petrarch all date from this period. Yet despite his early successes, his difficult temperament eventually alienated his friends and his extravagance consumed his earnings. He spent his last years living under assumed names in London slums. Following his death in 1827, Foscolo was buried in England. In 1871, his remains were transferred to Santa Croce, amid much fanfare, to be buried with the heroes of *The Sepulchres*.

Despite the many genres in which Foscolo wrote, certain themes recur: feminine beauty, freedom, death, art, imagination, the role of the great poets, and the importance of the past and its continuity with the present and future. Foscolo's dramas, including *Tieste, Aiace,* and *Ricciarda,* were briefly popular but now are considered his least successful writings. These works have excited little interest for either contemporary or modern scholars, who fault their obscure style, unnatural plots, poor construction, and ineffective characterizations. However, his translations of the works of such diverse authors as Callimachus, Homer, and Laurence Sterne met with more success. In particular, critics praise his *Esperimento di traduzione della "Iliade" di Omero* (Homer's *Iliad*) and *Viaggo sentimentale di Yorick lungo la Francia e l'Italia* (Sterne's *A Sentimental Journey*) for their fidelity to the originals; they also note Foscolo's accurate rendering of Sterne's satiric humor.

Foscolo wrote the majority of his essays while exiled in London. His method of composition was unusual; first, he composed in Italian, then translated the essays into French, and finally employed a translator to render the works into English. Modern critics lament the loss of many of the original Italian versions, since Foscolo was not always fortunate in his choice of a translator. In addition, many of the essays are considered fragmentary and incomplete, and scholars often fault Foscolo's bombastic and pedantic rhetoric. Yet other commentators praise Foscolo's erudition and lively style and credit him with inspiring English interest in little-discussed Italian writers. Critics note a dual purpose in Foscolo's essays. In addition to commenting on individual Italian authors, he advocated a historical scheme for the study and criticism of Italian literature that includes political and economic factors as well as literary history; this, according to René Wellek, is "Foscolo's chief importance" as a literary critic.

In his essays, particularly "Essay on the Present Literature of Italy" and "On the New Dramatic School in Italy," Foscolo clarified his views on the contemporary debate between the classic and romantic schools. He faulted romantic writers for their explicitly accurate historical dramas, which he claimed destroyed the poetic illusion by sacrificing imagination for history. He argued for the importance of mythology and other classical material and castigated the romantics for excluding such sources from their works. Yet his creative works contradict his anti-romantic stance. Critics point to his depiction of nature, passion, and the desire for freedom in *Letters of Ortis*

and the sonnets in *Poesie* as evidence of his romantic inspiration. It is this union of opposites that earned Foscolo the reputation as a transitional figure in Italian literature.

Although *Letters of Ortis* was widely acclaimed when first published, its appeal has diminished. Early critics noted its similarity to Johann Wolfgang von Goethe's *Die Leiden des jungen Werthers (The Sorrows of Young Werther),* but most agreed that Foscolo's novel was autobiographical rather than derivative. They praised its original presentation of the mood of the era and commended Foscolo's graceful style. The novel's popularity never extended beyond Italy, however, and today critics agree that Foscolo's importance rests on his poetry.

Foscolo revised his poems repeatedly and was rarely satisfied with his finished work. As a result, his poetic output was small, consisting of *The Sepulchres, Le grazie,* and the two odes and dozen sonnets published in *Poesie.* The odes and sonnets have been consistently praised since the nineteenth century for their blend of introspection and expert craftsmanship. It is these works, according to critics, that best demonstrate the influence of Alfieri. "A Luigia Pallavicini caduta da cavallo" and "All'amica risanata," both odes that celebrate feminine beauty, are renowned for their classical inspiration and neoclassical form. Critics also applaud the taut construction and emotional range of the sonnets and rank those written for Isabella Roncioni among the finest Italian love poems written since Petrarch.

Le grazie, Foscolo's unfinished poem, was never published as a whole during his lifetime. He continued to alter its organization until shortly before his death, and the majority of the poem was unknown until the mid-nineteenth century. The poem received little attention until recent critics noted that the absence of polemical discussions of contemporary political problems strengthens its appeal to a modern audience. Though scholars now laud its beauty, stylistic polish, and transformation of ancient myth into original, modern poetry, *Le grazie* has never attained the popularity of *The Sepulchres*.

Today, *The Sepulchres* is generally considered Foscolo's greatest achievement. Critics often compare the poem to the works of the English poets Thomas Gray, Edward Young, James Hervey, and Robert Blair, who also wrote on the theme of graveyards. For this work Foscolo drew heavily on mythological and classical sources and thus effectively combined ancient and modern themes in an exhortation to his contemporaries to live up to their inspired heritage. In addition, Foscolo celebrated the importance and permanence of art; poetry, according to Foscolo, "overcomes the silence of a thousand generations." The impact of *The Sepulchres* has been profound. Its patriotic sentiments greatly influenced the writers of the Risorgimento, a period following the 1820s when Italians were mainly concerned with political events and patriotic themes. The passages that praise Florence and Santa Croce as the home of the tombs of Michelangelo, Galileo, and Niccolò Machiavelli still inspire modern Italians. *The Sepulchres* ensures that Foscolo's name will endure among the great nineteenth-century Italian poets.

PRINCIPAL WORKS

Bonaparte liberatore (poetry) 1797
Tieste (drama) 1797
Orazione a Bonaparte pel Congresso di Lione (lecture)
  1802

Ultime lettere di Jacopo Ortis (novel) 1802; also
    published as *Ultime lettere di Jacopo Ortis* [revised
    edition], 1814
    [*Letters of Ortis*, 1813]
La chioma di Berenice [translator; from *The Locks of
    Berenice* by Callimachus] (poetry) 1803
*Poesie (poetry) 1803
Esperimento di traduzione della "Iliade" di Omero
    [translator; from the *Iliad* by Homer] (poetry) 1807
I sepolcri (poetry) 1807
    [*The Sepulchres*, 1820?; also published as *I sepolcri*,
    1928; and *On Sepulchres: An Ode to Ippolito
    Pindemonte*, 1971]
Dell' origine e dell' ufficio della letteratura (lecture) 1809
Aiace (drama) 1811
Ricciarda (drama) 1813
    [*Ricciarda*, 1823]
Viaggo sentimentale di Yorick lungo la Francia e l'Italia
    [translator, as Didimo Chierico; from *A Sentimental
    Journey* by Laurence Sterne] (novel) 1813
"Essay on the Present Literature of Italy" [with John Cam
    Hobhouse] (essay) 1818; published in *Historical
    Illustrations of the Fourth Canto of Childe Harold*
Essays on Petrarch (essays) 1821
"Discorso storico sul testo del *Decamerone*" (essay)
    1825; published in *Decamerone*
*Discorso sul testo e su le opinioni diverse prevalenti intorno
    alla storio e alla emendazione critica della
    "Commedia" di Dante* (essay) 1825
**"On the New Dramatic School in Italy" (essay) 1826?
Le grazie, carme (poetry) 1848
Opere edite e posthume di Ugo Foscolo. 12 vols. (poetry,
    novel, essays, and letters) 1850-90
Edizione nationale delle opere di Ugo Foscolo. 21 vols. to
    date. (poetry, novel, essays, and letters) 1933-
The J.C. Translations of Poems by Ugo Foscolo (poetry)
    1963

*Many of the poems in this work were originally published in the
journal *Nuovo giornale de' letterati* in 1802.

**Although most critics believe that Foscolo wrote this essay in 1826,
they are unable to establish when or where it was first published.

THE QUARTERLY REVIEW (essay date 1812)

[The letters of **Ultime Lettere di Jacopo Ortis**] derive much of
their interest from the mixture of truth and falsehood which
the story depicted in them contains, and yet more from the
singular character and circumstances of him who composed it.
(p. 438)

In the plot there is certainly not much pretence to novelty; nor
is the resemblance which it bears to that of [Johann Wolfgang
von Goëthe's *The Sorrows of Young Werther*] confined to the
mere outline of the story. The general tone of the two works
corresponds in a manner which cannot allow us to believe it
the result of an accidental coincidence. Much of the peculiar
cast of thinking, which characterizes Werter, is to be recognised in Ortis, and the cold and calculating disposition of the
husband of Charlotte, and her own more impassioned temperament, are revived in Odoardo and Teresa, who, it will be
recollected, stand in the same relation to him, which the two

former bear to the hero of the German romance. Yet though
without great pretence to novelty either in its story or even its
principal characters, the reproach of want of originality cannot
be applied to many parts of this singular production, where the
sentiments spring out of political circumstances wholly foreign
to those which existed in the time of Goëthe, and derive also
a peculiar cast from the national genius of the author. No where
is the southern character sketched with greater energy and truth.
The effect of a deep-seated grief on the mind, rendering it
morbidly susceptible to every little painful impression, 'putting,' as one of our old writers says, 'a sting in every fly which
buzzes about us,' is admirably kept up. There is also much
beautiful picturesque description, and Ugo Foscolo has the art,
like Madame de Staël, of rendering this happily subservient to
the suggestion and development of sentiment. Add to this, that
the muse of the Italian soars many a pitch above that of the
German novelist. In point of extravagance they are pretty fairly
matched; yet it must be confessed that there is a greater air of
truth in the story of Werter. . . . Again, if the pleasure we
receive from similar works depend upon a nice and modified
excitement of the passions, the author, if this be overwrought,
fails as much in overstepping his due limits, as if he fell short
of the end which he had proposed to himself. . . . We think
that in having stopt at the proper medium in this point, the
letters of **Ortis** have the advantage of [Goëthe's] romance; they
moreover exhibit another more striking superiority, they are
free from that grossness and perversity of sentiment, so remarkable in **Werter**, a sort of *sour krout*, which rises on our
stomach at almost every page of almost every German tragedy,
comedy, and romance. A very brilliant vein of eloquence also
runs throughout the whole, while the language is graced with
all the charms of the purest Tuscan phraseology. To those who
recollect with what difficulty Alfieri attained to that excellence,
this will be a sufficient subject of surprise. (pp. 441-42)

Though the author treats with great contempt that affectation
of general literature, which, as it should seem, is a folly not
confined to ourselves, many passages prove the extent of his
reading, and he appears to have no common acquaintance with
the English writers. A mind like his was calculated to receive
the impressions of our sovereign poet [Shakespeare]. . . .

It is but justice to state, that there is no baseness, and, if we
except the hero's too long indulgence in the society of Teresa,
no selfishness in the worst points of character justified in this
romance. The faults are those of an ardent and undisciplined
mind, acting upon the impulse of feeling, undirected by any
fixed and general principles of justice or propriety, and uncontrolled by the precepts of religion. (p. 444)

> *A review of "Ultime lettere di Jacopo Ortis," in* The
> Quarterly Review, *Vol. VIII, No. XVI, December,
> 1812, pp. 438-45.*

[UGO FOSCOLO] (essay date 1818)

[*The following excerpt is drawn from a survey of contemporary
Italian literature that was published as part of John Cam Hobhouse's book of illustrations for the fourth canto of Lord Byron's
Childe Harold. Authorship of the essay has been disputed. Although it was originally attributed to Hobhouse, modern critics,
notably E. R. Vincent (see Additional Bibliography), have ascer-
tained that most of the essay, including the critical portraits of
individual Italian authors, was written by Foscolo. In the following, Foscolo provides an overview of his own career, written in
the third person.*]

The learned of Italy speak neither well nor ill of the *Letters of Ortis,* which . . . has been more frequently reprinted in his own country than any other of Foscolo's works, and is certainly much more known on the other side of the Alps. The Germans have exhausted upon this little book all the metaphysics of criticism. . . . After all, it is but an imitation of [Goethe's] *Werter.* There is however this striking difference, that the object of the Italian is solely political. There is indeed something for all tastes in the politics, and the poetry, and the love of *Ortis.* The allusions to the downfall of the Venetian republic, and the introduction of living interlocutors, such as Parini at Milan, give a reality to the fable which must be highly interesting to the Italians, and is attractive even to strangers. There is a melancholy patriotism in every word in which he mentions Italy, that makes the author respectable in the eyes of every generous reader. There are some pictures of small objects that evince a considerable knowledge of the human heart, and are extremely affecting. . . . The author is in his proper element when he breaks forth into his ethical reflections: how truly he says, "That we are too proud to give our compassion when we feel we can give nothing else."

The love of Ortis is, perhaps, the least interesting portion of the work; there is not importance enough attached to his existence, to make it natural that so much importance should be attached to his end. It was difficult, perhaps, to give many attractions to the adventures of an obscure politician; but it is still possible that those of an age and sex more accessible to the tender feelings may be touched by the misfortunes and the heroic despair of the Italian Werter. But *Ortis* may boast of having been the first book that induced the females and the mass of readers to interest themselves in public affairs. (pp. 452-54)

The *Letters of Ortis* is the only work of the kind, the boldness of whose thoughts, and the purity of whose language, combined with a certain easy style, have suited it to the taste of every reader. It cannot be too often remarked, that it is principally the *style* which in all works attracts the admiration of the Italians; and it may here be mentioned, that their critics have laid it down as a rule, that the elements of their prose are to be collected only in the period between Dante and Machiavelli. This is the opinion of Alfieri.

Foscolo has followed this rule in his *Ortis,* and more scrupulously still in the *Sentimental Journey,* which he has translated with the words and phrases of the fourteenth century; not, however, to the prejudice of the conversational ease of our Yorick. This work, so popular in all foreign countries, had been twice before translated into Italian; but the torpidity of their style, and their repeated Gallicisms, had consigned these preceding versions to contempt. (p. 455)

[Foscolo] makes it an article of faith to vary his style according to his subject. Thus there is no less a difference between the letters, the romances, and the orations, than between the history and the epic or lyric poetry of these varied compositions. The *Ortis* and the *Sentimental Journey* resemble each other very little: notwithstanding that the author has followed the same rules of composition, and has always preserved the traits peculiar to his style. As for his *Discourse for the Congress of Lyons* [*Orazione a Bonaparte pel Congresso di Lione*], it appears evidently written by the same man, but in a different language.

He wrote this *Discourse* at the injunction of his government, when Bonaparte, in the year 1801, convoked at Lyons the *Notables* of the Cisalpine Republic. The directions given to the orator were to pronounce a panegyric; but Foscolo adopted a different course. He presented a moving picture of the wretched state of the laws, of the armies, of the finances, and of the moral condition of the new republic. The sects, both old and new, that distracted their country—the priests, the nobles, the democrats, the partisans of foreign usurpation, the adulatory writers, the libelists, the defrauders of the public revenue, the monopolists, who profited by the sale of the national property, are all handled with the same severity. (pp. 457-58)

[*Discourse for the Congress of Lyons*] is not more than eighty pages: and notwithstanding it is an historical composition, maintains a certain impetuosity and gravity of style which overwhelm and fatigue the attention. The events are hinted at, not detailed; the development concerns only their causes and their results. This brevity might be agreeable to those who had been spectators of, or actors in, the short and transitory scene; but foreign readers, and even those Italians removed by time or place from the original action, are left in the dark. It would be difficult to prove that the style of Tacitus, which Foscolo has not only copied but exaggerated with the devotion of a youth enchanted by his model, can be well adapted to this sort of composition. The English, who have perhaps run into the opposite extreme, will be astonished to hear that this *Discourse* was particularly esteemed by the critics, on account of its close resemblance to the Latin. We should call this pedantry: but it appears a meritorious exploit in the eyes of a nation, which, having for two hundred years diluted its language to insipidity, now lays it down for a maxim, that for the *graces* of style, the early Tuscan authors are to be consulted; and for the strength, and, if the word may be used, the nobility, of the language, the Latins are the only safe model. It must be confessed, that the origin of the language admits of this union. It is not unnatural that when they would discourse of liberty, they should have recourse to the manner of their Roman ancestors. (pp. 461-62)

Those who have criticised Foscolo's discourse on the [*Origin and the Duties of Literature* (*Dell'origine e dell'officio della letteratura: Orazione*)], have found all the beauties and all the defects of this author more strongly displayed in the discourse than in any other of his prose works. A strict propriety in the words, a severe grammatical exactness, and a scrupulous rejection of every thing not absolutely inherent in the genius of the language—these meritorious characteristics are apparent in every page: but on the other hand, the same composition is remarkable for an unusual method of connecting the phrases; for the perilous boldness of the metaphors; for the over-nice discrimination of the expressions, and the use of them in the primitive Tuscan sense in contradistinction to their modern acceptation; for a certain confusion of imagery with argument, a continual struggle between the natural impetuosity and the affected calm of the writer; for a union of objects very different in themselves, which are distinguished by a variety of colouring that dazzles and confounds the eye; and, lastly, for the crowd of ideas which together with the rapidity of expression overwhelm and fatigue the attention. (p. 469)

The political topics which have been generally selected for the subject of his performances, have, perhaps, induced [Foscolo] to leave us to guess that which he did not like to say openly. It is, however, equally true that the constant intensity of thought which he requires of his readers must be traced either to the peculiar mode in which his ideas are originally conceived, or to his wish to give them a new turn. Indeed all his writings bear the mark of meditation. . . . (pp. 470-71)

The published poetry of this writer is confined to two odes, and a little work called *I Sepolcri,* written when it was forbidden to bury the dead in family tombs. . . . The aim of Foscolo in this poem appears to be the proof of the influence produced by the memory of the dead on the manners and on the independence of nations. (p. 472)

This poem contains only three hundred lines, but it called forth pamphlets and criticisms in every shape, and from all quarters. The younger writers tried to imitate it: the critics pronounced it to have brought about a reform in the lyrical poetry of Italy. (pp. 473-74)

The blank verses of Foscolo are totally different from those of any other author. Each verse has its peculiar pauses and accents placed according to the subject described. His melancholy sentiments move in a slow and measured pace, his lively images bound along with the rapid march of joy. Some of his lines are composed almost entirely of vowels, others almost entirely of consonants; and whatever an Englishman may think of this imitation of sense by sound, (a decried effort since the edict of Dr. Johnson), the Italian poet has at least succeeded in giving a different *melody* to each verse, and in varying the *harmony* of every period.

It is perhaps necessary to be an Italian to feel the full effect of these combinations; but the scholar of every country may perceive that Foscolo has formed himself on the Greek model, not only in this particular, but in other branches of his art. (p. 476)

> [*Ugo Foscolo*], *"Essay on the Present Literature of Italy: Hugo Foscolo," in* Historical Illustrations of the Fourth Canto of "Childe Harold" *by John Hobhouse, second edition, John Murray, 1818, pp. 450-84.*

THE QUARTERLY REVIEW   (essay date 1820)

Signor Foscolo's dramatic career was opened by the tragedy of **'Thyeste,'** of which Alfieri is reported to have said, 'if the author be only nineteen he will surpass me.' A tragedy written at that age might naturally expect the indulgence of criticism, and **'Thyeste,'** in fact, is the work of a youth, but still that of a young poet. Considerable skill shewn in the management of a repulsive subject, great force and vehemence in the expression of passion, an attempt to relieve the general gloom of the piece by the excitement of a milder interest, that of the maternal affection of Erope, which is foreign indeed to the subject, but for which we are nevertheless grateful, and an animating spirit of enthusiasm, distinguish **'Thyeste'** from its less revolting, but tame and feeble rivals. (p. 90)

[Some may think the plot of **'Ricciarda'**] too horrible for legitimate tragedy, though we confess ourselves of a different opinion, the defects of the drama are too great an uniformity of situation, and an obscurity of style. Our terror is so often appealed to, lest the father should slay his child, that we become in some degree familiarised with the danger, and are of course less moved by it. . . . [Foscolo] displays indeed great mastery over the language, to comprise so many ideas in so few words; but when our feelings are addressed, we like not the having to dwell on sentences, the antithetical force and fullness of which occasionally remind us of Tacitus. We either hurry on without having received into our minds the whole meaning of the author, or we pause so long as to lose the spirit of the scene. But these defects are nobly counterbalanced by the general impression of poetic power which the whole piece bears; by the

conception and execution of the characters which appear to us truely tragic and original. There is something tremendous in Guelfo, whose vigilant suspicion finds aliment in the most trivial circumstances; and who is so deep in guilt, as to take pride in hardening himself in his atrocity. God to him, he thinks, must be a God of vengeance; he has sinned beyond hope of mercy, therefore he must go on; his is a fine exemplification of that faith of the devils, 'who believe and tremble.' Yet, even in him, nature sometimes speaks; gleams of parental affection pass across the gloom of his spirit; he wavers and is irresolute, till some new occurrence excites him again to frenzy, and he abandons himself to the guidance of furious passion. Ricciarda . . . is uniformly pleasing: willing to be the sacrifice, and only anxious that her father may escape the guilt of her death; for this, foregoing even her love for Guido—for this, offering herself to commit suicide. Guido, from his peculiar situation, is more inactive than we should have wished; but there is something imposing in his calm and uniform generosity. (p. 97)

> *"Italian Tragedy," in* The Quarterly Review, *Vol. XXIV, No. XLVII, October, 1820, pp. 72-102.**

SIR WALTER SCOTT   (journal date 1825)

> [*Scott was a Scottish novelist, poet, historian, biographer, and critic of the Romantic period who is best known for his historical novels, which were a great popular success.*]

London held some four or five years since one of those animals who are lions at first but by transmutation of two seasons become in regular course Boars. Ugo Foscolo by name, a haunter of Murray's Shop and of literary parties. Ugly as a baboon and intolerably conceited, he splutterd blusterd and disputed without even knowing the principles upon which men of sense render a reason and screamd all the while like a pig when they cut his throat. (p. 10)

> *Sir Walter Scott, in a journal entry on November 24, 1825, in his* The Journal of Sir Walter Scott, *edited by W.E.K. Anderson, fourth edition, Oxford at the Clarendon Press, Oxford, 1972, pp. 10-12.*

[ANDRÉ VIEUSSEUX]   (essay date 1832)

All [Foscolo's] writings bear the stamp of genius and of learning, all have faults characteristic of the man, but there is hardly any of them that is not interesting and instructive. Foscolo was a man of strong passions and of a most uneven temper. . . . There were three distinct epochs in our author's life: one of youthful enthusiasm and theory, which kept pace with the republican fever of those days; the next of cooler reflection, of cautious and almost sceptical investigation, under the reign of force and calculation which followed; the last an epoch of weariness and bitter despondency, which closed with his death. We see the first personified in his [**"Ultime Lettere di Jacopo Ortis"**]; the second in his **"Didymus the Clerk"** [in his translation of Laurence Sterne's "A Sentimental Journey"]; and the last exhibits itself in his essays and comments on Petrarch and Dante, with the latter of which poets, Foscolo, as well as Alfieri, held a strong sympathy. (p. 313)

[The great and lasting attraction of the letters in **"Ortis"**] lies in the political structures and the patriotic sentiments, in the living picture of the extraordinary epoch in which they were written, in the sarcastic exposure of the republican mimics of the time, the pungent satire on the corruptions of Italian society, the glow of indignation against injustice, hypocrisy and oppression, from whatever quarter they came, and in the lofty though desponding aspirations towards a better order of things, towards real and not nominal liberty. . . . (p. 318)

The language of the **"Ortis"** is impassioned but natural; full of life, and well suited to the times whose form and pressure it bears. It was a specimen of a new prose style, of which Italy had no model in her classic writers. The amatory part of the story has been considered a counterpart of [Goethe's "Werther"], but it differs from the latter in several essential particulars; though equally objectionable in its moral tendency and in its catastrophe, yet its principal character has more redeeming points about him than Werther. Teresa is also a more interesting person than Lolotte; and even the gloomy and unreasonable murmurs of Jacopo against the dispensations of Providence assume a less selfish and more generous tone than the maudlin sentimentality of his German prototype. As a work of fiction, there is, however, more unity in "Werther," in which the single passion of love produces the catastrophe: whilst Ortis, the representative of his age and country, is agitated by a tumult of feelings, and wishes, and disappointments, until he sinks under their accumulated weight.

But, as we have already said, it is in its national aspirations, and its descriptions of characters and events, that Foscolo's work bears the palm. The conversation of Jacopo with the venerable Parini under the shadowy trees of the Porta Orientale; the "dignified eloquence" of the sage, who, on the verge of the grave, with a body bent down by age, poverty and infirmity, but with a mind generous and firm in the purpose of virtue, looked with equal aversion on "ancient tyranny and modern licentiousness;" his deep toned lamentations over his country's blighted hopes, his grief at seeing "letters prostituted,—all the passions fast merging into one slothful channel of corruption and selfishness,—hospitality, benevolence and filial love discarded,—and despicable sciolists scared at the shadow of their own petty guilt;"—all these, terminating in the bitter memento—"the history of all ages teaches us that no liberty is ever to be expected from strangers, and that whoever meddles in the affairs of a conquered country works only for the public evil and his own infamy,"—exhibit a living picture of that remarkable man, whose modest worth Foscolo knew, and could appreciate. . . . These are moral touches, which show that the author's mind, even amidst the storms of passion and the general wreck of principle, had not altogether lost sight of the polar star of eternal truth. (pp. 318-19)

[Foscolo's translation of Sterne's "A Sentimental Journey"] is a masterpiece of its kind. The perfect ease and freedom of the style, the fidelity with which every thought and allusion of the original is rendered; the quaintness, the satire, the playfulness of Sterne, turned into genuine and current Italian humour, without ever appearing constrained or licentious; the sympathy of feeling that seems to have existed between the English traveller and his Italian translator; the short but lively and apposite notes which Foscolo has added to his version,—all these have combined to render the **"Viaggio Sentimentale di Yorick"** one of the most entertaining, we had almost said *original*, books in the language. It affords a complete refutation of the charge brought against it of being too stiff and formal for light entertaining prose. Foscolo has more than any of his contemporaries the merit of displaying the capabilities of Italian prose for every species of composition, when managed by a man of genius. . . . The sketch of **"Didymus the Clerk,"** which accompanies the **"Viaggio Sentimentale,"** is a double of Fo-

scolo himself in the mid-day of his life. The portrait is of course coloured; some features are altered for the sake of effect; but it gives a pretty correct idea of his temper, peculiarities, and favourite fancies. (pp. 335-36)

Foscolo wrote while in England, his **"Essays on the Love, Character and Writings of Petrarch"**—a work which we consider one of his best. . . . [His **"Historical Discourse on the Text of the Decamerone"** (**"Discorso storico sul testo del Decamerone"**)] is, like all his critical works, full of curious and uncommon erudition, illustrative of the manners of Italy during the middle ages, and exhibiting an impartial judgment on the too servilely worshipped Boccaccio, of whose style our author was by no means an admirer, whilst at the same time he did full justice to his talents and learning. (p. 342)

Foscolo's last work, the **"Discourse on the Text of Dante, and on the various Opinions concerning the History and the Corrections of the Divina Commedia"** [*Discorso sul testo e su le opinioni diverse prevalenti intorno alla storio e alla emendazione critica della Commedia di Dante*], is by far the best introduction to the study of that wonderful poem. It is of course a book of erudite research, intended for scholars—a book to be studied, and not merely run through; but at the same time it is wholly free from that dullness and languor which generally pervade the pages of ordinary commentators. The style of the author is lively, rapid and comprehensive; and when he occasionally indulges in long digressions, he has the art of rendering his narrative entertaining. He illustrates with great accuracy and judgment many disputed points of Dante's adventurous life; his political conduct, so variously interpreted; the character of his several patrons, and the state of parties in Italy at that interesting period; in the course of which he displays his deep acquaintance with that part of the history of the middle ages, with the unostentatious ease of a man to whom such matters were familiar. (pp. 342-43)

We cannot award Foscolo the merit of originality as an author. The few characters he drew were so many versions of his own. As a dramatist he utterly failed; but he was a most eloquent writer, an acute observer, an elegant poet, and a profound scholar and critic. He certainly did more to assert the independence of Italian literature than any writer for ages before. (p. 344)

[André Vieusseux], "Foscolo and His Times," in
The Foreign Quarterly Review, *Vol. IX, No. XXXIII,*
May, 1832, pp. 312-44.

[MARGARET DAVESIÈS DE PONTÉS]   (essay date 1859)

In many respects, Jacopi Ortis resembles [Goethe's] Werther. But in the German romance, love, and love alone, absorbs the mind of the hero and drives him to self-destruction. In the Italian, that passion is shared by another not less ardent, patriotism. In "Werther" there are few incidents; nothing to draw our attention from the principal figures and the main action. Werther destroys himself because she whom he loves is the bride of another. Not so Ortis. There are in him two men, as in Foscolo himself. It is the phantom of an expiring country, as well as that of a rival, which places the dagger in his hand. Thus, there is not the same degree of universal truth in the Italian as the German romance. . . . The success of [Foscolo's] romance was immense, for it touched the two chords that vibrate the most powerfully in the human heart; but that success was confined to Italy. The popularity of "Werther" was European. Foscolo's poems are less remarkable than his romances. They are powerful and fervid, like everything he wrote, but they are, generally speaking, turbid and exaggerated. From this censure, however, we may perhaps except the "**Sepulchri**," a poem in "versi scolti," or unrhymed, composed in memory of his friend, Parini. . . . The "**Sepulchri**" does not appear to us to merit all the eulogies lavished upon it. There is too little simplicity, too much erudition; allusions, mythological, historical, and literary, are heaped one upon the other; and these allusions are often so abstruse that the author is obliged to act as his own commentator. The verse, indeed, is exquisitely harmonious, and there are certainly here and there passages of considerable force and beauty, but they do not form the staple of the poem. The main characteristic is a reverent admiration, a deep regret for the days and the customs of antiquity. (pp. 431-32)

Foscolo's tragedies, though for a time most popular, are now nearly forgotten. The thoughts are noble and the language sonorous and eloquent, but the scenes and situations are generally forced and unnatural, and the personages deficient in warmth and passion. . . . Foscolo has not attained the *beauties* of his model [Vittorio Alfieri], while he has exaggerated his defects; but as his dramas, whatever their subject, always breathe patriotic ardour and national enthusiasm, they obtained great, if ephemeral success. (pp. 432-33)

Foscolo's correspondence is the image of the man himself; sometimes full of passion, energy, firm and serious convictions; sometimes doubt, uncertainty, and discouragement. It is his very soul which he pours forth to his friends, by turns eloquent and graceful, grave and witty. It breathes a heart at once burning with patriotism, and easily seduced by love, pleasure, and vanity. In this correspondence—not meant for the public—we find much to admire, much to pity—little to condemn. (p. 435)

> [Margaret Davesiès de Pontés], "Modern Poets and Poetry of Italy," in The Westminster and Foreign Quarterly Review, n.s. Vol. XVI, No. II, October 1, 1859, pp. 427-56.*

[H. T. TUCKERMAN]   (essay date 1860)

Sentiment and reflection, graceful expression, refined allusions, intense personality, give to [*Ultime Lettere d'Jacopo Ortis*] a singular charm. Its relation to the events of the time and the national sorrows, and occasional philosophic and poetic episodes, as well as picturesque descriptions, redeem it from the monotony of egotism; and it gradually becomes impassioned by unfolding, with the reality derived from experience alone, the birth, development, culmination, and catastrophe of love. It thus gave eloquent expression to the patriotic grief which then and afterward brooded over the nation's heart; and it did this while at the same time interweaving the graces of scholarship with the most colloquial simplicity, and depicting the hopes, fears, ecstasy, and anguish of an earnest and a frustrated love. It admits the reader so thoroughly into the consciousness of the writer, that he vibrates between the crises of the lover's emotion, the musings of the thwarted citizen, and the calm thoughts of the meditative scholar. . . . Here a quotation from Dante or Petrarch, there an interview with the venerable Parini, now a passing criticism, and again a glimpse of character, vary the otherwise morbidly conscious strain of the writer; but the tone is ever confidential,—the atmosphere of the whole that of sentiment; the effect on the reader who surrenders himself to the author is sometimes like that which

breathes from the pages of Rousseau, and sometimes reminds us of Jean Paul, and, but for the utter absence of humor, of Sterne. Obviously modelled on *Werther*,—then the favorite novel on the Continent,—its plan and framework are entirely subordinate to its sentiment, which is thoroughly Italian. Foscolo combined the incident and the impression of the suicide of one near and dear to him, and the actual political vicissitudes of his country, with his own recent impassioned experiences; and through these materials fused the glow of aspiration, tenderness, and despair, born in his own heart, with the expression thereof chastened by an art that heightened without overlaying candid and natural utterance.

Ortis, like its German prototype, has been condemned as immoral, because it indirectly justifies hopeless love and despairing suicide; but the scope and intent of the letters [that make up *Ortis*] in an aesthetic view, can scarcely be reduced to so narrow a significance. It is the love of country, the lament of patriotism, the cry of wounded humanity which forms the essential theme. The book was an ingenious and eloquent, and therefore an endeared, however extravagant, expression of a prevalent sentiment, climax, state of mind, and phase of destiny. . . . (pp. 223-25)

Represented as posthumous, and fragmentary in form, these letters gained in pathos what they lost by novelty, and this trait made them precious to those whose opinions on style were not fixed. Ostensibly published, and, when requisite, connected through a few words of explanation, by the friend to whom they were addressed, the *ruse* enhanced the effect. . . . The overture is national; but inwoven and permeating the whole is a personal theme. A lovely child, a peerless maiden, a faithful peasant, a conventional father, a magisterial bridegroom, with the hero, make up the *dramatis personae;* worldliness and pedantry are contemned, Nature adored, patriotism intensified; solitude, poetry, genius, and love, upheld as the normal elements that redeem and consecrate life. Music and art incidentally blend with politics and literature, and all is harmonized by a graceful, melodious utterance. There are passages of eloquent despair, of dramatic extravagance, of acute criticism, of intense and chastened melancholy, ending in passionate delight and suicidal calmness. (pp. 225-26)

[There is] a certain affinity between the sentiment of Foscolo and Sterne. It was especially at the point of tenderness that their natures coalesced, the difference being, that what in the Italian was profound and continuous, in the Englishman was casual and temporary, though none the less real. . . . In *Ortis,* Sterne is quoted, and the conviction expressed that the legitimate fruit of sorrow is pity and compassion, the only disinterested virtue. Herein we perceive a coincidence of feeling between Didimo and Yorick . . . ; but the verbal graces, the undercurrent of sentiment, what painters call the tone, and composers the theme, of the *Viaggio Sentimentale* [the translation of Sterne's *A Sentimental Journey*], brought it home to Foscolo's sympathies. Seldom has an author found a more apt foreign interpreter. So nicely reflected are the shades of meaning and pathetic touches of expression, that the work has been found the best prose guide to induce an intimate acquaintance on the part of Italians with our language, while the English reader, alive to the delicacies of verbal art, will seldom recognize a favorite author so instantly and completely under a foreign garb. (pp. 230-31)

I Sepolcri, in form, spirit, and design, was original. No Italian verse comes so near the higher household strain of our vernacular. The solemn cadence, the thoughtful pathos, the terse and erudite, yet melodious plea for the sanctities of death and the regrets of bereaved humanity, breathe a sentiment and a language akin to the elegiac verse of Gray. More learned, better sustained, and in purer taste, than the similar poems of Young and Blair, in tone it is not less contemplative than theirs, nor is the imagery, though more classical, less affecting. Nor are its English affinities confined to subject and tone; they equally extend to form; and seldom, if ever, have the most effective and choice traits of English blank verse been so admirably reproduced in Italian. The dignity and grace of the language intimately correspond with the solemn interest of the theme. It found an immediate echo in the thoughtful hearts of the poet's countrymen, and became a standard exemplar of elegiac verse. Yet in this case, as in that of the *Lettere d'Jacopo Ortis,* a swarm of verbal critics lighted upon the work, and extreme opinions were expressed as to its execution; though its sentiment was too genuine, humane, and pathetic not to win and awe as well as chasten and charm. (p. 235)

The first trait in the writings of Foscolo which commands our admiration and sympathy is his independence and moral courage; he proclaimed what he thought; he uttered what he felt; he was bravely true to his artistic conviction and the dignity of literature. In an age of servile imitation, academic compromise, and official patronage, this is no small distinction. He has "lived and written," says Hobhouse, "in a state of open warfare with the writers of the day, and the reigning political parties." Critics found fault with what they called the unmusical verse of *I Sepolcri,* not perceiving that the sweet monotony their enervated taste craved had sapped Italian poetry, and that this new precedent more than atoned, by energy of thought, sentiment, and expression, for the dulcet mediocrity it shamed.... The rhetoric of his Bonaparte oration and the "affected calmness" of his Inaugural have been complained of; yet the bold truthfulness of the one, and the philosophic severity of the other, were the most requisite lessons of the hour.

The versatility of his style is another prominent characteristic, and attests a rare mastery of the elements of literary art. What can be more diverse than the method, spirit, and form of *I Sepolcri* and the ode *All' Amica Risanata?* Or where do we find an Italian writer who alternates with such consummate ease from the oratorical to the didactic, from the eloquence of sentiment to the simplicity of narration, from unadorned logic to glowing apostrophe? Few professed lovers of ancient literature have better proved their wise allegiance to those standard exemplars; yet they do not overlay his individuality, trammel his native instincts, or pervert his sense of the progess of ideas and language. It is now conceded, by those capable of appreciating his example and influence, that he did more to emancipate the literature of his country from obsolete mannerism and pedantic trammels, and to exhibit the capabilities of his beautiful native language, than any other writer of his day except Parini. (pp. 255-56)

[*H. T. Tuckerman*], "Ugo Foscolo," in The North American Review, *Vol. XCI, No. CLXXXVII, July, 1860, pp. 213-58.*

FRANCESCO DE SANCTIS (essay date 1870)

[*Sanctis was a nineteenth-century Italian critic who regarded literature as the expression of a society's morals. His two volume* Storia della letteratura italiana, *first published in 1870 and excerpted below, is a survey of Italian literature through the late nineteenth century. This work, recognized by modern critics as one of the best histories of a national literature, also traces the development of Italian culture. In addition to the following critical comments on Foscolo, Sanctis describes the climate of contemporary Italian society: its political turmoil, longing for freedom, and worship of Napoleon. Sanctis was the first critic to note Foscolo's indebtedness to Giambattista Vico, the Italian Renaissance philosopher who found a consistent and identifiable pattern in the development of human institutions. Vico's influence on Foscolo is evident in* The Sepulchres, *which Sanctis describes as "a history of the living written by the dead."*]

[Ugo Foscolo] had begun, like Alfieri before him, by singing with lyrical enthusiasm of an unhoped-for liberty, but while the poet was singing of [Napoleon,] the hero-liberator of Venice, the hero changed into a traitor, and sold Venice to the Austrians. Ugo Foscolo became a homeless wanderer, without country, family, or illusions. From the fullness of his soul he produced his *Iacopo Ortis.* Its substance is the cry of Brutus: "O Virtue, thou art nothing but an empty word!" His illusions had withered like the leaves in autumn, and their death was his own death, was suicide.... There is a morbid strain in the *Iacopo.* The book is the easily provoked outburst of a very young man, not the mature expression of a world long and intimately communed with. It has a tendency to abstract reflection rather than to artistic development. The imaginative part is poor and monotonous, though the feeling is so highly exaggerated. (pp. 903-04)

The work that raised him to the level of the great was the *Sepolcri*—he was known henceforth simply as "the author of the *Sepolcri.*" And certainly this ode was the first lyrical voice of the new literature, the affirmation of the new consciousness, the birth of the new man. (p. 906)

The *Sepolcri* is a history of humanity written from a new point of view, a history of the living written by the dead. It has something of Vico in its inspiration. The world from its dark and formidable beginnings, natural and savage, is raised to a human and civilized state by the religion of sepulchres, the religion that educated Greece and Italy.... Though the story is old the perspective is new, therefore the colours and forms are original. Here, fused together, are Heaven and Hell, the vast Gothic shadow of the nothing and the infinite, and the tenderest and most delicate sentiments of the heart of man. And the whole has a solemn, as it were religious form, as of a hymn to the Divinity. (pp. 906-07)

The advent of the new literature was announced by the suppression of rhyme. The *terzina* and the *ottava rima* gave place to free verse. It was a reaction against the *cadenza* and the *cantilena.* Words were serious and important in themselves, so musical rhyme was done away with; the word was enough by itself. Foscolo does away even with the strophe, and not in a tragedy or a poem but actually in a lyrical composition, which he dares to rob of even rhythm and metre. Here [in the *Sepolcri*] certainly we get thought naked. The ideas are set alight in the depths of the imagination and break out impetuously as though warmed from their own heat, and with all their inner harmonies complete. The language, tamed and reduced as it is by hard effort, comes out, as it were, uneven, broken, with new textures and new sounds. It is the true and natural voice of the soul, the music of things, the grand manner of Dante. Even the type seems new. Instead of the sonnet and the canzone we have the ode, a free unmechanized form. It is the lyrical poem of a moral and religious world, the raising of the soul to the heights of humanity and history, the raising of the inner man above the passions of the day. It is man in his integrity—in his active life as a patriot and citizen and in the intimacy of his private affections. It is the dawn of the new century. The ode was the prelude to the hymn: Foscolo was knocking at the door of the nineteenth century.

He followed his ode with others—the *Alceo*, the *Sventura*, the *Oceano*. But the first inspiration had gone. These new odes were written deliberately, in the literary manner, so are only fragments, with nothing mature in them. At the end there appeared the *Grazie*. It has all the finish of an artistic work, but the poet has practically vanished. (pp. 908-09)

Foscolo opened the way to the new century. And there is little doubt that if human progress had but taken a logical and pacific form instead of the tumultuous form that it did, the last writer of the eighteenth century would have also been the first of the nineteenth century, and the head of the new school. But it happened that the world progressed under the appearance of reaction, and to Foscolo this seemed like a denial of the century he was conscious of belonging to. What he hated above all was the war on mythological forms, which he felt to be a denial of himself. It is true that later he moderated his opinions, both religious and political, to a great extent, adopted a truer conception of life, parted with many of his illusions, and threw in his lot with the new century. But the new century refused to accept him. Defamed and forgotten, and pulled unendingly back and forth by changing impressions, he ended sadly, bequeathing his *Grazie* to the new century like a challenge. It was the last flowering of Italian classicism. (pp. 909-10)

> Francesco de Sanctis, *"The New Literature," in his* History of Italian Literature, *Vol. 2, translated by Joan Redfern, Basic Books, Inc., Publishers, 1960, pp. 833-947.**

BENEDETTO CROCE (essay date 1923)

[*Croce was an Italian philosopher, historian, editor, and literary critic whose writings span the first half of the twentieth century. He founded and edited the literary and political journal* La critica, *whose independence, objectivity, and strong stand against fascism earned him the respect of his contemporaries. According to Croce, the only proper form of literary history is the* caratteristica, *or critical characterization, of the poetic personality and work of a single artist; its goal is to demonstrate the unity of the author's intention, its expression in the creative work, and the reader's response. In the following, Croce stresses "the close connection between [Foscolo's] life and poetry." Foscolo considered passion essential to writing and understanding poetry, and his depiction of deep and complex emotions earns Croce's warm praise. It is, according to Croce, "this whole-hearted feeling which ranks him among the great poets of the nineteenth century." This essay was first published in 1923 in* Poesia e non poesia: Note sulla letteratura europea del secolo decimonono.*]*

Foscolo's view of things was dark: he felt himself oppressed by an unknown violent power, which forces men into the world under the sun and obliges them to live out their life with that "fever" in their veins of which Shakespeare speaks, and then inexorably hurls them into the darkness of death and of oblivion. The thought of death, if it did not predominate in him, at any rate dominated. He liked to be at home with death since a boy, just like a character of Shakespeare, and not only with that form of death which comes upon us as fate, but also with that other form of it, which must be invited and desired, suicide, a way out of life that must always be kept open. This conception and disposition of spirit produces as a general idea the most different practical attitudes in life—asceticism and cynicism, ferocious renunciation and frivolous enjoyment, act-

ing and abstaining from action, quietistic self-abandonment and fervent labour and travail of spirit. This last form alone was possible to Foscolo, with his sensitive, energetic mind, requiring expansion and action, and open to generous impulses of all sorts. . . . His mind and thought enabled Foscolo to detect a light in the darkness of overpowering, unknown and external and therefore materialistic forces, which served as a rallying point from which he was able to regain his spontaneity, autonomy and freedom. What does it matter if he found this freedom in the beat of "pleasure" or of "pain"? What does it matter if he symbolized the negative yet dialectical and propulsive moment as *"ennui"* [boredom], *ennui* that obliges to action? What does it matter that he called the ideals of beauty, virtue, friendship, fatherland, humanity, "illusions"? By calling them so, he recognized their existence practically and asserted them theoretically, paying them homage and admitting their necessity. Hence his life as a citizen, a soldier, an artist, a learned man, a friend and a lover. He always felt and affirmed with pride the loftiness, the dignity and the profound excellence of this life, a view shared by all the youth of Italy at the period of the Risorgimento. . . . (pp. 80-1)

Foscolo held to a speculative position that was agnostic and materialistic and of great importance to him both practically and politically, but is of little importance and of little originality in the history of thought; this was his boundary in philosophy, the hemispheres of darkness which surrounded him. But Socrates also renounced philosophizing as to nature and the Cosmos, yet he produced, as is well known, something extremely philosophical, which has been fruitful in the course of centuries. I mean by this that Foscolo, although he limited his researches to the sphere of the human mind and declared that he did not wish to ascend to the origin of things, was yet the author of lively and fecund thoughts upon man, art, politics, morality, history and religion. (p. 82)

Foscolo was among the profound renewers, among the very first of those who profited by the doctrines which Vico had enunciated a century before on the theory of poetry and criticism. He was fully conscious of the close connection between life and poetry, denying the possibility of producing or of judging poetry to those who were learned in rules and models of art, but had never known human passions in their own hearts, nor fought the fights of the will, who had never quivered or suffered, loved or hated. Polemic, against academical writers, against desk writers and "cloister men," against the schools of old Italy, runs all through his pages. His remedy for all this is the historical interpretation of poetry, of true poetry, which, since it nourishes itself with the passions and affections of man at various times, can only be understood in that way. He was romantic in this respect and romantic in the best sense, culminating in admiration of the "primitive poet"; but he was also classical, because he did not like "the sentimental tinge" so "often artificial" of modern writers, preferring the naturalness of the ancients "who described things as they saw them, without desiring to magnify them before the eyes of satiated readers" and placing "harmony" at the summit of art. He always preferred the energetic, sober and condensed style of the Greek writers to the easy, flowing style of the modern French, which "dissolves one thought into ten periods." He met the romantic theories of "national drama" and of "historical drama" with the remark that poetry is by no means bound to "national subjects" and does not know what to do with historical exactitude. He possessed the most powerful possible sense of poetic form, which is not external form agreeing with rules and models, and the sense of great poetry. This enabled him to judge of Dante's poetry and of that of other poets in a new manner; he perceived that much of what men of letters of his day were still calling poetry was not poetry at all, and that Italy was almost without poetry during the two centuries, so rich in verse, which elapsed between Tasso and Alfieri. He assigned to poetry and the arts the end of potentializing life and making man sensible of it, effecting what might be described as an internal "catharsis" or "aesthetic education." Imperfections, hesitations and omissions can be noted in his theories and critical studies, but main lines, as we have indicated them, remain clear.

The same holds good of his other doctrines, and particularly of his view of movement, agitation, passion, action, as the sole reality, which he did not flee from or depreciate, but accepted. We see him altogether possessed of the spirit of the new times, which places salvation in action, happiness in creation, between pain and pain. For this reason, agnostic, pessimist and almost materialist as he was, he yet maintained the value of history, thus contradicting himself in a significant manner. His ideal of history was objective and substantial history, not erudition, anecdote or historical instances. He recalled Italians to the study of history. (pp. 83-4)

If all Foscolo were to be found . . . in his practical life and in his critical and political writings, he would nevertheless be a great man, an educator of manly generations to come, a renovator of the criteria both of ethical and of artistic life, and founder of Italy's new literary criticism. But he was a poet, a very pure poet, author of few but perfect and eternal lines. We are sensible of his poetic soul in his prose also, especially his early prose, where the impetus of the poet is such as not to permit the deliberate balance of prose, although endowing it with force and colour. Sometimes, too, it will impede the logical disposition and proportioning of his theses. . . . On one occasion he surprises himself in the midst of this shock of internal treasures, remarking in a letter: "I think this mode of writing prose comes from my having for so many weeks accustomed myself to think and to form images of my thoughts, singing them in my mind as though they were verses expressed in language quite different from prose." He added that "the Greeks and Latins were wiser when they devoted themselves entirely to verse or to prose and made no attempt as we do to embrace all trades." In this respect, Europe came to know, or knows Foscolo, in the very book which suffers most from this hybrid style, the juvenile *Ortis*. This very noteworthy book is not a simple literary imitation, but conveys, beneath the aspect of a literary imitation, important knowledge both of the author and of his times. It is a collocation of Foscolo's own thoughts and feelings during his first struggles in life. Its fault lies in an over-close realism of presentment of this world of thought and feeling, in its loudness of tone and hence in its rhetorical and emphatic form. (pp. 85-6)

We have said that Foscolo's poems are small in bulk, because we must certainly exclude the two tragedies, which he composed owing to that sort of attraction which the actual boards of the theatre with the crowd of spectators seem to exercise even upon great poets, as though it were a symbol of the other and greater theatre which they have in the hearts of the generations of mankind and which sometimes leads them astray towards what is external and does not correspond with their true inspiration. We must also exclude the bundle of juvenile verse, which the author himself had rejected, yet which the editors have had bad taste enough to unite in the volume of *Poesie,* with the addition of some later utterances and partly unfinished and unfelicitous burlesque epistles.

For this reason, the true and proper poetry of Foscolo is reduced to fourteen sonnets, of which only a few are of first-rate quality, to two odes, to a pair of brief compositions in unrhymed hendecasyllabics, to the poem of the *Sepulchres,* and to the fragments of the *Graces.* As regards the *Sepulchres* and the *Graces,* we must further bear in mind the didactic presupposition which was accepted by Foscolo, and which perhaps had its origin in him from Vico's idea of the "primitive poet," a master of civil and religious life. To this was due the didacticism which insinuates itself into the lofty lyrical poetry of the *Sepulchres* and prevents the *Graces* from becoming more than sketches and fragments. (pp. 89-90)

[Foscolo's] poetry contains the most intense manifestations of his soul: from it (as he once remarked when speaking of certain particular poems) "flows without any exterior aid that ethereal liquid which dwells in every man," of which "nature and heaven" had accorded him his share.

Four fundamental themes are to be discerned in this poetry: Death, in commemorating which is summed up all melancholy; Heroism, in which the value of the human will is asserted; Beauty, in which voluptuousness is present; Art and Imagination, which rescue human affections from death, making them immortal by pouring out upon them their balsam of eternity. These four themes are sometimes united and sometimes each one seems to rise above the others in turn, though they, too, are active or one feels them to be near at hand. These four themes are indeed inseparable, because they form the sole motive of life in its direct reality, not weakened by any thought of another world: they are life as fully expressed in Love, Sorrow, Death, Immortality. All that is one-sided and simply particular is here abolished. Is there perhaps in Foscolo that spasmodic horror of death which is to be met with in so many romantics and pre-romantics and amounts to desperate rebellion? Death is reflected and takes form in the image dear to him of the evening, of nocturnal shadow wherein his war-like, trembling heart finds assuagement and becomes softer, and everywhere throughout the *Sepulchres* is present the severe acceptation of death. But on the other hand, the feeling for death as that which destroys colour and extinguishes vigour, common in other writers, is not to be found there. The words and accents in which he sings the heroes of thought and action, voices his joy in beauty and pleasure, paints modes and aspects of feminine charm, or landscapes and scenes of nature, and celebrates the virtue of Poetry, are those of one who receives into his bosom all human passions, fully abandons himself to them and uses them as a means of self-expression. His verse is beautiful with that dolorous passionateness that is also joyous and amorous, and flows together there so as to form a sweet living being, soft and flexible, harmoniously resonant, seductive in every movement. The union of opposites is not with Foscolo a wise counsel of calm philosophic serenity, but the complexity of a soul richly endowed, which realizes all its riches. Those images that are the chilled material of thought operative in its own sphere, or memory of past conflicts, are not to be found in him: they are here active, living drama, which adapts itself to its own development. The final impression is not separation from life, but increased love of life: to think, to act, to enjoy, to know how to die, trusting oneself to the affection of the dear ones that remain and to the hearts of the poets.

The classic quality of Foscolo does not reside in his exquisite Graeco-Latin culture nor in his love of antique mythology, but in this whole-hearted feeling, which ranks him among the great poets of the nineteenth century. (pp. 90-2)

Benedetto Croce, ''Foscolo,'' in his European Literature in the Nineteenth Century, *translated by Douglas Ainslie, Alfred A. Knopf, 1924, pp. 79-95.*

ANTONIO CIPPICO (lecture date 1924)

[*This essay was originally presented as a lecture on January 30, 1924. Cippico uses an interdisciplinary approach: he weaves together biographical comments on Foscolo's life and love affairs, historical comments on contemporary political upheaval in Italy and throughout Europe. In addition, Cippico comments on the classical sources and themes of Foscolo's work, while demonstrating the effect of these influences on his poetry. Here, Cippico especially praises the Florentine sonnets, the two odes published in* Poesie, *and* The Sepulchres.]

[To Foscolo's love for Isabella Roncioni we owe his] admirable Florentine sonnets which are amongst the finest verses that Italy has had since the immortal love poems of Petrarch's *Canzoniere:*

Parchè taccia il rumor di mia catena,
Di lagrime, di speme, e di amor vivo,
E di silenzio; chè pietà mi affrena,
Se con lei parlo, o di lei penso e scrivo . . .

(To silence the din of my chain,
I live on tears, on hope, on love,
And on silence; seeing that pity restrains me,
If I speak with her, write to her or think of her.) . . .

The beauty of the beloved is refashioned in the depths of the poet's soul, and is mirrored in exquisite and nearly plastic music of imagery and words. This almost spiritual sensitiveness to beauty in Foscolo's verses is expressed more in relief than in colour, and therein lies the difference between his poetry and that of those non-Italian poets, his contemporaries—Byron, Hölderlin, Wordsworth, and Herder, among others. Although written when he was but twenty-two years of age, they are more passionately and intensely constructed than Petrarch's best ones. . . . (p. 18)

Equally plastic, but without that great lyrical inspiration which burns in every line of these verses, are his two great Odes—the one dedicated to *Luigia Pallavicini, Thrown from her Horse* . . . , on the Sestri Riviera, the other, *To My Convalescent Friend* . . . , dedicated to Antonietta Fagnani Arese, another of the poet's lady-loves. The first is poetry cut out in Parian marble, art for art's sake: in her infirmity, the Pallavicini at first reminds him of Venus wounded by a thorn, whilst weeping over the death of Adonis; then of Pallas emerging from her bath, and finally of Diana in her coach led by stags, rushing headlong down the slopes of Mount Etna. Three classical myths—yet three religious symbols: for Foscolo's artistic religion is that of ancient fables, which are a light veiling of truth.

It must not be forgotten that this Ode was written in the midst of the horrors and hunger of besieged Genoa, and therefore in its Parnassian tranquillity it is in vivid contrast with the tragic realities surrounding Foscolo at that time. With its mythological allegories, that are rather adherent than inherent, this Ode is a worldly and gallant parenthesis, an antithesis to the daily battle. It is a poem without love, exterior but not sensual. He drew his inspiration from the contrast between beauty and the disfiguration of beautiful forms. (p. 19)

In the second Ode, it is love, and not beauty alone, that awakens profoundest pity. The lady's is the languid beauty of a convalescent nor has it been disfigured. . . . (pp. 19-20)

It is true that this lyric gives no thought to virtue, still less to the senses. It is, rather, the exteriorization of all that is least transient and ephemeral in feminine beauty: the spiritual sense of beauty, which, if rebellious to colour, must necessarily be celebrated solely by a plastic artist. And very few of the greatest poets have ever been cleverer word sculptors than Ugo Foscolo. (p. 20)

'I have taken this style of poetry from the Greeks'—wrote Foscolo [of *I Sepolcri*]—'who were used to extract moral and political sentences from ancient traditions, presenting them not to the intellect of their readers, but to poetry and to the heart'.

Just as Pindar enthusiastically sang the praises of deities and heroes, so Foscolo endeavoured to treat his subject heroically and lyrically, imbuing it with a civil, moral, and educational spirit. (p. 21)

[The influence] of this poem—also described, correctly, as a *Hymn to Italy*—on the new generations of the peninsula was enormous. In fact, the primal idea of the poem is the mother country, that entity of life which ever renews itself even through the sanctity of death; the verses are pervaded with the conviction that an immortal love unites the living and the dead.

The doctrine that permeates through this great 'lyrical poem' does not spring from a conventional classical erudition. . . . If the poet's other lyrical works—the two **'Odes'**, *Alceo,* or the fragments of the hymns **The Graces**—show the solemn neo-Hellenic grace of the sculptorial art of his contemporary, Canova, there is nothing sugary in the marble fashioned by Foscolo. . . . The poet's classicism sprang from his intensely passionate existence of daily turbulence, and although differing widely from Germany's aesthetic romanticism, he shared its disdain for all archaeology. 'I am a world unto myself', affirmed Jacopo Ortis, the hero of the Foscolian novel. Therefore, his art, similar to that of the romantics, is a clear reflection of the *Ego;* it aspires to the fusion of ancient and modern, is anti-Christian and revolutionary, if only as a reaction against the restored catholicism of the Jesuits during the two centuries following on the Council of Trent. There is a profound difference between this catholicism and the ancient, especially as regards the consideration of death; for, whereas the ancients contemplated death with serenity, moderns viewed it with whimsical haughtiness and horror. Foscolo paganly puts the civil before the religious idea; he prefers terrestrial life to the celestial—as also love and glory to maceration and humility. (pp. 21-2)

[Foscolo's] classicism is purely personal, melancholy, yet eager with ill-restrained passion. For him death is the 'unknown calm' of Lucretius, 'the mysticism of oblivion', and it is this idea that runs all through the first part of [*I Sepolcri*]. In the second part, instead, he sings not of the immortality of the soul, but of the memory of men; these are represented by the great Italians who are buried in glory, in the Florentine Catholic Pantheon of Santa Croce: Michelangelo, Galileo, Alfieri. (p. 22)

I Sepolcri is the *epos* [epic] of great spirits, just as the *Inni Sacri* and the *Promessi Sposi* of Manzoni are that of humble ones. It celebrates the Pantheon of Italians. But in it the majestic shadows of Electra being kissed by a god, of Ajax and of Hector, sole conquerors of death, are outlined. There is no veil of mystery around this song of death. Death is considered politically, but with terror, following the example of Lucretius, Seneca, and Plato. Remembrance is prized only for the dead, and as constituting immortality. Remembered by Jove, Electra was immortalized, Hector by Homer. Foscolo disdains discussing the mystery of death, of that which was Tartar or Elysium for the masses of Hellas, 'oblivion' for Zeno and Epicurus, and purification for Plato. For him it gives but one consolation, remembrance, which means glory, the ultimate aim of life.

> Non di tesori eredità, ma caldi
> Sensi e di liberal carme l'esempie . . .

> (Not the heredity of treasures, but of warm
> Senses and the example of generous poems.)

In *I Sepolcri,* therefore, the classical world, with its myths and historical allusions, takes on an aspect of contemporary and tangible reality; Troy and Cassandra prophesying of the smoking ruins of the city from the tumulus of Ilus, are as real and present to us, in reading the great poem, as Florence, with her monuments and her hills. (pp. 22-3)

After having presented Italy with his great symphony on country and death, Foscolo, carried away by the fury of his restless and impassioned existence, by the vortex of his many love affairs, . . . and by the agitation of political battles, has left us little else in the way of poetry. The fragments of *The Graces* are the most important part of his latter production; they are of a purifying beauty, holy and sanctified, yet similar to detached and incomplete bas-reliefs, and for this reason it is next to impossible to gather them together into an organic unity of poetry. (pp. 23-4)

[Foscolo is] one of the greatest lyric poets of Italian literature since the days of Petrarch, . . . and to this day his word is a clarion call to all Italians to turn to their Immortals for example and inspiration in their efforts to give their nation an ever higher spiritual unity, ever worthier of her poets. (p. 24)

> *Antonio Cippico, "The Poetry of Ugo Foscolo," in* Proceedings of the British Academy, *Vol. XI, 1924-25, pp. 13-25.*

WALTER L. BULLOCK (essay date 1932)

[*Bullock examines three epistolary romances—Jean Jacques Rousseau's* La nouvelle Héloïse (The New Heloise), *Johann Wolfgang von Goethe's* The Sorrows of Young Werther, *and Foscolo's* Letters of Ortis—*to assess their interest to twentieth-century readers. While noting the thematic similarities of these three works, Bullock maintains that Foscolo was not greatly influenced by Rousseau or Goethe.*]

Foscolo's story is, in this twentieth century, perhaps the most readable of [*The New Heloise, The Sorrows of Young Werther,* and his own *Ortis*], though it certainly lacks the swift unity, and much of the art, of *Werthers Leiden.* The little things that tend to annoy us today in Werther—his oft-reiterated devotion to his Homer (through the first half of the story) though he shows no signs of knowing anything about what Homer wrote; his subsequent turn from Homer to that masterly and gifted faker Macpherson (whom he accepts as Ossian and quotes at agonizing length); his failure to meet the situation boldly, and to ask Lotte to consider and to wait—these are avoided by Foscolo. Jacopo's devotion to Plutarch, Dante, and Petrarch are obviously genuine; and occasional lines from the Italian poets annoy us far less than whole pages rendered from the "Ossian" by Werther. Again, such incidents in *Ortis* as the picture of the famous satirist Parini, an old man in Florence, have a very real interest today; while in the main story itself, Foscolo is the only one who really gives an adequate motive for the lovers' separation and the lady's marriage to another.

And Foscolo shrewdly adds verisimilitude to his tale by a number of minor touches: "Such and such a letter which Ortis must have written cannot now be found. . . ." "The other pages of this letter have been somehow lost. . . ." and the like.

Jacopo Ortis, however, is lacking indeed—we must repeat—in the unity of *Werther.* And this lack of unity is at bottom the result of an attempt to graft one hero upon another. For the *Ultime Lettere di Jacopo Ortis* was not conceived and composed as a single work; it represents a triple working over of material which presented itself to the author successively in quite different forms.

In one of the earlier versions Teresa was a widow with a little daughter, happily betrothed to a noble and affectionate Odoardo. And the hero of the earliest version had been a far more sentimental and far less violent individual, a man whose political activities and convictions seem to have been a very minor matter. One of the chief weaknesses in *Jacopo Ortis* lies in the fact that Foscolo did not always succeed in eliminating this earlier, more sentimental aspect of his hero; so that occasionally the character appears inconsistent. The fact that in its final version Foscolo's story shows the political element so strongly emphasized, pictures its hero as less sentimental and more forceful, and describes the heroine not as a widow with a little daughter but as a maiden, forced by circumstances and a father's will to marry one she did not love — . . . these changes are all caused by parallel changes in the author's circumstances. Between the first and last versions, the Italian political situation had entirely changed, reaching a crisis, and Foscolo himself had passed from comparative indifference to an active interest. . . . The lessening sentimentality and increasing force of Jacopo Ortis in the later version marks a corresponding change in the character of the author. . . . *Jacopo Ortis* went through three quite different forms, its author modifying and altering the story in accordance with his own changed outlook. (pp. 437-38)

> *Walter L. Bullock, "On Re-Reading Three Thwarted Romances: 'La nouvelle Héloïse', 'Die Leiden des jungen Werthers', 'Jacopo Ortis'," in* The Open Court, *Vol. 46, No. 913, June, 1932, pp. 431-40.**

ERNEST HATCH WILKINS (essay date 1954)

[*In this essay from his survey of Italian literature, Wilkins combines biographical and historical detail with critical commentary. Wilkins notes, through a discussion of Foscolo's varied writings, the duality of Foscolo's artistic personality in its alternately neoclassical and romantic manifestations.*]

[*Ultime lettere di Jacopo Ortis*] is based in part on Foscolo's own experiences, and in part on Goethe's *The Sufferings of Young Werther.* The sufferings of Werther, however, result only from his love: those of Ortis result both from his love and from the deplorable state of his fatherland. But the grief that permeates the novel is more than personal and more than political: it is a true *Weltschmerz* [world weariness], arising from a profound consciousness both of the transitoriness of all human achievement and of the inevitability of human suffering:

> I look out from my balcony now that the immense light of the sun is fading and the shadows are dispelling the faint rays that gleam on the horizon: and in the darkness of the sad and silent world I contemplate the image of the Destruction that devours all things. . . .

Men appear to be the makers of their own misfortunes; but their misfortunes derive from the
order of the universe, and the human race in
its pride and its blindness is a slave to fate. Our
talk is of things that have happened within a
few centuries: what are a few centuries in the
vast sweep of time?

(p. 380)

[The] novel is, fictionally, a recording of the emotions of its
hero, and, in actuality, an outpouring of the turbulent spirit of
its author. The style, consonant with that turbulence, is insistently tense and emphatic. The contrast between the *Ultime
lettere* and the odes of Foscolo is very striking. He is indeed,
in his creative life, a dual personality: in the odes he is an
objective neoclassicist, delighting in sunny classic memories
and concerned primarily with his artistry; while in the novel
he is a romantic—not as the adherent of a literary doctrine,
but because he is driven irresistibly to the utterance of the
stormy passions of his restless soul. (pp. 380-81)

Foscolo wrote also a number of lyrics, among them an ode
All' amica risanata, "To His Friend on Her Recovery," which
is of quite the same character and quality as the ode he had
written in Genoa [*A Luigia Pallavicini caduto da cavallo,* "To
Luigia Pallavicini Thrown from Her Horse"], and several excellent sonnets, which express the romantic phase of his poetic
being. . . .

The main elements in the thought of [*I Sepolcri*] are these: a
tomb, though it be beautiful and visited by mourning friends,
brings no comfort to the dead, but the sight and the care of it
lead to the cherishing of memories among the living; the law
is wrong in forbidding differentiation between the burial places
of the evil and the good, the illustrious and the infamous; the
cult of the tomb goes back to the beginnings of civilization
and has attended the whole course of its development; the sight
of the tombs of great men kindles the noble heart to glorious
deeds; and even though tombs may at last disappear the poet
renders the names of great men eternal. The poem proceeds,
however, not in the manner of a formal argument, but by a
series of surging lyric impulses, each giving inspired expression
to some one phase of the underlying thought. (p. 381)

[There are many] noble passages in the poem, and many lines
and brief sequences of lines that have as much poetic scope as
many an entire poem. The dignity of ancient burial ceremonies
and the beauty of English suburban cemeteries are made visible.
In the climax of the poem the blind Homer, groping his way
among Trojan tombs, learns from them the story of the rise
and fall of Ilium. Over the whole poem there broods a consciousness of the unending successions of life from the infinite
past to the infinite future, and a sense of the enduring sorrow
of the human lot: but through these shadows there gleams the
firm assurance of the grandeur of high achievement, and of
the immortality of heroism.

Foscolo was acquainted with Gray's *Elegy* and with other similar English poems, and traces of that acquaintance are discernible in *I sepolcri;* but Foscolo's purpose, as he himself
makes clear in one of his letters, was quite different from that
of the English poets. Young and Hervey, he says, wrote as
Christians, concerned with the ideas of resignation and immortality, and Gray wrote as a philosopher, praising simplicity
of life; whereas he, Foscolo,

considers tombs in their political significance;
and seeks to stimulate the political spirit of

Italians by adducing examples of nations that
honor the memory and the tombs of great men.

In the *Sepolcri,* also, one feels the presence of the spirit of
Vico. But Foscolo's poem, assuming into itself the essence of
all his learning, all his experience, and all his contemplation,
is wholly his own in its fullness and its power. Classic and
romantic elements are harmonized in its universality: Foscolo's
dual poetic personality is here perfectly unified. (pp. 382-83)

Foscolo wrote two tragedies, the *Aiace,* on the story of Ajax
and the *Ricciarda,* which tells a medieval story of Foscolo's
own invention. They are not lacking in eloquence; but they are
not well constructed, and they are ineffective in characterization. (p. 383)

Foscolo shows himself, in his essays, to be a master—the first
Italian master—of literary criticism, modern in its spirit and
in his judgments. He is in complete possession of the works
of which he writes; he is primarily concerned with their poetic
or other literary qualities; and he brings to his interpretation a
remarkable fund of historical learning and an amazingly comprehensive familiarity with the world's poetry. (p. 385)

> *Ernest Hatch Wilkins, "Foscolo and Other Writ-
> ers," in his* A History of Italian Literature, *Cam-
> bridge, Mass.: Harvard University Press, 1954,
> pp. 376-87.**

RENÉ WELLEK   (essay date 1955)

[*Wellek's* A History of Modern Criticism, *from which the following is drawn, is a major, comprehensive study of the literary
critics of the last three centuries. His critical method, as demonstrated in* A History, *is one of describing, analyzing, and evaluating a work solely in terms of the problems it poses for itself
and how the writer solves them. In the following, Wellek both
describes and evaluates Foscolo's critical approach. In concluding his discussion, he summarizes Foscolo's position as a critic
and praises Foscolo's contribution to Italian criticism: "In the
history of Italian criticism Foscolo will keep an important position
as the first critic who broke with neoclassicism and introduced a
historical scheme for the writing and criticism of Italian literature." However, Wellek adds that in the realm of European criticism "Foscolo is a latecomer."*]

[Ugo Foscolo], in the last year of his life, wrote an essay on
the "**New Dramatic School**" attacking Manzoni's theories and
his play *Il Conte di Carmagnola.* . . . Foscolo can argue in
great detail that Manzoni is quite mistaken in his favorable
view of the hero, the Count of Carmagnola, . . . and he can
show convincingly that Manzoni makes historical mistakes and
commits anachronisms even in small verbal matters. The attack
strikes more deeply when Foscolo argues against Manzoni's
distinction of ideal and historical figures. "In any work of
imagination everything depends on the incorporation and identification of reality and fiction." Illusion is achieved only when
"truth and fiction, facing each other and in contact, not only
lose their natural tendency of clashing but aid each other mutually to unite and fuse and to appear a single thing." Foscolo
holds up Shakespeare's *Othello* as an example of the poet's
power of emancipating himself from history. Italian romantic
theory is suspect to him as an attack on the rights of imagination, as a turn toward the actual, the dreary reality which
the poet should escape. . . . Foscolo even rejects all genre and
school distinctions, saying that "every great production is an
individual object which has different merits and distinct char-
actertistics." He protests against the lumping together of dif-

ferent, supposedly classical schools of drama: the Greeks, the French, and the Italians (Alfieri). They seem to him all perfectly distinct. (pp. 265-66)

The fine insights of this essay, its assertion of the power of imagination and the individuality of the work of art, are . . . the most brilliant flash of Foscolo's critical activity. The high level of the essay was never or very rarely reached before. Coming from it to an examination of the other critical writings, one must express a keen sense of disappointment. In part this is due simply to the external circumstances in which Foscolo's writing was produced. Much of his early criticism is in small prefaces or in formal orations at the University of Pavia which are full of fervid but bombastic academic oratory; much of the later writing, done in exile in England, sometimes preserved only in a wretched English translation, is heavily weighed down by a display of inert learning which Foscolo apparently felt to be demanded by the English periodicals or publishers for whom he was writing. His individuality is constantly cramped by his regard for the audience on which he felt dependent for his precarious living. . . . Foscolo's many grandiose schemes for a history of Italian literature and for a *European Review* which would be devoted to "comparative criticism" and to tracing "the reciprocal influence of literature and manners," came to nothing, though fragments of his plans are realized in his *Essays on Petrarch* . . .—his only book-form publication in English— in his editions, with long introductory dissertations, of the *Divine Comedy* and the *Decameron* . . . , and in scattered articles [published in English periodicals] on Dante, Tasso, and the "narrative and romantic poets of Italy."

But the fragmentariness and incompleteness, the heavy admixture of patriotic oratory and inert obsolete antiquarianism, are not the only causes of disappointment. It is rather a certain lack of coherence and sharpness in the choice of ideas which make Foscolo an eclectic, a figure of transition who, however great his importance in the history of Italian criticism, will never acquire great stature in a European context. One could even make a case for Foscolo's criticism as a repertory of neoclassical commonplaces. He can talk about "instruction by delighting." . . . He can define imagination in terms of 18th-century psychology as a power of visual recall. But most frequently Foscolo wavers between two concepts of poetry: one of them emotionalist, deriving from Dubos and Diderot, the other Platonic, deriving from a reading of Plato himself and from the 18th-century tradition of idealizing aesthetics. In the self-portrait he wrote for Hobhouse, Foscolo claims "he would tear his heart from his bosom if he thought that a single pulsation was not the unconstrained and free movement of his soul." The "flame of the heart" is his common phrase, and the purpose of poetry is defined as "making us strongly and fully feel our existence." But this view exists side by side with Platonic idealism. The early Pavia lectures . . . expound a curious concept of "eloquence" as the animating force behind all the arts and behind both prose and verse, which is identified with genius and inspiration in terms drawn from the polemics of Socrates against the sophistical rhetoricians. Later Foscolo can also say that the poet does not imitate but selects, combines, and perfects the scattered beauties of the world; he abstracts and embellishes in order to create the ideal. The ideal is the "universal secret harmony, which man strives to find again in order to strengthen himself against the burdens and pains of his existence." Poetry thus satisfies our need to "veil the unpleasant reality of life with the dreams of imagination." The poet is the man of feeling who expresses himself freely, and at the same time he is the creator of a world of ideals. He is

also the total man who proceeds not by analysis but by synthesis. "The poets," he says in the *Essays on Petrarch*, "transform into living and eloquent images many ideas that lie dark and dumb in our mind, and it is by the magic presence of poetical images that we are suddenly and at once taught to feel, to imagine, to reason, and to meditate."

Foscolo is saved from the consequences of mere emotionalism or Platonic idealism by his intense consciousness of the word, of the role of language and style in poetry. Many subtle comments on individual passages in Dante and Petrarch discuss the effect of single words. The detailed analyses of translations, either from Homer into Italian or Tasso into English, show Foscolo to be a true philologist, a "lover of words," whatever his technical shortcomings as an editor were. Foscolo knows the value of the study of revisions. "To develop the beauties of a poem the critic must go through the same reasonings and judgments which ultimately determined the poet to write as he has done. But such a critic would be a poet." . . . Foscolo knew that "literature is joined to language" and that style is joined to "the intellectual faculty of every individual." Words have a long history which is a "confluence of minor and accessory meanings," of feelings and images, which differ with every language and which the poet knows and uses for his purposes.

Foscolo's chief importance, especially for Italy, lies in his attempt to see this conception of poetry as part of history, of a philosophy of human development, and thus as the basis of a scheme for Italian literary history and a program for his own time. Foscolo's concept of history is, no doubt, influenced by Vico, but more directly it derives from 18th-century primitivism in the mode of Rousseau and Herder. An early age of mythic, bardic, heroic poetry is imagined when all the kinds were mixed and the poet was a prophet and philosopher. Foscolo does not envisage this original poetry very clearly. . . . Still, enough is known to Foscolo for him to justify the view that poetry was originally lyrical, lyrical-epic, and heroic and that it should become so again. Reviewing Monti's epic, *The Bard of the Black Forest,* he defends it with such historical arguments; his own *Grazie* he views as a mixture of the didactic, the lyric, and the epic. "Such perhaps was the first poetry." Such lyrical poetry is "the very summit of art." The ode celebrates gods and heroes and thus does not materially differ from ancient epic poetry. Heroic and lyric are confused or identified, since the aim of poetry is the exaltation of our existence and the poet is a hero himself.

In his criticism Foscolo always makes the genre distinction between "romantic" and "heroic" poetry to the disadvantage of "romantic." Thus in his mind Tasso surpasses every other Italian poet except Dante. The burlesque tradition of Italian poetry, especially its last stage in Casti, is constantly disparaged, and even Ariosto, though greatly admired, is to Foscolo only the master of an inferior, less noble kind of poetry. Tasso is definitely separated from Ariosto by emphasis on the historical character of his theme, which to Foscolo is a history of the Crusades written as an example for Tasso's own time. The main point of many of Foscolo's acute observations on Wiffen's English translation of Tasso is in the charge that Wiffen ignores Tasso's historical accuracy and makes him over into a poet of romance in the style of Spenser. Foscolo, for the sake of his lofty conception of the heroic, here runs counter to the evidence of the text and to the taste established since Hurd's plea for the Italians' "world of fine fabling."

The historical scheme which follows from primitivism is that of the decay of imagination with the progress of civilization. Foscolo sees this process in antiquity. Homer and Pindar are the great ancients, while Virgil and Horace are artificial, derivative, and courtly. The process is seen repeated during the Middle Ages. There Dante is the exemplar of the free, heroic poet, while Petrarch and Boccaccio indicate the beginnings of decadence. Foscolo's conception of Dante is, in its detail, untenable, for he ascribes to him heretical ideas and sees him as a reformer of the Church not only in morals but also in ritual and dogma. Nevertheless, Foscolo, in his article on Dante and the long dissertation on the text, makes a real effort, remarkable for the time, to place Dante in his historical and intellectual context. He pays close attention to Dante's theology and political ideas, to his life and to the tradition of the text. The theories are frequently mistaken or based on insufficient information, but the comments are often sensitive and new. . . . (pp. 266-70)

[Foscolo's comments on English literature are] very limited. His admiration for Shakespeare is qualified by his neoclassical prejudices. He explains that seeing Shakespeare on the stage always increases his resistance, because in the theater he cannot follow the verbal beauties and sees only the action and business. The reservation against Milton for lack of human interest is also conventional. . . . His interest in his English contemporaries seems quite perfunctory: for example, he was shocked by the impiety of Byron's *Cain*. There is a curious streak of the conventional and prudish in Foscolo's criticism which contradicts his own tumultuous erotic life and his exaltation of the strong and free man. But one must not forget that Foscolo had to struggle to keep his head above water in England and tried to make many adjustments to English respectability. He did not succeed, as witness the contemptuous comments in Sir Walter Scott's *Journal* [see excerpt above, 1825] or the quarrel with Hobhouse. Nobody in England knew then that the exile hunted by bailiffs would become the symbol of the Italian *Risorgimento*, would be solemnly reburied in Florence's Santa Croce alongside Michelangelo, Machiavelli, Galileo, and Alfieri, and would be, even more recently, exalted and closely studied as one of the very greatest Italian poets. In the history of Italian criticism Foscolo will keep an important position as the first critic who broke with neoclassicism and introduced a historical scheme for the writing and criticism of Italian literature. But in a European context Foscolo is a latecomer, an eclectic somewhere in the transition from a preclassical Platonic idealism to a romantic view of history. (pp. 271-72)

> *René Wellek, "The Italian Critics," in his* A History of Modern Criticism, 1750-1950: The Romantic Age, *Vol. 2,* Yale University Press, 1955, pp. 259-78.*

P. M. PASINETTI   (essay date 1960)

[*Pasinetti discusses the tone, structure, sources, and major themes of* The Sepulchres. *To this critic,* The Sepulchres *represents Foscolo's most successful attempt to achieve a balance "between the official and the personal, the public and the intimate."*]

A poet's vision of his *patria* [homeland], unless we mistake the texts of most national anthems for poetry, can be a very complex one. The way in which the *vates* [prophet or poet] handles the themes of allegiance, of communal sorrow, of glorious evocation, of exhortation, of prophecy, can among other things provide subtle insights into the very idea of the Nation as a cultural entity and a symbol of the human condition

in general. . . . It is extremely difficult to make this kind of poetry a success. The uniquely successful example I have in mind is Foscolo's *Dei sepolcri* . . . , a very compact poem of 295 unrhymed eleven-syllable lines, to Italians one of the most famous in the language and generally one of the most difficult.

How is a balance achieved here between the official and the personal, the public and the intimate? The poet's voice is, to a considerable extent, one of eloquent commemoration and exhortation; but at the same time we see that the poem exists also as a different kind of expression—as the personal musing, as the familiar address to a friend. If we should force it into a formula, we might say that the poem introduces the manner of the poetic epistle into a tissue largely woven out of "Romantic" materials. . . . (p. 4)

The main scene and the principal sources of the imagery are the burial ground, the sepulcher, the urn, the emblems in which the living preserve and honor the memory of the dead. The commemorative function of those objects is, in the end, identified with that of the poet as *vates,* for the poem is not only in the *vates* tradition, it is also *about* it: poetry establishes, and preserves for posterity, the memory of the great. The conventions of graveyard poetry are thus associated with the time-honored concept of the poet as preserver and solemnizer of the memories of heroes. . . . The image in which the central theme of the poem is most concisely stated (". . . le Muse . . . Siedon custodi de' sepolcri") [the muses sit and watch the tombs], suggests almost inevitably a neoclassic marble group, in so far as poetry can ever usefully recall sculpture. This aspect of the poem seems to justify the passages of high and solemn eloquence, the elaborate constructions, the Latinisms. All this, however, is constantly interwoven with other aspects and tones—that of personal meditation, that of the familiar address, and finally that of concretely "civic" poetry, *poesia civile.* The image of the poet himself corresponds to an image of the Nation both as idealized myth and as individual experience in a defined historical and social setting. (pp. 4-5)

The most immediate and localized elements are provided by the event which has given the poem its practical occasion. A decree, intended to place cemeteries out of the cities and to control the custom of inscriptions on graves, has been taken by the poet to signify decay of communal reverence toward the dead and of ritual piety. In so far as he claims that motif as his starting point (it becomes rather secondary in the actual working of the poem) the poet assumes his first rôle, indicating that he possesses certain practical "civic" connections and interests and singling himself out as the defender of higher values against the present rulers of his society. (p. 5)

The initial points of the poem are largely made through questions, partly rhetorical, aligned almost as variations and amplifications on the theme proposed by the first one—proposed, one would almost say, scholastically, as though to be debated and elaborated on by what will follow, in logical progression. . . .

There is the tone of solemn meditation on death, but it goes along with that of the familiar poetic musing addressed to a friend—a fellow-poet, Ippolito Pindemonte. So the questions acquire a conversational quality, the address is almost an exchange. . . . (p. 6)

The tone of the relationship existing between the two friends . . . aptly prepares us to the nature of the point which is finally made—the persistence of similar communions in friendship after death—a point which is developed in the lofty passage concluding what we may consider the first section of the poem (to line 50).

A second section can be singled out, comprising lines 51-151. After the general argumentative introduction has established the theme of the "corrispondenza" [correspondence] between the dead and the living as the humans' "celeste dote" [celestial gift], the oration, as it were, starts on its specific business. The "new law" on cemeteries is briefly mentioned at the start; then with an immediate transition, which is typical of the rather "telescoped" quality of the whole work, the unlamented grave of the poet Giuseppe Parini is given as instance of present abandonment and oblivion. It also occasions a passage in the moonlight-horror variety of Romantic night poetry, in a landscape of crosses . . . in the abandoned forgotten cemeteries where the hungry dog wanders. In contrast, a passage follows where the pious customs, the beliefs, the superstitions connected with burials are rehearsed. There may be a tone of eighteenth-century didacticism but it is tempered by the fact that those elements have an obvious function in the general pattern of the poem. Concreteness is maintained also through frequent transition from the general to the particular, and through shifts in the sharpness of vision and in verbal tenses. . . . (pp. 6-7)

Through such shifts the poem progresses even grammatically toward the suggestion that the poet's outlook is above time; there is a great fluidity in time levels; the scope of the poem and the outlook of the speaker are progressively and imperceptibly widened. (p. 7)

Firmly placed in the present tense is only the vision of the ruling society against which the poet addresses his most polemical passage. This is at the end of the second section (137-150): the rôle he assumes here is that of the poet-citizen, deprecating the false values of a governing class . . . whose cult of the dead is cold ostentation. He sets himself against that vain pomp and deceitful stability; in contrast to them, throughout the poem [he follows] . . . the tradition of Romantic patriotism where the pattern of exile is typical. . . . (pp. 7-8)

The not uncommon Romantic attitude of "looking forward to one's own death" had already made its appearance in the introductory section of the poem; . . . now that theme reappears in a more solemn and public connection, the stress being on the example and the message left after death.

The transition from this point is naturally to the section (151-197) where the poet assumes the function of the communal celebrator of heroes and evokes the memories of some of the country's great men of the past through the vision of their tombs in the church of the Holy Cross, in Florence. . . . (p. 8)

[Foscolo's] exclusive communion with the dead is brought out with particular sharpness as he recalls the image of his own more direct inspirer, Vittorio Alfieri, and some sort of identification between that noble and pale wanderer and himself is implicit. . . .

The memory of the poet Alfieri is proposed as the epitome of passionate allegiance to country. At that point the most sudden transition in the poem occurs. The passion . . . [speaks] to the present poet from the "religiosa pace" [religious peace] of the grave; and the idea that this was the same spirit which inspired the "virtue and wrath" of the Greeks at Marathon, in itself possibly a commonplace of patriotic poetry, is introduced, as it were, in mid-speech. . . .

The effect of the sudden transition, of course, is to suggest identity between the present and the remotely past. From here

to the end, the scene of the poem is occupied entirely by the world of ancient Greece and mythology. To simplify matters we may say that the earlier part of the poem is the more localized and time-bound and that it widens its scope as it progresses. (p. 9)

[The] final impression left by the poem as expression of "patriotic Romanticism" is that its *patria* is . . . , in fact, an "invention." Looking back at the whole poem we realize that the poet has attempted, with a conciseness probably unparalleled in the period, and in terms of the special taste, the cultural training, and the sensibility that were his own, to perform a synthesis which in very different ways presents itself in literary history when a conciliation is attempted between the personal, the "civic" and the mythical. (p. 12)

> *P. M. Pasinetti, "Notes Toward a Reading of Foscolo's 'Sepolcri'," in* Italian Quarterly, *Vol. 3, No. 12, Winter, 1960, pp. 3-12.*

KARL KROEBER (essay date 1964)

[*In his book-length study, Kroeber compares four early nineteenth-century poets whose works reflect and eventually transcend the political and social upheaval of their era. The organization of the study is topical, proceeding from "practical" works like* Letters of Ortis *to those that are "visionary" like* Le grazie. *In the following excerpt, Kroeber analyzes Foscolo's use of myth in* Le grazie *to depict the power of art and its ability to transform society.*]

[*The Graces (Le grazie)*] develops a fundamental motif of *Jacopo Ortis:* men need principles for transmuting their violent, primitive passions into finer, more enduring emotions. We should not try to disavow our most basic impulses but instead should render them what Foscolo calls "modest" or "discreet." Foscolo does not wish us to attenuate our emotions nor to back away from sensory experience. On the contrary, he wishes us to recognize that only a civilized man is capable of experiencing the most intense sensations and powerful emotions. . . .

[*The Graces* is not] unfinished in the sense that [John Keats's] *Hyperion* is unfinished, nor can *The Graces* properly be called a fragmentary poem, for, as [the Italian critic Michele] Barbi says, each apparently separable lyric part in fact contributes to a total and unified conception. Yet Foscolo never found an organization for the poem which entirely satisfied him. The main structure is firm; not all of the parts fit perfectly into it. This failure in perfect fit probably kept Foscolo from publishing his most ambitious work. He printed only a few excerpts, and the poem as a whole was unknown until the middle of the nineteenth century. (p. 154)

Foscolo's introduction to *The Graces* speaks of the three hymns composing the poem as if they were a temple.

> To the immortal Graces, the triplet daughters
> of Venus and the sisters of Love, the temple is
> sacred; born the day that Jove granted beauty,
> wisdom, and virtue to mortals, the goddesses
> serve to keep always enduring and always renewed those three celestial gifts, ever more
> modest as they are more praised. Enter and
> worship. . . .

Throughout *The Graces* one art form is made to express itself through a sister form, but there is no confusion and Foscolo's style is never "operatic." Singing, instrumental music, painting, sculpture, architecture, poetry, and the dance each makes its unique contribution to an ideal harmony of beauty, wisdom, and virtue which it is the purpose of *The Graces* as a whole to embody for our admiration and inspiration. The unity of *The Graces,* then, is created out of intricate diversity. The goddesses hymned are the graces of this life, not the grace of eternal life. They are the unified but diversified spirit of art, not in the narrow aesthetic sense but in the sense of civilization, the supranatural as opposed to the natural. They represent man's continual aspiration to achieve ever more intense and lasting beauty and wisdom and virtue.

In his invocation to the first hymn, to Venus, Foscolo prays to the Graces for the inspiration of their mysterious harmony so that he may depict their beauty. But his desire for the inner music which inspires beautiful figures is not an end in itself, is not the desire for mere self-expression. He wants his utterance to rejoice his country, Italy, afflicted by the tyranny of foreign oppressors. To Foscolo all true poetry is political poetry, because it inspires men to be free, and in his earlier verse Foscolo's politics tend to be specific and more or less practical. In *The Graces* he absorbs the particular tragedy of early nineteenth-century Italy into a more metaphysical schema. He does not minimize Italian difficulties and he is as resolute an opponent of tyranny as ever, but he now sees his country's travail as one moment in man's perpetual struggle to be free, to be civilized, to be wholly human. Foscolo's withdrawal from direct political polemic is an inevitable distancing which accompanies the deepening of his philosophic vision.

The first hymn tells of the birth of the Graces and of the early progress of mankind into civilization. The setting is the legendary land- and seascapes of prehistoric Greece. Foscolo's conception of mankind's earliest history derives from Vico, but in some important respects also contradicts Vico, since Foscolo sees human history as a single, unitary evolution: with the birth of the Graces civilization was born—a unique event, the most important in human history. (pp. 155-56)

An understanding of art is inseparable from an awareness of its artifice, its envisioned and created qualities which distinguish it from that which is purely natural. The heightened consciousness and sensibility demanded by art is central to Foscolo's conception of what constitutes civilization. The scheme of his conception may be summarized as follows: Venus, to whom the first hymn of *The Graces* is dedicated, is the spirit, the interior force, of the natural universe; it is she who brings the Graces to mankind. In other words, the arts and graces of civilized life arise in nature, for Venus is love and the sexual urge, she comes to man from the sea, from the very heart and womb of the natural world. In his vision of humane man Foscolo equates the growth of sexual attraction into transforming love—Venus—with the growth of the arts and civilities of society—the Graces. The parallel clarifies his conception of civilization emerging once for all time in human history. (pp. 156-57)

Thus Foscolo can be at the same time historical, tracing the progress of civilization from Greece to Rome to Renaissance Italy, and suprahistorical, portraying what the direction and goal of civilization's evolution will be. He sees civilization as a succession of discrete historical phenomena, and, simultaneously, as a single, unitary impulse or aspiration. Hence the arts are the supreme expression of civilization. Each work of art is a unique historical representative of the ideal, achieved through the artist's skilled, civilized handling of finite sensory

particularities, which constitutes a creation transcending the temporal and the material.

The second hymn of *The Graces,* to Vesta, who represents the crafts and skills of civil life, celebrates the transfer of the center of civilization from Greece to Italy, with special attention to the achievement of Italian poets from Dante to Tasso, concluding with verses complimentary to the wife of a Milanese leader of Foscolo's own day. Thus the subject of the first hymn is prehistory and the appearance of the Graces, and the subject of the second is human history up to the moment of writing. The third hymn carries us out of history to a metaphysical realm. This last hymn, to Minerva, who represents wisdom and spiritual tranquility, while more idealized and philosophical than its predecessors, is at the same time more personal and more specific. Here Foscolo is free to give full play to his projection of what the Graces might accomplish; hence the idealizations of the third hymn are not abstractions but concrete embodiments of his supranatural aspirations.

In his exordium of the final hymn, Foscolo prays for inspiration from the art of Amphion (with whom he associated the Homeric hymns), Pindar, and Catullus: "Sacred poets, give me your art, to me the spirit of your languages, and following in the Tuscan mode I shall more burningly embellish the celebrated stories." Only Foscolo's "mode" is new; his subject matter is old. Old and diverse materials shaped into an original unity of form, is the essence of his poetry. The "celebrated stories" are in fact the spirit of the older poets speaking to him from the sepulchre of the past, "illuminating with Elysian light the lonely fields where wandering Imagination led me to discern the truth." No passage in *The Graces* better illustrates the way in which Foscolo transforms the Neoclassic ideal of imitation of the ancients into a new ideal of inspiration from the ancients. Imagination is the key to this transformation. Imagination it is which enables the poet to create the new out of the old, to reanimate the spirit which binds all men in a union of diversities, and to annihilate the time and space barriers of the natural world. (pp. 157-58)

The climax of the third hymn is the weaving of the veil for the Graces. . . . (p. 159)

The veil of the Graces is imaginative creation. Depicting reality, it celebrates ideal loveliness. Protecting, preserving, itself figured with designs, it is yet transparent, revealing in all its inherent beauty the naked truth which it enfolds. The veil is woven of the stuff of dream and illusion and vision, but its insubstantial fabric is immortal, preserving as perpetual inspiration the beauty of life's inner vitality. So the veil, itself a creation of art, keeps free and effective the joyful inspirers of all the arts of civilized life, the Graces, who are the "daughters of Venus and the sisters of Love." Art cannot be disassociated from love, and love is a divine gift, a creative force. It is found in the sexual urge and the attraction to physical beauty, but it may surpass its beginnings, its goal being supranatural beauty and supranatural truth. This truth, like beauty, has its beginnings as physical truth, truth in nature. Through love this simple truth becomes "spiritualized," a process which is not outside nature but within nature, and supranatural truth, like supranatural beauty, is the fulfillment of natural truth, a fulfillment which transcends its origin.

> The Graces descend, clothed in their magic veil,
> upon poet, painter, and sculptor to inspire and
> illuminate them. But then,

The veil of the Goddesses suddenly sends forth a sound, like that of a distant harp, running softly on the wings of Zephyr; as an unknown harmony came among the islets from the Aegean, when the delirious Bacchantes tied to the severed head and fair hair of Orpheus the wonderful lyre, hurling it into the waves; and, sighing with nearby Ionia, the sacred Aegean sustained that harmony, and the islets, astonished, heard it, and the continents. . . .

This sound is produced by the veil itself, not by the Graces whom it enfolds. To Foscolo the veil possesses autonomous ''intermediate'' reality and vitality. Between the divine being of the Graces and the natural being of the artist floats the insubstantial but eternal harmony of art. The gods inspire man to make art, but its more-than-mortal beauty is man's creation. It is not accident that what Flora embroiders on the veil are scenes of ordinary human life, because art is natural reality made divine by human vision. The Bacchantes destroy Orpheus, but his song, sustained by the life of nature which he brought to intense fulfillment, lives on to touch with wonder the earth from which it emerged and which it now makes more beautiful, more delightful, more fit for creatures who may aspire to more than natural existence. (pp. 160-61)

> *Karl Kroeber, ''The Graces of Civility,'' in his* The Artifice of Reality: Poetic Style in Wordsworth, Foscolo, Keats, and Leopardi, *The University of Wisconsin Press, 1964, pp. 154-67.*

DOUGLAS RADCLIFF-UMSTEAD (essay date 1970)

[Radcliff-Umstead's book-length study, from which the following is drawn, provides a thorough introduction for the English-speaking reader to Foscolo's life and works. Radcliff-Umstead asserts in the preface that ''the major themes of all [Foscolo's] mature writings are contained in the youthful novel Last Letters of Jacopo Ortis''; *the following excerpt includes the critic's discussion of Foscolo's major themes as they are outlined in the novel and further developed in the odes and sonnets.]*

Despite its structural weaknesses, [*Last Letters of Jacopo Ortis*] does possess a degree of unity in the intense lyricism of Jacopo's letters, which move from prosaic narration to ecstatic meditation. Certain recurring themes fire the hero's imagination and momentarily distract him from sterile despair, such as: the glorification of Nature, adoration of feminine beauty and purity, the cult of tombs, the role of great poets, compassion for the misfortunes of mankind. Because the novel lacks a firmly constructed framework, these leitmotives often appear isolated and inoperative without a clear thematic orientation. One can, however, perceive an interior structure through the unifying vision of the protagonist. Thematic organization is not mathematically logical and mutually exclusive but is emotionally associative.

In the celebration of natural beauty the scattered elements in the novel acquire coherence. Nature provides more than a static and decorative background for the hero's reflections. Jacopo enjoys an intimate communion with physical Nature, which vibrates in sympathetic response to his sufferings. . . . Holding an essentially pagan outlook, the youth sees Nature as animated by a divine power. He envies the ancients who were able to live in harmony with natural deities. . . . Foscolo was striving toward a mythic explanation of Nature so that modern man, in spite of his psychological dualism and rejection of irrational

illusions, could recapture a oneness with the universe in moments of rapturous abandonment. (pp. 62-3)

Foscolo's treatment of the landscape often transcends the slavishly imitative picturesque tradition of the eighteenth century which viewed Nature as if it were a painting. . . . [He] desired to go beyond a literal transcription of the external world, for in *Last Letters* he depicted Jacopo's quest for a deeply satisfying spiritual experience in the adoration of Nature. During his solitary promenades and wanderings, Ortis is no tourist in search of the picturesque; instead, the sights along the way plunge his soul in reverie. (p. 64)

Ironically, the author's attempt to surpass the narrow confines of the picturesque school enabled him to combine a highly descriptive style with a symbolist interpretation of external reality. His treatment of trees is especially illustrative. Pines and cypresses abound throughout the letters, symbolizing death and immortality. Foscolo carefully observes the differences in green foliage of various trees: the somber hue of the cypress, for instance, reinforces the funereal stillness of cemeteries. . . .

Perhaps Jacopo's second Florentine letter (September 7, 1798) best exemplifies the emotions associated with trees. It starts with a pantheistic exclamation of joy: ''Throw open the windows, Lorenzo, and greet the hills from my room. On a fine September morning greet the sky, the lakes, the plains in my name; for they all recall my childhood.'' After this exuberant outburst of nearly complete oneness with Nature, the protagonist indulges in self-pitying melancholy while he reminisces over the native region which appears forever lost to him. Three kinds of trees occupy a prominent position in his recollections: lindens with their comforting shade; the weeping willow (the most beloved tree of the romantics); and a pine beside the ruins of a chapel. The picturesque elements of these scenes from his native province are arranged so as to create an atmosphere of increasing gloom. Sentiment, as evoked by trees, predominates over the pictorial element.

Since the hero lives in an era of social instability, he seeks in natural phenomena the permanence which is missing in man's creations. Seasons with their unfailing rhythm of death and rebirth arouse his wonder. Everyday occurrences assume dramatic importance for the youth. Sunrise appears miraculous to him for daily leading the earth out of nocturnal mystery. (p. 65)

Although natural spectacles can present an impression of eternity, their phenomenal flux also attests to this world's transitoriness. . . . [A] terrifying feeling of isolation sometimes distinguishes his attitude to Nature, which is perpetually transforming itself. Just as the dawn brings with it the promise of new life, the sunset bears a menace of universal decline and disintegration. In the letter of May 25, 1798, Jacopo reveals his awareness of the engulfing void that nightfall creates: ''I look out from my balcony now that the immense light of the sun is dying away and shadows are depriving the world of the languid rays that flash on the horizon; and in the darkness of the melancholy and silent world I contemplate the image of Destruction that devours all things.'' A dreadful nocturnal darkness threatens terrestrial dissolution. Nature for the protagonist either offers solace or portends destruction. (p. 66)

Nature in this novel represents an analogue of man's feelings. It mirrors the human psyche in its most gentle or violent moods. Nowhere is fierceness better expressed than in the tormented letter from Ventimiglia, February 19 and 20, 1799, when Jacopo decides not to continue his flight from Italy. Looking for relief from his desperation, he wanders about the desolate winter landscape near the French border until he catches sight of a stream. . . . The scene opens with a mimetic reproduction of the hero's agonizing emotions, for the Roja swells into a savage torrent with a crescendo of physical unrest that reflects the distress in Jacopo's soul. By standing on the bridge he is at the brink of destruction; ironically, his decision to turn from the frontier and go back to the Euganean Hills will carry him over the brink of life through his suicide. There occurs a tremendous collision between the grandiose calm of all-powerful Nature and the gigantic force of the swollen torrent which splits the mountains in two. This contrast of forces parallels the conflict within Ortis, who tries to repress the impetus of his anarchical emotions in order to enjoy a cheerless peace. The setting thus serves a metaphorical function to portray the explosive outburst of pent-up energies within the novel's protagonist. (pp. 67-8)

Of all the characters in the novel only one shares Ortis' appreciation of Nature. At the sunrise scene on the autumn promenade, Teresa alone joins the hero in thrilling to the radiant spectacle, letting a fullness of sublime emotions flood her heart. Her fiancé Odoardo remains totally insensitive to the beauty of dawn. It is then that Jacopo recognizes a kindred soul in the ''divine'' girl. . . . Teresa appears as more than human, acquiring a resplendent aura in the midst of the enthralling sunrise. Only she and Ortis are capable of enjoying a rapport with cosmic creation. (p. 69)

Jacopo's adoration of the ''divine'' girl should be understood in Neoplatonic terms where love is considered the desire for beauty. For this youth, love exercises a power which animates the world; every exalted feeling has its source in all-pervading love. Beauty is an essentialistic force that benevolently soothes mankind's sorrows. The hero sings Beauty's praises in the letter of April 29, 1798: ''Oh, Beauty, loving goddess of Nature! Wherever you show your friendly smile, joy plays and pleasure comes forth to perpetuate the life of the universe. The person who fails to recognize you and has no feeling for you is a disgrace to the world and to himself.'' Without the presence of chaste virtue, bodily beauty loses its luster. Teresa's outward loveliness is the manifestation of an unblemished soul that unswervingly obeys a sense of feminine modesty. (p. 70)

The theme of love in *Last Letters* derives from an amatory tradition in Italian literature called the Sweet New Style, which envisioned the beloved lady as an angelic creature who has come down to earth from heaven to lead mankind to salvation. She is an instrument of divine grace, making possible man's ascent to paradise. This tradition goes back to the late thirteenth and early fourteenth centuries and embraced poets like Guido Guinizelli . . . , Dante, and Petrarch without ever constituting a true school. (p. 72)

Teresa resembles the angelic ladies sung by the poets of the Sweet New Style since her beauty is of a celestial nature that ennobles the human race. The letters that speak of Ortis' adoration constantly re-echo the language of medieval Italian poets. . . . At times, Jacopo wonders if he has fallen in love with a creature of his imagination, for Teresa appears as a completely idealized figure. The hero almost commits blasphemy by preferring Teresa's beauty to God; this is the identical problem which the poet Guinizelli faced in one of his songs. Fortunately, the lady's mission of Christian charity removes any moral or religious crisis. Her physical presence embellishes the earth. By loving her, Ortis can bridge the gap between the sensual and the spiritual.

Out of the exalted love theme springs the motif of compassion. Foscolo viewed the earth as a vale of tears, where mankind can never experience happiness. Only in feeling compassion for another's misfortunes is there hope for alleviating this painful terrestrial existence. The letter from Ventimiglia sets forth the hero's theory about the consoling benefits of compassion: ''Lorenzo, do you know where true virtue still lives? In a few of us weak and unfortunate creatures who after having experienced all mistakes and calamities in life know how to deplore and work against them. Compassion is the sole virtue! All the other virtues are selfish.'' (pp. 72-3)

In Foscolo's opinion, compassion is so powerful, that it spans the gulf between the living and the dead. Although the novelist rejected the conventional Christian belief in an afterlife, he felt that an individual would continue to live as long as there were survivors who grieved for him. Consequently, death loses its frightening attributes for the hero and acquires a sad sweetness because he hopes to live in the memory of his beloved Teresa and his intimate friends. . . . Despite an Alfierian vision of the world dominated by brute force, Foscolo discovered in the theme of compassionate reverence for the dead a profound spiritual value. Death for the novel's hero cannot separate men from each other's affections.

In return for the respect shown to the departed, the living are inspired by the tombs of great men to perform heroic exploits. Tombs possess a moral and patriotic function to remind the present generation of former grandeur. . . . Through the efforts of a few superior men Italy once was in the front rank of nations for its artistic and scientific achievements. The tombs of Santa Croce serve as a monument to a proud tradition which should encourage the Italians of the Napoleonic era to resist mediocrity and oppression so as to bring about a national resurrection.

Foscolo upholds the primacy of poets among the great men of Italy's past. *Last Letters* is a hymn to poetry, with verses from Dante, Petrarch, and Alfieri cited throughout the text. The novelist believed that poetry was essential to embellish and enlarge drab reality with the veil of illusions. His work also celebrates individual poets who refused to prostitute their art to tyrannical governments. In Dante, the author saw the champion for truth, even at the cost of banishment from his homeland. . . . Jacopo places the Florentine exile with other sublime primitive poets like Homer and Shakespeare, whose immense genius embraced the wisdom of an entire age. The hero has learned the same bitter lessons of life in exile which Dante portrayed in the pages of the *Divine Comedy*.

While Dante always appeared as an austere figure to Foscolo, he considered Petrarch a spiritual father and consoling friend. In his novel, Jacopo remarks to Teresa that no poet better understood and expressed the effects of love than Petrarch. Several scenes in the work bear reminiscences to Petrarch's life. . . . Foscolo employs the historical facts from the lives of poets like Petrarch and Tasso to weave romantic myths.

With Tasso, Italian poetry perished only to be reborn in the late eighteenth century with the poets who inspired Foscolo with a love for Italy and an ardent desire for its political reform. . . . Alfieri is glimpsed in the work as a shadowy figure, in retreat from the revolutionary times which his dramas and treatises had anticipated. The most important poet is of course Parini, whose disillusionment with Napoleonic Italy is depicted in the letter of December 4, 1798. Disheartened by the radicalism of the Jacobin party and despondent over the duplicity of the liberals, the elderly poet has lost all hope for the future.

He attempts to restrain Jacopo's excessive idealism by pointing out how impotent the youth is in a debased society. Parini's advice is to withdraw from the struggle and preserve self-respect. The attention which the novelist draws to poets like Bertola, Alfieri, and Parini demonstrates his eagerness to prove that Italian letters could regain greatness once talented authors no longer courted the favor of monarchs but instead worked for the spiritual renewal of their nation.

Like the pieces of a shattered looking glass, the major themes in **Last Letters of Jacopo Ortis** suggest the impression of a possible whole that Foscolo did not succeed in realizing as a masterwork. These motives mark a point of arrival for the writer, who for the first time defined the subject matter of his artistic inquiry. The novel does not stand isolated from the productions of his maturity but should be regarded as a prelude to the poems and critical studies, where the same themes reappear in a harmoniously developed formulation. (pp. 73-6)

As a poet Ugo Foscolo insisted on perfection. He often reworked his poems, never being fully satisfied with the polished version. As a consequence of his striving toward absolute mastery over the technique of expression, the total number of Foscolo's poetic compositions from 1798 to 1802 was limited to merely two odes and a dozen sonnets. Those years witnessed an intense self-examination whereby the poet realized that original inspiration depended on the support of patient labor and extended reflection. During this period of spiritual exploration and discovery the youthful author came to see that poetry was more than the versified expression of unleashed emotions. By also seeking to overcome slavish adherence to the rhetorical tradition of Italian poetry, Foscolo channeled his creative powers to produce in his poems a condensation of his own thoughts and sentiments rather than a compilation of his readings. Although his desire to match genuine inspiration with consummate craftsmanship resulted in a paucity of poetic works, the author succeeded in surmounting the fragmentation that marred **Last Letters of Jacopo Ortis,** so that his poems arrived at a synthesis of controlled expression.

Mythic transformation of everyday reality distinguishes the two odes, **To Luigia Pallavicini Who Fell from Her Horse** and **To a Lady-Friend on Her Recovery.** The inspiration for both of these poems is feminine beauty threatened by an accident or illness. Foscolo therein depicts his compassion for afflicted beauty and his hope for its eventual triumph over catastrophe. (p. 77)

[In **To Luigia Pallavicini Who Fell from Her Horse,** it] was the poet's desire to fashion an Aeolian ode that would re-create the splendor of Hellenic verse. He proudly admitted classical inspiration. Although his poem displays a Pindaric love for the dance and chorus, it possesses none of the extravagant flights of imagination that characterize Grecian odes. Its firm structure and deeply meditative nature, instead, bear the obvious imprint of Horatian influence. Except for the frenzied accident scene, the Italian lyric follows the deliberately quiet, reflective system established by the Roman poet with its gentle nuances. . . . Foscolo successfully assimilated the various ancient sources and models into a work that became his own and not merely the product of a highly cultured but uninspired versifier.

In this poem, the author for the first time united Alfieri's verbal fierceness with Parini's neoclassical elegance. The expressive rapidity of the strophes which deal with the accident clearly re-echoes the nervous energy of verses in the Alfierian drama *Orestes.* Structurally the poem is a compromise between the strophic patterns of Parinian odes like *The Danger* and *Education;* rather than following the Sapphic and Alcaic schemes of Horatian odes, it is divided into eighteen sestets of seven-syllable verses with a varying rhyme for the first four lines and a rhymed couplet to conclude each strophe. Sometimes the similarities between Foscolo's verses and those of the Milanese poet are so striking as to deny any originality to the Pallavicini ode. . . . [Parini], however, did not go beyond observation of reality as captured in miniature. Although his verses possess a great variety with a Rococo love of ornamentation, Parini's supreme interest remained fixed on images abounding in picturesque and decorative details while Foscolo's imagination soars above daily reality to a transcendental mythic plane revealed in poetically vague ideas. In Parini's odes the reader is aware of gracious eighteenth-century compliments that are touched by a refined eroticism. With its nobler intonation, Foscolo's Genoese ode goes beyond gallant flattery and takes on the quality of a fervent pagan hymn to feminine beauty which does not reuqire Parinian sententious moralism and cultivated sensualism.

From the opening verse to the final strophe Luigia Pallavicini stands at the heart of the ode. The poet repeatedly employs the disjunctive pronoun *te* (you) in emphatic position to stress her importance. Nowhere does the poet individualize her features or explicitly refer to her disfigurement; rather commonplace adjectives conjure her feminine fragility. Like Dante's Beatrice, she is the ideal woman who symbolizes an eternal beauty. This injured noblewoman dwells in an indistinct sphere, a divine world of celestial beauty where the enchanting lady would be free of every impure contact. The gray mists and Northern melancholy of the Ossianic cycle, which frequently darkened the pages of **Last Letters,** vanish here in a limpid style that recaptures a luminous Hellenic serenity. Foscolo has surmounted fragmentation by constructing the ode around the unifying theme of adoration for beauty that is momentarily menaced but which is reborn in an aura of intensified ethereal glory. (pp. 81-2)

A detached lyrical serentiy characterizes the second of the odes that celebrate feminine beauty, for in **To a Lady-Friend on Her Recovery** there is the joyous certainty of the heroine's having regained her health and former loveliness. Rising to a religious contemplation, the poet isolates Antonietta Fagnani Arese in this ode from the rest of the universe; which cannot participate in the lady's superhuman existence. Her stellar solitude is made evident in the first two strophes, that open with a Vergilian-modeled simile (a rare device for Foscolo) which compares the lady's triumphantly rising from her sickbed to the splendid appearance of the star Venus at daybreak. In the same manner that the luminous morning star announces the dawn which dispels melancholy darkness, the renewal of Antonietta's good health after her winter-long illness restores to the world the vision of sovereign Beauty, the one true comfort for mankind's delirious raving. Here the poet formulates his own religion of Beauty that offers a refuge from human anguish. . . . In no respect [does this poem] fall to the level of frivolous compliments, for the poet seriously believes in the power of beauty to console mankind for life's insufficiencies. (pp. 82-3)

Whereas the poem to Luigia Pallavicini humanizes the gods of Olympus, the second ode develops a magical process that mythologizes terrestrial humanity. The central ninth sestet presents the author's appeal to the Graces to deny their kindly gaze to any person who might remind the heroine that her beauty is ephemeral since death forever threatens destruction.

With the hope of conquering the oblivion which death will bring, Foscolo moves brusquely in the tenth strophe to the second half of the ode; where he relates that Diana-Artemis, Bellona the Amazon, and Venus were originally mortal creatures until poets elevated them to the rank of deities. Herein is a major Foscolian theme: the role of art, particularly poetry, to surmount death. The author recognizes that it is his mission to insure Antonietta's immortality through the power of his verse. To other persons the Milanese noblewoman may appear as no more than a beautiful lady, the object of affection or envy; but for the poet she has become the priestess of Venus. . . . (p. 84)

Both of the neoclassical odes represent a yearning for eternity that is recaptured in a vision of serene Hellenic grace. It was in the smiling eyes of two beautiful women that Foscolo discovered an harmonious universe which recalled him to the splendor of ancient Greece. His second ode is able to pass from an allegorical representation of the impending Napoleonic war with England . . . to the spiritual reconstruction of an undying Hellas. This poem transcends a purely autobiographical expression of his love for Antonietta Fagnani Arese to arrive at a religious interpretation of the eternal feminine mystique. (p. 85)

While the two odes attain the atemporal harmony of Hellenic art, the poet's sonnets often reflect his tumultuous passions. A clear distinction must be made at once between the eight sonnets which appeared in the Pisan [journal] *Nuovo Giornale dei Letterati* in 1802 and the additional four that were published in the Milanese editions [of *Poesie*] of the following year. The first series represents a verse parallel to the tormented letters in *Jacopo Ortis*, expressing the author's anguish and disillusionment with the barbaric age in which he was forced to live; the final quartet of sonnets demonstrate Foscolo's mature comprehension of the adverse fate which befalls all mankind. In choosing the sonnet form the poet had two major traditions to inspire him: Petrarchan and Alfierian. . . . Although Petrarch's elegantly versified flight from a distressful present moment into a dreamlike vision of eternal love left a powerful impression on Foscolo, it was the strident verbal violence of Alfierian sonnets that excited his imagination with an implacable hatred for tyranny and a cult of the solitary genius. He saw that the sonnet with its strict simplicity could portray Petrarch's gentle melancholy or Alfieri's explosive wrath. His first eight sonnets mark an assimilation of these sources into an unique examination of the poet's own personality.

Each sonnet in the Pisan edition studies a particular mood of the author's. These sonnets resemble the pages of an intimate diary, where the writer feverously sketches his thoughts without arriving at the calmness of meditation. Although the poet later rearranged the sequence of the sonnets for the Milanese editions, by following their original order in the Pisan publication it is possible to trace Foscolo's spiritual crisis during the period 1798 to 1801—the years of active military service and his love for Isabella Roncioni. The opening two sonnets—"**I am not the man I used to be**" ("**Non son chi fui . . .**") and "**How are you?**" ("**Che stai?**")—respectively speak of the poet or to him. In the first poem Foscolo declares his discouragement over the psychological transformation which a soldierly career had effected in him. The initial octave laments how instead of dedicating himself to poetry and love he has turned his talents to massacring his fellow man. Regrettably, the images are academic and commonplace: the myrtle symbolizes love; the laurel, poetry; and Mars, war. This impersonal language shows no depth of feeling. (pp. 85-6)

Despite the interesting revelation of the poet's vacillating soul, [the first sonnet] fails to rise above mannerism. Its title is merely a translation of a line from an elegy by Maximian, and a banal phraseology characterizes the entire poem which never adequately renders the author's sense of horror and nausea under actual combat conditions. Along with its documentary value as a picture of the cleavage within Foscolo's heart, torn between an Alfierian conviction of his superiority and a fear of being compromised by his participation in the bloody wars of the period, the sonnet illustrates the pessimism of the youthful Italian generation in the early nineteenth century. (pp. 86-7)

[The second sonnet, "**How are you?**",] answers the sorrow of the first with a virile resolution. It is constructed on a series of contrasting parallel motives, with a heartrending repetition of the initial question to introduce the second tercet. Although melodramatic emphasis mars the effectiveness of the poem, it exemplifies Foscolo's attempt to overcome the suicidal inertia of a Jacopo Ortis. (p. 87)

In the Pisan edition sonnets IV through VII analyze Foscolo's adoration of the Roncioni girl. Generally the fourth sonnet bears the title "**To Florence,**" although it properly pays praise to the bank of the Arno River where Isabella used to take walks. Its first two lines "And you will have perennial life in poems, / shore, that the Arno greets in its journey," suggests in typical Foscolian fashion an abrupt interruption of a previously commenced discourse. The sonnet is carefully structured upon an antithesis between the octave, which treats of Florence's distant past; and the sestet, that sings a pagan hymn of joy in honor of feminine beauty. (p. 88)

Critics have often compared the picture of Isabella in the tercets to the "angelic lady" of the thirteenth- and fourteenth-century Sweet New Style. But instead of the hushed religious humility of the medieval poets before the vision of their lady, Foscolo evokes a voluptuous, ecstatic rapture when he looks into the divine eyes of his beloved or enjoys the fragrance of her golden tresses moving in the enamored breeze. The language of the final tercet strikingly resembles that of the two odes, with a similar sord *ambrosia* ("perfume") to designate an attribute of the terrestrial goddess. Isabella has undergone almost the identical process of deification as Luigia Pallavicini and Antonietta Arese. (pp. 88-9)

Foscolo's singular love sickness finds no relief in the sixth sonnet, "**Thus for entire days**" ("**Così gl'interi giorni . . .**"), which was recast from an earlier adolescent composition. . . . The reworked version sensitively blends Petrarchan reminiscences with an Alfierian pose of disdainful solitude. Here the central figure is the poet himself, described as passing his days in a state of ennui while during the nights he wanders the cold starless and moonless countryside hoping to find in the bleak landscape the image of his own disconsolate soul. A dark preromantic musicality suffuses the entire first quatrain, with the repetition of the vowel *u* (which Foscolo considered to possess a gloomy sound) in words like *bruna / Notte* (dark / Night), *la luna* (the moon), and *mute ombre* (mute shadows). The rhythm is slowed down by the use of two syllable substantives with the stress on the first syllable to reproduce mimetically the atmosphere of nocturnal stillness. There results a perfect correspondence between somber Nature and the hero's dismal spirit. (p. 90)

Remorse for leaving behind his beloved to follow the Napoleonic campaigns distinguishes the sonnet "**To his distant lady**" ("**Alla sua donna lontana**"). . . . The poem begins with an echo of elegies by Propertius and Ariosto: "Rightly, since I could / abandon you . . ."; the caesura in the first verse aids in suggesting the discontent of a lover who recognizes his grave error of preferring adventure over the joys of continual close contact with his lady. Now, as he stands on the shores of the Tyrrhenian Sea with the Maritime Alps in the background, the poet shouts out his plaints of regret. Nature, however, does not respond sympathetically to Foscolo's lament. Instead of the common romantic identification between the artist's tempestuous state of mind and stormy nature, this sonnet in the first quatrain displays a strikingly original discord between natural phenomena and the poet's sorrow. His anguished cries are lost as the waves strepitously lash the coast, and the marine winds scatter his words. The exterior storm drowns out the conflict within Foscolo's heart, as if to punish him for deserting his lady. Despite the similarity of their moods, Nature and the poet are in violent collision with each other. This picture of Nature insensitive and indifferent to the author's agony prefigures the principal situation in several of Leopardi's poems. For musical dissonance, the consonant *r* predominates to imitate the severity of the natural scene. (pp. 90-1)

Throughout the composition three elements [are] at work: amorous passion, which prevails; Nature, which remains deaf to the poet's suffering; and the artist's will power, which attempts in vain to repress the impetus of his emotions. With the final two verses the sonnet comes to a pessimistic conclusion. Immortal, omnipotent Love will relentlessly pursue Foscolo beyond the confines of life. After the originality of the earlier sections of the poem, the close sounds like a trite Petrarchesque echo. Like the other love lyrics, excepting the first, the sonnet displays a curious discrepancy between expression of an intensely romantic personality and an effete recourse to a conventional phraseology.

Last of the sonnets in the Pisan edition is the poet's "**Self-portrait**," which became the most worked-over of all of Foscolo's shorter lyrics. In 1803, 1808, and even during his exile in England, the author refashioned the verses, apparently never to his complete satisfaction. During the late eighteenth century and in the early years of the nineteenth there was a vogue of poetic self-portraiture. Alfieri had preceded Foscolo in this autobiographical genre, and Manzoni imitated their example. . . . Despite the pedestrian tendency to fall into prosaic enumerations of physical traits, these self-portraits in verse reflect a profound concern for understanding man in his often contradictory being. With the list of outward features the artist is forever painting an interior portrait of himself. The first verse in Foscolo's sonnet demonstrates a desire to study the torment in his soul as it is manifested in his face: "I have a furrowed brow; sunken, intent eyes." Constant reflection has wrinkled his brow, and deep-set eyes permit an observer to glimpse the passion within his mind. This line is reminiscent of a verse in the second sonnet, "**How are you?**" for both poems illustrate the writer's tendency to arrange concise details in symmetrical units. . . . Determined to explore his psyche thoroughly, he confesses to his many inconsistent traits: he is both prodigal and temperate, considerate and rude. (pp. 91-2)

The sestet perfects the moral portrait which was implicit in the physical description of the preceding verses. Here the poet is shown as melancholy and reserved, not easily deceived and unwilling to surrender to fear. . . . The poet agreed with Alfieri's belief that only in the act of dying was the truth about a man's life brought to light. In addition, he saw in death the just measure of the value that an individual's life has possessed.

Future generations may remember a man for his lofty deeds or noble writings. The final verse of the 1808 recasting of this sonnet starts with the poignant word "perhaps" (Italian *forse*) that lays bare the author's doubts about posterity's evaluation of his agonized existence.

As the emblem of the Pisan edition, Foscolo prefaced his works with the Horatian phrase, *sollicitae oblivia vitae* (forgetfulness of troubled life). That state of gentle oblivion remained an aspiration and not a fulfillment for the poet. Only in rare moments of rapturous enchantment with feminine beauty does the writer flee the tormented present. He never reaches a level of superior reflection that would free him from immediate personal grief and lead him to a comprehension of man's tragic destiny. But with the four sonnets of the Milanese editions, Foscolo transcends the solitary Alfierian struggle with a contrary world so that he can gaze serenely upon an eternal human drama. The Storm and Stress phase of his creative career is behind him now. No longer does the poet feel the necessity of maintaining a theatrical pose. Melodramatic emphasis yields to a sincerity and spontaneity of expression that constitute the essence of a true classicism. The poet now experiences a spiritual liberation whereby he is elevated from commonplace reality.

A mechanistic conception of the world and a romantic longing for the sleep of death are harmoniously fused in the sonnet "**To Evening**" ("**Alla Sera**"). This poem is the first in the Milanese editions, like a prelude to the dramatic alternation of despair and illusion in the other sonnets. It recalls the letters in Foscolo's novel that recapture the melancholy onset of nighttime. Here, however, the dread of engulfing darkness disappears as the poet momentarily finds peace with Nature. . . . Whether in the cheerful summertime or in dreary winter months, Foscolo affectionately greets evening's descent. Nature's attributes are personified by the cortege that clouds and breezes offer evening; this image is original to Foscolo, whose metaphors often express a striving toward a cosmic vision. Syntactically, the use of the coordinate conjunction "and" (Italian *e*) five times in six verses produces a fullness of melodic movement that expands the imagery in its representation of a natural phenomenon which renews itself every day at dusk. Syntactical arrangement of adjectives and the musicality of the Italian original result in giving the octave a powerful density. The poet, for instance, contrasts two opposing emotions by the rhyme *quiete* (rest, peace, tranquility) in the first verse with *inquiete* (restless, stormy as applied to wintry shadows) in the fifth line. Picturesque elements are intentionally lacking, as shown by the absence of adjectives of color inasmuch as this is not a poem of purely esthetic contemplation. An almost religious solemnity characterizes Foscolo's sympathetic response to the twilight hour. (pp. 92-4)

At the sonnet's close Foscolo has attained clarity of vision. This sense of placation cannot endure, for the poet does not become one with the whole of Nature. Meditation briefly lifts his soul out of the agitated world, but Foscolo never arrives at Leopardi's submergence of the ego in the infinite. Evening bears only the vague likeness of death's eternal rest. As long as life persists on according to inexorable Newtonian laws, the war within the poet's heart will continue to rage.

Tender nostalgia for his homeland is the opening theme of the sonnet "**To Zante**" ("**A Zacinto**"). Forced into banishment, the author views his faraway native island as hallowed territory. . . . Childhood memories, mythological reminiscences, and Homeric legends blend in an ever expanding movement across the octave and the first tercet, which form a single sentence. The poem begins with a soothing recollection of the author lying in his infant cradle, and it ends with a prophecy of his death in exile. Besides the natural devotion which the poet owes his native land, Zante is rendered holy for him by its ancient cult of immortal goddesses like Diana and Venus. Through the constant presence of protective deities the island has undergone a mythological transfiguration, so that it becomes the center of a luminous realm which life-giving Venus has endowed with a serene sky and verdant slopes.

Zante belongs to the same fabled Hellenic world which Foscolo celebrated in his second ode. The bard of that eternal Hellas was of course Homer, whose verses did not pass over in silence the island's beauties while they narrated the tale of Ulysses' wanderings across the Mediterranean. Foscolo felt a spiritual kinship with the Homeric hero since both of them had been condemned to travel incessantly in foreign lands. But in the final tercet the Italian poet establishes a painful antithesis between his destiny and that of Ulysses. Eventually, the Homeric hero was able to return home to the barren rocky shores of Ithaca, and his sufferings were immortalized in the *Odyssey.* By contrast, no honors will crown Foscolo's perpetual exile, and the foreigners in whose land he expects to die will not mourn his passing. Like Homer before him, he can offer only his poetry as tribute to his mother country. Never once, however, does Foscolo rebel against the tyranny of Fate. For, as a mature artist, he has resigned himself to an adverse destiny. (pp. 95-6)

It was the presence of death in Foscolo's own family that occasioned the poem to his brother, Gian Dionisio. Yet no maudlin sentimentality mars the elegiac harmony of the composition. . . . Structurally, the sonnet consists of four basic motives in a symmetrical arrangement: the imaginery picture of the poet before Gian Dionisio's gravestone; the representation of their lonely mother; Foscolo's confession of the difficulty in withstanding life's onslaughts; a final entreaty to the foreigners who will witness his death. The poem's central figure is not the brother who committed suicide but the mother who gave birth to the family and lived to bewail her children's troubled existence. Her presence lends unity to the sonnet's various motives. (p. 96)

Of all his sonnets the poet considered the one to his brother to be the best and included it in a later essay on the history of the Italian sonnet. With an intentional economy of expressive devices Foscolo depicted a domestic tragedy which he viewed as the consequence of an overruling universal fatality. Each section of the poem is densely constructed so that the sonnet does not display the expansive sweep of "To Zante." Three gerunds (*fuggendo, gemendo, traendo*) occur strategically in the rhyme scheme to reproduce the prolonged agony of flight, mourning, and old age. Single verses are architectonically designed so that the position of words heightens their significance, as in the sixth line with the contrast between the initial verb *parla* (she speaks) and the final adjective *muto* (mute). . . . Exile prevented Foscolo from carrying out the duties of fraternal affection. The political vicissitudes of the Napoleonic era cut the modern poet off from his family and made him an involuntary refugee from his country. Thus the grief of a bereaved brother is intensified by the bitterness of an exiled patriot who cannot embrace his loved ones. (pp. 96-7)

Doubts about his ability to continue the struggle of poetic creation characterize the final sonnet, **"To the Muse"** (**"Alla Musa"**). After the efforts necessary to achieve the technical perfection of the other three poems in the Milanese edition Foscolo felt spiritually desolate. It was as if his lyrical vein had dried up. The fourth sonnet starts off abruptly like the continuation of a dialogue between the author and the Aonian goddess (the Muse) who had earlier befriended him with the divine gift of poetic creativity. Throughout the first quatrain the verbs are in the imperfect tense, the period of Foscolo's productive past. A barren sense of sorrow marks a switch to the bewildered present tense in the second quatrain, where the author invokes the Muse's favor without receiving any response. . . . All of the poet's confusion at being abandoned by the Muse becomes evident in the first tercet with the verb *fuggisti* (you fled) in the merciless past-definite tense. Foscolo's sole souvenir of the goddess is sad recollection of the past and blind fear for the future. (pp. 97-8)

This creative aridity was not destined to endure. A productive resurrection would soon follow the passing phase of apparent sterility. Foscolo had merely exhausted the resources of the rigid sonnet form. The eleven-line opening sentence of the poem "To Zante" clearly illustrates an experiment at surpassing the traditional strophic patterns of the sonnet. In the final lines of "To the Muse," Foscolo explains his dissatisfaction with the limited possibilities of the sonnet structure:

> Therefore I realize, and Love repeats it for me,
>   that sparse labored rhymes can hardly give vent
>   to the pain which is to dwell within me.

By writing poems the author had sought to control and placate his passionate soul. His earlier sonnets had afforded him the opportunity to concentrate on the analysis of a particular emotional state. But the tendency of the sonnets in the Milanese edition, as also in the ode to Antonietta Arese, was toward a vast panoramic vision beyond all temporal barriers. Neither the fourteen verses of the sonnet structure nor the intricate schemes of the ode could adequately express Foscolo's mature longing to fashion a poem that would include lyric, epic, and didactic elements in a superior harmony. Blank verse, with the definitive abandonment of rhyme, eventually provided a solution. Thus, the poem "To the Muse" represents a moment of weariness which preceded the subsequent outburst of creative energy a few years later in the writing of the hymn, *Of Tombs.* (p. 98)

> *Douglas Radcliff-Umstead, in his* Ugo Foscolo, *Twayne Publishers, Inc., 1970, 147 p.*

ADDITIONAL BIBLIOGRAPHY

Cambon, Glauco. *Ugo Foscolo: Poet of Exile.* Princeton: Princeton University Press, 1980, 356 p.

   Examines the theme of exile in Foscolo's works. Cambon provides, in the introduction, a brief historical survey of earlier treatments of this theme, citing the Bible and the works of Ovid, Dante, Ezra Pound, T. S. Eliot, and James Joyce. A summary of the events that led to Foscolo's exile is also given. In succeeding chapters, Cambon discusses Foscolo's portrayal of exile in *Letters of Ortis,* the odes and sonnets, *The Sepulchres, Le grazie,* and the literary essays.

Canadian Journal of Italian Studies, Special Issue: On the 200th Anniversary of the Birth of Ugo Foscolo (1778-1978) I, No. 4 (Summer 1978): 249-328.

   A special issue devoted to Foscolo. All the articles are in Italian.

Forum Italicum, Special Issue: A Homage to Ugo Foscolo in the Bicentennial of His Birth 12, No. 4 (Winter 1978): 457-640.

A special issue devoted to Foscolo that contains two essays in English.

Franzero, Carlo Maria. *A Life in Exile: Ugo Foscolo in London, 1816-1827.* London: W. H. Allen, 1977, 127 p.

A biographical account of Foscolo's years in exile, from his departure for Switzerland until his death in England.

May, Frederick. "The Hughes-Foscolo Translation from Petrarch: Parts I, II, III, and IV." *Amor di libro: Rassegna di bibliografia e di erudizione* X, No. IV (October-December 1962): 195-202; XI, Nos. I, II, III (January-March 1963; April-June 1963; July-September 1963): 25-30, 97-101, 139-43.*

A close textual study of Foscolo's translation of one of Petrarch's poems. May contends that Foscolo collaborated with T. S. Hughes on this translation, and he supports his view with excerpts from their correspondence.

McCormick, C. A. "Ugo Foscolo: A Critical Theory of Translation." *AUMLA: Journal of Australasian Universities Language and Literature Association,* No. 5 (October 1956): 9-17.

Discusses the *Esperimento di traduzione della "Iliade" di Omero,* Foscolo's translation of Homer's *Iliad,* and his preface to that work, "Intendimento del traduttore," to elucidate the poet's theory of translation and criticism. McCormick finds that Foscolo advocated a historical approach: he sought to establish a link "between the individual poetic personality and the age in which it was formed."

————. "Ugo Foscolo and *Iacopo Ortis*; Creator and Character." *AUMLA: Journal of Australasian Universities Language and Literature Association,* No. 9 (November 1958): 22-35.

Analyzes successive versions of Foscolo's novel *Letters of Ortis* to determine the extent to which the character Jacopo Ortis accurately reflects its author.

————. "Foscolo's Two Theories of Translation and the Version of the *Sentimental Journey.*" *AUMLA: Journal of the Australasian Universities Language and Literature Association,* No. 18 (November 1962): 198-209.

Examines Foscolo's *Viaggo sentimentale di Yorick lungo la Francia e l'Italia,* a translation of Laurence Sterne's *A Sentimental Journey,* and cites its superiority over his *Esperimento di traduzione della "Iliade" di Omero,* a rendition of Homer's *Iliad.* In an earlier essay, McCormick explicated Foscolo's theories on translation and his approach to Homer (see annotation above, 1956).

O'Neill, Tom. *Of Virgin Muses and of Love: A Study of Foscolo's "Dei Sepolcri."* Publications of the Foundation for Italian Studies, University College Dublin, edited by David Nolan, no. 2. Dublin: Irish Academic Press, 1982, 219 p.

A line-by-line explication of *The Sepulchres* that includes detailed commentary on its genesis, composition, and critical reception.

Radcliff-Umstead, Douglas. "Foscolo and the Early Italian Romantics." *Italica: The Quarterly Bulletin of the American Association of Teachers of Italian* XLII, No. III (September 1965): 231-46.

Determines Foscolo's relation to the Italian Romantic school through an analysis of his critical writings.

Rudman, Harry W. "The First Generation of Italian Exiles in Great Britain: Foscolo, Rossetti, Panizzi." In his *Italian Nationalism and English Letters: Figures of the Risorgimento and Victorian Men of Letters,* pp. 179-208. Columbia University Studies in English and Comparative Literature, no. 146. New York: Columbia University Press; London: George Allen & Unwin, 1940.*

Discusses the positions of three Italian exiles in England. Rudman outlines the social and critical reaction to Foscolo and his works and describes those of his mannerisms that alienated London society.

Vincent, E. R. *The Commemoration of the Dead: A Study of the Romantic Element in the "Sepolcri" of Ugo Foscolo.* Cambridge: Cambridge at the University Press, 1936, 61 p.

An introduction to *The Sepulchres* that focuses on its romantic and classical elements and notes contemporary and ancient influences on the poem.

————. *Byron, Hobhouse and Foscolo: New Documents in the History of a Collaboration.* Cambridge: Cambridge at the University Press, 1949, 135 p.*

Draws upon previously unpublished letters and journal entries to document the collaboration between Foscolo and John Cam Hobhouse. Hobhouse had published a companion to the fourth canto of Lord Byron's *Childe Harold* that included an "Essay on the Present Literature of Italy." Vincent proves, to the satisfaction of modern critics, that Foscolo was the author of that essay (see excerpt above, 1818).

————. *Ugo Foscolo: An Italian in Regency England.* Cambridge: Cambridge at the University Press, 1953, 255 p.

A detailed account of Foscolo's life in London from 1816 to 1827. Vincent describes his work as a portrait of "the drama of the artist in society, the inner tragedy of a man who has seen a vision of reality and finds it impossible to reconcile it with his daily actions."

Wicks, Margaret C. W. "Ugo Foscolo, First Years in London, 1816-21" and "Ugo Foscolo (continued), Digamma Cottage and After, 1821-7." In her *The Italian Exiles in London: 1816-1848,* pp. 1-40, pp. 41-66. 1937. Reprint. Freeport, N.Y.: Books for Libraries Press, 1968.

A detailed biographical study of Foscolo's years in exile.

Aleksander Fredro

1793-1876

Polish dramatist, novelist, translator, and aphorist.

The most prominent Polish dramatist of the nineteenth century, Fredro is remembered today for his comedies which critics praise for their varied language, complex yet skillfully executed plots, and highly individualized characters. Although he composed his works during the height of the Romantic movement in Eastern Europe, Fredro refused to adopt Romantic literary tenets. Instead, he wrote classically inspired farces and comedies of manners for which he is often likened to the renowned seventeenth-century French dramatist Molière. His comedies *Maz i zona (Husband and Wife), Pan Jowialski,* known in English as *Mr. Joviality, Sluby panieńskie; czyli, Magnetyzm serca (Maidens' Vows; or, The Magnetism of the Heart),* and *Zemsta (Vengeance)* are considered his most enduring dramas.

Many of Fredro's works evoke his life in Austrian Galicia (now the Ukraine), where he was born to a family of Polish aristocrats. He was educated at his home in Suchorów and as a child demonstrated a natural gift for verse. In 1809, Fredro joined Napoleon Bonaparte's Grand Army. During a sojourn to Paris the young soldier became acquainted with the French Classical theater and wrote poetry that was published in *Pamiętnik Lwowski,* a Polish journal. When Fredro left the army in 1814, he settled with his family on their Galician estate and began reading the dramas of Molière and Carlo Goldoni and writing comedies in verse. After several unsuccessful stagings of his first work, *Intryga na prędce; czyli, Niema złego bez dobrego (An Improvised Intrigue),* another play, *Pan Geldhab,* was performed in Warsaw in 1821. The latter's populatiry assured public interest in his subsequent farces and comedies.

During a period of great productivity which lasted from 1821 to 1840, Fredro wrote what many commentators consider his best works, including *Vengeance, Maidens' Vows, Pan Jowialski,* and *Husband and Wife.* Although their witty dialogue, lively humor, and vivid characterizations have become hallmarks of Fredro's style, critics note that particular qualities of each demonstrate Fredro's dramatic skill. They cite the two squires, Raptusiewicz and Milczek of *Vengeance,* as examples of Fredro's ability to create comic characters who are both universal and individual. Scholars also praise his evocation of eighteenth-century Poland, asserting that he created a plausible atmosphere through the use of *ottava rima,* into which he incorporated old and modern Polish idioms. In addition, they mention his mastery of humorous dialogue in *Husband and Wife* and unromantic conception of love in *Maidens' Vows.* His writings were Classical in form, for unlike Romantic dramatists, who often dispensed with established structural principles, Fredro based his comedies on the unities of action, time, and place.

In 1835, the Romantic Polish poet Seweryn Goszczyński wrote a lengthy article that condemned Fredro's comedies as poor imitations of French and German models. He contended that they lacked national spirit, and he attributed Fredro's popularity to his comedies' superficial polish and wit. Because Fredro lived in an age when Polish authors were commonly political activists, several commentators have suggested that although

Goszczyński harshly criticized Fredro's writings, his attack was actually directed at the dramatist's alleged political conservatism. Although he continued to write, Fredro became increasingly reluctant to present his works to the public.

From 1840 until his death, Fredro managed his estate, involved himself in politics, and unbeknown to his contemporaries, wrote twenty comedies, among them *Pan Benet* and *Rewolwer.* These works of Fredro's "silent period" were posthumously published under the direction of his son, Jan Aleksander Fredro. Although considered less refined than his first comedies, Fredro's later works demonstrate the attributes associated with his successful comedies. Commentators note several differences, however, which include the use of prose instead of verse, greater attention to psychological realism, and a diminished interest in theatrical effect. While these works are occasionally performed in Poland, none are staged regularly.

Trzy po trzy, a collection of Fredro's memoirs, was written during the 1840s and published in 1877, despite his request that it not be made public. Modeled after Laurence Sterne's discursive novel *Tristram Shandy, Trzy po trzy* contains descriptions of episodes from Fredro's youth. Because the author deals primarily with his military career, the work's historical context is important. Poland was an independent nation prior to the eighteenth century, when its political and economic instability contributed to its eventual domination by Prussia, Russia, and Austria. Yet the Polish people never lost their desire for self-determination. When Napoleon began his military campaigns in Eastern Europe he was hailed by Poland's Romantic writers, including Adam Mickiewicz, who believed that Napoleon would liberate Poland. Fredro's satirical portrait of Napoleon in this work is seen by recent scholars as his attempt to debunk the messianic legend created by Romantic writers. Despite the topical content of Fredro's memoirs, they have garnered more praise from modern readers than from his contemporaries who criticized his disjointed narrative style. Modern scholars commend Fredro's narrative technique, power of observation, and subtle humor in *Trzy po trzy*. However, it is Fredro's large body of masterful comic works that have secured his reputation as the foremost Polish dramatist of the nineteenth century.

PRINCIPAL WORKS

Intryga na prędce; czyli, Niema złego bez dobrego (drama) 1817
Pan Geldhab (drama) 1821
Clavigo [translator, from *Clavigo* by Johann Wolfgang von Goethe; first publication] (drama) 1822
Mąż i żona (drama) 1822
    [*Husband and Wife* published in *The Major Comedies of Alexander Fredro*, 1969]
Damy i huzary (drama) 1825
    [*Ladies and Hussars*, 1925]
Pan Jowialski (drama) 1832
Śluby panieńskie; czyli, Magnetyzm serca (drama) 1833
    [*Maidens' Vows; or, The Magnetism of the Heart*, 1940]
Zemsta (drama) 1834
    [*Revenge*, 1946; also published as *Vengeance*, 1957]
Dożywocie (drama) 1835
    [*The Life Annuity* published in *The Major Comedies of Alexander Fredro*, 1969]
Nieszczęścicia najszczęśliwego męża (novel) 1841
Rewolwer (drama) 1877
Trzy po trzy (memoir) 1877
**Pan Benet* (drama) 1878
Pisma wszystkie. 10 vols. (dramas) 1955-58
The Major Comedies of Alexander Fredro (dramas) 1969
Komedie, wybor (dramas) 1972
Zapiski starucha (aphorisms) date unknown

*This work was written in 1861.

**This work was written in 1859.

Selections of Fredro's poetry in English translation have appeared in the following publications: *The Polish Land, A Golden Treasury of Polish Lyrics*, and *The Scarlet Muse: An Anthology of Polish Poems*.

[ALEXANDER (LESZEK) DUNIN-BORKOWSKI?] (essay date 1842)·

[Dunin-Borkowski was a Polish writer and revolutionary who, because he opposed Fredro's political conservatism, harshly criticized his comedies. This excerpt is drawn from a largely untranslated article "Uwagi ogolne nad literaturą w Galiciji" that was first published anonymously in 1842 in the Polish journal Tygodnik Literacki. *The essay has been attributed by modern critics to Dunin-Borkowski.*]

Educated superficially, since any other way was not possible in the country, disposed to glittering in salons rather than to the laborious pursuit of study, given over to military service under Napoleon and later to amusements and love affairs with the other youth of his class, amidst an idle life and landowners' pursuits, with a taste spoiled by French models, having experienced no misfortune or pain, which particularly excite the poetic mind, Alexander Fredro could not become an author except accidentally. For the companions of his youth, for the participants in his expeditions, his licentious and low pranks, he first composed an obscene drama . . . full of coarse humor and unbridled gaiety. Soon the work circulated widely in numerous transcriptions, seized with eagerness by the young people who learned the bawdiest places by heart and repeated them with great pleasure, and called the author's attention to his previously hidden talent that could have been used for something better.

His first thought then was to write comedies. But since such things cannot be shaken out of a sleeve because apart from talent some preparatory disposition was necessary, he threw himself into the reading of as many French and German comedies and happy tales of all kinds as possible. The traces of such study we can discern in all his works, for obviously swallowing too many models at one time he could not digest them and just threw them up whole. (pp. 32-3)

> *[Alexander (Leszek) Dunin-Borkowski?], in an extract from* The Major Comedies of Alexander Fredro *by Alexander Fredro, edited and translated by Harold B. Segel, Princeton University Press, 1969, pp. 32-3.*

ALEXANDER FREDRO (poem date 1872?)

[In the following fragment, Fredro reacts to the Polish poet Seweryn Goszczyński's unfavorable appraisal of his comedies. Although the poem was first published in 1877 in Fredro's memoirs Trzy po trzy, *it was probably written in 1872.*]

Some Minos rose up and barked madly,
He'd have liked my five volumes in five hells.
I wrote badly. Agreed. But to write badly's no crime;
It used to happen before and it still happens now.
I was more surprised by the anger than the contents,
And when nobody undertook my defense,
I couldn't understand, I couldn't guess,
Whether it was by counsel or treachery,
And understood only that I had to be silent.

                              (p. 35)

> *Alexander Fredro, in his* The Major Comedies of Alexander Fredro, *edited and translated by Harold B. Segel, Princeton University Press, 1969, 405 p.*

ALEXANDER FREDRO (essay date 1876?)

[This excerpt forms part of Fredro's memoirs Trzy po trzy *which, despite his wish that it not be made public, was posthumously published in 1877. Here Fredro disputes the assumption that an anonymously published article—possibly that of Dunin-Borkowski (see excerpt above, 1842)—was wholly responsible for his decision to no longer offer his comedies for production.]*

How many times I dissected myself morally, compared myself with other men, tried to fathom why I was almost always badly understood by others. Each simplest, clearest word of mine in the most indifferent conversation took on a different meaning in another person's understanding than it actually had, a meaning always harsh, always disparaging. My letters, usually written carelessly, became for me the cause of more than one deep pain for they fell subject to analysis just like some highly enigmatic utterances; they were interpreted, but always for the bad, never for the good. But my great single weakness was and is that I think out loud, that I express my opinion openly but always more to subject it to discussion than to pass judgment with it. The world does not understand frankness except in the case of someone stupid; on the part of an intelligent person, however, it is always taken for a well-calculated ghost. It's possible to renounce gratitude; every intelligent person should even avoid it. But always, continually, the purest intentions, the most eager favors, the most innocent words one sees twisted, changed into poison, and not being in a position to discover the reason in oneself this must ultimately rouse faith in some sort of unbreakable fatalism. This can repel me from this world that does not want me. Few are the walls between me and people so that I could enjoy the tranquility which is my only aim, that happiness which God has granted me in my domestic life. I broke my author's pen not, as it is supposed, on account of the bad as well as stupid article published anonymously, because the author of that article sold himself to an alien hostility, and to a hostility that was the reward for friendship and even for an important favor. I gave up my career where my self-love could have succumbed to the desire to pursue popularity. I tried, in a word, to remain stupid before the world. I hid myself in the shadow of stupidity before the slash, and before the still more unbearable clatter of human gnats, drones and gadflies—but in this thick shadow, however, I cannot avoid contact with a world that always remains the touch of electric current—annoying and often even painful. To blame the whole world—madness; to blame myself—unfair. It's best, then, to keep silent and not to think, just to keep on traveling farther the rough road, an exiled pilgrim! (pp. 34-5)

Alexander Fredro, in his The Major Comedies of Alexander Fredro, *edited and translated by Harold B. Segel, Princeton University Press, 1969, 405 p.*

ROMAN DYBOSKI (lecture date 1924)

[*Dyboski focuses on the characters in Fredro's farces, comedies of manners, and comedies representative of Polish life. He contends that the last group contains Fredro's best works and asserts that they "constitute the most perfect humorous embodiment of Polish national character and national spirit."*]

Fredro is the Polish Molière . . . , not in his qualities alone, but also in his limitations. Vainly would we look among his works for the prose of witty drawing-room dialogues, for highly individualized characters or modern social problems: we move throughout to the orderly stroke of rhymed repartee, among general types of human nature, and the conventional situations of the older comedy. Fredro rarely departs from the classic models which still held their ground in the distant days when he began to write. He takes no part in the conflict between the Classical Conservatives and the Romantic Revolutionaries. He does not even study for himself the theory of his literary art; like Shakespeare, he follows the beaten track of the accepted dramatic form as he found it in his early days, and gives full expression to his genius within its limits. He never forsakes

it, even many years later, when it has been deserted by the younger generation of writers. Indeed, he remained always somewhat outside the inner circle of the literary profession; a country squire throughout his life, he was content to be avowedly a dilettante in letters, and never up to date in literary fashions.

What secret of vitality, then, do these old-fashioned comedies contain, that their popularity should never have flagged, and should now be so powerfully renewed? We can only reply that they constitute the most perfect humorous embodiment of Polish national character and national spirit. . . . What power of stage effect he possessed was his by instinct. Sensational allusions to current events and persons of note are foreign to his art, as they were, indeed, precluded by the severe Austrian censorship of the time. Nor did the author's strength reside in his plots, which, like Molière, he took at random from what he chanced to read, and dramatized in a slap-dash, haphazard way, without despising the most time-honoured and outworn devices. Similarly, his characters are often taken with equal light-heartedness and directness straight from his observation of the surrounding world, and infused by his genius with immortal life.

However easy-going Fredro may appear to us in his technical work as a dramatist, and however careless in the choice and handling of his materials, he undoubtedly took his comic art very seriously, and was as deeply and subtly sensitive as most of the great humorists have been in the recesses of their souls. Among Fredro's comedies there is a one-act play which bears direct witness to this aspect of his nature: it is called *The Man-Haters and the Poet* [*Odludki i poeta*], and exhibits the enthusiasm of youthful idealism pitted against the cynicism of worldly-wise disillusionment. It displays a warmth of sympathy for the poetical idealist which shows Fredro, for once, openly on the side of Romantic exaltation against the narrow wisdom of the Classicist. (pp. 68-70)

His manner as a writer did not much change after the great crisis [that followed Seweryn Goszczyński's condemnatory essay], except in these respects: he had recourse to prose more frequently than hitherto, having in the past used verse almost exclusively; contemporary political and social developments were more openly alluded to, now that Galicia enjoyed home rule, than had been possible under the reactionary Austrian censorship; finally Fredro, not unlike Shakespeare, became with growing age more and more careless of theatrical effect and of the structure of his plays, and increasingly absorbed in psychological analysis and moral reflection. (p. 72)

Much of [Fredro's dramatic output] has proved too futile in its matter and workmanship to last, but there remains a considerable series of outstanding works, unequalled in the Polish tongue; and characters and quotations from them are as familiar in Poland as figures and sayings from Dickens are in England.

Fredro's principal productions may be surveyed in three groups: farces, comedies of manner of the traditional sort, and comedies peculiarly representative of Polish life. Of these, the first are his slightest work, the second the most typical of his manner, the third his highest and most permanent achievements.

The farces, which without much care for plot or character-drawing are intended to be frankly amusing, show Fredro's full possession of that most indispensable quality of a writer of comedy—the *vis comica* or power to make us laugh. His improbabilities and exaggerations carry all irresistibly before them. . . . In an early one-act play, *Grumbling and Contradiction* [*Zrzędnosc i przecora*], Fredro succeeds in spinning a series of brilliant scenes out of a very simple situation between a girl and her two guardians, a pair of brothers, who are inveterate grumblers and always quarrelling. . . . This little masterpiece is a *tour de force* in the almost infinite variety which it extracts from a quite primitive comic theme, such as might well soon weary an audience, presented, as it is in exactly the same shape by two characters who are almost continually on the stage.

Fredro's full-dress comedies have, of course, many features in common with the type of comedy which has been established in Europe since Molière, although the Polish character betrays itself at every turn, especially in the impulsive temper of his personages.

One of the best of the comedies, which are more international in type and less distinctly Polish in their peculiarities, is *Husband and Wife* [*Mąż i żona*]. . . . The play consists of conversation between only four persons; that the author can carry his audience through three acts of this without a dull moment is a testimony to his skill. His delicacy of expression and charming lightness help the play over many an ambiguous and daring situation, and altogether the comedy, his one excursion into frivolity, shows his mastery of witty dialogue at its highest. His other comedies have other excellences, but none approaches this play in the perfection of conversation, wrought in a gossamer-like verse.

Another comedy of human, and not specifically Polish, interest [*Mr. Moneyful (Pan Geldhab)*,] is more solid in its texture. . . . [In Mr. Moneyful] the author has standardized for Polish literature the type of the *nouveau riche*. With the Europe of today as full of men of this class as it was a hundred years ago, when the play was first produced, Fredro's hero has taken a new lease of vigorous life. . . . (pp. 72-4)

Another venerable type, the miser, is presented by Fredro in a comedy which also belongs to his recognized masterpieces, *The Life Interest* [*Dożywocie*]. The usurer, Patch, who is its central figure, has become as classic a character on the Polish stage as Molière's *Avare* on the French.

To these two types from Fredro's comedies—the upstart and the usurer—we may add a third, who completes the group of his best individual characters. It is that of *Mr. Joviality* [*Pan Jowialski*], who gives its title to another popular comedy. . . . [This hero] is one of those indomitably talkative and genial old gentlemen who abounded in the easy-going, convivial Poland of former times, and are not uncommon . . . , in fact, in all times and climes. He is as ready with proverbs as Cervantes' Sancho Panza or Dickens's Sam Weller, and he is equally full of stories which he insists on perpetually repeating to unwilling hearers.

As the hero of [*Mr. Joviality*] is such an inexhaustible talker, it is only natural that it should have given currency to more sayings than almost any other work by Fredro. But one of his plays has surpassed it in that special form of success, *The Mania for Things Foreign* [*Cudzoziemszczyzna; czyli, Nauka zbawienia*]. It is the ridiculous character in this comedy of a fanatical admirer of all foreign things, and particularly of everything English, which has perhaps contributed most liberally to Poland's treasury of familiar quotations. . . . (pp. 74-5)

The Mania for Things Foreign follows the tradition of the best eighteenth-century Polish satire and comedy in ridiculing a weakness which the Poles share with some of their Slavonic brethren, and particularly with the Russians: the uncritical admiration and imitation of foreign fashions, views, and insti-

tutions. This comedy, accordingly, has brought us by its national subject-matter to the third and highest sphere of Fredro's art. It takes its place among those theatrical masterpieces which have a distinctly Polish colouring, and while following Fredro's general practice of introducing comic characters of a universal and traditional type, yet invest them with peculiarities of conduct, habit, and speech only to be met with on Polish soil. It is among these, the most distinctly national comedies of Fredro, the comedies of Polish manners, that we find his greatest contributions to the classics of Polish literature, his two supreme works, *The Revenge* [*Zemsta*] and *Girlish Vows* [*Śluby panieńskie*]. (pp. 75-6)

By its half-critical, half-admiring attitude towards the national tradition, this masterpiece of Polish comedy [*The Revenge*] reminds us of its predecessor *The Old Polish Way* ('Sarmatyzm'), by the greatest of Poland's comic writers in the eighteenth century, Francis Zabłocki.

Fredro's other recognized masterpiece, placed higher by some of his admirers than *The Revenge,* is *Girlish Vows, or The Magnetism of the Heart.* The theme of [Shakespeare's] *Love's Labour's Lost* is reversed here: the vows of two girls to remain inexorable are overcome by the device of one of the two lovers, light-hearted, but good-natured and thoroughly lovable. Of the two heroines, the one who shows the more initiative and resolution reminds us of Shakespeare's Beatrice by her roguish wit and ready repartee; and like Beatrice she succumbs at last. Simple and unsophisticated in its plot, the play is less distinctly national in colouring than *The Revenge,* but the essential traits of the characters are typically Polish—especially their impulsiveness and generosity of heart. The glowing lyrics of the lovers' speeches stand as high in the range of Fredro's work as the poetry of Shakespeare in *Twelfth Night,* that sunniest production of his comic Muse.

Among the later comedies, written by Fredro after a pause of thirteen years, and never printed in his lifetime, one in particular deserves to be singled out for its popularity. *A Great Man for Little Affairs* [*Wielki cztowiek do matych interesbw*] is again the caricature of a type not uncommon in all ages and societies: the busybody who thinks himself the centre and mainspring of the affairs of every one about him. . . . Fredro was here glancing, with the ripe judgement of old age, at the self-importance of Austro-Polish politicians in self-governing Galicia. Political satire on a larger scale, exposing all the typical faults of Polish public life, was attempted by the author in this later period in a work which is unique among his comedies, in that it takes the form of an allegorical dramatic fable and the characters are all animals, as in Edmond Rostand's once-famous *Chantecler*. *The Watch Dog* [*Brytan Bryś*] . . . is perhaps more wise and morally sound in its speeches than entertaining in its plot; the verse has all the quality of the poet's highest art, but the difficulty of producing such a play has made it much less known than his other works.

Of the remaining sixteen comedies of the later period many are, in their peculiar excellence, quite equal to some of the earlier plays. *Mr. Benet* [*Pan Benet*], a farce written in admirable, ringing verse, shows undiminished spirit. In another one-act farce, *The Two Scars* [*Dwie blizny*], the author, by a *tour de force* recalling his previous one-act masterpiece, *Grumbling and Contradiction*, makes capital comedy out of the world-old theme of mistaken identity due to close resemblance. A third one-act play, *The Candle's Out* [*Świeczka zgasta*], has had a marked and unvarying success on the stage, which is seldom attained by the later and generally less vivid work of even popular dramatists. The scene of a fourth one-act farce, *On the Cracow-Vienna Line,* more modern in character than the majority of Fredro's plays, is laid in a railway waiting-room; and the subject—the reconciliation of a divorced couple—shows both the conservatism of old age and the kindliness peculiar to the author at every stage of his long life.

Among the longer comedies of this period, *Worthy of Pity* [*Godzien litości*] portrays an egoist who deceives and exploits his fellow men by playing the part of a persecuted victim. The character, subtly drawn, is considerably more complex in its structure than the standard types of the older comedy, and it shows even the art of Fredro tending, in its later phase, towards the modern form of comedy, which deals in individual characters rather than general types.

Fredro did not attain in old age the rounded and complete perfection displayed by his greatest works. But the individual qualities of his genius shine in each with unabated brilliancy, and we can scarcely speak of a twilight of his talent. He may, no doubt, like all the older comic poets, seem wanting in subtlety to a public intellectually more refined. But the zest and flow of his scenes, their abundant merriment, the soundness of his judgement on the fundamental aspects of human nature, finally his sterling Polish diction and golden verse, will appeal to his countrymen as long as Plautus and Molière are accounted masters by the world at large. (pp. 76-8)

> *Roman Dyboski, ''Modern Polish Dramatic Literature,'' in his* Modern Polish Literature: A Course of Lectures, *Oxford University Press, London, 1924, pp. 67-106.**

JULIAN KRZYŻANOWSKI   (essay date 1931)

Following the example of his eighteenth-century predecessors, Fredro began his career by a number of comedies in which he dealt with ridiculous characters well known in the history of the Italian and French stage. So, in his earliest play, *Mr. Moneyful* [*Pan Geldhab*] . . . , he introduced a sort of Monsieur Jourdain [from Molière's *Le Bourgeois Gentilhomme*], a stupid and boasting *nouveau riche* whose only ambition is to be admitted into the upper classes, though neither his education nor his manners are sufficiently refined to conceal his earlier road of life. So, later, in the character of Mr. Patch, the usurer (in *The Life Interest* [*Dożywocie*]), he gave an interesting analogy to Molière's immortal Harpagon [the miser in *L'avare*]. In these two comedies as well as in many others Fredro showed both his skill in reproducing traditional features of the comedy, borrowed from earlier generations of playwrights, and his gift for noticing the peculiarities of life in his own period. For, despite the obvious likeness of his characters to those created by his predecessors, all of them were given a real life and were closely bound up with the atmosphere which had produced them. Accordingly Fredro's Mr. Moneyful, besides the features which he had in common with the French *bourgeois-gentilhomme,* was a typical exponent of the times when, after the Napoleonic wars, there appeared in the drawing-rooms of Warsaw a number of clever *parvenus* who, as army contractors, had won enough money to climb the ladder of social distinctions. In this way the Polish playwright reconciled, as every true artist does, the two principles, the traditional inherited from his forerunners and the careful observation of his own surroundings. (p. 231)

The summit of [Fredro's] activity was represented by his three greatest comedies, the *Revenge* [*Zemsta*], *Girlish Vows, or the Magnetism of the Heart* [*Śluby panieńskie*], and *Mr. Joviality* [*Pan Jowialski*], each of which deals with a different subject and has a different character.

The first of them, the *Revenge* . . . , has much in common with the works of Fredro's predecessors and contemporaries; for as in the eighteenth-century comedy of Zabłocki called *The Old Polish Way (Sarmatyzm),* or as in [Mickiewicz's] *Pan Tadeusz,* its plot was based on the peculiar mania for litigation so profoundly characteristic of the old Polish gentry. As in *Les Romanesques* of Rostand, its subject is an old feud between two neighbours diametrically opposed in their characters, who finally are compelled to agree with each other as their children are united by marriage. (pp. 232-33)

The structure of [*Revenge*] is very vivid and skilful. The plot develops by means of the management of events in the hands of Czesnik, then in those of Rejent. It does not depend on the activity of the pair of young lovers; their fortunate marriage is nothing but a consequence of the policy of their guardians, who unconsciously work for their own disappointment and, therefore, make the comedy the more amusing. Consequently, even from the point of view of the plot itself, *Revenge* may be called a comedy of characters.

And, as a matter of fact, it is an unrivalled painting of the two opposite characters. [The Polish critic] Count Tarnowski, in his old but brilliant [untranslated] study of Fredro's comedies, said that the Polish playwright reflected in his work the most striking and true features of the two outstanding types of the old Polish gentry. There is no doubt that the critic was right; for in Poland's history one could meet men like Czesnik, tempestuous and full of energy and obstinacy, as much inclined to perform wonderful deeds of heroism as to commit villainies and crimes, according to their passing and changing tempers. . . . And just this wonderful medley of different traits makes Czesnik a living and true character, a ridiculous and yet quite serious exponent of the peculiarities of the Polish national character.

His enemy, Rejent, is likewise a masterpiece of skilful characterization. . . . In his own way he is the best Polish ''Tartuffe'', and entirely equal to his French brother. There is no doubt that in the rich gallery of lawyers, caricatured in literature, Rejent Milczek is one of the most interesting and significant. (pp. 233-35)

One more of the characters in the *Revenge,* that of the ''Polish Falstaff'', must be mentioned here because of his enormous and well deserved popularity. His name is Papkin, and he unites within himself the features of the traditional type, that of the braggart soldier with some peculiarities of his own, especially with ''those of an apish imitator of foreign fashions''. He contributes greatly to the comic effect of the play, particularly in the scene when, against his will, he is compelled to help his rival, Waclaw, to approach Klara.

The Polish character of the *Revenge,* evident enough in its characters, is strengthened by the verse form employed in it. Fredro availed himself here of the short octosyllabic verse, which was the favourite metre of Polish mediaeval poetry, and had survived in the Christmas plays and therefore appealed to the reader's ear as something familiar and associated with the well-known characters appearing in these plays. All these elements combine to establish the play's popularity with the Polish stage, on which it never fails to meet with success.

The second of Fredro's great comedies, *Girlish Vows or the Magnetism of the Heart* . . . , is quite different from the *Revenge* both in its plot and subject. (pp. 235-36)

Against the background of [a] simple plot, Fredro created a beautiful song of love and happiness, quite uncommon in his period, which was devoted to fierce and exaggerated love. Whilst his Romantic contemporaries considered love a destructive and dangerous power crushing the human heart and existence, Fredro tried to show its constructive and creative and beneficent influence on man, and he thoroughly succeeded. Sharing the general opinions on love and its importance, according to the Platonic conception of two spirits originating in the same source and, therefore, destined to meet each other in human forms, he regarded it as a fountain-head of permanent happiness, so abundant as to pour out in streams from the hearts of fortunate lovers.

A skilful playwright, he demonstrated its influence on noble human natures, developing within them new and unknown forces. Consequently the comedy is of great psychological interest, which again and again appeals to the public's attention and sympathy.

While in the *Revenge* the lovers are overshadowed by the characters of the two neighbours, and their love is handled as a commonplace convention furnishing the necessary material for the structure of the play, in *Girlish Vows,* in accordance with its subject, the lovers take the first place. Particularly noteworthy are the two girls; the sweet and grave Aniela who is radiant with the charm of her simplicity and goodness; her companion, Clara, "reminds us", Professor Dyboski rightly observes [see excerpt above, 1924], "of Shakespeare's Beatrice by her roguish wit and ready repartee". . . .

[One] might easily discover another and more striking analogy between the *Vows* and Goldsmith's comedy *She Stoops to Conquer*. Probably owing to the atmosphere of the French eighteenth-century comedy, to which both the Englishman and the Pole were indebted for the spirit of the jolly *genre,* the plot of the two plays, as well as their characters and their attitude to life give us the impression of something akin.

The last of Fredro's recognized masterpieces, called *Mr. Joviality* . . . , is bound up with an old literary tradition, on which were based both Shakespeare's *Taming of the Shrew* and Molière's *Le Bourgeois Gentilhomme*. But Fredro made a special use of it. While the writers mentioned introduced a churl into a society which mocked him for their amusement, in *Mr. Joviality* the disguised "sovereign" amuses himself at the cost of the people who clothe him in the garb of a pretended king. (pp. 237-38)

Very carefully Fredro drew an assortment of types for Mr. Joviality's family. All of them are eccentrics in some special manner. The manor becomes in truth a pathological museum of idiots and fools, with worthy Mr. Joviality at their head. . . . Nowhere has Fredro's underlying pessimism been given voice as in this play, which, to all outward appearances, is as sunny and joyful as his other pieces.

Moreover, he here gave vent to his satirical opinions on the Austrian Government and its bureaucratic policy; hidden under the guise of humour, they escaped the watchful eye of Austrian censorship. . . . (pp. 238-39)

[Fredro's] merits were duly appreciated by the Polish theatregoers, whereas the literary critics for a long time unconsciously sided with Goszczynski's exaggerated and false opinions [in his untranslated essay]. They considered Fredro as something less than his great contemporaries. It is easy to understand this narrow point of view. Polish nineteenth-century literature . . . was throughout national, or rather political, since it dealt with national problems, the existence and fight for independence. This element being missing in Fredro's comedies, they were naturally underrated. . . . [Recent] studies unanimously admit his greatness as a writer who depicted perfectly the common life and the common people of his period; and at the same time, as is customary with great writers, represented by ludicrous adventures and ridiculous characters the permanent elements of good and evil concealed in human nature. (pp. 239-40)

> *Julian Krzyżanowski, "Alexander Fredro and His Comedies," in his* Polish Romantic Literature, *E. P. Dutton and Company Inc., 1931, pp. 224-40.*

WIKTOR WEINTRAUB (essay date 1953)

[*Weintraub provides a brief overview of mid-nineteenth-century Polish Romanticism in verse and prose and examines Fredro's works, particularly* Trzy po trzy, *in relation to his era. He describes Fredro as outside the major literary current of his time and contends that his memoirs are markedly anti-Romantic because of their satiric treatment of Napoleon and lack of lyricism. Although* Trzy po trzy *was not published until 1877, critics agree that much of it was written by 1848, during the height of the Eastern European Romantic movement.*]

[In *Topsy Turvy Talk (Trzy po trzy),* Fredro] tells the story of his childhood and his military service in a rather queer way; he follows no chronological order. The episodes are scrambled; they are often interrupted by digressions, mostly lyrical, sometimes finished only after long intervals, and sometimes left altogether unfinished. The author gives the impression of following the free play of his fancy. (p. 538)

Older historians of literature frowned upon such structure. They enjoyed the charm of the book, its freshness and humor (it is difficult not to enjoy them), but they opined that Fredro spoiled his memoirs by disorderly and eccentric composition. Only relatively recently, since people have gotten used to more sophisticated ways of composition, have they begun to look at this whimsical form, not as an impediment to enjoyment, but as an additional source of charm.

Its model is, of course, Sterne's *Tristram Shandy*. Some thirty years ago, [the Polish critic Waclaw Borowy in his untranslated essay *Uwagi O 'Trzy po trzy'*] aptly analyzed Fredro's debt to Sterne for the zigzag method of composition, the frequent addresses to the reader, his taste for embarrassing situations, and the emphasis on what appear to be trivial details. . . . Fredro transplanted Sterne's method to memoirs. In all of Polish literary history, there is no other prose so deeply imbued with the spirit of Sterne as *Topsy Turvy Talk*.

Borowy examined the particular elements of Sterne's technique in Fredro's memoirs with his usual thoroughness and subtlety, but he stopped short of asking for the reasons which had compelled Fredro to choose just such an unusual technique of narration. They seem to be manifold. First of all, Fredro was a highly secretive man. There were matters about which he would not unbosom himself to the public for anything in the world. . . . Thus, in the memoirs, he passes in a few sentences over his Russian captivity in 1812, the memory of which was too painful to be revived. There is another significant omission in the book. Fredro wrote in detail about the circumstances of his joining the army in 1809. But he passed over the first three years of his military service, and wrote more extensively only about the Russian campaign of 1812. We know from other sources that they were gay years, of pretty loose morals. The older Fredro must have been a little ashamed of them. The Sternean manner permitted him not only to omit the events of those years but also to make the omission hardly noticeable.

But there was also another, more compelling, and more serious reason. Sterne's technique suited Fredro's vision of the world and especially his "truth" about the war. Sterne was a great "debunker." By dwelling on trifling details, by putting them in the forefront he destroyed the traditional hierarchy of value. He perversely attributed the greatest importance to the seemingly most insignificant details. (pp. 539-40)

Only if we [are aware of the cult of Napoleon in Poland], . . . can we grasp fully the impish character of Fredro's attitude towards Napoleon. The memoirs start with the following description of the author and Napoleon:

> On February 18, 1814, a man of middle age, rather corpulent, wearing a brown coat, buttoned up to the chin, and a three-cornered hat, on which there was no decoration except a little tri-colored rosette, was riding on a white horse. At a certain distance behind him, rode another man, far younger, also in a coat, but one of a dark green color, slouched as deeply as the first one or, perhaps, even more deeply. He was sitting on a roan horse. The white horse, of oriental origin, was small, mean-looking, but stout. The roan horse was . . . roan. It is difficult to say anything else about the horse. Not having as inducement the glory of his ancestors, or his own temper, he often stumbled on the road, which fate prepared for him day by day. The first of these riders was Napoleon, the second—me.

The quiet tone of the passage, which directs attention as much to the horses as to the men; the stressing of the all too human features of the God of War ("rather corpulent," "slouched")—all this gives a well-prepared "debunking" effect. Also worth mentioning is the fact that the author treats the Emperor on a plane with himself.

The same technique becomes even more clear a few pages later. The scene is, one would think, as Romantic as it could be: a meeting with the Emperor during the night at a bivouac. But Fredro makes use of every possible device to destroy the Romantic aura. First of all, the scene is told in nonchalant, colloquial language:

> From what I had the honor to tell you, Sir, you will perhaps guess that I must have been always close to the Emperor, Napoleon . . . And rightly so. Not only in my official papers does it say squarely that I took part in all the battles at which the Emperor himself was present, but at times we warmed ourselves at the same fire. True, it didn't happen often. The Emperor seldom appeared at a bivouac. And one must say that the fire for the Emperor was much, much bigger than the usual fires. It is also true that I always remained on the side towards which the wind blew the smoke . . .

And now in the best Sterne manner a trivial detail appears, which radically destroys any Romantic effect:

> . . . and, between us, it mostly happened that the Emperor turned his back toward the fire, and, thus, toward me, too. Moreover, he often lifted his coat-tails in order to warm himself better. In social life one might consider it a tactless gesture. But in wartime one does not observe etiquette so strictly, and I saw no reason to feel offended.
>
> (pp. 541-42)

Only once in the book does Fredro break out openly, inveighing in a passionate passage against the "infernal hypocrisy" and "devilish politics" of Napoleon toward Poland. The passage, however, is an exception. Usually, Fredro deals with the Napoleonic legend in quite a different way, through impish, irreverent commentaries. The tone set by Romantic poetry made them ring quite provocatively.

We find a similar contrary spirit in Fredro's war scenes. The Romantics saw war through a heroic, idealizing haze. Fredro's battle scenes are quite different. First of all, there is no general picture of the battlefield. . . . [What] we see are scenes of tumultuous chaos, confusion, disorder, where most discordant episodes, serious and trivial, are foisted up at every moment. That does not mean that Fredro's war scenes have anything in common with modern pacifist literature of the type of Barbusse or Romain Rolland. Any note of horror is absent from them. On the contrary, some of them are amusing, and we feel that young Fredro, in a way, enjoyed the tumult and disorder of battle. But the Romantic heroic halo is gone from these scenes. With Fredro we are far nearer to [the hero of Stendhal's *Chartreuse de Parme*] Fabrizio del Dongo on the battlefield of Waterloo or to *War and Peace* than, for instance, to Mickiewicz's *Ordon's Redoubt*.

The anti-Romantic note does not appear only in the war scenes, although it is most clear there. There is in ***Topsy Turvy Talk*** also the following scene. During the night, Fredro brings the report of victory at Montereau to the mayor of Fontainebleau:

> Then I woke the mayor. Frightened by the rattling of my saber, he started out of sleep with his wife, and I was filled with unworthy satisfaction that I could thus rouse someone from a comfortable bed. He entered the office, opened the mail which I handed him, put on the spectacles and read first of all in a low voice, then loudly. . . .
>
> (p. 543)

O honorable mayor! How beautiful you were at that moment! I remember your nose, remember the flowers of your nightgown. I see you as, leaning with one hand upon the official desk, you dropped the other with the letter, and, raising your eyes over your spectacles, you wept from joy. The actuary also started to blink in an effort to squeeze out some tears, and I fell asleep stretched in a rocking chair.

We see here the inversion of the traditional scale of values. It is the "bourgeois," traditionally despised by Romantic poetry, who is "beautiful," grand, moving, and it is the "bourgeois" with the traditional "bourgeois" attributes: a nightgown in flowers, a pair of spectacles, a comfortable family bed.

In connection with this persistent anti-Romantic note, very significant is Fredro's polemic against Mickiewicz's Parisian lectures, the same lectures in which the cult of Napoleon reached such a fantastic apogee. The point of departure of the polemic was not Napoleon, but the memoirs of General Kopeć. However, Fredro draws from this particular discussion far more general conclusions. (pp. 543-44)

The passage devoted to Kopeć is a kind of insertion. After having spoken of a madman whom he had met as a child, Fredro refers to Kopeć, another madman, collecting data to prove Kopeć's insanity, and then he switches to Mickiewicz:

> And this ill-fated creature left memoirs!!! And Mickiewicz expatiates upon them! And yet Mickiewicz met people who knew General Kopeć very well. How to believe the writers of that time! No, the writers of that time can provide merely materials, and only later enlightened opinion, after having cleared them from involuntary mistakes and from mistakes inspired by the partisan spirit, can bring forth the *truth* of history.

The passage is typical of Fredro's indirect attack on Romanticism. He does not call it by name. He deliberately speaks vaguely of "the writers of that time" *(owcześni pisarze),* and he appeals for judgment to "enlightened opinion," using an adjective so typical of eighteenth century Classical writers.

All these anti-Romantic notes are introduced discretely, without insistence, in a nonchalant way. But they appear again and again. And they give the memoirs a special coloring. In this respect they continue the tradition of Fredro's comedies.

A loose and capricious technique of narration served Fredro for another reason, too. It permitted him to break off the story at any moment for lyrical and reflective asides. When reading about the adventures of the young officer, we never forget the elderly gentleman who, some thirty-odd years later, is remembering things past, musing upon his youth, evaluating his adventures in the light of subsequent experience. One chronological plan continually passes into another. The reminiscences are vivid but we never forget the prism through which we see them. The melancholy of time passing is deeply felt throughout the whole book. This melancholy, together with humor, gives the book an emotional haze and a specific unity of tone. (pp. 544-45)

The seemingly nonchalant way of writing, and the number of humorous scenes, make one think of *Topsy Turvy Talk* as a work written in a light key. In a way, it is. But at the same time, it is the work of an independent and subtle observer, distinguishing fine shades of values, never following the beaten track. (p. 545)

The tone of the book is that of intimate chatter, conveyed not only through loose composition, but also through language, flowing easily, racy, full of idiomatic expressions, with the inflection of speech. But the intimacy is kept well under control. It would be completely misleading to assume . . . that the memoirs were written as a family souvenir only, intended for "private" consumption. The book contains no allusions that can only be understood by the initiated, no ciphers in a "family language," no indiscretions typical of such "private" reminiscences. When assuming the mask of an idle chatterer, Fredro was, in fact, an artist, well in command of his material and well conscious of the tools of his craft. (p. 546)

Wiktor Weintraub, "Alexander Fredro and His Anti-Romantic Memoirs," in The American Slavic and East European Review, *Vol. XII, No. 4, 1953, pp. 535-48.*

MANFRED KRIDL   (essay date 1956)

Though [Fredro's dramatic productions] coincided with the classical and romantic epochs, his works cannot be considered typical of either of these trends. Certain traits are present which may be classified as 'classical,' but there are also others which may, with reservations, be called 'romantic.' The essential nature of his output, however, has very little in common with the distinctly drawn traits of either movement; it stands beyond them as a highly original and autonomous production. (p. 321)

He began with pseudo-romantic ballads, but soon abandoned them for the comedy which was more suited for his talent. Even in his first works in this genre, in the one-act play *Intryga na predce (An Intrigue in a Hurry . . .)* and the three-act comedy *Pan Geldhab (Mr. Geldhab . . .),* he displayed great dramatic talent. Naturally, the dramatic values in these first comedies did not yet stand on the level of mature art, but they constituted a definite prognosis that a playwright of the first class was in the making, one who was to raise this genre, so neglected in Poland, to a high level. Of still greater promise was his next comedy . . . , *Mąż i żona (Husband and Wife).* It is, by comparison, the best of the Polish comedies written to that time. The plot is rather complex: it presents the love affairs of four persons, two of whom, a man and his wife, are unfaithful to each other: she with another man, he with the chambermaid; at the same time the other man is also enjoying intimate relations with the chambermaid. This erotic contredance was used to full advantage to fill three acts with lively scenes, carefree humor, and hidden satire, with seemingly incredible complications which, however, are psychologically and dramatically justified. Many scenes are full of paradoxical and comical situations, . . . and all the characters deceive and dupe one another. One could consider this play as a serious satire about the customs prevailing in certain circles of the gentry (and some satirical elements are undoubtedly there), were it not for the traditions of French comedy obvious in this play. Fredro's play, one may say, intensifies and even anticipates French tradition in this respect, for it was only later that the French comedy reached such subtlety and complications. The excellent dialogue is one of the outstanding virtues of this play; it holds the structure together, since the 'action' of the play can only in part take place on the stage. (p. 322)

There were among [Fredro's plays] works of different character and value, some light and unpretentious, such as *Damy i huzary (Ladies and Hussars . . .)*—which even today entertains the public with excellent human types and comical situations—and some more carefully worked out, which embrace complicated problems and display a greater wealth and variety of dramatic devices, such as *Śluby panieńskie (Maidens' Vows)* and *Zemsta (Vengeance)*. . . .

[*Maidens' Vows*] is different from Fredro's earlier works. While in the others his major concern had been to create comical and complex situations, in this one he turned his attention toward the spiritual experiences of his heroes, making their psychology and internal evolution the basis of this play. (p. 323)

The atmosphere of this comedy is cheerful, full of humor, charm, and subtlety; the characters are distinctly drawn and well presented dramatically; their experiences and spiritual evolutions are artistically justified; the structure of the play is transparent and compact.

Far more complex is the plot, or rather the several plots, of *Vengance,* the masterpiece of Fredro and of Polish comedy in general. Here the author went even further in the neglect of classical laws as he joined three or four dramatic plots in a truly masterful way. The structure of *Vengeance* is indeed one of the most thoroughly thought out and artfully conducted in Polish dramatic literature. (pp. 323-24)

[A schematic summary would demonstrate how the elements of the plot] join, overlap, and complicate one another and how they are solved. Fredro's mastery is displayed . . . in the way each of these matters goes through its own evolution, at the same time being closely connected with the others which also develop in their own directions. The spectator or the reader can never be sure that the ultimate result will be, for there are many possible solutions and almost every act leaves all these matters suspended. It is also quite frequent for an action to go in a given direction and then change suddenly, causing new complications and confusions in matters connected with it. All this makes the reading of *Vengeance,* and especially seeing it performed by outstanding actors, an esthetic delight. Everything in the play maintains the same high level: the vivid, individualized language, which sparkles with all the jewels of excellent Old Polish, the verse which flows freely, swiftly, and rhythmically and lends forcefulness and charm to current speech; finally the wonderful human types, specifically Polish, not at all idealized, splendidly presented, who characterize themselves right away in their first utterings and gestures and who are maintained uniformly by the author until the end. (pp. 324-25)

[*Pan Jowialski (Mr. Jovial),*] though not too interesting from the point of view of dramatic structure, is a veritable mine of proverbs, little sayings, anecdotes, fables, and jokes, unsurpassed in their kind. Besides we have here a satirical portrait of an old nobleman who is jovial, good, gentle, kind-hearted, but at the same time strangely not serious, unproductive, carefree, and, in the last analysis, soulless, as is also that whole life which surrounds him in a quiet nobleman's home, cut off from the world. It need not be added that these traits of the comedy do not make up for its structural deficiencies, for the aim of this literary genre can not be, of course, a simple accumulation of anecdotes and jokes, nor even the excellent characterization of the title character. Another comedy, *Dożywocie (Life Annuity),* has as its basis an original idea of selling his life annuity by a young squanderer, Leon Birbancki, to the usurer, Łatka. The latter is most interested, of course, that the young man should not ruin his health by revelry and that he should live as long as possible. He, therefore, persecutes him with excessive care, which brings about very comical scenes. The main interest and purpose of the author is centered on the usurer; he tries to characterize him from the largest number of points of view possible, and, for that purpose, creates situations which make such a characterization plausible. We can, therefore, justly call this play a comedy of character, modelled on many similar comedies by Molière. (p. 325)

Fredro was not only a great poet, but also an excellent prose writer. This is revealed in his memoirs published posthumously under the title *Trzy po trzy (Topsy Turvy Talk),* written in the Laurence Sterne manner, showing his intellectual superiority, his ironic attitude toward men and things, a subtle sense of observation, discreet humor and brilliant narrative style. . . .

As every great writer, Fredro took advantage of the age-old tradition of [Western European] comedy, especially of Molière and Goldoni; reminiscences of other French comedy writers have also been found. But these were only tools which Fredro used quite independently, which he adapted to his own artistic aims, creating entirely original Polish works which at the same time possess universal significance. (p. 326)

Manfred Kridl, "Literature at Home After 1831," in his A Survey of Polish Literature and Culture, *Mouton & Co., 1956, pp. 321-46.**

HAROLD B. SEGEL   (essay date 1969)

[*Segel identifies Fredro's place in the tradition of Polish and European comedy. In addition, he notes the influence of such writers as René de Pixerécourt, Augustan Scribe, Johann Nestroy, Ferdinand Raimund, and August Kotzebue and contends that Fredro's mastery of plot, characterization, and verse distinguish him from later dramatists. In contrast to many critics, Segel suggests that Fredro was not significantly influenced by Molière.*]

For the sake of neat categorization Fredro at times [has] been presented to the non-Polish world as the Polish Molière, or the Polish Goldoni, or even the Polish Musset. None of these appellations is particularly accurate. . . . (p. 49)

However fluent he may have been in Molière's comedy, however much he may have admired Molière, Fredro was not greatly in the French master's debt. This is quite evident in *The Life Annuity* [*Dożywocie*], which some consider his most Molièresque comedy after *Mister Moneybags* [*Pan Geldhab*]. Traces of Molière certainly can be found in *The Life Annuity,* as well as in *Mister Moneybags* and *Mister Joviality* [*Pan Jowialski*], but comparison of these comedies with Molière's work will show that the similarities are considerably less significant than the differences. Like *Husband and Wife* [*Mąż i żona*], *Ladies and Hussars* [*Damy i huzary*] and *The Vengeance* [*Zemsta*], these plays are original works which owe no more to Molière than to other sources of Fredro's genius: the old Polish burgher comedy of the sixteenth and seventeenth centuries, the comedy of Stanislavian Poland, the commedia dell'arte and Goldoni, Marivaux and Kotzebue.

During his stay in Italy Fredro . . . had a chance to become familiar with the traditions of Italian comedy and especially Goldoni, to whose plays he took an immediate liking. Polish scholarship . . . [has] demonstrated, quite convincingly, that while some motifs in Fredro may be traced to Goldoni, the two dramatists share only an ability to develop fine character studies within the context of the comedy of intrigue. In any less general way they have little in common.

Characterizing Fredro as a Polish Musset is even less sound than trying to make of him a Slavic Molière or a Slavic Goldoni. *Maidens' Vows* [*Śluby panieńskie*] is the only play of Fredro having anything of the aura of a Musset comedy about it, but here it would be more productive to look back to the inspiration of Marivaux—who was a source common to both Fredro and Musset—than to the kind of romantic comedy Musset's name has become identified with and from which Fredro was quite alien. (pp. 49-50)

Fredro was by no means aloof from the work of [the] artisans of comedy [including such minor dramatists as Pixerécourt, Scribe, Nestroy, Raimund, and Kotzebue]. This is reflected above all in his attention to plot and the reluctance to assume any discernible moral posture. But with these popular practitioners of the comic art Fredro ultimately shares little more than an admirable productive capacity and an almost total commitment to the genre of comedy at a time when in the history of European drama comedy had fallen from grace. What Fredro possessed that these writers did not was a genius that made him far more than a manufacturer of mediocre comedies and indeed placed him as a comic dramatist among the major talents of his time. In common with Grillparzer, Kleist, Gogol and Griboedov, Fredro sought to reaffirm the values of classical comedy in an age that for the most part spurned it. But his contribution in this respect must be measured not in terms of a single work or two but a substantial body of plays of considerable variety representing collectively a career of devotion to the art of comedy. This is where Fredro departs from these other dramatists and wherein his uniqueness for European drama is no less important than his uniqueness for Polish.

Comparing Fredro's work to that of his Polish and European predecessors and contemporaries, what can we isolate as the distinguishing characteristics of his comic genius? Fredro was, to begin with, a master of complex but skillfully executed plot design; this is evident in each play . . . where intrigue is as important as character. In his deft handling of plot, however, there is seldom the reliance on contrivance and straining of credulity that we have come to expect as somehow indispensable in comedy. The resolution of the plot flows plausibly from the course of the action and the relationships of the characters. Improbability enters rarely; some older Polish critics insisted on singling out *The Life Annuity* as the weakest of Fredro's better comedies from this point of view, but close examination of it discloses on the contrary a carefully and logically elaborated plot structure that shows up the author's sure hand as well as any other of his major plays. Writing about *The Life Annuity* in his introduction to the most recent edition of Fredro's collected works [*Pisma wszystkie*], the late Polish literary historian and critic Kazimierz Wyka was quite right when he said: "If Fredro thought in terms of action . . . , then *The Life Annuity* represents one of the very best examples of this kind of thinking, and not just in the history of Polish comedy."

Another area in which Fredro reveals a fine talent and in which he has few superiors in European comedy is characterization. Through all the intricacies of plot character is never neglected, with the result that the easily recognized comic types—the young lovers, cheating husbands and wives, husband-hunting widows and spinsters, servants, cantankerous old country squires, petty usurers, professional soldiers, bachelors and braggarts— are transformed into well-rounded, highly individualized creations who are rarely mere abstractions and rarely implausible.

In creating his own gallery of comic portraits Fredro was greatly aided by a feeling for language no less remarkable than let us say Gogol's. His characters, primary and secondary, have their own distinct idioms and it is through these idioms as much as through appearance and manner that the characters are recognized. The succulence, color, and variety of his language make Fredro a continuous source of delight to Polish audiences, but it is precisely this feature of his style that has denied him the recognition he deserves beyond the borders of his own country.

Like Kleist and Musset among his contemporaries Fredro also wrote comedies in verse. But here, no less than with his language, he again proved his considerable talent and originality. Whereas verse is most of the time a convention in European comedy, in Fredro's most impressive verse plays *(Maidens' Vows, The Vengeance, The Life Annuity)* it was a convention to which—like other comic conventions—he brought a new life. Breaking with the traditional verse pattern for comedy in **Husband and Wife**, Fredro went on to exploit verse as a technique of style in **Maidens' Vows** and as an instrument for effecting the light, vivacious tempo that remains one of the major sources of appeal of **The Vengeance** and **The Life Annuity** and without which it is difficult even to imagine these plays.

From the foregoing, we can see that the most outstanding characteristics of Fredro's technique—the sources of his appeal and impact as a comic dramatist—are the absence of moral tendentiousness and his welding of plot, character, and idiom into a single dramatic entity in which no one element carries greater weight than others. For this reason Fredro's best plays do not lend themselves to ready classification. The characters are usually so well drawn and so much individualized beyond mere types and the intrigue usually so ably structured that the traditional lines of comedy are blurred. Is **Husband and Wife** a comedy of intrigue, or a salon comedy of manners? Can we say that character is more important than situation in **Maidens' Vows?** Are **The Vengeance** and **The Life Annuity** primarily comedies of intrigue, or comedies of character? The questions are not easily answered because the plays are so composed that they cannot adequately be defined by one classification or the other. Even in the farce **Ladies and Hussars** the characters come off so well—with their own distinct personalities—that we feel we have gone beyond the traditional limits of the genre.

Fredro's importance in the total picture of European comedy rests then not only on the fact that he was a productive, talented writer of comedies who like Kleist, Gogol or Griboedov— though in a more substantial way—sought to preserve a classical comic art during the time of romanticism. In his dedication to classical comedy Fredro was not bound by its traditions. It had taught him the fundamentals of his craft, but he approached its traditions and conventions with a freshness and originality that enabled him to reshape it into something uniquely his own. In so doing he gave Polish drama a comic tradition it can take pride in and European drama a page in its history it has yet to appreciate. (pp. 51-4)

> Harold B. Segel, in an introduction to The Major Comedies of Alexander Fredro by Alexander Fredro, edited and translated by Harold B. Segel, Princeton University Press, 1969, pp. 3-54.

CZESŁAW MIŁOSZ (essay date 1969)

[*A celebrated Polish poet, essayist, and novelist, Miłosz was awarded the Nobel Prize for Literature in 1980. In the following excerpt from his comprehensive survey,* The History of Polish Literature, *Miłosz assesses Fredro's importance in the development of the Polish comic theater. He concludes that the Polish verse comedy, derived from the sixteenth- and seventeenth-century* komedia rybałtowska, *or realistic plebian comedies, reached its zenith with Fredro's works.*]

In a period of revolts, martyrdom, and flights of the imagination, Polish literature saw the birth of works that stand as the purest incarnation of Polish humor—Mickiewicz's *Pan Tadeusz* and the comedies of Aleksander Fredro. . . . Fredro was not a Romantic. His plays (though sometimes compared to Goldoni's) stemmed directly from the Polish comedy of the eighteenth century. With Fredro, therefore, the genre of Polish comedy in verse, whose origins go back to the *komedia rybałtowska,* reached its peak. In all probability, some works of the Polish Baroque theater were also known to him. He should not be regarded solely as an heir of the didactic Enlightenment trend. Fredro did not trouble with any thesis; he was simply possessed by a demon of laughter. In contrast to eighteenth-century comedy writers, who conceived of characters as types, Fredro built his as temperaments, individualizing them, making them visceral, as it were, and left the actor many possibilities to impersonate a given role through gestures, little signs, peculiar tics. . . . His verse has a classical clarity and neatness, but even though he adopted the versification of eighteenth-century comedy, he put it to quite a different use. He molded his meter perfectly to everyday speech—which explains why his idioms have become so much a part of the Polish language that they are quoted even by people who know nothing of their origin. (pp. 249-50)

Fredro's position as a major Polish comedy writer is well established, and his plays have formed an integral part of the repertoire of the Polish theater ever since the nineteenth century. (p. 254)

Czesław Miłosz, "Romanticism," in his The History of Polish Literature, *second edition, 1969. Reprint by University of California Press, 1983, pp. 195-280.**

JULIAN KRZYZANOWSKI (essay date 1972)

[*Krzyżanowski's* A History of Polish Literature *was originally published in Polish as* Dzieja Literatury Polskiej od początków do czasów najowszych *in 1972.*]

Aleksander Fredro's attitude towards Romanticism is one of the controversial questions of Polish literature, which was settled "on principle" without taking certain facts into consideration as a result of which [Fredro,] whose most intensive and prolific output coincided with the creative years of Adam Mickiewicz, was looked upon either as a precursor of Romanticism or as its opponent. The misunderstandings that arose because of this meant that the origin of Fredro's works was treated one-sidedly, for no consideration was given to the differences between the motives that led him to start his literary activity and the conditions in which his literary career developed. And it is precisely the interaction of these two factors that account for the specific and individual character of the works of this author.

As regards motive, his stay in Paris was behind his decision to write comedies, his imagination being stimulated by his first contact with the theatre in that city, where strains of the swan-song of the classicist comedy originating from the works of Molière were already sounding. . . . [When] he started writing his own comedies, he was living in quite different conditions, due to the emergence of the Romantic trend in Polish literature. The result of this duality was something quite unusual. The writer . . . looked at life with the eyes of his generation, a generation of romantics, and expressed his observations in the form of comedies of classicist structure. . . . (pp. 308-09)

[Fredro introduced] ideas into his works which were intended no so much to strengthen or improve the morals of his audiences as to evoke laughter, in other words, true comedies in the strict sense of the word. And for this reason he did not reject farcical ideas, which did not find favour with the Romantic critics, although it was not this element of his works that they attacked.

So in *Ladies and Hussars (Damy i huzary)* and *Good Lord! What the Devil is This! (Gwałtu, co sie dzieje)* Fredro gave us two excellent farces, composed of an unending chain of comic situations. In the former, these situations were created by the belated love affairs of sworn bachelors well advanced in years, caused by the "invasion of ladies" who arrived in a remote locality where a typical small garrison was stationed. The hilarious piling up of comic situations does not, however, become so farcical as to hide the truth of life. . . . [Through] all the complications of the farce, one senses a situation which is far from comic. A girl who wins the affections of an elderly officer is in love with his young nephew, so the farce contains elements of conflict that are no laughing matter. It is only in *Good Lord! What the Devil is This!,* where the scene is set in the little town of Osiek, known for the proverbial stupidity of its populace, and the action is based on the motif of "the rule of the fair sex" that we have pure situational comedy of the circus type. The heroines of this farce are the garrulous wives of the town, who make their unfortunate husbands do all the housework and take their place in managing the affairs of the town, only to return to their kitchens when danger allegedly threatens. The artistic aim of the author is the same as that of comedy through the ages—to make people roar with laughter.

But these excursions into the realm of comedy for comedy's sake, though repeated later too, were just excursions, for the author of *Ladies and Hussars* was influenced by the literary tradition that made comedy an instrument of instructing the reader or audience, making fun of bad habits and customs, so these accents are usually to be found in Fredro's works, although they are never brought to the fore to overshadow the scenes from life that he paints. They were more evident in his earliest works, in *Mr Moneyful (Pan Geldhab . . .)* and *Husband and Wife (Mąż i żona . . .).* (pp. 309-10)

The thing that makes *Husband and Wife* different from other comedies is the realistic approach to the whole problem [of infidelity], the new presentation of the soubrette originally created by Molière, as a participant in various intrigues on a par with her employers, or in other words, the use in comedy of the principle of realism, found rather in the romantic novels of the times than in plays.

This break-away from the conventions of the comedy determined the character of Fredro's next three works, which are generally regarded as his best. They are *Mr Jovial (Pan Jowialski),* *Maidens' Vows (Śluby panieńskie)* and *Revenge (Zemsta),* and a fourth, *Life Annuity (Dożywocie)* is usually included among Fredro's recognized masterpieces, which marked the close of the first period of Fredro's activity as a playwright. *Mr Jovial* is one of the most singular of his plays, for it is a complete departure from the first ones that had a simple one-thread plot and combines old and new motifs into a richly constructed whole. So we have the traditional story known from Baryka's little comedy *Peasant into King,* the only difference being that it is rather an upside-down version. . . . [The] old story is enriched by Fredro's ideas to such an extent that the comedy seems to be one with a multi-thread plot, a comedy showing Polish life. . . . Another thing increasing the impression of rich content is the large number of characteristic types going to make up the family of Mr Jovial, namely, the old gentleman himself, who loves telling anecdotes and quoting proverbs, his son, an idiot and the husband of a snobbish vixen, his daughter, a maiden lady whose head has been turned by reading romances. All of these characters live in a world of their own and each of them stands out distinctly against those surrounding them. Prominence is given to old Mr Jovial who has a proverb or a tale to tell on every occasion, a seemingly inexhaustible store of such entertaining anecdotes that they are enough to make a separate thread of the story by themselves. This comedy, which is one of the most amusing of Fredro's repertoire, in which laughter bubbles up constantly from beginning to end, is almost a farce, an effect heightened by the prosaic course of events, but it also contains certain satirical elements, and satire of a political nature. For there is undoubtedly some truth in the suggestion that *Mr Jovial* is a caricature of the systems prevailing in central and eastern Europe in the period of the Holy Alliance, though this side of the comedy should not be overestimated. (pp. 311-12)

The comedy of the salon, *Maidens' Vows or the Magnetism of the Heart (Śluby panieńskie czyli magnetyzm serca . . .)* is quite different, the very title indicating that it is linked with the Polish sentimental novel genre, from which one of its characters, the tender lover, is taken. It also contains accents of the romantic-magnetic notions of the birth of love and what causes it to flower, notions that the reader will have already have found in [Mickiewicz's drama] *Forefathers' Eve*. But it is not the sentiments of the romantic novel that are brought to the fore, rather a subtle and penetrating analysis of the awakening of feelings of love, the tone being a far cry from the romantic stereotypes and more like the light comedies of the 18th century in which "a dandy goes acourting", or a genre scene from the life of Napoleonic officers, excellently described by Fredro in his *Topsy Turvy Talk [Trzy po trzy]. . . . [Maidens' Vows]* is an unusual comedy, for contrary to *Mr Jovial*, it has very little action and the plot is built on [a thinly disguised] intrigue. . . . And if the preceding and following comedies by Fredro could be called "epic" comedies, *Maidens' Vows* is more of a lyrical comedy, on condition that this term is not understood to mean the sombre and passionate Romantic lyric poetry, but the serene and elegant love poems of earlier times. (p. 312)

[*Revenge*] is the epic type of comedy written at the same time as [Mickiewicz's poem] *Master Thaddeus* and, though this was unintentional, has some kinship with Mickiewicz's work, which was also based on a traditional motif known from the drama of earlier times: Shakespeare used this motif in his *Romeo and Juliet* and Zablocki based a comedy on it *(Sarmatism). . . .* It is the subject of stubborn antagonism between two neighbours, which is brought to an end by the marriage of their children. . . . Fredro might well have based his comedy on the story of the old castle of Odrzykoń, which his wife brought to him in her dowry, or on the tales told in the Lublin region, which were recorded by Koźmian, many years after the writing of *Revenge*, in his *Diaries (Pamiętniki)*. Wherever Fredro took the original plot from, he worked upon it in his own way, concentrating attention on two deadly enemies, neighbours who keep on picking quarrels with each other about very trifling matters. . . . [Fredro] was clearly aiming at preserving the "local colour". Among his papers a small dictionary of archaic words was found, compiled from Linde's dictionary. He makes such skilful and subtle use of these words in his octosyllabic verse that he obtains a specific atmosphere of the old times throughout the play, without any impression of artificiality. He links up his two antagonists [Mr Raptusiewicz and Mr Milczek] very ingeniously with another character Mr Papkin, a man who always pays visits at meal times, a liar, coward, humbug and braggart who brings into *Revenge* something of the atmosphere

of the old folk comedies of Italy—the commedia dell'arte— or similar Polish comedies modelled on them. In comparison with these strongly drawn characters, the lovers appear rather insipid. Their marriage, the result of the unsuccessful "revenge" of Mr Raptusiewicz, is actually a mechanical device to bring the action to the desired end, the "action proper" being the plots and counter-plots of the two antagonistic neighbours, who are typical characters of the old Polish culture, brought to life in two highly individual dramatic creations. (pp. 312-13)

[None of the plays Fredro wrote after his period of silence] attained the high artistic level of his earlier works and none of them won such great popularity as *Revenge* or *Maidens' Vows*. But there are among them some very good comedies, for instance, *The Revolver [Rewolwer]*, which is an excellent satire on the relations in a police state. . . . It tells of the adventures of the cowardly Baron Mortara, residing in a town where the possession of firearms in a punishable offence, whom malicious fate presents with a cigar lighter in the shape of a revolver. This motif is built up into a satire with grotesque and farcical accents and a wealth of comic situations reminiscent of the times of *Mr Jovial*. Another play written about the same time *The Fosterling (Wychowanka)* is quite different in character, being a comedy of customs and manners, which did not please the great admirers of the playwright, for it lacked the hilarious scenes they had come to expect from this author. . . . [It] is more like the "plays" of the end of the 19th century than the comedies usually written by Fredro, and even less like the plays in Molière's style. . . . But *The Fosterling* was an unusual example of Fredro's realism, which was heightened by the bitter experiences of the author, who intended shortly to publish his *Notes of an Old Man (Zapiski starucha)*, a collection of pungent aphorisms on various afflictions of human life. . . . (pp. 313-14)

[Although Fredro] allegedly turned his back on Romanticism, his works came very near to its realistic trend, which in Polish literature was only rarely found in epic and dramatic poetry, though it was fully evident in novels and comedies in prose. The attitude of the writer to the contemporary literary trends was a result of his particular kind of artistic talent, remarkable for his keen perception and observation of his surroundings, his great sense of the comic side of life and his predilection for a specific style of language. His comedies bring a rich gallery of pictures, large and small of the life of the landowner class [and] a wealth of details of customs and manners, which can equal the best novels of the times in which he lived. . . . (pp. 314-15)

Julian Krzyżanowski, "Polish Romantic Literature," in his A History of Polish Literature, *translated by Doris Ronowicz, PWN-Polish Scientific Publishers, 1978, pp. 220-353.**

ADDITIONAL BIBLIOGRAPHY

Majchrowski, Stefan. *Pan Fredro*. Warsaw, Poland: Ludowa Spółdzielnia Wydawnicza, 1965, 319 p.

   The only biography of Fredro. Majchrowski's work is a fictionalized account of Fredro's life written in Polish.

Pruska-Carroll, Malgorzata. ''Fredro's Memoirs—the *Gawęda* and Sterne's Technique.'' *Slavic and East European Journal* 23, No. 3 (Fall 1979): 362-70.*

An overview of the criticism of *Topsy Turvy Talk* in which the author compares Fredro's memoirs to Laurence Sterne's novel *Tristram Shandy*. Pruska-Carroll discusses the work of such Polish scholars as Kazimierz Wyka, Wiktor Weintraub, W. Borowy, Adam Grzymała-Siedlecki, and J. M. Rymkiewicz.

Segel, Harold B. ''The 'Awakened Sleeper' in Polish Literature.'' *Comparative Literature* XVI, No. 2 (Spring 1964): 138-57.*

Traces the theme of the awakened sleeper in world literature. Segel maintains that the character Mr. Joviality in *Pan Jowialski* is an ''interesting and original Polish contribution to the long history of the tale of the 'awakened sleeper' in European literature.''

Johann Gottfried von Herder

1744-1803

German critic, essayist, translator, editor, and dramatist.

One of the most prominent and influential critics in literary history, Herder is also well known as a primary theoretician of the *Sturm und Drang* (Storm and Stress) and Romantic movements. His essays on various topics, including religion, history, and the development of language and literature, are considered important to later studies on evolution and the development of the social sciences. Although his works are often faulted for their lack of organization, critics nevertheless praise Herder for his diversity and erudition.

Herder was born in Mohrungen, East Prussia, into a family of limited means. His father, a cantor, sexton, and schoolmaster, reared his three children in the Protestant faith and emphasized gentle discipline and manners. He encouraged his son to complete his education at the town school where the youth also mastered Latin and Greek studies. Following his graduation, Herder worked as a secretary to a manufacturer of religious pamphlets. He then entered the University of Königsberg where he studied medicine and theology. Herder remained at Königsberg until 1764, when he accepted a post as both master and minister at the Cathedral School of Riga.

Although Herder did not begin writing seriously until after his move to Riga, his later works reflect two major forces in his life at Königsberg: the influence of his professor, the philosopher Immanuel Kant, and his friendship with the religious writer Johann G. Hamann, who challenged the eighteenth-century school of rationalism. The significant influence of both these men is perhaps most evident in his *Über die neuere deutsche Litteratur*, a three-part essay in which Herder responded to Gotthold Ephraim Lessing's collection of literary letters, *Litteraturbriefe*. In his work, Herder defined his concept of literary historicism, stating that the current character of every nation is the culmination of an evolutionary process which can be traced through the development of that culture's literature and language. Herder further maintained that literature must be judged in light of this history and not by the standards represented by French Neoclassical literature or the Latin or Greek classics. Thus, with this work, Herder joined the movement against Neoclassicism.

In 1769, Herder left Riga and sailed to Brittany and Nantes, France, where he met the Prince of Holstein. Although he agreed to become the prince's tutor and accompany him on a grand tour of Italy, Herder remained with him for only a short time before a painful eye infection forced him to seek corrective surgery. During his recuperation Herder met Johann Wolfgang von Goethe and formed an influential and fortuitous friendship. He urged the young Goethe to study and value his German cultural heritage. By this time, Herder had come to be regarded as the leader and initiator of the *Sturm und Drang* movement, which is characterized by emotional intensity and which often derived its inspiration from folk legend. He also promoted the study and emulation of "natural" poets such as Homer and Shakespeare instead of the "artificial" poets of French Neoclassicism.

Herder's literary theories were also evident in the emerging German Romantic movement. His essay "Abhandlung über den Ursprung der Sprache, walche den von der Königl" *(Treatise upon the Origin of Language)* outlines Herder's concept of language, which he considers a natural development of every culture. Herder's continued interest in folklore, folksongs, and German sagas is further evidenced in his edition of *Volkslieder*, a collection of folksongs, some of which Herder translated into German. *Vom Geist der ebräischen Poesie (The Spirit of Hebrew Poetry)* is another historical and cultural study. In this essay he discusses the development of Hebrew literature and cites it as a primary example of the natural historical maturation of folklore. As in his other works, Herder's theories in this essay were informed by his love of primitive poetry.

Under the recommendation of Goethe, Herder became the general superintendent at Weimar Court in 1776, but felt disassociated from Goethe's literary and cultural circles and was unhappy. In 1784, he published the first part of *Ideen zur Philosophie der Geschichte der Menschheit (Outlines of a Philosophy of the History of Man)*, perhaps his most influential treatise. In the essay, Herder expanded his ideas from *Über die neuere deutsche Litteratur* and *Treatise upon the Origin of Language* and added a scientific component on organic evolution. These new ideas met with considerable disapproval from his colleagues, particularly from Goethe and the followers of

Kant. Although Goethe later insisted that he and Herder had remained on amicable terms, Herder considered the breach between them to be irreparable. Herder further isolated himself by challenging the doctrines of Kant's *Critique of Pure Reason*, a study in transcendental philosophy. He never reconciled with his former colleagues and in 1803 died in isolation at Weimar.

It is often stated that Herder's works lack both the style and shape that distinguish the creative efforts of his fellow German Romantics. He has been unfavorably compared with Johann Christoph Friedrich von Schiller, Goethe, and Lessing. In 1873, Karl Hillebrand noted that Herder's ideas often lacked order or system, a criticism which was echoed by later commentators. His genius, according to critics, rests in his ability to recognize in the folklore and myths of Germany and other cultures a literary heritage previously unstudied and unrecognized. James Sully remarked that while Herder never completed a work of lasting literary quality, his ideas have fostered a "modern historical attitude of mind," and have influenced many areas of German philosophy and literature.

Although Herder's methods of analysis are now considered somewhat dated, twentieth-century commentators generally agree that his importance lies in his influence rather than in the literary value of his works. According to Margaret Sherwood, his ideas concerning organic evolution and historicism have become the basis for a resurgence in the studies of the humanities. René Wellek considers Herder the "fountainhead of universal literary history" and calls him the "great initiator" of the study of primitive poetry.

Herder remains important for his contributions to both the *Sturm und Drang* and Romantic movements, as well as for his recognition of the import of German folklore and literature. While his works of literature will undoubtedly remain less important than those of succeeding German writers, his ideas remain central to German literature today. Goethe once remarked that Herder was "more inclined to examine and to stimulate than to direct and lead"; Margaret Sherwood reiterated this concept years later, writing that Herder was, indeed, a "pathfinder," and "like most geniuses . . . had but one thing, one great thing to say, and many ways of saying it. . . . [He] was a suggestor, rather than a demonstrator."

PRINCIPAL WORKS

Über die neuere deutsche Litteratur. Fragmente　(essays)
　　1767
Kritische Wälder　(essays)　1769
"Abhandlung über den Ursprung der Sprache, walche den
　　von der Königl"　(essay)　1772; published in *Von
　　deutscher Art und Kunst*
　[*Treatise upon the Origin of Language,* 1927]
"Shakespear"　(essay)　1773; published in *Von deutscher
　　Art und Kunst*
Volkslieder [editor]　(folk songs)　1778; also published as
　　Stimmen der Völker in Liedern, 1807
Vom Geist der ebräischen Poesie. 2 vols.　(essay)
　　1782-83
　[*The Spirit of Hebrew Poetry,* 1833]
Ideen zur Philosophie der Geschichte der Menschheit. 4
　　vols.　(essays)　1784-91
　[*Outlines of a Philosophy of the History of Man,* 1800]
Gott! Ein Gespräch　(essay)　1787
　[*God: Some Conversations,* 1940]

Briefe zu Beförderung der Humanität. 10 vols.　(epistles)
　　1793-97
Adrastea. 6 vols.　(dramas and poetry)　1800-04
Der Cid [translator; from *Cantàr de mio Cid*]　(poetry)
　　1805
J. G. Herders sämmtliche Werke. 45 vols.　(poetry, essays,
　　criticism, and folk songs)　1805-20
Journal meiner Reise im Jahr 1769　(journal)　1846
Herders sämmtliche Werke. 33 vols.　(poetry, essays,
　　criticism, and folk songs)　1877-1913

[THOMAS DE QUINCEY]　(essay date 1823)

[*An accomplished English essayist and critic of the early nineteenth century, De Quincey was also a student of German philosophy and a self-professed opium addict. In his appraisal of Herder excerpted below, De Quincey attributes to Herder a "morbid delicacy of temperament" which he feels may have shortened the author's life. It is unfortunate, says De Quincey, that Herder, a man of such a "voluptuousness," did not indulge in opium. "In fact," concludes De Quincey, "opium would, perhaps, have been a service to him."*]

Was Herder a great man? I protest, I cannot say. He is called the German Plato. . . . [I find it] difficult to form any judgment of an author so "many-sided" (to borrow a German expression)—so poly-morphous as Herder: there is the same sort of difficulty in making an estimate of his merits, as there would be to a political economist in appraising the strength and weakness of an empire like the Chinese, or like the Roman under Trajan: to be just, it must be a representative estimate—and therefore abstracted from works, not only many but also various, and far asunder in purpose and tendency. Upon the whole, the best notion I can give of Herder to the English reader, is to say that he is the German Coleridge; having the same all-grasping erudition, the same spirit of universal research, the same occasional superficiality and inaccuracy, the same indeterminateness of object, the same obscure and fanciful mysticism (*schwärmercy*), the same plethoric fulness of thought, the same fine sense of the beautiful—and (I think) the same incapacity for dealing with simple and austere grandeur. I must add, however, that in fineness and compass of understanding, our English philosopher appears to me to have greatly the advantage. (p. 373)

It appears that Herder rose from the very humblest rank; and, of necessity, therefore, in his youth, but afterwards from inclination, led a life of most exemplary temperance: this is not denied by those who have attacked him. . . . All this temperance, however, led to nothing: for he died when he was but four months advanced in his sixtieth year. Surely, if he had been a drunkard or an opium-eater, he might have contrived to weather the point of sixty years. In fact, opium would, perhaps, have been of service to him. For all his sufferings were derived from a most exquisite and morbid delicacy of nervous temperament: and of this it was that he died. With more judicious medical advice, he might have been alive at this hour. His nervous system had the sensitive delicacy of Cowper's and of Rousseau's, but with some peculiarities that belong (in my judgment) exclusively to German temperaments. I cannot explain myself fully on this occasion: but, in general, I will say, that from much observation of the German literature, I perceive a voluptuousness—an animal glow—almost a sensuality in the very intellectual sensibilities of the German, such as I find in the people of no other nation. (p. 374)

[Herder's letters to his wife and children] are delightful; especially those to the former, as they show the infinite—the immeasurable depth of affection which united them. Seldom, indeed, on this earth can there have been a fireside more hallowed by love and pure domestic affections than that of Herder. He wanted only freedom from the cares which oppressed him, and perhaps a little well-boiled opium, combined with a good deal of lemonade or orangeade (of which, as of all fruits, Herder's elegance of taste made him exceedingly fond), to have been the happiest man in Germany. With an angel of a wife, with the love and sympathy of all Germany, and with a medicine for his nerves,—what more could the heart of man desire? Yet not having the last, the others were flung away upon him; and, in his later years, he panted after the invisible world, merely because the visible (as he often declared) ceased to stimulate him. (p. 375)

[Thomas De Quincey], "Death of a German Great Man," in The London Magazine, Vol. VII, April, 1823, pp. 373-80.

[GEORGE BANCROFT]   (essay date 1825)

[In the following essay, Bancroft ascribes to Herder a poetic sensibility, but asserts that the author lacked the powers of invention and originality necessary to become a great literary figure. Instead, according to Bancroft, Herder became a critic who "knew how to estimate the excellence of others . . .".]

Of the men of letters in Germany, who contributed to elevate the reputation and improve the taste of their country, few were so distinguished for variety of attainments, industry, and the love of pure morality, as Herder. Without possessing great originality, he had still that power of genius, which gives life to acquisitions, and knew how to enrich and strengthen his mind by diligence in study and the faithful exertion of his faculties. The character of his mind was poetic; yet as nature had denied him the highest qualifications of the poet, and he was conscious of his own inability to tread firmly in the 'heaven of invention,' he contented himself with occupations suited to his capacities, taking the widest range through the literature of almost every age and nation, to which he could gain access, and returning from his excursions with noble spoils. He knew how to estimate the excellence of others; he could hold his mind aloof from the objects by which he was immediately surrounded, and enter upon the study of a foreign work, as if he had been of the country, for which it was originally designed. Being possessed of great skill in the use of his own language, he was able to transfer into it the lighter graces no less than the severe lessons of foreign poets. To turn over some parts of his works is as to walk in a botanical garden, where the rare and precious plants of other countries, which thrive in climates the most distant and most different, are artificially yet safely collected, and planted without injury in soils suited to their natures. (pp. 138-39)

[Some] of the volumes of his works may be compared to a fanciful piece of mosaic, composed of costly stones from all parts of the world, and if not always arranged in the very best taste, at least always rich in themselves, and well fitted to gratify the observer. He did more than translate. Wherever he found a beautiful idea, a just and happy image or allegory, he would seize upon it, and, giving it a form suited to his own taste, present it to the world anew. Deeply versed in biblical criticism, he often met amidst the rubbish of verbal commentators and allegorical expositors, many curious and instructive fables, narrations, proverbs, and comparisons. These he did not fail to select, to amplify and arrange, and thus put in currency again many a bright thought, which lay covered with the rust of learning, or buried under a mass of useless criticisms. He collected the ballads of the Spanish Cid, and formed of them a continued poem; he seized on ideas in the eastern as in the classic mythology, and wrought them into beautiful and instructive fictions; he selected from the writings of men, whose minds had an influence on their age, the thoughts which characterised them, and thus gathered a magazine of practical wisdom. In fables, dialogues, and familiar letters, in poems and allegories, imitated, translated, or original, he alike endeavored to please and to teach lessons of goodness. It may be said of Herder, that he passed his life in tranquil industry, possessed of a delicate perception of the beautiful, cherishing in himself and others a love of learning, creating as it were anew the thoughts of the wise and good, and always employed in disseminating a knowledge of what seemed to him the elements of virtue, and cherishing and promoting whatever can improve or adorn humanity. (pp. 139-40)

[Herder] not only wrote on subjects connected with letters, like a man of taste and feeling, but also on subjects of theology like a man of learning. His *Letters relating to the Study of Theology* are full of instruction and good sentiments, and his work *On the Spirit of the Hebrew Poetry,* though written subsequently to the lectures of Lowth, is full of original, profound, and interesting criticism, exhibiting the majesty of the Scriptures in many new views, and illustrating the rich imagery, the brilliant and sublime thoughts and language of the ancient prophets. Herder reverenced the inspired men as the oracles of God, only in so far as revelations of wisdom and goodness are common to all the superior minds, with which Providence has blessed the world. Whilst these views are rejected, there still can be but one opinion of the successful effort, which he has made to vindicate the character of the Hebrew Scriptures, and illustrate their claim to admiration for the beauties of their poetry. (p. 142)

Herder's reputation as a writer rests principally upon his works in prose. His mind . . . was of a poetic character, yet not inventive, and his sensibility to the beautiful and his lively and busy fancy never conducted him to high original efforts in verse. In his writings in prose everything is expressed with warmth and life. His thoughts are communicated under the most various forms and images; and his style would seem gorgeous, were it not at once clear and natural. There is in it a profusion of figures, but not a display of them; he makes use of them, because it was the most natural way for him to express his thoughts. They arose under such forms in his own mind, and he communicates them, as they existed within him. But for this he could be accused of an excess of ornament; but with him comparisons and the figures of rhetoric are not the efforts of art, but natural modes of expression, and he at all times pours them forth abundantly and in an interesting manner, yet not always with elegance, or taste. Few of his works can be recommended as finished performances, or of universal interest. His philosophical reflections on the history of man are written in a solemn and contemplative mood, and exhibit, perhaps, most fairly his private character not less than his merits as a writer. The influence of Herder on his age was wide, and entirely beneficial to the best interests of our race; he has been extensively read and admired, and always with results beneficial to morals and sentiments of philanthropy. A place cannot be assigned him among the great lights of the world; but he bore a high rank among his contemporaries, and was a blessing and an honor to his age. (p. 144)

[*George Bancroft*], "Writings of Herder," in The North American Review, *Vol. XX, No. XLVI, January, 1825, pp. 138-47.*

J. FREDERICK SMITH (essay date 1872)

[*The following essay was first published in April and October 1872 as "Herder As Theologian" in* The Theological Review.]

Herder was and still is one of the greatest teachers, and not least for the reason that he communicates his spirit as well as his doctrine to his disciples. (p. 72)

In few men's natures have so many conflicting elements been present as met in Herder's: thoughts and affections, strong clingings to the old and restless tendencies towards the new, a passion for improvement and a dread of innovation. As historian, he wrote bitter things against Christianity; as poet and Christian, he loved it with the fervour of a woman; as a lover of science, he studied physiology as the key to psychology; as husband, father, pastor, he cried for light to assure and guide him in that atmosphere in which the lights of science cannot live. His writings present him in conflict with nearly every class of students of his time, not from ignoble quarrelsomeness, but from the rich fulness, the fine sensitiveness, and grand breadth of his nature. He felt, with such rare sympathy, the truth of all error and the error of all truth, that he could not agree with even those who were most nearly one with him. Nay, he was bound, such was his nature, to contradict and condemn himself. (p. 73)

The prophets of the Old Testament were men acting and speaking with the whole energies of their natures combined. Herder possessed this peculiarity, but hardly acquired it from either the Hebrew prophets or Hamann. It was natural to him as to others like him. But his love of Hamann and the Old Testament nourished the peculiarity, and is explained by it. Herder does not always equally exhibit this characteristic. In his earlier works it is more predominant than in his later. But his life through, the keen steel of his intellect will glow and burn with the heat of his heart. He cannot help the light of his imagination playing bewilderingly about the path of an argument. His very style betrays him. Poetry breaks up and mars his prose. He argues with his feelings, and feels with his syllogisms. In all this, Hamann and Herder were brothers. And they were not alone in that *Sturm und Drang* period of German literature. (pp. 77-8)

Herder penetrated the recesses of that time when sense and spirit were one, because this was the secret of his own inward life. The outward and the inward were in his case, as in few others, but aspects of a harmonious whole. In his philosophical and theological thinking, therefore, we find that he has a deep-seated, invincible repugnance to all disunion. A dualism between mind and matter, God and nature, understanding and reason, natural and revealed religion, he cannot endure. All his labours, as philosopher, theologian, critic, historian, and scientific inquirer, have this as their aim, to bring man back to the point, whence he started as a child, of harmony within himself and between himself and the universe around him. It is especially the predominance of this aim and tendency in all his writings which, in our opinion, renders them so exceptionally productive. Wide of the mark as some of his views

are, he still knows in what direction the mark really lies, and the whole of the powers of his richly-endowed nature are striving to attain it. (pp. 131-32)

J. Frederick Smith, "Herder," in his Studies in Religion under German Masters, Williams and Norgate, *1880, pp. 71-132.*

KARL HILLEBRAND (essay date 1873)

[*While Hillebrand considers Herder an influential writer, he says that the author's theories are often "unclassified ideas, without order or system." Hillebrand maintains that this "chief defect" is responsible for Herder's inability to focus his thoughts and a tendency toward hasty conclusions. Further, he suggests that Herder was not an "apostle of cosmopolitanism" as many critics view him; rather, he was an "apostle of humanitarianism" who placed humanity above nationality, and who vehemently protested the divisive effects of nationalism.*]

In writing a history of German ideas, manners, and customs, it is impossible to lay too great a stress upon the close connection subsisting between the rise of German literature and the one great general principle which pervaded the whole of the eighteenth century, and which was, as we all know, the intellectual, moral, and social emancipation of the individual.

The entire age had been employed in resistance against every possible form of authority, whether Church, State, or Convention. Dogmas had become especially obnoxious, and, however skilfully they might be disguised, were speedily detected. For a time, at least, the adversaries of all established order were to be conquerors in this protracted struggle, and the close of the century was destined to witness the ruin of the traditional state as well as of positive religion in France, and of scholastic philosophy in Germany. Kant exercised the same influence over thought as the Revolution did over society. The individual was, or believed himself, forever released from the yoke of authority; everything was to begin again from the beginning; nor is this the place to narrate how many were the stones which had to be borrowed from the antique structure in order to prop up the new edifice. (p. 389)

Already, towards the commencement of the eighteenth century, a movement of resistance had made itself felt at different times against authority in literary matters, however firmly established it might seem. This authority, we are aware, was no other than that French classicism of which Boileau's *Art Poétique* contained the code, and the tragedy of the *Grand Siècle* represented the most perfect form, and which people were anxiously endeavoring to imitate in a language and with a natural inspiration utterly at variance with, and incapable of accommodating themselves to, its requirements. It was to Lessing that the task fell of freeing Germany from the despotism of a foreign rule; which he, however, accomplished, not by dethroning that authority to which Frenchmen had appealed, but, on the contrary, by re-establishing it in its true acceptation. He did, in fact, for Aristotle what Luther had done for the Bible. . . . Lessing had claimed the rights of individual genius to modify rule, and five years had hardly elapsed since the publication of his *Dramaturgie* when the literary *Montagne* already urged a radical abolishment of all literary legislation, and proclaimed the rights of genius to absolute self-government. Reform had drifted into Revolution, and Herder was marching at the head of the insurgents.

Herder, the dates of whose life and the tenor of whose intellect placed him midway between Lessing and Goethe,—Herder, who was neither a critic, like the former, nor a poet, like the latter, but who detected the hidden powers which were at work in history with a keener insight than either,—Herder was the real originator of the German civilization of the nineteenth century, the chief characteristic of which lies in its historical point of view. All that had been done in Germany previous to him since the awakening of the nation towards 1750 was mere preparatory work. Klopstock had succeeded in rehabilitating natural feeling and spontaneous enthusiasm which had been stifled beneath the formalism of all kinds then oppressing the German intellect. Wieland had done his best to import and acclimatize English and French culture. Winckelmann had, if we may be permitted to use the expression, blown away the dust from the ancients, thus revealing to view the purity of their outlines, buried as they were beneath a dense layer of rubbish. Lessing had exercised a purely negative influence; he had removed obstacles, cleared the ground, and sorted the imported merchandise, carefully rejecting what was not of pure alloy. It was with Herder that Germany's positive co-operation in the century's labors began. He it was who first gave utterance to the German idea, who began to form that capital which was to be Germany's contribution to the work of humanity. No one, Kant, perhaps, alone excepted, has contributed a larger amount to this stock; nor did any one ever exercise greater or more lasting influence over an age, a nation, or the world at large than Herder, who, like the genuine rebel he was, began by turning the then reigning science and literature upside down, as Kant did with the philosophical speculation of his time, and the French Revolution with the political world. (pp. 389-91)

Friedrich Schlegel was wont to call Herder the "mythologist of German literature"; nor could a better name have been found for him. He not only sought after the prophetic part of human nature, but sought for it in a prophetic way. We have no right to expect from Herder, the scholar, a decided method, any more than a definite dogma from Herder, the believer, an established system from Herder, the critic, or a precise form from Herder, the writer. While Lessing's clear intellect is employed in portioning out the ground with strict impartiality, drawing the boundaries between science and art, and forbidding poetry to trespass upon the domain of painting, Herder seeks poetry in all things, introducing it even into philosophy and science, while as a counterbalance he puts philosophy and science into his own poetry. He had the most delicate perception ever known for detecting and relishing the poetry of every nation, age, and description, added to an extremely pliable imagination, which rendered their assimilation easy to him. And when I say pliable, I do not mean creative or tempered. . . . Not one of his poems has become popular; not one of his personages is living; not a phrase of his has become proverbial. "My muse is wanting in that charming roundness with which you deceive the world," he himself wrote to Goethe. Herder abounds in ideas; but in unclassified ideas, without order or system. We feel that he preferred generalities to facts; hence arose his chief defect,—that of drawing hasty conclusions and forming superficial opinions. He never had the patience to collect solid materials as a foundation before proceeding to generalize. We owe to Herder all the numerous histories of poetry, languages, religions, and even of legislations which our century has produced; his own **"Ideas of a Philosophy of History"** . . . , unfinished, diffusely written in a loose, unconnected style, the style of a seer rather than of a thinker, still less of an historian, very insufficient if we look upon them as researches, form a book which is totally antiquated as far as form and materials are concerned; but as for the thoughts

contained in it, it seems written but yesterday; it might easily be taken for a sketch from the pen of M. Taine.

Herder's very universality itself was injurious to him. He embraced too wide an extent to allow of his grasping anything firmly. . . . His ever-wandering eye never could restrict itself to one narrow spot; and the flame of his enthusiasm bore a greater resemblance to the burning of a steppe than to the concentrated, persistent glow of a thoroughly heated fireplace. He caught glimpses,—we might almost say had visions,—of a genius upon all subjects, mastering none completely; and thus, while able to give the architect the most valuable suggestions, he was himself utterly at a loss to construct the smallest edifice. No man ever scattered abroad a greater quantity of fruit-bearing seeds than he; yet at the close of his life he found that he had not tilled a single corner of his own field according to rule. It is undeniable that his works are more remarkable for their variety than for the profundity of the learning they contain, as Herder himself was endowed with more imagination than good sense, more ardor than thoroughness.

It was precisely these defects, nevertheless, which determined his immense influence. He was certainly one of the greatest incentive powers the world has ever known. By dint of analyzing human nature and introducing into history the division of labor, people had come to such a point that, as Mephistopheles has it, "They held the parts in their hand, the intellectual link alone being wanting." It was Herder's unmethodical, visionary imagination which discovered the failing link, and reunited what intelligence had severed. "Everything that man undertakes to produce, whether by action, word, or in whatsoever way, ought to spring from the union of all his faculties; all that is isolated is condemnable." These were the words in which Goethe summed up the fundamental idea which inspired Hamann, that prophet of the gospel of nature, the mentor and initiator of Herder; an idea which his disciple adopted and adhered to steadily through life, and of which he became the missionary. (pp. 394-95)

Herder, who had . . . begun to bring primitive poetry into notice in his *Fragments* and *Sylvoe* . . . , did so henceforth still more forcibly in his *Blätter für Deutsche Art und Kunst* . . . with the aid and support of his disciple, Goethe. He it was who first established a fact subsequently confirmed by historical discovery, namely, that poetry always preceded prose in the annals of mankind, and who found out the superiority of ages in which genuine, entire natures still existed. (p. 397)

No book, since the appearance of Percy's "Antient Reliques," had produced so great a sensation as the *Stimmen der Völker,* a series of volumes containing popular poems, published by Herder . . . , and which became the model for all the numerous collections of the kind which have come out during the nineteenth century. Herder was eminently gifted for work of this sort. His delicate ear immediately distinguished the false from the true; it instantaneously seized the characteristics of melody, metre, and subject, while the pliability of his talent enabled him to render the whole in such forms of the German idiom as approached nearest to the original. These *Stimmen der Völker* contain specimens taken from every nation on the globe, every period of history, every class of society, written in every possible metre and on every imaginable subject. No one could have been better able to assimilate to himself, even occasionally to guess at the original tone of such productions, than Herder. He had no knowledge whatever of Sanscrit; yet, on reading *Sakuntala* in an English version towards the close of his career, he at once detected its true form, however transformed by the translation. The last and the most popular work he published, the *Cid,* a cycle of romances, was made from a French translation; and yet, whatever syllable-counters may say, its whole tone is deliciously and surprisingly Spanish, *chevaleresque* [chivalrous], and Catholic, like that of all true Castilian romances, although the outward form does not exactly render that of the originals. Surely Herder was not the first to point out the merits of popular verse, nor did he attempt for a moment to make the world believe him to be ignorant of the passages relating to this question which are to be found in Montaigne's writings; he was wont even readily to quote them. But there is surely a very great difference between a few hurried glimpses caught *en passant* [in passing] and a whole literary life dedicated to the cause. There is also a great difference between the effects produced by a vehement and persistent vindication of this cause in an age when it must of necessity at first sight have seemed paradoxical, and in which it ultimately succeeded in gaining the upper hand, and those produced by a scarcely noticed allusion of about half a page, written precisely at the time when the opposite tendency was about to triumph for the space of two centuries. (pp. 400-01)

In Herder's eyes, fables originally were, and would again become, were we to live less artificially, the poetical illustration of a lesson of experience by means of a characteristic trait drawn from animal life and developed by analogy. Now, Herder made this refutation of the mechanical theories then reigning throughout Europe from his point of view, i.e. that of poetical, spontaneous creation without special aim, not only on the domain of the fable, but on that of every other kind of poetry, small or large. To him material extension was of no consequence in works of art.... He studied the nature of epigrams as he had done that of fables, of the drama as of the epic poetry of the ancients; and to say the truth, it was he who showed his country the true Homer and the true Sophocles, as he was likewise to show it the true Shakespeare; the whole of the antique world has been looked upon with a different eye since Herder. (pp. 406-07)

[Herder] was a reader and a citizen of all ages. He deemed it necessary to know and appreciate the poetry of other countries, in order to be able duly to appreciate that of one's own; and that to be able to do this properly, it was indispensable that one should place one's self in the *milieu* which had produced it. Now, nature had endowed him for this purpose, with a pliability of intelligence, an acuteness of perception, a keenness of sight and hearing, and a refined delicacy totally unrivalled. This faculty of relishing and entering into the spirit of the most diverse countries and periods constitutes his chief and true grandeur. This was in reality his cosmopolitism, which has been so often misrepresented, and about which a legion of historians have been content to repeat stereotyped judgments, without attempting to subject them to the slightest criticism or control. But this cosmopolitism never for a moment prevented him from being the most German of all German writers in the general tone of his inspiration, still less from heralding the German idea to the world at large. In fact, Herder not only put an end to the remnants of reasoning, didacticism, and moralizing which Lessing had still admitted into the domain of poetry, leaving nothing at all beyond the arbitrary inspirations of the poet, but he also rose up against the idea of *rule,* which Lessing defended, in opposition to the essentially German conception of *individualism.* He gave back, if I may say so, its originality to German poetry, by putting a limit to the imitation of the ancients. (pp. 411-12)

However incomplete [Herder's **"Ideas of a Philosophy of History"**] may be, it made an epoch in German literature. It is still written even in the same poetical style which caused even his friend Hamann to shrug his shoulders, and which renders his critical studies so indigestible to a soberer generation. Besides, as in his literary *critiques,* he never directs his attacks upon details and errors of fact, but upon the general point of view, so also generality dominates in his **"Philosophy of History."** We find here, not exactly allegories in the Platonic acceptation, nor the prophetic visions to be met with in his earlier works, but still the same vagueness pervading the whole; general ideas have always more importance for him than positive facts. Herder's science and that of his time was incomplete, and the philosopher therefore frequently arrives at hasty conclusions. But there is one principal fact in his writings which made itself felt long after: Herder placed the history of civilization far above political history.... Herder was the first who ventured to leave the alleged aims of Providence in historical events out of the question, and, opposing himself alike to the idea of a preconceived plan and that of mere chance in history, refused to see anything in it beyond the development of given germs,— which has undoubtedly proved the most fertile of all modern ideas. (p. 416)

[In the **"Spirit of Hebrew Poetry,"** Herder] never tires of telling the world that the Bible is not only the basis of our own religion, but also contains that which is the most elevated and most ancient in the world.... It was Herder who opened the world's eyes anew to that poetry which had been hidden from its view by the mass of allegory, morals, dogmas, philosophical ideas, and law-texts with which it had been stifled. Herder had the boldness to treat the Bible like any other human document; and by doing so, he made the history of religions, which belongs essentially and exclusively to our age, possible; for nothing less than the example of Herder's deep and sincere religious feeling would have sufficed to enable men to study religion itself without placing themselves at the point of view of any given religion. The various forms under which mankind have successively or simultaneously tried to satisfy their craving for the infinite and the supernatural had to be duly respected and loved; but the point at which the believer no longer requires that the infinite and supernatural should have a definite conventional form, in order to adore and dread it, had also to be reached. An enthusiastic nature like Herder's, capable of understanding a mystical glow, and yet free-thinking enough not to attribute to himself and his sect alone the privilege of such mystical glow and the immediate conception of the Deity, was required. (p. 419)

It is usual to call Herder the apostle of humanitarian ideas, and not without reason, provided a contempt for nationalities be not implied. Herder placed humanity above nationality. In his eyes the title man was the noblest which can be imagined; and he belongs entirely to his essentially optimist age by this very exalted idea of man. In his eyes national prejudices were as contemptible as were religious and caste prejudices. He thought that the day would come when a single bond would unite all peoples, when a single, unwritten religion, a single civilization, a single morality, would bring men together in a common brotherhood. He protested vehemently against national exclusiveness, as he protested against every other species of exclusiveness. He did not wish that any people, not even his own, should be trumpeted forth as the elect; but he was not the less full of love and reverence for his country on that account.... Far from being a despiser of his native country, Herder was, perhaps, the most, I had almost said the only, patriotic German writer of the last century, as he undoubtedly was the one who understood best the degradation, and who most deplored the fragmentary condition, the slavery, and the political *décadence* of Germany. (pp. 420-21)

[This is the man who] has had the misfortune to become "the apostle of cosmopolitism" in the eyes of posterity. One ought far rather to say that, after having been the standard-bearer of the revolt of the Germanic against the Latin spirit of the eighteenth century, by his literary criticism, he was at once the first and most eloquent defender of that great nationality principle which has agitated our own century so deeply. By restoring national poetry to its place of honor, he contributed to the revival of patriotic sentiments; by formulating the German idea, he became the forerunner of those who, long after, created the German state. It is this universality, this breadth of horizon, which constitutes the real greatness of Herder. Understanding nationality as no one else in the century did and subordinating it to humanity, brought up in reverence for Hellenism and the first to point out its true character, he discovered the East by intuition; in heart a Christian, he knew how to assimilate all the pagan "humanism" in the Renaissance; full of admiration and intelligence for the classical authors, he found the secret of primitive and religious poetry; liberal in his political sympathies, he demonstrated the legality and undeviating consistency of history. . . . (p. 422)

Herder's ideas have penetrated our whole method of thinking in such a degree, his works are so incomplete and so disconnected, that it is hardly possible for us to account for the extraordinary effect these ideas and works produced in their day, or for the surprising influence exercised by Herder personally. From his twenty-fifth year he was indeed a sovereign. True, his actual and uncontested sway was not prolonged beyond a period of fifteen years, albeit his name still figured long after on the list of living potentates. The generation of the *Stürmer* and *Dränger*, or, as they were pleased to denominate themselves, the "original geniuses," looked up to Herder as their leader and their prophet. They turned from him later on, and went back to the exclusive worship of classical antiquity; but their very manner of doing homage to it bore witness to Herder's influence. The following generation threw itself no less exclusively into the Middle Ages; but, after all, what was it doing but following Herder's example when it raked up Dantes and Calderons out of the dust in order to confront them with and oppose them to Virgils and Racines? However they might repudiate, nay, even forget their teacher, his doctrines already pervaded the whole intellectual atmosphere of Germany, and men's minds breathed them in with the very air they inhaled.

Herder is certainly neither a classical nor a finished writer; he has gone singularly out of fashion, because his style is pompous and diffuse, his composition loose and disconnected, because his reasoning lacks firmness, and his erudition solidity. Still we repeat, that no other German writer of note toward the end of the last century exercised the important indirect influence which it was Herder's privilege to do. (pp. 422-23)

> *Karl Hillebrand, "Herder," in* The North American Review, *Vol. CXVI, No. CCXXXVIII, April, 1873, pp. 389-424.*

ROBERT FLINT (essay date 1874)

[*In the following essay, Flint faults Herder's major arguments in his* Ideas for a Philosophy of the History of Mankind. *According to Flint, Herder repudiates materialism but does not embrace spiritualism. Instead, says Flint, Herder's concept of the spirit is "poor and inadequate."*]

I can easily perceive various faults in ['**Herder's Ideas towards a Philosophy of the History of Mankind**']; the thoughts are often ill-defined, the language often over-exuberant, ultimate principles ignored or feebly grasped, analogies made too much of, the higher stages of civilisation unsatisfactorily treated; and yet I entertain the sincerest admiration for it, as displaying a breadth and truth of general view, a fulness of knowledge, and catholicity of feeling, of the rarest merit. It seems to me to be generally undervalued, because its author had no very eminent capacity for abstract speculation. I admit that he had not; in that respect he was not only far below a Kant or Hegel, but far below a Fichte or Herbert or Krause; yet none the less am I convinced that as regards the philosophy of history, after all that the illustrious chiefs of modern German philosophy have done or caused to be done, there is still need to go back to him, and there may still be found in him some things broader and better than in any of them. None of them had equal width and delicacy of mental susceptibility; in none of them did the relations between nature and man mirror themselves so faithfully on the whole.

It is very difficult to convey even a general notion of a work so comprehensive and rich as his; and, of course, utterly impossible to analyse its 20 books, its 118 chapters, all crowded with thoughts. (p. 376)

The great merit of '**Herder's Ideas towards a Philosophy of the History of Mankind**' is, as I have already hinted, their comprehensive and generally truthful exhibition of man's relationship to the rest of nature. No one before him had nearly equalled him in this respect; and the author who has since surpassed him most, Lotze, in his 'Mikrokosmos,' has avowedly imitated him. This merit must not be underrated. Geographical and climatic conditions and man's own organisation are undoubtedly factors which influence most powerfully all history, and which ought to be appreciated by the historical philosopher as completely as possible.

It is none the less especially to [this work] that whatever truth there is in the criticism of Gans, that '**Herder's Ideas towards a Philosophy of the History of Mankind**' contradict their title by not only banishing all metaphysical categories, but moving in an element of positive hatred to metaphysics," will be found to apply. I do not grant that there is the amount or kind of truth in it that Gans supposes; I deem it no fault or injury to have banished from the territory of historical science the sort of metaphysical categories to which Gans would give rights of citizenship and even of sovereignty; but certainly care must be taken that along with such categories no spiritual properties or powers be banished. And Herder, I fear, cannot be said to have exercised sufficient care in this respect. He repudiated materialism, but was far from adopting a decided spiritualism. He did not conceive of spirit otherwise than as an organic power, which is neither indeed identical with organism nor the function of organism; which, on the contrary, fashions and animates organic matter, yet which is originally the same with all the powers of matter, of irritability, of motion, of life, and merely acts in a higher sphere, in a more elaborate and subtle organisation. . . . With such a conception of spirit, Herder naturally represents it as entirely conditioned by its organism; he even goes so far as to argue in some pages which remind us unpleasantly of Helvetius and La Mettrie, that the *erect posture* of man is the grand characteristic which has determined the differences between his body, brain, mind, and those of the other animals. He supposes a complete coincidence between the spiritual power and the bodily instrument, so that there is nothing in the former which is not expressed in the latter; no innate properties, no latent wealth; that organisation is the full manifestation and measure of spirit. But he does not prove this, nor even try to remove the contradiction which appears to exist between such a supposition and two doctrines which he maintains as of fundamental importance,—viz., that man is free, and that history is a progress. He makes no effort to show how a power essentially identical with those of physical nature, and wholly incorporated in organisation, can be capable of free volition, nor that organic modification keeps pace with social evolution. He seems not to have felt that his conception of spirit made it imperative on him to vindicate his right to believe in liberty and progress. In my opinion his belief in them was as illogical as it was sincere.

His conception of spirit being thus poor and inadequate, he, notwithstanding his admission of liberty and progress, naturally ascribes to the external world and the bodily organisation an influence which is excessive. . . . Hence, as all his critics have remarked, his treatment of the lower and simpler stages of human life is immensely superior to his treatment of the higher; and his insight into the earlier forms of the development of speech, poetry, religion, and into the barbarian and oriental worlds generally, much deeper than that of any of his contemporaries; while his comprehension of the character of the classical nations was widely inferior to that of Lessing and Winckelmann. (pp. 378-80)

The interpretation which Herder gives of the two opening chapters of Genesis is good of its kind; but the kind . . . is radically bad, consisting of a surreptitious substitution of the professed interpreter's own ideas for those of his author.

Herder, in the last ten books of his work, marks the place in history of each nation and age, and this he does often with great truth, always with a noble freedom and breadth of judgment. In one most important respect he decidedly surpassed all his predecessors. He showed a far truer feeling of the rich variety of elements in human life, and of the duty of the historian of humanity to take account of all its aspects. The sympathetic character of his heart, and the synthetic character of his genius, preserved him from anything like narrowness or exclusiveness. And it is just this catholicity, as we may call it, of thought and sentiment, this breadth of conception and affection, which entitles Herder to the high place he must ever hold among those who have sought for a philosophy of history. He has, of course, treated each element and aspect of his subject in a way that seems superficial to the student of the present day who has the advantage of the light diffused by the special researches of eighty intervening years; he has neither adequately traced their separate developments, nor the relations of the separate developments to one another; each element, each epoch is very differently known now from what it was when he wrote; on all particular points—even in regard to art and poetry, which he treated with such wonderfully fine appreciation—Herder is out of date: but yet there is something in Herder which will never be out of date: yea, what is the very essence and life as it were of Herder, his catholicity, his comprehensiveness, can never be outgrown. The philosophy of history must always have incumbent on it as its first duty that of abiding faithful to his universality of spirit and aim. (pp. 381-82)

Humanity may mean the attributes which all human beings as such possess, or the culture of these attributes, or a state resulting from their culture, or an ideal to which human nature ought continually to be approximating although it can never reach it. Which of these does it mean in Herder? He does not tell us; nay, he passes from signification to signification, and interweaves and commingles them in the most hopelessly confused and inextricable way. It cannot reasonably be understood in the first sense, when said to be the end of human nature; for in that sense it is really the sum of the conditions of human nature, or the basis and beginning of human nature. What the highest of human beings aims at, cannot be what the lowest of human beings possesses. Taken in the second sense, humanity means self-cultivation. But is self-cultivation not essentially a means to an end? Does it not imply a standard above and a goal beyond itself? If by humanity be meant a state either actually realised or actually realisable, that state ought to be described. If by it be meant an unattainable ideal, its relation to the realised and realisable must stand in great need of elucidation. Now, Herder far from solving these and similar problems, does not even propose them. He leaves, that is to say, utterly vague and unsettled, the conception on which his whole historical philosophy revolves.

And unfortunately the remark must be extended. It is not only the central conception of his historical philosophy which he has left in this state, but all its general conceptions. He is constantly using such words as nature, fate, liberty, organism, &c., in the same loose, incoherent, and even inconsistent way as he uses the term humanity. In fact, although he had a great and rich intellect, he had not the sort of intellect fitted to deal satisfactorily with general conceptions, to analyse them with closeness and completeness, to separate them clearly and precisely from one another, and to trace with truthfulness their relations both to subordinate and co-ordinate conceptions. He was deficient in the logical qualities required for these exercises of mind.

It must also be acknowledged that he was not successful in his attempt to sum up his system in general theorems. The fifteenth book of his work—that in which he made the attempt—consists of five chapters, each intended to establish or illustrate an important proposition. These five propositions are the following:—

I. The end of human nature is humanity; and that they may realise their end, God has put into the hands of men their own fate.

II. All the destructive powers in nature must not only yield in time to the preservative powers, but must ultimately be subservient to the perfection of the whole.

III. The human race is destined to proceed through various degrees of civilisation, in various revolutions, but its abiding welfare rests solely and essentially on reason and justice.

IV. From the very nature of the human mind, reason and justice must gain more footing among men in the course of time, and promote the extension of humanity.

V. A wise goodness disposes the fate of mankind, and therefore there is no nobler merit, no purer or more abiding happiness, than to co-operate in its designs.

It is scarcely necessary to remark that these five propositions, even if thoroughly established, would be a very inadequate general expression of anything worthy of being called a philosophy of history. And they are far from sufficiently established, either by the speculative considerations, or the historical facts which Herder urges in support of them. The reasonings are feeble, the facts too few; and both reasonings and facts are not unfrequently irrelevant or inconsistent with other reasonings employed, or other uses made by him of the same facts elsewhere. (pp. 385-87)

Robert Flint, ''Herder,'' in his The Philosophy of History in France and Germany, *William Blackwood and Sons, 1874, pp. 375-87.*

JAMES SULLY (essay date 1882)

[*Although Sully does not rank Herder ''among the great European writers,'' he considers his influence in the nineteenth century of major importance. Herder's teachings, says Sully, are a ''step forward'' from rationalism. Sully concludes that Herder ''did much to foster the modern historical attitude of mind.''*]

Nobody would think of claiming for Herder a place among the great European writers. Neither in poetry nor in prose has he left a finished production of commanding literary quality. His chief poem, the *Cid,* is indeed said to be read by *der Gebildete;* [the educated person] but if so, it is not read as Lessing's *Nathan der Weise* is read. And among his voluminous prose writings there is none which approaches Lessing's *Laokoon* in that perennial charm which belongs to the skilful development of ideas and to a noble style. Yet, strange to say, there is hardly a German author—Kant and Goethe being, of course, left out of account—who has been more written about of late. . . .

This lively interest in Herder is due in part to the fact of his peculiar position in the history of German letters. The comparative smallness of this literature has one advantage, that it allows of the most detailed research into the events of its history. And one cannot wonder that among these events one of the most interesting and momentous should seem to be the work of a writer who took an equal part with Lessing in preparing the soil of German literature for its richest yield, who powerfully influenced both by his personal intercourse, and by his writings, the development of Germany's greatest poet, and whose ideas, generously scattered, have since borne fruit in all the leading developments of German thought.

Yet the significance of Herder's work in the history of the national literature, great as it undoubtedly is, does not, I think, fully explain the amount of pious thought which has been bestowed on it. There are some authors, below the rank of the greatest, whose utterances, though having little objective value as enduring literature, interest us profoundly as the revelation of a remarkable individuality. This is emphatically true of Herder. In the heap of ill-fashioned work that he has left we see recorded the upward strivings of an eager spirit into the empyrean of truth, the swift movements of a finely-gifted mind scattering brilliant sparks of thought into all the dark paths of human inquiry. These volumes of hasty pen-work are seen to be the outcome of a wide-ranging and energetic intellectual life. (p. 468)

In the *Fragmente* Herder followed up the attack of Lessing [in his *Literatur-briefe*] on the flimsy and lifeless performances of recent writers. In the introduction he paints the existing condition of German literature in no flattering colours. . . . But he did much more than this or he would not have produced the profound impression which he did. The burden of his message ran somewhat after this fashion. (p. 471)

Here [in the *Fragmente*] was the Rousseau doctrine, a return to the simplicity of nature, transplanted into the region of aesthetics and literary criticism. And looked at from our present point of view, it has the exaggerated look of Rousseauism as a whole. The idea of a poet moulded by all the traditions of culture deliberately setting to work to make himself spontaneous and indigenous after the manner of the primitive bard seems to argue the want of a sense of humour in its propounder. Nevertheless, Herder's teaching held a kernel of vital truth, and therefore turned out to be of lasting consequence. It was a decided step forward from the point of view of last century's rationalism. It was an eloquent plea for the rights of feeling as against those of intellect in matters of poetry, in a style quite above the reach of his teacher Hamann. It vindicated the importance of the primal and universal feelings as constituting the very life-blood of poetry, both early and late, rude and highly wrought. It inculcated the habit of looking at literature imaginatively from within, that is to say, by a reference to the motives and the historical conditions out of which it grew. It was an infusion into criticism of the modern spirit of large historical appreciation. (pp. 471-72)

[In Herder's essay, *On the Spirit of the Hebrew Language (Vom Geist der hebräischen Sprache),*] which, like all his later works, is a fuller development of ideas put forth in his early writings, he may be said to have almost discovered the spirit of early Hebrew literature for modern Europe. Nowhere is his fine appreciation of the first naïve expressions of human sentiment more strikingly exhibited; nowhere more conspicuous his ability to seize the particular shade of national feeling and imagery in its relation to the historical background. In this essay he laid the foundation of that truly historic mode of Biblical interpretation which has been brought to so high a degree of perfection by Ewald and others. (p. 478)

The aim of the [*Ideas for a Philosophy of the History of Humanity (Ideen zur Philosophie der Geschichte der Menschheit)*] is to exhibit human history as a natural process, to account for the stream of events apart from the supposition of external control, of any cause or purpose beyond itself, and solely by viewing man as organically connected with nature, as illustrating the action of the same forces and laws. It was thus a considerable step beyond Lessing's conception of an education of the human race. In working out his plan Herder shows his large penetrating insight into primitive ideas and institutions. And now and again he impresses us with his glimpses of the luminous principles of modern sociology. It is doubtless true that the *Ideen* illustrate Herder's characteristic faults, his want of accurate study, more especially in getting up the later periods of history, his vagueness in conception, his contentment with mere guesses based at most on obscure analogies in place of sound inductions. Nevertheless it remains a landmark in the history of thought. (pp. 478-79)

[In his life, Herder] had done much good work of the sort for which he was pretty certainly best fitted. He had stimulated the mind of his generation on the side of the imagination and the intellect as it is given to few to do. He had quickened those elemental feelings of human nature which are at the root of all vital poetry, and which only a one-sided and artificial culture tends to deaden. He had inspired his age with a larger sense of the worth of things human, and more particularly with an almost loving concern for the earliest records of human experience. He had done much to foster the modern historical attitude of mind, the habit of looking at the complex things of civilisation as a natural growth out of simple origins. In view of this informing spirit which he breathed into his age, it becomes a matter of less consequence that he never reached the rank of consummate master in the literary craft. (pp. 483-84)

James Sully, "Herder," in The Fortnightly Review, *n.s. Vol. XXXII, No. CXC, October 1, 1882, pp. 468-84.*

JOSEPH GOSTWICK   (essay date 1882)

[*Gostwick assesses Herder as a transitional figure between rationalism and Romanticism. Although he maintains that Herder's "genius might have been more creative" had his studies been "less comprehensive," he still believes that Herder "looked farther on and higher than all the poets who were his neighbors at Weimar."*]

The world will not hear of "potential great men"—men who "might have been great painters or great poets." Yet one is tempted to think that Coleridge, if he had not been buried in metaphysics, might have written a finer poem than "Christabel." And it seems probable that, if Herder's studies had been less comprehensive, his genius might have been more creative. But, whatever his rank may be, when he is distinctly estimated as a critic, or as a poet, or as a writer on the philosophy of history, it may be safely asserted, that in the general aim of all his life's work, he looked farther on and higher than all the poets and other literary men who were his neighbours at Weimar. For what was that aim?—Nothing less or lower than a union of practical life with the highest culture and with religion. The general purport of his writings on history, education, and religion cannot be given in a few precise words, but serves to suggest such questions as these:—"What is the use of an education that does not grasp the whole man? What is the worth of our civilization without a higher culture founded on religion? And what is the worth of religion, if it has not power to subdue this real world around us; power to permeate and transmute into a nobler form our common, practical, every day existence."

The souls of other men have been stirred by the same thoughts respecting the ultimate aims of educational religion; yet they especially belong to Herder. His general influence was favourable to the restoration of Christian belief, and his services—since his time too slightly estimated by certain critics—are remarkable, when we consider the character of the times in which he lived. He was well acquainted with Spalding, already named as one among the earliest and most respectable of the rationalists. Herder was Kant's pupil at a time when the "Kritik" was unknown; he lived to see its doctrine widely accepted, and then, with a characteristic courage, he wrote against it. Meanwhile he had done a great part of the work afterwards too largely ascribed to Kant's criticism. As to the general tendency of their work, Kant and Herder were alike in this—under the name of "humanity," they introduced ethical teaching far higher than the doctrine of utility, held by Spalding and other respectable men of his class; and this new ethical teaching was in fact borrowed from Christianity.

These remarks may serve to suggest an answer to a question that here might naturally arise—Why should Herder be noticed next to Lessing? Kant was twenty years older than Herder. The answer to the question is twofold. Lessing . . . had suggested this idea: that ethical Christianity—rightly accepted as a revelation of God's will and reason—may, in the last result of its own evolution, reduce itself to a clear, self-evident law for all men; a law written in the heart. The result so anticipated has

its systematic exposition in Kant's ethical books. . . . But Kant was a systematic philosopher, and it is obviously desirable that systems of philosophy—especially those of Kant, Fichte, Schelling, and Hegel—should be noticed in such an order as may show their true sequence. Moreover, we have to study the relations of culture with Christianity; and philosophy—strictly so called—is only one part of culture. . . . In the course of the years 1781-1803 a rapid transition was made, not alone in the tone in which religious questions were discussed, but also and almost contemporaneously in general culture, especially in poetical literature; and if—next to Lessing—any one man is to be named as the chief prophet of a higher culture, this man is Herder. It may be said that his work is in some respects not easily defined; but it is clear that his influence was great. (pp. 97-9)

[Turning] to Herder's prose writings—it is well known that he is no systematic or doctrinal writer. He speaks as one endowed with intuition, and sees the truth—so far as he sees it—as if by a kind of divination. Yet there are passages where he speaks clearly enough respecting the limitations of his belief. (p. 107)

[One] word cannot tell all that ought to be told, to show the true character and the importance of Herder's position as regards the union of Christianity and culture. He was not a clear writer; he mingled too often the free style and phraseology of poetry with the strict method and careful use of language required by scientific and didactic writing; he but partly unveiled some speculative views that, since his time, have been clearly displayed. All these items of adverse criticism, and many others like them, are true; yet they do not lessen the interest and importance of Herder's intermediate position as representative, partly of the age immediately preceding his own, and partly of that which followed.

That he retained traits of the earlier time is true. This humanitarian teaching might be vaguely described as a continuation and expansion of the utilitarian teaching found in the pages of such writers as Jerusalem, Spalding, and Zolliköfer; but Herder belonged not wholly to their school—a school including the most respectable of all the Lutheran pastors who were classed with the rationalists. Herder retained, with the ethics of the Christian religion, all the enthusiasm and glow of life that can remain united with its teaching, when its central tenet has been rejected. When he spoke, in terms that might be called Utopian, respecting the prospects of "humanity"—his favourite word—he was speaking of the highest results that in some far distant day may be visible, when ethical Christianity shall be united with a universal culture of mankind's highest faculties. (p. 109)

A critic possessing even Lessing's analytic skill, would find some difficulty in the task of giving a clear summary of Herder's religious views. In many instances, one of his passages might be set in contrast against another. In his ethical principles he remains Christian. His writings represent no system, but a world of thoughts, sentiments, and beliefs, where—as regards authority—there is no centre. . . . Taking his writings as a whole—their doctrine, or series of doctrines, their moral tone, their general tendency toward a union of high culture with practical religion—they especially deserve notice; they are at once characteristic of the time when he lived, and representative of tendencies that have been developed in our own age.

Few now read Herder's discursive writings, but it is clear that they have been extensively read, for almost the whole of the teaching contained in them has been repeated in clearer forms of expression. Setting aside books that may be called abstruse—

our lighter essays and reviews, of which the chief characteristic is a union of religion with some freedom of speculation, are to a large extent reproductions of Herder's own ideas, or of thoughts that have been suggested by his writings. (p. 111)

Joseph Gostwick, ''Herder,'' in his German Culture and Christianity: Their Controversy in the Time 1770-1880, *Frederic Norgate, 1882, pp. 88-113.*

W. SCHERER (essay date 1897)

[Herder's] first important works, which he published in Riga, were the **'Fragmente über die neuere deutsche Literatur'** . . . and the **'Kritische Wälder.'** . . . The former were meant to be a continuation of Lessing's 'Literaturbriefe,' while the latter stood in close connection with his 'Laokoon.' In the former Herder wrote like Hamann, in the latter he sometimes reminds us of Lessing. He showed himself throughout to be a careful, enthusiastic, but at the same time critical reader of Lessing, for whom he cherished all through life the greatest reverence. He continued to follow in Lessing's steps when he praised Shakspeare, Homer, and the popular songs. He showed Lessing's spirit too in the tolerance and wide human sympathies which prompted him to rescue barbarian nationalities, so-called dark ages, despised branches of poetry and forgotten poets from oblivion, and to give them their due honour. He sought to determine the boundaries of poetry and plastic art in a different manner from Lessing, and he went beyond Lessing in his endeavours to define the difference between plastic art and painting. He most successfully corrected and amended Lessing's theory of fables and epigrams, but he required, quite in Lessing's spirit, that lyric poetry as well as other kinds should above all be full of movement, progress, and action. But whereas Lessing was in the first place an art-critic, and only secondarily a historian of literature, of Herder the reverse was true: he was first and foremost a historian of literature, and only incidentally an art-critic. Lessing had recourse to his rich literary knowledge in order to find rules of composition and bases of criticism, but Herder studied the literature of all nations and periods for its own sake, and with enthusiastic appreciation. He tried to transport himself into the local and temporary conditions under which literary works had been produced, and to adopt the point of view then prevalent; he sought to be a Hebrew with the Hebrews, an Arab with the Arabs, a Skald with the Skalds, a Bard with the Bards; and in these endeavours, which were strengthened by kindred efforts among English writers of the same time, he proved himself a true pupil of Montesquieu and Winckelmann; their power of appreciating the past lived on in him, and bore new fruit in literature.

Herder showed his sympathetic appreciation of foreign poetry not only as a historian of literature, but also as a translator. His original poems, which evince a characteristic tendency towards didactic narrative, towards allegory, parable, and sacred legend, do not rise to any great merit, but his translations must be reckoned among the classical achievements of German literature. (pp. 87-8)

Herder's art, as a translator, was based on his deep insight into language and poetry in general, their origin, their development, and their relation to each other. In this especially he showed himself to be a disciple of Hamann. 'Poetry is the mother-tongue of the human race,' Hamann had said; a whole world of truth is indeed locked up in the pregnant word, and Herder

was the man to make it yield up its secret. Poetry is older than prose; poetry lives in language, lives in myth, and greets us at the threshold of history. Primitive poetry, the poetry of Nature, in which all Nature acts and speaks, being personified by man, who is all feeling and passion, poetry such as breathes in the songs of barbaric peoples—this, said Herder, is true poetry. The paradise of the Scriptures and Rousseau's ideal natural man meet us purified and transfigured in Herder's thought. He too is convinced that a return to Nature alone will regain us our original and ideal perfection. In his **'Literary Fragments,'** Herder sang the praises of his mother-tongue, its freedom and native force, and it was then already clear to him that the history of the human soul can only be deciphered from its language. His treatise on the **'Origin of Language'** cast the deepest glances into primitive times. His **'Spirit of Hebraic Poetry'** contained his ripest thoughts on the connection between language and poetry. His general views as a historian of literature were revealed in his prize essay on 'The causes of the lowering of taste amongst various nations once distinguished for it.' His fame as a man of universal sympathies, and as a versatile translator, was established by his collection of **'Popular Songs'**]. . . . All forms of lyric poetry were here represented, and the only principle of classification which Herder allowed of in this collection was an aesthetic one, namely, community of subject and sentiment. It is marvellous how Herder was able to appreciate the spirit of these songs, to strike the right note in his translations and retain it throughout, to reproduce exactly not only the feelings, but even the peculiar metre and style of each poem. The whole collection is a series of gems of poetry, all written in exquisite German, and free from the barrenness which meets us in most anthologies.

Herder's scientific work is marked by the same breadth of view and catholic sympathy as his poetry. Many of his thoughts had been uttered before, and few of them are thoroughly worked out; he furnished more suggestions than results, more questions than answers, bold hypotheses, but little argument. But we can well excuse in science the imperfection which is confined to details, and which is but the condition of rising to a wide view of the whole. It may be true that Herder looked at things only from a distance, where the eye deceives and forms melt into one another. Yet his point of view was so well chosen, that he could direct many people to their goals, and indicate the paths which are followed, even in the present day. He took in at a glance the limits and interrelation of the various sciences; and whoever advances to the highest problems in any of the sciences of the human mind, whoever studies history, or the science of language, mythology, or ethnology, whoever collects popular traditions or explores German or Hebrew antiquity, or would trace the development of national peculiarities in all spheres of life, and understand the formative influence of nature upon man—each one of these must reverence Herder as a seer of extraordinary powers. His work teaches on all sides the value which the union of separate departments of science has for the progress of knowledge. And more than this; if the example of Lessing proves how much criticism and poetic activity may advance each other, when combined in one man, the influence of Herder on Goethe shows how much benefit a clear-sighted young poet, thirsting for knowledge, may derive from an equally clear-sighted critic, who has all the resources of history and theory at his command. (pp. 88-90)

W. Scherer, ''Herder and Goethe,'' in his A History of German Literature, *Vol. II, edited by F. Max Muller, translated by Mrs. F. C. Conybeare, Charles Scribner's Sons, 1897, pp. 82-113.**

CHARLES J. LITTLE (lecture date 1904)

[*Little discusses Herder's presentation of the Bible as a "great historical product" and concludes that Herder is one of the first critics to recognize the Bible as a literary work. This excerpt was originally delivered as an address at Northwestern University.*]

Herder was essentially a talking genius; yet a talker moved more by the necessity of self-expression than by the desire to instruct; more by the disposition to compel his reader than to encourage him to independent thought. And especially in his theological writings does the whole man appear; not only *Geist und Vernunft und Verstand* but *Herz und Gemüth.* His **"Letters to Preachers,"** for example, were a fiery protest against reducing Christianity to a bare morality and the pastoral office to mere state service.... This view of the pastor's calling led Herder himself to a study of the Bible according to the law of his own soul. He brought to the Scriptures a sympathetic mind and a heart unchilled and unperverted; he gave the writers of the Bible a chance, as he had given Homer and Shakespeare a chance, to make their own impression. In this he resembled every great thinker who has shaped the thought of the world touching God's revelation of himself—Paul, Origen, Augustine, Luther, Pascal, Wesley; who never approach the sacred scriptures of mankind as analysts and critics merely, least of all the Christian Scriptures. To Herder the Bible was a great historical product; the fruitage of generations of life.... This life, this history, from which our religion has come, can of course be understood thoroughly only in connection with the large human life of which it is a part. All forms of light are forms of the same radiant energy, diverse though they be. Even so all forms of religion are forms of the same divine energy, diverse though they be.... [Herder] was the chief of those that led the way to the study of all religions in their essence and in their relations to each other; he grasped, as no one had done since the days of St. Paul, the fact that the whole world, not Israel only, had knowledge of the law of God.... (pp. 199-200)

[But Herder went farther] and in going farther anticipated the thought that has dominated these recent decades, the historical conception of nature, of life, of humanity—the tremendous thought of evolution; and this saved Herder from a purely natural theology. For he saw that nations as well as individuals have their peculiar endowments; that as the Greeks were the more artistic so the Hebrews were the more religious people, and this too by a divine arrangement. His *Archaeology of the Hebrews* combined the result of his researches in the early history of poetry and in the origins of religion....

He pursued this subject farther in his famous *Spirit of Hebrew Poesy.* Perhaps no single work has done so much as this one to transform conceptions of the Old Testament. It opened the way to the beauty of these remarkable writings and to the discovery of their sources. (p. 202)

> Charles J. Little, "Herder and Religious Thought," in Methodist Review, Vol. LXXXVI, No. 2, March-April, 1904, pp. 199-207.

GEORGE SAINTSBURY (essay date 1904)

[*Saintsbury was an English literary historian and critic of the late nineteenth and early twentieth centuries. A prolific writer, Saintsbury composed a number of histories of English and European literature as well as several critical works on individual authors, styles, and periods. Although he states that Herder's work "scarcely ever compresses and crystallises itself into a solid and fiery thun-*

derbolt of literary expression," Saintsbury still regards Herder as an important and influential critic. Further, he argues that Herder's most significant contribution was his comparative study of literature which emphasized the appreciation of folk songs. Herder's contribution as a teacher of the German people was, Saintsbury says, "invaluable."]

[There] is what I can only call a certain fearful *woolliness* about Herder's literary work. It scarcely ever compresses and crystallises itself into a solid and fiery thunderbolt of literary expression. He himself, in the very forefront of [the *Fragmente*], speaks of "Die liebe Göttin Langeweile," "the dear Goddess Ennui," as having "hunted many, if not most people, into the arms of the Muses." I am afraid it must be said that in his own case the dear Goddess did not understand where her mission as matchmaker ended, and is too frequently present at the interviews of man and Muse.

In the second place, that pedagogic instinct which has been noted, which is so excusable and so praiseworthy in him and in his contemporaries, when we consider their circumstances and *milieu,* interferes somewhat disastrously with the freedom and the lasting interest of his writing. The Latin nations, by their inheritance of real or supposed prerogative from Latin itself, we English by our alleged national self-sufficiency, escape this in greater or less degree. All the four, Italians, French, Spaniards, English, take themselves in their different degrees and manners for granted; they are "men," if only in the University sense. The Germans of the mid-eighteenth century are, and take themselves for, schoolboys: it is greatly to their credit, but it does not precisely make them good reading without a great deal of good will. Lastly Herder, as it seems to me (though, no doubt, not to others), in consequence of this sense of dissatisfaction with his own literature, climbs too rapidly to generalisations about the relation of literature itself to national character, and to the connection of literature, generally with the whole idea of humanity. All this is noble; but we are in a bad position for doing it. It will be a capital occupation for persons of a critical temperament when humanity has come to an end—which it has not even yet, and which it certainly had still less in Herder's time.

These general disadvantages are indeed compensated by general merits of a very eminent kind. Stimulated by Hamann, by Lessing, and by his own soul, Herder betook himself, as nobody had done before him, to the comparative study of literature, to the appreciation of folksong (perhaps his best desert), to the examination of Ancient, Eastern, Foreign literature in comparison with German. This is his great claim to consideration in the history of literature and of criticism: and it is so great a one that in general one is loath to cavil even at the most extravagant expressions of admiration that have been lavished upon him.

But individual examination of his works revives the objections taken above. For instance, the early *Fragmente zur Deutschen Litteratur* has an almost unique *relative* interest. I do not know where to look for anything like it as a survey (or rather a collection of studies) of a literature at a given period of its development. On the language; on the prosody; on the "rhetoric" in the narrow-wide sense, of German after the close of the Seven Years' War; on the chief authors and kinds of its literature; on a vast number of minor points, positive and comparative, in relation to it, Herder lavishes an amount of filial devotion, of learning, of ability, which is quite admirable. Taken *absolutely,* the value and the interest, and therefore the admiration, shrink a little.

The *Kritische Walder,* which followed the *Fragmente* in a couple of years, are occupied, first, with a sort of continuation of the work of Winckelmann and of Lessing in the *Laocoön* (a continuation which, like its forerunners, busied itself chiefly with the arts other than literature), and then with some work of Lessing's enemy, Klotz, somewhat more directly literary in kind. Klotz, however, had busied himself, and Herder necessarily busies himself in turn, with general questions of the moral-literary type, especially in reference to Homer and Virgil. The book is full of those curious *Rettungen* or "whitewashings." . . . But it has not very much for us.

There is some more, though the quality may be differently appreciated by different persons, in the Prize Essay of 1773 on the *Causes of the Decline of Taste in Different Nations:* and a great deal more in the twenty years later *Ideen zur Geschichte und Kritik der Poesie und bildenden Künste.* In the first, Herder develops (not of course for the first time, for Montesquieu had given the line long before, if he had not applied it much to literature, and Du Bos had started it before *him,* and Vico had in a manner anticipated both; but for the first time in a wide, and at the same time not loose, application to literature itself) the idea of Age- and Race-criticism—the close conjunction of a general conception of the characteristics of a time and a country with the phenomena observed or supposed to be observed in groups of literary production. In the second, at once generalising further, and descending to further particulars, we have an attempt to connect literature with general characteristics of humanity, and almost innumerable critical experiments of this process, on different authors and schools and kinds.

Anything that has to be said in general on these processes is for the Interchapters; but we may here repeat that no one can well exaggerate their historical importance or the influence that they have exercised since. Further, the merit of their combined precept and example, in directing study at once to those features which are common in all literature, and to the individual bodies by comparison of which the general features are discernible, is quite beyond question. The Prize Essay has perhaps the main defects of its kind, that of "figuring away" in plausible gyration, without bringing home any very solid sheaves, or even leaving any definite path. But the immense Miscellany of the *Ideen* more than makes up for this. Herder's general scheme, here, in the *Adrastea,* in that *Aurora* (suggested by the dawn of the nineteenth century) which he only planned, and which was but a small part of the huge adventures for which he died lamenting his lack of time, may be described as that of a mediaeval collection of *Quoestiones Quodlibetales,* methodised by the presence throughout of his leading practical and theoretic ideas. These were, as has been said, the necessity of enriching German literature with material, and furnishing it with patterns, "plant," and processes, by the study of *all* literature, ancient and modern, as a practical and immediate aim; and the working out of the notions of literature, as connected with the country, and literature, as connected with the general race, for ultimate goal.

But, owing to the enormous *dissipation,*—the constant flitting from flower to flower which his task imposed on him,—Herder was not and could not be a very important critic on particular points. He was bound to share the over-valuation of [James McPherson's] *Ossian*—for was not *Ossian* exactly what was wanted to dissolve and lubricate the *sècheresse* [dryness] of French-German enlightenment, and did it not appear to give a brilliant new example of "national" literature? So we must not overblame him for this, any more than we must overpraise

him—while praising him heartily—for having been undoubtedly the main agent in inoculating the Germans with Shakespeare. Elias Schlegel had begun the process, and Hamann had continued it; but the first was cut off too early for him to do more than make a beginning, and Hamann's mission was rather to send others, including Herder himself, than to work directly upon the general. It is also fair to say that, with all his soaring ideals and world-wide aspirations of mental travel, there was little *Schwärmerei* [worshipful enthusiasm] about Herder, except in a few semi-poetical passages, which can easily be skipped. His judgment is a pretty sound and sensible one, if his taste is not infallible—. . . and the equally modest and intelligent observations which follow on the impossibility of emulating or surpassing the special qualities of foreign literatures, however useful these literatures may be for study. To any nation Herder must have been a useful and stimulating teacher; to the Germans at this time he was simply invaluable. (pp. 355-59)

> *George Saintsbury, "Goethe and His Contemporaries," in his* A History of Criticism and Literary Taste in Europe from the Earliest Texts to the Present Day: Modern Criticism, Vol. III, *1904. Reprint by William Blackwood & Sons Ltd., 1935, pp. 351-405.*

MARTIN SCHÜTZE   (essay date 1921)

[*Unlike most commentators, Schütze defends Herder's methods of critical analysis. While Herder's theories are somewhat dated, Schütze says, his critical methods are "unassailable." Schütze particularly praises Herder's concept of personality based on character traits. In this theory, Herder synthesizes the idea that "every concrete individual is essentially different from every other and can never be replaced." Herder, Schütze concludes, "is the first to carry the principle of individualization to its proper conclusions."*]

[Herder] did not limit the principle of personality, as was the custom of eighteenth-century ideology, to an abstract, absolute atomic unit called man, but endeavored to trace it in every important, concrete relation which an unequaled gift of specific discernment revealed to him. All of which comes to this, that he was the first to realize and fully set forth the fundamental truth that the essence of personality can be found, not in any abstract conception of individuality, but only in a synthetic unity (which one might liken to the molecular entities of physics) of characteristic traits. The eighteenth-century atomism really destroyed the substance of individuality by eliminating the characteristic part of each concrete form of personality. It was Herder, in transforming Leibnitz' too abstract conception of the monad, who attained to the idea on which rests the fundamental belief of modern humanism, and which is its only fortress against the forces of regimentation which are growing ever stronger in the present age—the belief that every concrete individual is essentially different from every other and can never be replaced.

In Herder's view, the synthetic principle of personality as individuated spontaneity is primary but not absolute; it is universal, yet infinitely differentiated; it is an integral part of the general physical, physiological, biological, in short, the entire mechanical, organism of nature and yet embodies a wholly spontaneous, autonomous, and responsible force. The one problem at the roots of all his ideas was, therefore, to trace the empirical forms of personality in all their chief relations and to define the spontaneous part of each of these forms as the characteristic residue which could in no manner, except by overgeneralization and indiscriminate assumption, be reduced to the terms of mechanical science or rationalistic objective abstraction. He has thereby fixed the problem of personality in philosophy as well as in science. (pp. 113-14)

Herder's gift of specific discernment and virile sense of relevance in the interpretation of each concrete detail of these varying relations is unsurpassed. His fundamental problems are substantially the problems of present humanism. And with his extraordinary power of imagination and criticism he combined a tireless energy and an indefatigable zeal which have made him both the most philosophic and the most inspiring critic. Many of the details of his information are now obsolete, much of his history is wrong, many of his scientific hypotheses are now merely rudimentary guesses, as all concrete facts of information become either commonplace or false in the course of time, yet his methods of analysis, his standards of relevance and specific bearing, his genius for seizing upon the crucial part of the expressions of personality remain substantially unassailable. He has revealed the principal factors of individual spontaneity in its characteristic activities, and laid down, once for all, the essential forms of combination and the criteria of these entities. Thus he is, to a far higher degree and, above all, to a much more specific and definite effect than the present age realizes, the father of modern mechanism. . . .

Herder's greatest critical competence and principal imaginative interests lay in the field of literature. Regarding, as he did, language as the chief associative function of the mind, and literature as the "discourse of perfect sensibility," i.e., the discourse in which the activities of all the senses attained fullest unity, he could not but judge representative literature the truest and most characteristic expression and record of the spirit of man. (p. 115)

He was the first modern critic and poet to collect the best and most representative poetical productions of all the peoples to which he had access. This, the first international thesaurus, he translated with great skill and fidelity, and analyzed with the discriminating sympathy and the enthusiasm, both disinterested and purposeful, which distinguishes the great humanist. He hoped thus, by precept and example, to awaken the genius of his own people, and with it that of all the others, to a new springtide of creative idealism. (p. 117)

Herder's critical method, simple in principle but infinitely varied and flexible in application, is inherent in his theory of personality. He applies the test of individual integrity, not only to the matter of literary discourse, but to every part of form, from the general principles of structure and diction to every detail of technique. All form is secondary to the specific individuality which it invests and to which it holds an integral, organic relation analogous to that of the shape of a tree with respect to its nature. All fixed, external standards and rules of form are rejected. With this inevitable conclusion, the antagonism between his and the pseudo-classical or rationalistic theory of aesthetic becomes irreconcilable.

Some characteristic applications of the relativity, which he attributed to all parts of the genuine manifestations of personality, appear in the following conclusions: If an individual spirit, forming and appropriating a true expression, is rugged or savage, the form must be likewise; if simple and downright, so must be the utterance; if complex, like the "natures" of the personalities of the Shakespearean age, the form must be analogous; and so forth.

Herder thus is the first to carry the principle of individualization to its proper conclusions. (p. 121)

Herder's literary theory is a theory of organic relativity. It cannot be doubted that such a conception, provided it avoid the false simplicity and purely subjective conception of integrity pertaining to Romanticism, that is, provided it include, as in Herder's investigations it did, all the proper factors, both objective and subjective, is the ideal of a true interpretation of *Geistesgeschichte,* of the history of the characteristic manifestations of the human mind, which is the essence of humanism. For it is, as Herder never tires of asserting, in this creative method, that the production and the interpretation of folk literature in the highest sense, are identical.

This creative and critical identity of the personalities of author and audience is in Herder's view the specific character of classicity. This classicity Herder identified with "nature." (p. 122)

[Herder's] identification of folk literature with the classic or standard, i.e., the representative and best part of the literature of a people, and also with "nature," involves an idealization, i.e., a selection determined by a judgment of value. It also implies that the collective personality embodied in folk literature is the highest form of personality. We are here confronted with a very profound and interesting problem. It is impossible to dispose of it by the simple expedient of assuming, as is generally done, that Herder's final basis of judgment is aesthetic. For that term itself is not as simple as it appears to the rationalistic mind. Herder's conclusion of the integral union of all matters of literary and artistic substance and form with individual personality has removed aesthetics from its position of independence and isolation and made it an organic part of the entire problem of personality.

The idealization involved in Herder's results is therefore not of a purely formal character nor determined by a subjective choice, such as is supposed to be characteristic of a purely "aesthetic" judgment, but it is the verdict of the totality of one's judgment of the highest values of life itself. Herder's conclusions compel a fundamental synthesis of ultimate ethical with purely formal values, conditioned not by arbitrary subjective preference but by all the concrete facts of reality or the laws of nature. In other words, this idealization is itself the result of the same method and the same comprehensive reach of induction which are characteristic of Herder's other inquiries. They too are inherent in his primary principle of personality. (pp. 122-23)

Herder's identification of the individual peoples on the one hand, and of all humanity on the other, with nature, produces an apparent vagueness in the meaning of the latter. This vagueness, for which he has been much criticized, exists, however, only if we, as his critics do, assume in accordance with technical rationalistic philosophy the primacy of the general term, that is, in this case, if we suppose that an assumption of a general "nature" is the standard for all humanity and therefore for each "natural" individual. The matter becomes clear, however, if we bear in mind the essential principle in Herder's order of thought, which is inherent in his inductive method, to wit, that the more general is secondary to the more concrete conception, and therefore not absolute but relative. (p. 123)

His method of presentation in [his essays on poetry] differs from the first *Wäldchen* and from some others, as, for instance, that on the origin of language, in its extremely synthetic arrangement, which without the clue offered by the theory of personality is likely to lead to misunderstanding and to give an impression of confusion. His mind, passionate and creative, gifted with an immense capacity for assimilating knowledge and with a very vivid and energetic power of specific discernment, together with an extraordinary vision embracing a multiplicity of interconnections between details superficially far apart—a vision that, as it were, continually hovered over the whole range of knowledge and legitimate inference; sensitive to every glint of analogy and quick in the pursuit of the specific suggestions borne by the latter; ceaselessly illumined by flashes of insight and surprised and delighted by new avenues of surmise and combination; sparkling with the ever varying play of secondary but interesting detail, multitudinous as the ripples in a sunlit sea; prompted by an untiring and rich poetic imagination—a mind so abundant found a strictly analytic form of statement, in which each important idea could be expressed only once, too bald and rigid. He desired to assert the whole synthetic mass of his main ideas again and again in each group of its every augmenting combinations and ever ramifying distinctions. He craved to hold in one inspired, simultaneous image, in one living and continuous focus of unity, the sum of his knowledge.

Herder's statements, at their best, are clear and beautiful, rich and pregnant, and convey a fuller and more varied conception of the endless interrelation of the ideas pertaining to the focus of his interpretation than an analytic statement could make. It must be said, however, that at other times they are vexatious, requiring some efforts of simplification. A number of misinterpretations of his work have arisen from a complexity of presentation, caused not by the exigencies of the synthetic order, but rather by inadequacy of means of expression and arrangement, an inadequacy which is the inevitable burden of every thinker who leaves the beaten track to find new paths. By far the greater number of misunderstandings are, however, the results of attempts, inherited from the rationalistic and especially the Kantian critics of Herder, to force his interpretations and generalizations into the very forms of thought which it was the primary motive and character of Herder's critical labor to challenge. The theory of personality is fundamentally incompatible with the objective absolutism of Rationalism, and any attempt to subject it to the standards of the latter involves a *petitio principii*, i.e., an assumption of the principle at issue. Rationalism, before applying its characteristic tests to Herder's principle, is obliged to justify anew its primary assumptions in so far as they are at variance with the crucial tests demanded by Herder's view.

The blemishes adhering to Herder's mode of statement do not in themselves justify the common assumption, shared by both philosophical and literary critics of Herder, that his critical methods are confused. A synthetic, even a congested, form of statement is not necessarily proof of lack or confusion of analysis in critical method. Even in his most complex statements, patient scrutiny will reveal the persistence of his leading ideas and a power of discrimination, which rarely commits, and almost never persists in, essential errors. (pp. 125-27)

> *Martin Schütze, "The Fundamental Ideas in Herder's Thought: III," in* Modern Philology, *Vol. XIX, No. 2, November, 1921, pp. 113-30.*

MARGARET SHERWOOD (essay date 1934)

[*In the following excerpt, Sherwood traces Herder's conceptions of literature, art, and religion. She considers Herder a "pathfinder" and notes that his ideas concerning organic evolution prompted a resurgence in the study of the humanities. In conclusion, Sherwood states that Herder had "but one thing, one great thing to say, and many ways of saying it." She also notes the way in*

which his theories touched all areas and fields of study: literature and language, as well as scientific theory.]

There is exhilaration in tracing even a few of the ideas of Herder; it would be a brave person who would think that he could grasp or expound even a major part of the ideas that grew so swiftly in that teeming brain. No other name in the history of the German reaction in thought is more significant than his. There is cause for wonder that no one has, for English readers at least, put into brief form such an interpretation of Johann Gottlieb Herder as would make after generations conscious of their deep indebtedness to him. For that indebtedness of the whole of the nineteenth century, and, one would gladly add, the twentieth also, can hardly be overestimated. A bold and original thinker, already in his precocious youth, at twenty-two, in his *Fragments on the New German Literature, (Fragmente . . .),* he set forth ideas that were to revolutionize the study of language and literature, and other aspects of the intellectual and spiritual life of man, not only in Germany but in other lands. . . .

To Herder, more than to any other single thinker we owe those conceptions whereby the life of man, in its intellectual, its spiritual, its creative aspects, as expressing itself in language, in literature, in myth, in religion, is interpreted, not through rationalistic conceptions, in terms of the abstract, defined, limited, but in terms of life, of growth, development,—a conception which has since, increasingly, dominated the mind and imagination of the modern world, determined the methods of its scholarship. His first important utterances, made in *Fragmente,* affirm that the same law of change which operates in the physical life of individuals and of races, operates also in the intellectual and spiritual life of mankind. (p. 124)

In turning over the pages of the *Fragmente* one wonders at first, so familiar now are the ideas, why . . . they ran through Germany like a train of gunpowder, why the effect was so great. The work is fragmentary indeed, discursive, suggestive, no reasoned philosophical treatise with demonstration of a single theme. It touches on many topics and many writers; it is full of interpretations, and of thought-provoking assertions,— protests against the imitation, on the part of his countrymen, of the language and literature of the French; against the educational tyranny whereby a dead language, Latin, is made to crush living German speech. It is the work of a young man, groping his way toward those living conceptions of truth most ably presented years later in his *Outlines of a Philosophy of the History of Man (Ideen zur Philosophie der Geschichte der Menschheit).* (p. 125)

The idea that early human speech was a song, or poetry, springing from feeling, and that poetry is the common possession of all peoples, is the moving force in all Herder's interpretation of poetry, his special note in the eighteenth century cry of a return to nature. A lover of the poetry of the Bible, of primitive song,—in this influenced in youth by his friend, the prophet and sage Hamann, and by Percy's *Reliques* (1765), which made great stir in Germany, he set forth in his contribution to *Von deutscher Art und Kunst* . . . his plea for the beauty of primitive poetry, unstudied, irregular, emotional, unselfconscious. . . . Here is presented the idea, representing much of Herder's greatest service, of the worth, the significance of primitive song, which springs from the life, the whole life, of simple people, and from all the powers, not disintegrated by thought, reflection. In such poetry, life in its simplicity and its fulness is presented, with reality not found in the work of the present day,—wherein verses are polished and repolished which represent no genuine passion, thought, or imagining. . . . In Herder's thought, each individual race must keep through all phases of its development, something of its native genius, if poetry is to be poetry indeed.

It is true that he mistakes Macpherson's *Ossian* for pure, primitive poetry, but, if his example is wrong, his principle is right. Even Macpherson's *Ossian* did not deserve to be translated into German hexameters! One gains the impression that, for him, the music, the sound was the very self of folk song, an identity of form and content in indissoluble melody. (pp. 126-27)

In his remarkable translations in **Von Deutscher Art und Kunst** of Scotch and English ballads and of Shakespeare songs, and later in his great collection of songs of all people, **Volkslieder** . . . , Herder shows a skill that almost belies his creed as to the untranslateableness of poetry. For this he had a special gift; in feeling, diction, cadence these translations give charm for charm of the original. But there is irony in the fact that his original verse is stiff, didactic; it is only in translations that he can exemplify his theory of poetry, of simplicity, melody, outpouring of emotion in words that are feeling and combinations of words that are music, so far in him did the critical, and appreciative faculty outstrip the creative.

Working throughout Herder's early critical writings, curiously unifying remarks which have a tendency to become discursive, is his perception of vital process in all aspects of the life of humanity. He gives us not only new thought, but a new manner of thought; a new way of interpreting; it is as if his very mind breathed. Birth, growth, decay in all that pertains to the life of man,—this is one of those truths as obvious as breathing, so obvious that it takes genius to discover it! From first to last, through all his manifold studies of language, primitive poetry, literature, myth, his thought was tending in one direction, his mind, through intuitions, imaginative insight, reasoned opinions, was working one way. (pp. 127-28)

Herder's ideas are most fully presented in his **Outlines of a Philosophy of the History of Man (Ideen zur Philosophie der Geschichte der Menschheit)**. . . . (p. 131)

Book V of Herder's **Ideen** contains a fine plea for belief in immortality, as a necessary consequence of the logic of growth. No power can perish; there is no instance of it in nature. (pp. 132-33)

Herder was fully abreast with the most advanced scientific thought of his time, and contributed to it. His treatise may seem in many ways antiquated, but one finds there an interpretation of evolution that makes one feel the sweep of the one life through all the varied forms, in their inexhaustible fertile variety and individuality, their unceasing development. If scientists owe him a debt, poet and philosopher owe him a greater, for his deeper understanding of the import of the facts involved, his imaginative insight into their potential meaning. Significant on the physical side, the outstanding import of his work is spiritual. . . . In his suggestion of the trial and error method apparent in the development of both body and soul; in his idea that all destructive powers must yield in time to maintaining powers, and be ultimately subservient to the consummation of the whole; in his affirmation that "all the errors of man are mists of truth," ideas are expressed that have left their impress on philosopher and poet. (p. 133)

In reading the **Ideen** one has that freshness of intellectual experience that comes from following the steps of a pathfinder, and this delight, which is ever great, is never deeper than in

watching the changing phases of thought of this period, as man passed from a conception of himself as fixed, stationary, in a stationary universe, governed by inflexible, mechanical law, to an interpretation of himself as inextricably involved in the whole inner scheme of things, his fibres inwrought with the fibres of the universe, an organic part of a vast living, developing whole.

Herder makes a great, original and distinctive contribution to this conception, his greatest originality lying in his application of the idea of organic development to the intellectual, the spiritual, the creative life of man, and his influence is paramount in passing from static to dynamic conceptions in the interpretation of these aspects of human achievement. It is impossible to estimate accurately, perhaps impossible to overestimate, the work of Herder. When Hillebrand [see excerpt above, 1873] says that in his work "all the new ideas which have animated the intellectual world during fifty years are in germ"; and: "No one, Kant perhaps alone excepted, has contributed more to the stock of German thought, or has ever exercised a greater or more lasting influence over an age, a nation, or the world at large," adding that the *Ideen* has been the father to all the histories of poetry, religion, language, and law of our century, he probably does not exaggerate. If, earlier, Montesquieu had suggested the influence of environment in the development of human characteristics; if Winckelmann, and in slighter degree, Lessing, had employed something of the historical method; it remained for Herder to develop it, to relate it to a central conception of the organic nature of all life, and to broadcast this idea in manifold new applications. (pp. 133-34)

The "ideas" of Herder became philosophy, metaphysic, philology, history, comparative mythology, flashing, quicksilver-like, through all the world of thought. It was under the influence of the idea of organic evolution that the humanities came to life, and this idea has profoundly and permanently changed the way of interpreting man's life and man's thought. It is hardly possible to take up a treatise on any aspect of human existence or human activities without finding it permeated with these ideas of cohesion in the affairs of men, of organic development in their inner lives and their achievements, as throughout the universe.

Students of literature, in particular, owe Herder a greater debt than most of them realize. That belief in poetry as a natural growth among all races, the outcome of instincts common to all, has had far-reaching consequences in the regeneration of poetic theory in many lands, and in the inspiration of new poets. Equally potent has been his idea of the indissoluble nature of content and form in lyric verse, the soul of each race finding expression in its own peculiar rhythm of thought, feeling, and sound. Again, the idea of drama as having an inherent, living unity, grounded in nature, its form shaped by the imaginative insight of genius into the heart of great struggle, while it owed something to Lessing, contributed more to Schlegel and to Coleridge, and became the foundation of our later theory of drama. (pp. 135-36)

There is youth in the vitality, the vigor, the continual springing up of fresh ideas in Herder's mind, as in the pushing of green shoots through the earth, under the falling of spring rain. His feeling of life, growth,—his very temperament is an inherent part of the thought which was to work so potently in the intellectual revolution. His was a new and subtle consciousness of the inner working of nature in language, in literature, in all aspects of the intellectual and spiritual life of humanity; it is as if nature herself, finding a voice wherewith to express herself, were revealing her very mind and imagination, her secret, inner processes. *The life in things:* in apprehending this lies the originality of the man who was the leader of the leaders in the critics', the scholars' revolution. In whatever he touches, language, folk-song, the whole development of the human race, he puts his finger on the very pulse of life there, gets to the very springs of being; this is his peculiar genius.

In that world of dry rationalism, of dualism, of the eighteenth century, with little conception of the relation of mind to body, Herder's thought is marvel. (p. 146)

Like most geniuses, he had but one thing, one great thing to say, and many ways of saying it. His life work was the application of this idea in different fields: the laws of literary development, of the development of language, of myth, of religion, and, in his greatest work, the *Ideen,* the laws, physical, intellectual, spiritual, of all that is. In all this he was a suggestor, rather than a demonstrator; his manner was gentle, his voice was not strong, and his pen was unable to do justice to the fulness of his thought. (pp. 146-47)

Margaret Sherwood, "Herder and His Background: An Appreciation," in her Undercurrents of Influence in English Romantic Poetry, *Cambridge, Mass.: Harvard University Press, 1934, pp. 114-47.*

MARY M. COLUM (essay date 1937)

[Herder] had what Lessing lacked—the lyrical mind. Lessing was learned, witty, satirical, profound: he could analyze to the depths any type of literature except the lyrical, and this drawback made him somewhat lacking in the comprehension of every kind of poetry. He was never the equal of Herder in understanding the workings of the poetic mind. . . . [Herder] had the lyrical mentality, and because of this was naturally the poetic-critical mind as Lessing was the philosophical-critical mind. The aims of both critics were the same: to create a new German literature, to free the minds of their countrymen from the shackles of pseudo-classicism and the rule-making criticism of pedants. Both had the same belief that literature was the product of national conditions, both had the same dislike of classical French drama, the same passion for English literature and for Shakespeare. But where Lessing was guided by reason, Herder, who had a fiery, eager poet's mind, was guided by flashes of intuition; it was his glory and his defect that his mind worked in flashes. Where Lessing gave up his mind to the study of drama and the development of literary and aesthetic ideas, Herder gave his chiefly to the study of poetry, which he declared "ought to be the most impetuous and self-assured daughter of the human soul." (pp. 38-9)

[Herder] announced that the Greeks, after all, were only the Greeks, and that they had never been brought into the world to furnish artistic norms for all men to the end of time. The literature of the Greeks was like every other literature: a product of national conditions which could not be duplicated in another country, in another age. . . . Herder did for poetry a service that Lessing was not capable of doing: he awakened the latent lyricism of the Germans. He announced that poetry was the mother tongue of mankind, that the first authors of every nation are its poets, that the earliest poetry in a nation's history, being the most spontaneous, is the greatest: that is, the poetry of Homer, of the Bible, and, he added, the newly discovered poetry of Ossian. (pp. 39-40)

Strongly as he believed that literature, and especially poetry, was national and racial expression, it can be deduced from his work that there was one form of literature, at least, which from its very nature had to be international, and that was criticism. Literary ideas, no matter where they have had their rise, are equally the inheritance of all literatures that can avail themselves of them. Starting from this thought he became the initiator of the study of comparative literature, a necessary outgrowth of modern criticism. (pp. 42-3)

Not only did Herder start the study of comparative literature, he was one of the initiators of the modern manner of studying history, and his *Philosophy of History* played a great rôle in the method of writing history. No doubt he was influenced in this work by the ideas of that strange seventeenth-century philosopher, Vico. However, while no one can pretend that any new idea comes into being without antecedents, the fact remains that Herder exerted the greatest influence in starting people's minds on a new conception of history. "History has been transformed," said Taine, writing nearly a hundred years afterwards, "within a hundred years in Germany [that is, since Herder's *Philosophy of History*], within sixty years in France, and that by a study of their literatures." That is to say, the transformation was brought about by the application of Herder's thought. It is true that he was never able to outline his ideas with precision as Lessing could and did: his intuitions were often expressed in loose, cloudy, flowery language. Yet in its own loose way his mind sowed the seeds of as many ideas as did Lessing's. All those later critical theories explaining literature by the time and place, or accounting for it as an expression of society, are to be found in germ in Herder's work. His influence on the philosophers was marked; some of Hegel's aesthetics being simply certain ideas of Herder's, pondered over, systematized, and philosophically stated—notably, the idea of the race, milieu, and moment referred to previously, and which was taken over by Taine. Both Herder and Lessing, powerfully influenced a series of German philosophers, beginning with Hegel and Fichte—Fichte's famous *Addresses to the German Nation* being simply a metaphysical and political expression of the literary theories of these two great critics. (pp. 43-4)

While stressing the originality and power of both Herder and Lessing, it is not to be denied that they were deeply influenced by certain of their predecessors. . . . Where they found ideas that fitted in with theirs or could be used to help along the creation of the new literature they had in mind they took them over and formed their own construction on them. This is what all the important critics have done: those who came after Lessing and Herder in their turn used the ideas of these first modern critics as a foundation for their own contribution. For these two were the founders of a new school of literature, and that means the revealers of a new side of life; they emphasized a different side of man from the one which for so long had been exploited in literature: that product of the Enlightenment, the uniformitarian man, went into the background. A great renewal of life and literature had suddenly begun. (p. 46)

Mary M. Colum, "Modern Literature Begins: The Ideas of Lessing and Herder," in her From These Roots: The Ideas That Have Made Modern Literature, *1937. Reprint by Kennikat Press, 1967, pp. 18-46.**

A. GILLIES (essay date 1947)

Thanks to Herder, Romantic yearning became self-conscious. It became the subject of literature, along with every other aspect of the ''modern spirit'' which Romanticism endeavoured to portray. It was his doctrine that we should emulate the ancients by striving to reproduce in modern literature the whole range of modern civilization, as ancient literature—so he believed—reproduced all ancient civilization. Since modern meant post-classical, it was deemed to include medieval. It was Herder who in Germany pointed to the pulsing colour of the Middle Ages, to the romances and legends of kings and knights, popes and beggars, *jongleurs* [jugglers] and crusaders, monks and maidens in distress, all the change and variety and unrest which mark the progress of medieval life. No more comprehensive or fascinating picture of that epoch could have faced the young German Romanticists in their years of adolescence than that which he drew. (p. 402)

It is difficult to imagine what German literature would have been without Herder. He inspired the poetic evolution of Goethe, the balladry of Bürger; the whole spiritual atmosphere of the Storm and Stress; the basic philosophy of German Classicism and the teachings of Romanticism were alike the outcome of his work. His emphasis upon spontaneity and naturalness, his substitution of feeling for reason as the guide of poetical and human behaviour, his discovery of the historical sense began a revolution in German literature which has had no end. . . . Germany has been driven to probe more and more deeply into herself as she has struggled to find stability. Introspection has led to titanic despair, exaggerated over-sensitivity, and arrogant self-sufficiency by turns. The crisis which Herder initiated still awaits a permanent remedy.

Herder's own remedy, the fruit of his historical studies and his religious convictions, was the doctrine of *Humanität*—the fullest and finest flowering of the best in human nature; and unfortunately it has not endured. It did not endure, perhaps, because it represented too precarious a balance between the changeless dogma of the Christian and classical ethic and the relativistic teaching of his evolutionary history. It did not endure, moreover, because succeeding generations did not see ''the fullest and finest flowering of the best in human nature'' quite as Herder saw it. The historical approach was fundamental to all Herder's work, as it was to his literary criticism. He was always tracing origins and development, and it was quite logical that in the end his whole attention should be given to writing an all-embracing history of mankind, and to discovering what constitutes the sum total of human endeavour and human achievement. This he did in his ***Ideen zur Philosophie der Geschichte der Menschheit.*** It is a book which makes stimulating reading even today, and its influence, inside and outside Germany, has been incalculable. Indeed, the assumption is not unreasonable that modern history might well have shaped itself differently had it not been for this book, for it is not too much to say that from it has grown no small part of the problem of Eastern Europe.

Herder's purpose in studying human history was to explain it as illustrating and teaching the truths of religion, ''the progress of God in nature, the intentions which the Eternal has presented to us in the actuality of His works.'' The science of the philosophy of history became degenerate in later hands when this religious aspect was forgotten. In Herder it is fundamental. He studies the growth and manifestation of human effort in all times and places, in order to ascertain what is the purpose of life in the world. It is that man should discover all the gifts that nature has given him, and should develop them harmoniously and symmetrically, so that the result will be a positive, well-balanced, striving personality, solicitous about its own development and respectful of that of others. (pp. 402-03)

And Herder applied this same doctrine to a wider sphere, that of nationality. His total ideal was a future federation made up of national members all of whom had evolved in accordance with this general law, all equal and perfectly self-developed nationalities, each with complete freedom to immortalize itself by making to the common cause its own individual contribution, its own particular realization of *Humanität*. Each must, therefore, strive in its own way towards the ideal, and each will necessarily be drawn into harmonious co-operation with its fellows because of the basic qualities they all possess in common. Everywhere, he said, there is an endless variety striving towards a unity that lies in all things. The local and the universal in humanity are fused together. The real purpose of nationalism is to be the main pillar in the temple of humanity. It is a sad irony that he whose greatest ideal was peace, should have been enlisted against it in recent times. He declared that there was nothing worse than aggressive nationalism and he believed that the final function of the state was self-effacement.

Yet his work as a whole sowed the seed from which this national doctrine grew to proportions beyond his imagination. He founded the historical outlook in Germany, and it is this more than anything else that has marked off that country from Western Europe. . . . Herder retained the fundamental dogmas of Christianity in his historical system, but he created that which ultimately thrust them to one side—the sense of evolution in every sphere of human activity. The Germans have always had a sharper feeling of dependence upon nature than the Western countries—a deeper consciousness of unity with the infinite, a romantic absorption in the magic of historical vistas and speculations and mirages. . . . Other, and greater, historians had a keener historical sense than Herder, yet his—no doubt because of its very vagueness—has exercised an influence which Gibbon's and Hume's has not. The historical sense nourished that feeling of yearning and desire which we have noted as his contribution to German literature, and caused it to extend to other fields. For the march of history told that all things have their rise and fall, that those to whom the Germans felt inferior—and superior—would pass through this process and in the end the destiny of Germany would be fulfilled. A consoling doctrine, to be sure. Herder gave the Germans something to believe in—themselves. He taught them to look into their own powers and their weaknesses, and in this way contributed not a little to the uprising of that envy and self-pity and that confident self-assertion which have marked their historical evolution in modern times. (pp. 403-04)

He supported this comforting doctrine with the authority of religion. But it was a vague and undogmatic religion; for while Herder retained the ethical system of Christianity, his God was very much like Faust's, an all-embracing Godhead, of which the world is the ''living garment.'' (p. 404)

Herder taught the young poet [Goethe] how barren and artificial German literature had grown and how it could only revive by emulating the originality of other literatures, that is, by basing itself upon the memorials of its native past, its popular songs and legends. . . . Herder taught Goethe to be himself, and through Goethe he spoke to all generations to come.

Herder's teaching . . . [also] provided Goethe with much of the mature philosophy he later incorporated in the completed *Faust* and elsewhere. The basic difference between the English and the German Faust is that the English Faust is damned and exists as a warning, whereas in Germany, thanks to Goethe, salvation has come to be regarded as Faust's rightful destiny, and he is generally considered as an example. Because of his salvation Faust has become a symbolical figure, occupying a leading place in the national mythology. To Herder does not belong the credit of inventing Faust's salvation. What he did was to provide the theological background that made it possible in the form which we now know. Thanks to Herder Faust's salvation is fortified with the authority of religion. (p. 407)

Herder looked forward to an all-embracing rebirth of human culture in the sense of *Humanität.* He laboured in the service of a civilization which should be as complete in its own way as Greek civilization, the highest known, had been in its. He found ever new symbols for his doctrine: it is the renewal of vegetation in the spring-time, dawn after night, awakening after slumber, rejuvenation, palingenesis. There is a gradation of being in all the universe, through which man must make his pilgrimage, learning as he lives, improving as he errs, despising the passing beauty of the moment, rejecting indolence and inaction. "Idleness is the original sin of mankind," he said. Through striving, through tireless, balanced effort, we develop and preserve our personalities and make a lasting contribution to the progress of humanity.... Unless he strives man's fate will be that of the unfortunate handmaidens of Helena in the second part of *Faust,* who merge with nature, lose their identities upon leaving this earth, and become no more than disintegrated stone or ashes blown by the wind. (p. 408)

Germany has progressively ignored all but his earliest writings, consoling itself by the not incorrect if misleading belief that in them is contained the seed of all his later work—a strange commentary on German "thoroughness." The cure for it is "more Herder," the study of his work *in toto.* Then it will emerge that his creed was not one which taught disillusion, or titanic self-assertion, but harmonious, restrained, co-operative effort, developing every factor in human existence. The antidote to Faustianism in its negative sense is in Herder's radiantly optimistic view that a future of human greatness lies ahead. It has been tragic for Germany that he has been neglected. "Let us," he said, "toil with glad courageous hearts, even though we are clouded in darkness. For we are toiling towards a great future. And let us take for our goal all that is as pure, clear and free from dross as we can; for we walk in delusion, twilight and mist." It would be uncharitable to say that implicit in this aspiration is the willingness, even the determination, to hand over the present to a mythical and inscrutable future in the name of civilization, a factor which has been so unhappy a feature of German thought. Herder did not intend to preach such sacrifice of today to tomorrow. It has been his misfortune that so much of what he said has been capable of misapplication. His real message in all its fullness has yet to be grasped by his fellow-countrymen. They might do worse than turn to him in their disaster, provided they attend to the broad human essentials first and the details afterwards. (p. 410)

> *A. Gillies, "The Heritage of Johann Gottfried Herder," in* University of Toronto Quarterly, *Vol. XVI, No. 4, July, 1947, pp. 399-410.*

RENÉ WELLEK (essay date 1955)

[*Wellek's* A History of Modern Criticism, *from which the following is drawn, is a major, comprehensive study of the literary critics of the last three centuries. His critical method, as demonstrated in* A History, *is one of describing, analyzing, and evaluating a work solely in terms of the problems it poses for itself and how the writer solves them. Here, Wellek considers Herder's role not merely as an initiator of the movement against Neoclassicism, but also as the "fountainhead of universal literary his-*

tory." He faults Herder for the incoherent and incomplete style and structure of his literary works and views Herder's works as generalizations in which he makes no attempt to interpret a work of art as a "total organism." Regardless of these flaws, however, Wellek still recognizes Herder as a primary force in the resurgence of "natural poetry."]

There is scarcely any idea in Herder which could not be traced back to Blackwell or Harris, Shaftesbury or Brown, Blair or Percy, Warton or Young. Herder read them all, and of course he read his German predecessors and contemporaries, especially Lessing, Hamann, and Winckelmann. He sat at Hamann's feet and felt himself to be his personal disciple. He read the French—Rousseau, of whom he disapproved for a time, Diderot, and many others; and echoes of Vico's thought seem to have come to him through Cesarotti's notes to Ossian, which he read in the German translation by Michael Denis.

But it would be a mistake to consider Herder merely the synthesizer of what could be vaguely called preromantic criticism in Europe. He is not only a synthesizer whom none of his predecessors can approach in sweep and scope, he is also the first who sharply breaks with the neoclassical past, who abandons that curious double point of view which we found in writers such as Warton or Hurd. The whole scale of values is completely reversed, though even in Herder we can, of course, find survivals and accommodations to the older views. Herder differs from all other critics of the century not only in his radicalism but also in his method of presentation and argument. In his writings there is a new fervid, shrill, enthusiastic tone, an emotional heightening, a style which uses rhetorical questions, exclamations, passages marked by dashes in wearisome profusion, a style full of metaphors and similes, a composition which often abandons any pretense at argument and chain of reasoning. It is that of a lyrical address, of constant questions, cumulative intensifying adjectives, verbs of motion, of metaphors drawn from the movement of water, light, flame, and the growth of plants and animals. There is a constantly shifting use of terminology in which ancient words lose their original meaning, in which "drama," "ode," "elegy" may mean almost anything the author wants them to mean in his context. There is hardly a real book among the thirty-three volumes of Herder's **Collected Works.** Many of them are called quite rightly **Fragmente, Torso, Wälder, Briefe, Zerstreute Blätter, Ideen zur** ...; or they have fancy titles such as **Adrastea, Kalligone, Terpsichore,** which often conceal an extremely miscellaneous content. With the exception of a few treatises definitely devoted to theology, it is not safe to ignore any of his writings in a study of his literary criticism. Opinions and pronouncements on literary questions can occur in any context. Besides, Herder constantly rewrote what he had written: the second edition of the **Fragmente** differs profoundly from the first, and materials are often moved from one book to another. The exclamatory style, the shifting terminology, the fragmentariness of the arguments, the constant oscillation and flitting from one topic to another are extremely irritating ... but they do not justify a neglect of Herder. (pp. 181-82)

Not only is Herder of considerable intrinsic interest and, in spite of his incoherent style, of great inner intellectual cohesion and simplicity, but he has been enormously influential ...; it is obvious that Herder's ideas were the great quarry for the German romantics, for Jean Paul, for Novalis, and especially for the two Schlegels. It seems to me an exaggeration to claim that Herder was the first modern historian of literature and the first man with historical sense: but he is certainly the one who has most clearly been the fountainhead of universal literary history. He has also undoubtedly been the most influential force for stimulating interest in folk poetry and in establishing it as the ideal of poetry. . . . Herder's influence on the whole revival of folk poetry—its collecting and imitating, its interpretation and evaluation—is immeasurable, especially in the Slavic and Scandinavian countries. His influence was often indirect and anonymous, combined with that of predecessors, contemporaries, and followers; it is almost underground, for reasons which are in part due to the characteristics of Herder's writings and in part to extraneous circumstances such as the intermittent hostility of Goethe and Schiller. While his influence was obscured in the early 19th century, he has again been studied intensively in recent decades, especially in Germany, and has been played up as a sort of counterweight to Goethe and Schiller. The revival of Herder, which came originally from historians with religious interests (Nadler and Unger), was later taken up by the Nazis, who saw in him a source of German nationalism, of a national conception of literature and of the "blood and soil" ideology. They conveniently ignored or minimized his central teaching of *Humanität*. From the very nature of Herder's manner of thinking it is almost impossible to isolate his literary criticism and theory from the general body of his thought, from his philosophy of history, his theology, psychology, linguistic speculations, and aesthetic. (pp. 182-83)

[It has been suggested] that Herder's conception of the aim of criticism differs from that of the main neoclassicists, the whole tradition which attempted to build up a rational structure of coherent and systematic literary theory and of immutable standards of judgment. Herder conceives of criticism mainly as a process of empathy, of identification, of something intuitive and subrational. He constantly rejects theories, systems, faultfinding. In an early piece, the preliminary discourse to the second collection of *Fragmente über die neuere deutsche Literatur* . . . , he describes his views of the function of criticism: the critic should be a "servant of the author, his friend, his impartial judge. He should try to get acquainted with him, make a thorough study of him as a master, not seek to be your own master. . . . It is difficult but reasonable that the critic should transfer himself into the thoughts of his author and read him in the spirit in which he wrote." . . . In Herder we have the criticism of beauties rather than faults of which Chateaubriand is supposed to be the originator. It is actually not so much criticism as understanding, empathy (*Einfühlung*), submission to the author. . . . Thus "criticism without genius is nothing. Only a genius can judge and teach another." These were important sayings, salutary in their time for their stress on understanding, but they also contain the germs of much that is bad in criticism since Herder's time: mere impressionism, the idea of "creative" criticism with its pretensions to duplicating a work of art by another work of art, the critical errors of excessive attention to biography and the intention of the author, mere appreciation, and complete relativism.

This empathic conception of criticism is closely related to Herder's historical sense, his insistence that every work of literature needs to be seen and interpreted in its historical setting. . . . In the late *Briefe zur Beförderung der Humanität* . . . Herder expressly discusses methods of literary study. He rejects classification by genres and finds division into types such as "subjective" and "objective" (in Schiller) vague and unprofitable. The correct method is the "natural method, which leaves each flower in its place, and contemplates it there just as it is, according to time and kind, from the root to the crown. The most humble genius hates ranking and comparison. He would rather be the first in a village, than the second after

Caesar. Lichen, moss, fern, and the richest scented flower: each blooms in its place in God's order." The natural method is Herder's own, the historical method, which sees each work as part and parcel of its milieu and hence feels that each is in its place, fulfills its temporary function, and thus really needs no criticism. Everything had to be the way it has been: there is no need of judging, no need of standards, as all ages are equal. (pp. 183-85)

Herder's aesthetic is curiously sensualistic: he tried to deduce the individual arts from their respective senses, distinguishing sharply between painting—the art of the eye, music—the art of the ear, and sculpture—the art of touch. The last idea, later developed in a little work on *Plastik* . . . , was especially new at the time. At first Herder saw no way of reducing poetry to one of the senses and did not even classify it with the arts. Later he concluded that poetry has a special position in being the art of imagination, the "only fine art immediate for the soul," the "music of the soul" which "affects the inner sense, not the external eye of the artist." This view is effectively used in Herder's attempt at a refutation of the *Laokoon*, in the first *Kritisches Wäldchen* . . . , which, though diffuse, is one of his most impressive and coherent performances. He argues that Lessing's contrast between painting as an art of space and poetry as an art of time is specious. The mere succession in time is not central to the effect of poetry. Succession in time he assigns, unconvincingly, to music, forgetting about harmony and ignoring the fact that his arguments on poetry apply also to the forms of music. Sounds in poetry and language have meaning or soul. Poetry differs from the other arts by being energy, not work. . . . Herder's spontaneous energy is an obscure idea which removes poetry from the other arts, each correlated to a sense, merely on the analogy of the triad "time, space, and energy." He seems to mean an organizing power, a coherence of imaginative ideas, which makes it possible for poetry to express not only actions in succession but also bodies, images, pictures. (pp. 185-86)

Herder never gave up the view that poetry stands apart as the art of emotion, expression, and energy, appealing to the imagination. Nevertheless he recognized more and more its basis in language and in the sound of language. . . . He constantly stresses the sound and meter of poetry, and criticizes the inappropriate meter of Denis' German translation of Ossian. His own numerous verse translations all attempt first to imitate the sound, the tone, and the meter. Such a conception of poetry is, of course, lyrical. (pp. 186-87)

Language is associated in Herder's mind with literature from the very beginning. The first collection of the *Fragmente* opens with the statement that the "genius of a language is also the genius of the literature of the nation." Hence the origins of poetry and of language are one and the same. Herder's treatise *Über den Ursprung der Sprache* is thus a speculative history not only of language but also of poetry. The first language was nothing but a collection of elements of poetry. . . . [According to Herder, poetry] is naturally metaphorical and allegorical (Herder, it seems, does not distinguish between allegory and symbolism). Primitive man thinks in symbols, allegories, and metaphors, and their combinations make fables and myths. Thus poetry is not an imitation of nature but an "imitation of the creating, naming Godhead." The poet is a "second creator, *poietes,* maker," a saying which associates the poet with Prometheus and which comes from Shaftesbury. The poet is an original, an individual, and in Herder's mind this is not incompatible with his creating unconsciously and intuitively:

Shakespeare "paints passion to its deepest abysses without his knowing" of it and describes Hamlet "unconsciously" up to his hair. Later Herder became disgusted with the excesses of the *Sturm und Drang* cult of pure genius and began to reaffirm the role of reason and judgment, but he never gave up his view that genius is mainly instinctive, even sensuous. (pp. 187-88)

It is no chance, of course, that the concept of poetry and the poet . . . is seen in terms of a history of poetry in which the origins of poetry describe its nature. Herder is convinced that "it is absolutely impossible to have a philosophical theory of the beautiful in all arts and sciences without history." The concepts of a theory of literature "grow out of manifold concrete things, in many kinds and phenomena, in which genesis is the All-in-All." "If we want ever to achieve a philosophical poetics or a history of poetry, then we must begin with the individual genres and trace them back to their origins." He would say that as the "tree from the root, so must the progress and the flowering of an art be deduced from its origin. It contains the whole being of its product just as a whole plant is hidden with all its parts in a grain of seed." "Origins show the nature of a thing." This is the doctrine which the 19th century was to push to the extreme of neglecting the problems of description and evaluation in contemporary terms in favor of explanation by remote prehistory. It was to lead to an emphasis on Sanskrit and Proto-Indo-European rather than the study of contemporary speech, of Anglo-Saxon literature as compared to the study of the literature of our own time.

This evolution of literature is conceived of by Herder as literal evolution, as the growing of a germ, on a completely biological analogy. . . . Though this biological parallel permeates all of Herder's writings on literary history and history in general, he does not quite draw the fatalistic conclusions which are implied in any view of the growing, maturing, and aging of poetry. Actually Herder does not believe in uniform degeneration from the glories of the age of poetry. . . . (pp. 188-89)

The biological view of the evolution of poetry should logically produce resignation to an inevitable development. Poetry is the language of primitive man, of the childhood of mankind, and no return is possible since none of us can become young again. But Herder's view is not logical: first of all, he has recourse to the theory of cycles. Humanity is not conceived of as a single individual—there are as many humanities as there are nations. After the decline of Rome, there came the new flowering of the Middle Ages; after the degeneracy of the Renaissance and its artificial literature, there may come a new flowering of the imagination Moreover, Herder frequently forgets the implications of his deterministic biological point of view and simply appeals to the will to change the direction of development, asking for a return to the age of poetry. . . . In this view the Germans have a peculiar position. They seem to him in the greatest danger of losing their individuality and forgetting the treasures of their past. . . . Herder, after all, was a practical critic, a reformer who wanted to change the direction of literature and influence his time. It could not be done by resigned fatalism. The whole argument of the *Fragmente,* his first important publication, is directed against imitation, especially that of French and Latin literature. There also, for the first time, he publicly points to the regenerative power of folk poetry and recommends collecting it, not only in Germany but among "Scyths and Slavs, Wends and Bohemians, Russians, Swedes, and Poles." Thus a turn in the development of literature is possible if we return to our own past and to the past of humanity which lies all around us, in folk poetry, songs, legends, and

myths, even in superstitions and in the character of the language. Herder is one of those who believe that the German language is somehow peculiarly aboriginal because it is not derived from the Latin and is not a mixture of Latin and Germanic as is English. Thus Germans should cultivate its peculiarities, its idioms, its wealth of synonyms, its inversions, all its illogicalities, which are a source of poetry compared to the clarity, straightforwardness, poverty, and shallowness of the French language.

Throughout Herder's activity there runs this messianic desire to be a reformer and restorer of German poetry, and one must recognize that the advent of Goethe, who was Herder's personal pupil, seemed to justify his optimism and prophecy. One can understand how bitter was his disappointment when Goethe, and with him Schiller, turned to what Herder considered sterile classicism and aestheticism, thus denying all his teachings of a return to the folk and the national past. (pp. 189-90)

But it would be a mistake to think of Herder merely as a Teutonizing nationalist: his whole conception of the nation was that of a steppingstone toward "humanity." From a literary point of view the German nation was inferior to those which had preserved their individuality better and longer. Thus Herder constantly held up the example of other nations, and tirelessly translated, collected, and described the wealth of the world's literature. His *Volkslieder* . . . , now best known under the title given to them after Herder's death, *Stimmen der Völker in Liedern,* is the first comprehensive anthology of world literature, animated by a conception of folk poetry which was extremely broad and included much which we would not today think of calling by this term. Folk poetry is to Herder the fullest and most cherished embodiment of a people's soul. . . . Folk poetry is a highly inclusive concept: it includes Genesis, the Song of Songs, the Book of Job, the Psalms, in fact nearly all of the Old Testament. It includes Homer, Hesiod, Aeschylus and Sophocles, Sappho and the *Greek Anthology,* Chaucer, Spenser, Shakespeare, and the contents of Percy's *Reliques* (not only English and Scottish ballads but Elizabethan songs). It includes medieval romances, the German *Heldenbuch,* the troubadours, the *Minnesang,* Bürger's ballads, and Klopstock, whom Herder admired beyond any of the German poets. It includes even Dante and of course Ossian. (p. 192)

This conception of folk poetry is most conspicuous and most one-sided in Herder's view of Shakespeare. A paper entitled **"Shakespeare"** was contributed by Herder to a collection called *Von deutscher Art und Kunst.* . . . The Shakespeare piece is a most characteristic performance, a lyrical rhapsody rather than a piece of criticism. (p. 193)

In each [Shakespearean] play there is, according to Herder, a pervading mood which permeates it like the soul of the world. "Take the soil, the sap, and the energy from this plant, and you have planted it in air: take away place, time, individual status from these men, and you have taken away their breath and soul." How absurd is the question of the unity of time! What must be the illusion experienced by a man who after every scene will look at his watch to see whether it could have happened in the time elapsed. For a poet, a creator, a "dramatic God" no clock strikes on spire or temple: he has to make his own measures of space and time to produce a world which will move the audience. How Shakespeare has transformed a miserable romance, novel, or fabulous history into a living whole is the question Herder would consider the heart of the investigation. But he does not really attempt it and ends with a suggestion on the classification of Shakespeare's plays. They are all "history in the widest sense," the "greatly portentous happening of a world event, of a human fate." (p. 194)

It would be easy to criticize Herder's conception of folk poetry, or rather of nature poetry. The overrating of Ossian seems the most incomprehensible. . . . Herder certainly has a very one-sided conception of Shakespeare or Homer: he overrated or started the overrating of all kinds of folklore without being able to distinguish genuine productions from artificial derivatives and even fakes such as Ossian. His criticism of much neoclassical literature seems to us grossly unjust. His conception is too indulgent toward the purely naive, the mere lyrical cry, the merely spontaneous, and too inimical to great art, which may be intellectual, sophisticated, ironical, grotesque. But we must realize that Herder was struck with the novelty of his discoveries, which were fresh and appealing against the background of a decaying neoclassicism, while we are inured to many romantic charms by a century and a half of their vulgarization. We must not underrate the historical importance of Herder's conception of poetry, which certainly widened the horizon immeasurably and brushed aside many narrow or false conceptions of the neoclassical creed: its stress on the unities, its preoccupation with pure genres, its limitation to upper-class literature. In spite of the excesses of his primitivism and lyricism, Herder had a clearer and truer conception of poetry than all the critics we have discussed hitherto. His conception of poetry is centrally true: he is right in his stress on the role of metaphor, symbol, and myth, on poetry's essential function in a healthy society.

But Herder's importance lies not merely in his new conception of poetry or even in his general scheme of its origins. He is also, in many ways, the first modern historian of literature who has clearly conceived of the ideal of universal literary history, sketched out its methods, and written outlines of its development which are not merely an accumulation of antiquarian research, as the works of Warton and Tiraboschi, or the *Histoire littéraire de la France* tended to be. Herder certainly raised a great many of the problems of literary history and suggested what should be done and what questions should be answered. Literary history should trace the "origins, the growth, the changes and the decay [of literature] according to the different styles of the regions, times, and poets." . . . Herder's literary history is cultural history in the broadest sense. One sees its aim when he describes the procedure. In reading Dante or Petrarch, Ariosto or Cervantes he first sees only the poet, as a unique person; then he sees everything which has contributed to his formation or misformation. (pp. 195-96)

Literary history is thus conceived of primarily in sociological terms. There are impressionistic analyses of works of literature scattered through Herder's writings. The evocation of Sophocles' *Philoctetes* in the argument against Lessing is very suggestive and sensitive. *Vom Geist der ebräischen Poesie* . . . contains many penetrating, but also many fantastic, interpretations of the Old Testament. Elsewhere there are comments on the odes of Horace. The taste and sensitivity of Herder could be most amply demonstrated and investigated by an examination of his numerous poetic translations, which are, on the whole, extremely successful, though he suffered from a lack of access to the originals or from inadequate philological knowledge. But there is nowhere in Herder an attempt to interpret a work of art as a total organism, to analyze its structure or composition. His literary history is one of broad vistas, wide sweeps, bold generalizations.

He has been considered a forerunner of Taine in his stress on milieu. There is in Herder much about climate (hot, cold, and temperate), landscape, race (nations), customs, and even political conditions such as Athenian democracy in their relations to literature. One of his prize essays, called *Über die Wirkung der Dichtkunst auf die Sitten der Völker in alten und neuen Zeiten* . . . , is a survey of the history of literature with stress on its educative and civilizing function. But Herder rarely analyzes the environmental factors and never brings them into close relationship with the actual literature. He constantly argues in a circle: i.e., he explains a work of literature by history and then utilizes the work to throw light on history. (pp. 196-97)

But whatever the shortcomings of Herder's method—which to us, after 150 years of unparalleled accumulation of information and research, must appear dilettantish, arbitrary, and indiscriminate—the value for the times of his sketches of literary history cannot be doubted. What was needed was a premature synthesis, an asking of questions, without which literary history would have been totally swamped by antiquarianism. Indeed, the bold sketches of the Schlegels are directly inspired by Herder. (p. 198)

Herder has been acclaimed as the father of Germanistics. But his several attempts at histories of German literature are hardly systematic and well informed, even for the time. (pp. 198-99)

Herder is, of course, most disappointing when he discusses the French, for here his national and literary prejudices are greatest. He could not have known much of the French Middle Ages: he is obviously full of disgust for the "pomp" and "show" of the French drama of the 17th and 18th centuries. For the *Pucelle d'Orléans* Voltaire is praised only as a witty storyteller. Diderot, whom Herder met in Paris as a youth . . . , remained one of his favorite authors, and late in life he planned a translation of his writings which apparently would have extended to some of the novels, such as *Jacques le Fataliste*. Among the French writers Herder singles out for praise La Fontaine, as their "most original genius, whose charm will never become obsolete, as long as the French language lasts." Herder seems not to have known anything about the Spanish drama; but his last work, shortly before his death, was a free translation of the Cid romances, which unfortunately was based on a collection of late Spanish poetical versions and a French prose rendering. (pp. 199-200)

In Herder the poetics of neoclassicism is, if not dissolved completely, in the process of dissolution. He rejects all its main tenets: the imitation of nature, decorum, the unities, probability, propriety, clarity of style, purity of genre. Though he speculates a good deal on genre and of course uses the names of the genres, they constantly melt into one another in his discussions: epic, drama, and lyric are almost the same to him. Herder obviously was not much interested in Aristotle, whom he called once "a stiff man of bones like a skeleton: nothing but disposition, nothing but order." . . . In him we see then the ruins of a neoclassical poetics: he himself began to build a new romantic poetics on the conception of a natural poetry, sensuous, metaphorical, imaginative, spontaneous, with a standard of judgment based on historical relativism and an implicit distaste for the poetry of statement, reasoning, or reflection. But Herder's terminology is very loose: his concepts are shifting, his language is emotional and rhapsodical. While he was the great initiator, he left to others the task of formulating a new, coherent, systematic theory of poetry and literature. His first disciple was Goethe, who proved an unfaithful one. (p. 200)

René Wellek, "Storm, Stress, and Herder," in his
A History of Modern Criticism, 1750-1950: The Later
Eighteenth Century, Vol. 1, *Yale University Press,*
1955, pp. 176-200.

MARK JOEL WEBBER   (essay date 1980)

In discussing cultures both ancient and modern, Herder does
not shy away from comparisons, whether implicit or explicit.
Nor does he exclude the possibility of one culture's learning
from another. Nevertheless, his conception is still basically
relativistic, emphasizing the characteristic (and in some cases,
unique) traits of each culture without concluding that any nation
is better than another. (p. 517)

Taking the organic life-cycle as a natural law, Herder envisions
a "rise and fall" of language from the infantile stage of passion, sensuousness, and irregularity, to the senile stage of prosaic abstractness and correctness. Ironically, Herder's own inclination to analogical exposition—his preference for .the
"poetical" over the "philosophical" mode—results in an "infantile" lack of precision. He does not remain consistent in
the number of "ages" which make up the linguistic life-cycle,
nor does he indicate exactly which stage of language corresponds to the age of "excellence" or "manhood." Indeed, he
finds that both the poetic age and the succeeding age of prose
culminated in outstanding sub-periods. . . . If Herder is allowed
to speak through his imagery, he seems more attached to the
former period. He concedes, however, that the period of
"beautiful prose" has the advantage of combining the natural
beauty of early language with the utility and flexibility of later
language, and allows the modern writer the choice of which
aspect he wishes to emphasize and develop. By introducing
the possibility of interrupting or even reversing the natural flow
of linguistic evolution, Herder does violence to the .organicist
model. In the conclusion to the first collection of fragments
(**"Beschluß, über das Ideal der Sprache"**) Herder seems to
retreat still further from the teleology of the life-cycle analogy
to a more relativistic assessment of the various stages of linguistic development. . . . There are, then, difficulties of argument and interpretation in Herder's presentation of the laws
of linguistic development. No doubt part of the problem lies
in the fact that some of Herder's organic imagery originates in
the desire to write "poetically" and persuasively, rather than
with scientific objectivity. (p. 519)

How is [the post-Romantic] Young-German ideal of poetic
prose or prosaic poetry related to Herder's age of "beautiful
prose"? According to both Herder and the Young-German
mainstream, a period of prose, marked by a heightened capacity
for abstractness, succeeds one of poetry, some positive aspects
of which carry over into the new period. For Herder the epoch
of beautiful prose is most desirable because of its flexibility,
allowing development towards either poetic or philosophical
language. . . . The logic of Herder's argument runs counter to
his imagery throughout, and especially to the teleology inherent
in the organicist model. Herder's underlying sympathies come
through clearly: the advantages afforded by the flexibility of
"beautiful prose" are balanced, and perhaps outweighed, by
the potential disadvantages which come with a turning away
from nature to art, and with increased emphasis on rules and
correctness instead of on the free expression of emotion. To
the Young Germans, on the other hand, the new age is clearly
an advance, a return to nature from the art and artificiality of
the *Kunstperiode* and a reintroduction of vitality into an ossified

tradition. The difference of interpretation is indicative of a
fundamental difference in historical and aesthetic outlook.

Perhaps more remarkable than the discrepancy in attitudes is
the flexibility and self-sustaining power of the organic analogy,
which supplies both Herder and the Young Germans with criteria. Both the nature of analogical argument—the assumption
of an interconnection between two seemingly disparate realms—
and the main thrust of organicism—the assertion of totality
and uninterrupted development—point to an attempt to perceive or invent a unifying force which holds together all facets
of human existence. In this endeavor the Young Germans and
Herder are linked. But even here there is a characteristic difference between the organicism of Herder and that of the Young
Germans. Although both do use organicist categories and criteria polemically, Herder has a greater allegiance to the organicist model as a valid description of how the universe in
general and language in particular operate. (pp. 526-27)

The shift from Herder's philosophical organicism to the more
polemical use of organicist categories by the Young Germans
suggests the extent to which the relatively coherent world-view
of the eighteenth century disintegrated in the years between
Herder's **"Von den Lebensaltern einer Sprache"** and the writings of the Young Germans. Despite these differences, it becomes evident that Herder's concept of "beautiful prose" influenced the Young Germans' idea of poetic prose, which remains
. . . their most influential literary achievement. (p. 527)

Mark Joel Webber, "Towards a Natural History of
Language: Johann Gottfried Herder and Young-Ger-
man Theories of Poetic Prose," in Studies in Romanticism, *Vol. 19, No. 4, Winter, 1980, pp. 515-27.*

ADDITIONAL BIBLIOGRAPHY

Barnard, F. M. Introduction to *J. G. Herder on Social and Political*
Culture, by Johann Gottfried von Herder, edited and translated by
F. M. Barnard, pp. 1-60. Cambridge Studies in the History and Theory
of Politics, edited by Maurice Cowling, G. R. Elton, E. Kedourie,
J. R. Pole, and Walter Ullmann. Cambridge: Cambridge University
Press, 1969.
   A comprehensive look at the social and political forces which
   influenced Herder. Barnard characterizes Herder as "one of the
   first of modern thinkers to combine most effectively the historical
   and sociological method. . . ."

Berlin, Isaiah. "Herder and the Enlightenment." In *Aspects of the*
Eighteenth Century, edited by Earl R. Wasserman, pp. 47-104. Baltimore: Johns Hopkins Press, 1965.
   An extensive discussion which emphasizes Herder's role in the
   development of German nationalism. Berlin explains three particular aspects of Herder's theories: populism, expressionism, and
   pluralism.

Blackall, Eric A. "The Imprint of Herder's Linguistic Theory on His
Early Prose Style." *PMLA* LXXVI, No. 5 (December 1961): 512-18.
   Analyzes the variations in Herder's prose style.

Bowle, John. "The Originality of the Romantics: Herder, Hegel." In
his *Politics and Opinion in the Nineteenth Century: An Historical*
Introduction, pp. 27-50. New York: Oxford University Press, 1954.*
   Discusses the impact of Herder's theories on political thought.
   Bowle considers Herder's ideas "original and creative," but terms
   his political outlook "vague and unstable."

Burkhardt, Frederick H. Introduction to *God: Some Conversations,*
by Johann Gottfried Herder, translated by Frederick H. Burkhardt,
pp. 1-64. New York: Veritas Press, 1940.

A detailed introduction to Herder's works. Burkhardt traces the development of Herder's historical theories and discusses how his works reflect those theories. Burkhardt specifically concentrates on *God: Some Conversations*.

Clark, Robert T., Jr. *Herder: His Life and Thought*. Berkeley and Los Angeles: University of California Press, 1955, 501 p.
    The most complete Herder biography in English. Clark includes an extensive bibliography as well as informative notes on Herder's works.

"The Herder Centenary." *The Dial* XXXV, No. 420 (16 December 1903): 455-57.
    Compares Herder with Voltaire and discusses Herder's contribution to modern thought. The critic calls Herder "one of the pioneers in the modern movement which has made of literary criticism much more than a matter of judgment by fixed rules or of rhetorical analysis. . . ."

Ergang, Robert Reinhold. *Herder and the Foundations of German Nationalism*. 1931. Reprint. New York: Octagon Books, 1966, 288 p.
    A scholarly account of Herder's involvement in the German Nationalist movement.

Fugate, Joe K. *The Psychological Basis of Herder's Aesthetics*. The Hague: Mouton & Co., 1966, 303 p.
    A psychological approach to Herder's works. Fugate attempts to illustrate the relationship between Herder's "aesthetic" and the "perspective of his basic psychological presuppositions."

Gillies, A[lexander]. "Herder's Essay on Shakespeare: 'Das Herz Der Untersuchung'." *The Modern Language Review* XXXII, No. 2 (April 1937): 262-80.
    Analyzes the development of Herder's essay *Shakespear*. Gillies maintains that Herder placed Shakespeare "in the direct line of descent from the minstrels and ballad-mongers. . . ."

Gillies, Alexander. "Herder and *Faust*." *Publications of the English Goethe Society* n.s. XVI (1946): 90-111.*
    Discusses the impact of Herder's works on Johann Wolfgang von Goethe's *Faust*. Gillies suggests that Goethe employed Herder's theological theories in the development of the last version of his drama.

Hayes, Carlton J. H. "Contributions of Herder to the Doctrine of Nationalism." *The American Historical Review* XXXII, No. 4 (July 1927): 719-36.
    Maintains that Herder's contributions to cultural and political thought are not due to a clear, concise approach, but are a result of his prolific writings on various subjects.

Haym, Rudolf. *Herder, nach seinem Leben und seinem Werken dargestellt*. 2 vols. Berlin: Aufbau-Verlag, 1954.
    The definitive biography of Herder, written in German.

Hillebrand, Karl. "Herder." *North American Review* CXV, No. CCXXXVII (October 1872): 235-87.

An interpretation of the events leading to the dissolution of the friendship between Johann Wolfgang von Goethe and Herder. Hillebrand also highlights the rise of the influence of Kant during Herder's theological and literary careers.

Lovejoy, Arthur O. "Some Eighteenth Century Evolutionists." *The Popular Science Monthly* LXV, No. 4 (August 1904): 323-40.*
    A brief but thorough study of Herder's theory of evolution. Lovejoy delineates Herder's beliefs and cites lengthy examples from *Outlines of a Philosophy of the History of Man*.

Marks, Paul F. "The Application of the Aesthetics of Music in the Philosophy of the *Sturm und Drang:* Gerstenberg, Hamann, and Herder." In *Studies in Eighteenth-Century Culture: Racism in the Eighteenth Century,* Vol. 3, edited by Harold E. Pagliaro, pp. 219-38. Cleveland: Press of Case Western Reserve University, 1973.*
    An informative essay that discusses Herder's theory of the aesthetics of music.

McEachran, F. *The Life and Philosophy of Johann Gottfried Herder*. Oxford Studies in Modern Languages and Literature, edited by H. G. Fiedler. Oxford: Oxford at the Clarendon Press, 1939, 98 p.
    A biography which represents Herder's life and works from a philosophical viewpoint.

Noel, Thomas. "Herder and the Romantic Turn." In his *Theories of the Fable in the Eighteenth Century*, pp. 122-39. New York: Columbia University Press, 1975.*
    A summary of the works by Herder that challenge Gotthold Ephraim Lessing's concept of the fable in literature.

Schick, Edgar B. *Metaphorical Organicism in Herder's Early Works: A Study of the Relation of Herder's Literary Idiom to His World-View*. De Proprietatibus Litterarum, edited by C. H. Van Schooneveld, no. 20. The Hague: Mouton, 1971, 135 p.
    An in-depth study of Herder's theories of organicism.

Schütze, Martin. "The Fundamental Ideas in Herder's Thought: Parts I, II, and V." *Modern Philology* XVIII, Nos. 2, 6 (June 1920; October 1920): 65-78, 289-302; XXI, No. 1 (August 1923): 29-48.
    A series devoted to the delineation and explanation of Herder's philosophical and theological doctrines. Schütze discusses Herder's relationships with Johann Wolfgang von Goethe and Immanuel Kant as well as the political climate that influenced Herder's writings.

———. "Johann Gottfried Herder, August 25, 1744—December 18, 1803: His Significance in the History of Thought." *Monatshefte für Deutschen Unterricht* XXXVI, No. 6 (October 1944): 257-87.*
    A textual comparison of the works of Herder and Gotthold Ephraim Lessing. Schütze discusses Herder's historical significance and some of Herder's most important works, which he divides into five categories: letters, poetry, and language; art theories; theories of the organic unity of the mind; history of culture; theological and speculative works.

John Keats

1795-1821

English poet and dramatist.

Keats is considered a key figure in the English Romantic movement and a major poet in the English language. Critics note that though his creative career spanned only four years, he achieved remarkable intellectual and artistic development. His poems, notably the later works of *Lamia, Isabella, The Eve of St. Agnes, and Other Poems,* are valued not only for their sensuous imagery, simplicity, and passionate tone, but for the insight they provide into aesthetic and human concerns, particularly the conflict between art and life. The artistic philosophy delineated in Keats's poetry in such lines as those from the "Ode on a Grecian Urn"—"beauty is truth, truth beauty"— are illuminated by his correspondence, which critics place among the most sensitive ever written. In the letters, Keats set down poetic theories that have become standards of literary criticism, such as his theory of "*Negative Capability,* that is when man is capable of being in uncertainties, mysteries, doubts, without any irritable reaching after fact and reason." Despite Keats's present high status, however, recognition of his genius was slow in coming. His impassioned tone and sensual imagery appeared shockingly effusive to early nineteenth-century critics schooled in the neoclassical poetics of the eighteenth century. In addition, Keats's early affiliation with the so-called "Cockney School of Poetry," led by the liberal Whig poet and editor, Leigh Hunt, incited conservative Tory reviewers to malign his works, sometimes viciously. Therefore, in spite of the efforts of a loyal group of supporters, Keats's work was virtually unknown both during his lifetime and for twenty years after his death. It was not until the mid-nineteenth century that his writings began to draw a significant audience and to attract serious critical consideration. By the turn of the century, Keats was widely acknowledged as a poet of the first rank and often parallelled with William Shakespeare; since that time his superior reputation has remained undiminished.

Observers often comment on the fact that, unlike most outstanding artists', Keats's childhood provides no hint of the genius who was to emerge. The oldest of four children of a stable-keeper, Keats was raised in Moorfields, London. His father died when he was seven, followed six years later by his mother, and the Keats children were placed in the care of a guardian. Keats attended the nearby Clarke school, where he was distinguished only by his small stature (he was barely over five feet tall as an adult) and somewhat pugnacious disposition. At the Clarke school, Keats first encountered the works that influenced his early poetry, including Edmund Spenser's *The Faerie Queen* and *Lemprière's Classical Dictionary,* on which he based his knowledge of Greek mythology. At fifteen, he was placed as an apprentice to an apothecary and four years later entered Guy's and St. Thomas's Hospitals in London, where he completed medical courses and in 1816 passed the examinations to become a surgeon. As early as 1812, however, Keats had begun to compose poetry, and he opted after graduation to support himself on his small inheritance and to devote himself to writing.

An important impetus to Keats's decision was his meeting in 1816 with Hunt, who encouraged Keats and published his early

poems in his liberal journal, the *Examiner.* Keats was drawn readily into Hunt's circle, which included the poet John Hamilton Reynolds, the critic William Hazlitt, and the painter Benjamin Robert Haydon, who became Keats's intimates. *Poems,* a collection of Keats's immature and early efforts, was published two years later, but received little attention. His next work, *Endymion: A Poetic Romance,* a full-length allegory based on Greek mythology, was published the following year to mixed reviews. Soon after the appearance of *Endymion,* Keats began to experience the first symptoms of tuberculosis, the disease that had killed his mother and in 1818 took his brother Tom. Following Tom's death, Keats lived with his close friend Charles Armitage Brown in Hampstead, where he read avidly, particularly the works of William Wordsworth, John Milton, and Shakespeare, and continued steadily to write. Here Keats also began a passionate love affair with Fanny Brawne, a neighbor's daughter. The rigors of work, poor health, and constant financial difficulties prevented the two from fulfilling their ardent desire to be married. Keats's final publication, *Lamia, Isabella, The Eve of St. Agnes, and Other Poems,* included, in addition to the noted title poems, Keats's famous odes as well as *Hyperion,* an unfinished narrative based on Greek mythology. Keats later attempted a revision of this work, titled *The Fall of Hyperion,* which remained incomplete along with the poem "The Eve of St. Mark." Other uncollected writings include the dramatic experiments *Otho the Great* and *St. Stephen,* the humorous verse "Cap and Bells," and Keats's final sonnet, "Bright Star," all of which were first published in *The Life, Letters, and Literary Remains of John Keats,* compiled in 1848 by Richard Monckton Milnes. Keats, in a final effort to regain his health, sailed reluctantly in September 1820 away from Fanny, his family, and friends to Italy, where he died in Rome five months later. He was buried there beneath a gravestone which bore an epitaph that he himself composed: "Here lies one whose name was writ on water."

The history of Keats's early reputation is dominated by two hostile, unsigned reviews of *Endymion,* one by John Gibson Lockhart in *Blackwood's Edinburgh Magazine* and the other by John Wilson Croker in the *Quarterly Review.* Lockhart, a vociferous detractor of what he termed "The Cockney School," named for its members' ties to London and their alleged lack of refinement, attacked not only Keats's poem, which he abhorred on artistic and moral grounds, but the poet's lack of taste, education, and upbringing. While Croker was neither as vitriolic nor as personally cutting as Lockhart—critics acknowledge, in fact, the legitimacy of several of his critical complaints—his essay was singled out as damaging and unjust by Keats's supporters, who rushed to the poet's defense. While Keats was apparently disturbed only temporarily by these attacks, the story circulated after his death that his demise had been caused, or at least hastened, by Lockhart's and especially Croker's reviews. A chief perpetrator of this notion was Percy Bysshe Shelley, who composed his famous *Adonais: An Elegy on the Death of the Poet John Keats,* which was published with a bitter preface implicating Croker as the murderer of Keats. *Adonais,* in conjunction with the writings of Keats's well-meaning friends, effectively created a legend of Keats as sickly, swooning, and unnaturally delicate, a man so fragile that a magazine article was capable of killing him. Lord Byron commented wryly on Keats in a famous couplet in his poem *Don Juan:* "'Tis strange the mind, that very fiery particle. / Should let itself be snuffed out by an article."

The *Adonais* image of Keats as a frail flower lent credence to the view that dominated Keats criticism for forty years after his death and lingered into the twentieth century: that Keats was merely a poet of the senses, capable of evoking delicious sensations but incapable of conveying ideas. The critic responsible for initially establishing Keats as a poet of ideas who was worthy of serious critical consideration was Milnes, whose landmark biography, *Life Letters, and Literary Remains of John Keats,* presented Keats's own letters and poems as evidence of his intellectual maturity and artistic worth. The publication in 1880 of Matthew Arnold's essay identifying Keats as standing "with Shakespeare" marked the beginning of the flourishing of Keats's critical reputation as an intellectual poet. At the same time, however, such Pre-Raphaelites as William Morris, Dante Gabriel Rossetti, and William Holman Hunt sustained the old image of Keats by championing him as their artistic forebear because of his richly pictorial descriptions and lush imagery. Similarly, Arthur Symons admired Keats's poems for the "art for art's sake" quality that they evinced. Nevertheless, by the early twentieth century, such respected critics as Ernest de Sélincourt, A. C. Bradley, and Robert Bridges had confirmed Keats's status as an intellectual as well as an emotive or merely pictorial poet, and full-length works by Clarence DeWitt Thorpe and John Middleton Murry, among others, echoed their beliefs. Contemporary critics continue to find much to explore in Keats's complex intellectual nuances as well as in the beauties of his poetic technique. While early

nineteenth-century critics focused on *Endymion* in their discussions of the poet of sensations and later Victorian scholars often chose *Hyperion* as a subject of study, contemporary commentators frequently concentrate on the odes. Considered by many the most mature and highest expression of Keats's genius, the odes are also considered his most challenging works intellectually. The critical approaches employed by twentieth century commentators are numerous, however, and encompass such subjects as Keats's affiliation with other artists, including Shelley, Spenser, Wordsworth, and particularly Shakespeare; the evolution of Keats's aesthetic theory; and his use of various poetic images, such as metamorphosis and biological and nature imagery.

While his provocative intellect and stunning artistic ability form the basis of Keats's reputation, critics acknowledge the fact that, to many, the poet himself is as compelling as his work. The astonishing use he made of his brief creative life continues to awe readers. But above all, the earnestness with which he struggled against difficult circumstances to improve himself as a man and an artist has won the sympathy and imaginations of his readers. As Douglas Bush wrote: "No other English poet of the century had his poetic endowment, and no other strove so intensely. . . . However high one's estimate of what he wrote, one may really think—to use an often meaningless cliché—that Keats was greater than his poems."

PRINCIPAL WORKS

Poems (poetry) 1817
Endymion: A Poetic Romance (poetry) 1818
Lamia, Isabella, The Eve of St. Agnes, and Other Poems (poetry) 1820
Life, Letters, and Literary Remains of John Keats (letters and poetry) 1848
Another Version of Keats's "Hyperion" (poetry) 1856
Letters of John Keats to Fanny Brawne (letters) 1878
Letters of John Keats to His Family and Friends (letters) 1891
The Complete Poetical Works and Letters of John Keats (letters and poetry) 1899

[LEIGH HUNT]   (essay date 1816)

[*An English poet and essayist, Hunt is remembered as a literary critic who encouraged and influenced several young Romantic poets, especially John Keats and Percy Bysshe Shelley. Hunt produced volumes of poetry and critical essays and, with his brother John, established the* Examiner, *a weekly liberal newspaper. In his criticism, Hunt articulated the principles of Romanticism, emphasizing imaginative freedom and the expression of a personal emotional or spiritual state. Although his critical works were overshadowed by those of more prominent Romantic critics, Samuel Taylor Coleridge, William Hazlitt, and Charles Lamb, his essays are considered both insightful and generous to the fledgling writers he supported. The following excerpt originally appeared in the* Examiner *on December 1, 1816. Hunt enthusiastically introduces Keats, Shelley, and John Hamilton Reynolds as proponents of a new school of poetry which Hunt promises will restore "the same love of Nature, and of thinking instead of mere talking, which formerly rendered us real poets." Hunt reviews Keats's sonnet "On First Looking into Chapman's Homer," pronouncing it excellent. Literary historians believe that some critics responded negatively to Keats in reaction to what*] *they considered Hunt's excessive praise, particularly since Keats had not yet published his first book. Hunt's essay is significant also because it linked Keats inextricably with the controversial Hunt in the minds of Tory critics such as John Gibson Lockhart and John Wilson Croker (see excerpts below, 1818).*]

Many of our readers . . . have perhaps observed for themselves, that there has been a new school of poetry rising of late, which promises to extinguish the French one that has prevailed among us since the time of Charles the 2d. It began with something excessive, like most revolutions, but this gradually wore away; and an evident aspiration after real nature and original fancy remained, which called to mind the finer times of the English Muse. In fact it is wrong to call it a new school, and still more so to represent it as one of innovation, its only object being to restore the same love of Nature, and of *thinking* instead of mere *talking*, which formerly rendered us real poets, and not merely versifying wits, and bead-rollers of couplets. . . .

The object of the present article is merely to notice three young writers, who appear to us to promise a considerable addition of strength to the new school. (p. 426)

The last of [the] young aspirants whom we have met with, and who promise to help the new school to revive Nature and

> To put a spirit of youth in every thing,—

is, we believe, the youngest of them all, and just of age. His name is JOHN KEATS. He has not yet published any thing except in a newspaper; but a set of his manuscripts was handed us the other day, and fairly surprised us with the truth of their ambition, and ardent grappling with Nature. In the following Sonnet there is one incorrect rhyme, which might be easily altered, but which shall serve in the mean time as a peace-offering to the rhyming critics. The rest of the composition, with the exception of a little vagueness in calling the regions of poetry "the realms of gold," we do not hesitate to pronounce excellent, especially the last six lines. The word *swims* is complete; and the whole conclusion is equally powerful and quiet:—

> ON FIRST LOOKING INTO CHAPMAN'S HOMER.
>
> Much have I travel'd in the realms of Gold,
>   And many goodly States and Kingdoms seen;
>   Round many western Islands have I been,
> Which Bards in fealty to Apollo hold;
> But of one wide expanse had I been told,
>   That deep-brow'd Homer ruled as his demesne;
>   Yet could I never judge what men could mean,
> Till I heard Chapman speak out loud and bold.
> Then felt I like some watcher of the skies,
>   When a new planet swims into his ken;
> Or like stout Cortez, when with eagle eyes
>   He stared at the Pacific,—and all his men
> Looked at each other with a wild surmise,—
>   Silent, upon a peak in Darien. . . .
>
>   (pp. 426-27)

We have spoken with the less scruple of these poetical promises, because we really are not in the habit of lavishing praises and announcements, and because we have no fear of any pettier vanity on the part of young men, who promise to understand human nature so well. (p. 427)

> [*Leigh Hunt*], *in an extract from* The Romantics Reviewed, Contemporary Reviews of British Romantic Writers: Shelley, Keats, and London Radical Writers, Vol. I, *edited by Donald H. Reiman, Garland Publishing, Inc., 1972, pp. 425-27.**

[JOHN HAMILTON REYNOLDS?]   (essay date 1817)

[*Reynolds was a minor English poet and journalist who is noted chiefly for his close friendship with Keats. In the following review, which is attributed to Reynolds and which appeared in the* Champion *in March, 1817, Reynolds praised Keats's first book by invoking the names of William Shakespeare, John Milton, and Geoffrey Chaucer in comparison with the young poet. Reynolds's further attempt in this essay to link Keats with many of his better-known contemporaries was criticized as "injudicious" by George Felton Mathew (1817), who, faulting Reynolds for his excessive praise, wrote: "Too much praise is more injurious than censure." In this case, Mathews appears to have been correct, for literary historians often note that effusive reviews such as Hamilton's prompted in part the harsh attacks of later critics.*]

[*Poems*] is a little volume filled throughout with very graceful and genuine poetry. . . . At a time when nothing is talked of but the power and the passion of Lord Byron, and the playful and elegant fancy of Moore, and the correctness of Rogers, and the sublimity and pathos of Campbell (these terms we should conceive are kept ready composed in the *Edinburgh Review*-shop) a young man starts suddenly before us, with a genius that is likely to eclipse them all. He comes fresh from nature,—and the originals of his images are to be found in her keeping. Young writers are in general in their early productions imitators of their favourite poets; like young birds that in their first songs, mock the notes of those warblers, they hear the most, and love the best: but this youthful poet appears to have tuned his voice in solitudes,—to have sung from the pure inspiration of nature. . . .

We find in his poetry the glorious effect of summer days and leafy spots on rich feelings, which are in themselves a summer. He relies directly and wholly on nature. He marries poesy to genuine simplicity. He makes her artless,—yet abstains carefully from giving her an uncomely homeliness:—that is, he shows she can be familiar with nature, yet perfectly strange to the habits of common life. Mr. Keats is fated, or "we have no judgment in an honest face;" to look at natural objects with his mind, as Shakespeare and Chaucer did,—and not merely with his eye as nearly all modern poets do;—to cloth his poetry with a grand intellectual light,—and to lay his name in the lap of immortality. (p. 260)

[With] the exception of Milton's and Wordsworth's, we think [his Sonnets] the most powerful ones in the whole range of English poetry. (p. 261)

[*Poems*] is not without defects, which may be easily mentioned, and as easily rectified. The author, from his natural freedom of versification, at times passes to an absolute faultiness of measure:—. This he should avoid. He should also abstain from the use of compound epithets as much as possible. He has a few of the faults which youth must have:—he is apt occasionally to make his descriptions over-wrought.—But on the whole we never saw a book which had so little reason to plead youth as its excuse. The best poets of the day might not blush to own it. (p. 262)

> [*John Hamilton Reynolds?*], *in an extract from* The Romantics Reviewed, Contemporary Reviews of British Romantic Writers: Shelley, Keats, and London Radical Writers, Vol. I, *edited by Donald H. Reiman, Garland Publishing, Inc., 1972, pp. 260-62.*

G.F.M. [GEORGE FELTON MATHEW]   (essay date 1817)

[*Mathew was a childhood friend of Keats and the subject of a verse epistle included in Keats's* Poems. *Critics speculate that the following negative review of the volume was founded on more personal than aesthetic ground; it reflects Mathew's bitterness that Keats was spending far more time with the Leigh Hunt circle than with his old friends. In this review, which appeared in the* European Magazine *in May 1817, Mathew disputes John Hamilton Reynolds's comparison of Keats with well-known contemporary poets such as Lord Byron and Thomas Moore (see excerpt above, 1817). Responding to Hamilton's statement that Keats lacks the usual faults of a beginning poet, Mathew cites the "petty arguments" of Keats's principal poems as betraying a "youthful architect," and he terms another poem "pretty and innocent as childishness can make it." Mathew also accuses Keats of possessing the faults of his mentor, Leigh Hunt. Keats reportedly felt betrayed by Mathew's review, and its publication marked the end of their friendship.*]

[*Poems*] is full of imaginations and descriptions . . . [delicate and elegant]; but, although we have looked into it with pleasure, and strongly recommend it to the perusal of all lovers of real poetry, we cannot, as another critic has injudiciously attempted, roll the name of Byron, Moore, Campbell and Rogers, into the milky way of literature, because Keats is pouring forth his splendors in the Orient. . . .

Too much praise is more injurious than censure, and forms that magnifying lens, through which, the faults and deformities of its object are augmented and enlarged. . . .

We cannot then advance for our author equal claim to public notice for maturity of thought, propriety of feeling, or felicity of style. But while we blame the slovenly independence of his versification, we must allow that thought, sentiment, and feeling, particularly in the active use and poetical display of them, belong more to the maturity of summer fruits than to the infancy of vernal blossoms. . . . But if the gay colours and the sweet fragrance of bursting blossoms be the promise of future treasures, then may we prophecy boldly of the future eminence of our young poet, for we have no where found them so early or so beautifully displayed as in the pages of the volume before us.

The youthful architect may be discovered in the petty arguments of his principal pieces. These poetical structures may be compared to no gorgeous palaces, no solemn temples; and in his enmity to the French school, and to the Augustan age of England, he seems to have a principle, that plan and arrangement are prejudicial to natural poetry.

The principal conception of his first poem is the same as that of a contemporary author, Mr. Wordsworth, and presumes that the most ancient poets, who are the inventors of the Heathen Mythology, imagined those fables chiefly by the personification of many appearances in nature. . . . (p. 422)

[The fragment of a **"Tale of Romance"**] is as pretty and as innocent as childishness can make it, save that it savours too much,—as indeed do almost all these poems,—of the foppery and affectation of Leigh Hunt! (pp. 422-23)

We might transcribe the whole volume were we to point out every instance of the luxuriance of his imagination, and the puerility of his sentiments. With these distinguishing features, it cannot be but many passages will appear abstracted and obscure. Feeble and false thoughts are easily lost sight of in the redundance of poetical decoration. (p. 423)

> G.F.M. [George Felton Mathew], *in an extract from* The Romantics Reviewed, Contemporary Reviews of British Romantic Writers: Shelley, Keats, and London Radical Writers, Vol. I, *edited by Donald*

H. Reiman, Garland Publishing, Inc., 1972, pp. 421-24.

JOHN KEATS (essay date 1818)

[*In his preface to* Endymion, *excerpted below, Keats apologizes for the work's imperfections. Keats's modest acknowledgment of the book's weaknesses was used against him by critics such as John Wilson Croker (see excerpt below, 1818).*]

Knowing within myself the manner in which this Poem has been produced, it is not without a feeling of regret that I make it public.

What manner I mean, will be quite clear to the reader, who must soon perceive great inexperience, immaturity, and every error denoting a feverish attempt, rather than a deed accomplished. The two first books, and indeed the two last, I feel sensible are not of such completion as to warrant their passing the press; nor should they if I thought a year's castigation would do them any good;—it will not: the foundations are too sandy. It is just that this youngster should die away: a sad thought for me, if I had not some hope that while it is dwindling I may be plotting, and fitting myself for verses fit to live.

This may be speaking too presumptuously, and may deserve a punishment: but no feeling man will be forward to inflict it: he will leave me alone, with the conviction that there is not a fiercer hell than the failure in a great object. This is not written with the least atom of purpose to forestall criticisms of course, but from the desire I have to conciliate men who are competent to look, and who do look with a zealous eye, to the honour of English literature.

The imagination of a boy is healthy, and the mature imagination of a man is healthy; but there is a space of life between, in which the soul is in a ferment, the character undecided, the way of life uncertain, the ambition thick-sighted: thence proceeds mawkishness, and all the thousand bitters which those men I speak of must necessarily taste in going over the following pages.

I hope I have not in too late a day touched the beautiful mythology of Greece, and dulled its brightness: for I wish to try once more, before I bid it farewell. (pp. vii-ix)

> John Keats, *in a preface to his* Endymion: A Poetic Romance, *Taylor and Hessey, 1818, pp. vii-ix.*

[JOHN WILSON CROKER] (essay date 1818)

[*The following review appeared in an issue of the* Quarterly Review *dated April 1818, although the magazine was not actually issued until September of that year. Croker, its author, was a Tory politician and a regular contributor to the* Quarterly. *He is famous, or more accurately infamous, today for this derogatory notice of* Endymion, *which some of Keats's friends blamed for his early death (see excerpt below by Percy Bysshe Shelley, 1821). While Croker does acknowledge Keats's "powers of language, rays of fancy, and gleams of genius," he largely decries the work and provides extensive examples to illustrate his contention that Keats's versification is poor and his language faulty. Croker asserts that Keats shares the faults of Leigh Hunt, but expresses less meaning than Hunt because Keats, according to Croker, composes on the basis of sound rather than sense. Although Francis Jeffrey implicitly denounced Croker's review (see excerpt below, 1820), he echoed Croker's opinion that Keats appears to compose by following images rather than logic or plotline. Modern critics note that Croker did indeed make several valid criti-*

cisms of Keats's work, and that, in truth, his review was more carefully considered and far less personally vindictive than that of John Gibson Lockhart (see excerpt below, 1818). Yet owing perhaps to the prestige and influence of the Quarterly, *which was far more well-established than the relatively new, Scotland-based* Blackwood's, *Croker bore most of the blame for unfairly criticizing Keats. John Hamilton Reynolds defended Keats against Croker's review, which he termed a "wanton and empty attack" (1818), and John Scott in* London Magazine *(1820) called it "heartless" and "vindictive."*]

Reviewers have been sometimes accused of not reading the works which they affected to criticise. On the present occasion we shall anticipate the author's complaint, and honestly confess that we have not read [**Endymion: A Poetic Romance**]. Not that we have been wanting in our duty—far from it—indeed, we have made efforts almost as superhuman as the story itself appears to be, to get through it; but with the fullest stretch of our perseverance, we are forced to confess that we have not been able to struggle beyond the first of the four books of which this Poetic Romance consists. We should extremely lament this want of energy, or whatever it may be, on our parts, were it not for one consolation—namely, that we are no better acquainted with the meaning of the book through which we have so painfully toiled, than we are with that of the three which we have not looked into.

It is not that Mr. Keats, (if that be his real name, for we almost doubt that any man in his senses would put his real name to such a rhapsody,) it is not, we say, that the author has not powers of language, rays of fancy, and gleams of genius—he has all these; but he is unhappily a disciple of the new school of what has been somewhere called Cockney poetry; which may be defined to consist of the most incongruous ideas in the most uncouth language. . . .

[Mr. Keats] is a copyist of Mr. Hunt; but he is more unintelligible, almost as rugged, twice as diffuse, and ten times more tiresome and absurd than his prototype, who, though he impudently presumed to seat himself in the chair of criticism, and to measure his own poetry by his own standard, yet generally had a meaning. But Mr. Keats had advanced no dogmas which he was bound to support by examples; his nonsense therefore is quite gratuitous; he writes it for its own sake, and, being bitten by Mr. Leigh Hunt's insane criticism, more than rivals the insanity of his poetry.

Mr. Keats's preface [see excerpt above, 1818] hints that his poem was produced under peculiar circumstances.

> Knowing within myself (he says) the manner in which this Poem has been produced, it is not without a feeling of regret that I make it public.—What manner I mean, will be *quite clear* to the reader, who must soon perceive great inexperience, immaturity, and every error denoting a feverish attempt, rather than a deed accomplished. . . .

We humbly beg his pardon, but this does not appear to us to be *quite so clear*—we really do not know what he means—but the next passage is more intelligible.

> The two first books, and indeed the two last,
> I feel sensible are not of such completion as to
> warrant their passing the press. . . .
>
> (p. 768)

Thus 'the two first books' are, even in his own judgment, unfit to appear, and 'the two last' are, it seems, in the same con-

dition—and as two and two make four, and as that is the whole number of books, we have a clear and, we believe, a very just estimate of the entire work.

Mr. Keats, however, deprecates criticism on this 'immature and feverish work' in terms which are themselves sufficiently feverish; and we confess that we should have abstained from inflicting upon him any of the tortures of the *'fierce hell'* of criticism, which terrify his imagination, if he had not begged to be spared in order that he might write more; if we had not observed in him a certain degree of talent which deserves to be put in the right way, or which, at least, ought to be warned of the wrong; and if, finally, he had not told us that he is of an age and temper which imperiously require mental discipline.

Of the story we have been able to make out but little it seems to be mythological, and probably relates to the loves of Diana and Endymion; but of this, as the scope of the work has altogether escaped us, we cannot speak with any degree of certainty; and must therefore content ourselves with giving some instances of its diction and versification:—and here again we are perplexed and puzzled.—At first it appeared to us, that Mr. Keats had been amusing himself and wearying his readers with an immeasurable game at *boutsrimés* [a game in which the player improvises a poem from rhyme words that have been supplied]; but, if we recollect rightly, it is an indispensable condition at this play, that the rhymes when filled up shall have a meaning; and our author, as we have already hinted, has no meaning. He seems to us to write a line at random, and then he follows not the thought excited by this line, but that suggested by the *rhyme* with which it concludes. There is hardly a complete couplet inclosing a complete idea in the whole book. He wanders from one subject to another, from the association, not of ideas but of sounds, and the work is composed of hemistichs which, it is quite evident, have forced themselves upon the author by the mere force of the catchwords on which they turn.

We shall select, not as the most striking instance, but as that least liable to suspicion, a passage from the opening of the poem.

> Such the sun, the moon,
> Trees old and young, sprouting a shady boon
> For simple sheep; and such are daffodils
> With the green world they live in; and clear rills
> That for themselves a cooling covert make
> 'Gainst the hot season; the mid forest brake,
> Rich with a sprinkling of fair musk-rose blooms:
> And such too is the grandeur of the dooms
> We have imagined for the mighty dead; &c. &c. . . .
>
> (pp. 768-69)

Here it is clear that the word, and not the idea, *moon* produced the simple sheep and their shady *boon,* and that 'the *dooms* of the mighty dead' would never have intruded themselves but for the *'fair musk-rose blooms.'* . . .

We come now to the author's taste in versification. He cannot indeed write a sentence, but perhaps he may be able to spin a line. Let us see. The following are specimens of his prosodial notions of our English heroic metre.

> Dear as the temple's self, so does the moon,
> The passion poesy, glories infinite. . . .
> So plenteously all weed-hidden roots. . . .
> Of some strange history, potent to send. . . .
> Before the deep intoxication. . . .
> Her scarf into a fluttering pavilion. . . .

By this time our readers must be pretty well satisfied as to the meaning of his sentences and the structure of his lines: we now present them with some of the new words with which, in imitation of Mr. Leigh Hunt, he adorns our language.

We are told that 'turtles *passion* their voices,' . . . ; that 'an arbour was *nested*,' . . . ; and a lady's locks '*gordian'd* up,' . . . ; and to supply the place of the nouns thus verbalized Mr. Keats, with great fecundity, spawns new ones; such as 'men-slugs and human *serpentry*'. . . . (p. 769)

But enough of Mr. Leigh Hunt and his simple neophyte.—If any one should be bold enough to purchase this 'Poetic Romance,' and so much more patient, than ourselves, as to get beyond the first book, and so much more fortunate as to find a meaning, we entreat him to make us acquainted with his success; we shall then return to the task which we now abandon in despair, and endeavour to make all due amends to Mr. Keats and to our readers. (p. 770)

> [*John Wilson Croker*], *in an extract from* The Romantics Reviewed, Contemporary Reviews of British Romantic Writers: Shelley, Keats, and London Radical Writers, Vol. II, *edited by Donald H. Reiman, Garland Publishing, Inc., 1972, pp. 767-70.*

Z. [JOHN GIBSON LOCKHART] (essay date 1818)

[*Scots Lockhart wrote several novels, but his fame rests on his biography of Sir Walter Scott and his critical contributions to* Blackwood's Edinburgh Magazine *and the* Quarterly Review. *From 1817 to 1825, he was a principal contributor to* Blackwood's, *a Tory periodical which was founded to counter the influential Whig journal* The Edinburgh Review. *His trenchant wit contributed to the early success of the magazine and earned him the nickname of "The Scorpion." Later, as editor of the* Quarterly, *he was a less acerbic critic. Nevertheless, he is notorious for his series of scathing articles in* Blackwood's *on the "Cockney School" of poetry, in which he assailed John Keats and Leigh Hunt on the basis of political differences and, indirectly, for their inferior education and upbringing. In contrast, Lockhart recognized the talents of William Wordsworth, Samuel Taylor Coleridge, and Percy Bysshe Shelley, despite his aversion to their political principles. He is regarded a versatile, if somewhat severe, critic whose opinions of his contemporaries, though lacking depth, are generally considered accurate when not distorted by political animosities. In the following review, first published in* Blackwood's *in August, 1818, Lockhart continues the attack on what he termed the "Cockney School of Poetry," which he had initiated in October 1817. Attacking Keats personally rather than as a poet, Lockhart ridicules his medical training, his lack of education, and his friendship with Leigh Hunt and Robert Benjamin Haydon. While the review lacks technical criticism of the poetry, Lockhart does briefly revile the "loose, nerveless versification" of the Cockney School and stresses that the defects of Keats's verse are ten times those of his mentor, Hunt. Lockhart's emphasis on Keats's affiliation with the controversial Hunt indicates the extent to which this review was politically motivated. This review, along with that by John Wilson Croker (see excerpt above, 1818), was named by Keats's friends after his death as a chief cause of the poet's illness.*]

Of all the manias of this mad age, the most incurable, as well as the most common, seems to be no other than the *Metromanie*. The just celebrity of Robert Burns and Miss Baillie has had the melancholy effect of turning the heads of we know not how many farm-servants and unmarried ladies; our very footmen compose tragedies, and there is scarcely a superannuated governess in the island that does not leave a roll of lyrics behind her in her band-box. . . . [Mr John Keats] appears to have received from nature talents of an excellent, perhaps even of a superior order—talents which, devoted to the purposes of any useful profession, must have rendered him a respectable, if not an eminent citizen. His friends, we understand, destined him to the career of medicine, and he was bound apprentice some years ago to a worthy apothecary in town. But all has been undone by a sudden attack of the malady to which we have alluded. Whether Mr John had been sent home with a diuretic or composing draught to some patient far gone in the poetical mania, we have not heard. This much is certain, that he has caught the infection, and that thoroughly. For some time we were in hopes, that he might get off with a violent fit or two; but of late the symptoms are terrible. The phrenzy of the **"Poems"** was bad enough in its way; but it did not alarm us half so seriously as the calm, settled, imperturbable drivelling idiocy of **"Endymion."** (p. 90)

The readers of the *Examiner* newspaper were informed, some time ago, by a solemn paragraph, in Mr Hunt's best style, of the appearance of two new stars of glorious magnitude and splendour in the poetical horizon of the land of Cockaigne [see excerpt above, 1816]. One of these turned out, by and by, to be no other than Mr John Keats. This precocious adulation confirmed the wavering apprentice in his desire to quit the gallipots, and at the same time excited in his too susceptible mind a fatal admiration for the character and talents of the most worthless and affected of all the versifiers of our time. One of his first productions was the [opening sonnet in **"Poems,"**] *"written on the day when Mr. Leigh Hunt left prison."* . . . The absurdity of the thought in this sonnet is, . . . if possible, surpassed in another, *"addressed to Haydon"* the painter, that clever, but most affected artist, who as little resembles Raphael in genius as he does in person, notwithstanding the foppery of having his hair curled over his shoulders in the old Italian fashion. In this exquisite piece it will be observed, that Mr Keats classes together Wordsworth, Hunt, and Haydon, as the three greatest spirits of the age, and that he alludes to himself, and some others of the rising brood of Cockneys, as likely to attain hereafter an equally honourable elevation. Wordsworth and Hunt! what a juxta-position! The purest, the loftiest, and, we do not fear to say it, the most classical of living English poets, joined together in the same compliment with the meanest, the filthiest, and the most vulgar of Cockney poetasters. No wonder that he who could be guilty of this should class Haydon with Raphael, and himself with Spencer. . . . The nations are to listen and be dumb! and why, good Johnny Keats? because Leigh Hunt is editor of the *Examiner,* and Haydon has painted the judgment of Solomon, and you and Cornelius Webb, and a few more city sparks, are pleased to look upon yourselves as so many future Shakspeares and Miltons! The world has really some reason to look to its foundations! . . . At the period when these sonnets were published, Mr Keats had no hesitation in saying, that he looked on himself as "*not yet* a glorious denizen of the wide heaven of poetry," but he had many fine soothing visions of coming greatness, and many rare plans of study to prepare him for it. . . . [Having cooled a little], our youthful poet passes very naturally into a long strain of foaming abuse against a certain class of English Poets, whom, with Pope at their head, it is much the fashion with the ignorant unsettled pretenders of the present time to undervalue. Begging these gentlemens' pardon, although Pope was not a poet of the same high order with some who are now living, yet, to deny his genius, is just about as absurd as to dispute that of Wordsworth, or to believe in that of Hunt. Above all things, it is most pitiably ridiculous to hear men, of whom their country will always have reason to be proud, reviled by uneducated and flimsy striplings, who are not capable of understanding either their merits, or those of any other *men of power*—fanciful dreaming tea-drinkers, who, without logic enough to analyse a single idea, or imagination enough to form one original image, or learning enough to distinguish between the written language of Englishmen and the spoken jargon of Cockneys, presume to talk with contempt of some of the most exquisite spirits the world ever produced, merely because they did not happen to exert their faculties in laborious affected descriptions of flowers seen in window-pots, or cascades heard at Vauxhall; in short, because they chose to be wits, philosophers, patriots, and poets, rather than to found the Cockney school of versification, morality, and politics, a century before its time. After blaspheming himself into a fury against Boileau, &c. Mr Keats comforts himself and his readers with a view of the present more promising aspect of affairs; above all, with the ripened glories of the poet of Rimini [Hunt]. . . . So much for the opening bud; now for the expanded flower. It is time to pass from the juvenile **"Poems,"** to the mature and elaborate **"Endymion, a Poetic Romance."** The old story of the moon falling in love with a shepherd, so prettily told by a Roman Classic, and so exquisitely enlarged and adorned by one of the most elegant of German poets, has been seized upon by Mr John Keats, to be done with as might seem good unto the sickly fancy of one who never read a single line either of Ovid or of Wieland. If the quantity, not the quality, of the verses dedicated to the story is to be taken into account, there can be no doubt that Mr John Keats may now claim Endymion entirely to himself. To say the truth, we do not suppose either the Latin or the German poet would be very anxious to dispute about the property of the hero of the **"Poetic Romance."** Mr Keats has thoroughly appropriated the character, if not the name. His Endymion is not a Greek shepherd, loved by a Grecian goddess; he is merely a young Cockney rhymester, dreaming a phantastic dream at the full of the moon. Costume, were it worth while to notice such a trifle, is violated in every page of this goodly octavo. From his prototype Hunt, John Keats has acquired a sort of vague idea, that the Greeks were a most tasteful people, and that no mythology can be so finely adapted for the purposes of poetry as theirs. It is amusing to see what a hand the two Cockneys make of this mythology; the one confesses that he never read the Greek Tragedians, and the other knows Homer only from Chapman; and both of them write about Apollo, Pan, Nymphs, Muses, and Mysteries, as might be expected from persons of their education. . . . As for Mr Keats' **"Endymion,"** it has just as much to do with Greece as it has with "old Tartary the fierce;" no man, whose mind has ever been imbued with the smallest knowledge or feeling of classical poetry or classical history, could have stooped to profane and vulgarise every association in the manner which has been adopted by this "son of promise." . . . [We] must inform our readers that this romance is meant to be written in English heroic rhyme. To those who have read any of Hunt's poems, this hint might indeed be needless. Mr. Keats has adopted the loose, nerveless versification, and Cockney rhymes of the poet of Rimini; but in fairness to that gentleman, we must add, that the defects of the system are tenfold more conspicuous in his disciple's work than in his own. Mr Hunt is a small poet, but he is a clever man. Mr Keats is a still smaller poet, and he is only a boy of pretty abilities, which he has done every thing in his power to spoil. (pp. 90-3)

And now, good-morrow to "the Muses' son of Promise;" as for "the feats he yet may do," as we do not pretend to say, like himself, "Muse of my native land am I inspired," we shall adhere to the safe old rule of *pauca verba* [few words].

We venture to make one small prophecy, that his bookseller will not a second time venture £50 upon any thing he can write. It is a better and a wiser thing to be a starved apothecary than a starved poet; so back to the shop Mr John, back to "plasters, pills, and ointment boxes," &c. But, for Heaven's sake, young Sangrado, be a little more sparing of extenuatives and soporifics in your practice than you have been in your poetry. (p. 95)

> Z. [*John Gibson Lockhart*], *in an extract from* The Romantics Reviewed, Contemporary Reviews of British Romantic Writers: Shelley, Keats, and London Radical Writers, Vol. I, *edited by Donald H. Reiman, Garland Publishing, Inc., 1972, pp. 90-5.*

[JOHN HAMILTON REYNOLDS]   (essay date 1818)

> [*The following review originally appeared in the periodical* Alfred *and was reprinted in the* Examiner *on October 11, 1818. Here Keats's friend provides a strong defense against John Wilson Croker's attack (see excerpt above, 1818), acknowledging that it was politically motivated. It is noteworthy that Reynolds discusses how a negative review "in part generated the melancholy which ultimately destroyed" the aspiring author Kirk White. The story foreshadows charges that Keats was ruined by the* Quarterly.]

We have met with a singular instance, in the last number of the *Quarterly Review* [see excerpt above by John Wilson Croker, 1818] of that unfeeling arrogance, and cold ignorance, which so strangely marked the minds and hearts of Government sycophants and Government writers. The Poem of a young man of genius, which evinces more natural power than any other work of this day, is abused and cried down, in terms which would disgrace any other pens than those used in the defence of an *Oliver* or a *Castles.* We have read the poetic romance of **Endymion** (the book in question) with no little delight; and could hardly believe that it was written by so young a man as the preface infers. Mr. Keats, the author of it, is a genius of the highest order; and no one but a Lottery Commissioner and a Government Pensioner, (both of which, Mr. William Gifford, the Editor of the *Quarterly Review,* is) could, with a false and remorseless pen, have striven to frustrate hopes and aims, so youthful and so high as this young Poet nurses. The Monthly Reviewers, it will be remembered, endeavoured, some few years back, to crush the rising heart of Kirk White; and indeed they in part generated that melancholy which ultimately destroyed him; but the world saw the cruelty, and, with one voice, hailed the genius which malignity would have repressed, and lifted it to fame. . . .

The cause of the unmerciful condemnation which has been passed on Mr. Keats, is pretty apparent to all who have watched the intrigues of literature, and the wily and unsparing contrivances of political parties. This young and powerful writer was noticed some little time back in the *Examiner,* and pointed out, by its Editor, as one who was likely to revive the early vigour of English poetry [see excerpt above by Leigh Hunt, 1816]. Such a prediction was a fine but dangerous compliment to Mr. Keats: it exposed him instantly to the malice of this *Quarterly Review. . . .*

Lord Byron is a splendid and noble egotist . . . : no spot is conveyed to our minds that is not peopled by the gloomy and ghastly feelings of one proud and solitary man. It is as if he and the world were the only two things which the air clothed. . . . Mr. Keats has none of this egotism—this daring selfishness, which is a stain on the role of poesy. His feelings are full, earnest, and original, as those of the older writers were and are; they are made for all time, not for the drawing-room and the moment. Mr. Keats always speaks of, and describes nature, with an awe and a humility, but with a deep and almost breathless affection.—He knows that Nature is better and older than he is, and he does not put himself on an equality with her. You do not see him when you see her. The moon, and the mountainous foliage of the woods, and the azure sky, and the ruined and magic temple; the rock, the desert, and the sea; the leaf of the forest, and the embossed foam of the most living ocean, are the spirits of his poetry; but he does not bring them in his own hand, or obtrude his person before you, when you are looking at them. Poetry is a thing of generalities—a wanderer amid persons and things—not a pauser over one thing, or with one person. The mind of Mr. Keats, like the minds of our older poets, goes round the universe in its speculations and its dreams. It does not set itself a task. The manners of the world, the fictions and the wonders of other worlds, are its subjects: not the pleasures of hope, or the pleasures of memory. The true poet confines his imagination to no one thing—his soul is an invisible ode to the passions. (p. 438)

Mr. Keats has certainly not perfected any thing yet; but he has the power, we think, within him, and it is in consequence of such an opinion that we have written these few hasty observations. If he should ever see this, he will not regret to find that all the country is not made up of Quarterly Reviewers. All that we wish is, that our readers would read the Poem, as we have done, before they assent to its condemnation—they will find passages of singular feeling, force, and pathos. We have the highest hopes of this young Poet.... We think we see glimpses of a high mind in this young man, and surely the feeling is better that urges us to nourish its strength, than that which prompts the Quarterly Reviewer to crush it in its youth, and for ever. If however the mind of Mr. Keats be of the quality we think it to be of, it will not be cast down by this wanton and empty attack. Malice is a thing of the scorpion kind—it drives the sting into its own heart. The very passages which the *Quarterly Review* quotes as ridiculous, have in them the beauty that sent us to the Poem itself....

The turn of [some passages] is truly Shaksperian, which Mr. Keats will feel to be the highest compliment we can pay him, if we know any thing of his mind....

Does the author of such poetry as [*Endymion*] deserve to be made the sport of so servile a dolt as a Quarterly Reviewer?— No. Two things have struck us on the perusal of this singular poem. The first is, that Mr. Keats excels, in what Milton excelled—the power of putting a spirit of life and novelty into the Heathen Mythology. The second is, that in the structure of his verse, and the *sinewy* quality of his thoughts, Mr. Keats greatly resembles old Chapman, the nervous translator of Homer: His mind has "thews and limbs like to its ancestors." Mr. Gifford, who knows something of the old dramatists, ought to have paused before he sanctioned the abuse of a spirit kindred with them. If he could not feel, he ought to know better. (p. 439)

[*John Hamilton Reynolds*], *in an extract from* The Romantics Reviewed, Contemporary Reviews of British Romantic Writers: Shelley, Keats, and London Radical Writers, Vol. I, *edited by Donald H. Reiman, Garland Publishing, Inc., 1972, pp. 437-39.*

[CHARLES LAMB]   (essay date 1820)

[Lamb was an English poet, dramatist, and critic who was casually acquainted with Keats and reportedly admired his work a

great deal.. *In the following descriptive and somewhat impressionistic review of* Lamia, *Lamb isolates single images and phrases for praise. This demonstrates a common tendency of early Keats critics, noted by modern scholars, to stress the beauty of selected portions of Keats's poems rather than analyzing the significance and effect of the whole. This review was reprinted from the* New Times *in the July 30, 1820 issue of the* Examiner.]

[In *Lamia, Isabella, The Eve of St. Agnes, and Other Poems,* Mr. Keats describes] a high-born damsel, in one of the apartments of an old baronial castle, laying herself down devoutly to dream, on the charmed Eve of St. Agnes; and like the radiance, which comes from those old windows upon the limbs and garments of the damsel, is the almost Chaucer-like painting, with which this poet illumines every subject he touches. We have scarcely any thing like it in modern description. . . .

The finest thing in the volume is the paraphrase of Boccacio's story of the Pot of Basil. . . . [Isabella's arrival at her lover's grave], and digging for the body, is described in . . . stanzas, than which there is nothing more awfully simple in diction, more nakedly grand and moving in sentiment in Dante, in Chaucer, or in Spencer. . . . (p. 451)

More exuberantly rich in imagery and painting is the story of the Lamia. It is of as gorgeous stuff as ever romance was composed of. Her first appearance in serpentine form—

a beauteous wreath with melancholy eyes

her dialogue with Hermes, the *Star of Lethe,* as he is called by one of those prodigal phrases which Mr. Keats abounds in, which are each a poem in a word, and which in this instance lays open to us at once, like a picture, all the dim regions and their inhabitants, and the sudden coming of a celestial among them; the charming of her into woman's shape again by the God; her marriage with the beautiful Lycius; her magic palace, which those who knew the street, and remembered it complete from childhood, never remembered to have seen before; the few Persian mutes, her attendants, . . . the high-wrought splendours of the nuptial bower, with the fading of the whole pageantry, Lamia, and all, away, before the glance of Apollonius,—are all that fairy land can do for us. They are for younger impressibilities. To *us* an ounce of feeling is worth a pound of fancy; and therefore we recur again, with a warmer gratitude, to the story of Isabella and the pot of basil, and those nevercloying stanzas which we have cited, and which we think should disarm criticism, if it be not in its nature cruel; if it would not deny to honey its sweetness, nor to roses redness, nor light to the stars in Heaven; if it would not bay the moon out of the skies, rather than acknowledge she is fair. (p. 452)

[*Charles Lamb*], *in an extract from* The Romantics Reviewed, Contemporary Reviews of British Romantic Writers: Shelley, Keats, and London Radical Writers, Vol. I, *edited by Donald H. Reiman, Garland Publishing, Inc., 1972, pp. 450-52.*

[FRANCIS JEFFREY]   (essay date 1820)

[Jeffrey was a founder and editor (1803-1829) of the Edinburgh Review, *one of the most influential magazines in early nineteenth-century England. A liberal Whig and a politician, Jeffrey often allowed his political beliefs to color his critical opinions. His literary criticism, perhaps the most characteristic example of "impressionistic" critical thought dominant during the first half of the nineteenth century, stressed a personal approach to literature. Jeffrey felt that literature should be judged by his own conception of beauty (a beautiful work being that which inspires*

sensations of tenderness or pity in the reader), rather than by Neoclassical criteria such as restraint, clarity, order, balance, and proportion. Seeking a universal standard of beauty and taste, Jeffrey exhorted artists to "employ only such subjects as are the natural signs, or the inseparable concomitants of emotions, of which the greater part of mankind are susceptible." In addition, Jeffrey wanted literature to be realistic and to observe standards of propriety. Though he became famous for his harsh criticism of the Lake poets (Samuel Taylor Coleridge, William Wordsworth, and Robert Southey), Jeffrey was an exponent of moderate Romanticism and praised the work of John Keats, Lord Byron, and Walter Scott. Jeffrey was widely influential throughout his lifetime and helped to raise the status of periodical reviewing in nineteenth-century England. The following excerpt from an August 1820 article was the first review of Keats in the Edinburgh Review, *which was, after the* Quarterly Review, *the most influential literary magazine in Britain; its silence on Keats until almost 1820 had been generally taken as acquiescence to John Wilson Croker's essay in the* Quarterly *(1818). Jeffrey here attempts to correct that impression with a defense of Keats. He offers an appreciative review of* Endymion *in addition to a cursory mention of Keats's latest work,* Lamia. *While Jeffrey implicitly decries the review by Croker, he interestingly echoes Croker's complaint that Keats seems to compose by piling image upon image rather than by following a logical story line. Jeffrey perhaps realized that his attempt to boost Keats's reputation came a bit late. In a footnote to an 1844 reprint of the article, he wrote: "I still think that a poet of great power and promise was lost to us by the premature death of Keats . . . ; and regret that I did not go more largely into the exposition of his merits." For his part, Keats had been disappointed in the failure of the* Edinburgh Review *to review his works and wrote in 1819 to his brother George that "the cowardliness of the* Edinburgh *is more than the abuse of the* Quarterly."]

We had never happened to see either of these volumes [*Endymion* and *Lamia, Isabella, The Eve of St. Agnes, and Other Poems*] till very lately—and have been exceedingly struck with the genius they display, and the spirit of poetry which breathes through all their extravagance. . . . Mr. Keats, we understand, is still a very young man; and his whole works, indeed, bear evidence enough of the fact. They are full of extravagance and irregularity, rash attempts at originality, interminable wanderings, and excessive obscurity. They manifestly require, therefore, all the indulgence that can be claimed for a first attempt:—but we think it no less plain that they deserve it; for they are fleshed all over with the rich lights of fancy, and so coloured and bestrewn with the flowers of poetry, that even while perplexed and bewildered in their labyrinths, it is impossible to resist the intoxication of their sweetness, or to shut our hearts to the enchantments they so lavishly present. The models upon which he has formed himself, in the *Endymion,* the earliest and by much the most considerable of his poems, are obviously the Faithful Shepherdess of Fletcher, and the Sad Shepherd of Ben Jonson;—the exquisite metres and inspired diction of which he has copied with great boldness and fidelity—and, like his great originals, has also contrived to impart to the whole piece that true rural and poetical air which breathes only in them and in Theocritus—which is at once homely and majestic, luxurious and rude, and sets before us the genuine sights and sounds and smells of the country, with all the magic and grace of Elysium. His subject has the disadvantage of being mythological; and in this respect, as well as on account of the raised and rapturous tone it consequently assumes, his poetry may be better compared perhaps to the Comus and the Arcades of Milton, of which, also, there are many traces of imitation. The great distinction, however, between him and these divine authors, is, that imagination in them is subordinate to reason and judgment, while, with him, it is paramount and supreme—that their

ornaments and images are employed to embellish and recommend just sentiments, engaging incidents, and natural characters, while his are poured out without measure or restraint, and with no apparent design but to unburden the breast of the author, and give vent to the overflowing vein of his fancy. The thin and scanty tissue of his story is merely the light frame work on which his florid wreaths are suspended; and while his imaginations go rambling and entangling themselves everywhere, like wild honeysuckles, all idea of sober reason, and plan, and consistency, is utterly forgotten, and are 'strangled in their waste fertility.' A great part of the work indeed, is written in the strangest and most fantastical manner that can be imagined. It seems as if the author had ventured everything that occurred to him in the shape of a glittering image or striking expression—taken the first word that presented itself to make up a rhyme, and then made that word the germ of a new cluster of images—a hint for a new excursion of the fancy—and so wandered on, equally forgetful whence he came, and heedless whither he was going, till he had covered his pages with an interminable arabesque of connected and incongruous figures, that multiplied as they extended, and were only harmonized by the brightness of their tints, and the graces of their forms. In this rash and headlong career he has of course many lapses and failures. There is no work, accordingly, from which a malicious critic could cull more matter for ridicule, or select more obscure, unnatural, or absurd passages. But we do not take *that* to be our office;—and just beg leave, on the contrary, to say, that any one who, on this account, would represent the whole poem as despicable, must either have no notion of poetry, or no regard to truth.

It is, in truth, at least as full of genius as of absurdity; and he who does not find a great deal in it to admire and to give delight, cannot in his heart see much beauty in the two exquisite dramas to which we have already alluded, or find any great pleasure in some of the finest creations of Milton and Shakespeare. There are very many such persons, we verily believe, even among the reading and judicious part of the community . . . but utterly ignorant of the true genius of English poetry, and incapable of estimating its appropriate and most exquisite beauties. With that spirit we have no hesitation in saying that Mr. K. is deeply imbued—and of those beauties he has presented us with many striking examples. We are very much inclined indeed to add that we do not know any book which we would sooner employ as a test to ascertain whether any one had in him a native relish for poetry, and a genuine sensibility to its intrinsic charm. . . . Even in the judgment of a fitter audience, however, it must, we fear, be admitted, that, besides the riot and extravagance of his fancy, the scope and substance of Mr. K.'s poetry is rather too dreary and abstracted to excite the strongest interest, or to sustain the attention through a work of any great compass or extent. He deals too much with shadowy and incomprehensible beings, and is too constantly rapt into an extramundane Elysium, to command a lasting interest with ordinary mortals—and must employ the agency of more varied and coarser emotions, if he wishes to take rank with the seducing poets of this or of former generations. There is something very curious too, we think, in the way in which he, and Mr. Barry Cornwall also, have dealt with the Pagan mythology, of which they have made so much use in their poetry. Instead of presenting its imaginary persons under the trite and vulgar traits that belong to them in the ordinary systems, little more is borrowed from these than the general conception of their conditions and relations; and an original character and distinct individuality is bestowed upon them, which has all the merit of invention, and all the grace and attraction of the fictions on which it is engrafted. The antients, though they probably did not stand in any great awe of their deities, have yet abstained very much from any minute or dramatic representation of their feelings and affections.... The author before us, however, and some of his contemporaries, have dealt differently with the subject; and, sheltering the violence of the fiction under the ancient traditionary fable, have created and imagined an entire new set of characters, and brought closely and minutely before us the loves and sorrows and perplexities of beings, with whose names and supernatural attributes we had long been familiar, without any sense or feeling of their personal character. We have more than doubts of the fitness of such personages to maintain a permanent interest with the modern public;—but the way in which they are here managed, certainly gives them the best chance that now remains for them; and, at all events, it cannot be denied that the effect is striking and graceful. (pp. 385-87)

There is [in *Lamia, Isabella, The Eve of St. Agnes, and Other Poems*] a fragment of a projected Epic, entitled 'Hyperion,' ... of which we cannot advise the completion: For, though there are passages of some force and grandeur, it is sufficiently obvious ... that the subject is too far removed from all the sources of human interest, to be successfully treated by any modern author. Mr. Keats has unquestionably a very beautiful imagination, and a great familiarity with the finest diction of English poetry; but he must learn not to misuse or misapply these advantages; and neither to waste the good gifts of nature and study on intractable themes, nor to luxuriate too recklessly on such as are more suitable. (p. 390)

> [*Francis Jeffrey*], in an extract from The Romantics Reviewed, Contemporary Reviews of British Romantic Writers: Shelley, Keats, and London Radical Writers, Vol. I, *edited by Donald H. Reiman, Garland Publishing, Inc., 1972, pp. 385-90.*

[JOHN SCOTT] (essay date 1820)

> [*While acknowledging Keats's faults of obscurity and deliberate quaintness of phrase, Scott makes an appeal for recognition of Keats's genius. Modern critics note that Scott would have been perhaps more enthusiastic, but he was fearful of repeating the excesses of Leigh Hunt in the* Examiner *(see excerpt above, 1816).*]

The injustice which has been done to [Mr. Keats's] works, in estimating their poetical merit, rendered us doubly anxious, on opening [*Lamia, Isabella, The Eve of St. Agnes, and Other Poems*], to find it likely to seize fast hold of general sympathy, and thus turn an overwhelming power against the paltry traducers of a talent, more eminently promising in many respects, than any that the present age has been called upon to encourage. We have not found it to be quite all that we wished in this respect.... But we have found it of a nature to present to common understandings the poetical power with which the author's mind is gifted, in a more tangible and intelligible shape than that in which it has appeared in any of his former compositions. It is, therefore, calculated to throw shame on the lying, vulgar spirit, in which this young worshipper in the temple of the Muses has been cried-down; whatever questions it may still leave to be settled as to the kind and degree of his poetical merits. Take for instance, as a proof of the justice of our praise, the following passage from an **"Ode to the Nightingale"**:—it is distinct, noble, pathetic, and true: the thoughts have all chords of direct communication with naturally-con-stituted hearts: the echoes of the strain linger about the depths of human bosoms.

> Thou wast not born for death, immortal Bird!
> No hungry generations tread thee down;
> The voice I hear this passing night was heard
> In ancient days by emperor and clown:
> *Perhaps the self-same song that found a path*
> *Through the sad heart of Ruth, when, sick for home,*
> *She stood in tears amid the alien corn:*
> The same that oft-times hath
> Charm'd magic casements, opening on the foam
> Of perilous seas, in faery lands forlorn.
>
> (p. 318)

Let us [cite] also a passage of another sort altogether—the description [from **"The Eve of St. Agnes"**] of a young beauty preparing for her nightly rest, overlooked by a concealed lover, in which we know not whether most to admire the magical delicacy of the hazardous picture, or its consummate, irresistible attraction. "How sweet the moonlight sleeps upon this bank," says Shakspeare; and sweetly indeed does it fall on the half undressed form of Madeline:—it has an exquisite moral influence, corresponding with the picturesque effect. (pp. 318-19)

"Hyperion" [is] one of the most extraordinary creations of any modern imagination. Its "woods are ruthless, dreadful, deaf, and dull:" the soul of dim antiquity hovers, like a mountain-cloud, over its vast and gloomy grandeur: it carries us back in spirit beyond the classical age; earlier than "the gods of the Greeks;" when the powers of creation were to be met with visible about the young earth, shouldering the mountains, and with their huge forms filling the vallies. The sorrows of this piece are "huge;" its utterance "large," its tears "big."—Alas, centuries have brought littleness since then,—otherwise a crawling, reptile of office, with just strength enough to leave its slimy traces on the pages of a fashionable Review, could never have done a real mischief to the poet of the Titans! It is but a fragment we have of **"Hyperion"**: an advertisement tells us that "the poem was intended to have been of equal length with *Endymion,* but the reception given to that work discouraged the author from proceeding." Let Mr. Croker read the ... sublime and gorgeous personification of Asia, and be proud of the information thus given him [see excerpt above by John Wilson Croker, 1818].... (p. 319)

Will not our readers feel it as a disgrace attaching to the character of the period, that a dastardly attempt should have been made to assassinate a poet of power equal to these passages: that one should come like a thief to steal his "precious diadem;"—a murder and a robbery "most foul and horrible?" Cold-blooded conscious dishonesty, we have no hesitation to say, must have directed the pen of the critic of *Endymion* in the *Quarterly Review:* making every allowance for the callousness of a worldly spirit, it is impossible to conceive a total insensibility to the vast beauties scattered profusely over that disordered, ill-digested work. The author provokes opposition, as we have already fully said: not unfrequently he even suggests angry censure. We cannot help applying the word *insolent,* in a literary sense, to some instances of his neglectfulness, to the random swagger of occasional expressions, to the bravado style of many of his sentiments. But, coupling these great faults with his still greater poetical merits, what a fine, what an interesting subject did he offer for perspicacious, honourable criticism! But he was beset by a very dog-kennel; and he must be more than human if he has not had his erroneous tendencies hardened in him in consequence.

What strike us as the principal faults of his poetry, impeding his popularity, we would venture thus to specify.

1. His frequent obscurity and confusion of language. As an instance of the latter, we may mention, that he attaches the epithet of *"leaden-eyed,"* to despair, considered as a quality or sentiment. Were it a personification of despair, the compound would be as finely applied, as, under the actual circumstances, it is erroneously so. There are many, many passages too, in his last volume, as well as in his earlier ones, from which we are not able, after taking some pains to understand them, to derive any distinct notion or meaning whatever.

2. He is too fond of running out glimmerings of thoughts, and indicating distant shadowy fancies: he shows, also, a fondness for dwelling on features which are not naturally the most important or prominent. His imagination coquets with, and mocks the reader in this respect; and plain earnest minds turn away from such tricks with disgust. The greatest poets have always chiefly availed themselves of the plainest and most palpable materials.

3. He affects, in bad taste, a quaint strangeness of phrase; as some folks affect an odd manner of arranging their neckcloths, &c. This "shows a most pitiful ambition." We wish Mr. Keats would not talk of *cutting mercy with a sharp knife to the bone;* we cannot contemplate the *skeleton* of mercy. Nor can we familiarize ourselves pleasantly with the *dainties made to still an infant's cries:*—the latter is indeed a very round about way of expression,—and not very complimentary either, we think. Young ladies, who know, of course, little or nothing of the economy of the nursery, will be apt, we imagine, to pout at this periphrasis, which puts their charms on a level with baby-corals!

But we are by this time tired of criticism; as we hope our readers are:—let us then all turn together to the book itself. (pp. 320-21)

> [John Scott], in a review of "Lamia, Isabella, The Eve of St. Agnes, and Other Poems," in The London Magazine, Vol. II, No. IX, September, 1820, pp. 315-21.

THE LONDON MAGAZINE   (essay date 1821)

[*Modern critics suggest the author of the following eulogizing obituary was B. W. Procter, an intimate of Leigh Hunt who under the pseudonym Barry Cornwall wrote poetry, drama, and biographies.*]

We commence our article this month with but a melancholy subject—*the death of Mr. John Keats....*

Mr. Keats was, in the truest sense of the word, A POET.—There is but a small portion of the public acquainted with the writings of this young man; yet they were full of high imagination and delicate fancy, and his images were beautiful and more entirely his own, perhaps, than those of any living writer whatever. He had a fine ear, a tender heart, and at times great force and originality of expression; and notwithstanding all this, he has been suffered to rise and pass away almost without a notice: the laurel, has been awarded (for the present) to other brows: the bolder aspirants have been allowed to take their station on the slippery steps of the temple of fame, while he has been nearly hidden among the crowd during his life, and has at last died, solitary and in sorrow, in a foreign land.

It is at all times difficult, if not impossible, to argue others into a love of poets and poetry: it is altogether a matter of feeling, and we must leave to time (while it hallows his memory) to do justice to the reputation of Keats. There were many, however, even among the critics living, who held his powers in high estimation; and it was well observed by the Editor of the *Edinburgh Review*, that there was no other Author whatever, whose writings would form so good a test by which to try the love which any one professed to bear towards poetry [see excerpt above by Francis Jeffrey, 1820]. (p. 426)

A few weeks before [Mr. Keats] died, a gentleman who was sitting by his bed-side, spoke of an inscription to his memory, but he declined this altogether,—desiring that there should be no mention of his name or country; "or if any," said he, "let it be—*Here lies the body of one whose name was writ in water!*"—There is something in this to us most painfully affecting; indeed the whole story of his later days is well calculated to make a deep impression.... The public is fond of patronizing poets: they are considered in the light of an almost helpless race: they are bright as stars, but like meteors

> Short-lived and self-consuming.

We do not claim the *patronage* of the public for Mr. Keats, but we hope that it will now cast aside every little and unworthy prejudice, and do justice to the high memory of a young but undoubted poet. (p. 427)

> L., "Death of Mr. John Keats," in The London Magazine, Vol. III, No. XVI, April, 1821, pp. 426-27.

PERCY BYSSHE SHELLEY   (essay date 1821)

[*Shelley was a leading figure in the English Romantic movement and is regarded as a major English poet. His so-called "defense of poetry" and his investigation into its relation to the history of civilization was an important contribution to nineteenth-century aesthetics. Influenced by the French philosopher Jean-Jacques Rousseau and the German poet and pre-Romanticist Johann Gottfried Herder, Shelley viewed poetry, as he did human society, as a continuing evolution of ideas—in his words, as a "fountain forever overflowing with the waters of wisdom and delight," which when exhausted by one age, "another and yet another succeeds and new relations are ever developed." He argued that poetry was like a mirror to its age, the history of its manners, and as such he labeled all poets "legislators and prophets" who, even unconsciously or when in least prominence, as in the English Restoration, contributed to the spiritual and political evolution of humankind. Shelley knew Keats, although the two were not close friends, and he composed the poem* Adonais: An Elegy on the Death of the Poet John Keats *to express both his admiration of Keats's genius and his outrage at the critics' injustice to him. In the following preface to the poem, Shelley specifically implicates John Wilson Croker (see excerpt above, 1818) as Keats's murderer.* Adonais *and its preface were privately printed in Pisa in 1821 and by December of the same year had incited a critical controversy back in England. Modern critics note that* Adonais, *with such portrayals of Keats as a "pale flower by some sad maiden cherished," did much to perpetrate the popular Victorian image of Keats as frail and sentimental.*]

It is my intention to subjoin to the London edition of this poem a criticism upon the claims of its lamented object to be classed among the writers of the highest genius who have adorned our age. My known repugnance to the narrow principles of taste on which several of his earlier compositions were modelled prove at least that I am an impartial judge. I consider the fragment of ***Hyperion*** as second to nothing that was ever produced by a writer of the same years. (p. 430)

The genius of the lamented person to whose memory I have dedicated these unworthy verses was not less delicate and fragile than it was beautiful; and where cankerworms abound, what wonder if its young flower was blighted in the bud? The savage criticism on his **Endymion,** which appeared in the *Quarterly Review* [see excerpt above by John Wilson Croker, 1818], produced the most violent effect on his susceptible mind; the agitation thus originated ended in the rupture of a blood-vessel in the lungs; a rapid consumption ensued, and the succeeding acknowledgements from more candid critics of the true greatness of his powers were ineffectual to heal the wound thus wantonly inflicted.

It may be well said that these wretched men know not what they do. They scatter their insults and their slanders without heed as to whether the poisoned shaft lights on a heart made callous by many blows or one like Keats's composed of more penetrable stuff. One of their associates is, to my knowledge, a most base and unprincipled calumniator. As to **Endymion,** was it a poem, whatever might be its defects, to be treated contemptuously by those who had celebrated, with various degrees of complacency and panegyric, *Paris,* and *Woman,* and a *Syrian Tale,* and Mrs. Lefanu, and Mr. Barrett, and Mr. Howard Payne, and a long list of the illustrious obscure? . . . Miserable man! you, one of the meanest, have wantonly defaced one of the noblest specimens of the workmanship of God. Nor shall it be your excuse, that, murderer as you are, you have spoken daggers, but used none. (p. 431)

> *Percy Bysshe Shelley, in a preface to ''Adonais: An Elegy on the Death of John Keats,'' in his* The Complete Poetical Works of Percy Bysshe Shelley, *edited by Thomas Hutchinson, Oxford University Press, New York, 1933, pp. 430-31.*

BLACKWOOD'S EDINBURGH MAGAZINE (essay date 1821)

[In a review of Percy Bysshe Shelley's Adonais, *the anonymous reviewer derides Keats's high standing among his Cockney brethren and dismisses Shelley's contention that the* Quarterly *contributed to Keats's demise. The critic states that Keats's poetry, ''silly and presumptuous,'' got what it deserved. Until this review,* Blackwood's *had received Shelley's poetry warmly; however, the editors may have feared that his accusation in* Adonais *against the* Quarterly *could also be turned on them.]*

A *Mr John Keats,* a young man who had left a decent calling for the melancholy trade of Cockney-poetry, has lately died of a consumption, after having written two or three little books of verses, much neglected by the public. His vanity was probably wrung not less than his purse; for he had it upon the authority of the Cockney Homers and Virgils, that he might become a light to their region at a future time. But all this is not necessary to help a consumption to the death of a poor sedentary man, with an unhealthy aspect, and a mind harassed by the first troubles of versemaking. The New School, however, will have it that he was slaughtered by a criticism of the *Quarterly Review* [see excerpt above by John Wilson Croker, 1818]—''O flesh, how art thou fishified!''—There is even an aggravation in this cruelty of the *Review*—for it had taken three or four years to slay its victim, the deadly blow having been inflicted at least as long since. We are not now to defend a publication so well able to defend itself. But the fact is, that the *Quarterly* finding before it a work at once silly and presumptuous, full of the servile *slang* that Cockaigne dictates to its servitors, and the vulgar indecorums which that Grub Street Empire rejoiceth to applaud, told the truth of the volume, and

A sketch of Keats at the age of nineteen. Courtesy of Prints and Photographs Division, Library of Congress.

recommended a change of manners and of masters to the scribbler. Keats wrote on; but he wrote *indecently,* probably in the indulgence of his social propensities. He selected from Boccacio, and, at the feet of the Italian Priapus, supplicated for fame and farthings. (pp. 696-97)

> *''Remarks on Shelley's 'Adonais','' in* Blackwood's Edinburgh Magazine, *Vol. X, No. LVIII, December, 1821, pp. 696-700.*

LORD BYRON (poem date 1823)

[Byron was an English poet, dramatist, and satirist who is now considered one of the most important poets of the nineteenth century. Because of the satiric nature of much of his work, Byron is difficult to place within the Romantic movement. His most notable contribution to Romanticism is the Byronic hero: a melancholy man, often with a dark past, who eschews societal and religious strictures and seeks truth and happiness in an apparently meaningless universe. In the following stanza of his well-known poem Don Juan, *first published in 1823, Byron comments humorously on the demise of Keats, whom he was said to have disdained, although he did admire* Hyperion. *Leigh Hunt commented further on Byron's feelings towards Keats (see excerpt below, 1828).]*

John Keats, who was killed off by one critique,
    Just as he really promised something great,

If not intelligible, without Greek
  Contrived to talk about the gods of late,
Much as they might have been supposed to speak.
  Poor fellow! His was an untoward fate.
'Tis strange the mind, that very fiery particle,
Should let itself be snuffed out by an article.

> *Lord Byron, in an extract from "Canto XI," in his*
> Don Juan, *T. G. Steffan, E. Steffan, W. W. Pratt,*
> *eds., revised edition, Penguin Books, 1977, p. 412.*

LEIGH HUNT (essay date 1828)

[*In his* Lord Byron and Some of His Contemporaries, *Hunt provided the fullest biographical sketch to date of Keats. He also dismissed the notion that Keats had been killed by critics, although he allows that they "had perhaps hastened, and certainly embittered [his death]." Hunt proclaims prophetically that Keats's poetry will "take the applause two or three hundred years hence," but also criticized Keats's labored rhymes and his habit of allowing words to dictate the action of a poem, a tendency also noted by John Wilson Croker (1818) and Francis Jeffrey (1820).*]

[There] were political opinions in ["**Poems**"]; and these not according with the opinions of the then government authorities, the writer was found to be a very absurd person, and not to be borne. His youth, and the sincerity natural to youth, to say nothing of personal predilections, which are things that nobody has a right to indulge in but the affectionate followers of office, all told against instead of for him in the eyes of a servile weakness, jealous of independence in others, and (to say the truth) not very capable of discerning the greatest talent. To admire and comment upon the genius that two or three hundred years have applauded, and to discover what will partake of the applause two or three hundred years hence, are processes of a very different description. Accordingly, when Mr. Keats, in 1818, published his next volume, his poetic romance entitled "**Endymion**," the critical authority, then reigning at the west end, showed it no mercy. (p. 415)

"**Endymion**," it must be allowed, was not a little calculated to perplex the critics. It was a wilderness of sweets, but it was truly a wilderness; a domain of young, luxuriant, uncompromising poetry, where the "weeds of glorious feature" hampered the petty legs accustomed to the lawns and trodden walks, in vogue for the last hundred years. . . . (p. 416)

The great fault of "**Endymion**," next to its unpruned luxuriance, (or before it, rather, for it was not a fault on the right side,) was the wilfulness of its rhymes. The author had a just contempt for the monotonous termination of every-day couplets; he broke up his lines in order to distribute the rhyme properly; but going only upon the ground of his contempt, and not having yet settled with himself any principle of versification, the very exuberance of his ideas led him to make use of the first rhymes that offered; so that, by a new meeting of extremes, the effect was as artificial, and much more obtrusive than the one under the old system. Dryden modestly confessed, that a rhyme had often helped him to a thought. Mr. Keats, in the tyranny of his wealth, forced his rhymes to help him, whether they would or not; and they obeyed him, in the most singular manner, with equal promptitude and ungainness. "**Endymion**," too, was not without its faults of weakness, as well as of power. Mr. Keats's natural tendency to pleasure, as a poet, sometimes degenerated, by reason of his ill health, into a poetical effeminacy. There are symptoms of it here and there in all his productions, not excepting the gigantic grandeur of

"**Hyperion**." His lovers grow "faint" with the sight of their mistresses; and Apollo, when he is superseding his divine predecessor, and undergoing his transformation into a Divus Major, suffers a little too exquisitely among his lilies. But Mr. Keats was aware of this contradiction to the real energy of his nature, and prepared to get rid of it. What is more, he said as much in the Preface to "**Endymion**" [see excerpt above, 1818], and in a manner calculated to conciliate all critics who were worth touching his volume; but not such were those, from whom the public were to receive their notions of him. (pp. 418-19)

[Mr. Keats's] last and best volume of poems . . . [contained] *Lamia, Isabella,* the *Eve of St. Agnes,* and the noble fragment of *Hyperion.* I remember Charles Lamb's delight and admiration on reading this work [see excerpt above, 1820]; how pleased he was with . . . the description, at once delicate and gorgeous, of Agnes praying beneath the painted window. This last (which should be called, *par excellence,* the Prayer at the Painted Window) has been often quoted; but . . . I cannot resist repeating it. It throws a light upon one's book.

A casement high and triple-arch'd there was,
  All garlanded with carven imag'ries
Of fruits, and flowers, and bunches of knot-grass,
  And diamonded with panes of quaint device,
  Innumerable of stains and splendid dyes,
As are the tiger-moth's deep-damask'd wings;
  And in the midst, 'mong thousand heraldries,
And twilight saints, and dim emblazonings,
A shielded scutcheon blush'd with blood of queens and
  kings.

Full on this casement shone the wintry moon,
  And threw warm gules on Madeline's fair breast,
As down she knelt for heaven's grace and boon;
  Rose bloom fell on her hands, together press'd,
  And on her silver cross soft amethyst,
And on her hair a glory, like a saint:
  She seem'd a splendid angel, newly dress'd,
Save wings, for heaven.

The whole volume is worthy of this passage. Mr. Keats is no half-painter, who has only distinct ideas occasionally, and fills up the rest with commonplaces. He feels all as he goes. In his best pieces, every bit is precious; and he knew it, and laid it on as carefully as Titian or Giorgione. Take . . .

A DELICATE SUPPER.

And still she slept an azure-lidded sleep
In blanched linen smooth and lavender'd,
While he from forth the closet brought a heap
Of candied apple, quince, and plum, and gourd;
With jellies soother than the creamy curd,
And lucent syrops, tinct with cinnamon;
Manna and dates, in argosy transferr'd
From Fez: and spiced dainties, every one,
From silken Samarcand to cedar'd Lebanon.

These are stanzas, for which Persian kings would fill a poet's mouth with gold. . . . The melody is as sweet as the subject, especially at

Lucent syrops tinct with cinnamon

and the conclusion. Mr. Wordsworth would say that the vowels were not varied enough; but Mr. Keats knew where his vowels were *not* to be varied. (pp. 427-30)

It was Lord Byron, at that time living in Italy, drinking its wine, and basking in its sunshine, who asked me what was the meaning [in **"Ode to a Nightingale"**] of a beaker "full of the warm south." It was not the word beaker that puzzled him: College had made him intimate enough with that. But the sort of poetry in which he excelled, was not accustomed to these poetical concentrations. . . . When I told him, that Mr. Keats admired his "Don Juan," he expressed both surprise and pleasure, and afterwards mentioned him with respect in a canto of it [see excerpt above, 1823]. He could not resist, however, making undue mention of one of the causes that affected his health. A good rhyme about *particle* and *article* was not to be given up. I told him he was mistaken in attributing Mr. Keats's death to the critics, though they had perhaps hastened, and certainly embittered it; and he promised to alter the passage: but a joke and a rhyme together! Those Italian shrugs of the shoulders, which I hope will never be imported among us, are at once a lamentation and an excuse for every thing; and I cannot help using one here. At all events, I have kept my promise, to make the erratum myself in case it did not appear. (pp. 438-39)

[Keats was] as true a man of genius as these latter times have seen; one of those who are too genuine and too original to be properly appreciated at first, but whose time for applause will infallibly arrive with the many, and has already begun in all poetical quarters. I venture to prophesy . . . that Mr. Keats will be known hereafter in English literature, emphatically, as *the Young Poet;* and that his volumes will be the sure companions, in field and grove, of all those who know what a luxury it is to hasten, with a favourite volume against one's heart, out of the strife of commonplaces into the haven of solitude and imagination. (pp. 442-43)

> *Leigh Hunt, "Mr. Keats, with a Criticism on His Writings," in his* Lord Byron and Some of His Contemporaries: With Recollections of the Author's Life, and of His Visit to Italy, Vol. I, *second edition, Henry Colburn, 1828, pp. 407-50.*

RICHARD MONCKTON MILNES (essay date 1848)

[*Milnes, who became Lord Houghton, was an English politician, poet, critic, and essayist who is largely remembered today for his biography of Keats, from which the following is drawn. The* Life, Letters, and Literary Remains of John Keats *is regarded by many as marking the dividing line between Keats's obscurity and fame, because it successfully attracted a large audience for the poet. Moreover, Milnes's prestige helped eradicate the lingering air of vulgarity surrounding the image of Keats as the stable boy and apothecary. In addition, Milnes's arrangement of Keats's letters and poems interspersed with his own commentary allowed readers to observe first-hand Keats's intellectual maturity and poetic gift.*]

The impressible nature of Keats would naturally incline him to erotic composition, but his early love-verses are remarkably deficient in beauty and even in passion. Some which remain in manuscript are without any interest, and those published in [**"Poems"**] are the worst pieces in it. The world of personal emotion was then far less familiar to him than that of fancy, and indeed it seems to have been long before he descended from the ideal atmosphere in which he dwelt so happily, into the troubled realities of human love. Not, however, that the creatures even of his young imagination were unimbued with natural affections; so far from it, it may be reasonably conjectured that it was the interfusion of ideal and sensual life

which rendered the Grecian mythology so peculiarly congenial to the mind of Keats, and when the **"Endymion"** comes to be critically considered, it will be found that its excellence consists in its clear comprehension of that ancient spirit of beauty, to which all outward perceptions so excellently ministered, and which undertook to ennoble and purify, as far as was consistent with their retention, the instinctive desires of mankind. (p. 21)

Keats did not escape the charge of sacrificing beauty to supposed intensity, and of merging the abiding grace of his song in the passionate fantasies of the moment. Words indeed seem to have been often selected by him rather for their force and their harmony, than according to any just rules of diction; if he met with a word any where in an old writer that took his fancy he inserted it in his verse on the first opportunity; and one has a kind of impression that he must have thought aloud as he was writing, so that many an ungainly phrase has acquired its place by its assonance or harmony, or capability to rhyme, (for he took great pleasure in fresh and original rhymes,) rather than for its grammatical correctness or even justness of expression. And when to this is added the example set him by his great master Spenser, of whom a noted man of letters has been heard irreverently to assert "that every Englishman might be thankful that Spenser's gibberish had never become part and parcel of the language," the wonder is rather that he sloughed off so many of his offending peculiarities, and in his third volume [**"Lamia, Isabella, The Eve of St. Agnes, and Other Poems"**] attained so great a purity and concinnity of phraseology, that little was left to designate either his poetical education or his literary associates. (p. 27)

[The original manuscript of **"Endymion"**] betrays the leading fault of the composition, namely, the dependence of the matter on the rhyme, but shows the confidence of the poet in his own profusion of diction, the strongest and most emphatic words being generally taken as those to which the continuing verse was to be adapted. There was no doubt a pleasure to him in this very victory over the limited harmonies of our language, and the result, when fortunate, is very impressive. . . . (p. 58)

Let any man of literary accomplishment, though without the habit of writing poetry, or even much taste for reading it, open **"Endymion"** at random, (to say nothing of the later and more perfect poems,) and examine the characteristics of the page before him, and I shall be surprised if he does not feel that the whole range of literature hardly supplies a parallel phenomenon. As a psychological curiosity, perhaps Chatterton is more wonderful; but in him the immediate ability displayed is rather the full comprehension of and identification with the old model, than the effluence of creative genius. In Keats, on the contrary, the originality in the use of his scanty materials, his expansion of them to the proportions of his own imagination, and above all, his field of diction and expression extending so far beyond his knowledge of literature, is quite inexplicable by any of the ordinary processes of mental education. If his classical learning had been deeper, his seizure of the full spirit of Grecian beauty would have been less surprising; if his English reading had been more extensive, his inexhaustible vocabulary of picturesque and mimetic words could more easily be accounted for; but here is a surgeon's apprentice, with the ordinary culture of the middle classes, rivaling in aesthetic perceptions of antique life and thought the most careful scholars of his time and country, and reproducing these impressions in a phraseology as complete and unconventional as if he has mastered the whole history and the frequent variations of the English tongue, and elaborated a mode of utterance commensurate with his vast ideas.

The artistic absence of moral purpose may offend many readers, and the just harmony of the coloring may appear to others a displeasing monotony, but I think it impossible to lay the book down without feeling that almost every line of it contains solid gold enough to be beaten out, by common literary manufacturers, into a poem of itself. Concentration of imagery, the hitting off a picture at a stroke, the clear decisive word that brings the thing before you and will not let it go, are the rarest distinctions of the early exercise of the faculties. So much more is usually known than digested by sensitive youth, so much more felt than understood, so much more perceived than methodized, that diffusion is fairly permitted in the earlier stages of authorship, and it is held to be one of the advantages, amid some losses, of maturer intelligence, that it learns to fix and hold the beauty it apprehends, and to crystalize the dew of its morning. Such examples to the contrary, as the "Windsor Forest" of Pope, are rather scholastic exercises of men who afterwards became great, than the first-fruits of such genius, while all Keats's poems are early productions, and there is nothing beyond them but the thought of what he might have become. Truncated as is this intellectual life, it is still a substantive whole, and the complete statue, of which such a fragment is revealed to us, stands perhaps solely in the temple of the imagination. There is indeed progress, continual and visible, in the works of Keats, but it is towards his own ideal of a poet, not towards any defined and tangible model. All that we can do is to transfer that ideal to ourselves, and to believe that if Keats had lived, that is what he would have been. (pp. 252-53)

> *Richard Monckton Milnes, in an extract from* Life, Letters, and Literary Remains of John Keats, *edited by Richard Monckton Milnes, George P. Putnam, 1848, 393 p.*

[DAVID MASSON]   (essay date 1860)

[*Masson was a biographer, professor, and longtime editor of* Macmillan's Magazine. *In the following excerpt from a sensitive, often-noted review, Masson anticipates later critics in his conviction that Keats combines sensual imagery with great intellectual and moral beauty. Masson is also in advance of his time in his ranking of Keats as "very near indeed to our very best."*]

In virtue of that magnificent and universal sensuousness which all must discern in Keats, . . . he would certainly—even had there been less in him than there was of that power of reflective and constructive intellect by which alone so abundant a wealth of the sensuous element could have been ruled and shaped into artistic literary forms—have been very memorable among English poets. (p. 15)

But sensuousness alone, will not, nor will sensuousness governed by a reflective and fanciful intellect, constitute a great poet; and, however highly endowed a youthful poet may be in these, his only chance of real greatness is in passing on, by due transition and gradation, to that more matured state of mind in which, though the sensuous may remain and the cool fancy may weave its tissues as before, human interest and sympathy with the human heart and grand human action shall predominate in all. Now, in the case of Keats, there is evidence of the fact of this gradation—of a progress both intellectually and morally; of a disposition, already consciously known to himself, to move forward out of the sensuous or merely sensuous-ideal mood, into the mood of the truly epic poet, the poet of life, sublimity and action. There is evidence of this in his prose-letters. . . . In his poetry we have similar evidence.

Even in his earlier poems, one is struck not only by the steady presence of a keen and subtle intellect, but by frequent flashes of permanently deep meaning, frequent lines of lyric thoughtfulness and occasional maxims of weighty historic generality. . . . From *Endymion* itself, sensuous to very wildness as that poem is considered, scores of passages might be quoted proving that, already, while it was being written, intellect, feeling and experience were doing their work with Keats. . . . Seeing this, looking then at such of his later poems as *Lamia* and the *Eve of St. Agnes,* and contemplating last of all that wonderful fragment of *Hyperion* which he hurled, as it were, into the world as he was leaving it, and of which Byron but expressed the common opinion when he said "It seems actually inspired by the Titans, and is as sublime as Aeschylus," we can hardly be wrong in believing that, had Keats lived to the ordinary age of man, he would have been one of the greatest of all our poets. As it is . . . , I believe we shall all be disposed to place him very near indeed to our very best. (pp. 15-16)

> [*David Masson*], *"The Life and Poetry of Keats," in* Macmillan's Magazine, *Vol. III, No. 13, November, 1860, pp. 1-16.*

JAMES RUSSELL LOWELL   (essay date 1876)

[*Lowell was a celebrated nineteenth-century American poet, critic, essayist, and editor of two leading journals, the* Atlantic Monthly *and the* North American Review. *He is noted today for his satirical and critical writings, including* A Fable for Critics, *a book-length poem featuring witty critical portraits of his contemporaries. Often awkwardly phrased, and occasionally vicious, the* Fable *is distinguished by the enduring value of its literary assessments. Commentators generally agree that Lowell displayed a judicious critical sense, despite the fact that he sometimes relied upon mere impressions rather than critical precepts in his writings. Most literary historians rank him with the major nineteenth-century American critics. Lowell was influential in popularizing Keats among American readers. Because Americans were largely free from the political and class biases that hindered Keats's reputation in his own country, they were generally receptive to him from an early date. Lowell's appreciative overview typifies the contemporary American attitude toward Keats.*]

The faults of Keats's poetry are obvious enough, but it should be remembered that he died at twenty-five, and that he offends by superabundance and not poverty. That he was overlanguaged at first there can be no doubt, and in this was implied the possibility of falling back to the perfect mean of diction. It is only by the rich that the costly plainness, which at once satisfies the taste and the imagination, is attainable. (p. 322)

[Originality] has been denied to Keats because his poems take the color of the authors he happened to be reading at the time he wrote them. But men have their intellectual ancestry, and the likeness of some one of them is forever unexpectedly flashing out in the features of a descendant, it may be after a gap of several generations. . . . It is true that Keats has the accent of the men from whom he learned to speak, but this is to make originality a mere question of externals, and in this sense the author of a dictionary might bring an action of trover against every author who used his words. It is the man behind the words that gives them value, and if Shakespeare help himself to a verse or a phrase, it is with ears that have learned of him to listen that we feel the harmony of the one, and it is the mass of his intellect that makes the other weighty with meaning. Enough that we recognize in Keats that indefinable newness and unexpectedness which we call genius. (pp. 322-23)

Keats certainly had more of the penetrative and sympathetic imagination which belongs to the poet, of that imagination which identifies itself with the momentary object of its contemplation, than any man of these later days. It is not merely that he has studied the Elizabethans and caught their turn of thought, but that he really sees things with their sovereign eye, and feels them with their electrified senses.... He had an unerring instinct for the poetic uses of things, and for him they had no other use. We are apt to talk of the classic *renaissance* as of a phenomenon long past, nor ever to be renewed, and to think the Greeks and Romans alone had the mighty magic to work such a miracle. To me one of the most interesting aspects of Keats is that in him we have an example of the *renaissance* going on almost under our own eyes, and that the intellectual ferment was in him kindled by a purely English leaven. He had properly no scholarship, any more than Shakespeare had, but like him he assimilated at a touch whatever could serve his purpose. His delicate senses absorbed culture at every pore. Of the self-denial to which he trained himself (unexampled in one so young) the second draft of "**Hyperion**" as compared with the first is a conclusive proof. And far indeed is his "**Lamia**" from the lavish indiscrimination of "**Endymion**." In his Odes he showed a sense of form and proportion which we seek vainly in almost any other English poet, and some of his sonnets (taking all qualities into consideration) are the most perfect in our language. No doubt there is something tropical and of strange overgrowth in his sudden maturity, but it *was* maturity nevertheless. (pp. 324-25)

Keats rediscovered the delight and wonder that lay enchanted in the dictionary.... [He] had an instinct for fine words, which are in themselves pictures and ideas, and had more of the power of poetic expression than any modern English poet. And by poetic expression I do not mean merely a vividness in particulars, but the right feeling which heightens or subdues a passage or a whole poem to the proper tone, and gives entireness to the effect. (p. 325)

The poems of Keats mark an epoch in English poetry; for, however often we may find traces of it in others, in them found its most unconscious expression that reaction against the barrel-organ style which had been reigning by a kind of sleepy divine right for half a century.... The most profound gospel of criticism was, that nothing was good poetry that could not be translated into good prose, as if one should say that the test of sufficient moonlight was that tallow-candles could be made of it. We find Keats at first going to the other extreme, and endeavoring to extract green cucumbers from the rays of tallow; but we see also incontestable proof of the greatness and purity of his poetic gift in the constant return toward equilibrium and repose in his later poems. And it is a repose always lofty and clear-aired, like that of the eagle balanced in incommunicable sunshine. In him a vigorous understanding developed itself in equal measure with the divine faculty; thought emancipated itself from expression without becoming its tyrant; and music and meaning floated together, accordant as swan and shadow, on the smooth element of his verse. Without losing its sensuousness, his poetry refined itself and grew more inward, and the sensational was elevated into the typical by the control of that finer sense which underlies the senses and is the spirit of them. (pp. 326-27)

James Russell Lowell, "Keats," in his Among My Books, *second series, 1876. Reprint by Houghton, Mifflin and Company, 1894, pp. 303-27.*

MATTHEW ARNOLD   (essay date 1880)

[*Arnold is considered one of the most influential authors of the later Victorian period in England. While he is well known today as a poet, in his own time he asserted his greatest influence through his prose writings. Arnold's forceful literary criticism, which is based on his humanistic belief in the value of balance and clarity in literature, significantly shaped modern theory. Arnold's essay, first published in 1880, opens with an attack on Keats's letters to Fanny Brawne that many consider to be the most vilifying criticism he ever wrote. The body of his essay, however, is keenly appreciative of Keats, whom Arnold places "with Shakespeare." Arnold's essay was influential in gaining Keats wide acceptance as more than a poet of sensation alone. Using a method similar to Richard Monckton Milnes's in* The Life, Letters, and Literary Remains *of John Keats (see excerpt above, 1848), Arnold liberally quotes Keats's poems and letters as proof that he was more than the ill-bred sensualist he was sometimes called. Arnold ultimately concludes that "'the yearning passion for the Beautiful,' which was with Keats, as he himself truly says, the master passion, is not a passion of the sensuous or sentimental man, is not a passion of the sensuous or sentimental poet. It is an intellectual and spiritual passion."*]

Keats as a poet is abundantly and enchantingly sensuous; the question with some people will be, whether he is anything else. Many things may be brought forward which seem to show him as under the fascination and sole dominion of sense, and desiring nothing better. There is the exclamation in one of his letters: 'O for a life of sensations rather than of thoughts!' There is the thesis, in another, 'that with a great Poet the sense of Beauty overcomes every other consideration, or rather obliterates all consideration.' There is Haydon's story of him, how 'he once covered his tongue and throat as far as he could reach with Cayenne pepper, in order to appreciate the delicious coldness of claret in all its glory—his own expression.' (pp. 100-01)

Character and self-control, ... so necessary for every kind of greatness, and for the great artist, too, indispensable, appear to be wanting, certainly, to this Keats of Haydon's portraiture. They are wanting also to the Keats of the ***Letters to Fanny Brawne....*** [The publication of the letters] appears to me, I confess, inexcusable; they ought never to have been published. But published they are, and we have to take notice of them. Letters written when Keats was near his end, under the throttling and unmanning grasp of mortal disease, we will not judge. But here is a letter written some months before he was taken ill. It is printed just as Keats wrote it.

> You have absorb'd me. I have a sensation at the present moment as though I was dissolving—I should be exquisitely miserable without the hope of soon seeing you. I should be afraid to separate myself far from you. My sweet Fanny, will your heart never change? My love, will it? I have no limit now to my love.... Your note came in just here. I cannot be happier away from you. 'Tis richer than an Argosy of Pearles. Do not threat me even in jest. I have been astonished that Men could die Martyrs for religion—I have shuddered at it—I shudder no more—I could be martyred for my Religion—Love is my religion—I could die for that. I could die for you. My Creed is Love and you are its only tenet. You have ravished me away by a Power I cannot resist; and yet I could resist till I saw you; and even since I have seen you I have endeavoured often "to reason against

the reasons of my Love.'' I can do that no
more—the pain would be too great. My love
is selfish. I cannot breathe without you.

A man who writes love-letters in this strain is probably predestined, one may observe, to misfortune in his love-affairs;
but that is nothing. The complete enervation of the writer is
the real point for remark. We have the tone, or rather the entire
want of tone, the abandonment of all reticence and all dignity,
of the merely sensuous man, of the man who 'is passion's
slave.' Nay, we have them in such wise that one is tempted
to speak even as *Blackwood* or the *Quarterly* were in the old
days wont to speak [see excerpts above by John Gibson Lockhart, 1818, and John Wilson Croker, 1818]; one is tempted to
say that Keats's love-letter is the love-letter of a surgeon's
apprentice. It has in its relaxed self-abandonment something
underbred and ignoble, as of a youth ill brought up, without
the training which teaches us that we must put some constraint
upon our feelings and upon the expression of them. It is the
sort of love-letter of a surgeon's apprentice which one might
hear read out in a breach of promise case, or in the Divorce
Court. The sensuous man speaks in it, and the sensuous man
of a badly bred and badly trained sort. . . . [The] sensuous strain
Keats had, and a man of his poetic powers could not, whatever
his strain, but show his talent in it. But he has something more,
and something better. We who believe Keats to have been by
his promise, at any rate, if not fully by his performance, one
of the very greatest of English poets, and who believe also that
a merely sensuous man cannot either by promise or by performance be a very great poet, because poetry interprets life,
and so large and noble a part of life is outside of such a man's
ken,—we cannot but look for signs in him of something more
than sensuousness, for signs of character and virtue. And indeed the elements of high character Keats undoubtedly has,
and the effort to develop them; the effort is frustrated and cut
short by misfortune, and disease, and time, but for the due
understanding of Keats's worth the recognition of this effort,
and of the elements on which it worked, is necessary.

Lord Houghton, who praises very discriminatingly the poetry
of Keats, has on his character also a remark full of discrimination. He says: 'The faults of Keats's disposition were precisely the contrary of those attributed to him by common opinion.' And he gives a letter written after the death of Keats by
his brother George, in which the writer, speaking of the fantastic *Johnny Keats* invented for common opinion by Lord
Byron and by the reviewers, declares indignantly: 'John was
the very soul of manliness and courage, and as much like the
Holy Ghost as *Johnny Keats*.' It is important to note this testimony, and to look well for whatever illustrates and confirms
it. (pp. 101-06)

Signs of virtue, in the true and large sense of the word, the
instinct for virtue passing into the life of Keats and strengthening it, I find in the admirable wisdom and temper of what
he says to his friend Bailey on the occasion of a quarrel between
Reynolds and Haydon:—

> Things have happened lately of great perplex-
> ity; you must have heard of them; Reynolds
> and Haydon retorting and recriminating, and
> parting for ever. The same thing has happened
> between Haydon and Hunt. It is unfortunate;
> men should bear with each other; there lives
> not the man who may not be cut up, aye, lashed
> to pieces, on his weakest side. The best of men
> have but a portion of good in them. . . . The

sure way, Bailey, is first to know a man's faults,
and then be passive. If, after that, he insensibly
draws you towards him, then you have no power
to break the link. Before I felt interested in
either Reynolds or Haydon, I was well read in
their faults; yet, knowing them, I have been
cementing gradually with both. I have an affection for them both, for reasons almost opposite; and to both must I of necessity cling,
supported always by the hope that when a little
time, a few years, shall have tried me more
fully in their esteem, I may be able to bring
them together.

Butler has well said that 'endeavouring to enforce upon our
own minds a practical sense of virtue, or to beget in others
that practical sense of it which a man really has himself, is a
virtuous *act*.' And such an 'endeavouring' is that of Keats in
those words written to Bailey. It is more than mere words; so
justly thought and so discreetly urged as it is, it rises to the
height of a virtuous *act*. It is proof of character. (pp. 106-08)

What character, again, what strength and clearness of judgment, in his criticism of his own productions, of the public,
and of 'the literary circles'! His words after the severe reviews
of *Endymion* have often been quoted; they cannot be quoted
too often [see excerpt above by Keats, 1818]. . . . (p. 109)

Young poets almost inevitably over-rate what they call 'the
might of poesy,' and its power over the world which now is.
Keats is not a dupe on this matter any more than he is a dupe
about the merit of his own performances:—

> I have no trust whatever in poetry. I don't won-
> der at it; the marvel is to me how people read
> so much of it.

His attitude towards the public is that of a strong man, not of
a weakling avid of praise, and made to 'be snuff'd out by an
article' [see excerpt above by Lord Byron, 1823]:—

> I shall ever consider the public as debtors to
> me for verses, not myself to them for admi-
> ration, which I can do without.
>
> (p. 110)

[The] thing to be seized is, that Keats had flint and iron in
him, that he had character; that he was, as his brother George
says, 'as much like the Holy Ghost as *Johnny Keats*,'—as that
imagined sensuous weakling, the delight of the literary circles
of Hampstead. (p. 112)

[Nothing] is more remarkable in Keats than his clear-sightedness, his lucidity; and lucidity is in itself akin to character
and to high and severe work. In spite, therefore, of his overpowering feeling for beauty, in spite of his sensuousness, in
spite of his facility, in spite of his gift of expression, Keats
could say resolutely:—

> I know nothing, I have read nothing; and I mean
> to follow Solomon's directions: ''Get learning,
> get understanding.'' There is but one way for
> me. The road lies through application, study,
> and thought. I will pursue it.

And of Milton, instead of resting in Milton's incomparable
phrases, Keats could say, although indeed all the while 'looking
upon fine phrases,' as he himself tells us, 'like a lover'—

Milton had an exquisite passion for what is properly, in the sense of ease and pleasure, poetical luxury; and with that, it appears to me, he would fain have been content, if he could, so doing, preserve his self-respect and feeling of duty performed; but there was working in him, as it were, that same sort of thing which operates in the great world to the end of a prophecy's being accomplished. Therefore he devoted himself rather to the ardours than the pleasures of song, solacing himself at intervals with cups of old wine.

In his own poetry, too, Keats felt that place must be found for 'the ardours rather than the pleasures of song,' although he was aware that he was not yet ripe for it—

> But my flag is not unfurl'd
> On the Admiral-staff, and to philosophise
> I dare not yet.

Even in his pursuit of 'the pleasures of song,' however, there is that stamp of high work which is akin to character, which is character passing into intellectual production. *'The best sort of poetry*—that,' he truly says, 'is all I care for, all I live for.' It is curious to observe how this severe addiction of his to the best sort of poetry affects him with a certain coldness, as if the addiction had been to mathematics, towards those prime objects of a sensuous and passionate poet's regard, love and women. He speaks of 'the opinion I have formed of the generality of women, who appear to me as children to whom I would rather give a sugar-plum than my time.' He confesses 'a tendency to class women in my books with roses and sweet-meats—they never see themselves dominant'; and he can understand how the unpopularity of his poems may be in part due to 'the offence which the ladies,' not unnaturally 'take at him' from this cause. (pp. 113-15)

The truth is that 'the yearning passion for the Beautiful,' which was with Keats, as he himself truly says, the master-passion, is not a passion of the sensuous or sentimental man, is not a passion of the sensuous or sentimental poet. It is an intellectual and spiritual passion. It is 'connected and made one,' as Keats declares that in his case it was, 'with the ambition of the intellect.' It is, as he again says, 'the mighty *abstract idea* of Beauty in all things.' And in his last days Keats wrote: 'If I should die, I have left no immortal work behind me—nothing to make my friends proud of my memory; *but I have loved the principle of beauty in all things*, and if I had had time I would have made myself remembered.' He *has* made himself remembered. . . . (pp. 115-16)

For to see things in their beauty is to see things in their truth, and Keats knew it. 'What the Imagination seizes as Beauty must be Truth,' he says in prose; and in immortal verse he has said the same thing—

> Beauty is truth, truth beauty,—that is all
> Ye know on earth, and all ye need to know.

No, it is not all; but it is true, deeply true, and we have deep need to know it. And with beauty goes not only truth, joy goes with her also; and this too Keats saw and said, as in the famous first line of his *Endymion* it stands written—

> A thing of beauty is a joy for ever.

It is no small thing to have so loved the principle of beauty as to perceive the necessary relation of beauty with truth, and of

both with joy. Keats was a great spirit, and counts for far more than many even of his admirers suppose, because this just and high perception made itself clear to him. Therefore a dignity and a glory shed gleams over his life. . . . (pp. 116-17)

[By] virtue of his feeling for beauty and of his perception of the vital connection of beauty with truth, Keats accomplished so much in poetry, that in one of the two great modes by which poetry interprets, in the faculty of naturalistic interpretation, in what we call natural magic, he ranks with Shakespeare. 'The tongue of Kean,' he says in an admirable criticism of that great actor and of his enchanting elocution, 'the tongue of Kean must seem to have robbed the Hybla bees and left them honeyless. There is an indescribable *gusto* in his voice.' . . . This magic, this 'indescribable *gusto* in the voice,' Keats himself, too, exhibits in his poetic expression. No one else in English poetry, save Shakespeare, has in expression quite the fascinating felicity of Keats, his perfection of loveliness. 'I think,' he said humbly, 'I shall be among the English poets after my death.' He is; he is with Shakespeare.

For the second great half of poetic interpretation, for that faculty of moral interpretation which is in Shakespeare, and is informed by him with the same power of beauty as his naturalistic interpretation, Keats was not ripe. For the architectonics of poetry . . . he was not ripe. His *Endymion*, as he himself well saw, is a failure, and his *Hyperion*, fine things as it contains, is not a success. But in shorter things, where the matured power of moral interpretation, and the high architectonics which go with complete poetic development, are not required, he is perfect. [His poems] prove it,—prove it far better by themselves than anything which can be said about them will prove it. Therefore I have chiefly spoken here of the man, and of the elements in him which explain the production of such work. Shakespearian work it is; not imitative, indeed, of Shakespeare, but Shakespearian, because its expression has that rounded perfection and felicity of loveliness of which Shakespeare is the great master. To show such work is to praise it. (pp. 119-21)

> Matthew Arnold, "John Keats," in his Essays in Criticism, second series, The Macmillan Company, 1924, pp. 100-21.

F. M. OWEN (essay date 1880)

[*In the following excerpt from her* John Keats: A Study, *Owen provides a detailed analysis of* Endymion. *A. C. Bradley wrote in 1909 that Owen was the "first critic, I believe, who seriously attempted to investigate Keats's mind, and the ideas that were trying to take shape in some of his poems." Owen is recognized today particularly for her efforts to look beyond the surface decoration of* Endymion *to the meaning lying therein.*]

['*Endymion*'] is a more spiritual poem than [Keats] would have written a few years later, describing love as one who had not gained his knowledge from individual suffering but from a powerful imagination would be likely to describe it, and more interested in an ideal future than an absorbed present. The poem gains rather than loses from this fact. The spirit in a state of energy and activity, but free from self-concentration, would be winged for wider flight, and would see with clearer vision than when in its mortal pain it had

> To question heaven, and hell, and heart in vain,

though it might lack the wider sympathy of deepened and increased knowledge. (p. 46)

The openings of the four books are all remarkable, and worth studying apart from the poem itself. (p. 47)

With the exception of these openings, the hymns to Pan and to Neptune, the picture of the sleep of Adonis, the roundelay which introduces Bacchus and his train, and the hymn of Dian's festival, there are no digressions from the sequence and the regular development of the story, though the 'Edinburgh Review' asserted of it: 'The thin and scanty tissue of the story is merely the light framework on which his florid wreaths are suspended, and while his imaginations go rambling and entangling themselves everywhere, like wild honeysuckles, all idea of sober reason, plan, and consistency is utterly forgotten, and strangled in their waste fertility' [see excerpt above by Francis Jeffrey, 1820]. A more modern and appreciative critic [Walter Bagehot in his *Literary Remains* (see Additional Bibliography)] also says that in '**Endymion**' 'there are no complete conceptions, no continuance of adequate words.' But it was 'a vast idea' which was before the poet's mind, and from which he 'gained his liberty;' and as we trace the windings of the story we feel the inner meaning of it gleaming before us, as the fair shrine ever gleamed before Endymion. This 'ghost of melodious prophesying' comes to us with power even in the attractiveness of the narrative, and when we look beyond it, into the poet's hidden thought,—

> that moment have we stept
> *Into a state of oneness,* and our state
> Is like a floating spirit's. But there are
> Richer entanglements, *enthralments far*
> *More self-destroying,* leading by degrees
> To the chief intensity.

For the prophesying is of the ideal beauty which shall comprise not only the beauty already realised, but even the seeming ugliness and loss, and which will have had fused into its glowing splendour all reality.

> It is a ditty
> Not of these days, but long ago 'twas told
> By a cavern wind unto a forest old;
> And then the forest told it in a dream
> To a sleeping lake, whose cool and level gleam
> A poet caught as he was journeying
> To Phoebus' shrine.

It is a story so old that it is of no special time or date, but is ever new, for it is of an eternal truth—the story of an ideal filled with vast possibilities and limitless desires. It is the 'stretched metre of an antique song' reaching out to a great hope across ages of the world's restlessness and change. (pp. 48-50)

There is a deviation from the main thread of the poem [in the scene where Endymion finds himself in a chamber where Adonis is sleeping] for the purpose of describing this picture. It is one of the imaginations which Lord Jeffrey complained of as 'rambling and entangling themselves everywhere, like wild honeysuckles.' But there is probably subtle art in the digression, for it comes with exquisite relief of beauty between the under world of mystery through which Endymion has been wandering and the terror of the world of suffering to which he is passing. It is artistic, full of graceful outline, colour, and light. We can see the classic form of Adonis sleeping until Venus shall waken him to his summer life of beauty, the lilies above him, the green tendrils enmeshing him everywhere, the rich colouring of the convolvulus and velvet leaves.... (pp. 64-5)

'**Endymion**' is a consecutive whole with a distinct development, and very few digressions from its regular sequence; the next question we ask is, whether there is any underlying meaning in it? The story, exquisite as it is, is not of sufficient strength to stand on its merits as a story alone, and its very entanglements point to the supposition that its leading thoughts do not lie on the surface, and must be looked for deeper.

Many passages in the poem would lead us to believe that Keats was consciously expressing a vast idea in it, but genius is not of necessity conscious of what its inspirations convey to other minds, its varied capabilities of interpretation are one of the most distinctive signs of its prophetic power.

Perhaps the first interpretation and the most obvious which occurs to us is that Endymion himself is the Imagination in all time searching for the spirit of Beauty; that Cynthia, the enlightened side of the moon, represents the beauty of a bygone age, when the world was young; and the dark side, the Indian Princess, shows the newer phases on which Imagination has entered; Imagination at last discovering the eternal Unity of all Beauty, and becoming one with it for ever. This theory would be quite borne out by the poem, but there are parts of it which seem to point to a larger meaning still, a meaning of more widely human interest and therefore more abiding, and among the many interpretations which will be given to every work of genius, it may be worth suggesting this one. Let us take '**Endymion**' as a story of the Spirit of Man, the spirit which sleeps till wakened by higher spiritual power. Peona may represent the physical, or first developed side of man's nature, mechanically nursing and watching over the slumbering spirit, and aware that it possesses qualities beyond its own.

> Brother, 'tis vain to hide
> That thou dost know of things mysterious,
> Immortal, starry; such alone could thus
> Weigh down thy nature. Hast thou sinned in aught
> Offensive to the heavenly powers?

Endymion, touched with a higher knowledge, stands among his forest peers as one in a dream. He listens to their hopes and their beliefs, but they could not understand his if he expressed them. The spirit that has touched him is Love, but it is Love in the completed form of all 'completeness.' It is Love in its perfection. It is a vision which once seen makes it impossible that the spirit of man should ever be at rest again apart from its ideal. When it vanished the wind seemed to bring

> Faint fare-thee-wells and sigh-shrilled adieus,

as if its manifestation was far away from the unrest of the present. But Endymion must henceforth search for ever, the happy forest days are over. The spirit's life once stirred may sleep, indeed, but never unconsciously; it dreams, and its dreams are of its own existence. However much it tries to content itself with its former joys, it must for ever fail, for the fair shrine gleams before it, and the past holds nothing of the power which is drawing it on.

> Its higher hope
> Is of too wide, too rainbow-large a scope,
> To fret at myriads of earthly wrecks.
> Wherein lies happiness? In that which becks
> Our ready minds to fellowship divine.
> A fellowship with essence: till we shine
> Full alchemized and free of space. Behold
> The clear religion of heaven.

Can we be wrong in believing that, consciously or unconsciously, the thought which was in Keats's mind was of that refining fire through which the soul of man must pass?—that the purification from self, the beatitude of complete self-abnegation, is the hope which

> Is of too wide, too rainbow-large a scope,
> To fret at myriads of earthly wrecks?

From henceforth the true life of the spirit is hidden, but it is a waking reality, it is more than the sleep that is ended.

> My restless spirit never could endure
> To brood so long upon one luxury,
> Unless it did, though fearfully, espy
> A hope beyond the shadow of a dream!

It is a life of action, though of sadness—of undying hope, though steeped in suffering. The wakened spirit can neither 'love its life nor hate.'

> I'll smile no more, Peona; nor will wed
> Sorrow, the way to death; but patiently
> Bear up against it: so farewell, sad sigh;
> And come instead demurest meditation,
> To occupy me wholly, and to fashion
> My pilgrimage for the world's dusky brink.
> No more will I count over, link by link,
> My chain of grief: no longer strive to find
> A half-forgetfulness in mountain wind,
> Blustering about my ears; ay, thou shalt see,
> Dearest of sisters, what my life shall be:
> What a calm round of hours shall make my days.
> There is a paly flame of hope that plays
> Where'er I look.

But Endymion does not expect to be understood. He knows that the revelation he has had has made him alone for ever, as far as all former companionship is concerned, and he accepts his fate.

At first he is lured by the golden butterfly of pleasure, which changes, even when he seems to have tracked it home, into the nymph who says

> I am but as a child
> To gladden thee, and all I dare to say
> Is that I pity thee. . . .
> 　　　　　　Thou must wander far
> In other regions, past the scanty bar
> To mortal steps, before thou canst be ta'en
> From every wasting sigh, from every pain,
> Into the gentle bosom of thy love.
> Why it is thus one knows in heaven above.

Thus the light and early hours of the spirit's search begin with pleasure which promises greatly, and seems even in its passing to be sorry for the soul it leaves; and then life deepens, and the spirit passes from the cool mossy well and rose-trees to the city, with its feverish life, its restless hearts, its unresting days and nights. (pp. 84-90)

And the spirit, in the suffering of this new birth, wearies.

> 　　　　　　I can see
> Naught earthly worth my compassing, so stand
> Upon a misty jutting head of land
> Alone.

For what desolation is greater than that which is felt when for the first time the agony of the world is borne in upon the soul?

It stands alone in a mist upon a promontory, the waves of that sorrow of which it has become conscious breaking forlornly around it, its individual aims and hopes seeming for the time worthless.

Then hope revives with faith in the vision which shall yet harmonise the discords of this sorrow, and moments of wild and rapturous joy succeed to grief in thinking of the glimpse of beauty which has waked it to consciousness.

As each stage of life develops its power and rouses more fully the spiritual nature, the longing for the eternal beauty becomes more intense. (pp. 90-1)

But it is even at the moments when it has attained greatest altitude that the spirit is compelled to descend to the lowest depths, to look for the beauty which is hidden there. It was his highest dream which was interrupted by the voice which bade Endymion

> 　　　　　　descend where alleys bend
> Into the sparry hollows of the world.
> 　　　　　　　　　He ne'er is crowned
> With immortality who fears to follow
> Where airy voices lead; so through the hollow,
> *The silent mysteries of earth descend.*

Before all true ascending of the spirit there is descending too: there is a land of silent mystery which the soul must encounter alone, there are sorrows it must know, there are sufferings it must endure and see, before it can find that oneness of all beauty which is its eternal prize. (pp. 91-2)

It is by an irresistible impulse that the spirit is now led. Through winding passages, through giant ranges of sapphire columns, over bridges athwart a crystal flood, over jagged rocks and jutting ledges that overhang the deep abyss, on ridges so narrow that there seems to be no foothold, it makes its way, until, wearied, it rests at last before

> A wide outlet, fathomless and dim,
> To wild uncertainty and shadows grim.

And all this time it is alone, and its solitude magnifies the shadows.

> *And thoughts of self came on, how crude and sore*
> *The journey homeward to habitual self!*
> What misery most drowningly doth sing,
> In lone Endymion's ear, now he has caught
> The goal of consciousness?　Ah! 'tis the thought,
> The deadly feel of solitude: for lo,
> He cannot see the heavens, nor the flow
> Of rivers, nor hill flowers running wild
> In pink and purple chequer, nor, up-piled,
> The cloudy rack slow journeying in the west,
> Like herded elephants: nor felt nor prest
> Cool grass, nor tasted the fresh slumbrous air,
> But far from such companionship to wear
> An unknown time surcharged with grief away,
> Was now his lot.

This self-absorbment is destruction, the spirit must go deeper still, it must not rest, it cannot rest in *itself*, in its own sorrow or even its own terror. There is no help for it and no hope for it while it remains alone. (pp. 92-3)

Not seldom is the spirit tempted to think that it has reached the utmost limit possible, that there is neither light nor hope beyond, its path breaks off—

> he was indeed wayworn,
> Abrupt in middle air, his way was lost.

But here in the depths of its lonely sorrow the spirit is given another vision of the beauty which is to be, of the love which is the eternal truth though interpreted through the medium of its own passion. It was in his eagle descent through unknown things that Endymion found his jasmine bower, and saw once more the ideal whom he loved. Not yet can she raise him 'to starry eminence,' but she will 'tell him stories of the sky,' and his words, when she again vanishes from him, are the cry of every soul that has been touched with the larger love and eternal beauty. (p. 94)

It is now for the first time that Endymion emerges from himself and is touched with a sense of the sorrows of others. The sadness of Arethusa wakes pity in him, and breathing a prayer for her, he finds himself in the lowest depth of all, at the bottom of the sea of this world's sorrow. And it is here in the lowest depth, having sounded grief with its own plummet line, that the spirit begins to gain its truest life. It is moved with pity, and it labours to bring its own glad vision of love to hearts and lips that are cold and have grown weary of waiting. No sorrow is foreign to it, the suffering of others is its own, it believes in eternal love even here. Was there not a bright ray from Cynthia shining in 'that deep deep water world'? Was not the presence of him who believed in her as new life to those who had been living in darkness? (p. 95)

It was the might of the power of a strong belief—faith in eternal love—by which Endymion touched those cold dead hearts which seemed as if even love could not move them, and the fast-closed eyes that were shut to the beauty which Cynthia revealed to him.

And the spirit of man, when it goes into the depths of trouble and suffering, must go strong in this strong belief. It must lay the spell of its trust in eternal love and eternal beauty on the cold dead hearts and shut eyes of its brothers and sisters whom it finds there, and then shall be heard the noise of harmony, and those shall spring to each other whose love has not been dead but sleeping. For man too there shall be a writing in the starlight, for his heaven will be nearer and his completeness closer to its completed form.

And now the poem passes into a phase of mysterious vagueness. It necessarily must do so. The poet himself has come 'to the burthen of the mystery;' he can speak but vaguely of what he has found there. The spirit is led from the depths to the light of ordinary day with a new inspiration.

> Through the dark earth and through the wondrous sea

it passes to 'a new woe.'

The sad princess is represented as self-absorbed and full of sorrow. In loving her, Endymion loses sight of his ideal, and contents himself with a limited apprehension of real Beauty. For the time he becomes blind to all else. The mind that is wholly occupied with one side of an object must necessarily become untrue to its eager aspirations, and a great unrest and bewildering fills the soul. The poet represents Endymion in the fourth book as entering upon this phase of temptation. The world is darker, sadder than of old: sorrow is everywhere. Pan is dead, and the golden age is past. One fleeting dream of it

comes back in the pageant of Bacchus and his crew, and streams with sunset light across the present, then fades, leaving only the night to come, and the soul despairs.

> I have clung
> To nothing, loved a nothing, nothing seen
> Or felt but a great dream.

And such despair must paralyse all hope.

> I must be thy sad servant evermore.

Endymion will at last 'wed sorrow'—he will give up all attempts to reconcile his life and his aspirations, he will accept his fate, and, worse still, will joy in it.

The world is growing old, and there is nothing beyond it: he will content himself with that which is now and here. He will have no more of dreaming. The present is his; the present shall suffice him.

> *Woe!*
> *Woe! Woe* to that Endymion!   Where is he?

If he contents himself with life as it is he is lost. Was it for this that he had passed from the well and the rose-trees—that he had stood alone on the misty headland: that he had mastered his fate among the precipices, that he had sounded the depths of the ocean world—that his sorrow and his pity and his love should bring him to despair and the acceptance of a destiny which could never content him? (pp. 96-9)

It is the spirit's hour of keenest trial. It is undone for ever if it accepts inertly things as they are. The cry of its hopelessness is then—

> There never lived a mortal man who bent
> His appetite beyond his natural sphere,
> But starved and died.
>   • • • • •
>   Caverns lone, farewell!
> And air of visions, *and the monstrous swell*
> *Of visionary seas!*   No never more
> Shall airy voices cheat me to the shore
> Of tangled wonder.

But the soul has yet to learn its deepest spiritual lesson, that no love is true which does not realise itself as part of a greater whole—that all that is beautiful is One. The limited, sensuous love melts even in Endymion's grasp, leaving him unsatisfied and longing.

> By Nemesis! I see my spirit flit
> Alone about the dark.

And then he enters the wondrous cave. (p. 99)

There could not be a truer description of apathy [than the description of the cave]. But in touching earth again the earthly love is found, and the temptation once more asserts itself in all its strength. Yet

> I may not be thy love,
> I am forbidden,

says the sad princess, and Endymion knows it to be true, and is roused once more to higher aspirations.

> Not ignorant though
> That those deceptions which for pleasure go
> 'Mong men, are pleasures real as pleasures may be;
> But there are higher ones I may not see
> *If impiously an earthly realm I take.*

And the end of the story seems to slip from our grasp, shadowy, intangible, yet a glorious vision, with 'more of the music, and less of the words.'

It is only when Endymion has gained a wider power of vision, when he has learnt that true freedom is freedom from his own individual and limited desires and aims, and when he wishes thus to command his fate, that the Indian princess turns upon him with the face of his own beloved, and he knows that all love and beauty is one, that the truth of the finite is the truth of the infinite, that the fitful and dimly realised beauty in common life and the beauty gained through suffering is one with the beauty of light and of joy, and that it was necessary some change should spiritualise him into this belief. Being made one with eternal and universal love, the spirit is at rest for ever. (pp. 101-02)

> *F. M. Owen, in her* John Keats: A Study, *C. Kegan Paul & Co., 1880, 183 p.*

ALGERNON CHARLES SWINBURNE   (essay date 1882)

[*Swinburne was an English poet, dramatist, and critic. He was renowned during his lifetime for his lyric poetry, and he is remembered today for his rejection of Victorian mores. His explicitly sensual themes shocked his contemporaries; although they demanded that poetry reflect and uphold current moral standards, Swinburne's only goal, implicit in his poetry and explicit in his critical writings, was to express beauty. Here Swinburne offers a balanced overview of Keats's works. G. S. Fraser (see Additional Bibliography) credits Swinburne as the "first critic to give the odes a central position in Keats's work, and to emphasize Keats's Shakespearean quality. His relative placing of the other poems, and his sense of the extraordinary progress made by Keats between his second and third volumes, coincides remarkably with the general verdict of twentieth-century criticism." The following essay was originally published in 1882 in the* Encyclopaedia Britannica.]

[In *Poems*] there was little foretaste of anything greatly or even genuinely good; but between the marshy and sandy flats of sterile or futile verse there were undoubtedly some few purple patches of floral promise. The style was frequently detestable— a mixture of sham Spenserian and mock Wordsworthian, alternately florid and arid. His second book, *Endymion*, rises in its best passages to the highest level of Barnfield and of Lodge, the two previous poets with whom, had he published nothing more, he might most properly have been classed; and this, among minor minstrels, is no unenviable place. His third book [*Lamia, Isabella, The Eve of St. Agnes, and Other Poems*] raised him at once to a foremost rank in the highest class of English poets. Never was any one of them but Shelley so little of a marvellous boy and so suddenly revealed as a marvellous man. . . . Shelley, up to twenty, had written little or nothing that would have done credit to a boy of ten; and of Keats also it may be said that the merit of his work at twenty-five was hardly by comparison more wonderful than its demerit at twenty-two. His first book fell as flat as it deserved to fall; the reception of his second, though less considerate than on the whole it deserved, was not more contemptuous than that of immeasurably better books published about the same time by Coleridge, Landor, and Shelley. A critic of exceptional carefulness and candour might have noted in the first book so singular an example of a stork among the cranes as the famous and noble sonnet on Chapman's Homer; a just judge would have indicated, a partial advocate might have exaggerated, the value of such golden grain amid a garish harvest of tares as the hymn

to Pan and the translation into verse of Titian's Bacchanal which glorify the weedy wilderness of *Endymion*. But the hardest thing said of that poem by the *Quarterly* reviewer [see excerpt above by John Wilson Croker, 1818] was unconsciously echoed by the future author of *Adonais* [Shelley]— that it was all but absolutely impossible to read through; and the obscener insolence of the 'Blackguard's Magazine' [see excerpt above by John Gibson Lockhart, 1818], as Landor afterwards very justly labelled it, is explicable though certainly not excusable if we glance back at such a passage as that where Endymion exchanges fulsome and liquorish endearments with the 'known unknown *from whom his being sips such darling(!) essence.'* Such nauseous and pitiful phrases as these, and certain passages in his correspondence, make us understand the source of the most offensive imputations or insinuations levelled against the writer's manhood; and, while admitting that neither his love-letters, nor the last piteous outcries of his wailing and shrieking agony, would ever have been made public by merciful or respectful editors, we must also admit that, if they ought never to have been published, it is no less certain that they ought never to have been written. . . . But that there was a finer side to the man, even if considered apart from the poet, his correspondence with his friends and their general evidence to his character give more sufficient proof than perhaps we might have derived from the general impression left on us by his works; though indeed the preface to *Endymion* itself [see excerpt above, 1818], however illogical in its obviously implied suggestion that the poem published was undeniably unworthy of publication, gave proof or hint at least that after all its author was something of a man. . . . But if it must be said that he lived long enough only to give promise of being a man, it must also be said that he lived long enough to give assurance of being a poet who was not born to come short of the first rank. Not even a hint of such a probability could have been gathered from his first or even from his second appearance; after the publication of his third volume it was no longer a matter of possible debate among judges of tolerable competence that this improbability had become a certainty. Two or three phrases cancelled, two or three lines erased, would have left us in *Lamia* one of the most faultless as surely as one of the most brilliant jewels in the crown of English poetry. *Isabella*, feeble and awkward in narrative to a degree almost incredible in a student of Dryden and a pupil of Leigh Hunt, is overcharged with episodical effects of splendid and pathetic expression beyond the reach of either. *The Eve of St. Agnes,* aiming at no doubtful success, succeeds in evading all casual difficulty in the line of narrative; with no shadow of pretence to such interest as may be derived from stress of incident or depth of sentiment, it stands out among all other famous poems as a perfect and unsurpassable study in pure colour and clear melody. . . . Beside this poem should always be placed the less famous but not less precious *Eve of St. Mark,* a fragment unexcelled for the simple perfection of its perfect simplicity, exquisite alike in suggesting and in accomplishment. The triumph of *Hyperion* is as nearly complete as the failure of *Endymion;* yet Keats never gave such proof of a manly devotion and rational sense of duty to his art as in his resolution to leave this great poem unfinished. . . . Fortified and purified as it had been on a first revision, when much introductory allegory and much tentative effusion of sonorous and superfluous verse had been rigorously clipped down or pruned away, it could not long have retained spirit enough to support or inform the shadowy body of a subject so little charged with tangible significance. The faculty of assimilation as distinguished from imitation, than which there can be no surer or stronger sign of strong and sure original genius, is not more evident in the most Miltonic passages of the revised *Hyperion* than in the more Shakespearean passages of the unrevised tragedy which no radical correction could have left other than radically incorrigible. It is no conventional exaggeration, no hyperbolical phrase of flattery with more sound than sense in it, to say that in this boyish and fantastic play of *Otho the Great* there are such verses as Shakespeare might not without pride have signed at the age when he wrote and even at the age when he rewrote the tragedy of *Romeo and Juliet*. The dramatic fragment of *King Stephen* shows far more power of hand and gives far more promise of success than does that of Shelley's *Charles the First*. Yet we cannot say with any confidence that even this far from extravagant promise would certainly or probably have been kept; it is certain only that Keats in these attempts did at least succeed in showing a possibility of future excellence as a tragic or at least a romantic dramatist. In every other line of high and serious poetry his triumph was actual and consummate; here only was it no more than potential or incomplete. As a ballad of the more lyrical order, *La belle Dame sans Merci* is not less absolutely excellent, less triumphantly perfect in force and clearness of impression, than as a narrative poem is *Lamia*. In his lines on Robin Hood, and in one or two other less noticeable studies of the kind, he has shown thorough and easy mastery of the beautiful metre inherited by Fletcher from Barnfield and by Milton from Fletcher. The simple force of spirit and style which distinguishes the genuine ballad manner from all spurious attempts at an artificial simplicity was once more at least achieved in his verses on the crowning creation of Scott's humaner and manlier genius—Meg Merrilies. No little injustice has been done to Keats by such devotees as fix their mind's eye only on the more salient and distinctive notes of a genius which in fact was very much more various and tentative, less limited and peculiar, than would be inferred from an exclusive study of his more specially characteristic work. But within the limits of that work must we look of course for the genuine credentials of his fame; and highest among them we must rate his unequalled and unrivalled odes. Of these perhaps the two nearest to absolute perfection, to the triumphant achievement and accomplishment of the very utmost beauty possible to human words, may be that to Autumn and that on a Grecian Urn; the most radiant, fervent, and musical is that to a Nightingale; the most pictorial and perhaps the tenderest in its ardour of passionate fancy is that to Psyche; the subtlest in sweetness of thought and feeling is that on Melancholy. Greater lyrical poetry the world may have seen than any that is in these; lovelier it surely has never seen, nor ever can it possibly see. From the divine fragment of an unfinished ode to Maia we can but guess that if completed it would have been worthy of a place beside the highest. His remaining lyrics have many beauties about them, but none perhaps can be called thoroughly beautiful. He has certainly left us one perfect sonnet of the first rank; and as certainly he has left us but one.

Keats, on high and recent authority, has been promoted to a place beside Shakespeare [see excerpt above by Matthew Arnold, 1880]. . . . The faultless force and the profound subtlety of this deep and cunning instinct for the absolute expression of absolute natural beauty can hardly be questioned or overlooked; and this is doubtless the one main distinctive gift or power which denotes him as a poet among all his equals, and gives him right to a station near that of Coleridge and Shelley. . . . [The false Keats] whom Shelley pitied and Byron despised would have been, had he ever existed, a thing beneath compassion or contempt. That such a man could have had such

a genius is almost evidently impossible; and yet more evident is the proof which remains on everlasting record that none was ever further from the chance of decline to such degradation than the real and actual man who made that name immortal. (pp. 210-18)

Algernon Charles Swinburne, "Keats," in his Miscellanies, Worthington Company, 1886, pp. 210-18.

GERARD MANLEY HOPKINS (letter date 1887)

[Hopkins was a nineteenth-century English poet whose work was unknown until the twentieth century. A Roman Catholic priest, Hopkins composed his highly original verse without the knowledge of his superiors, for he felt that his work as a poet interfered with the role and responsibility of a Jesuit priest. Perhaps because of the isolation in which he wrote, Hopkins's work is characterized by its striking diction and unusual rhythmic structure. He was an experimental poet and invented a form he called "sprung rhythm" through which he endeavored to capture "the rhythm of prose, that is the native and natural rhythm of speech." In the following letter to Canon Dixon, Hopkins responds to Dixon's review of Sidney Colvin's 1887 biography of Keats (see Additional Bibliography). Here Hopkins disputes Dixon's claims that Keats is feminine and unlike Shakespeare, and he makes high claims for the poet which present-day critics identify as being very close to the views of modern criticism.]

During the summer examinations one of my colleagues brought in one day a *St. James's Gazette* with a piece of criticism he said it was a rare pleasure to read. It proved to be a review by you of Colvin's book on Keats. Still, enlightening as the review was, I did not think it really just. You classed Keats with the feminine geniuses among men and you would have it that he was not the likest but rather the unlikest of our poets to Shakspere. His poems, I know, are very sensuous and indeed they are sensual. This sensuality is their fault, but I do not see that it makes them feminine. But at any rate (and the second point includes the first) in this fault he resembles, not differs from Shakspere. For Keats died very young and we have only the work of his first youth. Now if we compare that with Shakspere's early work, written at an age considerably more than Keats's, was it not? such as *Venus and Adonis* and *Lucrece*, it is, as far as the work of two very original minds ever can be, greatly like in its virtues and its vices; more like, I do think, than that of any writer you could quote after the Elizabethan age; which is what the common opinion asserts. It may be that Keats was no dramatist (his *Otho* I have not seen); but it is not for that, I think, that people have made the comparison. The *Cap and Bells* is an unhappy performance, so bad that I could not get through it; senselessly planned to have no plan and doomed to fail; but Keats would have found out that. He was young; his genius intense in its quality; his feeling for beauty, for perfection intense; he had found his way right in his Odes; he would find his way right at last to the true functions of his mind. And he was at a great disadvantage in point of education compared with Shakspere. Their classical attainments may have been much of a muchness, but Shakspere had the school of his age. It was the Renaissance: the ancient Classics were deeply and enthusiastically studied and influenced directly or indirectly all, and the new learning had entered into a fleeting but brilliant combination with the medieval tradition. All then used the same forms and keepings. But in Keats's time, and worst in England, there was no one school; but experiment, division, and uncertainty. He was one of the beginners of the Romantic movement, with the extravagance and ignorance of his youth. After all is there anything in *En-*

dymion worse than the passage in *Romeo and Juliet* about the County Paris as a book of love that must be bound and I can't tell what? It has some kind of fantastic beauty, like an arabesque; but in the main it is nonsense. And about the true masculine fibre in Keats's mind Matthew Arnold has written something good lately [see excerpt above, 1880]. (pp. 49-50).

> *Gerard Manley Hopkins, in an extract from a letter to Canon Dixon on October 20, 1887, in* John Keats: 'Odes', a Casebook, *edited by G. S. Fraser, Macmillan, 1971, pp. 49-50.*

E. DE SÉLINCOURT (essay date 1905)

[*Sélincourt's is a study of the evolution of Keats's poetic style through an investigation of the various influences on his work. He notes that the artists who most affected Keats where those of his native England and he examines in particular the influence of Edmund Spenser, Leigh Hunt, William Shakespeare, William Wordsworth, John Milton, and John Dryden.*]

[It is] my object to attempt some further contribution to the study of Keats's poetic development and to direct attention to the principal forces which moulded his mind and art. In the case of Keats this study is of special interest, and, I think, of special importance. "The fair paradise of Nature's light" is, doubtless, the inspiration of all great poetry, but the mind which nature inspires may acquire its individuality by widely different processes. Whilst each of his great contemporaries owed no little debt to the influence of a culture either inherited or acquired naturally from early surroundings, and to a wide and generous training which stimulated the mind from many sources, Keats was educated almost exclusively by the English poets. . . . To his English predecessors he served a willing apprenticeship, detecting the deficiencies of each through his appreciation of the peculiar excellences of the rest, till he gained at last that complete unfettered independence which had always been the goal of his ambition (p. xx)

It is significant that Keats's earliest known composition is the *Imitation of Spenser,* written probably in 1813, and Spenser never lost hold upon his imagination. There was indeed an essential kinship between the two poets, and that brooding love of sensuous beauty, that frank response to the charm of nature and romance, that luxuriance of fancy and felicity of expression to which the *Faerie Queene* owes its irresistible fascination were soon to be re-echoed in the poems of Keats. But Keats was not the first poet to acknowledge that Spenser was his original. Apart from those who may justly claim so honourable a lineage, in every succeeding epoch there are to be found poetasters who have attempted to catch, though from afar, faint echoes of his melody, and to inform their own lifeless puppets with something of the spirit and the gesture of his magic world. Keats's literary education did not enable him to distinguish the essential qualities of Spenser from those of his latest imitators. Naturally, therefore, the influence of the eighteenth-century allegorists is paramount in his earliest writings. They were far easier to reproduce, and he could hardly be expected to realise when allegory devoid of imagination had become mere idle personification, and when a rich exuberance and easy grace of language had given way, in writers of a less intense and less continuous inspiration, to mere licentious fluency or empty verbiage. In this he was, doubtless, affected by the poetic taste of his time, which, as yet unconverted to the revolutionary doctrines of Wordsworth and Coleridge, still clung to the milder and more conventional romanticism countenanced by the age of reason. Of this period in his development he wrote later

"Beattie and Mrs. Tighe once delighted me," and at the same time he showed himself to be momentarily affected by the *Juvenilia* of Byron and the drawing-room melodies of Moore. A weak sonnet shows that already he had come under the spell of Chatterton, but it was not till later that Chatterton influenced his literary methods. For the present he was an eighteenth-century Spenserian, and traces of the diction and style of the eighteenth-century poets still linger even in that poem in which he most fiercely denounces them.

But this phase of his development, which has little relation with his later work, was soon followed by one of more lasting significance. Early in 1815 he came under the spell of Chapman's translation of *Homer,* of the early work of Milton, and of the poems of Fletcher and of William Browne, whilst his delight in the seventeenth-century Spenserians became inextricably blended with his admiration for the most prominent of Spenser's living disciples, the charming and versatile Leigh Hunt. (pp. xxii-xxiii)

[In the spring of 1816, just before Keats first met Hunt, Hunt's *Story of Rimini*] made its appearance with a preface in which he set forth at length his conception of poetic style and versification. The heroic couplet, he said, had been spoiled as a measure for narrative poetry by Pope and the French school of versification, who had mistaken smoothness for harmony, because their ears were only sensible of a marked and uniform harmony. He desired to return to its freer use, as it is to be found in the fables of Dryden, in Spenser, and in particular in Chaucer, its original master. (p. xxiv)

In upholding the restitution to the couplet of the Alexandrine, the double or feminine rhyme, the triplet and the run-on line or enjambement, Hunt set an example which was to be widely and on the whole satisfactorily followed, though he exaggerated into far too general a practice what was after all only an exceptional variation from the rule. But in his use of language his own interpretation of his theory led to most disastrous results. He had attacked Wordsworth, to whom he was obviously indebted for all that is really valuable in the preface, for the meanness of much of his poetry; but whereas Wordsworth was the most correct writer of his day, and was never led by his theories to treat of a great subject in other than a great manner, Hunt confused naturalness with triviality, and construed a freedom from the use of a specific poetic diction into the right to be slipshod in language and vague in thought. His addiction to abstract terms in his description of the concrete, his coinage of adverbs from present participles, or adjectives from nouns, and his reckless use of one part of speech for another can only be regarded as expedients by which to save himself the trouble of thinking clearly and definitely on any subject, whilst he forgot entirely his own proviso that the poet's vocabulary must be freed from all "mere vulgarisms, fugitive phrases and the cant of ordinary discourse".

But the language used by a poet cannot be considered to any purpose apart from the use to which he puts it, and it is here that Hunt reveals his own limitations with most fatal results. Absolutely sincere in his affections, and genuine in his convictions both in life and literature, he was lacking in real depth. . . . (p. xxv)

It is uncritical to father upon Hunt all the vices of Keats's early work. For Hunt could never have gained the same sway over his mind had there not been a natural affinity between them. Keats said of the cancelled preface to *Endymion*, "I was not aware that there was anything like Hunt in it, and if there is it is my natural way and I have something in common with Hunt'' and the remark expressed a truth of wider application than to the immediate case which evoked it. But it is certain that the theory and practice of his friend led him to accentuate all the worst features of his genius and encouraged him in those very failings which a sounder master might have taught him to overcome. And the superficial similarity between them made this influence all the more dangerous. Keats from the first went deeper than Hunt, but, reading into Hunt's light-hearted enthusiasm some of his own intenser feeling, came naturally enough to regard the language and style of *Rimini* as suited to the expression of that higher emotion of which its author had never dreamed.

Nowhere did the young poet need more guidance than in his treatment of romantic passion. His emotional temperament made it inevitable that he should be a love poet, and from his boyhood he had so idealised woman that he constantly found himself ill-at-ease in the presence of the reality. To this idealisation his reading of Spenser had given an impetus. It was as a poet of chivalrous love that Spenser had first appealed to him. (pp. xxvii-xxviii)

[It] was nothing short of disastrous that [Keats's] enthusiasm for Hunt led him to believe that the mantle of Spenser had fallen upon the shoulders of the poet of *Rimini*. For woman in Hunt's poetry was merely a lay figure over which to luxuriate a keen but often vulgar sense of the beautiful in art and nature, and chivalry was always more of an ecstasy than an activity. There is no wonder that Keats under his influence failed to realise that the intense sensuousness of Spenser's descriptions is only artistically justified by their spirituality, and instead of comprehending the full significance of Sir Calidore or the Red Cross Knight was satisfied to represent them as though they were lovesick tradesmen masquerading in a picturesque costume. Later Keats came to recognise this. "One cause," he writes, "of the unpopularity of my book is the tendency to class women in my books with roses and sweatmeats, they never see themselves dominant." Under other guidance, perhaps with no guidance at all, he might have discovered it earlier.

The first poem of the 1817 volume strikes at once the dominant note of the whole. Headed with a characteristic quotation from the *Story of Rimini*, "Places of nestling green for Poets made," it shows the influence of Hunt in its most pronounced form. It is inspired by a genuine love of nature, blended, as always in Keats, with an intensely real feeling for literature and for ancient legend, but after an opening of happy delicacy it degenerates into an indiscriminate catalogue of natural delights associated with the vulgar and mawkish sentiment and expressed with all the indefiniteness of the abstract style of Hunt. The poet

> straightway began to pluck a posey
> Of luxuries bright, milky, soft and rosy . . .

[The] whole poem is replete with adjectives of the delicious order by which he seeks to give utterance to his keen but vague delight, while its versification exhibits that negligence of form which had some precedent in Chapman and Browne, but received its special sanction from the theory and practice of Hunt. And yet notwithstanding such palpable faults of style and temper there are few poems in the volume which do not give some promise of future achievement; either in their imaginative suggestion, or in their strangely felicitous language, betokening

the poet who had already "looked upon fine phrases like a lover". Lines such as

> That distance of recognizance bereaves
> > (*Sonnet* . . .)

or

> Full in the speculation of the stars
> > (*I stood tip-toe* . . .)

have a ring about them which recalls the harmony of some old Elizabethan; the pictures of

> the moon lifting her silver rim
> Above a cloud, and with a gradual swim
> Coming into the blue with all her light
> > (*I stood tip-toe* . . .)

and of the sea that

> Heaves calmly its broad swelling smoothness o'er
> Its rocky marge, and balances once more
> The patient weeds; that now unshent by foam
> Feel all about their undulating home
> > (*Sleep and Poetry* . . .)

though missing the perfection of his later studies of moon and ocean are touched with the same tenderness, and lit up by the same magic, whilst the sonnet *On first looking into Chapman's Homer* proclaims him capable already of reaching, in supreme moments, the heights of song.

For the poet who could write like this the influence of Hunt could only be short-lived. (pp. xxviii-xxx)

[Already] side by side with the tendency to luxuriate in agreeable sensations, to "lose the soul in pleasant smotherings," had arisen within [Keats] the consciousness that if poetry was to absorb his whole life, to become a vocation rather than a pastime, it must correspond with his whole being and not merely with the least essential part of it. There were elements in his nature which had as yet found but partial or unsatisfactory expression, simply because they lay far deeper and were the harder to express. His was doubtless a supremely sensuous nature; such is the essential basis on which all poetry builds, and it was no more prominent in his early work than it was in the early work of Shakespeare; but the strong common-sense, the sound critical insight into the faults of himself and others, the habitual thoughtfulness of mind, the tender devotion to his family and friends, revealed in his letters and amply attested by all who knew him, are quite incompatible with a complete absorption in the luxury of his own sensations. (pp. xxx-xxxi)

[Keats] had a high conception not only of the pleasures but also of the duties of the poetic life and resolutely set himself to bring his own art into accord with his ideals. And though to the mind which craves for beauty there is an inherent shrinking from all that seems to combat it, yet, as his feeling for beauty deepened from sensation to emotion, and from emotion to a passion which embraced his whole moral and intellectual being, the conviction grew upon him that the artist, if only for the sake of his art, must be ready to open his heart and mind to receive all impressions that the world has to offer, even those that are in themselves unlovely. (p. xxxi)

Criticism, with its eye fixed on the development of style, has often failed to realise the deeper influences at work upon his mind of which, after all, his style is only the expression. Yet it is no insignificant fact that his intellect developed in the closest relation with two masters who in different ways could teach him what he needed most to learn. These were Shakespeare and Wordsworth. (p. xxxii)

Until the end of 1816 Shakespeare counted for little with Keats. Though he had doubtless read most of the plays, they had made no impression on his mind, and it is in keeping with the general character of his early work that apart from two superficial references to *Lear,* and a reminiscence of a famous passage in *As You Like It,* which he spoilt in the borrowing, all the allusions are to *A Midsummer-Night's Dream.* Shakespeare is to him the poet of Titania and fairyland. But the first use that he made of the retirement which followed on his dedication of his life to poetry, was to begin a real study of Shakespeare. The vocabulary and phraseology of *Endymion* differ chiefly from that of the 1817 volume in the influx of Shakespearian words, allusions and reminiscences, drawn from a large number of plays, whilst the influence of Shakespeare's poems is shown in the fact that though the larger number of Keats's sonnets are in Italian form, all the best, with the exception of the Chapman sonnet, which belongs to an earlier date, are written upon the model of Shakespeare.

But to say this is only to refer to the superficial signs of an influence which goes far deeper. . . . His letters shew that his passion for poetry was closely associated with his study, that it is Shakespeare who is educating him, inspiring him, comforting him. The line in *Lear,* "Do you not hear the sea," haunts him till he can give poetic utterance to his emotion. "Whenever you write," he tells Reynolds, of all his friends, perhaps, that one who had most intellectual sympathy with him, "say a word or two on some passage of Shakespeare that may have come rather new to you, which must constantly be happening, notwithstanding that we read the same play forty times; *e.g.,* the following never struck me so forcibly as at present:—

> urchins
> Shall for the vast of night, that they may work,
> All exercise on thee.

(pp. xxxii-xxxiv)

Shakespeare at once gives him an unapproachable standard, which prevents his thinking overmuch of his own productions, and at the same time keeps him from despondency. "I never quite despair and I read Shakespeare—indeed, I think I shall never read any other book much." It is in reference to Shakespeare [in the sonnet *On sitting down to read King Lear once again*] that he realises a truth fully applicable to his own poetry that the "excellence of every art is its intensity, capable of making all disagreeables evaporate from their being in close relationship with Beauty and Truth". (p. xxxiv)

At the same time that [Keats] was finding in Shakespeare the greatest examples of the imaginative presentation of life, he was turning to Wordsworth not only as the one living poet who was fully conscious of the dignity of his vocation, but even more than this as the inspired commentator on the poetic faculty, who traced its growth in the mind of the poet, and interpreted its significance to the world. Wordsworth's influence was never a personal one. It began to be exerted fully a year before the two poets had met, and even after their acquaintance it remained unchanged in character; it was never cemented by the ties of friendship. Still less was it a literary influence. Keats gives expression more than once to his antipathy to the artistic method by which Wordsworth chose to present his faith. "We hate poetry," he writes, "that has a palpable design upon us. Poetry should be great and unobtrusive, a thing which enters

into one's soul." To his eyes "the egotistical sublime" of Wordsworth contrasted unfavourably with "Shakespeare's great negative capability, his power of presenting uncertainties, mysteries and doubts without an irritable reaching after fact and reason". But just because much of Wordsworth's poetry seemed to be the studied expression of a definite philosophy of life and art rather than the cry of spontaneous emotion, it had all the more effect upon him. He stood in need of further poetic inspiration; what he desired was the direction of his intellect, and there is continual evidence of the deep hold which the teaching of Wordsworth had gained over his mind. The *Hymn to Pan* [from *Endymion*] might perhaps seem to Wordsworth "a pretty piece of paganism," yet it was Wordsworth's interpretation of Greek mythology which revealed to Keats the spirit which informed it. And Wordsworth affected him, too, in his attitude to subjects with which he is supposed to have been generally unconcerned. It is rarely, for example, that he touches on the politics of the hour. Yet his criticism sent to his brother George, to whom he communicated all his thoughts, could only have come from the student of Wordsworth's greatest political utterances. "The motives of our worst men," he writes, "are Interest and of our best Vanity. We have no Milton, no Algernon Sidney. Governors in these days lose the title of man in exchange for that of Diplomat and Minister. . . . All these departments of Government have strayed far from Simplicity, which is the greatest of strength" . . . and he goes on to disjoin himself from the Liberal party in a denunciation of Napoleon as "one who has done more harm to the life of Liberty than any one else could have done". It is evident from this passage how the cheery Radicalism of Hunt has been tempered by the spirit of [Wordsworth's] *Sonnets dedicated to National Independence and Liberty.*

Even more suggestive of the deep hold which the Wordsworthian creed had gained over his mind are the words in which he interprets to his brother, who is grieving with him over a common loss, the meaning of man's life in its relation with what is beyond.

> The common cognomen of this world among the misguided and superstitious is 'a vale of tears,' from which we are redeemed by a certain arbitrary interposition of God and taken to Heaven. What a little circumscribed notion! Call the world, if you please, the vale of Soul-making. Then you will find out the use of the world. . . . I will call the world a school instituted for the purpose of teaching little children to read—I will call the human heart the hornbook used in that school—and I will call the child able to read, the Soul made from that school and its horn-book. Do you not see how necessary a world of pains and troubles is to school an intelligence and make it a Soul? A place where the heart must feel and suffer in a thousand diverse ways.

This passage might well be taken as a commentary on Wordsworth's *Ode on Intimations of Immortality,* which, as Bailey tells us, "he was never weary of repeating". In Wordsworth, indeed, he saw a poet who, like himself, had drawn his first inspiration from the beauty of nature, but had only become conscious of

> how exquisitely
> The external world is fitted to the mind

after a deep and sympathetic study of humanity. Through a profound contemplation on the mysteries of being Wordsworth had at last attained to a resolution of the conflicting elements in his nature, in an impassioned philosophy in which "thought and feeling are one". This resolution was never attained by Keats, but he realised that the greatest poetry sprang from the desire for it, if not from its attainment; and both in his letters and in his poems there are continual signs that he was turning to Wordsworth for help and guidance. (pp. xxxv-xxxvii)

"Wordsworth," he writes, in a letter whose whole spirit is that of a disciple, "is explorative of the dark passages in the mansion of human life. He is a genius superior to us in so far as he can, more than we, make discoveries and shed a light in them. Now if we live and go on thinking, we too shall explore them."

The influence of Wordsworth appears in the poems of Keats before there are any traces of it in his correspondence. Several Wordsworthian echoes, which seem strangely incongruous with their surroundings, startle the reader of the 1817 volume into the conviction that even whilst the young poet was revelling in the luxuries of art and nature under the guidance of Leigh Hunt, he was gradually absorbing much of the poetry of Wordsworth [a footnote reads: *Cf. Specimen of an Induction* . . . with *I wandered lonely as a cloud.* . . . *Sonnet to Solitude* . . . with *Nuns fret not*. The *Sonnet to my Brothers* (1816) seems a reminiscence of Wordsworth's *I am not one who much or oft delights, etc. Sleep and Poetry,* . . . "The blue bared its eternal bosom" is both in thought and language a reproduction of Wordsworth's, *The world is too much with us*. It is worth noticing that all these poems of Wordsworth's are to be found in his 1807 volume. Lines like "A sense of real things comes doubly strong" and "Wings to find out an immortality" (*Sleep and Poetry* . . .) suggest the *Ode on Intimations, etc.* . . .]. It is significant that he associates the two men together, apparently unconscious of their essential antagonism, as the champions who have arisen to free English literature from the formalism and artificiality of the eighteenth century. *Sleep and Poetry,* with which the volume closes, is at the same time a glowing tribute to the sympathetic friendship which he had enjoyed at the Hampstead cottage and an attempt to express in the style of the *Story of Rimini* something of the spirit which had informed the *Lines written above Tintern Abbey*. Under the inspiration of this higher seriousness he becomes conscious that he too is "disturbed with the sense of elevated thoughts". "The realm of Flora and old Pan" in which he spent so many pleasant hours of comradeship "choosing each pleasure that the fancy sees" must now be renounced

for a nobler life
Where I may see the agonies, the strife
Of human hearts;

and the ideal of which he has been vouchsafed a vision is only to be attained by a deeper human sympathy and a more eager scrutiny of the mysteries of nature and of life.

In *Endymion* he strives to treat in a more highly poetic form the problem continually before his mind, and to present in a story whose beauty had long haunted him an allegory of the development of the poet's soul towards a complete realisation of itself. (pp. xxxviii-xl)

It is hardly safe to give a . . . detailed interpretation of the allegory, for as a whole *Endymion* is vague and obscure. But the vagueness and the obscurity do not prove that the poet's interest lay merely in the story and its decoration, they rather

point to that inability to portray his conceptions in clear outline, which accompanies an immaturity of artistic power. His mind at that time was, as he said later, like a pack of scattered cards. Thus much at least is certain, that in the dark wanderings of *Endymion* we may trace the groupings of the spirit after the ideal, and the episodes of Arethusa and of Glaucus could have no possible justification in the scheme of the poem had they not been introduced to emphasise the conception, already presented in *Sleep and Poetry,* that only by human sympathy can the poet reach the summit of his power.

In *Hyperion* the same strain of thought is present. The fruitless struggle of the Titans, types of the elemental energies of the world, against that dynasty whose rule was based on higher principle than mere brute force, is to Keats essentially concentrated in the fall of Hyperion, the flaming sun-god, before Apollo the god of light and song. And its fundamental conception that

'tis the eternal law
That first in beauty should be first in might

can only have one interpretation. For it is by "knowledge enormous" that Apollo has become a god, and if his knowledge has given him divinity, his perfect beauty and his power over song have come to him from the humanising influence of sympathy and suffering. . . . In *Lamia* [Keats] lays aside for the time the question of the place of human sympathy in art and concentrates his power upon a dramatic presentation of the antagonism between reason and emotion. Here we have no longer the calm reserve and self control of *Hyperion,* in its expression of a creed from which, in reality, Keats never wavered; but a passionate, almost morbid, expression of a conflict between those antagonistic forces which fought out their battle continually within his breast; and though with a true poetic feeling he keeps his own personality out of the poem, it lends additional passion to his treatment of the subject. The significance of *Lamia* in its relation to Keats's whole tone of thought is by no means summed up, as often represented even by his most sympathetic critics, in the well-known lines

Do not all charms fly
At the mere touch of cold philosophy?

for the poem is the utterance of a mood rather than of a settled conviction. True it is that the poet wishes to enlist our sympathies on the side of Lycius; that is essential, if the interest of the story is to be maintained; but it is possible for the emotional side of a nature to upbraid with bitterness the intellectual even while it recognises the right of the intellectual to supremacy. . . . [As Keats] follows the fate of his hero he represents the agony of the struggle in the soul of a man who clings to the false at the same time that he desires the true, who aspires after the ideal even whilst he is unable to relax his hold of those very shadows, not realities, which he knows well enough to despise. Keats realised the nature of the struggle from the very first and set himself to unify the conflicting emotions of his nature. He had no time to reach the perfect consummation of his genius; the widest sympathy with the world about him, the firmest grasp of the realities of human life and character were not yet his; but his whole work presents us with the struggle for it, and presents it with a passion and sincerity which is itself a constituent of the highest genius. For art itself represents a struggle after an infinite perfection, and in no one of our poets do we find this more vitally portrayed than in the work of Keats.

It is significant that in these three poems, which are the most ambitious of his works and reflect most fully his inner experience and his poetic ideals, he should turn for his source and much of his framework to the world of Greece, whose legends had fascinated his childhood, and had never lost their hold upon his imagination. There was much indeed in the Greek attitude to life, as he understood it, that made an irresistible appeal to him. The expression of truth in forms essentially beautiful, the spontaneous unquestioning delight in the life of nature and its incarnation in forms human but of more than human loveliness, made the pagan creed, outworn to Wordsworth, retain for Keats all its freshness and its vitality. (pp. xl-xliii)

But if at times [Keats] showed in his handling of classical legends a naïveté of feeling and a simple lucidity of expression sufficient to win the enthusiastic praise of Shelley, "He was a Greek!", his attitude to his subject and his presentation of it are as a rule far different from this. Nor can it be wondered at. Keats was no scholar, and of the literature in which the Greek spirit found true expression he could know nothing. But just as it was through his devotion to Spenser that he became a poet, so was it through his kinship, both in spirit and taste, with the Elizabethans, that he became the poet of ancient Greece. In his own day he was accused of versifying [the editor of the *Classical Dictionary*] Lemprière, and the *Dictionary* is still regarded as the main source of his classical inspiration. Yet it is highly probable that if he had found the legends of ancient mythology in Lemprière alone he would have left them there, and it is certain that if he had never seen a dictionary his debt to the world of Greece would have been the same. Homer had been known to him in the version of Pope, at least, one would have thought, as inspiring as Lemprière, but had left him cold; the Homer that he came to love appeared to him in the gorgeous but exuberant phraseology of Chapman. It seems indeed as if a story of the ancient world had to assume an Elizabethan dress before it could kindle his imagination. A careful examination of the legends which he employs in his poems will tend to show that though, doubtless, he became first acquainted with many of them in the dull pages of Lemprière or Tooke or Spence, and continued to make occasional use of the *Dictionary* as a work of reference, there is hardly an allusion that cannot be traced to an Elizabethan source. The legend of Endymion and Cynthia was well known to him in Lyly, in Fletcher, in Drayton; and of the main episodes and the wealth of illustration to which the poem owes much of its beauty, all that cannot be traced to Spenser or Chapman or Browne can be found in the *Metamorphoses* of Ovid, that book especially dear to the Renaissance and known to Keats in a late Elizabethan form. Keats possessed a copy of Ovid in the original, but the Ovid that he read and re-read was the famous version of George Sandys which delighted him as it had delighted the seventeenth century by "the sumptuous bravery of that rich attire" in which the translator had clothed it. Seeing then that Lemprière had no material to give him that he could not have met elsewhere, and often in the Sandys which we know him to have studied with assiduity, whilst Sandys supplied him with details of incident and phrase for which Lemprière may be searched in vain, we are justified in the inference that in cases where both Lemprière and Sandys are possible sources, Keats owed his inspiration to a living work of art and not to a museum of dead antiquities. (pp. xliv-xlv)

Endymion, the first fruits of [Keats's] whole-hearted devotion to his art, has no single definite model, but shows the natural influence of Spenser and the seventeenth-century Spenserians upon an immature, exuberant genius, which had already an intuitive sympathy with the laxer qualities of their style and method. It may indeed be regarded as the consummation of his early work, more ambitious in design than anything he had hitherto accomplished, and inspired by a greater purpose, but tainted with the same faults of style, execution and sentiment. "A trial," he calls it, "of my powers of imagination, by which I must make 4000 lines of one bare circumstance and fill them with poetry"; and the statement inevitably suggests that much of the poetry is independent of the real subject. For "the one bare circumstance" is embellished by incidents which retard the natural development of the action and by episodes which have no organic relation with the main story, but are only explicable after a full comprehension of their application and inner meaning. The progress of the involved allegory, itself sufficiently unclassical, finds ample precedent in seventeenth-century poets, and bears more resemblance to the rambling inconsequence of *Britannia's Pastorals* than to any work of more definitely artistic construction; and whilst the inner significance of the poem gives clear evidence of the spirit in which Keats had come to view his art, its general conduct shows him to be as yet far from attaining to the ideal which he sets forth in it. When he touches upon everyday life, as at the beginning of the third book, he is vague or trivial, and the general characterisation of Endymion in his relations with Peona, Cynthia and the Indian maiden, conceived with a delicate and imaginative insight into the ideal beauty of the legend, is vitiated throughout by the insipid sentimentality of expression, which the influence of Hunt, brought to bear upon his own lack of training, had led him to mistake for the universal language of the heart. (p. xlviii)

Yet notwithstanding its failure as a whole, its obscurity, its vicious lack of reticence, its banality, [*Endymion*] is redeemed by passages of glowing beauty which take their place with anything of their kind in our literature. Nowhere have the subtle influence of nature on the imaginative mind and a mystic yearning after her illimitable beauty found more impassioned expression, and however often the elaborate treatment of the main characters may fail in truth to life as a whole and to the Greek conceptions in particular, no poet has ever more fully possessed that creative power by which in a few lines, at times in a mere phrase, he can penetrate to the heart of a story long since dead and with magic touch bring it back to life, so that we see it in its essential and vital truth. (p. xlix)

[The] wonderful advance in style and treatment [in *Hyperion*] was due entirely to his subservience to a stricter model, and the change from *Endymion* to *Hyperion* is not the change from a romance to a classical epic, but the change from the influence of the Spenserians to the severer school of Milton. Milton's early poems had long been known to him; now for the first time he came under the potent spell of *Paradise Lost.* And now he learned his first great lesson in artistic concentration, and constructed his poem on a plan which bears obvious resemblance to Milton's Epic. His style, too, was deeply affected. Many a Miltonic echo can be caught in *Hyperion,* and in his vocabulary Keats replaces the limp and effeminate coinage and the exuberant wordiness of his former work by a virility of language and a stern compression of all superfluity. . . . It is only by the side of his great and unapproachable model that the blank verse of *Hyperion* seems at times to be monotonous, that the debate of the fallen Titans seems to lack something both in subtlety and passion; and if Keats cannot rival either the majesty or the stupendous range both of thought and melody that is the wonder of *Paradise Lost,* there is in *Hyperion* that glamour of romance, that same exquisite reading of the magic of nature which gave to *Endymion* its priceless charm. (pp. xlix-l)

Later, when the hand of death was already laid upon him, [Keats] took up *Hyperion* once more and attempted to remodel it in the form of an allegorical vision expounded to him by one of the fallen goddesses. Criticism is right in pointing out that the attempt was not successful, that he spoilt many lines in the process, and that the *Fall of Hyperion,* as it is called, shows a distinct decline of artistic power. But it is at least a question whether if his powers had remained at their height, he would not have done the same thing and succeeded, whether he would not have turned what is, after all, a magnificent literary *tour de force,* into a poem fully expressive of the essential qualities of his own peculiar genius. For an artist is never at his highest when he is forcing his art into an uncongenial channel, and if he spoiled some of his earlier lines it must also be remembered that some of those which he added in the *Vision* are among the finest that he ever wrote. For Keats, romantic to the core, could find no freedom in the restraint of a classical or even a Miltonic Epic.

For his model in *Lamia* he turned to the Fables of Dryden, the best modern example of the use of the heroic couplet in narrative verse. The versification and style of *Lamia* give clear evidence that he had made a careful study of Dryden. In contrast with the earlier couplets of the 1817 volume and of *Endymion* his employment of the run-on line and the feminine and weak endings is now carefully controlled, and he trusts to a careful use of the triplet and the Alexandrine to give his verse the necessary variety. Moreover, without direct imitation, such as would allow a comparison of special passages in the two poets, there are lines in *Lamia* which have caught with great effect the ring and the rapidity which are essential characteristics of Dryden's best work. Descriptions such as that of the nymph—

> At whose white feet the languid Tritons poured
> Pearls, while on land they wither'd and adored;

or of the angry god of love, who

> jealous grown of so complete a pair,
> Hover'd and buzz'd his wings, with fearful roar,
> Above the lintel of their chamber door,
> And down the passage cast a glow upon the floor;

or still more, perhaps, of the

> song of love, too sweet for earthly lyres,
> While, like held breath, the stars drew in their panting
> fires,

suggest the rhythmical use of language peculiarly remarkable in Dryden, whilst they are touched with a glowing imagination which is far beyond his reach.

Equally evident is the influence of Dryden on the construction of the poem. The story instead of being turgid, involved, incomprehensible, is related simply and effectively with emphasis only upon the more important dramatic effects. . . . It is a masterpiece of narrative, in construction not equalled elsewhere by Keats, whilst the conflict of emotion between the worship of beauty and the calls of higher reason gives a passionate force to the whole.

But his close study of Dryden was perhaps responsible for the recurrence of certain faults which mar the effect of an otherwise perfect work of art. His desire to attain to the masterly ease and fluency of Dryden's manner led him into frequent false rhymes and to some return of the unhappy characteristics of

his early vocabulary. And the careless levity expected of a Restoration poet in his treatment of love, and rarely present in Dryden without the compensating charm of urbanity and airy grace, appears in Keats in the form of that vulgarity which he seemed elsewhere to have out-grown. The execrable taste of the description of a woman's charms . . . and the feeble cynicism of the opening to the second book, both, in all probability, traceable to this cause, are alien to the whole spirit in which *Lamia* was conceived.

It is where *Lamia* is farthest removed from the Greek spirit, farthest too from the spirit of Dryden, that it is most characteristic of Keats. The brilliant picture of midnight Corinth, the glowing magnificence of the phantasmal palace are triumphs of romantic description; nor is there wanting to the poem that magical felicity of phrase, that singular power over the deeply charged epithet, something, too, of the mood which loves ''to touch the strings into a mystery'' and by its tender imaginative insight go straight to the heart of the situation. Such is the wistful thought of Hermes as he seeks for the nymph:—

> Ah, what a world of love was at her feet!
>
> (pp. li-liii)

These qualities find their fullest and most unfettered expression where Keats is freest from external restrictions of style and method, in the treatment of romantic themes drawn from mediaeval sources—in *Isabella,* in the *Eve of St. Agnes,* in the fragmentary *Eve of St. Mark* and in *La Belle Dame sans Merci.*

Of these *Isabella, or the Pot of Basil* was the first to be written and was finished only a month after the final revision of *Endymion.* . . . The poem is uneven in execution, and it would be easy to point out faults both in the taste and in the workmanship, which are all the more noticeable in comparison with their surroundings [in the 1820 volume]. Moreover the studied emphasis which he lays upon the avarice and pride of the wicked brothers and upon the limp ecstasy of Lorenzo's passion, serves in reality to weaken that very effect which he desired to intensify. But these flaws are easily outweighed by the vivid poetic feeling and essential truth with which he has grasped the fundamental emotion of the story. The opening stanzas, in their delineation of the delicate susceptibility of the lovers to each other's presence, are in their way perfect, and form a fitting prelude to the marvellous picture of the tragic climax. . . . Poetry such as [that describing the loneliness of the murdered lover], alike by its beauty of language and its sympathy with the subject, raises the tale which in Boccaccio is merely horrible, into the region of genuine tragedy.

But far more successful as a whole is the *Eve of St. Agnes,* which stands chronologically in the same relation to *Hyperion* as did *Isabella* to *Endymion,* and is faultlessly executed in the spirit of the legend which inspired it. In his revulsion from the magnificence of *Paradise Lost,* Keats had turned his thoughts once more to Chatterton, who had fascinated his youth; and it was Chatterton, doubtless, that guided him both here and in the companion fragment the *Eve of St. Mark,* to seek a subject in mediaeval legend and to invest it with an atmosphere of mystery and enchantment. To his admiration for the Rowley dialect may probably be traced the unfortunate attempt, in the later poem, to reproduce the actual language of the Middle Ages; in the *Eve of St. Agnes* he is content with catching an occasional cadence from the *Excellent Ballad of Charitie* and leaving the rest to his power over a diction chosen not for its antiquity but for its intrinsic beauty. But if he owed something to Chatterton he owed still more to Spenser, and there are clear indications both in the wealth of imagery and vivid colouring of the diction and in the use of the metre, never before seriously attempted by him, that he was renewing the study of his earlier master. The stanza is not merely formally Spenserian, it is employed with a truly Spenserian effect; and the subtle modulation of the melody, and in particular the lingering sweetness of the Alexandrine, are nowhere else so effective outside the *Faerie Queene*. With the form Keats has at last perhaps caught something of that spirit of chivalry inherent in Spenser which from the first he had desired to emulate. In his conception of Madeline, . . . [Keats] is free at last from the mawkish sentimentality and misdirected sensuousness of his early love-poetry.

To a full sympathy with the dominant emotion of the poem he attunes us by his consummate mastery over the nicest methods of romantic art, heightening the effect throughout by a series of vivid contrasts, and enveloping the whole in a dreamlike atmosphere of enchantment and wonder. . . . [Nowhere] is this sense of contrast more exquisitely developed than in the treatment of the shifting moonlight which pervades the poem, at times adding the last supreme touch of colour to a picture of carefully elaborated detail, at times, by its weird suggestiveness, rendering all detail superfluous. No description of the castle is given us, yet as Porphyro stands ''buttress'd from moonlight'' we see it outlined in black massiveness against the sky; languid shines the moon upon the little room, ''pale, lattic'd, chill,'' where he unfolds his plan to the beldame, and awaits the moment of its fulfilment; its full glory is veiled until it gleams upon the lustrous salvers of the mysterious feast, or bursts in magic splendour through the casement of the shrine of love. . . . (pp. liv-lvii)

In *La Belle Dame sans Merci* the mediaeval revival reaches its consummation. The depth of passion which it expresses, or rather implies, for there is not the least suspicion of raving, the intense lyrical feeling, though the poet's personality is absolutely merged in the dramatic conception, the exquisite art by which every detail of the weird landscape and every cadence of the wild but subtle melody contribute to the general effect of mystery and of desolation, produce together an effect elsewhere unequalled in the poetry of romance.

After reading such a work one is tempted to ask whether art can go further than this, or what room there is for development in an artist who at the age of twenty-four can produce such a masterpiece. And perhaps if art could be viewed in itself, apart from all other considerations, an answer would be difficult. But the greatest artists have always been in the fullest sense realists, have lit up with their imagination the real world and not been satisfied with reflecting, however beautifully, a world of dreams. . . . [For Keats, the] marvellous was still ''the most enticing and the surest guarantee of harmonious numbers''. But the marvellous alone no longer satisfied him. ''Wonders,'' he writes, ''are no wonders to me; I am more at home amongst men and women. I had rather read Chaucer than Ariosto. The little dramatic skill I may as yet have, however badly it might show in a drama, would I think be sufficient for a poem. I wish to diffuse the colouring of St. Agnes Eve throughout a poem in which character and sentiment would be the figures to such drapery. Two or three such poems, if God should spare me, written in the course of the next six years would be a famous *gradus ad Parnassum altissimum* [step toward Parnassian heights]. I mean they would nerve me up to the writing of a few fine plays—my greatest ambition.''

How far he might have realised this ambition it is difficult to conjecture. Genius for dramatic writing is never developed early, and it must be admitted that in the narrative poems that he had already written he had exhibited as subtle and sympathetic an insight into certain phases of human emotion as is exemplified in [Shakespeare's] *Venus and Adonis* or the *Rape of Lucrece,* and a far keener sense of dramatic propriety. *Otho the Great,* the only drama he lived to finish, was written in collaboration with Brown, under circumstances which precluded the possibility of successful characterisation; but its versification, at least, shows him to have studied with profit in the finest school of dramatic art, and he did not share that contempt for the stage under which not a few of our poets have veiled their chagrin at failure in dramatic composition. Lastly it must be admitted that of all his contemporaries he had the greatest objective power. ''As to the poetical character,'' he writes, ''(I mean that sort of which, if I am anything I am a member), it is not itself, it has no self, it has no character, it enjoys light and shade; it lives in gusto, be it foul or fair, high or low, rich or poor, mean or elevated. It has as much delight in conceiving an Iago as an Imogen. What shocks the virtuous philosopher delights the chameleon poet . . . a poet is the most unpoetical of anything in existence, because he has no identity—he is continually in for and filling some other body.'' This Protean quality of mind, an essential characteristic of the dramatic genius, he possessed in an eminent degree.

But whatever might have been his success in the drama, he had already discovered, in the Ode, a form of lyrical utterance well fitted to give expression to the essential qualities of his genius. In simple outbursts of unpremeditated art he could equal neither the spontaneity of the Elizabethan lyrist nor the glowing intensity of Shelley, and despite his success in using an occasional short line, he could never gain the lightness of touch which gave an unfailing sweetness and grace to the four-accent verse of Fletcher and Milton. But in his freedom from the faults that spring from too close a dependence on classic models—that stiffness of phraseology and over-elaboration of form which mar the verse of Dryden, of Gray, even at times of Collins—he stands without a rival as the poet of the richly meditative Ode. It is here that the long drawn out line which seems to brood over its own sweetness is used with most effect, that his poetry surprises with a fine excess, yet never cloys with exaggeration, that all the different elements that moulded or inspired his genius are completely harmonised in the imaginative expression of his present mood. The independence for which from the first he had striven is gloriously attained. In the Odes he has no master; and their indefinable beauty is so direct and so distinctive an effluence of his soul that he can have no disciple.

His first poem of sustained perfect loveliness had been the *Ode to Sorrow,* to be found in the fourth book of *Endymion,* and the exquisite fragment of an *Ode to Maia* had followed in the next year. The rest belong to 1819, the maturest period of his workmanship, and all but *Autumn* to the early months of the year. Bound together not only by a continual recurrence of phrase and cadence but by a similar train of thought and a unity of feeling they sum up his attitude to life. They are the expression in varying keys of emotion of a mind which has loved the principle of beauty in all things, and seeks in a world of change and decay, among the fleeting forms of loveliness, for something permanent and eternal. (pp. lvii-lx)

[The *Ode to Autumn*] could have been indeed his swan-song, as it is assuredly his last work of full and conscious power, if he could have been spared the agony of mind which can be read in the fevered attempts at self-expression and still more ominously in the months of silence that followed, when he could find no "heart-easing things" to allay the tortures of a posthumous life! It was otherwise decreed: yet the significance of the *Ode to Autumn* in its place among his poems should not be forgotten either in a consideration of what he might have become, or in a final estimate of what he had actually achieved. For as an interpreter of nature to the heart of man he was already, in his way, unapproachable. (p. lxii)

[Keats's] power of catching nature's mood must largely depend, not only upon his sympathy with nature, but also upon his wide and sympathetic understanding of humanity, and the effectiveness of his expression will depend upon his sympathy with both. And we may, in fact, trace in his poetry an ever growing sense of their intimate relationship. At first there is noticeable in his descriptions a definite and even awkward transition from a fresh and charming landscape to the human figure ill sorted with its environment; then, as his understanding of human life became more real and more intense, his insight into the heart of nature grew deeper, and his pictures of nature gathered emotional force, so that when he is at his greatest he can only speak of the one in terms of the other. Just as his feeling for nature can only find voice in language applicable to human emotion, so the beauty of nature is his unfailing resource for the expression of the deepest and subtlest emotions of the soul. (pp. lxiv-lxv)

[In his attitude to nature, Keats is] in the closest sympathy with the temper of his own day. For in an age whose ideals find fittest utterance in the "Renascence of Wonder," it was given to him, perhaps, most of all, to interpret the wonders of the natural world. Whether he leads us

> Through the green evening quiet in the sun,
> Through buried paths, where sleepy twilight dreams
> The summer time away   (*End*. ii. . . .)

or calls upon us to gaze with him

>   on the new soft fallen mask
> Of snow upon the mountains and the moors
>   (*Sonnet* . . .)

—whatever his imagination has touched thrills us with a sense of the mystery and awe which underlie the common things of earth; in all nature we read with him, as on the face of night, the symbols of a high romance, which finite language can never utter, but which answers none the less to the infinite longings of the human soul.

In all this there is no attempt at explanation. Even the most philosophic of our poets delighted to picture himself as

> Contented if he might enjoy
> The things which others understand,

and in the poetry of Keats this mood is entirely dominant. "Unless poetry comes like leaves to the tree it had better not come at all," he writes, and there is something of defiance in his tone when he claims as the inalienable prerogative of the poet identification with his subject rather than criticism of it.

> What sea-bird o'er the sea
> Is a philosopher the while he goes
> Winging his way where the great water throes?

Nature presents perforce analogies with human life, on which others may speculate as they will, it may even suggest lessons of direct bearing upon conduct; but the supreme truth to the poet is not to be found in the lessons of nature, but in her mysterious beauty, and in her never failing power, whencesoever it may spring, to respond to every mood of the changing heart of man. Nature does not call upon him to understand this, but simply to recognise it. The message of the thrust, heard by Keats in the glory of a February morning, was but the echo of Nature's voice:—

> O fret not after knowledge.   I have none,
> And yet my song comes native with the warmth.
> O fret not after knowledge!   I have none,
> And yet the evening listens.

Here lies the mystery: here, too, in a world of barren facts, of arid controversies, of idle speculations, the irresistible appeal. In moments of supreme enjoyment, when the heart seems to beat in consonance with the mighty heart of the universe, it is difficult to deny a belief in the conscious life and conscious sympathy of nature, but her sovereignty depends on no such faith. Even if she beam upon us in blank splendour,

>   like the mild moon,
> Who comforts those she sees not, who knows not
> What eyes are upward cast,   (*Fall of Hyp*. . . .)

the truth remains immutable, unassailed, that the eyes are still cast upward, that the splendour is there, that the comfort is never sought in vain. Keats knew, no less than Wordsworth, that "Nature never did betray the heart that loved her," and that the true worship of beauty, associated, as he had learnt to associate it, with a passionate sense of the sorrows of the world, is its own justification, and its own reward. (pp. lxvi-lxviii)

> *E. de Sélincourt, in an introduction to* The Poems
> of John Keats, *edited by E. De Sélincourt, Methuen*
> *& Co., Ltd., 1905, pp. xix-lxviii.*

PAUL ELMER MORE   (essay date 1906)

[*More was an American critic who, along with Irving Babbitt, formulated the doctrines of New Humanism in early twentieth-century American thought. The New Humanists were strict moralists who adhered to traditional conservative values in reaction to an age of scientific and artistic self-expression. In regard to literature, they believed that the aesthetic qualities of a work of art should be subordinate to its moral and ethical purpose. More was particularly opposed to Naturalism, which he believed accentuated the animal nature of humans, and to any literature, such as Romanticism, that broke with established classical tradition. His importance as a critic derives from the rigid coherence of his ideology, which polarized American critics into hostile opponents (Van Wyck Brooks, Edmund Wilson, H. L. Mencken) or devoted supporters (Norman Foerster, Stuart Sherman, and, to a lesser degree, T. S. Eliot). He is especially esteemed for the philosophical and literary erudition of his multi-volumed* Shelburne Essays *(1904-21). Like E. de Selincourt (1905), More explores the sources of and influences on Keats's poetry. He focuses on the inspiration of the Elizabethan poets on Keats, particularly in their shared preoccupation with the "marriage of the ideas of beauty and death."*]

["**On First Looking into Chapman's Homer**"] is the sonnet that to most people probably comes first to mind when Keats is named and his destiny remembered. There is about it the golden flush and wonder of youth—it was written in his twentieth year—and one catches in it also, or seems to catch, a certain quickness of breath which forebodes the rapture so soon quenched. The inspiration of unsoiled nature and of England's clear-voiced early singers is here mingled as in no other of our poets. (p. 100)

To call [Keats] a Greek, as Shelley did explicitly and as Matthew Arnold once did by implication [see excerpt above, 1880], is to miss the mark. "Keats was no scholar," says Mr. de Sélincourt aptly, "and of the literature in which the Greek spirit found true expression he could know nothing. But just as it was through his devotion to Spenser that he became a poet, so was it through his kinship, both in spirit and taste, with the Elizabethans, that he became the poet of ancient Greece" [see excerpt above, 1905].

I am inclined to think that the essential kinship of Keats to "The fervid choir that lifted up a noise of harmony," as he called them, rests upon something even deeper than similarity of language and poetic method or than "natural magic" [as Matthew Arnold termed it], that it goes down to that faculty of vision in his mind which, like theirs, beheld the marriage of the ideas of beauty and death. As an editor concerned with the minutiae of the poet's manner, Mr. de Sélincourt may well be pardoned for overlooking this more essential relationship; his services are sufficiently great after every deduction. It is not a small thing, for instance, to find in the Glossary a careful tabulation of the sources from which Keats drew his extraordinary vocabulary, and from the first word, "a-cold," to see how constantly he borrowed from Shakespeare and Milton and the writers that lie between, and how deliberately he sought to echo "that large utterance of the early Gods." The curious thing is that in the end all this borrowing should produce the impression of a fine spontaneity. Just as we are discovering more and more in the spaciousness of the Elizabethans a literary inspiration from foreign lands, so the freedom of diction in Keats was in large measure the influence of a remote age— which may be taken as another lesson in the nature of originality. The effect is as if the language were undergoing a kind of rejuvenation and no dulness of long custom lay between words and objects. Wordsworth's endeavour to introduce the speech of daily use is in comparison the mere adopting of another artifice.

It is scarcely necessary to add that this spontaneity in a mind so untrained as Keats's often fell into license and barbarism. From the days of the first reviewers his ill-formed compound terms and his other solecisms have, and quite rightly, been ridiculed and repudiated. Sometimes, indeed, his super-grammatical creations have a strange quality of genius that rebukes criticism to modesty. Thus in the familiar lines:

> As when, upon a trancèd summer-night,
> Those green-robed senators of mighty woods,
> Tall oaks, *branch-charmèd* by the earnest stars,
> Dream, and so dream all night without a stir,
> Save from one gradual solitary gust
> Which comes upon the silence, and dies off,
> As if the ebbing air had but one wave—

it is not easy to justify "branch-charmèd" by any common linguistic process; and yet who does not feel that the spell of the passage, the very mystery of its utter beauty, is concentrated in that one lawless word? It is the keystone of a perfect arch. By a stroke of rarer insight Keats, when he came to rewrite the scene for the later *Hyperion*, left that phrase untouched, though he changed, and in changing marred, nearly all the rest. But if occasionally these unlicensed expressions add to the magic of his style, more often they are merely annoying blemishes. There is no beauty in such a phrase as "unslumbrous

night," to take the first words that occur, no force in "most drowningly doth sing," and his elision (which occurs more than once) of perhaps into p'rhaps is of a sort to make even a hardened reader wince.

The fact is, Keats might learn from the Elizabethans almost every element of style except taste, and here where he most needed guidance they seemed rather to sanction his lawlessness. But there was a difference between their circumstances and his. When a language is young and expanding, the absence of restraining taste is not so much felt, and liberty is a principle of growth; whereas at a later stage the same freedom leads often to mere eccentricity and vulgarisms. So it is that in Keats's language we are often obliged to distinguish between a true Elizabethan spontaneity and a spurious imitation that smacks too much of his London surroundings. We resent justly the review of *Endymion* in *Blackwood's* in which the author was labelled as belonging to "the Cockney School of Poetry"; we take almost as a personal affront the reviewer's coarse derision: "So back to the shop, Mr. John, stick to 'plasters, pills, ointment boxes'" [see excerpt above by John Gibson Lockhart, 1818]; yet there is a hideous particle of truth in the insult which will forever cling to Keats's name. Great poets have come out of London, but only Keats among the immortals can be pointed at as "cockney." (pp. 101-05)

[Unfortunately, both Leigh Hunt and B. R. Haydon] reinforced the natural qualities of his mind with what may be called a kind of bastard, or cockney, Elizabethanism. It is painful to follow that influence, as so much in Keats's life is painful. In his maturity he could see the weakness of these friends and speak of them dispassionately enough. Of Leigh Hunt he wrote to his brother George . . . : "*Hunt does one harm by making fine things petty and beautiful things hateful. Through him I am indifferent to Mozart, I care not for white Busts—and many a glorious thing when associated with him becomes a nothing.*" So much Keats could see, but never, even in his greatest works, could he quite free himself from that malign influence; for it had laid hold of a corresponding tendency in his own nature. He was never quite able to distinguish between the large liberties of the strong and the jaunty flippancy of the underbred; his passion for beauty could never entirely save him from mawkish prettinesses, and his idea of love was too often a mere sickly sweetness. Never after the days of *Endymion,* perhaps, did he write anything quite in the character of "Those lips, O slippery blisses"; but even in the volume of 1820 [*Lamia, Isabella, The Eve of St. Agnes, and Other Poems*] he could not be sure of himself. There are too many passages there like these lines in *Lamia*:

> He, sick to lose
> The amorous promise of her lone complain,
> Swoon'd, murmuring of love, and pale with pain.

Not a little of this uncertainty of taste was due to Leigh Hunt.

And in the same way Haydon confirmed Keats on another side of his cockney Elizabethanism. Haydon himself was a man of vast and undisciplined, almost insane, enthusiasms, and he undoubtedly did much to keep the ambitious longings of Keats in a state of morbid fermentation. . . . [Unfortunately, Keats's] associations were not of a kind to help him to overcome the initial lack of training, by correcting his flaws of taste and egotistic enthusiasm, and by purging what I have called his Elizabethan spontaneity of its cockney dross. As Wordsworth wrote in his patronising way: "How is Keats? He is a youth of promise, too great for the sorry company he keeps."

The wonder of it is that he grew so rapidly, and that so large a part of the volume of 1820 should have attained the true and lofty liberties of the spirit. In many aspects he stands curiously apart from his age. One feels this in his attitude toward nature, which in his verse is still unsubjected to the destinies of mankind. With Wordsworth and Shelley, even with Byron, some thought of man's sufferings and aspirations rises between the poet's eye and the vision of Nature, but with Keats she is still a great primeval force, inhuman and self-centred, beautiful, and sublime, and cruel, by turns. One catches this note at times in the earlier poems, as in the largeness and aloofness of such a picture as this:

> On a lone winter evening, when the frost
> Has wrought a silence.

It speaks with greater clearness in the later poems—in the elfin call of the nightingale's song,

> The same that hath
> Charm'd magic casements, opening on the foam
> Of perilous seas, in faery lands forlorn;

and in the imagery, calling us back to times before man's feebler creation, of that "sad place" where

> Crag jutting forth to crag, and rocks, that seemed
> Ever as if just rising from a sleep,
> Forehead to forehead held their monstrous horns.

One has the feeling that the poet's mind is in immediate contact with the object described, and the imagination of the reader is shocked from self-complacency by a kind of sympathetic surprise. It is at bottom a mark of that unperverted and untheorised sincerity whose presence condones so many faults in the Elizabethan writers, and whose absence mars so many brilliant qualities in the contemporaries of Keats.

But more particularly I see this backward-reaching kinship of Keats in his constant association of the ideas of beauty (or love) and death. In the dramatists that association attained its climax in the broken cry of Webster, which rings and sobs like a paroxysm of jealous rage against the all-embracing power:

> Cover her face; mine eyes dazzle: she died young,—

but everywhere in them it is present or implied. Of their thirst for beauty there is no need to give separate examples; nor yet of their constant brooding on the law of mutability. They cannot get away from the remembrance of life's brevity:

> On pain of death, let no man name death to me:
> *It is a word infinitely terrible.*

But for the tedium of repetition one might go through Keats's volume of 1820, and show how completely the pattern of that book is wrought on the same background of ideas. Perhaps the most striking illustration may be found in those two stanzas which relate how Isabella in the lonely forest unearths the body of her buried lover:

> She gazed into the fresh-thrown mould, as though
>   One glance did fully all its secrets tell;
> Clearly she saw, as other eyes would know
>   Pale limbs at bottom of a crystal well;
> Upon the murderous spot she seem'd to grow,
>   Like to a native lily of the dell:
> Then with her knife, all sudden, she began
> To dig more fervently than misers can.

> Soon she turn'd up a soilèd glove, whereon
>   Her silk had play'd in purple phantasies,
> She kiss'd it with a lip more chill than stone,
>   And put it in her bosom, where it dries
> And freezes utterly unto the bone
>   Those dainties made to still an infant's cries:
> Than 'gan she work again; nor stay'd her care,
> But to throw back at times her veiling hair.

(pp. 108-15)

[In] these stanzas there is something that calls the mind back to the poetry of Webster and Ford. This poignant meeting of the shapes of loveliness and decay is the inheritance of the middle ages, which in England more especially was carried over into the new birth and made gorgeous with all the cunning splendours of the Renaissance. Keats did not learn his art from the real antiquity. The Greeks, too, had their version of the theme, and in the story of Persephone and Dis gave it its most perfect mythological form. But its interest with them lay primarily in its ethical associations, and the Powers of beauty and death were minor agents only in the great moral drama moved by the supreme unwritten laws. No Greek could have so gloated over the purely physical contrast of ideas—"A skull upon a mat of roses lying"—or put into it the same hungering emotion, as did Keats in these stanzas that follow the forest scene in *Isabella.* . . . To see how far Keats is from the spirit of Greece, we need only turn from this last stanza to the scene of Antigone, in the play of Sophocles, treading the last road for the love of one dead, and looking for the last time on the light of the sun and never again any more. She, too, bids farewell to the bright things of the world, the springs of Dirce and the grove of Thebes, but it is not in the language of Isabella.

The same music wrung from the transience of lovely things runs like a monotone through the other poems of Keats's great volume, but in a different key. The incongruity (as it appears, yet it lies at the bottom of human thought) intrudes even into *The Eve of St. Agnes,* with the opening image of the benumbed beadsman among the sculptured dead and with the closing return to the same contrast. In the Odes it is subdued to a musing regret—heard pensively in the *Ode to a Nightingale;* . . . speaking with a still more chastened beauty in the *Ode on a Grecian Urn;* . . . uttered with greater poignancy in the *Ode on Melancholy.* . . . (pp. 115-18)

It is the secret, for those who can read that mystery, of what is to many his most perfect work, the ballad of *La Belle Dame Sans Merci.*

From these ideal poems one turns naturally to the letters in which the fever and unrest, the glimpses of philosophy, and the broken hopes of Keats's actual life are expressed with such pathetic earnestness. The picture that results is of a strong man fighting against what he calls, with some self-depreciation, "a horrid Morbidity of Temperament." There is much to lament in this revelation never meant for the public; but in the end the sense of the man's greatness, the feeling of his reliance on the divine call, outweighs the impression of his painful susceptibility. . . . [The] truer Keats is to be found in his moments of proud independence: "I value more the privilege of seeing great things in loneliness than the fame of a Prophet." *Great things in loneliness!* These were to him, as almost every page of the letters would prove, *the mighty abstract Idea of Beauty* and the ever-present consciousness of death. The pity of it is that these relentless powers should have passed for him from the realm of reflection to the coarse realities of life, and that the experience of his few years (they were only twenty-five) should have been torn by them as by a warring destiny. It was inevitable that this contention should take the form of love. . . . The letters in which he pours out the agony of his love for Fanny Brawne resemble Hazlitt's *Liber Amoris* more than anything else in literature. They have the same uncontrolled passion, and the same unfortunate note of vulgarity, due not so much to the exuberance of his emotion as to the lack of any corresponding force in the woman. The flaccidity of her temperament deprives the episode of tragic ideality, and lowers it to the common things of the street. It even changes his mastervision to something approaching a sickly sentimentalism. (pp. 118-19)

As it seemed to [Keats] in those evil days when disease had laid hold of his body, Death was the victor in the contention of Fate. . . . But to the world, not Death but eternal Loveliness carried the palm. We think of him as the Marcellus of literature, who could not break through the *fata aspera* [harsh fate], and as one of "the inheritors of unfulfilled renown"; and still we know that he accomplished a glorious destiny. His promise was greater than the achievement of others.

And yet a word to avoid misunderstanding. . . . [In] pointing out the kinship of Keats to the Elizabethans, we should not forget that he is, like all men, still of his own age. By his depth and sincerity he differs, indeed, from certain other writers of the century who deal with the same subjects—from William Morris, for example, whose *Earthly Paradise* runs on the strange companionship of love and death with almost a frivolous persistence; but he is still far from the brave furor and exultation of the great passages in Marlowe. Again he has more than once imitated the simplicity of William Browne—notably in the *Ode on a Grecian Urn* where the lines to the "bold lover" . . . are evidently an echo of a passage in the *Pastorals*. . . .

> Here from the rest a lovely shepherd's boy
> Sits piping on a hill, as if his joy
> Would still endure, or else that age's frost
> Should never make him think what he had lost. . . .

But who does not feel that the young beauty of Keats is different from that first careless rapture, which has gone never to be recovered? Perhaps the very fact that he is speaking a language largely foreign to his own generation adds a personal eagerness, a touch at times of feverish straining, to his song.

I have already intimated that side by side with the superb zest of beauty there is another note in the dramatists which Keats rarely or never attains. That note is caught in such lines as Ford's

> For he is like to something I remember
> A great while since, a long, long time ago;

and always when it is struck, a curtain is drawn from behind the fretful human actors and we look beyond into infinite space. On the other hand, there is but little in Keats of the rich humanity and high passions that for the most part fill the Elizabethan stage. The pathos of *Isabella* is the nearest approach in him to that deeper source of poetry. Keats himself was aware that this background was lacking to his work, and harps on the subject continually. He perceived dimly that the motto of his faith,

> "Beauty is truth, truth beauty,"—that is all
> Ye know on earth; and all ye need to know,

was but a partial glimpse of the reality. Had he been sufficiently a Greek to read Plato, he might have been carried beyond that imperfect view; even the piteous incompleteness of his own life might have laid bare to him the danger lurking in its fair deception. As it is, his letters are filled with vague yearnings for a clearer knowledge; he is, he says, as one "writing at random, straining after particles of light in the midst of a great darkness." Unfortunately, inevitably perhaps, when he came to put his half-digested theories into practice, he turned, not to the moral drama of the Greeks or to the passionate human nature of the Elizabethans, but to the humanitarian philosophy that was in the air about him; and, accepting this, he fell into a crude dualism. "I find there is no worthy pursuit," he writes, "but the idea of doing some good to the world. . . . I have been hovering for some time between an exquisite sense of the luxurious, and a love for philosophy."

It has been generally supposed that Keats abandoned his unfinished *Hyperion,* and started to rewrite it in the form of a vision, through dissatisfaction with the Miltonic inversions of language in the earlier draft and through the influence of Dante's *Commedia.* That view is demonstrably true in part, but I think the real motive for the change goes deeper. There is, in fact, an inherent contradiction in his treatment of the theme which rendered a completion of the original poem almost impracticable. The subject is the overthrow of the Titans by the new race of gods—Saturn succumbing to the arms of his own child and Hyperion, Lord of the Sun, fleeing before Apollo of the golden bow and the lyre; it is the old dynasty of formless powers, driven into oblivion by the new creators of form and order. That was the design, but it is easy to see how in the execution the poet's dominant idea over-mastered him and turned his intended paean on the birth of the new beauty into a sonorous dirge for the passing away of the old. Our imagination is indeed lord of the past and not of the future. The instinctive sympathy of the poet for the fallen deities is felt in the very first line of the poem, and it never changes. Consider the picture of Hyperion's home:

> His palace bright,
> Bastion'd with pyramids of glowing gold,
> And touch'd with shade of bronzèd obelisks,
> Glared a blood-red through all its thousand courts,
> Arches, and domes, and fiery galleries;
> And all its curtains of Aurorian clouds
> Flush'd angrily—

or consider the apparition of Hyperion himself:

> He look'd upon them all,
> And in each face he saw a gleam of light,
> But splendider in Saturn's, whose hoar locks
> Shone like the bubbling foam about a keel
> When the prow sweeps into a midnight cove.
> In pale and silver silence they remain'd,
> Till suddenly a splendour, like the morn,
> Pervaded all the beetling gloomy steeps,
> All the sad spaces of oblivion,
> And every gulf, and every chasm old,
> And every height, and every sullen depth,
> Voiceless, or hoarse with loud tormented streams: . . .
> It was Hyperion;—

are there any words left in the poet's armory after this to describe the glory of Apollo? As a matter of fact, the third book in which he introduces the young usurper is distinctly below the other two in force and beauty, and Keats knew it and broke off in the middle. That was, probably, in September of 1819; about two months later he was engaged in reshaping his work into *The Fall of Hyperion*. . . . To compare this mutilated version with the poem Keats had written under the instinctive inspiration of his genius is one of the saddest tasks of the student of literature.

No, it was not any dislike of Miltonic idioms or any impulse from Dante that brought about this change in his ambition; it was the working of the ineluctable Time-spirit. His early associations with Leigh Hunt had prepared him for this treachery to his nature, but there was a poverty in the imagination of those cockney enthusiasts for progress which would have saved him ultimately from their influence. It was the richer note of Wordsworth, the still sad music of humanity running through that poet's mighty song, that wrought the fatal revolution. As early as May of 1818 he had written to a friend (and the passage is worthy of quoting at some length):

> My Branchings out therefrom have been numerous: one of them is the consideration of Wordsworth's genius . . . and how he differs from Milton. And here I have nothing but surmises, from an uncertainty whether Milton's apparently less anxiety for Humanity proceeds from his seeing further or not than Wordsworth: and whether Wordsworth has in truth epic passion, and martyrs himself to the human heart, the main region of his song. [After some wandering there follows the famous comparison of human life to a large mansion of many apartments, which may be used as a key to the symbolism of the later *Hyperion,* and then] We see not the balance of good and evil; we are in a mist, *we* are now in that state, we feel the "Burden of the Mystery." To this point was Wordsworth come, as far as I can conceive, when he wrote *Tintern Abbey,* and it seems to me that his genius is explorative of those dark Passages. Now if we live, and go on thinking, we too shall explore them. He is a genius and superior to us, in so far as he can, more than we, make discoveries and shed a light in them. Here I must think Wordsworth is deeper than Milton, though I think it has depended more upon the general and gregarious advance of intellect, than individual greatness of Mind.

The Fall of Hyperion is nothing less than the attempt of Keats, against the native grain of his genius, to pass from the inspiration of Milton and Shakespeare to that of Wordsworth. (pp. 120-28)

Paul Elmer More, "John Keats," in his Shelburne Essays, fourth series, *G. P. Putnam's Sons, 1906, pp. 99-128.*

A. C. BRADLEY   (essay date 1909)

[Bradley was a renowned Shakespearean scholar and influential literary critic. His focus in the excerpt below, originally published in 1909, is Keats's intellectual breadth as manifested in his letters, which for Bradley contain the key to the form and meaning of the poetry. According to Bradley, the letters reveal a Keats who defies the various accepted depictions: he is neither a pale, fragile creature, a sensualist, nor an aloof observer of life. Bradley stresses in particular the singular power of Keats's vision, stating that "It would not be easy to find anything written at the same age by another poet of the time which shows more openness of mind,

more knowledge of human nature, or more original power of thought. . .".]

My principal object is to consider Keat's attitude to poetry and his views about it. . . . But I wish to preface my remarks on this subject, and to prepare for them, by an urgent appeal, addressed to any reader of the poems who may need it, to study the letters of Keats. If I may judge from my experience, such readers are still far too numerous. . . . (p. 209)

The best of Keats's poems . . . can be fully appreciated without extraneous help; but the letters throw light on all, and they are almost necessary to the understanding of *Endymion* and of some of the earlier or contemporaneous pieces. They clearly reveal those changes in his mind and temper which appear in his poetry. They dispose for ever of the fictions once current of a puny Keats who was 'snuffed out by an article' [see excerpt above by Lord Byron, 1823], a sensual Keats who found his ideal in claret . . . and a mere artist Keats who cared nothing for his country and his fellow-creatures. Written in his last four years by a man who died at twenty-five, they contain abundant evidence of his immaturity and his faults, but they disclose a nature and character which command on the whole not less respect than affection, and they show not a little of that general intellectual power which rarely fails to accompany poetic genius. (p. 210)

[If] the reader has formed a notion of [Keats] as a youth with a genius for poetry and an exclusive interest in poetry, but otherwise not intellectually remarkable, this error will soon be dispelled by the letters. With Keats, no doubt, poetry and the hope of success in it were passions more glowing than we have reason to attribute to his contemporaries at the same time of life. The letters remind us also that, compared with them, he was at a disadvantage in intellectual training and acquisitions, like the young Shakespeare among the University wits. They show, too—the earlier far more than the later—in certain literary mannerisms the unwholesome influence of Leigh Hunt and his circle. But everywhere we feel in them the presence of an intellectual nature, not merely sensitive and delicate, but open, daring, rich, and strong; exceedingly poetic and romantic, yet observant, acute, humorous, and sensible; intense without narrowness, and quite as various both in its interests and its capacities as the mind of Wordsworth or of Shelley. Fundamentally, and in spite of abundant high spirits and a love of nonsense, the mind of Keats was very serious and thoughtful. It was original, and not more imitative than an original mind should be in youth; an intelligence which now startles by flashes of sudden beauty, and now is seen struggling with new and deep thoughts, which labour into shape, with scanty aid from theories, out of personal experience. In quality—and I speak of nothing else—the mind of Shakespeare at three and twenty may not have been very different. (pp. 212-13)

We shall have to consider . . . the meaning of his occasional outbreaks against 'thought,' 'knowledge,' 'philosophy.' It is important not to be misled by them, and not to forget the frequent expressions of his feeling that what he lacks and must strive to gain is this very 'knowledge' and 'philosophy.' Here I will only observe that his polemics against them, though coloured by his temperament, coincide to a large extent with Wordsworth's dislike of 'a reasoning self-sufficing thing,' his depreciation of mere book-knowledge, and his praise of a wise passiveness. And, further, what he objects to here is not the pursuit of truth, it is the 'Methodism,' the stubborn argument, and the habit of bringing to the argument and maintaining throughout it a ready-made theory. He offers his own thoughts and speculations freely enough to Bailey and to his brother—men willing to probe with him any serious idea—but not to Dilke. It is clear that he neither liked nor rated high the confident assertions and negations of Shelley and his other Godwinian friends and acquaintances. Probably from his ignorance of theories he felt at a disadvantage in talking with them. But he did not dismiss their theories as something of no interest to a poet. He thought about them, convinced himself that they were fundamentally unsound, and himself philosophises in criticising them. The following passage, from a letter to George and Georgiana Keats, is the nearest approach to be found in his writings to a theory of the world, a theology as he jestingly calls it: . . .

> I will call the *world* a School instituted for the purpose of teaching little children to read. I will call the *human heart* the horn-book read in that School. And I will call the *Child able to read,* the *Soul* made from that School and its horn-book. Do you not see how necessary a world of pains and troubles is to school an Intelligence and make it a Soul? A place where the heart must feel and suffer in a thousand diverse ways. Not merely is the heart a hornbook, it is the Mind's Bible, it is the mind's experience, it is the text from which the Mind or Intelligence sucks its identity. As various as the lives of men are, so various become their Souls; and thus does God make individual beings, Souls, identical Souls, of the sparks of his own essence. This appears to me a faint sketch of a system of Salvation which does not offend our reason and humanity.

Surely, when Keats's education is considered, this, with all its crudity, is not a little remarkable. It would not be easy to find anything written at the same age by another poet of the time which shows more openness of mind, more knowledge of human nature, or more original power of thought. . . . [We] are aware of a decided difference between the Keats of the earlier letters [before his illness] and the Keats of the later. The tour in Scotland in the summer of 1818 may be taken with sufficient accuracy as a dividing-line. The earlier Keats is the youth who had written the **Sonnet on first looking into Chapman's Homer,** and **Sleep and Poetry,** and who was writing **Endymion.** He is thoughtful, often grave, sometimes despondent; but he is full of the enthusiasm of beauty, and of the joy and fear, the hope and the awe, that accompanied the sense of poetic power. . . . This is the Keats who wrote 'A thing of beauty is a joy for ever'; who found 'the Religion of Joy' in the monuments of the Greek spirit, in sculpture and vases, and mere translations and mere handbooks of mythology; who never ceased, he said, to wonder at all that incarnate delight, and would point out to Severn how essentially modern, how imperishable, the Greek spirit is—a joy for ever. (pp. 220-24)

But after [the tour of Scotland] we feel a more decided change, doubtless hastened by outward events. The Blackwood and Quarterly reviews of **Endymion** appeared—reviews not less inexcusable because we understand their origin [see excerpts above by John Gibson Lockhart, 1818, and John Wilson Croker, 1818]. Then came his brother's death. A few weeks later he met Miss Brawne. Henceforth his youth has vanished. There are traces of morbid feeling in the change, painful traces; but they are connected, I think, solely with his passion. His brother's death deepened his sympathies. The reviews, so long as

health remained to him, did him nothing but good. He rated them at their true value, but they gave him a salutary shock. They quickened his perception, already growing keen, of the weaknesses and mannerism of Hunt's verse and his own. Through them he saw a false but useful picture of himself, as a silly boy, dandled into self-worship by foolish friends, and posturing as a man of genius. He kept his faith in his genius, but he felt that he must prove it. He became impatient of dreaming. Poetry, he felt, is not mere luxury and rapture, it is a deed. We trace at times a kind of fierceness. He turns against his old self harshly. Some of his friends, he says, think he has lost his old poetic ardour, and perhaps they are right. He speaks slightingly of wonders, even of scenery: the human heart is something finer,—not its dreams, but its actions and its anguish. His gaze is as intent as ever,—more intent; but the glory he would see walks in a fiery furnace, and to see it he must think and learn. He is young, he says, writing at random, straining his eyes at particles of light in the midst of a great darkness. He knows at times the 'agony' of ignorance. In one year he writes six or seven of the best poems in the language, but he is little satisfied. 'Thus far,' he says, 'I have a consciousness of having been pretty dull and heavy, both in subject and phrase.' Two months later he ends a note to Haydon with the words, 'I am afraid I shall pop off just when my mind is able to run alone.' And so it was.

It is important to remember this change in Keats in considering his ideas about poetry; but we have first to look at them in a more general way. Many of the most interesting occur in detached remarks or aphorisms, and these I must pass by. The others I intended at first to discuss in connection with Shelley's view of poetry; and, although that plan proved to be too large for a single lecture, I do not wish altogether to abandon it, because in the extracts which I have been reading the difference between the minds of the two poets has already appeared, and because it reappears both in their poetic practice and in their opinions about their art. Indeed, with so much difference, it might be thought unlikely that these opinions would show also a marked resemblance. For Keats, it may be said, was of all the great poets then alive the one least affected by the spirit of the time. . . . He did not concern himself, we may be told, with the progress of humanity, or with Manchester Massacres or risings in Naples. He cared nothing for theories, abstractions, or ideals. He worshipped Beauty, not Liberty; and the beauty he worshipped was not 'intellectual,' but visible, audible, tangible. 'O for a life of sensations,' he cried, 'rather than of thoughts.' He was an artist, intent upon fashioning his material until the outward sensible form is perfectly expressive and delightful. In all this he was at the opposite pole to Shelley. . . . And his practice, like his opinions, proves that, both in his strength and his limitations, he belongs to quite a different type.

In such a plea there would certainly be much truth; and yet it is not *the* truth, for it ignores other truths which must somehow be combined with it. There are great differences between the two poets, but then in Keats himself there are contending strains. Along with the differences, too, we find very close affinities. And these affinities with Shelley also show that Keats was deeply influenced by the spirit of his time. Let me illustrate these statements.

The poet who cried, 'O for a life of sensations,' was consoled, as his life withered away, by the remembrance that he 'had loved the principle of beauty in all things.' And this is not a chance expression; it repeats, for instance, a phrase used two years before, 'the mighty abstract idea I have of Beauty in all things.' If Shelley had used this language, it would be taken to prove his love of abstractions. How does it differ from the language of the *Hymn to Intellectual Beauty*? (pp. 224-27)

[Again, we notice] the likeness between *Alastor* and *Endymion*, each the first poem of any length in which the writer's genius decisively declared itself. Both tell the story of a young poet; of a dream in which his ideal appears in human form, and he knows the rapture of union with it; of the passion thus enkindled, and the search for its complete satisfaction. We may prefer to read *Endymion* simply as we read *Isabella*; but the question here is not of our preferences. If we examine the poem without regard to them, we shall be unable to doubt that to some extent the story symbolises or allegorises this pursuit of the principle of beauty by the poetic soul. This is one of the causes of its failure as a narrative. Keats had not in himself the experience required by parts of his design, and hence in them he had to write from mere imagination. And the poem, besides, shows in a flagrant degree the defect felt here and there in *Prometheus Unbound*. If we wish to read it as the author meant it, we must ask for the significance of the figures, events, and actions. Yet it is clear that not all of them are intended to have this further significance, and we are perplexed by the question where, and how far, we are to look for it.

Take, again, some of the most famous of the lyrical poems. Is it true that Keats was untroubled by that sense of contrast between ideal and real which haunted Shelley and was so characteristic of the time? So far is this from being the case that a critic might more plausibly object to his monotonous insistence on that contrast. Probably the best-known lyrics of the two poets are the stanzas *To a Skylark* and the *Ode to a Nightingale*. Well, if we summarise prosaically the subject of the one poem we have summarised that of the other. 'Our human life is all unrest and sorrow, an oscillation between longing and satiety, a looking before and after. We are aware of a perfection that we cannot attain, and that leaves us dissatisfied by everything attainable. And we die, and do not understand death. But the bird is beyond this division and dissonance; it attains the ideal;

> Das Unzulängliche,
> Hier wird's Ereigniss.
>
> [Here the Ineffable
> Takes on a Form]

This is the burden of both poems. In style, metre, tone, atmosphere, they are far apart; the 'idea' is identical. And what else is the idea of the *Ode to a Grecian Urn,* where a moment, arrested in its ideality by art and made eternal, is opposed to the change and decay of reality? And what else is the idea of the playful lines *To Fancy,*—Fancy who brings together the joys which in life are parted by distances of time and place, and who holds in sure possession what life wins only to lose? Even a poem so pictorial and narrative and free from symbolism as the *The Eve of St. Agnes* rests on the same feeling. The contrast, so exquisitely imagined and conveyed, between the cold, the storm, the old age, the empty pleasure and noisy enmity of the world outside Madeline's chamber, and the glow, the hush, the rich and dreamy bliss within it, is in effect the contrast which inspired the *Ode to a Nightingale.*

It would be easy to pursue this subject. It would be easy, too, to show that Keats was far from indifferent to the 'progress of humanity.' He conceived it in his own way, but it is as much the theme of *Hyperion* as of *Prometheus Unbound*. We are concerned however here not with the interpretation of his poems,

but with his view of poetry, and especially with certain real or apparent inconsistencies in it. For in the letters he now praises 'sensation' and decries thought or knowledge, and now cries out for 'knowledge' as his greatest need; in one place declares that an artist must have self-concentration, perhaps selfishness, and in others insists that what he desires is to be of use to his fellow-men. We shall gain light on these matters and on his relation to Shelley if I try to reduce his general view to a precise and prosaic form.

That which the poet seeks is Beauty. Beauty is a 'principle'; it is One. All things beautiful manifest it, and so far therefore are one and the same. This idea of the unity of all beauty comes out in many crucial passages in the poems and letters. I take a single example. The goddess Cynthia in *Endymion* is the Principle of Beauty. In this story she is also identified with the Moon. Accordingly the hero, gazing at the moon, declares that in all that he ever loved he loved *her:*

> thou wast the deep glen—
> Thou wast the mountain-top—the sage's pen—
> The poet's harp—the voice of friends—the sun;
> Thou wast the river—thou wast glory won;
> Thou wast my clarion's blast—thou wast my steed—
> My goblet full of wine—my topmost deed:—
> Thou wast the charm of women, lovely Moon!
> O what a wild and harmonised tune
> My spirit struck from all the beautiful!

When he says this he does not yet understand that the Moon and his strange visitant are one; he thinks they are rivals. So later, when he loves the Indian maid, and is in despair because he fancies himself therefore false to his goddess, he is in error; for she is only his goddess veiled, the shaded half of the moon.

Still the mountain-top and the voice of friends differ. Indeed, the one Beauty is infinitely various. But its manifestations, for Keats, tend to fall into two main classes. On the one hand there is the kind of beauty that comes easily and is all sweetness and pleasure. In receiving it we seem to suppress nothing in our nature. Though it is not merely sensuous, for the Principle of Beauty is in it, it speaks to sense and delights us. It is 'luxury.' But the other kind is won through thought, and also through pain. And this second and more difficult kind is also the higher, the fuller, the nearer to the Principle. That it is won through pain is doubly true. First, because the poet cannot reach it unless he consents to suffer painful sympathies, which disturb his enjoyment of the simpler and sweeter beauty, and may even seem to lead him away from beauty altogether. Thus Endymion can attain union with his goddess only by leaving the green hill-sides where he met her first, and by wandering unhappily in cold moonless regions inside the earth and under the sea. Here he feels for the woes of other lovers, and to help them undertakes tasks which seem to interrupt his search for Cynthia. Returning to earth he becomes enamoured of a maiden devoted to sorrow, and gains his goddess just when he thinks he has resigned her. The highest beauty, then, is reached through the poet's pain; and, in the second place, it has pain in itself, or at least appears in objects that are painful. In his early poem *Sleep and Poetry* Keats asks himself the question,

> And can I ever bid these joys farewell?

And he answers:

> Yes, I must pass them for a nobler life,
> Where I may find the agonies, the strife
> Of human hearts.

He felt himself as yet unequal to this task. He never became equal to it, but the idea was realised to some extent in *Isabella* and *Lamia* and *Hyperion.* The first two of these are tales of passion, 'agony,' and death. The third, obviously, is on one side a story of 'strife.'

Such, in its bare outline, is Keats's habitual view of poetry. What, then, are the points where, in spite of its evident resemblance to Shelley's, we feel a marked difference? The most important seem to be two. In the first place Keats lays far the heavier stress on the idea that beauty is manifested in suffering and conflict. The idea itself is to be found in Shelley, but . . . it is not congenial to him; it appears almost incidentally and is stated half-heartedly; and of the further idea that beauty is not only manifested in this sphere, but is there manifested most fully, we find, I believe, no trace. And this was inevitable; for the whole tendency of Shelley's mind was to regard suffering and conflict with mere distress and horror as something senseless and purely evil, and to look on the world as naturally a paradise entirely free from them, but ruined by an inexplicable failure on the part of man. To this world of woe his Intellectual Beauty does not really belong; it appears there only in flashes; its true home is a place where no contradictions, not even reconciled contradictions, exist. The idealism of Keats is much more concrete. He has no belief either in this natural paradise or in 'Godwinian perfectibility.' Pain and conflict have a meaning to him. Without them souls could not be made; and the business of the world, he conjectures, is the making of souls. They are not therefore simply obstacles to the ideal. On the contrary, in this world it manifests itself most fully in and through them. For 'scenery is fine, but human nature is finer'; and the passions and actions of man are finer than his enjoyments and dreams. (pp. 227-32)

The second point of difference between [Keats] and Shelley lies in this emphasis on beauty. The ideal with Shelley has many names, and one of them is beauty, but we hardly feel it to be the name nearest to his heart. The spirit of his worship is rather

> that sustaining Love
> Which, through the web of being blindly wove
> By man and beast and earth and air and sea,
> Burns bright or dim, as each are mirrors of
> The fire for which all thirst;

and 'love' is a word less distinctively aesthetic, if the term must be used, than 'beauty.' But the ideal for Keats is always and emphatically beauty or the 'principle of beauty.' When he sets the agonies and strifes of human hearts above a painless or luxurious loveliness, it is because they are the more beautiful. He would not have said that the *Midsummer Night's Dream* is superior to *King Lear* in beauty, but inferior to it in some other respect; it is inferior in *beauty* to *King Lear.* Let art only be 'intense' enough, let the poet only look hard enough and feel with force enough, so that the pain in his object is seen truly as the vesture of great passion and action, and all 'disagreeables' will 'evaporate,' and nothing will remain but beauty. Hence, though well aware how little he has as yet of the great poet's power of vision, he is still content when he can feel that a poem of his has intensity, has (as he says of *Lamia*) 'that sort of fire in it that must take hold of people some way.' And an earlier and inferior poem, *Isabella,* may show his mind. The mere subject is exceedingly painful, and Keats by no means suppresses the painful incidents and details; but the poem can hardly be called painful at all; for the final impression is that of beauty, almost as decidedly so as the final

impression left by the blissful story of *St. Agnes Eve.* And this is most characteristic of Keats. If the word beauty is used in his sense, and not in the common contracted sense, we may truly say that he was, and must have remained, more than any other poet of his time, a worshipper of Beauty.

When, then—to come to his apparent inconsistencies—he exalts sensation and decries thought or knowledge, what he is crying out for is beauty. The word 'sensation,' as a comparison of passages would readily show, has not in his letters its usual meaning. It stands for *poetic* sensation, and, indeed, for much more. It is, to speak broadly, a name for *all* poetic or imaginative experience; and the contents of the speech of Oceanus are, in kind, just as much 'sensation' as the eating of nectarines (which may well be poetic to the poetic). This is, I repeat, to speak broadly. For it is true that sometimes in the earlier letters we find Keats false to his better mind. Knowing that the more difficult beauty is the fuller, he is yet, to our great advantage, so entranced by the delight or glory of the easier, that he rebels against everything that would disturb its magic or trouble his 'exquisite sense of the luxurious.' And then he is tempted to see in thought only that vexatious questioning that 'spoils the singing of the nightingale,' and to forget that it is necessary to the fuller and more difficult kind of beauty. But these moods are occasional. He knew that there was something wilful and weak about them; and they gradually disappear. On the whole, the gist of his attitude to 'thought' or 'philosophy' may be stated as follows.

He was far from being indifferent to truth, or from considering it unimportant for poetry. In an early letter, when he criticises a poem of Wordsworth's, he ventures to say that 'if Wordsworth had thought a little deeper at that moment he would not have written it,' and that 'it is a kind of sketchy intellectual landscape, not a search after truth.' He writes of a passage in *Endymion*: 'The whole thing must, I think, have appeared to you, who are a consecutive man, as a thing almost of mere words, but I assure you that, when I wrote it, it was the regular stepping of Imagination towards a truth.' And many passages show his conviction that for his progress towards this truth 'thought,' 'knowledge,' 'philosophy,' are indispensable; that he must submit to the toil and the solitude that they involve, just as he must undergo the pains of sympathy; that 'there is but one way for him,' and that this one 'road lies through application, study, and thought.' On the other hand he had, in the first place, as we saw, a strong feeling that a man, and especially a poet, must not be in a hurry to arrive at results, and must not shut up his mind in the box of his supposed results, but must be content with half-knowledge, and capable of 'living in uncertainties, mysteries, doubts, without any irritable reaching after fact and reason.' And, in the second place, a poet, he felt, will never be able to rest in thoughts and reasonings which do not also satisfy imagination and give a truth which is also beauty; and in so far as they fail to do this, in so far as they are *mere* thoughts and reasonings, they are no more than a means, a necessary means, to an end, which end is beauty,—that beauty which is also truth. This alone is the poet's end, and therefore his law. 'With a great poet the sense of beauty overcomes every other consideration, or rather obliterates all consideration.' Thought, knowledge, philosophy, if they fall short of this, are nothing but a 'road' to his goal. They bring matter for him to mould to his purpose of beauty; but he must not allow them to impose *their* purpose on him, or to ask that it shall appear in his product. These statements formulate Keats's position more than he formulates it, but I believe that they represent it truly. He was led to it mainly by the poetic instinct in him, or because, while his mind had much general power, he was, more than Wordsworth or Coleridge or Shelley, a poet pure and simple. (pp. 232-36)

A. C. Bradley, "The Letters of Keats," in his Oxford Lectures on Poetry, *second edition, Macmillan and Co., Limited, 1934, pp. 209-44.*

ARTHUR SYMONS (essay date 1921)

[*An English critic, poet, dramatist, short story writer, and editor, Symons initially gained notoriety as an English decadent in the 1890s, and he eventually established himself as one of the most important critics of the modern era. His sensitive translations from the works of Paul Verlaine and Stéphane Mallarmé offered English poets an introduction to the poetry of the French Symbolists. Though he was a gifted translator and linguist, it was as a critic that Symons made his most important contribution to literature. His* The Symbolist Movement in Literature *provided his English contemporaries with an appropriate vocabulary with which to define their new aesthetic—one that communicated their concern with dreamlike states, imagination, and a reality that exists beyond the boundaries of the senses. Symons also discerned that the concept of the symbol as a vehicle by which a "hitherto unknown reality was suddenly revealed" could become the basis for an entire modern aesthetic, and he therefore laid the foundation for much of modern poetic theory. In the excerpt below, Symons demonstrates how Keats's poetry evinces the theory of "art for art's sake" and his affinity with the poets of the decadent movement.*]

John Keats, at a time when the phrase had not yet been invented, practised the theory of art for art's sake. The theory is almost infallible; it is certain that a poem must be written for the poem's sake simply; and that together with this there must be the rhythmical creation of beauty. Essential poetry is an essence too strong for the general sense; diluted, it can be endured; and for the most part the poets dilute it. Keats could conceive of it only in the absolute. "To load every rift with ore"; that to him was the essential thing; and it meant to pack

A sample of Keats's handwriting taken from his personal correspondence. Historical Pictures Service, Chicago.

the verse with poetry, with the stuff of the imagination, so that every line should be heavy with it. When I use the word "heavy" it contains many meanings. Keats was essentially luxurious; for, as he said at the last, with a last touch of luxuriousness in his apprehension of death: "I feel the flowers growing over me." There is something morbid in that sensual ecstasy—like something seized on with violence; as when his sense of beauty would quicken his pulses.

I am certain Baudelaire read and admired the poems of Keats; for there are certain characteristics in the versification and in the use of images in both poets. Keats had something feminine and twisted in his mind, made up out of unhealthy nerves—which are not to be found to the same extent in Baudelaire—which it is not the fashion to call decadent; Keats being much more than a decadent, but certainly decadent in such a line [from *Endymion*] as,

> One faint eternal eventide of gems,

which might have been written, in jewelled French, by Mallarmé. Keats luxuriates, almost like Baudelaire, in the details of physical discomfort, in all their grotesque horror, as when, in sleeplessness,

> We put our eyes into a pillowy cleft,
> And see the spangly gloom froth up and boil.

He is neo-Latin, again like Baudelaire, in his insistence on the physical symptoms of his lovers, the bodily translations of emotion. In Venus, leaning over Adonis, he notes:

> When her lips and eyes
> Were closed in sullen moisture, and quick sighs
> Came vexed and pouting through her nostrils small.

All this swooning of his lovers would at all events be very much at home in modern French poetry, where love is again, as it was to Catullus, a sickness, a poisoning. I find the same subtlety of expression in the Elizabethan Age, in John Donne, in William Morris, and in Rossetti. (pp. 180-81)

Matthew Arnold mentions the fact that Wordsworth said to him, "Goethe's poetry was not inevitable enough." (p. 181)

Can it be said that Keats was, on the whole, inevitable? Certainly, at his greatest; for he is one of our greatest, one of our most passionate poets; failing signally, however, in his lack of inspiration in regard to lyrics; but one who can call up atmosphere by the mere verse or remnant of a verse which seems to make a casual statement: one who never felt without passion; one whose *Lamia* is in its way as consummate as the magical *Eve of Saint Mark* and the unsurpassable ballad of *La Belle Dame sans merci*, which seems to contain the germ of both Morris and Rossetti. Only, so much of his verse is terribly unequal; immature and feverish. And in spite of the fact that perhaps no poet has ever packed so much poetic detail into so small a space—with perhaps the exception of Rossetti—metrically, he is often slipshod; with all his genius for words, he often uses them incorrectly; and he can write such nerveless lines as:

> Though the dull brain perplexes and retards;

and, in one of the greatest Odes ever written, for sheer lyrical genius, he can halt on the way so painfully as to commit this grievous error in metrical metre:

> Thou shalt remain, in midst of other woe
> Than ours, a friend to man, to whom thou say'st.

And yet, in spite of these faults and failures, Keats is, as I have written, unlike Wordsworth and Shelley, when they are not at their best, never prosaic and never out of key; for, as Shelley may have worshipped some star of unachieved desire, so Keats may have—with his Pagan instincts—worshipped in some obscure, some occult, chapel of the Moon. (pp. 181-82)

Arthur Symons, *"A Note on John Keats," in* The John Keats Memorial Volume, *edited by G. C. Williamson, John Lane Company, 1921, pp. 180-82.*

ROBERT BRIDGES   (essay date 1929)

[*Bridge's essay is an explication of Keats's poetic style, exploring the various artistic influences that inform the work and stressing Keats's imaginative power and intellectual complexity. This essay was first published in Bridges's* Collected Essays, Papers, & Etc. *in 1929.*]

If one English poet might be recalled to-day from the dead to continue the work which he left unfinished on earth, it is probable that the crown of his country's desire would be set on the head of John Keats; and this general feeling is based on a judgment of his work which we may unhesitatingly accept, namely, that the best of it is of the highest excellence, but the mass of it disappointing.

Nor is there any likelihood of this verdict being overset, although some may always unreservedly admire him on account of his excellences,—and this because his fault is often the excess of a good and rare quality,—and others again as unreservedly depreciate him on account of that very want of restraint, which in his early work, besides its other immaturities, is often of such a nature as to be offensive to good taste, and very provocative of impatient condemnation.

Among Keats' poems, too, a quantity of indifferent and bad verse is now printed, not only from a reverence for his first volume, which he never revised, and which is very properly reprinted as he issued it, but also from a feeling which editors have had, that since anything might be of value, everything was; so that any scrap of his which could be recovered has gone into the collections. Concerning which poor stuff we may be consoled to know that Keats himself would have had no care; for, not to speak of what was plainly never intended for poetry at all, he seems to have regarded at least his earlier work as a mere product of himself and the circumstances, now good now bad, its quality depending on influences beyond his control and often adverse, under which he always did his best. On one point only was he sensitive, and that was his belief that he sometimes did well, and would do better. The failures he left as they were, having too much pride to be ashamed of them, and too strong a conviction of an ever-flowing, and, as he felt, an increasing and bettering inspiration to think it worth while to spend fresh time in revising what a younger moment had cast off.

The purpose of this essay is to examine Keats' more important poems by the highest standard of excellence as works of art, in such a manner as may be both useful and interesting; to investigate their construction, and by naming the faults to distinguish their beauties, and set them in an approximate order of merit; also, by exhibiting his method, to vindicate both the form and meaning of some poems from the assumption of even his reasonable admirers that they have neither one nor other. (pp. 5-7)

[*Endymion* represents Keats'] youthful effort towards a reconstruction of English poetry on Elizabethan lines, in sympathy with the romantic and natural schools of his time, and in reaction against the poetry of the last century. A year passed before he began *Hyperion,* his other long poem, and in that time he fell under the influence of Milton, recognising in *Paradise Lost* the model of that workmanship, the neglect of which had spoiled his first attempt. (p. 32)

The opening promises well; we are conscious at once of a new musical blank verse, a music both sweet and strong, alive with imagination and tenderness. There and throughout the poem are passages in which Keats, without losing his own individuality, is as good as Milton, where Milton is as good as Virgil; and such passages rank with the best things that Keats ever did; but in other places he seems a little overshadowed by Milton, while definite passages of the *Paradise Lost* are recalled, and in some places the imitation seems frigid. Milton's grammar and prosody are apparently aimed at, but they are not strictly kept, nor is the poem maintained at the Miltonic elevation. Here and there, too, a fanciful or weak expression betrays the author of *Endymion.* . . . In his letters he attributes his dissatisfaction to the style; but one cannot read to the end without a conviction that the real hindrance lay deeper; for although we may say that this torso of Keats' is the only poem since Milton which has seriously challenged the epic place, it is to the style mainly that this is due; the subject lacks the solid basis of outward event, by which epic maintains its interest: like *Endymion,* it is all imagination; or, if we should accept Keats' personifications as sufficiently real for his purpose, even then the poem fails in conduct. The first two books describe the conditions of the older gods, and are impassioned with defeat, dismay, and collapse; the third introduces the new hierarchy, and we expect to find them radiant, confident, and irresistible; but there is no change in the colour of the poem; of the two deities introduced, Apollo is weeping and raving, and Mnemosyne, who has deserted the old dynasty for her hope in the new, "wails morn and eventide." It is plain that the story was strangling itself.

This failure is really the same in kind as the fault of *Endymion*: there is little but imagination, and a one-sidedness or incompleteness of that; a languor which, though it has now generally left the language, lingers in the main design. That Keats was conscious, too, that some of his earlier weaknesses were still visible will appear when we come to consider the *Revision of Hyperion*; but his own criticism of the poem was that it was Miltonic and artificial, and he confesses in a letter of September 1819 to a revulsion of taste. *Paradise Lost,* which not a month before had been "every day a greater wonder" to him, is now "a corruption of our language, accommodating itself to Greek and Latin inversions and intonations. I have but lately (he writes) stood on my guard against Milton. Life to him would be death to me." . . . But Keats' condemnation of grammatical inversion seems a going back from the great advance in style which he had made, and it is worth while to inquire what he meant. It might seem at first that he attributed to inversions the appearance of Miltonism in his poem, and that he could not afford to be imitative. But he had not abused inversion in *Hyperion,* nor is it absent from his revision, nor wholly from his other poems; and the truth is that it is of the essence of good style. In ordinary speech the words follow a common order prescribed by use, and if that does not suit the sense, correction is made by vocal intonation: but the first thing that a writer must do is to get his words in the order of his ideas, as he wishes them to enter the reader's mind; and when such an arrangement happens not to be the order of common speech, it may be called a grammatical inversion. . . . The best simple writers have the art of making the common grammatical forms obey their ideas, and Keats has usually a right order of ideas in a simple grammatical form, and a preference for this style over more elaborate constructions is no doubt what he intended to advocate, and this is well enough: but it must be remembered that he often gets good effect from the proper use of inversion, which is present where least suspected; and also that he does not refuse to invert the grammatical order for the sake of rhyme or metre, which, though it may occasionally be a beauty, is generally a license or abuse, a resource of bad writers. . . . (pp. 33-7)

If now, for the convenience of pursuing our subject, we consider the *Revision of Hyperion,* we must remember that we are passing over Keats' most important work,—for it was between his beginning the *Hyperion* in September 1818 to September 1819, when he discarded it, that is, when he was under the Miltonic influence, that almost all his best work was done,— and we shall now be dealing with what was really a transitional period. . . . (p. 37)

By some paradoxical devilry . . . [Keats] devoted the best hours of the day to supplying the market with a comic poem in the Byronic vein, *The Cap and Bells,* and worked in the evenings only, when fatigued and distracted, at the *Revision of Hyperion,* which might be in itself enough to account for any inferiority in the execution. This fragment is very interesting; first, it shows a new departure in style; secondly, a deliberate resumption of his old allegorising vein, which we found in *Endymion* and the early poems; thirdly, the most mature attempt that he ever made to express some of his own convictions concerning human life. It is in this third aspect that the chief interest lies, and it is strange that its matter should not have prevented the *Revision* from passing for a first draught, with such critics as might overlook the evidence of the form. The style, being evidently less mastered than in the longer poem, might at first sight deceive; but it should not have deceived, for, in spite of the inefficient execution, it is in some respects an advance; it aims at a greater severity and has a more thoughtful power than any of Keats' other work. But the evidence of the alterations of the passages common to the two versions is glaring. For instance, an old trick of Keats' is the abuse of invocation, as almost any page of *Endymion* will show: now in the *Revision of Hyperion* there is not a single vocative O admitted; and if we examine a passage which contained them in the original, and which is kept in the *Revision,* we shall see how their exclusion accounts for the alterations: for example. . . .

> Would come in these like accents; O how frail
> To that large utterance of the early gods!
> Saturn, look up! though wherefore, poor old king?
> I have no comfort for thee, no not one:
> I cannot say 'O wherefore sleepest thou?'
> For heaven is parted from thee, and the earth
> Knows thee not, thus afflicted, for a god.

The O's being proscribed, the first line is altered in *Revision* . . . to:

> Would come in this like accenting: how frail!

and the fifth line to

> Wherefore thus sleepest thou?

And this new *thus* drives out the original *thus* from line 7,

which now becomes *so afflicted.* He then sees the two *wherefores* and alters the third line to *and for what, poor lost king;* the change of *lost* for *old* being made to avoid the hackneyed *poor old.*

And besides this conscious correction of old faults, it is now for the first time that the influence of Dante appears, and that not merely in the gravity of the vision in this poem, which is unlike any other of his embodiments, and in the sort of connection conceived between his vision of doom and his own experience and poetic meaning, all which he might have come at through a translation, but in echoes of the Italian balance in passages where the sense is like Dante's, as in this—

> High prophetess, said I, purge off,
> Benign, if so it please thee, my mind's film.

And also where there is only the indefinable and individual touch to point to, as in—

> When in mid-day the sickening east-wind
> Shifts sudden to the south, the small warm rain
> Melts out the frozen incense from all flowers,

where the last line shows that Keats has now added to his style a mastery of Dante's especial grace: and such passages as this, or again when he calls written words

> The shadows of melodious utterance,

which is also Dantesque in thought, should, I think, have forbidden the later critics, who knew from external evidence when the *Revision* was written, from judging that the new style came from decay of poetic power. In these quotations there is certainly no falling off in the magic of his pen, while faults so foreign to him as the wrongness, lowness, and awkwardness in the diction of these lines—

> Therefore, that happiness be somewhat *shared,*
> Such *things* as thou *art* are admitted oft
> Into *like gardens thou didst pass* erewhile

show want of mastery in his new, not failure in his old manner, and are like fatigue.

To conclude this question of style, it may be added, that though the effect of an imitation of Milton is fairly got rid of from the *Revision,* and whole passages are excluded because they were too Miltonic, yet inversions and classicisms are used, and in the line—

> Saturn, sleep on; O thoughtless, why did I

a Latinism is actually introduced to supplant a mannerism of his own; for *O thoughtless* is changed to *me thoughtless.* (pp. 38-41)

There are four *Epistles* written in ten-syllable couplets:—

1. To Geo. Felton Mathew (Nov. 1815).

2. To my brother George (Aug. 1816).

3. To Ch. Cowden Clarke (Sept. 1816).

4. To Reynolds (March 1818).

(p. 66)

Though there are good things in these *Epistles,* their execution is in every respect very poor, and they are in so far more like letters written in rhyme than poems in the forms of letters, and they may all be taken with the apology which Keats sent with the fourth, to "excuse the unconnected subject and careless verse." The **"Epistle to Cowden Clarke"** is altogether far the worst, and though it has a rational argument, it is not worth defending from any condemnation for want of artistic form; but it is in my opinion wrong to include the other early epistles . . . in this judgment. . . . [The] 1st, 2nd, and 4th of the *Epistles* are, I should say, quite as well built. Their "argument" is perfectly clear, and if the form of it escapes the reader's attention, that is due to the lightness of the imaginative touch and flight, which is a welcome escape from the conscious pedantries of form, and, so long as the sense is clear, a great merit. Indeed, if the expression of these *Epistles* were at all worthy of their framework, they would be models of what such epistles should be. Nos. 1 and 2 must be passed over here. No. 4 is of great interest. Its argument (though Keats himself calls the poem unconnected) is a very beautiful artistic movement of thought, just short of caprice, returning at the end with great force to the apparent first motive, which is suddenly revealed as being much weightier than at first allowed to appear. (pp. 66-8)

If we include among the lyrical poems those written in seven-syllable couplets, we find three popular pieces, *Souls of Poets, Bards of Passion,* and *Ever let the fancy roam*. . . . These three poems have all of them the popular qualities of fluency and grace, and the statement of the subject is provocative of interest; yet, though the first sustains itself in a fine vein for six lines, there is little other merit either of thought or diction in the first two. . . . [There] can be no doubt that [*Fancy*] is by far the best of the three. It is maintained throughout at a fair level, and the simple descriptions of nature, recalling *L'Allegro,* are often very beautiful; and in the last division there is a sensuous passage done in the fine Miltonic manner, where the eight-syllable line is introduced with great effect, descriptively of Jove's languor.

Of the five other poems in this measure there is none worthy of praise as a whole.

There are left now only the lyrical poems in stanza, and easily first, holding a unique place in literature, stands *La belle dame sans merci*. . . . It would be impertinence to praise this poem, which charms alike old and young: and it stands above the reach of criticism. For other reasons it is better not to criticise, **"In a drear-nighted December,"** which, after a very long interval indeed, must be placed next. This poem is a great favourite, and perhaps deservedly so, both for its beauty and originality, but the latter quality proves expensive. And after this poem there is another gap, for if we mention the next best lyrics, we come to such poems as *Meg Merrilies,* and *Where be you going, you Devon maid?* which . . . is successful; and *I had a dove,* which could only have been written by a poet; and *Walking in Scotland,* of which the obscurity and strangeness of the sentiment described make it noteworthy. Mrs. Owen quotes the Faery song *Shed no tear!* as worthy of Keats, but we wonder how it was that there are not more better lyrics. Keats, one would have thought, would have excelled in them, and we can only suppose that we have his odes instead.

Success in lyrical verse requires a delicately strict subjection of imagination to one purpose, and this was not a part of Keats' poetic instinct; and though when he came to learn it, he wrote as it would seem almost unconsciously one of the best lyrics in the world; yet it is not improbable that he would still have regarded lyrics as a tract where he might cast off restraint. The fact remains that, with the exception of *La belle dame,* he never brought all his genius to "spend its fury in a song." (pp. 69-72)

Otho the Great is contemporary with *Lamia:* it was written July-September 1819, and should therefore be among Keats'

best work; but it is not, so that its failure must be specially accounted for: and it may, I think, be entirely laid to inexperience, and to the ugly and ill-shapen Elizabethan models to which Keats apparently looked in good faith for guidance; and among which, with their stagey fury, unnecessary confusions, rude manners, and occasional magnificences, his play might pass undistinguished. Unfortunately too this play turns on a question of maiden virtue, which he could not handle, and which he did not even choose for himself, for the plot was furnished him by a friend, who gave him the scenes across the table to versify or dramatise one by one—a most deadening situation. It is badly contrived: the antecedent conditions are very elaborate, and yet are never plainly stated; they have to be discovered from isolated, ill-managed and confused hints in the dialogue; so that the attention of an auditor, if it was not entirely put off by this riddle, would only be kept alive by a wish to come to a judgment of his guesses. The riddle, moreover, has no satisfactory solution. Then the scenes themselves are rather lacking in distinct dramatic point, independently of the uncertainty of the motive. But if these faults are not wholly due to Keats, he must yet have the blame of the lack of moral import, and of the imperfect delineation of the characters, whose manners are not good, and who seem to take a conscious interest in the plot. The style has the faults of cold magnificence, occasional flatness and common expressions, with careless grammar, and the use of childish tricks for impromptu effect. In spite of all this, there is a succinctness and force about the whole, which forbid one to conclude that Keats would not have succeeded in drama, and though it is commonly said that he lacked the essential moral grasp, his letters seem to me to refute this, and his determination would have been sufficient assurance of success. In fact, the fragment of *Stephen,* which he began on his own lines after finishing *Otho,* already shows an advance. This is written in a style midway between Marlowe and Shakespeare, and recalls the opening of the third part of *Henry VI.* The imitated magnificence is somewhat restless, but the narrative and purpose of the characters stand out fairly well amid the stir and freedom which was evidently the poet's aim.

It would be easy to quote from *Otho* some fine passages, and many fine lines and expressions, but they seem to be buried in a rubbish-heap from which one gladly turns back to the green tangle of *Endymion.* (pp. 72-4)

[There is one main quality of Keats' poetry] as yet unmentioned, which claims the first place in a general description, and that is the very seal of his poetic birthright, the highest gift of all in poetry, that which sets poetry above the other arts; I mean the power of concentrating all the far-reaching resources of language on one point, so that a single and apparently effortless expression rejoices the aesthetic imagination at the moment when it is most expectant and exacting, and at the same time astonishes the intellect with a new aspect of truth. This is only found in the greatest poets, and is rare in them; and it is no doubt for the possession of this power that Keats has been often likened to Shakespeare, and very justly, for Shakespeare is of all poets the greatest master of it; the difference between them here is that Keats' intellect does not supply the second factor in the proportion or degree that Shakespeare does; indeed, it is chiefly when he is dealing with material and sensuous subjects that his poems afford illustrations; but these are, as far as they go, not only like Shakespeare, but often as good as Shakespeare when he happens to be confining himself to the same limited field. Examples from Shakespeare are such well-known sayings as these—

> My way of life
> If faln into the sear, the yellow leaf.—*Macbeth.*

Lay not that flattering unction to your soul.—*Hamlet*

> We are such stuff
> As dreams are made on, and our little life
> Is rounded with a sleep.—*Tempest.*

Examples from Keats are—

> The journey homeward to habitual self.

> Solitary thinkings; such as dodge
> Conception to the very bourne of heaven.

> My sleep had been embroider'd with dim dreams.

In most of Keats' phrases of this sort there is a quality which makes them unlike Shakespeare; and if we should put into one group all those which are absolutely satisfactory, and then make a second group of those which are not so simply convincing, we should find in these last that the un-Shakespearian quality was more declared, and came out as something fanciful, or rather too vaguely or venturesomely suggestive; the whole phrase displaying its poetry rather than its meaning, and being in consequence less apt and masterly. This second group would contain many of the most admired lines of Keats, and these are very characteristic of him. Such are—

> Those green-rob'd senators of mighty woods,
> Tall oaks,

and—

> How tiptoe Night holds back her dark-grey hood.

The *Revision of Hyperion* shows that Keats himself was dissatisfied with his *senators;* and one can see the reason without condemning the passage or approving its omission. Finally, there would be left a third group of such-like phrases which plainly miss the mark.

Closely allied to these imaginative phrases, and perhaps more characteristic of Keats and peculiar to him, are the short vivid pictures which may be called his masterpieces of word-painting, in which with a few words he contrives completely to finish a picture which is often of vast size. Good examples of this are the sestet of the *Leander* sonnet; the last four lines of the *Chapman's Homer;* the passage beginning Golden his hair in *Hyperion*. . . ; and, to quote one from *Endymion*—

> The woes of Troy, towers smothering o'er their blaze,
> Stiff-holden shields, far-piercing spears, keen blades,
> Struggling, and blood, and shrieks.

For its wealth in such rare strokes of descriptive imagination Keats' poetry must always take the very first rank; and it is his imaginative quality of phrase which sets him more than any other poet of his time in creative antagonism to the eighteenth-century writers; for it was not only foreign to their style, but incomprehensible and repugnant to their pseudo-classic taste, which preferred a "reasonable propriety of thought," such as Hume found to be lacking in Shakespeare, to the shadowy powers of imagination, however godlike.

The limitation of Keats' faculty in this excellence—which, if it may be ascribed wholly to his youth, amply justifies the sentiment of the opening lines of this essay—leads us on naturally to another of his chief characteristics, and that is his close relationship with common Nature: he is for ever drawing his imagery from common things, which are for the first time represented as beautiful: and again in this we see his opposition to the eighteenth-century writers, who mainly contented themselves with conventional commonplaces for their natural imagery; whereas Keats discovers in the most usual objects either beauty or sources of delight or comfort, or sometimes even of imaginative horror, which are all new; and here his originality seems inexhaustible, and his wide poetic sympathies the strongest. Nor does he confine himself to matters of which he could have had much experience; he makes Nature the object of his imaginative faculty—Nature apart from man, or related to man as an enchantress to a dreamer. This is, I suppose, what he means when, comparing himself with Byron, he says, "There is this great difference between us: he describes what he sees,—I describe what I imagine. Mine is the hardest task: now see the immense difference." Here he shows a vast wealth which makes his poems a mine of pleasure. *Endymion* is crowded to excess with a variety of these images, and as they came up in his mind in an endless stream to illustrate his ideas, the ideas sometimes fare rather badly; for though they were no doubt generally held firm in his own mind, they are yet drowned by the images of their objective presentation; until these themselves at last lose even their own virtue, and fatigue the reader, who feels like a sightseer in a gallery overcrowded with pictures, which by degrees he ceases to regard with attention.

And in this devotion to natural beauty lies, I believe, one true reason of Keats' failure in the delineation of human passion. The only passion delineated by Keats is the imaginative love of Nature, and human love is regarded by him as a part of this, and his lover is happy merely because admitted into communion with new forms of natural beauty. This, which appeared in theory in the explanation of the allegory of *Endymion* . . ., is practically exposed in the 2nd stanza of the *Ode to Melancholy,* where, among the objects on which a sensitive mind is recommended to indulge its melancholy fit, the anger of his mistress is enumerated with roses, peonies, and rainbows, as a beautiful phenomenon, plainly without respect to its cause, meaning, or effect. And so in *Lamia*—

> He took delight
> Luxurious in her sorrows, soft and new,

and

> Fine was the mitigated fury.

How different is the parallel passage of Shakespeare, which at once occurs to one—

> O, what a deal of scorn looks beautiful
> In the contempt and anger of his lip!

This is not artistic admiration, but a lover's entire devotion. (pp. 83-9)

[We have to charge Keats with] lack of true insight into human passion. If this was wholly due to the absence of awakening experience, it is at least unfortunate that in *Lamia,* in which from its date we might have expected something mature, he should have chosen so low a type. Though perhaps suggested by the original of his story, it was not necessary to it: and even if he preferred to have his snake-woman bad, there was every reason why Lycius' passion should have been of a higher type. How unworthy it is is shown in the description of their meeting and in the following sentiment—

> But too short was their bliss
> To breed distrust and hate, that make the soft voice hiss.

This love is an association for mutual pleasure, the end of which is satiety and revulsion, and it is, I repeat, at least unfortunate that Keats, after he had known love, should, in his first attempt to delineate it, have been satisfied with so vulgar a type. The ideal passion in *Isabella* is insipid, and even in *The Eve of St. Agnes,* the passion . . . is at best of a conventional type, and has to have a good deal read into it by the light of the story.

But Keats' doctrine of beauty, which might be defended if it was spiritualised, which it never is by him, may often be reconciled with true feeling by the allowance which is due to his objective method; concerning this . . . I shall say no more here except to repeat that Keats' imagery probably always followed, if it did not always clearly picture, some train of ideas; and when he says in the Ode *To Fanny*

> My muse had wings,
> And ever ready was to take her course
> Whither I bent her force,
> *Unintellectual,* yet divine to me;—
> Divine, I say! What sea-bird o'er the sea
> Is a philosopher the while he goes
> Winging along where the great water throes?

these words should not be taken as a disavowal of meaning in "those abstractions which were his only life," but as an apology for immaturity, and they must be interpreted in the light of his high idea of philosophy. Keats was conscious, like Virgil, of a double inclination. He said of himself, April 1818: "I have been hovering for some time between an exquisite sense of the luxurious, and a love for philosophy. Were I calculated for the former, I should be glad; but as I am not, I shall turn all my soul to the latter." . . . [This is evidence] that Keats was unlikely to have depreciated the intellectual element of his art: but the intellectual element is always in league with emotion, and would have been, I imagine, considered by him as worthless in poetry without such mixture. In the *Epistle to Reynolds,* . . . even the unpleasantness of the consideration of what we call the struggle for existence would, simply presented, have been flat and commonplace; but he shows it as a "horrid mood," by which he is haunted, and uses great skill and a wealth of contrasted beauty in introducing it under this enhanced aspect, "wreathing a flowery band spite of the unhealthy ways made for his searching;" and in calling his Muse unintellectual, he was no doubt uttering his reiterated impatience for more knowledge, the expression of which recurs so often in his poems and letters, that it is needless to quote any one, and which rises to a sort of consummation in the *Revision of Hyperion,* where it seems as if he had imagined himself to have at length attained to an insight of the mystery.

There is less opposition, it seems to me, between Keats' true instinct for ideal philosophy and his luxurious poetry (which seems rather its young expression), than between these on the one hand and his practical human qualities, as revealed by his letters, on the other. The bond of all was an unbroken and unflagging earnestness, which is so utterly unconscious and unobservant of itself as to be almost unmatched. It is always present in his poetry both for good and ill, in the spontaneous and felt quality of his epithets, and the absence of any barrier even, it would sometimes seem, of consideration or judgment between his mind and his pen. Whether this earnestness is the account of his failure in his purely comic freaks I do not know, but it may certainly account for his want of humour, for which, in spite of some traces in his letters, it does not appear to have left any room. The best of the letters are serious and full of

good matter, a few are quite foolish, and a great number are written in a high-spirited jocular vein, which seems to be carelessly assumed for the double purpose of amusing his correspondent and relaxing his own mind. This chief charm in all of them is their unalloyed sincerity: there is nothing between the pen and the mind, not always even an effort or desire to write what should be worth reading: it is enough that it is he that writes, and his brother or friend that will read.

In spite of this earnestness and philosophy, it is certainly true that Keats' mind was of a luxurious habit; and it must have been partly due to this temperament that he showed so little severity towards himself in the castigation of his poems, though that was, as I said before, chiefly caused by the prolific activity of his imagination, which was always providing him with fresh material to work on. In this respect he is above all poets an example of what is meant by inspiration: the mood which all artists require, covet, and find most rare was the common mood with him; and I should say that being amply supplied with this, what as an artist he most lacked was self-restraint and self-castigation,—which was indeed foreign to his luxurious temperament, unselfish and devoted to his art as he was,—the presence of which was most needful to watch, choose, and reject the images which crowded on him as he thought or wrote.

And it is thus that Keats' best period was when he fell under the influence and example of Milton. He was a great deal influenced by other poets, and had an unequalled power of reproducing not only the style of any writer whom he imitated, but the mental attitude which informed the style, so that one is tempted to venture a bull of him, and say that if he had not been so original, he would have been only a plagiarist. But it was not until he came to rival Milton's epic that his originality seemed to be in danger; and no one would think of judging *Hyperion* by its likeness to *Paradise Lost.* If the two poems should be generally compared, though it is plain that Keats does not reach the sustained sonority and force of Milton (nor has he even shown as much skill in characterising his divinities, whose elemental personalities would seem to have offered him a more interesting and poetically rich opportunity than the biblical devils did to Milton), yet in one respect he is in my opinion superior to Milton, and that is for a warmth in his poetry of inestimable worth. To give an example, where he describes Asia, he has

> More thought than woe was in her dusky face.
> For she was prophesying of her glory.

Here there is a sympathetic touch in *dusky* which Milton would not have stopped to give, and it has the effect—at least it has to me—of warming the fine intellectual picture of Oriental slavery and metaphysics with an emotion that brings one at once into contact and sympathy with it.

So fragmentary and incomplete a treatise may break off abruptly. I began it with a due sense, as I thought, of responsibility, and with full admiration for the poet: I fine both increased at the end. (pp. 89-95)

Robert Bridges, in his John Keats: A Critical Essay, *Haskell House Publishers Ltd., 1972, 97 p.*

T. S. ELIOT (lecture date 1933)

[*Eliot, an American-born English poet, essayist, and critic, is regarded as one of the most influential literary figures of the first half of the twentieth century. As a poet, he is closely identified with many of the qualities denoted by the term Modernism, such as experimentation, formal complexity, artistic and intellectual eclecticism, and a classicist view of the artist working at an emotional distance from his or her creation. As a critic, he introduced a number of terms and concepts that strongly affected critical thought in his lifetime, such as his concept of the "objective correlative," which he defined in his* Selected Essays *as "a set of objects, a situation, a chain of events which shall be the formula of (a) particular emotion in the reader." His overall emphasis on imagery, symbolism, and meaning, and his shunning of extratextual elements as aids in literary criticism, helped to establish the theories of New Criticism. Eliot, who converted to Christianity in 1928, stressed the importance of tradition, religion, and morality in literature. In the following excerpt, taken from a lecture given in 1933, Eliot, like A. C. Bradley (1909), focuses on the letters, which he calls "certainly the most notable and the most important ever written by any English poet."*]

Keats [is] a singular figure in a varied and remarkable period.

Keats seems to me also a great poet. I am not happy about **Hyperion**: it contains great lines, but I do not know whether it is a great poem. The Odes—especially perhaps the **Ode to Psyche**—are enough for his reputation. But I am not so much concerned with the degree of his greatness as with its kind; and its kind is manifested more clearly in his Letters than in his poems; and in contrast with the kinds we have been reviewing, it seems to me to be much more the kind of Shakespeare. The Letters are certainly the most notable and the most important ever written by any English poet. Keats's egotism, such as it is, is that of youth which time would have redeemed. His letters are what letters ought to be; the fine things come in unexpectedly, neither introduced nor shown out, but between trifle and trifle. His observations suggested by Wordsworth's *Gypsey*, in a letter to Bailey of 1817, are of the finest quality of criticism, and the deepest penetration:

> It seems to me that if Wordsworth had thought a little deeper at that moment, he would not have written the poem at all. I should judge it to have been written in one of the most comfortable moods of his life—it is a kind of sketchy intellectual landscape, not a search for truth.

And in a letter to the same correspondent a few days later he says:

> In passing, however, I must say one thing that has pressed upon me lately, and increased my Humility and capability of submission—and that is this truth—Men of Genius are great as certain ethereal chemicals operating on the Mass of neutral intellect—but they have not any individuality, any determined character—I would call the top and head of those who have a proper self Men of Power.

This is the sort of remark, which, when made by a man so young as was Keats, can only be called the result of genius. There is hardly one statement of Keats about poetry, which, when considered carefully and with due allowance for the difficulties of communication, will not be found to be true; and what is more, true for greater and more mature poetry than anything that Keats ever wrote.

But I am being tempted into a descant upon the general brilliance and profundity of the observations scattered through Keats's letters, and should probably be tempted further into remarking upon their merit as models of correspondence (not that one should ever take a model in letter-writing) and their revelation of a charming personality. My design, in this very narrow frame, has been only to refer to them as evidence of a very different kind of poetic mind than any of those I have just been considering [William Wordsworth and Percy Bysshe Shelley]. Keats's sayings about poetry, thrown out in the course of private correspondence, keep pretty close to intuition; and they have no apparent bearing upon his own times, as he himself does not appear to have taken any absorbing interest in public affairs—though when he did turn to such matters, he brought to bear a shrewd and penetrating intellect. Wordsworth had a very delicate sensibility to social life and social changes. Wordsworth and Shelley both theorise. Keats has no theory, and to have formed one was irrelevant to his interests, and alien to his mind. If we take either Wordsworth or Shelley as representative of his age, as being a voice of the age, we cannot so take Keats. But we cannot accuse Keats of any withdrawal, or refusal; he was merely about his business. He had no theories, yet in the sense appropriate to the poet, in the same sense, though to a lesser degree than Shakespeare, he had a 'philosophic' mind. He was occupied only with the highest use of poetry; but that does not imply that poets of other types may not rightly and sometimes by obligation be concerned about the other uses. (pp. 100-02)

T. S. Eliot, "Shelley and Keats," in his The Use of Poetry and the Use of Criticism: Studies in the Relation of Criticism to Poetry in England, *Faber and Faber Limited, 1933, pp. 87-102.**

DOUGLAS BUSH (essay date 1937)

[*Bush explores Keats's intellectual seriousness and the inner conflict presented in his poetry regarding the role of the poet and the question of the relation of the artist to his art and to the world. Bush's essay was originally published in 1937.*]

Keats is probably the only romantic poet, apart from Blake, whose present rank is conspicuously higher than it was in the nineteenth century, and the rank given him by critics and poets of that period was not low. What is there in Keats that has enabled him to emerge from modern scrutiny a larger figure than ever before? In the first place, he carries relatively little excess baggage in the way of mediocre writing or "dated" ideas from which, in various ways and degrees, Wordsworth, Coleridge, Byron and Shelley must be cut loose. Keats speaks to us directly, almost as one of ourselves; we do not need to approach him through elaborate reconstructions of dead philosophies or dead poetical fashions. The romantic elements in him remained, so to speak, central, sane, normal—in everything but their intensity—and did not run into transcendental or pseudoromantic or propagandist excesses. It is one of Keats's essential links with some poetic leaders of our own age that he, alone among the romantic poets, consciously strove to escape from self-expression into Shakespearean impersonality.

Moreover, there is nowadays a much more general understanding of the solid strength of Keats's mind and character, of his philosophic attitude toward life and art, of his astonishing self-knowledge and capacity for growth, of his unceasing struggle to achieve poetic integrity. In all these respects, and especially in the last, he is linked with the serious poets of the present. Certain fundamental questions are always tormenting him; he can neither put them aside nor finally answer them. Has the artist a right to exist at all in the midst of chaos and wrong and suffering? If his existence is justified, can he allow his imagination to be self-centered, in the large sense "lyrical," or should it be dramatic and rooted in the heart of man and human life? Is truth, the truth which is the soul of poetry, to be won by sensuous intuition or by study and conscious thought? From first to last Keats's important poems are related to, or grow directly out of, these inner conflicts, conflicts which are all the more acute because his poetic ambitions are so often at odds with his poetic gifts. This central problem has been expounded many times of late years, but, in a chapter which necessarily reviews a large part of Keats's work, one can hardly take hold of any other thread. (pp. 13-14)

[The Epistle *To George Felton Mathew* (November, 1815)] contains the first embryonic statement of Keats's conflicting poetic impulses, though as yet they are scarcely in conflict. The more immediate pleasures are those of the eye and the realm of sense, but he goes on to speak of humanity, of the harsh treatment accorded poets, whose genius has helped to cure the stings of the pitiless world; and, as a good disciple of Clarke and "Libertas," he celebrates great champions of national freedom. The epistles addressed to George Keats and Clarke (August and September, 1816) show a similar mixture of themes and motives, from maidens with breasts of cream to the inevitable Alfred and William Tell. Sensuous delights and humanitarian aspirations follow one another in wayward alternation—the scarlet coats of poppies even suggest the pestiferous soldiery—and, though the two poetic worlds are not set in opposition, there is no doubt which is the more instinctive and congenial.

I Stood Tip-toe (1816) is the work of a young man who is literally in a transport of sensuous intoxication. At first sight the poem may appear only "a poesy of luxuries," sometimes described, however, with a new, sure delicacy and even largeness of expression, but the essential thing is Keats's first full affirmation of the identity of nature, myth, and poetry; hence the significance of the allusions to Psyche, Pan, Narcissus, and particularly Endymion and Cynthia, for the poem was, we remember, a first attempt on the theme of *Endymion*. Keats writes of Narcissus, for instance, almost as if he had himself invented the myth while gazing into a Hampstead pond, and when one thinks of his progressive adaptation of myth to humanitarian symbolism one may say, by way of definition, not disparagement, that he is as yet a self-centered Narcissus. (p. 15)

In *Sleep and Poetry*, written in the autumn and winter of 1816, [Keats's] contradictory impulses and ambitions reveal the beginnings of genuine conflict. The exposition of the three stages of poetic development, taken over from *Tintern Abbey* (and later paralleled, with deeper understanding, in the letter on the mansion of life), leads from the glad animal movements of the carefree schoolboy through the adolescent passion for the finer joys of nature and sense. Keats's symbols for this passion, however, are not the cataract, the rock, the mountain and the wood, but the realm of Flora and old Pan, and kisses won from white-shouldered nymphs. It is in this world, amid this store of luxuries, that he is now delightedly dwelling. The third stage, partly retrospective for Wordsworth, is for Keats an anticipation of the future, and he almost has to goad himself on. He "must pass" these joys for a nobler kind of poetry, that which deals with the agonies, the strife of human hearts. The poem has all the varieties of style that we expect in Keats's earlier work, from the Titianesque Bacchus and the pretty descriptions of Hunt's pictures to the sculptural massiveness of "might half slumb'ring on its own right arm." In *Venus and Adonis* Shakespeare's Ovidian and Italianate mythology is only tapestry in comparison with the dew-bedabbled hare, the lark, and the snail, and in *Sleep and Poetry* the picture of Diana

bathing is far inferior to that of the sea, which Keats had lately beheld with his own eyes, and the weeds that "Feel all about their undulating home." Our old friends Alfred and Kosciusko appear, for a moment, sandwiched between Sappho and Petrarch and Laura, for in Keats's heart liberty is a noble but somewhat remote and chilly ideal compared with love. His desire to interpret sterner themes is wholly sincere, yet, for a poet untried by life, it is less strong than ardent youthful instinct for "the most heart-easing things." (pp. 16-17)

Endymion was Keats's most serious early attempt to answer fundamental questions about the relation of the artist to his art and to the world. Shelley had asked similar questions in *Alastor*, and, without losing sight of other factors, one may perhaps understand *Endymion* best by taking it in part as a reply to Shelley, a reply which includes imitation and adaptation as well. Shelley's hero is a romantic idealist who finds no satisfaction in the unlovely world of humanity, and, frustrated in his quest, dies in solitude; but it is better, says Shelley, so to pursue the vision and perish than to live, a finished and finite clod, untroubled by a spark. No search for ideal love and beauty could be unattractive to Keats, and there is something of Shelley's hero in Endymion. Yet that hero, for all his powers of locomotion, inhabited, as Keats would see, an ivory tower. It is a fundamental source of Keats's strength, and of his hold upon us, that he, despite his love of poetic luxuries and devotion to art, shared and understood the common experience of mankind as Shelley, with all his humanitarian zeal, never did. Although, then, Endymion does not learn his lesson until the very end, his whole previous pilgrimage has been leading him away from purely visionary idealism to the knowledge that the actual world of human life must be accepted, not denied, and that only through participation in that life can the ideal be realized. That thoroughly Wordsworthian doctrine is, to be sure, the moral Shelley expounded in the preface to *Alastor* (which ends with some lines from *The Excursion*), but Shelley seems to have largely forgotten it in the poem, which is in effect a glorification of the unique and isolated visionary. (p. 18)

Endymion's abandonment of active life and public service, and Peona's censure of such conduct, along with her brother's plea for the contemplative ascent to reality, reflect Keats's uncertain view of the predicament of the artist. Can writing poetry be included among the ways of doing good to the world? And, in poetry, what are the just claims of the senses and of humanity at large? When *Endymion* was passing through the press, Keats wrote to Taylor: "I have been hovering for some time between an exquisite sense of the luxurious and a love for Philosophy—were I calculated for the former I should be glad—but as I am not I shall turn all my soul to the latter." In this particular utterance there is no doubt which is Keats's primary instinct (however mistaken he is, for once, in his judgment of himself), but, as countless other utterances show, his sterner ambitions were fundamental and lasting. We may remember that by "philosophy" Keats means not so much philosophical and literary learning, though that is included, but "a comprehension (and a comprehension of a peculiar kind) of the mystery of human life." He wanted to be Shakespearean, and the thought of all he could never be did not comfort him, it left him perpetually dissatisfied with what his special gifts enabled him to do best.

The dream-goddess seems, in Keats's intention, to represent the supreme aspect of ideal beauty which is ideal love; what he mainly describes is in fact the sensuous earthly passion which, at least in its earlier stages, brings torment with it. A major part of his plan is to show love progressing from selfish passion to spiritual altruism, but his instincts partly defeat his purposes; love does not, even in the case of the Indian maiden, rise so far as it should above the warm embracements of Endymion and his goddess and Venus and Adonis. When the goddess is an abstraction in the background, she is a chaste ideal Diana; when with her worshiper, she is more like Venus. As in *Alastor* the imagination of a young man and a poet cannot help presenting the ideal as a breathing, desirable woman rather than a principle of beauty. A deliberately colorless outline of the poem should have made clear, so far as an outline can, the consistently earthly and sensuous character of Endymion's passion. The staid Bailey deplored the "indelicacy," and wished that Keats had not been inclined toward "that abominable principle of Shelley!—that sensual love is the principle of things." Though Miss Lowell's refusal to see symbolism in the poem was mere temperamental wrongheadedness, she did discern Keats's preoccupation with normal, youthful, amorous emotion. The dream-goddess is a symbol of the ideal, which Keats sincerely worshiped, but she is nine parts flesh and blood and one part Platonic. For Endymion, as for Philip Sidney, "Desire still cries, 'Give me some food,'" and he cannot, with high resignation, turn to a religious and philosophic second-best: "Leave me, O love which reachest but to dust." (pp. 19-20)

If the dream-goddess had been kept wholly on the level of ideal love, the appearance of the Indian maiden would have been more logical; the goddess herself, however, comes so close to being a human love, except in her prolonged absences from her votary, that Keats might be said to have almost proved his case before the Indian maiden is introduced. But the episode makes the fourth book much clearer than the second and third. As Mr. Leonard Brown points out, the Arab maiden of *Alastor* was quite neglected by the hero, who had no thought for a mere human girl who loved him; but in Keats's parable the value of a human love must be made of central significance. While Shelley's self-centered poet found solitude and death, Endymion, in achieving selflessness, finds love and service and more abundant life. Ideal love or beauty is a transcendent divinity not to be immediately apprehended by man, or by man isolated from his fellows; mortals can win that heaven only through intermediaries, through experience of human love and sympathy with sorrow. (The altruistic motive ought to govern this incident, but, in spite of the maiden's situation and her song, it is her beauty rather than her distress that seems to excite Endymion.) The idealist thinks that the abstract and the concrete, the spirit and the flesh, are remote from and opposed to each other, that in loving the Indian maiden he has forfeited his highest hopes. But, after much painful vacillation, he learns that apparent defeat was real victory, that earthly love and beauty are identical with the divine; he learns, in short, "the holiness of the Heart's affections and the truth of Imagination." This, a primary article in Keats's creed, we may if we like label as only another statement of the romantic doctrine of the beautiful soul, but Keats was too normal and sane to hold such a faith in any extravagant or half-spurious way; he wrote no *Epipsychidion*.

Thus, while Keats's hopes and confessions and beliefs are sometimes blurred and obscure, sometimes waywardly decorative, one can hardly fail to see the outlines of a large and really impressive symbolic plan. Nor, on the other hand, can one slight the earthly and sensuous emotions in order to keep a young poet on the plane of abstract or even humanitarian philosophizing. The Platonism of the poem, so far as it goes, is entirely sincere and fundamental, but, whatever he had absorbed from Spenser and others, there is little more in *Endy-*

mion than an instinctive personal devotion to the ideal which is in some degree, like amorous passion, the birthright of any youthful poetic nature. Keats would not be what he is if he were not kindled by an authentic beam from the white radiance of the One, but his habitation is the dome of many-colored glass. He has grown immensely since *Sleep and Poetry,* where he had looked forth from the realm of Flora and old Pan to contemplate the agonies of human hearts, yet his humanitarian and Platonic faith, however sincere an affirmation, is still beyond his experience, and, in general, the more spiritual parts of the poem are less real than the sensuous. The harmony of the solution comes home to us less than the author's troubled and ever-present consciousness of discord. . . . (pp. 20-1)

If Shakespeare was always the deity in Keats's poetic heaven, Wordsworth and Milton were saints under the throne. Shakespeare was the very opposite of the egotistical sublime, the great exemplar of negative capability, of undogmatic, unobtrusive, impersonal art, but Wordsworth and Milton were more approachable and more imitable. Keats's vacillating allegiance to these two poets is one of the clearest testimonies to the conflict in himself, the conflict he discerned in Milton, between the ardors and the pleasures of song. The letters record so many changes of attitude, so many fluctuating moods, sometimes ripples on the surface, sometimes not, that it is difficult to generalize, but, with reservations, it may be said that when Wordsworth is in the ascendant Keats's mind and poetic ambition are turned to the human heart, the mysteries of pain and existence, the improvement of the world; and the ascendancy of Milton, though he sometimes appears as a humanitarian and champion of liberty, means that Keats is enjoying great art and fine phrases with the passion of a lover. But this is all a matter of emphasis and shading, not a clear-cut division. Keats was always striving for unity; in *Endymion* he had attempted to unite the ideal and the real, and in the two *Hyperions* he was to do so again. Where the odes stand in relation to that problem we may try to see. (pp. 23-4)

At first sight Keats's theme in the *Ode to a Nightingale* and the *Ode on a Grecian Urn*—the two cannot be separated—is the belief that whereas the momentary experience of beauty is fleeting, the ideal embodiment of that moment in art, in song, or in marble, is an imperishable source of joy. If that were all, these odes should be hymns of triumph, and they are not. It is the very acme of melancholy that the joy he celebrates is joy in beauty that must die. Even when Keats proclaims that the song of the bird is immortal, that the sculptured lover feels an enduring love that is beyond the pains of human passion, his deepest emotions are fixed on the obverse side of his theme. He tries to believe, and with part of his mind he does believe and rejoice, in the immortality of ideal beauty, but he is too intense a lover of the here and now, of the human and tangible, to be satisfied by his own affirmations. It is the actual moment that is precious, that brings ecstasy with it, and the moment will not stay. The truth that Keats embraces is not that of his large humanitarian aspirations, nor the smaller measure of truth granted to the philosophic intellect, it is the truth, that is, the reality, apprehended through the senses. The author of these odes hears the still, sad music of humanity, but he tries to escape from it. The bird's song, poetry, carries him away from the lazar-house of life and above the level of the dull, perplexing brain; the urn is a symbol of untroubled beauty in the midst of human woe and it teases him out of thought. Was it the ecstasies and torments of love that intensified and decided the conflict, or was it that in poetry the senses had for the time won the victory and released him from the half-paralyzing claims of "higher" poetry? At any rate, as in *Endymion*, Keats is not wholly happy with the ideal, his instinct seeks the particular object and experience. And his instincts are more honest than Shelley's, for he is always aware of the cleavage in himself. He may grasp at the ideal as an authentic and inspiring sanction for his love of the actual, but he does not deceive himself, or us, when he endeavors, with more than Shelley's occasional misgivings, to bridge the gap between them. He cannot so easily rhapsodize about Intellectual Beauty when he is thinking of holding the hands of Harriet or Mary or Emilia or Jane. Neither beauty nor truth is for Keats a real abstraction, a Platonic Idea; beauty is something beautiful, the "material sublime." When he tries to generalize from a melancholy ecstasy, he remains at odds with himself. The urn is a joy for ever, but the marble figures are cold. (pp. 25-6)

Whether or not it was his original intention, Keats gave [*Lamia*] a meaning, so that it takes its place among the many poems which embody the inward struggle between the claims of self and the senses and the claims of the world and "philosophy." But here Keats does not seem to know which side he is on, and a plausible case can be, and has been, made out for *Lamia* as a condemnation of philosophy, as a condemnation of the senses, and as a condemnation of a divorce between the two. Each of these interpretations can be supported by chapter and verse from Keats's other poems and from his letters, yet each leaves difficulties in *Lamia* itself.

On the one hand Lamia is a sinister serpent woman; the house to which she takes her lover is a "purple-lined palace of sweet sin"; she is afraid when he hears the heroic sound of trumpets from the outside world, for she knows "that but a moment's thought is passion's passing bell." . . . On the other hand Keats obviously sympathizes with the sensuous or sensual passion, the "unperplex'd delight," of the young lovers; Apollonius the sage is the ghost of folly haunting the sweet dreams of his former disciple; and at the end, when Apollonius is about to cast a blight upon Lamia, the author lets himself go in an attack on "cold philosophy." Thus Lamia is at the same time a beautiful woman who loves and should be loved, and a evil embodiment of the wasting power of love, a *belle dame sans merci*.

Such central contradictions cannot be reconciled. Spenser, with the easy flexibility of a Renaissance poet, could first exploit the sensuous and then condemn it; that compromise was impossible for Keats, a modern poet driven to seek for unity in himself and the world, yet we wonder, as we do in reading of the destruction of the bower of bliss, if Keats's stern conclusion expresses as much of himself as had gone into the tale of amorous enchantment. There is the essential difference, however, that Spenser was dealing largely with the world of imagination, as Keats was in *Endymion*. There Keats had arrived at a solution, a harmonizing of his instincts and his aspirations, yet the former element is so much the stronger, at that stage in the author's growth, that we doubt if the solution is final. The dilemma that faced Endymion, compared with that of Lycius, was esthetic and theoretical. The trouble in *Lamia* is that, despite the exotic story and trappings, the poem is a too immediate transcript of actual experience; despite the technical skill, it is, spiritually, the raw material of a poem. The conflict has been interpreted wholly in terms of poetry, of the senses and the intellect, and the attack on cold philosophy certainly belongs to poetic theory; it embodies not only one of Keats's own moods but something of the general romantic protest against a purely scientific view of the world. Yet the fire that Keats

was aware of in *Lamia* was not merely born of opposed literary desires, however intense, it came from the divided soul of a lover. The struggle between passion and the craving to escape from passion is felt too keenly and rendered too literally—the literalness is that of Keats, not of D. H. Lawrence—to result in a unified, integrated poem. . . . We may be moved, if we are not put off by the glittering surface, but we are moved in much the same way as we are in reading the letters to Fanny Brawne, which are after all the best commentary on the poem. (pp. 27-9)

[*Hyperion* and *The Fall of Hyperion*] are the culmination of Keats's poetic progress, the last and greatest statement of his conflicting instincts and ambitions. (p. 31)

The chief reason for the abandonment of *Hyperion* may well have been, as Mr. Abercrombie in particular has said, that Keats perceived his poem to be mainly façade, that his elaboration of a semi-Miltonic pattern, though grand in itself, was smothering his idea under decoration. He must have known as well as we do that for stately elevation and beauty the first two books had no superior or equal since Milton, but, to a man of Keats's poetic conscience, it would have meant more that he was not getting his theme expressed. When the poem takes a fresh start in the fragmentary third book, he seems determined to come to grips with his central story, to set forth his "message"; by that time, however, if the poem was to comprise four books, the architecture was so much out of proportion that Keats did not see his way to a satisfactory ending or recasting. Milton and Wordsworth had been the two poles of Keats's poetical orbit, and, to change metaphors, the wedding of Miltonic technique to Wordsworthian inwardness was almost bound to be an unequal union.

If *Endymion* was in the philosophic sense Keats's *Prelude*, *Hyperion* was his *Excursion*. Apollo, like Endymion, is John Keats. But the author of *Hyperion* has emerged from the chamber of maiden-thought. The untried idealism of *Endymion* has not weakened; it has, under the stress of realities, become stronger, sterner, less self-centered. The facts of death and love have been proved on the author's pulses. "Sensations" without knowledge have ripened and deepened into sensations with knowledge. Although the mere "poetical" beauty of the fragment is completely satisfying even now, when so much merely beautiful poetry has faded, description is not simply description; it carries a weight of magnanimity and compassion which the author of *Endymion* could not yet have felt or expressed. And Keats has not, like the elder Wordsworth, cut himself off from some of his youthful and essential roots; even though Keats did not solve his problem, the two *Hyperions* represent the consummation of his growth. (pp. 33-4)

From a world of medieval fixities . . . , he contemplated the melancholy spectacle of endless change, and he arrived at a compromise half Christian, half scientific, the doctrine that all things work out their own perfection under divine control, until the process of change shall give way to the changelessness of eternity. Keats was no "Godwin perfectibility Man," and in *Hyperion* his faith in progress was put in a way peculiarly his own. The Jupiter whom Shelley overthrows is a wholly evil embodiment of superstition, tyranny, and custom, whose reign must give way to the rule of universal love. Keats's Titans, though beneficent rulers of the world, must yield to a race of gods superior in beauty and magnanimity. However familiar the speech of Oceanus, it must be partly quoted:

> And first, as thou wast not the first of powers,
> So art thou not the last; it cannot be:
> Thou art not the beginning nor the end. . . .

Then thou first-born, and we the giant-race,
Found ourselves ruling new and beauteous realms.
Now comes the pain of truth, to whom 'tis pain;
O folly! for to bear all naked truths,
And to envisage circumstance, all calm,
That is the top of sovereignty. Mark well!
As Heaven and Earth are fairer, fairer far
Than Chaos and blank Darkness, though once chiefs;
And as we show beyond that Heaven and Earth
In form and shape compact and beautiful,
In will, in action free, companionship,
And thousand other signs of purer life;
So on our heels a fresh perfection treads,
A power more strong in beauty, born of us
And fated to excel us, as we pass
In glory that old Darkness: nor are we
Thereby more conquer'd, than by us the rule
Of shapeless Chaos. . . .
        . . . for 'tis the eternal law
That first in beauty should be first in might.

The passage hardly needs corroboration, but one may quote two more personal bits of prose. In the important letter of May 3, 1818, Keats had compared Milton and Wordsworth in regard to their zeal for humanity and their knowledge of the human heart, and he had put Wordsworth first, not because of individual superiority but because of a general advance among mankind. "What is then to be inferr'd? O many things—It proves there is really a grand march of intellect—, It proves that a mighty providence subdues the mightiest Minds to the service of the time being, whether it be in human Knowledge or Religion." On September 18, 1819, Keats wrote: "All civil[iz]ed countries become gradually more enlighten'd and there should be a continual change for the better." One might add some brief queries from *The Excursion* which epitomize a good deal of Wordsworth:

Is Man
A child of hope? Do generations press
On generations, without progress made?

If Keats's notion of the enlightened progress of the race is partly Wordsworthian, still more so is the ideal of individual progress summed up in the speech of Oceanus, the power to bear all naked truths and face circumstance with calm. All through *The Excursion* Wordsworth is pleading for self-discipline achieved through reason and the law of duty, and for the "pagan" Keats, Wordsworth's stoicism would be detachable from his Christian faith. The soul, says Wordsworth, craves a life of peace, "Stability without regret or fear," the central peace subsisting at the heart of endless agitation. Possessions, opinions, passions change, but duty remains, "by the storms of circumstance unshaken." Reason is "A crown, an attribute of sovereign power," and a life of discipline may enable Age, "in awful sovereignty," to sit on a superior height, disencumbered from the press of near obstructions. One may dismiss all this as Polonian moralizing and say that Keats had no such stuff in mind when he named *The Excursion* as one of the three things in the age to rejoice at. But one can hardly read **Hyperion** or the letters and not believe that the attaining of such stability of soul was a reality to him. Again I must limit myself to two inadequate scraps. "The best of Men have but a portion of good in them—a kind of spiritual yeast in their frames which creates the ferment of existence—by which a Man is propell'd to act and strive and buffet with Circumstance." "Circumstances are like Clouds continually gathering and bursting—

While we are laughing the seed of some trouble is put into the wide arable land of events—while we are laughing it sprouts [it] grows and suddenly bears a poison fruit which we must pluck."

The words of Oceanus are no incidental exhortation, they cast back to the speech of Coelus in the first book, and they are essential to Keats's whole conception of the Titans and the significance of their defeat. He does not think of them as primitive deities of brute force and tyranny. Saturn laments that he is

buried from all godlike exercise
Of influence benign on planets pale,
Of admonitions to the winds and seas,
Of peaceful sway above man's harvesting,
And all those acts which Deity supreme
Doth ease its heart of love in.

Even Enceladus gives similar testimony. The myth of a steady decline from the golden age is not for Keats. The Titans are superior to their predecessors; they are one link, not the first, in the upward succession. Indeed the principal Titans are so completely majestic and sublime that Keats would have been sorely tried in creating gods who could win our sympathy away from them. But his intention is clear. The Titans, however benign and beneficent, had in a crisis behaved not like deities but like frail mortals; they had lost, and deserved to lose, the sovereignty of the world because they had lost the sovereignty over themselves.

Divine ye were created, and divine
In sad demeanour, solemn, undisturb'd,
Unruffled, like high Gods, ye liv'd and ruled:
Now I behold in you fear, hope, and wrath;
Actions of rage and passion; even as
I see them, on the mortal world beneath,
In men who die.—This is the grief, O Son!
Sad sign of ruin, sudden dismay, and fall!

Coelus, who belongs to the old order and does not understand the situation, exhorts Hyperion, the one unconquered Titan, to use force. Later we see Saturn himself,

the supreme God
At war with all the frailty of grief,
Of rage, of fear, anxiety, revenge,
Remorse, spleen, hope, but most of all despair.

Thus, even though the Titans were

symbols divine,
Manifestations of that beauteous life
Diffus'd unseen throughout eternal space,

they failed to justify the continuance of their reign. Hence the larger vision and wisdom of Oceanus, who alone among them has "wandered to eternal truth," and who now is able to envisage circumstance, all calm. He alone, except weak Clymene, whose glimpse of truth is only sensuous and emotional, can see the glow of superior beauty in the eyes of his successor and acknowledge the rightness of defeat.

When Apollo passes from aching ignorance to knowledge, the god, the true poet, is born.

Knowledge enormous makes a God of me.
Names, deeds, gray legends, dire events, rebellions,

Majesties, sovran voices, agonies,
Creations and destroyings, all at once
Pour into the wide hollows of my brain,
And deify me, as if some blithe wine
Or bright elixir peerless I had drunk,
And so become immortal.

The most important passage in the first book of *Endymion*—the answer to the question "Wherein lies happiness?"—contained a similar list of symbols of human history, but there the emphasis was on the clear religion of heaven, the "oneness" enjoyed by the soul that felt a bond with nature and legend, and that oneness was the first stage of experience leading to friendship and love. The lines in *Hyperion* have less of nature and of self, and more of the rise and fall of nations, the whole chaotic story of man's troubled past. Keats is not here concerned with the source of happiness, or with love, but with the knowledge that is sorrow, the sorrow that is wisdom. And the bright elixir that Apollo has drunk is no opiate that carries him Lethewards, away from the fever and fret of the world of man, for Keats has attained, potentially, his poetic manhood. (pp. 34-8)

The Fall of Hyperion was [Keats's] last effort to integrate his faculties and impulses, and to set forth his conception of the poet and the poet's function in the world. In *Hyperion* the meaning of Apollo's spiritual birth-pangs had been left somewhat obscure; the objective manner of presentation was not natural to one who had always written directly out of his own feelings, and perhaps he did not quite know what to do with the god when he had got him. The narrative in the *Fall* seems to carry out the general intention of *Hyperion,* but, by the late summer of 1819, Keats's failing health, the prolonged fever of his love for Fanny Brawne, pecuniary troubles, perhaps most of all the conviction that the topmost heights of poetry were not to be won by a divided soul, such causes as these had deepened and embittered his despair over himself, his past and his future. In the symbolism of the garden, the temple, and the shrine, we have perhaps another variation on the three Wordsworthian stages of development, from sensuous pleasure to humanitarian concern for the world. But the sketch of poetic evolution is not now, as in *Sleep and Poetry,* partly wishful prophecy. Keats is here looking back on what seem to him to be the facts of his brief career, and he condemns himself, with harsh sincerity, for having dwelt in an ivory tower, for having given to men the illusive balm of dreams, whereas true poets, by intense effort, seize upon the reality which is not illusive. To them, as to active benefactors of humanity, the miseries of the world are misery, and will not let them rest.

One need not be a sentimentalist to feel the profound personal tragedy not only in the self-laceration of this last effort to feel the giant agony of the world, but also in Keats's turning aside from the *Fall* to enjoy a last serene "sensation" in *To Autumn.* We do not endorse his condemnation of a large part of his work, but we can understand his attitude, can even see that the whole course of his development made it inevitable. As he said himself, the genius of poetry must work out its own salvation in a man, and we cannot guess, if he had had health and some measure of contentment, what would have been his ultimate solution and achievement. His house was, most of the time, divided against itself, but his consciousness of the fissure, his unceasing endeavor to solve the problem of sense and knowledge, art and humanity, are in themselves an index of his stature. No other English poet of the century had his poetic endowment, and no other strove so intensely to harmonize what may, without undue stretching of the terms, be called the Apol-

lonian and the Faustian ideals of poetry. However high one's estimate of what he wrote, one may really think—to use an often meaningless cliché—that Keats was greater than his poems. (pp. 39-40)

Douglas Bush, "Keats," in Keats: A Collection of Critical Essays, *edited by Walter Jackson Bate, Prentice-Hall, Inc., 1964, pp. 13-40.*

KENNETH ALLOTT   (essay date 1958)

[*Allott's focus is Keats's "Ode to Psyche." He examines the poem's structure, which he calls "architectural," and its tone, which he deems one of "defensive happiness."*]

'To Psyche' is neither unflawed nor the best of Odes, but to me it illustrates better than any other Keats's possession of poetic power in conjunction with what was for him an unusual artistic detachment—besides being a remarkable poem in its own right. This may be another way of saying that it is the most architectural of the Odes, as it is certainly the one that culminates most dramatically. (p. 74)

'To a Nightingale' and 'On a Grecian Urn' have in common a pattern suggesting mounting sexual excitement and its relief—the point being that at an early stage in these poems the poet ceases to choose where he is going. This is not true of 'To Psyche', for which, as I have already said, an architectural metaphor seems best.

Yes, I will be thy priest, and build a fane
In some untrodden region of my mind . . .

The poem itself is a Corinthian detail in the 'fane' promised to the goddess. . . . [There] is more detachment in the less-familiar ode, and it gives the poem a peculiar interest. Of course why 'To Psyche' should 'hit so hard' is left unexplained by these remarks, and to understand how our feelings have been engaged we need to go much further into it. (pp. 75-6)

If we try to forget the other odes and look at 'To Psyche' freshly, two immediate impressions seem normal. The first is that the poem opens badly but warms up rapidly after a weak start; the second is that, while the poem is a happy one, its tone is more exactly described if the happiness is thought of as defensive or defiant.

Robert Bridges observed that 'the beginning of this ode is not so good', and it needs no special insight to see that Keats could have produced a more arresting opening by deleting his first quatrain with its tasteless echo of 'Lycidas' and the displeasing phrase 'soft-conched ear' (Elizabethan for the cliché 'shell-like ear'). Again, later in the first stanza, the repetition of 'grass' in ll. 10 and 15 is clumsy, and the reader is nagged by the distracting survival of the rhymes for a further two lines after the sense has closed in:

A brooklet, scarce espied.

Some of these faults probably came from working over the poem too often and at first, perhaps, too coolly—the price that Keats paid for his 'peaceable and healthy spirit' may have been that his 'pains' fixed his first stanza against further correction while its elements were still imperfectly combined. . . . Here the practical result is that several layers of composition appear to be cobbled together, not inexpertly, but without the ruthlessness of exclusion of otherwise acceptable phrase or rhyme that would have been given by a firm sense of poetic direction. The weakness disappears after the first stanza, which seems to confirm that Keats discovered his real subject in the process of writing—the rise in poetic temperature at the beginning of the third stanza ('O brightest! though too late for antique vows') may announce his full awareness of this discovery. I differ from Bridges about the value of this central section of the ode. He considers that the poem climbs with a steady improvement towards its conclusion and that its middle is only 'midway in excellence'. I find the first half of the third stanza at least the equal in excellence of the final stanza so admired by Bridges, particularly if his comment is kept in mind that 'the imagery is worked up to outface the idea' in the ode's last section. The observation has, of course, a wider and more general application to Keats's poetry—it is simplest to ascribe the 'outfacing' to his infatuation with a luxurious Elizabethan diction (as Lady Chatterley remarked to her husband, whom circumstances compelled to prefer Art to Life, 'The Elizabethans are so upholstered'). Against the overloaded imagery of the fourth stanza and some weak phrasing earlier, it is fair to set the successful rhyming. **'To a Nightingale'**, for example, has a bad rhyme in stanza six and forced expressions for the sake of rhyming in the first and last stanzas.

The other immediate impression, that of the Ode's defensive happiness, is not easy to pin down, but Keats seems to be rejoicing because of

> . . . having to construct something
> Upon which to rejoice.

There is a defiant assertion that unaided he can put the clock back, that the ode itself proves that his is 'a fond believing lyre' in spite of an age

> . . . so far retir'd
> From happy pieties . . .

Positively, one relates this conviction to the nearness of Fanny Brawne [Keats was living next door to Fanny Brawne while writing the poem]—Keats is in love and for lovers 'happy pieties' are still possible.

In any move to go beyond these immediate impressions it is natural to examine carefully the serial letter to George and Georgiana Keats . . . in which an unrevised version of **'To Psyche'** is copied out. It cannot, surely, be an accident that this copy of the ode should closely follow Keats's reflections on the world as a 'vale of Soul-making'. 'Do you not see', says Keats, 'how necessary a World of Pains and troubles is to school an Intelligence and make it a Soul?' We can hardly fail to link the intelligent 'Spark' struggling to become a soul as a result of a 'World of Pains and troubles' with the Psyche who achieves apotheosis and happiness after long wanderings and sufferings in search of Cupid. (pp. 81-3)

We need to be aware how closely ideas on the meaning and function of myth were bound up with Keats's attempt to make sense of the human situation. He tells George and Georgiana that his system of soul-making 'may have been the Parent of all the more palpable and personal Schemes of Redemption, among the Zoroastrians the Christians and the Hindoos'. . . . That is to say, in these intimate speculations Psyche has for him much the same degree of reality and unreality as 'their Christ their Oromanes and their Vishnu'. Figures drawn from religious myths—and to Keats Christianity was simply the last of the great mythologies—may be understood sympathetically, he thinks, as personifications of certain kinds of human need or self-knowledge (people 'must have the palpable and named Mediator and Saviour'). This is Keats's personal extension of

a mode of mythological explanation then a commonplace. It has been conveniently summarised by Hazlitt [in the first of his *Lectures on the English Poets*].

> If we have once enjoyed the cool shade of a tree, and been lulled into a deep repose by the sound of a brook running at its foot, we are sure that whenever we can find a shady stream, we can enjoy the same pleasure again, so that when we imagine these objects, we can easily form a mystic personification of the friendly power that inhabits them, Dryad or Naiad, offering its cool fountain or its tempting shade. Hence the origin of the Grecian mythology.

Keats first met these ideas powerfully in Book IV of Wordsworth's *The Excursion* (see, especially, ll. 847-87), a poem which in one mood he hailed as among the 'three things to rejoice at in this Age'. . . . Though Wordsworth's influence on Keats's thought has not been fully traced—Book IV of *The Excursion* is quarry for much more in the Odes than is generally realized—it is, of course, accepted that Keats expounded Greek myths with a Wordsworthian accent in much of his early poetry, including **Endymion**.

Echoes of Milton's 'On the Morning of Christs Nativity' have been noted in the second stanza of **'To Psyche'**. De Selincourt [see excerpt above, 1905], followed by Finney and others, cites the nineteenth stanza of the hymn:

> The Oracles are dumm,
> No voice or hideous humm
>   Runs through the arched roof in words deceiving.
> *Apollo* from his shrine
> Can no more divine,
>   With hollow shreik the steep of *Delphos* leaving
> No nightly trance, or breathed spell,
> Inspire's the pale-ey'd Priest from the prophetic cell . . .

and finds a parallel in the ode's

> No voice, no lute, no pipe, no incense sweet
>   From chain-swung censer teeming;
> No shrine, no grove, no oracle, no heat
>   Of pale-mouth'd prophet dreaming.

This, however, does not quite do justice to Keats's memory. Milton's influence is active earlier in stanza two and also extends more subtly to the first half of the ode's third stanza. Thus one line from the twenty-first stanza of the hymn—

> The *Lars*, and *Lemures* moan with midnight plaint . . .

—should be set beside Keats's

> Nor virgin-choir to make delicious moan
>   Upon the midnight hours;

and Milton's two preceding lines—

> In consecrated Earth,
> And on the holy Hearth . . .

—lend the force of 'consecrated' and 'holy', as applied to the elements of earth and fire, to reinforce 'haunted' in his twentieth stanza:

> From haunted spring, and dale
> Edg'd with poplar pale,
>   The parting Genius is with sighing sent . . .

—and so, I believe, help to inspire Keats's nostalgic

> When holy were the haunted forest boughs,
> Holy the air, the water, and the fire.

It is all much simpler than it sounds in the telling. Only three stanzas of Milton's hymn are involved and their splintering and telescoping in recollection suggest that Keats was not conscious of pastiche.

The chief Miltonic echoes have been recorded, but nobody has stopped to explain why Keats thought of Milton at this point in his poem. Clearly what happened was that 'faded' in l. 25 started a train of thought—to which a strong feeling-tone of regret was compulsively attached—about the end of the old Greek world with its 'happy pieties' (thought and feeling become explicit in the poem some ten lines later at the beginning of the third stanza). By literary association ideas of the fading of belief in the Olympian gods and of a lost numinous nature recalled Milton's description of the departure of the heathen deities of the Mediterranean world at the birth of Christ. The difference in tone between the two poems could hardly be wider. Milton writes of the end of heathendom with an almost fierce satisfaction (though it is certainly possible to detect an undercurrent of tenderness for the 'parting Genius' and 'Nimphs in twilight shade' of the classical world). Keats's tone is throughout one of unmixed regret for 'the fond believing lyre', for primitive times with their supposed simplicity and wholeheartedness of feeling. 'To Psyche' is now becoming something more than the celebration of a neglected goddess—it projects a nostalgia for an imagined wholeness of being once possible, . . . but now, it would seem, impossible (except at lucky moments for the poet and lover). The nostalgia has also a direct personal application. Keats's regret for the realm of Flora and old Pan is at the same time a regret for an earlier phase of his own mental growth before the disenchantment produced by reflection on a darkening experience of the world. A critic should move as delicately in these matters as if he were treading on eggshells, but this double reference is unmistakable. It would be an oversimplification to think of Keats's attitude as 'purely escapist'. By the spring of 1819 he was not trying to avoid thoughts of 'Whirlpools and volcanoes'—he had worked his way through at least to a theoretical acceptance of the value of heartbreaking experience: what he found it hard to bear was that moments of joy and well-being should be poisoned by self-consciousness.

> The point at which Man may arrive is as far as the paral[l]el state in inanimate nature and no further—For instance suppose a rose to have sensation, it blooms on a beautiful morning it enjoys itself—but there comes a cold wind, a hot sun—it cannot escape it, it cannot destroy its annoyances—they are as native to the world as itself.

Men ought not to be less happy than roses, Keats might have said; and he believed that those who had—in a phrase from *Endymion*—'culled Time's sweet first-fruits' had been able to live in the immediate present and were much to be envied. His own power to live in the present, which lay close to the sources of his poetry, depended for survival, as he knew, on his skill in preventing the withering of instinctive enjoyment by reflection.

If Keats thought that sun was exchanged for shadow at some necessary stage in the development both of the individual and of human society as a whole, what was it on the universal plane that corresponded in his view to the over-balance of the reflective power that he feared in himself? The answer is to be found in 'Lamia'—the dangerous respect given to science (natural philosophy) at the expense of the imagination.

> Do not all charms fly
> At the mere touch of cold philosophy? . . .
> Philosophy will clip an Angel's wings,
> Conquer all mysteries by rule and line,
> Empty the haunted air, and gnomed mine—
> Unweave a rainbow . . .

It is known that this passage leans heavily on a paragraph in the first of Hazlitt's *Lectures on the English Poets*. The paragraph concludes:

> . . . the history of religious and poetical enthusiasms is much the same; and both have received a sensible shock from the progress of the experimental philosophy.

Keats was less simple-minded than Hazlitt, but he accepted this judgement in essence. I do not think he was ever interested in discovering when this historical change had taken place or begun to take place; and, in saying so, I do not forget in how many ways he was a child of the Enlightenment or how mutually antagonistic were some of the 'prose' feelings with which he saluted the March of Mind. But Keats could not doubt that the poetic experience was valuable, or fail to suppose that in forgetting Pan men had lost something which they would not find in the *Transactions* of the Royal Society (the 'Fall' had taken place somewhere between the days of 'the fond believing lyre' and the present). He felt that currents of thought, among the most reputable and influential of his age, were inimical to the kind of poetry that he was writing and perhaps to all poetry; and that he needed to develop his resistance to their influence, and to the influence of the reflective traitor within himself, if he was to remain wholehearted, i.e. keep his capacity for responding poetically to experience.

These ideas and feelings seem relevant to the fourth stanza of 'To Psyche'. Against the background that I have sketched the

>   . . . fane
> In some untrodden region of my mind

becomes the 'Great Good Place' where the experimental philosophy rumbles as harmlessly as distant thunder. Keats is constructing a mental landscape for wholehearted enjoyment, and it is fitting that the scenery should recall the natural setting of the Pan festival in *Endymion* and 'Time's sweet first-fruits' under the side of Latmos. The similarity of setting can be shown by quotation.

> Far, far around shall those dark-cluster'd trees
>   Fledge the wild-ridged mountains steep by steep;
> And there by zephyrs, streams, and birds, and bees,
>   The moss-lain Dryads shall be lull'd to sleep;
> And in the midst of this wide quietness
> A rosy sanctuary will I dress
>
> Upon the sides of Latmos was outspread
> A mighty forest . . .
>
> And it had gloomy shades, sequestered deep,
> Where no man went . . .
>
>   . . . Paths there were many,
> Winding through palmy fern, and rushes fenny,

And ivy banks; all leading pleasantly
To a wide lawn, whence one could only see
Stems thronging all around between the swell
Of turf and slanting branches: who could tell
The freshness of the space of heaven above,
Edg'd round with dark tree tops? . . .

    Full in the middle of this pleasantness
There stood a marble altar, with a tress
Of flowers budded newly . . .

In this 'green remote Cockagne', which mixes the scenery of Latmos with the delectable valley in Apuleius, Keats will be able to preserve the visionary poetic experience from marauding analysis—the 'shadowy thought' expended for Psyche's delight is the gardener's creative reverie, opposed antithetically to the matter-of-fact operations of scientific logic. And Keats recognizes that keeping one part of the self simple and direct in its receptiveness is a matter intimately linked with the experience of love—the soul's sanctuary is rosy, Milton's 'celestial rosie red, love's proper hue'. We may note here that both the meeting of Cupid and Psyche in the first stanza and the description of the sanctuary in the fourth stanza have diffuse echoes of Spenser's Garden of Adonis (*Faerie Queene*, Bk. IV, Canto vi) and of the nuptial bower in Eden in *Paradise Lost*.

Since we have to do with a mental landscape, the introduction of Fancy as the gardener is apt enough (though it jars many readers at first). It follows easily as an idea from the Renaissance and neoclassic doctrine that fancy has the power of 're-taining, altering and compounding' the images supplied by the senses. The phrase quoted is from No. 411 of *The Spectator*, and in another paper Addison comes very close to thinking of fancy as a gardener when he says that the poet 'has the modelling of nature in his own hands' (No. 418). The same doctrine of art's ability to improve on nature may be found earlier in Sidney, Bacon and others; and Puttenham invents his own gardener:

> . . . arte is not only an aide and coadiutor to
> nature in all her actions, but an alterer of them,
> and in some sort a surmounter of her skill, so
> as by meanes of it her owne effects shall ap-
> peare more beautifull or straunge or miraculous
> . . . the Gardiner by his arte will not onely make
> an herbe, or flowr, or fruite, come forth in his
> season without impediment, but will also em-
> bellish the same . . . that nature of her selfe
> woulde never have done . . .

Puttenham, Sidney, Bacon and Addison express a stock idea—they are not, of course, in any sense sources of Keats's image, though I suspect that 'feign' in

> With all the gardener Fancy e'er could feign

may be a generalized Elizabethan echo. For example, Burton's discussion of Phantasy in *The Anatomy of Melancholy* mentions that it 'feigns infinite other unto himselfe' from the images furnished by daily experience. It is an amusing coincidence that Burton should choose 'Psyche's palace in Apuleius' as one example of fancy's power. I do not want to make too much of a last remark about 'the gardener Fancy', but I think it probable—since Fancy is the true creator of the mental landscape in this stanza—that Keats is glancing at the idea of God as the gardener who designed Eden. Indeed the association

seems inevitable if we remember that Adam and Eve cull Time's first-fruits and that **'To Psyche'** is about a kind of Fall.

If this attempt to understand **'To Psyche'** is correct in outline, the poem moves through three stages. In the first stage (st. I, ll. 1-23) Keats sets out to praise Psyche as the neglected goddess whose sufferings and mistakes represent the inevitable conditions of human experience. She has achieved 'identity' and lasting happiness. Love is her companion. Keats uses the convention of a sudden vision or waking dream, which comes to him when he is wandering 'thoughtlessly', because he had learned to speak in one breath of 'the most thoughtless and happiest moments of our Lives', . . . because Spenser's mythological poetry seemed to him a kind of waking dream, and because he knew that poetic experience was to be wooed by opening the mind receptively, not by concentrating its conscious powers. The vision of Psyche and 'the winged boy' in their Eden-like retreat draws some of its richness, as I have said, from descriptions of embowered lovers in Spenser and Milton. The tone of this first stanza is contented, even cool, except for the touch of feeling conveyed by the repetition 'O happy, happy dove', which measure the irksome distance between the actual world and the happiness that Psyche has already won.

The second stage of the poem spreads itself over the second and third stanzas (ll. 24-49). Keats passes easily from the neglect of Psyche (born as a goddess too late for the fervours of primitive worship) to the fading and wearing-out of belief in the Olympians, and then to a nostalgic outpouring of feeling for the magnanimity of life in an age when all nature was still 'holy' (full of the anthropologist's *mana*), all enjoyment wholehearted, and every herdsman or shepherd the poet of his own pleasure. The contrast is not with the age of Apuleius, but with a present which is a twilight for poetic and mythological modes of thought—the March of Mind has upset the balance of our natures, making the simple enjoyment of an experience in an 'eternal moment' an almost heroic achievement. Keats's regret embraces his own loss of an earlier innocence. After the first quatrain of the third stanza we have his defiance of these tendencies and changes in the age and in himself ('Yet even in these days . . . I see, and sing, by my own eyes inspired'). At this point the repetition of the catalogue of worship from the ode's second stanza is a way of suggesting the poet's firmness or obstinacy. Psyche's worship will not be skimped or abbreviated by him in an age of unbelief.

The third and final stage of the poem consists of the fourth stanza (ll. 50-67). Here Keats gets his second wind. The movement introduced by the emphatic

    Yes, I will be thy priest . . .

represents an accession of strength. The tread is more measured than in anything that has gone before, but there is no loss of smoothness or pace, and the whole stanza, consisting of a single long but quite coherent sentence, develops its momentum quietly at first, then confidently, and finally with exultation at its climax in the last quatrain. The defiance of the third stanza gives way to confidence as Keats comes to see how he can worship Psyche (the repetition of 'shall' and 'will' is extraordinarily positive). Briefly, he will do so by keeping 'some untrodden region' of his mind as a safe refuge where Psyche or the soul may unfold all her powers in a landscape and climate wholly benign and friendly. The stanza constructs the remoteness and peaceful seclusion of a valley:

> Far, far around shall those dark-cluster'd trees
>   Fledge the wild-ridged mountains steep by steep;
> And there by zephyrs, streams, and birds, and bees,
>   The moss-lain Dryads shall be lull'd to sleep.

The succession of pictorial details moves in and down from the dark mountains and forests to the humming warmth of the valley floor with its streams and pastoral drowsiness, and the description comes to a focus on Psyche's refuge or shrine:

> And in the midst of this wide quietness
> A rosy sanctuary will I dress . . .

A complex image, accumulated from these details, is being offered as the equivalent of a mental state, which may be negatively defined by what it excludes. Calculation, anxiety and deliberate activity are shut out. The 'wide quietness' of the valley symbolizes a mood in which the soul will be able to breathe freely, and in which poetry, here defined as 'the wreath'd trellis of a working brain' may be coaxed to put forth its buds and bells and nameless stars. The soul is promised a rich indolence which will safeguard its natural gift for delight and restore to wholeness whatever the world beyond the mountains has broken down. In this luxurious sanctuary, a place made lovely and inviting with all the resources of a poetic imagination—and these resources are infinite, for Fancy

> . . . breeding flowers, will never breed the same . . .

—Psyche will be disposed to welcome the visits of love (whose 'soft delight' was still for Keats the soul's 'chief intensity'). Perhaps the final implications are that wholeheartedness can never be lost while Psyche is willing to welcome love in at her casement, and, less directly, that love, poetry and indolence are the natural medicines of the soul against the living death it must expect from 'cold philosophy'. (pp. 85-94)

> Kenneth Allott, "The 'Ode to Psyche'," in John Keats: A Reassessment, edited by Kenneth Muir, Liverpool University Press, 1958, pp. 74-94.

JACK STILLINGER (essay date 1961)

[In his explication of "The Eve of St. Agnes," Stillinger challenges the "metaphysical" interpretation of the poem, which finds the work a chronicle of the spiritual pilgrimage of the character Porphyro. He suggests instead that Porphyro represents life's "ordinary cruelties" and that Madeline's deception by him is actually self-deception. Indeed, Stillinger sees Madeline as representative of Keats's "hoodwinked dreamers," characters who do not distinguish between the ideal and the real and whose folly he often exposes in his poems. This essay first appeared in Studies in Philology in 1961.]

The commonest response to *The Eve of St. Agnes* has been the celebration of its "heady and perfumed loveliness." . . . For many readers, as for Douglas Bush, the poem is "no more than a romantic tapestry of unique richness of color"; one is "moved less by the experience of the characters than . . . by the incidental and innumerable beauties of descriptive phrase and rhythm." (p. 71)

The only serious attempt to make something of the poem has come from a small group of critics whom I shall call "metaphysical critics" because they think Keats was a metaphysician. To them the poem seems to dramatize certain ideas that Keats held a year or two earlier about the nature of the imagination, the relationship between this world and the next, and

the progress of an individual's ascent toward spiritualization. (p. 72)

The events [of the poem] are thought to relate to a passage in the well-known letter to Benjamin Bailey, 22 November 1817, in which Keats expressed his faith in "the truth of Imagination": "What the imagination seizes as Beauty must be truth—whether it existed before or not. . . . The Imagination may be compared to Adam's dream—he awoke and found it truth." For the metaphysical critics, just as Adam dreamed of the creation of Eve, then awoke to find his dream a truth—Eve before him a beautiful reality—so Madeline dreams of Porphyro and awakens to find him present and palpably real. (p. 73)

The other main strand of the critics' thinking concerns the apotheosis of Porphyro. By relating the poem to Keats's simile of human life as a "Mansion of Many Apartments," the critics would persuade us that the castle of Madeline's kinsmen allegorically represents human life, and that Porphyro, passing upward to a closet adjoining Madeline's bedchamber, and thence into the chamber itself, progresses from apartment to apartment in the mansion of life, executing a spiritual ascent to heaven's bourne. For a number of reasons, Keats's simile confuses rather than clarifies the poem. But the idea of spiritual pilgrimage is not entirely to be denied. Porphyro says to the sleeping Madeline, "Thou art my heaven, and I thine eremite" . . . , and when she awakens, after the consummation, he exclaims to her: "Ah, silver shrine, here will I take my rest / After so many hours of toil and quest, / A famish'd pilgrim,—saved by miracle." . . . (pp. 73-4)

In brief summary, the main points of the metaphysical critics' interpretation are that Madeline's awakening to find Porphyro in her bedroom is a document in the validity of the visionary imagination; that Porphyro in the course of the poem makes a spiritual pilgrimage, ascending higher by stages until he arrives at transcendant reality in Madeline's bed; and that there the lovers re-enact earthly pleasures that will be stored up for further, still more elevated repetition in a finer tone. If these ideas seem farfetched and confused, the fact should be attributed in part to the brevity of my exposition, and to the shortcomings of any attempt to abstract ideas from a complicated poem, even when it is treated as allegory. Yet one may suggest reasons for hesitating to accept them.

For one thing, when the imaginative vision of beauty turns out to be a truth—when Madeline awakens to find Porphyro in her bed—she is not nearly so pleased as Adam was when he awoke and discovered Eve. In fact, truth here is seemingly undesirable: Madeline is frightened out of her wits, and she laments, "No dream, alas! alas! and woe is mine! / Porphyro will leave me here to fade and pine." . . . For another, it is a reversal of Keats's own sequence to find in the poem the spiritual repetition of earthly pleasures. In Madeline's dream the imaginative enactment of pleasure comes first; it is an earthly repetition of spiritual pleasure that follows, and perhaps in a grosser, rather than a finer, tone. That the lovers are consciously intent on experiencing the conditions of immortality—consciously practising for the spiritual repetition of pleasure at an even higher level of intensity—implies, if one reads the critics correctly, that both Madeline and Porphyro have read *Endymion,* Keats's letters, and the explications of the metaphysical critics.

Much of the critics' interpretation rests on the religious language of the poem. Madeline is "St. Agnes' charmed maid," "a mission'd spirit" . . . , "all akin / To spirits of the air"

. . . , "a saint," "a splendid angel, newly drest, / Save wings, for heaven," "so pure a thing, so free from mortal taint." . . . To Porphyro, her "eremite," she is "heaven" . . . , and from closet to bedchamber he progresses from purgatory to paradise. Finally, Porphyro is "A famish'd pilgrim,—saved by miracle." . . . (pp. 74-5)

What is perhaps most telling against the critics, in connection with the religious language of *The Eve of St. Agnes,* is that when Porphyro calls himself "A famish'd pilgrim,—saved by miracle," his words must be taken ironically, unless Keats has forgotten, or hopes the reader has forgotten, all the action leading to the consummation. The miracle on which Porphyro congratulates himself is in fact a *stratagem* that he has planned and carried out to perfection. Early in the poem, when he first encounters Angela, she is amazed to see him, and says that he "must hold water in a witch's sieve, / And be liege-lord of all the Elves and Fays, / To venture" into a castle of enemies. . . . Although Porphyro later assures Madeline that he is "no rude infidel" . . . , the images in Angela's speech tend to link him with witches and fairies rather than with the Christian pilgrim. By taking a closer look at the poem, we may see that Keats had misgivings about Porphyro's fitness to perform a spiritual pilgrimage and arrive at heaven.

Porphyro's first request of Angela, "Now tell me where is Madeline" . . . , is followed by an oath upon the holy loom used to weave St. Agnes' wool, and it is implied that he is well aware what night it is. "St. Agnes' Eve," says Angela, "God's help! my lady fair the conjuror plays / This very night: good angels her deceive!" . . . While she laughs at Madeline's folly, Porphyro gazes on her, until "Sudden a thought came like a full-blown rose . . . then doth he propose / A stratagem." . . . The full force of "stratagem" comes to be felt in the poem—a ruse, an artifice, a trick for deceiving. For Angela, the deception of Madeline by good angels is funny; but Porphyro's is another kind of deception, and no laughing matter. She is startled, and calls him "cruel," "impious," "wicked" . . . ; the harshness of the last line of her speech emphasizes her reaction: "Thou canst not surely be the same that thou didst seem." . . . (pp. 75-6)

Porphyro swears "by all saints" not to harm Madeline: "O may I ne'er find grace / When my weak voice shall whisper its last prayer, / If one of her soft ringlets I displace." . . . He next enforces his promise with a suicidal threat: Angela must believe him, or he "will . . . Awake, with horrid shout" his foemen, "And beard them." . . . Because Angela is "A poor, weak, palsy-stricken, churchyard thing" . . . , she presently accedes, promising to do whatever Porphyro wishes—

> Which was, to lead him, in close secrecy,
> Even to Madeline's chamber, and there hide
> Him in a closet, of such privacy
> That he might see her beauty unespied,
> And win perhaps that night a peerless bride,
> While legion'd fairies pac'd the coverlet,
> And pale enchantment held her sleepy-eyed. . . .

At this point our disbelief must be suspended if we are to read the poem as an affirmation of romantic love. We must leave our world behind, where stratagems like Porphyro's are frowned on, sometimes punished in the criminal courts, and enter an imaginary world where "in sooth such things have been." . . . [Angela] leads Porphyro to Madeline's chamber, "silken, hush'd, and chaste," where he takes "covert." . . . In the first draft Stanza XXI is incomplete, but two versions that can be pieced

together call Porphyro's hiding-place "A purgatory sweet to view love's own domain" and "A purgatory sweet to what may he attain." The rejected lines, mentioning "purgatory sweet" as a stage toward the "paradise" . . . of Madeline's chamber, are documents in Porphyro's spiritual pilgrimage, perhaps. The ideas of viewing love's own domain, or what he may attain, are documents in the peeping-Tomism that occupies the next few stanzas. As Angela is feeling her way toward the stair, she is met by Madeline, who turns back to help her down to "a safe level matting." . . . If the action is significant, its meaning lies in the juxtaposition of Madeline's unselfish act of "pious care" . . . with the leering overtones just before of Porphyro's having hidden himself in her closet, "pleas'd amain" . . .—pleased exceedingly by the success of his stratagem— and with the tone of the narrator's words immediately following: "Now prepare, / Young Porphyro, for gazing on that bed; / She comes, she comes again, like ring-dove fray'd and fled." . . . (pp. 76-7)

The mention of "ring-dove" is interesting. Porphyro has taken "covert"—the position of the hunter (or perhaps merely the bird-watcher). There follows a series of bird images that perhaps may be thought of in terms of the hunter's game. In a variant to the stanza Madeline is "an affrighted Swan"; here she is a "ring-dove"; in the next stanza her heart is "a tongueless nightingale" . . . ; later in the poem she is "A dove forlorn" . . . ; still later Porphyro speaks of robbing her nest . . . , and in a variant says, "Soft Nightingale, I'll keep thee in a cage / To sing to me." (p. 77)

Porphyro tries to awaken Madeline, or so it seems. . . . It is curious that in the proposition . . . , "Open thine eyes . . . Or I shall drowse beside thee" . . . , Porphyro does not wait for an answer: "Thus whispering, his warm, unnerved arm / Sank in her pillow." . . . "Awakening up" . . . , he takes Madeline's lute and plays an ancient ditty, which causes her to utter a soft moan. It would seem that she does at this point wake up: "Suddenly / Her blue affrayed eyes wide open shone. . . . Her eyes were open, but she still beheld, / Now wide awake, the vision of her sleep." . . . Not unreasonably, we might think, she weeps, sighs, and "moan[s] forth witless words." . . .

We shall see in a moment, however, that she has not after all awakened from her trance. The "painful change" she witnesses—the substitution of the genuine Porphyro for the immortal looks and voice of her vision—"*nigh* expell'd / The blisses of her dream" . . . , came near expelling them, but did not in fact do so. Apparently she is to be thought of as still in her trance, but capable of speaking to the Porphyro before her. . . . At the end of Stanza XXXVI, the image of "St. Agnes' moon" combines the notions of St. Agnes, the patron saint of maidenhood, and Cynthia, the goddess of chastity, and the symbolic combination has "set," gone out of the picture to be replaced by a storm: "Meantime the frost-wind blows / Like Love's alarum pattering the sharp sleet / Against the window-panes; St. Agnes' moon hath set." . . . (p. 80)

Keats's final manuscript version of the consummation, rejected by his publishers on moral grounds, as making the poem unfit to be read by young ladies, is more graphic. For a rather lame conclusion to Madeline's speech . . . , he substituted the lines, "See while she speaks his arms encroaching slow / Have zon'd her, heart to heart—loud, loud the dark winds blow." Then he rewrote Stanza XXXVI:

> For on the midnight came a tempest fell.
> More sooth for that his close rejoinder flows
> Into her burning ear;—and still the spell
> Unbroken guards her in serene repose.

With her wild dream he mingled as a rose
Marryeth its odour to a violet.
Still, still she dreams—louder the frost wind blows
Like Love's alarum pattering the sharp sleet
Against the window-panes; St. Agnes' moon hath set.

The revised version makes clearer that Madeline is still dream-ing: "still the spell / Unbroken guards her in serene repose." And it makes clearer the connection between the sexual con-summation, the setting of St. Agnes' moon, and the rising of the storm. When Porphyro's "close rejoinder flows / Into . . . [the] burning ear" of Madeline, we may or may not recall Satan "Squat like a Toad, close at the ear of *Eve*" . . . ; but one would go out of his way to avoid a parallel between the advent of the storm in Keats's poem and the change in Nature that comes about when our first mother in an evil hour reached forth and ate the fruit. . . . Unlike Eve, however, rather more like Clarissa, Madeline by this time has no choice; the revision heightens the contrast between her innocent unconsciousness and the storm raging outside: "Still, still she dreams—louder the frost wind blows." (pp. 80-1)

[When Madeline finally does wake up, her] speech shows a mixed attitude toward what has happened, but above all it is the lament of the seduced maiden: "No dream, alas! alas! and woe is mine! / Porphyro will leave me here to fade and pine.— / Cruel! what traitor could thee hither bring?" . . . She will curse not, for her heart is lost in his, or, perhaps more accu-rately, still lost in her romantic idealization of him. But she is aware that her condition is woeful: Porphyro is cruel; Angela is a traitor; and Madeline is a "deceived thing;— / A dove forlorn and lost." . . . (pp. 81-2)

After giving so much space to Porphyro, in admittedly exag-gerated fashion portraying him as peeping Tom and villainous seducer, I must now confess that I do not think his stratagem is the main concern of the poem. I have presented him as villain in order to suggest, in the first place, that he is not, after all, making a spiritual pilgrimage, unless the poem is to be read as a satire on spiritual pilgrimages; in the second place, that the lovers, far from being a single element in the poem, are . . . [protagonist and antagonist]; and in the third place, that no matter how much Keats entered into the feelings of his characters, he could not lose touch with the claims and re-sponsibilities of the world he lived in. (p. 82)

From now on . . . it may be best to think of Porphyro as representing, like the storm that comes up simultaneously with his conquest, the ordinary cruelties of life in the world. Like Melville, Keats saw

Too far into the sea; where every maw
The greater on the less feeds evermore. . . .
Still do I that most fierce destruction see,
The Shark at savage prey—the hawk at pounce,
The gentle Robin, like a pard or ounce,
Ravening a worm.

Let Porphyro represent one of the sharks under the surface. And to borrow another figure from Melville, let the main con-cern of the poem be the young Platonist dreaming at the mast-head: one false step, his identity comes back in horror, and with a half-throttled shriek he drops through transparent air into the sea, no more to rise for ever. There are reasons why we ought not entirely to sympathize with Madeline. She is a victim of deception, to be sure, but of deception not so much by Porphyro as by herself and the superstition she trusts in. Madeline the self-hoodwinked dreamer is, I think, the main

concern of the poem, and I shall spend some time documenting this notion and relating it to Keats's other important poems—all of which, in a sense, are about dreaming.

If we recall Keats's agnosticism, his sonnet "Written in Disgust of Vulgar Superstition" (Christianity), and his abuse in the *Letters* of "the pious frauds of Religion," we may be prepared to see a hoodwinked dreamer in the poem even before we meet Madeline. He is the old Beadsman, so engrossed in an ascetic ritual that he is sealed off from the joys of life. After saying his prayers, he turns first through a door leading to the noisy revelry upstairs. "But no. . . . The joys of all his life were said and sung: / His was a harsh penance on St. Agnes' Eve." . . . And so he goes another way, to sit among rough ashes, while the focus of the narrative proceeds through the door he first opened, and on into the assembly of revellers, where we are introduced to Madeline and the ritual she is intent on following. In the final manuscript version, between Stanzas VI and VII, Keats inserted an additional stanza on the ritual, in part to explain the feast that Porphyro sets out:

'Twas said her future lord would there appear
Offering as sacrifice—all in the dream—
Delicious food even to her lips brought near:
Viands and wine and fruit and sugar'd cream,
To touch her palate with the fine extreme
Of relish: then soft music heard; and then
More pleasure followed in a dizzy stream
Palpable almost: then to wake again
Warm in the virgin morn, no weeping Magdalen.

Then the poem, as it was printed, continues describing Made-line, who scarcely hears the music, and, with eyes fixed on the floor, pays no attention to anyone around her.

Several things deserve notice. By brooding "all that wintry day, / On love, and wing'd St. Agnes' saintly care" . . . , and by setting herself apart from the revellers, Madeline presents an obvious parallel with the Beadsman. Both are concerned with prayer and an ascetic ritual; both are isolated from the crowd and from actuality. A second point is that the superstition is clearly an old wives' tale: Madeline follows the prescription that "she had heard old dames full many times declare." . . . It is called by the narrator a "whim"; "Full of this whim was thoughtful Madeline." . . . The irony of the added stanza en-forces the point. Madeline's pleasures turn out to be palpable in fact. When she awakens to find herself with Porphyro, she is anything but warm: rather, she wakes up to "flaw-blown sleet" and "iced gusts" . . . ; it is no virgin morn for her; and she is a "weeping Magdalen," who cries, "alas! alas! and woe is mine!" . . . But at this point, early in the poem, "she saw not: her heart was otherwhere: / She sigh'd for Agnes' dreams, the sweetest of the year." . . . Perfunctorily dancing along, she is said to be "Hoodwink'd with faery fancy; all amort, / Save to St. Agnes and her lambs unshorn." . . .

The superstition is next mentioned when Angela tells that Madeline "the conjuror plays / This very night: good angels her deceive!" . . . Porphyro thinks of the ritual in terms of "enchantments cold" and "legends old." . . . Proceeding to her chamber, Madeline is called "St. Agnes' charmed maid," "a mission'd spirit, unaware." . . . When she undresses, "Half-hidden, like a mermaid in sea-weed" . . . , she is perhaps linked briefly with the drowning Ophelia, whose spreading clothes momentarily support her "mermaid-like" upon the water; like Ophelia, she is engrossed in a fanciful dream-world. "Pensive awhile she dreams awake, and sees, / In fancy, fair St. Agnes in her bed, / But dares not look behind, or all the charm is fled.'' . . . This last line carries a double meaning: in following her ritual, Madeline must look neither ''behind, nor sideways'' . . . ; but the real point is that if she did look behind, she would discover Porphyro, and then ''the charm'' would be ''fled'' for a more immediate reason.

Asleep in bed, Madeline is said to be ''Blissfully haven'd both from joy and pain . . . Blinded alike from sunshine and from rain, / As though a rose should shut, and be a bud again.'' . . . Her dream is ''a midnight charm / Impossible to melt as iced stream,'' ''a stedfast spell.'' . . . It is while she is in this state of stuporous insensibility—while ''still the spell / Unbroken guards her in serene repose,'' ''Still, still she dreams—louder the frost wind blows''—that Porphyro makes love to her. On awakening to learn, ''No dream, alas! alas! and woe is mine,'' she calls herself ''a deceived thing,'' echoing Angela's words earlier, ''good angels her deceive!'' Her condition is pitiful, yet at the same time reprehensible. Her conjuring (perhaps like Merlin's) has backfired upon her, and as hoodwinked dreamer she now gets her reward in coming to face reality a little too late. The rose cannot shut, and be a bud again.

Whether *The Eve of St. Agnes* is a good poem depends in large part on the reader's willingness to find in it a consistency and unity that may not in fact be there. But however it is evaluated, it stands significantly at the beginning of Keats's single great creative year, 1819, and it serves to introduce a preoccupation of all the major poems of this year: that an individual ought not to lose touch with the realities of this world.

In the poems of 1819, Keats's most explicit, unequivocal statement about the conditions of human life comes in the *Ode on Melancholy.* Life in the world, we are told in the third stanza, is an affair in which pleasure and pain are inseparably mixed. Beauty and the melancholy awareness that beauty must die, joy and the simultaneous fading of joy, ''aching Pleasure'' and its instant turning to poison—all are inextricably bound up in life. There is no pleasure without pain, and, conversely, if pain is sealed off, so also is pleasure. One accepts the inseparability of pleasure and pain, or one rejects life entirely, and suffers a kind of moral and spiritual emptiness amounting to death. (pp. 83-6)

In bed, under the delusion that she can achieve bliss in her dream, yet wake up in the virgin morn no weeping Magdalen, [Madeline] is ''Blissfully haven'd both from joy and pain'' . . .—for all practical purposes in the narcotic state rejected by the *Ode on Melancholy,* experiencing nothing. Keats reiterates the idea two lines later, ''Blinded alike from sunshine and from rain,'' and the folly of her delusion is represented by the reversal of natural process, ''As though a rose should shut, and be a bud again.'' . . . As generally in Keats's poems, dreaming is attended by fairy-tale imagery: under the spell of ''faery fancy,'' Madeline plays the conjuror, and Porphyro is linked in several ways with fairy-lore, witchcraft, and sorcery, as well as pagan sensuality. It is possible that Madeline never completely awakens from her fanciful dream; for she believes Porphyro when he tells her that the storm is ''an elfin-storm from faery land'' . . . , and she imagines ''sleeping dragons all around'' . . . when they hurry out of the castle.

The heroine of *The Eve of Saint Mark,* written a week or so after the completion of *The Eve of St. Agnes,* in some ways resembles Madeline. Among the ''thousand things'' perplexing Bertha in the volume she pores over are ''stars of Heaven, and angels' wings, / Martyrs in a fiery blaze, / Azure saints in

silver rays.'' . . . Enwrapped in the legend of St. Mark, ''dazed with saintly imag'ries'' . . . , she ignores the life in the village around her, and cuts herself off from reality—a ''poor cheated soul'' . . . , ''lost in dizzy maze'' and mocked by her own shadow.

The wretched knight-at-arms in *La Belle Dame Sans Merci* is similarly a hoodwinked dreamer. La Belle Dame is ''a faery's child''; she sings ''A faery's song,'' speaks ''in language strange,'' and takes him to an ''elfin grot.'' When he awakens from his vision he finds himself ''On the cold hill's side.'' But he is still the dupe of his dream, still hoodwinked, because he continues, in a barren landscape, ''Alone and palely loitering,'' hoping for a second meeting with La Belle Dame. And he denies himself participation in the actual world, which, against his bleak surroundings, is represented as a more fruitful scene, where ''The squirrel's granary is full, / And the harvest's done.''

In *Lamia,* the hoodwinked dreamer is of course Lycius, who falls in love with the serpent woman Lamia, in whose veins runs ''elfin blood,'' who lingers by the wayside ''fairily,'' with whom he lives in ''sweet sin'' in a magical palace with a ''faery-roof.'' . . . ''She seem'd, at once, some penanced lady elf, / Some demon's mistress, or the demon's self.'' . . . What she promises to do for Lycius is what, according to the *Ode on Melancholy,* cannot be done for mortal men: ''To unperplex bliss from its neighbour pain; / Define their pettish limits, and estrange / Their points of contact, and swift counterchange.'' The inseparability of pleasure and pain is for her a ''specious chaos''; she will separate them ''with sure art'' . . .—or so the blinded Lycius thinks. But ''Spells are but made to break,'' wrote Keats, in a passage subsequently omitted from the text. ''A thrill / Of trumpets'' reminds Lycius of the claims of the ''noisy world almost forsworn'' . . . , and he holds a wedding feast, at which ''cold philosophy,'' in the form of his old tutor Apollonius, attends to put ''all charms'' to flight. The ''foul dream'' Lamia vanishes under the tutor's piercing gaze, and Lycius, too engrossed in his dream to survive, falls dead. (pp. 87-8)

The metaphysical critics are right in asserting Keats's early trust in the imagination. What they sometimes fail to recognize, themselves eager for glimpses of heaven's bourne, and to an extent hoodwinked with their own rather than Keats's metaphysics, is that before Keats wrote more than a handful of poems we would not willingly let die, he in large part changed his mind. Late in January 1818, on sitting down to read *King Lear* once again, he wrote a sonnet bidding goodby to romance: ''Let me not wander in a barren dream.'' A few days later he called it ''A terrible division'' when the soul is flown upward and the body ''earthward press'd.'' In March he wrote, ''It is a flaw / In happiness to see beyond our bourn,'' and about the same time he recognized that ''Four seasons''—not just eternal spring, as the visionary might conjure up—''Four seasons fill the measure of the year.'' Similarly ''There are four seasons in the mind of man,'' who ''has his Winter too of pale misfeature, / Or else he would forego his mortal nature.'' . . . ''Fancy,'' said Keats to Reynolds, ''is indeed less than a present palpable reality.'' It would be a distortion of fact to maintain that he always held this later view, but it is worth noting that even when he and his fancy could not agree, he declared himself ''more at home amongst Men and women,'' happier reading Chaucer than Ariosto.

The dreamer in Keats is ultimately one who turns his back, not merely on the pains of life, but on life altogether; and in the poems of 1819, beginning with *The Eve of St. Agnes,* his dreaming is condemned. If the major concern in these poems is the conflict between actuality and the ideal, the result is not a rejection of the actual, but rather a facing-up to it that amounts, in the total view, to affirmation. It is a notable part of Keats's wisdom that he never lost touch with reality, that he condemned his hoodwinked dreamers who would shut out the world, that he recognized life as a complexity of pleasure and pain, and laid down a rule for action: achievement of the ripest, fullest experience that one is capable of. These qualities make him a saner if in some ways less romantic poet than his contemporaries, and they should qualify him as the Romantic poet most likely to survive in the modern world. (pp. 89-90)

> Jack Stillinger, "The Hoodwinking of Madeline: Scepticism in 'The Eve of St. Agnes'," in Keats: A Collection of Critical Essays, edited by Walter Jackson Bate, Prentice-Hall, Inc., 1964, pp. 71-90.

HAROLD BLOOM (essay date 1961)

[Bloom, an American critic and editor, is best known as the formulator of "revisionism," a controversial theory of literary creation based on the concept that all poets are subject to the influence of earlier poets, and that, to develop their own voice, they attempt to overcome this influence through a deliberate process of "creative correction" which Bloom calls "misreading." Bloom also extended this theory, introduced in 1973 in his The Anxiety of Influence, to include the critic or reader as another willful misreader of literary texts. His theories are largely based on his readings of English poetry from the Romantic period to the present. His essay below focuses on Keats's imaginative faculty as evidenced in the odes.]

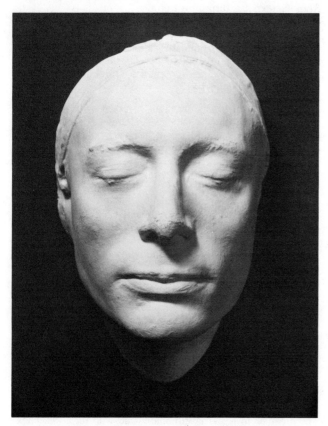

Plaster cast of Keats's life mask. The Granger Collection, New York.

Keats [is] a hero of the imagination in his unwavering insistence that an increase in consciousness need not be an increase in the despair of actuality, and in his stubborn identification of imagination with the potential of consciousness. (pp. xiv-xv)

That Keats had the healthiest of imaginations, balanced at last in a harmony of its own impulses, is now generally and rightly believed. The world of Keats is our world as Shakespeare's is, at once actual and visionary, sensuous, probable, yet open to possibility. From the Ode to Psyche on, it is accurate to say of Keats that his consciousness and imagination were one, and his sense of actuality absolute. He was refreshingly free of [what Wallace Stevens termed] existing conceptions of the world, and free also of apocalyptic desire, the inner necessity that compelled Blake and Shelley to create their radical but open conceptions of possible worlds. The presence of death heightened Keats's imaginative naturalism by giving it relentless urgency, without persuading Keats that the earth was less than enough. (p. xv)

The Ode to a Nightingale opens with the hammer beats of three heavily accented syllables—"My heart aches"—signaling the sudden advent of a state of consciousness unlike the Beulah state of "indolence," soft, relaxed, and feminine, which marks Keats's usual mode of heightened awareness and creativity. Like Shelley in the Skylark, Keats is listening to an unseen bird whose location he cannot specify—it is "In some melodious plot / Of beechen green, and shadows numberless." But the sharp immediacy of its song is nevertheless emphasized, for it sings "of summer in full-throated ease." The effect of the song on Keats is dual and strongly physical, indeed almost deathly. His heart aches, and his sense is pained with a drowsy numbness that suggests, first, having been poisoned; next, having taken a narcotic. Not the sound alone of the song, but Keats's empathizing with the bird, has done this. He is not envious of the bird, but is "too happy" in its happiness. He cannot sustain his own "negative capability" in this case; he has yielded his being too readily to that of the bird.

And yet, he welcomes this dangerous vertigo, for the next stanza of the poem seeks to prolong his condition by its wish for drunkenness, for "a beaker full of the warm South." The slackening intensity from poison to narcotic to wine is itself a return to an ordinary wakeful consciousness, a sense of the usual reality from which Keats here would "fade away into the forest dim," to join the nightingale in its invisibility and enclosed joy; to leave behind the world of mutability, where every increase in consciousness is an increase in sorrow. But the leave-taking is the contrary of Keats's expectation; the flight is not an evasion, but an elaboration of waking reality:

> Away! away! for I will fly to thee,
>   Not charioted by Bacchus and his pards,
> But on the viewless wings of Poesy,
>   Though the dull brain perplexes and retards:
> Already with thee!

Suddenly, having put aside the last aid to invocation, but by the act of writing at his poem, he is where he wills to be, with the nightingale. The wings of Poesy are "viewless," not just because they are invisible, but because the flight is too high for a vision of the earth to be possible. And the state that now commences is a puzzle to the retarding "dull brain." The sweep of the imagination here is more than rational in its energy. Between the ecstatic cry of "Already with thee!" and the bell-like tolling of the word "forlorn" at the poem's climax, Keats enters the inner world of his poem, that highest state of the imagination which Blake called Eden. The mystery of Keats's unresolved contraries is in his quite anti-Blakean association of this state of more abundant life with what seems to be the death impulse. What for Blake is a state of greater *vision* is for Keats the realm of the *viewless:*

> Already with thee! tender is the night,
> And haply the Queen-Moon is on her throne,
>   Cluster'd around by all her starry Fays;
>   But here there is no light,
> Save what from heaven is with the breezes blown
>   Through verdurous glooms and winding mossy ways.

It is the night that is tender, the paradoxical darkness of the Keatsian vision constituting the mark of that tenderness. Nature is not blacked out; moon and stars may be present, but their light must first submit to the diminishing maze through which the night winds are blown.

Sight goes; the other senses abide in this trance, which at once equals nature and poetry. He cannot see, but odor, taste, and sound, in an instructive ordering, are called upon to describe the phenomena of the world he has at once entered and created. First, odor and taste, in the form of "soft incense" and "dewy wine":

> I cannot see what flowers are at my feet,
>   Nor what soft incense hangs upon the boughs,
> But, in embalmed darkness, guess each sweet
>   Wherewith the seasonable month endows
> The grass, the thicket, and the fruit-tree wild;
>   White hawthorn, and the pastoral eglantine:
>   Fast fading violets cover'd up in leaves;
>   And mid-May's eldest child,
> The coming musk-rose, full of dewy wine,
>   The murmurous haunt of flies on summer eves.

The sensuous imagery here is the luxury of the lower paradise, of the Gardens of Adonis or of Beulah, but set in a context more severe. The odors and tastes are almost those of a more abandoned Milton, a blind poet intensifying the glory he cannot apprehend. But this is closer to the blindness of faith, the evidence of things not seen. Keats cannot see the flowers, but they do him homage at his feet. The "soft incense hangs upon the boughs" for him; and the darkness is "embalmed," a hint of the death wish in the next stanza. The month has kept faith; it is seasonable, and so aids Keats in guessing the identity of each odor. The significance of the "musk-rose" is that it is "coming," still a potential, for it is "mid-May's eldest child" and Keats is writing his ode early in May. Even as he anticipates the taste of the "musk-rose, full of dewy wine," Keats empathizes in advance with the insects, tasting of that wine on still-to-come summer eves. The rose as "*murmurous* haunt of flies" summons in the sense of hearing:

> Darkling I listen; and, for many a time
>   I have been half in love with easeful Death,
> Call'd him soft names in many a mused rhyme,
>   To take into the air my quiet breath

He listens, in the nightingale's own darkness, to the ecstasy of the bird's song. A clue to the poet's deliberate blinding of himself is heard here in a slight but haunting echo of a plangent passage of Milton. In the great invocation to light which opens Book III of *Paradise Lost,* the blind poet prepares himself to describe the glory of God the Father, "bright effluence of bright essence increate," a light so intense as to put out our earthly

sight. As he reflects on his own sightless eyes, Milton's thoughts turn to the nightingale singing in darkness:

> Then feed on thoughts, that voluntary move
> Harmonious numbers; as the wakeful Bird
> Sings darkling, and in shadiest Covert hid
> Tunes her nocturnal note.

How consciously Keats remembered this passage one cannot say, but it contains the whole kernel of the *Ode to a Nightingale,* including the identification of poet and bird in their situations; involuntary in Milton, voluntary in Keats.

As he listens in the bird's own darkness, Keats approaches that supreme act of the Romantic Imagination so prevalent in his master, Wordsworth, the fluid dissolve or fade-out in which the limitations of time and space flee away, and the border between being and non-being, life and death, seems to crumble:

> Now more than ever seems it rich to die,
>   To cease upon the midnight with no pain,
>   While thou art pouring forth thy soul abroad
>   In such an ecstasy!
> Still wouldst thou sing, and I have ears in vain—
>   To thy high requiem become a sod.

Two attitudes toward death, the first shading into the second, are involved in this beautiful but disturbed stanza. Previous to the occasion this ode celebrates, the poet says, he has frequently invoked Death, under his "soft names" of ease, calling on Death to take his breathing spirit "into the air," that is, to die by the very act of exhaling. As he has called upon Death in "many a mused rhyme," this exhaling is equivalent to the act of uttering and composing his poem, and we are reminded that spirit means both soul and breath, and that the poet invoking his muse calls upon a breath greater than his own to inspirit him. Death, then, is here a muse, but this was previously only partly the case:

> I have been *half* in love with easeful Death

But:

> Now more than ever seems it rich to die,
>   To cease upon the midnight with no pain

"Rich" and "cease" are marvelously precise words. Now, in the shared communion of the darkness out of which the nightingale's song emerges, it seems rich to die, and he is *more than half* in love with easeful Death. For he has reached the height of living experience, and any descent out of this state into the poverty of ordinary consciousness seems a death-in-life, a pain to be avoided, in contrast to the life-in-death "with no pain" to be maintained were he "to cease upon the midnight." "To cease," suddenly not to be, and thus to cross over into non-being attended by the "requiem," the high mass of the nightingale's song. For the nightingale itself is pouring forth its soul abroad in an ecstasy that transcends the division between life and death; the bird lives, but its breath-soul is taken into the air as it gives itself freely in the extension of its ecstasy.

Two notes deliberately jar within this passion: "and I have ears in vain—" and "become a sod." At the very moment of Keats's most exultant self-surrender to the bird's song, he yet intimates his own mortality, his separateness from the immortality of the song:

> Thou wast not born for death, immortal Bird!
>   No hungry generations tread thee down;

The voice I hear this passing night was heard
  In ancient days by emperor and clown:
Perhaps the self-same song that found a path
  Through the sad heart of Ruth, when, sick for home,
    She stood in tears amid the alien corn;
      The same that oft-times hath
Charm'd magic casements, opening on the foam
  Of perilous seas, in faery lands forlorn.

The sadness of this stanza is double, for there is the explicit burden of Keats as he explores his separateness from the bird's song, and the implicit lament in the stanza's coming to rest upon the fateful word "forlorn," the repetition of which serves to shatter the inner world of the nightingale's song. The pathos of the reference to Ruth becomes tragic in its implied transference to the poet, through whose heart the self-same song now finds its path to indicate *his* coming alienation, not from home, but from the song itself. The closing lines of the stanza, with their hint of the Spenserian world, to Keats the universe of poetry itself, are a final presage of the loss that is to come. The "faery lands" are forlorn, not that the poet has forsaken them, but that, like the bird's song, they have abandoned him:

Forlorn! the very word is like a bell
  To toll me back from thee to my sole self!
Adieu! the fancy cannot cheat so well
  As she is fam'd to do, deceiving elf.
Adieu! adieu! thy plaintive anthem fades
  Past the near meadows, over the still stream,
    Up the hill-side; and now 'tis buried deep
      In the next valley-glades:
Was it a vision, or a waking dream?
  Fled is that music:—Do I wake or sleep?

The double tolling of "forlorn" converts the nightingale's song into a "plaintive anthem," a requiem for the shattered communion between poet and song, as it rings the poet back to the isolation of his sole self. The movement of imagination becomes the deception of an elf, like the Belle Dame, Keats's triple mistress, Poetry, Consumption, and Death. The song fades with the unseen flight of the bird, until it is "buried deep." There remains only the resolution of the nature of the poetic trance—fully manifest, as in a vision, or merely the latent content of a waking dream? The answer is uncertain, for "fled is that music." At the close, Keats is left pondering the contraries: is the act and state of creation a heightening or merely an evasion of the state of experience? Once back in experience, the honest answer is only in the continued question, both as to fact and to will: "Do I wake or sleep?"

The difficulties of the **Ode on Melancholy** are infrequently realized because the poem is not often closely read. Yet even a superficial reading involves us in Keats's deliberately unresolved contraries. The admonition of the first stanza is against false melancholy, courted for the sake of the supposed oblivion it brings. But oblivion is not to be hired; for Keats true melancholy involves a sudden increase in consciousness, not a gradual evasion of its claims.

Keats canceled the initial opening stanza of this ode presumably because he saw that the poem's harmony was threatened if fully half of it were concerned with the useless quest after "the Melancholy." His sense of proportion did not fail him in this, and yet something went out of the poem with the exclusion of that stanza:

Though you should build a bark of dead men's bones,
  And rear a phantom gibbet for a mast,
Stitch shrouds together for a sail, with groans
  To fill it out, blood-stained and aghast;

Although your rudder be a dragon's tail
  Long sever'd, yet still hard with agony,
    Your cordage large uprootings from the skull
Of bald Medusa, certes you would fail
  To find the Melancholy—whether she
  Dreameth in any isle of Lethe dull.

The "whether" in the ninth line may be read as "even if." This remarkable and grisly stanza is more than the reverse of an invitation to the voyage. Its irony is palpable; its humor is in the enormous labor of Gothicizing despair which is necessarily in vain, for the mythic beast, Melancholy, cannot thus be confronted. The tone of the stanza changes with the dash in line 9; with it the voice speaking the poem ceases to be ironical. With the next stanza, the first of the received text, the voice is passionate, though its message is the same. By excluding the original first stanza, Keats lost a grim humor that finds only a thin echo at the poem's close. That humor, in juxtaposition to the poem's intensities, would have been parallel to successful clowning in a tragedy.

As the poem stands, the idle quest after the Melancholy is yet inviting:

No, no, go not to Lethe, neither twist
  Wolf's-bane, tight-rooted, for its poisonous wine;
Nor suffer thy pale forehead to be kiss'd
  By nightshade, ruby grape of Proserpine;
Make not your rosary of yew-berries,
  Nor let the beetle, nor the death-moth be
    Your mournful Psyche, nor the downy owl
A partner in your sorrow's mysteries;
  For shade to shade will come too drowsily,
  And drown the wakeful anguish of the soul.

What is most important here is "*too* drowsily" and "*wakeful* anguish." The truest parallel is in the first stanza of the **Ode to a Nightingale**. There the drowsiness is not excessive; it numbs, but the soul's anguish remains wakeful. The properties of questing after the Melancholy are there also; hemlock, a dull opiate, Lethe, but only in the form of "as though." The melancholy is genuine there, as it is here. It is as though Keats had quested after the epiphanies of these poems, but he has not. The negative grace of the state of being these odes embody falls suddenly, comes with the sharp immediacy of a blow. "My heart aches"; the three heavily accented syllables begin the poem by battering three times at the poet's and our consciousness. "But when the melancholy fit shall fall / Sudden from heaven . . ." is the equivalent in this ode. But when it falls without one's having provoked it, "Then glut thy sorrow"; one need show no restraint in feeding it further. On what? The melancholy fit has fallen as the rains of April fall, to "foster the droop-headed flowers," to cover the hills with green. The shock is that this green fostering, for all its beauty, *is* like the fall of melancholy, for April's green is here called "an April shroud." The enduring color of fresh life is only a grave color, and so your sorrow can also be glutted on the loveliness of such supposedly non-sorrowful emblems as a morning rose, a shore rainbow, or the wealth of globed peonies. To complete the complexity, Keats offers as food for sorrow the *wealth* of one's beloved's "rich anger."

The force of this second stanza is that it is inexplicable, unresolved, until it is suddenly clarified by the first line of the final stanza:

She dwells with Beauty—Beauty that must die

The line relies on its immediate expository force after the puzzle of the preceding stanza; it requires a long pause after reading. The emphasis needs to be put upon "*must* die"; the anger of the mistress, which so delights the sadism-hunting scholar, is significant only in its richness, not in any sexual implication. It is rich because it offers a possibility of feeding deeply upon an animated beauty that is doomed to lose all motion, all force. Animation, as in its root meaning, here reveals the living soul in full activity, with the special poignance that in this poem is definitive of true melancholy, consciousness of mutability and death. Like Wallace Stevens in *Sunday Morning, Esthétique du Mal* (especially Section XV, the poem's conclusion), and *The Rock,* Keats is insisting on the mingled heroic ethic and humanist aesthetic that the natural is beautiful and apocalyptic precisely because it is physical and ephemeral. Keats's contrast is in his tense insistence that *something* in nature *must* prevail, and his final despair that nothing can, even as the parallel and contrast to Stevens is Yeats, in his insistence (however ironic) that Byzantine realities are superior to mere natural beauties. Spenser in the *Mutabilitie* Cantos and Milton throughout his work resolve these conflicts by a cosmic dialectic. It remained for Blake and Wordsworth, in their very different ways, to humanize these resolutions. With younger and modern Romantics it has been too late in the day to offer full measure in these conflicts; bitterness, however visionary, necessarily keeps breaking in.

The magnificence of the ***Ode on Melancholy***'s final stanza is in its exactness of diction as it defines the harmony of continued apprehension of its unresolved contraries. Only Beauty that *must* die is beauty; Joy cannot be present without simultaneously bidding adieu: and *aching* Pleasure (the adjective triumphantly embodies a pair of contraries) is immanent only by turning to poison for us, even as we sip its real (not supposed) honey. For, like the rest of Keats's odes, this poem is tragic, it reaches beyond the disillusionments of a state of experience into the farther innocence of a poet's paradise, as in the shrine of Moneta in the ***Fall of Hyperion,*** to which this is surely a reference (the "has" helps establish it):

> Ay, in the very temple of delight
> Veil'd Melancholy has her sovran shrine

And, as in the ***Fall of Hyperion,*** this truth is seen by none except those who earn the poet's melancholy, which is not to be usurped. The *strenuous* tongue does not simply sip the grape's juice; it *bursts* the grape of Joy, with the inevitable double consequence of tasting might and the sadness of might, Moneta's or the Melancholy's double aspect, the Goddess as Muse and as Destroyer:

> And be among her cloudy trophies hung.
>
> (pp. 397-406)

> *Harold Bloom, "Introduction" and "John Keats,"*
> *in his* The Visionary Company: A Reading of English
> Romantic Poetry, *1961. Reprint by Faber and Faber,*
> *1962, pp. xiii-xv, 354-427.* *

GEOFFREY H. HARTMAN   (essay date 1973)

[In the following excerpt, Hartman focuses on Keats's ode "To Autumn" and his more lengthy Fall of Hyperion. *This essay was originally published in 1973 in* Literary Theory and Structure: Essays in Honor of William K. Wimsatt.*]*

"Most English great poems have little or nothing to say." Few do that nothing so perfectly, one is tempted to add, as Keats's

"To Autumn." Our difficulty as interpreters is related to the way consciousness almost disappears into the poem: the mind, for once, is not what is left (a kind of sublime litter) after the show is over. "To Autumn" seems to absorb rather than extrovert that questing imagination whose breeding fancies, feverish overidentifications, and ambitious projects motivate the other odes. (p. 124)

In what follows I suggest, daringly, that "To Autumn" has something to say: that it is an ideological poem whose very form expresses a national idea and a new stage in consciousness, or what Keats himself once called the "gregarious advance" and "grand march of intellect." (pp. 124-25)

My argument runs that "To Autumn," an ode that is hardly an ode, is best defined as an English or Hesperian model which overcomes not only the traditional type of sublime poem but the "Eastern" or epiphanic consciousness essential to it. The traditional type was transmitted by both Greek and Hebrew religious poetry, and throughout the late Renaissance and eighteenth century, by debased versions of the Pindaric or cult hymn. Only one thing about epiphanic structure need be said now: it evokes the presence of a god, or vacillates sharply between imagined presence and absence. Its rhetoric is therefore a crisis-rhetoric, with priest or votary, vastation or rapture, precarious nearness or hieratic distance ("Ah Fear! Ah frantic Fear! I see, I see thee near!"). As these verses by William Collins suggest, epiphanic structure proceeds by dramatic turns of mood and its language is ejaculative (Lo, Behold, O come, O see). Keats's "Hesperianism" triumphs, in "To Autumn," over this archaic style with its ingrained, superstitious attitude toward power—power seen as external and epochal. The new sublimity domesticates with the heart; the poet's imagination is neither imp nor incubus. Though recognizably sublime, "To Autumn" is a poem of *our* climate.

Climate is important. It ripens wits as well as fruits, as Milton said in another context. The higher temperature and higher style of the other odes are purged away: we have entered a temperate zone. What is grown here, this "produce of the air," is like its ambience: Hesperian art rather than oriental ecstasy or unnatural flight of the imagination. Autumn is clearly a mood as well as a season, and Stevens would have talked about a weather of the mind. Yet "mood" and "weather" have an aura of changeableness, even of volatility, while the Autumn ode expresses something firmer: not, as so often in Stevens or in the "Beulah" moments of other poets, a note among notes but, as in Spenser, a vast cloud-region or capability. The very shape of the poem—firm and regular without fading edges but also no overdefined contours—suggests a slowly expanding constellation that moves as a whole, if it moves at all.

Its motion is, in fact, part of the magic. Time lapses so gently here; we pass from the fullness of the maturing harvest to the stubble plains without experiencing a cutting edge. If time comes to a point in "To Autumn" it is only at the end of the poem, which verges (more poignant than pointed) on a last "gathering." The scythe of time, the sense of mortality, the cutting of life into distinct, epochal phases is not felt. We do not even stumble into revelation, however softly—there is no moment which divides before and after as in the "**Ode to Psyche**" with its supersoft epiphany, its Spenserian and bowery moment which makes the poet Psyche's devotee despite her "shadowy thought" nature. The Autumn ode is nevertheless a *poesis,* a shaped segment of life coterminous with that templar "region of the mind" which the other poems seek, though they may honor more insistently the dichotomy of inside and out, fane and profane. Poetry, to change "the whole habit of the mind," changes also our view of the mind's habitat. To say that **"To Autumnn"** is ideological and that its pressure of form is "English" has to do with that also. (pp. 126-28)

In the odes of Keats there is a strong, clearly marked moment of disenchantment, or of illusion followed by disillusion. Fancy, that "Queen of shadows" (Charlotte Smith), becomes a "deceiving elf"—and although the deception remains stylized, and its shock releases pathos rather than starker sentiments, it is as pointed as the traditional turn of the Great Ode. (Compare the turn, for example, from one mode of music to another in Dryden's *Alexander's Feast* or the anastrophe "He is not dead, he lives" in pastoral elegy.) The transition leading from stanzas 7 to 8 in the Nightingale ode is such a turn, which results in calling imagination a "deceiving elf." An imaginative fancy that has sustained itself despite colder thoughts is farewelled.

There is, exceptionally, no such turn in **"To Autumn."** The poem starts on enchanted ground and never leaves it. This special quality becomes even clearer when we recall that **"La Belle Dame sans Merci,"** with its harvest background and soft ritual progression, ends in desolation of spirit on the cold hillside. But because the final turn of the Nightingale ode, though clear as a bell, is not gross in its effect, not productive of coital sadness, a comparison with Autumn's finale is still possible. In **"To Autumn"** birds are preparing to fly to a warmer clime, a "visionary south," though we do not see them leave or the cold interrupt. In **"To a Nightingale"** the poet is allowed a call—adieu, adieu—which is birdlike still and colors the darker "forlorn," while his complete awakening is delayed ("Do I wake or sleep?") and verbal prolongations are felt. There is no complete disenchantment even here.

"To Autumn," moreover, can be said to have something approaching a strophic turn as we enter the last stanza. With "Where are the songs of Spring? Aye, where are they?" a plaintive anthem sounds. It is a case, nevertheless, where a premise is anticipated and absorbed. The premise is that of transience, or the feel of winter, and the rest of the stanza approaches that cold threshold. The premise is absorbed because its reference is back to Spring instead of forward to Winter; by shifting from eye to ear, to the music-theme, Keats enriches Autumn with Spring. We remain within a magical circle where things repeat each other in a finer tone, as Autumn turns into a second Spring: "While barred clouds *bloom* the soft-dying day." The music now heard is no dirge of the year but a mingling of lullaby and aubade. For the swallows a second summer is at hand (aubade). For us—if we cannot follow them any more than the elusive nightingale—what comes next is not winter but night (lullaby). We go gently off, in either case, on extended wings.

Thus **"To Autumn,"** like Stevens's "Sunday Morning," becomes oddly an Ode to Evening. The full meaning of this will appear. But in terms of formal analysis we can say that the poem has no epiphany or decisive turn or any absence/presence dialectic. It has, instead, a *westerly drift* like the sun. Each stanza, at the same time, is so equal in its poetical weight, so loaded with its own harvest, that westering is less a natural than a poetic state—it is a mood matured by the poem itself. **"To Autumn,"** in fact, does not explicitly evolve from sunrise to sunset but rather from a rich to a clarified dark. Closely read it starts and ends in twilight. "Season of mists and mellow fruitfulness"—though the mists are of the morning, the line links fertility and semidarkness in a way that might be a syntactical accident were it not for the more highly developed

instance of "I cannot see what flowers are at my feet . . . ," that famous stanza from the Nightingale ode where darkened senses also produce a surmise of fruitfulness. The Autumn ode's twilight is something inherent, a condition not simply of growth but of imaginative growth. Westering here is a spiritual movement, one that tempers visionariness into surmise and the lust for epiphany into finer-toned repetitions. We do not find ourselves in a temple but rather in Tempe "twixt sleepe and wake." We can observe the ode unfolding as a self-renewing surmise of fruitfulness: as waking dream or "widening speculation" rather than nature-poem and secularized hymn. (pp. 128-29)

The opening stanza is so strongly descriptive, so loaded with told riches, that there seems to be no space for surmise. A desire to fill every rift with Autumn's gold produces as rich a banquet as Porphyro's heap of delicates in **"The Eve of St. Agnes."** Thesaurus stanzas of this kind are self-delighting in Keats; but they also have a deeper reason. Porphyro knows that Madeline will find reality poorer than her dream and enhances his value by serving himself up this way. The sumptuous ploy is to help him melt into his lady's waking thought. So Autumn's banquet, perhaps, intends to hold the awakening consciousness and allow the dream to linger. Not only the bees are deceived; the dream "Warm days will never cease" is not in them alone; it is already in Autumn, in her "conspiring." On this phrase all the rich, descriptive details depend; they are infinitives not indicatives, so that we remain in the field of mind. "Conspiring how to load and bless . . . To bend with apples . . . fill all fruit . . . To swell the gourd." As we move through Autumn's thought to the ripening of that thought, we cease to feel her as an external agent.

Thus, the descriptive fullness of the first stanza turns out to be thought-full as well: its pastoral furniture is a golden surmise, imagination in her most deliberate mood. By moving the point of view inward, Keats makes these riches mental riches, imaginative projects. He does not, at the same time, push the mental horizon to infinity: the mood remains infinitive, looking onto "something evermore about to be."

Once we see that what is being satisfied is empathy or in-feeling, and that to satisfy it Keats (like Autumn) fills outside with more and more inside, the structure of the poem as a progressive surmise becomes clear. In-feeling, in Keats, is always on the point of overidentifying; and even here it demands more than the first stanza's dream of truth. However glowing a prospect Autumn paints, it must still, as it were, come alive. This happens in the second stanza where the drowsy ponderer meets us in person. Now we are in the landscape itself; the harvest is now. The figure of Autumn amid her store is a moving picture, or the dream personified. Yet the two stanzas are perfectly continuous; in-feeling is still being expressed as the filling-up of a space—a figure like Autumn's was needed to plump the poem. Though we approach epiphanic personification in the figure of Autumn, the casualness of "sometimes" "sometimes," together with the easy mood of the opening question, gives us a sense of "widening speculation" and prevents a more than cornucopial view of the goddess.

But the dream is almost shattered at the end of the stanza. The word "oozings" extends itself phonically into "hours by hours," a chime that leads to the idea of transience in "Where are the songs of Spring?" Though immediately reabsorbed, this muted ubi sunt introduces the theme of mutability. Oozings—hours —ubi sunt. . . . A single word, or its echoes, might have disenchanted Keats like the turn on "forlorn" in the Nightingale ode. Disenchantment, however, does not occur: there is no reverse epiphany as in **"La Belle Dame sans Merci,"** no waking into emptiness.

We have reached, nevertheless, the airiest of the stanzas. Does a chill wind not brush us, an airiness close to emptiness? Do we not anticipate the "cold hill's side"? Even if the mood of surmise is sustained, it might well be a surmise of death rather than fruitfulness.

Here, at the consummate point of Keats's art, in-feeling achieves its subtlest act. Keats conspires with autumn to fill even the air. Air becomes a granary of sounds, a continuation of the harvest, or *Spätlese*. In this last and softest stanza, the ear of the ear is ripened.

More than a tour de force or finely sustained idea is involved. For at the end of other odes we find an explicit *cry*, which is part of their elegiac envoi. Here that cry is uttered, as it were, by the air itself, and can only be heard by an ear that knows how to glean such sounds. . . . In lyric poetry the cry is a sign of subjective feelings breaking through and in the cult-hymn of being possessed by divine power. It signifies in both a transcendence absent from this "final finding of the air." Lyricism, in **"To Autumn,"** frees itself for once of elegy and ecstasy: it is neither a frozen moment of passion nor the inscription that prolongs it.

The Grecian urn's "Beauty is Truth, Truth Beauty" remains an extroverted, lapidary cry. However appropriate its philosophy, its form is barely snatched from a defeat of the imagination. **"To Autumn"** has no defeat in it. It is the most negative capable of all of Keats's great poems. Even its so-called death-stanza expresses no rush toward death, no clasping of darkness as a bride, or quasi-oriental ecstasy. Its word-consciousness, its mind's weather—all remains Hesperian. As its verses move toward an image of southerly flight (the poem's nearest analogue to transcendence), patterns emerge that delay the poet's "transport to summer." Perception dwells on the border and refuses to overdefine. So "fullgrown lambs" rather than "sheep." Add such verbal ponderings or reversing repetitions as "borne aloft . . . hilly bourn," a casual chiastic construction, playing on a mix of semantic and phonetic properties. Or the noun-adjective phrase "treble soft" which becomes an adjective-noun phrase when "treble" is resolved into the northern "triple." And consider the northernisms. The proportion of northern words increases perceptibly as if to pull the poem back from its southerly orientation. There is hardly a romance language phrase: sound-shapes like sallows, swallows, borne, bourn, crickets, croft, predominate. And, finally, the poise of the stanza's ending, on the verge of flight like joy always bidding adieu. (pp. 131-33)

Keats's respect for the sublime poem does not have to be argued. There is his irritation with the "egotistical sublime" of Wordsworth, his admiration for Milton who broke through "the clouds which envelope so deliciously the Elysian field of verse, and committed himself to the Extreme," his anguished attempt to write the *Hyperion*. . . . I must now make clear what kind of problem, formal and spiritual, the sublime poem was.

A first difficulty centers on the relation of romance to sublime or epic. The romance mode, for Keats, is now presublime (and so to be "broken through") and now postsublime. Where, as in the first *Hyperion*, Keats wishes to sublimate the sublime he turns with relief to the "golden theme" of Apollo after the Saturnine theme of the first two books. In the *Fall of Hyperion*, however, romance is an Elysium or Pleasure-garden to be transcended. While in **"La Belle Dame sans Merci"** romance becomes sheer oxymoron, a "golden tongued" nightmare.

It is best to find a view beyond this special dialectic of romance and epic in Keats, all the more so as that is complicated by the dream-truth, or vision-reality split. No formal analysis will disentangle these rich contraries. It can only reduce them to the difference suggested in the *Fall of Hyperion* between "an immortal's sphered words" and the mother-tongue. This is the dichotomy on which Keats's epic voyage foundered: the opposition between Miltonic art-diction and the vernacular. "Life to him [Milton] would be death to me." "English must be kept up." Yet such a distinction is no more satisfying than one in terms of genre. Vernacular romance is perhaps more feasible than vernacular epic—but we get as mixed up as Keats himself when we define each genre in family terms and put romance under mother, epic under father. (pp. 134-35)

A solution is to consider both romance and epic—or the high-visionary style in general—as belonging to an older, "epiphanic" structuring of consciousness. Against it can be put a nonepiphanic structuring; and if the older type is primarily associated with the East, the modern would be with the West or, at its broadest, Hesperia. It is possible to treat this distinction formally as one between two types of structuring rather than two types of consciousness. Eventually, however, Keats's charge of superstition or obsolescence against the earlier mode will move us into ideology and beyond formalism. A man who says, like Keats, that life to Milton is death to him is concerned with more than formal options.

Epiphanic structure implies, first of all, the possibility of categorical shifts: of crossing into . . . and even, I suppose, out of ordinary human consciousness into something else. Apotheosis (as at the end of *Hyperion*), metamorphosis, and transformation scenes are type instances of such a crossing. It is accompanied by a doctrine of states, a philosophy of transcendence, and a formulary for the "translation" of states. Epiphanic structure can bear as much sophistication as an author is capable of. Take the sequence, based on *Paradise Lost*, Book VIII, which haunted Keats: "The Imagination may be compared to Adam's Dream: He awoke and found it truth." This refers chiefly to Adam seeing Eve first in dream and, upon waking, in the flesh. Keats will often use it ironically rather than not use it at all. So in the **"Eve of St. Agnes"** Madeline wakes into Imagination's truth and finds it—how pale, how diminished! She melts the reality—Porphyro—back into her dream in a moment of, presumably, sexual union.

A more complex instance is the dark epiphany in **"La Belle Dame sans Merci"** where the enchanted knight wakes, as it were, into the arms of the wrong dream and cannot find his way back to the right one. Whereas, in Milton, one cunning enjambment expresses the intensity of the quest springing from imaginative loss,

> *She [Eve] disappear'd, and left me dark, I wak'd*
> *To find her*

a moment Keats repeats faintly in the Autumn ode,

> *Sometimes whoever seeks abroad may find*
> *Thee*

in **"La Belle Dame"** there is nothing—no natural food—can satisfy the knight. He starves for his drug, like Keats so often for the heightened consciousness of epiphanic style.

In *Paradise Lost,* Adam's dream prepares him for the truth he is to meet. Truth is conceived of as a fuller, perhaps more difficult, dream; and God seeks to strengthen Adam's visionary powers by engaging him in these dream-corridors. Instead of a single dramatic or traumatic change there is to be a gradual tempering of the mind. This modification of epiphanic structure may have inspired a favorite speculation of Keats, that happiness on earth would be enjoyed hereafter "repeated in a finer tone and so repeated." Miltonic tenderness, by allowing Adam's consciousness to develop, by giving it time for growth, lightens the all-or-nothing (sometimes, all-and-nothing) character of epiphanic vision. Though the end remains transport and deification, the means are based, at least in part, on a respect for natural process. (pp. 135-37)

Can we see the gods die in **"To Autumn,"** the epiphanic forms dissolve, as it were, before our eyes? Autumn is, by tradition, the right season for this dissolution, or dis-illusion.

> *Let Phoebus lie in umber harvest*

Stevens writes in "Notes toward a Supreme Fiction,"

> *Let Phoebus slumber and die in autumn umber*
> *Phoebus is dead, ephebe.*

But, in tradition also, a new god treads on the heels of the old, and loss figures forth a stronger presence. In Hesperian poetry, from Collins to Keats to Stevens, this entire absence/presence vacillation does no more than manure the ground of the poem, its "sensible ecstasy."

Consider the invocation "Season of mists and mellow fruitfulness." The odic O is hardly felt though the verses immediately fill one's mouth with rich labials extended in a kind of chiastic middle between "Season" and "sun." Nothing remains of the cultic distance between votary and personified power: we have instead two such powers, autumn and sun, whose closeness is emphasized, while the moment of hailing or petitioning is replaced by a presumptive question ("Who hath not seen thee") suggesting availability rather than remoteness. The most interesting dissolve, however, comes with the grammatical shift, in the opening line, from mythic-genealogical to descriptive-partitive "of," which effectively diffuses autumn into its attributes. Compare "Season of mists and mellow fruitfulness" with the following apostrophes:

> *Thou foster-child of silence and slow time.*

Here the poet uses clearly and finely a formula which alludes to the high descent of the apostrophized object. In our next example

> *Nymph of the downward smile, and side-long glance*

the grammatical form is analogous, but the "of" has moved from genealogical toward partitive. The nymph is eminently characterized by these two attributes: they *are* her in this statuesque moment. The opening of **"To the Nile"**:

> *Son of the old moon-mountains African*
> *Stream of the pyramid and crocodile*

actually brings mythic-genealogical and partitive-descriptive together. Against this background we see how beautifully dissolved into the ground of description is the mythical formula of **"To Autumn"**'s first line.

We do, of course, by what appears to be a regressive technique, meet Autumn personified in the second stanza. If the poem approaches a noon-point of stasis—of arrest or centered revelation—it is here. The emergence of myth serves, however, to ripen the pictorial quality of the poem rather than to evoke astonishment. The emphasis is on self-forgetful relaxation (at most on "forget thyself to marble") not on saturnine fixation. No more than in **"To Evening"** is nature epiphanic: Keats's autumn is not a specter but a spirit, one who steals over the landscape, or "amid her store" swellingly imbues it. The poet's mind is not rapt or astonished and so forced back on itself by a sublime apparition.

It is essential, in fact, to note what happens to mind. In the cult hymn the invocation merges with, or is followed by, the god's *comos:* an enumeration of his acts and attributes. But Keats's first stanza becomes simply the filling up of a form, a golden chain of infinitives hovering between prospect and fulfillment, until every syntactical space is loaded and the poet's mind, like the bees', loses itself in the richness. The stanza, in fact, though full, and with its eleven lines, more than full, is not a grammatical whole but a drunk sentence. The poet's mind, one is tempted to say, has entered the imagined picture so thoroughly that when the apostrophe proper is sprung at the opening of stanza 2, and the grammatical looseness corrected, it simultaneously opens a new speculative movement. And when the generative figure of Autumn appears in the second stanza, it is self-harvesting like the poet's own thoughts. The last stanza, then, leaves us in a "luxury of twilight" rather than dropping us into a void where "no birds sing."

The demise of epiphanic forms in **"To Autumn"** raises a last question: is not the sequential movement of the whole poem inspired by a progressive idea with Enlightenment roots? There seems to be, on the level of sensation, something that parallels the first **Hyperion**'s progress from heavier to lighter, from Hyperion to Apollo, and from fixed burdens to a softer oppression. Several key phrases in Keats's letters suggest an "enlightenment" of this kind. The poet talks of "widening speculation," of "the regular stepping of Imagination toward a Truth," and of easing the "Burden of the Mystery." Magical moments like the fourth stanza of **"Ode on a Grecian Urn"**

> *Who are these coming to the sacrifice?*
> *To what green altar, O mysterious priest*

are surely related to this lightening. Mystery survives, but in a purged, airy, speculative form. The "overwrought" questions of the ode's beginning, which sought to penetrate or fix a symbol-essence, are purified into surmise and evoke a scene of "wide quietness" rather than bacchic enthusiasm.

There is a progress then; but is it toward a truth? We know what the conclusion to the Grecian Urn ode suggests. "Beauty is Truth, Truth Beauty" is a chiastic phrase, as self-rounding as the urn. No ultimate turn or final step toward a truth occurs. Though there are turns in the poem, they are more musical than epiphanic, and the very notion of "the turn" merges with that of the art-object: Keats turns the urn in his imagination until the urn is its turnings. The poet's speculation is circular.

Keats's rondure, his counterprogression, subverts without rejecting the received idea of "enlightenment." Poetry clearly has its own progress, its own lights. Formalistic or art-centered terms have, therefore, a certain propriety. But they cannot suffice for Keats any more than for Wordsworth, who also seeks to ease the "burthen of the mystery" ("Tintern Abbey" . . .). Consider the profound difference between these poets, who both believe in a dispersion of older—poetical or religious—superstitions. Such qualities as decorum, impersonality, symbolic adequacy are a function mainly of the concenteredness of **"To Autumn"**: the poem turns around one image like a ''leaf-fring'd legend.'' Though Wordsworth's poems may also have a center of this kind (Lucy's death, a peculiar landscape, a remembered scene), it rarely appears as picturesque symbol or image. Wordsworth's kernels are mysteries: charged spiritual places which confront and confuse a mental traveler who circles their enchanted ground—or who, like a policeman, tries to cordon off the disturbance. This too is an important ''enlightenment'' form, delimiting a romance apparition or sublime feelings—yet how different from Keats! In Wordsworth the spirit must find its own containment, and never quite finds it; those ''spots of time'' erupt from their hiding-places like the Hebraic God; the structure of his poems expresses various attempts at containment which accrete with difficulty into a personal history (''Tintern Abbey'') or an eschatological and cultural one (''Hart-Leap Well''). But Keats's experience is limited from the outset by Greek or picturesque example. What perplexes his imagination is a mysterious picture rather than a mystery.

Keats's formal a priori takes us back to Greece and where, according to Hegel, modern consciousness began. Formal beauty mediates ''between the loss of individuality . . . as in Asia, where spiritual and divine are totally subsumed under a natural form, and infinite subjectivity.'' Greek character is ''individuality conditioned by beauty'' and in its respect for divine images modern and free, rather than Asiatic and superstitious. ''He [the human being] is the womb that conceived them, he the breast that suckled them, he the spiritual to which their grandeur and purity is owing. Thus he feels himself calm in contemplating them, and not only free in himself, but possessing the consciousness of his freedom.''

That Hegel's description can fit Keats makes one cautious about the whole enterprise of dividing consciousness into historically localized phases. All the more so as Hölderlin has his own myth of the Hesperian character, which is said to begin when Homer moderates oriental pathos or ''fire from heaven.'' I make no claim for the historical exactness of either Hegel or Hölderlin. Historical speculation and criticism stand, as Professor Wimsatt has observed, in a highly problematic relationship.

Yet there is something like ''Hesperian'' freedom in **"To Autumn,"** a poem which becomes—in Hegel's words—the womb for the rebirth of an astral or divine image. Such a divine image is certainly there; we should not exaggerate the absence of poetical superstition in Keats. Though his central figure is picturesque its star quality glimmers through.

Much has been written on Autumn's affinities to Demeter or other harvest deities. The divinity, however, that haunts Keats early and late is Apollo: sun-god, god of song, and ''foreseeing god.'' The difference between Hyperion and Apollo is, in good part, that the former is now doomed to live under ''the burden of the mystery.'' Hyperion cannot dawn any more; he remains darkling. But Apollo in **Hyperion,** even though that poem breaks off and leaves the young god's metamorphosis incomplete—even though he too must shoulder the mystery—should break forth like the sun to ''shape his actions'' like ''a fore-seeing god.'' In the Autumn ode the major theme of clairvoyance—at once foreseeing and deep-seeing (deep into the heart or maw of life)—is tempered. Yet it is far from absent.

For Autumn's ''conspiring'' function is comparable to that of the guardian genius. . . . An idea of poetic or personal destiny enters, in however veiled a form. The poet who writes this ode stands under the pressure of an omen. As summer passes into autumn (season of the year or human season), his dreaming deepens into foresight:

> When I have fears that I may cease to be
> Before my pen has glean'd my teeming brain,
> Before high-piled books, in charact'ry,
> Hold like rich garners the full-ripen'd grain . . .

> Herr: es ist Zeit. Der Sommer war sehr gross

> [Lord, it is time. The summer was very great.]

In fear of early death, and sensing riches his pen might never glean, Keats evokes a figure of genial harvests. Three times he renews his surmise of fruitfulness, three times he grasps the shadow without self-defeating empathy. Even fruitfulness is not a burden in **"To Autumn."** This, at last, is true impersonality. (pp. 141-46)

> Geoffrey H. Hartman, ''Poem and Ideology: A Study of Keats's 'To Autumn','' in his The Fate of Reading and Other Essays, *University of Chicago Press,* 1975, pp. 124-46.

STUART M. SPERRY   (essay date 1973)

[*In his essay on* Lamia, *Sperry discusses the poem's satirical and self-mocking tone and interprets the Hermes episode as a possible self-parody of Keats's philosophy of the creative process.*]

The apparent playfulness of [**Lamia**'s] opening only lends greater edge to a bitterness verging at times on sarcasm, a disconcerting quality of self-mockery. We have the sense of a poet pondering a major dilemma not with the end of resolving it but rather delighting perversely in its difficulties and embarrassments. Virtually from its beginning the poem is permeated by a sense of comic fatality—the sharp, unpleasant ring of old Apollonius's undeluded laughter: '' 'twas just as he foresaw.'' . . . In a number of respects **Lamia** is a work written by a poet against his better self. (p. 292)

Time and reflection had shown Keats the need, above all, for greater detachment and control—the virtues of a new and necessary defensiveness. In the past he had approached the end of major poems overly involved in the process of composition only to find himself unsure of his final objectives, conscious of new possibilities and complications. Now, however, it was possible to anticipate such a state of affairs. Even better, one could convert the familiar predicament to positive advantage by accepting it frankly from the outset, by adopting the dilemma as the nucleus for a drama of divided impulses and sympathies whose very point would lie in its insolubility. Through a sharpening of aim and focus, through a superior degree of self-consciousness, it was possible to turn irony back upon itself. (pp. 292-93)

Toward this end, as well as to avoid past confusions, the subject matter and its range of implication were kept tightly in hand from the outset. The story of Lycius and Lamia in Burton's *Anatomy of Melancholy,* a work he had read with an unhealthy fascination, as he himself realized, was from the first strikingly relevant to his own predicament, and its ending—its mixture of destruction and inconclusiveness—was ideally suited to the kind of satirical effect he could foresee. The very vulnerability and lack of depth of Burton's characters constituted a positive asset. His own talent had never been for strong characterization, and for what he wanted to achieve it was sufficient to play the weakness of one figure off against another. The way

to succeed with the poem was by remaining deliberately ambivalent and detached, refusing to take sides while encouraging
others (critics for example) to do so at their own cost. . . . It
would be, as he hoped, purely in dramatic terms the most
successful of the works he had composed.

Other advantages of such a plan were apparent. There was no
need, as there had been in the past, to struggle for an original
assimilation of a given legend, to force the work toward the
realization of some difficult and partly hidden significance. It
was possible to conceive of the project, even, like one of
Dryden's fables, as primarily a work of adaptation, and to
encourage this impression the appropriate passage from Burton
was printed directly after the poem in the 1820 volume. In line
with his broader aim, he was beginning more and more to
relish the control and detachment of Dryden's style and sensibility, a poet whose wit and urbanity, inseparable from a
subtlety of versification within the tight limits demanded by
the closed couplet, he had been intensively studying as a model.
Rather than plunging impulsively into a subject or a theme,
letting it shape itself, as it were, from the inside out, there
were real advantages in beginning with a deliberate irony of
stance and manner, in keeping on top of one's material simply
by staying outside it. (pp. 293-94)

The poem does not begin with the events described by Burton
but with the so-called Hermes episode, a piece of narrative
chiefly of Keats's own invention which, while it has alternately
perplexed critics and been dismissed by them as a mere curtain
raiser, is vital to our understanding of the whole drama. . . .
The very emblems that characterize [Lamia] are bewilderingly
varied and contradictory, from the coolness of her silver moons
and stars to the heat of her more passionate and dazzling colors,
from the gentleness and pathos of her complaint to the incongruous mixture of feminine seductiveness and serpent guile
with which she utters it. The range of implication that surrounds
her extends from the earthly to the visionary, from the sensual
to the spiritual, from the deceptive to the revelatory. It is not
until she breathes upon Hermes' eyes that the god, whatever
his own powers, can see his Nymph; yet she requires the touch
of his serpent rod in order to escape from the labyrinth of her
prison. Whereas she opens Hermes' eyes to a new range of
experience, she later casts her beguiling spell over Lycius.

The chief effect of the episode is to establish at the outset a
distinct perspective for viewing Lamia's ambivalence. For one
must not overlook the fact that, unlike Lycius, we see her first
before her metamorphosis, in her serpent form, and in part, at
least, through Hermes' eyes. Indeed the particular cynicism of
the episode, within the larger fatality of the poem, lies in the
fact that the god's success in using Lamia's power to fulfill
his own desire directly sets the stage through her release and
transformation for Lycius's subsequent disaster. For it is difficult to explain why Hermes succeeds while Lycius fails except
through the kind of priority he enjoys within the poem. Often
in the past critics have distinguished between the two purely
on the basis of the god's divinity, as if it were some isolated
phenomenon, as if Hermes' immortality were not, as the introduction to the poem testifies, only the most obvious manifestation of a more significant advantage. True the god is more
purposeful and aggressive than the relatively passive Lycius,
though Keats pokes gentle fun at the signs of his amatory
distress. Yet his chief advantage lies not only in the fact that
he sees Lamia first but that he sees her when the diverse values
she suggests are in a special sense undifferentiated. Her serpent
condition, that is to say, comprehends a potential power for

sensuous or spiritual enjoyment, for revelation or deception,
for truth or falsehood. Yet these qualities, as she embodies
them, are, whatever subtle overtones of antithesis may play
about her, not clearly separated or distinguishable. They subsist
together, however uneasily, as aspects of a larger potentiality;
they account for the striking mobility and fluctuation of her
serpent appearance. Hermes is never confused or deceived by
her, for he understands and accepts, if only instinctively, the
instability of her nature, the range of possibility that surrounds
her. . . . Hermes is concerned simply to attain the Nymph, and
if he wins her only in dreams, the point, for him at least, has
no significance:

> It was no dream; or say a dream it was,
> Real are the dreams of Gods, and smoothly pass
> Their pleasures in a long immortal dream. . . .

Clearly we are dealing in the case of Hermes with a realm of
awareness where our habitual distinctions between reality and
dream, consciousness and unconsciousness, truth and error,
are simply irrelevant, while the narrator's tone of affected
nonchalance contains more than a trace of bitterness. Hermes
draws on Lamia's power to substantiate his vision of sufficient
joy and truth while permitting her, by way of compensation,
the freedom to assert herself more ambitiously, to exercise her
power independently and, later, more dubiously on Lycius.

One cannot study the relationships between the actors in the
Hermes episode without becoming aware both of their psychological complexity and of their close connection with Keats's
larger concern with the nature of the poetic process—more
specially, with the changes that have come about in its effect
through time and the evolving character of human awareness.
Virtually every critic has agreed that later in the poem Lycius
comes to represent the poet as well as the lover. Moreover the
famous passage in which Keats juxtaposes the symbol of imaginative transformation, the "awful rainbow" of the past, against
its present dissolution at the killing touch of "cold philosophy"
. . . , provides certain authority for interpreting the anguish of
his situation—his divided allegiance to both Lamia and his
harsh old tutor, Apollonius—as a comment on the predicament
of the contemporary poet. . . . Indeed from the outset of the
poem it seems clear that the "rainbow-sided" Lamia, in all
her shifting lights and colors, her capacity for transformation,
her ability first to conceal and then reveal, represents a power
closely akin to the imagination. The drift of one set of implications of the episode seems unmistakable. As we have seen,
Hermes derives his primary advantage from his mythological
nature, from a state of awareness in which the divisions that
haunt the modern consciousness do not exist. Like the earliest
poets, the prototype of Homer or Ovid, he ventures upon the
imagination in its full range of potentiality, when the ambiv-
alences that characterize it for a later time are submerged or,
at most, present only latently. He may, to be sure, require its
intensifying energies but only to realize his own dream of
beauty and truth. In drawing on its power, however, he also
gives it a kind of necessary activation and, in performing his
own part of the bargain, grants Lamia an autonomous existence,
deceptively purged of her uglier but more material elements.
One might say the result of Hermes' conquest is to release into
the world the disembodied essence of romance, a power of
mere enchantment by which Lycius, the later, weaker, characteristically "Romantic" poet, is seduced and, partly through
the indecisiveness of his own nature, destroyed. There seems
to be a fatal principle of compensation at work. On one level
the drama of the episode depicts the transformation and atten-

uation of imaginative power from its first discovery to its modern degeneration to mere charm or spell. (pp. 295-99)

In *Lamia,* as (in a more diffuse way) in *Endymion,* the poetic and sexual themes, both broadly imaginative in their concern, are inseparable. One can, for example, interpret Hermes' serpent rod, the means by which Lamia gains her release, as the poet-magician's control over the powers of the unconscious without gainsaying those who may want to read it, more obviously, as a phallic symbol. Throughout the poem such different kinds of interpretation are complementary rather than exclusive. Nothing better illustrates this fact than part of the comment Keats penned into the margin of his copy of Burton's *Anatomy* in disgust at the worldly mingling of "goatish winnyish lustful love with the abstract adoration of the deity." "Has Plato separated these loves?" he wrote. "Ha! I see how they endeavor to divide—but there appears to be a horrid relationship." . . . [The annotation] takes us to the heart of . . . [an] imaginative conflict of the poem and the root of Lamia's ambivalence, a quality that the self-confident Hermes is able to ignore or take for granted but that proves fatal to the poet-scholar Lycius, caught between "phantasy" and "reason" in a "twilight of Platonic shades." . . . Throughout the poem the glance of dazzled wonder and the voyeur's piercing stare are increasingly at odds. Nevertheless the dawning rapture of the lovers' union, the moment when the god first turns upon the "printless verdure" to discover the Nymph before him, perpetuates through its intermingling of chastity and voluptuousness what had for long been a major ideal of Keats's art. . . . That he now chose to approach such ideals through the light intrigues of a mythological escapade, to subject them to a partly playful, partly caustic irony, is no evidence that he took them any less seriously than before. The new detachment bears witness, rather, to a recognition that former goals—"the yearning Passion I have for the beautiful, connected and made one with the ambition of my intellect" . . .—were no longer achievable in the way he had once imagined them for reasons the poem goes on to demonstrate.

The pivotal importance within the poem of Keats's whole involvement with the creative process emerges if we pause to look more closely at what is in many ways the center of the Hermes episode—Lamia's metamorphosis. . . . [The] transformation Lamia undergoes when touched by Hermes' rod draws its significance, and much of its tone of subtle mockery, from its correspondence to some of Keats's favorite analogies for poetic creation. As she writhes, convulsed by heat and flame, emitting, rather ludicrously, sharp sparks of phosphorus, her brighter colors are quickly inundated:

> Her mouth foam'd, and the grass, therewith besprent,
> Wither'd at dew so sweet and virulent;
> Her eyes in torture fix'd, and anguish drear,
> Hot, glaz'd, and wide, with lid-lashes all sear,
> Flash'd phosphor and sharp sparks, without one cooling
> tear.
> The colours all inflam'd throughout her train,
> She writh'd about, convuls'd with scarlet pain:
> A deep volcanian yellow took the place
> Of all her milder-mooned body's grace. . . .

The description resembles nothing so much as the effects of a violent chemical reaction. Both in what it depicts and what it implies, the passage is marked by a brilliant, mocking irony. A sort of chemical analysis or separation of elements takes place. Lamia's bright emblems and colors are overrun and dwindle to a little pile of charred remains: "Nothing but pain

and ugliness were left." . . . As we soon discover, however, she has only dissolved to ascend from the throes of her ordeal transformed. A moment later we hear her voice ringing softly through the trees as, "Borne aloft" like a vaporous distillation, she flies off, changed to a radiant but almost incorporeal lady, to lie in wait for Lycius:

> Still shone her crown; that vanish'd, also she
> Melted and disappear'd as suddenly;
> And in the air, her new voice luting soft,
> Cried, "Lycius! gentle Lycius!" . . .

Feigning aversion to his sudden love, she complains how "finer spirits cannot breathe below / In human climes, and live" and longs for "purer air" to soothe her "essence." . . . While promising a secret power to "unperplex bliss from its neighbour pain," she nevertheless denies that the "subtle fluid" in her veins is different from the blood of human hearts. . . . (pp. 300-03)

Viewed in one way, the episode is a brilliantly comic if somewhat bitter parody of Keats's whole early sense of the nature of poetic creation. It unmistakably suggests his discovery of the ironic possibilities latent in those "compositions and decompositions which take place" before "that trembling delicate and snail-horn perception of Beauty" . . . and that intensity that makes "all disagreeables evaporate, from their being in close relationship with Beauty & Truth." . . . To compare the fiery pangs of Lamia's etherealization with the "fierce convulse" and "wild commotions" of Apollo's dying into life at the end of *Hyperion* is to understand how a serious conception had become a subject for deliberate travesty. Indeed the Hermes episode and its aftermath can be taken in no small measure as a caricature of the "Pleasure Thermometer," of the whole notion of "intensity" that Keats had long pondered as an ideal leading to the achievement of happiness and truth. However fascinating, Lamia's beauty is too fragile and attenuated to survive for long in contact with the world—at least the world into which Lycius is bent on leading her, the world as Apollonius represents it.

Lamia's metamorphosis and the central logic of its governing metaphor are fundamental and determining factors in the larger rhythm of the poem. For if Lamia is transformed, however dubiously, at the outset, she is methodically and somewhat pathetically destroyed at the conclusion. By helping Hermes she gains the impetus necessary to free herself from the baser and anomalous elements that compose her nature. Her fiery distillation explains the fairy brilliance and intoxicating charm Lycius at first finds so irresistible. Yet it also leaves her weak and susceptible to the power of Apollonius's analytic gaze. When his withering glance looks through her and she vanishes with a scream, she does not seem to die so much as to evaporate. Both the mystery and potential tragedy of her sudden disintegration are comically subverted by the realization, if only implicit, of the virtually scientific logic that dominates the phases of her various transformations. Indeed Lycius's old tutor best fits the epithet most frequently applied to him if we take the word "philosopher" in its older sense of "natural philosopher" or man of science. He is, of course, the unlyric Apollo, the power of science and healing isolated from any saving touch of humor, compassion, or genuine benevolence, a cross between Apollo and Polonius. As he makes his way toward Lamia's palace and the bridal chambers, chuckling to himself like someone who has just solved "some knotty problem" . . . , we are reminded of the self-satisfied researcher who has just discovered the solution to some puzzling phenomenon, ready now to elucidate the whole mystery before the common multitude with, like Linus Pauling, a flair for the dramatics of the occasion.

While the key to the significance of Lamia's transformation and rebirth is Keats's favorite image of the thermometer—the instrument essential to chemists for determining those intensities at which specific reactions occur—the image fundamental to her dissolution, as the major interpolation of the poem makes clear, is equally scientific—the prism. (pp. 303-04)

The thermometer and the prism . . . frame the beginning and the end of *Lamia,* just as in many ways they span the beginning and the end of the poet's career. At the time of *Endymion* he could acclaim his discovery of the "Pleasure Thermometer" as "of the greatest Service to me" for "set[ting] before me at once the gradations of Happiness" . . .—an image that comprehended the creative possibilities latent in his whole commitment to the ideal of "intensity." In *Lamia,* however, the instruments of science play a more analytic, eventually destructive, role, while Keats's insight into the nature of the poetic process is not only more penetrating but, to say the least, ambivalent. Everyone knows the story of Haydon's "immortal dinner" when Keats and Lamb agreed that Newton "had destroyed all the poetry of the rainbow by reducing it to its prismatic colours." Thereupon they drank "Newton's health, and confusion to mathematics," and the equivocal nature of the toast is reflected in the divided sympathies of Keats's poem. The account of how Newton had demonstrated that when a single ray of light passes through a triangular prism it divides into the various constituent colors—red, orange, yellow, green, blue, indigo, and violet—in accordance with a fixed mathematical ratio was by Keats's day legendary. Doubtless it was just these facts the poet had in mind when he wrote:

> There was an awful rainbow once in heaven:
> We know her woof, her texture; she is given
> In the dull catalogue of common things. . . .

Yet Keats must also have known how one of his boyhood heroes, Sir William Herschel, had carried Newton's discovery one step further by showing that the various colored rays of light differed in their power of rendering objects visible and how, by placing thermometers in different parts of the spectrum, it could be proved that they differed in their caloric intensities. The story of Herschel's demonstration that the greatest heat was actually produced in an area beyond the red rays where there was no visible light was virtually as well known as Newton's discovery. Both the thermometer and the prism provided complementary means for measuring the intensity of those closely related concepts, heat and light. In *Lamia* the metaphor operates with a thoroughly ironic precision: what it creates it as readily destroys.

The consistency with which throughout his career Keats adopts analogies from contemporary science to express his own sense of the imagination and its creative processes is indeed striking. Yet the continuity of metaphor should not blind one to the radically shifting emphasis it comes in time to serve, especially in such a work as *Lamia.* In *Endymion* the scientific metaphor, so fundamental to the argument of the first book and, indeed, to the anticipated thrust of the poem as a whole, is largely affirmative and progressive in what it suggests. Even as late as May 1818, when Keats was looking forward to returning to his medical books, he could conceive of a useful and productive alliance between the arts and sciences. "Every department of knowledge we see excellent," he wrote, "and calculated to-

wards a great whole." . . . In *Lamia,* however, the fundamental scientific analogies serve the uses of the comic spirit, and, even more, of a pervasive skepticism and controlling irony. Lamia, taken as the essence of imaginative perception, is first distilled and then evaporated with all the brilliance of an experiment in chemistry but with little of the happy exuberance that characterizes Shelley's "The Cloud." Her appearance, indeed her value and significance, are relative to the changing circumstances of the poem, to the different viewpoints of the characters that surround her. For while the poem derives, from beginning to end, a balance and symmetry from the logic of the thermometer-prism metaphor, it moves at the same time between the quite different historical poles represented by Hermes and Apollonius. Indeed the poem achieves its principal effect through the way in which it develops the poet's ambivalence toward science within a pessimistic view of history and the progress of human culture that is in sharp contrast to major aspects of *Hyperion.* Within Hermes' world, the lost domain of mythic unity and timelessness, Lamia's power of imaginative revelation possesses genuine effect. In Apollonius's world of science and analysis, she is no longer able to survive. The weak cunning of her "sciential brain," her power to "Intrigue with the specious chaos, and dispart / Its most ambiguous atoms with sure art". . . , is child's play compared with the exact calculations of the molecular chemist or atomic physicist.

The pessimism of the poem's historical perspective, the steady polarization it establishes between science and the imagination, controls the movement of a drama where the play of character is quite secondary to a basic irony of situation. (pp. 305-08)

The characters are throughout merely the creatures of the poem's framework and the changing stresses it brings to bear upon them, and they react predictably. The poet's invitation to the reader to join him in choosing and awarding wreaths to the three principals is partly tongue-in-cheek and partly a deliberate trap. For any reasoned balance of sympathies, not to mention taking sides, is out of the question. The characters and the attitudes they represent are all hopelessly inadequate. The dilemma they together represent is one which, within the terms the poem itself sets out, can have no conceivable resolution. The predicament, moreover, is clearly one of major relevance to Keats's whole approach to art and to experience. Of all his longer works, *Lamia* is the most patently and self-consciously—at times bitterly—ironic. (p. 309)

> *Stuart M. Sperry, in his* Keats the Poet, *Princeton University Press, 1973, 350 p.*

HELEN VENDLER   (essay date 1983)

[In her book-length study, excerpted below, Vendler examines Keats's odes.]

The *Ode on a Grecian Urn* squarely confronts the truth that art is not "natural," like leaves on a tree, but artificial. The sculptor must chisel the stone, a medium external to himself and recalcitrant. In restricting itself to one sense, the *Urn* resembles *Nightingale,* but in the *Urn* the sense is sight, not hearing. The *Urn* suppresses hearing, as the *Ode to a Nightingale* had suppressed sight (and as both suppress the "lower senses" of touch and taste). If *Nightingale* is an experiment in thinking about art in terms of pure, "natural," nonrepresentational music prolonged in time, the *Urn* is an experiment in thinking about art in terms of pure, "artificial," representational visuality extended in space (a space whose extension, in Keats's special case, rounds on itself—the urn is a self-limiting frieze). . . . [Precisely] because the nightingale's song is nonrepresentational it can ignore that world "where men sit and hear each other groan"; because it is nonconceptual or nonphilosophical it can avoid those sorrows and leaden-eyed despairs inseparable from thought. The *Ode to a Nightingale* can therefore bypass (until the questions which break its trance end the poem) the question of truth, and expatiate in its consideration of sensation and beauty, suggesting, by its darkness, that the more indistinct and dim and remote that beauty, the better. Beauty, in the form of the bird's song without words, stimulates the reverie of the musing Fancy, which endlessly projects itself on a perfect void—the essentially vacant, if transfixing, song of the nightingale.

All of this changes with the *Ode on a Grecian Urn*. Keats now proposes, with respect to art as he understands it and wishes to practice it, that art is a constructive and conscious shaping of a medium, and that what is created is representational, bearing some relation to "Truth." He proposes to examine this premise through a deliberately invented vehicle for understanding, a carved marble Hellenic urn. Recognizable represented forms—male, female, and animal—appear on the urn (crowding to the borders of composition the leaves and grass so dear to decoratively breeding Fancy; the leaves are the nostalgic tribute to the earlier naive view of the artist as one who puts forth leaves as naturally as trees). The attitudes conferred by Keats on his represented forms are also clearly recognizable and unambiguous: they are attitudes of sexual pursuit and flight, of music-making and courtship, and of communal religious performance. Instinctive and civilized actions alike are represented: human beings—and perhaps even the gods themselves (though they are here indistinguishable from human beings)—are the natural inhabitants of this medium. The forms, and the attitudes in which they are displayed, are beautiful—in the largest sense of that word (a sense Keats had imbibed from the Elgin marbles), a sense which includes the striking, the conflictual, and the memorable as well as the graceful and decorous. The urn seems in fact remarkably like life, framing as it does vivid moments of action or feeling.

This advance in Keats's conceiving of what art is like—an advance over the less complex (because instinctually expressive and nonrepresentational) postulate of the nightingale ode—requires a different response to the artifact. The actions represented on the urn excite in the beholder an empathy like that solicited in the listener by the *melos* [sweetness] of the nightingale, but they, unlike the birdsong, are allowed to provoke him to early questions. The constitutive trope of the *Urn* is interrogation, that trope of the perplexed mind.

Three times the poet "enters" a scene on the urn; but, as I see the progress of the poem, he enters each successive scene with a different view, as spectator, of what the urn is and what it does. Each entrance can be represented conceptually as a different Keatsian hypothesis about what is offered us by aesthetic experience, each provoking a different conclusion on our part about propriety of response. Keats once again plays the part of "audience," as he had in *Nightingale*; but he has turned from listener to spectator (or so we at first believe—the terms were always problematic to him, since his own art of written poetry entails in its audience both a seeing and a listening). Keats has, by eliminating a live self-expressive artist (like the bird), turned his attention more profoundly to what an artifact, in and of itself, without first-person expressive or biographical context, may be said to convey. And by making his symbol not ambiguously "natural" (as was the "music" of the Dryad-

bird) but unarguably man-made in a highly intellectual and conventionalized form, he can examine the question of the capacities and limits of an aesthetic medium far more exactly than he could in *Nightingale*.

Keats's first hypothesis about aesthetic experience, evoked by the orgiastic first scene on the urn, is that art tells us a story, a history, about some people who are not ourselves. The proper response to the urn in this instance is then to question it, to ask of it, "Who are these people, and what are they doing?"—the question of a believer in a naive mimetic art, in art as illustration. (pp. 116-18)

Keats's second hypothesis about aesthetic response is evoked by the second scene, which shows a piper accompanying a youth courting a maiden. This second hypothesis (prompted by his own use of allegorical frieze in *Indolence* and *Nightingale*) proposes that the urn represents not mythologically or historically identifiable figures acting out some known (if lost) legend, but rather what would nowadays be called a universal or archetypal "Truth"—in this instance, the truth of the unity of Love, Beauty, and Art, symbolized by the classic icon of a lover courting a maiden to music. The archetype is idealized—that is to say, it represents a human fantasy: that the lover will forever love, and the beloved be forever fair, and their courtship give rise to, and be accompanied by, an eternally refreshed art, "songs forever new." In this hypothesis, the urn is not representing other people, mythological or historical, but is allegorically representing ourselves and our feelings—except that it shows us ourselves and our actions "in a finer tone." Our proper response to the urn is, under this hypothesis, to give up useless questions of what historical or mythological story it illustrates, rejoice in its extreme beauty, regret the discrepancy that exists between the fantasized and the real, and yet recognize the truth of our aspirations (here, toward a "happy" art accompanying constancy in love and perpetuity of beauty) represented in the actualized fantasy. Keats is now attempting to reverse his declaration in *Nightingale* that "Beauty cannot keep her lustrous eyes, / Or new Love pine at them beyond tomorrow." If not in life, at least in the truthful allegorical representation of our idealism, "For ever wilt thou love, and she be fair!"

The response stimulated by the second hypothesis—a response of sympathy with an idealized human state—is incompatible with the response solicited by the first hypothesis, that query about historical or legendary names and places. In the second response, the speaker is not exercised to discover originating legend or narrative, but naively once again enters wholly into the pictured scene, temporarily "forgetting" that he is contemplating a vase, and taking in the sculptured spectacle purely as life: "More happy love! more happy, happy love! . . . / For ever panting, and for ever young."

Keats, I believe, saw both of these naive responses (in which he shows his spectator of the vase fully participating) as in themselves alone not adequate to art. Art does not exist to offer historical truth alone, whether social or divine or sylvan; neither is it created primarily to offer the moral truth of accessible archetypal ideals. Consequently, in exhibiting each of these two responses, Keats does not permit the excitement generated by them to survive. The mind cannot rest in either hypothesis. In the first instance, the questions rise to a frenzy—"What pipes and timbrels? What wild ecstasy?"—but the frenzy toward specification is instantly quieted by a change of orchestration, as Keats allows the excited mind which posed the questions to abandon historical inquiry and try to begin, ra-

tionally, to consider the import of art. Keats turns to generalization and to philosophical diction, introducing a new movement, one of thought rather than empathy, as he meditates on
the relative capacities of music, poetry, and the visual arts.

This new movement rejects the "heard melodies" so praised
in the ode Keats had just completed on the nightingale (those
melodies addressing the sensual ear) in favor of spatial and
visual melodies which address the spirit. However, the criterion
of aesthetic praiseworthiness here is still "sweetness" or *melos*. The bitterly truthful or the dissonant seem as yet to have
no place in Keats's conception of this sculptural art, which is
said to have "sweeter" melodies than music, and to express
a "flowery" tale (like that embowered one of Cupid and Psyche, perhaps) "more sweetly" than Keats's own art of poetry
could do.

This philosophical meditation on the superiority of spiritual to
sensual melody interrupts the speaker's naive participation in
the initial orgiastic scene; in the same way, a reflection on
earthly passion and its putative inferiority to sculptured passion
interrupts his second naive entry, this time an entry into the
love on the urn. Once again, Keats draws a hierarchical comparison—not, now, one favoring visual art over sensual music
or "our" rhyme, but rather one favoring the love on the urn
over our "breathing human passion" far below it. To recapitulate: neither the naive factual questioning nor the naive
thoughtless empathy is allowed to continue undisturbed: one
is checked by a debate on the relative sweetness of music,
rhyme, and sculpture, the other by a bitter intellectual recollection of the realities of human passion. In each case, the
poet's self—first the self as artist in a putatively deficient
medium (since rhyme, like music, is addressed to the sensual
ear), and second the self as embittered lover—rises to pit itself
in some "philosophic" way against its own spontaneous, immediate, and "naive" response to the urn.

Undaunted, the speaker attempts a third time to "enter" the
urn, and Keats proposes, in his fourth stanza, a new and more
adequate hypothesis about the aesthetic experience offered by
an artifact, and our aesthetic response. The urn, he suggests,
is not just the illustration of a legend or tale about other people;
nor is it just a representation, in archetypal and idealized form,
of our human aspirations. Rather, it is most truly described as
a self-contained anonymous world, complete in itself, which
asks from us an empathic identification supremely free both
of factual inquiry and of self-interest. Naive museum-goers
demand either a known story, or the representation of a state
visibly analogous to one of their own. It is easy to be merely
narratively curious: "What men or gods are these?" It is even
easier, by analogy with ourselves, to love a lover: "More happy
love! more happy, happy love!" To the first of these naive
responders, art is like a newspaper photograph, in need of an
explanatory caption; to the second, art is like a mirror, in which
he narcissistically luxuriates. But Keats, contemplating his third
scene—a ritual sacrificial procession—foreign, ancient, remote
from anything he has himself known—asks not about an antecedent legend but investigates instead the boundaries of representation: What group has the artist now selected? To what
altar is the heifer being led? From what town does the procession issue? (pp. 119-22)

While this third hypothesis—in which the audience, prompted
by the visible artifact, engages by its interrogation in an act of
cooperative mutual creation with the artist—is more satisfying
than the purely mimetic, historical hypothesis of the artifact-
as-illustration given in the first stanza, or the purely expressive

and allegorical one of the artifact-as-mirror proposed in the
second and third stanzas, it is also, because the most sophisticated hypothesis, the most alienating. We might be grateful
to the urn while it was instructing us in historical or legendary
truths about divine or human action; we might warm to it while
it represented, through a universal archetype, truths of emotion
at once eternal and personal. But once we recognize that it is
primarily neither culturally instructional (a "sylvan historian")
nor flatteringly truthful to our narcissistic wishes—that it is
neither about someone else nor about us, but rather about its
own inventions into which we are enticed and on which we
exercise our own pathos in return—we see it as necessarily
artificial, a work in a given medium by a given hand. The
return out of trance into consciousness, exhibited once in *Nightingale,* is here deliberately made to occur three times, with
each exit from a scene into which one has entered. While we
are "within" the urn, we are not outside it; while we are outside
reflecting on it, we are not "within" it. Like the figures on
the urn, we cannot at once be in the town where we live and
on the urn.

I have been speaking, on the whole, as though Keats, looking
at an urn, were pressed, by the intensity of his feelings, to
three successively more complex and intelligent responses. In
point of fact, of course, Keats invents his three urn-scenes—
of orgiastic pursuit to music, of courtship to music, and of
religious observance—to which his three hypotheses of response will be attached. The first turbulent scene is invented
as one likely to stimulate archaeologic questions which could
be satisfied by the "truths" of a museum notice: "This scene
represents a ceremonial orgy in honor of the god such-and-
such; participants attempted ecstatic sexual experience by the
use of intoxicants, and ritual music was played on the kind of
pipe represented here," and so on. The second idyllic scene
is invented as one which has the tendency to evoke psychological "truth" of an easy reductiveness: "In every civilization
we find the eternal pair, youth and maiden; we recognize here
the idealized posture of youthful first love and pastoral song."
But the third religious scene is invented as one presenting the
real test of aesthetic response. Once we pass (as museum visitors) beyond a wish for the explanatory factual truths of historical or cultural captions, and beyond the narcissistic stage
of being interested only in "lyric" art which we can see as a
reflection of something in ourselves, we can confront art as it
is in itself, in its ultimate formal anonymity and otherness. It
is not "they"—men or gods. It is not "I" or "we." Or it is
not primarily these. It is itself. And, by its nature, it draws us
to itself; we do not impose our concerns upon it.

Keats's triple hypothesis engenders the compositional rhythm
of the poem, its large structural form. Whereas *Nightingale*
traces first a withdrawal from the world, then an engagement
with the music of the bird, and later an involuntary disengagement at the admission of thought (a single parabolic tra-
jectory), the *Urn,* as I have said, repeats a comparable form
three times, once for each scene. I recapitulate here in formal
terms what I have already described thematically. The opening
address to the urn—grateful, but equilibrated and archaeolog-
ical—gives way to a mounting voyeuristic excitement, as the
beholder surrenders to the orgiastic scene. This excitement is
not allowed a gradual subsidence. Instead, at the very moment
of its interrogatory climax, it is admonished by a reproof of
the sensual, as the wild ecstasy is replaced, in a striking whit-
ening of voice, by soft pipes which play "not to the sensual
ear" but rather "to the spirit ditties of no tone." Yet a second
time, while seeing the young lovers on the urn, the speaker's

excitement is heightened; he feels, this time, not the excitement of a voyeur, but that of a passionate sympathizer. This fever of identification, defensively over-prolonged through an extra stanza, is suddenly cooled, in the midst of its exclamatory *accelerando* [acceleration] (just as the earlier factual questions had been broken into in mid-career), by the memory of human passion, with its paradoxical simultaneous cloying and persisting thirst. In both of these cases, the irruption of the reflective mind is sudden, unforeseen, and apparently unpreventable: mind bursts in—whether in questions or in reflection—on receptive sensation as a force no longer able to be repressed. Keats's easy sense of being able to outwit the "dull brain"—with its perplexing questions and its retarding of trance—has vanished forever. The brain breaks in; and what is more, Keats welcomes it, and entertains it; he is genuinely interested in meditating on the relation between heard and unheard melodies, on art addressed to the ear vis-à-vis art addressed to the spirit. And in fact the brain is never really banished; even to the orgiastic figures it had addressed its intellectual questions; even in describing the lovers it incorporates its knowledge of earthly change in the elegiac and contrastive language through which the sympathy for them is addressed.

When, the third time, the speaker bends to the urn, he has lost his voyeuristic and narcissistic motives. The speaker is—really for the first time—the truly aesthetic spectator, viewing the scene with a speculative curiosity which is no longer idle nor hectic. He no longer makes a self-absorbed, contrastive referral to his own human case, but rather extends himself in a generous loss of self in the other. He enters into the life of the religious scene, prolonging it forward and backward with tenderness and feeling, investing the procession with the weight of life's mysteries of whence and whither without altering its otherness, both cultural and historic. The priest remains mysterious, a figure for Fate leading life on (derived as he is from the priest in *Psyche,* he is yet the devotee of no one deity); the little town remains unknowable, a figure for the invisibility of origins; the green altar remains unseen, and undescribed (unlike Psyche's fane), a figure for a veiled end.

When this last intensity of engagement with the urn fails (as, like the preceding ones, it must), it fails because Keats has seen too far into the core of an eternal destruction. This destruction is not melodramatic and fierce, like the mutual ravening of all created beings which Keats had flinched at in his epistle to Reynolds. That earlier destruction was something outside aesthetic experience, which nonetheless blighted that experience—"It forces us in summer skies to mourn: / It spoils the singing of the nightingale" (**Dear Reynolds . . .**). Here, in the **Urn,** no such sensational interference from the outside is envisaged: the destruction of aesthetic reverie arises rather from the necessary obliteration inherent in process itself. All processions, by the very fact of their existence as processions, leave their origins behind; all travel is sacrificial of its origins. . . . The mysterious priest has something of the folk-tale force of a pied piper: we are all led willingly on, by many pieties, into life and then out of it. Life's sadness does not lie in the bitterness of sexual rhythms with their ultimate exhaustion, those rhythms underlying the Nightingale ode; it does not even lie, as Keats had thought, in the perplexing intellect which interrupts or retards sensual reverie; rather, it lies in the very existence of origins, processions, and ends, in the fact of process.

These precocious insights left Keats with a poem four-fifths complete, with its great fourth stanza—expressing his furthest reach—already written. The poem had begun, we recall, with

a comparison of the urn with rhyme—to the disadvantage of rhyme. The urn's whole and simultaneous visual art, where everything can be present (and presented) at once, seemed to Keats, fresh from his disillusion with the nightingale, sweeter than a temporally experienced art like music or poetry. The reason for this preference is exposed in the second and third stanzas: what is seen whole and simultaneously need never come to an end, whereas the defect of a temporal art, like the song of the nightingale or the rhyme of the poet, is that it bids adieu, and fades. Visual art is not fugitive—or so it would at first appear.

But as Keats explores his successive responses to visual art through his invented scenes on the urn, he discovers that there is a rhythm of engagement and disengagement by which the mind imposes its own temporality on the stasis of visual art. To the first scene, the beholder attributes a rhythm of pursuit and escape, a more excited version of the rhythm of the later procession. The inflamed men or gods come from somewhere; the maidens loth are struggling to escape to some haven. This invention of origins (Tempe? Arcady?) and ends (escape) accounts in part for the rhythms of engagement and disengagement. But a far more powerful force toward disengagement resides in every spectator's intermittent awareness, in contemplating any work of art, that the scene before his eyes is not a real but a represented one. Keats's first involuntary disengagement is caused by this knowledge; having seen the pipes and timbrels represented, he knows that they are *not* real, that they pipe unheard except to the spirit. This art is a dumbshow, and the pipes are in fact silent; but Keats, in an effort to mitigate the strict knowledge of disengagement, avoids the uncompromising word "silent" and calls the pipes, instead, "soft." We of course know that they are so soft as to be "unheard"; they play ditties "of no tone." The word "silent," though here repressed, waits in the wings and appears, insistently, in the last two stanzas.

Keats's response to the urn therefore becomes a classic case of the dilemma which the psychologists of perception (using the classic figure of the duck-rabbit) call the dilemma of figure and ground. If the spectator focuses on one aspect, the other recedes into the background, and vice versa. In this case, the dilemma is that of subject matter and medium, of "men" and "marble." While Keats pressingly interrogates the urn's figures, he cannot think of them as other than real: "What men or gods are these? . . . For ever wilt thou love . . . O mysterious priest . . ." On the other hand, as soon as he allows his consciousness of the marble medium to arise, he loses his sense of the figural representations as "real," and a disjunction in tone marks the breaking of the spell. There are, as I have said, three such disjunctions in the poem (I italicize the moment of the tonal reversal):

> What pipes and timbrels? What wild ecstasy?
> *Heard melodies are sweet . . .*

> For ever panting and for ever young;
> *All breathing human passion far above . . .*

> What little town . . .
> Is emptied of this folk, this pious morn?
> *And, little town, thy streets for evermore*
> *Will silent be.*

In concluding his poem Keats wished, it seems to me, to give equal credence to each side of these junctures, to recognize fully both his participation in the represented "reality" and his awareness of the constituting medium removing those representations from actual life. Since, in Keats's view, one cannot experience sensory participation in the represented scene and intellectual awareness of the medium at one and the same time, and since attention can change focus so rapidly from what is being represented to the medium of representation and back again, Keats has to affirm two wholly incompatible responses, never simultaneous, one always canceling the other, but both of them authentic, both of them provided by the artifact, both of them "aesthetic."

It was in his second stanza that Keats had most wonderfully allowed the two responses, to matter and to medium, free play. He permits there a rapidly alternating perception first of one and then of the other, and he uses identical language for the two experiences in order to show that they compete on identical terrain. Commentary often refers to the impossibility of deciding which are "bad" and which "good" of the many "can's" and "cannot's" in this stanza. To the piper and the youth, Keats says in turn, "Thou canst not leave thy song," which is meant to be good but has overtones of coercion; "Never, never canst thou kiss," which is surely bad; and "She cannot fade," which is surely good. In this stanza, the poet still sees medium and subject matter in (to quote Wordsworth) "a constant interchange of growth and blight." The marble medium confers certain benefits ("She cannot fade") and certain limitations ("Thou hast not thy bliss"). The lines focus alternately on life matter—the beauty of the maiden, the ardor of the lover—and on the coercions of the marble medium—"Never, never canst thou kiss." The quick shuttling back and forth in the speaker's mind between immersion in the fervent matter and recognition of the immobile medium represents a tension as yet unconceptualized in the poem (that is, one yet "philosophically" or "reflectively" analyzed).

In the following stanza, the third, Keats defensively attempts to suppress interrogation by suppressing one half of his response, his awareness of the limits of the medium. Thus he hopes to enter wholly into the static happiness of the represented matter, which attempts a return to Psyche's timeless bower: "Ah, happy, happy boughs! . . . And happy melodist . . . More happy love! More happy, happy love! / For ever warm . . ." The difference between this bower and that of Psyche is that into this bower has intruded the vocabulary of time, in the thoughts of shed leaves and springs that have been bidden adieu. And the undistinguished nature of the language of this stanza demonstrates the necessary failure of invention when the momentum of the poem is deliberately halted, stalled in its most recent perception. The needle of receptive sensation sticks, we might say, in its last phrase. The strain of maintaining timelessness in the vocabulary of time climaxes in the return of the repressed, as the sexual consummation prohibited by the atemporal visual medium of the urn takes place violently in Keats's recollection, leaving "a burning forehead, and a parching tongue."

Keats returns to the problem of subject matter and medium at the end of his poem. Shocked by the "deceiving" ability of representational art to persuade his belief not only in the represented procession but equally in the green altar and the fantasized town, he recoils intellectually from participation in subject matter into pure awareness of medium, becoming the apparently detached, but in reality the cheated, spectator. He no longer anthropomorphizes the urn into bride, child, or historian—all names which had been prompted by a wish to assimilate the artifact itself to its representational function—but rather addresses it as pure medium, as an Attic shape, a fair

attitude, embroidered by the chisel of its carver with marble men and maidens. But, as in the earlier attempt to suppress the intellect in the third stanza, one half of the response-field cannot be maintained alone. Marble men and maidens suddenly "swell into reality" and walk on real earth "with forest branches and the trodden weed." It is hopeless to try to maintain a detached attitude: the scene *is* cold marble and it *is* trodden weeds, both and each, one moment the carved, the next the real.

The dilemma the urn presents is one insoluble to description. We can, if we like, see the whole ode as Keats's extreme test of his negative capability, in a moment when "Things cannot to the will / Be settled, but they tease us out of thought." (pp. 122-29)

Perhaps there is no formulation adequate to the alternating awareness of subject matter and medium, of "nature" and "artifact" in aesthetic response. But it seems to me that the ending of the *Urn* has been unfairly criticized because neither Keats's intention nor his accomplishment has been entirely understood. (Though Keats's leaving his intent obscure may represent a flaw in execution, it does not excuse us from attempting to penetrate that intent.) The fiction of the ode is that of a poet coming, in woe, to a work of art, interrogating it, and being solaced by it. . . . Instead of repudiating, as he had done in the Nightingale ode, the tranced Fancy which makes illusion swell into reality, he now thinks of conscious representational artifice as a refuge, enabling man to "enter into the existence" of other modes of being, as he entered into the existence of the sparrow picking about the gravel (*Letters* . . .). (It is significant that the word "Fancy" is not used here, nor in subsequent odes; that word does not denote the truth value that Keats is now attributing to art.)

There are lesser and better ways of entering into the existence of other beings. Keats had already explored one mode, which precluded all memory of the world left behind, in his meditation in *Nightingale* on lyric as pure, spontaneous, nonrepresentational melodiousness evocative of rich sensations. Now, by adding the truth of representation, and the truth of "unnatural" artifice consciously shaping a form, to the beauty of sensation, Keats can explore more complicated modes of aesthetic response—those which I have here named, too crudely, as voyeuristic, narcissistic, and disinterestedly aesthetic. All of them, however, cause that journey outward from habitual self into some other thing which seems, such is the force of creation, to swell into reality. On the other hand, the philosophic mind knows that in truth—at least in the truth of "consequitive reasoning" as Keats called it—the art object (here the urn) exists in a given medium (here the carved marble). "A complex mind," says Keats, is "one that is imaginative and at the same time careful of its fruits—who would exist partly on sensation partly on thought—to whom it is necessary that years should bring the philosophic Mind" (*Letters* . . .). Sensation and Thought are respectively aligned, in this famous letter to Bailey, to Beauty and Truth. Truth is, for Keats, the property of the conscious or waking mind, that mind which both sees aspects of life and meditates on them conceptually, Adam's mind which woke to the truth of Eve. (I use Keats's own vocabulary, however imprecise, as the one least falsifying to his thought: "The Imagination may be compared to Adam's dream—he woke and found it truth," as he explained to Bailey.) Keats had decided to omit the question of truth from his poem of sensation, *Nightingale*, but he found he could not continue to write without admitting to the precincts of verse the perplexities of the brain as well as the delights of sensation. The urn's original charming names of bride, child, and sylvan historian, fictively naturalizing metaphors, are all projects of sensation rather than of thought; thought must treat the urn as artifact. When Keats allows philosophical thought to accompany his sensations of visual response, that thought sees the emotions and acts of the beautiful represented forms, but also recognizes the gap in psychological continuity between perception of matter and perception of medium. Allowing thought as well as sensation full play, Keats recognizes that his own voluntary submission to the art object entails not only empathy but also the detached recognition of its specific medium—causing that successive rhythm of entrance and exit which he had found so painful when he believed it to be caused exclusively by the deceptive cheating of a temporally dissolving Fancy. Now, seeing the dialectic between empathy and reflection as an ineluctable process of consciousness, he can regain an equilibrium of feeling before the urn, and give it a self-elucidating speech which will be true to its paradoxical union of stimuli to sensation and thought alike.

The urn, as we last see it, is not a historian but rather an epigrammatist. It is, astonishingly, no longer silent, as it had been during Keats's prolonged interrogation. It finally speaks because the speaker has ceased to ask it those historical and extrapolatory questions which it is not equipped to answer. The urn is only a "silent form" when the wrong kinds of truth are asked of it. As soon as Keats sees it as a friend of man (rather than as a historian or an archaeologist) it speaks, and becomes an oracular form, saying (as oracles often do) two things equally true. It says "Beauty is Truth" when we are looking at it with the eyes of sensation, seeing its beautiful forms as actual people, alive and active. It says "Truth is Beauty" when we are looking at it with the eyes of thought, seeing it, as the mind must see it, as a marble inscribed by intentionality, the true made beautiful by form. The two messages do not coincide; they alternate. Like a lighthouse, the urn beams one message, then the other, as we respond alternately to its human verisimilitude (which solicits our empathy) or to its triumphant use of its resistant medium (which solicits our admiration). The urn can speak of nothing but itself, and its self-referentiality is nowhere clearer than in the interior completeness of its circular epigram, which encounters our ironic sense of its limitation. When the urn says, commenting on its own motto, that that is all men know on earth and all they need to know, we realize that it makes that announcement from the special perspective of its own being, the timeless being of the artwork in the Platonic realm where Truth and Beauty are indistinguishable. It speaks to us from its own eternity, at once so liberating and so limited. Keats's choice of a circular frieze, rather than a linear one, confirms the urn's self-enclosing and self-completing form.

Nonetheless, the urn, unlike the uncaring, "natural" Nightingale, speaks to man. It is, in the phrase Keats used as well for Milton, "a friend to man," and it exemplifies the "great end" attributed, in *Sleep and Poetry*, to poetry, "that it should be a friend / To soothe the cares, and lift the thoughts of man." . . . The art of the urn-sculptor is, like the art of the poet in *Psyche*, mimetic, but it is mimetic in a philosophical way, not a photographic one; it does not copy some lost historical model, but rather it chooses evocative human postures. It is beautiful, like the song of the nightingale, but it is, in a way the bird's song cannot be, representationally true. Although it is expressive, it is not solely self-expressive, like the bird's song; although it has been made by an artist, it does not exhibit his

motives (as Keats's earlier urn, in *Indolence*, had borne his motives Love, Ambition, and Poesy). Rather, it expresses a variety of cultural motives, not a homogeneous or personal set, and is therefore a broadly socially expressive form. And it is deliberate, a reworking of nature with tools, even a violation (by its chiseling) of nature, not a spontaneous ecstatic outpouring or budding.

The poet himself utters the closing words in which the urn's motto and commentary are encapsulated as a quotation:

> When old age shall this generation waste,
>   Thou shalt remain, in midst of other woe
> Than ours, a friend to man, to whom thou say'st,
> "Beauty is truth, truth beauty,"—that is all
>   Ye know on earth, and all ye need to know.

The last two lines are spoken by the urn, which places special emphasis on the mottolike epigram before going on to comment on its unique worth. But the whole last sentence of the poem is the sentence of the speaker who, in his prophecy, recounts what the urn will say to succeeding generations. The speaker has reached, by the end of the poem, a prophetic amplitude of statement, looking before and after. With his philosophic mind, he foresees the time when his own generation will be wasted by old age, as previous generations have been in their turn; in that time to come, another young generation will be feeling woe as he has felt it, and will come to the urn, as he has come, for refuge and solace. In its generosity this picture of parallel relations between generations represents an advance over the cruel representation, in *Nightingale*, of hungry filial generations each treading the past parental generation down. In his closing stanza, Keats is now above and beyond his own past immediate encounters with the urn-scenes; his detachment is now comparable to the detachment of the urn itself. But his mind is more capacious, in this last stanza, than the being of the urn is. Keats's mind here encompasses past, present, and future; youth, woe, age, the wasting of time, and the coming of another generation—all those horrors from which he had so strenuously averted his gaze in *Nightingale*. Keats's mind judges and places the single experience of seeing the urn in the total human experience of the life and death of generations. The sublimity—and ecstasy—of art is therefore granted as one moment along the span of life, a moment in which, by the intensity of art, all disagreeables are made to evaporate "from their being in close relationship with Beauty & Truth" (*Letters* . . .). The disagreeables—age, death, woe—have reasserted themselves in the mind of the speaker both during the poem (in his reflective moments) and at the end of the poem. But he gives the last, solacing word to the urn, because it utters that word afresh to each new generation—yet he encapsulates that last word in his own last overarching sentence of praise for art.

The divinity physically worshiped in this ode is the art object, the urn. The divinities conceptually celebrated are the twin divinities of Beauty *and* Truth, Sensation *and* Thought. The divinity imaginatively celebrated is that greeting of the spirit that takes place between the audience and the art object. The object provides the beautiful carved forms of the three scenes; the spirit moves to enter into and share the life of each scene, and even, in the third instance, helps to extend that life into imagined new creation. Together the object and the spirit create the aesthetic reverie, real and unreal at once. If it is true that, as we read Keats's fourth stanza, our sense of a beautiful train of anonymous figures led by a mysterious priest from obscure origins to an ultimate sacrificial rite in an unknown place is all we know of beauty and truth on earth and all we need to know, then Keats's urn has kept its promise to our generation as to his. (pp. 130-35)

Helen Vendler, in her The Odes of John Keats, *Cambridge, Mass.: The Belknap Press, 1983, 330 p.*

ADDITIONAL BIBLIOGRAPHY

Allott, Miriam. *John Keats*. Writers and Their Works, edited by Ian Scott-Kilvert. Essex: Longman Group, 1976, 62 p.
Concise overview in which Allott traces the evolution of Keats's thought. Allott's essay succeeds Edmund Blunden's contribution to the same series (see annotation below).

Balslev, Thora. *Keats and Wordsworth: A Comparative Study*. Munskaard: Norwegian Universities Press, 1962, 192 p.*
Traces William Wordsworth's influence upon Keats's poetry and analyzes the relationship between various aspects of the two poets' art, including symbol and imagery.

Bate, Walter Jackson. *The Stylistic Development of Keats*. New York: Humanities Press, 1962, 214 p.
A largely prosodic study in which Bate seeks "to give a precise description of the unfolding and development of a great poet's stylistic craftsmanship, and to ally this technical progression with the changing bents of mind which gave it rise and direction."

———. *John Keats*. Cambridge, Mass.: Harvard University Press, Belknap Press, 1963, 732 p.
Detailed biography that is considered the most reliable and comprehensive modern source. Bate incorporates the biographical information that came to light subsequent to World War II, particularly the material included in Hyder Edward Rollins's *The Keats Circle: Letters and Papers, 1816-1878* (see annotation below).

———, ed. *Keats: A Collection of Critical Essays*. Englewood Cliffs, N.J.: Prentice-Hall, 1964, 177 p.
Four general discussions and seven contemporary essays on specific poems: each of the five odes, the two *Hyperions*, "Lamia," and "The Eve of St. Agnes." Critics represented include Earl Wasserman, David Perkins, D. G. James, and Harold Bloom.

Beaudry, Harry R. *Romantic Reassessment: The English Theatre and John Keats*. Edited by James Hogg. Salzburg Studies in English Literature, edited by Erwin A. Stürzl. Salzburg: Universität Salzburg, 1973, 240 p.
A conscientious, detailed study of the contemporary theater of Keats's time and his relation to it. Beaudry concludes his work with an analysis of *Otho the Great* and *King Stephen* as they relate both to the theater of Keats's day and to the poet's artistic development.

Bernbaum, Ernest. "John Keats." In his *Guide through the Romantic Movement*, 2d ed., pp. 86-110. New York: Ronald Press, 1972.
An introductory guide to the history of Keats criticism.

Blackstone, Bernard. *The Consecrated Urn: An Interpretation of Keats in Terms of Growth and Form*. London: Longmans, Green, 1959, 426 p.
A provocative study of Keats's poetic and philosophical growth based on his use of biological images. As Blackstone states in his preface, he approaches his subject from a "botanico-physiologico-cosmogonical" slant.

Blunden, Edmund. *John Keats*. Rev. ed. Writers and Their Works, edited by Geoffrey Bullough, no. 6. London: Longmans, Green, 1966, 40 p.
An excellent biographical and critical introduction.

———, ed. *Shelley and Keats as They Struck Their Contemporaries*. London: C. W. Beaumont, 1925, 94 p.*
Offers several brief, seldom-noted allusions to Keats culled from the writings of such contemporaries as Lord Byron and William Wordsworth.

Brown, Charles Armitage. *Life of John Keats*. Edited by Dorothy Hyde Bodurtha and Willard Bissell Pope. London: Oxford University Press, 1937, 129 p.
Recognized as the first full-length biography of Keats, although not published until this date. The editor includes an introduction in which he outlines the genesis of the work, which was written by Keats's close friend. Much of the material is considered merely invective against Keats's detractors, although it is valued as a record of Keats's life from 1818 to 1821, a period during most of which Keats and Brown lived together in Hampstead.

Bush, Douglas. *John Keats: His Life and Writings*. Masters of World Literature Series, edited by Louis Kronenberger. New York: Macmillan, 1966, 224 p.
Concise and readable biography. Bush's work is somewhat less comprehensive than Walter Jackson Bate's earlier *John Keats* (see annotation above).

Clarke, Charles Cowden. "Recollections of Keats." *The Atlantic Monthly* VII (January 1861): 86-100.
Affectionate reminiscences by Keats's childhood friend, who was the son of Keats's schoolmaster. Clarke offers an interesting account of the authors and books that influenced Keats as a schoolboy and youth.

Colvin, Sidney. *Keats*. London: Macmillan & Co., 1964, 240 p.
A biography, first published in 1887, that helped to expose a broader audience to Keats's life and works. Colvin expanded on this book in a later, more detailed study (see annotation below).

———. *John Keats: His Life and Poetry, His Friends, Critics, and After-Fame*. New York: Octagon Books, 1970, 598 p.
Standard biographical source based on Colvin's earlier biography (see annotation above).

Courthope, W. J. "Romanticism in English Poetry: Keats." In his *A History of English Poetry: The Romantic Movement in English Poetry, Effects of the French Revolution, Vol. VI*, pp. 320-56. London: Macmillan and Co., 1910.
A somewhat cursory critical overview notable because Courthope upholds the view that Keats is a merely pictorial and therefore inferior poet. Courthope was one of the most influential critics—indeed, one of the only critics—of his day to maintain this stance.

Danzig, Allan, ed. *Twentieth Century Interpretations of "The Eve of St. Agnes": A Collection of Critical Essays*. Englewood Cliffs, N.J.: Prentice-Hall, 1971, 120 p.
Six essays reprinted from the works of such critics as Earl Wasserman, Bernard Blackstone, and Walter Jackson Bate in addition to an original piece by Clifford Adelman.

D'Avanzo, Mario. *Keats's Metaphors for the Poetic*. Durham, N.C.: Duke University Press, 1967, 232 p.
Examines within the context of Keats's entire oeuvre recurring metaphors for imagination and poetic creativity. Among the images D'Avanzo examines are woman as poetry, sleep and dreams, the bower, and images of reality. D'Avanzo notes as particularly important Keats's use of all forms of art, such as painting, poetry, sculpture, and architecture, as subjects for his poems.

Dickstein, Morris. *Keats and His Poetry: A Study in Development*. Chicago: University of Chicago Press, 1971, 270 p.
A chronological reading of Keats's development in terms, according to the critic, "of his changing attitude toward 'consciousness,' what Keats calls 'the thinking principle,' by which he means not pure intellection so much as self-awareness. . . ." Dickstein's study is representative of recent academic criticism.

Empson, William. *Seven Types of Ambiguity*. Rev. ed. London: Chatto & Windus, 1949, 258 p.*
Landmark modernist work that includes in chapter seven a brief discussion of "Ode to Melancholy." The ode, which Empson says "pounds together the sensations of joy and sorrow until they

combine into sexuality," is cited as exhibiting what Empson defines as a "seventh type ambiguity," or that which is "full of contradiction, marking a division in the author's mind."

Finney, Claude Lee. *The Evolution of Keats's Poetry.* 2 vols. New York: Russell & Russell, 1963.
> Detailed biographical criticism. The author related only those facts of Keats's life that relate to his poetry in an attempt "to reconstruct the environment in which Keats lived and to present and explain the personal, social, and practical forces which inspired and influenced his poems."

Fogle, Richard Harter. *The Imagery of Keats and Shelley: A Comparative Study.* Hamden, Conn.: Archon Books, 1962, 296 p.*
> A comparison of the imagery of Keats and Percy Bysshe Shelley focusing on imagery of sensation in addition to synaesthetic, empathetic, concrete, and abstract imagery.

Ford, George H. *Keats and the Victorians: A Study of His Influence and Rise to Fame, 1821-1895.* Yale Studies in English, vol. 101. Hamden, Conn.: Archon Books, 1962, 197 p.*
> A study of how Keats influenced the Victorians and an examination of their attitudes toward him. The book is chiefly devoted to Alfred, Lord Tennyson, Matthew Arnold, Dante Gabriel Rossetti, and Algernon Charles Swinburne.

Ford, Newell F. *The Prefigurative Imagination of John Keats: A Study of the Beauty-Time Identification and Its Implications.* Hamden, Conn.: Archon Books, 1966, 168 p.
> An analysis of Keats's identification of beauty and truth based primarily on a concordance of the occurrence of the word "truth" throughout his writings. After Ford discusses his study, he reinterprets many of Keats's major writings in light of his findings.

Garrod, H. W. *Keats.* Oxford: Oxford at the Clarendon Press, 1926, 157 p.
> Overview of Keats's poetry, excluding *Endymion,* based on a series of lectures. Garrod generally adheres to the nineteenth-century view that Keats is at his best as a poet of the senses.

Gittings, Robert. *John Keats: The Living Year, 21 September 1818 to 21 September 1819.* Cambridge, Mass.: Harvard University Press, 1954, 247 p.
> An account of the single year of Keats's life during which, according to the critic, he wrote "nearly all" his greatest poetry. Gittings focuses on the events and sources that provided Keats's inspiration and prologue and epilogue provide the details of the other periods of Keats's life.

———. *The Mask of Keats: A Study of Problems.* London: William Heinemann, 1956, 177 p.
> Discusses various biographical and literary subjects that were either not treated in Gittings's earlier *John Keats: The Living Year, 21 September 1818 to 21 September 1819* (see annotation above) or that fell outside its time scheme. Of particular concern to the critic are the questions of Keats's debt to Dante and the exact date of the composition of his sonnet "Bright Star."

———. *John Keats.* London: Heinemann, 1968, 469 p.
> Scholarly biography that is considered the most factually accurate account of Keats's life. The book contains extensive illustrations and illuminating footnotes.

Goellnicht, Donald C. *The Poet-Physician: Keats and Medical Science.* Pittsburgh: University of Pittsburgh Press, 1984, 291 p.
> Traces the influence of Keats's medical knowledge and training on his letters and poems. After recounting the biographical details of the poet's medical training, Goellnicht links specific images and metaphors from the poems as well as broader attitudes and ideas to Keats's studies.

Goldberg, M. A. *The Poetics of Romanticism.* Yellow Springs, Ohio: Antioch Press, 1969, 186 p.
> Examines Keats's poetic theory as delineated in his poems and letters and attempts to place it in literary history from Plato to Sigmund Freud, James Joyce, and T. S. Eliot.

Green, David Bonnell, and Wilson, Edwin Graves, eds. *Keats, Shelley, Byron, Hunt, and Their Circles: A Bibliography, July 1, 1950-June 30, 1962.* Lincoln: University of Nebraska Press, 1964, 323 p.*
> A collection of bibliographies originally published in volumes I through XII of the *Keats-Shelley Journal.* The collection lists all books and articles dealing with Keats, Percy Bysshe Shelley, Lord Byron, Leigh Hunt, and their circles, and the editors frequently supply helpful brief descriptions of the material. See annotation below by Robert A. Hartley for the continuation of the bibliography.

Hartley, Robert A., ed. *Keats, Shelley, Byron, Hunt, and Their Circles: A Bibliography, July 1, 1962-December 31, 1974.* Lincoln: University of Nebraska Press, 1978, 487 p.*
> A continuation of the earlier edition edited by David Bonnell Green and Edwin Graves Wilson (see annotation above).

Hewlett, Dorothy. *Adonais: A Life of John Keats.* Indianapolis: Bobbs-Merrill Co., 1938, 415 p.
> A biography in which Hewlett attempts to "set Keats against the Georgian background." As part of her attempt to present Keats's life in relation to his era, Hewlett excerpts liberally from contemporary reviews of Keats's works. The book was revised in 1970 as *A Life of John Keats.*

Kauvar, Gerald B. *The Other Poetry of Keats.* Rutherford, N.J.: Fairleigh Dickinson University Press, 1969, 238 p.
> Focuses on Keats's lesser known and less frequently studied works, particularly the early and late poems, for their intrinsic artistic value as well as for the light they shed on Keats's development.

The Keats House Committee. *The John Keats Memorial Volume.* London: John Lane, the Bodley Head, 1921, 276 p.
> A centenary compilation of critical essays and biographical articles on Keats and his circle as well as a bibliography of Keats's writings and several translations of his poems into various languages. The volume includes contributions, in both English and foreign languages, from ninety British, American, European, and Eastern critics and scholars, including George Saintsbury, Amy Lowell, Clement Shorter, A. C. Bradley, and Robert Bridges.

Little, Judy. *Keats As a Narrative Poet: A Test of Invention.* Lincoln: University of Nebraska Press, 1975, 167 p.
> An analysis of Keats's longer narrative works, such as *Endymion,* "Lamia," and the two versions of *Hyperion.* Little attempts to demonstrate the intelligence and virtuosity of the larger structures of Keats, "whose sensitive control of the smaller elements in his work," she states, "has long been recognized."

Lowell, Amy. *John Keats.* Boston: Houghton Mifflin Co., Riverside Press, 1929, 662 p.
> A controversial biography that, in addition to meticulously recounting the details of Keats's life, urges Keats's acceptance as a representative of the spirit of modern poetry.

Lyon, Harvey T. *Keats' Well-Read Urn: An Introduction to Literary Method.* New York: Henry Holt and Co., 1958, 118 p.
> A superb introduction to Keats's "Ode to a Grecian Urn." In an attempt "to introduce the student to poetry through criticism, and to criticism through poetry," Lyon offers excerpts from significant textual, scholarly, and critical commentary on the odes by eight writers, from Keats's contemporaries to modern scholars.

MacGillivray, J. R. *Keats: A Bibliography and Reference Guide with an Essay on Keats' Reputation.* University of Toronto Department of English, Studies and Texts, no. 3. Toronto: University of Toronto Press, 1949, 210 p.
> A bibliography through 1946 of primary sources, including first editions and later editions of Keats's poetry, letters, and prose, translations, and creative writings inspired by Keats's life and works, as well as criticism from periodicals and books. MacGillivray also provides a lengthy, useful overview of the rise of Keats's reputation through 1946.

Matthews, G. M., ed. *Keats: The Critical Heritage*. The Critical Heritage Series, edited by B. C. Southam. New York: Barnes & Noble, 1971, 430 p.

An anthology of Keats criticism drawn from books, magazines, letters, and journal entries from the first reviews through 1863. Informative annotations preface each critical piece, and the editor has contributed a helpful introductory overview of Keats's reputation.

Mayhead, Robin. *John Keats*. Cambridge: Cambridge University Press, 1967, 127 p.

Helpful introductory study aimed primarily at the general reader and at students who are unfamiliar with Keats's work. The author integrates a summary of recent Keats criticism into the discussion.

Muir, Kenneth, ed. *John Keats: A Reassessment*. Liverpool English Texts and Studies, no. 5. Liverpool: Liverpool University Press, 1958, 182 p.

Significant collection of ten essays by such noted scholars as Kenneth Muir, Miriam Allott, R. T. Davies, and David I. Masson. Topics explored include Keats's debt to the Elizabethans and his relationship with William Hazlitt, but the majority of the essays are on single poems.

Murry, John Middleton. *Keats and Shakespeare: A Study of Keats' Poetic Life from 1816 to 1820*. London: Oxford University Press, 1926, 248 p.*

A sensitive, influential account of four years of the "inward life" of Keats with special emphasis on Keats's spiritual affinity with and artistic debt to William Shakespeare. Murry supplemented his study with a volume of essays that was revised and expanded several times and was ultimately titled *Keats* (see annotation below).

———. *Keats*. New York: Noonday Press, 1955, 322 p.

Important essays in which Murry discusses various biographical and critical concerns, including Keats's relationship to John Milton, William Blake, and William Wordsworth, his ideas on friendship, and his various poetic theories. This collection was originally published in 1930 as *Studies in Keats* and appeared in revised and enlarged editions as *Studies in Keats: New and Old* in 1939 and *The Mystery of Keats* in 1949. *Keats*, the final incarnation, is intended, as are the earlier volumes, as a companion to Murry's *Keats and Shakespeare: A Study of Keats' Poetic Life from 1816 to 1820* (see annotation above).

Notcutt, H. Clement. Introduction to *Endymion: A Poetic Romance*, by John Keats, pp. xi-lxi. London: Oxford University Press, 1927.

A discussion of the genesis and meaning of *Endymion* that is especially useful for students approaching the poem for the first time.

O'Neill, Judith, ed. *Critics on Keats*. Readings in Literary Criticism, edited by Judith O'Neill, no. 1. Coral Gables, Fla.: University of Miami Press, 1972, 115 p.

Anthology of brief excerpts of commentary on Keats by major critics.

Patterson, Charles I., Jr. *The Daemonic in the Poetry of John Keats*. Urbana: University of Illinois Press, 1970, 258 p.

Examines and demonstrates the effect on Keats's poetry of his awareness of the pre-Christian Greek and Celtic conceptions of the non-malicious demon. Of particular interest to Patterson in this regard are "La Belle Dame sans Merci," "Lamia," "Ode on Indolence," and *Endymion*.

Pettet, E. C. *On the Poetry of Keats*. 1957. Reprint. Cambridge: Cambridge at the University Press, 1970, 395 p.

An examination of Keats's poetry from various viewpoints. While most of Keats's poetry is discussed, the ode "To Autumn" and *The Fall of Hyperion* are considered only briefly. The greatest attention is reserved for *Endymion*, particularly in an effort to discourage its interpretation as evidence that Keats was a metaphysical writer.

Reiman, Donald H. "John Keats." In his *English Romantic Poetry, 1800-1835: A Guide to Information Sources*, pp. 167-83. American Literature, English Literature, and World Literatures in English Information Guide Series, vol. 27. Detroit: Gale Research Co., 1979.

A concise bibliography of collected, selected, and translated editions of Keats's works as well as key textual and critical material. Reiman includes useful descriptive annotations.

Richardson, Joanna. *The Everlasting Spell: A Study of Keats and His Friends*. London: Jonathan Cape, 1963, 255 p.

A study of Keats's relationship with his friends and his influence on them. Richardson also examines how those who survived Keats kept his reputation alive. Fullest attention is granted to Fanny Brawne and to Keats's close friend and first biographer, Charles Armitage Brown (see annotation above).

———. *Keats and His Circle: An Album of Portraits*. London: Cassell, 1980, 127 p.

A collection of portraits and likenesses of Keats, his family, and friends.

Rollins, Hyder Edward. *Keats's Reputation in America to 1848*. Cambridge, Mass.: Harvard University Press, 1946, 147 p.

An exhaustive study of a somewhat limited subject: Keats's reception and reputation in America before 1850.

———, ed. *The Keats Circle: Letters and Papers, 1816-1878*. 2 vols. Cambridge, Mass.: Harvard University Press, 1948.

Exhaustive collection of documents from Keats's circle offering valuable information about both the poet and his friends.

Rossetti, William Michael. *Life of John Keats*. London: Walter Scott, 1887, 217 p.

Brief, sympathetic biography more notable for its perceptive critical commentary than for its now obsolete factual data. Rossetti was the brother of Dante Gabriel Rossetti, the Pre-Raphaelite painter who in the latter part of the nineteenth century promoted Keats as a decorative poet.

Schwartz, Lewis M. *Keats Reviewed by His Contemporaries: A Collection of Notices for the Years 1816-1821*. Metuchen, N.J.: Scarecrow Press, 1973, 362 p.

Reprints of critical essays on Keats that were originally published from 1816 to 1821 as well as material occasioned by his death and by the publication of Percy Bysshe Shelley's *Adonais*.

Sharp, Ronald A. *Keats, Skepticism, and the Religion of Beauty*. Athens: University of Georgia Press, 1979, 198 p.

A consideration of the relationship between skepticism and aestheticism, viewing the latter as the solution to all the problems posed by the former. Sharp discounts the common notion that Keats's impulses toward the real and ideal conflicted, and he attempts to demonstrate through Keats's writings that these two notions were, in fact, compatible.

Slote, Bernice. *Keats and the Dramatic Principle*. Lincoln: University of Nebraska Press, 1958, 229 p.

A consideration of how Keats's awareness of the dramatic principle of objectivity, as well as his interest in playwrighting and in the theater itself, informed both his life and art. Slote believes that Keats achieved greater and greater dramatic objectivity in his poetry, and she concludes her study with a detailed discussion of *Lamia* as a dramatic poem.

Sperry, Stuart M. *Keats the Poet*. Princeton: Princeton University Press, 1973, 350 p.

An overview combining recent scholarship and criticism with Sperry's own observations. Sperry's study is useful as a starting point for upper level students.

Stillinger, Jack. *The Hoodwinking of Madeline and Other Essays on Keats's Poems*. Urbana: University of Illinois Press, 1971, 185 p.

Eight critical essays chiefly written between 1961 and 1971. Included is commentary on *Endymion*, "Isabella," *Hyperion*, "Lamia," "The Eve of St. Mark," and the odes, as well as the title essay on "The Eve of St. Agnes" (see excerpt above, 1961).

Stillinger states that the collection is directed primarily at students rather than scholars.

———. *The Texts of Keats's Poems*. Cambridge, Mass.: Harvard University Press, 1974, 297 p.
A technical study of the various manuscripts and editions of Keats's poems.

———, ed. *Twentieth Century Interpretations of Keats's Odes: A Collection of Critical Essays*. Englewood Cliffs, N.J.: 1968, 122 p.
Eighteen modern interpretations of and viewpoints on Keats's five odes. The editor provides an introduction in which he discusses the style and development of the odes as well Keats's life and other writings.

Talbot, Norman. *The Major Poems of John Keats*. Sydney: Sydney University Press, 1968, 108 p.
A tri-part introductory guide for the student offering a consideration of Keats in relation to the Romantic movement, an analysis of four major poems ("Ode to a Nightingale," "Ode on a Grecian Urn," *The Fall of Hyperion*, and "To Autumn"), and a summary of Keats's criticism.

Tate, Allen. "A Reading of Keats." In his *The Hovering Fly and Other Essays*, pp. 52-70. 1949. Reprint. Freeport, N.Y.: Books for Libraries Press, 1968.
Analyzes Keats's use of the pictorial method in "Ode to a Nightingale." Tate integrates a discussion of late nineteenth and early twentieth-century Keats criticism into his discussion.

Thorpe, Clarence D[e Witt]. "Keats." In *The English Romantic Poets: A Review of Research*, edited by Thomas M. Raysor, pp. 191-241. New York: Modern Language Association of America, 1950.
A selective guide to research aimed primarily at graduate students.

Thorpe, Clarence De Witt. *The Mind of John Keats*. New York: Russell & Russell, 1964, 209 p.
The first and most significant arguments that Keats was an intellectual poet as well as merely one of sensations.

Trilling, Lionel. Introduction to *The Selected Letters of John Keats*, by John Keats, edited by Lionel Trilling pp. 3-41. Great Letters Series, edited by Louis Kronenberger. New York: Farrar, Straus and Young, 1951.
A key analysis of the artistic, biographical, and psychological interest of Keats's correspondence.

Van Ghent, Dorothy. *Keats: The Myth of the Hero*. Rev. ed. Edited by Jeffrey Cane Robinson. Princeton: Princeton University Press, 1983, 277 p.
Traces the myth of the hero archetype through Keats's works. The study is an edited and revised version of an unfinished manuscript left by Van Ghent at her death in 1967.

Ward, Aileen. *John Keats: The Making of a Poet*. New York: Viking Press, 1964, 450 p.
Considered among the best modern biographies. Ward's study is a critical account written from a subtly psychological perspective.

Wasserman, Earl R. *The Finer Tone: Keats' Major Poems*. Baltimore: Johns Hopkins Press, 1953, 228 p.
Influential analysis of Keats's philosophic tendencies and his poetic technique. Wasserman discusses five poems: "Ode on a Grecian Urn," "La Belle Dame sans Merci," "The Eve of St. Agnes," "Lamia," and "Ode to a Nightingale."

Williams, Meg Harris. *Inspiration in Milton and Keats*. Totowa, N.J.: Barnes & Noble Books, 1982, 212 p.*
Traces the development of Keats's and John Milton's poetic inspiration through a chronological discussion of their works.

Wilson, Katharine M. *The Nightingale and the Hawk: A Psychological Study of Keats' Ode*. London: George Allen & Unwin, 1964, 157 p.
A Jungian interpretation of Keats's poetic imagery in "Ode to a Nightingale."

Wolff, Lucien. *An Essay on Keats' Treatment of the Heroic Rhythm and Blank Verse*. Paris: Hachette et Cie, 1909, 154 p.
Meticulous analysis of Keats's early poems "Lamia" and *Hyperion*.

Zillman, Lawrence John. *John Keats and the Sonnet Tradition: A Critical and Comparative Study*. Los Angeles: Lyman House, 1939, 209 p.
Explores the formal and technical aspects of Keats's sonnets in relation to the English sonnet tradition from Sir Thomas Wyatt and Henry Howard.

Ignacy Krasicki

1735-1801

(Also wrote under the pseudonym of Michael Mowiński) Polish poet, novelist, dramatist, editor, essayist, and short story writer.

Krasicki is renowned as one of the greatest Polish writers of the Enlightenment. His highly polished concise verse and prose were influential in the development of the Polish language. Krasicki helped establish Polish as a viable literary language by excluding foreign and vulgar phrases from his writings. In addition, he is admired for his mastery of several genres and for his influence on the development of the Polish novel, fable, and poetry. In his works, Krasicki often uses satire both to entertain and instruct his audience.

The descendant of an impoverished aristocratic family, Krasicki was born in Dubieko, in southern Poland. As a child he demonstrated his developing literary talent at the Jesuit school in Lwów and later at the Warsaw Catholic Seminary. In 1751, Krasicki was ordained a priest and rose quickly through the ranks of the ecclesiastical hierarchy to become a friend and personal chaplain of the Polish king, Stanisław August Poniatowski. At the suggestion of the king, Krasicki promoted the arts and helped improve the Polish educational system. He also contributed essays to the periodical *Zabawy przyjemne i pozyłeczne,* and in 1764, at the king's invitation, he became the editor of the *Polish Monitor,* a moralistic periodical patterned after the London *Spectator.* In the *Monitor,* which was one of the first Polish literary periodicals, Krasicki published many of his own writings as well as those he adapted from foreign sources. He was appointed the Bishop of Warmia in 1776, during a period of political uncertainty that strongly affected Krasicki's career. Though Poland was a united nation during much of the eighteenth century, its increasing political and economic instability allowed its powerful neighbors Prussia, Russia, and Austria to gradually absorb what had been Polish territory. This occurred in three phases, known as partitions. When the First Partition took place in 1772, Krasicki's diocese was ceded to Prussia. As a subject of the Prussian king Frederick the Great, Krasicki did not remain politically active; instead, he directed his energy to writing. The year 1775 marks the beginning of Krasicki's greatest period of literary productivity, when he wrote many of his most celebrated poems, fables, parables, and his two novels *Mikołaja Doświadczyńskiego przypadki* and *Pan Podstoli.* In 1795, the year that Krasicki was consecrated the Archbishop of Gniezno, the Third Partition dismembered the Polish nation. Krasicki lived at the court of the Prussian king Frederick William until shortly before his death.

Krasicki was a remarkably prolific writer, whose critically acclaimed writings include epics, novels, fables, and satires, yet several of his works, including his epistles, dramas, and fictional history, are neglected by English-language critics. His mock-heroic epic poem *Myszeidos* is derived from an old Polish legend. It depicts a war between cats and mice, and is often interpreted as a parody of the political squabbles of Poland's provincial assemblies and national parliament. While acknowledging its excellent versification, many scholars assert that the poem is monotonous and unsuccessful as an allegory. In *Monachomachija; czyli, Wojna mnichow (Monachologia; or,*

Handbook of the Natural History of Monks), Krasicki depicted a dispute between the Dominican and Carmelite monastic orders. His satirical portraits of the sloth and ignorance of individual monks are considered evidence of his didactic intent: to alleviate superstition, drunkenness, and pedantry from monastic life. Because it was written by a clergyman, *Monachologia* caused a great sensation and was harshly criticized in Poland when first published; today, the poem's witty and vividly drawn portraits are generally thought to outweigh its antiquated style and uninteresting plot. *Antymonachomachija,* its sequel, is also an attack on life in the monastery, although critics concur that Krasicki intended this poem to appear as a refutation of his earlier work.

Krasicki's novels *Mikołaja Doświadczyńskiego* and *Pan Podstoli* are among the first Polish examples of that genre. *Mikołaja Doświadczyńskiego* comprises three parts, or books, in which Krasicki criticizes the faults of his age. In Part I he describes the protagonist Doświadczyński's education and entrance into society, and in Parts II and III he presents a utopian society and outlines his plan for the betterment of humanity. Throughout its detailed plot and vividly sketched scenes, Krasicki uses his economical, concentrated prose to satirize many facets of Polish life. *Pan Podstoli* consists of conversations recounted by the narrator, Pantler, in which Krasicki treats such varied subjects as bribery, prodigality, and ignorance. Here, the author advocates moderation and stresses the importance of art over politics. Though scholars generally praise the realism of *Pan Podstoli*, they dispute its genre. Several contend that because it lacks plot and characterizations, it cannot be labeled a novel. Most agree, however, that the work's basic flaw is the character of Pantler, whose lack of human frailties is considered unbelievable. Both *Mikołaja Doświadczyńskiego* and *Pan Podstoli* were popular in Poland in the eighteenth century and were widely imitated. In addition, they spurred public interest in the novel which led to the Polish publication of works by such novelists as Henry Fielding, Oliver Goldsmith, and Abbé Prévost. Despite their immediate popularity and importance as early examples of the Polish novel, *Mikołaja Doświadczyńskiego* and *Pan Podstoli* have received only limited critical attention by English language critics.

Among Krasicki's best-known works are his collections of approximately two hundred fables contained in *Bajki i przypowieści* and *Bajki nowe*. These fables depict both people and animals in their struggle between vice and virtue. While Krasicki borrowed their themes and format from the works of such fabulists as Aesop and Jean de la Fontaine, most critics contend that by placing them in the particular context of contemporary Poland and imbuing them with his satirical humor, he made the fables uniquely his own. Scholars praise their concision, versification, and dramatic power; several suggest, however, that his style is too austere. Like many Enlightenment poets, Krasicki also wrote satires, collected in *Satyry*, in which he ridiculed the Polish gentry by focusing on their vices, including gambling, drunkenness, usury, and avarice. In *Satyry*, he skillfully combined lyrical, dramatic, and didactic elements to create what commentators describe as masterful satire. They note that while Krasicki continued to write in his elegant verse style, the tone of his satires is more bitter than previous writings. Of Krasicki's many works, the fables and satires have received the most sustained critical attention. These short verse works, in addition to his mock-heroic epics and novels, have secured Krasicki's reputation as one of the greatest Polish authors of the eighteenth century.

PRINCIPAL WORKS

Myszeidos (poetry) 1775
Mikołaja Doświadczyńskiego przypadki (novel) 1776
Monachomachija; czyli, Wojna mnichow (poetry) 1778
 [*Monachologia; or, Handbook of the Natural History of Monks*, 1852]
Pan Podstoli (novel) 1778
Bajki i przypowieści (fables) 1779
Historia na dwie księgi podzielona (fictional history) 1779
Satyry (satires) 1779
Antymonachomachija (poetry) 1780
Listy (epistles) 1780
Wojna Chocimska (poetry) 1780
 [*The War of Chocim* published in *Specimens of the Polish Poets*, 1827]
Satyry (satires) 1784
Bajki nowe (fables) 1802
Dopełnienia. 8 vols. (poetry) 1830-32
Pisma wybrane. 4 vols. (poetry, novels, letters, essays, and short stories) 1954
Komedie (dramas) 1956
Korespondencja I. Krasickiego, 1734-1801 (letters) 1958
Pisma poetyckie (poetry) 1975

Selections of Krasicki's fables and poetry in English translation have appeared in the following publications: *An Argosy of Fables, A Collection of Polish Verse, Five Centuries of Polish Poetry,* and *Poets and Poetry of Poland.*

STANISLAS KOŹMIAN (essay date 1838)

Ignatius Krasicki, Bishop of Warmia, is by common consent placed at the head of [Polish] poets. Though the validity of his title to sovereignty might, perhaps, be questioned, I shall still abide by it, feeling that in none of our writers are combined so many and varied excellencies. In any period, in any literature, his works must have been remarkable for their purity of taste, and classic finish: how much the more so, when it is remembered that they have been produced in Poland, and under so many adverse circumstances. . . .

The chief characteristic of his genius was its wit, and hence he excelled chiefly in the composition of fables, satires, and serio-comic poems. His fables alone are almost two hundred in number; they are in the mouth of every child in Poland. The French critics, in the fulness of their admiration for Lafontaine, say, that having painted nature so well, he destroyed his pencil. The Polish might amend their remark by saying, that he lent it to Krasicki.

His wit shows itself as a sharper and more powerful weapon in his satires. In these, his panegyrists have praised him for combining the delicacy and the sprightliness of Horace with the force of Juvenal. To our thinking, Krasicki could hardly be more justly lauded, than by quoting what Blair says of the Roman writer, ''that he reproves with a smiling aspect, and while he moralizes like a sound philosopher, discovers at the same time the politeness of a courtier;'' or still more delicately to express the gentleness, decorum, and elegance with which our satirist points out national faults and prejudices, we may borrow the simile of the German, who said of Horace, that ''he laughs with white teeth.'' . . . It was, however, in the serio-comic poem, that Krasicki's humour found its freest scope; three of the four compositions of this kind, which owe their authorship to him, are considered as his finest works. The first of these is **'Myszeis'** ['**Myszeidos'**], the Polish Batrachomyomachia (Homer's poem), wherein is told the tale, possessed by the Poles in common with many other nations, of a king being devoured by mice. The poet in his ingenious account of the war between the mice and the rats, ridicules the dissensions, which then prevailed in the councils of Poland. Another of Krasicki's serio-comic poems originated in the circumstance of [King] Frederick having once . . . [asked] him to write something after the sarcastic manner of the French philosopher [Voltaire]. In compliance with his request the bishop composed his **'Monachomachia,'** or the War of Monks. Nor could he have paid a better compliment to a Protestant king, or have better trodden in the footsteps of the French sage, than by thus holding up to ridicule the peculiarities of monkish life. (p. 493)

Besides being distinguished as an original writer, our poet was excellent as a translator. His version of Ossian, to the delight of the whole Polish nation, attests [to] his powers in this branch of authorship. The smaller pieces of his poetry, his poetical epistles, and descriptions of his journeys, in which he relieved prose with poetry, are also full of beauty. His prose works are less eminent. Two of his novels, however, are still read and admired, not for any great power of invention which they display, but for their faithful descriptions and poignant satire on national errors and prejudices. (p. 494)

> *Stanislas Koźmian, "Literature of the Nineteenth Century," in* The Athenaeum, *No. 559, July 14, 1838, pp. 491-95.**

THE NORTH AMERICAN REVIEW (essay date 1848)

[Krasicki's] works are distinguished for their piquant wit and easy gracefulness of style, rather than for depth of feeling or glow of fancy; yet there are times when a higher spirit seems to kindle in him, when the patriotic ardor never wanting in any Pole lends a temporary glow to his pencil. There are passages in his **"Wojna Chocimska"** eloquent and stirring, and though this work cannot claim to be regarded as a great poem, it rises, in many parts, far above the level of modern epics. The fables of Krasicki [in **"Bajki i przypowieści"** and **"Bajki nowe"**] are gracefully and pleasantly written, and have deservedly enjoyed great popularity; but the most esteemed of his works, and those which have the best preserved their first reputation, are his satires [in **"Satyry"**]. To this style of composition his powers were peculiarly adapted; for satire addresses itself to the intellect, and, making no demand upon the feelings, leaves us the less sensible of the absence of enthusiasm. (p. 333)

> *"Living Writers of Poland," in* The North American Review, *Vol. LXVI, No. CXXXIX, April, 1848, pp. 323-48.**

[W. R. MORFILL] (essay date 1879)

It must be confessed that the **"War of Chocim"** [**"Wojna Chocimska"**] written to celebrate a Polish victory in the earlier part of the seventeenth century, is at best but a dull affair; dull, however, as it is, it is made even more pale and colourless in the tame version [given in] . . . **"Specimens of Polish Poets."** The mock heroics of Krasicki are, to say the least, amusing: poems in the style of the "Rape of the Lock" [by Alexander Pope] are more likely to be genuine productions in the eighteenth century than an epic. (p. 372)

> *[W. R. Morfill], "Polish Literature," in* The Westminster Review, *n.s. Vol. LV, No. II, April 1, 1879, pp. 359-86.**

PAUL SOBOLESKI (essay date 1883)

Krasicki occupied a high place in Polish literature. He was very witty, and although he did not display great creative powers in his comic composition, he had a way of his own to sing with the harmony of a bird, adding to it a precision and a consummate finish. Being an excellent judge of the human heart, he had a happy faculty of seeing men and things exactly as they were; hence he was pertinent and practical. He was an excellent delineator of the faults and foibles of the living pictures of society.

Among the poetical works of Krasicki his satires are entitled to the first place and consideration; except their pungency they have no real bitterness in them, and always a tendency to correct the existing state of things. In them he paints in a humorous manner the customs, ways, and manners so precisely that such a description was something very uncommon in those days. (pp. 123-24)

His **"Monachomachia, or the War of the Monks,"** was written when he and [the French philosopher] Voltaire lived together at the Palace of Sans-Souci. It was a happy occurrence that when Krasicki embraced Voltaire's philosophical ideas he did not reach as deeply as Voltaire himself. . . . [Krasicki] was by nature true to himself, and did not possess that virulence of character. . . . In this production he distinguishes himself in pleasant but harmless wit, nice imagery, accuracy, and grace of expression. Throwing the mantle of fun, and even ludicrousness, over high thoughts, the author exerted great power and influence in that direction. (pp. 124-25)

Besides the satirical writings of Krasicki we can place his **"Letters"** [**"Listy"**]—the subject matter and the style of which very much approach his satires. These, being written in verse after French models, palpably remind us of the haste and defects of the literature of that period.

In his **"Doświadczyński"** (the man of experience), a moral tale written in prose, Krasicki paints the social defects of that time. Thoughtlessness, prodigality, litigation, bribery, the law intrigues, court eloquence, are pictured in vivid colors. This jocular but highly interesting production hits somebody or something every time, and shows in the author an uncommon talent and discrimination of how and where to castigate national blemishes.

From all of Krasicki's writings his **"Fables"** [**"Bajki i przypowieści"** and **"Bajki nowe"**] were perhaps the most popular; they all contain truths, expressed with great conciseness and wit, comprising at the same time deep meaning, sound practical philosophy, replete with the spirit of reflection, humanity, and frequently patriotism. They are all short, practical tales, allegories, or witty anecdotes. (pp. 125-26)

His **"Pan Podstoli"** we consider a valuable depository, and it stands as a living monument of Polish ancestry. In this work Krasicki rises higher in philosophical tendency than any painters of characters or novel-writers have ever led us. In the representation of Mr. Podstoli he did not follow any especial ideal, or the originality of any person; he simply and plainly painted a characteristic portrait of a citizen, husband, father, and neighbor. . . . (p. 126)

Krasicki is the man of his epoch, not only of the age he lived in, but for all ages to come, so long as we will think, feel, and write in Polish. Krasicki had within him every quality to raise him to so high a sphere. He possessed immense creative powers, an original mind, and original ways of looking at things,—qualities which in reality constitute a true poet. He created a sphere to which he attracted the people without any resistance on their part,—so much so that his poetry became a necessary element in their existence.

The great archbishop stands on the borders of the eighteenth and nineteenth centuries; but the creation and preparation of a boundless poetical sphere, and bringing a general use of his ideas into different strata of society, make him a poet not only of his age, but also of the present time. (pp. 126-27)

> *Paul Soboleski, "Krasicki," in* Poets and Poetry of Poland: A Collection of Polish Verse, *edited by Paul Soboleski, second edition, Knight & Leonard, Printers, 1883, pp. 123-28.*

STANISLAW DOBRZYCKI (essay date 1922)

[Throughout his chronological survey of Krasicki's works, Dobrzycki stresses the author's influence on Polish literature. Ac-

cording to this critic, Krasicki had a profound impact on Polish as a literary language and on the development of several genres, including the novel, satire, and fable. Dobrzycki also focuses on the increasing didacticism of Krasicki's works and his attempt to combat sarmatism, which critics describe as the archaic traditions and values of the eighteenth-century Polish gentry. Sarmatism was a legacy of the "Saxon chaos," a period at the beginning of the eighteenth century during the rule of Augustus II of Saxony when the nation's economy, education, and literature deteriorated.]

Within a few years, from 1773 to 1780, [Krasicki] produced his finest works—those which place him incontestably at the head of contemporary letters, by which he exercised the greatest influence upon the subsequent development of literature, and in which he at the same time revealed himself best, both as a thinker and as a literary artist.

The first in date (1775) is a poem which became all the rage at the time, but in no way excites the same admiration to-day. This mock-heroic poem bears the title of *Myszeis* [*Myszeidos*] . . . , and in it he celebrates the battle of the rats and mice against the cats. People have tried to explain this odd and puerile theme, wholly out of harmony with the age, by saying that it is, or was intended to be, nothing more or less than an allegorical political satire. If such was indeed the poet's intention, we can only say that he did not carry it out properly, or that he blunted all its points on purpose. But neither explanation appears to be the truth. The *Myszeis* obviously belongs to the category of those mock-heroic poems in which the seventeenth and eighteenth centuries delighted, to those burlesque productions which were the degenerate descendants of the great epics. . . . It is impossible for us to-day to translate the *Myszeis* into terms of politics, though in a number of details and sketches from life it has a very marked air of topical satire, and conforms in this respect to the general tendency of contemporary literature. Its wit, however, is not so sparkling, nor its sallies so entertaining as to make us overlook the triviality of the subject and the poverty of invention displayed. Still, to do it justice, we must admit that, if the public of the time took such keen delight in the *Myszeis*, they had some reason for it: it was long since Polish literature had heard so ringing a line, so winged and harmonious a stanza, so pure and restrained a language, just as it had never beheld so much charm, ease and general lightness. Trivial in substance and barren of thought, this poem is yet in its form the first irrefutable proof that Polish poetry, after escaping from the chaos of the Saxon period, has learnt to assume the embroidered mantle of the bard.

In 1778, Krasicki brought out a second poem, still in the same humorous vein, but this time profounder in thought and more trenchant in its wit: the *Monachomachia*. . . . [It] is a criticism of the dull intelligence of some monks, of their purely vegetable existence altogether given over to the pursuit of comfort and material pleasures, and altogether barren of higher spiritual aspirations. When we have allowed for the exaggeration and coarsening demanded by this style of composition, which amounts to complete misrepresentation and caricature (and these are defects from which no burlesque or mock-heroic poems in European literatures are exempt in this period), we see that the *Monachomachia* is an excellent work of its kind. Of its kind—for in these days we no longer greatly appreciate this style of composition, and if any poet should happen to attempt a subject of the sort, he would approach it in quite another spirit and execute it in quite another form. The psychology of the characters is too summary, uniform and monotonous, and differing only in external signs. Thus the comic element does not grow

out of the characterisation, as in the great humourists, but only out of the situation and material contrasts. None the less, the poem is full of charming details, animated scenes, vigorously-drawn satirical pictures and just and sensible criticisms. The author never gets angry or loses his temper—such a thing would have been quite contrary to his nature—he jests, rather, with the joyous humour of our ancestors, or else arms himself with an irony void of gall or bitterness, smiling and light, yet sharp and caustic.

The *Monachomachia* is not only interesting as a manifestation of the talent of Krasicki, but also assumes a much greater significance if we look at it in its context and in relation to the tendencies then dominant among Polish society.

As far as it is a satire on monastic customs and ignorance in general, it is very much of its period, of the century of rationalism and free-thought. It is related to the whole literature of Europe (especially to French literature), which expended so much energy in attacking the religious Orders, and discrediting them by force of satire, irony, ridicule and malice. It is thus probable that the root-idea of this work was not inspired in Krasicki by life itself, but rather by books and other literature, and that in writing it he had had no other intention than to sketch an amusing caricature. But the poet's penetrating observation and his powerful instinct for reality have introduced into the *Monachomachia,* side by side with the purely literary elements, others which are essentially alive; thus he is not content with making what might be called a general satire on Europe: it is the life of Polish monks which he depicts for us, a life which he had the opportunity of observing for himself at short range. . . . [He] takes up his pen with the declared intention of urging his contemporaries into the path of reform, as being the only one which could lead them to a higher culture, he mingles in his poem more lofty and pregnant thoughts with the element of entertainment: his aim is not only to distract and amuse, but to instruct and correct. (pp. 344-46)

[Let] us now examine for a moment the quality of the subject-matter which this satire had to deal with: it is essentially comic; it presents us with absurdities rather than vices, absurdities which pointed the contrast between the modern civilisation and that of the Saxon period, which were weaknesses, but not crimes, defects, but not the shameful perversities of corrupt characters, such as, for example, treachery, hypocrisy or debauchery. Hence, for all its caustic quality, the satire is merry and facetious rather than malicious or virulent. And if we look more closely, we may even see that it is directed less against the monks than against the Saxon period itself; the poem in fact mocks and holds up to scorn ignorance, idleness, drunkenness—things which, in Polish satire of this period, are inseparable from "sarmatism" in general. (pp. 346-47)

Almost at the same time as the two poems we have mentioned, there appeared Krasicki's two best prose works—two novels: The *Adventures of Nicholas Doświadczyński* [(*Mikołaja Doświadczyńskiego przypadki*) and *The Podstoli* (*Pan Podstoli*)]. . . . These novels reveal a new Krasicki. His horizon has widened, his thought has become profounder, his field of observation more extended, the "motifs" he treats, more numerous and varied. In fact, *Doświadczyński* marks an important date in the history of the modern novel, that of the first appearance of the *genre* in Polish letters. (p. 347)

[*Doświadczyński*] is a didactic and moral composition: to attain this double end, the author sends his hero—and the reader—to the school of life, and skilfully draws lessons therefrom. He starts off with a bad upbringing at home and subsequently at school, and shows the inevitable result to be indecision and vagueness of thought and a weak, wavering character, and hence, a moral downfall for the lad thus ill-equipped for life's pilgrimage. Then, to provide some sunshine to dispel these clouds of gloom, Krasicki goes on to narrate the events and circumstances which together bring about the moral salvation and regeneration of Doświadczyński, and lead to a harmonious conclusion, in all respects, mental and material, of the course of his "adventures" and his destiny.

In this respect, the *Adventures of Doświadczyński* are a Polish specimen of that type of novel which was enjoying so great a vogue in all Western European literature at that period. . . . [We] owe to Krasicki the introduction of this genre into his native letters. If, however, we scrutinise the work in detail, we find that it suffers from lack of unity, being composed of various different elements and materials derived from a number of separate sources.

The three parts of the novel have the same general tendency running through them, but they differ perceptibly in the way this tendency is brought out in the vicissitudes of the story, in the mental process by which it is disengaged, and, finally, in artistic value.

The best, both in form and substance, is incontestably the first part, because in it the poet keeps closer to life and reality. Here, the better to set forth his ideas and compose his scenes, he makes use of the medium which was the most appropriate to the theme, the medium of satire. With a fine irony, supported by an acute observation, the author makes his characters move and speak, and paints wonderful and unforgettable pictures: we have the paternal home, the environment in which Doświadczyński is brought up, the band of adventurers and intriguers with whom he wastes his youth, the extravagant life he leads after coming into his magnificent inheritance, his stay in Warsaw, when he is initiated into the code of etiquette and into social elegance, the episode of the Court of Justice at Lublin . . . , finally his foreign travels, and his wild doings in Paris. . . . All these scenes, sketched in with extraordinary vivacity and vividness, sparkle with verve and wit, and a wit undoubtedly far more subtle and refined than that of the *Monachomachia*. Besides, the subject is a much wider one, and consequently gives much freer scope for thought. Hence in this satire almost the whole panorama of contemporary Polish life is unrolled before our eyes: here the author attacks Sarmatism (Doświadczyński's parents, his education, school discipline, justice and justices, and the frivolous, debauched, lazy and stupid life of many rich country nobles), as also at the same time the evils inherent in the new customs (gaming, dissipation, display, futility, fashionable education and the whole superficial veneer of civilisation). This satire shows us how, in the country as in town, in the old days as in modern times, characters were bound to become corrupted under the disastrous influence of ignorance, frivolity and failure to understand life. . . . [*Doświadczyński*] is also an admirable mirror of the manners of the period. (pp. 347-49)

The only accusation that might be made against the first book of *Doświadczyński* is that it is rather brief and summary in method. It is true that the principal events and circumstances which it is important to throw into relief are clearly rendered by the author in high light and with all possible truth and brilliance. But in a novel of this kind we should prefer a rather less headlong pace; we should like to linger over a few details and small incidents which might give the tale something of

what is called epic quality and make the picture clearer, more comprehensive and more nearly complete. This breadth which we observe in the English novels of the eighteenth century is wanting in *Doświadczyński*, and excellent as it is, Part I is still only a sketch of the novel of manners.

The sequel of the work [in Parts II and III], in which the author offers for our contemplation the progressive amendment of his hero, does not keep up to the level of the first book. . . . Except for the last pages, where Doświadczyński is back in his native land, and which contain an excellent satire on political life, Krasicki has here involved himself in an undertaking quite foreign to the bent of his talent and in these last two parts of his work has abandoned the firm ground of reality to float in a sea of "literature." Nothing but literary suggestion in the taste of the day can account for the Utopian isle of the Nipouans, brooded over by the shade of Rousseau, and who knows whether Krasicki, in painting this chimerical Eden, was not poking ironical fun at himself, thus struggling with a task so incongruous in form and idea with his whole moral and intellectual organisation? . . .

[We] must note a certain deviation and break in the original and logical idea of the work. Under the stress of circumstance Doświadczyński changes and becomes a better man. But the improvement is only an individual one. . . . Krasicki did not see that the principal aim, the essential point of the first part of the novel is to show up the evils preying upon society, and that the conclusion we come to, in reading it, is that those evils must be put right here and now, in the country itself. On his return to Poland Doświadczyński is no longer the man he was when he left home; he is changed, but we do not find him taking any action to combat the evil of which he was once the victim. (p. 349)

In histories of literature, *The Podstoli* is classed as a novel, but this is merely an approximate description, because it must have a label of some kind. The book, as a matter of fact, is not a novel. Certainly things happen in it; indeed, there is a great deal of action and a vast number of characters to carry it on. But we do not find in it that definite plan of action which the novel demands, action with a beginning, a development and an end: nor do we find the character-drawing usual in a novel. It is rather a series of detached episodes, serving to acquaint us with the character of the principal hero and intermingled with his innumerable speeches and disquisitions, all jumbled together anyhow, without preamble or *dénouement*. In *The Podstoli*, the author intends to show us a decent man and a good citizen. In fact, we are dealing with a moral treatise, like those of which ancient literature has bequeathed us many examples, such as Rej's *Life of a Good Man*, and Górnicki's *Courtier*; but the form is no longer the same. The taste of the public had altered in the meantime; people no longer cared for lessons conveyed directly in the severe and rigic guise of a dissertation or a treatise on morality; it was now necessary to wrap up the precepts in an attractive form, to clothe them in all the graces of style, as did the French novel. . . . Thus, as regards literary form, *The Podstoli* also derives from French literature.

In substance and tendency it is, however, pre-eminently Polish, and reproduces a specifically Polish aspect of life. Krasicki is not here concerned with human psychology in general, or the ideal man. His object is to create a type and model by which his own fellow-citizens may take example. Thus he places him among exclusively Polish conditions and eliminates all out-of-the-way contingencies, fortuitous occurrences and accidents such as still play a great part in the history of Doświadczyński; he shows us the Podstoli pursuing the even tenor of his daily life in all its simplicity and verisimilitude, with no extraordinary incidents: in short, in constructing this ideal personage he never for a moment forgets to make him perfectly accessible and imitable.

It is just this that constitutes the great value of the work: its artistic value in the first place, thanks to the exactitude, realism and sincerity of the pictures. And this value is increased still further by the mastery with which the secondary characters are presented, the subsidiary figures which supplement the picture of the Podstoli himself. These personages are either, each in his own sphere, replicas of the Podstoli, duplicates, so to speak, of the decent man of the world, or else they form a contrast to him. It goes without saying that Krasicki draws the latter with satiric strokes, and if we take them in the abstract, these are perhaps the most living of all the portraits. We should notice, as a trait which helps us in placing Krasicki as a satirist and redresser of the errors and abuses of society, that he takes these antitheses of the Podstoli from the ''sarmatist'' world quite as frequently as from the world of modern society. This further accentuates the Podstoli as the type of the ''golden mean,'' the true ideal, the faithful incarnation of Krasicki's inmost thought.

It is a fact that in *The Podstoli* the fantastic and unreal find no place; they are wholly excluded from it. The work gains great historic importance thereby, and becomes for us to-day an interesting document, a valuable repository of information about the period. This also gives it moral value, since the ideal proposed is within the range of possibility, and may be attained. We must not forget, however, that this possibility refers more to details, less to the whole: the Podstoli in his entirety is, indeed, too ideal for a simple mortal; he is too impeccable, too exempt from human frailty: and this is the great weakness of the book. In detail it is very life-like and very true, whereas in the conception and presentment of the chief character it is too theoretical and too machine-made. It certainly looks as though the author could hardly have avoided this drawback: in a novel one can represent man just as he is in real life, with all his good qualities and weaknesses, whereas in a moral treatise one can only hold up an example for imitation, which must consequently be complete, perfect, without spot or wrinkle. (pp. 350-51)

Still, with all its defects, *The Podstoli* is one of the most interesting and remarkable works of its kind. It has no sparkling fancy, it does not move us, it does not impress us with the profundity of its psychology, but if we wish to know all about Krasicki himself and his period, we could not find a better guide than *The Podstoli.* (p. 352)

The *Adventures of Doświadczyński* and the *Podstoli,* welcomed enthusiastically by the public, constitute an important event in the literature of this closing century, both as to their matter and their form. They are the first prose works of the period which are written in a renovated, chastened, pure and elegant language. The finer modern prose, like the finer modern poetry only comes in with Krasicki. Moreover these two works decide the shape and structure of the Polish novel. Thus they begin a new era in the development of this form, and . . . they may be said to introduce it into Poland. As soon as these novels appeared they gave rise to imitations.

The works we have mentioned represent the first phase in the literary activity of Krasicki when it has reached its full ex-

pression. His best work was soon to follow, it is the masterpiece of Polish Pseudo-classicism, the *Satires* [*Satyry*]. . . . (p. 353)

Krasicki had had many forerunners in this literary form, but he may be considered as the creator of modern Polish satire. In his hands it reached its typical, classical form and attained to its highest artistic expression. His satires, and there are twenty-two, are first of all masterpieces of form and composition, and under this aspect they can vie with the productions of the greatest satirists in the whole of literature. The language is admirably suited to the form as to the matter; it is ''literary'' from one end to the other of the work, crystal-clear, elegant and at the same time exquisitely simple and natural. The essential principles of right expression are never ignored or neglected; there is no affectation, no grandiloquence, nor is there any vulgarity. In them are revealed in a striking manner all the characteristic merits of Krasicki, of his temperament, his art and his turn of mind.

The art of the composition also contributes to the perfection of the satires; it is faultless, clear and condensed. The verse runs easily, light and unencumbered. It is on the skilful combination of divers elements, such as the lyrical, the epic, the dramatic and the didactic, that the internal disposition of the satire depends and this is what determines, in a great measure, the impression it creates. From this point of view, too, the satires of Krasicki offer first of all a great variety and then a happy combination of the several elements we have mentioned.

Sentiment, it must be admitted, is not the dominant characteristic of Krasicki. The rationalism of the time did not encourage its growth, nor did the poet's own disposition favour its manifestation. Nevertheless it is in his *Satires* that there is relatively the greatest display of emotion, and that the poet's sensitiveness comes out most strongly.

But the *Satires,* with all the wit that flashes in them, with all the gaiety they display, and with all their elegant trifling, leave on the whole an impression of sadness. In any case we are here in quite another atmosphere from that of the *Myszeis* and the [*Monachomachia*] with their elvish pranks and laughter. . . . Even when, as in the born satirist, liveliness, irony, malice seem to dominate, the time comes when such a writer harks back to seriousness and even to melancholy and despondency. Krasicki is no exception to the rule. (pp. 353-54)

If the *Satires* are Krasicki's best work, the *Fables* [*Bajki i przypowieści* and *Bajki nowe*] are his most popular one, and the one that has penetrated most widely into the life of the Polish nation. Like La Fontaine in France and Krilow in Russia, Krasicki is in Poland the standard fable-writer. (p. 355)

[It] is to Krasicki that must be ascribed the rapid success of fable in the Polish literature of the period. It was he who gave to that form of poetry, as he had given to satire, the perfect, definitive, artistic form which was henceforth to stand as a model and which, as a matter of fact, was imitated by all others.

Krasicki had at first dealt with immediate actuality, the men and things of the Poland of his time; but he gradually extended his purview and his studies and turned to problems lying beyond the bounds of local observation, to universal human problems. Thus it was that the [*Monachomachia*] was succeeded by *Doświadczyński* and *The Podstoli,* that these were followed by the *Satires* and finally, as the crowning work, by the *Fables,* in which the general element, characteristic of humanity as a whole, asserts its supremacy. Here the author has not chiefly or exclusively in view the transformation of the ''Sarmatian''

Polish world into a modern society on the same level as the other nations of Europe. His teaching goes further. It is addressed not so much to his fellow-countrymen as to man in general.

The *Fables* are written in a pure, correct and classical language, which is even, perhaps, a little too severe in form, that is to say devoid of those inequalities which sometimes add an agreeable variety to turns of phrase and expressions, and makes them richer in colour and more individual. The construction of Krasicki's *Fables* is excellent: extremely neat, concise and logical, bringing out all that is essential in the expression as well as in the ideas and consequently answering perfectly to the double object of a work of art. By this close texture and logical arrangement, by the wonderful painting of the characters, Krasicki's *Fables* attain to a dramatic quality which is also revealed in the organising of the action. Here the fabulist often employs methods similar to those used for the stage. For these many reasons, the *Fables* are worthy, as we have said, to figure among the masterpieces of their kind in all literature. If a fault were to be found in Krasicki, it would be a certain parsimony of details. The tendency to give us a bare sketch becomes more marked in the *Fables,* and there is perhaps here some loss of value in the effect produced. Consequently, though Krasicki is nowise inferior to La Fontaine in vivacity of action, in the freshness and originality of his situations, he remains behind him in dramatic power and as a painter of manners. (pp. 355-56)

After the Saxon chaos, Krasicki reformed the language of literature and above all the poetic speech. Krasicki's own style is perhaps a little pale, it is without any marked individuality. This is, however, peculiar to the epoch and to Pseudoclassicism in general. It lacks colour and vigour. On the other hand, it is polished, concise, clear, logical; it is really a "literary" language and not the vulgar tongue, common, rough, sometimes stronger and more expressive, but devoid of artistic perfection. It is the impulse given by Krasicki which has chiefly contributed to raise the standard of the literary tongue of his time and to give it polish. . . .

The influence of Krasicki was also deeply felt in the various literary forms. The poet had given a classical shape to the mock-heroic poem, to satire, to the epistle, to the fable. Apart from a few insignificant modifications the types of each kind that he introduced into Polish literature were destined to subsist till the Romantic period, and, in the case of the fable, even beyond its time. Krasicki is also the creator of the modern novel. Soon, it is true, new elements were to appear, in the sentimental and in the historical novel, but Krasicki is none the less the true inventor of that form of composition. (p. 358)

> Stanislaw Dobrzycki, "Pseudo-Classicism: First Period," in Polish Encyclopaedia: The Polish Language, History of Literature, History of Poland, Vol. I, *The Committee for the Polish Encyclopaedic Publications, 1922, pp. 232-370.**

MANFRED KRIDL (essay date 1956)

[Krasicki's writing] is rich and varied and of an excellence that entitles him to be considered the greatest poet of the eighteenth century—the most distinguished after Kochanowski and before Mickiewicz. (pp. 147-48)

[Krasicki] set Polish poetry at a level it had not known since the 'golden age.' His work is imbued with the spirit of the age and represents one of its favorite precepts (derived from Hor-

The title page of the 1776 edition of Mikotaja Doświadczyńskiego przypadki.

ace), that literature should both 'amuse and instruct,' or teach through entertainment. Both the entertaining and didactic elements are strong in Krasicki's poetry, as among all the contemporary poets, but it should not be assumed that such deliberate intention to instruct makes his works artistically inferior. Krasicki's poetry generally does not directly recite any moral lessons. It does not force morality on the reader, insisting on what is good and bad, nor does it give any advice on how people should act or think; instead it attempts to represent the world, its people, and its problems in such a way that the lesson emerges, as it were, of its own accord, through a deeper comprehension of the facts which poetry has the power to promote. . . . With a poet of such talent as Krasicki, endowed with a sharp sense of observation, a subtle irony, and an ability to characterize people and their attributes in a few deft, synthesizing strokes, the moral effect of his work was all the more striking and effective. No wonder then that Krasicki's influence was great, especially among the enlightened circles of society, and that quite early in his writing career he was acclaimed as the greatest writer of his epoch.

Krasicki's fables count among his masterpieces. He wrote two collections: *Bajki i przypowieści* (*Fables and Parables* . . .) and *Bajki nowe* (*New Fables* . . .). The versified *Wstęp do bajek* (*Preface to the Fables*) may give us some idea of the poet's mastery. This small poem is composed of ten parallel sentences, beginning with the anaphora: 'there was' (there was a young man, there was an old man, there was a rich man, and so on); each line contains one or two sentences, which in turn present certain highly condensed, paradoxical formulations of various human types. The paradox consists in the poet's attribution to these types certain traits which they normally do not possess; thus, there is a young man, who led a moderate life, an old man who never scolded, a generous millionaire, . . . and finally a poet 'who never made up stories.' Having enumerated all these improbabilities, the poet ends his preface as follows:

> What kind of a fable is this? Anything can happen!
> That's true, nevertheless I shall include this among
>   fables.

In this way Krasicki suggests not so much the themes of his fables (for they naturally do not treat the types described in the preface), but their general tone, a tone in which irony mingles with humor, satire with objectivity, skepticism about human nature with a certain sympathetic understanding and tolerance.

Like all fable-writers, Krasicki borrowed the subjects for his fables from all the accessible ancient and modern sources, and, like every distinguished fabulist, he elaborated these traditional themes in a new way. His writing shows originality and, among other things, considerable independence from his models, even (at least in the first collection) from such a popular and attractive model as Lafontaine. He resembles rather Phedrus and Lessing in his compact structure and economy of language, but even these and other similarities are at most fragmentary. The sources of approximately one third of the *Fables and Parables* are known; but even when Krasicki takes a known motif he often transforms it completely, changing the characters and situations and drawing completely original conclusions from them. So, for instance, Aesop's fable about the fox who teases a goat in order to get out of a pit is changed by Krasicki in such a way that the fox, trapped in the pit, cannot find a savior and, in addition, has to listen to a moral disquisition from a wolf (*Lis i wilk—The Fox and the Wolf*). . . . Because of this treating of known motifs, and because very often the subject itself is Krasicki's own invention, many of his fables constitute a completely distinct type in the genre, quite unknown in other literatures.

Krasicki's compactness of structure is sometimes taken to extremes. Only the essence of a problem is given, and the characters and their traits are portrayed by one or two details. This is the case of [*Pan i pies (The Master and the Dog)*], which is composed of four lines and contains the whole story of the poor dog and his inhuman master. (pp. 148-50)

In his longer fables the poet devotes more space to the characterization of the heroes who are presented with greater detail; he makes more precise descriptions, but even here he is punctilious in the logical, compact structure which restricts the account to the most essential elements. A good example is found in the popular fable *Przyjaciele (Friends)*, with its description of exquisite human types in the guise of different animals, who find every excuse not to help a hare that is being persecuted by dogs. To the hare's ardent plea the horse simply answers 'I cannot' and sends the poor animal to others. The bull advises him to wait a while (although the dogs are right behind him) because he (the bull) has an appointment with a cow. The goat would be only too happy to help him, but he claims to have a hard back on which the hare would be very

uncomfortable. The sheep maintains that although he could carry the hare, the dogs would catch up with them and devour them both. Finally the calf evades the question in a truly calf-like manner: 'How can I take you, when the elder ones wouldn't?' The fable ends with a sentence which became proverbial: 'Among cordial friends the dogs devoured the hare.' (pp. 150-51)

The style and versification of the fables are in perfect harmony with their structure. The style is simple and clear; it avoids all unusual expressions, but makes precise use of the common words and phrases of Polish. This exact sense of language enabled Krasicki to construct within the slim framework of the fables complete and substantial stories and dramas. The verse structure is characterized by the same purposeful precision. Whether the rhythmic pattern is uniform (a great number have the thirteen-syllable line) or varied, it always fulfills its structural task, which is to bind the individual sentences firmly together and stress the important words by accent, rhyme, and caesura.

In the *Satyry (Satires)* Krasicki perfected on Polish ground a genre already known in antiquity and cultivated in Poland and in the West for many centuries. They are generally long, sometimes reaching several hundred lines, and give a more elaborate picture of human life; each satire concentrates on one human trait or vice such as drunkenness, greediness, cheating, hypocrisy, debauchery, card-playing, usury, avarice, prodigality, snobbishness of fashion, and the like. In the satire entitled *Pijaństwo (Drunkenness)*, two friends meet in the street. One of them, who is so weak and has such a headache that he can scarcely walk, gives an account of how he got drunk the day before. His narrative reveals an excellent psychological picture of drunkards and the gradual process of addiction which becomes second nature. (pp. 151-52)

In another satire, entitled *Żona modna (The Fashionable Wife)*, Krasicki traces a broader picture of the troubles of a young nobleman married to a fashionably educated young lady, brought up in the French taste, who despises everything domestic, is lazy and whimsical, and thinks only of parties and travel, depreciating and exploiting her husband. (p. 153)

Both these satires are written in the form of a dialogue; but in both one character is set in the foreground: in the first the drunkard, in the second the unfortunate husband of the fashionable lady. Their interlocutors play a secondary part, which is somewhat larger in *Drunkenness* . . . and slight in *The Fashionable Wife*. Within this general framework other reported dialogues take place, particularly the conversations, which are so well individualized linguistically, between the young couple, and vivid, amusing scenes are presented. Krasicki also wrote some satires with a different structure, in which the account is given either directly by the author, or in a series of sketches devoted to various human types, or in the form of ironic congratulations.

The characters are necessarily drawn only in outline, but they are very much alive, set in a slightly ironical light, and treated in a way which exposes brilliantly their comic characteristics. The language of the satires is the same as that of the fables: clear, natural, and flowing. The verse moves with equal ease and fulfills its structural function.

Krasicki's satires resemble the satires of Horace and Boileau with regard to the subject matter and the universality of the human types portrayed. Their themes, however, have their own local color, and although some motifs are borrowed from foreign authors, their elaboration is as original as that of the fables. (p. 154)

Manfred Kridl, ''The Eighteenth Century,'' in his A Survey of Polish Literature and Culture, Mouton & Co., 1956, pp. 123-90.*

CZESŁAW MIŁOSZ (essay date 1969)

[*A celebrated Polish poet, essayist, and novelist, Miłosz was awarded the Nobel Prize for Literature in 1980. In the following excerpt, drawn from his comprehensive survey* The History of Polish Literature, *Miłosz discusses Krasicki's role in Polish literature.*]

As a poet, [Krasicki] was responsible chiefly for that distillation of the language which for a while toned down the chaotic richness of the Baroque. In a way, he returned to the clear and simple language of Kochanowski, and his role in Polish poetry may be compared to that of Alexander Pope in English poetry. A hard worker, he conceived of literature as a specific vocation, namely, to intervene as a moralist in human affairs. Since he was not pugnacious by temperament (contrary to one of his masters, Voltaire), his moralizing, rarely distinguishable from sheer play, lacks vitriolic accents. (p. 177)

Among Krasicki's works employing the shorter poetic forms, his *Satires* (*Satyry* . . .) fills a prominent place. Here the author shows himself to be an observer and psychologist of human folly. . . . Many details of everyday life, revealed through dialogue, verge on the grotesque, and much that is effective in the presentation of various patterns of social behavior is achieved through the device of parody. One satire, using a somewhat different device, **''Felicitations''** (**''Powinszowania''**), praises lavishly the most common human vices. Krasicki in his *Satires* practices the difficult art of presenting vivid characters while using only the simplest words.

But the most durable among Krasicki's poems are those in his *Fables and Parables* (*Bajki i przypowieści* . . .). Here particularly we feel the ''light touch'' of a man of the Enlightenment. The ambition of such a writer was not to force his way toward the formulation of a newly discovered truth, but, since Reason is universal, to give form to a general, commonly known wisdom. Poetry for him was a more concise and elegant prose, and originality of subject had no importance. Thus, Krasicki unhesitatingly borrowed the subjects of his fables from the enormous body of fabular literature starting with Aesop and finishing with his own French contemporaries. He also borrowed from La Fontaine, especially in the second volume of his collection *New Fables (Bajki nowe),* . . . but whatever he took was always completely transformed. His extreme conciseness is best seen if one counts the number of words in the original author's version and compares it to that of Krasicki's on the same subject. The pleasure not only for the poet but for the reader as well is probably due to the squeezing of a whole story, sometimes even a novella, into a few lines, and among Krasicki's best are those fables which consist of only one quatrain where the author's pen moves in one rush toward the final *pointe* [climax]. The title *Fables and Parables* is explained by the division into parts, the first dealing with presumed animals, the second with people. Krasicki's philosophy is dry and sober. His is a world where the strong win and the weak lose in a sort of immutable order recognized as such without protest. A certain cynicism seems to be an ingredient of eighteenth-century thinking, and some fables are even cruel. Reason is exalted

as the human equivalent of animal strength: the wise survive, the stupid perish. (p. 178)

Czesław Miłosz, ''The Second Half of the Eighteenth Century—The Enlightenment,'' in his The History of Polish Literature, second edition, 1969. Reprint by University of California Press, 1983, pp. 159-94.*

DAVID J. WELSH (essay date 1969)

[*In this descriptive study, Welsh provides historical information and discusses several of Krasicki's works that are neglected by English-language critics, including the epistles, comedies, and letters. Here, he focuses on the didacticism, characters, and themes in the novels* Mikołaja Doświadczyńskiego *and* Pan Podstoli.]

Krasicki's purpose in writing the **Adventures of Nicholas Find-Out** [**Mikołaja Doświadczyńskiego przypadki**] was partly to counteract the pernicious effects of romances (he portrays Nicholas indulging a taste for them, with ludicrous consequences) and in addition to provide a ''cure for the age.'' Krasicki was always a skilful judge of contemporary taste, and knew how to hit on a topic that would interest his readers—whether they read the novel as an adventure story or as lightly veiled satire. In any case, the popularity of the novel was such that three further editions were published by 1779 and printers in Warsaw and elsewhere were sufficiently encouraged to commission and publish novels by Fielding, Goldsmith, Prévost and others. The circulation of romances declined, and in this way the development of the novel proper in Poland can be traced directly to Krasicki's *Nicholas.* In effect, Krasicki brought about the sudden forward leap that brought Polish fiction to the level of Voltaire's *Candide* and Dr. Johnson's *Rasselas.*

Krasicki was an attentive reader of the English novelists, and his *Nicholas* is related to both Defoe's *Robinson Crusoe* and Swift's *Gulliver.* (pp. 70-1)

Krasicki's Nicholas tells his own story in the first person, looking back from a comfortable middle-age on the adventures and follies of his youth. As he claims, he is writing his **Adventures** ''not for vain praise or self-humiliation, but to warn my descendants.'' This artless remark sets the novel's tone, and acts as a signal that we may expect Krasicki to employ one of his favorite weapons—irony—in Nicholas's narrative.

The relationship between Nicholas on the one hand, and Gulliver and Robinson Crusoe on the other is apparent in the way they are all ''outward-looking'' characters, not highly individualized. The world in which such characters live is clear-cut and unambiguous, the differences between right and wrong, wisdom and folly, virtue and vice are well distinguished, even though characters may err. All the situations in which these characters are placed are designed by the novelist to illuminate moral, ethical, social and other matters, from education, manners, corruption in the Polish law-courts, foreign travel, to agriculture and ''natural religion.'' Nicholas's adventures can usefully be considered, in effect, as a series of examples, during which Krasicki discourses satirically and ironically on topics that interested him and his contemporaries. Nicholas's tale provides a framework for these two modes.

The wide range of other characters who appear and disappear as the novel proceeds function in much the same way as Nicholas. They are puppets directed by the novelist's all-powerful hand to illustrate and prove his points. They are of three types: the positive virtuous characters, the negative foolish or vicious characters, and those who are introduced for comic effect. By our standards, perhaps, these characters lack the vitality to live apart from Krasicki's stated opinions of them: but by eighteenth-century standards, such characters were interesting precisely because they are types in which readers could believe. The unusual, the complex, and the abnormal were deliberately sacrificed in the interests of plausibility and verisimilitude. (pp. 71-2)

In addition to being the first Polish novel in the modern sense of the word, the *Adventures of Nicholas Find-Out* is also an index to Krasicki's eminence as a stylist in prose. This is eighteenth-century prose at its most characteristic, marked by concentration and economy. The plain, unadorned language derives its effect, in the main, from Krasicki's unfailing ability to order and arrange what he has to say, so that the logical connections are immediately grasped by the reader. Each word knows its own place, and Krasicki clearly knows how each word got there. (p. 81)

Although *The Squire* [*Pan Podstoli*] is a work of fiction, it is hardly a novel like *Nicholas*. Many elements which we usually look for in a novel are absent: there is little characterization, and plot is lacking. To compensate, the work contains a vast deal of talk. (p. 82)

Essentially, the work looks back to a literary genre practiced during the Renaissance in Poland, as elsewhere in Europe at that time. This was the *speculum*, or "mirror," in which writers provided readers with a model for their own lives. (p. 83)

Just as the books of Gornicki and Rej had provided sixteenth-century Polish readers with pictures of somewhat idealized "courtiers" and "honest men," so Krasicki's *The Squire* was read by eighteenth-century readers as depicting an ideal way of life. The Squire's hospitable, temperate, and industrious mode of life on his prosperous country estate was one that these readers would have wished for themselves. The Squire is an example of "how things ought to be" in contemporary Poland—one of the themes of *Nicholas*.

The Polish gentry at this time was the most influential class in the Republic. The king himself, the aristocracy, and the magnates were aware of this—and, like Krasicki, they were aware that the gentry were, for the most part, still firmly rooted in the reactionary and obscurantist traditions of the Saxon past. The gentry was the class which most needed the benefits of enlightenment, and Krasicki's *Squire* was shrewdly designed to reach and appeal to this very class.

There was considerably more to the popularity of *The Squire* than this depiction of an ideal way of life, however. Krasicki provides a hint towards this other reason in the epigraph with which he furnished the book: "Moribus antiquis." In full, this motto signifies "The Roman Republic endures thanks to ancient ways and men." (pp. 83-4)

Krasicki is signalizing the patriotic motives which lie behind his book, and regarded in this light, the figure of the Squire becomes a symbol of an enduring and stable way of life in a nation already a prey to internal strife and a victim to external pressures that led to the collapse and disappearance of the Polish State as an entity for longer than a century. . . .

Although Krasicki's *The Squire* lacks the poetic quality that makes Mickiewicz's *Pan Tadeusz* (1834) a work of great literary artistry, there is a similar atmosphere prevailing in both books, though the first is in many ways an epitome of the Age of Enlightenment, and the other an epitome of Romantic art. *Pan Tadeusz* celebrates Poland's vanished past: the action takes place in 1811-1812, when Napoleon's campaign against Russia had convinced many Poles that there was hope for the re-establishment of an independent Poland. (p. 84):

The Squire and *Pan Tadeusz* are both, in their own ways, "realistic" works, in that they depict a range of characters, settings and themes that are representative of a given social class at a specific point in time. . . . Krasicki's Squire and the other characters are not exceptional or heroic individuals involved in heroic or exceptional actions: they are presented as typical of eighteenth-century Polish society as it "ought to be." Significantly, Krasicki's characters do not have individual names, but are spoken of and addressed by their rank or social status: so the narrator meets the Squire, the Priest, the Chamberlain, the Colonel and the Colonel's Wife, just as many characters in *Pan Tadeusz* are referred to throughout the poem simply as the Count, the Usher, the Judge or the Steward. In both novel and poem the characters are occupied for most of the time in ordinary, everyday, even prosaic occupations—eating and drinking, taking walks, visiting, and celebrating private occasions such as birthdays or wedding feasts. (p. 85)

Krasicki's characters in *The Squire* cannot be said to share the vitality and humanity of the protagonists of *Pan Tadeusz*, because their function is entirely different. Like the characters in *Nicholas Find-Out* they are little more than pretexts, introduced so that the Squire and his author can expatiate at length on a wide range of topics, on most of which . . . Krasicki had already expressed his opinions in the *Monitor*, the *Satires*, *Nicholas* and elsewhere.

Krasicki's characters look back to the "character sketches" of the seventeenth century, as practiced by La Bruyère and others. They are not to be regarded as individuals but as human types. . . . As a rule they are briefly described on their first appearance: the narrator's meeting with the Squire when the book starts is characteristic of Krasicki's method, as we are informed that the Squire was "dressed in a white jacket, with a leather belt and wide straw-hat," and has a "serious countenance, ruddy complexion and grey mustache." (p. 86)

The wretched state of the Polish peasantry at this time is one of the topics to which Krasicki reverts time and again. As we know, he was an author who never minded saying the same thing twice (or more often), providing he thought it true and useful. But by present-day standards, his attitude to serfdom is ambiguous: genuinely concerned with the miserable lot of the Polish peasantry—as were many of his enlightened contemporaries—Krasicki never recommended that serfdom be abolished in Poland. The institution was, to his mind, part of the natural order of things, though it was the moral duty of the gentry to improve the lot of their serfs. (p. 89)

Apart from the digressions and moralizing, *The Squire* contains much information on manners and customs in eighteenth-century Poland. We learn, for example, that Polish gentry, when travelling to visit relatives or friends, usually took their own beds with them; that visitors might be welcomed by the host firing a cannon in their honor; . . . and that it was not uncommon for carriage wheels to break, whereupon travelers were forced to seek refuge in squalid inns. (p. 90)

To be sure, Krasicki was not concerned with providing his readers with information of this kind: primarily they, after all, regarded *The Squire*, with is type-characters and settings, as an almost inexhaustible fount of moralizing. Today, moralizing is an acquired taste, and it must be admitted that in any case Krasicki's is not of a very high order. Though well-meant, it is moralizing that comes less from the heart than from decorum and good manners. The Squire's morality derives from respectability, which deplores excess and has no place for the passions, for conflict, hope, frustration or despair. No one, at the present time, would describe *The Squire* (as Dmochowski, Krasicki's first editor, did) as "the most beautiful and useful work in any language." Nevertheless, for all the change in literary taste since that time, it is difficult to imagine the Polish Age of Enlightenment without Krasicki's *Squire*. (pp. 90-1)

> *David J. Welsh, in his* Ignacy Krasicki, *Twayne Publishers, Inc., 1969, 150 p.*

JULIAN KRZYŻANOWSKI (essay date 1972)

[*The following excerpt is drawn from Krzyżanowski's comprehensive* History of Polish Literature *which was originally published in Polish as* Dzieja Literatury Polskiej od poczatków do czasów najnowszych *in 1972. Krzyżanowski analyzes Krasicki's epic poems, fables, and satires and concludes that their didactic elements are successful only when coupled with humor.*]

The best of Krasicki's literary output . . . are his works in prose and verse, which though they do not cover an extensive period chronologically . . . are extremely versatile, artistically almost perfect, and of great social importance. . . . He introduced variety into his didactic writings with a large dose of humour, which came naturally to him, and it is precisely in this sphere that he had his greatest achievements; on the other hand, where his works were purely didactic and serious in tone, they were very average, even mediocre, although they were generally read eagerly, praised and quoted in his lifetime.

Krasicki's fame as the greatest Polish poet in the times of [King] Stanisław Augustus was due first and foremost to the works in which his exceptional talent as a humorist was combined with the didacticism of the age of Enlightenment, that is, his satirical-humorous writings. Mention is due above all to his mock-heroic poems. (pp. 182-83)

As mock-heroic poems are bound to contain a lot of nonsense, making known situations absurd by mockery, it can hardly be assumed that Krasicki, in proclaiming the principle "To teach, 'tis not enough, thou shouldst also amuse" in *Mouse-iad [Myszeidos]*, had entirely given up the idea of learning and only wanted to produce a witty poetic trifle. True, some readers did look for hidden allusions to people and events in *Mouse-iad* and there were some who wanted to treat it as a political satire on the relations in the times of Stanisław Augustus, but ideas of this kind are not confirmed by the poem itself. Of course, Krasicki was attacking various public vices of the times, he mocks the influence of women on politics . . . ; he also makes fun of the tendencies towards drunkenness inherited from the Saxon times. . . . All this makes *Mouse-iad* just a bubbling up of good humour in an excellent writer, whose fancy was taken by a comic idea and who made every effort to convey this idea in excellent artistic language. It is an effort to show the world what can be done with subjects that have been treated seriously for centuries, if they are presented in an unexpected way, in a comic light. For instance, poets had been describing bloody scenes of battle in an accepted stereotype way for centuries. In Krasicki's work, this traditional and accepted way takes another form.

The beginning of the stanza is maintained in the traditional, serious tone, one might forget that this is a mock war of four-legged warriors, but the last two lines bring one down from

the realms of imagination, shatter the illusion of an epic, reminding the reader that this is only a mock battle. Another epic tradition, from the times of Homer, dictated that the participation of the gods in the battle should be emphasized; this eternal "mythological mechanism" is also found in *Mouse-iad*, represented by "the old hag", the Witch of fairy tales. . . . The same applies to the traditional speeches made by the heroes of epics and the descriptions of the funeral rites of the fallen knights, etc. They appear in a distorted form in *Mouse-iad*, and by this device a comic effect is obtained, which was obviously what the author was aiming at.

The same approach can be seen in Krasicki's next, even more famous work *Monachomachia, or the War of the Monks (Monachomachia albo wojna mnichów)*. (pp. 184-85)

But in *Monachomachia* [unlike in *Mouse-iad*], it was not laughter that imparted character to the whole work. The man of the age of Enlightenment was sensitive to all manifestations of absurdity, particularly when such absurdities were hidden under the veil of religious immunity. Hence the aversion felt towards the religious orders. . . . *Monachomachia* was a pungent satire against the "reverend absurdity . . . under the ancient protection of the temple," against "the pious idlers," who loved the drinking cup more than books. In a number of exquisite pictures, like the search for the monastic library scattered about in remote corners, like the preparations for the disputation in the mediaeval mode, the debate and its interruption by a fight Krasicki was attacking the intellectual ignorance of the average monk and evoked a lot of protest. In answer to these protests, the bishop of Warmia produced *Antimonachomachia*, allegedly a withdrawal of what "a capricious writer had written, emboldened by his simplicity", "persuaded to do so by impious ones", but he did not withdraw his charges. . . . (pp. 185-86)

[Both] poems about "the war of the monks"—being a characteristic example of how the man of the Enlightenment age dealt with the things in religious life he did not agree with, and also an example of the method used by Voltaire and his followers—show Krasicki as a satirist. A rather unusual satirist, for the humorist was present too. . . . Krasicki looks at human weaknesses with the smile of man deeply interested in the manifestations of human follies and who uses these follies to achieve the greatest possible literary effect, and this is seen above all in *Mouse-iad* and then in *Monachomachia*. Human follies seen from this point of view are not so much evil as amusing and the moralist is ousted by the amused observer.

But the author of *Mouse-iad* was soon to change his attitude and become much more severe. This new view of people gave birth to another two works, much more mature and of greater artistic excellence, namely, his [*Fables and Stories (Bajki i przypowieści)*] and *Satires (Satyry)*. (pp. 186-87)

While using ideas that had been known for as long as people could remember [in his *Fables and Stories*], Krasicki succeeded in creating something that was specifically his own, giving them new values and presenting them in the simple form of unusually eloquent epigrams. In this he was doing the same as Kochanowski had done before him in his *Fraszki*. Limiting himself to the most essential elements of the tale, he constructed his stories according to very simple and artistic devices so that the moral was evident from the very action of the fable. One of the devices he used most often was a forceful contrast of happenings, which explains things with the utmost clarity without any comment from the writer. The fable *The Master and His Dog (Pan i pies),* for instance, goes as follows:

> All night long the dog did bark, kept the thief at bay,
> Master woke, dog was beaten on the following day,
> Dog awaited not the thief next night, slept soundly,
> House was robbed, the dog barked not, was beaten
>   roundly.

(p. 187)

Because of this restraint and concentration of attention on the course of events, the action, Krasicki's fables have great dramatic impact. . . .

However, fables in epigrammatic form did not satisfy Krasicki. Following in the footsteps of La Fontaine, . . . he attempted to write longer fables too, with a more extensive plot, presented in epic form, like the story of the shepherd who cried "Wolf!" to fool his companions . . . ; but this collection of *New Fables [Bajki nowe],* as he called them, were not marked for the utter simplicity of the previous ones and the lack of this simplicity could not be compensated by the wealth of details about customs and manners to which the European reader had been accustomed by La Fontaine's fables. (p. 188)

[Krasicki's] *Satires* were not a brilliant novelty, for the poet applied the literary form already known from the works of Naruszewicz, one which was very popular at that time, namely, pictures in verse, interspersed with comments on these pictures or simply the form of treatises dealing with some moral problem or another. But what was brilliant was the new content the bishop brought into the old form.

Hurling thunderbolts at the most common faults of the "corrupt world": hypocrisy, waste, drunkenness, the pursuit of costly novelties, cruelty towards servants and subjects, card playing, the fashionable mania for travel and many many others, Krasicki limited himself exclusively to matters of customs and manners, leaving aside the "public sins". . . . (p. 189)

[The detailed picture he gave in his *Satires* of the general background] has its limits, for it is confined only to the life of the magnates or the wealthy gentry, but he shows their life from ever different aspects, in country and town residences, at the royal court, in the salons of the capital, in travels round the country and abroad, and shows them in constant movement, among a great multitude of people comprising not only the "men of property", but also their servants of higher and lower rank; he shows them with their guests and with acquaintances, and thanks to this the *Satires* are a sort of unrivalled poetic sketch-book. . . . (p. 191)

Krasicki attains this unequalled wealth of description in a rather mechanical way, which he uses in most of his satires. In attacking some human fault, he describes it not by theoretical deliberations but illustrates it by practical examples showing how this fault becomes evident in life. So in his satire *The Gambler (Gracz)* aimed against card playing and showing "Mark, Count of Clubs", who makes a fortune at cards by all kinds of cheating and then opens and runs a gambling den where landowners from the country lose their annual "income" at the tables, he portrays all sorts of men. One of the players throws a fatal card into the fire, another scatters the whole pack of cards, others plaintively tell the story of their misfortunes to anyone who cares to listen, while others, having played the very shirts off their backs, despairingly sink ever deeper into debt. The satire ends with the story of the career of the

trickster, for whom there is nothing left in life but to swindle naive partners.

Krasicki's mastery and ingenuity consists in the fact that each of these genre scenes is unique, he does not repeat himself and if the same kind of scene does occur it is so changed that there is always a new element in it. At the same time this ingenuity reaches its peak in the frames put round the different satires previously outlined by a series of sketches. In one case the frame might be a dialogue, in another, the advice given to a friend, but the most interesting are those in which the author uses other literary forms to gain his satirical effects. For instance, *The Happiness of the Jokers (Szczęśliwość filutów)* begins with New Year's wishes to all kinds of persons who are not particularly respected. This satire revives the old custom of preachers at the New Year, when the preacher jokingly wished his listeners everything calculated to cure them of their faults. The construction of *The Gambler* is even more entertaining, for it is given the frame of a parody of a mock-heroic poem on cards, the history of their invention, all done with ceremonious exaggeration, full of apostrophes and the no less solemn remarks of the author himself.

Satires of mixed construction linking the sketch and treatise, are incomparably more frequent, for Krasicki rarely wrote picture-satires of exclusively epic content, in fact there are only two of them—*A Wife of Fashion (Żona Modna)* and *Drunkenness (Pijaństwo).*

A Wife of Fashion is an excellently constructed image of a lady of fashion bringing ruin upon her miserly husband, who chose the elegant lady with an eye to her dowry, only to see too late that the extravagant woman is costing him more than he gained from the fortune she brought with her. The chain of scenes form a distinct and complete whole, based on the contrasting of two different characters and the mutual grudges the lady of fashion and the miserly Sarmatian bear each other because of this. *Drunkenness,* on the other hand, is the story of a gentleman who is ill because of drinking too much and is an extensive and vivid picture of a company of tipsy men quarrelling and brawling about matters of no consequence born in minds benumbed with drinking. This satire has a magnificent ending, for the narrator does not spare the drunkards, heaping upon their heads his accusations and then proclaiming a tirade on sobriety, and then, when asked where he is going, he says: "To have a glass of vodka"

Apart from the characteristic features of the *Satires* already mentioned, there is one more which distinguishes them from other works by Krasicki and ranks them quite separately in the historical development of the Polish poetic style. Krasicki makes large-scale use of irony, little known to his predecessors, or at least very rarely applied. Instead of expressing his indignation, thundering his disapproval or at least writing reproaches, the bishop uses elegant language to praise all that he considers deplorable, but expresses his praise in such a way that it is a sharper attack than a severe reproof. (pp. 191-92)

The greatest masterpiece of irony is his satire *To the King (Do króla),* which is given pride of place in the collection. This great admirer of King Stanisław Augustus gathered all the accusations of the gentry against the king and mocked these charges mercilessly by skilful use of irony. One of the charges against the king was that he was too young; Krasicki speaks these words of comfort: "But thou hast improved. Already thy throne, by our grace, has given you grey hairs". . . .

However, Krasicki's irony shows that a characteristic change had taken place in the attitude of the poet; we no longer see in his works the old amusement at the absurdities of men, but a certain bitterness in looking upon these things, although he does not express this. Irony helped him to rise to Olympic heights and, having mastered his own impulses, or even his tastes and likings, looked down on the empty vanity of the "corrupt world" from the heights of his attitude of reason, free of prejudice. (p. 193)

> *Julian Krzyżanowski, "Literature of the Enlighten-ment Period," in his* A History of Polish Literature, *translated by Doris Ronowicz, PWN-Polish Scientific Publishers, 1978, pp. 164-219.**

ADDITIONAL BIBLIOGRAPHY

Bain, R. Nisbet. "Decadence and Demoralisation." In his *The Last King of Poland and His Contemporaries*, pp. 93-114. New York: Arno Press & The New York Times, 1971.*

A brief character sketch.

Čiževskij, Dmitrij. "Classicism." In his *Comparative History of Slavic Literatures*, edited by Serge A. Zenkovsky, translated by Richard Noel Porter and Martin P. Rice, pp. 105-17. Nashville: Vanderbilt University Press, 1971.*

An outline of Slavic Classicism. Čiževskij cites Krasicki's works as noteworthy examples of Polish Classicism.

Hoisington, Thomas H. "Travels to the Lands of Xaoo and Pande-sówna: The Beginnings of a Nonrealistic Tradition in Polish Prose." *The Polish Review* XXII, No. 1 (1977): 29-36.*

Discussion of the utopian elements in *Mikołaja Doświadczyń-skiego*. Hoisington considers Krasicki and Jan Potoki, the founders of the nonrealistic tradition in Polish letters.

Najder, Zdzislaw. "The Development of the Polish Novel: Functions and Structure." *Slavic Review* 29, No. 4 (December 1970): 651-62.*

Traces the development of the novel in Poland. Najder maintains that Krasicki's *Mikołaja Doświadczyńskiego* and *Pan Podstoli* are characteristic and influential examples of the early Polish novel.

Emma Lazarus

1849-1887

(Also wrote under the pseudonym of Esther Sarazal) American poet, essayist, novelist, dramatist, and translator.

Lazarus achieved prominence in the 1880s as the literary champion of the Jewish people. Confronted with the spectacle of thousands of Jewish exiles seeking refuge in the United States from pogroms, or widespread anti-Jewish attacks, in Russia and eastern Europe, she became an ardent activist, exhorting American Jews to unite with the refugees under the banner of Judaism and proclaiming the nobility of the Judaic tradition to Jews and non-Jews alike. For these efforts, she has been hailed as a modern counterpart to the biblical heroine Deborah, who led the Israelites in battle and song, and she is widely regarded today as the most talented late-nineteenth-century American Jewish writer. Lazarus is also acclaimed as a pioneer Zionist, though many of her works attest to her faith in the United States as a haven for expatriated Jews and other exiles. "The New Colossus," her famous sonnet welcoming the "huddled masses yearning to breathe free" to the shores of America, is inscribed on the base of the Statue of Liberty in New York harbor.

In contrast to her Jewish activism in the 1880s, Judaism played a relatively inconspicuous part in Lazarus's early life and literary career. Raised in a prosperous and socially prominent family, she was educated privately at her family's home in New York City. Exhibiting unusual precocity as a poet and linguist, Lazarus published two volumes of original verse and translations, *Poems and Translations* and *Admetus, and Other Poems*, by the time she was twenty-one. Although critics often commented that the former volume was marred by a strain of adolescent melancholy, Lazarus's verse was strong enough to attract the attention of Ralph Waldo Emerson, who subsequently praised several of the manuscript poems that later appeared in *Admetus*. Emerson eventually retracted his praise and discouraged Lazarus from publishing these poems, but her perseverance was rewarded in 1871 when reviewers hailed the author of *Admetus* as a promising young poet. In the following decade Lazarus devoted herself almost exclusively to literary pursuits. While she contributed poems to *Lippincott's* and other national magazines, her major publications were a novel based on Johann Wolfgang von Goethe's relationship with Frederika Brion entitled *Alide: An Episode of Goethe's Life*, and *The Spagnoletto*, a tragic drama set in seventeenth-century Italy.

Although Lazarus published translations of the medieval Spanish Hebrew writers Solomon Ibn Gabirol and Judah Halevi in the *Jewish Messenger* in 1879 and issued a highly regarded volume of translations from the works of the German-Jewish poet Heinrich Heine, most critics agree that her Jewish consciousness was largely quiescent prior to the onset of the Russian pogroms. Indeed, she appears to have published only two original poems on Jewish topics—"In the Jewish Synagogue at Newport" and a memorial verse for Reverend J. J. Lyons— during the 1860s and 70s. Explaining her position to Rabbi Gustav Gottheil in 1877, Lazarus observed: "My interest and sympathies . . . [are] loyal to our race, although my religious convictions (if such they can be called) and the circumstances of my life have led me somewhat apart from our people."

Lazarus's Jewish sympathies were aroused in April 1882 when the *Century Magazine* published an article by Madame Z. Ragozin defending the Russian pogroms of 1881. Having witnessed the effects of these persecutions while visiting the refugees' camp on Ward's Island, New York, Lazarus rose to her people's defense and published a forceful rebuttal of Ragozin's anti-Jewish arguments entitled "Russian Christianity versus Modern Judaism" in the May issue of the *Century*. Shortly thereafter she arranged for the serial publication of *The Dance to Death*, her historical tragedy based on the fourteenth-century persecution of the Jewish community in Nordhausen, Germany. This drama, which Lazarus published so as to "arouse sympathy and to emphasize the cruelty of the injustice done to our unhappy people," was reprinted in 1882 in *Songs of a Semite: The Dance to Death, and Other Poems*. Featuring "The Banner of the Jew," a militant call for Jewish unity, *Songs of a Semite* earned Lazarus critical and popular recognition as the literary champion of her people. Lazarus also became deeply involved in contemporary Jewish affairs during this period; in addition to contributing a series of weekly essays (later collected under the title *An Epistle to the Hebrews*) to the *American Hebrew* magazine in 1882-83, she worked in aid of the Jewish refugees and became a leading force in the establishment of the Hebrew Technical Institute, a school providing vocational retraining for dispossessed immigrants. Lazarus's benevolence ultimately insured her fame, for she composed the moving verses of "The New Colossus" in 1883 for a literary auction benefitting a pedestal fund for the Statue of Liberty.

Unfortunately, Lazarus did not live to see her fame realized. Shortly after returning home from a trip to France and England, she was stricken with a grave sickness and then experienced the emotional shock of losing her beloved father. Her subsequent attempt to relieve her grief by traveling in England and Europe was abbreviated by illness: she returned to the United States two years later, fatally ill with cancer. Lazarus died in New York City in 1887 at age thirty-eight.

Directness and clarity of vision are the distinguishing qualities of Lazarus's writings on Jewish themes. Guided by an ever-deepening appreciation of the attainments and mission of her people, she shared her vision with Jews and non-Jews in moving verse and cogent prose. Lazarus's essays clearly set forth the major thematic concern of her poems, which is the need for Jewish pride and unity. It was to this end that she urged American Jews to organize and help alleviate the sufferings of less fortunate expatriated Jews in *An Epistle to the Hebrews;* it was also this motive which led her to argue for the establishment of an independent national Jewish homeland in the 1883 essay "The Jewish Problem." In her poems, Lazarus's advocacy sometimes took on martial tones, as when she recalled the heroic activism of the Maccabees in "The Banner of the Jew," but she was generally less strident. Two representative Lazarus poems are "Gifts" and "The Choice," in which she characterizes zeal for divine truth as the imperishable, if costly, legacy of the Jewish people. Many critics regard Lazarus's "By the Waters of Babylon: Little Poems in Prose," a magazine publication collected posthumously in *The Poems of Emma Lazarus,* as the culmination of her work and thought. Written in bold verse recalling the style of Walt Whitman, the work opens with an affecting depiction of the expulsion of the Jews from Spain in 1492; this passage is followed by a more hopeful, but equally telling, description of the condition of modern Jewish exiles in America. Accomplished Jews throughout the ages are then enumerated for the reader, to whom Lazarus issues the final challenge of her poetic career, writing:

> But thou—hast thou faith in the fortune of Israel? Wouldst
>   thou lighten the anguish of Jacob?
> Then shalt thou take the hand of yonder caftaned wretch
>   with flowing curls and gold-pierced ears;
> Who crawls blinking forth from the loathsome recesses
>   of the Jewry;
> Nerveless his fingers, puny his frame; haunted by the
>   bat-like phantoms of superstition in his brain.
> Thou shalt say to the bigot, "My Brother," and to the
>   creature of darkness, "My friend."

Lazarus's critical reputation reached its apogee in 1871, when *Admetus, and Other Poems* elicited predictions of her future greatness from contemporary critics. Since then she has been in a critical twilight, often honored as a valiant activist but rarely analyzed as a legitimate literary talent in her own right. Indeed, the most vigorous discussion involving her writing career has been a mild, extra-literary controversy provoked by Josephine Lazarus's remark that Judaism had been but a "dead letter" to her sister before the onset of the Russian pogroms. This point of view prevailed for many years, until Morris U. Schappes, Albert Mordell, and other modern critics argued for an earlier date for the beginning of Lazarus's Jewish sympathies. Max Baym tended to concur with Josephine Lazarus's assessment, but even he noted that Lazarus's literary reputation was not well served by the narrow focus of the critics' discussion. Some later commentators, most notably Joseph Lyons and Sol Liptzin, have broadened the scope of Lazarus commentary by relating her work to the twentieth-century issue of Jewish-American assimilation.

Lazarus's current literary reputation is modest but respectable: Dan Vogel and Edward Wagenknecht devoted recent studies to her career, and she continues to inspire the admiration of appreciative Jewish Americans. Perhaps Louis Harap provided the fairest appraisal of Lazarus's stature and achievement when he wrote: "She has won a minor place in the history of American literature because she embodied a valid fusion of genuine poetic sensibility with inspired advocacy of her calumniated and persecuted people. Her career demonstrates once again that poetry enlisted in a cause need not be ephemeral, but may be art in its own right."

PRINCIPAL WORKS

Poems and Translations (poetry and translations) 1866
*Admetus, and Other Poems (poetry and translations) 1871
Alide: An Episode of Goethe's Life (novel) 1874
The Spagnoletto [first publication] (drama) 1876
Poems and Ballads of Heinrich Heine [translator] (poetry and ballads) 1881
"Russian Christianity versus Modern Judaism" (essay) 1882; published in journal *The Century Magazine*
Songs of a Semite: The Dance to Death, and Other Poems (poetry, drama, and translations) 1882
"The Jewish Problem" (essay) 1883; published in journal *The Century Magazine*
**The Poems of Emma Lazarus. 2 vols. (poetry, dramas, and translations) 1889
An Epistle to the Hebrews (essays) 1900
Emma Lazarus: Selections from Her Poetry and Prose (poetry, essays, drama, and translations) 1944
The Letters of Emma Lazarus, 1868-1885 (letters) 1949

*This work includes the poem "In the Jewish Synagogue at Newport."

**This work includes the poems "Gifts," "The Choice," and "The New Colossus."

THE NEW YORK TIMES (essay date 1867)

[In the following review of Lazarus's first published work, Poems and Translations, *the critic emphasizes Lazarus's youthfulness and notes the derivative character of her verse.]*

The poems and translations by Emma Lazarus are chiefly remarkable from the fact stated upon the title-page of the volume, that they were written by a girl—we beg pardon, by a young lady under seventeen, and during the three years preceding her arrival at that age. Yet the volume, which is a small octavo, contains no less than 300 well-filled pages; and among the poems are quite passable translations from Heinrich Heine, Dumas, Victor Hugo, and it might be added, from Tennyson. It could not be expected that one so young could create anything strikingly original herself, and it is easy to tell what authors were her favorites before Miss Lazarus began to write. Properly restrained and guided, the precocity of which this volume is the fruit might have produced creditable results; but this premature rushing into print almost invariably proves fatal to the one who is persuaded into it.

A review of "Poems and Translations," in The New York Times, *February 23, 1867, p. 2.*

R[ALPH] W[ALDO] EMERSON   (letter date 1868-69)

[An American essayist and poet, Emerson founded the Transcendental movement and shaped a distinctly American philosophy which embraced optimism, individuality, and mysticism. His philosophy stresses the presence of ongoing creation and revelation by a god apparent in all things, who exists in everyone, as well as the essential unity of all thoughts, persons, and things in the divine whole. Emerson was one of the most influential figures of the nineteenth century. In February, 1868, Lazarus sent Emerson a gift copy of her Poems and Translations. *Emerson's encouraging reply, excerpted in the first letter below, marked the beginning of a correspondence during the course of which Emerson assumed the role of Lazarus's literary advisor. As the following letters indicate, Emerson eventually expressed ambivalence regarding Lazarus's verse, admonishing her to excise numerous "feeble lines & feeble words" from 'Admetus" before attempting to publish it. Yet when he later learned that William Dean Howells had rejected the work for publication in the* Atlantic Monthly, *Emerson claimed that he would have "thankfully and proudly" printed the poem. Lazarus dedicated "Admetus" to Emerson when it was published in 1871, but their relationship foundered in 1874 when Emerson excluded Lazarus's verse from* Parnassus, *an anthology of American verse edited by him. The following excerpts are taken from letters dated February 24, 1868, November 19, 1868, June 7, 1869, July 9, 1869, and October 6, 1869.]*

[Your] poems have important merits, & I observe that my poet gains in skill as the poems multiply, & she may at last confidently say, I have mastered the obstructions, I have learned the rules: henceforth I command the instrument, & now, every new thought & new emotion shall make the keys eloquent to my own & to every gentle ear. . . . Perhaps I like best the poems in Manuscript. Some of those in [*Poems and Translations*] are too youthful, & some words & some rhymes inadmissable. "Elfrida" & "Bertha" are carefully finished, & well told stories, but tragic & painful,—which I think a fault. You will count me whimsical, but I would never willingly begin a story with a sad end. Compensation for tragedy must be made in extraordinary power of thought, or grand strokes of poetry. But you shall instantly defy me, & send me a heart-breaking tale, so rich in fancy, so noble in sentiment that I shall prefer it to all the prosperities of time. (pp. 3-4)

• • • • •

I write immediately on closing my first entire reading of "Admetus," to say, All Hail! You have written a noble poem, which I cannot enough praise. You have hid yourself from me until now, for the merits of the preceding poems did not unfold this fulness & high equality of power. I shall not stop to criticise, more than to say that it is too good than that the reader should feel himself *detained* by speeches a line too long. And the only suggestion I dare offer is that you shall read for the tone of Teutonic humanity Act III. Scene 1. of [William Shakspeare's play] "Measure for Measure," as the only corrective of your classic sympathies. I think I shall return the treasured sheets by tomorrow's mail, secure that the eternal Apollo & the placated Fates will guard them to you. (p. 9)

• • • • •

"Heroes" is good to write & to read. . . . The tone & sentiment of the poem are noble, & the voice falters in reading it aloud.

And yet Mr Lowell is right, if by rough judgment he can drive you to a severer pruning of your verses, & mainly to a severer ear. This poem is so free of fault, however, that you can well afford to put the 10th stanza into the smelting-pot again, & save the stanza, which is essential, by mending its melody. Did you ever read such a word as "'gainst" in Tennyson? here it occurs twice in this stanza: then "intense" is a dangerous word which we avoid in conversation for its flatness,— but that is venial: but the verse fails by absence of all force & melody in the last line. You must change that & its correspondent rhyme. Having made this rude beginning, is there not hope that I may now presently arrive at the older & more peremptory duty of restoring to you **"Admetus"** & [**"A Masque of Venice,"**] with notes? (p. 11)

• • • • •

I ought long ago to have taken a decided part either to work out my criticism on your poems—as I doubted not at first to do,—or to have sent them back, & committed them to your own. But I still believed that my preoccupations were temporary, & the freedom would presently return—which does not return. . . . For **"Admetus,"** I had fully intended to use your consent & carry it to Mr Fields for the *Atlantic.* But on reading it over carefully, I found that what had so strongly impressed me on the first reading was the dignity & pathos of the story as you have told it, which still charms me. But the execution in details is not equal to this merit or to the need. You permit feeble lines & feeble words. Thus you write words which you can never have spoken. Please now to articulate the word "smileless,"—which you have used twice at no long interval. You must cut out all the lines & words you can spare & thus add force. . . . The dialogue of Hyperion & the Fates is not good enough. Cut down every thing that does not delight you to the least possible. I have marked a few heedless words. "Doubt" does not "ravage" nor [can it] be "revenged."

But I hate to pick & spy, & only wish to insist that, after reading Shakspeare for fifteen minutes, you shall read in this MS. a page or two to see what you can spare. (pp. 11-12)

For [**"A Masque of Venice,"**]—I had it in mind when I first brought it home to indicate some capital scraps of pastoral poetry in Ben Jonson, to show you what a realism those English brains attained when gazing at flowers & pheasants. . . .

And now that I may pour out all my vitriol at once, I will add that I received the poem on Thoreau, but that I do not think it cost you any day-dawn, or midnight oil. But the poem [**"Heroes"**] keeps all its value. (p. 12)

I decide to inclose the two Manuscripts to you by mail today, & I am not without hope that I may find an opportunity to talk with you about them when you have forgiven me my bilious mood. (pp. 12-13)

• • • • •

Mr Howells declines printing [**"Admetus,"**] & leaves us only the doubt whether he or we are in the wrong. I should have printed it thankfully & proudly. . . . I am at a loss to find the imitation of Tennyson & Morris that the editor remarks. I am glad you had the courage & diligence to condense the piece, and now the more, that our Aristarchus still finds you too expansive. One of the things I owe to India is the proverb of the Pundits, "that an author rejoiceth in the economizing of half a short vowel as much as in the birth of a son." You can well afford to receive back the fable, but when will the *Atlantic* give me one as noble?

If I never write, pity me still as an anxious worker. (p. 13)

R[alph] W[aldo] Emerson, from five letters to Emma Lazarus from February 24, 1868 to October 6, 1869, in Letters to Emma Lazarus in the Columbia University Library, *edited by Ralph L. Rusk, Columbia University Press, 1939, pp. 3-4, 9, 11-13.*

[J. R. WISE] (essay date 1871)

[Admetus, and Other Poems *was well received by contemporary reviewers: in praising the volume, Wise greeted Lazarus as a writer of great potential, as did reviewers for the* Illustrated London News *(1871), the* Galaxy *(1872), and the* Nation *(1872). Lazarus's critical reputation was never greater, for several critics compared "Admetus" favorably with Robert Browning's treatment of the Admetus/Alcestis myth in "Balaustion's Adventure," and others granted that certain elements of her "Tannhäuser" were superior to William Morris's "The Hill of Venus," a redaction of the Tannhäuser legend published in* The Earthly Paradise.]

We give a hearty welcome to Miss Lazarus. Her [*Admetus, and Other Poems*] has been a thorough surprise. . . . Admirers of [Robert] Browning will, we know, think that we are uttering something akin to blasphemy when we say that the **"Admetus"** of Miss Lazarus will in some points bear comparison with "Balaustion's Adventure." We do not for one moment compare the setting of the story by the American writer with that of Browning, nor do we find the same depth of philosophic reflection in her as in our own favourite poet. But here is a description which may be put side by side with the most beautiful passages in our English version of the story, and not fear comparison:—

> To river-pastures of his flocks and herds
>   Admetus rode, where sweet-breathed cattle grazed,
> Heifers and goats and kids and foolish sheep;
> Dotted cool spacious meadows with bent heads,
> And necks' soft wool broken in yellow flakes,
> Nibbling sharp-toothed the rich, thick-growing blades. . . .

This is thoroughly pastoral, and smells, as Shakspeare would say, of April and May. The touch of the "bent heads," reveals at one stroke the sheep feeding. The next line, "the soft wool broken in yellow flakes," gives us a perfect picture of what everybody must have seen, but few noticed—the way in which the wind, when the sheep hold their heads down, lifts up the wool upon their necks, showing the locks underneath quite yellow, in contrast with those above, which have been bleached by the rain. Then lastly, mark the epithet "sharp-toothed," not broken-toothed, as we for the most part see sheep's teeth, from their having to gnaw the scanty herbage close to the ground, amongst the flints—for here the grass was "rich and thick-growing." We think, too, that the description of Hercules in **"Admetus,"** will bear comparison with that in "Balaustion's Adventure." (pp. 563-64)

It must not, however, be concealed that Miss Lazarus is very unequal. She appears to write much of her poetry, as Americans eat their dinners, in hot haste. . . . Yet we cannot help saying that we have not for a long time seen any volume of poetry which, in so many various ways, gives such promise as the present. We most sincerely trust that the author may not be spoilt by the flattery of friends. She has still very much to learn, but still more to unlearn. (p. 564)

[J. R. Wise], in a review of "Admetus, and Other Poems," in The Westminster Review, *n.s. Vol. XL, No. II, October 1, 1871, pp. 563-64.*

THE ILLUSTRATED LONDON NEWS (essay date 1871)

Mrs. or Miss Lazarus—for the American lady's position is quite unknown to us—must be hailed by impartial literary criticism as a poet of rare original power. She has unconsciously caught from admiring perusal more, perhaps, of the style of Tennyson's Arthurian Idylls, in her narrative and drámatio pieces, than would seem fitly to attend the perfectly fresh and independent stream of her thought. The tone, the phrases, the turns of melody in her blank-verse lines too often remind us of the English master whom she follows in her craft of rhythmic diction. But her conceptions of each theme, and the whole compass of her ideas and emotions, differ essentially from those of preceding or contemporary poets. In her treatment of the story of Alcestis and Admetus, one of the two Greek subjects among the poems in [*Admetus, and Other Poems*], she is far happier than Mr. Browning in his half adaptation of Euripides. The motive of Alcestis in dying to preserve the life of her lord is here not a mere blind womanly fondness. It is rather an exalted persuasion that he, as the best of men and kings, the saviour and wise ruler of his country, as a person honoured of the gods, as a monarch gratefully and trustfully obeyed by the people, is an object most worthy of her noble self-sacrifice. . . . The conflict afterwards between Hercules and Death, and the return of life to Alcestis, are represented with more force, as well as more grace, in this poem than in that of Mr. Browning. . . . [**"Orpheus"**] is a not less pathetic and beautiful version of . . . the story of Orpheus and his wife Eurydice. But she leaves these fine reproductions of the Hellenic mythology for the picturesque figures and scenery of the Middle Ages and the romances of chivalry. She takes up the narratives of Sir Lohengrin and Sir Tannhaüser, those famous allegories of the ordeal of Christain heroism in a wicked world. In the treatment of such fables, it appears to us, but more especially in **"Tannhaüser,"** there is a risk of over-describing the qualities attractive to the senses—physical beauty of females, gorgeous dresses, jewels, and furniture, meats, drinks, and perfumes, with their luxurious enjoyment. It is true that the seductive presence of these objects, and their effect on the knight led captive by Venus, are essential to the moral of the tale. But the reader's taste is cloyed by their excessive abundance, which is a fault that we find in some parts of Mr. William Morris's "Earthly Paradise," and in some of Spenser's "Faerie Queen." . . . It may of course be replied that this effect of disgust with the excessively multiplied means of delight in the enchanted palace of the temptress, Venus, or Armida, or whatever name she may bear, is the very lesson to be taught by the poetical fiction. But if the story lack zest from the accumulation of too many luscious ingredients, the author's purpose will fail of success. Emma Lazarus, it must be said, has avoided this error better than Mr. Morris. She has supplied an efficient corrective in the toilsome wanderings of the knight over the rugged mountains; in his doleful, penitential confession to the friar at the rustic chapel, and again to the Bishop, in his pensive journey to Rome, where the Pope condemns him, instead of saving and blessing; lastly, in the hour of solitary prayer, which yields his soul relief. The whole narrative of this spiritual disease and its cure is related with profound sympathy, and in an interesting and lifelike manner, which reminds us of Mr. Tennyson's treatment of Lancelot and Guinevere.

Yet we prefer the shorter meditative poems in this volume, which are composed in various forms of rhymed stanzas, to the ancient stories told so impressively in the blank-verse compositions we have noticed. [The verses **"On a Tuft of Grass"**] are very touching.... For the truth of observation and description, in [the author's] views of familiar natural objects, and for the exquisite finish of each picture, with its appropriate expression of feeling, the first four **"Epochs"** can hardly be overpraised....

[Emma Lazarus] is heartily patriotic, like Mr. Longfellow and Mr. Lowell, devoting several of her best lyrical pieces to the cause of the Union in the late Civil War and to the fidelity of its brave defenders. **"Heroes,"** the men who fought and fell, the men who fought and suffered, or were maimed, yet who survive, and they who have quietly gone back to the plough, the loom, the shop, or the desk, as valiant in peaceful industry as in the shock of battle are worthily glorified by her muse. **"The Day of Dead Soldiers"**—namely, May 30, 1869, the sabbath which was appointed by Congress for a religious service in remembrance of all those killed in the United States armies—is the subject of another very impressive poem. Emma Lazarus may well ask, in her final appeal, entitled **"How Long?"** whether the history of the great English-American Republic will not henceforth yield to her countrymen some more suitable themes of epic poetry than those of the European nations. We trust that she will follow her own counsel and the example of Longfellow's "Evangeline," in selecting an American topic for her next poetic narrative. It will be no surprise to us, after the present volume, if she hereafter take a high place among the best poets in this age of our common English tongue.

> *A review of "Admetus, and Other Poems," in* The Illustrated London News, *Vol. LIX, No. 1674, October 14, 1871, p. 359.*

THE GALAXY (essay date 1872)

We welcome a genuine poetic talent in Miss Lazarus. There are fine qualities in her verse that distinguish it broadly from the ordinary work of women, and from the best work of most young writers. Her lines flow with a subtle melody revealing an innate sense of music that needs very little critical training, only some half dozen of more than four thousand failing in perfect rhythm. Her subjects are removed from every-day life without being lifeless, for the atmosphere shed around them, whether of classic clearness or of misty medieval romance, harmonizes with their age, and the figures show through it undistorted and well grouped. And she begins, as all true natural singers have begun, with simple objects and emotions, and not with the intricate puzzles and anomalies of inner life. Where spasm and convulsion inspire so many immature analysts, only great confidence in her own powers could embolden a young author to choose such plain serene themes, in her **"Admetus"** and **"Orpheus,"** as the story of fate yielding up its prey to the passion of pure heroic love. (p. 136)

With a touch not less firm and delicate, the story of knightly constancy and submissive faith is wrought out in **"Lohengrin,"** from a few shimmering hints of romance, an aerial palace, a swan, a sunlit stream such as flows through Cole's Voyage, all woven into the wonder and grace of a life spent for duty, in some region away from the world, yet not withdrawn from human pains and sacrifices. It teaches how the inspiration of such a life, near and possible to the quick superstitious imagination of chivalric days, may still exist under modern prosaic

conditions. The **"Tannhäuser"** shows the same qualities of sustained vigorous verse, enriched with picturesque description and apt suggestive epithets, haunted with the horror of a crime too simple in its greatness to tolerate poses, or strain for contortions in utterance. The subject naturally provokes comparison with [William Morris's] "The Hill of Venus," but the treatment is too unlike to leave any room for the charge of plagiarism. There are passages indeed in this poem, such as the entrance to the enchanted mountain, and the parting from the angry goddess, finer than similar descriptions in Morris's more elaborate one. But for the rest, the subject in its depths is one that only a man can deal with. The virile raptures and the sensuous swoons of a supernatural passion are too gross for a woman's pen. To analyze the remorse and exhaust the bitter flavor of the disappointment is to come too close to the sin. Yet within the limitations prescribed by feminine instinct, the author finds ample range for great beauty of description both of persons and objects, and for all the abasement, the penitence, and the horror that the changes of the story demand. It is not less a powerful picture of erring human nature because all veils are not dropped.

Of the minor poems, **"On a Tuft of Grass," "Dreams,"** and **"In Memoriam"** are remarkable for fineness of thought, showing through very delicate expression. **"Epochs"** is the only one purely subjective, and not affectedly so, reading like a glimpse of personal life, with very real utterance of suffering and consolation. The translations from [Johann Wolfgang von Goethe's drama] "Faust" are correct and flowing, but rather nerveless. Indeed we believe there are reasons, which want of space does not allow us even to glance at, why a great translation, involving close patience and various learning, can never be made easy for a woman by the widest extension of her rights. The choruses might certainly be better rendered on a revision by the skill which managed the lyrical passages of the **"Orpheus"** so well that the author should not need to be reminded how strict a frame of fourteen lines the sonnet demands. And the general elevation of her diction, most spontaneous and unsought, causes regret for the occasional use of a word such as "trudge" that cannot be made poetic, and for the negligence of grammar that permits the second person to be dismissed from the verb in several instances. Trifles like these detract very little from the uncommon merit and promise of these poems, and are not only worth pointing out in aid of that completeness which the author's many excellences gives us the right to expect she will attain in her future performances. (pp. 136-37)

> *A review of "Admetus, and Other Poems," in* The Galaxy, *Vol. XIII, No. 1, January, 1872, pp. 136-37.*

THE NATION (essay date 1872)

[In *Admetus, and Other Poems,*] Miss Emma Lazarus gives us a volume of poetry nearly all of which is of promise either for what it is or what it is not. Among the pieces of the latter sort we count the greater number of poems in her volume, because of their freedom from the common faults of youthful writers of verse, and especially youthful female writers of verse. In each case, either her selection of her subject, or else her grasp of it and her thoughtful way of dealing with it, whether wisely chosen or not, indicate more than common ability, and separate her from the writers of the ordinary sentimental verses adorned with imagery more or less successful. Among the pieces which we think are to be praised for positive merits of their own are those composing a series which the author names **"Epochs."**

These are in a way sentimental poems; but there is in them a naturalness of sentiment, a force and apparent honesty, united with a certain artistic reserve, of expression, a firm hold on the realities of feeling amid temptations of morbidness of feeling, which altogether seem to us worthy of marked praise and to augur well for the writer's future. Of the **"Admetus,"** the **"Tannhäuser,"** the **"Lohengrin,"** and the **"Orpheus"** the execution is to be commended, we think, rather than the choice of subject or anything that the author imports of her own into the old tales. Like her translation, they probably have done her more good as practice pieces than they will do any one else.

A review of "Admetus, and Other Poems," in The Nation, *Vol. XIV, No. 345, February 8, 1872, p. 92.*

I[VAN] TOURGUÉNEFF (letter date 1874)

[*In 1874, Lazarus sent Tourguéneff, the noted Russian novelist, a copy of* Alide: An Episode of Goethe's Life. *His response is excerpted below.*]

I have just finished [*Alide: An Episode of Goethe's Life*]—and though, generally speaking, I do not think it advisable to take celebrated modern men—especially poets and artists—as a subject for a novel—still I am truly glad to say I have read your book with the liveliest interest: It is very sincere and very political at the same time; the life and spirit of Germany have no secret for you—and your characters are drawn with a pencil as delicate as it is strong.—I feel very proud of the approbation you give to my works—and of the influence you kindly attribute to them on your own talent: an author, who writes as you do— is not a "pupil in art" any more; he is not far from being himself a master.

I[van] Tourguéneff, in a letter to Emma Lazarus on September 2, 1874, in Letters to Emma Lazarus in the Columbia University Library, *edited by Ralph L. Rusk, Columbia University Press, 1939, p. 17.*

THE CENTURY (essay date 1882)

[*In the following review of Lazarus's* Poems and Translations of Heinrich Heine, *the critic assesses Lazarus's performance as Heine's translator and biographer.*]

Miss Lazarus has many precursors [as a translator of Heine], and of Heine's cleaner work there is little left that has not found a translator before this. But she brings to the task a strong enthusiasm in the man and his work, and confirms her right to be heard by a delicate appreciation of the quality of Heine's verse. Perhaps of more use than the translations is the preface giving a short sketch of the poet's life: it is both sympathetic and well expressed.

The renderings from the original are remarkably close, and enjoy the same freedom from involution or straining after effect that makes most of Heine's work limpid, and places some of it at the very front of German literature. At times, Miss Lazarus does not succeed in giving the full shade of meaning to a line, not because she does not understand the original, it appears, but on account of the needs of rhythm or rhyme. The exceedingly generous use that the Germans are able to make of double or feminine rhymes is one of the greatest stumbling-blocks in the way of the conscientious translator who strives after a rendering which will give word for word, accent for accent; rhyme for rhyme. In the unrhymed and most charming little poem, "The Asra," all goes well until we reach the last line,

where a slight, but yet important change has been made. Heine wrote:

> Und der Sklave sprach: ich heisse
> Mohamet, ich bin aus Yemmen,
> Und mein Stamm sind jene Asra
> Welche sterben, wenn sie lieben.

In the answer of the dying slave the translation loses the fineness of the point—the delicacy of his declaration—by directing the thought to himself, instead of to his whole tribe, as will be seen:

> Spake the youthful slave: My name is
> Mahomet, I come from Yemen;
> And by birth I am an Asra,
> One who dieth when he loves.

By throwing the blame of his death on a peculiarity of his tribe, Heine gave to the young Arab the dignity that belongs to the hand of fate. It invests his hopeless love with a wonderful pathos. It explains and condones his temerity; it also shields the princess from remorse. A light is thrown backward on his life, and we see him pining away without a word, although, by a sort of ancestral curse, he must surely die. Whether taken as spoken in good faith, or merely as the ruse of a detected lover, it is necessary to a complete appreciation of the poem to have this shade of meaning brought out, airy though it may at first sight appear.

Many such slips have not been noticed; they are themselves of the most pardonable kind, and testify to the difficulty of the task. (pp. 785-86)

Two features we have regretfully missed from the biographical sketch, viz., the consideration of Heine from the stand-point of an Israelite, and something authoritative as to his position in Germany, both as student and exile. We want something more definite than indignation for German discriminations against the Jews. And how do orthodox Jews regard the scoffing poet? What position has he really in German literature? What did his burlesques do in the way of enlightenment? Now that the *Judenhetze* [Jew-baiting] is aroused once more in Prussia and Russia, it is the time for a well-informed co-religionist to be heard on these questions. Here is a chance for one so well-fitted by birth, education, and a poetical nature as Miss Lazarus. (p. 786)

"Miss Lazarus's Translation of Heine," in The Century, *Vol. XXIII, No. 5, March, 1882, pp. 785-86.*

WILLIAM JAMES (letter date 1882)

[*An American philosopher of the late nineteenth century, James was the founder of Pragmatism as a philosophical school. In opposition to the tenets of scientific materialism and philosophic idealism, which had prevailed in Western philosophy throughout the eighteenth and nineteenth centuries, James attempted to comprehend and describe human life as it is actually experienced, rather than formulating models of abstract reality far removed from lived reality. Evidently prompted in a letter from Lazarus to familiarize himself with her works, James recorded his impressions of* Poems and Translations *in the letter excerpted below. James's remark that poetry ought to be "the overflowing of a life rich in other ways" alludes to the thematic limitations of Lazarus's early verse. Critics unanimously maintain that Lazarus overcame this shortcoming when she embraced the Judaic cause.*]

The only volume of yours I have found in Boston is your earliest one [*Poems and Translations*]—and even that I have hardly had a propitious moment to read; but taking the shorter ones that begin the book all together, they leave a most beautiful impression of a young girl making her way securely towards deep and rich things. . . . I think the power of *playing* with thought and language that such as you possess is the divinest of gifts. You should not be too much professional artists at it, I mean too exclusively bound to it,—it ought to be the overflowing of a life rich in other ways. To tell you the truth, able as the Shelley & Byron poem was, and beautiful as were many of its stanzas, I don't think I enjoyed it quite as much as some of the simpler little things. Don't you rather overdo Byron? Vide [Witness] his life! And big and careless as is his power, isn't it essentially *rhetorical* power, the power of words that are often but echoes of other words, a harmony of word-associations instead of definite thoughts definitely and fatally creating just their own exact expression. *This* seems to me almost always the case with Shelley. However far be it from me to play the poetical critic. (pp. 48-9)

> *William James, in a letter to Emma Lazarus on August 26, 1882, in* Letters to Emma Lazarus *in the Columbia University Library, edited by Ralph L. Rusk, Columbia University Press, 1939, pp. 48-9.*

THE NEW YORK TIMES   (essay date 1882)

Whatever may be the judgment as to the quality of the performances [in Miss Lazarus's *Songs of a Semite: The Dance to Death, and Other Poems*], whether translations or of original design, the project enlists the sympathy of any one who believes that no fresh venture in letters is without its modicum of good, and that in the case of a race which has suffered, and in some countries yet suffers, great injustice, attention drawn to its achievements in literature will encourage such respect and admiration as it deserves.

[It] is clear that [in "**The Dance to Death**"] Miss Lazarus has made a work of no little strength. At the same time, there appears to be a too anxious adherence to the facts of history. It would have been better to change the course of events so as to avoid the numerous improbabilities. The reader wants more certainty that Süsskind von Orb was a good man. Why did he keep Liebhaid from her father? And was he not the author of the ruin of Schnetzen's castle? Caskets supposed to contain immense riches are not left unopened by ecclesiastics or greedy nobles of the fifteenth century. When a lover is told that it contains safety for his true love he does not forget about it and then give it to a third person not on his side. For this there may be documentary evidence, but in a work of art it is better to alter facts, seeing that the record is already in history and the work of art is meant to excite emotion, not to write history. For this reason some of the shorter pieces of the pamphlet are more attractive than the "**Dance to Death**," although it should be remembered that the ability to handle a matter of this scope is rare, and that Miss Lazarus has come very near to making a masterpiece of it. "**The Crowing of the Red Cock**" and "**The Banner of the Jew**" are original poems full of spirit and vigor. . . . Full of curious and beautiful passages are the translations from the Hebrew poets of mediaeval Spain. But the fullest, sweetest, and highest note struck by this young lady will be found in the memorial verses in honor of Rabbi Lyons, who died recently in New-York. Any one who writes from the heart such verses as this [poem contains] may be safely held to have the true poetic gift. . . .

> *A review of "Songs of a Semite: The Dance to Death, and Other Poems," in* The New York Times, *October 8, 1882, p. 5.*

THE CENTURY   (essay date 1883)

It is a very curious fact that the Jews, who seem as a race to be possessed of much more than ordinary intelligence, . . . should have done little in literature to record the oppressions to which they have been subject. Even Heine, with his diamond wit and extraordinary attainments, was never the champion of his race in any manly, vigorous fashion. (p. 471)

[Miss Emma Lazarus], after writing prose and verse of a high grade on topics having to do with anything but Hebrew matters, has recently developed in a line which cannot help exciting the finest indignation of which she is capable; and which in fact has called out her very best resources. Her success hitherto has been among Christians rather than her own folk, but now she appeals to her race. Perhaps her studies of Heine, . . . may have pointed the way. But much more must the inexcusable misery inflicted on Jews in Russia have sharpened her pen. The fine ringing lines of "**The Banner of the Jew**" could only have been written under the stress of righteous wrath at the infamies perpetrated under the eyes, and sometimes with the covert approval of, Russian officials. . . .

Strange that it should be a woman to say that word: "Strike! for the brave revere the brave!" It invests this little pamphlet ["**Songs of a Semite**"] with an interest that will go on deepening, if the call is heard, until it may, perhaps, attain some day to the place of a classic phrase among the Jews; for who shall say in these days what a race cannot do that has the domestic virtues, the ability, and the wealth of the Jews, and, behind all, a real grievance that strengthens their hands and makes every liberal and conscientious thinker their ally? In "**The Crowing of the Red Cock**" there is another cry of agony for the maltreatment of Russian co-religionists, but the mood is softer:

> What oceans can the stain remove
> From Christian law and Christian love?
>
> Nay, close the book; not now, not here,
>   The hideous tale of sin narrate,
> Reëchoing in the martyr's ear,
>   Even he might nurse revengeful hate;
> Even he might turn in wrath sublime,
> With blood for blood and crime for crime.

Nevertheless, she has not closed the book, for Miss Lazarus has given time and talents to a five act drama ["**The Dance to Death**"] in which she narrated one "hideous tale of sin," full of the lurid glare of holocaust of innocent merchants, their wives and babes, and of the fantastic love for the horrible that existed in the humor of the Gothic ages. . . . The drama has fine passages, and the plot itself does much to awaken and fascinate the attention. It has also weak parts that might be left out. . . . Meantime it is a fact to be noted that in "**Songs of a Semite**" this talented young authoress has struck on solid ground. Her ability to write works *de longue haleine* argues exceedingly well for her future fame in letters. Her appearance as a champion of her race is to be hailed with pleasure. A writer could not have better material from the past or a stronger stimulus in the present. (p. 472)

A review of "Songs of a Semite: The Dance to Death and Other Poems," in The Century, *Vol. XXV, No. 3, January, 1883, pp. 471-72.*

J[AMES] R[USSELL] LOWELL   (letter date 1883)

[*Lowell was a celebrated nineteenth-century American poet, critic, essayist, and editor. He is noted today for his satirical and critical writings, including* A Fable for Critics, *a book-length poem featuring witty critical portraits of his contemporaries. Lowell considered "The New Colossus" to be a finer achievement than the work which it commemorates, the Statue of Liberty. He expressed his admiration for the sonnet in the letter excerpted below.*]

I must write . . . to say how much I liked your sonnet about the Statue ["**The New Colossus**"]—much better than I like the Statue itself. But your sonnet gives its subject a *raison d'être* [reason for being] which it wanted before quite as much as it wants a pedestal. You have set it on a noble one, saying admirably just the right word to be said, an achievement more arduous than that of the sculptor.

> *J[ames] R[ussell] Lowell, in a letter to Emma Lazarus on December 17, 1883, in* Letters to Emma Lazarus in the Columbia University Library, *edited by Ralph L. Rusk, Columbia University Press, 1939, p. 74.*

JOHN G[REENLEAF] WHITTIER   (letter date 1887)

[*A noted poet, reformer, journalist, and critic, Whittier was the most quoted American author of the post-Civil War era and was the first American poet to encourage purely descriptive narration. Whittier's works are noted for their moral content and simple sentiment. As a critic, he employed an approach to literature which praised the moralistic efforts of obscure writers and condemned sensational, "immoral" attempts by better-known writers, such as Lord Byron. Whittier submitted the following remarks for publication in the Emma Lazarus memorial number of the* American Hebrew *magazine.*]

With no lack of rhythmic sweetness, [Emma Lazarus] has often the rugged strength and verbal audacity of Browning. Since Miriam sang of deliverance and triumph by the Red Sea, the Semitic race has had no braver singer. "**The Crowing of the Red Cock,**" written when the Russian sky was red with blazing Hebrew homes, is an indignant and forceful lyric worthy of the Maccabean age. Her "**Banner of the Jew,**" has the ring of Israel's war trumpets. Well may those of her own race and faith lament the loss of such a woman. They will not sorrow alone. Among the "mourning women" at her grave the sympathizing voice of Christian daughters will mingle with the wail of the daughters of Jerusalem.

> *John G[reenleaf] Whittier, in a letter to the editor of* The American Hebrew *on November 28, 1887 in* The American Hebrew, *Vol. 33, No. 5, December 9, 1887, p. 67.*

EDMUND CLARENCE STEDMAN   (letter date 1887)

[*A major nineteenth-century American critic and anthologist, Stedman gained wide critical influence as the author of* Victorian Poets *and* Poets of America, *published in 1875 and 1885 respectively. In conjunction with his popular* American Anthology, *published in 1900, the latter work helped to establish a greater interest in and appreciation for American literature. A foe of the "heresy of the didactic," Stedman wrote criticism which is often*

informed by his belief that "a prosaic moral is injurious to virtue by making it repulsive." Stedman was fairly close to Lazarus, for the two writers lived in neighboring homes and met frequently between 1879 and 1881. Indeed, he claimed to have been Lazarus's confidant during this period, urging her to take advantage of her Jewish roots when she revealed to him that she felt as though she had as yet "accomplished nothing to stir, nothing to awaken, to teach or to suggest, nothing that the world could not equally well do without." In the following essay, originally published as a letter to the editor in the Emma Lazarus memorial number of the* American Hebrew *magazine, (dated December 9, 1887), Stedman pays tribute to her, noting with some surprise that the journal had earlier described Lazarus as an enthusiastic adherent of Judaism.*]

[Emma Lazarus] was—though without the slightest trace of pedantry—the natural companion of scholars and thinkers. Her emotional nature kept pace with her intellect; as she grew in learning and mental power, she became still more earnest, devoted, impassioned.

These advances marked her writings—especially her poetry, which changed in later years from its early reflection of the Grecian ideals and took on lyrical and veritably Hebraic fire and imagination. . . . [There] was a contagious inspiration in her Semitic ardor, her satire, wrath and exaltation. That she was able to impart these qualities to sustained creative work is shown by her strangely powerful drama '**The Dance to Death,**' unique in American poetry. Viewed merely on the literary side, her abilities were so progressive, under the quickening force of a lofty motive, that her early death is a deplorable loss in a time when so much verse, if not as sounding brass, seems to come from tinkling cymbals.

During the last few years, . . . I met Miss Lazarus less frequently, and I scarcely knew what inference to derive from your feeling biographical sketch, as to her religious attitude and convictions. That she was aglow with the Jewish spirit, proud of her race's history and characteristics, and consecrated to its freedom from oppression throughout the world,—all this is finely manifest; yet her intellectual outlook was so broad that I took her to be a modern Theist in religion, and one who would not stipulate for absolute maintenance of the barriers with which the Mosaic law isolated the Jewish race, in certain respects, from the rest of mankind. Taking into account, however, the forces of birth and training, I could understand how our Miriam of today, filled with the passion of her cause, should return to the Pentateuchal faith—to the Mosaic ritual in its hereditary and most uncompromising form. Nor would any lover of the heroic in life or literature, if such had been her course, desire to have it otherwise. (pp. 264-65)

> *Edmund Clarence Stedman, "Emma Lazarus," in his* Genius and Other Essays, *Moffat, Yard and Company, 1911, pp. 264-67.*

THE CRITIC, NEW YORK   (essay date 1887)

[*The author of the following posthumous assessment of Lazarus's life and literary work concludes by suggesting that American Jews were not entirely sympathetic to Lazarus's message and that Lazarus lived "as much a Christian as a Jewess." The reviewer supports the latter assertion in part by citing Lazarus's association with the liberal rabbi Dr. Felix Adler. Subsequent critics have addressed both of these issues. Joseph Lyons (1961) and Sol Liptzin (1966) commented at length on the "Jewish consciousness" of Lazarus's fellow American Jews, each maintaining that Lazarus's call for Jewish unity often went unheeded by complacent Jews who were anxious to assimilate into the American cultural mainstream. While Edmund Clarence Stedman (1887) and Louis Ruchames (see Additional Bibliography) noted Lazarus's early attraction to other religious beliefs, Morris U. Schappes (1944) emphasized her disinterest in theology, observing that "her concern was not so much with the articles of Jewish faith as the plight of the Jewish people."]*

[Emma Lazarus's *Poems and Translations*] is now very rare, having been soon outlawed by the fastidiousness of the writer. Yet it may be questioned whether she ever surpassed some of these early pieces in the merely literary quality of her work, although with a wider experience of life she gave attention to themes of greater weight. A curious contradiction, to find a girl of fifteen, totally inexperienced in anything save books, writing a poem ['**On a Lock of My Mother's Hair**'] . . . on the famous theme 'Ich habe gelebt und geliebet,' and putting herself in the place of a gray-haired woman! . . .

Most remarkable was the grasp of mind which could construct and carry through with great artistic skill the long narrative poems '**Bertha**' and '**Elfrida.**'

'**Admetus**' has in workmanship a touch of the Tennysonian *morbidezza* . . . ; yet there is evidence in [*Admetus, and Other Poems*] that the young writer, hardly out of her teens, realized the weakness of looking over-seas for inspiration. The verse of Emerson was too harsh and masculine to impress itself on her style, but in '**How Long?**' she exclaimed

> How long, and yet how long
> Our leaders will we hail from over seas,
> Masters and kings from feudal monarchies,
> And mock their ancient song
> With echoes weak of foreign melodies? . . .

The yearning expressed in this poem was put in force by its writer very rarely. Only at one period did she free herself from the trammels of a literature alien to America and the ideals of Americans who are not content to be echoes of European thought. (p. 293)

[*Admetus, and Other Poems*] had a timid allusion to Judaism, in '**The Jewish Synagogue at Newport.**'

> What prayers were in this temple offered up
>   Wrung from sad hearts that knew no joy on earth,
> By these lone exiles of a thousand years
>   From the fair sunrise land that gave them birth!

A Christian might have penned these quiet lines. But in the same year she wrote '**The Banner of the Jew,**' . . . a singular outburst from a woman of a race whose latter mission appears to be to amass wealth and bend the head under oppressions more or less practical, more or less severe.

The same martial spirit that moved Emma Lazarus to patriotic verse in childhood . . . kindles again at the injustice with which her race has been treated in the past. For the theme, she had a strong recollection of the fight of the Maccabees for freedom from Grecian tyrants; and for the metre, perhaps unconsciously had in mind Drake's spirited 'American Flag.' Another glowing piece, full of indignation at the sufferings of her race, is '**The Crowing of the Red Cock.**' More sustained, but perhaps less effectual in calling attention to a woman who dared, timid as by nature she was, to reprove bigotry and stir her fellows, is '**The Dance to Death.**' . . .

It is a great leaf in Emma Lazarus's chaplet to have taken the stand she did in regard to her race. Yet if the whole truth must be told, there was a counterblast when she found herself in contact with the practical view of the matter. In America there is little or nothing tangible for Jews to resent; there is no crusade (if the irony be forgiven) to make against the Cross; at worst, such Hebrews as lack self-respect are treated with the severity that arises in consequence of bad manners, not from their Judaism. But she wrote for *The American Hebrew*, the *Century* and *THE CRITIC* letters, essays and poems which had their effect. . . . Where a practical result was possible, she met with response from the Hebrews. The race did not fail to appreciate the fervor of a gifted woman, but with characteristic shrewdness and moderation did not follow her more excited directions. . . .

[When her death was imminent, Emma Lazarus] sent for Dr. Felix Adler, but not for the Rabbi of her synagogue; yet it was her wish that Jewish rites should be used at her burial. She died as she lived, as much a Christian as a Jewess—perhaps it would be truer to say, neither one nor the other; yet singular in the love for her race and its amazing history, and in the vigorous assertion of the right of that race to be treated like other men, on individual merits, not on those of race. (p. 294)

> *"Miss Lazarus's Life and Literary Work," in* The Critic, *New York, n.s. Vol. VIII, No. 206, December 10, 1887, pp. 293-95.*

[JOSEPHINE LAZARUS]   (essay date 1888)

[Josephine Lazarus's critical account of her sister's life and works, excerpted below, gained wide currency when it was reprinted in 1889 as a preface to The Poems of Emma Lazarus. *For many years commentators accepted Josephine Lazarus's contention that Judaism had been a "dead letter" to the poet previous to the publication of Madame Z. Ragozin's defense of the Russian pogroms in 1882, and few critics have objected to her criticism of her sister's works. However, some modern commentators, most notably Morris U. Schappes (1944) and Albert Mordell (1949), have argued that Emma Lazarus exhibited an interest in her people in works written well in advance of both the pogroms and Ragozin's defense of them.]*

The story of [Emma Lazarus's] life is the story of a mind, of a spirit ever seeking, ever striving, and pressing onward and upward to new truth and light. Her works are the mirror of this progress. In reviewing them the first point that strikes us is the precocity, or rather the spontaneity, of her poetic gift. She was a born singer; poetry was her natural language, and to write was less effort than to speak. . . . ["**Poems and Translations**"] constituted her first published volume. Crude and immature as these productions naturally were, and utterly condemned by the writer's later judgment, they are, nevertheless, highly interesting and characteristic, giving, as they do, the key-note of much that afterwards unfolded itself in her life. One cannot fail to be rather painfully impressed by the profound melancholy pervading the book. The opening poem is "**In Memoriam**"—on the death of a school friend and companion; and the two following poems also have death for theme. "**On a Lock of my Mother's Hair**" gives us reflections on growing old. These are the four poems written at the age of fourteen. There is not a wholly glad and joyous strain in the volume, and we might smile at the recurrence of broken vows, broken hearts, and broken lives in the experience of this maiden just entered upon her teens, were it not that the innocent child herself is in such deadly earnest. The two long narrative poems, "**Bertha**," and "**Elfrida**," are also tragic in the extreme. . . . We have said that Emma Lazarus was a born singer, but she did not sing, like a bird, for joy of being alive; and of being young, alas! there is no hint in these youthful effusions, except inasmuch as this unrelieved gloom, this ignorance of "values," so to speak, is a sign of youth, common especially among gifted persons of acute and premature sensibilities, whose imagination, not yet focused by reality, overreaches the mark. With Emma Lazarus, however, this somber streak has a deeper root; something of birth and temperament is in it—the stamp and heritage of a race born to suffer. But dominant and fundamental though it was, Hebraism was only latent thus far. It was classic and romantic art that first attracted and inspired her. She pictures Aphrodite the beautiful, arising from the waves, and the beautiful Apollo and his loves—Daphne, pursued by the god, changing into the laurel, and the enamored Clytie into the faithful sunflower. Beauty, for its own sake, supreme and unconditioned, charmed her primarily and to the end. Her restless spirit found repose in the pagan idea—the absolute unity and identity of man with nature, as symbolized in the Greek myths, where every natural force becomes a person, and where in turn persons pass with equal readiness and freedom back into nature again.

In this connection a name would suggest itself even if it did not appear—Heine the Greek, Heine the Jew, Heine the Romanticist, as Emma Lazarus herself has styled him; and already in this early volume of hers we have trace of the kinship and affinity that afterwards so plainly declared itself. Foremost among the translations are a number of his songs, rendered with a finesse and a literalness that are rarely combined. Four years later, at the age of twenty-one, she published her second volume, "**Admetus and Other Poems.**" . . . Of classic themes we have "**Admetus**" and "**Orpheus**," and of romantic, the legend of Tannháuser and of the saintly Lohengrin. All are treated with an artistic finish that shows perfect mastery of her craft, without detracting from the freshness and flow of her inspiration. While sounding no absolutely new note in the world, she yet makes us aware of a talent of unusual distinction, and a highly endowed nature—a sort of tact of sentiment and expression, an instinct of the true and beautiful, and that quick intuition which is like second-sight in its sensitiveness to apprehend and respond to external stimulus. But it is not the purely imaginative poems in this volume that most deeply interest us. We come upon experience of life in these pages; not in the ordinary sense, however, of outward activity and movement, but in the hidden undercurrent of being. . . . [Her poem "**Epochs**"] marks a pivotal moment in her life. Difficult to analyze, difficult above all to convey, if we would not encroach upon the domain of private and personal experience is the drift of this poem, or rather cycle of poems, that ring throughout with a deeper accent, and a more direct appeal, than has yet made itself felt. It is the drama of the human soul—"the mystic winged and flickering butterfly," "flitting between earth and sky, in its passage from birth to death." (pp. 875-76)

In "**Epochs**" we have, doubtless, the impress of a calamity brought very near to the writer and profoundly working upon her sensibilities; not, however, by direct, but by reflex, action, as it were, and through sympathetic emotion—the emotion of the deeply stirred spectator, of the artist, the poet, who lives in the lives of others and makes their joys and their lives his own. (p. 876)

For some years [after the publication of *Admetus, and Other Poems*] almost everything that she wrote was published in "Lippincott's Magazine,". . . and we shall still find in her poems the method and movement of her life. Nature is still the fount and mirror, reflecting, and again reflected, in the

soul. We have picture after picture almost to satiety, until we grow conscious of a lack of substance and body and of vital play to the thought, as though the brain were spending itself in dreamings and reverie, the heart feeding upon itself, and the life choked by its own fullness without due outlet. Happily, however, the heavy cloud of sadness has lifted, and we feel the subsidence of waves after a storm. . . . Nature is the perpetual resource and consolation. "'T is good to be alive!" she says [in "**Matins**"], and why? Simply,

> To see the light
> That plays upon the grass, to feel (and sigh
> With perfect pleasure) the mild breezes stir
> Among the garden roses, red and white,
> With whiffs of fragrancy. . . .

"**Phantasies**" (after Robert Schumann) is the most complete and perfect poem of this period. Like "**Epochs**," it is a cycle of poems, and the verse has caught the·very trick of music—alluring, baffling, and evasive. This time we have the landscape of the night, the glamour of moon and stars—pictures half real and half unreal, mystic imaginings, fancies, dreams, and the enchantment of "faërie," and throughout the unanswered cry, the eternal "**Wherefore**" of destiny. Dawn ends the song with a fine clear note, the return of day, night's misty phantoms rolled away, and the world, itself again green, sparkling and breathing freshness. (p. 877)

"**The Spagnoletto**" has grave defects that would probably preclude its ever being represented on the stage. The dénouement especially is unfortunate and sins against our moral and æsthetic instinct. The wretched, tiger-like father stabs himself in the presence of his crushed and erring daughter, so that she may forever be haunted by the horror and retribution of his death. We are left suspended, as it were, over an abyss, our moral judgment thwarted, our humanity outraged. But "**The Spagnoletto**" is nevertheless a remarkable production, and pitched in another key from anything the writer has yet given us. Heretofore we have only had quiet, reflective, passive emotion: now we have a storm and sweep of passion for which we were quite unprepared. Ribera's character is charged like a thundercloud with dramatic elements. Maria Rosa is the child of her father, fired at a flash, "deaf, dumb, and blind," at the touch of passion. (pp. 878-79)

Exquisitely tender and refined are the love scenes—at the ball and in the garden—between the dashing prince-lover in search of his pleasure and the devoted girl with her heart in her eyes, on her lips, in her hand. Behind them, always like a tragic fate, the somber figure of the Spagnoletto, and over all, the glow and color and soul of Italy.

["**Poems and Ballads of Heinrich Heine**"] was generally accepted as the best version of that untranslatable poet. Very curious is the link between that bitter, mocking, cynic spirit and the refined, gentle spirit of Emma Lazarus. Charmed by the magic of his verse, the iridescent play of his fancy, and the sudden cry of the heart piercing through it all, she is as yet unaware or only vaguely conscious of the real bond between them—the sympathy in the blood, the deep, tragic, Judaic passion of eighteen hundred years that was smoldering in her own heart, soon to break out and change the whole current of her thought and feeling. (p. 879)

All this time she had been seeking heroic ideals in alien stock, soulless, and far removed; in pagan mythology and mystic, medieval Christianity, ignoring her very birthright—the majestic vista of the past, down which, "high above flood and fire," had been conveyed the precious scroll of the Moral Law. Hitherto Judaism had been a dead letter to her. . . . [It] was only during her childhood and earliest years that she attended the synagogue and conformed to the prescribed rites and usages which she had now long since abandoned as obsolete and having no bearing on modern life. Nor had she any great enthusiasm for her own people. As late as April, 1882, she published . . . [an article entitled] **"Was the Earl of Beaconsfield a Representative Jew?"** in which she is disposed to accept as the type of the modern Jew the brilliant, successful, but not overscrupulous *chevalier d'industrie*. In view of subsequent, or rather contemporaneous, events, the closing paragraph of the article in question is worthy of being cited:

> Thus far their religion [the Jewish], whose mere preservation under such adverse conditions seems little short of a miracle, has been deprived of the natural means of development and progress, and has remained a stationary force. The next hundred years, will in our opinion, be the test of their vitality as a people; the phase of toleration upon which they are only now entering will prove whether or not they are capable of growth.

(pp. 879-80)

["**Russian Christianity verses Modern Judaism,**" published in 1882, marks the beginning of] the crusade that she undertook in behalf of her race, and the consequent expansion of all her faculties, the growth of spiritual power which always ensues when a great cause is espoused and a strong conviction enters the soul. Her verse rang out as it had never rung before—a clarion note, calling a people to heroic action and unity; to the consciousness and fulfillment of a grand destiny. When has Judaism been so stirred as by "**The Crowing of the Red Cock**" and ["**The Banner of the Jew**"]. . . .

Her whole being renewed and refreshed itself at its very source. She threw herself into the study of her race, its language, literature, and history. (p. 880)

While under the influence of all the emotions aroused by [a] great crisis in the history of her race she wrote the "**Dance to Death,**" a drama of persecution of the twelfth century, founded upon authentic records—unquestionably her finest work in grasp and scope and, above all, in moral elevation and purport. . . .

The action is without surprise, the doom fixed from the first; but so glowing is the canvas with local and historic color, so vital and intense the movement, so resistless the "internal evidence," if we may call it thus, penetrating its very substance and form, that we are swept along as by a wave of human sympathy and grief. In contrast with "**The Spagnoletto,**" how large is the theme and how all-embracing the catastrophe. In place of the personal we have the drama of the universal. Love is only a flash now—a dream caught sight of and at once renounced at a higher claim.

> Have you no smile to welcome love with, Liebhaid?
> Why should you tremble?
> Prince, I am afraid!
> Afraid of my own heart, my unfathomed joy,
> A blasphemy against my father's grief,
> My people's agony!

> What good shall come, forswearing kith and God,
> To follow the allurements of the heart?

asks the distracted maiden, torn between her love for her princely wooer and her devotion to the people among whom her lot has been cast.

> O God!
> How shall I pray for strength to love him less
> Than mine own soul!
> No more of that,
> I am all Israel's now. Till this cloud pass,
> I have no thought, no passion, no desire,
> Save for my people.

Individuals perish, but great ideas survive—fortitude and courage, and that exalted loyalty and devotion to principle which alone are worth living and dying for. (p. 881)

[What Emma Lazarus accomplished] has real and peculiar significance. It is the privilege of a favored few that every fact and circumstance of their individuality shall add luster and value to what they achieve. To be born a Jewess was a distinction for Emma Lazarus, and she in turn conferred distinction upon her race. To be born a woman also lends a grace and a subtle magnetism to her influence. Nowhere is there contradiction or incongruity. Her works bear the imprint of her character, and her character of her works. The same directness and honesty, the same limpid purity of tone, and the same atmosphere of things refined and beautiful. The vulgar, the false, and the ignoble—she scarcely comprehended them, while on every side she was open and ready to take in and respond to whatever can adorn and enrich life. (p. 884)

> [*Josephine Lazarus*], *"Emma Lazarus," in* The Century, *Vol. XXXVI, No. 6, October, 1888, pp. 875-89.*

THE LITERARY WORLD (essay date 1889)

[As we lay *The Poems of Emma Lazarus*] aside there is perhaps a touch of disappointment on our spirits. It is inevitable that in the case of a figure so attractive, so commanding as Miss Lazarus, the first interest of the reader should be personal. We look for herself in her poems, but the search is not fully rewarded. The nature of Emma Lazarus, as revealed in her work, has a curious reticence. Grave, ardent, sensitive, it is also elusive; a certain dignity, even in the most intimate poems, bids us not intrude too far. Yet this very reserve has its own significant charm, and our respect for the woman deepens, though we crave for a greater abandonment on the part of the poet.

In her earlier work, produced before her Hebrew awakening, there is, besides this characteristic reticence, a slight vagueness, an uncertainty of touch and aim. The chief artistic fault is a frequent langour of movement that corresponds to this dimness of conception. We find a tremulous responsiveness to beauty, expressed now in sympathetic rendering of old legend, now in graceful nature studies illumined by poetic fancy. We find a tendency to deal in delicate effects, in evanescent phases of oversubtilized thought and emotion. All this is in a sense the birthright of every finely organized child of the century. But there is an individual element in the work of Emma Lazarus, a genuineness, a moral earnestness, a groping after reality, that make themselves felt through all her fine-spun imaginative tissue. When a subject once possesses her she treats it clearly and loftily. The early poem "**Epochs**" . . . possesses strength, insight, harmony. Some of the strophes, as "**Regret,**" "**Grief,**" "**Loneliness,**" "**Victory,**" contain really memorable lines. "**Phantasies,**" less ambitious in theme, yet equally true to music and to life, is a rare and exquisite record. Already the poet is swayed more potently by national than by personal enthusiasm, and her noble sonnet ["**The New Colossus**"] on the Bartholdi statue has thrilled many a cold and indifferent nature to its first apprehension of the glory in even the more sordid elements of our American life. On the whole, the poems of this first era always respond to the sympathy which they cannot perhaps command. They leave us with the sense of a fine nature touched to fine issues, yet searching to discover its true self in some faith as yet unrealized, imperative, adequate. . . .

[The poems that Miss Lazarus wrote after her Hebrew awakening] glow with light clear because intense. Less poetic to a superficial glance than the earlier work, the breadth and simplicity of their treatment bear witness to the definite strength of their inspiration. . . . The drama "**The Dance to Death**" sweeps the reader on, merged in its mighty current, oblivious of all besides. He cannot stop to inquire whether he be carried away by the lurid conception, by the knowledge of its historic truth, or by pure poetic power. In such a poem as "**Gifts**" the vigor of the thought uplifts the treatment to a severe nobility. Greatest of all in their strange cadence and visionary power are the short prose-poems. Is it too much to say that a gleam of the solemn fire of the Hebrew prophets shines through the work of this latest child of their race?

> *A review of "The Poems of Emma Lazarus," in* The Literary World, *Vol. XX, No. 3, February 2, 1889, p. 36.*

SOLOMON SOLIS-COHEN   (essay date 1889)

The writings of Emma Lazarus may be divided into two groups, corresponding very closely to two periods of her soul-life; whereof the dividing line is the year (1879-80) of the revival of anti-Jewish demonstrations throughout Northeastern Europe, and especially and most cruelly in Russia. (p. 295)

This division is indicated in the arrangement of the two volumes [of *The Poems of Emma Lazarus*] wherein the sisters of the dead singer have reproduced . . . such of her verses as they had reason to believe she would not have been unwilling to have preserved in permanent form. . . . We could have wished . . . that the criticism of the poet or of her literary executors, had spared such of the earlier poems as "**Orpheus**," "**The Garden of Adonis**," "**Dreams**," "**Wings**," "**Realities**"; which, with a little of the crudity but much more of the vigor and freshness of youth, exhibit the same purity and singleness of thought, delicate fancy, human sympathy, and refined grace of diction, that in "**Admetus**" and "**Tannhäuser**" won the instant admiration and grateful recognition of critics and lovers of pure English verse at home and abroad. The "**Admetus**" of Emma Lazarus will not suffer by comparison with either Browning's or William Morris's treatment of the same theme. Perhaps it is the truer insight of her woman's nature that makes her represent the king as an unconscious and unwilling recipient of the new life gained by the sacrifice of his queen's. Her Alcides too, lightly and delicately yet withal vigorously sketched, is an original creation; and to our mind, by far the noblest delineation of the hero.

"**Epochs**," a thoughtful and thought-awakening cycle of poems, . . . takes for its motto, a sentence from the poet's friend, Emerson: "The epochs of our life are not in the visible facts, but in the silent thoughts by the wayside as we walk." Full of the poet's subjectivity, they clearly reveal the exquisite sen-

sitiveness of her soul, the richness of its inner life, and its power of intimate communion with nature; together with a hint of the passionate sympathy with suffering, that later, fired her Jewish poems. . . .

Of later poems, the most powerful is that entitled "**A Masque of Venice**." . . . It is a weird but nevertheless gracefully wrought fantasy, reminding us of Poe at his best.

But had Emma Lazarus given us only beautiful remodellings of Grecian myth and mediaeval legend, sweet, sympathetic pictures of the inner life, poetic descriptions of nature that gild the "**Fog**" and glorify the "**Morning**,"—even patriotic lyrics and elegies like "**Heroes**," "**How Long?**," "**The South**," "**Sunrise**," which breathe a profound love of country, and a lofty aspiration for its future,—her place in the history of song would not have been that eminence whereto her response to the call of a stern hour suddenly lifted her. From the savage land of the Tsar came the despairing cry of a people over whom once again swept the terrible tide of undeserved hatred and bitter persecution. . . . [To] Emma Lazarus, that cry of despair came with an unusual force. . . .

It came to her, as of old the cry of the oppressed people to Deborah: "'*Uri!* '*uri! dabberi shir!*—Awake! Awake! Pour forth thy song!" The Jewess that had slumbered in the groves of Arcadia, forgetting Zion, forgetting the exiles by the rivers of Babel, did indeed "awake and sing." Rang out a burst of impassioned prophecy, whereof the like had not been heard since the Spain of Torquemada dashed from Israel's hand the harp the kindly Moor had bidden him lift from off the willow-bough. No longer was the mocking, cynical Heine . . . the chief poet of Judaic blood—but prophet and psalmist, Gabirol, Ben Ezra, Hallevi, spoke to her and inspired her word. . . .

In "**The New Year**," written for the Jewish festival of Rosh-Hashanah, 5643 (1882), she sings with glowing enthusiasm of what she had before deemed lifeless forms, and pictures the steadfast heroism of the martyrs to whom these forms were indeed a living inspiration.

> High above flood and fire ye held the scroll,
> Out of the depths ye published still the Word.
> No bodily pang had power to swerve your soul:
>   Ye in a cynic age of crumbling faiths
> Lived to bear witness to the living Lord,
>   Or died a thousand deaths.
>
> Kindle the silver candle's seven rays,
> Offer the first fruits of the clustered bowers
> The garnered spoil of bees. With prayer and praise
> Rejoice that once more tried, once more we prove
> How strength of supreme suffering still is ours
>   For Truth and Law and Love.

The identification of the poet with her people is complete. It is "we," who perform the prescribed festal rites, who suffer, and who rejoice in the choice of suffering rather than betrayal of a divine trust.

"**The Banner of the Jew**" is a trumpet call for the restoration of Palestinian nationality, which became the enthusiastic hope of the now ardent Jewess, the everpresent dream of the poet. . . .

["**The Dance to Death**"] is but an episode in a single scene of the perpetual tragedy of Israel's persecutions. It exhibits both dramatic power, and a lofty poesy; and would alone give the author an enduring name. The final catastrophe, where the Jews of Nordhausen, condemned to perish by fire, pass to the platform above the flames, carrying in procession the sacred scrolls of the Law and singing hymns of joy, is portrayed by direct and indirect action with surpassing skill, and conveys an impression of indescribable majesty—up to the very moment of the stage direction: "Music ceases; a sound of crashing boards is heard and a great cry—HALLELUJAH!" The love episode of gentle Liebhaid Von Orb and the noble Prince William of Meissen, is given too, with tender grace and sweetness; inviting literary contrast with the equally well-drawn love scenes between the pleasure-seeking John of Austria and the passionate Maria, in the poet's earlier drama, **"The Spagnoletto."**

"Gifts" and **"The Choice"** set forth in different ways the same idea: The Egyptian prays for wealth, the Grecian for beauty, the Roman for power—they obtain their wishes and decay with their perishing gifts. The Hebrew asks for Truth, and though at the cost of unending martyrdom, receives with Truth unending life. . . .

[**"By the Waters of Babylon: Little Poems in Prose"**] is the culmination of her power as a writer, and merely from a literary standpoint we must regret that she could not have been spared to enrich the English anthology with other poems in the same prose form. (p. 296)

Emma Lazarus, as shown in the volumes before us, must be given high and unique place in the choir of English singers; but more than this, she has an exalted station among the lofty spirits who have voiced the sublime passion and inspiring hope of Israel. (p. 297)

> *Solomon Solis-Cohen, "The Poems of Emma Lazarus," in* The American, *Vol. XVII, No. 446, February 23, 1889, pp. 295-97.*

THE SPECTATOR   (essay date 1889)

The execution [of Emma Lazarus's **"The Dance to Death"**] is somewhat unequal. Miss Lazarus seems to have written in haste, and to have felt that dislike of the labour of correction which often goes with imperfect physical power, and the dialogue is often wanting in dramatic propriety; but the plot is well contrived, and the interest admirably sustained. The customary motives that bring about such tragedies—private greed or vengeance, popular prejudices and superstitions, and religious tests—are skilfully combined, and made to work up together to a striking catastrophe. (p. 608)

Emma Lazarus's verse was wanting in some of the qualities which go to make up greatness of the first class; but there is much of genuine power about it, and it is interesting as coming from a race which, while in many respects as vigorous as ever, has shown for many years but little literary power. Henry Heine is, of course, a conspicuous exception; nor could there be a more curious contrast than that between these two representatives of the Hebrew race. (p. 609)

> *A review of "The Poems of Emma Lazarus," in* The Spectator, *Vol. 63, No. 3201, November 2, 1889, pp. 608-09.*

ISRAEL ABRAHAMS   (essay date 1920)

[Emma Lazarus] wrote much as a Hellenist, but her genuine outbursts were stimulated by two crises: the American War of North and South in the sixties, and the Russian Persecutions in the eighties. In a sense it is unfortunate that the May Laws came so late. Emma Lazarus had but few years to live after the promulgation of the legislation which sent forth, from their country, those myriads of Russian Jews, whose presence has so profoundly altered Jewish conditions in various lands. Her Jewish poems are full indeed of fire, but it is the fire of an immature passion. When she died, she had only begun to find herself as the singer of Israel's cause.

Even so, however, her songs will not die. For she realized that Israel is "the slave of the Idea." She did not fully grasp what the Idea was, however. Israel's migrations . . . were all, she felt, towards a destined end, and that end—Freedom. . . . Freedom is part of Israel's Idea; it is not the whole of it.

In her new-found enthusiasm for the Hebrew language she translated much from the medieval poets. But she will always come to one's mind as the bard of Hanukkah. There [in such works as **"The Feast of Lights"**] she comes nearest to the Idea of which Israel is the missioner. (pp. 319-21)

[Her] hand is always firmest when her theme is the Maccabaean heroism. This subject gave her the opportunity which her nationalistic mood needed. (p. 322)

[**"The Banner of the Jew"**] is bold and moving, but the reader cannot fail to observe that the metre and the passion are derived from Byron's "Isles of Greece". The Hebrew's protest *against* Greece must, forsooth, owe its form and sentiment to the Saxon's plea *for* Greece! The Jewish muse is still in leading strings. The true, full song of Israel's hope is yet to come. None the less, the genius of Emma Lazarus struck truly the key-note to that song. We hear its echo still. (p. 324)

> *Israel Abrahams, "The Poems of Emma Lazarus," in his* By-Paths in Hebraic Bookland, *The Jewish Publication Society of America, 1920, pp. 319-24.*

RACHEL COHEN   (essay date 1927)

Among Jewish women writers of all ages, among Jewish writers who have used the English tongue as their medium of expression, for force, power and sincerity and pure literary worth Emma Lazarus stands pre-eminent: she is in direct line of descent to the Prophets and the great Hebrew poets. Her greatest value to us lies in the Jewish spirit so manifest in her writings: the prophetic utterances that see beyond the present deep into the heart of the future: the past its foundation, knowledge its weapon, history its safeguard, the honest intention its soul; with the sorrows of the past to make possible the glorious future. A rare insight, the courage of conviction, a virile power of expression, that urge that made Moses work to free his bonded brethren—all this was the power of Emma Lazarus, the greatest Jewess of modern times. (p.184)

"Russian Christianity v. Modern Judiasm" is a splendid work, not a justification nor an accusation. Emma Lazarus merely takes Madame Ragozin's statements and tears them to pieces, hurls each argument down to the depths of ridicule, and bravely stands her ground against all comers. The reply is well written, it is logical, it is damaging. With **"Songs of a Semite"** she declared herself a National Jewess; and was a forerunner of Zionism. Her [subsequent] works, now all of Jewish interest, follow close on one another, and are invaluable to the Jew who takes a conscious pride in his birth and the ancient people from which he sprung. (p. 186)

The [poetry] of Emma Lazarus has its message for this age as it had for her own. She felt the tragedy of the Jew, and sought to alleviate his hard lot. All her poems breathe the spirit, and the message of Judaism; the need for the national re-establishment that would mean the new creative spirit that would be based on the fine traditions of the past. (p. 188)

Emma Lazarus, with the power of her pen, helped to regenerate her people. Her endeavors helped to make easier the way for those who, following in her footsteps, came years after her. She foresaw and foretold what no other Jewess had seen. She wrote in English for the world to read. She was at one with the meanest Jewish refugee, the greatness of kin that knows of no barriers. . . . It is, indeed, small wonder that one who had felt with all intensity the sufferings of the terror, pogrom-hounded Jews, was able to pen the spirit of that Colossus, the immense woman who stands, with uplifted lamp in hand, waiting to welcome, with mother-love, the sufferers and weary of the Old World to the glorious promise of the New. . . . (p. 189)

Rachel Cohen, "Emma Lazarus," in The Reform Advocate, Vol. LXXIV, No. 8, September 24, 1927, pp. 184-89.

MORRIS U. SCHAPPES (essay date 1944)

[*Schappes provides an overview of Lazarus's contribution as a proponent of the Jewish cause. Significantly, he traces Lazarus's Jewish consciousness back to "her earliest days as a young writer," characterizing her transformation in the 1880s as a change from passive sympathy with her people to active sympathy. He also broaches the subject of Lazarus's interest in socialism. For a further discussion of the development of Lazarus's Jewish consciousness, see Max I. Baym (1949) and Albert Mordell (1949).*]

Most of those who have written about Emma Lazarus, both in her own time and more recently, have fallen prey to a confusing exaggeration. To dramatize a point that has its own sufficient drama, they have resorted to melodrama. They would have us believe that until the Russian pogroms of the 1880's she had no interest in Jews or the problems of Jews, that she had virtually no consciousness of being a Jew. (p. 11)

The record as I read it, however, shows that a Jewish consciousness was present in Emma Lazarus from her earliest days as a young writer. There is her poem, written at the age of eighteen, **"In the Jewish Synagogue at Newport,"** published in her volume, *Admetus and Other Poems,* and immediately reprinted in "The Jewish Messenger." There is her life-long interest in Heine, whose position as a Jew she so thoroughly understood and so brilliantly analyzed. There are her translations from Gabirol and Halevy, published in "The Jewish Messenger" early in 1879. There is the aid she gave Dr. Gustav Gottheil of Temple Emanu-El "for some years before 1882" in his work on a collections of hymns and anthems adapted for Jewish worship. And, perhaps most significant, there is the fact that she wrote her profoundly moving play, **"The Dance to Death,"** a "few years" before it was published in 1882.

Then what was the character of the transformation that Emma Lazarus underwent? It was not from no interest in Jewry or a lack of interest to a sudden espousal of the cause of the Jew. Consciousness and interest there had always been, but it was an interest in Jewry distant and past, not present and American. (p. 12)

[Her] interest in Jewry was extensive but placid. She felt herself confronted with no *problems* that she and other Jews had to solve. No action was required. The persecuted Jews of fourteenth century Germany, whose condition and courage she dramatizes in **"The Dance to Death,"** were long dead, and

conditions in Germany had been changed. In general the extension of democracy was easing the burden of the Jew. Her sympathies were all with the oppressed, whose history she was reading, but it was a passive sympathy because she saw no present issue. Such an issue was presented, to the world and to Emma Lazarus, by the Russian pogroms that began in 1879 and increased in extent and ferocity during the next years. The pogroms evoked a passionate reaction she had not known before, and led her into active struggle against the brutalities abroad that her imagination rendered so vivid and her conscience made so personal. (p. 13)

She developed a passion for Jewish history, but not for theology. Her concern was not so much with the articles of Jewish faith as with the plight of the Jewish people. She rewrote in prose and sang in poetry the vital lessons that could solve the problems of the Jews of the 1880's. The heroes, scholars and poets of the Jewish people—Bar Kochba and Raschi, Gabirol and Halevy—she made more than ever her own, and shared them with her people. To Jew and non-Jew she presented with eloquence her concept of, and findings about, the Jews.

The Jews needed and loved freedom. She wrote: "Until we are all free, we are none of us free." . . . Jews sought learning first, and wealth only secondarily, and that generally when they felt wealth was their only protection against insult. Their banner bore the democratic word Justice rather than the condescending or sentimental word Charity. Jews were rebels, not dogmatists.

> The Jew (I say it proudly rather than deprecatingly) is a born rebel. He is endowed with a shrewd, logical mind, in order that he may examine and protest; with a stout and fervent heart, in order that the instinct of liberty may grow into a consuming passion, whereby, if need be, all other impelling motives shall be swallowed up.

Jews would follow the truth, therefore, wherever it lead, despite the fact that for the Jew it so often led to persecution. Maybe others—non-Jews—also shared these ideals. But they were the *dominant* Christians and could have applied their principles—yet so often did not—and oh so often hounded the Jews for trying to do so. These things she learned and these she taught in words noble and stark. (p. 14)

In words without malice but sharp and stinging she told the rich American Jew that his freedom depended on the state of the pogrom-ridden Jews of the Caucasus. The American Jews may have squirmed, but they heeded her, when she issued the challenge: where is the American Ezra who will lift the Banner of the Jew and use it as an international battle-standard? Perhaps some of them even reflected that the American Ezra might be named Emma. . . .

With Heine she noted that each country gets the Jews it deserves or the Jews that it makes (a theme that recurs: see **"Raschi in Prague"** and **"Russian Christianity versus Modern Judaism"**). What Jews would our country make, and get? In the United States the Jew was "the free citizen of a Republic." Several times she noted the fateful fact that 1492 was the year in which the Jews were driven from Spain while Columbus was discovering America to "bequeath a Continent to Freedom." (See **"1492"** and **"By the Waters of Babylon."**) The more conscious of her Jewishness Emma Lazarus became, the prouder she grew of America. (p. 15)

For her America was to be free, its democracy to be thoroughly tested. American Jews, . . . [the] new immigrants especially, must do everything—not only those few things allowed them in European despotisms—they must farm and work and build and trade and learn and create and teach. . . . What Booker T. Washington was preaching to the Negro people she taught the Jews. They must conquer new forms of labor. Interest in her idea spread. She lived to see the founding of The Hebrew Technical Institute, of which she was acknowledged to be the original inspiration. . . .

With democracy so limited in Europe—Czars, Kaisers, tyrants regnant so widely—Jews needed a home of their own, a state where they could become a nation again. . . . [Emma Lazarus began to discuss this idea] with her special vigor in "The American Hebrew." Her solution was not intended for American Jews, who, she made it clear, would, could, and should stay here. But the . . . oppressed and haunted millions of Europe—they needed it. It was her answer to the lack of democracy on the Continent. Herzl's concept, to become known as Zionism, was still unheard of when she expressed her aspiration for the conditions of a normal national life for the Jews. (p. 16)

[She] looked where it was forbidden and daring to look. In the Mosaic Code she had found the ethics and foundation of the idea then so fresh—Socialism. She disputed with surprised Christians their claim to having originated Socialist ideals. The basis was in the Mosaic Code, she insisted. And wasn't Marx, weren't other leaders of the Socialist movement, Jews? Proudly she claimed her own.

In England, there was a poet, whom she had long admired imitated, and emulated, William Morris. He was a Socialist, a Marxian. When she went to England in the spring of 1883 she made sure to seek him out, spending a day with him at his factory in Surrey, and wrote about it for "The Century" on her return home. Morris and Socialism were being misrepresented. In the article ["**A Day in Surrey with William Morris**"] she set out to explain how good and sincere Morris was, how his poetry had led him to his politics, and what his politics were. . . . Moses, Marx, and William Morris—she claimed them all. (p. 17)

[**"By the Waters of Babylon"**] is the beautiful summation of her character and ideals, and of her most mature style. In an earlier poem, **"Echoes,"** Emma Lazarus had expressed the feeling that she was handicapped because she was a woman and alone. "Late-born and woman-souled," she was "one in love with solitude and song." She dared not "cope . . . with the world's strong-armed warriors." Not hers to "recite the dangers, wounds, and triumphs of the fight." She thought then she was one "who veiled and screened by womanhood must grope." But in the last five or six years of her life she strode from solitude into a fighting fraternity with her people that made her a leader of Jews on two continents and of the American people as a whole too. (p. 18)

> *Morris U. Schappes, in an introduction to* Emma
> Lazarus: Selections from Her Poetry and Prose *by*
> *Emma Lazarus, edited by Morris U. Schappes, Co-*
> *operative Book League, 1944, pp. 7-20.*

MAX I. BAYM   (essay date 1949)

[*In the following essay, Baym suggests that, much to the detriment of her critical reputation, Lazarus has been inappropriately characterized as a "singer with a special cause." To support this*

contention, he proposes a relatively late date for the inception of her Jewish consciousness and emphasizes Lazarus's earlier struggle to be accepted within the mainstream of American literature. Lazarus's sister Anne Humphreys Johnstone, to whom Baym refers in the essay, was a convert to Roman Catholicism who at one time refused to permit republication of her sister's writings on Jewish topics.]

The second phase [of Emma Lazarus's literary career] really begins with the *Songs of a Semite,* containing the poetic drama, **"The Dance of Death,"** and ends with **"By the Waters of Babylon."** This phase is marked particularly by . . . a progressive prose series dealing with Jewish questions, the final term of which was her essay on **"Renan and the Jews."** But even here the authorities she bases herself on are people like Sylvestre de Sacy, Secrétan, Montégut, Claude Fauriel, Gabriel Charmes, Edgar Quinet, Émile de Lavelaye, Joseph Salvador and Renan among the French, and George Eliot and Laurence Oliphant among the English,—all non-Jews, excepting Salvador who was of a Jewish father and a Catholic mother.

There is at least room for reasonable doubt whether there would have been that second phase in her poetic career, had she attained a place in [Emerson's 1874 anthology] *Parnassus,*—had she truly and actually been accepted by Lowell, Howells and Emerson. Those who persisted in that doubt a score of years ago had it reinforced by a letter [written in 1926 by Emma's sister Anne Humphreys Johnstone]. . . . In this communication Mrs. Johnstone maintained that had her sister not been cut off in mid-career, the latter's Jewishness would now be regarded in a different light.

> There has been a tendency [Mrs. Johnstone
> wrote] on the part of some of her public to
> overemphasize the Hebraic strain in her work,
> giving it thus a quality of sectarian propaganda,
> which I greatly deplore, for I understood this
> to have been merely a phase in my sister's
> development, called forth by righteous indig-
> nation at the tragic happenings of those days.
> Then, unfortunately, owing to her untimely
> death, this was destined to be her final word.

Indirectly, then, those who have denied her admittance to *Parnassus* have helped to make her a singer with a special cause. And, the subsequent estimate of her as a poet has been obfuscated by three pervasive interested parties: those who would present her as an orthodox Jewess interested in the dates of holidays and memorials; those who would link in her character and work Jewish ardour with social revolution; and those who, like her sister [Anne], would suppress her Jewishness and true origin. As a result, she has fared ill indeed at the bar of accredited literary history even in the very year when some celebrate the centenary of her birth. . . . Poor Emma is given short shrift indeed in the recently published volume *Literary History of the United States* [1948]. In [the second volume], . . . she is dismissed amiably as a supporter of Zionism and as a tendencious writer influenced by the events in Eastern Europe towards 1881. In the third volume only three sentences are spent on her, in which her filiopietism is stressed when we are told that she is best known for her *Songs of a Semite* and her own insignificance is implied when her correspondence is evaluated as "*important for the stature of her correspondents*" (italics ours).

It is high time, we submit, that Emma Lazarus as a literary personality were saved from parochialism *in aula academics* [in academic halls] as well as from those zealots who throw her true worth out of historic focus in one way or another. A calm and collected study of her work would reveal her as deserving of a respectable place in American literary history. (pp. 278-80)

Max I. Baym, "Emma Lazarus and Emerson," in *Publications of the American Jewish Historical Society, Vol. XXXVIII, Part 4, June, 1949, pp. 261-87.**

ALBERT MORDELL (essay date 1949)

[*Mordell's account of Lazarus's efforts as a proponent of the Jewish cause features a detailed account of her early interest in Jewish themes as well as a critical analysis of her judgment in matters relating to the Jews.*]

In evaluating Emma Lazarus's writings, the first misapprehension to be cleared up is that unwittingly fostered by her sister Josephine . . . [when she stated] that Judaism had been a dead letter to Emma before the Russian wave of pogroms in the early eighties [see excerpt above, 1888]. This has led to a belief that the literary range of her early work was purely cosmopolitan and that she devoted herself to her own people only in the last five years of her life. Contrary to the general impression, however, Emma Lazarus had made her translations from the German versions of poems by Solomon Ibn Gabirol and Yehudah Halevi before the pogroms and had contemplated their inclusion in a volume together with essays about their authors. The translations from Gabirol appeared in *The Jewish Messenger* for January 17, January 31, and August 18, 1879. Those from Yehudah Halevi were printed in the same periodical on January 24, February 7, February 14 and February 21, 1879. These are the poems that were later reprinted in *Songs of a Semite* . . . and again in the second volume of *The Poems of Emma Lazarus*. . . . As a matter of fact her play, *The Dance to Death*, . . . which first appeared in the *American Hebrew* (beginning with June 30 to September 3, 1882) and was later included in both *Songs of a Semite* and *Poems of Emma Lazarus*, was composed . . . a few years previously. Poems like her elegy on the death of her uncle, the Reverend Jacques J. Lyons in 1877, and **"In the Jewish Synagogue at Newport,"** written at the age of eighteen, attest to Emma's awareness of her Jewish connections. (pp. 79-80)

[It is true, however, that with her response to Madame Ragozin's defence of the Russian pogroms, a] great change had come over Miss Lazarus. She was transformed into a literary champion of her people. . . . Shy as she was, she would emerge from her ivory tower, take up the trumpet and blow a blast that all Christendom would hear. . . . [**"The Banner of the Jew,"**] printed in the *Critic*, June 3, 1882, marks a new period in the life of Miss Lazarus and reflects the new era in the life of her people as well. . . . For the next three years and intermittently thereafter, products from her pen appeared in the pages of the *American Hebrew*. These included her previously mentioned masterpiece *The Dance to Death*. . . . When Miss Lazarus wrote this story of Jewish martyrdom and courage, she was merely dramatizing an episode far away from her in time and distance. She attached no obtruding moral, for the implications were clear. She was writing as an artist, not ever believing that the conditions in her play would be repeated in her own days. This however actually happened when the Russian pogroms broke out, and the play thus became timely.

Next to this play, the most important contribution of Emma Lazarus to the *American Hebrew* was **"An Epistle to the He-**brews," a series of articles which ran from November 3, 1882 to February 23, 1883. . . . Naturally she wrote here about alleviating the sufferings of the Jews, but she suggested the organization of a fraternal and practical movement. She also sought to have Jews return to varied economic pursuits and follow the intellectual education of their ancestors. She called for a wider study of Hebrew literature and history. Above all she demanded recognition of certain principles of religion and law upon which Judaism is founded. Thus she anticipated to some degree the views of Ahad Ha'am. She sought the support of every Jew for Zionism; she urged upon him "a patriotic and unselfish interest in the sufferings of his oppressed brethren of less fortunate countries, sufficient to make him promote by every means in his power the establishment of a secure asylum." (pp. 82-3)

Miss Lazarus was now committed to Zionism. She realized that pleas for toleration, statistics about Jewish ability, social data showing comparative freedom from crime, clear evidence of Jewish patriotism, and demands for emancipation were surface remedies for injustice to the Jews in foreign lands. . . . She penned an article for the *Century Magazine* of February 1885, called **"The Jewish Problem"** in which she maintained that the Jews were driven into [their] position by intolerance and ignorance and were forced to enter upon a vigorous and concerted action of defense.

It is remarkable that she should have been fermenting with ideas from the contemporary writings of Perez Smolenskin with whose works she was not familiar. In her **"New Ezekiel"** printed in the *American Hebrew* for January 19, 1883, . . . she wrote:

> The Spirit is not dead, proclaim the word,
> Where lay dead bones, a host of armed men stand!
> I open your graves, my people, saith the Lord,
> And I shall place you living in your land.

Her Zionism became militant and she was fascinated by the figure of Bar Kokhba. On November 12, 1884, . . . Emma Lazarus read a paper **"The Last National Revolt of the Jews."** In it, this Jewish liberator was portrayed as a hero and even compared to Washington. . . . A poem on Bar Kokhba apparently written about this time or shortly before is to be found in her collected poems. Historians have not all been in accord with her in her estimate of the well-intentioned patriot who was the cause of one of the greatest disasters in Jewish history. Her final efforts in behalf of the Jewish cause was **"By the Waters of Babylon."** . . . In one section she listed the great Jewish names from Maimonides to Montefiore and then called on the American Jew to welcome the despised Russian Jew as a brother. One does not however escape the feeling that there was at times an air of patronage and condescension in Emma Lazarus as among many others toward the immigrants whom she described as "haunted by the bat-like phantoms of superstition."

Emma Lazarus of course was not always right in her judgment in matters relating to the Jews. . . . [In the essay **"M. Renan on the Jews"**] she showed herself ready to abandon all the national and traditional concomitants of historical Judaism for an emasculated "pure ideal Jewish religion." In **"An Epistle to the Hebrews"** she opposed the revival of the Jewish Sabbath which in her opinion was more adapted to the needs of a simple agricultural society than to the conditions of a complex civilization. In her Beaconsfield essay [**"Was the Earl of Beaconsfield a Representative Jew?"**] she practically accepted some non-Jewish appraisals of Jews as narrow, arrogant, subject to a passion for revenge, vanity, and love of pomp.

Emma Lazarus was after all better acquainted with English than Hebrew literature. Being a liberal and much taken with reform movements in the air, such as Single Tax, Socialism and Ethical Culture, all of which she traced to the Bible, she underestimated the power of tradition and custom. Hence she succumbed to the casual compliments of Renan to Judaism in his statements about the value of the Jewish religion residing solely in its moral generalities. Had she read his bitter attacks upon the Talmud and his criticisms of the Jews for their alleged lack of originality, she might have reserved her eulogy upon him in the prize essay she wrote. But it must be remembered that she did not err less than other Jewish contemporaries. She must be given credit for her self-sacrifice and services to a cause then unpopular. (pp. 83-5)

While to us Jews Miss Lazarus is of particular interest, we must remember she belongs to American Literature at large, occupying the place of a more than minor poet. Her command of technique and vocabulary, her brimming with thought and seething with emotion, mark her a true daughter of the muses. She was a follower of Emerson and Thoreau, of Wordsworth and Shelley, of Tennyson and Browning, no less than of Moses Ibn Ezra and Heine. Her magnificent translations of the two famous love poems of Alfred de Musset, "The May Night" and "The October Night" would be enough to give her an immortal name. Yet historians of American literatures have often passed her by or casually referred to her. Edmund Clarence Stedman and Whittier, however, included poems by her in their anthologies. One of the lesser tragedies of her life was that the man she worshipped, Emerson, did not include any poem by her in his anthology *Parnassus . . .* , in spite of an admiration for her talents expressed in letters to her, and of years of friendship. (pp. 86-7)

> Albert Mordell, "The 100th Birthday of Emma Lazarus: July 22, 1849—November 19, 1887," in Jewish Book Annual: 1948-49, Vol. 7, Abraham G. Duker, Pinkhos Churgin, Moshe Starkman, eds., Jewish Book Council of America, 1949, pp. 79-88.

AARON KRAMER   (essay date 1956)

[*Kramer traces Lazarus's artistic development through an examination of "her relationship with the writings of Heinrich Heine."*]

One of the most remarkable features of Emma Lazarus' career is her dramatic transformation, in a very short span of years, from a thin-voiced, imitative echo, into a flaming prophetess whose lines reverberated across the continents.

In tracing her development, one can scarcely find a better gauge than her relationship with the writings of Heinrich Heine. . . . [Heine was] one of the first poets she chose to translate. *Poems and Translations,* written between the ages of fourteen and sixteen . . . contains a number of these efforts. . . . [In the 1871 collection *Admetus and Other Poems*], too, the translations from Heine predominate. Archaic, and sometimes stilted, these lyrics are nevertheless sensitively, sympathetically rendered. Her choice of poems for translation is illuminating—corresponding to the mood of her own work at this period: romantic, morbid, fanciful, other-worldly. (pp. 248-49)

It is not surprising that she failed to tackle even one of Heine's poems inspired by Jewish themes. Her attitude is made quite clear in the lines written **"In the Jewish Synagogue at Newport."** Although she treats her subject with sympathy and respect, she expresses not a word of kinship. The Hebrew tongue she calls "a language dead," the Judaic idea "spent."

Five years later, a new note was struck in the writings of Emma Lazarus. On February 18, 1876, she published in the *Jewish Messenger* a different type of translation from the kind she had specialized in before. It was Heine again, but no longer the Heine of romantic song. Her inspirer now was Heine, the Jew. She had come to a phase in her development when she could be moved by the story of an anti-Semitic Spanish lady's love for a rabbi's son.

Not only was she stirred to translate this ironic gem, "Donna Clara," but to go beyond it, and produce two sequels based on suggestions in Heine's own notes: **"Don Pedrillo,"** in which this son of Donna Clara and the Jew expresses his hatred of Jews to the rabbi whom he does not know as his father; and **"Fra Pedro,"** in which the boy, now an abbot, persecutes the Jews. These poems revealed not merely her great imitative talent, but an uncanny ability to recreate an age and country known to her through books alone.

This ability had been proved before. The Greece of **"Admetus"** and **"Orpheus,"** the Germany of **"Tannhäuser"** and *Alide* . . . , and the Italy of the *Spagnoletto* . . . had all come to life, in a variety of centuries; but her poems of Israelite Spain were expressed with perhaps more bite, more personal feeling, than anything she had previously done. (pp. 249-50)

[1881 was] a noteworthy year for Emma Lazarus, since it marked the publication of her Heine translations, with a biographical sketch, marking the twenty-fifth anniversary of the master-poet's death. (p. 250)

Many of the songs [in *Poems and Ballads of Heinrich Heine*] hold up remarkably well, although the language often strikes one as old-fashioned. She succeeded in capturing the mood of Heine as a romantic poet, and seldom did violence to his meaning. What she selected for translation, however, would give the uninitiated reader a wholly inadequate notion of Heine's range in theme and technique. Preponderant are his early love-sick verses which, although perhaps most popular, can hardly be called representative of his life work.

Not a single political poem is included, although his *Songs for the Times* contain at least a dozen of Germany's outstanding political poems. Not a single excerpt is given from his *Hebrew Melodies* and *Romancero*. Neither from *Germany—A Winter's Tale*, nor from *Atta Troll—A Midsummernight's Dream*, is a single passage presented, although these monumental satires had immeasurable influence in their time.

Where in her 1881 selection do we find the bitterness, the earthy humor, the merciless exposure of society, the clarion-call to revolt, the exaltation of folk-heroes, the identification with Jewish suffering and glory? All these are essential parts of Heine, and all are missing from Emma Lazarus' selection.

It is interesting to discover that, in tackling Heine's irreverent version of the Tannhäuser legend, she left out the final section with a cryptical little note: "There are eight more verses to this poem, which I take the liberty of omitting." Perhaps she was shocked by the violent cynicism of Heine's attack, and by the off-color impishness of his writing, which certainly was a far cry from her own relatively tame treatment of the same legend ten years before. Perhaps she felt that this kind of poetry was simply not her forté. It does, after all, lack the high dignity which is never absent—even for a moment—from Emma Lazarus' work. Yet the modern reader, who wants to get the Heine poem that the translator has promised, is likely to find her little piece of censorship more shocking than even those eight stanzas of vitriol could be.

If her translation is incomplete, and a bit safe, no such complaint can be registered against the seventeen-page biographical sketch which precedes the poetry. It shows profound sympathy with and understanding of the man and his work, as well as of his times. She is completely absorbed in her subject. Unlike the prefaces of many translators, not a single personal reference is made. Her scholarship is flawless; exhaustive research must have gone into the preparation of her sketch. (pp. 251-52)

She skilfully compares Heine's problems with those faced by her former idol, Goethe. Heine's Jewishness is discussed at length, and a reasonable approach to his apostasy is presented. She points out that he was "no enthusiast for the Hebrew faith, but he was none the less eager to proclaim himself an enthusiast for the rights of the Jews and their civil equality." (pp. 252-53)

The evaluation of Heine's *Rabbi of Bacharach* indicates her standards and appreciations at that time. It explains in large measure both her choice of *The Dance to Death* as a subject for artistic treatment and her method of treatment. It makes quite clear the fact that Heine, more than any other writer outside of Emerson, was her spiritual and aesthetic guide. He, too, in writing the *Rabbi of Bacharach*, was illustrating "the persecution of his people during the middle ages." He

> treats this theme in a purely objective manner. He does not allow himself a word of comment, much less of condemnation concerning the outrages he depicts. He paints the scene as an artist, not as the passionate fellow-sufferer and avenger that he is. But what subtle eloquence lurks in that restrained cry of horror and indignation which never breaks forth, and yet which we feel through every line, gathering itself up like thunder on the horizon for a terrific outbreak at the end!

Her own poetry had long before shown the influence of Heine as lyricist, especially marked in such pieces as **"Off Rough Point"** and **"Song, Venus"** which are almost translations of specific Heine songs. It was only in *The Dance to Death*, however, that she finally achieved parity with him as a chronicler of Jewish martyrdom. (pp. 253-54)

In December of 1884, *Century Magazine* published a long essay by Emma Lazarus, **"The Poet Heine."** . . . This article is more than a vital supplement to her 1881 biographical sketch.

Her new, illustrative translations of political poems such as "The Spinners," and Hebraic poems such as "Prologue to the Rabbi of Bacharach" and an excerpt from "Judah Halevi," indicate that she might have been on the way to fulfilling her role as complete Heine translator. . . . The unrhymed, paragraph form used for some of these poems appears closely related to the form of her last work, **"By the Waters of Babylon,"** and may indeed be a clue to her change in technique.

In this paper she treated of Heine's "fatal and irreconciliable dualism"—half-Hebrew and half-Greek—which had been a painful problem with her as well. More sympathetically than in the earlier study, she traced his love for "the possible Germany of the future." She quoted some pungent prose passages of political satire, and some which glorified the ancient proph-

ets, especially Moses: "the great emancipator, the valiant rabbi of liberty, the terrible enemy of all servitude!" She pointed out that, later in life, Heine confessed (as she herself might have confessed), "that in his youth he had never done justice to this great master, nor to the Hebrew people."

After giving in full her fine rendering of his revolutionary poem, "The Spinners," she exclaimed:

> Compared with these ringing, burning words, how cold seems the detached cosmopolitanism of Goethe, the serene pagan, the courtier and companion of princes, who, from his lofty heights of indifference, accused Heine, the embittered enthusiast, of a "want of love."

(Could such words have been written by the devoted *Faust* translator, by the author of that Goethe idyll, *Alide*?) (pp. 255-56)

One hundred years after Heine's death, and almost seventy after Emma Lazarus'—the phenomenon of their kinship remains striking. It may be termed a classic illustration of cultural interweaving—and of that unbroken continuity, from epoch to epoch, by which the flame of art is made immortal. (p. 257)

Aaron Kramer, "The Link between Heinrich Heine and Emma Lazarus," in Publications of the American Jewish Historical Society, *Vol. XLV, No. 4, June, 1956, pp. 248-57.*

JOSEPH LYONS (essay date 1961)

[Lyons asserts that Lazarus "was never a poet"; instead, he describes her as "perhaps the finest prose writer of her time" and praises her as a dedicated and articulate spokesperson for the Jews.]

It is easy to conclude that, contrary to the judgement of critics since her day, [Emma Lazarus] was really a great poet who died unrecognized. In truth, however, she was never a poet. On occasion—and only under the influence of the one passion of her life, the cause of the Jews and the meaning of their tragedy—she wrote some good lines or coined a striking phrase. But her writing has not the stamp of greatness. It may be intelligent, often skillful, even moving, but no more. These are characteristics belonging to the best of prose writing, and this is just what she was, perhaps the finest prose writer of her time. She might even have made her reputation independently with her fine essays on contemporary events. Some of her major works, such as the long epic **"Tannhäuser,"** read as though excellent prose had been broken up into pentametric lines; and her superb celebration of the Hebraic tradition which she called **"By the Waters of Babylon"** is subtitled **"Little Poems in Prose"** and is actually composed in the form of paragraphs. The literary artist whom she most admired was not a poet but the novelist George Eliot. Since she was primarily an essayist rather than a dramatist, the melodramatic tragedies which she persisted in writing were quite artificial; their conflict was thematic rather than dramatic, the characters mere figures or symbols rather than personalities, and the lines a series of set orations rather than living dialogue. As Emily Dickinson . . . was totally a poet, so Emma Lazarus may best be summed up as primarily a writer. This may be why the Victorian maiden of New England did not leave her home but poured out her soul in self-contained jewels of poetry—meanwhile referring to publication as "the auction of the mind"—while her New York counterpart discovered herself, and finally exhausted herself, only when she learned to use her writing as a weapon in a pre-eminently social cause.

Granted this much, then, the picture seems clear. We see the dedicated and gifted Jewess who is aroused to defend the rights of her fellow Jews. In her exaltation as a writer she expressed better than any literary figure of her time the ringing theme of freedom from oppression; and by her talent she became one of the first articulate champions of a Zionist homeland for all Jews. But matters are seldom this clearcut, not in personal lives nor in the affairs of groups. If we look more closely at the inner structure of Emma Lazarus' life and career, particularly as she revealed it in her published work, we will find pairs of opposites. In their clashing they light up and therefore reveal the complex truth of her roles as person, citizen, writer, and Jewess.

She was a sum of contradictions. Although her active public life revealed her as committed to defending the homeless and pauperized wandering Jews of Eastern Europe, she was personally an aristocratic member of the oldest Jewish congregation in America, a wealthy socialite, a snob whose most deeply felt speeches in all her plays were the ones she put in the mouths of her villains as they cursed the "cringing, accursed, Oriental Jew." By temperament an essayist and writer of prose, she wrote almost exclusively verse and poetic tragedies. A Victorian maiden lady to the core, she yet chose to be the translator of Heine. Finally, although shy by disposition and retiring on the basis of her background, she became an active political leader, traveled widely, and spent the last years of her life away from her home and family. But beyond all these dual aspects of her personal life, she expressed through her writings a more basic contradiction, an inner division which is still alive for us today. It has to do with America and its role as haven for the oppressed and with the consequent discordance which lies at the heart of the Jew's life in America today. Emma Lazarus was perhaps the first Jewish writer in modern times to sense this problem, and it may be that in this rather than in her better known works lies her enduring contribution to Jewish culture.

She very early became fascinated by the image of America as the open port toward which harried exiles might turn, expressing it first in her sonnet . . . ["**The New Colossus**"] and at about the same time in a poem with the title "**1492**":

> Thou two-faced year, Mother of
>   Change and Fate,
> Didst weep when Spain cast forth
>   with flaming sword,
> The children of the prophets of the
>   Lord . . .
> No anchorage the known world could
>   afford,
> Close-locked was every port, barred
>   every gate.
> Then smiling, thou unveil'dst, O
>   two-faced year,
> A virgin world where doors of sun-
>   set part . . .

Similarly, in a description of the expulsion of the Jews from Spain on August 3, 1492, she wrote in one of her "**Little Poems in Prose**": "O bird of the air, whisper to the despairing exiles, that today, today, from the many masted, gayly bannered port of Palos, sails the world-unveiling Genoese, to unlock the golden gate of sunset and bequeath a continent to

Freedom!" As she clearly saw, this was the stroke by which history had at once cast the Jews out from the best civilization they had known in the Diaspora and also sent forth an explorer to discover a land in which the scattered Jews might finally find a new home. It was indeed a two-faced year, one which drove the Jews eastward in their wanderings even as it marked out the first path for their journey to the West.

Her recognition, however, was of even more than this. Somehow she achieved an insight into the historic role of the Jews themselves as carriers of this "two-faced" history of recent centuries. For the High Holy Days in the autumn of 1882 she wrote a poem, "**The New Year—Rosh Hashanah, 5643,**" in which she celebrated the Jews as those who, "In a cynic age of crumbling faiths, Lived to bear witness to the living Lord, Or died a thousand deaths." To this she added a summary of their role and fate:

> In two divided streams the exiles
>   part,
> One rolling homeward to its ancient
>   source,
> One rushing sunward with fresh will,
>   new heart,
> By each the truth is spread, the law
>   unfurled,
> Each separate soul contains the na-
>   tion's force,
> And both embrace the world.

We may find in this verse a capsule description which brilliantly sums up the place of the Jew in a Gentile world. There are those Jews who, like Emma Lazarus' own family, choose America, and here they are constantly faced with the problem of being both Jew and American. It is the problem of assimilation—or else, as she learned in her own year of discovery, the problem of being brother to those Jews who seem alien and strange. The Jew in America has repeatedly to learn that the higher he rises in a land of opportunities, the greater his risk of being revealed as no more than the lowliest, most alien Jew. Just as the German government boasts of its payment of reparations to the state of Israel, the Jew in America is called upon to live through once more the horror story created by Eichmann as a loyal servant of the German government. Emma Lazarus, too, was acutely aware of this knife edge of history which makes of each Jewish group a divided stream, for in her own family she saw one sister carry on the tradition which she herself had started while another renounced the struggle and became a Catholic. She would have recognized, though perhaps not sympathetically, the choice made today by those who call themselves Americans first and Jews a poor second, who dissociate themselves from other Jews who are less typically or excellently American, who keep trying to push away the intruding past and finally even turn away in embarrassment at contemporary reminders offered by the trial of Eichmann.

Then there is the other "stream" of Jewry. If the first represents a journey "sunward," toward the land of the future, the second surely stands for a return "homeward," toward that great source which has sustained a people as a nation down the centuries. Together the two streams do "embrace the world." But also, together they represent both the past, with its constraint and its necessity, and the future, with all its hope and danger. Those Jews who choose to create a state in Israel where nation, race, and culture will fuse, find that as they build a community on their ancient traditions they must compromise with the exigencies of the present. As they build toward the future and exist responsibly in the present, they must begin to temper the meaning and the practices of the traditional past. . . . The Israeli is history's new model for the Jew; but the question to be pondered is whether this is more than a one-sided resolution of the Jew's eternal fate, that he is the world's past and its future, both and not simply one. (pp. 82-5)

Joseph Lyons, "In Two Divided Streams," in Midstream, *Vol. VII, No. 4, Autumn, 1961, pp. 78-85.**

SOL LIPTZIN (essay date 1966)

Emma Lazarus, the third of the women-poets who pioneered in the Jewish lyric, was by far the most talented and the most influential. (p. 60)

Not until after the appearance of George Eliot's *Daniel Deronda* in 1876, with its call for Jewish rejuvenation and ingathering in the Holy Land, did Emma Lazarus become aware that she no longer had to seek "heroic ideals in alien stock, soulless and far removed, in pagan mythology and mystic, medieval Christianity, ignoring her very birthright—the majestic vista of the past, down which high above flood and fire had been conveyed the precious scroll of the Moral Law" (see excerpt above by Josephine Lazarus, 1888). (p. 61)

[In Liebhaid von Orb, the heroine of **"The Dance to Death"** who was] torn between love for a princely suitor who offered unfathomed joy and her devotion to a persecuted people who were about to undergo martyrdom, the poetess dramatized her own inner conflict between the radiant Anglo-American world of letters which beckoned and lured and the Jewish masses who were in desperate need of an articulate voice to give utterance to their agony and hope. Her decision was made: "I am all Israel's now. Till this cloud pass—I have no thought, no passion, no desire, save for my people." (pp. 62-3)

[In **"Russian Christianity** *versus* **Modern Judaism"** she] expressed her pride in belonging to a people that was the victim of massacres rather than to one that perpetrated massacres. She held that it required heroism to choose to remain a Jew when every bribe, spiritual and secular, was held out by modern society to persuade Jews to become converts to the dominant faith. . . . [The] despoiled exiles were heroes and not degenerates. They were her brothers, despite their shabby dress and strange jargon. (p. 63)

Emma Lazarus was prepared to accept the burden and the blessing of a prophetess. She felt that the time had come for Jews to undertake vigorous and concerted action to reestablish themselves as an independent nationality. She asked them to awaken from their assimilationist delusions, to raise again the banner of the Jew, to let resound once more the battle-anthems that led them to victory over pagans and idolators and that ennobled them even in defeat, when, as the smallest of nations, they took up arms under Bar Kochba against the moral tyranny of the greatest of nations. The martial stanzas of her lyric **"The Banner of the Jew"** demanded of her lethargic Jewish contemporaries that they exchange their comfortable but unheroic life for a more difficult but more meaningful existence. . . . In a lyric **"The New Ezekiel,"** she prophesied that the dead bones of her people, whose sap was dried by twenty scorching centuries of wrong, would soon revive and take on flesh. Jews would resume a national existence on their hallowed soil. She tried to open Jewish eyes to the beauty and grandeur of the Hebraic past and to the opportunities that could arise for a Jewish future. If Jews were to experience a national revival,

vast vistas would open up for all mankind. The historic group from whose hands dropped the seed out of which grew Christianity and Islam would again sow seeds for humanity's future growth. (pp. 64-5)

[Emma Lazarus's] native, well-adjusted, prosperous, coreligionists [were indifferent] to her breath-taking visions of Jewish national redemption in Palestine. The immigrants who were streaming from the Eastern European Pale to America's shores would have reacted more vigorously to her stimulating ideas, if they had known of them. But their language of communication was still Yiddish and not English. Decades were to pass before they were to attain to supremacy on the American Jewish scene and before they were able to embody the dreams of the Sephardic poetess Emma Lazarus and the thoughts of the Viennese aesthete Theodor Herzl in concrete deeds and mass activities. (p. 67)

Sol Liptzin, "The Nineteenth Century Jewish Lyric," in his The Jew in American Literature, *Bloch Publishing Company, 1966, pp. 53-67.**

LOUIS HARAP (essay date 1974)

Of the Jewish writers in the last half of the nineteenth century, the most talented was unquestionably Emma Lazarus. To be sure, her competition among Jewish Americans was not keen. Yet she has won a minor place in the history of American literature because she embodied a valid fusion of a genuine poetic sensibility with inspired advocacy and defense of her calumniated and persecuted people. Her careeer demonstrates once again that poetry enlisted in the service of a cause need not be ephemeral, but may be art in its own right. In her poetry and prose the Jewish people found an effective voice against the incoming tide of anti-Semitism abroad and at home. (p. 284)

The tributes from leading literary figures after her death give some indication of her quality and the deep impression she made on contemporaries. . . .

Yet despite her sensitivity to modern currents, she never quite cast off the language of an outmoded tradition. Only in the last poem published in her lifetime, **"By the Waters of Babylon,"** . . . did she depart from traditional structure. To the end she persisted in using to excess the hyphenated adjective (e.g., "ivory-pale"). Although her language lost some of its stiffness after she became a defender of her people, traces of traditional poetic diction remained. But she so infused her later poetry with intensity of feeling and conviction as to raise it above conventionality. Deeper research needs to be done to bring her more fully to our knowledge. From what we do know, however, she merits a permanent place in American literature as a talented, humane poet. (p. 299)

Louis Harap, "Emma Lazarus," in his The Image of the Jew in American Literature: From Early Republic to Mass Immigration, *The Jewish Publication Society of America, 1974, pp. 284-99.*

DAN VOGEL (essay date 1980)

[Vogel's assessment of Lazarus's achievement, excerpted from the last chapter of Emma Lazarus, *his full-length study of Lazarus's writing career, features a discussion of her impact on twentieth-century American Jewish writers.]*

[Emma Lazarus] left to her literary progeny an American public prepared and willing to accept the writings of American Jews and other Americans from minority groups. . . . The conditioning of the American public to interest itself in—indeed, to *see* itself in—the troubles and victories of the Jew began with Emma Lazarus's essays and poems.

On the other hand, the shift from the genre of poetry to the genre of fiction symbolizes the gap between the genteel Romanticism of Lazarus and the humanistic Realism of those who followed her. For all the immediacy and anger of Lazarus's Jewish poems, her vision of heroism is apt for an age of innocence. She was a Romantic who hoped for a Maccabean Byron to rise and fight the dragons enslaving her people.

It is a concept out of step with our generation of American Jewish writers of fiction. Except for the later Saul Bellow and Meyer Levin, most see heroism in mere endurance. If the schlemiel can survive, he has achieved victory. (p. 161)

To find a closer literary inheritance pertaining to Jewish heroism, we must turn to American Jewish poetry. Muriel Rukeyser, Linda Pasten, Charles Reznikoff, Karl Shapiro, and Hyam Plutzik are some who had the courage of an Emma Lazarus to declare that the Jew is more than a schlemiel. They are impressed with his persistence throughout the Exile, with his irrefrangible clutching at a meaningful, creative future. They, like Lazarus, write poems of indignation, pride, and hope. In their work there is no resignation to mere survival. Heroism resounds through their verse because the cadences of the Bible and the medieval visionaries are heard there as in Lazarus's verse. But the genre of poetry is today distinctly minor compared to the fiction. (pp. 161-62)

[If] her poetry will receive further study, Emma Lazarus will not be served by acolytes to John Donne and T. S. Eliot. Her images are not metaphysical; her paradoxes not clever. She is devoid of ambiguities. A comparison with Emily Dickinson for technique or with Robert Frost for covert complexity would simply be fruitless. She belongs in that special section of the Poets' Valhalla reserved for those who are beloved more than studied, like Longfellow, Whittier, Sandburg, E. A. Robinson. With them, she is the spokesman, not of the head, but of the heart, where, in addition to love, courage resides. (p. 162)

Dan Vogel, in his Emma Lazarus, *Twayne Publishers, 1980, 183 p.*

ADDITIONAL BIBLIOGRAPHY

The American Hebrew: Emma Lazarus Memorial Number 33, No. 5 (9 December 1887): 65-96.
    Tributes to Lazarus by such noted contemporaries as Robert Browning and John Hay, as well as Edmund Clarence Stedman and John Greenleaf Whittier (see excerpts above, 1887).

Angoff, Charles. *Emma Lazarus: Poet, Jewish Activist, Pioneer Zionist.* Publications of the Jewish Historical Society of New York, no. 3. New York: Jewish Historical Society of New York, 1979, 12 p.
    A brief monograph that focuses on Lazarus's contributions as a Jewish activist. Angoff praises Lazarus's talents and energy in defending Jewish interests, lauds her role as a pioneer Zionist, and asserts that she was "the first Jewish-American poet" to produce "poems of genuine beauty and force."

Baym, Max I. "A Neglected Translator of Italian Poetry: Emma Lazarus." *Italica* XXI, No. 4 (December 1944): 175-85.
    Argues for greater recognition of Lazarus's prowess as a translator of Italian poetry.

———. "Emma Lazarus' Approach to Renan and Her Essay, 'Renan and the Jews'." *Publications of the American Jewish Historical Society,* No. 37 (1947): 17-29.
    An informative essay describing the circumstances surrounding Lazarus's composition of "M. Renan and the Jews" and the sources that she drew on in writing it. As an aid to the reader, Baym provides a reprint of Lazarus's essay.

Cohen, Mary M. "Emma Lazarus: Woman; Poet; Patriot." *Poet Lore* V, Nos. 6,7 (1893): 320-31.
    An early biographical-critical essay recalling Lazarus's virtues as a woman, poet, and American patriot.

"Pride of Birth." *The Commonweal* XL, No. 1 (21 April 1944): 18-19.
    A review of Morris U. Schappes' introduction to *Emma Lazarus: Selections from Her Poetry and Prose,* which is excerpted above. Emphasizing the minority status of American Jews in the 1880s, the reviewer discusses the sociological significance of Lazarus's efforts to foster self-pride among her coreligionists.

Cowen, Philip. "Emma Lazarus." In *Autobiographies of American Jews,* edited by Harold U. Ribalow, pp. 27-37. Philadelphia: Jewish Publication Society of America, 1965.
    An excerpt from Cowen's 1932 autobiography, *Memories of an American Jew.* Cowen recounts Lazarus's connection with his influential journal the *American Hebrew* and hails her as "the one poet of first rank American Jewry has yet produced."

Frank, Murray. "Emma Lazarus—Symbol of Liberty." *The Chicago Jewish Forum* 6, No. 4 (Summer 1948): 251-56.
    A concise literary biography, written in commemoration of the sixtieth anniversary of Lazarus's death.

Jacob, H. E. *The World of Emma Lazarus.* New York: Schocken Books, 1949, 222 p.
    An interpretative biography. Jacob places great emphasis on Lazarus's "fixation upon her father" and maintains that she experienced a complete breakdown when Ralph Waldo Emerson excluded her work from *Parnassus,* his 1874 anthology of American verse.

Lesser, Allen. "Emma Lazarus: Poet and Zionist Pioneer." In his *Weave a Wreath of Laurel: The Lives of Four Jewish Contributors to American Civilization,* pp. 55-69. New York: Coven Press, 1938.
    A sympathetic biographical sketch reprinted from the April-June, 1938 issue of the *Menorah Journal.*

Liptzin, Sol. "Call to Heroism." In his *Generation of Decision: Jewish Rejuvenation in America,* pp. 114-36. New York: Bloch Publishing Co., 1958.
    Discusses Lazarus's efforts to rally American Jews to a "Jewish rebirth" in the midst of the "dreary, dessicated, vague Jewish consciousness of the eighteen-eighties."

Merriam, Eve. *Emma Lazarus: Woman with a Torch.* New York: Citadel Press, 1956, 160 p.
    A full-length laudatory biography.

Morais, Henry Samuel. "Emma Lazarus." In his *Eminent Israelites of the Nineteenth Century: A Series of Biographical Sketches,* pp. 186-92. Philadelphia: Edward Stern & Co., 1880.
    A contemporary biographical sketch that focuses on Lazarus's early literary career.

Mordell, Albert. "Some Final Words on Emma Lazarus." *Publications of the American Jewish Historical Society,* No. XXXIX, Part 3 (March 1950): 321-27.
    Reviews the work of Max I. Baym, Morris U. Schappes, and other Lazarus scholars.

Pauli, Hertha. "The Statue of Liberty Finds Its Poet." *Commentary* I, No. 1 (November 1945): 56-64.
    A popularized account of Lazarus's life and literary endeavors.

Price, Warwick James. "Three Forgotten Poetesses." *The Forum* XLVII (March 1912): 361-76.*
    A synopsis of Lazarus's life and work. Although Price relegates her writing to the class of "secondary literature," he makes fa-

vorable comparisons between Lazarus's verse and the poems of
Emily Dickinson and John Greenleaf Whittier.

Ruchames, Louis. "New Light on the Religious Development of Emma
Lazarus." *Publication of the American Jewish Historical Society* XLII,
No. 1 (September 1952): 83-8.
     A discussion of Lazarus's 1872 poem "Outside the Church."
     Ruchames argues that the poem reveals Lazarus to be a fervent
     pantheist at this stage of her development, thus belying her rep-
     utation for personal religious indifference.

Rusk, Ralph L., ed. *Letters to Emma Lazarus in the Columbia University Library*. New York: Columbia University Press, 1939, 84 p.
     A valuable collection of correspondence which includes letters
     from Robert Browning, William Morris, Ralph Waldo Emerson,
     and other prominent contemporaries.

Schappes, Morris U. Review of *The World of Emma Lazarus,* by H.
E. Jacob. *American Literature* 21, No. 4 (January 1950): 506-08.
     A condemnatory review of H. E. Jacob's biography (see anno-
     tation above). Itemizing numerous factual inconsistencies and not-
     ing the lack of documentation in the book, Schappes advises
     readers to approach *The World of Emma Lazarus* with "great
     caution."

Wagenknecht, Edward. "Emma Lazarus." In his *Daughters of the
Covenant: Portraits of Six Jewish Women,* pp. 25-54. Amherst: University of Massachusetts Press, 1983.
     Studies Lazarus's work, character, and personality.

Whicher, George F. "Poetry After the Civil War." In *American Writers on American Literature,* edited by John Macy, pp. 374-88. New
York: Horace Liveright, 1931.*
     Draws on Lazarus's example to illustrate the distinctive contri-
     butions of Roman Catholic and Jewish poets to late nineteenth-
     century American poetry.

William Maginn

1794-1842

(Also wrote under the pseudonyms of Morgan O'Doherty, Oliver Yorke, P. J. Crossman, P. P. Crossman, C. J. Crossman, Morgan Rattler, Oehlenschlaeger, Luctus, Dr. Olinthus Petre, Timothy Tickler, C. O. C., O. P., P. P. P., and R. T. S.) Irish essayist, short story writer, poet, translator, journalist, critic, editor, and novelist.

One of the most prominent journalists in England during the first half of the nineteenth century, Maginn wrote prolifically for a variety of English periodicals and was the founding editor of *Fraser's Magazine for Town and Country*. In addition, he was a principal early contributor, under the pseudonym of Morgan O'Doherty, to *Blackwood's Edinburgh Magazine*. Many critics believe that Maginn invented the *Noctes Ambrosianae*, a popular series of dialogues published in *Blackwood's* between 1822 and 1835 in which contemporary issues and personalities are treated in turn with levity, gravity, and pungent satire. Maginn's articles range from burlesques in verse to literary criticism and contain a rich blend of farcical humor, classical allusions, and political commentary. Renowned during his lifetime for his versatility, wit, and scholarship, he was often referred to by his contemporaries as the "modern Rabelais."

Maginn was the eldest son of Dr. John Maginn, a schoolmaster in Cork. By the age of eleven, he was sufficiently proficient in classical literature to enter Trinity College in Dublin. He returned to Cork after graduating from college, and upon his father's death in 1813, he assumed charge of the school. When he was just twenty-five, he received a doctorate in law from Dublin University. This accomplishment, combined with his fluency in a number of languages, including Latin, Greek, French, Hebrew, Spanish, and Portuguese, caused his admiring friends to nickname him "The Doctor." In 1819, in order to relieve the tedium of conducting the school, Maginn began sending gratuitous contributions under a variety of pseudonyms to several English and Irish periodicals as well as to the Scottish *Blackwood's*. *Blackwood's* afforded a medium for the vigorous, anecdotal style in which Maginn excelled, and he rapidly became one of the magazine's most valued contributors. Yet it was not until 1821, during a visit to Edinburgh, that he introduced himself to *Blackwood's* publisher, William Blackwood, and its other leading writers, John Wilson and John Gibson Lockhart.

Eager to pursue a literary career, Maginn relinquished the management of the academy to one of his brothers in 1823 and moved with his wife to London. His *Blackwood's* articles, the authorship of which was well known by this time, had won him a considerable reputation, and he was quickly invited to write for some of London's most noted journals, among them the *Quarterly Review, John Bull,* and the *Literary Souvenir*. Perhaps the greatest evidence of the esteem in which Maginn was held is that John Murray, the publisher of the *Quarterly*, selected him to compose Lord Byron's biography after the poet's death in 1824. However, Maginn declined the task when Murray refused to allow him to publish Byron's often controversial letters and memoirs in their entirety. The biography was eventually written by Thomas Moore, who suppressed much of Byron's correspondence. After briefly serving as Paris

correspondent for the *Representative*, a short-lived morning newspaper, Maginn was appointed joint editor, with Stanley Lees Giffard, of the *Standard*, which soon became London's leading conservative daily.

In 1830, differences arose between Maginn and the publisher of *Blackwood's* which culminated in Maginn's departure from the magazine. Shortly afterwards, he persuaded Hugh Fraser to join with him in establishing *Fraser's*, a monthly periodical which Maginn edited from its inception until 1836. Not only was *Fraser's* an immediate financial success, but its staff included some of England's most gifted writers, including William Makepeace Thackeray and Thomas Carlyle. One of the most popular features in *Fraser's* was *A Gallery of Illustrious Literary Characters, 1830-1838*. Published in the magazine between June, 1830 and April, 1838, the *Gallery* comprises a series of portraits drawn by Daniel Maclise of prominent literary figures of the time, each accompanied by a brief, witty, biographical sketch. With a few exceptions, all of the thumbnail biographies were written by Maginn.

Maginn reached the height of his prestige and prosperity during the initial years of *Fraser's* publication. By the mid-1830s, although his *Fraser's* salary was augmented by his income from the *Standard* and his miscellaneous periodical contributions, he was constantly in debt. He freely loaned money to destitute acquaintances and lavishly entertained friends on credit. Increasingly, Maginn relied on liquor to sustain him in bursts of literary energy. His intemperance alienated some of his employers: in 1834, he was dismissed from the *Standard* for neglecting his duties, and he resumed his connection with *Blackwood's* in order to supplement his income. To add to Maginn's difficulties, his attack on the novel *Berkeley Castle*, which appeared in *Fraser's* in August, 1836, resulted in a duel with its author, Grantley Berkeley. Neither man was injured, but Maginn's reputation was damaged by the scandal, and many harsh reviews that were later published anonymously in *Fraser's* were erroneously attributed to him. Maginn's problems were further aggravated in 1838, when his sorrow at the death of his close friend, the popular poet Letitia Elizabeth Landon, precipitated rumors that he had engaged in an extramarital affair with her. In the same year, nevertheless, Maginn began to write two of his best-known works: *Shakespeare Papers*, a collection of critical essays on William Shakespeare's plays that first appeared in *Bentley's Miscellany* and *Fraser's*, and *Homeric Ballads*, a series of translations of Homer's poetry that was originally published in *Fraser's* between January, 1838 and October, 1842. While the pieces in *Homeric Ballads* were admired by early critics for their fidelity to the original ballads, later commentators often complain that the ballad form is unsuited to Homer's poetry in English translation. The essays in *Shakespeare Papers*, particularly ''Lady Macbeth'' and ''Dr. Farmer's 'Essay on the Learning of Shakespeare' Considered,'' are consistently praised for their critical insight; at least one commentator, Malcolm Elwin, ranks the work ''among the finest Shakesperian criticism of the nineteenth century.''

In 1839, Maginn was hired as editor of the *Lancashire Herald*, a new weekly newspaper in Liverpool. Within a few months the paper failed, and he returned to London, where he spent most of his time eluding creditors and writing for the *Age*. Early in 1842, Maginn was imprisoned for debts incurred in the publication of *Magazine Miscellanies*, a collection of his periodical contributions that sold poorly. Critics speculate that this period in Maginn's life inspired Thackeray's portrait of Shandon, the imprisoned Irish journalist in *The History of Pendennis: His Fortunes and Misfortunes, His Friends and His Greatest Enemy*. Maginn was released from jail in May, 1842, after declaring bankruptcy. His health ruined, he died three months later of tuberculosis at Walton-on-Thames.

On the whole, Maginn's works have received little critical attention. In the twentieth century, it is generally agreed that Maginn was, in Elwin's words, ''the victim of his own versatility,'' the same quality that prompted his close friend Edward Vaughan Kenealy to describe him as ''a man so various that he seems to be not one, but all mankind's epitome.'' Many critics, among them Michael Monahan and Elwin, lament that Maginn, by not fully developing his talents, left a body of work incommensurate with his abilities. Most modern commentators single out *Maxims of Sir Morgan O'Doherty, Bart.*, a collection of comic observations on eating and drinking that originally appeared in *Blackwood's*, as the best expression of his genius. They also note that the rollicking Irish humor which distinguishes *Maxims* is also displayed in *Whitehall; or, The Days of George IV*, a satire on contemporary historical novels, as well as in Maginn's parodies, drinking songs, and short stories. Today Maginn's works are considered dated, but he is remembered for his contribution to early nineteenth-century periodical writing. In her detailed account of Maginn's involvement with *Fraser's*, Miriam M. H. Thrall asserts that ''Maginn was before all else a great magazinist, without question the greatest

of his day.'' He is most appreciated by later critics for his erudition and humor. His admirers share George Saintsbury's opinion that ''many of the greatest wits have had nothing like his learning; and hardly any man of very great learning has had anything like his wit.''

PRINCIPAL WORKS

Whitehall; or, The Days of George IV [with John Gibson Lockhart] (novel) 1827
Magazine Miscellanies (essays, short stories, poetry, maxims, and ballads) 1841
Maxims of Sir Morgan O'Doherty, Bart. [as Morgan O'Doherty] (maxims) 1849
Homeric Ballads [translator] (ballads) 1850
Noctes Ambrosianae [with John Wilson, John Gibson Lockhart, James Hogg, et al.] (essays) 1854
Miscellaneous Writings of the Late Dr. Maginn. 5 vols. (essays, short stories, poetry, maxims, ballads, and translations) 1855-57
Shakespeare Papers (essays) 1860
A Gallery of Illustrious Literary Characters, 1830-1838 (essays) 1873
Miscellanies: Prose and Verse. 2 vols. (essays, short stories, poetry, ballads, and maxims) 1885
Ten Tales (short stories) 1933

[J. G. LOCKHART] (essay date 1828)

[*Lockhart wrote several novels, but his fame rests on his biography of Sir Walter Scott and his critical contributions to* Blackwood's *and the* Quarterly, *which he edited from 1825 to 1853. He is regarded as a versatile, if somewhat severe, critic whose opinions of his contemporaries, though lacking depth, are generally considered accurate when not distorted by political animosities. Lockhart's derogatory review of* Whitehall; or, The Days of George IV, *in which he complains that ''the author has spoiled a laudable joke by wire-drawing it to 330 pages,'' has prompted critics to speculate on the nature of Lockhart and Maginn's collaboration on the novel. Ralph M. Wardle draws upon this review, along with Lockhart's correspondence with William Blackwood, to support his contention that Lockhart was primarily responsible for the novel's conception. According to Wardle, Lockhart composed a brief parody of contemporary historical novels in 1827 which Maginn later expanded upon and published anonymously as* Whitehall *(see Additional Bibliography).*]

The conception of [**'Whitehall; or, George IV'**] is better than its execution: the author has spoiled a laudable joke by wiredrawing it to 330 pages; and, what is much worse, by engrafting malice, sometimes coarseness into the bargain, on a stock which ought to have borne no fruits but those of sheer merriment. The object is to laugh down [Horace Smith's] 'Brambletye House' species of novel—and for this purpose we are presented with such an 'historical romance' as an author of 'Brambletye House', flourishing in Barbadoes 200 or 2000 years hence, we are not certain which, nor is the circumstance of material moment, might fairly be expected to compose of and concerning the personages, manners, and events of the age and country in which we live. We have no desire to analyze the structure of so mere an extravaganza; but humbly recommend [it] as it stands, to the study of those well-meaning youths who imagine that a few scraps of blundered antiquarianism, a prophetical beldame, a bore, and a rebellion, are enough to make [one of Sir Walter Scott's Waverly novels]. The book is, in fact, a series of parodies upon unfortunate Mr. Horace Smith—and it is paying the author no compliment to say that his mimicry (with all its imperfections) deserves to outlive the ponderous original. (p. 87)

> [*J. G. Lockhart], in a review of ''Whitehall; or, The Days of George IV,'' in* The Quarterly Review, *Vol. XXXVII, No. LXXIII, January, 1828, pp. 87-8.*

J. G. LOCKHART   (epitaph date 1842)

[In this frequently quoted epitaph composed for his friend and colleague shortly after his death, Lockhart describes Maginn's character and literary career.]

Here, early to bed, lies kind William Maginn,
   Who with genius, wit, learning, life's trophies to
      win,
Had neither great lord, no rich cit.[izen] of his kin,
   Nor discretion to set himself up as to ''tin''—
So, his portion soon spent (like the poor heir of Lynn);
   He turned author ere yet there was beard on his chin,
And, whoever was out, or whoever was in,
   For your Tories his fine Irish brains he would spin,
Who received prose and rhyme with a promising grin
   ''Go ahead, you queer fish, and more power to your
      fin,''
But to stave from starvation stirred never a pin,
   Light for long was his heart, though his breeches
      were thin,
Else his acting, for certain, was equal to Quin:
   But at last he was beat, and sought help of the bin,
(All the same to the Doctor, from claret to gin)
Which led swiftly to gaol, and consumption therein.
   It was much when the bones rattled loose in the skin,
He got leave to die here, out of Babylon's din.
   Barring drink and the girls, I ne'er heard of a sin:
Many worse, better few, than bright broken Maginn.

> *J. G. Lockhart, in an epitaph to William Maginn, in* Notes and Queries, *Vol. 176, No. 3, January 21, 1939, p. 49.*

[EDWARD VAUGHAN KENEALY]   (essay date 1844)

[Kenealy was one of Maginn's closest friends during the last years of his life. In this highly commendatory essay, he praises Maginn's writings for their originality, variety, humor, and decorum and hails him as an ''inimitable'' parodist and an accomplished scholar. Kenealy expresses admiration for Shakespeare Papers *and favorably compares* Homeric Ballads *to Alexander Pope's translations of Homer's poetry, but he maintains that the* Gallery *is the ''most original and sparkling'' of his works. He differs from the majority of critics in his opinion that Maginn's writings are an ample expression of his genius.]*

[The variety of Maginn's writings] proves the amazing versatility of his mind—their excellence is an emblem of its wealth and beauty. Poetry, romance, and criticism, parody, translation, and burlesque—of these there are enshrined amid the vast collection of his compositions, examples as perfect and splendid as any in the language, and such as if presented to the world at one view could not fail to astonish, to gratify, and to instruct it. (p. 73)

There is scarcely a single point of view in which we contemplate the intellectual character of Maginn, that we are not struck with admiration, with reverence, and with regard. As a poet, he has left behind him writings that breathe of the divinity of genius, and would be sure to immortalise his name, had he bequeathed no other memorials of his intellect, realising as they do, almost to the letter, the praise of Proclus in his dissertation on Plato . . ., *the lineaments of poetry in all their lustre!* As a scholar he was perhaps the most universal of his time, no subject being unknown to him, or beyond the reach of his reading; far more various in his learning than Voltaire, far more profound and elegant than Johnson; rivalled, perhaps, only by Peter Bayle, or that erudite old man, James Roche of Cork, whose wonderful memory and riches of scholarship, now comparatively unknown, will be the delight of some future time. As a political writer he was once pronounced, by no mean authority, to be ''the greatest in the world,'' and although perfection in that attainment is scarcely worth the ambition of a lofty mind, it would be hard to name any other author of the present time, except Sydney Smith, who was at once so witty, so philosophical, so elegant and earnest in political discourses. (p. 74)

Originality, the distinctive attribute of genius, he possessed in no ordinary degree; and whether we examine his criticisms or his maxims, grave or gay, his translations or his songs, his tales or his humorous compositions, we shall find that to no one preceding writer is he much indebted for his mode of thought and style. He resembles Aristophanes, or Lucian, or Rabelais, more perhaps than any modern author; he has the same keen and delicate raillery, the withering sarcasm, the strange and humorous incident, the quaint learning, the bitter scorn of quackery and imposture, the grave and laughable irony, the profound and condensed philosophy of this illustrious triad; but the grossness and obscenity, the loose and depraved sentiments, the utter defiance of modesty and decorum, which their ordinary imitators substitute for wit and wisdom, he does not possess in the slightest degree. Nothing can be more sly than his satire—nothing, when he wishes it, more terrific or more scathing; but it is always clothed in the robe of decency, and does not ever disgust. Even Swift has not equalled him in sarcasm, though in the power of irony he may be entitled to more praise, as having preceded Maginn. Read any subject on which the Doctor has written, and afterwards examine how it is treated by other men; then will be seen the superiority of his intellect. For although his view of it be different from that of any other person—an eccentric or a satirical one for instance—he still clothes it with such new light, he illuminates it so brilliantly from the golden lamp of his own intellect, and displays withal such admirable common sense in all he says, that the reader will derive from his odd, hasty, but masterly delineations, a more perfect idea of the matter in question, than from the most profound and laboured, and even learned disquisitions of others. As instances of this quality, may be cited his famous Essay on Dr. Farmer's *Learning of Shakespeare,* and his still more famous papers on Southey's strange performance, *The Doctor.* Contrast either of these with any other compositions on the same theme, and then indeed you will be convinced of what we have advanced. . . . So that if ever any man after Rousseau was entitled to Sir William Jones's elegant summary of that fine genius, ''whose pen, formed to elucidate all the arts, had the property of spreading light before it on the darkest subject, as if he had written with phosphorus on the sides of a cavern,'' most assuredly that man was William Maginn.

As a scholar he has been compared to Porson, but, extensive as were his acquirements and deep his knowledge of the dead languages, he did not equal, or indeed approach, that renowned critic. Neither could he have hoped to do so, without devoting a life to the study and his whole heart to the single object—a thing, it need not be added, to be expected from any man in the world sooner than Maginn; for his genius was too noble, his mind too volatile, to chain itself down to such miserable drudgery; and the most dazzling prospects would scarcely have kept him steady in one pursuit for a twelvemonth. But few men, apart from those who are cloistered from year to year in the learned solitude of colleges, and whose especial profession is scholastic literature, possessed a more deeply-founded acquaintance with the standard writers of Greece and Rome or a more extensive knowledge of the best authors in the modern continental languages; and this wealth of erudition it was which enabled him so beautifully to decorate those papers which he composed the quickest, and make them, in the words of Thucydides . . . , "treasures for all posterity, rather than exercises for present and temporary perusal." His fine knowledge of the Greek is best demonstrated by his admirable and witty translations from Lucian and his *Homeric Ballads,* which for antique dignity and faithfulness are unsurpassed by any versions in our language, and will carry his name down to all time with that of Pope; the one being like a sculptor who relies solely on the simply and unstudied grandeur of the naked figure; the other resembling a statuary who enchants every eye by the gorgeous drapery in which he invests the marble, and the picturesque adjuncts with which he surrounds it. Both are entirely distinct, and both inimitable in their way. One is a translation—the other a paraphrase. Those who wish to know *what* and *how* Honor wrote, must read Maginn—those who seek to be delighted with *the Iliad,* must peruse Pope. The first may be illustrated by the Parthenon of Athens, a model of severe beauty, standing alone upon its classic hill, amid the wild olives, and under the crystal skies of Hellas; the second by the Church of St. Peter's at Rome, where every extraneous ornament of price or brilliancy—painting, sculpture, cameos of gems and gold, perfume and stately arras—is added to give lustre to the temple. No one but a scholar could have completed the former—Pope was able to accomplish the latter. (pp. 75-6)

[Maginn] was versed in Hebrew, he was a master of Italian, French, and German; and so well acquainted was he with the leading writers of these countries, that he could tell you in a moment, and with unerring correctness, the characteristics for which each was distinguished. He was more attached to scholia and scholiasts than might have been expected, and was a most excellent judge of meters. . . . He possessed an almost inexhaustible fund of quotation from old writers; but of late years, when his fame and reputation for knowledge were fully established, he drew upon it sparingly; yet the allusions in which he indulges, as if inadvertently, betray the wonderful research of his studies, and render his works worthy of the praise which Fabricius passed upon the *Bibliotheca* of Photius. . . . "[Not] a book, but an immortal treasury."

His poetical compositions are of the sparkling order of Swift, and possess much of the sprightliness of Lafontaine, without any of the immodesty which tarnishes it. No writing did he ever publish which might make a mother curse his memory for the errors of her child, or husband attribute to him the destruction of a once virtuous wife. All his songs are modest and decorous, flashing with radiant fun, insphering, as it were, the very spirit of jest and humour; and though many are marked by [a] vein of exquisite libel . . . , we believe the very first to

laugh at their prodigality of wit would be the persons who are themselves made the objects of his arrows. But he was occasionally written in a higher spirit, and for grander ends; and several of his more serious lyrics are worthy of a Tyrtaeus, or Burns, or Proctor, the greatest of all living song writers. . . . Perhaps the English language does not contain any thing more terse or noble [than "**The Soldier Boy**"]: it is worth a hundred Irish melodies, and a thousand Oriental Romances. To this may be added his third part of [Samuel Taylor Coleridge's] *Christabel,* which is a more spirited and weird-like conclusion than the author himself might have drawn, and perhaps it was a consciousness that he could not exceed this finale of the Doctor, which prevented Coleridge from attempting the completion. As a parodist he was inimitable—perhaps the greatest that ever lived. (pp. 76-7)

His habits of composition were such as only would suit a man of real mind, and that a granary of thought and learning. For he wrote with rapidity, never pausing over his paper for words or ideas—never resorting to those thought-provoking scratches of the head, in doing which Hogarth (the Fielding of the pencil) has depicted his poor poet; seldom revising or altering what he had once penned, but finishing the subject in an off-hand way . . . infinitely more pleasing than belongs to the most elaborate and polished style. Not of him, indeed, could be said, as it was by Pythias of Demosthenes . . . , that his discourses smelled of the lamp. . . . But his writings, though struck off thus at a heat, lose little of beauty or nervousness thereby, but derive even a new charm from this characteristic—because they plainly appear to be the unstudied efforts of his genius; and the merest reader will at once discover, that it is nature, not art, which speaks. . . . [From] his candour, much of his excellence was derived. The leaders which he wrote for the newspapers were usually finished in half an hour, or perhaps less; but the masculine understanding that dictated them, the terseness and vehemence, darting, like sturdy oak trees, in every sentence, the sparks of wit, or the thrust of sarcasm—these give value to the article, and atone for its haste. The writings on which he appears to have bestowed most care were the *Homeric Ballads.* . . . (p. 79)

[In all Maginn's contributions to *Blackwood's Magazine*] there was a profusion of wit and learning which flashed on the public with a splendour to which they were unused. Scarcely one appeared in which there was not something libellous; but the sting was so beautifully applied, and so mitigated by the surrounding fun, that it was difficult seriously to quarrel with the author. . . . (p. 81)

A highly popular and delightful feature in [*Fraser's Magazine*], was the *Gallery of Literary Portraits.* . . . These were entirely original in plan and execution, and created a sensation in literary circles, not often paralleled. . . . As a whole, they are, we think, the most original and sparkling of the doctor's productions; and when we remember that they were hit off at a moment's notice, we shall be easily able to fancy how meteoric was the intellect from which they emanated. Wit was their principal recommendation. "This," as Sir William Jones said of Dunning, "relieved the weary, calmed the resentful, and animated the drowsy; this drew smiles even from such as were the objects of it; scattered flowers over a desert; and, like sunbeams sparkling on a lake, gave vivacity to the dullest and least interesting theme." And we never read them, without involuntarily thinking we hear the doctor speak, for they are perfect resemblances of what his conversation was. (p. 88)

The **"Fraser Papers"** form the next feature of interest and importance in the magazine. Though written on subjects generally of a temporary nature, and every one of them hastily struck off in Fraser's back parlour, over such supplies of liquid as would totally incapacitate all other men from work . . . , the doctor and his associate in the task, Mr. C, (a writer of no mean ability,) have flung into the essays such radiant fun, blended with such sound reasoning, that they seem destined to avoid the fate which overtakes most political writings, and has consigned those of Swift and Addison already to oblivion. They do not, it is true, contain much of what is called "the philosophy of history;" they do not aspire to such august thought as invests the pamphlets of Burke, and will convey them in triumph down to all posterity; for such ends they were not designed or written; but as speculations flung off to win some temporary advantage—to gall some political adversary, or celebrate some triumph of party, they are inimitable, and are impregnated with as much of the true Rabelaisian fire as will keep them vigorous for ever. (p. 89)

[Maginn's *Shakespeare Papers* consist] of some of the ablest and most beautiful dissertations on the characters of our dramatist that adorn the language. They incline a little to much, perhaps, to paradox, but their great ability is universally admitted. Combined with his **"Essay on Dr. Farmer,"** and sundry reviews and criticisms on Shakespeare, which have appeared in [*Fraser's*], they form a most valuable and interesting body of facts, surmises, and annotations on our great poet. In the ninety-sixth, ninety-seventh, and ninety-ninth numbers of [*Fraser's*], was published that strange medley of wit and learning entitled **"The Doctor"**. It was a review of Southey's fantastical work, and the cleverest of any that appeared. (p. 91)

> [Edward Vaughan Kenealy], "William Maginn, LL.D.," in The Dublin University Magazine, *Vol. XXIII, No. CXXXIII, January, 1844, pp. 72-101.*

THE IRISH QUARTERLY REVIEW (essay date 1852)

[*This anonymous critic is one of the first to express the opinion, often echoed by later commentators, that Maginn's work was not commensurate with his abilities.*]

In all the sad instances of misapplied genius amongst the literary men of the nineteenth century, [William Maginn] is the most glaring and the most pitiable. "When the funeral pyre was out, and the last valediction over, men took a lasting adieu of their interred friends, little expecting the curiosity of future ages should comment upon their ashes." So writes Sir Thomas Brown, and as we look back through the life of William Maginn, we wish that he had borne in mind this quaint thought of the old moralist, and had felt with him, that we must all "make provision for our names," because, "to subsist in bones, and be but pyramidally extant, is a fallacy in duration." Had Maginn thought thus he would have saved himself many a heart-sickening pang, many a weary hour of depression, and of penitence for days cast away, in which he had been prodigal of that which would have been to him wealth, honor, fame—his glowing, brilliant, glorious genius. (p. 596)

The chief fault in Maginn's criticisms is, that party spirit and cliqueism too often rendered him wilfully blind to the merits of those whose works were under review. His dislike of Byron and of Moore is a proof of the former; his continued abuse of Leigh Hunt and Barry Cornwall is a clear exemplification of the latter. He had a most decided hatred of all meanness, and a most unmitigated contempt of all false, and clinquant sentimentality. Real feeling, and genuine pathos, he understood well, and appreciated deeply, but mock sentiment, or sentimentality was, in his eyes, like that damsel who sang,

> I sits with my feet in a brook;
>   If any one asks me for why,
> I hits him a lick with my crook,
>   And says, sentiment kills me, says I.

Maginn's genius was peculiar; we know of but three men to whom he can be compared—Lucian—Rabelais—Fielding. (p. 622)

> "Doctor Maginn," in The Irish Quarterly Review, *Vol. II, No. VII, September, 1852, pp. 593-625.*

WILLIAM JERDAN (essay date 1853)

[*From 1817 to 1850, Jerdan was editor of the* Literary Gazette, *one of the first English periodicals to which Maginn contributed. In this laudatory excerpt from his autobiography, Jerdan praises Maginn's versatility, scholarship, humor, and originality.*]

Of Maginn, the precocious, the prolific, the humorous, the eccentric, the erratic, the versatile, the learned, the wonderfully endowed, the Irish,—how shall I attempt to convey any idea? There is hardly any species of literature in which he has not left examples as masterly as any in the language. Romancist, parodist, politician, satirist, linguist, poet, critic, scholar—preeminent in all and in the last all but universal—the efflux of his genius was inexhaustible; and were even the approach to a considerable collection of his productions accomplished, I am convinced that the world would be more than ever astonished by the originality, learning, fancy, wit, and beauty with which he illuminated the widest circle of periodical literature. For he was at all, and wrote everywhere. He jested, and he mystified, and he laughed. He played with pebble-stones and nuggets of gold; pelting with the one, and hitting hard with the other. A sprite or a gladiator as the maggot took—a warm-hearted Irishman, though a fearful literary antagonist, his career was devious, zigzag, corruscating, here, there, and everywhere, flashing with the electric force agreeable to his nature, or working with the regulated toil which graver occasions demanded from his vigorous intellect. (p. 82)

> William Jerdan, "The 'Gazette'—New Contributors—Mr. Pyne, Wine and Walnuts—Dr. Maginn," in his The Autobiography of William Jerdan: With His Literary, Political, and Social Reminiscences and Correspondence During the Last Fifty Years, *Vol. III, Arthur Hall, Virtue, & Co., 1853, pp. 77-102.*

MATTHEW ARNOLD (lecture date 1861?)

[*Arnold is considered one of the most influential authors of the later Victorian period in England. While he is well known today as a poet, in his own time he asserted his greatest influence through his prose writings. Arnold's forceful literary criticism, which is based on his humanistic belief in the value of balance and clarity in literature, significantly shaped modern theory. Here, he terms* Homeric Ballads *"vigorous and genuine poems in their own way." However, the critic contends that the ballad form is unsuited to Homer's poetry in English translation, an argument that is repeated by Miriam M. H. Thrall (1934). Arnold's discussion of* Homeric Ballads *was originally included in a lecture most likely delivered at Oxford in 1861.*]

[Maginn's] *Homeric Ballads* are vigorous and genuine poems in their own way; they are not one continual falsetto, like the pinchbeck *Roman Ballads* of Lord Macaulay; but just because they are ballads in their manner and movement, just because, to use the words of his applauding editor, Dr. Maginn has 'consciously realised to himself the truth that Greek ballads can be really represented in English only by a similar manner,'—just for this very reason they are not at all Homeric, they have not the least in the world the manner of Homer. There is a celebrated incident in the nineteenth book of the *Odyssey,* the recognition by the old nurse Eurycleia of a scar on the leg of her master Ulysses, who has entered his own hall as an unknown wanderer, and whose feet she has been set to wash. 'Then she came near,' says Homer, 'and began to wash her master; and straightway she recognised a scar which he had got in former days from the white tusk of a wild boar, when he went to Parnassus unto Autolycus and the sons of Autolycus, his mother's father and brethren.' This, 'really represented' by Dr. Maginn, in 'a measure similar' to Homer's, becomes:—

> And scarcely had she begun to wash
> Ere she was aware of the grisly gash
>   Above his knee that lay.
> It was a wound from a wild boar's tooth,
> All on Parnassus' slope,
> Where he went to hunt in the days of his youth
> With his mother's sire,—

and so on. That is the true ballad-manner, no one can deny; 'all on Parnassus slope' is, I was going to say, the true ballad-slang; but never again shall I be able to read [the nineteenth book of the *Odyssey*] . . . without having the detestable dance of Dr. Maginn's,—

> And scarcely had she begun to wash
> Ere she was aware of the grisly gash,—

jigging in my ears, to spoil the effect of Homer, and to torture me. To apply that manner and that rhythm to Homer's incidents, is not to imitate Homer, but to travesty him. (pp. 51-3)

> *Matthew Arnold, in his* On Translating Homer, *Smith, Elder, & Co., 1896, 178 p.**

THE SPECTATOR   (essay date 1886)

Maginn was a consummate *littérateur* of the journalist type. He acquired easily, had a retentive memory, a love of literature rather than of knowledge, and that facility of composition that so often lends to minds essentially mediocre the appearance of genius. He wrote a novel, called *Whitehall in the Days of George IV.,* . . . displaying little power but great literary dexterity, out produced no other work of any importance. [His] *Miscellanies* contain no contribution of permanent value to literature properly so called; but many of the articles reprinted in them are very entertaining, even at the present day, when the allusive point in them is, in a great measure, lost. Of such men as Maginn it is not unfrequently asserted that they only want some solidity of character or purpose to be geniuses. But the quality in question is a moral rather than an intellectual one, and in all probability had Maginn possessed it, the result would simply have been that his literary work would have proved less fragmentary and much more remunerative, but not a whit more attractive. He had neither true depth of insight nor real force of imagination. His **"Man in the Bell"** . . .—a story reminding us somewhat of Poe's "Pit and the Pendulum"—is an admirable bit of writing, but nothing more. His review of "Farmer's Essay on the Learning of Shakespeare"

was certainly not worth reprinting. It is a mere academic exercise at the best, based on no extent of research, throwing no new light on contested points, and absolutely wrong in its main theory, that Shakespeare used the original texts of the Greek and Latin classics in constructing his plays, whereas these are full of proofs that he depended wholly upon translations. . . . The review is equally at fault in its minor guesses, as, for instance, where the writer sneers at the notion of Shakespeare having held horses at the theatre door. . . .

Nor has Maginn's humour anything of the rich quality of Thackeray's. The vein of tenderness that crops out in almost every page of *The Newcomes, Pendennis,* and even *Vanity Fair,* and makes Thackeray so intensely human in his great pity by giving a pathetic tinge to his bitterest satire, will not be found in anything Maginn has written. The "Doctor," who was the best of fellows at a symposium, and ever generous and kindly in deed, took a good-natured view enough of the world he lived in, but would never have seen anything but villainy in villains. Thackeray, on the contrary, had a word to say even for such a mean rascal as Barnes Newcome, if not by way of defence, by way of extenuation,—so human, knew the great master, is it to err, so pitiable the lot of even the successful scoundrel. But if he had less humour, Maginn, in his prose at all events, had more fun than Thackeray, and was a keen though superficial observer of society within less narrow limits. On the whole, he reveals himself most fully in his *Maxims,* which may still be read with amusement. They recall . . .—it must be owned—La Bruyère, though commonly differing from the *Characters* in matter. They are mostly of an Epicurean cast, for Maginn was no Stoic—it is a marvel, indeed, how he contrived to afford himself almost every gastronomic and bacchic indulgence he felt a fancy for. A few may be cited by way of example. "Man and wife," writes the Doctor, who knew what he was talking about, "generally resemble each other in features, never in disposition." "Mediocrity," it is keenly observed, "is always disgusting, except of stature in a woman." Perhaps, too, it may be in some measure true that "in making an estimate of a man's character, we should always lay out of view whatever has any connection with the womankind." And it is still more true that "the next best thing to a really good woman is a really good-natured one;" while "the next worst thing to a really bad man is a really good-natured one" (in Maginn's sense of the latter expression). Lastly, poetry, in the Doctor's day, at all events, might not inaptly be compared with claret,—"You enjoy it only when very new or very old."

Of course the Doctor was a nimble versifier. He was particularly fond of translating popular songs and ballads into Greek and Latin verse, a vain pastime that has a curious fascination for clever minds of a certain cast. Such productions, as a rule, give no pleasure whatever save to their author, and the present case is no exception. Nor was Maginn a scholar; though he had a considerable acquaintance with the classics, it was not probably beyond what a clever young fellow carries away with him from College. Another of his tastes was for turning the poetry of the day into parody or burlesque. Thus he treated "The Ancient Mariner" and "Christabel" of Coleridge, and Scott's "Eve of St. John"—not without some success. The success is most marked, perhaps, in the case of "Christabel;" but the comic idea is not sufficiently sustained. Maginn had no notion of poetry. His criticisms of Byron, Keats, and Shelley are as absurd as they are coarse and ill-natured,—ill-natured, we make no doubt, in language only, and not in intention, for the Doctor harboured no hatreds, though he often wrote as though he were animated by the deadliest hostility, which, perhaps, he really felt against the Whigs, the Liberals of those days. His ballads and songs are not to be compared with Thackeray's, either in matter or form. The best of them is **"The King of Achen's Daughter,"** a tragi-comic performance of some merit, and one or two of his rhymed Latin pieces are notable as *tours de force*. But Maginn really only dabbled in literature. He is to be judged by his work as a journalist, and of that only his contemporaries could form a just judgment. Their verdict was favourable, and by it we may be content to abide. The [two volumes of *Miscellanies*] are well edited, the selection being good and typical; only the process might have been carried further. A single volume would have well held all that was worth reviving of the Doctor's writings. (p. 53)

"William Maginn, LL.D.," in The Spectator, *Vol. 59, No. 3002, January 9, 1886, pp. 52-3.*

GEORGE SAINTSBURY (essay date 1893)

[*Saintsbury was a prominent English literary historian and critic of the late nineteenth and early twentieth centuries. A prolific writer, he composed a number of histories of English and European literature as well as several critical works on individual authors, styles, and periods. In Saintsbury's opinion, Homeric*

Portrait of Maginn drawn by Daniel Maclise that accompanied his biographical sketch in the Gallery. *Mary Evans Picture Library.*

Ballads *are unduly praised by critics, and he calls for greater recognition of "Memoirs of Ensign and Adjutant Odoherty" which Saintsbury calls* Memoirs of Morgan O'Doherty, Maxims, *"Dr. Farmer's 'Essay on the Learning of Shakespeare' Considered," and Maginn's miscellaneous writings in prose and verse. Expressing particular admiration for Maginn's short stories, among them "The Man in the Bell," "Bob Burke's Duel with Ensign Brady," and "A Story without a Tail," Saintsbury laments that his "incurably reckless and random nature and habits" prevented him from developing his talent for this genre. Saintsbury's essay originally appeared in* Macmillan's Magazine *in December, 1893.*]

The work of Maginn, though easier to appreciate than it was a few years ago, is even yet hid as a whole from the general cognisance. I do not even know that it would be possible to recover it entirely; and I am quite sure that if it were so recovered it would suffer from the fatal drawback of being almost entirely Journalism, and of a consequent inequality all the greater that its author was the least gifted of all men with the senses of responsibility and hesitation. . . . Since the pious care of Mr R. W. Montagu collected in 1885 his *Miscellanies* in two volumes, it has been possible by adding the letterpress of the *Fraser Gallery* to them to obtain something like a conspectus of Maginn's extraordinary faculty. It is not a complete conspectus: and yet it is a conspectus which shows us the flaws in the work and makes us pretty certain that they would widen if the area of collection were extended.

It shows us, however, at the same time the great and multifarious gifts of the man. In one respect I own I am a heretic. I cannot away with Maginn's Homeric translations in ballad form. Mr Gladstone, I believe, thinks their tone Homeric; I should say it was as much like Homer, though in a different way, as Pope is. Mr Matthew Arnold [see excerpt above, 1861?] thought them "genuine poems in their own way.". . . However, no more of this. In the case of such as Maginn it is important not to blame the small fragment of his work which for some reason or other has been unduly praised, but to bring forward the far greater part of it which has never been praised enough. It is astonishing how various and how vivid the lights of that part are.

As for the letterpress of the *Fraser Gallery,* I own that, clever as it is, I have no great affection for it. It is one of the earliest and one of the best examples of a kind of journalism for which there has since been greater and ever greater demand,—the brief biography, smart in style and somewhat swaggering in manner, of "Celebrities of the Day," "Men of the Time," and what not. Maginn knew a great deal: he was sufficiently on an intellectual equality with most of his subjects for his treatment not to be merely impertinent; and it is certain that he had at this particular time a coadjutor in Lockhart, whose knowledge and whose competency were even greater than his own, though Lockhart's actual literary faculty might not be quite so versatile. So the things are amusing enough and sometimes more than amusing; also, which is not common in this kind of thing, they contain a rather unusual amount of positive biographical and miscellaneous information, not no doubt to be accepted quite unverified, but often extremely useful in the way of setting one on tracks. It is unlucky that in addition to their other faults they contain a great deal of the tedious and obsolete newspaper mannerism of the time, a mannerism of knowing and braggart assumption, which had been started in *Blackwood's Magazine,* which was to obtain for many years, and which is not quite dead yet. It must, I suppose have appealed to some taste, have hit some cranny of the human mind, but it certainly seems very unengaging to me.

This defect and others appear, but are less notable, in the miscellanies of all kinds which Mr Montagu has collected. In so far as there is any direct original for the tricks which Maginn began to play directly he became one of *Blackwood's* contributors, I am rather disposed to see it in the . . . combinations of fanciful divagation, scholarly parallel, and scurrilous personal attack which distinguished that celebrated periodical. . . . There are in [the *Memoirs of Morgan O'Doherty*] all the traits which Wilson subsequently elaborated and perfected in the *Noctes*,—the interspersions of verse, serious and comic, the studied desultoriness, the critical, social, and literary vagaries. Indeed there is no doubt that this famous series did owe its origin to Maginn. . . . (pp. 291-95)

The *Memoirs* themselves are filled with parodies and patter songs of singular liveliness, and characterised, as Maginn's writings generally are, by odd, but by no means unhappy lapses into the serious. They also show that wide familiarity with literature, especially with classical literature, by which the author was honourably distinguished. Since the comparative disuse of a classical education, these Greek and Latin freaks of Maginn's have probably become something of a stumbling block to the generation which is now sent into the world unfurnished with the keys to some of the world's best things. . . . But if the habit is thus to some a disqualification, it is, of course, to others an additional charm. And I do not know that any one has ever managed this particular style of academical wit better than Maginn. He may not have been an extremely profound or accurate scholar but few men have had more knowledge of the classics . . .—the knowledge which enables a man to talk and write in "the tongues" almost as freely as in his own language, and which leaves him rarely at fault for a quotation from or a quip in them. Yet few men could be more vernacular. . . . (pp. 295-96)

[*The Maxims of Sir Morgan O'Doherty*] are very well worth knowing. With not a few of what seem now, and a few of what should surely have seemed at any time, breaches of good manners and good taste, they contain a great deal of wisdom on the first principles of literature, feeding, and philosophy, with a picture of Fourth-Georgian manners which, used with discretion, is instructive, and, used with or without discretion, entertaining. Maginn should not have spelt Château Grillet, Château *Grillé,* which is absurd; but it is greatly to his credit that he pronounced that too little known wine to be delicious. It shows that he had no vulgar taste.

His most serious and solid work in matter and manner, if not also in actual bulk, is the rather famous *Consideration of Farmer's Essay on the Learning of Shakespeare.* With some quite astonishing slips (such as "Nugae Curialiae," which perhaps is due to carelessness in correcting his proofs) it contains probably as much sound learning, shrewd wit, and acute criticism as can be found in any single contribution to the enormous, and too often worthless library of Shakesperian comment. (p. 297)

[In Maginn's miscellaneous writings in verse and prose] there may be thought to be too much . . . parody and burlesque criticism. *The Rime of the Ancient Waggonere, The Third Part of Christabel, Mooreish Melodies,* and so forth, though all very well in their own way and in small doses, are apt to become a little tiresome when collected in volumes. Nevertheless Maginn did some of his best work in these forms. *The Pewter Quart* is an admirable thing, the most spirited and genuine drinking-song perhaps of this century, if not the most poetical. Nor are the burlesque commentaries on *The Leather Bottell* and *The Black Jack* which follow by any means ungracious fooling,

though they may be thought to have been carried on a little too long. There is great merit, both political and sentimental, in the variations which he founded on that most beautiful old song which begins "Let's drink and be merry." Some of his Latin versions in *The Embalmer* and elsewhere are excellent, and indeed it is difficult to dip anywhere into this class of his writing without finding pasture, though perhaps it is not wise to browse too long at one time thereon, and though not all the herbs are suited to all tastes. For instance I have never been able myself to take much delight in his exercises in jargon and thieves' Latin; but they please others.

A gift which Maginn must have had in extraordinary measure, but which, for some reason or other, he seems to have left for the most part uncultivated, was his talent for prose fiction in little. A long story I do not suppose he could ever have managed, and his longest known to me, *The Last Words of Charles Edwards,* is dreary enough. But the man who wrote three such masterpieces, by no means in the same kind, as *The Man in the Bell, Bob Burke's Duel with Ensign Brady,* and, best of all, *A Story without a Tail,* must have had it in him to write a great many more. There are many instances on record of men who have produced only one or two poems of value; very few I think of men who have produced one or two extraordinarily good prose-tales and no more. The sole explanation that occurs to me is that work of actual invention required a certain amount of planning and thinking, which Maginn's incurably reckless and random nature and habits refused to give. If it be so, the loss inflicted in this respect by his foibles is greater than any other. I have read *A Story without a Tail* literally scores of times and never without fresh enjoyment.

Indeed in "the chronicle of wasted time" (to play on words in his own manner) there are few more melancholy histories than Maginn's. Many of the greatest wits have had nothing like his learning; and hardly any man of very great learning has had anything like his wit; while it cannot be said that he wanted opportunity. Yet not only did he make a mess of his life, but he also, in a way which by no means necessarily follows, made a mess of his genius. It is hardly possible to open a page of his without finding something that seems like indisputable evidence of that quality; yet in twenty years of literary production he did no great thing, and not more than one or two small things that are perfect. Neither drink nor debts, neither want of method nor even want of industry, will fully account for this. And perhaps after all the truth is here, as in so many other cases, that Maginn did give the best that was in him to give, that his talents were more showy and versatile than solid, that the appearance in him was greater than the real capacity, and that in furnishing forth the part of a brilliant journalist and improvisatore he performed his day's work as it was appointed for him. (pp. 297-300)

With Hood, who surpassed [Maginn, Theodore Hook, and Richard Harris Barham] in originality of wit and quality of poetry, and Praed, who in his smaller scale and sphere excelled them all in fineness of touch, they are perhaps the chief of all such [humorists] as amused the town during the third and fourth decades of this century. Nothing that they did except [Barham's] *The Ingoldsby Legends* can be called individually important, and nothing with that exception is destined, I should suppose, to a long lease of life or a probable hope of resurrection. . . . [The] strongest of Maginn's claims,—the delusive and elusive air of genius frustrated which somehow clings to his work—is to be found chiefly in his mixture of classical learning and farcical humour, a mixture which I fear is less and less likely to be appreciated until the slow wheel of time has made a pretty long revolution. (pp. 300-01)

George Saintsbury, "Three Humourists: Hook, Barham, Maginn," in his Essays in English Literature: 1780-1860, *J. M. Dent & Co., 1895, pp. 270-302.*

P. A. SILLARD (essay date 1904)

"In the bowl," as [Maginn] said himself, "he sought sweet oblivion of all woe"; and that such a brilliant genius and profound scholar should have done such great injustice to his marvellous intellect is all the more to be regretted when we regard the excellence of his serious work. His **"Homeric Ballads"** prove him to have been a scholiast of worth, and his less-known **"Lucianic Comediettas"** . . . were unmistakable masterpieces. . . . His Shakespeare papers are almost all excellent, that on **"Lady Macbeth"** especially being full of fine thoughts felicitously expressed. He displayed a surprising range of reading in criticising the "Essay on the Learning of Shakespeare," that extraordinary farrago by old Farmer, Master of Emmanuel College, upon whose "peddling pedantry" and "fatheaded and scornful blockheadism" he poured a full measure of his contempt. (pp. 291-92)

[Consistency] in the sense of being tied down to one particular set of views was a virtue to which Maginn laid no claim. He always spoke out what he had in his mind to say, and said it in the raciest manner. (p. 293)

[While he illuminated] the pages of "Fraser" with his genius month after month, he kept the readers of "Blackwood" convulsed with laughter with **"A Story without a Tail,"** "Bob Burke's Duel with Ensign Brady of the 48th" (which is not only one of the raciest Irish stories ever written, but is a masterpiece of humorous fiction), and various other contributions, amongst which mention must be made of the **"Tobias Correspondence,"** a remarkably clever production. . . . In it he assures us will be found set forth from his own experience "the whole art and mystery of editing a newspaper." There can be no question but that his experience was both large and varied enough to qualify him to instruct others to their profit. The pity of it was that it brought him neither riches nor wisdom; . . . he lives for all time in Thackeray's "Pendennis" as Captain Shandon, "the learned and thriftless, the witty and unwise." (p. 294)

P. A. Sillard, "Doctor Maginn," in The Gentleman's Magazine, *Vol. CCXCVI, No. 2079, March, 1904, pp. 286-95.*

D. J. O'DONOGHUE (essay date 1904)

Maginn held religiously to the tradition that liquor is the chief attraction in life, and the only possible theme for a wit after exhausting his pleasantries about persons. Maginn, however, was very much in earnest and did not respect the tradition simply because it was one, but solely on account of his belief in its excellence. There can be no question, it seems to me, of Ireland's supremacy in the literature devoted to Bacchus. Whether any credit attaches to the distinction is, of course, another matter. All the bards were not so fierce as Maginn in their likes and dislikes when the liquor was on the table. (p. x)

Maginn's great service in exposing the true character of the wretched rubbish often palmed off on the English public as Irish songs deserves to be noticed. . . . He proved most con-

clusively that the stuff thus styled Irish, with its unutterable refrains of the "Whack Bubbaboo" kind, was of undoubted English origin; topography, phraseology, rhymes, and everything else being utterly un-Irish. (p. xii)

Of parodists, Maginn may be considered the best. He was a great humorist in every way, and may be claimed as the earliest writer who showed genuine rollicking Irish humor. He could be both coarse and refined; and his boisterous praise of the bottle was not a sham. But his occasional apparent delight in savage personal criticism was really quite foreign to his character, as he was a most amiable man, much loved by those who knew him. (p. xiv)

D. J. O'Donoghue, "Irish Wit and Humor," in Irish Literature, Vol. VI, *edited by Justin McCarthy and others, John D. Morris & Company, 1904, pp. vii-xv.*

MICHAEL MONAHAN (essay date 1914)

[Maginn's] translations, serious and burlesque, sufficiently attest his mastery of the classic tongues. His essays on the plays and learning of Shakespeare show his command of the splendid resources of our English speech. (p. 212)

Unhappily for Maginn's status in literature, [his] enormous versatility was purchased at the cost of more enduring performance. The Doctor did too many things well to achieve a surpassing success in any single line. As he himself would have said, with whimsical pedantry, the labour was "too autoschediastical." (p. 213)

The carelessness with which he regarded the fate of his productions, may be paralleled only in the case of Shakespeare. He rarely gave the authority of his name to any of his writings, which he threw off with incredible ease and fertility. Yet if only the pencil sketches accompanying the **"Gallery of Literary Characters"** were to survive, they would insure the fame of Maginn as the most brilliant and audacious wit of his generation. (p. 214)

Maginn in his most surprising feats of genius and scholarship must always remain "caviare to the general." It is not difficult to see that he could not have produced his incomparable burlesques in the classic languages by simply swallowing lexicons through a long course of years. You may have little Latin, but, with a small share of trouble, you can't miss the heroic effect of Maginn's rendering of the famous old English ballad of **"Chevy Chase"** into the tongue of Virgil. (p. 217)

The gentle art of literary "roasting" seems to have declined in virulence since the days of Maginn. He was easily the first practitioner of his time. . . . The papers in which he pretended to expose the plagiarisms of Tom Moore are among the most learned and ingenious. (p. 223)

Michael Monahan, "Doctor Maginn," in his Nova Hibernia: Irish Poets and Dramatists of Today and Yesterday, *1914. Reprint by Books for Libraries Press, Inc., 1967, pp. 203-31*

THE TIMES LITERARY SUPPLEMENT (essay date 1928)

[*A Story without a Tail*] tells of a party of gay and impecunious young men who met to dine in "Jack Ginger's chambers in the Temple." Food—they ate a sirloin of beef on top of a leg of pork—drink and conversation are given an heroic air consonant with the age. The story is definitely a voice from the past, showing that nothing changes so completely from one generation to another as the flavour of jollity. Would anyone describing the modern equivalent of such a party, if there is such a thing, lay emphasis on the great amount of cheese the men ate and the rapidity with which they ate it? But it is very well done, if here and there with too much polysyllabic humour. But the story has a point: a mysterious ending. There is a strange contrast between the protracted and robust description of the young men's appetites for food and drink, and the delicacy with which the mystery at the end is managed. It is a slight piece, a curiosity of literature, but well worth the revival.

> *A review of "A Story without a Tail," in* The Times Literary Supplement, *No. 1398, November 15, 1928, p. 863.*

THE TIMES LITERARY SUPPLEMENT   (essay date 1933)

[The stories in *Ten Tales*] are a revelation in their skill, charm and high spirits. . . .

Two of the stories, "**The Man in the Bell**" and "**A Night of Terror**," are of the sensational order, with no stamp of nationality upon them. A third, "**Jochonan in the City of Demons**," is founded upon an Egyptian legend, and is a good specimen of its kind. The other seven are Irish of the Irish, and it is certainly in them that the writer's talents are best displayed. There are touches in them which help to explain why Maginn's fame has disappeared: why Nationalist and Catholic Ireland, which could have done most to keep it alive, has not been concerned about it. Maginn was a Tory in politics to begin with. In his stories, too, he handles Irish saints with small respect; in "**A Vision of Purgatory**" we actually find St. Patrick in the chair of a masonic lodge, supported by St. Declan, St. Finbar, St. Brandon and the rest of the brotherhood. Yet Maginn shows himself a fine Irishman in these tales. The longest, "**Bob Burke's Duel**," is somewhat in the vein of Lever, but more highly finished. "**The Two Butlers of Kilkenny**" is a little masterpiece in technique, the secret being revealed to the reader from the first—a method which in the hands of a writer of this calibre is really more effective than the surprise ending. But it is the old Southern Irish fairy-stories, "**The Legend of Bottle Hill**," "**The Legend of Knocksheogowna**," "**The Legend of Knockgrafton**," in which Maginn has his greatest triumphs. He takes these tales, revitalizes them, adds a fresh touch of humour from his own plentiful store, and yet preserves their strangeness and whimsical fancy. One has heard more than one version of the legend of Knockgrafton without ever realizing that it could be more than one of those stories related by earnest students of folk-lore, a little of which goes a long way with their victims, the laymen in such matters. How the sweet-voiced hunchback joined in the fairies' song, "raised" it with a new phrase, delighted the singers and was relieved by them of his hump: how the second hunchback, sent to get rid of his in the same way, joined in with a bawl, "never minding the time or the humour of the tune," and was rewarded by having the last man's hump clapped on top of his own—Maginn stamps this with his personality. If he left much more in the vein of these legends, he was indeed a very fine artist.

> *"William Maginn," in* The Times Literary Supplement, *No. 1656, October 26, 1933, p. 722.*

P. S. O'H[EGARTY]   (essay date 1934)

With the exception of the four fairy stories, of which more anon, the six tales . . . which this Volume [*Ten Tales*] contains, are tales well worth reprinting, but they are not the sort of thing upon which a reputation can be made. They are brilliant, extravagant, fanciful, witty, coruscating, and irresponsible, but not great art. They have the marks of their time, and any reader with an acquaintance with nineteenth century literature would at once place these, reading them at random, in the first half of the nineteenth century, without at the same time being able to allocate them to an individual.

Maginn was brilliant at many things, and the most extravagant tributes were paid to him by his contemporaries. What he did he did well. But he did nothing so superlatively as to leave any mark upon any time save his own. He had the instability and the jumpiness of very great talent not under control, and not adequately directed. His tales, in their quippishness, have a curious similarity to those of Mangan, and his other work was of his time, akin to that of those other contemporaries of his with equal wayward talent—Prout and Kenealy. . . . (p. 78)

[Maginn] has been almost forgotten. Yet [his work] is very good. . . . *The Shakespeare Papers,* the *Homeric Ballads,* and various of his critical and fanciful sketches are meritorious and ought to be given finality in a proper collected edition.

With the fairy stories, however, one comes to quite another thing. Each of the four tales claimed for Maginn in this volume is a gem of the purest literary merit. (p. 79)

> *P. S. O'H[egarty], in a review of "Ten Tales," in* The Dublin Magazine, *n.s. Vol. IX, No. 1, January-March, 1934, pp 78-80.*

MIRIAM M. H. THRALL   (essay date 1934)

[*Thrall's* Rebellious "Fraser's": Nol Yorke's Magazine in the Days of Maginn, Thackeray, and Carlyle *is a well-researched, comprehensive study of Maginn's involvement with* Fraser's. *In addition to discussing Maginn's various contributions to* Fraser's, *and his influence upon the magazine's staff, Thrall provides an account of Maginn's life in which she emphasizes the more controversial aspects of his reputation, including his association with Letitia Elizabeth Landon. The first critic to question Maginn's right to be considered the sole author of* Whitehall, *Thrall proves to the satisfaction of modern commentators that Lockhart collaborated with him on the novel. Here, Thrall underscores Maginn's importance as a magazinist, arguing that he was a "generative force" in the periodicals to which he contributed.*]

With isolated exceptions, only [Maginn's *Shakespeare Papers*] were lifted above their own time, and here the style is excellent. In these more careful essays Maginn's prose has an easy rectitude and simplicity which is unusual in his day. Without a trace of the precious, it is cultivated, carrying lightly its knowledge of diction and manners. Something of the same guarded wisdom is to be found in his *Maxims of Sir Morgan O'Doherty,* his introduction to the *Homeric Ballads,* the *Gallery of Literary Characters,* and in passages scattered through his articles. If Maginn anticipated much that is cheap in modern writing, he also anticipated much that is best. (pp. 229-30)

Maginn's translations of Homer are themselves less commendable than his introduction and notes. He adopted the unfortunate theory that the great epics could be most nearly represented in English by hexameters and by the ballad form—with a result which met with enthusiastic approval in his own day of much Greek and more Latin, but which is difficult to associate with Homer. (pp. 233-34)

Of more general interest today are the burlesques in verse, which are sufficient in quantity and fineness to place Maginn among the best parodists in the English language. . . . His stinging ridicule of Moore, if not able to undermine that facile poet's popularity, left no room for doubt that less sentimental writing also had its great advantages. Among the most destructive of these **"Moore-ish Melodies"** were **"Billingsgate Music," "Rich and Rare,"** and the two parodies of the ''Last Rose of Summer,'' under the inebriate titles of **"'Tis the Last Glass of Claret,"** and **"The Last Lamp of the Alley."**

As a creative writer Maginn's fame is likely to rest on his downright honesty. His songs, such as **"The Pewter Quart," "The Wine-Bibber's Glory,"** and **"A Twist-imony in Favour of Gin-Twist"** do for drink what his absurd **"Irishman and the Lady"** does for the Irish drinker; they exaggerate to substantial truth. His satiric ballad, **"The Powldoodies of Burran,"** has a burly realism that harks back to Swift. It shows his faith in the Irish vernacular and his control over its outer reaches of thought and sound. (p. 235)

[*Whitehall*] shows not only the irritation which two exceedingly keen critics felt at the abuses of their own day; there is an opening of satire within satire with preposterous but medicinal buffoonery. . . . Like Bernard Shaw's remedial mixtures, it tumbles together governors and governed, the noble Negro, the popular poet, the sacrificial servant, the fainting maiden, in a series of fantastic juxtapositions not less true because distorted. (p. 243)

[It] is well to remember that [Maginn's] real achievement does not lie in his contributions to any one type of writing—neither in his burlesques and parodies, skillful as they often are, nor in his scholarly criticism, though that in its turn deserves attention; nor even in his fine Irish work. Rather it lies in the rapid development of the periodicals to which he so abundantly contributed. Maginn was before all else a great magazinist, without question the greatest of his day. For over twenty years he was a generative force in the organs with which he was most closely connected. His incredible vitality quickened their method, and widened their interest and observation. The very ease with which he could be imitated lifted the level of the ordinary contributions. He taught the facilities of direct expression and made directness fashionable. His own work has the quality of surprise and search, a curiosity for the things of the time that had not been expressed, and above all a wholesome predilection for plain dealing. (pp. 243-44)

> *Miriam M. H. Thrall, "Literary Work," in her* Rebellious "Fraser's": Nol Yorke's Magazine in the Days of Maginn, Thackeray, and Carlyle, *Columbia University Press, 1934, pp. 229-44.*

LOGAN PEARSALL SMITH (essay date 1937)

[Maginn's writings] are excellent reading, for Maginn was a sound scholar and possessed an admirable and racy style. His paper on Farmer's *Essay on the Learning of Shakespeare* is full of critical insight, and of an accurate, exquisite pedantry which I find delightful; and in an essay on Lady Macbeth he gives a luminous survey, which I have never seen equalled, of the treatment given to women in the literatures of Greece, of Rome, of Italy and England. He translated Homer also in a way that won the praise of Matthew Arnold; and in the writing

of stories about Irish adventurers he beat on his own field Thackeray, who owed more to him than has ever been acknowledged. In looking through his amusing essays, I found one of special interest to those who try to see things as past generations saw them.

We are all familiar with the abhorrence, nausea and contempt felt by Byron and his friends for what Byron called the 'p———a-bed' poetry of Keats, of that 'pretentious and ill-bred Cockney poet, that miserable self-polluter of the human mind'; but Maginn, being a sound Tory of the school of Lockhart and Wilson, gives us in a review of *Adonais* the essence of the disgust of another group of good writers for what he calls the 'poetico-metaphysical maniac' Shelley, who, with the Godwinian colony of licentious atheists at Pisa was 'playing the Bacchanal beside the Tuscan Sea.' With gusto, wit and indignation, he writes of the dreary nonsense of *P. B. Shelley's* lamentations for the death of a *Mr. J. Keats*, 'a poor sendentary man of unhealthy aspect who left a decent calling for the melanchol. trade of Cockney-poetry,' and who, after writing two or three little books of silly, presumptuous, verse, full of servile Cockney slang, and recently died of a consumption caused (so his friends alleged) by what right-minded people regarded as the undisputably just sentence of the *Quarterly Review*.

After a careful examination of *Adonais*, Maginn finds in this great poem only five readable lines; the rest of this 'odoriferous, colourific, daisy-enamoured style,' being a mere wild waste of words, upon which, in his own opinion, he greatly improved in an elegy on a tom-cat, which he prints with pride.

> O bard-like spirit! beautiful and swift!
> Sweet lover of pale night!—
> The dazzling glory of thy gold-tinged tail,
> Thy whisker-wavering lips—

Surely lines like these were much better, much less nonsensical and inflated than those of P. B. Shelley's lament! Thus Maginn writes with honest conviction and total unawareness of the crushing Day-of-Judgment reversal which was fated to make ridiculous, before the tribunal of Posterity, this contemporary judgment.

But among Maginn's writings there is one sweet-tempered and infinitely witty book, which ought to make Posterity willing to forgive all his literary and other misdemeanours. In this little volume, which was entitled **The Maxims of Sir Morgan O'Doherty, .Bart.**, our kindly tippler has embodied the sparkling essence of his convivial life. (pp. 188-89)

[Maginn's *Maxims*], being concerned as they mostly are with the three of the main interests of his life, eating and drinking and making love (though shrewd observations on literature and human nature are mingled with them), possess one of the most important merits of this aphoristic way of writing: they are unmistakably his own—no one else could have written them. . . . (p. 191)

> *Logan Pearsall Smith, "Captain Shandon," in his* Reperusals and Re-Collections, *Harcourt, Brace and Company, 1937, pp. 185-93.*

J. LYLE DONAGHY (essay date 1938)

[*Donaghy maintains that in Maginn's writings, the principle characteristics of early nineteenth-century English periodical literature—"arrogant controversialism, pedantry," and "headlong blunder"—are tempered by his scholarship, religious faith, and sense of humor. Maxims and Ten Tales are, according to Don-*

*aghy, Maginn's only works of enduring merit. Nevertheless, he
expresses admiration for ''Dr. Farmer's 'Essay on the Learning
of Shakespeare' Considered,'' ''Lady Macbeth,'' and the introduction to* Homeric Ballads.]

Maginn had one of those swift and powerful intellects, almost
overbearing in its tendencies. He would not have been overbearing to meet; but when he took his pen in his hand he at
once adopted something of a domineering and aggressive attitude. Whence was this? Naturally power must express itself
and Maginn's was a powerful intellect; naturally scholarship
must take to itself something of the tone of the ruler and Maginn
was a scholar. But the bluster, the bullying, the brow-beating,
whence were these? Why, they were of Fleet Street, and they
were of the age. The impatience, the over-running of diverse
intellectual fields in confidence of a general scholarship—
weighty-seeming theses, the erudite paraphernalia of blunder—
these were of the journalism of Maginn's age. Look in the
quarterlies of the period: in *Blackwood's,* the *Edinburgh Review,* the *Cornhill*—here in philosophical-sounding article after
article protracted to great length, is the very genius of Doctor
Foolishness. . . . On such Maginn was bred. (p. 44)

Hence these main ingredients of Maginn's literary manner—
arrogant controversialism, pedantry, headlong blunder. But in
Maginn these were modified by (1) a native sense of humour;
(2) a faith in the fundamental teachings of orthodox religion;
(3) a genuine scholarship. All three qualities, in combination
with the literary vices of his epoch, operated both well and
ill—ill sometimes; for, of course, ''Lilies that fester smell far
worse than weeds.'' His humour carried the day with a large
stride, or it aggravated crudity and gave boredom another arm.
When he was work-tired or drink-exhausted it mostly did the
latter. His orthodox faith rallied their own weapons (along with
better) against contemporary cant and bunkdum, less successfully against vice; but it also prejudiced his philosophical vision
and led him to impute some Puritan motives to Homer and
Shakespeare, of which they were in all probability—and thank
God!—guiltless. His genuine learning gave worth to his criticism, brightened the sparkle, or it made inanity ponderous,
turned the smile into a yawn.

Two of Maginn's longest and most learned critical articles are
his **''Farmer's 'Essay on the Learning of Shakespeare' considered,''** and his article on **''Lady Macbeth''** which appear
in *Miscellanies.* Both these articles are in many ways brilliant;
but they are both partially unsatisfactory from a critical point
of view. The latter, especially. Now, it is true that, even in
opposition, a certain degree of soundness and worth in the
opponent improves the standard of the debate, and that a reviewer will write best and produce more valuable materials,
deliver sounder and more considered judgments, where some
commencement has been made in integrity and depth in the
work which he reviews.

It is well to remember this in estimating Maginn's review of
Farmer. Farmer's essay, showing that Shakespeare had no
knowledge of the classical languages, and was dependent, as
regards classical materials, entirely upon translations, is the
work of a pedantic half-learned nasty-natured imbecile. There
is really no more to be said about it. Maginn, however, was
invited to write a review of the essay—and did so. The effect
is something like that which would be produced by a tank
going over an assortment of empty canned-meat tins. Truly,
as a demonstration of the tank's power it is neither very interesting nor very edifying, for empty canned-meat tins are
only empty canned-meat tins though you adduce all science to

their demolition. The tank, however, remains interesting even
although it is no fortress which it demolishes.

Maginn's method in this review is not positive. He contents
himself on the whole with demolishing his opponent's arguments against Shakespeare's having been learned linguistically.
He does not on the other side himself adduce proofs in favour
of Shakespeare's having been learned. In the case in hand, the
negative method was sufficient for his purpose. He takes Farmer's main points and one after one exposes them in all their
pitiful puerility. Enough of Farmer; let us consider the tank.
Even in such mean employ, the tank has already left a clear
road; for not only did it crush the tins, but such was its weight
that it has inevitably left a broad smooth path behind it. When
Maginn laid down his pen, not only Farmer was gone, but
much popular misunderstanding and musty nonsense. (pp. 45-7)

[There] is much minor criticism in Maginn's review which is
unsound, and his textual emendations of Shakespeare do not
by any means recommend themselves to me. It is however,
considering the worthlessness of its occasion (Dr. Farmer's
Essay) a great and brilliant review.

Almost equally brilliant in a different way is the article on
Lady Macbeth. Here, however, the fundamental critical po-
sitions seem to me to be as unsound as in the review of the
Farmer Essay, they are sound. (p. 48)

But though I think that the fundamental critical positions in
the article on Lady Macbeth are unsound, much of the rest of
Maginn's observations on the dramatic progress of the play,
and on the character of Lady Macbeth is interesting.

To turn to other work of Maginn: his critique on Lord Byron
is severe but not unmerited; on the other hand his criticism of
Shelley's ''Lament for Adonais'' is a half-truth and palpably
unfair. He seems also to have under-rated, surprisingly, Coleridge's ''Christabel.'' With most of his trifles and smaller
pieces I am almost entirely out of sympathy. Such things as
his Latin rendering of ''Chevy Chase'' I think are dull and
only indifferent clever. It is not clever to do them for they only
contribute to hackney a fine poem. Maginn had not the lightness
of touch and grace which make Father Prout's relics pleasing,
to this day. Of course, much of the stuff I refer to was inevitably
ephemeral and was never intended by its author to be anything
else. Yet, absolve me, O world, of all priggery when I assert
here my all-embracing incompetence to get into sympathy with
the appalling vacuity of mind—barren it seems to me of spontaneous humour and only spontaneously dull—which issued in
Mangan's ''Apostrophe to the Comet,'' and in many of Maginn's smaller poems and articles, and which with kindred
blatancy speaks its nothing in full many a wit of their epoch.

Maginn's ballad renderings of passages of [Homer's] *Odyssey*
are interesting but not to my mind successful—they are too
hard in their expression and miss both the beauty and nobility
of the Homeric poems—Maginn was not a poet; but if the
translations are unsuccessful, the brief introduction to them,
vigorous and perspicuous, is of the very best of Maginn. Good,
too, is his prefatory note on the ''Return from Troy.''

And now I have carped and condemned and mixed praise with
blame; there remain, for a monument to the native genius of
one of the most learned of the literary men of last century, two
light works which seem to me completely successful and of
enduring merit. These are *The Maxims of Sir Morgan O'Doherty, Bart.,* and the *Ten Tales.* In the *Maxims,* a vein of
vigorous humour distinctly Maginn's is exploited to the full.

Here even his prejudices come forth in a rollicking guise that moves to mirth, and mix with sage reflection in the mask of comedy and frank folly. Here through a hundred and forty-two maxims a strong style almost boisterously humorous full of resource, moves carelessly and consistently to the end with no failing of the materials of humour. (pp. 49-51)

[*The Ten Tales*] are of that order of narrative, which includes the last phase of the folk-tale in Ireland, and the anecdote of the West; but they are of the cream of that degenerate world, and Maginn has made of them fine tales, humorous in conception and execution, with a sure and easy movement—they are simply latter-day folk tales made or retold by a scholar who had the art of story-telling. None but would enjoy them, though they are not very well known. These are the best memorial of William Maginn, a name darkly familiar to all in Mangan's poem, one of the many brilliant wits flung up by a benighted nation, and who have squandered their genius in the metropolis of London. (p. 51)

J. Lyle Donaghy, "William Maginn," in The Dublin Magazine, *n.s. Vol. XIII, No. 3, July-September, 1938, pp. 43-51.*

ADDITIONAL BIBLIOGRAPHY

"Dr. Maginn." *Chamber's Edinburgh Journal* n.s. I, No. 6 (10 February 1844): 92-4.
    Brief biographical sketch.

Cooke, A. K. "William Maginn on John Keats." *Notes and Queries* CCI (March 1956): 118-20.*
    Uses several of the letters that Maginn wrote to William Blackwood following John Keats's death as a springboard for a brief discussion of the political nature of a series of essays in *Blackwood's* in which Keats's poetry was virulently attacked.

Elwin, Malcolm. "Wallflower the Second: 'The Doctor' (William Maginn)." In his *Victorian Wallflowers: A Panoramic Survey of the Popular Literary Periodicals*, pp. 85-127. 1934. Reprint. Port Washington, N.Y.: Kennikat Press, 1966.
    Appreciative essay in which Elwin argues that Maginn was the "victim of his own versatility" and laments that he "settled to no concentrated work worthy of his powers. . . ." Elwin's *Victorian Wallflowers* is, according to the critic, a study of nine "central and representative figures—or 'wallflowers',", whose writings typify Victorian periodical literature.

Herd, Harold. "'Bright, Broken Maginn'." In his *Seven Editors*, pp. 69-88. 1955. Reprint. Westport, Conn.: Greenwood Press, 1977.
    Biographical study that focuses on the more controversial aspects of Maginn's reputation. Herd concentrates on Maginn's intemperance, his duel with Grantley Berkeley, and his association with Letitia Elizabeth Landon.

[John Gibson Lockhart]. "The Gallery of Illustrious Literary Characters: No. VIII, The Doctor." *Fraser's Magazine* II, No. XII (January 1831): 716.
    A colorful portrait of Maginn's character and personality.

Mackenzie, Shelton. "Memoir of William Maginn, LL.D." In *Miscellaneous Writings of the Late Dr. Maginn: The Fraserian Papers, Vol. V.*, by William Maginn, edited by Shelton Mackenzie, pp. ix-cx. New York: Redfield, 1857.
    Laudatory account of Maginn's life in which Mackenzie quotes freely from Maginn's writings and from contemporary critical estimates of his literary career. Mackenzie discredits the commonly held belief that Maginn's literary talent gradually deteriorated as a result of his intemperance. He insists that *"Dr. Maginn was not an habitual drunkard"* and notes that his "really *best*

things—the *Shakespeare Papers,* and *Homeric Ballads*—were the very latest of his productions."

Maginn, William. "The Last of the Homeric Ballads: No. XVI, Nestor's First Essay in Arms." *Fraser's Magazine* XXVI, No. CLIV (October 1842): 439-46.
    Contains an introduction by Edward Vaughan Kenealy in which Kenealy affectionately describes his last visit with Maginn.

Montagu, R. W. "Memoir." In *Miscellanies: Prose and Verse, Vol. I,* by William Maginn, edited by R. W. Montagu, pp. vii-xix. London: Sampson Low, Marston, Searle, & Rivington, 1885.
    Sympathetic account of Maginn's life and literary career.

O'Donoghue, D. J. "Maginn, William, LL.D. "In his *The Poets of Ireland: A Biographical and Bibliographical Dictionary of Irish Writers of English Verse*, pp. 295-97. 1912. Reprint. Detroit: Gale Research Co., 1968.
    Provides bibliographical information.

Oliphant, [Margaret]. *Annals of a Publishing House: William Blackwood and His Sons, Their Magazine and Friends*. 2 vols. New York: Charles Scribner's Sons, 1897.*
    A detailed account of Maginn's involvement with *Blackwood's* that includes correspondence between Maginn and William Blackwood. Oliphant relegates her discussion of Maginn to a chapter not immediately following those devoted to John Wilson and John Gibson Lockhart, commenting that "we are by no means proud of the part Maginn took in the Magazine, nor of himself or the connection so speedily formed, and to place him immediatley after the Great Twin Brethren who formed it is too honourable a place."

Ralli, Augustus. "England, 1832-1840: Maginn." In his *A History of Shakespearian Criticism, Vol. I*, pp. 193-97. 1932. Reprint. New York: Humanities Press, 1965.
    Briefly summarizes Maginn's commentary on several characters in William Shakespeare's plays, including Falstaff, Jacques, Romeo, and Lady Macbeth.

Sadleir, Michael. *Bulwer, A Panorama: Edward and Rosina, 1803-1836, Vol. I*. Boston: Little, Brown, and Co., 1931, 409 p.
    Speculates on the causes of the hostility between Maginn and Edward Bulwer-Lytton in a chapter focused on Maginn's association with various periodicals and an appendix. Angered by Bulwer's efforts to encourage Letitia Elizabeth Landon to repel his flirtatious advances, Sadleir writes, Maginn attacked the novelist in a series of essays that appeared in *Fraser's,* between April, 1830 and February, 1833. In an additional appendix, Sadleir provides a bibliography of Maginn's works.

"Biographical Sketch of Dr. Maginn." In *Shakespeare Papers: Pictures Grave and Gay,* by William Maginn, pp. 1-22. London: Richard Bentley, 1859.
    Biographical portrait that includes a personal reminiscence of Maginn by Robert Macnish and a character sketch of the author by David Macbeth Moir.

Stevenson, Lionel. "Romanticism Run to Seed." *The Virginia Quarterly Review* 9, No. 4 (October 1933): 510-25.*
    Views the "riotous improvisation" that characterizes English literature of the late 1820s and 1830s as an inevitable result of the Romantics' defiance of traditional rules of theme and technique. According to Stevenson, the writings of Maginn, John Wilson, John Gibson Lockhart, Theodore Hook, Francis Sylvester Mahony, and Letitia Elizabeth Landon typify English literature of this period. Stevenson provides a brief description of Maginn's literary career that focuses on his association with *Blackwood's* and *Fraser's.*

Strout, Alan L[ang]. "Concerning the *Noctes Ambrosianae*." *Modern Language Notes* LI, No. 8 (December 1936): 493-504.*
    Describes the origin and development of the *Noctes Ambrosianae*.

Strout, Alan Lang. "William Maginn as Gossip." *Notes and Queries* CC (June 1955): 263-65.

Presents a selection of Maginn's letters to William Blackwood in which he discusses *Blackwood's* and its contributors. Maginn's letters, Strout contends, display his "facile facetiousness" and offer "fascinating" commentary on London society.

"A Brief Account of Dr. William Maginn." In *Ten Tales*, by William Maginn, pp. 7-14. London: Eric Partridge, 1933.
Concise biographical portrait.

"Tragedy of a Writer: William Maginn, 1794-1842." *The Times Literary Supplement*, No. 2116 (22 August 1942): 418.
Attributes Maginn's "contemporary evanescence" to his versatility, critical integrity, and lack of ambition.

Wardle, Ralph M. "The Authorship of *Whitehall* (1827)." *Modern Language Notes* LVI, No. 3 (March 1941): 207-09.*
Confirms Miriam M. H. Thrall's conclusion that John Gibson Lockhart collaborated with Maginn on *Whitehall* (see excerpt above, 1934) and speculates on the nature of their collaboration. Wardle suggests, on the basis of Lockhart's correspondence with William Blackwood and his review of *Whitehall* (see excerpt above, 1828), that Lockhart composed a brief parody of contemporary historical novels in 1827 which Maginn later expanded upon and published anonymously as *Whitehall*.

———. "Outwitting Hazlitt." *Modern Language Notes* LVII, No. 6 (June 1942): 459-62.*
Reprints passages from a series of articles that appeared in *Blackwood's* between August, 1823 and September, 1824 in which

Maginn harshly reviewed several of William Hazlitt's critical essays. Maginn's attacks on Hazlitt, Wardle states, were written in response to Hazlitt's threat to sue William Blackwood for libel.

———. "Timothy Tickler's' Irish Blood." *The Review of English Studies* XVIII, No. 72 (October 1942): 486-90.*
Argues that Maginn often wrote under the pseudonym of Timothy Tickler for *Blackwood's* although the pseudonym is commonly identified with John Gibson Lockhart. According to Wardle, Maginn was a frequent contributor to a series of essays entitled "Letters of Timothy Tickler to Eminent Men of Letters of the Day" that appeared in *Blackwood's* between July, 1823 and December, 1824. Wardle supports his conclusion with excerpts from Maginn's correspondence with William Blackwood.

———. "Who Was Morgan Odoherty?" *PMLA* LVIII, No. 3 (September 1943): 716-27.*
Discusses the extent to which the pseudonym Morgan Odoherty was used interchangeably by the contributors to *Blackwood's*. Wardle complains that Shelton Mackenzie, the editor of *Miscellaneous Writings of the Late Dr. Maginn*, erred in attributing a number of articles in *Blackwood's* signed Morgan O'Doherty, including "The Rime of the Auncient Waggonere," to Maginn. Wardle also argues that "Christabel, Part Third," which appears in *Miscellanies: Prose and Verse*, was written by David Macbeth Moir.

Robert Southey

1774-1843

(Also wrote under the pseudonym of Don Manuel Alvarez Espriella) English poet, historian, biographer, essayist, short story writer, translator, and editor.

Though often overlooked by modern scholars, Southey is recognized by literary historians as a significant member of the Lake School of poetry, a group which numbered among its more outstanding exponents William Wordsworth and Samuel Taylor Coleridge. In his own day Southey was considered a prominent literary figure, and his writings received serious critical assessment from his contemporaries. As a poet, he composed short verse, ballads, and epics and experimented extensively with versification and meter. Southey's prose writings include ambitious histories, biographies, and social commentaries; critics often praise these writings more than his poetry. In addition, he frequently contributed essays on social reform to the *Quarterly Review* and worked both as a translator and editor. While critics of his era generally acclaimed his prose writings, few applauded his verse, and its merits are still debated. Despite the variety and size of Southey's oeuvre, only "The Story of the Three Bears" has achieved enduring fame; ironically, few readers associate this classic children's tale with his name.

Born in Bristol, England, Southey spent much of his youth in Bath under the care of his mother's half-sister. He was a sad, neglected child with a sensitive nature. In 1788, he entered school in London but was expelled in 1792 for condemning corporal punishment in an article in *The Flagellant*, a journal he had founded. This breach of justice aroused in him a rebellious spirit and an enthusiasm for the French Revolution. The same year, Southey entered Oxford University, where he met Coleridge. Together, they agreed that their distaste for the English governmental system could be alleviated only by the creation of their own utopian society. Southey and Coleridge outlined a plan for a "pantisocracy," or egalitarian agricultural society, to be founded in Kentucky. Though these ideas never became reality, for a time both men were absorbed by their concepts of revolution. They composed radically oriented verse, engaged in demonstrations, and wrote a drama, *The Fall of Robespierre.* However, as their lives became financially secure, their dreams of utopia faded. Southey left Oxford and traveled to Spain and Portugal. There he wrote *Letters Written during a Short Residence in Spain and Portugal,* a series of letters that details Southey's political transition from revolutionary to conservative Tory. Upon his return to England, Southey married, studied law in London, and composed poetry. When he received a substantial inheritance, he abandoned his legal studies and devoted himself to literature. In 1801, Southey moved to the English Lake District, the home of Wordsworth and Coleridge.

Southey has come to be associated with the Lake School partly as a result of Francis Jeffrey's scathing review in the *Edinburgh Review* in 1802 of Southey's epic poem, *Thalaba the Destroyer.* This review, which Jeffrey included within the context of a general condemnation of the Lake School, stated that the poetry of the Lake School displayed "a splenetic and idle discontent with the institutions of society." In particular, Jef-

frey singled out Southey's taste as "perverted" and criticized the fantastic elements of *Thalaba*. Though Jeffrey overestimated the closeness of Southey's literary relationship with Wordsworth and Coleridge, in his review he often displayed acute perception. Jeffrey noted that Southey's inspiration usually stemmed from books rather than life, a point often reiterated in subsequent analysis. Southey found the "attempt at Thalabacide" unjust, but expressed to a friend, "such public censure . . . attracts attention, and will make the subject remembered when the censure itself is forgotten." In fact, Jeffrey's attribution of Southey to the Lake School enhanced Southey's stature as a poet. While his verse shares traits in common with that of Wordsworth and Coleridge, such as love of nature and concern for the sufferings of common people, Southey's early work also displays his innate desire for controversy. The mixed reception afforded his early epic poems developed largely from his experiments in prosody and meter. Many critics have found his versification, which was inspired by classical poetry, to be at odds with his purported subject of social reform. Of Southey's epics, the best known are *Joan of Arc, Madoc,* and *The Curse of Kehama;* these poems extol his belief in courage and strength as humanity's most admirable qualities and depict their fearless heroes in exotic settings. His epics are noted primarily for their extensive and graphic violence; though Southey maintained that the works were social as well as artistic statements, his colorful battle scenes most fully display his creative abilities. He based these sequences on his own vivid and horrifying dreams, which he recorded with considerably more passion than the actual historic battles incorporated in his verse. Southey considered poetry a most noble profession and devoted himself to it; however, most critics find his verse technically correct but, with the exception of the battle episodes, devoid of spirit or emotion.

As Southey's family grew, his financial responsibilities increased, and he turned his pen to ventures more lucrative than poetry. He composed the extensive *History of Brazil* and, in 1809, became a steady contributor to the Tory *Quarterly Review*. In the *Quarterly* essays, Southey developed his plans for social reform and often wrote of the need for economic and social services for the poor. In 1813, Sir Walter Scott secured Southey's appointment as Poet Laureate of England. While Southey hoped to compose poetry that would embrace his concepts of decorum and patriotism, his official poems were largely received as cumbersome and inappropriate. Of these, his best known is *A Vision of Judgment*, written to mark the death of King George III in 1820. Though the poem tells only of the King's triumphant ascent into heaven, Southey prefaced the work with a harsh condemnation of the poet Lord Byron. Although Byron had earlier poked fun at Southey in his *English Bards and Scotch Reviewers* and in his preface to *Don Juan*, his comments did not have the sting of Southey's preface, in which he denounced Byron as a member of the "Satanic School" of poetry and called his verse "loathsome and lascivious." In a rage, Byron retaliated with his own "Vision of Judgment," a satire which critics agree far outshines Southey's poem. In this work, Byron referred with mockery and bitterness to Southey's poem *Wat Tyler*, an early, radical work that contrasted sharply with Southey's later political beliefs. The publication of *Wat Tyler* in 1817, which was unauthorized by Southey, had created a furor; many people felt that a man capable of such controversial work had no right to be Poet Laureate. Byron, with his fellow countrymen, resented Southey's apparently expedient change of political doctrine and its espousal in his new writings. Though Southey remained Laureate until his death, he wrote little poetry after *A Vision of Judgment*.

Though critics praise Southey's prose works more than his poetry, few are remembered today with the exception of his highly praised biography, *The Life of Nelson*. Southey's penchant for research and reporting was well suited to the task of biographical writing. Critics note an empathy between Southey and the British admiral Horatio Nelson; in Nelson, Southey recognized traits of leadership and fortitude that he aspired to himself, and his recreation of Nelson is generally considered the finest characterization in all of Southey's work. Scholars also concur that military biographies and histories were better suited to his later conservative beliefs and direct prose style. While his social commentary in *Sir Thomas More; or, Colloquies on the Progress and Prospects of Society* was harshly criticized in 1830 by Thomas Babington Macaulay, later commentators admired Southey's political and religious insights. Others maintained, as did John Gibson Lockhart, that he often wrote extensively on obscure subjects for the sole purpose of trumpeting his own knowledge.

Southey's best known work, "The Story of the Three Bears," did not appear until the end of his career. He included the tale in *The Doctor,* an eclectic collection of short stories and essays written in a relaxed, humorous tone. Published anonymously, *The Doctor* caused a controversy among scholars who were puzzled as to its authorship. Several critics, including John Gibson Lockhart, maintained steadfastly that Southey had not composed the work. Though some critics faulted its light mood, modern scholars consider *The Doctor* one of Southey's finest achievements. "The Story of the Three Bears" displays his best traits as a prose writer. Masterly and smooth, the style is reminiscent of that of Jonathan Swift and Daniel Defoe. Following the publication of *The Doctor,* Southey's health failed and, in 1840, he lost his mental faculties. After years of an active literary life, Southey was unable to speak or read, and he remained in this condition until his death in 1843.

While interest in Southey's social theories has increased since his death, his reputation as a creative writer—especially as a poet—continues to decline. Literary historians remember him for his association with the early Romantics and for his position in contemporary literary society. Ultimately, his tireless work schedule marked him as a quintessential working man of letters, rather than an artist; most scholars agree with his editor, Robert Gittings, who stated that Southey's genius "was not truly literary, not truly creative, but almost purely academic and factual."

PRINCIPAL WORKS

The Fall of Robespierre [with Samuel Taylor Coleridge] (drama) 1794
Joan of Arc (poetry) 1796
Letters Written during a Short Residence in Spain and Portugal (letters) 1797
Poems. 2 vols. (poetry) 1797-99
Thalaba the Destroyer (poetry) 1801
Madoc (poetry) 1805
Letters from England [as Don Manuel Alvarez Espriella] (letters) 1807
The Curse of Kehama (poetry) 1810
History of Brazil. 3 vols. (history) 1810-19
History of Europe. 4 vols. (history) 1810-13
The Life of Nelson (biography) 1813
Roderick: The Last of the Goths (poetry) 1814
The Minor Poems (poetry) 1815
The Lay of the Laureate: Carmen Nuptiale (poetry) 1816
The Poet's Pilgrimage to Waterloo (poetry) 1816
Wat Tyler (poetry) 1817
The Life of Wesley and the Rise and Progress of Methodism (biography) 1820
A Vision of Judgment (poetry) 1821
Sir Thomas More; or, Colloquies on the Progress and Prospects of Society (essays) 1829
The Devil's Walk [with Samuel Taylor Coleridge] (poetry) 1830
Essays Moral and Political (essays) 1832
Selections from the Prose Works (prose) 1832
Lives of the British Admirals. 5 vols. (biography) 1833-40
*The Doctor. 7 vols. (short stories and essays) 1834-47
Poetical Works. 10 vols. (poetry) 1837-38
Life and Correspondence of Robert Southey. 6 vols. (letters) 1849-51
New Letters (letters) 1965

*This work includes the short story "The Story of the Three Bears."

[JOHN AIKIN] (essay date 1796)

[We] do not hesitate to declare our opinion that the poetical powers displayed in [*Joan of Arc*] are of a very superior kind, and such as, if not wasted in premature and negligent exertions, promise a rich harvest of future excellence. Conceptions more lofty and daring, sentiments more commanding, and language more energetic, than some of the best passages in this poem afford, will not easily be found:—nor does scarcely any part of it sink to languor; as the glow of feeling and genius animates the whole. The language is, for the most part, modelled on that of Milton, and not unfrequently it has a strong relish of Shakspeare: but there are more defective and discordant lines than might be wished, either owing to carelessness, or to that piece of false taste, as we think it, the copying of harsh sounds or images in harsh versification. Indeed, the author, in his preface, expressly imputes his defects of this kind to design: but surely the loose prosody of English blank verse is neither too difficult, nor too melodious, to render a close adherence to its rules an indispensable law of poetry. Another frequent cause of halting measure is the false pronunciation of French proper names, which the writer commonly accents on the first syllable, after the English manner. We confess that we are also offended with the frequency of alliteration, often when the repeated sound is most harsh and unmusical. Nor can we praise the licentious coinage of new verbs out of nouns, in which our poet, in common with many other modern lovers of novelty, too much indulges. Indeed, there are few pages in which there is not somewhat to be mended in the diction or versification,—clearly accusing the hurry with which so great a work has been completed.

With respect to the *sentiments,* they are less adapted to the age in which the events took place, than to that of the writer; being uniformly noble, liberal, enlightened, and breathing the purest spirit of general benevolence and regard to the rights and claims of human kind. In many parts, a strong allusion to later characters and events is manifest; and we know not where the ingenuity of a crown lawyer would stop, were he employed to make out a list of inuendos. In particular, War, and the lust of conquest, are every where painted in the strongest colours of abhorrence.—Far be it from us to check or blame even the excesses of generous ardour in a youthful breast! Powerful antidotes are necessary to the corrupt selfishness and indifference of the age. (pp. 362-63)

> [*John Aikin*], "Southey's 'Joan of Arc, an Epic Poem'," *in* The Monthly Review, *London, Vol. XIX, April, 1796, pp. 361-68.*

[JOHN AIKIN] (essay date 1796)

No one who possesses a true relish for poetry, we conceive, will open with indifference a volume by the author of *Joan of Arc.* He will, perhaps, be prepared to expect somewhat of negligence and inequality, but he will certainly look for examples of that vivid force of imagination, and that warm colouring of expression, which essentially distinguish the Poet from the artificial measurer of syllables. Nor will such a reader be disappointed by the publication before us [*Poems*]. It contains abundant variety of style and subject, and consists of pieces very differently valued by the author himself. Of the lyric compositions, (which, indeed, are not numerous,) he speaks in terms of disparagement which may lead us to wonder that they should have been admitted; nor can we forbear to repeat a hint which we formerly ventured to give this youthful writer,—

that a little more deference for the public, and a greater sensibility towards his own permanent fame, would be useful in directing the efforts of his genius [see excerpt above, 1796]. (pp. 297-98)

The volume begins with a piece of some length, intitled *The Triumph of Woman.* . . . It is an elegant and pleasing composition, though perhaps less spirited than the subject would seem to demand. The joyous affections do not appear to be those that are most congenial to the writer's mind. (p. 298)

It can scarcely be necessary for us, after . . . the general view that we have given, formally to recommend this volume to the notice of our poetical readers, and its author to their esteem. Genius is a despotic power, and irresistibly commands homage. (p. 302)

> [*John Aikin*], "Southey's 'Poems'," *in* The Monthly Review, *London, Vol. XIX, April, 1796, pp. 297-302.*

THE BRITISH CRITIC (essay date 1801)

The process of *writing himself down* is [in *Thalaba the Destroyer*] fully performed by Mr. Southey, if it be allowed that he had ever written himself up. A more complete monument of vile and depraved taste no man ever raised. In his Preface he has the absurdity to speak of the verse of Dryden and Pope, that is, the English heroic couplet, in the following ridiculous terms: "Verse is not enough favoured by the English reader; perhaps this is owing to the obtrusiveness, the regular *Jews-harp twing twang,* of what has been foolishly called heroic measure." He has, therefore, given a rhapsody of Twelve Books in a sort of irregular lyric, so unlike verse or sense, that if it were worth while to present our readers with a tissue of so coarse a texture, we could fill whole pages with specimens of its absurdity. We will have mercy, and give only a single example, which may be taken at random, for no part seems to be better than the rest.

> In the eve he arrived at a well,
> The acacia bent over its side,
> Under whose long light-hanging boughs
> He chose his night's abode.
> There due ablutions made and prayers performed,
> The youth his mantle spread,
> And silently produced
> His solitary meal.
> The silence and the solitude recalled
> Dear recollection; and with folded arms
> Thinking of other days, he sate, till thought
> Had left him, and the acacia's moving shade
> Upon the funny sand
> Had caught his idle eye,
> And his awakened ear,
> Heard the grey Lizard's chirp,
> The only sound of life. . . .

This is really *chirping like a Lizard!*—and the writer of this wretched stuff has the vanity to censure the approved verse of his country; this unharmonious stuff—which, were not the lines divided by the printer, no living creature would suspect to be even intended for verse; for this execrable performance, loaded with notes, often brought in without necessity, often as nonsensical as the text itself, the purchaser is modestly required to pay 14s. We can only say that, if fourteen copies are sold, and thirteen of the buyers do not repent their bargain, the world is more foolish than we could imagine. The work may be characterized in five words, "Tales of Terror, run mad." (pp. 309-10)

> *A review of "Thalaba the Destroyer," in* The British Critic, *Vol. XVIII, September, 1801, pp. 309-10.*

THE MONTHLY MAGAZINE LONDON (essay date 1802)

To those who have been long accustomed to the swing of rime and the see-saw of couplets, the irregular verse, or measured prose, in which [*Thalaba*] is composed, will appear to have been adopted rather for the accommodation of the writer than of the reader—rather to elude the abecedary drudgery of spelling *ban, can, dan, fan, &c. bare, care, dare, fare, &c.* till the desiderated syllable arrives, than to invite from the second gate of the palace of pleasure a new charmer of the ear. . . . But those who delight in the narrative odes of Pindar, or the descriptive odes of Stolberg, will perceive that ages have sanctioned and nations have admired a similar structure of metre.

The fable or story of *Thalaba* is perhaps too marvellous: every incident is a miracle; every utensil, an amulet; every speech, a spell; every personage, a god; or rather a talismanic statue; of which destiny and magic overrule the movements, not human hopes and fears—not human desires and passions, which always must excite the vivid sympathy of men. It offers, however, scope beyond other metrical romances, for a splendid variety of description, which . . . shifts, with the cameleon capriciousness of lyric inspiration, and with the versatile instantaneity of pantomime scenery, from the blasted wilderness, to caverns of flame; from bowers of paradise, to cities of jewelry; from deserts of snow, to aromatic isles; and from the crush of worlds, to the bliss of heaven. As in shuffling tarocco-cards, figures, motley, new, and strange, causing palpitation, dance before the eye, and thwart the anxious grasp; so here portentous and alarming forms glare on the wonder, without enabling the spectator to form any guess about their approaching influence over the play, by an speculation of probability. Whatever loss of interest this poem may sustain, as a whole, by an apparent driftlessness of the events and characters, is compensated by the busy variety, the picturesque imagery, and striking originality of the parts. . . . (pp. 581-82)

> *A review of "Thalaba, a Metrical Romance," in* The Monthly Magazine, *London, Vol. XII, No. 82, January 20, 1802, pp. 581-84.*

[FRANCIS JEFFREY] (essay date 1802)

[Jeffrey was a founder and editor (1803-1829) of the Edinburgh Review, *one of the most influential magazines in early nineteenth-century England. A liberal Whig and a politician, Jeffrey often allowed his political beliefs to color his critical opinions. Here, Jeffrey attacks the Lake School of poetry and lists what he considers its unappealing traits. He criticizes the poets' "affectation of great simplicity and familiarity of language," and he calls Southey's taste "perverted." Though Jeffrey's* Thalaba *enraged Southey, his treatment of him as a major representative of a new poetic movement brought Southey further into the public eye. Most scholars believe that it is because of Jeffrey's association of Southey with the Lake School that he came to be known as a Lake Poet.]*

[Mr. Southey] belongs to a *sect* of poets [the Lake Poets], that has established itself in this country within these ten or twelve years, and is looked upon, we believe, as one of its chief champions and apostles. The peculiar doctrines of this sect, it

would not, perhaps, be very easy to explain; but, that they are *dissenters* from the established systems in poetry and criticism is admitted, and proved, indeed, by the whole tenor of their compositions. Though they lay claim, we believe, to a creed and a revelation of their own, there can be little doubt, that their doctrines are of *German* origin, and have been derived from some of the great modern reformers in that country. Some of their leading principles, indeed, are probably of an earlier date, and seem to have been borrowed from the great apostle of Geneva. As Mr Southey is the first author, of this persuasion, that has yet been brought before us for judgment, we cannot discharge our inquisitorial office conscientiously, without premising a few words upon the nature and tendency of the tenets he has helped to promulgate.

The disciples of this school boast much of its originality, and seem to value themselves very highly, for having broken loose from the bondage of ancient authority, and re-asserted the independence of genius. Originality, however, we are persuaded, is rarer than mere alteration; and a man may change a good master for a bad one, without finding himself at all nearer to independence. That our new poets have abandoned the old models, may certainly be admitted; but we have not been able to discover that they have yet created any models of their own; and are very much inclined to call in question the worthiness of those to which they have transferred their admiration. The productions of this school, we conceive, are so far from being entitled to the praise of originality, that they cannot be better characterised than by an enumeration of the sources from which their materials have been derived. The greatest part of them, we apprehend, will be found to be composed of the following elements: 1. The antisocial principles, and distempered sensibility of Rousseau—his discontent with the present constitution of society—his paradoxical morality, and his perpetual hankerings after some unattainable state of voluptuous virtue and perfection. 2. The simplicity and energy . . . of Kotzebue and Schiller. 3. The homeliness and harshness of some of Cowper's language and versification, interchanged occasionally with the *innocence* of Ambrose Philips, or the quaintness of Quarles and Dr Donne. (pp. 63-4)

[The Lake Poets] have, among them, unquestionably, a very considerable portion of poetical talent, and have, consequently, been enabled to seduce many into an admiration of the false taste (as it appears to us) in which most of these productions are composed. They constitute, at present, the most formidable conspiracy that has lately been formed against sound judgment in matters poetical; and are entitled to a larger share of our censorial notice, than could be spared for an individual delinquent. (p. 64)

Their most distinguishing symbol is undoubtedly an affectation of great simplicity and familiarity of language. They disdain to make use of the common poetic phraseology, or to ennoble their diction by a selection of fine or dignified expressions. There would be too much *art* in this, for that great love of nature with which they are all of them inspired; and their sentiments, they are determined, shall be indebted, for their effect, to nothing but their intrinsic tenderness or elevation. There is something very noble and conscientious, we will confess, in this plan of composition; but the misfortune is, that there are passages in all poems that can neither be pathetic nor sublime; and that, on these occasions, a neglect of the establishments of language is very apt to produce absolute meanness and insipidity. (pp. 64-5)

The followers of simplicity are . . . at all times in danger of occasional degradation; but the simplicity of this new school seems intended to ensure it. *Their* simplicity does not consist, by any means, in the rejection of glaring or superfluous ornament,—in the substitution of elegance to splendour,—or in that refinement of art which seeks concealment in its own perfection. It consists, on the contrary, in a very great degree, in the positive . . . rejection of art altogether, and in the bold use of those rude and negligent expressions, which would be banished by a little discrimination. (p. 65)

In making these strictures on the perverted taste for simplicity, that seems to distinguish our modern school of poetry, we have no particular allusion to Mr Southey, or [*Thalaba,*]: On the contrary, he appears to us to be less addicted to this fault than most of his fraternity. . . . (p. 68)

At the same time, it is impossible to deny that the author of the '**English Eclogues**' is liable to a similar censure; and few persons, we believe, will peruse the following verses (taken, almost at random, from the *Thalaba*) without acknowledging that he still continues to deserve it.

> At midnight Thalaba started up,
> For he felt that the ring on his finger was moved.
> He called on Allah aloud,
> And he called on the Prophet's name.
> Moath arose in alarm:
> "What ails thee, Thalaba?" he cried,
> "Is the robber of night at hand?"
>
> "Dost thou not see," the youth exclaimed,
> "A Spirit in the tent?"
> Moath looked round, and said,
> "The moon-beam shines in the tent,
> I see thee stand in the light,
> And thy shadow is black on the ground."
> Thalaba answered not.
> "Spirit!" he cried, "what brings thee here?" &c.
>
> (pp. 68-9)

Now, this style, we conceive, possesses no one character of excellence; it is feeble, low, and disjointed; without elegance, and without dignity; the offspring, we should imagine, of mere indolence and neglect, or the unhappy fruit of a system that would teach us to undervalue that vigilance and labour which sustained the loftiness of Milton, and gave energy and direction to the pointed and fine propriety of Pope.

The *style* of our modern poets, is that, no doubt, by which they are most easily distinguished; but their genius has also an internal character; and the peculiarities of their taste may be discovered, without the assistance of their diction. Next after great familiarity of language, there is nothing that appears to them so meritorious as perpetual exaggeration of thought. There must be nothing moderate, natural, or easy, about their sentiments. . . . [All] their characters must be in agonies and ecstasies, from their entrance to their exit. To those who are acquainted with their productions, it is needless to speak of the fatigue that is produced by this unceasing summons to admiration, or of the compassion which is excited by the spectacle of these eternal strainings and distortions. Those authors appear to forget, that a whole poem cannot be made up of striking passages; and that the sensations produced by sublimity, are never so powerful and entire, as when they are allowed to subside and revive, in a slow and spontaneous succession. It is delightful, now and then, to meet with a rugged mountain, or a roaring stream; but where there is no sunny slope, nor

shaded plain, to relieve them—where all is beetling cliff and yawning abyss, and the landscape presents nothing on every side but prodigies and terrors—the head is apt to grow giddy, and the heart to languish for the repose and security of a less elevated region. (pp. 69-70)

The first thing that strikes the reader of *Thalaba* is the singular structure of the versification, which is a jumble of all the measures that are known in English poetry, (and a few more), without rhyme, and without any sort of regularity in their arrangement. Blank odes have been known in this country about as long as English sapphics and dactylics; and both have been considered, we believe, as a species of monsters, or exotics, that were not very likely to propagate, or thrive, in so unpropitious a climate. Mr Southey, however, has made a vigorous effort for their naturalization, and generously endangered his own reputation in their behalf. The melancholy fate of his English sapphics, we believe, is but too generally known; and we can scarcely predict a more favourable issue to the present experiment. Every combination of different measures is apt to perplex and disturb the reader who is not familiar with it; and we are never reconciled to a stanza of a new structure, till we have accustomed our ear to it by two or three repetitions. This is the case, even where we have the assistance of rhyme to direct us in our search after regularity, and where the definite form and appearance of a stanza assures us that regularity is to be found. Where both of these are wanting, it may be imagined that our condition will be still more deplorable; and a compassionate author might even excuse us, if we were unable to distinguish this kind of verse from prose. In reading verse, in general, we are guided to the discovery of its melody, by a sort of preconception of its cadence and compass; without which, it might often fail to be suggested by the mere articulation of the syllables. (p. 72)

The subject of [*Thalaba*] is almost as ill chosen as the diction; and the conduct of the fable as disorderly as the versification. (p. 74)

[*Thalaba*] consists altogether of the most wild and extravagant fictions, and openly sets nature and probability at defiance. In its action, it is not an imitation of any thing; and excludes all rational criticism, as to the choice and succession of its incidents. (p. 75)

Though the tissue of adventures through which Thalaba is conducted in the course of this production, be sufficiently various and extraordinary, we must not set down any part of the incidents to the credit of the author's invention. He has taken great pains, indeed, to guard against such a supposition; and has been as scrupulously correct in the citation of his authorities, as if he were the compiler of a true history, and thought his reputation would be ruined by the imputation of a single fiction. There is not a prodigy, accordingly, or a description, for which he does not fairly produce his vouchers, and generally lays before his readers the whole original passage from which his imitation has been taken. In this way it turns out, that the book is entirely composed of scraps, borrowed from the oriental tale-book, and travels into the Mahometan countries, seasoned up for the English reader with some fragments of our own ballads, and shreds of our older sermons. The composition and harmony of the work, accordingly, is much like the pattern of that patch-work drapery that is sometimes to be met with in the mansions of the industrious, where a blue tree overshadows a shell-fish, and a gigantic butterfly seems ready to swallow up Palemon and Lavinia. The author has the merit merely of cutting out each of his figures from the piece where its inventor had placed it, and stitching them down together in these judicious combinations.

It is impossible to peruse this poem, with the notes, without feeling that it is the fruit of much reading, undertaken for the express purpose of fabricating some such performance. The author has set out with a resolution to make an oriental story, and a determination to find the materials of it in the books to which he had access. Every incident, therefore, and description,—every superstitious usage, or singular tradition, that appeared to him susceptible of poetical embellishment, or capable of picturesque representation, he has set down for this purpose, and adopted such a fable and plan of composition, as might enable him to work up all his materials, and interweave every one of his quotations, without any *extraordinary* violation of unity or order. When he had filled his common-place book, he began to write; and his poem is little else than his common-place book versified.

It may easily be imagined, that a poem constructed upon such a plan, must be full of cumbrous and misplaced description, and overloaded with a crowd of incidents, equally unmeaning and ill assorted. The tedious account of the palace of Shedad, in the first book—the description of the Summer and Winter occupations of the Arabs in the third—the ill-told story of Haruth and Maruth—the greater part of the occurrences in the island of Mohareb—the paradise of Aloadin, &c. &c.—are all instances of disproportioned and injudicious ornaments, which never could have presented themselves to an author who wrote from the suggestions of his own fancy; and have evidently been introduced, from the author's unwillingness to relinquish the corresponding passages in D'Herbelot, Sale, Volney, &c. which appeared to him to have great capabilities for poetry.

This imitation, or admiration of Oriental imagery, however, does not bring so much suspicion on his taste, as the affection he betrays for some of his domestic models. The former has, for the most part, the recommendation of novelty; and there is always a certain pleasure in contemplating the *costume* of a distant nation, and the luxuriant landscape of an Asiatic climate. We cannot find the same apology, however, for Mr Southey's partiality to the drawling vulgarity of some of our old English ditties. (pp. 77-8)

[From the] observations which we have hitherto presented to our readers, it will be natural for them to conclude that our opinion of this poem is very decidedly unfavourable; and that we are not disposed to allow it any sort of merit. This, however, is by no means the case. We think it written, indeed, in a very vicious taste, and liable, upon the whole, to very formidable objections: But it would not be doing justice to the genius of the author, if we were not to add, that it contains passages of very singular beauty and force, and displays a richness of poetical conception, that would do honour to more faultless compositions. There is little of human character in the poem, indeed; because Thalaba is a solitary wanderer from the solitary tent of his protector: But the home-group, in which his infancy was spent, is pleasingly delineated; and there is something irresistibly interesting in the innocent love, and misfortunes, and fate of his Oneiza. (pp. 79-80)

All the productions of [Southey], it appears to us, bear very distinctly the impression of an amiable mind, a cultivated fancy, and a perverted taste. His genius seems naturally to delight in the representation of domestic virtues and pleasures, and the brilliant delineation of external nature. In both these departments, he is frequently very successful, but he seems to want

vigour for the loftier flights of poetry. He is often puerile, diffuse, and artificial, and seems to have but little acquaintance with those chaster and severer graces, by whom the epic muse would be most suitably attended. His faults are always aggravated, and often created, by his partiality for the peculiar manner of that new school of poetry, of which he is a faithful disciple, and to the glory of which he has sacrificed greater talents and acquisitions, than can be boasted of by any of his associates. (p. 83)

> [*Francis Jeffrey*], *"Southey's 'Thalaba',"* in The Edinburgh Review, *Vol. I, No. I, October, 1802, pp. 63-83.*

WILLIAM WORDSWORTH   (letter date 1805)

[*An English poet and critic, Wordsworth was central to English Romanticism. His literary criticism reflects his belief that neither the language nor the content of poetry should be stylized or elaborate and that the purpose of the poet was to feel and express the relation between man and nature. As a close friend and contemporary of Southey, Wordsworth encouraged him in his writing and expressed admiration for his work. In the following letter, Wordsworth concedes that* Madoc *"fails in the highest gifts of the poet's mind . . . ," but praises Southey's descriptive talents.*]

We have read **Madoc** and been highly pleased with it; it abounds in beautiful pictures and descriptions happily introduced, and there is an animation diffused through the whole story though it cannot perhaps be said that any of the characters interest you much, except perhaps young Llewellyn whose situation is highly interesting, and he appears to me the best conceived and sustained character in the piece. His speech to his Uncle at their meeting in the Island is particularly interesting. The Poem fails in the highest gifts of the poet's mind Imagination in the true sense of the word, and knowledge of human Nature and the human heart. There is nothing that shows the hand of the great Master: but the beauties in description are innumerable; for instance that of the figure of the Bard towards the beginning of the convention of the bards, receiving the poetic inspiration, that of the wife of Tlalalu the Savage going out to meet her husband; that of Madoc and the Aztecan King with the long name preparing for battle, everywhere, indeed, you have beautiful descriptions, and it is a work which does the Author high credit. . . . (p. 595)

> *William Wordsworth, in a letter to Sir George Beaumont on June 3, 1805, in* The Letters of William and Dorothy Wordsworth, the Early Years: 1787-1805, *Vol. I by William Wordsworth and Dorothy Wordsworth, edited by Ernest De Selincourt and Chester L. Shaver, Oxford at the Clarendon Press, Oxford, 1967, pp. 593-95.*

THE ECLECTIC REVIEW   (essay date 1805)

The leading character of [*Madoc*] is *horror*. It presents a hyperbolical description of the manners and superstitions of the wildest savages in the wildest parts of America, long before Europe had planted her standard among them. We have piles of skulls—skulls for drinking bowls—beads of human hearts incased with gold, and hung round the necks of chiefs and heroes. One of [Mr. Southey's] heroes, Coanocotzin, hangs up the skeleton of his enemy, a neighbouring prince, and makes it hold a lamp, in the hall where he sups and revels. Others of his heroes strip off the skins of the slain, and dance before us, as they wear them, all dropping with blood. Others make their drums out of them. Of cannibals, and human sacrifices, we are sickened almost in every page. (pp. 900-01)

Almost the first thing, that struck us as a defect in the poem, is the author's unfortunate selection of names. But, Aelgyvarch, Gwynon, Gwynodil, Goervyl, (for a *lady*!), Coanocotzin, and Yuhidthiton, though they may be truly Welch or American, are hardly more poetical than [Jonathan Swift's] Brobdignag, or [Henry Carey's] Chrononhotonthologos. We are sorry to observe, in this, as in most of Mr. S.'s performances, expressions which border closely on impiety. . . .

Before we quit the subject of verbal criticism, we remark an absurd partiality for crowding in technical terms and phrases, especially naval and military terms. (p. 902)

Mr. S. seems to be enamoured of any thing either very old, or very new-fashioned, so that it be only out of the common way. . . . As compound epithets, we have "the-every-where" and "the-for-ever-one," "dwindling our all-too-few;" and an orator is called a "mouth-piece." . . .

We have, in other places, *yeugh*, for yew; to *belate*, for to benight; *wonderment*, for wonder; *attent*, for attention; *desperate*, for despairing (*desperate of their country's weal*); *guidage*, for guidance; and many other things, for—we know not what. Mr. S. at other times, is enamoured of alliterations, with sundry nameless fopperies and singularities. . . . (p. 903)

But let us take a more comprehensive view of the forty and five chapters into which Mr. S. has distributed a myriad of *wild and wonderous* verses. [*Madoc*] is grossly improbable; for, of such an important expedition as that of first colonising a new world, would no more traces have reached us, than a few worse than Rabbinical traditions? In *conducting* his fable, Mr. S. has *judiciously*, though not in the most *modest* way, disclaimed the title of epic. The manners, and minor historical facts, are most barbarously romantic. At so much snake-worship; so much human sacrifice; at such diabolical painting of savages; and such deification of a marauder, possibly almost as savage as the Indians themselves; at such eulogia on human nature in one case, and such libels on it in the other, we turn away disgusted. . . . The poem closes with an act of the most premeditated suicide by an American chief; a very favourite catastrophe with modern poets: and the hero, Madoc, being thus delivered from his last implacable foe, is left with his followers, in peaceable possession of a domain, which the natives had been miraculously deterred from attempting to recover. (p. 904)

[We dismiss *Madoc*] with our sincere wishes that Mr. S. would no longer disgrace the talents and genius, which he evidently possesses, by an affectation of singularity which is so much beneath him. . . . If he tells us, that antiquated, obsolete language suits an ancient story, why did he not write in Welsh? His unpardonable *innovations* upon his native language, in giving us words and expressions never heard of before, deserve the severest reprehension. His story is considerably too long, and is too much deficient in incident and character, to be interesting. There are some good things in it: but he would do well to reflect, that a diamond among rubbish does not always repay the search. We cannot, therefore, advise our readers to expend their two guineas on this volume. . . . (p. 908)

> "Southey's 'Madoc'," in The Eclectic Review, December, 1805, pp. 899-908.

ROBERT SOUTHEY   (letter date 1806)

[*In the following letter, Southey defends himself against charges made by a reviewer of* Madoc *that his poetic diction is faulty. Though* Thalaba *may not be perfect, Southey states,* Madoc *contains "not a single instance of illegitimate English."*]

Thalaba is faulty in its language. *Madoc* is not. I am become what they call a Puritan in Portugal, with respect to language, and I dare assert, that there is not a single instance of illegitimate English in the whole poem. The faults are in the management of the story and the conclusion, where the interest is injudiciously transferred from Madoc to Yuhidthiton; it is also another fault, to have rendered *accidents* subservient to the catastrophe. . . . I acknowledge no fault in the execution of any magnitude, except the struggle of the women with Amalahta, which is all clumsily done, and must be rewritten. Those faults which are inherent in and inseparable from the story, as they could not be helped, so are they to be considered as defects or *wants* rather than faults. I mean the division of the poem into two separate stories and scenes, and the inferior interest of the voyage, though a thing of such consequence. But as for unwarrantable liberties of language—there is not a solitary sin of the kind in the whole 9,000 lines. Let me be understood: I call it an unwarrantable liberty to use a verb deponent, for instance, actively, or to form any compound contrary to the strict analogy of the language—such as *tameless* in *Thalaba*, applied to the tigress. I do not recollect any coinage in *Madoc* except the word *deicide;* and that such a word exists I have no doubt, though I cannot lay my finger upon an authority, for depend upon it the Jews have been called so a thousand times. That word is unobjectionable. It is in strict analogy—its meaning is immediately obvious, and no other word could have expressed the same meaning. Archaisms are faulty if they are too obsolete. *Thewes* is the only one I recollect; that also has a peculiar meaning, for which there is no equivalent word. But, in short, so very laboriously was *Madoc,* rewritten and corrected, time after time, that I will pledge myself, if you ask me in any instance why one word stands in the place of another which you, perhaps, may think the better one, to give you a reason . . . which will convince you that I had previously weighed both in the balance. Sir, the language and versification of that poem are as full of profound mysteries as [the English satirist Samuel Butler]; and he, I take it, was as full of profundity as the great deep itself.

I do not know any one who has understood the main merit of [*Madoc*] so nearly as I wished it to be understood as yourself: the true and intrinsic greatness of Madoc, the real talents of his enemies, and (which I consider as the main work of skill) the feeling of respect for them;—of love even for the individuals, yet with an abhorrence of the *national* cruelties that perfectly reconcile you to their dreadful overthrow. (pp. 8-10)

> *Robert Southey, in a letter to Grosvenor C. Bedford on January 1, 1806, in his* The Life and Correspondence of Robert Southey, Vol. III, *edited by Rev. Charles Cuthbert Southey, Longman, Brown, Green, and Longmans, 1850, pp. 8-10.*

LORD BYRON   (essay date 1809)

[*Byron was an English poet and dramatist who is now considered one of the most important poets of the nineteenth century. Because of the satiric nature of much of his work, Byron is difficult to place within the Romantic movement. His most notable contribution to Romanticism is the Byronic hero: a melancholy man, often with a dark past, who eschews societal and religious stric-*

tures and seeks truth and happiness in an apparently meaningless universe. Byron composed his full-length satirical poem English Bards and Scotch Reviewers *after his first volume of poetry,* Hours of Idleness, *was harshly attacked in the* Edinburgh Review. *English Bards and Scotch Reviewers is considered accomplished and witty, though unjustly vicious in its treatment of authors and critics alike. The following section on Southey, though berating the fantastic nature of his epics, does not contain the venom of Byron's later writings on the author (see excerpts below, 1819 and 1822). In fact, Byron's journal entry of 1813 (see excerpt below), indicates that he initially admired Southey's writing, especially his prose.*]

The time has been, when yet the Muse was young,
When Homer swept the lyre, and Maro sung,
An Epic scarce ten centuries could claim,
While awe-struck nations hailed the magic name:
The work of each immortal Bard appears
The single wonder of a thousand years.
Empires have mouldred from the face of earth.
Tongues have expired with those who gave them birth,
Without the glory such a strain can give,
As even in ruin bids the language live.
Not so with us, though minor Bards content,
On one great work a life of labour spent;
With eagle pinion soaring to the skies,
Behold the Ballad-monger Southey rise!
To him let Camoens, Milton, Tasso, yield,
Whose annual strains, like armies, take the field.
First in the rank see Joan of Arc advance,
The scourge of England, and the boast of France!
Though burnt by wicked Bedford for a witch,
Behold her statue placed in Glory's niche;
Her fetters burst, and just released from prison,
A virgin Phoenix from her ashes risen.
Next see tremendous Thalaba come on,
Arabia's monstrous, wild, and wond'rous son;
Domdaniel's dread destroyer, who o'erthrew
More mad magicians then the world e'er knew.
Immortal Hero! all thy foes o'ercome,
For ever reign—the rival of Tom Thumb!
Since startled metre fled before thy face,
Well wert thou doomed the last of all thy race!
Well might triumphant Genii bear thee hence,
Illustrious conqueror of common sense!
Now, last and greatest, Madoc spreads his sails,
Cacique in Mexico, and Prince in Wales;
Tells us strange tales, as other travellers do,
More old than Mandeville's, and not so true.
Oh! Southey, Southey! cease thy varied song!
A Bard may chaunt too often and too long:
As thou art strong in verse, in mercy spare!
A fourth, alas! were more than we could bear.
But if, in spite of all the world can say,
Thou still wilt verseward plod thy weary way;
If still in Berkley Ballads most uncivil,
Thou wilt devote old women to the devil,
The babe unborn thy dread intent may rue:
"God help thee," Southey, and thy readers too.

(pp. 14-18)

> *Lord Byron, in an extract from his* English Bards, and Scotch Reviewers: A Satire, *1809. Reprinted by James Cawthorn, 1810, pp. 14-18.*

THE ECLECTIC REVIEW   (essay date 1810)

[The exploits of the adventures in *The History of Brazil*], and the incidents connected with them, by no means merited so

accurate and minute a delineation, as Mr. S. has thought proper to furnish. We do not mean to say that he has written a dull or an useless book; but his success would unquestionably have been far more splendid, had the subject been equal to his talents. It is no slight proof, indeed, of his genius, that he has been able so completely to carry his reader's attention through such a train of unimportant and monotonous details, and compel them to afford him so much delight.

As far as the knowledge subservient to research on this subject can be considered of importance, it may be safely affirmed, perhaps, that no one among his countrymen was nearly so well qualified as Mr. Southey, by an acquaintance with the Portuguese language and literature, for writing a history of Brazil. The work before us affords abundant evidence that he has not been sparing of his labour in the accumulation of facts. The most authentic sources, at least as far as printed books, and not these alone, extend, were open to his inspection, and have been carefully explored. No fact, we are satisfied, which could greatly interest the inquirer in the history of the formation of the settlements in Brazil, has escaped his research. To say this, is to pronounce no ordinary panegyric; and yet we see no indication, in the present work, that Mr. Southey was endowed with the most important qualities of a great historian. The comprehensive views of the great philosopher do not appear to predominate in his mind. We are far from presuming to say that he is not intitled to rank, and rank highly, among enlightened men. But with his good intentions, with his industry, and his talent for composition, we could wish that his depth and originality of thinking were still more conspicuous.

The subject Mr. Southey has undertaken, did not call, perhaps, for many very important exertions of thought; and for that very reason it might not have been selected by a man of greater powers. But of those occasions which it did present, we do not think that Mr. Southey has made the most advantage. Amidst all the details, for example, respecting tribes of savages with which the work abounds, no assistance is offered to the reader in generalizing the phaenomena of savage life; scarcely any in tracing the causes of the peculiarities among different tribes, of which his narrative makes mention; no attempt is made to illustrate the springs of human nature, as exhibited in those unfavourable circumstances; to trace the points of agreement and diversity between this the most unhappy state of society, and that which is presented at all the different stages of civilization. Had Mr. Southey avoided those lengthened statements and explanations, which a full treatment of the subject would have required (though they would have been more instructive and more interesting, too, than so much repetition of the details respecting the particular tribes), comprehensive reflections drawn from a profound insight into the subject, however shortly expressed, would have thrown a light upon his pages, for which the work at present contains nothing to compensate. (pp. 789-90)

Many of the situations in this history are very striking, and are well described by Mr. Southey. His style of narrative is simple, and sometimes even approaching the colloquial familiarity, but never vulgar; and well supplied the want of dignity and ornament by its liveliness and variety. Quaint expressions occasionally present themselves, but not obtrusively; nor are these blemishes very general. We do not imagine that much labour has been employed in putting the materials of the work into form. They are disposed, however, with considerable skill; and though few parts of the book are so wrought up as to produce a very lasting impression, the whole is read with untired attention. (pp. 796-97)

To sum up our opinion of [*The History of Brazil*], we do not think it is either a very splendid or very profound production. The state of knowledge respecting the regions and the history of the American continent, is, it must be confessed, so imperfect, that there is scarcely any man who will not derive instruction from a perusal of the present work. But after all, the settlements in Brazil were far from deserving so many fine paragraphs. And though a considerable portion of the inferences to which the facts here related give occasion, are no less true with regard to a great part of the Spanish conquests than to the Portuguese, yet the history of Brazil is still an obscure and subordinate portion of the history of America; and when once the history of America, or of the Spanish part of it, shall be well written, little will remain to attract notice or yield instruction in the history of Brazil. (p. 800)

"Southey's 'History of Brazil'," in The Eclectic Review, Vol. VI, September, 1810, pp. 788-800.

[JOHN FOSTER]   (essay date 1811)

[We] think the two mortal sins of [*The Curse of Kehama* are] absurdity and irreverence. . . . There is not any thing that can properly be called *characters* in the work. Kehama is a personage so monstrous, that nothing extravagant could be said to be out of character in him. There is much ability evinced in giving Ladurlad more of what we can sympathize with, more of purely *human* dignity, amiableness, and distress, than would have been supposed practicable in a representation of human beings under such strange and impossible circumstances. We need not say one word more of the wonderful power of description, displayed in every part of the poem. It appears with unabated vigour in the concluding canto or section, which exhibits Padalon, the Hindoo hell. This exhibition, however, has a kind of coarse hideousness, which would be very remote from any thing awful or sublime, even if it included much less of the clumsy, uncouth monstrosity of the Hindoo fables; and if the measureless power and terrors of Kehama, and his making himself into eight terrible gods, did not appear so insipidly and irksomely foolish. There is too much sameness of fire, steel, and adamant; and there is in the whole scene a certain flaring *nearness*, which allows no retirement of the imagination into wide, and dubious, and mysterious terrors. This puts it in unfortunate contrast with the infernal world of Milton, and the difference is somewhat like that between walking amidst a burning town, and in a region of volcanoes. We must not bring even into thought, any sort of comparison between the display of mind in Milton's infernal personages and those of Padalon.

The general diction of [*The Curse of Kehama*] is admirably strong, and various, and free; and, in going through it, we have repeatedly exulted in the capabilities of the English language. The author seems to have in a great measure grown out of that affected simplicity of expression, of which he has generally been accused. The versification, as to measure and rhyme, is a complete defiance of all rule, and all example; the lines are of any length, from four syllables to fourteen; there are sometimes rhymes and sometimes none; and they have no settled order of recurrence. This is objectionable, chiefly, as it allows the poet to riot away in a wild wantonness of amplification, and at the very same time imposes on him the petty care of having the lines so printed, as to put the letter-press in the form of a well adjusted picture. (pp. 349-50)

[*John Foster*], *"Southey's 'Curse of Kehama',"* in The Eclectic Review, Vol. VII, April, 1811, pp. 334-50.

LITERARY PANORAMA   (essay date 1811)

[*The following essay was originally published as an unsigned review in the* Literary Panorama *in June 1811.*]

Mr. S. was determined to produce something extraordinary [with *The Curse of Kehama*], and something extraordinary he has produced. His poetry affords the finest possible scenery and subjects for the pencil of art: in fact it is a series of shifting pictures. But to do them justice demands conceptions of immense magnificence; colours of superlative brilliancy; a canvas of endless extent:—in fact, a PANORAMA. If any ask for a moral,—it is to be found, we suppose, in the immortality of woe which ingulphs Kehama, the vicious tyrant: while to the suffering but virtuous Kailyal, and the tormented but undismayed and indefatigable Ladurlad, are assigned an immortality of bliss.

If we were desired to name a poet whose command of language enables him to express in the most suitable and energetic terms the images which agitate his mind, we should name Mr. Southey: if we were requested to point out a poem which to a freedom of manner in the construction of its stanzas, united a condensation of phrase, with a happy collocation of words, thereby producing force, we should recommend *Kehama;*—it contains lines never excelled for vigour, or surpassed in rhythm. Its descriptions are so charming, or so powerful, so delightful, or so tremendous, that we are engrossed by the incident under our perusal, and willingly endeavour to suspend our recollection of the incongruities by which it was introduced or to which it leads. *They* may be too shocking to our faith, or too abhorrent from our knowledge, to be tolerated, while *this* may repay our rivetted attention with delight. (p. 146)

Mr. Southey's *Thalaba* proved his acquaintance with the manners of Arabia, and the genius of the Arab poets; his *Madoc* brought before us, the feelings, the superstitions, and the natural objects of the new world: having exhausted earth, he has now had recourse to heaven and hell:—where will be his next adventure? we, for our parts, could wish that he would 'homeward bend his weary way,' and treat us with a subject in which the sympathy of the human heart, the interior of man, may afford a scope to the powers of his genius; a triumph worthy of immortality to his art and his talents. (p. 147)

An extract from a review of "Kehama," in Robert Southey: The Critical Heritage, *edited by Lionel Madden, Routledge & Kegan Paul, 1972, pp. 146-47.*

THE BRITISH CRITIC   (essay date 1813)

Mr. Southey's idea of a *Life of Nelson* so exactly corresponds with our own, that we subjoin his concise, but satisfactory description of the impression under which he compiled it, adding as our opinion, that all that was undertaken has been successfully accomplished.

> Many lives of Nelson have been written: one is yet wanting, clear and concise enough to become a manual for the young sailor, which he may carry about with him, till he has treasured up the example in his memory and in his heart. In attempting such a work, I shall write the eulogy of our great naval Hero; for the best eulogy of Nelson is the faithful history of his actions: the best history, that which shall relate them most perspicuously. . . .

The reader therefore is here presented with a plain narrative of events and actions which, though familiar to us all, we are all delighted to peruse again. The history is, beyond all question, faithful. The great and splendid achievments of the Hero are detailed with vigour, accompanied with a circumstantial attention to the incidents and anecdotes which they involve. His defects and follies, for alas the greatest, the wisest, and the best, have their proportion of these, are neither overlooked nor descanted upon with unbecoming severity. The great error of all, the unfortunate and unjustifiable infatuation in favour of Lady Hamilton, to the prejudice of the natural and legitimate claim on his affection and his honour, is introduced with much feeling and delicacy. That other momentous deviation also from the path of rectitude which took place in the Bay of Naples, equally discreditable to Nelson's prudence, honour, and humanity, is introduced with some, though not quite its due share of animadversion. (p. 360)

If we have not protracted this article by animadverting upon many of the compiler's private and political opinions, Mr. Southey must not think that they were either unobserved, or approved. In the first place, they do not often obtrude themselves, and whether the part which the English government took at the commencement of the French revolution, was as this writer thinks, "a miserable error," or whether, as many politicians, as sound and as wise as Mr. Southey, believe it to have been, not only judicious, but unavoidable; it can hardly, at this period, be worth while to argue. We are, on the whole, exceedingly well pleased with the performance, and think it admirably adapted to answer the purpose for which it was intended. (p. 366)

> "*Southey's 'Life of Nelson*'," *in* The British Critic, *Vol. XLIII, October, 1813, pp. 360-66.*

LORD BYRON   (journal date 1813)

[*The following excerpt from Byron's journal indicates that he at one time admired Southey's talent despite his earlier, negative comments in* English Bards and Scotch Reviewers *and his later, venomous writings (see excerpts above, 1809, and below, 1819, 1822). Here Byron describes* The Life of Nelson *as "beautiful" and states that Southey's "prose is perfect."*]

Southey, I have not seen much of. His appearance is *Epic;* and he is the only existing entire man of letters. All the others have some pursuit annexed to their authorship. His manners are mild, but not those of a man of the world, and his talents of the first order. His prose is perfect. Of his poetry there are various opinions: there is, perhaps, too much of it for the present generation; posterity will probably select. He has *passages* equal to any thing. At present, he has *a party,* but no *public*—except for his prose writings. The *Life of Nelson* is beautiful.

> *Lord Byron, in an extract from a journal entry on November 22, 1813, in* Robert Southey: The Critical Heritage, *edited by Lionel Madden, Routledge & Kegan Paul, 1972, p. 157.*

[JOHN HERMAN MERIVALE]   (essay date 1815)

[We have no scruple in declaring our opinion that Mr. Southey's *Roderick, the Last of the Goths*] will contribute to the advancement of the author's legitimate fame more largely than any of his former poems. Its principal faults are that it is too long by half, too declamatory, and consequently often cold

and spiritless where it ought to be most impassioned, and that it is incumbered by a pervading affectation of scriptural phraseology:—but these defects are counterbalanced by a well chosen subject, happily suited to the prevailing enthusiasm of the author's mind in favour of Spanish liberty, by a deep tone of moral and religious feeling, by an exalted spirit of patriotism, by fine touches of character, by animated descriptions of natural scenery, (the effect of which is often injured, however, by a too great minuteness of detail,) and by an *occasional* excellence of versification worthy of the best and purest age of English poetry. We are sorry to be obliged to qualify this praise by repeating that it applies to the work before us only in part, the remainder being mere prose, divided off into feet, and not unfrequently by a very blundering measure. (pp. 226-27)

[To the plan of the poem, we have something] to object. The minor personages are too frequently introduced, and made too prominent, considering the very little diversity that is thrown into their characters and circumstances. Alphonso, for instance, is an ardent young soldier, with nothing to distinguish him from that very numerous tribe, and he conduces no more to the interest of the drama than any one individual patriot in the whole host of Pelayo's adherents; yet he is brought almost as much forward on the canvas as Pelayo himself. Roderick's mother also acts a very poor though a long part, considering the importance attached to her . . . ;—it would have been much better to have killed her before the period of Roderick's emigration from his cell. The nature of Roderick's crime renders the subject peculiarly difficult to manage, with a view to the interest which it is necessary to attach to his character; and yet almost any deviation from the generally received historical fact is certain of being attended with a greater or less degree of incongruity. We do not think that Mr. Southey's plan of representing it as the effect of a vehement (though in its origin a virtuous) passion, returned with the most devoted affection by the unfortunate object of it, but wrought to a temporary delirium by the force of conflicting circumstances, is by any means exempt from this charge; and, whatever effect may in some respects be thus obtained, it is at least attended with this faulty consequence, that the despair and penitence of Roderick, almost unexampled in severity and duration, are thus made to bear no proportion to an offence in which, extenuated as it now appears, the will can scarcely be said to have had any part. It also makes the vengeance of Julian for a fault not only in great measure reparable, but which the perpetrator had the most ardent wish to repair as far as it was possible, little less than diabolical, and the conduct of the lady, by her outrageous virtue actuating that vengeance, much more than mischievously perverse. In short, according to our way of contemplating it, Mr. Southey has sacrificed all the moral, as well as the actual, probability of the story to the design of extenuating the fault of his hero, when in fact the strength of the subject consists in the very enormity of the crime. (pp. 239-40)

> [*John Herman Merivale*], *in a review of "Roderick, the Last of the Goths," in* The Monthly Review, *London, Vol. LXXVI, March, 1815, pp. 225-40.*

[JOHN TAYLOR COLERIDGE]   (essay date 1815)

[Mr. Southey's] name is one, which, we confess, we dwell on with peculiar pleasure; in all the ranks of contemporary literature, there is none more honourably, or more enviably distinguished. Whether considered as a biographer, historian, or poet, it will be found that his writings breathe uniformly the same excellent spirit, and are calculated to produce the same good effect. Whatever be their fate or popularity now, (and this depends so much on whim and fashion, that we venture on no predictions,) from them all he will hereafter derive a higher praise than that which is due to the mere exhibition of talent; for they display a pure singleness of heart, actively disposed to benevolence and justice; and their tendency is to encourage in each sex of our fellow-citizens their appropriate virtues—to make our men bold, honest, and affectionate, and our women meek, tender, and true. (pp. 353-54)

Mr. Southey is eminently a moral writer; to the high purpose implied in this title [*Roderick, the Last of the Goths*], the melody of his numbers, the clear rapidity of his style, the pathetic power which he exercises over our feelings, and the interesting manner of telling his story, whether in verse or prose, are all merely contributive. It would therefore be no less useful than pleasant, if we had time, or opportunity, or if we could do the subject justice, to contemplate him rising independently and virtuously from small beginnings; in many temptations, and under many difficulties, still cherishing the pure light that was within him; always fearless and full of cheerful hope; never pausing for a moment to decide between faulty indulgence and self-denying sacrifice; sometimes ridiculed and despised, sometimes condemned or forgotten, yet ever self-justified, and in the end rewarded. He now stands extorting respect from the scorner, and honourable acquittal from the judge;—from the world he receives fame, and is blessed with more intense affection from those who watched his progress with anxiety, but never doubted of his final success. (pp. 354-55)

The subject [of *Roderick, the Last of the Goths*] is the foundation of the Spanish monarchy in the mountainous province of Asturia on the overthrow of the Moorish invaders; its hero is Roderick, the last of the Gothic dynasty. The name of this personage is already familiar to our readers, from the spirited poem of Walter Scott, which bears it for its title, but they are not to expect the same character. Nothing can be more different; though both, we believe, are founded on sufficient authority for all the purposes of poetry; in the one case, without any palliation for his fault, we are presented with a semi-barbarian chief, struggling with remorse, and beat by circumstances, rather than by conviction, to an unwilling and ineffectual repentance. . . . Mr. Southey's Don Roderick, on the other hand, is a man, who with some excuse to plead for a guilty act, is yet so overpowered by its fatal consequences, and so properly sensible of its own foulness, that all the energies of a powerful mind become directed to a sincere effectual penitence, and to compensation for the evils of which he has been the author. In this light we look upon him as new among the heroes of poetry; had Spenser written the poem, he would have been the hero of the Legend of Penitence; in the course of it, without forgetting the frailty of human nature, is displayed one constant triumph of principle over the most besetting temptations; and before it ends, there is not a turbulent, unruly feeling of an ill regulated mind, that is not subdued into "the perfect peace, the peace of Heaven."

There are some of our readers, whom such a declaration will alarm; they are so accustomed to divest poetry of its moral, that when they hear of a hero with grey locks in a friar's gown, they will apprehend that the poem is but a sermon in blank verse. Courage, however, *chers enfans* [dear children]; here is plenty of sword and dagger, war-horse and chariot, a bugle or two, some little love, several beauties, and even a marriage in *prospectu* [prospective], with all other ingredients of a "charm-

ing poem.'' If any one doat so desperately on "love and glory," that this does not content him, we are very sorry, but we cannot honestly recommend Don Roderick to his attention. (pp. 355-56)

> [John Taylor Coleridge], *"Southey's 'Roderick, the Last of the Goths',"* in The British Critic, *n.s. Vol. III, April, 1815, pp. 353-89.*

WILLIAM HONE   (essay date 1817)

[*Hone's notice indicates the generally negative reaction to the unauthorized publication of Southey's poem* Wat Tyler. *Hone stresses that the quality of Southey's artistic output diminished considerably from the time of his appointment as Poet Laureate. Reviews such as the following, which was originally published on February 22, 1817 in* Reformists' Register and Weekly Commentary, *did much to influence public opinion against Southey.*]

Wat Tyler is attributed by the *Morning Chronicle*, to no less a person than the Poet Laureate, one Mr. Robert Southey, a gentleman of credit and renown, and, until he became Poet Laureate, a Poet. The present poem appears to have been written many years ago, when Mr. Southey had not merely reforming opinions, but very wild notions indeed. In consideration of a Court pension, he now regularly inflames his muse, in praise of official persons and business, at certain periods throughout the year, as precisely stated and rehearsed in verse, as the days whereon his pension is made payable and receivable. His present muse, however, is no more like to that which he formerly courted, than the black doll at an old rag shop is like Petrarch's Laura. Poor Southey! a pensioned Laureate! compelled to sing like a blind linnet by a sly pinch, with every now and then a volume of his old verses flying into his face, and putting him out!

> *William Hone, in an extract from* Robert Southey: The Critical Heritage, *edited by Lionel Madden, Routledge & Kegan Paul, 1972, p. 232.*

LITERARY GAZETTE   (essay date 1817)

[*The following essay, which was originally published in the* Literary Gazette *on March 29, 1817, was one of the few which defended* Wat Tyler.]

Sarah, Duchess of Marlborough, having an electioneering object to carry against Lord Grimstone, got into her possession the manuscript of a foolish play, called *Love in a Hollow Tree,* written by that noble man when a boy at school. This comedy she published and circulated with great industry, and at a considerable expense, for the purpose of covering her opponent with ridicule; but all that her Grace gained by the vindictive manoeuvre was the raising a laugh against his Lordship and herself. The artifice of the Duchess, however, was a harmless piece of pleasantry, compared with the rancorous malevolence or wicked cupidity of those persons who have, contrary to all honour and honesty, sent the poem of *Wat Tyler* into the world, without the consent of the author. Whether their intention has been to hold him up to public ridicule, or to put money into their own pockets, at his expense, the inference drawn by every liberal mind will be equally decisive in reprobating the nefarious transaction. But if this conduct be so reprehensible, what apology can be made for those legislators (we speak without the slightest reference to party, with which we have nothing to do, and for which we feel only contempt,) who, forgetful of their intimate connexion with the laws and constitution of the country, have dragged this surreptitious piece into their political debates, with the view of wounding the feelings of the author still more severely, and of aggravating an injury which was already sufficiently enormous. (pp. 240-41)

> *A review of "Wat Tyler," in* Robert Southey: The Critical Heritage, *edited by Lionel Madden, Routledge & Kegan Paul, 1972, pp. 240-41.*

S[AMUEL] T[AYLOR] COLERIDGE (essay date 1817)

[*An English poet and critic, Coleridge was central to the English Romantic movement. Besides his poetry, his most important contributions include his formulation of Romantic theory, his introduction of the ideas of the German Romantics to England, and his Shakespearean criticism, which overthrew the last remnants of the Neoclassical approach to Shakespeare and focused on Shakespeare as a portrayer of human nature. As Southey's first literary partner and lifelong friend, Coleridge is an especially noteworthy commentator on his achievements. In the following excerpt from his* Biographia Literaria, *originally published in 1817, Coleridge assesses Southey both as a friend and colleague. Unlike Southey's detractors, Coleridge declares that no other literary or historical figure is as accomplished as Southey.*]

[By what have Southey's works] been characterized, each more strikingly than the preceding, but by greater splendor, a deeper pathos, profounder reflections, and a more sustained dignity of language and of metre? Distant may the period be, but whenever the time shall come, when all his works shall be collected by some editor worthy to be his biographer, I trust that an excerpta of all the passages, in which his writings, name, and character have been attacked, from the pamphlets and periodical works of the last twenty years, may be an accompaniment. Yet that it would prove medicinal in after times I dare not hope; for as long as there are readers to be delighted with calumny, there will be found reviewers to calumniate. (p. 40)

I have in imagination transferred to the future biographer the duty of contrasting Southey's fixed and well-earned fame, with the abuse and indefatigable hostility of his anonymous critics from his early youth to his ripest manhood. But I cannot think so ill of human nature as not to believe, that these critics have already taken shame to themselves, whether they consider the object of their abuse in his moral or his literary character. For reflect but on the variety and extent of his acquirements! He stands second to no man, either as an historian or as a bibliographer; and when I regard him as a popular essayist, (for the articles of his compositions in the reviews are for the greater part essays on subjects of deep or curious interest rather than criticisms on particular works) I look in vain for any writer, who has conveyed so much information, from so many and such recondite sources, with so many just and original reflections, in a style so lively and poignant, yet so uniformly classical and perspicuous; no one in short who has combined so much wisdom with so much wit; so much truth and knowledge with so much life and fancy. His prose is always intelligible and always entertaining. In poetry he has attempted almost every species of composition known before, and he has added new ones; and if we except the highest lyric, (in which how few, how very few even of the greatest minds have been fortunate) he has attempted every species successfully: from the political song of the day, thrown off in the playful overflow of honest joy and patriotic exultation, to the wild ballad; from epistolary ease and graceful narrative, to the austere and impetuous moral declaration; from the pastoral claims and wild

streaming lights of the "**Thalaba,**" in which sentiment and imagery have given permanence even to the excitement of curiosity; and from the full blaze of the "**Kehama,**" (a gallery of finished pictures in one splendid fancy piece, in which, notwithstanding, the moral grandeur rises gradually above the brilliance of the colouring and the boldness and novelty of the machinery) to the more sober beauties of the "**Madoc**"; and lastly, from the "**Madoc**" to his "**Roderic,**" in which, retaining all his former excellencies of a poet eminently inventive and picturesque, he has surpassed himself in language and metre, in the construction of the whole, and in the splendour of particular passages. (pp. 45-6)

Publicly has Mr. Southey been reviled by men, who, (as I would fain hope for the honor of human nature) hurled firebrands against a figure of their own imagination, publicly have his talents been depreciated, his principles denounced; as publicly do I therefore, who have known him intimately, deem it my duty to leave recorded, that it is Southey's almost unexampled felicity, to possess the best gifts of talent and genius free from all their characteristic defects. . . . That scheme of head, heart, and habitual demeanour, which in his early manhood, and first controversial writings, Milton, claiming the privilege of self-defence, asserts of himself, and challenges his calumniators to disprove; this will his school-mates, his fellow-collegians, and his maturer friends, with a confidence proportioned to the intimacy of their knowledge, bear witness to, as again realized in the life of Robert Southey. But still more striking to those, who by biography or by their own experience are familiar with the general habits of genius, will appear the poet's matchless industry and perseverance in his pursuits; the worthiness and dignity of those pursuits; his generous submission to tasks of transitory interest, or such as *his* genius alone could make otherwise; and that having thus more than satisfied the claims of affection or prudence, he should yet have made for himself time and power, to achieve more, and in more various departments than almost any other writer has done, though employed wholly on subjects of his own choice and ambition. But as Southey possesses, and is not possessed by, his genius, even so is he master even of his virtues. The regular and methodical tenor of his daily labours, which would be deemed rare in the most mechanical pursuits, and might be envied by the mere man of business, loses all semblance of formality in the dignified simplicity of his manners, in the spring and healthful chearfulness of his spirits. . . . As son, brother, husband, father, master, friend, he moves with firm yet light steps, alike unostentatious, and alike exemplary. As a writer, he has uniformly made his talents subservient to the best interests of humanity, of public virtue, and domestic piety; his cause has ever been the cause of pure religion and of liberty, of national independence and of national illumination. When future critics shall weigh out his guerdon of praise and censure, it will be Southey the poet only, that will supply them with the scanty materials for the latter. They will likewise not fail to record, that as no man was ever a more constant friend, never had poet more friends and honorers among the good of all parties; and that quacks in education, quacks in politics, and quacks in criticism were his only enemies. (pp. 47-9)

> *S. T. Coleridge, "The Author's Obligations to Critics and the Probable Occasion—Principles of Modern Criticism—Mr. Southey's Works and Character," in his* Biographia Literaria, Vol. I, *edited by J. Shawcross, Oxford University Press, 1958, pp. 34-49.*

LORD BYRON   (poem date 1819)

[*In this preface to his* Don Juan, *first published in 1819, Byron details his disgust with Southey's appointment as Poet Laureate of England. Byron expresses not only his resentment of Southey's newly conservative political stance, but further dismisses Southey's "trash of phrase" as "ineffably, legitimately vile." This indictment is much harsher than Byron's early writings on Southey (1809 and 1813), and foreshadows his final condemnation of Southey (see excerpt below, 1822). T. S. Eliot called this preface "one of the most exhilarating pieces of abuse in the language."*]

Bob Southey! You're a poet, poet laureate,
   And representative of all the race.
Although 'tis true that you turned out a Tory at
   Last, yours has lately been a common case.
And now my epic renegade, what are ye at
   With all the lakers, in and out of place?
A nest of tuneful persons, to my eye
Like 'four and twenty blackbirds in a pye,

'Which pye being opened they began to sing'
   (This old song and new simile holds good),
'A dainty dish to set before the King'
   Or Regent, who admires such kind of food.
And Coleridge too has lately taken wing,
   But like a hawk encumbered with his hood,
Explaining metaphysics to the nation.
I wish he would explain his explanation.

You, Bob, are rather insolent, you know,
   At being disappointed in your wish
To supersede all warblers here below,
   And be the only blackbird in the dish.
And then you overstrain yourself, or so,
   And tumble downward like the flying fish
Gasping on deck, because you soar too high, Bob,
And fall for lack of moisture quite a dry Bob.

And Wordsworth in a rather long *Excursion*
   (I think the quarto holds five hundred pages)
Has given a sample from the vasty version
   Of his new system to perplex the sages.
'Tis poetry, at least by his assertion,
   And may appear so when the Dog Star rages,
And he who understands it would be able
To add a story to the tower of Babel.

You gentlemen, by dint of long seclusion
   From better company, have kept your own
At Keswick, and through still continued fusion
   Of one another's minds at last have grown
To deem, as a most logical conclusion,
   That poesy has wreaths for you alone.
There is a narrowness in such a notion.
Which makes me wish you'd change your lakes for
     ocean.

I would not imitate the petty thought,
   Nor coin my self-love to so base a vice,
For all the glory your conversion brought,
   Since gold alone should not have been its price.
You have your salary; was't for that you wrought?
   And Wordsworth has his place in the Excise.
You're shabby fellows—true—but poets still
And duly seated on the immortal hill.

Your bays may hide the baldness of your brows,
   Perhaps some virtuous blushes; let them go.
To you I envy neither fruit nor boughs,
   And for the fame you would engross below,
The field is universal and allows
   Scope to all such as feel the inherent glow.
Scott, Rogers, Campbell, Moore, and Crabbe will try
'Gainst you the question with posterity.

For me, who, wandering with pedestrian Muses,
   Contend not with you on the wingèd steed,
I wish your fate may yield ye, when she chooses,
   The fame you envy and the skill you need.
And recollect a poet nothing loses
   In giving to his brethren their full meed
Of merit, and complaint of present days
Is not the certain path to future praise.

He that reserves his laurels for posterity
   (Who does not often claim the bright reversion)
Has generally no great crop to spare it, he
   Being only injured by his own assertion.
And although here and there some glorious rarity
   Arise like Titan from the sea's immersion,
The major part of such appellants go
To—God knows where—for no one else can know.

If fallen in evil days on evil tongues,
   Milton appealed to the avenger, Time,
If Time, the avenger, execrates his wrongs
   And makes the word *Miltonic* mean *sublime*,
He deigned not to belie his soul in songs,
   Nor turn his very talent to a crime.
He did not loathe the sire to laud the son,
But closed the tyrant-hater he begun.

Think'st thou, could he, the blind old man, arise
   Like Samuel from the grave to freeze once more
The blood of monarchs with his prophecies,
   Or be alive again—again all hoar
With time and trials, and those helpless eyes
   And heartless daughters—worn and pale and poor,
Would he adore a sultan? He obey
The intellectual eunuch Castlereagh?

Cold-blooded, smooth-faced, placid miscreant!
   Dabbling its sleek young hands in Erin's gore,
And thus for wider carnage taught to pant,
   Transferred to gorge upon a sister shore,
The vulgarest tool that tyranny could want,
   With just enough of talent and no more,
To lengthen fetters by another fixed
And offer poison long already mixed.

An orator of such set trash of phrase,
   Ineffably, legitimately vile,
That even its grossest flatterers dare not praise,
   Nor foes—all nations—condescend to smile.
Not even a sprightly blunder's spark can blaze
   From that Ixion grindstone's ceaseless toil,
That turns and turns to give the world a notion
Of endless torments and perpetual motion.

A bungler even in its disgusting trade,
   And botching, patching, leaving still behind
Something of which its masters are afraid,
   States to be curbed and thoughts to be confined,

Conspiracy or congress to be made,
   Cobbling at manacles for all mankind,
A tinkering slave-maker, who mends old chains,
   With God and man's abhorrence for its gains.

If we may judge of matter by the mind,
   Emasculated to the marrow, it
Hath but two objects, how to serve and bind,
   Deeming the chain it wears even men may fit,
Eutropius of its many masters, blind
   To worth as freedom, wisdom as to wit,
Fearless, because no feeling dwells in ice;
Its very courage stagnates to a vice.

Where shall I turn me not to view its bonds,
   For I will never feel them. Italy,
Thy late reviving Roman soul desponds
   Beneath the lie this state-thing breathed o'er thee.
Thy clanking chain and Erin's yet green wounds
   Have voices, tongues to cry aloud for me.
Europe has slaves, allies, kings, armies still,
And Southey lives to sing them very ill.

Meantime, Sir Laureate, I proceed to dedicate
   In honest simple verse this song to you.
And if in flattering strains I do not predicate,
   'Tis that I still retain my buff and blue;
My politics as yet are all to educate.
   Apostasy's so fashionable too,
To keep *one* creed's a task grown quite Herculean.
Is it not so, my Tory, ultra-Julian?

(pp. 41-5)

Lord Byron, in a dedication to his Don Juan, *T. G. Steffan, E. Steffan, W. W. Pratt, eds., Penguin Books, 1978, pp. 41-5.*

QUEVEDO REDIVIVUS [PSEUDONYM OF LORD BYRON] (essay date 1822)

[*The following is taken from Byron's preface to his "Vision of Judgment" and from the poem itself, which he composed after Southey prefaced his poem of the same name with a harsh indictment of Byron as a member of the "Satanic School of Poetry." Southey's poem, which depicts the triumphant ascent of King George III to heaven, was largely regarded by critics as an inappropriate and awkward failure, and Byron parodied its faults in his own "Vision of Judgment." Byron's poem condemns Southey's lack of ability and judgment, and it is the belief of most critics that the satire is more successful than its model. This is considered the culmination of Byron's varied critical commentary on Southey (see excerpts above, 1809, 1813, and 1819).*]

It hath been wisely said, that "One fool makes many;" and it hath been poetically observed,

   That fools rush in where angels fear to tread.
—*Pope.*

If Mr. Southey had not rushed in where he had no business, and where he never was before, and never will be again, ["The Vision of Judgment"] would not have been written. It is not impossible that it may be as good as his own ["**Vision of Judgment**"], seeing that it cannot, by any species of stupidity, natural or acquired, be *worse*. The gross flattery, the dull impudence, the renegado intolerance and impious cant of the poem by the author of "**Wat Tyler,**" are something so stupendous as to form the sublime of himself—containing the quintessence of his own attributes. (pp. i-ii)

If there is any thing obnoxious to the political opinions of a portion of the public, in the following poem, they may thank Mr. Southey. He might have written hexameters, as he has written every thing else, for aught that the writer cared—had they been upon another subject. But to attempt to canonize a Monarch, who, whatever were his household virtues, was neither a successful nor a patriot king,—inasmuch as several years of his reign passed in war with America and Ireland, to say nothing of the aggression upon France,—like all other exaggeration, necessarily begets opposition. In whatever manner he may be spoken of in this new "Vision," his *public* career will not be more favourably transmitted by history. Of his private virtues (although a little expensive to the nation) there can be no doubt. (p. iii)

He had written praises of a regicide;
   He had written praises of all kings whatever;
He had written for republics far and wide,
   And then against them bitterer than ever;
For pantisocracy he once had cried
   Aloud, a scheme less moral than 'twas clever;
Then grew a hearty antijacobin—
Had turn'd his coat—and would have turn'd his skin.

He had sung against all battles, and again
   In their high praise and glory; he had call'd
Reviewing "the ungentle craft," and then
   Become as base a critic as ere crawl'd—
Fed, paid, and pamper'd by the very men
   By whom his muse and morals had been maul'd:
He had written much blank verse, and blanker prose,
And more of both than any body knows.

(pp. 35-6)

Quevedo Redivivus [pseudonym of Lord Byron], "'*The Vision of Judgment*'," *in* The Liberal, *Vol. I, No. 1, 1822, pp. i-39.*

[JOHN GIBSON LOCKHART] (essay date 1824)

[*Lockhart, a Scottish critic and novelist, wrote several novels, but his fame rests on his biography of Sir Walter Scott and his critical contributions to* Blackwood's Edinburgh Magazine *and the* Quarterly Review. *He is regarded as a versatile, if somewhat severe, critic whose opinions of his contemporaries, though lacking depth, are generally considered accurate when not distorted by political animosities. Lockhart had few kind words for Southey. While he admits in the following review that* The Life of Nelson *is a masterpiece, he considers all Southey's other works failures. To Lockhart, Southey's works are both unreadable and pretentious. In particular, he cites Southey's* Life of Wesley *as an overly ponderous work and charges that Southey wrote such books only to flaunt his own knowledge. Lockhart comments further on Southey in an excerpt below (1834).*]

The worthy Laureate is one of those men of distinguished talents and industry, who have not attained to the praise or the influence of intellectual greatness, only because they have been so unfortunate as to come too late into the world. Had Southey flourished forty or fifty years ago, and written half as well as he has written in our time, he might have ranked . . . with the first of modern critics, of modern historians, perhaps even of modern poets. The warmth of his feelings and the flow of his style would have enabled him to throw all the prosers of that day into the shade—His extensive erudition would have won him the veneration of an age in which erudition was venerable—His imaginative power would have lifted him like an eagle over the versifiers who then amused the public with their feeble echoes of the wit, the sense, and the numbers of Pope. He could not have been the Man of the Age; but, taking all his manifold excellencies and qualifications into account, he must have been most assuredly *Somebody*, and a great deal more than somebody.

How different is his actual case! As a poet, as an author of imaginative works in general, how small is the space he covers, how little is he talked or thought of! The Established Church of Poetry will hear of nobody but Scott, Byron, Campbell: and the Lake Methodists themselves will scarcely permit him to be called a burning and a shining light in the same day with their Wordsworth—even their Coleridge. In point of fact, he himself is now the only man who ever alludes to Southey's poems. We can suppose youngish readers starting when they come upon some note of his in the *Quarterly,* or in these new books of history, referring to ''*the Madoc,*'' or ''*the Joan,*'' as to something universally known and familiar. As to criticism and politics of the day, he is but one of the *Quarterly* reviewers, and scarcely one of the most influential of them. He puts forth essays half antiquarianism, half prosing, with now and then a dash of a sweet enough sort of literary mysticism in them— and more frequently a display of pompous self-complacent simplicity, enough to call a smile into the most iron physiognomy that ever grinned. But these lucubrations produce no effect upon the spirit of the time. A man would as soon take his opinions from his grandmother as from the Doctor. The whole thing looks as if it were made on purpose to be read to some antediluvian village club—The fat parson—the solemn leech—the gaping schoolmaster, and three or four simpering Tabbies. There is nothing in common to him and the people of this world. We love him—we respect him—we admire his diligence, his acquisitions, his excellent manner of keeping his note-books—If he were in orders, and one had an advowson to dispose of, one could not but think of him. But good, honest, worthy man, only to hear him telling of his opinion of Napoleon Buonaparte!—and then the quotations from Coleridge, Wordsworth, Lamb, Landor, Withers, old Fuller, and all the rest of his favourites—and the little wise-looking maxims, every one of them as old as the back of Skiddaw—and the delicate little gleams of pathos—and the little family-stories and allusions— and all the little parentheses of exultation—well, we really wonder after all, that the Laureate is not more popular.

The first time Mr Southey attempted regular historical composition he succeeded admirably. His *Life of Nelson* is truly a masterpiece;—a brief—animated—glowing—straightforward—manly English work, in two volumes duodecimo. That book will be read three hundred years hence by every boy that is nursed on English ground.—All his bulky historical works are, comparatively speaking, failures. His *History of Brazil* is the most unreadable production of our time. Two or three elephant quartos about a single Portugueze colony! Every little colonel, captain, bishop, friar, discussed at as much length as if they were so many Cromwells or Loyolas—and why?—just for this one simple reason, that Dr Southey is an excellent Portugueze scholar, and has an excellent Portugueze library. The whole affair breathes of one sentiment, and but one— Behold, O British Public! what a fine thing it is to understand this tongue—fall down, and worship me! I am a member of the Lisbon Academy, and yet I was born in Bristol, and am now living at Keswick.

This inordinate vanity is an admirable condiment in a small work, and when the subject is really possessed of a strong interest. It makes one read with more earnestness of attention

and sympathy. But carried to this height, and exhibited in such a book as this, it is utter nonsense. It is carrying the joke a great deal too far.—People do at last, however good-natured, get weary of seeing a respectable man *walking* his hobby-horse.

Melancholy to say, the **History of the Peninsular War** is, in spite of an intensely interesting theme, and copious materials of real value, little better than another Caucasus of lumber, after all. If the campaigns of Buonaparte were written in the same style, they would make a book in thirty or forty quarto volumes, of 700 pages each. He is overlaying the thing completely—he is smothering the Duke of Wellington. The underwood has increased, is increasing, and ought without delay to be smashed. Do we want to hear the legendary history of every Catholic saint, who happens to have been buried or worshipped near the scene of some of General Hill's skirmishes? What, in the devil's name, have we to do with all these old twelfth century miracles and visions, in the midst of a history of Arthur Duke of Wellington, and his British army? Does the Doctor mean to write his Grace's Indian campaigns in the same style, and to make them the pin whereon to hang all the wreck and rubbish of his commonplace book for **Kehama,** as he has here done with the odds and ends that he could not get stuffed into the notes on **Roderick** and [his translation of] **My Cid**? Southey should have lived in the days of 2000 page folios, triple columns, and double indexes—He would then have been set to a *corpus* [body] of something at once, and been happy for life. Never surely was such a mistake as for him to make his appearance in an age of restlessly vigorous thought, disdainful of originality of opinion, intolerance for longwindedness, and scorn of mountains in labour—Glaramara and Penmanmaur among the rest.

In all these greater histories, the Laureate has been much the worse for some unhappy notion he has got into his head, of writing *à la* Clarendon. Clarendon is one of the first English classics, and one of the first historical authors the world can boast; but nobody can deny that he is, nevertheless, a most prolix penman. . . . [Now, the Doctor] brings really but a slender image of the Chancellor's qualifications. He writes not about things and persons that he has seen, and if he did, he has extremely little insight into human character, and a turn of mind altogether different from that which is necessary for either transacting or comprehending the affairs of active life. He has the prolixity—without the graphic touches, the intense knowledge, the profound individual feeling, of a writer of memoirs. He reads five or six piles of old books, and picks up a hazy enough view of some odd character there, and then he thinks he is entitled to favour us with this view of his, at the same length which we could only have pardoned from some chosen friend, and life-long familiar associate of the hero himself.

Perhaps Southey's **Life of Wesley** is the most remarkable instance extant, of the ridiculous extremities to which vanity of this kind can carry a man of great talents and acquirements. Who but Southey would ever have dreamt that it was possible for a man that was not a Methodist, and that had never seen John Wesley's face, nor even conversed with any one of his disciples, to write two thumping volumes under the name of a **Life of Wesley** without turning the stomach of the Public? For whom did he really suppose he was writing this book? Men of calm sense and rational religion, were certainly not at all likely to take their notion of the Founder of the Methodists, from any man who could really suppose that Founder's life to be worthy of occupying one thousand pages of close print. The

Methodists themselves would, of course, be horrified with the very name of such a book, on such a subject, by one of the uninitiated. Probably, few of them have looked into it at all; and, most certainly, those that have done so, must have done so with continual pain, loathing, and disgust. But our friend, from the moment *he* takes up any subject, no matter what it is, seems to be quite certain, first, that that subject is the only one in the world worth writing about; and, secondly, that he is the only man who has any right to meddle with it. (pp. 208-10)

The truth is, that a real historian, either a Hume, or a Clarendon, or a Du Retz, or a Tacitus, would have found no difficulty in concentrating all that really can be said, to any purpose, about Wesley, Zinzendorf, Whitefield, and all the rest of these people, in, at the most, fifty pages. And then the world would have read the thing and been the better for it. At present, the Methodists stick to their own absurd Lives of Wesley and there exists no Life of him adapted for the purposes of the general reader, or composed with any reference to the ideas of any extensive body of educated men whatever.

Nevertheless, who will deny, that in these two thick volumes a great deal both of instruction and amusement is to be found? The hero being what he was, it was indeed quite impossible that this should be otherwise. And the complaint is not of the materials, nor of the manner in which the most interesting part of them is made use of, but of the wearisome mass of superfluous stuff with which the Laureate has contrived to overlay his admirable materials, and to make his fine passages the mere oases in a desert; and of that portentous garrulity, for the sake of indulging in which, he has *not* drawn the extraordinary man's character. (pp. 210-11)

> [*John Gibson Lockhart*], "*Southey's 'Life of Wesley','' in* Blackwood's Edinburgh Magazine, *Vol. XV, No. LXXXV, February, 1824, pp. 208-19.*

BLACKWOOD'S EDINBURGH MAGAZINE (essay date 1825)

We fear that Mr Southey has greatly over-rated the merits of ["**Tale of Paraguay**"], and that it is unworthy of his high genius and reputation. He takes his motto from Wordsworth—

> Go forth, my little book,
> Go forth, and please the gentle and the good.

Now, perhaps Mr Southey will not acknowledge those readers to be among "the gentle and the good," who are not pleased with his little book. For our own parts we have been pleased—considerably pleased with it—but our admiration of Mr Southey's powers cannot blind us to that which the whole world, himself excepted, will speedily pronounce to be a somewhat melancholy truth—namely, that the **"Tale of Paraguay"** is, with many paltry, and a few fine passages, an exceedingly poor poem, feeble alike in design and execution. (p. 370)

Undoubtedly there is a good deal in it to please—even to delight—"the gentle and the good." But it is a faint, feeble, and heavy composition; and the "gentle and the good" will act prudently in perusing it before night-fall; for if read late on in the evening, it will be apt to set the "gentle and the good" to sleep without a night-cap. (p. 377)

> "*Southey's 'Tale of Paraguay'," in* Blackwood's Edinburgh Magazine, *Vol. XVIII, No. CIV, September, 1825, pp. 370-77.*

[WILLIAM HAZLITT] (essay date 1825)

[*One of the most important commentators of the Romantic age, Hazlitt was an English critic and journalist. He is best known for his descriptive criticism in which he stressed that no motives beyond judgment and analysis are necessary on the part of the critic. A critic must start with a strong opinion, Hazlitt asserted, but he must also keep in mind that evaluation is the starting point—not the object—of criticism. The following essay originally appeared in 1825 in Hazlitt's* The Spirit of the Age; or, Contemporary Portraits, *which was published anonymously. In the excerpt below, Hazlitt praises Southey's "natural" prose style but concedes that he was not a great intellect; rather, his mind was "the recipient and transmitter of knowledge [rather] than the originator of it."*]

Mr. Southey's mind is essentially sanguine, even to over-weeningness. It is prophetic of good; it cordially embraces it; it casts a longing, lingering look after it, even when it is gone for ever. He cannot bear to give up the thought of happiness, his confidence in his fellowman, when all else despair. It is the very element, 'where he must live or have no life at all.' While he supposed it possible that a better form of society could be introduced than any that had hitherto existed, while the light of the French Revolution beamed into his soul (and long after, it was seen reflected on his brow, like the light of setting suns on the peak of some high mountain, or lonely range of clouds, floating in purer ether!) while he had this hope, this faith in man left, he cherished it with child-like simplicity, he clung to it with the fondness of a lover, he was an enthusiast, a fanatic, a leveller; he stuck at nothing that he thought would banish all pain and misery from the world—in his impatience of the smallest error or injustice, he would have sacrificed himself and the existing generation (a holocaust) to his devotion to the right cause. But when he once believed after many staggering doubts and painful struggles, that this was no longer possible, when his chimeras and golden dreams of human perfectibility vanished from him, he turned suddenly round, and maintained that 'whatever *is,* right.' Mr. Southey has not fortitude of mind, has not patience to think that evil is inseparable from the nature of things. His irritable sense rejects the alternative altogether, as a weak stomach rejects the food that is distasteful to it. He hopes on against hope, he believes in all unbelief. (p. 245)

[Not] truth, but self-opinion is the ruling principle of Mr. Southey's mind. The charm of novelty, the applause of the multitude, the sanction of power, the venerableness of antiquity, pique, resentment, the spirit of contradiction have a good deal to do with his preferences. His inquiries are partial and hasty: his conclusions raw and unconcocted, and with a considerable infusion of whim and humour and a monkish spleen. His opinions are like certain wines, warm and generous when new; but they will not keep, and soon turn flat or sour, for want of a stronger spirit of the understanding to give a body to them. . . . He is more the creature of impulse, than he is of reflection. He invents the unreal, he embellishes the false with the glosses of fancy, but pays little attention to 'the words of truth and soberness.' His impressions are accidental, immediate, personal, instead of being permanent and universal. Of all mortals he is surely the most impatient of contradiction, even when he has completely turned the tables on himself. Is not this very inconsistency the reason? Is he not tenacious of his opinions, in proportion as they are brittle and hastily formed? Is he not jealous of the grounds of his belief, because he fears they will not bear inspection, or is conscious he has shifted them? Does he not confine others to the strict line of orthodoxy, because he has himself taken every liberty? Is he not afraid to look to the right or the left, lest he should see the ghosts of his former extravagances staring him in the face? (pp. 245-46)

We must say that 'we relish Mr. Southey more in the Reformer' than in his lately acquired, but by no means natural or becoming character of poet-laureat and courtier. He may rest assured that a garland of wild flowers suits him better than the laureat-wreath: that his pastoral odes and popular inscriptions were far more adapted to his genius than his presentation-poems. He is nothing akin to birth-day suits and drawing-room fopperies. 'He is nothing, if not fantastical.' In his figure, in his move-ments, in his sentiments, he is sharp and angular, quaint and eccentric. Mr. Southey is not of the court, courtly. Every thing of him and about him is from the people. He is not classical, he is not legitimate. He is not a man cast in the mould of other men's opinions: he is not shaped on any model: he bows to no authority: he yields only to his own wayward peculiarities. He is wild, irregular, singular, extreme. He is no formalist, not he! All is crude and chaotic, self-opinionated, vain. He wants proportion, keeping, system, standard rules. . . . With him every thing is projecting, starting from its place, an episode, a digression, a poetic license. He does not move in any given orbit, but like a falling star, shoots from his sphere. He is pragmatical, restless, unfixed, full of experiments, beginning every thing a-new, wiser than his betters, judging for himself, dictating to others. He is decidedly *revolutionary*. He may have given up the reform of the State: but depend upon it, he has some other *hobby* of the same kind. Does he not dedicate to his present Majesty that extraordinary poem on the death of his father, called *The Vision of Judgment*, as a specimen of what might be done in English hexameters? In a court-poem all should be trite and on an approved model. He might as well have presented himself at the levee in a fancy or masquerade dress. Mr. Southey was not *to try conclusions* with Majesty—still less on such an occasion. The extreme freedoms with departed greatness, the party-petulance carried to the Throne of Grace, the unchecked indulgence of private humour, the assumption of infallibility and even of the voice of Heaven in this poem, are pointed instances of what we have said. . . . Look at Mr. Southey's larger poems, his *Kehama*, his *Thalaba*, his *Madoc*, his *Roderic*. Who will deny the spirit, the scope, the splendid imagery, the hurried and startling interest that pervades them? Who will say that they are not sustained on fictions wilder than his own Glendoveer, that they are not the daring creations of a mind curbed by no law, tamed by no fear, that they are not rather like the trances than the waking dreams of genius, that they are not the very paradoxes of poetry? All this is very well, very intelligible, and very harmless, if we regard the rank excrescences of Mr. Southey's poetry, like the red and blue flowers in corn, as the unweeded growth of a luxuriant and wandering fancy; or if we allow the yeasty work-ings of an ardent spirit to ferment and boil over—the variety, the boldness, the lively stimulus given to the mind may then atone for the violation of rules and the offences to bed-rid authority; but not if our poetic libertine sets up for a law-giver and judge, or an apprehender of vagrants in the regions either of taste or opinion. Our motley gentleman deserves the strait-waistcoat, if he is for setting others in the stocks of servility, or condemning them to the pillory for a new mode of rhyme or reason. Or if a composer of sacred Dramas on classic models, or a translator of an old Latin author (that will hardly bear translation) or a vamper-up of vapid cantos and Odes set to music, were to turn pander to prescription and palliater of every dull, incorrigible abuse, it would not be much to be wondered at or even regretted. But in Mr. Southey it was a lamentable

falling-off. It is indeed to be deplored, it is a strain on genius, a blow to humanity, that the author of *Joan of Arc*—that work in which the love of Liberty is exhaled like the breath of spring, mild, balmy, heaven-born, that is full of tears and virgin-sighs, and yearnings of affection after truth and good, gushing warm and crimsoned from the heart—should ever after turn to folly, or become the advocate of a rotten cause. After giving up his heart to that subject, he ought not (whatever others might do) ever to have set his foot within the threshold of a court. He might be sure that he would not gain forgiveness or favour by it, nor obtain a single cordial smile from greatness. All that Mr. Southey is or that he does best, is independent, sponta-neous, free as the vital air he draws—when he affects the courtier or the sophist, he is obliged to put a constraint upon himself, to hold in his breath, he loses his genius, and offers a violence to his nature. His characteristic faults are the excess of a lively, unguarded temperament. . . . We declare we think his former poetical scepticism was not only more amiable, but had more of the spirit of religion in it, implied a more heartfelt trust in nature and providence than his present bigotry. We are at the same time free to declare that we think his articles in the *Quarterly Review,* notwithstanding their virulence and the talent they display, have a tendency to qualify its most per-nicious effects. They have redeeming traits in them. 'A little leaven leaveneth the whole lump'; and the spirit of humanity (thanks to Mr. Southey) is not quite expelled from the *Quarterly Review.* At the corner of his pen, 'there hangs a vapourous drop profound' of independence and liberality, which falls upon its pages, and oozes out through the pores of the public mind. There is a fortunate difference between writers whose hearts are naturally callous to truth, and whose understandings are hermetically sealed against all impressions but those of self-interest, and a man like Mr. Southey. *Once a philanthropist and always a philanthropist.* No man can entirely baulk his nature: it breaks out in spite of him. In all those questions, where the spirit of contradiction does not interfere, on which he is not sore from old bruises, or sick from the extravagance of youthful intoxication, as from a last night's debauch, our 'laureate' is still bold, free, candid, open to conviction, a re-formist without knowing it. (pp. 246-49)

Mr. Southey's prose-style can scarcely be too much praised. It is plain, clear, pointed, familiar, perfectly modern in its texture, but with a grave and sparkling admixture of *archaisms* in its ornaments and occasional phraseology. He is the best and most natural prose-writer of any poet of the day; we mean that he is far better than Lord Byron, Mr. Wordsworth, or Mr. Coleridge, for instance. The manner is perhaps superior to the matter, that is, in his *Essays and Reviews.* There is rather a want of originality and even of *impetus:* but there is no want of playful or biting satire, of ingenuity, of casuistry, of learning and of information. He is 'full of wise saws and modern' (as well as ancient) 'instances.' Mr. Southey may not always con-vince his opponents; but he seldom fails to stagger, never to gall them. In a word, we may describe his style by saying that it has not the body or thickness of port wine, but is like clear sherry with kernels of old authors thrown into it!—He also excels as an historian and prose-translator. His histories abound in information, and exhibit proofs of the most indefatigable patience and industry. By no uncommon process of the mind, Mr. Southey seems willing to steady the extreme levity of his opinions and feelings by an appeal to facts. His translations of the Spanish and French romances are also executed *con amore* [with love], and with the literal fidelity and care of a mere linguist. (p. 250)

Mr. Southey's conversation has a little resemblance to a commonplace book; his habitual deportment to a piece of clockwork. He is not remarkable either as a reasoner or an observer: but he is quick, unaffected, replete with anecdote, various and retentive in his reading, and exceedingly happy in his play upon words, as most scholars are who give their minds this sportive turn. We have chiefly seen Mr. Southey in company where few people appear to advantage, we mean in that of Mr. Coleridge. He has not certainly the same range of speculation, nor the same flow of sounding words, but he makes up by the details of knowledge, and by a scrupulous correctness of statement for what he wants in originality of thought, or impetuous declamation. The tones of Mr. Coleridge's voice are eloquence: those of Mr. Southey are meagre, shrill, and dry. Mr. Coleridge's *forte* is conversation, and he is conscious of this: Mr. Southey evidently considers writing as his stronghold, and if gravelled in an argument, or at a loss for an explanation, refers to something he has written on the subject, or brings out his port-folio, doubled down in dog-ears, in confirmation of some fact. He is scholastic and professional in his ideas. He sets more value on what he writes than on what he says: he is perhaps prouder of his library than of his own productions—themselves a library! He is more simple in his manners than his friend Mr. Coleridge; but at the same time less cordial or conciliating. . . . Had [Southey] lived a century or two ago, he would have been a happy as well as blameless character. But the distraction of the time has unsettled him, and the multiplicity of his pretensions have jostled with each other. No man in our day (at least no man of genius) has led so uniformly and entirely the life of a scholar from boyhood to the present hour, devoting himself to learning with the enthusiasm of an early love, with the severity and constancy of a religious vow—and well would it have been for him if he had confined himself to this, and not undertaken to pull down or to patch up the State! However irregular in his opinions, Mr. Southey is constant, unremitting, mechanical in his studies, and the performance of his duties. . . . He passes from verse to prose, from history to poetry, from reading to writing, by a stopwatch. He writes a fair hand, without blots, sitting upright in his chair, leaves off when he comes to the bottom of the page, and changes the subject for another, as opposite as the Antipodes. His mind is after all rather the recipient and transmitter of knowledge, than the originator of it. He has hardly grasp of thought enough to arrive at any great leading truth. His passions do not amount to more than irritability. With some gall in his pen, and coldness in his manner, he has a great deal of kindness in his heart. Rash in his opinions, he is steady in his attachments—and is a man, in many particulars admirable, in all respectable—his political inconsistency alone excepted! (pp. 250-52)

[*William Hazlitt*], *"Mr. Southey," in his* Lectures on English Poets & The Spirit of the Age, *J. M. Dent & Sons, Ltd., 1910, pp. 244-52.*

[THOMAS BABINGTON MACAULAY]   (essay date 1830)

[*The following essay is the most extensive attack made upon Southey's social and economic ideas. In his vitriolic review of* Sir Thomas More; or, Colloquies on the Progress and Prospects of Society, *Macaulay, a noted historian and statesman, asserts that Southey is devoid of philosophical knowledge and understanding and that he is unqualified to write about many of his subjects. Macaulay later referred to Southey's concepts as "nonsense" and called him arrogant "beyond any man in literary history." William Maginn disputed Macaulay (see excerpt below, 1830).*]

It would be scarcely possible for a man of Mr Southey's talents and acquirements to write two volumes so large as [those which make up *Sir Thomas More; or Colloquies on the Progress and Prospects of Society*], which should be wholly destitute of information and amusement. Yet we do not remember to have read with so little satisfaction any equal quantity of matter, written by any man of real abilities. We have, for some time past, observed with great regret the strange infatuation which leads the Poet-laureate to abandon those departments of literature in which he might excel, and to lecture the public on sciences of which he has still the very alphabet to learn. He has now, we think, done his worst. The subject which he has at last undertaken to treat is one which demands all the highest intellectual and moral qualities of a philosophical statesman,—an understanding at once comprehensive and acute,—a heart at once upright and charitable. Mr Southey brings to the task two faculties which were never, we believe, vouchsafed in measure so copious to any human being,—the faculty of believing without a reason, and the faculty of hating without a provocation.

It is, indeed, most extraordinary that a mind like Mr Southey's,—a mind richly endowed in many respects by nature, and highly cultivated by study,—a mind which has exercised considerable influence on the most enlightened generation of the most enlightened people that ever existed—should be utterly destitute of the power of discerning truth from falsehood. Yet such is the fact. Government is to Mr Southey one of the fine arts. He judges of a theory or a public measure, of a religion, a political party, a peace or a war, as men judge of a picture or a statue, by the effect produced on his imagination. A chain of associations is to him what a chain of reasoning is to other men; and what he calls his opinions, are in fact merely his tastes. (p. 528)

[In] the mind of Mr Southey, reason has no place at all, as either leader or follower, as either sovereign or slave. He does not seem to know what an argument is. He never uses arguments himself. He never troubles himself to answer the arguments of his opponents. It has never occurred to him, that a man ought to be able to give some better account of the way in which he has arrived at his opinions than merely that it is his will and pleasure to hold them,—that there is a difference between assertion and demonstration,—that a rumour does not always prove a fact,—that a fact does not always prove a theory,—that two contradictory propositions cannot be undeniable truths,—that to beg the question, is not the way to settle it,—or that when an objection is raised, it ought to be met with something more convincing, than 'scoundrel' and 'blockhead.'

It would be absurd to read the works of such a writer for political instruction. The utmost that can be expected from any system promulgated by him is that it may be splendid and affecting,—that it may suggest sublime and pleasing images. His scheme of philosophy is a mere day-dream, a poetical creation, like the Domdaniel caverns, the Swerga, or Padalon; and indeed, it bears no inconsiderable resemblance to those gorgeous visions. Like them, it has something of invention, grandeur, and brilliancy. But like them, it is grotesque and extravagant, and perpetually violates that conventional probability which is essential to the effect even of works of art.

The warmest admirers of Mr Southey will scarcely, we think, deny that his success has almost always borne an inverse proportion to the degree in which his undertakings have required a logical head. His poems, taken in the mass, stand far higher than his prose works. The *Laureate Odes*, indeed, among which the *Vision of Judgment* must be classed, are, for the most part, worse than Pye's, and as bad as Cibber's; nor do we think him generally happy in short pieces. But his longer poems, though full of faults, are nevertheless very extraordinary productions. We doubt greatly whether they will be read fifty years hence,— but that if they are read, they will be admired, we have no doubt whatever.

But though in general we prefer Mr Southey's poetry to his prose, we must make one exception. The *Life of Nelson* is, beyond all doubt, the most perfect and the most delightful of his works. The fact is, as his poems most abundantly prove, that he is by no means so skilful in designing, as in filling up. It was therefore an advantage to him to be furnished with an outline of characters and events, and to have no other task to perform than that of touching the cold sketch into life. No writer, perhaps, ever lived, whose talents so precisely qualified him to write the history of the great naval warrior. There were no fine riddles of the human heart to read—no theories to found—no hidden causes to develope—no remote consequences to predict. The character of the hero lay on the surface. The exploits were brilliant and picturesque. The necessity of adhering to the real course of events saved Mr Southey from those faults which deform the original plan of almost every one of his poems, and which even his innumerable beauties of detail scarcely redeem. The subject did not require the exercise of those reasoning powers the want of which is the blemish of his prose. It would not be easy to find in all literary history, an instance of a more exact hit between wind and water. John Wesley, and the Peninsular War, were subjects of a very different kind,—subjects which required all the qualities of a philosophic historian. In Mr Southey's works on these subjects, he has, on the whole, failed. Yet there are charming specimens of the art of narration in both of them. The *Life of Wesley* will probably live. Defective as it is, it contains the only popular account of a most remarkable moral revolution, and of a man whose eloquence and logical acuteness might have rendered him eminent in literature, whose genius for government was not inferior to that of Richelieu, and who, whatever his errors may have been, devoted all his powers, in defiance of obloquy and derision, to what he sincerely considered as the highest good of his species. The *History of the Peninsular War* is already dead:—indeed, the second volume was dead-born. The glory of producing an imperishable record of that great conflict seems to be reserved for Colonel Napier.

The *Book of the Church* contains some stories very prettily told. The rest is mere rubbish. The adventure was manifestly one which could be achieved only by a profound thinker, and in which even a profound thinker might have failed, unless his passions had been kept under strict control. In all those works in which Mr Southey has completely abandoned narration, and undertaken to argue moral and political questions, his failure has been complete and ignominious. On such occasions, his writings are rescued from utter contempt and derision solely by the beauty and purity of the English. We find, we confess, so great a charm in Mr Southey's style, that, even when he writes nonsense, we generally read it with pleasure, except indeed when he tries to be droll. A more insufferable jester never existed. He very often attempts to be humorous, and yet we do not remember a single occasion on which he has succeeded farther than to be quaintly and flippantly dull. (pp. 529-31)

The extraordinary bitterness of spirit which Mr Southey manifests towards his opponents is, no doubt, in a great measure

to be attributed to the manner in which he forms his opinions. Differences of taste, it has often been remarked, produce greater exasperation than differences on points of science. But this is not all. A peculiar austerity marks almost all Mr Southey's judgments of men and actions. We are far from blaming him for fixing on a high standard of morals, and for applying that standard to every case. But rigour ought to be accompanied by discernment, and of discernment Mr Southey seems to be utterly destitute. His mode of judging is monkish; it is exactly what we should expect from a stern old Benedictine, who had been preserved from many ordinary frailties by the restraints of his situation. No man out of a cloister ever wrote about love, for example, so coldly and at the same time so grossly. His descriptions of it are just what we should hear from a recluse, who knew the passion only from the details of the confessional. Almost all his heroes make either like seraphim or like cattle. (pp. 531-32)

[If] we except some very pleasing images of paternal tenderness and filial duty, there is scarcely any thing soft or humane in Mr Southey's poetry. What theologians call the spiritual sins are his cardinal virtues—hatred, pride, and the insatiable thirst of vengeance. These passions he disguises under the name of duties; he purifies them from the alloy of vulgar interests; he ennobles them by uniting them with energy, fortitude, and a severe sanctity of manners, and then holds them up to the admiration of mankind. This is the spirit of Thalaba, of Ladurlad, of Adosinda, of Roderick after his regeneration. It is the spirit which, in all his writings, Mr Southey appears to affect. 'I do well to be angry,' seems to be the predominant feeling of his mind. (p. 532)

We have always heard, and fully believe, that Mr Southey is a very amiable and humane man; nor do we intend to apply to him personally any of the remarks which we have made on the spirit of his writings. Such are the caprices of human nature. . . . [When] Mr Southey takes up his pen, he changes his nature as much as Captain Shandy when he girt on his sword. The only opponents to whom he gives quarter are those in whom he finds something of his own character reflected. (pp. 532-33)

Mr Southey's political system is just what we might expect from a man who regards politics, not as a matter of science, but as a matter of taste and feeling. All his schemes of government have been inconsistent with themselves. In his youth he was a republican; yet, as he tells us in his preface to these *Colloquies*, he was even then opposed to the Catholic claims. He is now a violent Ultra-Tory. Yet while he maintains, with vehemence approaching to ferocity, all the sterner and harsher parts of the Ultra-Tory theory of government, the baser and dirtier part of that theory disgusts him. Exclusion, persecution, severe punishments for libellers and demagogues, proscriptions, massacres, civil war, if necessary, rather than any concession to a discontented people,—these are the measures which he seems inclined to recommend. A severe and gloomy tyranny—crushing opposition—silencing remonstrance—drilling the minds of the people into unreasoning obedience,—has in it something of grandeur which delights his imagination. But there is nothing fine in the shabby tricks and jobs of office. And Mr Southey, accordingly, has no toleration for them. (p. 533)

In the preface [to these *Colloquies*], we are informed that the author, notwithstanding some statements to the contrary, was always opposed to the Catholic Claims. We fully believe this; both because we are sure that Mr Southey is incapable of publishing a deliberate falsehood, and because his averment is in itself probable. It is exactly what we should have expected that, even in his wildest paroxysms of democratic enthusiasm, Mr Southey would have felt no wish to see a simple remedy applied to a great practical evil; that the only measure which all the great statesmen of two generations have agreed with each other in supporting, would be the only measure which Mr Southey would have agreed with himself in opposing. He has passed from one extreme of political opinion to another, as Satan in Milton went round the globe, contriving constantly to 'ride with darkness.' Wherever the thickest shadow of the night may at any moment chance to fall, there is Mr Southey. (pp. 533-34)

Mr Southey has not been fortunate in the plan of any of his fictitious narratives. But he has never failed so conspicuously, as in the work before us; except, indeed, in the wretched *Vision of Judgment.* (p. 534)

[In these *Colloquies*], in the *Vision of Judgment,* and in some of his other pieces, his mode of treating the most solemn subjects differs from that of open scoffers only as the extravagant representations of sacred persons and things in some grotesque Italian paintings differ from the caricatures which Carlile exposes in the front of his shop. We interpret the particular act by the general character. What in the window of a convicted blasphemer we call blasphemous, we call only absurd and ill-judged in an altar-piece. (p. 536)

There is nothing which [Mr. Southey hates so bitterly as the manufacturing system]. It is, according to him, a system more tyrannical than that of the feudal ages,—a system of actual servitude,—a system which destroys the bodies and degrades the minds of those who are engaged in it. He expresses a hope that the competition of other nations may drive us out of the field; that our foreign trade may decline, and that we may thus enjoy a restoration of national sanity and strength. But he seems to think that the extermination of the whole manufacturing population would be a blessing, if the evil could be removed in no other way.

Mr Southey does not bring forward a single fact in support of these views. . . . (p. 538)

It is not from bills of mortality and statistical tables that Mr Southey has learned his political creed. He cannot stoop to study the history of the system which he abuses—to strike the balance between the good and evil which it has produced—to compare district with district, or generation with generation. (p. 539)

Mr Southey has found out a way, he tells us, in which the effects of manufactures and agriculture may be compared. And what is this way? To stand on a hill, to look at a cottage and a manufactory, and to see which is the prettier. Does Mr Southey think that the body of the English peasantry live, or ever lived, in substantial and ornamented cottages, with box-hedges, flower-gardens, beehives, and orchards? If not, what is his parallel worth? (p. 540)

The signs of the times, Mr Southey tells us, are very threatening. His fears for the country would decidedly preponderate over his hopes, but for his firm reliance on the mercy of God. Now, as we know that God has once suffered the civilised world to be overrun by savages, and the Christian religion to be corrupted by doctrines which made it, for some ages, almost as bad as Paganism, we cannot think it inconsistent with his attributes that similar calamities should again befal mankind.

We look, however, on the state of the world, and of this kingdom in particular, with much greater satisfaction, and with better hopes. Mr Southey speaks with contempt of those who think the savage state happier than the social. On this subject, he says, Rousseau never imposed on him even in his youth. But he conceives that a community which has advanced a little way in civilisation is happier than one which has made greater progress. The Britons in the time of Caesar were happier, he suspects, than the English of the nineteenth century. On the whole, he selects the generation which preceded the Reformation as that in which the people of this country were better off than at any time before or since.

This opinion rests on nothing, as far as we can see, except his own individual associations. He is a man of letters; and a life destitute of literary pleasures seems insipid to him. He abhors the spirit of the present generation, the severity of its studies, the boldness of its enquiries, and the disdain with which it regards some old prejudices by which his own mind is held in bondage. He dislikes an utterly unenlightened age; he dislikes an investigating and reforming age. The first twenty years of the sixteenth century would have exactly suited him. They furnished just the quantity of intellectual excitement which he requires. The learned few read and wrote largely. . . . This is a state of things in which Mr Southey would have found himself quite comfortable; and, accordingly, he pronounces it the happiest state of things ever known in the world. (pp. 556-57)

It is not strange that, differing so widely from Mr Southey as to the past progress of society, we should differ from him also as to its probable destiny. He thinks, that to all outward appearance, the country is hastening to destruction; but he relies firmly on the goodness of God. We do not see either the piety, or the rationality, of thus confidently expecting that the Supreme Being will interfere to disturb the common succession of causes and effects. We, too, rely on his goodness,—on his goodness as manifested, not in extraordinary interpositions, but in those general laws which it has pleased him to establish in the physical and in the moral world. We rely on the natural tendency of the human intellect to truth, and on the natural tendency of society to improvement. (p. 562)

> [*Thomas Babington Macaulay*], "Southey's 'Colloquies on Society'," in The Edinburgh Review, *Vol. L, No. C, January, 1830, pp. 528-65.*

[WILLIAM MAGINN]   (essay date 1830)

[*Maginn, a Tory and the editor of* Fraser's Magazine, *responds to Thomas Babington Macaulay's negative assessment of* Sir Thomas More; or, Colloquies on the Progress and Prospects of Society *(see excerpt above, 1830). After Maginn attacks both Macauley's career and the* Edinburgh Review, *a Whig publication, he defends Southey's political stance and affirms his public influence.*]

Mr. Southey has read much, has written much, and, by [Thomas Babington Macauley's] confession, has "exercised considerable influence on the most enlightened generation of the most enlightened people that ever existed." Now, this "most enlightened generation of the most enlightened people that ever existed" have not been led to believe in Mr. Southey's mere assertion, from any persuasion of his being a prophet or an evangelist—they have believed in him, and been influenced by his writings, from the thorough and heartfelt conviction of their truth. Men are not apt to lend their credulity to their fellows merely on the strength of flat and naked positions; and the greater the enlightenment of such men, the stiffer is the

stubborness of their pride and obstinacy in yielding their faith as converts to new promulgations of opinions. . . . How stands it, therefore, with Mr. Southey? What is his intellectual position in this "most enlightened generation?" Even his enemy, Mr. Thomas Babington Macauley, confesses that he has exercised "*considerable* influence." This phrase holds a self-contradiction. In points of understanding there can be no half measures,—there can be no qualifications—no divisions or subdivisions of beliefs or leanings; it must be entirely, or in nowise. Either a teacher enjoys influence, or he does not. . . . If our reasoning be worth a rush, [Mr. Thomas Babington Macauley's] admission as to Mr. Southey's "influence on the most enlightened generation of the most enlightened people that ever existed," pulls him one way, whilst his hollow assertion that "in the mind of Mr. Southey reason has no place at all," necessarily pulls him in the opposite direction. . . .
(pp. 590-91)

Mr. Southey is one of the most accomplished scholars of which this country has ever boasted—and accomplished scholarship predicates very pointedly, we think, years of deep study, various reading, thought, and reflection. General history, moreover, has been Mr. Southey's favourite branch of study—and *"History is Philosophy teaching by example."* (p. 591)

The Laureate has, moreover, been noted as one of the most effectual controversial writers of his day; and as controversy cannot be carried on without argument, and *general* reputation for any quality is not to be acquired by charlatanism—and as the Laureate has gained a general reputation for his feats as such controversial writer, we need say no more on this subject.

Mr. Thomas Babington Macauley is eternally crowing up his own logical efficiency, and the illogical and common-place arguments of every other individual. Could he persuade the world of these facts, it were well . . .—but, alas! his assertions pass by his auditory even as the idle wind to which they pay not the slightest observance. In reference to Mr. Southey's alleged weakness in argumentation, thus stands the fact:—That the Laureate is not a keen disputant, cannot be denied—that his writings are not stuck full of philosophical knottinesses and metaphysical intertwistings, is equally so;—but it is also undeniable, that, in the most beautiful style of which the English language is susceptible, and of which our literature can boast, the theories which his mind has conceived, the actions of past ages which his patience and industry have attained, and those other actions which (his existence having been cast at the period which witnessed the most remarkable circumstances and events that mankind were ever fated to behold) his wondering eyes have witnessed, have been severally noted down and recounted to the world at large, whilst his philanthropic bosom glowed with the ardent and Christian hope that his fellow-creatures would employ his narratives in practical and beneficial adaptation. Such has been the tendency of all Mr. Southey's literary exertions. With such views, therefore, the mode of composition and method of argument which he has employed have been well selected. Mankind are contented to receive instruction in *intelligible* language, and are fain to turn their backs on the fantastic tricks and incomprehensible cackle of logomachising ganders and self-vaunting pseudo-persifleurs and jargonists—leaving them to the contemplation of their own egregious contortions of body, their own super-exquisite jaw openings and oral crookedness, in the respective mirrors of their own vanity.
(pp. 591-92)

"Mr. Southey's political system," says his critic, "is just what we might expect from a man who regards politics not as a matter of science, but as a matter of taste and feeling. All his schemes of government have been inconsistent with themselves. In his youth he was a republican; yet, as he tells us in his preface to these *Colloquies,* he was, even then, opposed to the Catholic claims," &c.—we have already given the whole of the paragraph. In answer, we reply briefly: 1. Although Mr. Southey may regard politics "not as a matter of science, but as a matter of taste and feeling," it behoves not Mr. Macauley to bring the charge of inconsistency against the Laureate in particular—but rather against those members of his own House who have wantonly and impudently forfeited their pledged faith to their country—and apostatised and ratted from their own confiding party for a worse motive than defect of taste or misapplication of feeling—for base wordly emolument and a hireling stipend.—2. To say of a young man that in his youth he was a republican, is almost the best praise that can be yielded to the purity and goodness of his nature. A ripened judgment is a thing unnatural for youth—and, without a ripened judgment, it is impossible to say to a certainty that republicanism is one of those errant false lights which have worked infinite woe to the world. But it is natural that a youth, even in his youngest years, should, if he be possessed of quick feelings and warmth of heart, have some bias; and it is, further, natural that he should lean towards that, whatever it may be, which is brought nearest to a heart so liable to excitation. Now, the story of republican Rome and republican Greece (in the usual course of study) is forced upon him as a subject for every day's, every hour's consideration, until his imagination becoming inflamed by contemplating the actions of a Miltiades, and Themistocles, and Aristides,—of an Epaminondas, Phocyon, and Thrasybulus,—of a Coriolanus and Cincinnatus,—of a Scipio and Regulus;—he imagines that all blessings and all glory in governments must flow from republics; and, consequently, he is induced to become a warm republican, until a further knowledge of the constitution and essence of happiness induces an alteration in his opinions. Viewing the matter in this light, we are confident that every reader will consider the republicanism of boyhood and early youth as not only venial, but praiseworthy.—3. Though Mr. Southey be an ultra-Tory, there is no necessity for following precisely along the ruts and in the footmarks made by every other ultra-Tory that ever preceded him.—4. That Mr. Southey bears not mortal enmity to those individuals who have been politically opposed to him, may be proved from his recent *Life of John Bunyan*. The amplest justice has been done to that obstinate, yet honest non-conformist; and the kindness of feeling which he has evinced towards the old offender and scurrilist, Mr. Hone, has drawn upon himself the displeasure of his own party.—5. Democracy does not predicate the removal of religious distinctions. The religion of Rome, and the schools of ancient philosophy, continued in vigour, notwithstanding the existence of democracy.

We now turn to that paragraph wherein is contained Mr. Southey's confession against butchers. And, 1. Because butchers are in an employment which is beneficial to society, is no reason why they, by the wear and tear of that employment, should not be divested of all humanity, as much as coal-heavers are rendered unfit for the society of the Duke of Wellington, or nightmen or scavengers for associating with Sir Robert Peel, or Mr. Dawson, or the Bishop of London.—2. Though "the certain law or custom" prejudicial to the milky characters of butchers, "may never have existed but in the imaginations of old women," still the very inference from its being, by Mr. Macauley's own acknowledgment, habitual to the imaginations of old women—who, Heaven knows, form perhaps a larger portion of the community than the *Athenian* critic will allow—

is, that it has somewhat of the character, and therefore somewhat of the truth, of a popular proverb.—3. "Looking with favour on a soldier" argues not, in respect to Mr. Southey, "that human blood is by no means an object of so much disgust as the hides and paunches of cattle;" or that he loves the stench of human carnage, because, "in 1814, he poured forth poetical maledictions on all who talked of peace with Buonaparte." If this were true of the Laureate, Mr. Pitt, and the late Lord Melville, and his present Majesty, and his immortal father, and the late Lords Liverpool and Castlereagh, and the Duke of Wellington, and Sir Walter Scott, and Mr. Wordsworth, with every man who ever lighted a farthing rushlight in illumination of the glorious successes of our national armies, would severally be fiends of equal magnitude with the quiet, unobtrusive, placable Mr. Southey.—4. The ecstasy which broke forth in *The Poet's Pilgrimage* is very good "poetical inspiration," notwithstanding the shallow-pated Mr. Thomas Babington Macauley's naked assertion to the contrary; and if the magpie-tongued criticaster had turned up to the poem, he would have paused, and *perhaps* felt, a secret shame at bringing his atrocious charge against the gentle laker;—first, because his opening motto from Pindar shews that his poetical mind was rhapsodising over the brilliance of national triumphs.—Secondly, because the proem would have presented as sweet a family picture as the kindest-hearted of poets ever drew. The man who can without hesitation—nay, with pleasure—participate in the youthful frolics of children, and who, even after having arrived at the maturity of human life, still retains in his bosom the desire for self-improvement, and the unsubdued spark of youthful emulation, is not exactly the individual whose nostrils are to be delighted by the fetid effluvia steaming over a field of slaughtered bodies. . . . (pp. 595-96)

Mr. Thomas Babington Macauley is a quack and a pseudo-philosopher, and accordingly, no two of his opinions or actions will be found to tally or coincide.

But why should he have singled out Mr. Southey for his fierce and foul vituperation? No one can impugn the harmless tenure of Mr. Southey's life, or his retiring nature (particularly since he refused a seat in that very sapient assembly, of which Mr. Macauley is so bright and particular a star), or the sincerity of his faith, or his earnest wish to further the improvement of his fellow-creatures, or the soundness of his scholarship. Now, for any, or all these reasons, however Mr. Macauley may differ from the Laureate, surely the latter . . . or deserves respectful consideration and fair usage, to say nothing of love, charity, mercy, and forbearance—qualities which, by their beauty of conduct on all occasions, the saints have identified with themselves. But his false reasonings and low abuse of the Laureate prove Mr. Thomas Babington Macauley to be no whit better than the general run of his sinful fellow-creatures. The Laureate has made for himself a fair reputation— . . . the moral beggar, therefore, hates his richer neighbour, and that hatred is manifested in the exquisite piece of criticism, the beauties of which we have done all that in us lay to shew forth to the admiration of an enraptured world. (p. 600)

[William Maginn], "Mr. Thomas Babington Macauley and Mr. Southey," in Fraser's Magazine, Vol. V, No. 1, June, 1830, pp. 584-600.

JOHN STUART MILL (letter date 1831)

[*An English essayist and critic, Mill is regarded as one of the greatest philosophers and political economists of the nineteenth*

century. Early in his political career, Mill was recognized as a leading advocate of the utilitarian philosophy of Jeremy Bentham, and he was a principal contributor to the Westminster Review, an English periodical founded by Bentham that later merged with the London Review. During the 1830s, after reading the works of William Wordsworth, Samuel Taylor Coleridge, and Auguste Comte, he gradually diverged from Bentham's utilitarianism. As part owner of the London and Westminster Review from 1835-40, Mill was instrumental in modifying the periodical's utilitarian stance. He is considered a key figure in the transition from the rationalism of the Enlightenment to the renewed emphasis on mysticism and the emotions of the Romantic era. In the following excerpt from his letter to John Sterling, Mill illuminates what he discerns as Southey's central problem as a political thinker. He writes: "Southey is altogether out of place in the existing order of society: his attachment to old institutions & his condemnation of the practices of those who administer them, cut him off from sympathy & communion with both halves of mankind."]

I never could understand [Southey] till lately; that is, I never could reconcile the tone of such of his writings as I had read, with what his friends said of him: I could only get rid of the notion of his being insincere, by supposing him to be extremely fretful and irritable: but when I came to read his *Colloquies,* in which he has put forth much more than in any other work, of the natural man, as distinguished from the writer aiming at a particular effect, I found there a kind of connecting link between the two parts of his character, & formed very much the same notion of him which I now have after seeing & conversing with him. He seems to me to be a man of gentle feelings & bitter opinions. His opinions make him think a great many things abominable which are not so; against which accordingly he thinks it would be right, & suitable to the fitness of things, to express great indignation: but if he really feels this indignation, it is only by a voluntary act of the imagination that he conjures it up, by representing the thing to his own mind in colours suited to that passion: now, when he knows an individual & feels disposed to like him, although that individual may be placed in one of the condemned categories, he does not conjure up this phantom & feels therefore no principle of repugnance, nor excites any. No one can hold a greater number of the opinions & few have more of the qualities, which he condemns, than some whom he has known intimately & befriended for many years: at the same time he would discuss their faults & weaknesses or vices with the greatest possible freedom in talking about them. It seems to me that Southey is altogether out of place in the existing order of society: his attachment to old institutions & his condemnation of the practices of those who administer them, cut him off from sympathy & communion with both halves of mankind. Had he lived before radicalism & infidelity became prevalent, he would have been the steady advocate of the moral & physical improvement of the poorer classes & denouncer of the selfishness & supineness of those who ought to have considered the welfare of those classes as confided to their care. Possibly the essential one-sidedness of his mind might then have rendered him a democrat: but now the evils which he expects from increase of the power wielded by the democratic spirit such as it now is, have rendered him an aristocrat in principle without inducing him to make the slightest compromise with aristocratic vices and weaknesses. Consequently he is not liked by the Tories, while the Whigs and radicals abhor him. (pp. 82-3)

John Stuart Mill, in a letter to John Sterling, October 20-22, 1831, in his The Earlier Letters of John Stuart Mill: 1812-1848, Vol. XII, edited by Frances E. Mineka, University of Toronto Press, 1963, pp. 82-3.

EDWARD LYTTON BULWER   (essay date 1833)

[*Bulwer-Lytton was a popular, versatile nineteenth-century author who wrote under several variations of his name, including the form with which he signed this piece. He is remembered today for his prolific literary output, which included his fashionable novel* Pelham; or, The Adventures of a Gentleman. *The following essay was originally published in 1833.*]

[The] most various, scholastic, and accomplished of such of our literary contemporaries as have written works as well as articles, and prose as well as poetry—is, incontestably, Dr. Southey. **"The Life of Nelson"** is acknowledged to be the best biography of the day. **"The Life of Wesley"** and **"The Book of the Church,"** however adulterated by certain prepossessions and prejudices, are, as mere compositions, characterized by an equal simplicity and richness of style,—an equal dignity and an equal ease. No writer blends more happily the academical graces of the style of last century, with the popular vigour of that which distinguishes the present. His **"Colloquies"** are, we suspect, the work on which he chiefly prides himself, but they do not seem to me to contain the best characteristics of his genius. The work is overloaded with quotation and allusion, and . . . seems crushed beneath the weight of its ornaments; it wants the great charm of that simple verve which is so peculiarly Southeian. Were I to do justice to Southey's cast of mind—to analyse its properties and explain its apparent contradictions, I should fill . . . [two volumes] with Southey alone. Suffice it *now* (another occasion to do him ampler justice may occur elsewhere,) to make two remarks in answer to the common charges against this accomplished writer. He is alleged to be grossly inconsistent in politics, and wholly unphilosophical in morals. I hold both these charges to spring from the coarse injustice of party. If ever a man wrote a complete vindication of himself—that vindication is to be found in Southey's celebrated [letter to William Smith defending himself against Smith's attack on **"Wat Tyler"**]; the triumphant dignity with which he puts aside each successive aspersion—the clearness with which, in that letter, his bright integrity shines out through all the mists amidst which it voluntarily passes, no dispassionate man can mark and not admire. But he is not philosophical?—No,—rather say he is not logical; his philosophy is large and learned, but it is all founded on hypothesis, and is poetical not metaphysical. (pp. 59-60)

Edward Lytton Bulwer, "Literàture," in his England and the English, *Vol. II, Gregg International Publishers Limited, 1971, pp. 51-113.**

[JOHN GIBSON LOCKHART]   (essay date 1834)

[*Here the critic asserts that the anonymously published* The Doctor, *a mixture of "dross" and "gems," could not be attributed to Southey: "The gross errors, both in the conception and in the execution, . . . could never have been supposed to have come from him."*]

['**The Doctor**'] has excited more attention than any one belonging, or approaching, to the class of *novels*, which has appeared in England for a considerable number of years; and we are not at all disposed to wonder that such should have been the case. It is broadly distinguished from the mass of books recently published in the same shape and form, both by excellencies of a very high order, and by defects, indicating such occasional contempt of sound judgment, and sense, and taste, as we can hardly suppose in a strong and richly cultivated mind, unless that mind should be in a certain measure under the influence of disease. The author says of one of his characters:—'He was born with one of those heads in which the thin partition that divides great wit from folly is wanting.' The partition in his own head would seem to be a moveable one. A clearer or a more vigorous and understanding than he in his better parts exhibits, we have seldom encountered; but two-thirds of his performance look as if they might have been penned in the vestibule of Bedlam. The language, however, even where the matter is most absurd, retains the ease, the strength, and the purity of a true master of English; and there occur, ever and anon, in chapters over which no human being but a reviewer will ever travel for the second time, turns of expression which would of themselves justify us in pronouncing the author of this 'apish and fantastic' nondescript to be a man of genius.

The writer is often a wise one—but his attempts at what is now called *wit* are, in general, unsuccessful: nor can we speak much better of his humour, though he has undoubtedly a few passages which might make Heraclitus chuckle. With these rare exceptions, his jocularity is pedantic and chilling—his drollery wire-drawn, super-quaint, Whistlecraftish. The *red* letters and mysterious monogram of his title-page—the *purple* German-text of his dedication to *the Bhow Begum Redora Niabarma*—his division of chapters into ante-initial, initial, and post-initial—his inter-chapters—his post-fixed preface, &c. &c.—what are all these things but paltry imitations of the poorest sort of fun in [Laurence Sterne's] *Tristram Shandy.* All his jesting about bells, and 'the manly and English art' of bell-ringing, . . . appears to us equally dolorous. As for his bitter sneers at Lord Byron—his clumsy and grossly affected contempt for Mr. Jeffrey—and the heavy magniloquence of his own self-esteem—we dismiss them at once in silence. They mark as evidently the disruption of the 'thin partition,' as his prolix babble on the garden-physic of his great-grandmother, the drivelling of the alchemists, and the succession of the mayors of Doncaster—or his right merry and conceited elaboration of one of the dirtiest of all the practical jokes in Rabelais.

If we were not quite serious in our suspicion that '**The Doctor**' is the work of a man who stands more in need of physic than of criticism, we should have felt it our duty to illustrate, by citations, the justice of the language which we have not hesitated to apply to so great a portion of these volumes. As it is, we willingly spare ourselves a thankless piece of trouble, and our readers a dose or two of dullness—and, indeed, of disgust. Let us henceforth drop a veil upon the mountain of dross and rubbish, and keep all our daylight for the gold and gems, which have made it worth the sifting.

One word only as to the outline. The author does not seem to have reflected that Rabelais adopted the broad grotesque of his plan—(and execution also)—because it would have been impossible for any man of that age, above all for a curé of Meudon, to satirize the baseness of French courtiers, and the hypocrisy of Romish priests—in any direct shape; or to have perceived that, after all, the great French humorist would have been infinitely more popular than he is, had he not pushed the system of *rambling* to such an extent as he has done. The same sort of thing might have been the result of a very little reflection on the personal position and character of the author of *Tristram Shandy,*—which work, of course, has been the more immediate prototype of '**The Doctor.**' Sterne was to the last, what we have no reason to believe that Rabelais was in the more advanced part of his life,—a profligate priest; and his buffoonery of manner was the shield rather than cloak of his licentiousness.

Moreover, there is one very important particular in which Sterne's *plan,* with all its wildness, stands contrasted, to its own infinite advantage, against that of his anonymous imitator. The strange farrago of odd, yet often second-hand learning, for the purpose of exhibiting which *Tristram Shandy* was, no doubt, first conceived, is all, by the art of Sterne, poured out dramatically: the character of *My Father* is a most original conception, most happily worked out with a skill which can convert materials, apparently the most incongruous, to the one main design. . . . **'The Doctor'** seems to have been framed with exactly the same primary view—that of furnishing a pretext for the clearance of a rich common-place book; but the author, after a few awkward attempts to avail himself, for this purpose, of the instrumentality of *his* hero's father and tutor, takes the office of showman openly into his own hands—and thenceforth the 'curiosities of literature,' of which **'The Doctor'** presents certainly a sequence not unworthy of being classed . . . with that in Southey's **Omniana,** are brought forth, so as hardly to help in any degree the development of any one of the characters in the book. (pp. 68-70)

Be this author who he may, the names which conjecture has banded about in connexion with his work imply, all and each of them, a strong impression of the ability and erudition which it evinces. At first, suspicion lighted almost universally, we believe, on the Poet Laureate himself; and certainly the moral, political, and literary doctrines of the book are such, in the main, as might have countenanced such a notion—nor do we hesitate to pay the language of the book the extraordinary compliment of saying that much of it also might have done even Mr. Southey no discredit; but surely, of all the gross errors, both in the conception and in the execution, to which we have already alluded, the least could never have been supposed to have come from him,—unless, perhaps, in some merely juvenile prolusion, casually dug up out of a long-forgotten cabinet; and their catalogue contains some items which even that theory could never have reconciled us to affiliate upon him. Of the real author of the work we happen to know he is ignorant. . . . (p. 95)

> [*John Gibson Lockhart*], "'The Doctor'," in The
> Quarterly Review, *Vol. LI, March, 1834, pp. 68-96.*

[WILLIAM MAKEPEACE THACKERAY] (essay date 1860)

[*A famed Victorian author, Thackeray is best known for his satiric sketches and novels of upper- and middle-class English life, and he is credited with bringing a simpler style and greater realism to English fiction. The following brief tribute indicates the generally positive attitude of his fellow writers towards Southey following his death. Like many of his contemporaries, Thackeray expresses admiration for Southey's industry rather than his poetic genius.*]

[I will take a man of letters whose life I admire],—an English worthy, doing his duty for fifty noble years of labour, day by day storing up learning, day by day working for scant wages, most charitable out of his small means, bravely faithful to the calling which he had chosen, refusing to turn from his path for popular praise or princes' favour;—I mean *Robert Southey.* We have left his old political landmarks miles and miles behind; we protest against his dogmatism; nay, we begin to forget it and his politics: but I hope his life will not be forgotten, for it is sublime in its simplicity, its energy, its honour, its affection. In the combat between Time and Thalaba, I suspect the former destroyer has conquered. Kehama's curse frightens very few readers now; but Southey' private letters are worth piles

of epics, and are sure to last among us, as long as kind hearts like to sympathize with goodness and purity, and love and upright life. (pp. 401-02)

> [*William Makepeace Thackeray*], "The Four Georges:
> Sketches of Manners, Morals, Court, and Town Life,"
> in The Cornhill Magazine, *Vol. II, No. 10, October,
> 1860, pp. 385-406.**

EDWARD DOWDEN (essay date 1876)

[*An Irish critic and biographer, Dowden is known for his once influential criticism of William Shakespeare. As a biographer, Dowden interpreted literary works as a personal record of the author's mind and character. His biography of Southey is among the best known, though many critics feel that Dowden exaggerated Southey's talent in his depiction of him as a saintly artist.*]

After thirty Southey seldom cared to utter himself in occasional verse. . . . Still, he could apply himself to the treatment of large subjects with a calm, continuous energy; but as time went on his hand grew slack, and wrought with less ease. Scarcely had he overcome the narrative poet's chief difficulty, that of subduing varied materials to an unity of design, when he put aside verse, and found it more natural to be historian than poet.

The poetry of sober feeling is rare in lyrical verse. This may be found admirably rendered in some of Southey's shorter pieces. Although his temper was ardent and hopeful, his poems of pensive remembrance, of meditative calm, are perhaps the most characteristic. Among these his **Inscriptions** rank high. Some of those in memory of the dead are remarkable for their fine poise of feeling, all that is excessive and transitory having been subdued; for the tranquil depths of sorrow and of hope which lie beneath their clear, melodious words.

Southey's larger poetical works are fashioned of two materials which do not always entirely harmonize. First, material brought from his own moral nature; his admiration of something elevated in the character of man or woman—generosity, gentleness, loyalty, fortitude, faith. And, secondly, material gathered from abroad; mediaeval pomps of religion and circumstance of war; Arabian marvels, the work of the enchanters and the genii; the wild beauties and adventure of life amid New-World tribes; the monstrous mythology of the Brahman. With such material the poet's inventive talent deals freely, rearranges details or adds to them; still Southey is here rather a *finder* than a *maker*. His diligence in collecting and his skill in arranging were so great that it was well if the central theme did not disappear among manifold accessories. One who knows Southey, however, can recognize his ethical spirit in every poem. Thalaba, as he himself confessed, is a male Joan of Arc. Destiny or Providence has marked alike the hero and the heroine from mankind; the sheepfold of Domremi, and the palm-grove by old Moath's tent, alike nurture virgin purity and lofty aspiration. Thalaba, like Joan, goes forth a delegated servant of the Highest to war against the powers of evil; Thalaba, like Joan, is sustained under the trials of the way by the sole talisman of faith. (pp. 187-89)

The word *high-souled* takes possession of the mind as we think of Southey's heroic personages. Poetry, he held, ought rather to elevate than to affect—a Stoical doctrine transferred to art, which meant that his own poetry was derived more from admiration of great qualities than from sympathy with individual men or women. Neither the quick and passionate tenderness of Burns nor the stringent pathos of Wordsworth can be found in Southey's verse. . . . In **Kehama,** a work of Southey's mature years, the chivalric ardour of his earlier heroes is transformed into the sterner virtues of fortitude and an almost despairing constancy. The power of evil, as conceived by the poet, has grown more despotic; little can be achieved by the light-winged Glendoveer—a more radiant Thalaba—against the Rajah; only the lidless eye of Seeva can destory that tyranny of lust and pride. *Roderick* marks a higher stage in the development of Southey's ethical ideal. Roderick, too, is a delegated champion of right against force and fraud; he too endures mighty pains. But he is neither such a combatant, pure and intrepid, as goes forth from the Arab tent, nor such a blameless martyr as Ladurlad. He is first a sinner enduring just punishment; then a stricken penitent; and from his shame and remorse he is at last uplifted by enthusiasm, on behalf of his God and his people, into a warrior saint, the Gothic Maccabee.

Madoc stands somewhat away from the line of Southey's other narrative poems. Though, as Scott objected, the personages in *Madoc* are too nearly abstract types, Southey's ethical spirit dominates this poem less than any of the others. The narrative flows on more simply. The New-World portion tells a story full of picturesque incident, with the same skill and grace that belong to Southey's best prose writings. . . . Those, however, who opened [*Madoc*] were few: the tale was out of relation with the time; it interpreted no need, no aspiration, no passion of the dawn of the present century. And the mind of the time was not enough disengaged to concern itself deeply with the supposed adventures of a Welsh prince of the twelfth century among the natives of America.

At heart, then, Southey's poems are in the main the outcome of his moral nature; this we recognize through all disguises—Mohammedan, Hindoo, or Catholic. (pp. 189-90)

Though his materials are often exotic, in style Southey aimed at the simplicity and strength of undefiled English. If to these melody was added, he had attained all he desired. . . . On the whole, judged by the highest standards, Southey's poetry takes a midmost rank; it neither renders into art a great body of thought and passion, nor does it give faultless expression to lyrical moments. But it is the output of a large and vigorous mind, amply stored with knowledge; its breath of life is the moral ardour of a nature strong and generous and therefore it can never cease to be of worth.

Southey is at his best in prose. And here it must be borne in mind that, though so voluminous a writer, he did not achieve his most important work, the *History of Portugal,* for which he had gathered vast collections. It cannot be doubted that this, if completed, would have taken a place among our chief histories. The splendour of story and the heroic personages would have lifted Southey into his highest mood. We cannot speak with equal confidence of his projected work of second magnitude, the *History of the Monastic Orders.* Learned and sensible it could not fail to be, and Southey would have recognized the more substantial services of the founders and the brotherhoods; but he would have dealt by methods too simple with the psychology of religious emotions; the words enthusiasm and fraud might have risen too often to his lips; and at the grotesque humours of the devout, which he would have exhibited with delight, he might have been too prone to smile.

As it is, Southey's largest works are not his most admirable. *The History of Brazil,* indeed, gives evidence of amazing patience, industry, and skill; but its subject necessarily excludes it from the first rank. At no time from the sixteenth to the nineteenth century was Brazil a leader or a banner-bearer among

lands. The life of the people crept on from point to point, and that is all; there are few passages in which the chronicle can gather itself up, and transform itself into a historic drama. Southey has done all that was possible; his pages are rich in facts, and are more entertaining than perhaps any other writer could have made them. (pp. 191-93)

History as written by Southey is narrative rendered spiritual by moral ardour. There are no new political truths, he said. If there be laws of a nation's life other than those connected with elementary principles of morality, Southey did not discover these. What he has written may go only a little way towards attaining the ultimate ends of historical study, but so far as it goes it keeps the direct line. It is not led astray by will-o'-the-wisp, vague-shining theories that beguile night wanderers. Its method is an honest method as wholesome as sweet; and simple narrative, if ripe and sound at first, is none the less so at the end of a century.

In biography, at least, one may be well pleased with clear and charming narrative. Here Southey has not been surpassed, and even in this single province he is versatile; he has written the life of a warrior, of a poet, and of a saint. His industry was that of a German; his lucidity and perfect exposition were such as we rarely find outside a French memoir. There is no style fitter for continuous narrative than the pedestrian style of Southey. It does not beat upon the ear with hard, metallic vibration. The sentences are not cast by the thousand in one mould of cheap rhetoric, nor made brilliant with one cheap colour. Never dithyrambic, he is never dull; he affects neither the trick of stateliness nor that of careless ease; he does not seek out curiosities of refinement, nor caress delicate affectations. Because his style is natural, it is inimitable, and the only way to write like Southey is to write well. (pp. 194-95)

> *Edward Dowden, in his* Southey, *Harper & Brothers Publishers, 1876, 197 p.*

LESLIE STEPHEN (essay date 1902)

[*Stephen is considered one of the most important literary critics of his age. In his moral criticism, Stephen argues that all of literature is nothing more than an imaginative rendering, in concrete terms, of a writer's philosophy or beliefs. It is the role of criticism, he contends, to translate into intellectual terms what the writer has told the reader through character, symbol, and plot. Stephen's analyses often include biographical judgments of the writer as well as of the work. As Stephen once observed: "The whole art of criticism consists in learning to know the human being who is partially revealed to us in his spoken or his written words." Here, Stephen provides a favorable assessment of Southey's letters, describing them as "the self-portraiture of a man whose good qualities are seconded by super-abundant vivacity." While Stephen believes that the letters are examples of excellent correspondence, he adds that Southey's stoical and overly businesslike attitude prevented him from creating a complete picture of himself.*]

I read somewhere the other day a contemptuous reference to Southey's letters. It gave me a shock, and yet, upon reflection, I had to admit that from a purely literary point of view it had some justification. In spite of this, I can always turn with pleasure to the ten volumes of correspondence. . . . His letters are the self-portraiture of a man whose good qualities are seconded by superabundant vivacity. I am afraid, however, that this does not quite sum up the impression which they make. Southey was not exactly the typical saint—the man whose talents serve only to give lustre to the beauty of holiness. . . .

He is good enough (if I may speak as a member of the craft) to serve as the patron saint of men of letters by profession, though we must humbly confess that he would be a little out of place in a more exalted sanctuary. A man who lives by his pen must renounce some pretensions of lofty morality; he cannot expect to be on a pedestal beside the great philanthropists and prophets and statesmen. He confesses himself to belong to a lower class of humanity; but he may be a good specimen of his class, as a cab-horse may be a good cab-horse though he does not expect to win the Derby. If he pays his bills and is kind to his family, and does not sell his pen to the enemy, he deserves respect in his life, and may at least claim the usual complimentary epitaph. Southey is interesting to me because he represents the high-water mark in that direction during his own generation. He is the most complete type of the man fitted by nature for this peculiar function, which one must sorrowfully admit not to be the highest. (pp. 45-7)

[We] are content to pass Southey's poems with the admission that they are not so unreadable as Glover's *Leonidas,* or Wilkie's *Epigoniad.* The characteristic point is Southey's complacent and indomitable faith in his own performances. There is something sublime in his self-confidence. He commends the judicious critic who had said that *Madoc* was the best English poem since *Paradise Lost.* 'This is not exaggerated praise, for unfortunately there is no competition.' *Madoc* must, indeed, be compared with the *Odyssey,* not with the *Iliad,* but it is a good poem, and must live. He objects to being called the 'sublimest poet of the age,' for on that point Wordsworth and Landor are 'at least his equals.' But this statement is not to be suspected of 'mock-modesty,' as he sufficiently proves by adding that he 'will have done greater things than either,' though not because he possesses 'greater powers.' In fact, there are different classes of excellence. His mind, he admits, is wholly unlike Milton's, whose proper analogue is Wordsworth. For himself, he may be fairly compared with Tasso, Virgil, or Homer. Every generation, he observes elsewhere, will afford some half-dozen admirers of *Kehama,* 'and the everlasting column of Dante's fame does not stand upon a wider base.' Meanwhile, he points out that contemporary popularity can only be won by compliance with the faults of the time—a consoling doctrine which he shared with Wordsworth and Landor. Unfortunately, there are other roads to unpopularity besides simple excellence. Southey, however, was able to preserve the pleasant belief that he was one of the few fixed stars of his time, though differing from other stars in glory, and that his light would be recognised through the ages to come.

This failing, if it be rightly called a failing, is clearly an essential characteristic. If a man is to be condemned because he has a calm conviction of his own undeniable merits, no case can be made out for Southey. His self-confidence is written in the very character of his face. (pp. 56-8)

It was happy for Southey that he had hardly more humour than Milton or Wordsworth or Shelley or Miss Brontë. In spite of his defect, or his immunity, shall we say, from this morbid propensity, Southey was certainly no prig. He could enjoy nonsense and was proud of it, though his nonsense, it must be confessed, is poor enough in quality. It is amusing to read his correspondence with Grosvenor Bedford upon his *Doctor.* . . . [The] *Doctor* is a very delightful book; a book 'for the bedside,' which is always entertaining without endangering sleep. Like Burton's *Anatomy,* it is, of course, a commonplace book in disguise. But, besides its collection of 'curiosities of literature,' it has really charming interludes when Southey is not tempted into too deliberate facetiousness. A great author would not like, I imagine, to rest his fame upon a perfect nursery story, and yet, if 'literary immortality' be desirable, the immortal story of the *Three Bears* is more likely to secure that result than *Madoc* or *Roderick.* To add a new legend fit to take place amidst the old legendary stories is surely a remarkable feat. This is the gem of the *Doctor;* but it is one outcome of a playful and tender sentiment which, amidst some obvious defects, often shows the real charm of Southey's domestic atmosphere. . . . To read the *Doctor* is to spend an hour with Southey in his library; and, if here and there to be a little overdosed with an author's pedantry, yet to be made aware of his domestic charm. There was a nursery in his house as well as a library; and the *Three Bears* must have been told to the precocious boy whose early death almost broke his father's heart. (pp. 61-5)

The *Doctor,* indeed, shows the limitations of Southey's intellect, which have led critics to condemn him as a mere fossil in politics and his enemies to denounce him as a renegade and a timeserver. (p. 66)

Southey constantly insisted upon the doctrine, consoling for some authors, that the secret of good writing is to be concise, clear, and pointed, and not to think about your style at all. 'Style' must come unconsciously. You must aim at the mark without thinking about your attitude. The method is excellent when you are writing a plain statement of fact or argument, and is so far applicable in letter-writing that self-consciousness or deliberate attempts at literary elegance is the worst of all faults. Yet really first-rate letters should imply a certain detachment. The writer should be able to play a little with his subject: to tell a bit of news so as to give the picturesque aspects; to insinuate a humorous or melancholy reflection without falling into sermonising; and, in short, to put into a few lines the effect of a whole evening of spontaneous and discursive chat. Southey, having to squeeze in a letter between an epic and a quarterly review, is too eager and impetuous. He goes to the point at once like a good man of business, and cannot give the effect of leisurely and amused reflection. The reader has to supply a good deal from independent knowledge, or to gather it from the general result of the correspondence. . . . He takes up one burthen after another as all in the day's work so simply that we may fail to notice the energy implied in his forty years of unremitting labour. It is quite natural, when one comes to think of it, that his brain should have given way at last: but at any given moment he seems to be working as smoothly and unconsciously as a well-oiled steam-engine. There are no creaks and groans and whinings, and one can forget that there was any strain. So he makes few protestations; but the old friendships go on from schoolboy days to the end without a cloud. . . . Of all the charges made by his enemies, the most absurd was that of servility. He always says what he thinks, and though he had never a year's income in advance, never condescended to unworthy flattery of patrons or the public. If he estimates his work too highly, he takes it as a mere matter of course that he should be independent and plain-spoken. The letters after the death of the son who was to have inherited his genius, are almost the only ones in which Southey allows himself to utter the strong domestic affections in which we see, on reflection, that he found his real happiness. Even in the midst of this grief he is, perhaps, a little overanxious to insist upon his power of preserving a stoical calm; but for once he cannot conceal the emotions which he generally keeps in the background. . . . When, however, one tries to form a picture of Southey's life and to supply the side which he leaves in obscurity, one begins to hope that even a journalist may save his soul. That the letters do not give up that secret at the first glance is, perhaps, the reason why they are not more generally valued; but to those who have been immersed in the same element, it should not be difficult to supply the gaps. (pp. 81-5)

Leslie Stephen, ''Southey's Letters,'' in his Studies of a Biographer, second series, Duckworth & Co., 1902, pp. 45-85.

ARTHUR SYMONS (essay date 1909)

[An English critic, poet, dramatist, short story writer, and editor, Symons initially gained notoriety as an English decadent in the 1890s, and he eventually established himself as one of the most important critics of the modern era. His sensitive translations from the works of Paul Verlaine and Stéphane Mallarmé offered English poets an introduction to the poetry of the French Symbolists. Though he was a gifted translator and linguist, it was as a critic that Symons made his most important contribution to literature. His The Symbolist Movement in Literature provided his English contemporaries with an appropriate vocabulary with which to define their new aesthetic—one that communicated their concern with dreamlike states, imagination, and a reality that exists beyond the boundaries of the senses. Symons praises the ''ease and flexibility'' of Southey's writings but maintains that his work is devoid of spirit. His epics are failures, according to Symons, with the exception of Roderick: The Last of the Goths. Symons concludes that Southey was best suited to write humorous verse.]

In his 'Table-Talk' Coleridge is reported to have spoken of Southey's English prose as 'next door to faultless.' It is that, and it has most negative merits; but it is, like his verse, uninspired, without any great or exquisite qualities; without magic. It has ease and flexibility; it is, as he said of it, contrasting it scornfully with Coleridge's, 'perspicuous and to the point.' As a style of all work it is incomparable; as Southey is the ideal of the 'well-read' man, so his style is the ideal of the 'readable' style. His 'Life of Wesley' is remarkable as a psychological study, and that, like the 'Life of Nelson,' is a marvel of clear, interesting, absorbing narrative. We remember it, not for any page or passage, but as a whole, for its evenness, proportion, and easy mastery of its subject. But in that unique subject, which gave him the opportunity of his life, a subject absolutely 'made to his hand,' can it be said that Southey found, any more than in his criticism of literature, the vraie vérité, the essential thing? The portrait of Wesley he gives us, but does he give us anywhere the secret of Wesley?

In one of his books, 'The Doctor,' which was published anonymously, volume by volume, Southey has tried for once to give us what he could of the secret of himself. It is his most personal work in prose; and it is personal partly for this reason, that it is a compilation, a collection of curiosities, a farrago, yet thrown together, one realises, by a man of order, who lets nothing escape him unawares, tells just what he chooses to tell. . . . 'I see in "The Doctor,"' wrote Southey, who, in the course of his book, refers, rather more often than is necessary for purposes of disguise, to Southey, 'Southey and Wordsworth' (never 'Wordsworth and Southey'), 'a little of Rabelais, but not much; more of Tristram Shandy, somewhat of Burton, and perhaps more of Montaigne.' . . . The influences are there, it is true, and the personal quality; but can the book, with all its quaintness, pleasantness and variety, bear the least of these comparisons, or stand by itself with any firmness? Perhaps the best thing in it is the nursery story of 'The Three Bears,' and that is one of Southey's real successes, one of his successes in comedy; but how few of the other more serious pages leave

so deep an impression on the memory as this piece of engaging nonsense?

As a writer of verse Southey had a small but genuine talent of a homely and grotesque order; and if he had had less ambition, and a keener sense of his own limitations, he might have appealed with more likelihood of final satisfaction to 'that Court of Record' which, sooner or later, as he says, with his imperturbable self-confidence, 'pronounces unerringly upon the merits of the case.' But he was revolutionary, where no revolt was needed; original, at his own expense; an inventor of systems, not a discoverer of riches. (pp. 153-54)

If we wish to find an infallible test of Southey's ear for rhythm, we shall find it in the 'short passages of Scripture rhythmically arranged or paraphrased' which are printed among his 'poetical remains.' One example will suffice. Here is the text as we find it in Jeremiah: 'Give glory unto the Lord your God, before he cause darkness, and before your feet stumble upon the dark mountains, and, while ye look for light, he turn it into the shadow of death, and make it gross darkness.' And this is what seemed to Southey a finer rhythmical arrangement:—

Give glory to the Lord your God!
Lest, while ye look for light,
He bring the darkness on,
And the feet that advanced
With haughty step,
Marching astray in their pride,
Stumble and fail
In the shadow of death. . . .

[We] see him deliberately, and with complete unconsciousness of what he is doing, turning a solemn and measured prose into unevenly jigging verse. . . . (pp. 156-57)

Then, Southey was not only an innovator in regard to metre, but in regard to the subject-matter of poetry. His great ambition was to write epics, and he wrote five or six immense narratives, of which the two most characteristic were founded on Arabian and Indian mythology. . . . [These poems are] empty frameworks, gaudy with far-fetched rags of many colours, which collapse at a touch or breath. . . . We see him reaching wildly after the local colour of the East, and yet, while trying to weave an Eastern pattern, boasting that 'there was nothing Oriental in the style.' It is as if a traveller brought back foreign fripperies from far countries, and hung himself all over with them, not in manner native to them, or to him. For all his deliberate heapings up of horror and amazement, his combinations of violence without heat and adventures without vital motion, Southey was no born romantic, but the solitary seeker after romance, writing among his books, and seeking in them the atmosphere, and in his subjects the imagination, which he should have brought with him, for they are to be found in no books and in no subjects. His incidents are impossible, but have none of that strangeness which is one of the properties of beauty; his seminary of sorcerers, his Glendoveers and Azyoruca, his demons and deities of Indian and Arabian mythology, have no power over the mind or the senses; in the horrors of his slaughtering and suffering immortals there is no thrill. A shadow on the wall, a footstep on an empty road, is enough material for the true master of terrors to chill the soul with. Southey wrecks many heavens and many hells, and does not quicken a pulse. (pp. 157-58)

'Roderick, the Last of the Goths' [is] the latest and perhaps the best of the epics. . . . [The] verse is quiet, and might contain good poetry, if it were not presented as a substitute for it. It is the rarest thing for a narrative poem, unless the narrative is an excuse and not an object, to be anything but prose disguised; here the narrative is everything, and we can but wonder why it has been written in blank verse rather than in prose. No unexpected beauty, light or music, ever comes into it; but one reads on, placidly interested, as if one were reading history. . . . But there is not in the whole long poem a single line by which one could recognise it at sight as poetry. . . . (p. 159)

When I ask myself if there is not in all Southey's work in verse anything which might not as well have been written in prose, I find myself hesitating a little over one section of ['**The Doctor**'], a section in which homely quaintness is sometimes combined with a grotesque or ironical humour. 'Take my word for it, Sir,' said Mr. Edgworth to Southey, 'the bent of your genius is for comedy'; and I think Mr. Edgworth was right. There is real metrical fun in '**The Cataract of Lodore,**' and in '**The Old Woman of Berkeley**' a real mastery of the gruesome. In the verses on '**The Holly Tree**' there is a certain measure, and in the verses written in his library there is more, of a pungent homeliness, through which for once the real man seems to speak, and to speak straight. But better than any of these, because it combines in one the best of their qualities, is '**The Battle of Blenheim,**' where the irony is at once naïve and profound, and where the extreme simplicity of the form is part of the irony. All the other poems may be compared with other better things of the same kind, as '**The Cataract of Lodore**' with '**The Bells**' and '**The Old Woman of Berkeley**' with '**The Witch of Fyfe**'; but in this poem Southey is himself, and no one has done a better poem of the kind. It is a poem of the pedestrian sort, but it is good of its sort. Southey's talent was pedestrian, and it was his misfortune that he tried to fly, with wings made to order, and on his own pattern, and a misfit. (p. 160)

Arthur Symons, "Robert Southey (1774-1843)," in his The Romantic Movement in English Poetry, *Archibald Constable & Co. Ltd., 1909, pp. 148-60.*

OLIVER ELTON (essay date 1912)

[*The two-volume survey from which the following excerpt is taken was originally published in 1912.*]

Southey's prose is much more voluminous, and much better, than his verse; yet little of it has lived. It is better, because the negative excellences of his verse—such as the level, workmanlike diction, so lacking in salience—become positive virtues in his prose. Here his subject is given to him; he seldom has to create one. And where there is greatness in the subject, as in the *Life of Wesley* or the *Life of Nelson* there is, then the style is a perfect medium. We look through it as through pure gently-flowing water; it does not distract our attention from the subject, and this is Southey's merit. It is pure eighteenth-century English, ranking high in its own high order. But whether that order be the highest or no, Southey's prose is not supreme within it. His mind is receptive and impressible rather than originative, and this deficiency is mirrored in his language. Swift has all the classical virtues, lucidity, measure, adaptiveness; but he also moulds and colours his subject. Southey does not; he has little genius; and his achromatic prose, with all its effortless ease and rightness, leaves us impatient and dissatisfied. . . . [However, there] is room for a pleasing and varied anthology from his prose works. Many delightful passages could thus be saved from the mass of lumber. The *Life of*

Nelson, at any rate, is secure; it need not figure in such a treasury. This process could be well applied, for instance, to *The Doctor,* where the style is not achromatic, but tinted, wilful, and humoristic, and which Southey wrote to please himself and wrote from his heart. In *The Doctor,* however, he becomes tedious; a little of it goes a long way; and it is a book to be 'tasted,' not 'chewed and digested.' Besides, much of it is imitative. Southey has taken on, by second nature, a comic rich Rabelaisian manner, or a whimsical excursive Sterne-like manner, and becomes the creature of his chameleon reading. We hardly feel, as we do with his favourite Burton, whose vast learning colours his very essence, that he is original in spite of it. But most of Southey's books fall into the former class, and are in his even, limpid style.

Otherwise, they almost defy classification. Some of them, such as *Omniana* . . . and the *Commonplace Book,* are immense collections of 'notes and queries,' such as three ordinary scholars do not gather in a lifetime. They give a vivid picture of Southey's mental furniture, and of the kind of material, ever easily at command, that he was ready to give out, woven and shot and broidered, in *The Doctor.* (pp. 8-9)

[The *Life of Nelson,*] designed as a manual 'for the young sailor, which he may carry about with him,' and therefore studiously simple in language, was written before the materials for a true biography were sifted or available, and founded on authorities which are now pronounced most unsafe. . . . Southey shows his usual incapacity for appreciating Napoleon and the French, and he was not conversant with the science of naval warfare. Yet he achieved a classic memoir, which is not merely a romance. He has an intuition of Nelson's genius and greatness as a man, he writes with a noble measure and reserve, and the skill of his narrative, interweaving as it does history and biography without confusion, and unfolding the character of his hero from point to point through his actions, is memorable enough.

The *Life of Wesley and the Rise and Progress of Methodism* . . . , which is also a life of Whitfield and of many lesser lights, is not a work of art like the *Nelson,* but is a more durable piece of historical scholarship, and calls out many of Southey's rarer gifts. It is written, to begin with, from without; that is, from the standpoint of his strict Anglicanism, here noticeably liberalised, and also in the spirit of a calm detachment which is wholly inaccessible to, and condemnatory of, the more passionate and violent forms of enthusiasm. . . . Southey works from the printed sources with much diligence, suffers Wesley to speak for himself, and if necessary to condemn himself, and leaves a most luminous impression of his work and genius.

Of his other memoirs little need be said; of the *Lives of the Admirals,* or of the briefer ones of Cromwell and Bunyan. The *Cromwell* is bigoted and unintelligent; the *Bunyan* hardly worthy of the theme, though not disfigured in the same way. Southey was more at home with Cowper, his *Life* of whom is full of charm and kindness, though somewhat rambling. . . . (pp. 11-12)

If most of Southey's prose has fallen out of sight, the reason is less to be found in its mass and its air of taskwork than in a certain intellectual stiffness and sterility of view. His conservatism is unbending; yet this is no bar to permanence, for the same might be said of Wordsworth, of Coleridge, and of Scott. But Southey's conservatism has not the geniality, the romantic chivalrousness, of Scott's; nor has it the august stamp of fervid meditation which at times distinguishes Wordsworth's. Nor is it, like Coleridge's, rooted in a philosophic play of thought, which is alive to the last whatever we may think of the conclusions; it is fixed and unreflective. In the same way Southey, though his enjoyment of books is deep, indeed is perhaps his master-passion, is not a critic of mark; beside Coleridge he seems lifeless. In his endless quotations and accompanying expressions of relish we miss that reaction of thought upon the subject, that penetrative power as of radium-rays, which is felt in every page of the *Table Talk* or of *Anima Poetae* [both by Coleridge]. For all this, Southey, if not in any strict sense a great writer, is often, nay, is instinctively, a sound and a good one, and is repeatedly a delightful one; and he left the status of men of letters, and the tradition of their calling higher than he found it. His correspondence, with its dignity, its naturalness, and its playful, affectionate touches of home, has all the virtues of his best writing. . . . (p. 12)

> Oliver Elton, "Southey and Landor," in his A Survey of English Literature: 1780-1830, Vol. II, Edward Arnold (Publishers) Ltd., 1920, pp. 1-48.*

THOMAS R. LOUNSBURY (essay date 1915)

[Southey's] prose, though lacking in the very highest graces of style, and by no means deserving of the excessive laudation sometimes bestowed upon it, is generally delightful and fully merited the favor with which it was regarded. It was simple, clear, and unaffected, and was frequently marked by felicities of phrase which arrest the attention and enforce the idea. It is even now always read with pleasure save when he sought to play the part of a humorist. The drollery of Southey is one of the most depressing things in literature. It excites a distrust in human nature, almost a sense of shame, that anything so preposterous should ever have been mistaken for facetiousness by any civilized man, still more by a man of a high order of ability. Yet it has further to be said that even in his prose his success was largely due to works which he himself regarded as comparatively unimportant. These were the little sketches, essays, and reviews which he produced merely as potboilers. (p. 344)

But there was one field in the department of prose which he purposed to make peculiarly his own. This was history. To build upon it a great name was one of his most ardent ambitions. To one work in particular he devoted his attention at an early period and labored at it more or less during his whole life. This was a history of Portugal. It was never completed and no portion of it was ever published. An offshoot of it, indeed—the history of Brazil—came out between the years 1810 and 1819 in three very bulky volumes. I have never read it—a peculiarity I share with nearly all the members of the English-speaking race—and therefore have not a right to express an opinion as to its merits. . . .

The truth is that Southey was unfitted both by temperament and training for a historian. By nature he was the intensest of partisans. To every investigation he made or question he considered, he brought a bundle of prejudices and preconceived views. He lacked entirely the judicial cast of mind which is never swerved from the truth by the merely plausible. He lacked still more that high historical imagination which gives to its possessor an almost intuitive insight into the motives which sway both individuls and masses of men. (p. 345)

One purely literary production of his of some notoriety, if not of much importance [was the work entitled **"The Doc-**

tor"]. . . . There are, it may be said, interesting passages in it, but it is not interesting as a whole. Worse than anything else, it is everywhere deformed by that terrible facetiousness in which Southey took delight, and in that bastard wit which relies for its effect not upon the idea which is sought to be conveyed but upon the variations of type in which the words are printed. Literature in fact has little more depressing than the ghastly attempts at humor found here. An elephant playfully endeavoring to gambol like a kitten may give one a physical counterpart to the mental feats of Southey in his desperate struggles to be jocose. (pp. 346-47)

[Southey's reputation] has slowly but steadily sunk since his death, in spite of occasional efforts to revive it; and that posterity, which in his opinion was to revere his memory, is already beginning to come dangerously near to forgetting his name. (p. 351)

> Thomas R. Lounsbury, "Southey As Poet and Historian," in The Yale Review, Vol. IV, No. 2, January, 1915, pp. 330-51.

JACK SIMMONS (essay date 1945)

[*Simmons's biography, which was originally published in 1945, is considered the definitive twentieth-century study of Southey's life. Simmons provides an overview of the poet's career and an appreciative survey of Southey's major works.*]

In his own time [Southey] was thought of primarily as a poet. Wordsworth and some other discerning judges might consider that his prose had higher and rarer merits: for the general public his reputation was founded by *Joan of Arc,* established by the four succeeding epics, and crowned by his appointment as Poet Laureate. Nowadays, those long poems are condemned out of hand, and they are seldom read; but they were none the less the corner-stone of his fame.

There is little to be said for *Joan of Arc,* except from a historical point of view: the poem is mainly interesting as an early manifesto of the Romantic Movement. It has none of the tender beauty of Wordsworth's *Evening Walk* . . .; nor can it match [his] *Lyrical Ballads,* which followed it by two years, in arresting power. But it was a portent in 1796 all the same, from the political views it expressed. . . . The epic poem had never been used before to preach the doctrines of pacifism. . . . (pp. 207-08)

In a literary sense, however, *Joan of Arc* is a conservative piece of work, strongly marked with the character of the late eighteenth century. Book IX (the Maid's Vision) is a pure Gothic tale of horror, such as Mrs. Radcliffe or "Monk" Lewis might have conceived; while there are occasional descriptive passages after—but a very long way after—the manner of Thomson and Gray:

> 'Twas now the hour
> When o'er the plain the pensive hues of eve
> Shed their meek radiance, when the lowing herd,
> Slow as they stalk to shelter, draw behind
> The lengthening shades; and seeking his high nest,
> As heavily he flaps the dewy air,
> The hoarse rook pours his not unpleasing note.

As we should expect in the work of a man of twenty-one, the poem is full of echoes, particularly of Milton and Spenser. Its only artistic merit consists in the forthright vigour with which the story is told, wishy-washy though the language and sentiment often are; and the bland, *naïve* tone of the whole thing is disarming and sometimes attractive.

The next of the epics to be written, though not to be published, was *Madoc,* the longest, the least successful, the most tedious of the five. It need not detain us. The story is highly involved, and it is impossible to feel the smallest interest in the cardboard characters with their outlandish names—Yuhidthiton, Tlalala, Tezozomoc and the rest of them. The poem is unlikely to find readers now, except among specialist students of Romantic literature, and perhaps Welsh or Mexican nationalists.

Its successor, *Thalaba,* is a great deal more attractive and interesting. The poem was written in almost exactly a year . . . , [much of it in very pleasant circumstances]. Something of this happiness seems to be reflected in *Thalaba,* which is sunny and gracious in tone. . . . As in all Southey's mythological pieces, the episodes fail to convince the reader because they are at once incredible in a human sense and uninteresting as miracles. They happen with too much ease: thousand-mile journeys through ice-bound passes and burning deserts occur almost casually—we are not made to feel their difficulty at all. (pp. 208-09)

But though the plot may be uninteresting, *Thalaba* has many incidental quiet beauties. . . . And there are some charming descriptive passages. In the fourth book, for instance, during his journey over the desert to Bagdad, Thalaba sees a mirage:

> But oh the joy! the blessed sight!
> When in that burning waste the Travellers
> Saw a green meadow, fair with flowers besprent,
> Azure and yellow, like the beautiful fields
> Of England, when amid the growing grass
> The blue-bell bends, the golden king-cup shines,
> And the sweet cowslip scents the genial air,
> In the merry month of May!

If only Southey had written more of England, which he knew and loved devotedly, instead of dealing with remote subjects for which neither he nor we can really feel any deep sympathy, he might have been an important poet.

Technically, *Thalaba* is of interest as an experiment in un-rhymed irregular stanzas. To be successful, a poem in such a form must pulsate with a strong rhythm. Unhappily, rhythmical drive was not among Southey's qualities. He tried to supply the deficiency by the frequent repetition of phrases, which becomes an irritating trick; and too often the verse of *Thalaba* lapses into prose in consequence. In language, the poem shows a great advance on *Joan.* There are still some passages of an artificial eighteenth-century character, such as that at the beginning of Book V about the pelican and the tiger (incorrectly described as ''the spotted prowler of the wild''); but altogether the language of *Thalaba* is far purer, simpler, less derivative.

With *The Curse of Kehama* we reach the finest of the epics, a poem of real distinction and even splendour. Like *Thalaba,* it is written in irregular stanzas; but they are rhymed, and that makes all the difference. It is a Hindu fable this time, hardly more interesting in detail than its predecessor, but incomparably grander in execution and scope. . . . It works up to an impressive climax at the end, and there is a very fine passage in Book XIX, where Ereenia, one of the Glendoveers (''the most beautiful of the Good Spirits'') and the real hero of the story, flies to the top of Mount Calasay. (pp. 209-11)

Thalaba was written in a year: *Kehama* took shape very much more slowly. . . . That may be why it is a better poem. With

Southey, difficulties and hesitation are usually a sign of good work (this is often true of his prose as well: the *Life of Nelson* cost him immense trouble in its details). The things he wrote fluently seldom have any power. *The Curse of Kehama*—there can be no doubt of it—stands with [Walter Landor's] *Gebir* at the head of English oriental poems of the Romantic period, a very much more distinguished work than [Thomas Moore's] *Lalla Rookh* or [George Gordon, Lord Byron's] *The Giaour.*

Its successor, the fifth of the series, was *Roderick, the Last of the Goths.* Some good judges, such as Coleridge [see excerpt above, 1817] and Lamb, have given it the highest place among Southey's long poems. It is true that it boasts much the most interesting plot; the central theme, Roderick's penitence and expiation, is a noble one; and the King himself comes near to being a real character. But the poem is not very easy reading all the same. It is written in blank verse, in some respects admirably handled; but the metre has not the charm of the light irregular rhythms of *Kehama,* thickly interspersed with rhymes. The modern reader who wishes to sample Southey's epic poetry at its most attractive will do best to begin with *Kehama* or *Thalaba* rather than *Roderick.* (p. 212)

First place among [Southey's shorter pieces] must go to the ballads and metrical tales: he had in him a true vein of the grotesque, which finds its best expression here. **''The Old Woman of Berkeley,'' ''The Inchcape Rock'',** and the story of Bishop Hatto were familiar to most of us as children, and they do not lose their charm. The same is true of the subtler **''Battle of Blenheim''.** Nor are these the only good ones: **''Queen Orraca and the Five Martyrs of Morocco'',** for instance, is a fine story. In these pieces Southey is in his element: nobody has ever equalled him in the peculiar *genre* of the comic-grotesque, except Barham in the *Ingoldsby Legends*—and they are an altogether more elaborate affair. His pure comic pieces are also very entertaining. The best of them show extraordinary metrical dexterity: that indeed is the main point of **''The Cataract of Lodore''** and **''The March to Moscow''.**

The historical poems are of less interest. They include a group of some fifty inscriptions and epitaphs, modelled on those of Akenside and the Italian poet Chiabrera, both of whom were favourites with Southey. One might have expected this form to suit him, for the very defects of his verse—a certain stiffness and impersonality—can become virtues in an inscription. Yet on the whole these pieces are disappointing. They are diffuse, they lack pith. . . . The best of them are those referring to episodes in the Peninsular War. Among the other historical pieces, only one is remarkable: the **''Funeral Song for the Princess Charlotte of Wales''.** . . . (pp. 212-13)

There still remains a handful of small lyrical poems, and these comprise Southey's most charming contribution to English verse. They all have one feature in common: they describe the peace and pleasure of domestic life. That is what he most deeply loved: it is not surprising that it should have called forth his best poetry. Two of these pieces are famous, and have often appeared in anthologies: **''The Holly Tree''** and **''My Days Among the Dead are Passed''.** But there are other poems in the same spirit too, and at least one of the same calibre—the sonnet on Winter. . . . Or again, the gentle ballad **''Brough Bells'',** and the graceful inscription for his daughter's album, **''Little Book, in Green and Gold''.** (pp. 213-14)

The central defects of Southey's poetry are two. In the first place it has no magic: it does not *sing.* The second defect is even more important than the first: indeed, it is probably responsible for it. . . . Southey found that poetical composition excited him too much, upsetting the delicate balance of his mind and breaking into his sleep. (It was linked, one cannot doubt, with his weird, astonishing dreams, of which he has left a fascinating record that a modern psychiatrist might with advantage explore.) His first thought had always to be of his family and of the bread and butter he must earn for them. . . . The disturbance of composing poetry with concentration—the difficult, and sometimes agonising, process . . .—was a luxury he could not afford. He chose rather to write tales in verse and light pieces, which he threw off with a fatal facility. Presently he found even that too exciting, and he turned over almost completely to prose.

This does not imply a claim that he was a potential Wordsworth or Coleridge: it only means that he did not let himself go, or give his poetical talent full scope. Of set purpose, he kept it within constricting limits, never allowing it the time or the concentrated energy that great poetry demands. Instead, verse took turn and turn about with history, politics, and reviewing: the four last epics were almost entirely written before breakfast. Whether one considers that he did his duty best by bringing up a family and providing for them at the expense of his poetry, or that in doing so he sinned against the light, failing to use the talent committed to him, must depend upon one's point of view.

One might feel more inclined to judge him harshly on this issue if he had not left us something besides his verse: the huge, delightful legacy of his prose. Here he is a master beyond dispute, an artist of a high order.

To understand his achievement fully, it must be looked at in a historical as well as an aesthetic light. In poetry, it is a commonplace to say that the *Lyrical Ballads* marked a revolutionary departure from eighteenth-century practice. (pp. 214-15)

We are accustomed to speak of the "clarity" of eighteenth-century prose. The Romantics would have thought that an odd and mistaken judgment, at best no more than a half-truth. They were for ever decrying the style of the second half of the century, of Johnson and Gibbon, with its periods and regular rhythms. (p. 215)

The Romantic prose-writers reacted from the Johnsonian style in two ways. Wordsworth, Coleridge, and Lamb turned to the seventeenth century for their models. [Wordsworth's] *Tract on the Convention of Cintra* is impregnated with the style and spirit of Milton, Coleridge's prose was deeply influenced by the great Caroline divines, Lamb's by Fuller and Sir Thomas Browne. All of them have one thing in common: they are essentially poetical styles, intensively evocative and musical. Southey did not hark back so far. His closest affinities are with Swift, and still more with Defoe. This was quite natural, for the problems that faced them were the same: they were all three voluminous authors, writing constantly for the press. And it is significant that each of them wrote a children's classic: Defoe in *Robinson Crusoe*, Swift in *Gulliver's Travels*, Southey in **"The Story of the Three Bears"**. That is a difficult feat, which few great writers have achieved, for a single false note is fatal—nothing will do short of complete simplicity, sincerity, and truth.

But whereas the terse style of Swift and Defoe was in harmony with the spirit of their age (it developed from the masters of the preceding generation, from Dryden and pamphleteers like Halifax), Southey was an almost unique practitioner of the art

in the early nineteenth century. The nearest parallel to him among the writers of his own time is to be found in Cobbett; but admirable though Cobbett's work is, it cannot compare with Southey's in variety or poetic feeling. Contrast him, on the other hand, with Hazlitt, another prolific writer. Hazlitt's style is far more elaborate and highly wrought, enriched with every kind of device of quotation and inversion. It is an instrument of greater power than Southey's, perhaps of greater range; but on the other hand it has less clarity and ease. Above all, it is an obviously self-conscious style, whereas Southey's is completely self-effacing.

Yet the art is there all the same. Coleridge observed that "in the very best styles, as Southey's, you read page after page, understanding the author perfectly, without once taking notice of the medium of communication; it is as if he had been speaking to you all the while"; and more recently it has been well said that "we look through it as through pure gently-flowing water". But nothing could be more incorrect than to suppose that because his style is so quiet and unassuming it was easily achieved or can easily be imitated. (pp. 215-16)

During the course of his life [Southey] forced himself out of the debased eighteenth-century manner in which he began to write into a crisp, nervous style of his own. In his prose he pursued a lonely path, of a piece with the stubborn independence of his career. The Romantic tendency was in general towards ornament: the object he set before himself was above all to be plain and brief. He was thus at variance with Coleridge and Lamb and Hazlitt; but also, in writing as much as in politics, with the *Edinburgh Review*. Jeffrey and his young disciple Macaulay still looked back to the late eighteenth century for their models. Their rotundity, the regular rise and fall of their sentences, has little parallel in Southey, whose style is altogether lighter and more pliant. But those are the very qualities that give it special value for us to-day; for it stands nearer to our ideals and needs than that of any other of his contemporaries. (p. 216)

> *Jack Simmons, in his* Southey, *Yale University Press, 1948, 256 p.*

V. S. PRITCHETT (essay date 1952)

[*Pritchett, a modern British writer, is respected for his mastery of the short story and for what critics describe as his judicious, reliable, and insightful literary criticism. He writes in the conversational tone of the familiar essay, and he approaches literature from the viewpoint of an informed but not overly-scholarly reader. Pritchett's critical method is to stress his own experience, judgment, and sense of literary art as opposed to following a codified doctrine derived from a school of psychological or philosophical theory. Here he praises Southey's* Letters from England *for their historical and literary value.*]

Southey's **Letters from England** is one of the curiosities of the early literature of tourism. It was written in the first decade of the 19th century when travelling in England for pleasure had become possible—it had begun with the improvement in the roads two generations before—and when the taste for the picturesque was strong. Southey continued the tradition that dated from Defoe's *Tour,* and the journeys in Smollett's *Humphrey Clinker;* though in using the satirical device of the foreign visitor—Southey's traveller was a firm Spanish Catholic—the book had the chance of being another *Citizen of the World* [by Goldsmith] or another *Lettres Persanes* [by Montesquieu]. With these works it cannot be compared. Southey had his opinions and information, but he was no satirist. He could conceive respectability but not innocence. The *Letters* are a mild miscellany of accurate impressions and the product of an agreeable but rather literal and industrious mind. His account of the English universities, for example, is documentary. As he was young when he wrote this book it has freshness, and the picture we get of the England of 1805 is valuable and vivid in its living detail; but what we know of his subsequent life as a prolific and successful literary personage, gives a pathos to this early work. Southey had the infinite capacity for taking pains, but zest took the place of genius; and upon his talent there lies the discreet gleam of eager, anxious and limited natures who seem to have turned to literature in order to feel socially secure and presentable. He succeeded in his two ambitions: happy family life and respectable eminence. Literature, for him, was something habitable. . . .

[At the time he wrote the *Letters*] Southey had just spent more than a year in Spain and Portugal and he used more ingenuity than was really necessary in putting his narrative into the mouth of a Spanish Catholic. This gentleman is unnecessarily well-drawn for, from the reader's point of view, he is a mere mystery and conundrum. The curious thing is that Southey had been converted in Portugal to passionate hatred of the Roman Catholic church; why was he at such pains to assume the Roman Catholic point of view? I think Southey, like many men who are bent on moderation at all costs, enjoyed intrigue with his own convictions and, as a writer, liked to paralyse the extremism that was buried in his nature. . . .

[The] *Letters* are too well-written to pass as concocted translations. His prose is light, supple, fluent, clear and perfectly adapted to the movement of travel and informative observation. He is never tedious; one can complain only that he is unadventurous. He certainly speaks out about the horrible conditions of life of the industrial poor; he has his go at the "wicked pride" of Pitt; he is a tender spirit who loathes horseplay, brutality and cruelty; and he can never leave a religious sect alone. But we pick our way through this industrious compilation looking rather for the human instance than for opinion, for the anecdote, the scene at the inn, the landscape. He has the gift of putting down people in movement: the coachman waiting for the stroke of the Minster bell in York before he cracks his whip, the children jeering at an old man, the innkeeper diddling him on the turnpike, people pushing for the window seat on the coaches, the accident on the road and the men shovelling snow off the London roofs. . . . At its best, Southey's prose has [an] easy power of disengagement and connection, so that even in the descriptions of landscape, the scene is caught as it changes under the eye, is held on some detail, and then released once more until the new sight is picked up. The description of the Lake Country has been greatly praised for this agreeble mixing of simple topography and impression, but his scenery is always good. There sticks in my mind that brief picture of an island in the fens with its four enormous willows at the end of it—"planted no doubt by a gentleman of taste." And noted by one: the conjunction is very English in its feeling for the countryside. Southey's prose is not closely written, majestic or rich; it means no more than it says. He aims at transparency so that we might be looking through the clear water to the brown pebbles of a lively northern beck. It is the prose of a mild, critical mind and occasionally Southey's triteness has its own irony. . . .

Southey took pains to crowd his narrative. The moans of the Napoleonic wars have a contemporary echo; the small gentry

and the professional classes are being ruined; a government that employs snoopers is undermining morality, high prices and taxes are killing the best; who can afford to educate his children?—this was to be Southey's lasting cry: he was to have seven of his own and there were the Coleridges to support as well; he liked the martyrdom of responsibility. The picturesque side makes up for this. We hear that glass windows for shops have come in, that the art of window-dressing has begun. In one shop he sees a sturgeon two yards long; next door a chemist displays bottles of intestinal worms with the name and address of the one-time host and the infallible cure. (p. 406)

The *Letters* make a long book, but one can see why the historians have not disdained to dip in it. Southey had his helpers and correspondents; he was a mass-observer before his time, a collector of miscellany. His England was a cross-grained place but Southey was well on his way to the conviction that it was better suited to the profession of authorship than were the banks of the Susquehanna. (p. 408)

> *V. S. Pritchett, in a review of "Letters from England," in* The New Statesman & Nation, *Vol. XLIII, No. 1100, April 5, 1952, pp. 406, 408.*

BRIAN WILKIE   (essay date 1965)

[*In the following excerpt from his full-length study of the epic tradition in Romantic poetry, Wilkie delineates the distinctions between what he considers Southey's three "genuine" epics, Madoc, Roderick, and Joan of Arc, and his romances, Thalaba and The Curse of Kehama. He categorizes them according to their versification, moral intent, and historical value. Wilkie further asserts that while Southey intended the romances to preach, his epics possessed more noble aspirations in their roles as moral tales.*]

Southey's epic conscience, his solemn belief that the epic ought to have high seriousness and observe an old-fashioned and stately decorum, is reflected in the careful distinction he generally made between his three genuine epics [*Madoc, Roderick,* and *Joan of Arc*] and his romances—*Thalaba* and *The Curse of Kehama.* To lump all these poems together under the general heading of epics, as is sometimes done, is to lose sight of the more conservative approach which Southey generally adopts in his true epics. At times he used the word *epic* in a rather loose way. . . . But almost always Southey distinguished scrupulously between his own epics and romances. Most neoclassical epic theorists had granted fabulous material a place in the epic, though often uneasily; they had, after all, Aristotle's sanction for admitting probable impossibilities. But on this score Southey is often more royalist than the king, for his epics, unlike his romances, are basically naturalistic, despite their exoticism. The romance, Southey claimed, might dispense with "epic laws." Furthermore, romance had the prerogative of digression, and loose construction he seems to have accepted as almost the definitive mark of the form. In such attitudes Southey shows himself to be the heir of countless critical discussions of epic unity and the function of "episode."

Another important mark of the distinction Southey made between his epics and his romances was their versification. The epics were to be written in blank verse, the romances in a less pure, more bizarre strain. He seems to have thought of blank verse as a perspicuous medium to be used when the inherent grandeur of a subject was to be allowed to shine through the verse without distortion—in other words, when the poet was attempting the sublime, a quality which critics of the preceding

age had often linked with simplicity. . . . [However,] Southey's avoidance of blank verse in *Thalaba* and *Kehama* was, in
fact, a kind of protection for the true epics; the distinction
between blank verse and the meters used in his romances was
to mark outwardly the superior dignity and loftier intentions
of the epics.

Southey considered his epics more important than his romances, but the distinction between the two forms is not the
simple distinction between the serious and the frivolous. The
romances belong to a comprehensive plan whose value is independent of the individual subjects of the poems, the plan
which Southey conceived during his school days of illustrating
the various mythologies of the world in a series of narrative
poems. The plan is primarily educational and has something
of the quality of a tour de force, like playing a number of
themes in the same musical style. The greater importance of
the epics is a literary rather than a moral distinction. The romances, in fact, are more forthrightly didactic; they are closer
to Spenser than to Ariosto, and Southey sometimes thought of
them in allegorical terms. (pp. 36-7)

The importance of *Thalaba* and *Kehama* is qualified by their
being installments in a plan whose general documentary value
meant more to Southey than any of the component parts; individually the romances are in many ways virtuoso entertainments. Yet their strong moral emphasis is an important link
between them and Southey's epics. All of Southey's long poems
contain the same central moral idea—the confidence in Faith,
the self-reliance which scorns external events as by their nature
foreign to the soul and unable to affect it in any important way.
The romances differ from the epics, however, in the way they
express this moral. To the extent that the epics are moral (a
large extent), they are so in an exemplary way; their purpose
is to present, not lessons, but images, of heroism. This fact
probably explains their more naturalistic approach. The romances, though not true allegories, have something of the
artificial, masquelike quality of allegory. The actions of the
heroes—Thalaba's destruction of the evil Domdaniel, the overthrow of Kehama and his enchantments—are projections on a
thoroughly fanciful supernatural plane of the values which
Southey believes in. The immediate application of these values
is not spelled out; they are abstract, like the cardinal virtues.
The romances do not sound rallying-cries; they preach sermons.
Their values are meant to be relevant to life, but the reader
must generalize an abstract moral from the exotic tale and then
re-interpret and apply the moral in familiar human terms. Like
typical allegory, Southey's romances operate on two levels,
that of narrative action and that of ideals. But Southey inverts
the usual relationship of these levels; the narrative vehicle is
a supernatural, wildly fabulous tale, while the underlying message is moral—usually, in fact, domestic. The emphasis on
domestic values is one of the most characteristic strains in
Southey. . . . In Southey vice is conquered with regularity and
supreme ease.

There is an important statement by Southey which indicates
his basic moral intention in *Thalaba* and points toward his more
sentimental notion of heroism, both in his romances and his
epics. "It would be well," he writes, "to make Thamama's
[that is, Thalaba's] most painful obstacles arise from those
domestic feelings which in another would be virtue." Here,
as he does in *Joan* . . . , Southey introduces the kind of conflict
which runs back through all the definitive literary epics—the
conflict between duty and happiness. But, as both his statement
and his poems indicate, he substitutes domestic contentment

for voluptuous pleasure as the alternative to duty, instead of
posing the problem in the familiar form of duty versus carnality.
In *Joan* this modification of the traditional conflict serves a
functional purpose, since there the peace of domesticity contrasts with the horror of war and therefore emphasizes that
horror. But in *Thalaba* the new version of the old struggle is
less useful; here the conflict is a typically puritan one, a conflict
between two kinds of righteousness, one easy and pleasant,
the other stern and bitter. Southey's abhorrence of sensuality
prevents him from posing the problem in the traditional way,
even in a semi-allegorical romance where the pleasures of the
flesh could be used to best symbolic advantage. (pp. 38-9)

Southey's romances occasionally resemble his epics in using
elements copied in some detail from traditional epic. Some of
these elements are among the recurrent accessories of older
romances as well as of the epic or romantic epic—one recalls
Southey's somewhat permissive epic canon and the unselfconscious inclusion of Ariosto in it—but they do add something
of epic dimension and atmosphere. To put it another way, epic
and romance were different forms for Southey, but they were
not in every way mutually exclusive.

In Southey's general attitude toward literature of the past, and
especially in his attitude toward epic, one finds not only the
inconsistencies which are, after all, to be expected from a
person as outspoken as he was, but also the sharply ambivalent
attitude toward tradition which is typical of epic poets. Southey
is atypical of them, however—apart from his obvious inferiority as a poet—in his serious preoccupation with the legalisms
of epic *theory*. Sometimes Southey scornfully rejects the theory, but by and large he observes it, and sometimes he pretends
to reject it while in fact following it. In any event, he uses
epic *theory* as a point of departure much more systematically
than the great epic poets or his own contemporaries usually
did. . . . Greater epic poets have imitated their models but
have not generally felt so much conditioned, one way or the
other, by rules, since their main concern has been with the
values preached by their poetic predecessors and not with pre-
scriptive formulas. This distinction between Southey and other
epic poets is significant. . . . (pp. 40-1)

To express his antipatriotism and the quasi-religious values
that were his in 1795 Southey could hardly have chosen a better
vehicle than the story of [*Joan of Arc,*] especially in view of
his tendentious interpretation of her character. The fifteenth-
century English wars in France are associated with the names
of great English heroes, and for Southey to depict these wars
as adventures in greedy imperialism fought against a pastoral
people led by a sweet-tempered young girl was a brilliant tour
de force of propaganda. (p. 44)

Through Joan the young Southey expresses not only his views
on English opposition to the French Revolution but also a
system of religious values which are at times Wordsworthian
in their emphasis on natural piety. This religious note, perhaps
accidentally, also serves Southey's propagandistic purpose, for
Joan is like the revolutionary French patriots in being opposed
both by the English and by the religionists of the Old Re-
gime. . . . In fact, though, the religious message is not mere
occasional propaganda. The entire scheme of religious and
moral values in the poem hints at the general ethical concept
which is to remain fairly constant through Southey's later long
narrative poems, whether they be epics or romances—the confident belief in the ultimate triumph of the righteous cause. In
these later poems Southey is to emphasize continually that
righteousness will prevail by virtue of its own invincible force,

whatever merely external obstacles it encounters. In *Joan* this confidence is more directly connected with divine aid, but the heroine's serene rejection of merely circumstantial obstacles is as great as it is ever to be for Southey's later heroes. . . . [However, because of] simple resolutions of conflicts, *Joan* loses something in dramatic effectiveness; the young peasant girl, like all of Southey's heroes, conquers too easily for her victories to have anything more than a mechanically exemplary value, as in pious cautionary tales. (pp. 44-6)

[*Joan of Arc*] challenges the conventional idea of heroism. The sophisticated, literary epic had made heroism more than mere martial prowess, but it had always included and (sometimes grudgingly) praised such prowess; even in Milton the angels are great warriors. In *Joan* the whole value of fighting is questioned, and the grim necessity of war for the freedom of one's homeland is established only after the issue has been explored at some length. . . .

During the time when Southey was writing and publishing *Joan of Arc,* his attitude toward traditional epic seems to have been inconsistent and fluctuating. The Preface which accompanies the 1796 edition treats the standard epics and their heroes with cavalier independence, but many years later he acknowledged some kind of debt to them; his intention, he stated, had been not to imitate but to follow. This statement may well be an old man's pious rationalization in retrospect; it would be more accurate to say that the poem *does* imitate but does *not* follow. It is true, though, that some of Southey's choicest youthful invective was directed at what he considered epic poetasters and their servile imitations. (p. 46)

Yet Southey wanted *Joan of Arc* to be, in an important and publicly recognizable way, an epic. Looking back much later on his early life, he wrote that to compose an epic had been, during his youth, the highest ambition possible, and that it had been the earliest of his own daydreams. It was not simply that he had certain ideas which seemed to demand the epic framework for their expression; his attraction was partly to the form for its own sake. But . . . an epic is not really identifiable by a lofty tone or certain general literary objectives or the poet's reverential attitude toward his subject. For an epic to be recognizable as such, it must have some of the devices which mark it as a lineal descendant of other epics, superficial as these devices may seem in isolation. Consequently, despite his alleged independence of rules and refusal to imitate, Southey does what Milton, despite a similar declaration of disdainful independence, does in *Paradise Lost:* he imitates.

Most of the imitations in *Joan* are obvious. The central situation in the poem is the siege of Orleans, a familiar enough setting. The poem begins in the middle of things: the war between France and England has been going on for some years. . . . There are obvious attempts at Miltonic style.

But *Joan of Arc* uses the epic associations most ingeniously through deliberate or pointed departures from standard epic devices or by occasional adoption of such devices with a twist which alters them for Southey's own purpose, usually political propaganda. Thus, *Joan* is in a very real sense a national poem, as many neoclassic theorists believed an epic should be, for although Southey aggressively chooses not to glorify his own country, the message of the poem is directed at the English and concerns English ideals. Southey tries to reveal to his countrymen, for their edification, a heroic standard which is defined negatively—that is, by English departures from it. (pp. 47-8)

Southey denounces war through another free adaptation of an epic device: the thumbnail sketch of a warrior during a scene describing his fight and death; the author uses this Homeric technique, but for his own ends. He takes an unknown soldier and tries to give him individuality by describing his background. . . . More specifically, he takes a single soldier and sketches his life before the war, a life of peaceful domestic bliss [or of rustic cheer, or of convivial hospitality, or of peaceful enjoyment of the comforts of life]. . . . The effect is to underline the pathos of war and to disparage the false glory of heroic exploits. Southey does not preach peace at any price, but he does stress the suffering and disorder caused by war. And again a traditional epic device is used, somewhat ironically, to drive home the point.

Perhaps the most striking way in which Southey uses the epic tradition as a springboard is in his choice of a woman as hero. . . . [This] departure from precedent has powerful propaganda value. It is true that Southey had a number of epic precedents for Joan in the warrior maidens who figure in almost every important model. . . . But in Southey's poem the warrior maiden is the central figure. . . . Nevertheless, Southey's substitution of heroine for epic hero would have seemed a blatant repudiation of the tradition of epic virility, a pointed request that the reader compare basic human values with merely martial or brutal ones. Here it is the critical clichés which make Southey's propaganda point possible; the reader is asked to accept the much oversimplified view (shared by some falsely nostalgic people today) in which earlier epic heroism consists in mere strength and derring-do; if the reader thinks of epic so simple-mindedly, the shock value of Southey's reversal of precedent is obviously heightened. In preferring the "good herdsman Eumaeus" to "a thousand heroes" Southey is expressing both his sentimentalism and his dismay at the epic's thirst for blood; his choice of a woman as hero of his first epic expresses the same two feelings. In his later epics the quasi-pacifist leanings first weaken and then (in *Roderick*) completely disappear, but in *Joan* Southey is still an extreme liberal.

Joan, as epic heroine, is faced with the same problem as are many epic heroes—the problem of the conflicting demands of her love and her vocation. Of course, there is never any possibility that she will neglect her mission; Southey's protagonists are almost as superior to temptation as they are to sin. She may regret her stern duty and the renunciation it demands, but she does not waver. Still, we are given some sense of Joan's sacrifice, as well as her lover's, and thus the pathos of war is again emphasized. But her temptation does not involve unruly passions. . . . For Joan heroism in war is a hard alternative to something which is good in itself—namely, a retired life of domestic happiness. There is no moral question involved, only the question of the heroine's having sufficient heroic stature. (pp. 49-50)

In *Joan of Arc* Southey preaches radical political values and reinforces them with an iconoclastic attitude toward the epic and its tradition. In his later epics, *Madoc* and *Roderick,* the political radicalism largely disappears, and in general the approach to epic mellows toward conservatism; that is, the epic devices are generally used in a straightforward way, without irony or restiveness—this despite Southey's continuing progressivism about literature as a whole. There are exceptions, however, especially in *Madoc,* the composition of which spans both the years of Southey's youthful radicalism and the first years of his retreat from that position. *Madoc* is thus a transitional work in Southey's career as an author of epics. It is

filled with self-conscious reminiscences of the standard epics. . . . [However] there is one revealing incident in the poem
wherein Southey strategically reverses epic precedent. Just as
Joan had rejected the vision of the future, so Madoc rejects
heroic precedent by declining a challenge to decisive single
combat. The reason, apparently, is that Southey wants to distinguish Madoc's noble, quasi-religious cause from the less
elevated ones celebrated in earlier epics. (p. 55)

Through the third and last of his epics Southey preaches [a]
somewhat impersonal, highly idealized kind of heroism. In
Roderick it takes a strange and very repellent form, one that
seems in some ways to depart from the older heroic values but
in even more emphatic ways is old-fashioned enough—certainly that if blood is the criterion. In the poem Southey manages to combine exactly the kind of operatically mawkish heroism which by some lights typifies the Romantic betrayal of
earlier epic with a militaristic zeal that seems the more ap-
pallingly fierce and cruel for its merger with high-sounding,
suprapersonal values. The reconciliation is accomplished in
much the same way as in the "Battle Hymn of the Republic."
But, putting aside this ambiguous idea of heroism, Southey's
approach to epic in the two later poems is fairly conservative;
if we refuse the title of conventional epic to **Madoc** and **Roderick,** we do so mainly on the score of quality, for the poems
have many of the traditional features of epic, used in fairly
conventional ways. Both as polemic and as a document in the
history of epic **Joan of Arc** is much the most interesting of the
three works. It is not squarely in the epic tradition, but the
reasons that ultimately disqualify it tell us more about the way
epic works than do the more pallid efforts with which Southey
followed it up.

Joan of Arc fails of genuine epic status not only because, like
Madoc and **Roderick,** it is not good enough, but also because
its targets include the epic tradition itself and not merely earlier,
inadequate visions now to be superseded. Through his career
as a whole, Southey generally felt veneration for the epic; he
might sense and occasionally resent the pressure of neoclassic
rules, but he also felt a reverent sense of guidance by the
organic continuum represented in the great epics themselves.
The Preface to **Madoc,** a poem that tries, however unsuccess-
fully, to carry forward the epic tradition, attacks indignantly
the *rules* of Aristotle; the Preface to **Joan,** a truly anti-epic
poem, claims to repudiate the very texture, the recurrent devices, of the epic tradition. Not that this disclaimer is conclusive in itself, for epic poets tend to indulge in exactly such
rhetoric; what matters is that in **Joan** Southey really does what
he threatens, he tries to undermine what epic has stood for, to
cut the lifeline of the tradition. The poem, however, is a youthful outburst eccentric to his epic career. (pp. 56-7)

If it is necessary to classify **Joan of Arc,** . . . [call it a noncomic
mock-epic]. It is certainly more than coincidence that the eighteenth century, the age of relative critical consensus about the
epic, is also the great age of mock-epic. All mock-epic depends
on the widespread acceptance of a rigid traditional pattern,
whether the pattern has been absorbed through the kind of
desperate simplifications fed to schoolboys or through critical
theory at large. The true epic imitates in order to dramatize
through the familiarity of the setting a new and loftier heroic
ideal that has allegedly surpassed the old ideals by way of
growing out of them; mock-epic takes as at least one of its
targets the epic vehicle itself, which it ridicules, often gently,
by substituting for an oversimplified traditional heroism an
absurdly incongruous version of it. *Comic* mock-epic depends

on an inflexible view of epic because the more inflexible and
narrow-minded the reader's stereotype, the funnier the joke at
the epic's expense. (p. 57)

> Brian Wilkie, "'Epomania': Southey and Landor,"
> in his Romantic Poets and Epic Tradition, *University
> of Wisconsin Press, 1965, pp. 30-58.*

MICHAEL N. STANTON (essay date 1974)

[*Stanton analyzes Southey's theory of autobiography as revealed
in his* Life and Correspondence. *The critic maintains that Southey
was not attempting to compose an inward narrative in the Romantic tradition, but rather to objectively record his life as a
"kind of genre-painting in words."*]

[As his *Life and Correspondence* begins, Southey seeks] to
recall a social fabric of the past, weaving skeins of detail
together to suggest the textures of a period, "a stage of society." And it is in the accumulation of details, the small facts
and individual threads, that the pattern of the fabric becomes
evident. . . .

For Southey the value of the past does not lie in the insights
it can yield into one's own heart and mind as in part it does
for Wordsworth. Nor does it lie in the contrast of past and
present. . . . (p. 115)

Rather Southey finds value in trying to recreate the past as an
integral structure, through a textured accumulation of numerous
and richly varied details. A total recall or total grasp of the
past—the personal interwoven with the social—is itself a guard
against time and the chances of mortality. At the beginning of
his twelfth letter Southey writes, "I have sometimes fancied,
when dreaming upon what may be our future state, that in the
next world we may recover a perfect recollection of all that
has occurred to us in this". . . . This suggests that a complete
encompassment of the past can represent a triumph over time;
he immediately qualifies this handsome fancy with the notion
that everyone probably has something he would *like* to forget.

In suggesting that the past has some imaginative hold over
Southey, I do not wish to de-emphasize his avowed and explicit
purpose of creating a social history. That record is more important as an end in itself than is the re-capture of the past as
an experiment in imaginative regeneration. For it seems clear
that in spite of his faithful efforts to record a total past, time
oppresses Southey; or rather, *because* of this large and impossible attempt, *we know* it oppresses him.

Time did oppress him of course in a very practical way, for
he had to live by his pen, and there was much writing to be
done. It also weighed upon him as a barrier to personal achievement. . . . And time and the past, in their usual roles as sen-
tinels of man's mortality, are oppressive; many years after his
time at Westminster Southey meets the son of a schoolfellow,
and the chance meeting becomes for him "one of those incidents in life that bring home to us the lapse of time with most
effect". . . . (pp. 115-16)

But these are subordinate themes in Southey's reminiscences.
He shares a concern with time and the past with writers who
are called Romantics; but that concern is hardly exclusive to
Romanticism. . . . Southey in these letters, that is, the recollection of emotionally significant private experience, is to a
great extent what he claims to be, a historian of domestic
society. He sees his childhood background and education as
individual, certainly, but hardly as unique or even atypical.

Southey's recollections of his boyhood are not suffused with passion; rather they are tinged with nostalgia. Describing his grandmother's house at Bedminster, he writes, "I have seen the gazebo [on the roof] since, from the windows of a stage coach; and this is probably the last view I shall ever have of a place so dear to me. Even the recollections of it will soon be confined to my own breast". . . . This kind of mild and wistful regret, relieved occasionally by a gentle hopefulness, is characteristic of Southey's tone as he contemplates the passing of time.

Clearly, Southey's autobiography is not a revelation, but an exercise in control and selection. Such critical remarks as he makes in the course of his narrative show how this approach carries over into literary theory. The true basis of a good poem, Southey says, is planning and organization, not spontaneous utterance. In a passage which is itself one of the most emotional in the autobiography, he rails against poets who speak from emotional inspiration. . . . (pp. 116-17)

But this emphasis on rational control arises from an excess, rather than a deficiency, of emotion. It is a conscious effort to guard against feeling. Many of his contemporaries noted the quickness and sensitivity of Southey's emotional nature. . . .

This passionate side of Southey is scarcely displayed on the surface of his autobiography, but is revealed there, I think, in a curious way: by the fact that he never finished it. . . .

Two themes evident in the autobiography itself combine to produce its cessation. The first is Southey's concern with time, or with perfect and immortal recapitulation of the past. The second, really the obverse of the first, is his preoccupation throughout the letters with death and disaster—a preoccupation which shows forth, as perhaps nothing else could, the buried emotional side of Southey.

"I have lived in the sunshine," he writes in the first letter, "and am still looking forward with hope". . . . The latter part of this statement is very likely true, but Southey's own account belies the first. He had written just above this, speaking of the whole autobiographical project, "here I begin . . . hoping . . . that I may find leisure and courage to pursue it to the end,— courage I mean to live again in remembrance with the dead". . . . He did not of course pursue it to the end, . . . and part of the reason he did not was the agony of living again with the dead. As the letters proceed, their emphasis on death, and on recollections of dead friends and schoolmates, increases, until the seventeenth is almost a meditation on the waste of talent and promise that death brings. . . . (p. 117)

For many of the deaths Southey records, deaths which to him were real and grievous losses, are to be compensated for by the oft-repeated hope of a meeting in a better world. Even here, the hope of immortality is inescapably bound into a hope for reunion, for a coming together of the scattered and shattered fragments of the past, and for a re-weaving of that whole fabric of time which will overcome time.

Two major features of the letters need to be re-emphasized in order to make clear what individualizes them, and sets off the kind of autobiography Southey was trying to write from other possible kinds, or from what we would consider more centrally Romantic documents. The first feature is their relative objectivity: their lack of any kind of inward dimension, any accounting for the growth and shaping of the imagination. They give us a great deal of information about Southey, and about his times, but little insight into the Southeyan psyche. Only indirectly, through analysis of Southey's personal concerns, his selections among possible subjects, can we arrive at a sense of the contours of his mind as they define themselves in his autobiography.

The second feature is the obverse of this, for it has to be understood that Southey was not trying to write an inward narrative. To say that his autobiography is external and objective, and to that extent "un-Romantic," is to describe it, not evaluate it. He was attempting, as he himself says, to write a minor history of the society which existed in his younger days, and to re-create, for a variety of reasons, the social past of his boyhood. And he was writing that history and that re-creation for their own sake, not merely as they impinged on him, or shaped him.

This then is Southey's implicit theory of autobiography as his account of his own life exemplifies it. It is a kind of genre-painting in words. . . . (pp. 118-19)

> *Michael N. Stanton, "Southey and the Art of Autobiography," in* The Wordsworth Circle, *Vol. V, No. 2, Spring, 1974, pp. 113-19.*

ADDITIONAL BIBLIOGRAPHY

Bernbaum, Ernest. "Robert Southey." In his *Guide through the Romantic Movement*, 2d ed., pp. 154-63. New York: Ronald Press Co., 1949.
    An overview of Southey's life and writings. Bernbaum ranks Southey as "among those Romantics who are historically interesting but . . . of secondary importance."

Beyer, Werner W. "Southey, Orientalism, and *Thalaba*." In his *The Enchanted Forest*, pp. 234-45. Oxford: Basil Blackwell, 1963.
    Traces the Oriental motif in Southey's epic poem *Thalaba*.

Brandes, George. "The Lake School's Oriental Romanticism." In his *Main Currents in Nineteenth Century Literature: Naturalism in England, Vol. IV*, pp. 90-101. London: William Heinemann, 1905.*
    An analysis of the Oriental elements found in Southey's poetry, with special attention paid to *Thalaba*.

Carlyle, Thomas. "Appendix: Southey; Wordsworth." In his *Reminiscences, Vol. II*, edited by James Anthony Froude, pp. 307-41. 1881. Reprint. St. Clair Shores, Mich.: Scholarly Press, 1971.*
    A personal reminiscence of Southey emphasizing his assiduous working habits.

Carnall, Geoffrey. *Robert Southey and His Age: The Development of a Conservative Mind*. Oxford: Oxford at the Clarendon Press, 1960, 233 p.
    An analysis of the development of Southey's political ideas. Carnall investigates little-studied aspects of Southey's life and work and concludes that Southey's reaction to the events of his era is representative of that period's conservatism.

———. *Robert Southey*. Bibliographical Series of Supplements to 'British Book News' on Writers and Their Work, edited by Geoffrey Bullough. London: Longmans, Green & Co., 1964, 40 p.
    Brief biography and critical outline of Southey's major works.

Curry, Kenneth. *Southey*. Routledge Author Guides, edited by B. C. Southam. London: Routledge & Kegan Paul, 1975, 191 p.
    An introduction to Southey's life and work. In his preface, Curry states that he has tried to present Southey's "career and his works in a favorable light in terms of the difficulties of his own life as a professional man of letters."

Elia [pseudonym of Charles Lamb]. "Letter of Elia to Robert Southey, Esquire." *The London Magazine* VIII (October 1823): 400-07.

A letter in which Lamb defends himself and his writings against the attacks of Southey.

English Opium-Eater, The [pseudonym of Thomas De Quincey]. "Lake Reminiscences, from 1807 to 1830: No. IV—William Wordsworth and Robert Southey." *Tait's Edinburgh Magazine* VI, No. LXVII (July 1839): 453-64.*
    A fond reminiscence of Southey as a companion and spirited conversationalist.

Haller, William. *The Early Life of Robert Southey: 1774-1803*. New York: Octagon Books, 1966, 353 p.
    Considered an influential overview of Southey's early career. Haller suggests that Southey deserved to fail as a poet. The reasons for his justified failure, according to Haller, include his inability to achieve a unique poetic style and his misconception of the new world, which Southey used as the basis of his narrative poetry.

Morgan, Peter F. "Southey on Poetry." *Tennessee Studies in Literature* XVI (1971): 77-89.

Studies Southey's commentary, reprinted from his essays in the *Quarterly Review*, on the general nature of English poetry.

Saintsbury, George. "Robert Southey." In his *Essays in English Literature, second series*, pp. 1-37. London: J. M. Dent & Co., 1895.
    A complimentary overview of Southey's poetic career. Saintsbury pays special attention to *The Curse of Kehama*, which he considers "the greatest thing by far that Southey did, and a thing, as I think, really great, without any comparatives and allowances."

Sanderson, David R. "Robert Southey and the Standard Georgian Style." *The Midwest Quarterly: A Journal of Contemporary Thought* XII, No. 3 (April 1971): 335-52.
    An analysis of Southey's prose style. Sanderson considers Southey's narrative to be admirable in its descriptive powers; however, he adds that Southey fails to convey the sense of action necessary for successful fiction.

Schilling, Bernard N. "Southey." In his *Human Dignity and the Great Victorians*, pp. 61-73. New York: Columbia University Press, 1946.
    An analysis of Southey's views of English politics in the 1820s.

John Greenleaf Whittier

1807-1892

American poet, journalist, essayist, editor, and hymn writer.

A noted abolitionist and social reformer in his own time, Whittier is now remembered for his simple, old-fashioned poetry. In his most popular works, Whittier utilized a refined sense of rural and biblical imagery to demonstrate his genuine appreciation for nineteenth-century New England life. His best-loved poem, *Snow-bound: A Winter Idyl,* assured Whittier's popular success and placed him in the company of such other enduring American poets as William Cullen Bryant, Oliver Wendell Holmes, and Henry Wadsworth Longfellow. Whittier's reputation has suffered in the twentieth century because of the didacticism and dated nature of his works; his significance in American literary history, however, is still acknowledged today.

Whittier was born on a farm in Haverhill, Massachusetts to Quaker parents. Though he had little formal education, Whittier devoted himself to the study of the Bible and the works of John Milton, Sir Walter Scott, Lord Byron, and Robert Burns. Plagued with a nervous condition that hindered him throughout his life, Whittier was unsuited to farm life and longed for a career as a poet. In particular, he enjoyed the works of the Scottish poet Burns, whom he sought to emulate in his own early poems. In 1826, Whittier's sister anonymously sent his poem "The Exile's Departure" to the *Newburyport Free Press* for publication. The poem so impressed editor and noted social reformer William Lloyd Garrison that he encouraged Whittier to contribute more verse to the newspaper. With Garrison's influence, Whittier became the editor of another popular New England publication, the *American Manufacturer.* By 1830, Whittier's reputation as a skilled editor had earned him a job editing the most powerful northern Whig journal of the era, the *New England Weekly Review.* During this time, Whittier also published his first literary collection, *Legends of New England in Prose and Verse,* which reflected the poet's love of New England tradition and romantic folklore. Though the volume was well received, Whittier suppressed later editions, stating that his literary inexperience was all too apparent in the collection's prose and verse.

After editing a number of successful journals, Whittier was forced to resign from the *New England Weekly Review* because of his father's death and his own ill health. In 1832, he returned to Haverhill, where he concentrated on his literary career while trying to salvage the failing family farm. Again, Garrison became an influential force in Whittier's life when he enlisted the poet as a spokesman for the foundering abolitionist movement. Whittier became a lobbyist for the movement in Boston and Washington and a delegate to the first American Anti-Slavery meeting. Had he not been ineligible because of his youth, Whittier later said, he would have campaigned as a candidate for the United States Senate.

Whittier considered his antislavery tracts his most significant contributions to society. For nearly twelve years, he devoted himself exclusively to abolitionist issues, publishing an essay entitled *Justice and Expediency; or, Slavery Considered with a View to Its Rightful and Effectual Remedy, Abolition* and a

collection of poetry, *Poems Written during the Progress of the Abolition Question in the United States, Between the Years 1830 and 1838.* Although praised by abolitionists, the work drew an irate response from the general public, who criticized its didactic tone and political nature. Whittier countered these arguments with the contention that, although his literary reputation would suffer as a result of his political involvement, the antislavery movement was a just and noble cause. According to Whittier, his abolitionist poetry would survive on its merit as a historical document. The poet did not, however, remain in the ranks of the Garrisonian anti-slavery movement; rather, Whittier broke with his former mentor, condemning his desire to promote a military resolution to the political differences between the northern and southern states as an unacceptable solution to a moral issue. Instead, Whittier preferred to work for change through political channels and, although he continued to write occasionally for the abolitionist cause, he also campaigned extensively for candidates who proposed legislative answers to antislavery issues. "Ichabod," one of Whittier's final abolitionist poems, reflected his shock and anger at the decision made by his personal friend, the politician Daniel Webster, to support southern slaveholders.

Although Whittier's antislavery works are now considered dated because of their limited scope and subjects, most critics agree that his poetry possesses merit. In 1843, Whittier resumed his literary career with the popular collection of poetry, *Lays of My Home, and Other Poems*. He contributed to the noted American poet James Russell Lowell's *Pioneer Magazine* and published several more volumes of poetry, including *Voices of Freedom* and *The Supernaturalism of New-England*. Later, Whittier suppressed the latter work after Nathaniel Hawthorne faulted his inept treatment of Gothic themes. Whittier fared better with his only novel, *Leaves from Margaret Smith's Journal in the Province of Massachusetts Bay*. The work, in the form of a fictional journal, depicts life in the New England colonies through the eyes of a young English girl. This and other works have prompted critics to praise Whittier for his ability to convey accurately the conflicts between New England Quakers and Puritans.

In the following years, Whittier composed most of his ballads, which many critics consider his finest poetic achievements. Of these works, ''Skipper Ireson's Ride'' and ''Barbara Frietchie'' are two of the most enduring. They are admired for their simple versification and sensitive portrayal of the commonplace. Although his early ballads inspired critical acclaim, it was not until 1866, with the publication of his most successful ballad *Snow-bound*, that Whittier achieved renown as a literary figure. In *Snow-bound*, Whittier nostalgically describes the interactions of a family while ''snowbound'' by an unexpected winter storm. The poem's emotional depth is thought to have derived from Whittier's grief over the deaths of his mother and sister. Contemporary critics praised the ballad's directness and realistic depiction of the past. Today, the work is considered a precursor of the pastoral poems of such twentieth-century poets as Robert Frost. *Snow-bound* was also a crucial financial success for the author: he realized ten thousand dollars from the sale of the ballad and was able to live comfortably until his death in 1892.

Critical appraisal of Whittier's work is generally divided into four distinct periods. In the first phase, through the end of the Civil War, Whittier's critics expressed admiration for the emotional impact of his verse, but pointed to numerous technical flaws. Specifically, commentators often criticized the poet's clumsy prose, grammatical errors, and faulty rhyme scheme. James Russell Lowell commended Whittier's boldness and sincerity, yet never considered him a first-rate poet. Similarly, Edgar Allan Poe called Whittier a ''fine versifier,'' but refused to elevate the poet's name to equal status with that of other American poets of his era. Nonetheless, Whittier was one of the most popular and respected writers of his time and, following the publication of *Snow-bound*, enjoyed widespread acclaim.

The overwhelming popularity of *Snow-bound* marked the beginning of the second phase of critical reaction to Whittier's work. During this period, which climaxed in the early 1920s, Whittier was esteemed as one of America's most admired literary figures. The poet's saintly life, as described by biographies of the era, became inseparable from the evaluation of his work and his death prompted an outpouring of loving remembrances and fond memorials, few of which accurately assessed the quality of the poet's work.

The late 1920s saw a dramatic shift in the consideration of Whittier as poet. Instead of the adulation of the turn of the century critics, such commentators as Howard Mumford Jones and Norman Foerster suggested that Whittier was too staunchly moralistic and sentimental to represent accurately nineteenth-century American thought. However, these early twentieth-century critics agreed that Whittier's importance derives from

his reputation as the social reformer. Although few critics discussed Whittier during the 1930s and 1940s, in the 1950s there was a resurgence of interest in the author and his work. This fourth phase of Whittier criticism is characterized by the writings of such contemporary critics as Hyatt H. Waggoner, who reevaluated Whittier's work in terms of its religious strength and significance. Many critics, including the acknowledged Whittier scholar John B. Pickard, considered the poet a paradoxical blend of success and failure and insisted that Whittier deserved to be remembered for his significance as a historical figure rather than for his literary works.

If Whittier has not retained his early reputation as one of America's greatest poets, he remains an instrumental voice in American literary development. His early works survive mainly as historical documents which represent a turbulent era in American history, but a few of his best-loved works, such as *Snow-bound*, endure as nostalgic pastorals which are studied today. Whittier often referred to his role in the development of American literature, and critics today concur with his appraisal of his place in history: ''I am not one of the master singers and don't pose as one. By the grace of God, I am only what I am and don't wish to pass for more.''

(See also *Dictionary of Literary Biography*, Vol. I: *The American Renaissance in New England*.)

PRINCIPAL WORKS

''The Exile's Departure'' (poetry) 1826; published in newspaper *Newburyport Free Press*

Legends of New England in Prose and Verse (legends) 1831

Moll Pitcher (poetry) 1832

Justice and Expediency; or, Slavery Considered with a View to Its Rightful and Effectual Remedy, Abolition (essay) 1833

Mogg Megone (poetry) 1836

Poems Written during the Progress of the Abolition Question in the United States, Between the Years 1830 and 1838 (poetry) 1837; also published as *Poems* [revised edition] 1838

Lays of My Home, and Other Poems (poetry) 1843

The Stranger in Lowell (criticism) 1845

Voices of Freedom (poetry and essays) 1846

The Supernaturalism of New-England (poetry and legends) 1847

Leaves from Margaret Smith's Journal in the Province of Massachusetts Bay (fictional journal) 1849

Old Portraits and Modern Sketches (poetry and biographical sketches) 1850

Songs of Labor, and Other Poems (poetry) 1850

The Chapel of the Hermit, and Other Poems (poetry) 1853

**The Panorama, and Other Poems* (poetry) 1856

The Poetical Works of John Greenleaf Whittier. 2 vols. (poetry) 1857

***Home Ballads and Poems* (ballads and poetry) 1860

In War-Time, and Other Poems (poetry) 1864

Snow-bound: A Winter Idyl (poetry) 1866

The Tent on the Beach, and Other Poems (poetry) 1867

Among the Hills, and Other Poems (poetry) 1868

Ballads of New-England (ballads) 1870

Child Life: A Collection of Poems [editor; with Lucy Larcom] (poetry) 1872

The Pennsylvania Pilgrim, and Other Poems   (poetry)
     1872
Child Life in Prose [editor; with Lucy Larcom]   (short
     stories)   1873
The Complete Works of John Greenleaf Whittier. 7 vols.
     (poetry, legends, essays, tales, biographical sketches,
     and historical sketches)   1876
****The Writings of John Greenleaf Whittier.* 5 vols.
     (poems, ballads, legends, tales, biographical sketches,
     historical sketches, and criticism)   1888-89
At Sundown   (poetry)   1890
The Complete Poetical Works of John Greenleaf Whittier
     (poetry)   1894
*Whittier on Writers and Writing: The Uncollected Critical
     Writings of John Greenleaf Whittier*   (criticism)   1950
The Letters of John Greenleaf Whittier   (letters)   1975

*This work includes the poem "Ichabod."

**This work includes the poems "Maud Muller" and "Barbara Friet-
chie."

***This work includes the poem "Skipper Ireson's Ride."

****This work also includes poetry written by Elizabeth H. Whittier.

JOHN GREENLEAF WHITTIER   (essay date 1831)

[*In the following preface to* Legends of New England in Prose
and Verse, *Whittier explains his purpose in writing the volume.
Although Whittier affirms here his reasons for recreating the
popular folklore of New England, in later years he refused to
allow* Legends of New England *to be reprinted because he felt
the work revealed his inexperience.*]

[In *Legends of New England*] I have attempted to present in an
interesting form some of the popular traditions and legends of
New-England. The field is a new one—and I have but partially
explored it. New-England is rich in traditionary lore—a thousand associations of superstition and manly daring and romantic
adventure, are connected with her green hills and her pleasant
rivers. I leave the task of rescuing these associations from
oblivion to some more fortunate individual; and if this little
volume shall have the effect to induce such an effort, I shall
at least be satisfied, whatever may be the judgment of the public
upon my own humble production.

I have in many instances alluded to the superstition and bigotry
of our ancestors—the rare and bold race who laid the foundation
of this republic; but no one can accuse me of having done
injustice to their memories. A son of New-England, and proud
of my birth-place, I would not willingly cast dishonor upon its
founders.—My feelings in this respect, have already been expressed, in language, which I shall be pardoned I trust for
introducing in this place:

> Oh—never may a son of thine,
> Where'e his wandering steps incline,
> Forget the sky which bent above
> His childhood like a dream of love—
> The stream beneath the green hill flowing—
> The broad-armed trees above it growing—
> The clear breeze through the foliage blowing:—
> Or, hear unmoved the taunt of scorn,
> Breathed o'er the brave New-England born;

> Or mark the stranger's Jaguar hand
>   Disturb the ashes of thy dead—
> The buried glory of a land
>   Whose soil with noble blood is red,
>   And sanctified in every part,
> Nor feel resentment, like a brand,
>   Unsheathing from his fiery heart!

An apology is even in worse taste than a preface; but I would
simply state that this volume was written during the anxieties
and perplexing cares attendant upon the management of a political and literary periodical. (pp. xix-xx)

> *John Greenleaf Whittier, in a preface to his* Legends
> of New England, *1831. Reprint by Scholars' Fac-
> similes & Reprints, 1965, pp. xix-xx.*

THE NEW-YORK MIRROR   (essay date 1831)

There could scarcely be a more imposing title to an American
public than that of ["**Legends of New-England**"]. It has been
generally believed that our country labours under an immense
disadvantage in its inferiority to other nations in traditionary
lore, and in those materials of history which, imperfectly seen
through the dim mist of time, are calculated to arouse the most
interesting associations. This is partially true; but we have
scarcely yet a right to complain, as those materials which do
actually exist among us, have by no means been exhausted. . . .
The hallowed influence of ages is not upon our cities, our
temples, or our institutions; and it would be useless to deny
that we have had no Shakspeares and Miltons to hallow the
spots where they have lived, and where their ashes repose; yet
we are by no means destitute of themes for the writer, both
curious and interesting, although they are of a different description, and the title of the volume now before us is precisely
of a kind to awaken expectation. Mr. Whittier has very happily
chosen his subject; but he has not availed himself to a very
great extent of the advantages which it affords. Indeed in his
preface he frankly declares that he has no hope but to call the
attention of others to the legends upon which he has only
slightly touched [see excerpt above, 1831]. We can scarcely
forgive him for having shuffled off his task in so careless a
manner, especially as the few trifles contained in his work are
exceedingly well wrought up, are clothed in the language of a
practised and able writer, and touch upon the most curious
features in the history of New-England, viz. the Indian traditions, and the dark and bloody period of witchcraft. He offers
no satisfactory apology for having opened the mine, without
exploring more thoroughly its treasures. It betrays that absence
of literary enthusiasm, for which perhaps the public is more
to blame than the author; and that exclusive devotedness to the
mere business transactions of life, which may create good merchants and rich men, but which will never make successful
writers. He is on the spot, and probably within reach of the
best sources of information at present in existence, and is hardly
excusable for having used so little research in preparing the
present collection. His little volume, however, will be acceptable to the public. It consists of several sketches, in prose
and verse, all of which we have read with pleasure. As a poet
Mr. Whittier possesses undoubted genius; and his prose efforts,
although apparently thrown off without labour, are evidently
the offspring of a ready pen. (p. 292)

The reader will discover in the "**Rattle-snake Hunter,**" a page
of animated and beautiful description, which will impress him
with an exalted opinion of the author's versatility of talent. It

seemed at first difficult to decide whether he is more fluent in prose or poetry, but the **"Weird Gathering"** turns the scale in favour of the latter.

"Metacom" . . . opens with a glowing and truly poetic picture of sunset, and a fine portraiture of the red hero.

"The Spectre Ship" is a poem, imbued with the spirit of [Samuel Taylor Coleridge's] "Rime of the Ancient Mariner."

The **"Spectre Warriors,"** the **"Human Sacrifice,"** the **"Indian's Tale,"** the **"Powwaw,"** and the **"Last Norridgewock,"** are beautiful and original Indian sketches. The rest of the volume consists of the **"Midnight Attack,"** the **"Murdered Lady,"** the **"Unquiet Sleeper,"** the **"Haunted House,"** the **"White Mountains,"** the **"Mother's Revenge,"** and the **"Aerial Omens,"** all founded on some legend of New-England. Several of them are productions of superior merit. . . .

We cannot conclude without a few observations respecting the tone of modern criticism, which has been so long practised by persons of all classes of information and intellect, as to render its phrases unmeaning, its censure harmless, and its praise mere puffing, without either influence or value. In considering Mr. Whittier's book we have, perhaps, in a measure checked the enthusiasm of our admiration, in order to avoid the inflated style which too universally prevails. Books, infinitely inferior to the **"Legends of New-England,"** have been introduced to the public in terms of unlimited rapture, until all the phraseology of critical applause has been exhausted upon the most insipid and meretricious offsprings of vanity, ignorance, and dullness. The volume before us, if it is to be compared with many others with which the teeming press inundates the community, and if it is to be reviewed in the same spirit, is justly deserving of a much more exalted style of praise than it has received at our hands; for, without exaggeration, we may assert that, with only one or two exceptions, it is decidedly the most agreeable work of the kind we have read since the days of [Irving's "Sketch Book"]. Before we opened it, from our previous knowledge of the literary abilities of the author, we anticipated much pleasure, but our expectations were more than realized; and though we will not, in the usual style, inform the public that he is equal to Scott or Irving, we can assure them that the **"Legends of New-England"** is no trifling addition to the stock of American literature. (p. 293)

> A review of "Legends of New-England," in The New-York Mirror, Vol. VIII, No. 37, March 19, 1831, pp. 292-94.

EDGAR ALLAN POE (essay date 1841)

[*Considered one of America's most outstanding men of letters, Poe was a distinguished poet, novelist, essayist, journalist, short story writer, editor, and critic. Poe stressed an analytical rather than emotive approach to literature and emphasized the specifics of style and construction in a work, instead of concentrating solely on its ideological statement. Although Poe and his literary criticism aroused controversy in his own lifetime, he is now valued for his critical theories. Here, Poe echoes his contemporaries in praising Whittier's subjects and versification, yet he contends that the poems lack imagination.*]

J. Greenleaf Whittier, is placed by his particular admirers in the very front rank of American poets. We are not disposed, however, to agree with their decision in every respect. Mr. Whittier is a fine versifier, so far as strength is regarded independently of modulation. His subjects, too, are usually cho-

Considered the earliest likeness of Whittier. Believed to depict Whittier at twenty-one, this photograph was taken by W. G. Thompson, Whittier's "official" photographer.

sen with the view of affording scope to a certain *vivida vis* [vivid force] of expression which seems to be his forte; but in taste, and especially in *imagination*, which Coleridge has justly styled the *soul* of all poetry, he is even remarkably deficient. His themes are *never* to our liking. (p. 286)

> *Edgar Allan Poe, "A Chapter on Autography," in* Graham's Magazine, *Vol. XIX, No. 6, December, 1841, pp. 273-86.**

[C. C. FELTON] (essay date 1843)

Mr. Whittier commands a vigorous and manly style [in his *Lays of My Home*]. His expression is generally simple and to the point. Some passages in his poems are highly picturesque; and at times his imagery is bold and striking. But he is deficient in the sense of proportion. His pieces seem to be the chance sallies of a strong imagination, irregularly excited and roused to fitful action, rather than the well planned and artfully finished works of the accomplished poet. In his poems, thoughts frequently are but loosely connected with each other; indeed, the associating link is sometimes wholly imperceptible. At times, a poem continues long after the sense is completed; then again, the strain suddenly ceases, why or wherefore we know not. From this it happens, that the reader carries away from the perusal of his works a vague recollection of poetical phrases, but no image of an entire and perfected poem. Mr. Whittier is not yet completely master of English versification. With many passages of fine harmony, he has written more that are deformed by harshness, and forced turns of accentuation. The spirit of most of his pieces is highly to be commended; and yet the violence of the partisan introduces here and there a disagreeable discord. What right, for instance, has Mr. Whittier to speak in the virulent tone, which he sees fit to employ, against those clergymen who hold different opinions from his on the disputed question of capital punishment? There is no taste, no Christianity, and no poetry in all this: if Mr. Whittier supposes there is, he mistakes all three.

The most vigorous, finished, and the best conceived pieces in this volume are the **"Norsemen," "Raphael,"** and **"Massachusetts to Virginia."** These three are worth all the rest of the volume together. The lines are musical almost without a fault; and the imagery and expression are noble and spirit-stirring. (pp. 509-10)

> [C. C. Felton], *"Whittier's 'Poems',"* in The North American Review, *Vol. LVII, No. CXXI, October, 1843, pp. 509-10.*

THE SOUTHERN QUARTERLY REVIEW (essay date 1843)

Mr. Whittier is the writer of verses which it would be proper, in customary parlance, to describe as respectable. But in truth they rank in that class, which, we are told by unquestionable authority, is unendurable by gods, men or columns. The sin of mediocrity is at their doors. With tolerable smoothness of flow, and occasional energy of expression, Mr. Whittier's verses are distinguished by nothing so much as their wondrous frigidity. He is called the Quaker poet, and his poetry is the very pink of broad-brimism. It lacks, very equally, tenderness and felicity. Its chief, or only, merits, are plain good sense, general correctness, and a very fair and commendable appreciation of morals and propriety. Beyond this, [*Lays of My Home and Other Poems*] is a blank. It possesses neither originality nor warmth,—unless, indeed, when the author falls into a fury (as he does) with Virginia, and for no better reason that we can see, but because our very excellent senior sister thought proper to adopt certain measures to prevent philanthropic persons from the Bay State—Quakers, in all probability,—from stealing and carrying back the slaves which they (or their ancestors) had previously sold her. These proceedings of Virginia do make our poet worthy, and thus enable him to display—what otherwise we should scarcely have supposed him to possess—a due proportion of the *genus irritabile* [sensitive nation]. To confess a truth, we have been quite confounded by the perusal of this volume. Giving due credit to the lavish tongues of certain of the critics, and forgetting the monstrous penchant on the part of our Northern brethren, to mistake all their own geese as swans, we took for granted—in our own ignorance of Mr. Whittier's writings,—that he was a genuine son of Phoebus,—blasted, in very tolerable degree, with the poetic fire. But this volume throws cold water on our former faith. It proves that our author's claim to be the divine afflatus is exceedingly small. He makes verses, it is true,—very tolerable verses, as the world goes,—but sadly deficient in glow and inspiration. (pp. 516-17)

> *"Whittier's Poems,"* in The Southern Quarterly Review, *Vol. IV, No. 8, October, 1843, pp. 516-19.*

THE NORTH AMERICAN REVIEW (essay date 1844)

John Greenleaf Whittier is one of our most characteristic poets. Few excel him in warmth of temperament. . . . He seems, in some of his lyrics, to pour out his blood with his lines. There is a rush of passion in his verse, which sweeps every thing along with it. His fancy and imagination can hardly keep pace with their fiery companion. His vehement sensibility will not allow the inventive faculties fully to complete what they may have commenced. The stormy qualities of his mind, acting at the suggestions of conscience, produce a kind of military morality which uses all the deadly arms of verbal warfare. When well intrenched in abstract right, he always assumes a hostile attitude towards the champions or practisers of abstract wrong. He aims to give his song "a rude martial tone,—a blow in every thought." His invective is merciless and undistinguishing; he almost screams with rage and indignation. Occasionally, the extreme bitterness and fierceness of his declamation degenerate into mere shrewishness and scolding. Of late, he has somewhat pruned the rank luxuriance of his style. The **"Lines on the Death of Lucy Hooper," "Raphael," "Follen," "Memories,"** . . . are indications that his mind is not without subtle imagination and delicate feeling, as well as truculent strength and fierce energy. There is much spiritual beauty in these little compositions. (pp. 30-1)

Whittier has the soul of a great poet, and we should not be surprised if he attained the height of excellence in his art. The faults of his mind, springing from excessive fluency and a too excitable sensibility, exaggerated as they have been by the necessities of hasty composition, have prevented him from displaying as yet the full power of his genius. It is by no means unlikely, that, when he has somewhat tamed the impetuosity of his feelings, and brooded with more quiet intensity over the large stores of poetry which lie chaotically in his nature, he may yet produce a work which will rival, and perhaps excel, the creations of his most distinguished contemporaries. He has that vigor, truthfulness, and manliness of character,—that freedom from conventional shackles, . . .—that native energy and independence of nature,—which form the basis of the character of every great genius, and without which poetry is apt to be a mere echo of the drawing-room, and to idealize affectations instead of realities. (p. 32)

> *"Griswold's 'Poets and Poetry of America',"* in The North American Review, *Vol. LVIII, No. CXXII, January, 1844, pp. 1-39.**

JOHN GREENLEAF WHITTIER (poem date 1847)

[*"Proem"* was originally published as a preface to the 1847 collection of Whittier's works, The Supernaturalism of New-England. *In the poem, Whittier acknowledges his lack of literary education, but claims that his verse has served its purpose in the noble cause of abolition. "Proem" has prefaced all subsequent collections of Whittier's works.*]

    I love the old melodious lays
Which softly melt the ages through,
      The songs of Spenser's golden days,
      Arcadian Sidney's silvery phrase,
Sprinkling our noon of time with freshest morning dew.

    Yet, vainly in my quiet hours
To breathe their marvellous notes I try;
      I feel them, as the leaves and flowers
      In silence feel the dewy showers,
And drink with glad, still lips the blessing of the sky.

    The rigor of a frozen clime,
The harshness of an untaught ear,

The jarring words of one whose rhyme
    Beat often Labor's hurried time,
Or Duty's rugged march through storm and strife, are
    here.

Of mystic beauty, dreamy grace,
No rounded art the lack supplies;
    Unskilled the subtle lines to trace,
    Or softer shades of Nature's face,
I view her common forms with unanointed eyes.

Nor mine the seer-like power to show
The secrets of the heart and mind;
    To drop the plummet-line below
    Our common world of joy and woe,
A more intense despair or brighter hope to find.

Yet here at least an earnest sense
Of human right and weal is shown;
    A hate of tyranny intense,
    And hearty in its vehemence,
As if my brother's pain and sorrow were my own.

O Freedom! if to me belong
Nor mighty Milton's gift divine,
    Nor Marvell's wit and graceful song,
    Still with a love as deep and strong
As theirs, I lay, like them, my best gifts on thy shrine!

> *John Greenleaf Whittier, "Proem," in his* The Complete Poetical Works of John Greenleaf Whittier, *Houghton Mifflin Company, 1894, p. 63.*

[NATHANIEL HAWTHORNE]   (essay date 1847)

[Hawthorne is considered one of the greatest American fiction writers. His The Scarlet Letter, *with its balanced structure, simple, expressive language, and superb use of symbols, is a recognized classic of American literature. In Hawthorne's review of* The Supernaturalism of New-England, *he disagrees with some of Whittier's premises and states that his style "has not quite the simplicity that the theme requires." Further, Hawthorne criticizes the author for revealing to readers his own disbelief in the tales. Although it was not entirely negative, this review prompted Whittier to suppress later editions of* The Supernaturalism of New-England.]

Mr. Whittier's literary name has been little other than an accident of exertions directed to practical and unselfish purposes—a wayside flower, which he has hardly spared the time to gather. In the dedication of [*The Supernaturalism of New England*] to his sister, he well expresses the feeling of relief, and almost self-reproachful enjoyment, with which he turns aside from his "long, harsh strife with strong-willed men," to converse with ghosts and witches, and all such legendary shadows. We doubt not, he will return to the battle of his life with so much the more vigor, for this brief relaxation; but we are bound to say that, if he could have more entirely thrown off the mental habit of a man writing under a stern sense of duty, he might have succeeded better in such a labor of love and idleness, as the present. In spite of himself, Mr. Whittier stoops to the theme with the austere dignity of a schoolmaster at his amusements; a condescension that may seem exaggerated, when we consider that the subject will probably retain a human interest, long after his more earnest efforts shall have lost their importance, in the progress of society.

In the first chapter of the book, there are some good remarks on the spiritual tendencies that lie beneath the earthy surface of the Yankee character. Such spirituality certainly does exist; but we cannot perceive that its indications are, or ever have been, so peculiar as to form any system that may come fairly under the title of New England Supernaturalism. The contrary is rather remarkably the fact; the forest life of the first settlers, and their intercourse with the Indians, have really engrafted nothing upon the mythology which they brought with them from England—at least, we know of nothing, although Mr. Whittier intimates that these circumstances did modify their English superstitions. We should naturally look for something duskier and grander in the ghostly legends of a wild country, than could be expected in a state of society where even dreams are covered with the dust of old conventionalisms. But, if there be any peculiarity, it is, that our superstitions have a more sordid, grimy, and material aspect, than they bore in the clime from which they were transplanted. A New England ghost does not elevate us into a spiritual region; he hints at no mysteries beyond the grave, nor seems to possess any valuable information on subjects of that nature. He throws aside even his shroud, puts on the coat and breeches of the times, and takes up the flesh-and-blood business of life, at the very point where he dropt it at his decease. He so mingles with daily life, that we scarcely perceive him to be a ghost at all. If he indeed comes from the spiritual world, it is because he has been ejected with disgrace, on account of the essential and inveterate earthiness of his substance.

This characteristic of a New England ghost story should by all means be retained; else the legend will lose its truth. Mr. Whittier has sometimes caught the just effect, but occasionally allows it to escape, by aiming at effects which are inconsistent with the one alluded to. He has made a fine ballad of the **"New Wife and the Old;"**—its only defect is, indeed, that he has made it too fine, at the sacrifice of the homeliness which was its essence. His style, in fact, throughout the volume, has not quite the simplicity that the theme requires; it sparkles a little too much. The proper tone for these legends is, of course, that of the fireside narrative, refined and clarified to whatever degree the writer pleases, but still as simple as the Bible—as simple as the babble of an old woman to her grandchild, as they sit in the smoky glow of a deep chimney-corner. Above all, the narrator should have faith, for the time being. If he cannot believe his ghost-story while he is telling it, he had better leave the task to somebody else. Now, Mr. Whittier never fails to express his incredulity either before or after the narrative, and often in the midst of it. It is a matter of conscience with him to do so.

One other criterion must be allowed us. Mr. Whittier has read too much. He talks too learnedly about the "Ahriman of the Parsee, the Pluto of the Roman mythology, the Devil of the Jew and the Christian, the Shitan of the Mussulman, the Machinito of the Indian;" and quotes some black letter mystic or modern poet on every page. There is nothing in his treatment of the subject that requires such an array of authorities, nor any such depth in the well of his philosophy, that we can descend into it only by a flight of steps, constructed out of old folio volumes.

But, how much easier it is to censure than to praise, even where the merits greatly outweigh the defects! We conclude, with the frank admission that we like the book, and look upon it as no unworthy contribution from a poet to that species of literature which only a poet should meddle with. We hope to see more of him, in this, or some other congenial sphere. There are many legends still to be gathered, especially along the sea-

board of New England—and those, too, we think, more original, and more susceptible of poetic illustration, than these
rural superstitions. (pp. 247-48)

[*Nathaniel Hawthorne*], ''Supernaturalism,'' *in* The
Literary World, *Vol. 1, No. 11, April 17, 1847,
pp. 247-48.*

[JAMES RUSSELL LOWELL]   (poem date 1848)

[*Lowell was a celebrated nineteenth-century American poet, critic,
essayist, and editor of two leading journals: the* Atlantic Monthly
and the North American Review. *He is noted today for his satirical
and critical writings, including* A Fable for Critics, *a book-length
poem featuring witty critical portraits of his contemporaries. Often
awkwardly phrased, and occasionally vicious, the* Fable *is distinguished by the enduring value of its literary assessments. In
the following excerpt from that work, Lowell praises Whittier as
a ''true lyric bard'' and expresses his appreciation for Whittier's
involvement in the cause for abolition. For additional commentary
by Lowell, see excerpts below, 1864 and 1866.*]

There is Whittier, whose swelling and vehement heart
Strains the strait-breasted drab of the Quaker apart,
And reveals the live Man, still supreme and erect
Underneath the bemummying wrappers of sect;
There was ne'er a man born who had more of the swing
Of the true lyric bard and all that kind of thing;
And his failures arise, (though perhaps he don't know
    it,)
From the very same cause that has made him a poet,—
A fervor of mind which knows no separation
'Twixt simple excitement and pure inspiration,
As my Pythoness erst sometimes erred from not
    knowing
If 'twere I or mere wind through her tripod was
    blowing;
Let his mind once get head in its favorite direction
And the torrent of verse bursts the dams of reflection,
While, borne with the rush of the metre along,
The poet may chance to go right or go wrong,
Content with the whirl and delirium of song;
Then his grammar's not always correct, nor his rhymes,
And he's prone to repeat his own lyrics sometimes,
Not his best, though, for those are struck off at white-
    heats
When the heart in his breast like a trip-hammer beats,
And can ne'er be repeated again any more
Than they could have been carefully plotted before:
Like old what's-his-name there at the battle of Hastings,
(Who, however, gave more than mere rhythmical
    bastings,)
Our Quaker leads off metaphorical fights
For reform and whatever they call human rights,
Both singing and striking in front of the war
And hitting his foes with the mallet of Thor;
Anne haec, one exclaims, on beholding his knocks,
Vestis filii tui, O, leather-clad Fox?
Can that be thy son, in the battle's mid din,
Preaching brotherly love and then driving it in
To the brain of the tough old Goliath of sin,
With the smoothest of pebbles from Castaly's spring
Impressed on his hard moral sense with a sling?

All honor and praise to the right-hearted bard
Who was true to The Voice when such service was
    hard,

Who himself was so free he dared sing for the slave
When to look but a protest in silence was brave;
All honor and praise to the women and men
Who spoke out for the dumb and the drown-trodden
    then!
I need not to name them, already for each
I see History preparing the statue and niche;
They were harsh, but shall *you* be so shocked at hard
    words
Who have beaten your pruning-hooks up into swords,
Whose rewards and hurrahs men are surer to gain
By the reaping of men and of women than grain?
Why should *you* stand aghast at their fierce wordy war,
    if
You scalp one another for Bank or for Tariff?
Your calling them cut-throats and knaves all day long
Don't prove that the use of hard language is wrong;
While the World's heart beats quicker to think of such
    men
As signed Tyranny's doom with a bloody steel-pen,
While on Fourth-of-Julys beardless orators fright one
With hints at Harmodius and Aristogeiton,
You need not look shy at your sisters and brothers
Who stab with sharp words for the freedom of others;—
No, a wreath, twine a wreath for the loyal and true
Who, for sake of the many, dared stand with the few,
Not of blood-spattered laurel for enemies braved,
But of broad, peaceful oak-leaves for citizens saved!

(pp. 42-4)

[*James Russell Lowell*], *in his* A Fable for Critics:
A Glance at a Few of Our Literary Progenies, *second
edition, G. P. Putnam, 1848, 80 p.**

J.G.F. [J. G. FORMAN]   (essay date 1849)

It is not our purpose, in this review [of *Poems*], to go into
criticism of the comparative merits of Whittier as a poet. This
is a work for abler pens. Like all others who possess superior
excellences, he doubtless has his defects. There is one proof,
however, that the former far surpasses the latter, which cannot
fail to be appreciated by all. It is the wide-spread popularity
of his poems, and the prominent place they already occupy in
the literature of our country. It is of some of these excellences
we would speak, and with the more confidence, because the
great heart of Humanity, which is generally in the right place,
is on his side.

Among the characteristics, of Whittier's style, his vigor, truthfulness, and simplicity, are marked and striking. His descriptive powers are of a high order, though he displays them rather
in presenting a strong outline, and the general features on a
subject, than in giving minute details. His pictures, therefore,
are most agreeable to the reader, and leave a strong impression
on the mind, while something is left for the imagination to
supply. The creative or imaginative faculty is probably less
active than in some of his contemporaries, but in fidelity of
description, and a delicate appreciation of all forms of beauty,
he is unsurpassed. His poetry is the poetry of human life, of
truth and pure sentiment, rather than of fiction. In his descriptions of New England scenery, of familiar landscapes, and the
associations he connects with them, there is a tenderness and
beauty that captivates the heart. He combines more of boldness
and strength, with gentleness and delicacy of sentiment, than
any author whom it has been our pleasure to read.

His descriptions of Indian life and character are remarkable for their strength and fidelity. Two of his longest poems are founded on incidents in the history of the Indian tribes that inhabited that portion of New England where Mr. Whittier has spent much of his early life. These are, the **"Bridal of Pennacook"** and **"Mogg Megone."** In both these poems a tragic interest is maintained throughout; the events, the scenes where they occurred, and the Indian character and mode of life, are brought before the mind with wonderful fidelity and power of description. There is no exaggeration, and no excess of imagery and verbiage encumbers these poems. The delineations are faithfully drawn, and the narratives given in language strong and vigorous, yet chaste, and flowing as a mountain stream. The style does not abound in similes, but when they do occur, they are always beautiful and perfect of their kind. . . .

Another characteristic of Mr. Whittier is, the strong current of moral and religious sentiment that flows through all his poems. Occasionally, he indulges a vein of ridicule, as in **"The Hunters of Men;"** sometimes he uses a keen and powerful sarcasm, as in **"The Response,"** and some other pieces; and again he burns with holy indignation, and utters the most writhing rebukes—but they are all for a good purpose, and sanctified by the end in view. These are called forth by the wrongs and sufferings of the oppressed and down-trodden slave, as though he would, by every means in his power, awaken his countrymen to a sense of injustice and the shame of which we stand guilty before God and man. His sympathies are all on the side of Humanity. Oppression and cruelty find no apologist in him. His heart is in all the great reforms of the age. No poet of our times, or of any time, has accomplished more for Truth and Man than he. . . .

The popularity of his poems will cause them to be read by thousands whose ears would otherwise be closed against all appeal, and their hearts will be moved to feel, and their understandings opened to perceive, the injury inflicted on this portion of the human race. These **"Voices of Freedom"** fill one-third of the volumes, and will continue to make themselves heard until the oppressor shall let go his hold, and the slave be restored to his rights and liberty. How many have these **"Voices"** aroused to a sense of the deep and cruel sin of slavery! They have come from the mountains, and echoed along the valleys, like the blast of the bugle on the night air, awakening the inhabitants of the land to the danger and the sin of the nation in upholding this uprighteous system of oppression. What a thrilling voice is that which speaks in poems entitled **"The Slave Ships,"** and **"Our Countrymen in Chains!"** And in **"The Christian Slave!"** . . .

The position which Whittier has attained is one which reflects a moral beauty upon his life and fame. It was, in some respects, an untried path in the walks of literature which he selected, and promises little in the way of reputation, though it has yielded much. It requires a high degree of moral courage to walk in it, but it has crowned his rising fame with unfading laurels. That it put his moral courage to the test is indicated in the following lines:

> Deep as I felt, and stern and strong;
> In words which Prudence smothered long,
> My soul spoke out against the wrong.

His abhorrence of that moral cowardice which fears to utter an honest truth, is thus strongly expressed:

> For thy self, while wrong and sorrow
>   Make to thee their strong appeal,
> Coward wert thou not to utter
>   What the heart must feel.

> Earnest words must need be spoken,
>   When the warm heart bleeds or burns
> With its scorn of wrong, or pity
>   For the wronged, by turns.

Notwithstanding the influence of the slave power upon the literature of our country, on which its blighting influence has been felt, as upon everything else, the merits of Whittier, as a poet, must meet with universal acknowledgment, though it be yielded tardily by those who have no sympathy with the man. He has struck out a bolder path than any of his contemporaries, and seized upon greater and loftier themes than they. And this fact, itself, together with the vigor and beauty of his style, will give him a position in the front rank of American poets. With less of artistic skill than some of them, the greatness of his themes, and the outpourings of his generous spirit, will more than offset all his deficiencies. If he is not equal in the fertility and brilliancy of his imagination, he is unsurpassed in the simplicity, the beautiful flow and harmony, and the pure sentiment, of some of his miscellaneous poems. He possesses, too, a deep spirituality, and you feel that his mind is in intimate communion with the beautiful and true in all things. His **"Raphael"** and the lines on Follen and Channing are equal to anything in the English language of their kind. . . .

Some of the poems of Whittier are founded on events in the history of the Friends, but in none is there the least exhibition of bigotry or intolerance. He has too strong a repugnance to either, to fall into the same errors himself. The persecution of the Quakers is brought to our recollection, but not in such a way as to indicate a spirit of hatred towards those who were guilty of this wrong, or towards their descendants. The intolerance and bigotry of the priesthood, and the part they took in those persecutions, are made quite prominent, but not more so than was necessary to the truthfulness of his narrations. No one who reads him can fail to admire the beautiful ballad in which he recites the treatment of **"Cassandra Southwick,"** and the fine poem entitled **"Barclay of Ury."** The beautiful spirit of meekness and submission which distinguished so many of the early Quakers forms a fine theme for Whittier's pen, while it enables us to frame an excuse for the extravagances of some who did not know so well how to bear the persecutions which they endured for conscience's sake. Some of his verses indicate a sympathy wide and deep enough to embrace the whole world of Humanity. He seems to connect himself with the destiny of his race, with which his and all other individual destinies are interwoven. . . .

One valuable and interesting feature in the book remains to be noticed. It contains a fine steel engraving of the author, which will render it doubly dear to those who prize both the poet and the man. Those who have enjoyed his personal acquaintance say it is an excellent likeness. It is very much like the ideal image of the man who had formed it from reading the productions of his mind; so far do we associate mental character with organization. It is a face full of thought and kindly sentiment. The features are finely chiseled, and the eye is full of calm, reflective passion. It is a face expressive of the finest sensibilities and feelings, in which gentleness and dignity of soul are harmoniously blended, indicating the warm and generous friend and the moral hero. In that thoughtful-looking eye, there dwells the perception and the love of beauty. The harmonies of the outward world—the beautiful in thought and deed, of love, religion, and the soul—are all reflected there. And then there arises above that face a head. . . . The Perceptive faculties and Language are full, but it is in the superior regions of the forehead that the strength and vigor of his mind are seen. There the Reflective powers stand out prominently, and Ideality swells its rounded form above the hollow temples, partially concealed beneath the hair. Then in the unusual height of the head you perceive the fulness of the moral region—of Benevolence, and Conscience, and Firmness—the Sentiments of Justice, Freedom, and Humanity. There are the sources of his moral power, and give direction to his mind.

> J.G.F. [J. G. Forman], "Whittier's 'Poems'," in The National Era, Vol. III, No. 5, February 1, 1849, p. 17.

[ORESTES BROWNSON] (essay date 1850)

[In the following attack on Whittier, the critic attempts to undermine the poet's character, criticizing his reputation as "a Quaker, an infidel, an Abolitionist, a philanthropist, . . . a Red Republican." Brownson concedes that Whittier has some of the attributes of a true poet, but asserts that he uses these gifts for the wrong reasons.]

Mr. Whittier has some of the elements of a true poet, but his poems, though often marked by strength and tenderness, are our abomination. He is a Quaker, an infidel, an Abolitionist, a philanthropist, a peace man, a Red Republican, a non-resistant, a revolutionist, all characters we hold in horror and detestation, and his poems are the echo of himself. God gave him noble gifts, every one of which he has used to undermine faith, to eradicate loyalty, to break down authority, and to establish the reign of anarchy, and all under the gentle mask of promoting love and good-will, diffusing the Christian spirit, and defending the sacred cause of liberty. He approaches us in the gentle and winning form of an angel of light, and yet, whether he means it or not, it is only to rob us of all that renders life worth possessing. If he believes himself doing the will of God, he is the most perfect dupe of the Evil One the Devil has ever been able to make. He is silly enough, after having denounced Pius the Ninth in the most savage manner, and canonized the assassins and ruffians who founded the Roman republic, to think that he can pass with Catholics as not being their enemy, because, forsooth, he favored the Irish rebellion! Whoever denounces our Church or its illustrious chief is our enemy, and we would much sooner hold the man who should seek to deprive us of life to be our friend, than the one who should undertake to deprive us of our religion. With this estimate of Mr. Whittier, how can we praise his poems, or commend them to the public?

> [Orestes Brownson], in a review of "Songs of Labor, and Other Poems," in Brownson's Quarterly Review, n.s. Vol. IV, No. IV, October, 1850, p. 540.

MOTLEY MANNERS [PSEUDONYM OF AUGUSTINE J.H. DUGANNE] (essay date 1851)

[Duganne was a nineteenth-century soldier and author noted primarily for his widely circulated paperback novels. His Parnassus in Pillory: A Satire was an imitation of James Russell Lowell's A Fable for Critics (see excerpt above, 1848), but Duganne's satire never achieved the enduring fame of Lowell's work. In the following excerpt from Parnassus in Pillory, Duganne expresses admiration for the spirit of Whittier's poetry, but criticizes the lack of revision in his works. He recommends that Whittier correct more of his grammatical and syntactical errors, and shorten his lengthy ballads.]

Hark! Whittier's sledge upon the hearts of men
Beats in continual music—"ten-pound-ten!"
Sworn foe of "institutions patriarchal,"
Black ground, he finds, gives gems a brighter sparkle.
Lo! how he comes, with earnest heart and loyal,
Flanked by his ordnance for a battle royal;
Swinging a club might stagger Hercules,
To dash the mites from off a mouldering cheese;
Roaring like Stentor from his brazen throat,
To drown some snappish spaniel's yelping note;
Ah, Whittier! Fighting Friend! I like thy verse—
Thy wholesale blessing and thy wholesale curse;
I prize the spirit which exalts thy strain,
And joy when truth impels thy blows amain;
But, really, friend! I cannot help suspecting
Though writing's good, there's merit in correcting!
Hahnemann likes best "the thirtieth dilution,"
But poetry scarce bears so much diffusion;
The homoeopathic thought (though truth sublime)
Dies through materia medica of rhyme;
So, Whittier, give less lexicon, and more
Good thought—of which no doubt thou hast a store.
Give us, if thou wouldst sing a flying slave,
Just as few bars as he or she would crave;
And if on "Ichabod" thou launchest malison,
Make it no longer than two books of Alison.
And, further, Whitter, "an thou lovest me,"
Let thy chief subject for a while go free;—
Or else, (how frail "Othello's occupation!")
When slavery falls, will fall thine avocation!
Living the black man's friend, i'faith, thou'lt die so:
A paraphrase of Wilmot's great proviso!
Whittier, adieu! my blows I would not spare,
For when I strike, I strike who best can bear;
Oft in this rhyme of mine I lash full hard
The man whom much I love, as friend and bard;
Even as the leech, inspired by science pure,
Albeit he probe and cauterize—must cure!

(pp. 70-2)

> Motley Manners [pseudonym of Augustine J.H. Duganne], in his Parnassus In Pillory: A Satire, 1851. Reprint by Kennikat Press, 1971, 96 p.*

[WILLIAM SYDNEY THAYER] (essay date 1854)

[In one of the first reviews to mention Whittier's Biblical allusions, Thayer provides a detailed discussion of the poet's literary strengths. Specifically, Thayer notes Whittier's intensity and "strong religious fervor" and remarks that while his verse sometimes bears evidence of "extreme haste," the fault is overcome by the "strength and simplicity of his conceptions." Thayer also praises Whittier's use of proper names even though, when overused, they result in stiff, pedantic writing. Like Edgar Allan Poe (1841), Thayer asserts that Whittier's poems lack imagination.]

In considering Whittier's merits as an author, it is quite manifest that we should mention, first, his intensity,—that vivid force of thought and expression which distinguishes his writings. His verses sometimes bear marks of extreme haste, but the imperfections which would result from this cause are in a great measure obviated by the strength and simplicity of his conceptions. He begins to write with so clear an apprehension of what he intends to say, that in many cases his poems come out at first heat with a roundness and perfection which would lead one to suppose that they had passed through the fires of revision. But at times this vehemence is overdone, and needs a restraint which longer consideration would have supplied. This vividness, which Whittier possesses in a greater degree than any other living author with whom we are acquainted, is in part a natural peculiarity of his mind, and in part arises from the urgent circumstances under which he wrote. His object was to produce an immediate effect upon the popular mind,—to stimulate his readers to immediate action,—and in consequence his productions have a business-like directness and cogency which do not belong to ordinary poetic effusions. Whittier's genius is essentially lyrical. It would be out of his power to write in a strain so purely imaginative as that of Keats "To a Grecian Urn," or other similar productions. Besides, mere devotion to the poetical art, mere exercise of the imagination for its own sake, seems inappropriate to him who considers, as he says,

> Life all too earnest, and its time too short,
> For dreamy ease and Fancy's graceful sport.

One short, vigorous blast suffices him. (pp. 42-3)

Like every other true lyric poet, Whittier does not lack his multitude of friendly critics, who advise him to concentrate his efforts upon some great work, instead of dissipating his energy upon what they consider mere ephemerals,—to devote himself to some gigantic undertaking, which shall loom up like the Pyramids to tell posterity his fame. But in our opinion the author has unwittingly best consulted his genius and reputation in the course which he has adopted. His shortest productions are his happiest. There is no doubt that the writing of long poems is sanctioned by many eminent examples; but they are the least read of an author's works, and are known to most people only by certain favorite extracts. (pp. 43-4)

The Quakerism in which Whittier was reared, and which he has always professed, stands . . . in strange conflict with the belligerent tone of many of his writings. We should hardly have expected so rude and martial a strain from the quiet, drab-coated professor of the mild tenets of his sect. (p. 47)

We are naturally led, from the consideration of our author's Quakerism, to that strong religious fervor which is manifested in every part of his writings. So deeply rooted is it, and apparently so blended with his imaginative powers, that, in some of his productions, one can hardly tell which predominates. His religious views embrace a simple faith in the Quaker doctrine of the inward light, combined with an intense apprehension of the brotherhood of man. In order to show his devotional spirit, we quote the concluding stanza of **"The Quaker of the Olden Time."**

> O, spirit of that early day,
> So pure and strong and true!
> Be with us in the narrow way
> Our faithful fathers knew.
> Give strength the evil to forsake,
> The cross of Truth to bear,
> And love and reverent fear to make
> Our daily lives a prayer!

The poems entitled **"Follen," "Questions of Life," "My Soul and I,"** and others of a similar kind, are exquisite in their delicacy of thought and expression, and show a wrestling with some of the gravest and most perplexing questions that come under the consideration of meditative minds.

Whittier rarely writes without being so impressed with some strong feeling, that he cannot fail to awaken a corresponding emotion in his reader. Of this, his verses written in memory of his friends bear witness. We would refer emphatically to the **"Lines to a Friend on the Death of his Sister,"** and to the perfect poem entitled **"Gone."** For the same reason, he writes with such energy, as not to give himself much concern about the customary ornaments of poetical diction. His imagery, when he introduces it, comes without an effort, as the natural accompaniment of his verse, never obtruding itself on the reader's attention, or seeming other than an essential part of the whole. (pp. 47-8)

One peculiarity of Whittier's imagery is, that so much of it is drawn from the Bible. This book is so the common property of Christendom, that to resort to it for purposes of poetical illustration is as justifiable as to resort to the book of Nature. He shows a very great familiarity with every part of holy writ, and an exceeding aptness in its citation. Of a brother reformer and poet he speaks as

> Like Nehemiah, fighting as he wrought.

The conjunction of the clergy and laity against the Abolition agitation he characterizes as

> Pilate and Herod friends!

The free and dexterous use of proper names is another characteristic of our poet. With an affluence of these his extensive knowledge supplies him, and he displays uncommon skill in weaving them harmoniously into his verse. Even the long sesquipedalian Indian words present no insuperable difficulties. There is something strangely impressive in the effect of the introduction of a melodious or sonorous name, particularly if it indicates a place of which we have no personal knowledge. The imagination is touched in that vague and mysterious way in which it delights, and the burden is put upon the reader of supplying the requisite beauty or sublimity to fill out the supposed conception of the author. (p. 49)

[The] introduction of proper names, generally felicitous in Whittier's writings, is in some instances overdone, and gives an air of stiffness and pedantry; as in the enumeration of nations in **"The World's Convention."**

As a consequence of the seeming haste in which many of these poems are written, the author is betrayed into occasional inaccuracies of grammar and rhyme. Many of these, which we had observed in his earlier volumes, we are glad to see corrected in the revised collection. But some still remain. Speaking of the tendency of youth to look on the best side of everything, he says:—

> Turning, with a power like Midas,
> All things into gold.

The first line is not in accordance with the idiom of the language, and even if it should be corrected by the addition of an apostrophe after Midas, it would remain clumsy. An obvious improvement would be to substitute

> Turning with the power of Midas.

We have noticed several inadmissible rhymes,—"dawn" with "scorn," "curse" with "us," "war" with "saw" and "draw," &c.

Instances of anything resembling the use of other people's thoughts are seldom to be found in Whittier's poems. The following, from **"The Chapel of the Hermits,"** is hardly a plagiarism:—

> That all of good the Past hath had
> Remains to make our own time glad.

But Lowell's version is better:—

> The Present moves attended
> By all of brave and excellent and fair,
> That made the old time splendid.

In closing our notice of Whittier's poetry, we forbear extended remark upon the great variety of his metres, and his unusual success and facility in the management of them.

Of his prose style we have already spoken at some length. It is classical, vigorous, and never dull, with a vein of humor running through it, which lacks *abandon* and seems somewhat inflexible and metallic. (pp. 50-1)

Whittier is a writer whose sentiments are thoroughly American;—not that he is always in harmony with the prevalent opinion of his countrymen, but that his productions are deeply imbued with the spirit of our institutions. They contain the genuine American doctrines of freedom and humanity, brought up to the latest and highest standard. His unmeasured sympathy for his kind has led him into a field new and entirely his own, and given him an unquestionable title to the name of an original author. (p. 52)

> [William Sydney Thayer], "John G. Whittier and His Writings," in The North American Review, Vol. LXXIX, No. CLXIV, July, 1854, pp. 31-53.

J.G.W. [JOHN GREENLEAF WHITTIER]   (essay date 1857)

[*In this preface to the 1857 collection,* The Complete Poetical Works of John Greenleaf Whittier, *Whittier apologizes for his lack of revision, a fault cited by Augustine J. H. Duganne (1851) and John Vance Cheney (1892). Whittier acknowledges that the collection contains works that he would "willingly let die."*]

In these volumes, for the first time, a complete collection of my poetical writings has been made. While it is satisfactory to know that these scattered children of my brain have found a home, I cannot but regret that I have been unable, by reason of illness, to give that attention to their revision and arrangement which respect for the opinions of others and my own afterthought and experience demand.

That there are pieces in this collection which I would 'willingly let die,' I am free to confess. But it is now too late to disown them, and I must submit to the inevitable penalty of poetical as well as other sins. There are others, intimately connected with the author's life and times, which owe their tenacity of vitality to the circumstances under which they were written, and the events by which they were suggested.

The long poem of **'Mogg Megone'** was in a great measure composed in early life; and it is scarcely necessary to say that its subject is not such as the writer would have chosen at any subsequent period. (p. xxi)

> J.G.W. [John Greenleaf Whittier], in an introduction to his The Complete Poetical Works of John Greenleaf Whittier, Houghton Mifflin Company, 1894, pp. xxi-xxii.

An oil painting of Whittier at age twenty-six. This portrait was painted in 1833 by Robert Peckham.

[DAVID ATWOOD WASSON]   (essay date 1860)

[Mr. Whittier] is, on the whole, the most representative poet that New England has produced. [In his **Home Ballads and Poems,** he] sings her thoughts, her prejudices, her scenery. He has not forgiven the Puritans for hanging two or three of his cosectaries, but he admires them for all that. . . . Whatever Mr. Whittier may lack, he has the prime merit that he smacks of the soil. It is a New England heart he buttons his strait-breasted coat over, and it gives the buttons a sharp strain now and then. Even the native idiom crops out here and there in his verses. He makes *abroad* rhyme with *God, law* with *war, us* with *curse, scorner* with *honor, been* with *men, beard* with *shared.* For the last two we have a certain sympathy as archaisms, but with the rest we can make no terms whatever,—they must march out with no honors of war. The Yankee lingo is insoluble in poetry, and the accent would give a flavor of *essence-pennyr'y'l* to the very Beatitudes. It differs from Lowland Scotch as a *patois* from a dialect.

But criticism is not a game of jerk-straws, and Mr. Whittier has other and better claims on us than as a stylist. There is true fire in the heart of the man, and his eye is the eye of a poet. A more juicy soil might have made him a Burns or a Béranger for us. New England is dry and hard, though she have a warm nook in her, here and there, where the magnolia grows after a fashion. It is all very nice to say to our poets, "You have sky and wood and waterfall and men and women,—in short, the entire outfit of Shakspeare; Nature is the same here as elsewhere"; and when the popular lecturer says it, the popular audience gives a stir of approval. But it is all *bosh,* nevertheless. Nature is *not* the same here, and perhaps never will be, as in lands where man has mingled his being with hers for countless centuries, where every field is steeped in history, every crag is ivied with legend, and the whole atmosphere of thought is hazy with the Indian summer of tradition. Nature without an ideal background is nothing. We may claim whatever merits we like, (and our orators are not too bashful,) we may be as free and enlightened as we choose, but we are certainly not interesting or picturesque. We may be as beautiful to the statistician as a column of figures, and dear to the political economist as a social phenomenon; but our hive has little of that marvellous bee-bread that can transmute the brain to finer issues than a gregarious activity in hoarding. (pp. 637-38)

Mr. Whittier himself complains somewhere of

The rigor of our frozen sky,

and he seems to have been thinking of our clear, thin, intellectual atmosphere, the counterpart of our physical one, of which artists complain that it rounds no edges. We have sometimes thought that his verses suffered from a New England taint in a too great tendency to metaphysics and morals, which may be the bases on which poetry rests, but should not be carried too high above-ground. Without this, however, he would not have been the typical New England poet that he is. In the present volume there is little of it. It is more purely objective than any of its forerunners, and is full of the most charming rural pictures and glimpses, in which every sight and sound, every flower, bird, and tree, is neighborly and homely. . . . Every picture is full of color, and shows that true eye for Nature which sees only what it ought, and that artistic memory which brings home compositions and not catalogues. There is hardly a hill, rock, stream, or sea-fronting headland in the neighborhood of his home that he has not fondly remembered. Sometimes, we think, there is too much description, the besetting sin of modern verse, which has substituted what should be called wordy-painting for the old art of painting in a single word. The essential character of Mr. Whittier's poetry is lyrical, and the rush of the lyric, like that of a brook, allows few pictures. Now and then there may be an eddy where the feeling lingers and reflects a bit of scenery, but for the most part it can only catch gleams of color that mingle with the prevailing tone and enrich without usurping on it. This volume contains some of the best of Mr. Whittier's productions in this kind. **"Skipper Ireson's Ride"** we hold to be by long odds the best of modern ballads. There are others nearly as good in their way, and all, with a single exception, embodying native legends. In **"Telling the Bees,"** Mr. Whittier has enshrined a country superstition in a poem of exquisite grace and feeling. **"The Garrison of Cape Ann"** would have been a fine poem, but it has too much of the author in it, and to put a moral at the end of a ballad is like sticking a cork on the point of a sword. (pp. 638-39)

This last volume has given us a higher conception of Mr. Whittier's powers. We already valued as they deserved his force of faith, his earnestness, the glow and hurry of his thought, and the (if every third stump-speaker among us were not a Demosthenes, we should have said Demosthenean) eloquence of his verse; but here we meet him in a softer and more meditative mood. . . . The half-mystic tone of **"The Shadow and the Light"** contrasts strangely, and, we think, pleasantly, with the warlike clang of **"From Perugia."** The years deal kindly with good men, and we find a clearer and richer quality in these verses where the ferment is over and the *rile* has quietly settled. We have had no more purely American poet than Mr. Whittier, none in whom the popular thought found such ready

and vigorous expression. The future will not fail to do justice to a man who has been so true to the present. (p. 639)

> *[David Atwood Wasson], in a review of "Home Ballads and Poems," in The Atlantic Monthly, Vol. VI, No. XXXVII, November, 1860, pp. 637-39.*

LYDIA MARIA CHILD   (letter date 1862)

[Child was a noted American humanitarian writer, editor, and abolitionist. Her Appeal in Favor of That Class of Americans Called Africans, *one of the first antislavery volumes to appear in the United States, helped to advance the abolitionist cause and firmly established the role of women in the antislavery movement. Here, Child praises Whittier's expression of "African humor." For additional commentary by Child, see excerpts below, 1874 and 1877.]*

I was moved to write you my thanks for **"The Two Watchers;"** but I was busy working for the "contrabands" at Fortress Monroe, and so I kept the thanks warm in my heart, without giving them an airing. But that Negro Boat Song at Port Royal! How I have chuckled over it and sighed over it! I keep repeating it morning, noon, and night; and, I believe, with almost as much satisfaction as the slaves themselves would do. It is a complete embodiment of African humor, and expressed as they would express it, if they were learned in the mysteries of rhyme and rhythm. I have only one criticism on the negro dialect. They would not say, "He 'leab' de land." They would say, He "'leff'" de land. At least, so speak all the slaves I have talked with, or whose talk I have seen reported.

What a glorious, blessed gift is this gift of song, with which you are so lavishly endowed! Who can calculate its influence, which you exert always for good! My David, who always rejoices over your writings, was especially pleased with the Boat Song, which he prophesies will be sung ere long by thousands of darkies. He bids me say to you that

One bugle note from Whittier's pen
Is worth at least ten thousand men.

So you see that you are at least equal to a major-general in the forces you lead into the field, and your laurels are bloodless. (pp. 159-60)

> *Lydia Maria Child, in a letter to John G. Whittier on January 21, 1862, in her* Letters of Lydia Maria Child, *Houghton, Mifflin and Company, 1883, pp. 159-62.*

[JAMES RUSSELL LOWELL]   (essay date 1864)

[In the following review of Whittier's In War-Time, and Other Poems, *Lowell calls attention to the fervor of his verse and describes Whittier as "the most American of our poets." Lowell also notes that although Whittier is a Quaker and therefore a pacifist, he has provided the "keenest expression" of the Civil War. For additional commentary by Lowell, see excerpts above, 1848, and below, 1866.]*

It is a curious illustration of the attraction of opposites, that, among our elder poets, the war we are waging finds its keenest expression in the Quaker Whittier. Here [in *In War Time, and Other Poems*] is, indeed, a soldier prisoner on parole in a drab coat, with no hope of exchange, but with a heart beating time to the tap of the drum. Mr. Whittier is, on the whole, the most American of our poets, and there is a fire of warlike patriotism in him that burns all the more intensely that it is smothered by his creed. (pp. 290-91)

Mr. Whittier is essentially a lyric poet, and the fervor of his temperament gives his pieces of that kind a remarkable force and effectiveness. Twenty years ago many of his poems were . . . vigorous stump-speeches in verse, appealing as much to the blood as the brain, and none the less convincing for that. By regular gradations ever since his tone has been softening and his range widening. As a poet he stands somewhere between Burns and Cowper, akin to the former in patriotic glow, and to the latter in intensity of religious anxiety verging sometimes on morbidness. His humanity, if it lack the humorous breadth of the one, has all the tenderness of the other. In love of outward nature he yields to neither. His delight in it is not a new sentiment or a literary tradition, but the genuine passion of a man born and bred in the country, who has not merely a visiting acquaintance with the landscape, but stands on terms of lifelong friendship with hill, stream, rock, and tree. In his descriptions he often catches the *expression* of rural scenery, a very different thing from the mere *looks*, with the trained eye of familiar intimacy. A somewhat shy and heremitical being we take him to be, and more a student of his own heart than of men. His characters, where he introduces such, are commonly abstractions, with little of the flesh and blood of real life in them, and this from want of experience rather than of sympathy; for many of his poems show him capable of friendship almost womanly in its purity and warmth. One quality which we especially value in him is the intense home-feeling which, without any conscious aim at being American, gives his poetry a flavor of the soil surprisingly refreshing. Without being narrowly provincial, he is the most indigenous of our poets. In these times, especially, his uncalculating love of country has a profound pathos in it. He does not flare the flag in our faces, but one feels the heart of a lover throbbing in his anxious verse.

Mr. Whittier, if the most fervid of our poets, is sometimes hurried away by this very quality, in itself an excellence, into being the most careless. He draws off his verse while the fermentation is yet going on, and before it has had time to compose itself and clarify into the ripe wine of expression. His rhymes are often faulty beyond the most provincial license even of Burns himself. Vigor without elegance will never achieve permanent success in poetry. We think, also, that he has too often of late suffered himself to be seduced from the true path to which his nature set up finger-posts for him at every corner, into metaphysical labyrinths whose clew he is unable to grasp. The real life of his genius smoulders into what the woodmen call a *smudge*, and gives evidence of itself in smoke instead of flame. Where he follows his truer instincts, he is often admirable in the highest sense, and never without the interest of natural thought and feeling naturally expressed. (pp. 291-92)

> [*James Russell Lowell*], "Whittier's 'In War Time'," in The North American Review, *Vol. XCVIII, No. CCII, January, 1864, pp. 290-92.*

THE ATLANTIC MONTHLY   (essay date 1864)

[*In the following panegyric to Whittier as a "born" poet, the reviewer divides Whittier's poetry into three periods and labels the latest, comprising the ballads, the best.*]

[Had **"In War-Time"** been no more] than a mere private reminiscence, it should, at present, have remained private. But have we not here a key to Whittier's genius? Is not this Semitic centrality and simplicity, this prophetic depth, reality, and vigor, without great lateral and intellectual range, its especial characteristic? He has not the liberated, light-winged Greek imagination,—imagination not involved and included in the religious sentiment, but playing in epic freedom and with various interpretation between religion and intellect; he has not the flowing, Protean, imaginative sympathy, the power of instant self-identification with all forms of character and life, which culminated in Shakspeare; but that imaginative vitality which lurks in faith and conscience, producing what we may call *ideal force of heart,* this he has eminently; and it is this central, invisible, Semitic heat which makes him a poet.

Imagination exists in him, not as a separable faculty, but as a pure vital suffusion. Hence he is an *inevitable* poet. There is no drop of his blood, there is no fibre of his brain, which does not crave poetic expression. Mr. Carlyle desires to postpone poetry; but as Providence did not postpone Whittier, his wishes can hardly be gratified. Ours is, indeed, one of the plainest of poets. He is intelligible and acceptable to those who have little either of poetic culture or of fancy and imagination. Whoever has common sense and a sound heart has the powers by which he may be appreciated. And yet he is not only a real poet, but he is *all* poet. The Muses have not merely sprinkled his brow; he was baptized by immersion. His notes are not many; but in them Nature herself sings. He is a sparrow that half sings, half chirps, on a bush, not a lark that floods with orient hilarity the skies of morning; but the bush burns, like that which Moses saw, and the sparrow herself is part of the divine flame.

This, then, is the general statement about Whittier. His genius is Hebrew, Biblical,—more so than that of any other poet now using the English language. In other words, he is organically a poem of the Will. He is a flower of the moral sentiment,— and of the moral sentiment, not in its flexible, feminine, vine-like dependence and play, but in its masculine rigor, climbing in direct, vertical affirmation, like a forest-pine. In this respect he affiliates with Wordsworth, and, going farther back, with Milton, whose tap-root was Hebrew, though in the vast epic flowering of his genius he passed beyond the imaginative range of Semitic mind.

In thus identifying our bard, spiritually, with a broad form of the genius of mankind, we already say with emphasis that his is indeed a Life. Yes, once more, a real Life. He is a nature. He was *born,* not manufactured. Here, once again, the old, mysterious, miraculous processes of spiritual assimilation. Here, a genuine root-clutch upon the elements of man's experience, and an inevitable, indomitable working-up of them into human shape. To look at him without discerning this vital depth and reality were as good as no looking at all.

Moreover, the man and the poet are one and the same. His verse is no literary Beau-Brummelism, but a *re*-presentation of that which is presented in his consciousness. First, there is inward vital conversion of the elements of his experience, then verse, or version,—first the soul, then the body. His voice, as such, has little range, nor is it any marvel of organic perfection; on the contrary, there is many a voice with nothing at all in it which far surpasses his in mere vocal excellence; only in this you can hear the deep refrain of Nature, and of Nature chanting her moral ideal.

We shall consider Whittier's poetry in this light,—as a vital effluence, as a product of his being; and citations will be made, not by way of culling "beauties,"—a mode of criticism to which there are grave objections,—but of illustrating total growth, quality, and power. Our endeavor will be to get at, so far as possible, the processes of vital action, of spiritual assimilation, which go on in the poet, and then to trace these in his poetry.

God gave Whittier a deep, hot, simple, strenuous, and yet ripe and spherical, nature, whose twin necessities were, first, that it *must* lay an intense grasp upon the elements of its experience, and, secondly, that it *must* work these up into some form of melodious completeness. History and the world gave him Quakerism, America, and Rural Solitude; and through this solitude went winding the sweet, old Merrimac stream, the river that we would not wish to forget, even by the waters of the river of life! And it is into these elements that his genius, with its peculiar vital simplicity and intensity, strikes root. Historic reality, the great *facts* of his time, are the soil in which he grows, as they are with all natures of depth and energy. (pp. 331-32)

Whittier's poetic life has three principal epochs. The first opens and closes with the **"Voices of Freedom."** We may use Darwin's phrase, and call it the period of Struggle for Life. His ideal itself is endangered; the atmosphere he would inhale is filled with poison; a desolating moral prosaicism springs up to justify a great social ugliness, and spreads in the air where his young hopes would try their wings; and in the imperfect strength of youth he has so much of dependence upon actual surroundings, that he must either war with their evil or succumb to it. . . .

Our poet, too, conversing with God's stars and silence, has come to an understanding with himself, and made up his mind. That Man's being has an ideal or infinite value, and that all consecrated institutions are shams, and their formal consecration a blasphemous mockery, save as they look to that fact,—this in his Merrimac solitudes has come forth clearly to his soul, and, like old Hebrew David, he has said, "My heart is fixed." Make other selections who will, he has concluded to face life and death on this basis. (p. 333)

These **"Voices of Freedom"** are no bad reading at the present day. They are of that strenuous quality, that the light of battle brings to view a finer print, which lay unseen between the lines. They are themselves battles, and stir the blood like the blast of a trumpet. What a beat in them of fiery pulses! What a heat, as of molten metal, or coal-mines burning underground! What anger! What desire! And yet we have in vain searched these poems to find one trace of base wrath, or of any degenerate and selfish passion. He is angry, and sins not. The sun goes down and again rises upon his wrath; and neither sets nor rises upon aught freer from meanness and egoism. All the fires of his heart burn for justice and mercy, for God and humanity; and they who are most scathed by them *owe* him no hatred in return, whether they *pay* him any or not. (p. 334)

In the year 1850 appeared the **"Songs of Labor, and other Poems"**; and in these we reach the transition to his second epoch. Here he has already recognized the pure ground of the poem,—

> Art's perfect forms no moral need,
> And beauty is its own excuse,—

but his modesty declines attempting that perfection, and assigns him a lower place. He must still seek definite uses, though this use be to lend imagination or poetic depth to daily labor:—

> But for the dull and flowerless weed
> Some healing virtue still must plead,
> And the rough ore must find its honors in its use.

> So haply these my simple lays
> Of homely toil may serve to show
> The orchard-bloom and tasselled maize
> That skirt and gladden duty's ways,
> The unsung beauty hid life's common things below.

Not pure gold as yet, but genuine silver. The aim at a definite use is still apparent, as he himself perceives; but there is nevertheless a constant native play into them of ideal feeling. It is no longer a struggle for room to draw poetic breath in, but only the absence of a perfectly free and unconscious poetic respiration. Yet they are sterling poems, with the stamp of the mint upon them. And some of the strains are such as no living man but Whittier has proven his power to produce. **"Ichabod,"** for example, is the purest and profoundest *moral* lament, to the best of our knowledge, in modern literature, whether American or European. . . .

Two years later comes the **"Chapel of the Hermits,"** and with it the second epoch in Whittier's poetic career. The epoch of Culture we name it. The poet has now passed the period of outward warfare. All the arrows in the quiver of his noble wrath are spent. (p. 335)

Our poet's is one of those deep and clinging natures which hold hard by the heart of bygone times; but also he is of a nature so deep and sensitive that the spiritual endeavor of the period must needs utter itself in him. (p. 336)

"The Panorama and other Poems," together with **"Later Poems,"** having the dates of 1856 and 1857, constitute the transition to his third and consummate epoch. Much in them deserves notice, but we must hasten. And yet, instead of hastening, we will pause, and take this opportunity to pick a small critical quarrel with Mr. Whittier. We charge him, in the first place, with sundry felonious assaults upon the good letter *r*. In the **"Panorama,"** for example, we find *law* rhyming with *for*! You, Mr. Poet, you, who indulge fastidious objections to the whipping of women, to outrage that innocent preposition thus! And to select the word *law* itself, with which to force it into this lawless connection! Secondly, *romance* and *allies* are constantly written by him with the accent on the first syllable. These be heinous offences! A poet, of all men, should cherish the liquid consonants, and should resist the tendency of the populace to make trochees of all dissyllables. In a graver tone we might complain that he sometimes—rarely—writes, not by vocation of the ancient Muses, who were daughters of Memory and immortal Zeus, but of those Muses in drab and scoop-bonnets who are daughters of Memory and George Fox. Some lines of the **"Brown of Ossawatomie"** we are thinking of now. We can regard them only as a reminiscence of his special Quaker culture.

With the **"Home Ballads,"** published in 1863, dawns fully his final period,—long may it last! This is the epoch of Poetic Realism. Not that he abandons or falls away from his moral ideal. The fact is quite contrary. He has so entirely established himself in that ideal that he no longer needs strivingly to assert it,—any more than Nature needs to pin upon oak-trees an affirmation that the idea of an oak dwells in her formative thought. (pp. 336-37)

It is this poetic realism that Whittier has now, in a high degree, attained. Calm and sure, lofty in humility, strong in childlikeness,—renewing the play-instinct of the true poet in his heart,—younger now than when he sat on his mother's knee,—chastened, not darkened, by trial, and toil, and time,—illumined, poet-like, even by sorrow,—he lives and loves, and chants the deep, homely beauty of his lays. He is as genuine, as wholesome and real as sweet-flag and clover. Even when he utters pure sentiment, as in that perfect lyric, **"My Psalm,"** or in the intrepid, exquisite humility—healthful and sound as the odor of new-mown hay or balsam-firs—of **"Andrew Rykman's Prayer,"** he maintains the same attitude of realism. He states God and inward experience as he would state sunshine and the growth of grass. This, with the devout depth of his nature, makes the rare beauty of his hymns and poems of piety and trust. He does not try to *make* the facts by stating them; he does not try to embellish them; he only seeks to utter, to state them; and even in his most perfect verse they are not half so melodious as they were in his soul. (p. 337)

It is, however, in his ballads that Whittier exhibits, not, perhaps, a higher, yet a rarer, power than elsewhere,—a power, in truth, which is very rare indeed. Already in the **"Panorama"** volume he had brought forth three of these,—all good, and the tender pathos of that fine ballad of sentiment, **"Maud Muller,"** went to the heart of the nation. In how many an imagination does the innocent maiden, with her delicate brown ankles,

> Rake the meadow sweet with hay,

and

> The judge ride slowly down the lane!

But though sentiment so simple and unconscious is rare, our poet has yet better in store for us. He has developed of late years the precious power of creating *homely beauty*,—one of the rarest powers shown in modern literature. Homely life-scenes, homely old sanctities and heroisms, he takes up, delineates them with intrepid fidelity to their homeliness, and, lo! there they are, beautiful as Indian corn, or as ploughed land under an October sun! He has thus opened an inexhaustible mine right here under our New-England feet. What will come of it no one knows.

These poems of his are natural growths; they have their own circulation of vital juices, their own peculiar properties; they smack of the soil, are racy and strong and aromatic, like ground-juniper, sweet-fern, and the *arbor vitae*. Set them out in the earth, and would they not sprout and grow?—nor would need vine-shields to shelter them from the weather! They are living and local, and lean toward the west from the pressure of east winds that blow on our coast. **"Skipper Ireson's Ride,"**—can any one tell what makes that poetry? This uncertainty is the highest praise. This power of telling a plain matter in a plain way, and leaving it there a symbol and harmony forever,—it is the power of Nature herself. And again we repeat, that almost anything may be found in literature more frequently than this pure creative simplicity. . . .

Our deep-hearted poet has fairly arrived at his poetic youth. Never was he so strong, so ruddy and rich as today. Time has treated him as, according to Swedenborg, she does the angels,—chastened indeed, but vivified. Let him hold steadily to his true vocation as a poet, and never fear to be thought idle, or untrue to his land. To give imaginative and ideal depth to the life of the people,—what truer service than that? And as for war-time,—does he know that **"Barbara Frietche"** is the true sequel to the Battle of Gettysburg, is that other victory which the nation *asked* of Meade the soldier and obtained from Whittier the poet? (p. 338)

> *"Whittier," in The Atlantic Monthly, Vol. XIII, No. LXXVII, March, 1864, pp. 331-38.*

[JAMES RUSSELL LOWELL] (essay date 1866)

[In his review of Whittier's Snow-bound, *Lowell praises the poem for its warmth and its vivid recreation of a New England winter. In comparing* Snow-bound *to Whittier's earlier work, Lowell concludes that the poet's "fire glows more equally and shines on sweeter scenes" as he ages. Lowell's recognition of* Snow-bound *as a valuable cultural record presages early twentieth-century opinion. For additional commentary by Lowell, see excerpts above, 1848 and 1864.]*

We are again indebted to Mr. Whittier, as we have been so often before, for a very real and a very refined pleasure. The little volume before us ["**Snow-Bound. A Winter Idyl"**] has all his most characteristic merits. It is true to Nature and in local coloring, pure in sentiment, quietly deep in feeling, and full of those simple touches which show the poetic eye and the trained hand. Here is a New England interior glorified with something of that inward light which is apt to be rather warmer in the poet than the Quaker, but which, blending the qualities of both in Mr. Whittier, produces that kind of spiritual picturesqueness which gives so peculiar a charm to his verse. There is in this poem a warmth of affectionate memory and religious faith as touching as it is uncommon, and which would be altogether delightful if it did not remind us that the poet was growing old. Not that there is any other mark of senescence than the ripened sweetness of a life both publicly and privately well spent. There is fire enough, but it glows more equally and shines on sweeter scenes than in the poet's earlier verse. It is as if a brand from the camp-fire had kindled these logs on the old homestead's hearth, whose flickering benediction touches tremulously those dear heads of long ago that are now transfigured with a holier light. The father, the mother, the uncle, the schoolmaster, the uncanny guest, are all painted in warm and natural colors, with perfect truth of detail and yet with all the tenderness of memory. Of the family group the poet is the last on earth, and there is something deeply touching in the pathetic sincerity of the affection which has outlived them all, looking back to before the parting, and forward to the assured reunion.

But aside from its poetic and personal interest, and the pleasure it must give to every one who loves pictures from the life, **"Snow-Bound"** has something of historical interest. It describes scenes and manners which the rapid changes of our national habits will soon have made as remote from us as if they were foreign or ancient. Already, alas! even in farmhouses, backlog and forestick are obsolescent words, and close-mouthed stoves chill the spirit while they bake the flesh with their grim and undemonstrative hospitality. Already are the railroads displacing the companionable cheer of crackling walnut with the dogged self-complacency and sullen virtue of anthracite. Even where wood survives, he is too often shut in the dreary madhouse cell of an air-tight, round which one can no more fancy a social mug of flip circling than round a coffin. Let us be thankful that we can sit in Mr. Whittier's chimney-corner and believe that the blaze he has kindled for us shall still warm and cheer, when a wood fire is as faint a tradition in New as in Old England.

We have before had occasion to protest against Mr. Whittier's carelessness in accents and rhymes, as in pronouncing "lý-ceum," and joining in unhallowed matrimony such sounds as *awn* and *orn*, *ents* and *ence*. We would not have the Muse emulate the unidiomatic preciseness of a Normal schoolmistress, but we cannot help thinking that, if Mr. Whittier writes thus on principle, as we begin to suspect, he errs in forgetting that thought so refined as his can be fitly matched only with an equal refinement of expression, and loses something of its charm when cheated of it. We hope he will, at least, never mount Pegásus, or water him in Helícon, and that he will leave Múseum to the more vulgar sphere and obtuser sensibilities of Barnum. Where Nature has sent genius, she has a right to expect that it shall be treated with a certain elegance of hospitality. (pp. 631-32)

> *[James Russell Lowell], in a review of "Snow-Bound,"
> in* The North American Review, *Vol. CII, No. CCXI,
> April, 1866, pp. 631-32.*

LYDIA MARIA CHILD (letter date 1874)

[In the following letter, Child thanks Whittier for the emotional impact and beauty of his poetry. For additional commentary by Child, see excerpts above, 1862, and below, 1877.]

I cannot help writing to thank you for the Lines you have written to the memory of Charles Sumner. They are very beautiful, and nothing could be more appropriate. . . .

I was reading over several of your poems last week, and for the thousandth time I felt myself consoled and strengthened by them, as well as delighted with their poetic beauty. It was a very precious gift you received, dear friend, to be such a benefactor to the souls of your fellow-beings. I know of no one man who I think has done so much in that way. That immortality you are sure of. (p. 228)

> *Lydia Maria Child, in a letter to John G. Whittier
> on June 18, 1874, in her* Letters of Lydia Maria
> Child, *Houghton, Mifflin and Company, 1883,
> pp. 228-29.*

PAUL H. HAYNE (poem date 1877)

[Whittier's seventieth birthday in 1877 was a celebrated literary event. The Atlantic Monthly *hosted a testimonial dinner in his honor, and the* Literary World *included a special section devoted to poems, essays, and letters of tribute contributed by Whittier's contemporaries. Hayne's remarks and the following seven excerpts were taken from the commemorative issue of the* Literary World.]

From this far realm of Pines I waft thee now
   A Brother's greeting, Poet, tried and true;
So thick the laurels on thy reverend brow
   We scarce can see the white locks glimmering through!

O, pure of thought! Earnest in heart as pen,
   The tests of time have left thee undefiled;
And o'er the snows of three-score years and ten
   Shines the unsullied aureole of a child.

> *Paul H. Hayne, "To the Poet in Whittier," in* The
> Literary World, *Vol. VIII, No. 7, December 1, 1877,
> p. 120.*

HENRY W. LONGFELLOW (poem date 1877)

[An American poet, novelist, and critic, Longfellow was one of the most popular American writers of the nineteenth century. Yet after his death, his reputation suffered a serious decline. The very characteristics which made his poetry popular in his own day— gentle simplicity and a melancholy reminiscent of the German Romantics—are those that fueled the posthumous debate against his work. Despite the continuing debate over Longfellow's stature,

he is considered instrumental in introducing European culture to the American readers of his day. In the following excerpt, Longfellow attributes to Whittier a spiritual quality. For additional information, see explanatory notes for Paul H. Hayne (1877).]

Three Silences there are; the first of speech,
   The second of desire, the third of thought;
   This is the lore a Spanish monk, distraught
With dreams and visions, was the first to teach.
These Silences, commingling each with each
   Made up the perfect Silence, that he sought
   And prayed for, and wherein at times he caught
Mysterious sounds from realms beyond our reach.
O thou, whose daily life anticipates
   The life to come, and in whose thought and word
   The spiritual world preponderates,
Hermit of Amesbury! thou too hast heard
   Voices and melodies from beyond the gates,
   And speakest only when thy soul is stirred!

> *Henry W. Longfellow, "The Three Silences," in* The
> Literary World, *Vol. VIII, No. 7, December 1, 1877,
> p. 120.*

EDMUND C. STEDMAN (poem date 1877)

[A major nineteenth-century American critic and anthologist, Stedman gained wide critical influence as the author of Victorian Poets *and* Poets of America. *In conjunction with his popular* American Anthology, Poets of America *helped to establish a greater interest in and appreciation for American literature. A foe of the "heresy of the didactic," Stedman wrote criticism which is often informed by his belief that "a prosaic moral is injurious to virtue by making it repulsive." In the following poetic tribute, Stedman laments Whittier's mortality, but rejoices in the immortality of the author's verse. For additional commentary by Stedman, see excerpt below, 1898. For additional information, see explanatory notes for Paul H. Hayne (1877).]*

Whittier! the Land that loves thee, she whose child
Thou art,—and whose uplifted hands thou long
Hast stayed with song availing like a prayer,—
She feels a sudden pang, who gave thee birth
And gave to thee the lineaments supreme
Of her own freedom, that she could not make
Thy tissues all immortal, or, if to change,
To bloom through years coeval with her own;
So that no touch of age nor frost of time
Should wither thee, nor furrow thy dear face,
Nor fleck thy hair with silver. Ay, she feels
A double pang that thee, with each new year,
Glad Youth may not revisit, like the Spring
That routs her northern Winter and anew
Melts off the hoar snow from her puissant hills.
She could not make thee deathless; no, but thou,
Thou sangest her always in abiding verse
And hast thy fame immortal—as we say
Immortal in this Earth that yet must die,
And in this land now fairest and most young
Of all fair lands that yet must perish with it.
Thy words shall last: albeit thou growest old,
Men say; but never old the poet's so-
Becomes; only its covering takes on
A reverend splendor, as in the misty fall
Thine own auroral forests, ere at last
Passes the spirit of the wooded dell.

And stay thou with us long! vouchsafe us long
This brave autumnal presence, ere the hues
Slow fading,—ere the quaver of thy voice,
The twilight of thine eye, move men to ask
Where hides the chariot,—in what sunset vale,
Beyond thy chosen river, champ the steeds
That wait to bear thee skyward? Since we too
Would feign thee, in our tenderness, to be
Inviolate, excepted from thy kind,
And that our bard and prophet best-beloved
Shall vanish like that other: him that stood
Undaunted in the pleasure-house of kings,
And unto kings and crowned harlots spake
God's truth and judgment. At his sacred feet
Far followed all the lesser men of old
Whose lips were touched with fire, and caught from him
The gift of prophecy; and thus from thee,
Whittier, the younger singers,—whom thou seest
Each emulous to be thy staff this day,—
What learned they? righteous anger, burning scorn
Of the oppressor, love to humankind,
Sweet fealty to country and to home,
Peace, stainless purity, high thoughts of heaven,
And the clear, natural music of thy song.

> Edmund C. Stedman, "Ad Vatem," in The Literary
> World, Vol. VIII, No. 7, December 1, 1877, p. 120.

WILLIAM C. BRYANT   (essay date 1877)

[Bryant is considered one of the most accomplished American poets of the nineteenth century. His treatment of the themes of nature and mutability identifies him as one of the earliest figures in the Romantic movement in American literature. In his essay commemorating Whittier's birthday, excerpted below, Bryant extols Whittier's life, which he calls "as beautiful as his verse". For additional information, see explanatory notes for Paul H. Hayne (1877).]

I should be glad to celebrate in verse the seventieth return of John Greenleaf Whittier's birthday, if the thoughts and words fitting for such an occasion would come at call, to be arranged in some poetic form, but I find that I must content myself with humble prose. Let me say then that I rejoice at the dispensation which has so long spared to the world a poet, whose life is as beautiful as his verse, who has occupied himself only with noble themes, and treated them nobly and grandly, and whose songs in the evening of life are as sweet and thrilling as those of his vigorous meridian. If the prayers of those who delight in his poems shall be heard, that life will be prolonged in all its beauty and serenity, for the sake of a world which is the better for his having lived; and far will be the day when all that we have of him will be his writings and his memory.

> William C. Bryant, in a tribute to John Greenleaf
> Whittier, in The Literary World, Vol. VIII, No. 7,
> December 1, 1877, p. 121.

L. MARIA CHILD   (poem date 1877)

[Child's tribute focuses on Whittier's optimism. For additional commentary by Child, see excerpts above, 1862 and 1874. For additional information, see explanatory notes for Paul H. Hayne (1877).]

I thank thee, friend, for words of cheer,
That made the path of duty clear,
When thou and I were young, and strong
To wrestle with a mighty wrong.
And now, when lengthening shadows come,
And this world's work is nearly done,
I thank thee for thy genial ray,
That prophesies a brighter day,
When we can work, with strength renewed,
In clearer light, for surer good.
God bless thee, friend, and give thee peace,
'Till thy fervent spirit finds release!
And may we meet in worlds afar,
My Morning and my Evening Star!

> L. Maria Child, "Sentiment," in The Literary World,
> Vol. VIII, No. 7, December 1, 1877, p. 121.

WILLIAM LLOYD GARRISON   (poem date 1877)

[Garrison, a nationally recognized leader in the abolitionist movement, was a key figure in Whittier's initial journalistic success and in his decision to become involved in the antislavery movement. In the following poetic tribute, Garrison ranks his friend with the "choicest poets of all time" and praises Whittier for his role in the fight against slavery. For additional information, see explanatory notes for Paul H. Hayne (1877).]

This is the tribute that I fain would pay
To him whose friendship I have closely shared,
Whose genius marked, from early youth till now
He counts his three-score years and ten complete;
But still erect in form, in mind as bright,
In heart as tender, and in soul as warm
As in mid-life, untouched by lapse of time;
Whom "troops of friends" this day unite to crown;
To proffer gratulations; to express
That high respect and admiration strong,
That deep affection and entwining love,
Which modest worth, and purity of life,
And noble aims to serve the public weal,
And scathing testimonies bravely borne
'Gainst popular sins, at loss of all repute,
So well deserve, so widely have secured.

Poets there are of various moods and gifts,
Each striking chords best suited to his ear,
And choosing themes concurrent with his taste;
But prone too oft to deal in phantasies,
In amatorial strains of carnal taint,
In passionate appeals to warlike deeds,
In bacchanalian medleys to be sung
Where congregate the maudlin votaries
Of the accursèd demon of the still,
Drowning their reason in the poisoned bowl.

How shall we rank the poet of our love?
A birthright Quaker—one in spirit, too,
Yet catholic beyond the bounds of sect.
Not his the highest reach of the sublime,
Nor loftiest flight on fancy's airy wings,
Nor strongest power of genius to conceive,
Invent, portray, with an enchanter's skill,
Nor best attainment in poetic art,
Nor precedence in rhythmic melody;

Yet, if excelled in these by famous bards
From Homer down to those of our own times,
With nobler claims he stands without his peer
In all that true affection can express,
Or purest love can prompt to gracious acts;
In tenderest sympathy for his suffering race,
Wherever in the wide world needing aid,
All caste and class distinctions giving way
To the strong ties of human brotherhood;
In carrying comfort unto mourning hearts
Bowed down by sore bereavement, teaching well
The lesson of a higher life beyond,
And a divine compassion over all;
In perfect chastity of thought and speech,
And an uplifting moral power to bless
And strengthen frailty through the inner light;
In breathing "peace on earth, good will to men,"
That so the sword no longer may devour,
And desolating war forever cease.
But, signally, in this he takes the palm,
As hero-bard in Freedom's struggling cause,
When millions in our guilty land were held
In chattel servitude, and bought and sold
Along with cattle in the market-place;
Poets there are of various moods and gifts,
Each striking chords best suited to his ear,
And choosing themes concurrent with his taste;
But prone too oft to deal in phantasies,
In amatorial strains of carnal taint,
In passionate appeals to warlike deeds,
In bacchanalian medleys to be sung
Where congregate the maudlin votaries
Of the accursèd demon of the still,
Drowning their reason in the poisoned bowl.

How shall we rank the poet of our love?
A birthright Quaker—one in spirit, too,
Yet catholic beyond the bounds of sect.
Not his the highest reach of the sublime,
Nor loftiest flight on fancy's airy wings,
Nor strongest power of genius to conceive,
Invent, portray, with an enchanter's skill,
Nor best attainment in poetic art,
Nor precedence in rhythmic melody;
Yet, if excelled in these by famous bards
From Homer down to those of our own times,
With nobler claims he stands without his peer
In all that true affection can express,
Or purest love can prompt to gracious acts;
In tenderest sympathy for his suffering race,
Wherever in the wide world needing aid,
All caste and class distinctions giving way
To the strong ties of human brotherhood;
In carrying comfort unto mourning hearts
Bowed down by sore bereavement, teaching well
The lesson of a higher life beyond,
And a divine compassion over all;
In perfect chastity of thought and speech,
And an uplifting moral power to bless
And strengthen frailty through the inner light;
In breathing "peace on earth, good will to men,"
That so the sword no longer may devour,
And desolating war forever cease.
But, signally, in this he takes the palm,
As hero-bard in Freedom's struggling cause,

When millions in our guilty land were held
In chattel servitude, and bought and sold
Along with cattle in the market-place;
And they who sought by flight to escape their doom
Were tracked by bloodhounds, seized, and carried back
To added stripes and tortures; none allowed
To give them food or shelter, at the risk
Of fine, imprisonment, or being lynched;
In that dark hour, with Church and State combined
To keep them in their chains, and stigmatize
As "madmen and fanatics" all who sought
Emancipation as their rightful due,
He manfully stood forth, with dauntless front,
Zealous in their behalf; in thrilling verse
Rehearsed the dreadful story of their wrongs,
Summoned with trumpet-tones the true and brave
To rally to the rescue, well equipped
With spiritual weapons for the fight,
And with unwavering faith in Him whose arm
Is strong to smite, omnipotent to save.
Read, read his spirit-stirring strains, unmatched
For power and pathos, making sluggish blood
Tumultuous in the beatings of the heart,
Strengthening the inner man to stand erect,
Heedless of private hate and public scorn,
In full assurance that the end is near—
Oppression's ignominious defeat,
And Liberty victorious through the land!

Yes! he has lived to see (rich recompense!)
The suffering bondmen from their chains set free;
To hear their grateful songs to heaven ascend,
With merry chimings of the jubilee bell.
What wrongs they suffer now are done to men
And citizens, and not to slaves; and these
Must be redressed, and all their rights secured.

From youth to manhood, manhood to old age—
If age at seventy years is counted old—
His is a life to honor and extol,
Entitling him to take conspicuous rank
Among the benefactors of mankind,
And with the choicest poets of all time.

> *William Lloyd Garrison, "The Poet of Our Love,"
> in* The Literary World, *Vol. VIII, No. 7, December
> 1, 1877, p. 121.*

WILLIAM S. SHURTLEFF (poem date 1877)

Dear Whittier: When the Muses unto thee
Gave, in largess, the power of poesy,
They laid no limit to thy minstrelsy;
    But made thee apt, at thy occasion's need,
    To deftly use or lute or lyre or reed,—
    All music's means; but, bade thee ever heed
These two behests: that, using each at will,
Whate'er thy instrument or theme, thou still,
By every song, some human want should'st fill;
    And that, whate'er reward should lure thy song,
    Thou ne'er should'st be the laureate of Wrong!

So hast thou sung! So was thy matin lay,
Thy noon-tide psalm, the vesper of thy day,
True unto Truth, O, blameless bard! alway.

So now thou singest, on the hither shore
That banks the wave too soon must bear thee o'er
To that fair realm thy song has reached before.
So may'st thou sing, until thy last note—dies?
Nay! is translated, through the choral skies,
To mingle with the heavenly harmonies.
So shall thy earliest celestial song
Thy latest earthly melody prolong!

> *William S. Shurtleff, in a tribute to John Greenleaf Whittier, in* The Literary World, *Vol. VIII, No. 7, December 1, 1877, p. 121.*

H[ARRIET] B[EECHER] STOWE   (essay date 1877)

[Stowe was an important nineteenth-century abolitionist and writer. Her famous novel, Uncle Tom's Cabin; or, Life among the Lowly, *is noted for its humanitarian tone and antislavery focus; it became one of the most popular and profoundly influential novels of the nineteenth century. Here, Stowe commends Whittier for his compassionate and inspirational verse. For additional information, see explanatory notes for Paul H. Hayne (1877).]*

I am glad that there is to be a tribute of affectionate remembrance, on the seventieth birthday of our friend Mr. Whittier. He is the true poet whose *life* is a poem, and our friend has received grace of the Father to live such a life. His life has been a consecration, his songs an inspiration, to all that is highest and best. It has been his chief glory, not that he could speak inspired words, but that he spoke them for the despised, the helpless, and the dumb; for those too ignorant to honor, too poor to reward him. Grace was given him to know his Lord in the lowest disguise, even that of the poor hunted slave, and to follow him in heart into prison and unto death. He had words of pity for all—words of severity for none but the cruel and hard-hearted. Though the land beyond this world be more beautiful and more worthy of him, let us pray the Father to spare him to us yet more years, and to fill those years with blessing.

> *H[arriet] B[eecher] Stowe, in a tribute to John Greenleaf Whittier, in* The Literary World, *Vol. VIII, No. 7, December 1, 1877, p. 122.*

R. H. STODDARD   (essay date 1881)

[Stoddard's assessment of Whittier's verse contains both praise and censure. Stoddard appreciates Whittier's use of subjects that are not normally considered poetical, like shoemaking and cattle herding. Yet while commending the "literary workmanship" of Whittier's later works, Stoddard ultimately does "not rank him high as an artist." For additional commentary by Stoddard, see excerpt below, 1899.]

The writings of Mr. Whittier have . . . confined themselves to three phases of our national life and history, viz.: to the picturesque savagery of the red men, to episodes of the colonial life of the Puritans and Quakers, and to the consideration of the evils of slavery. His Indian poems are not remarkable, though they are as good as any we have, with the exception, perhaps, of some of Bryant's, which hardly rise above the level of lyrics. His legendary poems are glimpses of the struggle between a set form of faith and the freedom of conscience, and, while they are poetically just to both sides, they leave no doubt in the mind on which side the poet's sympathies are ranged. (What part could a Quaker take, pray, but the part of the wronged and the opposed—the part of his ancestors and brethren? I say brethren advisedly, for the New England Quaker

of forty years ago was rather a tolerated than a respected member of the community.) His anti-slavery poems were earnest and indignant; earnest in their maintenance of the freedom of all men without regard to color, and indignant at the persecutions of those who sought to restore the rights which had been wrested from them. It was not necessary to be an abolitionist to be moved by these anti-slavery productions of Mr. Whittier; but it was necessary to be a very ardent one in order to find them, or make them, poetical. They were wrung from his heart—torn from his soul; but, strange to say, they made no mark in our literature; they contained no unforgetable verse— no line which the world would not willingly let die. The poet was so overpowered by his inspiration that he forgot to deliver his message. (p. 122)

Mr. Whittier was wiser than he knew, I think, when he resolved to be the poet of Labor [in his volume **"Songs of Labor and Other Poems"**]. A lesser poet would not have ventured to do so, for he would not have considered it poetical, and, even if he could have persuaded himself that it was, he would not have been able to distinguish its poetic from its prosaic element. It belongs to a class of subjects which are not in themselves poetical, though they are made so when the imagination is brought to bear upon them. There is nothing poetical in the act of making shoes, or of driving cattle. (p. 124)

Mr. Whittier is given to the writing of occasional poems, and, if he is not so successful in this journalistic walk of verse as some of his contemporaries, it is because his cleverness is not equal to his genius. When he does succeed, as in his lines on **"Randolph of Roanoke,"** and in **"Ichabod,"** he ranks among the greatest masters of poetic portraiture. A great man sat for his portrait in **"Ichabod"**—a man whom New England still delights to honor for his great intellectual endowments, but who fell from his high estate because he dared to differ with New England in a question of political morals. How far he was right, and how far he was wrong, is a problem which does not concern me. (p. 127)

The ethical or moral element which is the motive and inspiration of such poems as **"The Chapel of the Hermits"** is never absent for any length of time from Mr. Whittier's poetry. I do not place it among high poetic endowments, though it may be allied to them; nor do I think it is always wisely employed by Mr. Whittier. If there ever was a time when poets were moral teachers, that time has long since past. They are at most lay preachers now, and that not of set purpose, but by indirection. Mr. Whittier did not perceive this as clearly as could be wished, and his poetry has suffered in consequence. (pp. 129-30)

It is not given to many poets to know what they do best, and the few who possess that knowledge are seldom content to be guided by it. The weakness of modern poets—or one of their weaknesses—is the desire to write long poems, as if poetry were measured by quantity and not quality. Another weakness is a studied avoidance of simple every-day themes. Mr. Whittier has mistaken his powers as little as any American poet, but he has not always cultivated them wisely, or he would have written ten narrative poems where he has written one. (pp. 130-31)

Mr. Whittier is one of the few American poets who have succeeded in obtaining the suffrages of the reading public and of the literary class. Men of letters respect his work for its sincerity, simplicity, and downright manliness, and average readers of poetry respect it because they can understand it. There is not a grown man and woman in the land who does not readily enter into the aspiration and discontent of **"Maud Muller,"** and into the glowing patriotism of **"Barbara Frietchie."** Whether the incident which is the inspiration of the latter ever occurred, is more than doubtful; nevertheless, the poem is one that the world will not willingly let die. The reputation of such poems is immediate and permanent, and beyond criticism, favorable or otherwise; the touch of nature in them is beyond all art. (p. 131)

[**"Snow-bound"**] has no prototype in English literature, unless Burns's "Cotter's Saturday Night" be one, and it will be long, I fear, before it has a companion-piece. It can be fully appreciated only by those who are New England born, and on whose heads the snows of fifty or sixty winters have fallen. One must have been snow-bound in order to recognize the faithfulness of Mr. Whittier's pictures of winter life and landscape, and to enjoy the simple pleasures of a country homestead in a great snow-storm. (pp. 132-33)

The materials upon which **"Snow-bound"** is based are of the slightest order, and the wonder is that any poet, even the most skillful one, could have made a poem out of them. I should not say that Mr. Whittier was a skillful poet, but he has made a poem which will live, and can no more be rivaled by any winter poetry that may be written hereafter than [William Cullen Bryant's] "Thanatopsis" can be rivaled as a meditation on the universality of death. The characters in this little idyl are carefully drawn, and the quiet of the homestead during the storm is in striking contrast to the outdoor bustle which succeeds it. There is no evidence anywhere that the poem cost a moment's labor; everything is naturally introduced, and the reflections, which are manly and pathetic, are among the finest that Mr. Whittier has ever written. **"Snow-bound"** at once authenticated itself as an idyl of New England life and manners.

In **"The Tent on the Beach, and Other Poems,"** . . . we had Mr. Whittier in his character of a story-teller again, with a wider range than he had hitherto shown in his choice of subjects. He added variety to the tales that were told in **"The Tent on the Beach"** by a framework of verse similar to that employed by Mr. Longfellow in his "Tales of a Wayside Inn," but he added nothing to the poetic value of the tales themselves by this framework, or by the conversation which his summer guests held in the intervals of narration. (p. 134)

The literary workmanship of Mr. Whittier has improved, I think, from year to year, and in reading [**"Songs of Labor and Other Poems"**] we may be sure that we have the best art of which he is capable. I do not rank him high as an artist, though he has art enough to answer his purposes generally. Poetry seems never to have been a pursuit with him, but a charge which was intrusted to him, and which he was to deliver when the spirit moved him, well or ill, as it happened, but honestly, earnestly, and prayerfully. He has a noble vein of sacred poetry in his nature, and, had he chosen, might have enriched the world's store of hymnology as no other living poet could have done. His seriousness of soul, the intense morality of his genius, accounts, I think, for his defects as a poetical artist in such poems as **"The Chapel of the Hermits,"** for example, in **"Among the Hills, and Other Poems,"** . . . in **"Miriam, and Other Poems,"** . . . and in **"The Pennsylvanian Pilgrim, and Other Poems."** . . . The motives of these poems, especially the last, seem to me too slight for the superstructures which he had builded upon and around them. (p. 135)

R. H. Stoddard, "John Greenleaf Whittier," in The Homes and Haunts of Our Elder Poets *by N. H.*

Powers, R. H. Stoddard, and F. B. Sanborn, D. Appleton and Company, 1881, pp. 105-36.

J.G.W. [JOHN GREENLEAF WHITTIER]   (essay date 1887)

[*In his preface to the 1887 edition of* The Complete Poetical Works *of John Greenleaf Whittier,* Whittier *says that he has spent little time in revising his work, for he has "neither strength nor patience to undertake correction." He also defends his abolitionist poetry as suitable for its purpose and historically valuable, despite its artistic weaknesses.*]

After a lapse of thirty years since [the preface to the 1857 volume of my collected works (see excerpt above)] was written, I have been requested by my publishers to make some preparation for a new and revised edition of my poems. I cannot flatter myself that I have added much to the interest of the work beyond the correction of my own errors and those of the press, with the addition of a few heretofore unpublished pieces, and occasional notes of explanation which seemed necessary. I have made an attempt to classify the poems under a few general heads, and have transferred the long poem of **"Mogg Megone"** to the Appendix, with other specimens of my earlier writings. I have endeavored to affix the dates of composition or publication as far as possible.

In looking over these poems I have not been unmindful of occasional prosaic lines and verbal infelicities, but at this late day I have neither strength nor patience to undertake their correction.

Perhaps a word of explanation may be needed in regard to a class of poems written between the years 1832 and 1865. Of their defects from an artistic point of view it is not necessary to speak. They were the earnest and often vehement expression of the writer's thought and feeling at critical periods in the great conflict between Freedom and Slavery. They were written with no expectation that they would survive the occasions which called them forth: they were protests, alarm signals, trumpet-calls to action, words wrung from the writer's heart, forged at white heat, and of course lacking the finish and careful word-selection which reflection and patient brooding over them might have given. Such as they are, they belong to the history of the Anti-Slavery movement, and may serve as way-marks of its progress. If their language at times seems severe and harsh, the monstrous wrong of Slavery which provoked it must be its excuse, if any is needed. In attacking it, we did not measure our words. "It is," said Garrison, "a waste of politeness to be courteous to the devil." But in truth the contest was, in a great measure, an impersonal one,—hatred of slavery and not of slave-masters. (pp. xxi-xxii)

After the great contest was over, no class of the American people were more ready, with kind words and deprecation of harsh retaliation, to welcome back the revolted States than the Abolitionists; and none have since more heartily rejoiced at the fast increasing prosperity of the South.

Grateful for the measure of favor which has been accorded to my writings, I leave this edition with the public. It contains all that I care to republish, and some things which, had the matter of choice been left solely to myself, I should have omitted. (p. xxii)

J.G.W. [John Greenleaf Whittier], in an introduction to his The Complete Poetical Works of John Greenleaf Whittier, *Houghton Mifflin Company, 1894, pp. xxi-xxii.*

ATHENAEUM AND LITERARY CHRONICLE (essay date 1892)

The chorus of voices which lately in the evening and the morning papers attested English sympathy with the loss sustained, perhaps more by the general body than the literary minority of his countrymen, in the death of the poet Whittier, had in it, naturally, less of the minor than the major key. The death of a potent wielder of true-tempered literary weapons in a righteous contest, who rests, full of years and honour, after he has seen the cause he loved triumphant, is no matter for regret; and that a long period of rest from polemical activity intervened between the contest and the grave is probably well for the purely literary fame of the writer whose death we record.

For though on the great question of slavery, and kindred matters of national interest,

> Against injustice, fraud, or wrong,
> His heart beat high—

and this . . . righteous indignation, produced stirring metrical arguments, full of passionate rhetoric, which appeal to his larger audience and are admirable in their kind, the poetic student will recur with more pleasure to what may be generally classed as Whittier's poems of nature. In these he often shows unrestrained pathos, natural observation, simplicity, purity, charity. Yet it is probably by the more impassioned strains of his martial music, the pugnacity and aggressiveness which he shared with his admirer and co-religionist John Bright, that his fame will live; and it is, perhaps, no injustice to his reputation to say that he will be remembered as the literary mouthpiece of political justice on a memorable occasion, rather than as a poet of the higher, though not the highest class among writers of English. (p. 354)

> *"John Greenleaf Whittier," in* The Athenaeum and Literary Chronicle, *No. 3385, September 10, 1892, pp. 354-55.*

THE LITERARY WORLD (essay date 1892)

The value of Mr. Whittier's literary work, its place and time considered, is quite inestimable. He was the poet of America. Free from self-consciousness, never mistaking roughness for strength, he expressed the highest thought and purest ideals of the people in verse that appealed irresistibly to them by its vigor, simplicity, beauty and warm human sentiment. He wrote from a great heart overflowing with benevolence and faith. He waited for the word of the Spirit, and delivered with glowing lips the divine message. . . . Mr. Whittier had the true gift of the balladist, the spontaneous narrative and the ringing notes; his descriptive and legendary poems are penetrated with the atmosphere of his native region near the Merrimac; and when he sometimes chose a foreign theme, he filled it with his own beautiful spirit. He had great felicity in the choice of words, instinctively adopting those which gave color and clearness to the thought; his metrical sense was natural and delicate. In prose his work, though of minor value, was admirable, written in a characteristic style, composed, sensitive, harmonious, with bright touches of gentle humor which often illuminated the noble and serious pages.

The beautiful idyl, *Snow-Bound,* will survive, like the pastorals of Theocritus, as a picture of rural life. Its brilliantly poetic temper, its simple verity, and its glowing celebration of the family and the home, render it a perfect presentation of New England ideals. It is a masterpiece, profoundly felt and beautifully uttered.

In Mr. Whittier's later poems is heard again the voice of the prophet, this time foretelling the glorious liberty of the children of God in another world. He never doubted that all must turn to good in the end. His imaginations of the future life were divinely human; for him heaven was to be

> The harvest-gathering of the heart,

where the affections of earth would be continued in all their tenderness and without fear of any change. How many sorrows he comforted, how many hopes he inspired, can only be inferred from the universal expression of love and veneration that his death has called forth. Crusader of humanity, poet and saint—his compatriots may say to him in his own words:

> Hail and farewell! We go our way;
> Where shadows end, we trust, in light;
> The star that ushers in the night
> Is herald also of the day.

> (p. 332)

> *"John Greenleaf Whittier," in* The Literary World, *Vol. XXIII, No. 20, September 24, 1892, pp. 332-33.*

GEORGE EDWARD WOODBERRY (essay date 1892)

[*Woodberry discusses both the stylistic deficiencies and the popularity of Whittier's work.*]

[It should not be forgotten] that Whittier began as a poet, and not as a reformer, and it may be added that the poet in him was, in the long run, more than the reformer. He did not resort to verse as an expedient in propagandism; rather, wearing the laurel,—to use the good old phrase,—he descended into the field just as he was. He had begun with those old Indian legends in lines which still echoed with Byron's tales, and he had with them much the same success that attended other aboriginal poetry. It seems, as one reads the hundred weary epics, from which Whittier's are hardly to be distinguished, that the curse of extinction resting on the doomed race clung also to the Muse that so vainly attempted to recompense it with immortality in the white man's verse. These were Whittier's juvenile trials. He came early, nevertheless, to his mature form in the ballad and the occasional piece; his versification was fixed, his manner determined, and thenceforth there was no radical change.

This is less remarkable inasmuch as it is a commonplace to say that he owed nothing to art; the strength of his native genius was all his secret, and when he had freed a way for its expression the task of his novitiate was done. He had now a mould in which to run his metal, and it satisfied him because he was not exacting of perfect form or high finish; probably he had no sense for them. This indifference to the artistic workmanship, which a later day prizes so much as to require it, allowed him to indulge his natural facility, and the very simplicity of his metres was in itself a temptation to diffuseness. The consequence was that he wrote much, and not always well, unevenness being usually characteristic of poets who rely on the energy of their genius for the excellence of their work. To the artist his art serves often as a conscience, and forces him to a standard below which he is not content to fall. Whittier, however, experienced the compensations which are everywhere to be found in life, and gained in fullness, perhaps, more than he lost in other ways. The free flow of his thought, the simplicity of his structure, the willingness not to select with too nice a sense, but to tell the whole, all helped to that frankness of the man which is the great charm of his works, taken together, and assisted him in making his expression of old New

England life complete. . . . In Whittier, Nature reminds us, as she is wont to do from time to time, that the die which she casts exceeds the diploma of the schools. Art may lift an inferior talent to higher estimation, but genius makes a very little art go a long way. This was Whittier's case. The poetic spark was inborn in him, living in his life; and when academic criticism has said its last word, he remains a poet, removed by a broad and not doubtful line from all stringers of couplets and filers of verses.

Whittier had, in addition to this clear native genius, character; his subject, too, New England, had character; and the worth of the man blending with the worth of the life he portrayed, independent of all considerations of art, has won for him the admiration and affection of the common people, who know the substance of virtue, and always see it shining with its own light. (p. 643)

The secret of his vogue with the plain people is his own plainness. He appeals directly to the heart, as much in his lesser poems as in those which touch the sense of right and wrong in men with stinging keenness, or in those which warm faith to its ardor. He has the popular love of a story, and tells it more nearly in the way of the old ballad-makers. He does not require a tragedy, or a plot, or any unusual action. An incident, if it only have some glamour of fancy, or a touch of pathos, or the likeness of old romance, is enough for him; he will take it and sing it merely as something that happened. . . . It is to be acknowledged, too, that the material for these romances was just such as delights the popular imagination. The tales of the witches, notwithstanding the melancholy of the delusion, have something of the eeriness that is inseparable from the thought of the supernatural, and stir the dormant sense of some evil fascination; and the legends of spectral shapes that haunted every seacoast in old times, and of which New England had its share, have a similar quality. Whether they are told by credulous Mather or the make-believing poet, they have the same power to cast a spell. When to this sort of interest Whittier adds, as he often does, the sights of religious persecution, or some Lochinvar love-making, or the expression of his faith in heaven, his success as a story-teller is assured. In reality, he has managed the ballad form with more skill than other measures; but it is because he loves a story and tells it for its own sake, with the ease of one who sits by the fireside, and with a childish confidence that it will interest, that he succeeds so well in pleasing. In his sea-stories, and generally in what he writes about the ocean, it is observable that he shows himself to be an inland-dweller, whose acquaintance with the waves is by distant glimpses and vacation days. He is not a poet of the sea, but this does not invalidate the human truth of his tales of voyaging, which is the element he cared for. Perhaps the poetic quality of his genius is most clear in these ballads; there is a freer fancy; there are often verses about woman's eyes and hair and cheeks, all with similes from sky and gold and roses, in the old fashion, but not with less naturalness on that account; there is a more absorbing appeal to the imagination both in the characters and the incidents. If these cannot be called his most vigorous work, they are at least most attractive to the purely poetic taste.

In the ballads, nevertheless, one feels the strong undertow of the moral sense dragging the mind back to serious realities. It is probably true of all the English stock, as it certainly is of New England people, that they do not object to a moral, in a poem or anywhere else. Whittier's moral hold upon his readers is doubtless greater than his poetic hold. He appeals habitually

to that capacity for moral feeling which is the genius of New England in its public life, and the explanation of its extraordinary influence. No one ever appeals to it in vain; and with such a cause as Whittier took up to champion, he could ring out a challenge that was sure to rank the conscience of his people upon his side. (pp. 643-44)

It is not without perfect justice that **"Snow-Bound"** takes rank with [Burns's] "The Cotter's Saturday Night" and "The Deserted Village"; it belongs in this group as a faithful picture of humble life. It is perfect in its conception and complete in its execution; it is the New England home, entire, with its characteristic scene, its incidents of household life, its Christian virtues. . . . It is, in a peculiar sense, the one poem of New England,—so completely indigenous that the soil has fairly created it, so genuine as to be better than history. It is by virtue of this poem that Whittier must be most highly rated, because he is here most impersonal, and has succeeded in expressing the common life with most directness. All his affection for the soil on which he was born went into it; and no one ever felt more deeply that attachment to the region of his birth which is the great spring of patriotism. In his other poems he had told the legends of the country, and winnowed its history for what was most heroic or romantic; he had often dwelt, with a reiteration which only emphasized his fondness, upon its scenery in every season, by all its mountains and capes and lakes and rivers, as if fearful lest he should offend some local divinity of the field or flood; he had shared in the great moral passion of his people in peace and war, and had become its voice and been adopted as one of its memorable leaders; but here he came to the heart of the matter, and by fitly describing the homestead, which was the unit and centre of New England life, he set the seal upon his work, and entered into all New England homes as a perpetual guest. (p. 646)

It is impossible to think of [Whittier] and forget that he is a Christian. It is not rash to say that it is probable that his religious poems have reached many more hearts than his antislavery pieces, and have had a profounder influence to quiet, to console, and to refine. Yet he was not distinctly a poet of religion, as Herbert was. He was a man in whom religion was vital, just as affection for his home and indignation at wrong doing were vital. He gave expression to his manhood, and consequently to the religious life he led. There are in these revelations of his nature the same frankness and the same reality as in his most heated polemics with the oppressors of the weak; one cannot avoid feeling that it is less the poet than the man who is speaking, and that in his words he is giving himself to his fellow-men. This sense that Whittier belongs to that class of writers in whom the man is larger than his work is a just one. Over and above his natural genius was his character. At every step of the analysis, it is not with art, but with matter, not with the literature of taste, but with that of life, not with a poet's skill, but with a man's soul, that we find ourselves dealing; in a word, it is with character almost solely: and it is this which has made him the poet of his people. . . . (p. 647)

No one of his contemporaries has been more silently beloved and more sincerely honored. If it be true that in him the man was more than the poet, it is happily not true, as in such cases it too often is, that the life was less than it should have been. The life of Whittier affects us rather as singularly fortunate in the completeness with which he was able to do his whole duty, to possess his soul, and to keep himself unspotted from the world. . . . Lovers of New England will cherish his memory as that of a man in whom the virtues of this soil, both for public and for private life, shine most purely. On the roll of American poets we know not how he may be ranked hereafter, but among the honored names of the New England past his place is secure. (p. 648)

George Edward Woodberry, "John Greenleaf Whittier," in The Atlantic Monthly, Vol. LXX, No. CCCCXXI, November, 1892, pp. 642-48.

OLIVER WENDELL HOLMES (poem date 1892)

[Holmes was a prominent physician, scientist, poet, essayist, and novelist of the nineteenth century. Today, his poetry is valued primarily for its social commentary, as well as for its tone and language. In the following memorial to Whittier, Holmes laments the death of his close friend.]

Thou, too, hast left us. While with heads bowed low,
    And sorrowing hearts, we mourned our summer's
        dead,
The flying season bent its Parthian bow,
    And yet again our mingling tears were shed.

Was Heaven impatient that it could not wait
    The blasts of winter for earth's fruits to fall?
Were angels crowding round the open gate
    To greet the spirits coming at their call?

Nay, let not fancies, born of old beliefs,
    Play with the heart-beats that are throbbing still,
And waste their outworn phrases on the griefs,
    The silent griefs that words can only chill.

For thee, dear friend, there needs no high-wrought lay,
    To shed its aureole round thy cherished name,—
Thou whose plain, home-born speech of *Yea* and *Nay*
    Thy truthful nature ever best became.

Death reaches not a spirit such as thine,—
    It can but steal the robe that hid thy wings;
Though thy warm breathing presence we resign,
    Still in our hearts its loving semblance clings.

Peaceful thy message, yet for struggling right,—
    When Slavery's gauntlet in our face was flung,—
While timid weaklings watched the dubious fight
    No herald's challenge more defiant rung.

Yet was thy spirit tuned to gentle themes
    Sought in the haunts thy humble youth had known.
Our stern New England's hills and vales and streams,—
    Thy tuneful idyls made them all their own.

The wild flowers springing from thy native sod
    Lent all their charms thy new-world song to fill,—
Gave thee the mayflower and the golden-rod
    To match the daisy and the daffodil.

In the brave records of our earlier time
    A hero's deed thy generous soul inspired,
And many a legend, told in ringing rhyme,
    The youthful soul with high resolve has fired.

Not thine to lean on priesthood's broken reed;
    No barriers caged thee in a bigot's fold;
Did zealots ask to syllable thy creed;
    Thou saidst "Our Father," and thy creed was told.

Best loved and saintliest of our singing train,
    Earth's noblest tributes to thy name belong.
A lifelong record closed without a stain,
    A blameless memory shrined in deathless song.

Lift from its quarried ledge a flawless stone;
    Smooth the green turf and bid the tablet rise,
And on its snow-white surface carve alone
    These words,—he needs no more,—HERE WHITTIER
        LIES.

(pp. 648-49)

Oliver Wendell Holmes, "In Memory of John Greenleaf Whittier," in The Atlantic Monthly, Vol. LXX, No. CCCCXXI, November, 1892, pp. 648-49.

T. CUTHBERT HADDEN (essay date 1892)

[In the fight for abolition, Whittier] was unknown, this young poet, he was obscure, he was without influence. It was all true; but the young poet was not without zeal, and so he fought on, never despairing, till at last the head of the hydra was crushed— and in view of the band of evil prophets, many of them, strange to say, hailing from our own land, he sheathed the sword and put on the victor's crown.

It was a glorious triumph, but that it was bought at the cost of much excitement and nervous strain we can easily see from the poet's **"Voices of Freedom."** There we have many powerful if sometimes not too poetical verses, struck off as it were at white heat, like the **"Marseillaise,"** and full of the most impassioned pleading and burning denunciation. (p. 471)

[The moral purpose of Whittier's early work] is perhaps the most important element for the critic who would duly determine his ultimate position as a singer. And in that connection . . . , one cannot miss the resemblance between him and the other two distinguished American poets whom after so short an interval he has followed to the Silent Land. The names of Lowell, of Whittier, and of Whitman are all associated more or less with the Abolition struggle. . . . As with Whitman, so with Whittier, these enthusiasms were the inspiration not only of the poet's lyrics, but of his life as well. His whole man was enlarged and formed into a permanent mould by the influence of these early days of struggle; and it is undoubtedly as one of the last veterans of this struggle that he has merited the praise and the reverence that are receiving expression now that he has passed away.

And yet there is very little, if, indeed, there is anything at all, among these anti-slavery productions that is destined to live. They served but a passing need, and have already lost much of their value as literature. . . . His last work came from those later days passed in the quiet of great peace, when the poet had already entered on the reward which comes from the consciousness of duty well done. There are times when the spirit of poetry seems to have possessed him utterly, when the best thought is worked out in a terse and telling form, with all the true fire and magic of genius. There are lines where the musical effect, the seemingly effortless and inevitable aptness of word and rhythm, with their perfect and crystalline clearness of thought, disclose the highest quality of poetical art. They move with the same unconscious volition as when the bird hovers over the meadow's surface, or darts with unerring swiftness at its mark. On the other hand, as even the kindly American critic has admitted, there are whole pages which resemble the same bird with folded wings, hopping aimlessly here and there upon the ground—pages of purely commonplace and mechanical jingle, such as any versifier with an ordinary metrical ear can produce by the ream.

No writer, however, should be judged by his least successful efforts, and it is enough that Whittier has left us a number of poems which for musical charm, for lyric passion, for concentrated and exquisite expression of high poetic feeling, are equal to anything which America has produced. There is, as some one has remarked, a haunting melody about many of his verses which comes back to us like the scent of birches and bog-myrtle.

> The pines were dark on Ramoth hill,
> Their song was soft and low;
> The blossoms in the sweet May wind
> Were falling like the snow.

This beautiful poem, by the way, serves to remind us how little of the inspiration of love there is in the Quaker poet. The only poem, besides **"My Playmate,"** in which he refers to the tender passion is that entitled **"Memories."** Mr. Whittier has been in love, and for a moment he takes us into his confidence. The glimpse is valuable, if only to assure us of his common clay. As has been said, there is something unhuman if not inhuman about a man who has never been in love, but the American poet has been "there," and has profited by the experience, as all good men, especially old bachelors, do. (pp. 472-73)

His poems dealing with individual characters are notable . . . for their individuality and their graphic force. Take **"Cassandra Southwick"** for example, where we see portrayed a veritable woman, noble in her tribulations and glorious in her triumph; or **"Randolph of Roanoke,"** a splendid tribute to the memory of a great man, and all the more praiseworthy that it was wrung from the lips of an opponent. The Quaker poet saw the Virginian slave-holder as he was—a man to be known and respected. Some of his ballads are among the best that the century has given us, full of charm and pathos, and as pure and fresh as the mountain breezes. That one of **"Annie and Rhoda"** brims over with the feeling which appeals most strongly to the emotions. (p. 473)

[Whittier's] work, if not great, has at least been earnest and genuine, and there is surely enough in it to hand down his name to future generations along with the names of Longfellow and Lowell, Bryant and Poe, Whitman and Holmes. In any case, he will always be entitled to the honor of having used his talents in the highest service to which it was possible to put them. (p. 474)

> *T. Cuthbert Hadden, "The Quaker Poet," in The Living Age, Vol. LXXX, No. 2525, November 19, 1892, pp. 469-74.*

JOHN VANCE CHENEY (essay date 1892)

[*Cheney, like many other critics of his time, predicts that Whittier's poetry will endure.*]

[One distinguished critic] laments Whittier's turning from the quiet scenes of the hearthside and of the home fields,

> Making his rustic reed of song
> A weapon in the war with wrong.

I cannot share the sentiment. Excellent as prove the "homely idyls" and "summer pastorals" of the after days, I think too

An etching of Whittier produced from a daguerreotype dated 1844-45. The Bettmann Archive, Inc.

much cannot be said in praise of the judgment that deferred these till the fire and irony, the tenderness and invective, of the **"Voices of Freedom"** should have helped to work out their great purpose, until the prayers of the patriot should have been answered, and his hope satisfied. The country has certainly been the gainer, and I question the loss to song. Whittier's range is not wide; he has gone the ground over, and perhaps no other preparation than that chosen could have served better as a prelude to the last happy work,—

> [The] free and pleasant thoughts, chance sown,
> Like feathers on the wind.

If Whittier was by nature and training fitted to sing the life and nature of New England, he was equally equipped for the "war with wrong"; and in this, the stormier field, there was none to stand beside him, his voice had no second in those dark days. Not handicapped by scholarship, pricked by the sense of duty that goaded the prophets of old, his and his only was the stroke that brought the fire.

> Leave studied wit and guarded phrase
> For those who think but do not feel;
> Let men speak out in words which raise
> Where'er they fall, an answering blaze
> Like flints which strike the fire from steel.

Such was the one voice and the only voice in America that could blend with Garrison's in the battle for the slave. (p. 300)

The effect of [Whittier's abolitionist] trumpet blast . . . is sufficient justification for forgetting all the rules of art save those that go to its making. Whether it be the torrent of scorn poured

Whittier at age fifty-six. This photograph was taken by F. K. Clarkson in 1860.

on the "paid hypocrites" in their "tasseled pulpits," or the wail of the broken-hearted slave-mother for her daughters sold into bondage,—whatever haps to the fane of poesy, the temple of freedom is ringed to the spire-tip with fire as of the lightning. Most of these pieces written, not for the future and for the author, but for the hour and for the cause, have little attraction now; still while there are few notable poems among them, there are many choice lines and not a few fine stanzas. . . .

In the last half of volume three [of the first volume of Whittier's collected works entitled **"The Writings of John Greenleaf Whittier"**] we have the **"Songs of Labor."** The author of these songs, writing of things of which he is a part, exhibits quite another sort of authorship than the cataloguing of the various kinds of labor that drift into the ken of the professional idler while observing a spear of grass. (p. 301)

New England is not America, but it is the corner of America that the poets happen to deal with; and such American life and manners and landscape as the muses have seen fit to sanction are to be found mainly in the work of Bryant, Emerson, Whittier, Longfellow, Holmes, and Lowell. It is said that Whittier is restricted to the hills and valleys of his birth-spot; and it is said, again, that Whitman, of all our poets, is the one to voice the sea. Well, I am content to take Whittier where he is least at home, and Walt [Whitman] where he is most at home; and see from which we get "the breath of a new life, the healing." (p. 302)

In the first volume of [**"The Writings of John Greenleaf Whittier"**] we find Whittier in a favorite field of our home poetry. Here, among the familiar poems first published under the title,

"Ballads of New England," are **"Telling the Bees"** and **"My Playmate,"** replete with pure pathos, with human interest the most close and tender; **"The Wreck of Rivermouth"** and the other direct, spirited narratives leading on to the brisk bit of novelty, **"Skipper Ireson's Ride."** The simplest measures, adorned chiefly by the inner beauty of thought, spontaneous as birdsongs, straight from the heart and to the heart,—such are these poems, the fame of which far enough exceeds the ambition of the author.

Some one has regretted the lack of display of the poet's inner life; but could there be a better showing of this than the steady undercurrent of high, invincible spirit flavoring every line, ay, prompting it? There is no need of explicit announcement of this and that; the soul of the man and the music of the bard flower together, telling their story plainly and sweetly as the common blossoms of the native fields and byways. There is something inflexible in Whittier, he is stiff; but so was Wordsworth. While with both it is a stubborn defect, it yields to the rich inheritance and experience of spirit that refuses to be held, that, despite all bonds, will leap in the freedom of the mountain brook, take the sunshine, and run with grace and music down into the valley where wake and sleep, where toil and rest, the multitude of the children of men. Patient endurance, self-sacrifice, all the mind and heart devoted to a high cause—this is the soil from which the fadeless flowers of song have always blown, and from which they will forever blow. In the term of years that suffices the most of us for a lifetime at the post of duty, in the long solemn watch upon the jeopardy of a mighty cause,—in this deep past of the patriot lies the secret of Whittier's choicer poems, simple, heart-felt, sweet as the common light and air.

> So fall the weary years away;
> A child again, my head I lay
> Upon the lap of this sweet day.

Here is the secret,—the simple faith, the trust and repose of the child; this, after the toil, the trial as by fire, of that small band of immortals that stood for the inalienable birthright of man. . . .

Whittier is stiff; he is also provincial. Provincial he may be, for the greater part; but he has his lifts into universality as surely as certain things in the human heart hold, the world over. If the bleakness of the old Haverhill birth-spot is on many a page, a goodly number lie in the warmer light everywhere recognized and rejoiced in. The simplest forms of verse structure are the rule, but there is, too, freedom of melody no mere master of meters can hope to waken. There is, moreover, originality of a higher order than that of intricate technics,—the originality of naked simplicity. (p. 303)

Sometimes I think we do not see Whittier quite as he is. Deficient in the enchantment possible only to the highest order of genius, somewhat bald, somewhat crude and narrow, impatient of revision, so careless that he can rhyme "banner" with "Susquehanna," and "cotton" with "fortune," so reckless, indeed, as to try to force "onward" and "looking" into a union of sweet sound—this is one side of the equation; but what is the other? If he leads his contemporaries in faults, does he not also lead them in certain essentials, in the primal virtues of simplicity, sinew, enthusiasm, and spontaneity? With less imagination and with but a fraction of the learning, a tithe of the versatility, of Lowell, he is more direct and telling. The Quaker poet, far more than Lowell, has been the poetic power of his time. With as much imagination as Longfellow, he has more grip and fire; unequal to him as an artist, he has qualities even rarer than the instinct of form,—enthusiasm and spontaneity. Deficient in imagination, again, as compared with Bryant, he has fervor and the lyric gift. While Bryant is letting his imagination wing serenely over the world and the fate of the race, Whittier, at a stroke, catches some happy expression on the face of nature or sets in vibration those heart-strings that suffer the breath of the elder bard to pass over them without a tremor. While Bryant is spreading his energy, thinning it on the long stretch, Whittier is husbanding his for the one decisive stroke, for the thrust to the quick. In short, by means of the first of the poetic virtues,—simplicity, enthusiasm, and virility, by the virtues of temperament and voice that take the heart even before the mind, perhaps Whittier is not only the representative American poet, but a poet as sure as any among us to endure. When the gold of his work has been cleared of the dross by one who shall be to him what Arnold was to Wordsworth, it is among the possibilities that the result will be a contribution to American poetry as characteristic and lasting as any thus far produced. There will be neither the soaring of Bryant, the subtle penetration, the indescribable flavor of Emerson, the scholastic finish, the literary art of Longfellow, nor the reaches that in a few instances ally Lowell with the immortals; but there may be a residuum strong, very strong, against the wear and waste of time. (p. 304)

> *John Vance Cheney, "Whittier," in* The Chautauquan, *Vol. XVI, No. 3, December, 1892, pp. 299-306.*

THE LONDON QUARTERLY REVIEW (essay date 1893)

[*In addition to praising Whittier as a reformer, the anonymous critic contrasts Whittier's life and work with that of the English poet William Cowper.*]

As a religious poet, Whittier has been compared to Cowper; but the points of contrast seem more numerous than those of resemblance. Both, it is true, have gained, through their devotional verse, extensive popularity with the large class of readers to whom the religious "motive" is of more importance than the quality of its poetic embodiment. Whittier, like Browning, though for a different reason, might be called "the poet of the unpoetical," and the same remark, though in a minor degree, applies to [Cowper]. . . . Both, again, had that sensibility to natural beauty which often accompanies a retiring disposition and a delicate physical organisation. But here the likeness ends. Cowper was gently born and bred, a man of elegant culture. Whittier began life as a farm-labourer, and what culture he had was picked up at odd moments in a newspaper-office. Cowper was a frail hypochondriac, shrinking, with more than a woman's sensitiveness, from the mere notion of facing the rough work of active life. Whittier, in spite of his delicate health, was one of the hardest workers and fighters of his generation.

Moreover, there was a fundamental difference in their way of regarding the great truths, to the enforcement of which each, in his own sphere, had devoted himself. To Whittier the love of God was the one salient fact of the universe. The sunny optimism of his creed pervades everything he wrote. The mystery of sin, the problems of man's fallen nature, the inscrutability of the Divine will—all these points, which exercised so profoundly some of the finest minds of his time, seem to have troubled him very little. (p. 242)

[Whittier's] death leaves Dr. Wendell Holmes as the sole survivor of that group of gifted men [The Fireside Poets], whose works are the inheritance not only of America, but of the whole English-speaking race. They all of them came to maturity in the midst of that great process of moral and social regeneration known as "the Anti-Slavery movement." They were all of them baptised in the fire of that conflict; and all in their separate ways witnessed for the right as they saw it.

As a mere man of letters, Whittier could hardly sustain a comparison with his compeers. We miss in him the artist-soul of Longfellow, the wit and fancy of Holmes, the keen satire and wide culture of Lowell; but there is, in his best work, an intensity of conviction, a white heat of enthusiasm, a trumpet-note of courage and faith, that cannot be paralleled in the work of his contemporaries. It may well be that, when his poems are lying untouched on the shelves of our libraries, the work that he did for the poor and the friendless will be spoken of for a memorial of him; and whether, or not, he lives as a poet in the memory of future ages, he has earned at any rate this praise—than which there is no greater—that he "served his generation by the Will of God." (pp. 243-44)

> *"John Greenleaf Whittier," in* The London Quarterly Review, *Vol. XIX, No. 11, January, 1893, pp. 224-44.*

MARIA S. PORTER (poem date 1893)

[*A long-time friend of Whittier, Porter was a popular nineteenth-century writer.*]

No purer record have we seen
  Than his upon whose bier to-day
With mourning hearts and reverent mien
  These lilies white and fair we lay;

Fit types are they of spotless life
  Through nearly fourscore years and ten,
With every manly virtue rife,
  Peaceful, yet strong with speech and pen.

His verse is known in every land;
  By countless lips his hymns are sung;
From Bay State to Pacific strand
  His words have like a prophet's rung.

When Slavery's cloud, so fraught with fate,
  Hung black upon the nation's sky,
From Casco Bay to Golden Gate
  Was heard a spirit-stirring cry;

And notes of warning, clear and strong,
  Rang out when Whittier grasped the pen,
Till Right, triumphant over Wrong,
  Upraised the slaves and made them men.

Through seas of blood and Treason's hate,
  Justice at last o'ercame her foe;
Still did his pen their wrongs relate,
  That rights of freemen they should know.

No smallest leaf can we to-day
  Add to the green of laurel crown,
Only our grateful tribute pay
  To one who meekly wore renown,

And tell how much his songs have wrought
  In hours of pain and days of gloom,
What balm, what blessing they have brought,
  How filled our lives with light and bloom.

Can sculptor carve or limner paint
　　"The Hero" as his pen hath done,
The "Cadmus of the blind," the saint
　　Who light from deepest darkness won;

The lovely **"Playmate"** neath the pine—
　　"The pines so dark on Ramoth hill"—
The bashful boy who fed the kine
　　And plucked the flowers of Folly Mill?

We see the sweetbrier and the flowers,
　　And hear the moaning of the pines,
And singing through the golden hours
　　The birds atilt on swaying vines.

We see the dear New England home,
　　The tender scenes in **"Snow-Bound"** given;
The tyrant 'neath Saint Peter's dome,
　　Whose papal cloak his scorn hath riven

Till all men view his hidden wrong
　　Who bound on Rome her "cast-off weight"—
A figure drawn in colors strong,
　　Forever for the world to hate.

"Eternal Goodness" holds a creed
　　Embodied in a holy hymn
To comfort hearts in sorest need
　　When eyes with grief and loss are dim.

How vain the effort to rehearse
　　His gifts to us of tongue and pen—
The wondrous power of his verse,
　　His lifelong work for fellow-men.

In loyalty to all that's good,
　　In stern rebuke of every wrong,
And manly faith in womanhood,
　　Without a peer he stands in song.

　　　　　　　　　　　　　　　(pp. 55-6)

Maria S. Porter, "Memorial Poems: John Greenleaf Whittier," in her Recollections of Louisa May Alcott, John Greenleaf Whittier, and Robert Browning, Together with Several Memorial Poems, *The New England Magazine Corporation, 1893, pp. 55-6.*

EDMUND CLARENCE STEDMAN　　(essay date 1898)

[*Stedman remarks that Whittier "became dearer for his very shortcomings." Stedman attributes Whittier's literary flaws to his lack of education and suggests that if Whittier had been a more scrupulous critic of his own work, he could have overcome some of his stylistic flaws. Yet Stedman also considers Whittier the most natural balladist of his time. For additional commentary by Stedman, see excerpt above, 1877.*]

It would not be fair to test Whittier by the quality of his off-hand work. His verse always was auxiliary to what he deemed the main business of his life, and has varied with the occasions that inspired it. His object was not the artist's, to make the occasion serve his poem, but directly the reverse. Perhaps his *naïveté* and carelessness more truthfully spoke for his constituents than the polish of those bred in seats of culture; many of his stanzas reflect the homeliness of a provincial region, and are the spontaneous outcome of what poetry there was in it. His feeling gained expression in simple speech and the forms which came readily. Probably it occurred somewhat late to the mind of this pure and duteous enthusiast that there is such a thing as duty to one's art, and that diffuseness, bad rhymes,

and prosaic stanzas are alien to it. Nor is it strange that the artistic moral sense of a Quaker poet, reared on a New England farmstead, at first should be deficient. A careless habit, once formed, made it hard for him to master the touch that renders a new poem by this or that expert a standard, and its appearance an event. His ear and voice were naturally fine, as some of his early work plainly shows. **"Cassandra Southwick," "The New Wife and the Old,"** and **"The Virginia Slave Mother"** were of an original flavor and up to the standards of that day. If he had occupied himself wholly with poetic work, he would have grown as steadily as his most successful compeers. But his vocation became that of trumpeter to the impetuous reform brigade. He supplied verse on the instant, often full of vigor, but often little more than the rallying-blast of a passing campaign. . . . It is safe to assume that if he had been more discriminating, or had cherished the resolve of Longfellow or Tennyson to make even conventional pieces artistic, many occasions would have escaped him. . . . Whittier emphatically became [a journalist poet], though in every way superior to the band of temperance, abolition, and partisan rhymesters that, like the shadows of his own failings, sprang up in his train. He wrote verses very much as he wrote editorials, and they were forcible only when he was deeply moved by stirring crises and events. Some of his best were tributes to leaders, or rebukes of great men fallen. But he was too apt to write weak eulogies of obscurer people; for every friend or ally had a claim upon his muse.

His imperfections were those of his time and class, and he was too engrossed with a mission to overcome them. He never learned compression, and still is troubled more with fatal fluency than our other poets of equal rank,—by an inability to reject poor stanzas and to stop at the right place. . . . [Elizabeth Barrett Browning and Whittier] were so much alike, with their indifference to method and taste, as to suggest the question (especially in view of the subaltern reform-verse-makers) whether advocates of causes, and other people of great moral zeal, are not relatively deficient in artistic conscientiousness and in what may be called aesthetic rectitude.

An occasional looseness in matters of fact may be forgiven one who writes from impulse. We owe **"Barbara Frietchie"** to the glow excited by a newspaper report; and the story of **"Skipper Ireson's Ride,"** now challenged, if not true, is too well told to be lost. Whittier became, like a mother's careless, warm-hearted child, dearer for his very shortcomings. But they sometimes mar his bravest outbursts. Slight changes would have made that eloquent lyric, **"Randolph of Roanoke"** a perfect one. Feeling himself a poet, he sang by ear alone, in a somewhat primitive time; but the finest genius, in music or painting for example, with the aid of a commonplace teacher can get over more ground in a month than he would cover unaided in a year; since the teacher represents what is already discovered and established. There came a period when Whittier's verse was composed solely with poetic intent, and after a less careless fashion. . . . His ruder rhymes of a day bear witness to an experience which none could better illustrate than by citing the words of the poet himself:

　　　　Hater of din and riot,
　　　　He lived in days unquiet;
　　　　And, lover of all beauty,
　　　　Trod the hard ways of duty.

In prose he soon became skilled. His letters often are models of epistolary style; the best articles and essays from his pen are written with a true and direct hand, though rather barren of the epigram and original thought which enrich the prose of Lowell, Holmes, and Emerson. *Margaret Smith's Journal* is . . . a trifle thin in plot, but such a quaint reproduction of the early colonial period—its people, manners, and discourse—as scarcely any other author save Hawthorne, at the date of its production, could have given us.

His metrical style, except in certain lyrics of marked individuality, is that of our elders who wrote in diffuse measures, and whose readers favored sentiment more than beauty or wit. It is a degree more old-fashioned than styles which are so much older as to become new by revival; that is to say, its fashion was current within our own recollection and is now passing away. Some forms put on a new type with each successive period, such as blank-verse and the irregular ode-measures in which Lowell, Taylor, and Stoddard have been successful. Whittier uses these rarely, and to·less advantage than his balladverse. He has conformed less than any one but Holmes to the changes of the day. . . . Even his recent sonnets, **"Requirement,"** **"Help,"** etc., are little more than fourteen-line homilies. Those who know their author find something of him in them, but such efforts do not reveal him to a new acquaintance. A poet's voice must have a distinct quality to be heard above the general choir. (pp. 107-11)

The poet's distinctive touch first appears in the legendary ballads which now precede the **"Voices of Freedom"** in his late editions. **"The New Wife and the Old"** is almost our best specimen of a style that Mrs. Hemans affected, and which Miss Ingelow, Mrs. Browning, and others have employed more picturesquely. It is a weird legend, musically told, and clearly the lyric of a poet. The early Quaker pieces are as good, and have all the traits of his verse written forty years afterward. His first ballads give the clew to his genius, and now make it apparent that most of his verse may be considered without much regard to dates of production. **"Cassandra Southwick,"** alone, showed where his strength lay: of all our poets he is the most natural balladist, and Holmes comes next to him. (p. 112)

On the whole, it is as a balladist that Whittier displays a sure metrical instinct. . . . Whittier's successes probably have been scored most often through ballads of our eastward tradition and supernaturalism, such as those pertaining to witchcraft,—a province which, from **"Calef in Boston"** to **"The Witch of Wenham,"** he never has long neglected. Some of his miscellaneous ballads are idyllic; others, in strong relief, were inspired by incidents of the War, during which our non-combatant sounded more than one blast, like that of Roderick, worth a thousand men. His ballads vary as much in excellence as in kind; among the most noteworthy are **"Mary Garvin,"** **"Parson Avery,"** **"John Underhill,"** and that pure bit of melody and feeling, the lay of **"Marguerite."** Yet some of the poems which he classes in this department properly are eclogues, or slow-moving narratives. He handles well a familiar measure; when aiming at something new, as in **"The Ranger,"** he usually is less at ease, despite the fact that the nonpareil of his briefer pieces is thoroughly novel in form and refrain, and doubtless chanced to come to him in such wise. **"Skipper Ireson's Ride"** certainly is unique. Dialect poems are too often unfaithful or unpoetic. Imagination, humor, and dramatic force are found in the ballad of the Marblehead skipper's dole, and its movement is admirable. The culmination is more effective than is usual in a piece by Whittier. We have the widow of the skipper's victim saying "God has touched him! why should

we?"—an old dame, whose only son has perished, bidding them "Cut the rogue's tether and let him run"; and

> So, with soft relentings and rude excuse,
> Half scorn, half pity, they cut him loose,
> And gave him a cloak to hide him in,
> And left him alone with his shame and sin.
> Poor Floyd Ireson, for his hard heart,
> Tarred and feathered and carried in a cart
> By the women of Marblehead!

The change of feeling in indicated by the single word "poor." This is only a minor piece, but quantity is the plane, and quality the height, of lyrical verse. (pp. 113-14)

A balladist should be a good reciter of tales. Our poet's prose work on **"The Supernaturalism of New England"** was devoted to the ghost and witch stories of his own neighborhood. In general design his chief story-book in verse, **"The Tent on the Beach,"** like Longfellow's "Tales of a Wayside Inn,"—the first series of which it post-dated and did not equal,—follows the oft-borrowed method of Boccaccio and Chaucer. The home tales of this group are the best, among them **"The Wreck of Rivermouth"** and **"Abraham Davenport."** Throw out a ballad or two, and, but for a want of even finish, **"The Tent on the Beach"** might be taken for a portion of Longfellow's extended work. As a bucolic poet of his own section, rendering its pastoral life and aspect, Whittier surpasses all rivals. (pp. 114-15)

Those who criticise [Whittier's] pastoral spirit as lacking Bryant's breadth of tone, Emerson's penetration, and Thoreau's detail, confess that it is honest and that it comes by nature. His most vivid pictures are of scenes which lie near his heart, and relate to common life. . . . Lyrics such as **"Telling the Bees,"** **"Maud Muller,"** and **"My Playmate"** are miniature classics; of this kind are those which confirmed his reputation and still make his volumes real household books of song. (p. 116)

[**"Snow-Bound. A Winter Idyl"**] is not rich in couplets to be quoted for their points of phrase and thought. Point, decoration, and other features of modern verse are scarcely characteristic of Whittier. In **"Snow-Bound"** he chose the best subject within his own experience, and he made the most of it. Taken as a whole, it is his most complete production. . . . Here is that air which writers of quality so often fail to capture. . . . Whittier found his idyl already pictured for him by the camera of his own heart. . . . From the key struck at the opening to the tender fall at the close, there is a sense of proportion, an adequacy and yet a restraint, not always observed in Whittier. (pp. 117-18)

The song of the Quaker bard is almost virginal, in so far as what we term the master-passion is concerned. Its passion comes from the purpose that heated his soul and both strengthened and impeded lyrical expression. . . . Three-fourths of Whittier's anti-slavery lyrics are clearly effusions of the hour; their force was temporal rather than poetic. There are music and pathos in **"The Virginia Slave Mother,"** and **"The Slave-Ships"** is lurid and grotesque enough. . . . The poet's deep-voiced scorn and invective rendered his anti-slavery verse a very different thing from Longfellow's, and made the hearer sure of his "effectual calling." . . . A little of this, however, goes quite far enough in poetry. As a writer of personal tributes, whether paeans or monodies, the reform bard, with his peculiar faculty of characterization, has been happily gifted. . . . One of his memorable improvisations was **"Ichabod,"** the lament for Webster's defection and fall,—a tragical subject handled with lyric power. In after years, his passion tempered by the flood of time, he breathes a tenderer regret in **"The Lost Oc-**

casion."... But the conception of "Ichabod" is most impressive; those darkening lines were graven too deeply for obliteration. In thought we still picture the deserted leader, the shadow gathering about his "august head."... (pp. 121-22)

Whittier is the Galahad of modern poets, not emasculate, but vigorous and pure; he has borne Christian's shield of faith and sword of the Spirit. His steadfast insistence upon the primitive conception of Christ as the ransomer of the oppressed had an effect, stronger than argument or partisanship, upon the religiously inclined; and of his lyrics, more than of those by his fellow-poets, it could be averred that the songs of a people go before the laws. (p. 124)

His occasional and personal pieces reveal his transcendental habit of thought. We find him imagining the after-life of the good, the gifted, the maligned. (p. 125)

Whittier's religious mood is far from being superficial and temporary. It is the life of his genius, out of which flow his ideas of earthly and heavenly content. In outward observance he is loyal to the simple ways of his own sect.... (p. 126)

The basic justification of Whittier's religious trust appears to be the "inward light" vouchsafed to a nature in which the prophet and the poet are one. This solvent of doubt removes him alike from the sadness of Clough and Arnold and the paganism of certain other poets. In the striking "Questions of Life," a piece which indicates his highest intellectual mark and is in affinity with some of Emerson's discourse, he fairly confronts his own share of our modern doubts.... (pp. 127-28)

Whittier's audience has been won by unaffected pictures of the scenes to which he was bred, by the purity of his nature, and even more by the *earnestness* audible in his songs, injurious as it sometimes is to their artistic purpose. (p. 129)

> *Edmund Clarence Stedman, "John Greenleaf Whittier," in his* Poets of America, *1898. Reprint by Scholarly Press, 1968, pp. 95-132.*

R. H. STODDARD   (essay date 1899)

[*Although Stoddard acknowledges the spirit and purpose of Whittier's abolitionist writing, he pronounces it unsuccessful as poetry. He suggests that Whittier was attracted to the "darker features of the Puritan character" which he presented in his ballads. The ballads, the critic concludes, will endure. For additional commentary by Stoddard, see excerpt above, 1881.*]

I do not blame Whittier for being an Abolitionist, for it was a dangerous honor to be one when he was, but I wish he had written less Abolition verse. It may have encouraged his brother Abolitionists, if they needed encouragement,—which was hardly the case, I think, since fanaticism thrives when persecuted and the blood of martyrs is the seed of the church,—and it may have made more Abolitionists, but all the same it was not poetry. (p. 811)

[The poems in "**Voices of Freedom**"] are not pleasant reading, the themes which they celebrate being of a melancholy character, as may be imagined from some of their titles: "**The Slave-Ships**," "**Our Countrymen in Chains**," "**The Hunters of Men**," "**The Christian Slave**," "**The Farewell of a Virginia Slave Mother**," "**The Branded Hand**," "**The Slaves of Martinique**."... The feeling in these pieces was potent enough to give them a vogue in the anti-slavery journals to which they were contributed and other journals in which they were copied.... There was an undeniable spirit and vigor in them, a

vehemence of expression and a profusion of rhetoric, which, restrained, would have made them more effective. They read as if they were improvised, many are too long, and all need revision. (pp. 811-12)

["**Mogg Megone**" and "**The Bride of Pennacook**"] abounded in vivid descriptions of forest scenery and the stock properties of Indian life, but they were not remarkable, for considered as stories they were not worth the telling, and considered as poems they were not poetical. The reading which led to them was valuable, however, in that it was in historical directions, and if Whittier missed his way therein when he struck the Indian trail, he found it when he ventured into the by-ways of colonial tradition, as in "**Cassandra Southwick**," "**The Exiles**," and other of his early ballads. In balladry he discovered the clue of his genius, but, not seeing whither it would lead him, he suffered it to slip from his fingers and went on without it, following whatever *ignis fatuus* [foolish fire] crossed his path. What most strongly attracted him to our colonial period were the darker features of the Puritan character, its narrowness of vision and its fierce intolerance, the cruelty that persecuted men of his faith for their peaceable ways, the fanaticism that hanged women and children of its own faith for being witches. This was an important element in American life, which demanded recognition in American literature, and which obtained it in the ballads of Whittier as surely as its strangely supernatural element obtained recognition in the tales of Hawthorne. (pp. 812-13)

["**The Barefoot Boy**," "**Maud Muller**," "**Telling the Bees**," "**Snow-Bound**," "**Skipper Ireson's Ride**," and "**Barbara Frietchie**"] and a few others of the same class, are to me more purely and distinctively American than anything else that Whittier has written; and I wish he could have persuaded himself to write more like them. They reflect, they depict, they embody, the individuality of the people, their lives, their customs, their ways of thinking; and centuries hence, when these shall have changed, as no doubt they will through the introduction of strains of other blood than our own, students of social history as well as students of national poetry will read them as they now read the songs of Burns and the poems of Chaucer. (p. 814)

> *R. H. Stoddard, "John Greenleaf Whittier," in* Lippincott's Monthly Magazine, *Vol. LXIII, June, 1899, pp. 808-16.*

PAUL ELMER MORE   (essay date 1905)

[*More was an American critic who, along with Irving Babbitt, formulated the doctrines of New Humanism in early twentieth-century American thought. The New Humanists were strict moralists who adhered to traditional conservative values in reaction to an age of scientific and artistic self-expression. In regard to literature, they believed that the aesthetic qualities of a work of art should be subordinate to its moral and ethical purpose. More was particularly opposed to Naturalism, which he believed accentuated the animal nature of humans, and to any literature, such as Romanticism, that broke with established classical tradition. He is especially esteemed for the philosophical and literary erudition of his multi-volumed* Shelburne Essays *(1904-21). In the following essay on Whittier, More suggests that the poet suffered from a lack of self-criticism, a "canon of taste" that might have motivated him to revise his work, making it more poetical and less moralistic. Whittier's poetry, however, is unique in its recreation of the English concept of homeliness, and* Snow-bound *is, according to More, unsurpassed in its emotional and nostalgic effect. Furthermore, More says that Whittier's ballad* The Penn-*]

sylvania Pilgrim *is successful even though the ballad reflects the same flaws which he finds in Whittier's early poetry.*]

What [Whittier] needed above everything else, what his surroundings were least of all able to give him, was a canon of taste, which would have driven him to stiffen his work, to purge away the flaccid and set the genuinely poetical in stronger relief—a purely literary canon which would have offset the moralist and reformer in him. . . . Byron had written verse as vacillating and formless as any of Whittier's; Shelley had poured forth page after page of effusive vapourings; Keats learned the lesson of self-restraint almost too late; Wordsworth indulged in platitudes as simpering as "holy Eva"; but none of these poets suffered so deplorably from the lack of criticism as the finest of our New England spirits. The very magnificence of their rebellion, the depth and originality of their emotion, were a compensation for their licence, were perhaps inevitably involved in it. The humbler theme of Whittier's muse can offer no such apology. . . . (pp. 35-6)

[Whittier's] reward is not that he showed "a hate of tyranny intense" or laid his gifts on the shrine of Freedom, but that more completely than any other poet he developed the peculiarly English *ideal of the home* which Cowper first brought intimately into letters, and added to it those *homely comforts of the spirit* which Cowper never felt. (p. 36)

Perhaps something in his American surroundings fitted him peculiarly for this humbler rôle. The fact that the men who had made the new colony belonged to the middle class of society tended to raise the idea of home into undisputed honour, and the isolation and perils of their situation in the earlier years had enhanced this feeling into something akin to a cult. America is still the land of homes. That may be a lowly theme for a poet; to admire such poetry may, indeed it does, seem to many to smack of a bourgeois taste. And yet there is an implication here that carries a grave injustice. For myself, I admit that Whittier is one of the authors of my choice, and that I read him with ever fresh delight; I even think there must be something spurious in that man's culture whose appreciation of Milton or Shelley dulls his ear to the paler but very refined charm of Whittier. If truth be told, there is sometimes a kind of exquisite content in turning from the pretentious poets who exact so much of the reader to the more immediate appeal of our sweet Quaker. (pp. 36-7)

There, to me at least, and not in the ballads which are more generally praised, lies the rare excellence of Whittier. True enough, some of these narrative poems are spirited and admirably composed. Now and then, as in *Cassandra Southwick*, they strike a note which reminds one singularly of the real ballads of the people; in fact, it would not be fanciful to discover a certain resemblance between the manner of their production and of the old popular songs. . . . The very atmosphere that surrounded the boy in a land where the traditions of border warfare and miraculous events still ran from mouth to mouth prepared him for such balladry. (p. 38)

No doubt this legendary training helped to give more life to Whittier's ballads and border tales than ordinarily enters into that rather factitious form of composition; and for a while he made a deliberate attempt to create out of it a native literature. But the effect was still deeper, by a kind of contrast, on his poetry of the home. . . . In *Snow-Bound* his memory called up a picture of the old Haverhill homestead, unsurpassed in its kind for sincerity and picturesqueness; in poem after poem he celebrated directly or indirectly "the river hemmed with lean-

ing trees," the hills and ponds, the very roads and bridges of the land about these sheltered towns. On the one hand, the recollection of the wilder life through which his parents had come added to the snugness and intimacy of these peaceful scenes, and, on the other hand, the encroachment of trade and factories into their midst lent a poignancy of regret for a grace that was passing away. (p. 39)

[It] must be seen that the crudeness of Whittier's education, and the thorny ways into which he was drawn, marred a large part, but by no means all, of his work. There are a few poems in his collection of an admirable craftsmanship in that genre which is none the less difficult—which I sometimes think is almost more difficult—because it lies so perilously near the trivial and mean. There are others which need only a little pruning, perhaps a little heightening here and there, to approach the same perfection of charm. Especially they have that harmony of tone which arises from the unspoiled sincerity of the writer and ends by subduing the reader to a restful sympathy with their mood. No one can read much in Whittier without feeling that these hills and valleys about the Merrimac have become one of the inalienable domiciles of the spirit—a familiar place where the imagination dwells with untroubled delight. Even the little things, the flowers and birds of the country, are made to contribute to the sense of homely content. (p. 40)

[The] emotion that furnishes the loudest note to most poets is subdued in Whittier to the same gentle tone. To be sure, there is evidence enough that his heart in youth was touched almost to a Byronic melancholy, and he himself somewhere remarks that "Few guessed beneath his aspect grave, What passions strove in chains." But was there not a remnant of self-deception here? Do not the calmest and wisest of us like to believe we are calm and wise by virtue of vigorous self-repression? Wordsworth, we remember, explained the absence of love from his poetry on the ground that his passions were too violent to allow any safe expression of them. Possibly they were. Certainly, in Whittier's verse we have no reflection of those tropic heats, but only "the Indian summer of the heart." The very title, *Memories,* of his best-known love poem . . . suggests the mood in which he approaches this subject. It is not the quest of desire he sings, but the home-coming after the frustrate search and the dreaming recollection by the hearth of an ancient loss. In the same way, his ballad *Maud Muller,* which is supposed to appeal only to the unsophisticated, is attuned to that shamelessly provincial rhyme,

> For of all sad words of tongue or pen,
> The saddest are these: "It might have been!"

It is a little so with us all, perhaps, as it was with the judge and the maiden; only, as we learn the lesson of years, the disillusion is likely to be mingled strangely with relief, and the sadness to take on a most comfortable and flattering Quaker drab—as it did with our "hermit of Amesbury." (pp. 41-2)

[It may be] that too complete a preoccupation with the reforming and political side of Whittier's life has kept the biographers from recognising that charm in what he himself regarded as his best poem. In 1872, in the full maturity of his powers and when the national peace had allowed him to indulge the peace in his own heart, he wrote his exquisite idyl, *The Pennsylvania Pilgrim.* (p. 48)

Here the faults of taste that elsewhere so often offend us are sunk in the harmony of the whole and in the singular unity of impression; and the lack of elevation that so often stints our praise becomes a suave and mellow beauty. All the better elements of his genius are displayed here in opulent freedom. The affections of the heart unfold in unembittered serenity. The sense of home seclusion is heightened by the presence of the enveloping wilderness, but not disturbed by any harsher contrast. Within is familiar joy and retirement unassailed—not without a touch of humour, as when in the evening, "while his wife put on her look of love's endurance," Pastorius took down his tremendous manuscript—

> And read, in half the languages of man,
> His *Rusca Apium,* which with bees began,
> And through the gamut of creation ran.

> (pp. 49-50)

> *Paul Elmer More, "Whittier the Poet," in his Shel-burne Essays, third series, Houghton Mifflin Company, 1905, pp. 28-53.*

ERNEST D. LEE (essay date 1908)

[*In this overview of Whittier's work, Lee attributes to Whittier the homely dignity as well as the faults of a genuine native poet.*]

Few poets afford a more striking illustration of the untrust-worthiness of contemporary fame than Whittier. At the close of the American Civil War his countrymen unanimously assigned him the foremost place among American poets. To-day he ranks below Longfellow, Poe, Walt Whitman, and Emerson. Yet it is in his very limitations that we must seek for the explanation of his influence. . . . His talent was a genuine prod-

An engraving of Whittier by William Adolph. Although the portrait is dated 1899, the engraving was taken from an 1880 photograph by Notman. Whittier was seventy-three.

uct of American soil, and his verse is instinct with the spirit of American life and American nature. "These painted autumn woods," says young Mr. Jordan to Margaret Smith [in **"Margaret Smith's Journal"**], "and this sunset light, and yonder clouds of gold and purple, do seem to me better fitted to provoke devotional thoughts and to awaken a becoming reverence and love for the Creator, than the stained windows and lofty arched roofs of old minsters." Here we have the key to the judgment of his contemporaries. Whittier was essentially a national poet; Longfellow was too fond of worshipping in the old minsters. (p. 78)

[Whittier] was a journalist and politician first, and a poet afterwards. He regarded the abolition of slavery as his lifework and verse but as a ready means of heightening his appeal to Northern sentiment. His anti-slavery poems are for the most part hasty impromptus, written in a white heat of passion for immediate publication. Their chief merit is their absolute sincerity. But they are frankly emotional; they make no appeal to the intellect, and are full of glaring technical defects. Yet they stirred men's pulses and swayed men's hearts. Much of their power is due to the tone of deep religious earnestness that underlies them. But it is the power of the popular preacher rather than of the poet; witness these lines from the third stanza of **"Expostulation"**:—

> What ho! Our countrymen in chains!
> The whip on woman's shrinking flesh!
> Our soil yet reddening with the stains
> Caught from her scourging, warm and fresh!
> What! Mothers from their children riven!
> What! God's own image bought and sold!
> Americans to market driven,
> And bartered as the brute for gold!

Such verse is not poetry; its realism is too intense; nothing is left to the imagination. But it is very effective rhetoric, and its impassioned indignation went straight to the hearts of its readers; line after line striking home like a rapier-thrust. Equally effective is the pathos of **"The Farewell of a Virginia Slave Mother to her Daughters Sold into Foreign Bondage."** It is an eloquent picture of a mother's despair, and of the horrors of a Southern rice-swamp. . . . But its pathos is entirely due to its descriptive power; the mother has no individuality; her feeling is purely objective; we never get a glimpse into her heart. The poem lacks the inspired ideality and woman's intuition of Mrs. Browning's "Runaway Slave." (pp. 79-80)

The cause of humanity always had a warm sympathiser in Whittier. His heart was with the people, and in his **"Songs of Labour and Reform,"** he sings the praise of honest work in rousing, if common place stanzas, which, though below the level of art, won a wide popularity among the sturdy, unso-phisticated New Englanders. **"The Gallows,"** and **"The Human Sacrifice,"** contain an eloquent appeal for the abolition of capital punishment; with much bitter irony at the expense of its Calvinist advocates, who seem to have argued for its efficacy as a deterrent on the ground that the criminal dies without hope of salvation. . . . Perhaps the best of these poems—certainly the most vigorous—is **"From Perugia,"** in which the barbarities sanctioned by the Papacy while struggling to uphold the last vestiges of temporal power are described with a passionate indignation at suffering and wrong that is eminently characteristic. But with the possible exception of Juvenal, the fiercest satire never attains to any great poetic heights. And the attempt to give poetic expression to "the unsung beauty hid life's common things below,'' often results in a mere reproduction of their plain exterior. (p. 81)

As the typical national poet, Whittier is quite at home among the national legends, and in spite of common-place conception and phrases, his ballads met with as much success, at least in America, as those of Longfellow. One of the best is **"Cassandra Southwick."** . . . We have here the impetuous rhythm and the democratic sentiment of **"Virginia,"** with a strong Hebrew colouring. Very different in character is the ballad of **"Maud Muller"**—a simple, unaffected story of a judge and a bare-footed haymaker, of love sacrificed to ambition and pride of station, and of vain regrets for the "might have been." Less popular, perhaps, but more satisfying to the critical sense, is **"Skipper Ireson's Ride,"** with its straightforward telling of a plain tale, and its quaint dialect refrain. . . . It is a fine ballad, and not less so for the difficulty in determining wherein its beauty consists. Enough that it does not contain a single jarring note, and that it strikes one as a living poem—its thought embodied in a living form. But probably the most popular of all Whittier's ballads, especially in America, is **"Barbara Frietchie."** (p. 82)

[Whittier] had not Longfellow's wide culture and travelled experience, and his tales, though interesting, lack the graceful charm of [Longfellow's] ''Wayside Inn'' stories. **"The Wreck of Rivermouth"** is a fine piece of realism, but it fails to grip one like the thrilling narrative of storm and shipwreck in the ''Ballad of Carmilhan.'' Far better, in our opinion, is [Whittier's] **"Kallundborg Church"**—an old Norse legend of a daring lover, who seeks the aid of a Troll to build the church that is to win him his bride. . . . The pulse of human sympathy beats strongly throughout. And the poem is quite free from the padding and superfluous introductory matter that disfigures so much of Whittier's work.

But when Whittier is deeply moved, his thoughts seem to fall naturally into terse and trenchant language. This is especially noticeable in the most powerful of his personal poems. Even in **"Isabel,"** a youthful poem in which the earnestness of the rebuke to a beautiful, but heartless woman, is veiled beneath gentle banter and delicate raillery, there is not a superfluous word. The same conciseness of expression lends vigour to the simple pathos and broad charity of the lines to Brown of Ossawatomie. And it makes **"Ichabod"** one of the most powerful protests in literature. The occasion was the betrayal of the hopes of the anti-slavery men through the support given by Daniel Webster to the Fugitive Slave Law in 1850. The structure of the poem is perfect; not a line, not a syllable could be deleted without spoiling the harmony. And it is not mere eloquence; it is poetry, and satisfies feeling and intellect alike. . . . The effect is heightened by the impression of reserved power which is suggested by a restraint that is the more remarkable in Whittier as it is so rare. We are reminded of Browning's ''Lost Leader''; there is the same slow, dignified movement, the same moral inspiration, and the same skilful, harmonious blending of sublimity and pathos. But for once the superiority must be conceded to the American poet; the strength of **"Ichabod"** is enhanced by its greater simplicity; the feeling is even more intense, and the imagery even more felicitous. And the expression is a perfect embodiment of the thought; as we read the lines we seem to penetrate the depths of the writer's soul. (pp. 84-5)

There is a homely simplicity in Whittier's descriptive poetry which appeals to us by its entire absence of affectation. For though incapable of rising to Wordsworth's heights, he never

sinks to the bathos of [Wordsworth's ballads] ''The Pet Lamb,'' or ''The Idiot Boy.'' What a contrast to these is afforded by **"Telling the Bees"**—a charming account of the quaint old custom of draping the hives in black upon a death in the family, with a realistic description of the Whittier homestead. And the pathos in **"A Sea Dream"** is genuine; we feel that we are in the presence of some hidden sorrow in the lines:—

> But turn to me thy dear girl-face
> Without the angel's crown,
> The wedded roses of thy lips,
> Thy loose hair rippling down
> In waves of golden brown.

Here is no mawkish sentimentality, such as we find in Wordsworth's ''Ruth,'' but a simple yet dignified expression of feeling that appeals to everyone. And the setting of the song is quite in keeping with its mysterious sadness; the scene—the beach with the waves beating their accompaniment to the sad, sweet strain; the singer—an unromantic city man, whose hard, shrewd face gave no clue to the secret hinted at in his song. It is Whittier at his best, when he is able to give us a glimpse beneath the surface of things. Such insight is rarely found, save in one who has himself experienced the bitter-sweetness of disappointed love. (p. 87)

[**"Memories"**] is a beautiful tribute from a great-hearted man to a noble woman. And a poet who can write like this has fathomed some at any rate of the secrets of soul-communion:—

> Yet hath thy spirit left on me
> An impress Time has worn not out,
> And something of myself in thee,
> A shadow from the past, I see,
> Lingering, even yet thy way about. . . .

And rarely has Whittier used the simple ballad metre with greater effect than in this poem. The beautiful description of local scenery and wild flowers, the singing of the birds and the moaning of the pines, harmonise with the sentiment and the parting; there is an indefinable sadness even in such purely descriptive lines as—

> The lilies blossom in the pond,
> The bird builds in the tree,
> The dark pines sing on Ramoth hill
> The slow song of the sea.

In **"The Henchman,"** the theme of unrequited love is handled more explicitly, and with something of the old-world grace and dainty tenderness of Sir Philip Sidney's Sonnets. It is a charming ballad of devoted love which seeks no recompense, and is free from any taint of selfishness; which renders unobtrusive homage, content, if need arise, to die for the beloved—and thus exacting from mankind ''the reverence due to holy things.'' Yet, it was personal experience that had taught Whittier to feel

> The assurance strong,
> That love, which fails of perfect utterance here,
> Lives on to fill the heavenly atmosphere
> With its immortal song.

More characteristic, perhaps, of Whittier's Muse than these revelations of personal feeling is the sustained descriptive realism of **"Snow-Bound."** It is generally regarded as his masterpiece. And though we must confess to a preference for the pervasive idealism of **"Memories,"** and **"A Sea Dream,"** or even for the delightful child-romance of **"In School-days,"** the importance of **"Snow-Bound"** from a national point of view can hardly be over-estimated. True, it lacks imaginative power, and has little claim either to symmetry of structure or to charm of style. But it is an authentic picture of New England life, and the sentiment, if commonplace, is sincere. Whittier has here done for the New England farmer what Burns did for the Scottish peasant in "The Cotter's Saturday Night." He has made him the subject of a national poem, simple, homely, and appealing directly to the patriotism of the people. But **"Snow-Bound"** has not the majestic musical cadences of Burns's poem. Its chief merit is an unmistakable impress of truth and accuracy in detail. . . . In some respects **"Snow-Bound"** is more like the analytic realism of the eighteenth century than the more imaginative nature-poetry of the nineteenth. The description of the snow-storm which forms the setting of the poem recalls that of a winter storm in Thomson's "Seasons." . . . But just because the realism of [these] poems is so excellent, and their historic value as representing phases of life that have passed away is so lasting, they fall short of the highest art through a certain lack of ideality. They are mimetic rather than interpretative; an imitation, not a criticism of life. For the highest art is the product of a judicious union of the real and the ideal. Drawing its materials from nature, it transmutes them in the mind of the artist as in a crucible; and the resultant masterpiece is a new creation; Matter has been informed by Mind. (pp. 87-9)

No American poet is so thoroughly imbued with the Spirit of the Age as Whittier. The Gospel of Human Freedom permeated everything he wrote. Its practical manifestation in his own country—the Abolitionist movement—held unchallenged possession of his brain and heart, and swept him irresistibly before it. . . . The chief sources of his power are the intensity of his emotion and his moral earnestness. Great qualities, these; they enabled him to fight effectively against the commercial selfishness and political time-serving that, for so many years, stood in the way of Emancipation. But they do not suffice to lift a man out of his environment, and to free his mind from the trammels of custom. The prejudices of the Quaker sect clung to Whittier all his days. (p. 90)

To the same cause—to his inability to get beyond the Quaker groove—we must attribute his lack of artistic sensibility. For with Whittier, as we have seen, poetry was not an end, but a means—a convenient vehicle for a preacher's message. Hence he never succeeded in mastering the technique of his art. His indifference to melody is sufficiently shown by his rugged rhythms and slovenly rhymes. He shows a distinct preference for the plain sing-song of the four-line ballad; and much of his verse gives one the impression of being measured out by the footrule. His facile expression was a snare to him; he never learnt to condense, and rarely knew when to stop. And we could dispense with the obvious moral, that is usually emphasised at the close. (p. 91)

Ernest D. Lee, *"John Greenleaf Whittier,"* in The Westminster Review, *Vol. CLXIX, No. 1, January, 1908, pp. 78-92.*

EDMUND GOSSE (essay date 1912)

[*A distinguished English literary historian, critic, and biographer, Gosse wrote extensively on seventeenth- and eighteenth-century English literature. His commentary in* Seventeenth-Century Studies, A History of Eighteenth-Century Literature, Questions at Issue, *and other works is generally regarded as sound and suggestive, and he is also credited with introducing the works of Norwegian dramatist Henrik Ibsen and other Scandinavian writers to English readers. In his assessment of Whittier, Gosse says that Whittier deserves to be remembered for his individuality and simplicity rather than his artistic talents.*]

Mr. Whittier was composing verses all his life, and the difference of quality between those he wrote at twenty and at eighty is remarkably small. He was a poet in the lifetime of Gifford and Crabbe, and he was still a poet when Mr. Rudyard Kipling was already famous. During this vast period of time his style changed very little; it had its ups and downs, its laxities and then its felicities, but it bore very little relation to passing conditions. There rose up beside it Tennyson and Browning, Rossetti and Swinburne, but none of these affected Whittier. His genius, or talent, or knack—whichever we choose to call it—was an absolutely local and native thing. It was like the Indian waters of strange name of which it sang, Winnepesaukee and Merrimac and Katahdin; it streamed forth, untouched by Europe, from among the butternuts and maples of the hard New England landscape. The art in Whittier's verse was primitive. Those who love his poetry most will wish that he had possessed a better ear, that he could have felt that "mateless" does not rhyme with "greatness." In all his books there is a tendency to excess, to redundancy; he babbles on, even when he has nothing very inspired to say.

But when all this is acknowledged, none but a very hasty reader will fail to recognise Whittier's lasting place in the history of literature. He is not rich, nor sonorous, nor a splendid artist; he is even rather rarely exquisite, but he has an individuality of his own that is of durable importance. He is filled with moral enthusiasm, as a trumpet is filled with the breath of him who blows it. His Quaker quietism concentrates itself till it breaks in a real passion-storm of humanity, and when Whittier is roused he sings with the thrilling sweetness of a wood-thrush. By dint of simplicity and earnestness, he frequently hits upon the most charming phrases, instinct with life and truth; so that the English poet with whom it seems most natural to compare him in the lyrical order is the epic and didactic Crabbe. If the author of "The Borough" had been dowered with the gift of writing in octosyllabics and short stanzaic measures, and had been born of stern Puritan stock in Massachusetts, and had been roused by the sight of a public iniquity, such as slavery, recognised and applauded in society, he might have presented to the world a talent very much resembling that of Whittier. But, as it is, we look around in vain for an English or American poet of anything like the same merit who shares the place of Whittier.

The grave of the admirable Quaker poet at Amesbury is hemmed in by a hedge of vigorous arbor vitae. His memory, in like manner, depends for its protection, not on the praise of exotic communities which can never, though they admire, rightly comprehend it, but on the conscience of New England, shy, tenacious, intrepid, to which, more than any other poet has done, Whittier made a direct and constant appeal. (pp. 145-47)

Edmund Gosse, *"A Visit to Whittier,"* in his Portraits and Sketches, *1912. Reprint by Scholarly Press, Inc., 1971, pp. 135-47.*

JOHN MACY (essay date 1913)

[*Macy, like many critics of his era, praises Whittier for the gentle humility and authenticity of his verse while acknowledging its limitations.*]

Whittier's good sense and modest dignity are nowhere better expressed than in the verses introductory to his collected work. (p. 111)

[In his verse entitled **"Proem"** (see excerpt above, 1847), this] New England Quaker, confessing that he could not achieve poetry, has in the act of confession made a beautiful poem, sound in stanzaic structure, and not unmelodious. Whittier compels admiration in spite of the undeniable crudities of his lyre, crudities that he so charmingly acknowledged. Spontaneity, sincerity, passion, these are his high gifts; they triumph over all his verbal difficulties. They lift him not among the great poets, whose company he humbly knew he could not join, but among the genuine poets, who have said their heart in English words, who are true to the earth though they do not rise upon the earth-spurning wings of absolute song. Whittier's earliest inspiration was the anti-slavery fervour, and of this passion, the tensest, most noble, that swept over New England and roused its dull muse to ecstasy, Whittier was the authentic laureate.

It is impossible . . . to detach Whittier's ruggedly heroic verses from the harsh soil of history, to see them except through the noon air of his pacific and serene personality. To hear his verses, as it were from his own lips, gives them double dramatic force. His shy Quaker voice is hoarse with rage, the lips of innocence are white with scorn. The casual reader of "**Ichabod**" might be unimpressed, for the verses are plain, ordinary, lighted by no flash of self-explanatory beauty. But when the poem is understood as the divine indignation of a benevolent Quaker at Webster's surrender to the slave power, it becomes incandescent, and one imagines that Webster, cynical politician who bent his shaggy brows histrionically upon his opponents, must have shrivelled beneath those lyric curses of naïve righteousness. It is the devastating wrath of a peaceful man! . . . Poems on current events are as a rule ephemeral; emotion that is strong enough to make such poems permanent is a mighty fact in literature. In Whittier's occasional verses the vehicle of the emotion seems to have been heated by its very resistance to the idea. He is so intense in his meaning that his technically defective verses are not quite bad, certainly never ludicrous. Sometimes his fiery challenge dashes against the stubborn hardness of his words like the dissonance of swift water over rocks. For example the lines from "**Toussaint L'Ouverture**":

> To hear above his scar-worn back
> The heavy slave-whip's frequent crack.

"Frequent" is a feebly mischosen word. But the two lines and the verses in which they are set are powerful. "**The Slave Ships**" is naïvely terrible. One stanza has the naked simplicity of genius:

> Red glowed the western waters—
>   The setting sun was there,
> Scattering alike on wave and cloud
>   His fiery mesh of hair.
> Amidst a group of blindness
>   A solitary eye
> Gazed from the burdened slaver's deck
>   Into that burning sky. . . .

The reader's patriotic sympathies cannot fill utterly bad verses with the breath of life. The noblest enthusiasm cannot flame in wholly unpoetic verse. All the earnest belief in the world will not forge poetry. The abundance of dead unremembered verses by others on the same themes that Whittier rushed into rough rhythms is proof of his individual genius. It may be that

our knowledge of his seraphic gentleness throws into relief the Hebraic violence of his prophecies; it may be that the facts of biography lend adventitious merit to his poetry; but even so, the failure of other equally sincere enthusiasts, and his almost unfailing success in striking out some white hot lines in poem after poem on the same subject, acclaim his genius when all temporal and historic prejudices are deducted.

The difference between a good hymn and a bad hymn lies not in a difference of religious sincerity, and the reader's accessible emotions will be the same in both cases; the difference is in the psalmists' poetic powers. (pp. 112-15)

Most of the singers of liberty in America have been beneath their task. . . . Whittier, shy and gentle, nurtured in a childlike faith and untrained, unperplexed by culture, sends the tones of his trumpet across the world, to England, the arch-hypocrite mouthing liberty and defending slavery, and to the Pope, vicar of the prince of peace entangled in cowardly and murderous politics. . . . [Whittier,] cradled in an unwarlike creed, blazes forth in bellicose rebuke, strikes again and again at the smooth brow of evil with verses virile and aflame. His single purpose overwhelms the obstacles of his verbal hesitations. There is no mistaking him, even when the ear protests against his unintentional dissonances. Whether his work is poetry or rhymed propaganda, it is literature, for it expresses a man and events in words that are to-day alive with emotion. One who by temperament and by the habit of other reading feels himself out of sympathy with Whittier's hoarse verses has but to open his mind and present fresh surfaces to the impact of Whittier's intensity in order to be smitten by it.

Whittier's religious verse is a mixture of banality and exaltation. At its worst it is but the grotesque psaltery with which Protestant Christianity from Doctor Watts to Doctor Moody has offended the sensitive ear. At its best it is the passion of worship which transcends particular belief or doubt and imparts immediately the religion of the singer. "**Laus Deo**" is a moving song of adoration; its triumphant ecstasy is instantly contagious. His less inspired hymns are sweet and manly, in spite of their childishness, and now and again their childishness becomes rather a childlike simplicity which is near to poetry.

Of Whittier's narratives and ballads, some, like "**The Witch's Daughter**," are of good substance but unpoetic in expression. Others, like "**Maud Müller**," are simply bad, as Whittier, with his mischievous modesty, was the first to admit. "**Cassandra Southwick**" is a good ballad; it has swing and rush and a lively pictorial effect. "**Skipper Ireson's Ride**" is excellent; it has the haunting ring of true balladry; it repeats itself over and over in the reader's ears; and whatever is of unforgettable rhythm, of a rhythm that carries and continually reminds one of the content, is true poetry. Chant this over once and it will stay in the memory:

> Old Floyd Ireson, for his hard heart,
> Tarred and feathered and carried in a cart
>   By the women of Marblehead.

The best of poets is he who dreams something that the rest of mankind would never, never think of and makes it real—Dante, Shakespeare, Shelley. A lesser type of poet, but a genuine poet, is he who celebrates the actual land on which he lives, the daily scenes familiar to many eyes, the people among whom he moves. Whittier is the unrivalled portrayer of the New England landscape. Burden him with every disability that criticism can impute to a poet; unfrock him from the priesthood of perfect singers; reduce him to the plain common ground of minor poets, where he placed himself, the simplest, most un-deluded common citizen in the democracy of letters; remember every *gaucherie* of which he is innocently guilty: he still keeps "on Yankee hills immortal sheep."

His masterpiece is **"Snow-Bound."** The placid fidelity of the poem, the justice of the details, the apparently unsought felicity of the words identify it inevitably and forever with the experience of every one who has lived in New England. (pp. 116-19)

Many aspects of the world out the window are unlike anything that Whittier saw. And yet **"Snow-Bound"** is true; it describes yonder landscape. The poem stands through all changes permanent as one of the granite boulders sheeted in snow. The fingers of life moulded the words. Through the plain verses actuality said itself, and actuality is immortal. If one who had been brought up in a New England village should be stricken blind, **"Snow-Bound"** would give him eyes again for all that Whittier describes. (pp. 119-20)

The sketches of character are good portraits, not too highly praised when they are compared to Chaucer's Prologue; the faces are alive and ruddy in the firelight, homely-beautiful like "Flemish pictures" (Whittier's own just analogy)—the father, a "prompt, decisive man," the uncle "innocent of books," and the aunt—was ever more charming tribute to the elderly maiden?

> The morning dew, that dried so soon
> With others, glistened at her noon;
> Through years of toil and soil and care,
> From glossy tress to thin gray hair,
>   All unprofaned she held apart
>   The virgin fancies of the heart.

Then the sister

>   Keeping with many a light disguise
>   The secret of self-sacrifice.

And the strongest portrait of all (strange that Whittier of all men could draw it so richly!), is that of the cultivated passionate woman:

>   A certain pardlike, treacherous grace
>   Swayed the lithe limbs and dropped the lash,
>   Lent the white teeth the dazzling flash,
>   And under low brows, black with night,
>   Rayed out at times a dangerous light;
>   .   .   .   .   .   .
>   A woman tropical, intense.

Whittier's art is restricted. He never achieved the final majesties of the grand style. But within his limits he is genuinely good. His verse lacks some of the virtues, and by compensation it is free from some of the vices, of his university-bred contemporaries, who wrote so often with the pens of the ages that they did not learn firmly to grasp their own. Whittier's poems are indigenous to the soil as lilacs and elm trees, and they are also the voice of a very great man. Through a medium which he did not fully master, he did manage to convey with power and vividness his fiery convictions, blazes of passion across the blue serenity of his faith. With the sureness that plain simple vision gives to an imperfect draughtsman, he made pictures of his landscape that are unsurpassed, if not unsurpassable. If the day comes when they are no longer enjoyed, on that day the last Yankee will have died. (pp. 120-21)

John Macy, "Whittier," in his The Spirit of American Literature, *Doubleday, Page & Company, 1913, pp. 111-22.*

WINFIELD TOWNLEY SCOTT   (essay date 1934)

There was little of the true dramatist in Whittier, as his early prose tales reveal. Here he could undoubtedly have improved with training; but he never acquired that skill except in the swift strokes of a few ballads. Still, his main direction was correct, the errors were avoided when he turned to *Snow-Bound*; the country which he knew well was at last peopled with human beings whom he knew intimately. Added to all this was a seemingly-artless simplicity of line and phrase. *Snow-Bound* was not a phenomenon; given the circumstances, it was inevitable. . . . For Whittier, this poem was redolent with nostalgia—it is for us, too—so well has he reproduced his mood with his scene. *Snow-Bound* has all the reality of life, and is alive.

As far as literary craftsmanship is concerned, the first reason for this lies in Whittier's unusual power of description. His descriptions of nature are among his chief claims as a poet. When these are underscored by an interest beyond themselves, they exhibit a loveliness both individual and simple. They create half the charm of *Snow-Bound* and *The Pennsylvania Pilgrim*. They touch a large number of his poems and enrich them just so far. They were an entirely natural product of his talent, for his love of the out-of-doors was genuine and he possessed an unusually pictorial mind. Again and again the good things of his poetry are the pictures, whether they be of a group at a fireside or a tarred and feathered captain in a cart. The chief joy of these pictures is rapidity of manner. Sometimes the poems themselves are long-winded, tiresomely repetitious, and have little to say; but his descriptions always run true. Even in his early work this ability was notable. Lines in **"Moll Pitcher"** . . . bear witness. Again and again he describes completely and with the utmost artlessness—too often to be anything less than a good poet. (pp. 265-66)

[Whittier's] quality of swift delineation made his ballads successful. There are faulty places in the longer ones, and they sometimes become as loquacious and loose as ballads are liable to be. But though they rise and fall in merit, their peaks are memorably fine and generally finer than any other poetry produced by that New England group which Longfellow figuratively headed. Such a ballad as **"Mabel Martin"** is too direct and strongly created altogether to permit sections to spoil it; that poem, and **"Kathleen,"** and **"The Countess"** are nearly as robust as **"Skipper Ireson's Ride"** and far better, in parts, than anything in those better-known poems, **"The Captain's Well"** and **"Barbara Frietchie."**

"Kathleen" and the ballad . . . **"The Sycamores"**—Whittier's favorite—have in common a weird mood, rather Irish, and delightfully achieved. His material for his narrative and legendary poems, however, is largely American in source; in this Whittier deserves pioneer credit. Occasionally his interest wandered to foreign legends—probably under the guidance of Longfellow's example—and the resultant poems are surprising. **"The Dead Feast of the Kol-Folk"** and the **"Brewing of Soma"** belong among his most interesting and commendable work. Occasionally his material came from original balladry. This is true of **"Skipper Ireson,"** whose rolling rhythms and sharp strength make it unforgettable. (pp. 267-68)

Whittier's people, except in a few notable instances, are not often successful save in his ballads, where the primary interest of story leads us somewhat away from considering them over-long as characters. One striking exception, however, is the poem **"Abram Morrison."** . . . [In Whittier] we find a spiritual directness of mood and treatment. His colloquial blank verse occasionally seems Frostian to a later ear; in his portraits he stands definitely as an ancestor. In his poem about the Irish Quaker, Whittier represents, to a really striking degree, an antecedent to Robinson and his Tilbury Town characters. . . . (p. 269)

Too many minor poets have tried to cut pebbles as if these were diamonds, and with ineffective success. Whittier's talents were consistent; there was little surprising and eventful in them; his best course was his slow, steady growth. Whittier himself knew that his work showed growth. No one acknowledged his early crudities more fully than himself; many of them caused him pain. Such a poem as **"Mogg Megone,"** which he would have thrown away entirely—and been right in so doing—was dragged into his collected works by the requests of well-meaning friends whose kindliness, so conceived, obscured their vision. (pp. 270-71)

The limitations of his craftsmanship are well known, and he himself was "not unmindful" of them. He wrote under inspiration, spasmodically. Scribbling rapidly on all kinds of scrap paper, often in illegible scrawls, he worked diligently at composition. Though at times he wrote easily and swiftly, his manuscripts most often show crossings and discardings and new attempts in considerable number. He sometimes had the town printer set a poem up for him, the better to correct it in print. . . .

Whittier knew better than most of the self-appointed critics and carpenters at poetry, who were always ready to offer their suggestions as to how he might improve and polish. (p. 271)

He was a man with something to say who became aware of the importance of craftsmanship, but less keenly aware than was Longfellow, for example. If he chose to stick a moral cork on the end of his sword, time after time, we can just as often forget the fact. Such silly verse as his elegy on **"Conductor Bradley,"** such prosaic verbosity as he sometimes exhibited was almost as bad as Wordsworth's less graceful moments. But nobody of consequence rests a critical judgment of Wordsworth on "Peter Bell." The only difference, in the case of the American, is that school children are still forced to read Whittier's less fortunate poetry; while the truly worthy things stand untouched or forgotten. They who know **"In School-Days"** are not often aware of a better poem, **"The Last Walk in Autumn."** They who can recite **"Barbara Frietchie"** have never heard of **"Abram Morrison;"** to read any "moral" poem will serve—not the beautiful **"What the Birds Said."** Which of us knows **"The Henchman"**—or could even guess that the author was an old man of seventy? . . . This poem is dissimilar from anything else Whittier ever wrote, good and bad; it belongs among his very best things. Its purity of line, its chaste control of the art of lyric singing make it strangely beautiful. (pp. 271-72)

Whittier's religious verse has received little attention from literary criticism. We all know he was a Quaker and a liberal and staunch upholder to the last of the fundamentals of his faith. The moral-pointing habit of so many of his immediate predecessors and contemporaries he found congenial enough, to the misfortune of many of his poems. In certain of his poems,

however, he achieved a simplicity of religious expression that is at once beautiful and universal. He wrote some of the finest hymns we have. . . . In the contemplation of God as found in nature, Whittier missed the fervor and exaltation, the religious ecstasy of Donne and Marvell. If he saw a "spiritual symbolism" in the world about him, rarely did he lift it to the level of great mysticism.

Yet this American Quaker of the nineteenth century had something else, as valid, perhaps, as excellent, and as expressive in its way—an atmosphere of quiet trust and reliance. His use of the word "peace"—intense, ultimate peace—is reminiscent of Keats's employment of "quiet." The best of this part of his poetry requires no religious sympathy for us to appreciate its grace and felicity. The fortunate results of setting his religious verse to music have made his hymns more widely known among Americans than those of any other writer. . . . Such verse as that, as **"The Eternal Goodness,"** as the stanzas of the great hymn beginning "Dear Lord and Father of mankind," as several of his most reverent poems—these have something which colors them with an individual loveliness, essentially minor but none the less fine. His individual felicities need not hold us long, except as they point to summary truths about his verse. The commendable accuracy of his descriptions, the precision and simplicity of his best lines, the directness of his thought are all characteristic of his most finished work. His excellencies and faults at times run together. His field of expression varied little, and what was good and what was bad had often the same tune. He found certain forms of verse which suited him and rarely did he stray very far from these. Thus he who runs may read but he will not easily discover the perfection of Whittier's art. In two or three poems, such as **"Telling the Bees,"** this art is complete and flawless. In certain others, it seems likely to immortalize whole sections of sturdy verse. Yet even as an old man he was liable to unfortunate lines and he was bedeviled with a feeling of worthlessness if his work did not find some reason beyond itself for its existence. To-day he shares the momentary, if fashionable, depreciation which is visited on almost every one who was so unlucky as to have lived, on whichever side of the water, in the reign of Victoria. (pp. 272-74)

In his *Songs of Labor,* he antedated Whitman's celebration of the workingman by ten years. In looking for American legends, he anticipated Hawthorne. He was far in advance of most of his contemporaries in his intuitive search for material of every kind. Many poets two generations later, who still have their ears stopped to native sounds by the strains of a remote, if courtly, muse, might do well to learn of him. He created a handful of enduring poems out of the lure of New England, rather than the faery lore of some far East; his was the authentic goldenrod, rather than exotic flowers transplanted from foreign lands; not the lark and the nightingale, but the jay and the nuthatch, sing in his verse. All of it is instinct with his honesty and his integrity; much of it shows his clear-sightedness; the precious part of it is an American inheritance. (p. 275)

Winfield Townley Scott, "Poetry in American: A New Consideration of Whittier's Verse," in The New England Quarterly, *Vol. VII, June, 1934, pp. 258-75.*

DESMOND POWELL (essay date 1937)

[*Unlike many critics who praise Whittier's realism, Powell claims that "Whittier pledged himself to the theory of art as escape from life."*]

Whittier in his study. Courtesy of Prints and Photographs Division, Library of Congress.

It is true that Whittier is read by the children, because they are made to read him in school; that does not mean he is a children's poet. It is true that the trend is away from him; but it is away from a host of good writers. It is true that he is a minor poet: the intensity, the mastery, the opulence of major poets are not his. The history of literature, however, seems to prove that writers can live for qualities other than these. And it is also true that a large part of Whittier's work is sectional. Perhaps the most severe charge that can be brought against his nature poems is that so many of them depend upon the reader's knowledge of a landscape that most of us do not know and that is beginning to disappear before the eyes of those who do. But lines like

> And through the war march of the Puritan
> The silver stream of Marvell's music ran

are not sectional. Nor are most of the other lines upon which his fame will ultimately depend.

True, the adverse criticism which Whittier has received is justified. Most of his work is bad. He could not restrain his faculty for jogging verse. He could not concentrate his powers. He could not recognize a bad stanza even when it occurred between two good ones. He could spoil a lyric by tacking a moral on the end as readily as Bryant. He could accept the popular canons of taste, and thereby enervate his work, as thoroughly as Long-

fellow. He could rely on what he deemed to be the truth, rather than upon his ability to express it in terms of life and beauty, as completely as Lowell. Yet despite all these and other stultifying restrictions he managed to write well, occasionally by transcending them, but more often by doing his best within their narrow limits.

Whittier's nature poetry offers a good example of his achievement within a restricted field. Much as it has been praised, its peculiar quality has been little recognized. It was conditioned on the great sensory limitation of color-blindness. To speak of him as painting a scene is inexact; rather he etches it. *Snow-Bound* is memorable largely because it gave full play to his powers as an artist in black and white. It is the sharp ravine cutting the expanse of snow, the ducks' black squadron lying beneath the gray November cloud, the cat's dark silhouette crouching on the wall that we remember when we think of this poem. Even the angel invoked at the end has wings of ashen gray. Though at times Whittier employed conventional color associations to good advantage, such successes are rare. Seldom did he make an adjective of his own like that of the "crimson-blooded maples" in **"The Ranger."** In his best pictures he let color go and concentrated on things that could be revealed in black and brown and gray. Thus it is that he dealt so much with the pattern of light and shade in summer woods, with autumn eves when the spectrum began to disappear, with the sea when shadows fell dark upon its face. Within this narrow range he gave us some unforgettable poetry, the somber quality of which is the chief component of its beauty. Although he was often able to suggest sounds felicitously, his imagery was chiefly visual. In **"Summer by the Lakeside"** there is not an auditory image, and in nearly a hundred descriptive lines only two color adjectives. His achievement becomes the more remarkable when we recognize these facts.

The study of Whittier is a study of limitations. In order to understand them it is necessary to take into account the theory of poetry within which he worked. He never stated it in detail, but in the introduction to **"Amy Wentworth"** he wrote a brief defense of the art:

> Let none upbraid us that the waves entice
> Thy sea-dipped pencil, or some quaint device
> Rhythmic and sweet, beguiles my pen away
> From the sharp strifes and sorrows of today.
> Thus while the east-wind keen from Labrador
> Sings in the leafless elms, and from the shore
> Of the great sea comes the monotonous roar
> Of the long-breaking surf, and all the sky
> Is gray with cloud, home-bound and dull, I try
> To time a simple legend to the sounds
> Of winds in the woods, and waves on pebbled bounds,—
> A song for oars to chime with, such as might
> Be sung by tired sea-painters, who at night
> Look from their hemlock camps, by quiet cove
> Or beach, moon-lighted, on the waves they love.

These lines, I think, explain why Whittier, who was a born poet, was in the main such a futile one.

We think of Whittier, when we think of him at all, as a quiet old Quaker in white whiskers and black pants, who spent his time walking in the country around Amesbury and drinking tea with the temperance ladies of the neighborhood. We forget the ardent young abolitionist of the thirties, who was stoned out of Concord and rotten-egged out of Newburyport. A true spiritual descendant of Roger Williams, Whittier for many years fought for an unpopular cause. He saw his beliefs held up to ridicule, his name defamed, his office sacked and burnt by the mob. He went on fighting until in the end, for reasons which he did not understand, his cause prevailed. Despite the uneventful later years there was action, there was heroism in Whittier's life. Except for a few feeble successes among the anti-slavery poems he was unable to transmute these experiences into literature. His statements about art in poems like **"Amy Wentworth"** furnish us with an explanation of this. Looked at more closely the tragedy of Whittier becomes a tragedy of the intellect. He was a bad poet because he was a bad critic. He could challenge injustice, but he could not challenge untruth. He could not even perceive it.

Long before the phrase was coined, Whittier pledged himself to the theory of art as escape from life. That much great poetry can be explained by this theory is doubtful. . . . [Whittier] accepted the escape theory in its simplest form without recognizing that it was inadequate to explain the great poetry he most admired. Although he wrote that Luther's pen was mightier than von Seckingen's mailed fist, he could not see what made that pen powerful. Although he gave himself utterly to the abolitionist cause, he failed to sing the songs of justice and liberty as Shelley had sung them. His excuse in **"Proem"** [see excerpt above, 1847] was that life got in the way, that duty and labor made his song unskilled and harsh. He could not see that duty and labor had made the song of Milton clear and

strong. . . . He believed poetry should be something plaintive and sweet which would charm the world away from its memory of bitter things. . . . [Whittier produced a] long line of stories which now so weary the reader, not so much because he lacked the narrative gift as because he refused to make his characters convincing. That he could depict character when he wished, he proved in *Snow-Bound*; that he could tell a story when he was not bogged down by the devising of romantic atmosphere, he proved in **"Skipper Ireson's Ride."** But in the ballads he was trying to get away from reality, to write about faint far-off things that would soothe rather than arouse.

> And then, as is my wont, I told
> A story of the days of old,
> Not found in printed books,—in sooth
> A fancy with slight hint of truth. . . .

Statements like this occur in half a dozen places. One can see how such an intention must have reacted on those poems in which his intenser emotions were engaged. He could not give himself to them utterly as poet; he lost his strength when he needed it most.

This is why the anti-slavery poems fail to interest us any more. I wish that Whittier could have achieved the feeling of **"To a Southern Statesman"** in more of them. I wish he could have made use of the experiences of his life as inciting forces for poetry. I wish he could have poured out on the people of Concord and Newbury the wrath that Jones Very once visited on the folk of Salem. But wrath and indignation are only two of the emotions and the anti-slavery poems only a small part of our loss. More important is the effect of Whittier's theory on the rest of his work. Hate and scorn were weakened, the other passions were killed by it. The result is an impersonal quality that sticks in the throat. Actually he was a poor romantic; he kept the best part of himself out of his work. The statement that his most intimate poems lack vigor and masculinity is true. The charge that his nature poetry contains too much nature and too little Whittier is just. The suggestion that his love poems prove he never experienced love is only too plausible. Yet Whittier is not cold; he is rather the warmest poet in the whole New England group. He gives the impression not of a man who lacks fire, but of one who banks it. This was a conscious process dictated by his belief.

Even while holding this view, however, one must recognize that the emotional content of some of Whittier's finest poems is as much the result of the limits of his theory as his nature pictures are the result of the limits of his color-blindness. Take, for example, that much-admired poem **"Telling the Bees."** Whittier's approach to his theme grew directly out of that attitude which we now derisively label "Victorian sentimentality." In **"Marguerite," "The Countess,"** and **"The Bridal of Pennacook"** he dealt with the same theme. We usually say we cannot read those poems because they are sentimental. But **"Telling the Bees"** we are able to read, even though we *do* find it sentimental. Why? In truth it is not because **"Marguerite"** is sentimental that we dislike it, but because it is a bad poem. **"Telling the Bees"** is a good poem, one in which Whittier has induced in us Coleridge's "suspension of disbelief." Whether we share his feeling in general or not is of little importance to our appreciation of the poem. For some he has preserved a mood that has gone out of literature; for others he has expressed a mood that has not gone out of life. Whichever it is, it is something that few poets can do today because they are incapable of Whittier's approach. **"Telling the Bees"** is a good poem not in spite of its sentimentality but in part because of it.

In the same way his successful treatment of some of the lesser emotions may be due to his flight from the greater ones. There is a special tenderness in his work, special because it exists apart from passion. Foregoing the expression of love between the sexes, he became pre-eminently the poet of friendship. This is the emotion of **"My Playmate,"** of **"Benedicite,"** of half a dozen other minor masterpieces. Meeting it in **"Lucy Hooper,"** we forget our objections to worn-out rhymes and conventional images. There is in him, too, a childlike innocence that may be the result of turning his back on life. He preserves all of the kindliness of Christianity and none of its fanaticism. With two or three exceptions his religious poems are imitative and without distinction; but throughout his other work occur lines of religious verse of exceptional grace. He was able also to suggest many vague feelings that are too tenuous for exact phrasing: the nearly pleasurable sadness aroused in old grave-yards, the melancholy of autumn twilights, the stilling effect of "the sea's long level dim with rain." (pp. 335-40)

> *Desmond Powell, "Whittier," in* American Litera-
> ture, *Vol. 9, No. 3, November, 1937, pp. 335-42.*

GEORGE ARMS (essay date 1953)

[*Arms provides a detailed analysis of Whittier's poetry, including "Maud Muller," "Skipper Ireson's Ride," and "The Tent on the Beach." He proposes that the success of some of Whittier's poetry depends on the poet's ability to fuse the subject matter with his own experiences. According to Arms, Whittier's treatment of legends is ineffective because of his lack of historical authority.*]

With everyone else we would admit that for prosiness, emotional flatness, and intellectual emptiness some of Whittier's poems can be surpassed only by diligent search. Yet in one long poem [*Snow-Bound*] his "largeness" is questioned by few, and for other poems a rereading may lead to the admission that we have good reason to remember him. The poet is seldom more imperfectly and infrequently a poet than are those of us who write about him inadequate as critics.

Customarily scholars have divided Whittier's poems into the legendary, antislavery, personal, and religious. Though a simplification of the ten divisions in the collected works, the categories are more logical and useful as a description of subjects than are Whittier's own. Yet both classifications are delusive, for all the poems are personal and transform into personal reminiscence even matter that is remote. We should not confuse this personalizing with romantic confession, for neoclassical restraint made Whittier hesitate to publish poems too "near my heart." But without seeking to unveil the intimately personal, at his best Whittier must make his material relevant to himself. Against his stated preference for "farmer boy and barefoot girl" in the poem on Robert Burns, he frequently writes of "lands of gold and pearl, Of loving knight and lady." Yet he always brings the foreign home and brings the local to his heart—often, it must be admitted, by plain didacticism, but at his most successful with intensity. Thus the New England custom of *Telling the Bees* is presented in terms of the poet's own experience; the antislavery *Ichabod*, one of the few propaganda poems that retain power, transforms a public betrayal into an occasion for private pity; and *The Brewing of Soma* concludes, after eleven stanzas describing Asiatic religious ritual, with the devotional hymn, **"Dear Lord and Father of Mankind."** The poems are not better because they are about

the author; rather Whittier could make them better only when they fuse with his own experience. (pp. 33-4)

Dilution [of Whittier's concept of inner light] did exist, for Whittier was affected by the romanticism of his time, traces of which we most easily discern in the relationship he felt between man and nature and in his view of evil. The healing and rejuvenating power of nature, expanded fitfully to identification and even pantheism, finds place in many of the poems. . . . [Unlike Wordsworth, Whittier] uses nature as little more than the basis of hope. Too often, as in *Summer by the Lakeside,* he expresses the hope with a wearying verboseness; once (*Storm on Lake Asquam*) the hope so permeates the description that he almost suppresses prose exegesis; and upon another occasion (*Pentucket*) he wistfully contrasts the hope of nature with human depravity and achieves greater effectiveness for not trying to explain. Thus in spite of his titling a large section of the collected work "Poems of Nature" and in spite of the presence of many other poems indulging in natural description and philosophizing, neither Wordsworth nor other more radical romantic thinkers entered deeply into Whittier's pages. (pp. 34-5)

In treating evil Whittier shows less the challenge of romantic-transcendental concepts than the superficial benignity of his age. To read *The Reformer* against Hawthorne's *Earth's Holocaust* or *The Fisherman* against *Moby-Dick* makes it plain that Whittier belongs with the easy theologians of the time. He recognized evil, but in the narrative poems he thrust it aside or treated it melodramatically. In the poems on Robert Burns he admits moral faults, and then goes on to declare that they are inessential or to ask forgiveness. Yet when it does not suggest failure to recognize man's full nature, the sense of man's glory in the face of his debasement conveys solid belief at best. Whatever shortcomings we may find here, Whittier does not offend for his affirmation of human dignity and for his ideal of man. His favorite bywords are "order" and "symmetry"—"calm beauty of an ordered life," "the flawless symmetry of man." (p. 35)

Whittier is an uneasy poet in spite of frequent pronouncements which limit, and hence might strengthen, the scope and practice of his muse.

Probably the main trouble is not didacticism, for although Whittier indulges in digressive moralizing he shows no more of it than his background might lead us to expect. In theory he does not incline toward it at all. His critical writing thus neglects and even spurns didactic elements: a review of *Evangeline* commends Longfellow for not displaying social censure; one on Holmes recognizes without rebuke that, far from being a reformer, Holmes almost sympathizes with folly; and an essay on Marvell praises the Puritan poet for being genial, polite, and fashionable. Though Whittier defends didacticism in his own poetry, he also recognizes its limitations. In *The Tent on the Beach* the Traveller (Bayard Taylor) upbraids him because

> You check the free play of your rhymes, to clap
> A moral underneath, and spring it like a trap.

True art, according to the *Proem* and *Dedication*, requires no direct moralizing, though that may find place in lower levels. Morality can get along without the didactic tag: "The whisper of the inward voice Is more than homilies."

Whether Whittier was willing to accept art as an essential expression of life remains at best an open question. No doubt his modest recognition of his own shortcomings influences his scale of values for others. Speaking of an illustrated edition of his poems, he found the pictures "often better than the verses they illustrate." (pp. 35-6)

As a part of this self-sacrificing modesty, one finds a depreciation of art which not only tends to place it low on a scale of values but to split it off altogether.... Whittier's poetry opens the gap still further: art there is the "mockery" of nature. In tributes to contemporary poets the men are divorced from their work, and of himself Whittier wrote, "I am a *man* and not a mere verse-maker." (p. 36)

The sense of dedication [found in his *Proem* (see excerpt above, 1847)] rescues Whittier from what could be an offensive artistic position. Though the split is there, though all too often the Quaker garb hanging loosely over his "restless wings of song" keeps him from happy flights, the man and poet have secured a reconciliation.

Still, the gifts of which Whittier wrote in *Proem* are not those for which we enjoy knowing him. Mostly he was thinking of his antislavery poems, to which he insistently gave a large part of his volumes. At the time he was not justifying such poems as *Telling the Bees, Skipper Ireson's Ride*, and *The Pennsylvania Pilgrim,* for none of these had yet been written. But in retrospect he probably saw, as the retaining of the *Proem* in later collections suggests, that these poems were more acceptable gifts at the shrine of freedom than antislavery propaganda.

The "legendary" poems, however, immediately raise another problem. Just as Whittier was uneasy with art, so he was uneasy with the past that was so much a part of him. He believed in the epic quality of his own age and saw "ancient myth and song and tale" as inadequate to the great political question of his time. The unbalance of this attitude may account for the ludicrous attempt to heroicize a certain Conductor Bradley for his actions at a railroad wreck and for the smug praise of the "moral steam enginery" of his age. Perhaps because he lacked an integrated view of the past, he often introduced the legendary poems with long preludes. These afford a dramatic setting and prepare the readers' emotion for the story that follows, but primarily (as he hints in *The Bridal of Pennacook*) they serve to justify the stories by the personal associations of their scenes. (p. 37)

[Whittier's] most memorable poems of character present no stock figures of virtue or evil, but people to whom Whittier gives depth and solidity of understanding, even while he passes moral judgment. Most are "bad" characters, yet bad characters redeemed by nobility. Webster, in *Ichabod* ..., is the most moving, because he is worst and greatest. This poem on his betrayal in the Seventh of March speech has its inconsequential oratory ("Revile him not, the Tempter hath A snare for all"); but for the greater part diction and imagery are used with dignity. What sustains the poem is the central image of the fallen angel, not presented with metaphorical outspokenness as ornament, but slowly expanded from the "So fallen! so lost!" of the first line to the "fallen angel" in the latter part.

> Of all we loved and honored, naught
>   Save power remains;
> A fallen angel's pride of thought,
>   Still strong in chains.
>
>   (p. 39)

[In *Skipper Ireson's Ride*] one feels solid structure.... Perhaps this happens because the material springs from an evil man

and situation and because Whittier has drawn upon his own boyhood.... It is well to point out that the mob action against Ireson does not receive the moral approval of Whittier, himself by the time of this poem's composition a man who had experienced mob violence. Mediating thus between two forces of evil, Whittier takes time for little more than vivid presentation of the action in the early stanzas. The first stanza with its allusions to the Golden Ass of Apuleius, to the Arabian Nights, and to Mohammed highlights the picturesque with an irresponsible humor that is carried into the later stanzas and the whole tone of the poem:

> The strangest ride that ever was sped
> Was Ireson's, out of Marblehead!
>   Old Floyd Ireson, for his hard heart,
>   Tarred and feathered and carried in a cart
>   By the women of Marblehead!

Until the last two stanzas, all is vigor, and the reader is allowed to draw his own conclusion of the horror beneath it. But at the end Whittier comes close to negating his fine effect when the skipper, crying that the sense of his own evil is greater punishment than tar and feathers, repents with a confession that works well as an indirect plea for his liberation. Though it may be argued that Whittier in thus ending the story merely follows such historical source as he knew, one suspects that if this is so he would not have chosen the story had it ended otherwise. But I am not sure that the genteel intention, made plain by the shift in refrain from "old Floyd" to "poor Floyd," is conveyed in the poem.... After the skipper's supposed repentance the refrain still speaks of his hard heart; and it is with "half scorn, half pity" that the women give him his freedom. The modern reader, at least, skeptically wonders whether the repentance of this Son of Wrath is for the sake of his eternal life or immediate escape, and the poem retains its brutally humorous effect without weakening. (pp. 40-1)

[Most readers] would solidly agree in the dismissal of *Maud Muller*. Furthermore they would have close sympathy with its own author's judgment—for losing patience at the persistent questions of well-intentioned readers, Whittier once wrote that he didn't think the poem worth "serious analysis." To most readers today the poem has become the epitome of all that is bad in Whittier. The contrast between this critical situation and the esteem which the nineteenth century had for the poem suggests *Maud Muller* ... as an important exhibit in Whittier's treatment of character.

Probably the average reader did make an emotional debauch of the poem. What is more, the materials in the poem lent themselves to the same kind of attitude in Whittier. The poor unbred country dweller rescued by a rich and cultivated lover appears close to what he had earlier wished for himself and to what he later piously endorsed in *Among the Hills*. But in *Maud Muller* he shows consciousness of the corrosive sentimentality implicit in such a situation. Of this view, the reputedly infamous couplet is at the heart:

> For of all sad words of tongue or pen,
> The saddest are these: "It might have been!"

For the casual reader the words are sad because a country Cinderella has missed her chance, but in the context they are sad because of the emotional waste that the judge and Maud suffer by giving these words their allegiance. In the lines that go before, Whittier says this as plainly as he needs to:

> Alas for maiden, alas for Judge,
> For rich repiner and household drudge!

God pity them both! and pity us all,
Who vainly the dreams of youth recall.

The qualification that immediately follows the crucial "might have been" ("Ah, well! for us all some sweet hope lies Deeply buried from human eyes") does not weaken by excuse. Rather, it strengthens by urging an extenuation of vain mortality as an imperfect type of spiritual yearning. In the characterization of the man and girl, Whittier has prepared us for this with an insight that commands respect. At the time he does it one is not altogether sure whether he attempts irony in having the judge look back at Maud and think of her wisdom and goodness just when she indulges in an egocentric daydream of herself as a grand lady. But as the story continues and as the judge and Maud marry with members of their classes, the suspicion becomes a certainty. Not desiring to make his heroine a monster, he still makes her an object of pity—and this not for her rural marriage but for her false dream.

For our own delight as well as for the poet's repute, it is a pity that Whittier could not treat his good characters more often in this mood. On one or two other occasions he does it less sharply, as with the members of the family circle in *Snow-Bound* or with Pastorius in *The Pennsylvania Pilgrim*. But in the better of these two poems, it must be remembered that the picture of rural innocence secures effective relief from the exotic Harriet Livermore. In many others, whether the characters are out of a legendary past or out of childhood experience, unrelieved sweetness causes the reader to fret not only for that in itself but for the apparent license to artistic abandonment that it bestows upon the poet. *In School-Days* shows what may happen, and is a better spot for making an attack against Whittier than *Maud Muller*. (pp. 41-2)

On the other hand, when character is realized, the whole poem emerges integral and direct. Something more might be desired for *Skipper Ireson's Ride*, but within their kind *Ichabod* and *Maud Muller* are perfect. In the poem on Webster we have seen Whittier's ability in sustaining his metaphor; and in that on Maud he shows precision in his handling of the main issue. Given the ingredients, Whittier can make a poem on many counts, and in *Maud Muller* we may properly suspect a pun when the girl dreams, thinking of the judge as taking the place of her real husband, that "joy was duty and love was *law*." Also in this poem we find a sense of narrative technique that could hardly be bettered. Instead of the long introductory description typical in Whittier, the scene is set in a single couplet.

Maud Muller on a summer's day
Raked the meadow sweet with hay.

To the "meadow sweet with hay" in the first stanza, a "mock-bird" and a "far-off town" are added in the next few, both properties that anticipate the demands of the drama. The judge enters, talks with Maud, rides away. Paralleling the immediate response of the two, glimpses are given of their later regret. And the story, with a quotation drawn from Maud's own musing, is quickly concluded.

Something about economy of narrative has already been said for *The Pennsylvania Pilgrim*, and a good deal more will be said for *Snow-Bound*. But perhaps *Barbara Frietchie* . . . affords the most convincing example. The setting, a little more discursive than that of *Maud*, is still far from leisurely. Rather than using properties with symbolic intent, Whittier mostly prepares for the story by a remarkable use of prepositions: "*Up* from the meadows," "*Round about* them," "*Over* the mountains." With another step toward the main action, we come

back to the first preposition and get it three times more—"*Up* rose old Barbara Frietchie," "She took *up* the flag," "*Up* the street came the rebel tread"—and conclude the sequence with its reverse as Stonewall Jackson appears:

Under his slouched hat left and right
He glanced; the old flag met his sight.

In eight rapid couplets the flag is fired upon, rescued, and its rescuer defended by the general. In the remaining nine, day ebbs, the two protagonists die, and the poem concludes with an elegiac fitness that contrasts the repose with the earlier action, the evening with the "pleasant morn" that began the story, and the stars of the flag with those of the scene. In this closing couplet the vertical movement of the "up" prepositions is also recalled:

And ever the stars above look down
On thy stars below in Frederick town!

The poem has blemishes—why Whittier had to resort to such wooden phrasing to achieve rhyme as "fruited deep" and "royal will" when in the same poem he rhymed "staff" and "scarf" challenges explanation. Nor can I excuse Whittier for attributing to Jackson "a blush of shame," in spite of the later couplet honoring Jackson and the sense that throughout the poem Jackson plays a more interesting part than Barbara Frietchie and emerges the better from it. Yet with its faults, the poem seems to me as fine as any done of a Civil War episode, belonging with Melville's *Sheridan at Cedar Creek* and with no other narrative poem of the war. (pp. 42-4)

The one poem by which Whittier is almost universally esteemed, even in our reaction against him, remains for consideration. With *Snow-Bound* . . . he reached for once on a large scale that harmony in art which he seems to have achieved during the greater part of his life only in spirit. For this poem belonged to his being as much as *Huckleberry Finn* to Mark Twain's, and we shall not err by regarding it with the same love and honor. (pp. 44-5)

Beyond the realistic details [of the poem] but arising from them is a symbolic richness . . . , though not in an immediately accurate way. Epigraphs—the woodfire of Cornelius Agrippa that "drives away dark spirits" and the radiant fireplace of Emerson's *Snow Storm* that provides a haven against the cold—make plain the major symbol. The building of the fire on the third night expands it, as does the covering of the fire when the evening ends. . . . But if the hearth gives us the major symbol and scene of the central action, the poem does not limit itself to this. So completely has the poet felt his material that all is fused. Even the coat of "homespun stuff" and the "low rhythm" of the ocean in the first strophe take on overtones. Furthermore, the poet shows so much certainty in his use of the fireplace as symbol that he is able to suggest qualification when at the end of the week the family is no longer a unit in its isolation.

The chill embargo of the snow
Was melted in the genial glow,

but the glow this time belongs to the world and not the domestic hearth.

The poem has led into this insight—one which prevents it from being disposed of as sentimental—by the mother's prayer for uncomforted strangers and by the summons she receives to help a neighbor. The schoolmaster and the eccentric guest have also furnished preparation in their contrast with the family group. Both represent a culture which though indigenous contrasts with the rustic family's "common unrhymed poetry Of simple life and country ways." (pp. 45-6)

There are three major passages in which [Whittier's anti-slavery sentiment] appears: the first, at the beginning of the characterizations of the family circle when a schoolbook poem that is recited allows digression into the poet's later abolitionist activity; the second, when the schoolmaster is described as the type of those who will lead the postwar settlement of the issue; and the third, in the epilogue, when social responsibilities are contrasted with private reverie. The first passage is most out of context and can only be justified by its shock of surprise and by its later reinforcement. The last passage is stated in terms so general that if we did not see the connection between its closing line ("The century's aloe flowers to-day") and the aloe of the later *Pennsylvania Pilgrim,* its reference to the slavery issue might escape us.

The second passage is the crucial one and explains why the others are not outside the bounds of the poem. The schoolmaster and the eccentric are both of the world and both destined to play an important part in it. One enters into a course that represents a sterile and self-indulgent religious fanaticism, while the other vigorously rights social wrong. Though we may well wish that Whittier had followed Emerson in recognizing the potential self-indulgence of reformers and though the second coming of Christ (which Harriet Livermore prophesied) has more potential significance than the Thirteenth Amendment, we should recognize that for Whittier and most of his contemporaries slavery was the moral issue of the age, "the century's aloe," just as the absolute state is of ours. Even if we differ from his implication that the moral issue must be public or from his choice of this particular issue, we may regard it as a poetical counter that serves its purpose in the poem. Using both the genial glow of the world and its sufferings as countersuggestion to domesticity, Whittier has also modified the idyllic dream for one of "larger hopes and graver fears."

It might be urged against the poem that the elegiac meditations, which like the antislavery passages appear on three occasions, are excrescences too. That so far as I know they have not been thus regarded makes a direct defense unnecessary. But they may help us to see how intensely the poem is organized. Though upon two occasions they come just before the antislavery lines (a juxtaposition that has its point), we have even less right to dismiss them as clichés of nineteenth-century emotion. The central intent of the poem is not to memorialize a way of life (whether agrarian or domestic) that has been lost to an urban world, but rather to memorialize life that is always lost to death. (pp. 46-7)

> George Arms, "Whittier," in his The Fields Were Green: A New View of Bryant, Whittier, Holmes, Lowell, and Longfellow, with a Selection of Their Poems, *Stanford University Press, 1953, pp. 33-89.*

HOWARD MUMFORD JONES (essay date 1957)

[*A distinguished twentieth-century American critic, humanist, and literary scholar, Jones is noted for his illuminating commentary on American culture and literature. Awarded the Pulitzer Prize for his study of the formation of American culture in* O Strange New World, *he is also acclaimed for his criticism in* The Theory of American *and similar works in which he examines the relationship between America's literary and cultural development. In the following assessment of Whittier's writing, Jones concedes that Whittier is given to elaborate sentimentality, but points to a* "vein of honest simplicity" *in the poet's work which* "anticipates and parallels . . . Robert Frost." *Jones also analyzes Whittier's religious verse, which he considers his greatest achievement. Unlike many critics, however, Jones asserts that Whittier's ballads are not successful.*]

Is Whittier no more than a producer of rhymed rhetoric that, however effective in its time, has lost its fire and energy? Is there no portion of his work that can still give aesthetic pleasure? If we will but remember Pater's injunction that beauty has been produced in many periods in many styles and in many forms, I think one can find even today a small but permanent portion of beauty in Whittier. That portion is not, I think, in popular and facile successes like **"Maud Muller"** and **"Barbara Frietchie,"** but is rather found in three sorts of poems: those in which he writes about nature in New England; those in which (alas, too rarely!) he presents character; and those which concern—how shall I put it?—his notion of the relation of God and man.

One must distinguish between sentimentality and simplicity. Whittier, however manly in his private life, is incorrigibly given to sentimentality—far more so than is Longfellow. But there is in him likewise a vein of honest simplicity, particularly when he looks at the natural world about him, that anticipates and parallels the later effects of Robert Frost. (pp. 236-37)

The secret of the excellence of [Whittier's poem] **"Abraham Davenport"** lies in its fusion of low relief with salient observations. The metrical tone is faint, like Crabbe's, but the pattern is always *there,* is always gently persistent so that it can carry even the formal description of the threatening sky without melodrama. Against its gentle beat various important observations seem projected by an impulse that is partly respect, partly humor. We laugh at what we love, and, obviously, Whittier loves Abraham Davenport and can therefore afford to laugh at him a little. Note the amusing repetition of verbs placed first in the line, towards the end of the second section— "roosted," "lowed," "flitted," and then the variation that follows—"men prayed and women wept." The deliberate simplicity of

> "Bring in the candles." And they brought them in,

cannot be bettered in its place, nor can the contrast between the husky voice and shaking hands of the Speaker and the mock solemnity of

> An act to amend an act to regulate
> The shad and alewise fisheries.

The writer is so at ease with his material, he can take time out for a little play with figures of speech and figures of arithmetic; and even the last line, which in another poem—say, **"Conductor Bradley"**—might be tedious, is caught up in the wonderful atmosphere of irony and heroism, admiration and anticlimax Whittier achieves. Indeed, the irony of the penultimate

> A witness to the ages as they pass

might be that of Frost or Robinson.

Whittier's ballads seldom come off, but *Snow-Bound: A Winter Idyl* remains a delight to those capable of reading it. I say "capable of reading it" for the reason that Whittier, like Mendelssohn, cannot be approached as if he were Bartok or Ives. The poem overcomes its flaws. The little sketches of personalities and the reflections they occasion are admirable in their kind; and, somehow, the final address to the "Angel of the backward look," despite its obviousness, does not offend, it fits the mood of the poem, placing "these Flemish pictures of old days" in right perspective. The work *is* an idyl (we commonly overlook the sub-title) and is therefore entitled to its mood of idyllic nostalgia for something lovely and lost. The opening is properly famous; and the line-by-line heaping up of detail about the storm and about the effect of the storm upon human life has the ring of truth and simplicity. . . . The [reader] hears an admonition in *Snow-Bound*: an admonition not too hastily to throw away the past. In the poem the beauty of memory is made the more poignant because of the

> restless sands' incessant fall,

the importunate hours that bid

> The dreamer leave his dream midway.

> (pp. 242-43)

Religious verse of the first water by American writers is small in quantity, but to this small anthology of Christian utterance Whittier contributes. The instinct that breaks **"The Eternal Goodness"** into smaller units and uses these for singing in our Protestant churches is, I think, sound. To be sure, God is also a mighty fortress, but there are many mansions in heaven with room for gentleness and peace. In such poems Whittier is at his best unsurpassed. What writer in English can better the serenity of stanzas like these?

> And so beside the Silent Sea
>   I wait the muffled oar;
> No harm from Him can come to me
>   On ocean or on shore.
>
> I know not where His islands lift
>   Their fronded palms in air;
> I only know I cannot drift
>   Beyond His love and care.

Whittier has, I suppose, only so much of mysticism as the Quaker faith allows. His poetry expresses no dark night of the soul; yet, believing that

> God should be most where man is least,

he has his flashes of marvelous quietude:

> Where pity dwells, the peace of God is there,

he writes in one poem, and in another:

> Here let me pause, my quest forego;
> Enough for me to feel and know
> That He in whom the cause and end,
> The past and future, meet and blend,—
> Who, girt with his Immensities,
> One vast and star-hung system sees,
> Small as the clustered Pleiades,—
> Moves not alone the heavenly quires,
> But waves the spring-time's grassy spires,
> Guards not archangel feet alone,
> But deigns to guide and keep my own.

There are too many S-sounds in the antepenultimate line in this passage, but this, one of the best portions of **"Questions of Life,"** seems to me finely fashioned. Here again, however, diffuseness is the fatal flaw. **"Andrew Rykman's Prayer,"** which has all the potentialities of a notable religious expression, goes on and on. The present state of literary criticism is indifferent or hostile to religious poetry unless it take the form of high church Anglicanism; and so we forget that no American writer has more finely phrased a trust in the goodness of God. (pp. 243-44)

[In Whittier's works] Time is incessant, Time takes away the loveliest and the best, Time closes the school-house by the road, and Time occasions the much quoted "moral" of **"Maud Muller."** There is here no originality of thought or of interpretation, but Whittier again and again avails himself of what I may call the temporal fallacy to achieve his poetical effects. Thus *Snow-Bound* is seen, as it were, down a long tunnel of Time, its colors the clearer, its outlines the sharper by reason of the fact that the poet is almost sixty; and Whittier most applauds those who can look through the veil of Time and know it for illusion. . . . Contrasts of time and eternity are the commonplaces of poetry; my point is only that in so far as he is mystic, Whittier, troubled by the "harder task of standing still," as he somewhere says, meets the implications of time more immediately as a part of his problem of faith and progress than careless readers perceive. You can see him at his obvious worst on this theme in a poem like **"The New Year,"** but you can also find his unexpected excellence in a poem like **"The Prayer of Agassiz:"**

> Him, the endless, unbegun,
> The Unnamable, the One
> Light of all our Light the Source,
> Life of life, and Force of force.

But one returns, as one must always return in this category of his art, to the marvel of stanzas like these from **"Our Master:"**

> But warm, sweet, tender, even yet
>   A present help is He;
> And faith has still its Olivet,
>   And love its Galilee.
>
> The healing of His seamless dress
>   Is by our beds of pain;
> We touch Him in life's throng and press,
>   And we are whole again.

Not even the seventeenth century can surpass this simple perfection of religious statement. (pp. 245-46)

> *Howard Mumford Jones, "Whittier Reconsidered,"*
> in Essex Institute Historical Collections, *Vol. XCIII,*
> *No. 4, October, 1957, pp. 231-46.*

HYATT H. WAGGONER (essay date 1959)

[*In the following excerpt, Waggoner assesses Whittier's religious poetry and argues that its value exceeds that of devotional verse; instead, it is "readable as poetry." The one aspect that most dates Whittier's poems, according to Waggoner, is his unremitting belief in progress. For additional commentary by Waggoner, see excerpt below, 1984.*]

Whittier's poetry most typically is not simply "old-fashioned:" it is almost the exact counterpart of the kind of poetry that the modern poets have taught us to like and to think of as good. If James's idea that what is stated is not literature and what is literature is not stated is the whole truth, then most of Whittier's poetry is not literature. It states, emphatically. It aims to convey truth and to influence moral attitudes. It is relaxed, ruminative, placid, unambiguous, "thin." It is almost never dramatic even when it deals, as it so often does, with people, and irony is generally confined to the unread poems of reform. In the classroom most of the poetry is, unfortunately, useful in a way that does Whittier's memory no good: it illustrates what Eliot meant by the concept of the "dissociation of sensibility." . . . Anthology pieces like **"The Barefoot Boy"** and **"Barbara Frietchie"** have become children's classics, but we are likely to feel that the absence in them of any sign of the critical intelligence at work is fatal. (pp. 32-3)

Whittier's own self-estimate in **"Proem"** [see excerpt above, 1847] as an "untaught" versifier whose only claim to fame is that he put his verse, such as it was, to work in the service of Duty and offered it at Freedom's shrine, is too modest. Unless we are prepared to argue that typically contemporary taste and critical theory are the only defensible taste and theory, unless we are ready consciously to absolutize the relative, we had better admit that poetry which generally lacks distinction on the purely verbal level, as *style,* may yet have other qualities that make it memorable as poetry. Only if we can bring ourselves to grant that a lack of irony, ambiguity, and other hallmarks of the modern mind, and a fondness for plain statement, are qualities not necessarily fatal to poetry, can we attain a position from which it is possible to make even a limited claim for Whittier as a poet. If we can assume that a taste in poetry catholic enough to include the best of Whittier need not be a sign of confusion or lack of critical standards we need say no more at the moment of his failures and move on to consider what he accomplished at his best.

Whittier's contemporaries read him chiefly as a religious poet, and I think we shall have to also, if we are to continue to read him at all. He is I think one of a rather small number of religious poets in America whose work is still readable as poetry and not just as devotional exercise. (pp. 33-4)

One large section of the final edition of his poetry arranged by Whittier himself is labelled "Religious Poems," but most of his best poetry might very appropriately have been so labelled, and much of his best religious poetry is to be found in other sections of his book, in "Poems of Nature," for instance, and "Anti-Slavery Poems" and "Poems Subjective and Reminiscent." Paradoxically, it might be said that Whittier's poetry is most effectively religious when it is not explicitly "religious poetry," and that his poems of nature and reform are seldom memorable except when they are informed by a strongly religious feeling. The very flat songs of labor are a case in point, and the poems of nature written after the Civil War are another. Only when the objects of nature serve as "attendant angels to the house of prayer" do the nature poems generally rise much above the level of the honest and conscientious. In short, the well-known hymns like **"Dear Lord and Father of Mankind"** express a feeling that is almost never absent from the best poetry but seldom well expressed directly.

Whittier shared, of course—both as a devout Quaker and as a man of his time and place—the tendency of nineteenth-century Protestantism to reduce religion to a matter of feeling and action in good causes, to deny the validity of religious *thought* and create a "religion of the heart." Anti-intellectualism frequently makes the positive religious affirmations in his poetry seem sentimental. His deep piety and his detestation of "the husks of creed" often combine to produce mere emphatic exhortations to faith instead of successful communications of religious thought or experience. But when he writes not of faith as such but of what he sees as the Christian demand for justice and love, he speaks with passion, with fire, and often with a fine control. Whittier's conscience was not just sensitive, it was informed, grounded in and directed by a deep understanding of the whole Gospel that he never, despite the doubts that troubled him, ceased to hold up as the controlling image in his

life. He fully anticipated the Social Gospel movement on its positive side without falling into its religious negativism. He saw formal creeds separating men and repudiated them for this and other reasons, but he felt that an untheological Biblical faith could draw men together and constituted the only unanswerable argument for reform.

Some of the finest invective poetry ever written in America resulted from his feeling of what was demanded by his faith. (pp. 34-5)

His authentic voice comes through to us very clearly, and without suffering by comparison with any other poet in America in the nineteenth century, in such poems as **"Clerical Oppressors," "Official Piety," "The Gallows," "Lines on the Portrait of a Celebrated Publisher," "Letter: From a Missionary of the Methodist Episcopal Church South, in Kansas, to a Distinguished Politician,"** and **"On a Prayer-book: With Its Frontispiece, Ary Scheffer's 'Christus Consolator,' Americanized by the Omission of the Black Man."** The voice here is angry, even outraged, but never self-righteous or shrill or merely moralistic. Here for once Whittier is even capable of a kind of humor, as he registers the gap between word and deed and explores the characteristics of a "dead" faith. The result is a group of jeremiads that often rise to thoroughly effective satire and usually contain at least a few lines of memorable invective. (pp. 35-6)

[The prelude to **"Among the Hills"**] is good didactic poetry. Though it is above Whittier's average performance in its succinct wit, there is a good deal more like it. To dismiss Whittier's poems of reform as versified propaganda, as we have tended to do, is easier if we have not read them than if we have. In Whittier's best work we have an expression of the religious conscience at its purest and best. If all the reformers of the age had had Whittier's humility and his faith and vision, Hawthorne might not have been moved to satirize reformism in *The Blithedale Romance* or James in *The Bostonians*. Whittier's anti-slavery poems are not irrelevant to us because legal slavery no longer exists, nor is their relevance simply a function of the fact that the fight for justice and freedom and brotherhood is never ended. The poems themselves supply the explanation of their continuing vitality: they are not propaganda verse so much as they are visions of the great society. . . . (p. 36)

Perhaps the aspect of the thought in Whittier's poems that most dates them today is the unfailing faith in progress. When he writes of progress in the abstract, that is, of Progress, the result is usually no better than **"The Psalm of Life."** On this subject Whittier had no guide but what he once called the "moral steam-enginery" of his age. But these passages are easy to winnow out, and they are not a good enough reason for forgetting the rest of his work. Whittier had more Hope than we generally have in this unhopeful age, in both the strict Pauline and the Quaker sense. But though we find it difficult to respond readily to cheerful writing, we ought to recognize that Whittier is, at his best at any rate, saved from the inanities of a too easy faith by his belief that social progress and individual redemption are not unrelated and that neither is automatic or inevitable. He knew that man had to choose, and that choice was not easy or success guaranteed. His life-long devotion to "liberal" causes can only be fully understood when we realize the extent to which he was "conservative"—in the only viable sense of the term. The "eternal step of Progress" that resounds through his poetry is finally reducible to faith in God's finding willing hands to do His work. We need not share this faith to agree that it is not inane or necessarily unintelligent. (p. 38)

[There were] two subjects on which Whittier could feel without distrusting his feelings, think without distrusting his thought, and write without distrusting his symbols—the demands of the religious conscience, and the experiences of childhood. **"Snow-Bound,"** which is certainly his finest poem, but which has been widely enough and well enough appreciated so that it has seemed unnecessary to add any further comment of my own— **"Snow-Bound"** shows us what he could do with the latter subject: he could create out of it one of the most memorable poems in nineteenth century American literature. The familiar **"Ichabod"** or **"Massachusetts to Virginia"**—or, perhaps better because fresher for us, **"Official Piety"**—show us what kind of poetry he could make out of moral feeling. These and others like them are distinguished works of art, for which no apology whatever is needed. Whether they are "great" poems or not is arguable, but they certainly seem to me very much alive.

Whittier's claim for himself was typical of the man, modest and just and true. "What I had I gave." I think we should decide that what he had was no major poetic talent, and the talent he had was weakened a good deal of the time by an outlook that made him distrust symbolization, but what he had was well worth the giving. Not just American life but American poetry too is richer because he lived and wrote. (pp. 39-40)

> *Hyatt H. Waggoner, "What I Had I Gave: Another Look at Whittier," in* Essex Institute Historical Collections, *Vol. XCV, No. 1, January, 1959, pp. 32-40.*

JOHN B. PICKARD (essay date 1960)

[*A noted Whittier critic, Pickard is a descendant of Whittier's "official" biographer, Samuel T. Pickard. Pickard considers Whittier's ballads his greatest achievement, but admits that they are often marred by "digressions and extravagant romantic phrasing." "Skipper Ireson's Ride" is, according to Pickard, the most outstanding ballad in nineteenth-century American literature. Pickard also provides a detailed analysis of Whittier's ballads and concludes that these poems enable Whittier to claim a place among "America's finest creators of historical and traditional narrative."*]

[Whittier's] first collection of poems and tales, *Legends of New England,* dealt entirely with local traditions and superstitions. They are marred by digressions and extravagant romantic phrasing and employ the typical Gothic devices of doomed lovers, ghostly ships, and hidden horrors. However, one ballad, **"The Black Fox,"** has a sure poetic beat and adapts its subject and content to the ballad tradition of simplicity. The introduction to the poem re-creates the atmosphere of a winter's evening in rural New England with a clearness of language and simplicity of diction that indicate Whittier's ballad capabilities:

> Around an ancient fireplace,
>   A happy household drew;
> A husband and his own good wife
>   And children not a few;
> And bent above the spinning wheel
>   The aged grandame too.

The grandmother is an excellent choice as a narrator with her homespun descriptions and superstitious nature, while her account of the mysterious activities of the black fox effectively conveys rural delight in the supernatural. Though the story is artificial, even sentimental in parts, it minimizes Gothic horror and eliminates moralizing—a marked improvement on Whittier's other ballad attempts.

Another early ballad was **"The Song of the Vermonters."** . . . Its theme, a rallying cry for all patriotic Vermonters to defend their state during a revolutionary invasion, is an obvious imitation of Scott's border romances; while its form, rhyming couplets with a basic anapestic beat, give a martial ring to the whole:

> Ho—all to the borders! Vermonters, come down,
> With your breeches of deerskin and jackets of brown;
> With your red woolen caps, and your moccasins, come,
> To the gathering summons of trumpet and drum.

The poem's local color descriptions of the countryside, boastful praise of Vermont's qualities, and defiant challenge to "all the world" are conscious attempts to present the song as an authentic ballad. In fact, Whittier predated the poem, 1779 [although it was first published in 1833]. Despite its rhetorical air, characteristic moralizing, and poetic language, many sections do accord with good ballad presentation. This poem indicates how close Whittier was to having the right medium for expressing his deep-rooted feelings about the New England past. (pp. 58-9)

[**"The Hunters of Men"**] is a caustic satire on the newest Southern amusement, the tracking down of escaped slaves. Opening his poem in the best chivalric manner, Whittier establishes the atmosphere of a medieval chase with his invitation for all to come hunting:

> Have ye heard of our hunting, o'er mountain and glen,
> Through crane-brake and forest,—the hunting of men?
> The lords of our land to this hunting have gone,
> As the fox-hunter follows the sound of the horn;
> Hark! the cheer and the hallo! the crack of the whip.

The archaic words, the courtly adjectives, and the titling of the hunters as "lords" are all devices of olden romances; while the use of a refrain, "the hunting of men," and the conscious repetitions of similar phrases and sound patterns are part of established ballad technique. These gracious phrases and romantic images are ironically contrasted with the inhuman end of the hunt—the killing of men. With heavy-handed satire Whittier continues this romantic pretense throughout the poem: "Gay luck to our hunters," "Oh, goodly and grand is our hunting to see," and "Ho, alms for our hunters." The irony fails when Whittier depicts priests, politicians, mothers, and daughters merrily hunting the slaves—Whittier had not yet learned the restraint and understatement necessary for finished satiric art and essential to valid ballad creation.

One of his first real ballads was **"The Exiles."** . . . It shows how a decade of abolitionist work had matured him; and, conversely, how far he had yet to go for poetic maturity. Certainly his abolitionist writing had enlarged his sense of the dramatic, developed his awareness of emotional appeal, and taught him the necessity of direct statement and common words. The plot of **"The Exiles"** was aptly suited to ballad demands for an exciting, realistic narrative, since it was the tale of Thomas Macy's flight down the Merrimack River to escape persecution for harboring Quakers. Its theme, the dramatic struggle of one man against existing injustice, stressed the value of inner principle over outward law. Everything was within the range of Whittier's talents and interests, for he had grown up in the Merrimack valley and the greater part of his life had been spent fighting for freedom and resisting intolerance. Yet he failed to develop the poem artistically. In the first place the poem is overly long (sixty stanzas); it abounds in digressions and numerous pious interjections by the author; and finally, its labored

The Whittier homestead, located outside Haverhill, Massachusetts. This homestead is depicted in Whittier's Snow-bound: A Winter Idyl.

comparisons and sentimental tone ignore the realism and simplicity of good balladry. Over half the poem deals with a wordy description of the fleeing Quaker, his being sheltered by Macy, and eventual capture—all of which distract from the central drama of Macy's courage and flight. Throughout there are numerous lapses into poetic diction, such as "plashing on its pebbled shore," "How pale Want alternated / with Plenty's golden smile," and "vile scoffer." Structurally the poem fails to preserve dramatic suspense as Whittier interjects his own personal views, like "of his bondage hard and long . . . it suits not our tale to tell" and of Macy's trials on Nantucket after his escape, "Behold is it not written / In the annals of the isle."

On the credit side is the fine ballad meter used by Whittier and touches in the story demonstrate how naturally he could portray characters and how realistically he could sketch in background settings. The inner serenity of the old Quaker is described as the covering of "autumn's moonlight," while the frustrated priest is seen with his "grave cocked hat" gone and his dishevelled wig hanging behind him "like some owl's nest . . . upon a thorn." The flight of Macy down the Merrimack is simply presented through selected scenes of nearby communities:

> The fisher wives of Salisbury—
> The men were all away—
> Looked out to see the stranger oar
> Upon their waters play.

Deer Island's rocks and fir-trees threw
> Their sunset-shadows o'er them,
And Newbury's spire and weathercock
> Peered o'er the pines before them.

"Cassandra Southwick" . . . shows a considerable advance over **"The Exiles"** in dramatic structure and presentation. Here, too, the incident is one culled from the history of Quaker persecutions; but, instead of trying to relate the complete story behind Cassandra's imprisonment, Whittier concentrates on the attempt of Governor Endicott to have the maid sold as a slave. The early section of the poem as Cassandra waits in prison sentimentalizes her devout nature and overuses Biblical phrasing and allusion. However, once dawn breaks and she leaves for the wharves, the movement is swift and dramatic. The small details like the hoar frost melting on the walls, the laughter and idle words of the crowd, Cassandra's maiden shame under the hostile gaze of the assembled mob, and her pathetic prayer for aid convey the tenseness of the moment as she walks toward the docks. The next two stanzas show Whittier's art at its best, precise, exact, and selective. With briefest possible detail the atmosphere of a seaport town is presented. . . . All the characters are generalized, but their very indefiniteness adds to the mood of suspense and uneasiness. . . . [The] nucleus of the story is well told and it does have a swift narrative movement. Whittier's use of the first person narrator gives an immediacy and interest to the whole; while the repetitions of key words, the series of "and" connectives, and the parallelisms of adjectives and nouns create a definite folk flavor in the poem.

The imagery is of the simplest kind: the captain growls back his answer "like the roaring of the sea," Rawson's cheek is "wine-empurpled," and Endicott looks at the disapproving crowd with a "lion glare." Though the poem is overlong, a bit didactic and melodramatic, it is a long step from the discursive and dramatically weak **"The Exiles."** Whittier had found his proper subject matter and was now approaching surety of presentation.

Another ballad of the same year, **"The New Wife and the Old,"** deals with a local superstition which Whittier had heard as a child about the power of dead spirits. Though its consciously set mood of terror is somewhat reminiscent of Gothic narrative, its excellent style holds the reader's interest:

> Dark the halls, and cold the feast
> Gone the bridemaids, gone the priest.
> All is over, all is done.
>
> . . . . .
>
> Hushed within and hushed without,
> Dancing feet and wrestlers' shout;
> Dies the bonfire on the hill;
> All is dark and all is still.

The repetitions of similar verb patterns and the balance of phrases with their recurrence in later stanzas establishes a mood of waiting and anxiety. The resulting drama does not quite live up to this effective introduction as the young bride has her wedding ring and bracelet melodramatically stolen by the ghost of a former wife. Near the end of the story, interest switches from the terror and wonder of the new bride to an examination of the sinful conscience of the older husband. Also Whittier upsets the unity of the story by musing on the supernatural reasons for the dead wife's action. Still, the ballad technique is sure and the story does concentrate on the one main incident without undue digression or moralizing. (pp. 59-63)

[The ballad **"Kathleen"**] shows Whittier's complete mastery of ballad technique. Purporting to be a tale of old Ireland and sung by a wandering Irish scholar, the poem does not have a local theme, but its content and style are handled in traditional ballad manner. Briefly, the story relates the selling of a beautiful Irish girl to the American colonies by her cruel stepmother, a later rescue by a young lover, and a safe return to her sorrowing father. The first stanzas immediately begin the narrative with the marriage of the "mighty lord" of Galaway to another wife, while the second stanza marks out the conflict in the ballad, the new wife's favoring of her own kin to the neglect of Kathleen. A few stanzas later, Kathleen is introduced and warning is given of her coming doom. In traditional ballad fashion dialogue is used throughout to convey feeling and action; no motivation is given for the stepmother's sudden decision to sell Kathleen; and there is no plausible explanation for her triumph over the old lord's love for his daughter. The art in these following stanzas is a thing of utmost simplicity.

> He smoothed and smoothed her hair away,
>   He kissed her forehead fair;
> "It is my darling Mary's brow,
>   It is my darling's hair!"
>
> Oh, then spake up the angry dame,
>   "Get up, get up," quoth she,
> "I'll sell ye over Ireland,
>   I'll sell ye o're the sea!"

This simple, objective tone is preserved throughout and the scholar's final summation, in perfect keeping with his function

as a wandering minstrel, provides the desired happy ending. Noticeable, too, is the absence of sophisticated imagery; only the most conventional descriptions are given, as the girl is "fair" and "the flower of Ireland"; her arm is "snowy-white" and her hand, "snow-white"; while the stepmother is seen as "angry" and "evil." This ballad readily illustrates the progress Whittier had made from his early uneven, discursive ballads. (pp. 63-4)

[Whittier's **"Skipper Ireson's Ride"** can be considered] his masterpiece and the best American ballad of the nineteenth century.

The ballad opens slowly, comparing the strangeness and wonder of Floyd Ireson's ride out of Marblehead to all the other famous rides of story and rhyme. The refrain at the end, which is repeated in each stanza with slight variations, gives the essence of the story, though it does not tell us why the skipper was driven out. The second stanza puts the reader immediately *in medias res,* as we watch the tarred and feathered skipper driven through the main streets of Marblehead by the enraged populace. The description is precise and graphic. (p. 65)

The ballad succeeds because of its dramatic structure, sure handling of details, definite localization, simplicity of diction, and the "psychology" indigenous to New England. The whole poem centralizes on one incident, Skipper Ireson's ride from Marblehead. Like "Sir Patrick Spens," the story is based on a conflict of loyalties and gives us no description of the central incident; the sinking of the ship is merely indicated by a brief dialogue, while its effects are seen in the actions of the women. Throughout, the author is impersonal, employing terse dialogue to keep the action objective and straightforward. And there is no moral attached; for it is organic with the story itself. The variations within the ballad, from the outward crowd scene to a flashback, then to the crowd again and to the final sudden psychological twist, are masterful; and they sustain interest. Whittier was to write other fine ballads—some more famous—but none were to equal the harmony of content and form which he achieved here. . . .

Whittier's most famous ballad, **"Barbara Frietchie,"** perfectly exemplifies . . . the ballad approach. The incident—the courage of an old lady in waving a Union flag before the conquering rebel troops—was supposedly a true one. It was written in the heat of the crucial battle year of 1863 and embodied Whittier's passionate belief that fundamentally many Southern rebels loved the Union as he did. (p. 67)

The story is told in the simplest of all verse forms, rhyming couplets of four beats a line, separated into stanzas. The stage for the drama is set by the few suggestive details, evoking the environs of Frederick town and the luxuriant land, ripe for harvest: "meadows rich with corn," and "apple and peach tree fruited deep." The action proper begins with the entrance of the "famished rebel horde" into the town and the disappearance of the Union flags:

> Forty flags with their silver stars,
> Forty flags with their crimson bars,
>
> Flapped in the morning wind: the sun
> Of noon looked down, and saw not one.

These lines have a perfect ballad movement, and a continuing economy of detail sweeps the drama along: the ranks of soldiers are "dust-brown"; and their leader, Stonewall Jackson, is characterized by his "slouched hat" and impetuous order to shoot the flag down. Barbara Frietchie's act in waving the torn flag and her address to the rebels, "Shoot if you must this old grey head, / But spare your country's flag," are melodramatic, as is Jackson's blush of shame and order to his troops to spare the woman. Yet, the unpolished and highly emotional presentation of the scene is in keeping with the manner of true balladry, where subtlety is a thing unknown. The theatrical nature of Barbara Frietchie's and Jackson's acts heightens the climax and strikingly illustrates the theme. Her successful defense of the flag is underscored by Whittier's picture of it waving over the heads of the rebel host, and leads to the ending tribute, "Flag of Freedom and Union, wave." By means of this simple story, Whittier echoed the thoughts and emotions of an entire country. No other Civil War poem, save Walt Whitman's "Oh Captain, My Captain," was so definitely the product of an hour and so quickly recognized by the people as an expression of their feelings. (pp. 68-9)

["**The Henchman**"] demonstrates his mastery of ballad techniques. . . . [It] has no moral, but it is entirely different in tone and presentation. The poem is a love song, chanted exultantly and hopefully by the lover in praise of his lady. The imagery is rich and set, heightened by a lover's exaggerations. The comparisons centralize on the joyous things of spring and summer, birds, flowers, sun, and wind, and make the lady superior to them all.

> My lady walks her morning round,
> My lady's page her fleet greyhound,
> My lady's hair the fond winds stir,
> And all the birds make songs for her.
>
> . . . . .
>
> The hound and I are on her trail,
> The wind and I uplift her veil;
> As if the calm, cold moon she were,
> And I the tide, I follow her.

The repetition of certain phrases and syntactical patterns enhance the tone and convey the reverence of the lover's devotion with their litany of praise. The action of the ballad is slight, though there is an undercurrent of conflict—his adoration versus her proud disdain. However, this is never developed and the lyric and decorative effects dominate.

This type of ballad is the exception rather than the rule for most of Whittier's later pieces. Some of his other ballads, like "**The Brown Dwarf of Rügen**," "**King Volmer and Elsie**," and "**Kallundborg Church**," also convey the charm of a foreign land and create a fairy tale atmosphere by the techniques used in "**The Henchman**" (in much the same manner as Longfellow's ballads). In general, Whittier's later ballads tend to take a concrete historical incident or some local tradition and to dramatize it, using actual locale for realistic background setting. These tales fit in perfectly with his critical belief that there was romance underlying the simplest of incidents and that the writer should utilize the materials within his own experience. "**The Wreck of Rivermouth**" is typical of these ballads. The story is based on the historical character of Goody Cole of Hampton, who was persecuted for being a witch in the latter half of the seventeenth century. . . . The ballad proper begins with the boat full of "goodly company," sailing past the rocks for fishing outside the bay. The idyllic atmosphere of the summer's day is conveyed by the picture of the mowers in the Hampton meadows, who listen to the songs coming from the passing boat and who longingly watch the joyous young girls. As the boat rounds the point where Goody Cole lives, the laughing group taunts her and sails on, but only after she answers their jibes with a bitter proverb: "'The broth will be

cold that waits at home; / For it's one to go, but another to come.'" Inadvertently her prophecy proves true, as a sudden storm sweeps upon the ship, driving it to destruction on Rivermouth Rocks. In one brief moment all are lost, and the next stanzas mournfully re-echo their previous happiness. . . . A stunned and broken Goody Cole is left behind, pathetically cursing the sea for fulfilling her wish. Her tragedy, like Skipper Ireson's, is an inner thing—the torment she will have for the rest of her life, wondering if her angry words actually caused the death of the group. The final scene in church highlights the community's silent condemnation of those who dare to transgress its conventions. This scene is overlong and marred by the needless introduction of another outcast, the Reverend Stephen Bachiler, and by the heavy moral tone of the conclusion, "Lord, forgive us! we're sinners all."

The poem illustrates Whittier's successes and failures in ballad presentation. The story itself is typical and probable, and Whittier's handling of it is realistic. He places it exactly in Hampton, New Hampshire, by employing details characteristic of that locale: fishing for haddock and cod, the scent of the pines of Rye, the mowing of salted grass, and Goody Cole's use of familiar native proverbs. There is a keynote of drama in the situation, as well as good narrative appeal, that fits into ballad presentation; for, Whittier allows us to view a Goody Cole who is human and natural, and to see her as an old woman tragically destroyed by a village's narrow hate. Yet, like so many of his ballads, this one needs more concentration especially in ending before the dramatic effect is lost. Also, there is a hint here of his overreaching for sentimental and emotional effect, which is so clearly seen in his ballads, like "**The Witch of Wenham**" and "**How the Women went from Dover**."

On the whole, Whittier's ballads represent his chief poetic achievement. Like Longfellow, he was a pioneer in the development of native American ballads; yet, he understood the true function of good balladry and refused to write ballads based on European models. Whittier took moments from American history and local legends and presented them in a realistic, natural manner that was strengthened by his wide knowledge of past times and lifelong familiarity with the locale. Whittier composed these poems not for a moral or social purpose, but because of an irrepressible desire to express his feelings for his section—its history, legends, and special characteristics. And in these poems, Whittier attained the rank of one of America's finest creators of historical and traditional narrative. (pp. 70-2)

> *John B. Pickard, "Whittier's Ballads: The Maturing of an Artist," in* Essex Institute Historical Collections, *Vol. XCVI, No. 1, January, 1960, pp. 56-72.*

ROY HARVEY PEARCE (essay date 1961)

Whittier is the central figure among [the People's Poets: Bryant, Longfellow, Lowell, and Holmes]. For, unlike the others, he had to earn his status; he could not, as they did, assume it and then act and write on the assumption. Yet the influence was at least to a degree mutual. For Whittier read them, Longfellow in particular; and their example encouraged him to do what he had to do. In turn they admired him for having done it, and in the process saw that he exemplified ideally the history of the poor farm boy become patriarch of popular culture. Speaking to his popular audience, Whittier spoke to his own kind—strong, forthright, always instinctively making the proper poem for the proper occasion, never beyond his readers' range of comprehension. If his fellows had not loved him so, they surely would have envied him. (p. 226)

Listening always to his Voice, Whittier composed his career accordingly. There are the fiercely abolitionist poems—the one to Garrison, **"Massachusetts to Virginia,"** **"The Reformer,"** **"The Rendition,"** **"Ichabod"** and the rest. These are essentially like Lowell's and Holmes's "public" poems—occasional, ode-like, affirming, reinforcing in memorable language a noble sentiment which already exists and then editorializing on it. Their strength lies in the degree of moral responsibility they directly evoke; their weakness consists in the fact that once the occasion for the exercise of that responsibility has passed, the poems exist only as monuments to the nobility of purpose of the poet and his great audience. Such poems comprise aspects at once of Whittier's biography and his readers'—the biography of a community held together by its devotion to a common cause. Likewise, Whittier's "historical" poems—**"Cassandra Southwick,"** **"Barclay of Ury,"** **"Skipper Ireson's Ride,"** for example. In these, the poet chooses to memorialize a moment of moral decision; but he puts between the moment and those who read of it the form of the ballad (or an approximation to it); and he sets his account of the moment in a self-consciously ballad-like meter; so that the form and the meter define the moment as one out of times long gone by. Whittier does not re-create the moment but rather looks back at it. In the narratives as in the ode-like poems, what comes through is a sense of moral principle, not moral experience.

If the diaphanous curtain of folk-memory (which Whittier renders so beautifully) does not in fact intervene between poet (and with him, his readers) and subject, Whittier arranges that it does. When he writes of natural scenes, it is (like Bryant and Lowell) as an onlooker who may learn all he must by observing, not by willing himself into a kind of meditative participation. When he writes of his favorite poets, Wordsworth and Burns, the effect is just the same. He softens them and their poetry, suffusing it all with the gently flowing inner light of his own being. He knew what he was doing; he would surely have been unconcerned about the consequences it would have for the staying-power of his poetry. He had a task: to reach just that sort of reader that he himself was. (pp. 227-28)

[The] greatest example of Whittier's accommodation of fantasy to reality is his undoubted masterpiece **"Snow-Bound."** It might well be that this is the only great poem written by the Fireside Poets; that in it Whittier builded much greater than he knew. For his handling of the fantasy-reality problem is such as in its dexterity to constitute a mode of art in itself. We may take pleasure as much in Whittier's sheer artistry as in what that artistry produces. The setting, a lonely farmhouse whose inhabitants feel the oncoming storm to be a "portent," not a "threat," makes a proper occasion for memories of what might have been. Indeed, after the storm, it is hard to distinguish between what might have been and what actually was:

> And, when the second morning shone,
> We looked upon a world unknown,
> On nothing we could call our own.

At this point, with the hypnotic meter and the unusual triplet reinforcing the effect of the description, we are in another world. That world has its own realities—gathering wood for the fire, tending the farm animals, keeping warm; but, by virtue of being realities in a world detached from the one of common-

sense day-to-day experience, they too partake of fantasy. The storm continues; likewise does the journey to the interior world of Whittier's fantasies. But we are, as the poem continues, always aware that this is a poet, here and now, looking backward, regretting the loss of those who, there present; are now dead.

Thus our fantasies are all the more intensified for being available to us, at the poet's command, here and now. Yet there is a fantasy within the fantasy, memory within memory. We are told, in succession, how the adults in the family each recalled his own history, a snow-bound state within a snow-bound state; and we sense, however dimly, the power of an infinite regression into the comforts of fantasy, even as we know that all this *is* fantasy (or, if you like, memory softened) and therefore at best offers us only temporary surcease from the trials of our day-to-day lives. The adults all take on the qualities of characters out of folklore; their memories are superhumanly rich; they are almost rural shape-shifters as Whittier makes them tell their stories, and they have the magical power to transport their auditors as they will; the auditors identify with, lose themselves in, the being of the storytellers. . . . The family is snow-bound for a week, we are told. Then reality supervenes, but gradually. Teamsters have broken through; the doctor has been making his rounds. Now comes the village newspaper and the world of wars—*wars*, be it noted:

> We saw the marvels that it told.
> Before us passed the painted Creeks,
>   And daft McGregor on his raids
>   In Costa Rica's everglades.
> And up Taygetos winding slow
> Rode Ypsilanti's Mainote Greeks,
> A Turk's head at each saddle-bow!

The contrast seems to be complete: a fantasy world made by love and a real world made by hate. Yet family love—this is not fantasy; and war is not everything. Or did Whittier believe at some depth of his Quaker consciousness that in the modern world it just might possibly be this way? For soon, too soon, ". . . all the world was ours once more!" . . . Dream as he might, guide his readers in their dreaming as he might, Whittier had always to listen to **"What the Voice Said."** As a very young man he declared that he wanted to write "Yankee pastorals." He did. His glory was that he not only knew their limitations but put a sense of those limitations into them. (pp. 230-31)

Roy Harvey Pearce, "American Renaissance (2): The Poet and the People," in his The Continuity of American Poetry, *Princeton University Press, 1961, pp. 192-252.**

HYATT H. WAGGONER (essay date 1984)

[*In the following appraisal, Waggoner addresses the moralistic nature of Whittier's poetry and claims that this quality subjects his work to ridicule. According to Waggoner, Whittier's poetry reflects three major aspects of his life: religious conscience, childhood memories, and nature. Whittier unites these three elements most perfectly, Waggoner says, in* Snow-bound. *Waggoner also discusses the life and death imagery in Whittier's works. For additional commentary by Waggoner, see excerpt above, 1959.*]

No famous nineteenth-century American poet offers greater obstacles to a just evaluation today. None of the "schoolroom poets," except perhaps Longfellow in his several worst poems, is easier to ridicule. More so even than Longfellow's, Whittier's poetry is "old-fashioned," and old-fashioned precisely in the way recent criticism has taught us to consider inferior. . . . Why read [Whittier] when we already know that he is generally moralistic, sermonizing at almost every opportunity? When it is clear that he distrusts and often undercuts his own symbols; worse, that he distrusts *all* symbols and ultimately poetry itself, extending his Quaker preference for unmediated apprehension of Reality to all experience? Why read a poet who thought that "The outward symbols disappear / For him whose inward sight is clear"?

Poetry for Whittier, as for the Puritans, is a concession to the flesh, an expedient of words and meters required only because man's spiritual sense is still so imperfect. "The world will have its idols, / And flesh and sense their sign." In a fallen world, truth must be conveyed in the "trappings" of form, but poetry aspires to the "deepest of all mysteries, silence." A very old-fashioned idea! But doesn't it, in some sense? Can a poet say *all* in a poem? (pp. 70-1)

Though he seems to have been incapable of distinguishing between the moral and the moralistic, his best antislavery poems are moral satire and invective, with nothing moralistic about them. Though he was capable at his worst of outrageous sentimentality, as **"The Barefoot Boy"** or **"Barbara Frietchie"** may remind us, there is nothing in the least sentimental about **"Snowbound."** Whittier was able to respond poetically to three areas of his experience. When he wrote about the demands made by the religious conscience, about memories of his own childhood, or about nature considered as symbolic revelation, he quite frequently wrote better than he knew, better than his theory or his taste should have permitted him to write. (pp. 71-2)

In general, the least readable of Whittier's poems are those he devoted to his "great cause," the abolition of slavery. Yet even his poems of reform deserve, at their best, to be read as *poems*. Denouncing slavery, they raise what we might be inclined to see as an archaic and long-since corrected evil to a level of universal meaning where it requires no effort on our part to see it as still *our* problem. Prompted by specific events or prepared for specific occasions, a number of these poems transcend their interest as historical documents to remind us powerfully of the timeless discrepancy between what we are and what we ought to be, between profession and deed, between our faith and our works.

On this last subject Whittier most often wrote at his best level in the pre-Civil War poems. Since for him conscience was the voice of God, his chief scorn was directed at those "clerical oppressors" who were either blind to the implications of their faith or actively perverted what seemed to him its clear meaning in their defense of an institution of which, as he noted, they were the beneficiaries. Though even on this subject Whittier's diction often fails, there are enough fine lines and passages to make it worth our while to reread occasionally such long unread poems as **"Clerical Oppressors," "Letter from a Missionary of the Methodist Church South, in Kansas, to a Distinguished Politician,"** and **"On a Prayer-Book, with its Frontispiece, Ary Scheffer's 'Christus Consolator,' Americanized by the Omission of the Black Man."**

The better-known, because more often anthologized, poems of reform like **"Massachusetts to Virginia," "Ichabod," "The Haschish," "The Panorama,"** and **"Laus Deo!"** contain passages of some of the best invective verse in our literature. The

voice in them is righteous but not self-righteous, angry but not shrill; not moralistic so much as prophetic in the great tradition. **"Massachusetts to Virginia"** is a merely sectional poem only to those who miss its moral meaning, and **"Ichabod"** is so enriched by its Biblical allusions that Daniel Webster, whom the poem attacks, becomes the type of any betrayer of any high cause. (pp. 72-3)

[**"Telling the Bees"**] is strengthened by Whittier's handling of visual imagery. In it, as in the greater **"Snowbound,"** both black and white suggest death, and colors suggest life. With a reliance upon implication all too rare in his work, Whittier here makes both the imagery and the action dramatic. The speaker in the poem is one to whom things happen. He and the reader together share a gradual revelation.

The effect is rare in Whittier, but by no means limited to this one poem, as **"The River Path"** will illustrate. Here the speaker finally states explicitly the consolation he finds in nature, but not before he has experienced fully the darkness in which he has walked. The ending, with its support for the hope of immortality, gains force from the extended emphasis on "the damp, the chill, the gloom" in which, reading the poem, we too find ourselves immersed as we gaze with the speaker out of the darkness toward the light. (p. 73)

In **"Snowbound"** nature speaks, but not to console. It speaks in the sound of the "mindless wind." Man is now not only "more" than his abode, as he was in **"Monadnock from Wachuset,"** he is actively threatened by a hostile environment and brought to know his essential humanity by that threat. In the attitude it implies toward nature, **"Snowbound"** is closer to Stephen Crane than to most of Whittier's contemporaries. It is not only a fine poem; it is a document of considerable importance in nineteenth-century intellectual history.

"Snowbound" is surely the finest American pastoral poem before the pastorals of Frost. It is a true pastoral, not an idyl, despite Whittier's misleading subtitle. It pictures rural life under simplified conditions, not in order to idealize it but to find out what its meaning is for us. Comments on the poem have too often ignored the conclusion, with the unfortunate result that we have been taught to read the poem as an expression of simple nostalgia. There is nostalgia in the poem, to be sure, but the nostalgia exists in tension with judgment. Though we do not associate Whittier with complexity of feeling or subtlety of thought, in his greatest poem he expressed more meaning than his critics have been patient enough to grasp. (pp. 76-7)

In Whittier's poem nature clarifies human life by threatening it. Nature's *mindlessness* suggests to Whittier that man is *not* mindless, or loveless. Though he begins by describing the storm at length, his real concern is for people. The storm is important for him only as the occasion of the family's enforced companionship around the fire. More than two-thirds of the poem is taken up with the portraits of those present. More significantly, the poem culminates in the long religious meditation beginning "Clasp, Angel of the backward look," in which the "Flemish pictures of old days" that have been presented are offered as having more than sentimental value: They may touch the heart of the "worldling" and move him beyond his secularism, and they strengthen the speaker's resolution to continue to work for a better world. (pp. 77-8)

If one of the functions of memory as it has been exercised in the poem is to make us see more clearly the full implications of the "green hills of life that slope to death," and so to deepen our faith beyond that of the worldlings, another is to remind us that the past provides resources that can help us do our duty in the present:

> I hear again the voice that bids
> The dreamer leave his dream midway
> For larger hopes and graver fears:
> Life greatens in these later years,
> The century's aloe flowers to-day!

That is, things we have long worked for have come to fruition, but the voice of conscience will not let us go on dreaming. When the storm was over there was work to do; now that it has been relived in memory, there is work of another kind to do. The final lesson nature has to teach us is the necessity of moral commitment.

This becomes clearer when we notice the changes in point of view as the poem proceeds. At first the voice is generalized and impersonal as the coming of the storm is objectively described. Then, on the first morning after the storm, as the father and the boys start to shovel the paths, the point of view of childhood becomes dominant and the whole experience becomes an exciting adventure. This is the only part of **"Snowbound"** that should remind us of Emerson's poem ["Snow Storm"]. Memory lets Whittier for the moment simply relive his childhood as though nothing has happened since: This is how it seemed *then*. The childish speaker looks outward, as Emerson's mature speaker had looked, and is similarly entranced by the "marvelous shapes" the snow has assumed. He is "well pleased" with this escape from the routine life of the household. For two verse paragraphs there are no references to nature as a threat. But then as these images return and we hear once again "the shrieking of the mindless wind," we become aware of a more mature point of view being counterpointed with the childish one. We are prepared thus for the conclusion, in which we discover that all this took place long ago in the speaker's youth; that all but one besides the speaker of those who gathered around the hearth are now dead; and that these memories should not be sentimentally dwelt upon but be put to use so that life may prevail over death.

The implications of the imagery are wholly consistent, throughout this very long poem, with such an interpretation of its meaning. In other poems Whittier had sometimes lamented nature's silence. Now nature seemed, as it spoke through the storm, to be *alien*. He describes it as "dark," "cheerless," "sad," "ominous," "a threat," "cold," "hard," "dreary," "bitter," and "gray." The images imply that it is also *blind* and *dead*.

Not that Whittier has changed his mind and given up his Quaker Christianity for naturalism; rather, he is writing as a *poet* of his memories of a specific event and of the particular face nature showed in that event. Looking out into the storm, the speaker saw a world previously "unknown"; he could see in it "nothing we could call our own." The snow obliterates all signs of those values that have given meaning to the speaker's life:

> No church-bell lent its Christian tone
> To the savage air, no social smoke
> Curled over woods of snow-hung oak.
>
> (pp. 78-9)

[Whittier's emphasis is] on the "dead" nature outside as motivating a turn inward to the light and warmth of the fireside. Hawthorne many years before in "Night Sketches: Beneath an Umbrella" had explored a nature that revealed itself as a "black impenetrable nothingness," before returning to the hearth. For both writers the images of *circle* and the *hearth* counter the isolation induced by a feeling that human values may not be backed by nature. As Whittier puts it now, the "human tone" is wholly absent from this "solitude." (p. 79)

The contrast between life-imagery and death-imagery is maintained consistently throughout the poem, not simply in the initial description of the storm. Life is "unfading green," a "pleasant circle," characterized by "warmth and light" and "green hills"; death is imaged as snow on graves and the blackness of a "bitter night." By the time we are told, late in the poem, that death has now claimed all but one of those who made that human circle, we are thoroughly prepared for the meditation on the hope of reunion in another world.

The question has become, which of nature's several voices speaks the ultimate truth, the "mindless" voice or the voice that pronounces, at other times, what seems like a "benediction of the air." We cannot *know*, Whittier implies, we can only *hope* that at the foot of the green hill of life the "mournful cypresses" have "white amaranths" in bloom beneath them. We have stretched "the hands of memory forth / To warm them at the wood-fire's blaze." The very intensity of the cold has made it the more necessary to seek and treasure warmth. Nowhere is Whittier closer to Hawthorne than in this expression of one of Hawthorne's commonest themes, in some of Hawthorne's favorite images. But Whittier's religious faith was firmer than Hawthorne's, and there is nothing guarded or ambiguous about the imagery of his conclusion. Faith, for him, restores the "circle" broken by time. The fragrance blown in the end from "unseen meadows" by a wind no longer cold and mindless was foretold in the beginning by the "circling race / Of life-blood in the sharpened face." The meditation with which the poem concludes, far from being "tacked on," merely makes explicit what the images have been saying all along.

Whittier never wrote so well again, but **"Snowbound"** was no lucky accident. If we have understood, for example, the religious position expressed by the other poems, we are prepared for the way he paints his portraits of the people in this poem. As we might expect of a devout Quaker who, in **"Haverhill,"** counseled his fellow-townsmen to

> Hold fast your Puritan heritage,
> But let the free thought of the age
> Its light and hope and sweetness add
> To the stern faith the fathers had,

he loves these people but he does not idealize or sentimentalize them. (pp. 80-1)

Uniting as it does the three subjects on which he could write best, memories of childhood, nature, and the demands of a religious conscience, **"Snowbound"** gave Whittier his best, perhaps his only perfect, chance to be a good poet without ceasing to be a good Quaker. It gave him a chance to utilize his best resources as a poet, his quite personal memories, and yet to raise them to national, if not universal, significance, just because he was fortunate enough to share the background of most Americans. **"Snowbound"** is replete with "metre-making" arguments. Its style could hardly be plainer, less embellished. It passes Emerson's test of the true American poem. (pp. 82-3)

Hyatt H. Waggoner, "Five New England Poets: The Shape of Things to Come," in his American Poets: From the Puritans to the Present, *revised edition, Louisiana State University Press, 1984, pp. 69-85.**

ADDITIONAL BIBLIOGRAPHY

Allen, Gay Wilson. "John Greenleaf Whittier." In his *American Prosody*, pp. 127-53. New York: American Book Co., 1935.

An informative discussion of Whittier's prosody. Allen maintains that Whittier's inconsistent style indicates his indifference to developing his own personal manner of versification. His detachment, according to Allen, does not detract from Whittier's writing; rather, Allen argues, Whittier achieves individuality in his works because he violates basic rules of grammar and syntax.

B[allou], H. "Whittier's Poems." *Universalist Quarterly* VI (April 1849): 142-60.*

A comparison of Whittier's and William Cullen Bryant's poetry. Ballou argues that Whittier's genius does not rival that of Bryant and suggests that his works need more refinement and polish.

Cady, E[dwin] H[arrison]. Introduction to *Whittier on Writers and Writing: The Uncollected Critical Writings of John Greenleaf Whittier*, by John Greenleaf Whittier, edited by Edwin Harrison Cady and Harry Hayden Clark, pp. 1-14. Syracuse, N.Y.: Syracuse University Press, 1950.

A rare glimpse of Whittier's critical writings. Cady traces the development of his critical theories and concludes that he was "not a great critic." However, Cady considers his social commentary to be of interest historically and to students of Whittier because of the insight it offers on "the man and the world of experience he knew."

Carpenter, George Rice. *John Greenleaf Whittier*. American Men of Letters. Boston: Houghton, Mifflin and Co., Riverside Press, 1903, 311 p.

A biography which maintains that Whittier's life was dominated by political motivation rather than humanitarian passion. According to Carpenter, Whittier was most effective in reaching the public through his writings as a journalist and pamphleteer.

Christy, Arthur. "Orientalism in New England: Whittier." *American Literature* 1, No. 4 (January 1930): 372-92.

A study of Oriental themes in Whittier's works.

Foerster, Norman. "Whittier." In his *Nature in American Literature: Studies in the Modern View of Nature*, pp. 20-36. New York: Russell & Russell, 1958.

Outlines Whittier's representation of natural elements in his literature.

Fowler, William J. "Whittier and Tennyson." *The Arena* VII, No. XXXVII (December 1892): 1-11.*

A comparison of the lives and careers of Whittier and Alfred, Lord Tennyson.

Hall, Donald. "Whittier." *The Texas Quarterly* III, No. 3 (Autumn 1960): 165-74.

A comparison of Whittier's stylistic techniques with those of William Butler Yeats and W. H. Auden. Hall finds similarities in the writings of the three authors, but notes one major difference: Whittier is both optimistic and nostalgic, believing in the triumph of goodness.

Kennedy, W. Sloane. *John Greenleaf Whittier: His Life, Genius, and Writings*. Boston: D. Lothrop Co., 1886, 311 p.

The first biography to be written about Whittier. Unauthorized and published at the height of the poet's popularity, the work was not well accepted because of its subtle degradation of Whittier's art.

Leary, Lewis. *John Greenleaf Whittier*. New York: Twayne Publishers, 1961, 189 p.

An extensive discussion of Whittier both as an individual and as a poet. Leary suggests that Whittier has been "victimized" by earlier critical treatments which do not grant him the stature he deserves.

A Memorial of John Greenleaf Whittier from His Native City Haverhill, Massachusetts. Cambridge, Mass.: Riverside Press, 1893, 106 p.

A commemoration of Whittier's life as a Haverhill native. The volume contains testimonials by city officials, as well as a biographical sketch and an ode to Whittier.

Miller, Lewis H., Jr. "The Supernaturalism of *Snow-Bound*." *The New England Quarterly* LIII, No. 3 (September 1980): 291-307.

An analysis of *Snow-bound* as an example of New England supernaturalism.

Mordell, Albert. *Quaker Militant: John Greenleaf Whittier*. 1933. Reprint. Port Washington, N.Y.: Kennikat Press, 1969, 354 p.

A psychoanalytic study of Whittier. Mordell provides an extensive examination of Whittier's unpublished letters and reminiscences and argues that Whittier was the victim of a tragic love affair. According to Mordell, Whittier's ill-fated romance resulted in his becoming a "frustrated celibate and vain philanderer."

"Editor's Table." *The New England Magazine* VII, No. 4 (December 1892): 539-43.

A brief overview of Whittier's major prose pieces. The essay contains extensive excerpts from Whittier's works.

Parrington, Vernon Louis. "The Mind of New England, the Rise of Liberalism: Certain Militants, John G. Whittier." In his *The Romantic Revolution in America: 1800-1860*, pp. 361-70. New York: Harcourt, Brace and Co., 1927.

Chronicles Whittier's participation in the antislavery movement.

Pickard, John B. "Imagistic and Structural Unity in *Snow-Bound*." *College English* 21, No. 6 (March 1960): 338-43.

A structural and thematic analysis of *Snow-bound*.

——. *John Greenleaf Whittier: An Introduction and Interpretation*. New York: Holt, Rinehart and Winston, 1961, 145 p.

The most complete study of Whittier's writings and political career. Pickard is considered the foremost contemporary Whittier scholar.

——, ed. *Memorabilia of John Greenleaf Whittier*. Hartford, Conn.: Emerson Society, 1967, 167 p.

A collection of photographs, commemorative poetry, and essays about Whittier.

Pickard, Samuel T. *Life and Letters of John Greenleaf Whittier*. 2 vols. Boston: Houghton, Mifflin and Co., Riverside Press, 1894.

The "official" biography sanctioned by Whittier before his death. Although Pickard's biography greatly romanticizes Whittier's political motivation, the work is still considered a standard source for its broad survey of Whittier's letters and memoirs.

Pollard, John A. *John Greenleaf Whittier: Friend of Man*. Boston: Houghton Mifflin Co., Riverside Press, 1949, 615 p.

A lengthy biography of Whittier which provides several helpful appendices. Pollard includes a bibliography, as well as extensive notes concerning Whittier's lineage.

Quynn, Dorothy Mackay, and Quynn, William Rogers. "'Barbara Frietschie'." *The Maryland Historical Magazine* XXXVII, No. 3 (September 1942): 227-54.

Explores the historical inaccuracies found in Whittier's ballad "Barbara Frietchie."

Ringe, Donald A. "The Artistry of Whittier's *Margaret Smith's Journal*." *Essex Historical Collections* 108, No. 3 (1972): 235-43.

An appraisal of Whittier's *Leaves from Margaret Smith's Journal in the Province of Massachusetts Bay*. Ringe concludes that the prose is a "unified work of art" and that Margaret Smith is a "consistently developed character."

Schaedler, Louis C. "Whittier's Attitude toward Colonial Puritanism." *The New England Quarterly* XXI, No. 3 (September 1948): 350-67.

Analyzes Whittier's treatment of Puritans and Quakers in his writing. In particular, Schaedler examines *Leaves from Margaret Smith's Journal in the Province of Massachusetts Bay*.

Trawick, Leonard M. "Whittier's *Snow-Bound*: A Poem about the Imagination." *Essays in Literature* I, No. 1 (Spring 1974): 46-53.

Assesses the importance of Whittier's *Snow-bound* as a Romantic poem. The poem's place in Romantic tradition, according to Trawick, is firmly established by the ''act itself of transcending the limitations of time and space through imagination.''

Underwood, Francis H. *John Greenleaf Whittier: A Biography*. Boston: Houghton, Mifflin and Co., Riverside Press, 1893, 413 p.

A biography written with Whittier's knowledge, but not with his approval. Underwood expresses great admiration for Whittier throughout the work.

Wagenknecht, Edward. *John Greenleaf Whittier: A Portrait in Paradox*. New York: Oxford University Press, 1967, 262 p.

Discredits Albert Mordell's accounts of Whittier's love life (see annotation above) and argues that Whittier never married because of his extreme poverty and obligations to his mother and younger sister.

Warren, Robert Penn. ''Whittier.'' *The Sewanee Review* LXXIX, No. 1 (Winter 1971): 86-135.

A discussion of the Biblical allusions and allegories in Whittier's works.

Waters, Rev. Thomas F. ''Whittier, the Poet, As Historian.'' *The Massachusetts Magazine* 1, No. 1 (January 1908): 3-10.

Addresses the historical inaccuracies of Whittier's works. Waters specifically examines Whittier's depictions of Quaker persecution and the Salem witch trials.

Appendix

The following is a listing of all sources used in Volume 8 of *Nineteenth-Century Literature Criticism*. Included in this list are all copyright and reprint rights and acknowledgements for those essays for which permission was obtained. Every effort has been made to trace copyright, but if omissions have been made, please let us know.

THE EXCERPTS IN NCLC, VOLUME 8, WERE REPRINTED FROM THE FOLLOWING PERIODICALS:

The American, v. XVII, February 23, 1889.

The American Hebrew, v. 33, December 9, 1887.

American Literature, v. 9, November, 1937. Copyright © by Duke University Press, Durham, N.C. Reprinted by permission of the Publisher.

American Quarterly, v. XXIV, May, 1972 for ''The Nursery Tales of Horatio Alger'' by Michael Zuckerman. Copyright 1972, Trustees of the University of Pennsylvania. Reprinted by permission of the publisher and the author.

The American Scholar, v. 34, Winter, 1964-65. Copyright © 1965 by the United Chapters of Phi Beta Kappa. By permission of the publishers, the United Chapters of Phi Beta Kappa.

The American Slavic and East European Review, v. XII, 1953.

The Antioch Review, v. XXI, Spring, 1961. Copyright © 1961 by the Antioch Review Inc. Reprinted by permission of the Editors.

The Athenaeum, n. 559, July 14, 1838; v. 2, September 17, 1853; n. 3385, September 10, 1892; n. 3718, January 28, 1899.

The Atlantic Monthly, v. VI, November, 1860; v. XIII, March, 1864; v. XVIII, August, 1866; v. LXX, November, 1892.

Blackwood's Edinburgh Magazine, v. III, June, 1818; v. III, August, 1818; v. X, December, 1821; v. XV, February, 1824; v. XV, June, 1824; v. XVIII, September, 1825; v. CLXXXV, September, 1831.

Blackwood's Magazine, v. 258, August, 1945.

The British Critic, v. XVIII, September, 1801; v. XLIII, October, 1813; n.s. v. III, April, 1815; n.s. v. X, July, 1818.

Brownson's Quarterly Review, n.s. v. IV, October, 1850.

The Catholic Presbyterian, v. IV, November, 1880.

The Century, v. XXIII, March, 1882; v. XXV, January, 1883; v. XXXVI, October, 1888.

The Champion, March 9, 1817.

The Chautauquan, v. XVI, December, 1892.

The Christian Observer, v. XVII, May, 1818; v. XVIII, February, 1819.

The Cornhill Magazine, v. II, October, 1860.

The Critic, New York, n.s. v. VIII, December 10, 1887; v. XVI, December 5, 1891; v. XXIII, June 29, 1895.

The Critical Review, v. LX, October, 1785.

Dickens Studies, v. I, September, 1965. © copyright, 1965, by the Trustees of Emerson College. Reprinted by permission.

The Dickensian, v. LXIX, January, 1973. Reprinted by permission.

The Dublin Magazine, n.s. v. IX, January-March, 1934; n.s. v. XIII, July-September, 1938.

Dublin University Magazine, v. XXIII, January, 1844.

The Eclectic Review, December, 1805; v. VI, September, 1810; v. VII, April, 1811.

The Economist, v. V, November 27, 1847.

The Edinburgh Review, v. I, October, 1802; v. II, April, 1803; v. IV, July, 1804; v. XXXIV, August, 1820; v. L, January, 1830; v. CL, January, 1842.

Education, v. XLIX, September, 1928.

ELH, v. 29, June, 1962. Reprinted by permission of *ELH* and the Johns Hopkins Press.

Essays in Criticism, v. VI, July, 1956 for "Keats's 'Ode to Psyche'" by Kenneth Allott. Reprinted by permission of the publisher and the Literary Estate of Kenneth Allott./ v. X, July, 1960. Reprinted by permission of the publisher.

Essex Institute Historical Collections, v. XCIII, October, 1957; v. XCV, January, 1959; v. XCVI, January, 1960. Copyright, 1957, 1959, 1960, by the Essex Institute, 132-134 Essex Street, Salem, MA. All reprinted by permission.

European Magazine and London Review, v. LXXI, May, 1817.

The Examiner, n. 466, December 1, 1816; n. 563, October 11, 1818; n. 657, July 30, 1820; n. 2078, November 27, 1847; n. 2384, October 8, 1853.

Foreign Quarterly Review, v. IX, May, 1832.

The Fortnightly Review, v. XXXI, March 1, 1882; n.s. v. XXXII, October 1, 1882.

Fraser's Magazine, v. V, June, 1830.

The Galaxy, v. XIII, January, 1872.

The Gentleman's Magazine, v. 296, January-June, 1904.

German Life & Letters, n.s. v. XXX, October, 1976. Reprinted by permission.

Graham's Magazine, v. XIX, December, 1841; v. XXXII, May, 1848.

The Hudson Review, v. XII, Winter, 1959-60. Copyright © 1960 by The Hudson Review, Inc. Reprinted by permission.

Illinois Quarterly, v. 39, Fall, 1976. Copyright, Illinois State University, 1976. Reprinted by permission.

The Illustrated London News, v. LIX, October 14, 1871.

The New-York Mirror, v. VIII, March 19, 1831.

The New York Times, February 23, 1867; October 8, 1882.

The Nineteenth Century and After, v. XCII, August, 1922.

Nineteenth-Century Fiction, v. 20, December, 1965 for ''From Portrait to Person: A Note on the Surrealistic in 'Jane Eyre' '' by Lawrence E. Moser; v. 31, March, 1977 for ''Resistance, Rebellion, and Marriage: The Economics of 'Jane Eyre' '' by Nancy Pell. © 1965, 1977 by The Regents of the University of California. Both reprinted by permission of The Regents and the respective authors./ v. VII, September, 1952 for '' 'Bleak House': The Anatomy of Society'' by Edgar Johnson. © 1952, renewed 1980, by The Regents of the University of California. Reprinted by permission of The Regents and Georges Borchardt, Inc., as agents for the author.

The North American Review, v. II, January, 1816; v. XIX, October, 1824; v. XX, January, 1825; v. XXXVIII, January, 1834; v. LVII, October, 1843; v. LVIII, January, 1844; v. LXVI, April, 1848; v. LXVII, October, 1848; v. LXXIX, July, 1854; v. XCI, July, 1860; v. XCVIII, January, 1864; v. CII, April, 1866; v. CXVI, April, 1873.

Notes and Queries, v. 176, January 21, 1939.

The Open Court, v. 46, June, 1932. Copyright by The Open Court Publishing Company, 1932, renewed 1960. Reprinted by permission of The Open Court Publishing Company, La Salle, Illinois.

The Personalist, v. XLI, October, 1960. Reprinted by permission.

PM Daily, September 16, 1945.

PMLA, v. LXXXII, September, 1957. Copyright © 1957 by the Modern Language Association of America. Reprinted by permission of The Modern Language Association of America.

The Port Folio, v. XIX, February, 1825.

Proceedings of the British Academy, v. XI, 1924-25. Reprinted by permission.

Publications of the American Jewish Historical Society, v. XXXVIII, June, 1949./ v. XLV, June, 1956. Reprinted by permission.

Putnam's Magazine, v. II, July, 1868.

Putnam's Monthly, v. II, November, 1853.

The Quarterly Review, v. VIII, December, 1812; v. XVI, October, 1816; v. XIX, April, 1818; v. XXIV, October, 1820; v. XXXVII, January, 1828; v. LI, March, 1834.

The Reform Advocate, v. LXXIV, September 24, 1927.

Reformist's Register and Weekly Commentary, v. I, February 22, 1817.

The Reporter, v. 37, September 7, 1967 for ''The Homilies of Horatio'' by Marcus Klein. © 1967 by The Reporter Magazine Company. All rights reserved. Reprinted by permission of the author.

The Saturday Review, London, v. 53, January 21, 1882; v. 53, February 18, 1882.

The Saturday Review of Literature, v. XVIII, September 17, 1938.

The Sewanee Review, v. LI, Summer, 1943. Published 1943 by The University of the South. Reprinted by permission of the editor.

The Southern Quarterly Review, v. IV, October, 1843.

The Southern Review, v. V, April, 1969 for '' 'Bleak House': Structure and Style'' by Albert J. Guerard. Copyright, 1969, by Albert J. Guerard. Reprinted by permission of the author.

Southwest Review, v. XXV, July, 1940.

The Spectator, v. 21, November 6, 1847; v. 26, September 24, 1853; v. 55, February 4, 1882; v. 59, January 9, 1886; v. 63, November 2, 1889./ v. 148, January 16, 1932. © 1932 by *The Spectator.* Reprinted by permission of *The Spectator.*

Abrahams, Israel. From *By-Paths in Hebraic Bookland*. Jewish Publication Society of America, 1920.

Adams, Maurianne. From "'Jane Eyre': Woman's Estate," in *The Authority of Experience: Essays in Feminist Criticism*. Edited by Arlyn Diamond and Lee R. Edwards. University of Massachusetts Press, 1977. Copyright © 1977 by The University of Massachusetts Press. All rights reserved. Reprinted by permission.

Ainger, Alfred. From *Lectures and Essays, Vol. I*. Macmillan, and Co., 1905.

Arms, George. From *The Fields Were Green: A New View of Bryant, Whittier, Holmes, Lowell, and Longfellow, with a Selection of Their Poems*. Stanford University Press, 1953. Copyright 1953 by The Board of Trustees of the Leland Stanford Junior University. And renewed 1981 by George Warren Arms. Excerpted with the permission of the publishers, Stanford University Press.

Arnold, Matthew. From *On Translating Homer*. Longman & Co., 1861.

Arpad, Joseph J. From an introduction to *A Narrative of the Life of David Crockett of the State of Tennessee*. By David Crockett, edited by Joseph J. Arpad. College & University Press, 1972. Copyright © 1972 by College and University Press Services, Inc. All rights reserved. Reprinted by permission.

Bagehot, Walter. From "William Cowper," in *Estimates of Some Englishmen and Scotchmen*. Chapman and Hall, 1858.

Bailey, J. C. From an introduction to *The Poems of William Cowper*. By William Cowper, edited by J.C. Bailey. Methuen & Co. Ltd., 1905.

Baillie, J. From a letter to Susan Ferrier in May, 1831, in *Memoir and Correspondence of Susan Ferrier: 1782-1854*. Edited by John Ferrier and John A. Doyle. Eveleigh Nash & Grayson Limited, 1929.

Bennett, E. K. From *A History of the German "Novelle:" From Goethe to Thomas Mann*. Cambridge at the University Press, 1934. Reprinted by permission.

Blackwood, William. From a letter to Susan Ferrier on May 6, 1817, in *Memoir and Correspondence of Susan Ferrier: 1781-1854*. Edited by John by John Ferrier and John A. Doyle. Eveleigh Nash & Grayson Limited, 1929.

Bloom, Harold. From *The Visionary Company: A Reading of English Romantic Poetry*. Doubleday & Company, Inc. 1961. Copyright © 1961 by Harold Bloom. Reprinted by permission of the author.

Blount, Trevor. From "Dickens and Mr. Krook's Spontaneous Combustion," in *Dickens Studies Annual, Vol. I*. Edited by Robert B. Partlow, Jr. Southern Illinois University Press, 1970. Copyright © 1970 by Southern Illinois University Press. All rights reserved. Reprinted by permission of Southern Illinois University Press.

Bradley, A. C. From *Oxford Lectures on Poetry*. Second edition. Macmillan and Co., Limited, 1909. Reprinted by permission of Macmillan, London and Basingstoke.

Bridges, Robert. From *Collected Essays Papers &c. of Robert Bridges: A Critical Introduction to Keats, Vol. IV*. Oxford University Press, London, 1929.

Brontë, Anne. From *Poems*. By Currer, Ellis, and Acton Bell. Aylott & Jones, 1846.

Brooke, Stopford A. From *Theology in the English Poets: Cowper, Coleridge, Wordsworth & Burns*. E. P. Dutton & Co., 1910.

Bulwer, Edward Lytton. From *England and the English, Vol. II*. Richard Bentley, 1833.

Bush, Douglas. From *Mythology and the Romantic Tradition*. Cambridge, Mass.: Harvard University Press, 1937. Copyright © 1937 by the President and Fellows of Harvard College. And renewed 1964 by Douglas Bush. Excerpted by permission.

Byron, Lord. From an extract from "Canto XI," in *Don Juan*. By Lord Byron, edited by T. G. Steffan, E. Steffan, and W.W. Pratt. Revised edition. Penguin Books, 1982. Text, introduction and notes copyright © T. G. Steffan, E. Steffan and W. W. Pratt, 1973, 1977, 1982. All rights reserved. Reprinted by permission of Penguin Books Ltd.

Byron, Lord. From an extract from *English Bards and Scotch Reviewers: A Satire*. James Cawthorn, 1805.

Byron, Lord. From *Don Juan: Cantos I and II*. Thomas Davison, 1819.

Byron, Lord. From *Letters and Journals, 6 Vols*. Edited by R. E. Prothero. n.p., 1898-1901.

Cawelti, John G. From *Apostles of the Self-Made Man*. University of Chicago Press, 1965. © 1965 by the University of Chicago. All rights reserved. Reprinted by permission of The University of Chicago Press and the author.

Chesterton, G. K. From an introduction to *Bleak House*. By Charles Dickens. Everyman's Library Series. J. M. Dent & Co., 1907. All rights reserved. Reprinted by permission of the publisher, J. M. Dent & Sons Ltd., London.

Chesterton, G. K. From "Charlotte Brontë As a Romantic," in *Charlotte Brontë, 1816-1916: A Centenary Memorial*. Edited by Butler Wood. T. Fisher Unwin Ltd., 1917. All rights reserved. Reprinted by permission of Miss D. E. Collins.

Chesterton, G. K. From *Varied Types*. Dodd, Mead and Company, 1903. Reprinted by permission of Miss D. E. Collins.

Child, Lydia Maria. From letters to John G. Whittier on January 21, 1862 and June 18, 1874 in *Letters of Lydia Maria Child*. Houghton Mifflin Company, 1883.

Cockshut, A.O.J. From *The Imagination of Charles Dickens*. New York University Press, 1962. Copyright © 1961 by A.O.J. Cockshut. Reprinted by permission of New York University Press.

Cody, William F. From *Story of the Wild West and Camp-Fire Chats*. R. S. Peale & Co., 1888.

Colby, Vineta. From *Yesterday's Woman: Domestic Realism in the English Novel*. Princeton University Press, 1974. Copyright © 1974 by Princeton University Press. All rights reserved. Excerpts reprinted with permission of Princeton University Press.

Coleridge, S. T. From *Biographia Literaria, Vol. I*. Rest Fenner, 1817.

Colum, Mary M. From *From These Roots: The Ideas That Have Made Modern Literature*. Charles Scribner's Sons, 1937, Columbia University Press, 1944. Copyright © 1937 by Charles Scribner's Sons. Copyright renewed © 1965 by Columbia University Press. Reprinted by permission of Columbia University Press.

Cowley, Malcolm. From "The Real Horatio Alger Story" in *A Many-Windowed House: Collected Essays on American Writers and American Writing*. By Malcolm Cowley, edited by Henry Dan Piper. Southern Illinois University Press, 1970. Copyright © 1970 by Malcolm Cowley and Southern Illinois University Press. All rights reserved. Reprinted by permission of Southern Illinois University Press.

Craig, G. Armour. From "The Unpoetic Compromise: On the Relation between Private Vision and Social Order in Nineteenth-Century English Fiction," in *Society and Self in the Novel: English Institute Essays, 1955*. Edited by Mark Schorer. Columbia University Press, 1956. Copyright 1956, Columbia University Press, New York. Reprinted by permission of the publisher.

Craik, W. A. From *The Brontë Novels*. Methuen, 1968. © 1968 W. A. Craik. Reprinted by permission of Methuen & Co. Ltd.

Craik, Wendy. From "Susan Ferrier," in *Scott Bicentenary Essays*. Edited by Alan Bell. Scottish Academic Press, 1973. © 1973 Institute for Advanced Studies in the Humanities, University of Edinburgh. All rights reserved. Reprinted by permission of the author and Scottish Academic Press, Ltd.

Croce, Benedetto. From *European Literature in the Nineteenth Century*. Translated by Douglas Ainslie. Alfred A. Knopf, 1924. Reprinted by permission of the Literary Estate of Benedetto Croce.

Crockett, David. From a preface to *A Narrative of the Life of David Crockett of the State of Tennessee*. By David Crockett. E. L. Carey and A. Hart, 1834.

Crouse, Russel. From an introduction to *Struggling Upward, and Other Works*. By Horatio Alger, Jr. Crown, 1945. Copyright © 1945 by Crown Publishers. And renewed 1972 by Anna E. Crouse, Timothy Crouse & Lindsay Ann Crouse. Used by permission of Crown Publishers, Inc.

De Sélincourt, E. From an introduction to *The Poems of John Keats*. Edited by E. De Sélincourt. Methuen, 1905. Reprinted by permission of Methuen & Co. Ltd.

Dobrzycki, Stanislaw. From "Pseudo-Classicism: First Period," in *Polish Encyclopaedia: The Polish Language, History of Literature, History of Poland, Vol. I*. Committee for the Polish Encyclopaedic Publications, 1922.

Douglas, Sir George. From *The Blackwood Group*. Oliphant Anderson & Ferrier, 1897.

Dowden, Edward. From *The French Revolution and English Literature*. Charles Scribner's Sons, 1897.

Dowden, Edward. From *Southey*. Harper & Brothers Publishers, 1876.

Duganne, Augustine J. H. From *Parnassus In Pillory: A Satire*. Adriance, Sherman & Co., 1851.

Dunin-Borkowski, Alexander (Leszek)? From an extract in *The Major Comedies of Alexander Fredro*. By Alexander Fredro, edited and translated by Harold B. Segel. Princeton University Press, 1969. Copyright © 1969 by Princeton University Press. All rights reserved. Excerpts reprinted with permission of Princeton University Press.

Dyboski, Roman. From *Modern Polish Literature: A Course of Lectures*. Oxford University Press, London, 1924. Reprinted by permission of Oxford University Press.

Eliot, George. From a letter to Charles Bray on June 11, 1848, in *The George Eliot Letters: 1836-1851, Vol. I*. Edited by Gordon S. Haight. Yale University Press, 1954. Copyright, 1954, by Yale University Press. And renewed 1982 by Gordon S. Haight. All rights reserved. Reprinted by permission of The Beinecke Rare Book and Manuscript Library, Yale University.

Elton, Oliver. From *A Survey of English Literature: 1780-1830, Vols. I and II*. Edward Arnold (Publishers) Ltd., 1912.

Emerson, Ralph Waldo. From five letters to Emma Lazarus from February 24, 1868 to October 6, 1869, in *Letters to Emma Lazarus in the Columbia University Library*. Edited by Ralph L. Rusk. Columbia University Press, 1939. Copyright 1939, renewed 1967, Columbia University Press. Reprinted by permission of the publisher.

Fadiman, Clifton. From *Any Number Can Play*. The World Publishing Company, 1957. Copyright © 1957 by Clifton Fadiman. All rights reserved. Reprinted by permission of Harper & Row, Publishers, Inc.

Fink, Rychard. From an introduction to *Ragged Dick and Mark, the Match Boy*. By Horatio Alger, Jr. Collier Books, 1962. Copyright © 1962 by Macmillan Publishing Co., Inc. All rights reserved. Reprinted with permission of Macmillan Publishing Company.

Flint, Robert. From *The Philosophy of History in France and Germany*. William Blackwood and Sons, 1874.

Foltinek, Herbert. From an introduction to *Marriage: A Novel*. By Susan Ferrier, edited by Herbert Foltinek. Oxford University Press, London, 1971. Introduction, notes, select bibliography, and chronology © Oxford University Press 1971. Reprinted by permission of Oxford University Press.

Foscolo, Ugo. From "Essay on the Present Literature of Italy: Hugo Foscolo," in *Historical Illustrations of the Fourth Canto of "Childe Harold."* By John Hobhouse. Second edition. John Murray, 1818.

Fredro, Alexander. From *The Major Comedies of Alexander Fredro*. Edited and translated by Harold B. Segel. Princeton University Press, 1969. Copyright © 1969 by Princeton University Press. All rights reserved. Excerpts reprinted with permission of Princeton University Press.

Garis, Robert. From *The Dickens Theatre: A Reassessment of the Novels*. Oxford at the Clarendon Press, Oxford, 1965. © Oxford University Press 1965. Reprinted by permission of Oxford University Press.

Garland, Hamlin. From an introduction to *The Autobiography of David Crockett*. By David Crockett. Charles Scribner's Sons, 1923. Introduction copyright 1923. And renewed 1951 by Zulime Taft Garland. Reprinted with permission of Charles Scribner's Sons.

Gilbert, Sandra M., and Susan Gubar. From *The Madwoman in the Attic: The Woman Writer and the Nineteenth-Century Literary Imagination*. Yale University Press, 1979. Copyright © 1979 by Yale University. All rights reserved. Reprinted by permission.

Gilfillan, Rev. George. From "The Poetry of William Cowper," in *The Poetical Works of William Cowper, Vol. II*. By William Cowper, edited by Rev. George Gilfillan. James Nichol, 1854.

Gissing, George. From *The Immortal Dickens*. Cecil Palmer, 1925.

Golden, Morris. From *In Search of Stability: The Poetry of William Cowper*. Bookman Associates, 1960. Copyright © 1960 by Twayne Publishers. Reprinted with the permission of Twayne Publishers, a division of G. K. Hall & Co., Boston.

Gosse, Edmund. From *Portraits and Sketches*. Charles Scribner's Sons, 1912.

Gostwick, Joseph. From *German Culture and Christianity: Their Controversy in the Time 1770-1880*. Frederick Norgate, 1882.

Harap, Louis. From *The Image of the Jew in American Literature: From Early Republic to Mass Immigration*. Jewish Publication Society of America, 1974. Copyright © 1974 by The Jewish Publication Society of America. All rights reserved. Reprinted by permission.

Hardy, Barbara. From *The Appropriate Form: An Essay on the Novel*. The Athlone Press, 1964. © Barbara Hardy, 1964. Reprinted by permission.

Hartman, Geoffrey H. From "Poem and Ideology: A Study of Keats' 'To Autumn'," in *Literary Theory and Structure: Essays in Honor of William K. Wimsatt*. Frank Bradley, John Palmer and Martin Price, eds. Yale University Press, 1973. Copyright © 1973 by Yale University. Reprinted by permission of Yale University Press.

Hauck, Richard Boyd. From *Crockett: A Bio-Bibliography*. Greenwood Press, 1982. © 1982 by Richard Boyd Hauck. All rights reserved. Reprinted by permission of Greenwood Press, a Division of Congressional Information Service, Inc., Westport, CT.

Hazard, Lucy Lockwood. From *The Frontier in American Literature*. Thomas Y. Crowell Company, 1927.

Hazlitt, William. From *Lectures on the English Poets*. Second edition. Taylor and Hessey, 1819.

Hazlitt, William. From *The Spirit of the Age; or, Contemporary Portraits*. H. Colburn, 1825.

Hopkins, Gerard Manley. From a letter to Canon Dixon on October 20, 1887, in *The Correspondence of Gerard Manley Hopkins and Richard Watson Dixon*. Edited by Claude Colleer Abbott. Oxford University Press, London, 1935.

Hughes, Glyn Tegai. From *Romantic German Literature*. Holmes and Meier, 1979. Edward Arnold, 1979. © Glyn Tegai Hughes 1979. All rights reserved. Reprinted by permission of Holmes & Meier Publishers, Inc., IUB Building, 30 Irving Place, New York, NY 10003. In Canada by Edward Arnold (Publishers) Ltd.

Hunt, Leigh. From *Lord Byron and Some of His Contemporaries: With Recollections of the Author's Life, and of His Visit to Italy, Vol. I*. Second edition. Henry Colburn, 1828.

Hutchings, Bill. From *The Poetry of William Cowper*. Croom Helm, 1983. © 1983 Bill Hutchings. Reprinted by permission of the publisher and the author.

Irving, William Henry. From *The Providence of Wit in the English Letter Writers*. Duke University Press, 1955. Copyright © 1955 by Duke University Press, Durham, N.C. Copyright renewed 1983 by William Henry Irving. Reprinted by permission of the Publisher.

James, William. From a letter to Emma Lazarus on August 26, 1882, in *Letters to Emma Lazarus in the Columbia University Library*. Edited by Ralph L. Rusk. Columbia University Press, 1939. Copyright 1939, renewed 1967, Columbia University Press. Reprinted by permission of the publisher.

Jerdan, William. From *The Autobiography of William Jerdan: With His Literary, Political, and Social Reminiscences and Correspondence During the Last Fifty Years, Vol. III*. Arthur Hall, Virtue, & Co., 1853.

Jones, Howard Mumford. From a foreword to *Davy Crockett: American Comic Legend*. Edited by Richard M. Dorson. Rockland Editions, 1939.

Keats, John. From a preface to *Endymion: A Poetic Romance*. By John Keats. Taylor and Hessey, 1818.

Ker, W. P. From "Lecture-Talk: The English Poets," in *On Modern Literature: Lectures and Addresses*. Edited by Terence Spencer and James Sutherland. Oxford at the Clarendon Press, Oxford, 1955. Reprinted by permission of Oxford University Press.

Knies, Earl A. From *The Art of Charlotte Brontë*. Ohio University Press, 1969. Copyright © 1969 by Earl A. Knies. All rights reserved. Reprinted by permission of Ohio University Press, Athens.

Knox, Alexander. From "Cowper, I," "Cowper II," and "Cowper, III," in *Eighteenth-Century Critical Essays, Vol. II*. Edited by Scott Elledge. Cornell University Press, 1961.

Kridl, Manfred. From *A Survey of Polish Literature and Culture*. Mouton, 1956. Copyright 1956 by Mouton & Co., Publishers, Inc., The Hague, The Netherlands. All rights reserved. Reprinted by permission of The Estate of Manfred Kridl.

Krieger, Murray. From *The Tragic Vision: Variations on a Theme in Literary Interpretation*. Holt, Rinehart and Winston, 1960. Copyright © 1960 by Murray Krieger. All rights reserved. Reprinted by permission of Holt, Rinehart and Winston, Publishers.

Kroeber, Karl. From *The Artifice of Reality: Poetic Style in Wordsworth, Foscolo, Keats, and Leopardi*. The University of Wisconsin Press, 1964. Copyright © 1964 by the Regents of the University of Wisconsin. Reprinted by permission.

Krzyżanowski, Julian. From *A History of Polish Literature*. Translated by Doris Ronowicz. PWN-Polish Scientific Publishers, 1978. Copyright © 1978 by PWN-Polish Scientific Publishers-Warszawa.

Krzyżanowski, Julian. From *Polish Romantic Literature*. E. P. Dutton and Company, Inc., 1931.

Leavis, Q. D. From '''Bleak House': A Chancery World,'' in *Dickens the Novelist*. By F. R. Leavis and Q. D. Leavis. Chatto & Windus, 1970. Pantheon Books, 1971. Copyright © 1970 by F. R. Leavis and Q. D. Leavis. All rights reserved. Reprinted by permission of Pantheon Books, a division of Random House, Inc. In Canada by permission of the authors and Chatto & Windus.

Lindsay, Jack. From *Charles Dickens: A Biographical and Critical Study*. Andrew Dakers Ltd., 1950. Reprinted by permission of the author.

Liptzin, Sol. From *The Jew in American Literature*. Bloch, 1966. Copyright 1966, by Bloch Publishing Co., Inc. Reprinted by permission.

Lowell, James Russell. From *Among My Books, second series*. J. R. Osgood and Company, 1876.

Lowell, James Russell. From *A Fable for Critics: A Glance at a Few of Our Literary Progenies*. Second edition. G. P. Putnam, 1848.

Lowell, James Russell. From a letter to Emma Lazarus on December 17, 1883, in *Letters to Emma Lazarus in the Columbia University Library*. Edited by Ralph L. Rusk. Columbia University Press, 1939. Copyright 1939, renewed 1967, Columbia University Press. Reprinted by permission of the publisher.

Lowell, James Russell. From *Literary Essays, Vol. III*. Houghton Mifflin Company, 1890.

Lucas, John. From *The Melancholy Man: A Study of Dickens's Novels*. Methuen & Co. Ltd., 1970. © 1970 John Lucas. Reprinted by permission of the author.

Lynn, Kenneth S. From *The Dream of Success: A Study of the Modern American Imagination*. Little, Brown and Company, 1955.

MacLean, Kenneth. From ''The Poets: William Cowper,'' in *The Age of Johnson: Essays Presented to Chauncey Brewster Tinker*. Yale University Press, 1949. Copyright, 1949, by Yale University Press and renewed 1977 by Mrs. Frederick W. Hilles. All rights reserved. Reprinted by permission.

Macy, John. From *The Spirit of American Literature*. Doubleday, Page & Company, 1913.

Mann, Thomas. From *Reflections of a Nonpolitical Man*. Translated by Walter D. Morris. Ungar, 1983. English translation copyright © by Frederic Ungar Publishing Co., Inc. Reprinted by permission.

Masefield, Muriel. From *Women Novelists from Fanny Burney to George Eliot*. I. Nicholson and Watson, Ltd., 1934.

Mill, John Stuart. From an extract from a letter to Mrs. Richard Watson in March, 1854, in *Charles Dickens: A Critical Anthology*. Edited by Stephen Wall. Penguin Books, 1970. Copyright © Stephen Wall, 1970. Reprinted by permission of Penguin Books Ltd.

Mill, John Stuart. From a letter to John Sterling, October 20-22, 1831, in *The Earlier Letters of John Stuart Mill: 1812-1848, Vol. XII*. Edited by Frances E. Mineka. University of Toronto Press, 1963. Copyright, Canada, 1963 by University of Toronto Press. Reprinted by permission.

Miller, J. Hillis. From an introduction to *Bleak House*. By Charles Dickens, edited by Norman Page. Penguin Books, 1971. Copyright © Penguin Books, 1971. Reprinted by permission of Penguin Books Ltd.

Milnes, Richard Monckton. From an extract from *Life, Letters, and Literary Remains, of John Keats*. Edited by Richard Monckton Milnes. George P. Putnam, 1848.

Milosz, Czeslaw. From *The History of Polish Literature*. Second edition. University of California Press, 1983. Copyright © 1969, 1983 by Czeslaw Milosz. Reprinted by permission of the University of California Press.

Monahan, Michael. From *Nova Hibernia: Irish Poets and Dramatists of Today and Yesterday*. M. Kennerley, 1914.

Mordell, Albert. From ''The 100th Birthday of Emma Lazarus: July 22, 1849-November 19, 1887,'' in *Jewish Book Annual: 1948-49, Vol. 7*. Edited by Solomon Grayzel. Jewish Book Council of America, 1949.

More, Paul Elmer. From *Shelburne Essays, third series*. Houghton Mifflin, 1905. Copyright, 1905, by Paul Elmer More. Reprinted by permission of Houghton Mifflin Company.

More, Paul Elmer. From ''John Keats,'' in *Shelburne Essays, fourth series*. G. P. Putnam's Sons, 1906. Copyright, 1906 by Paul Elmer More.

Moses, Belle. From *Charles Dickens and His Girl Heroines*. Appleton, 1911. Copyright, 1911, by D. Appleton and Company. And renewed 1938 by Belle Moses. Reprinted by permission of E. P. Dutton, Inc.

Nabokov, Vladimir. From *Lectures on Literature*. Edited by Fredson Bowers. Harcourt Brace Jovanovich, 1980. Copyright © 1980 by the Estate of Vladimir Nabokov. All rights reserved. Reprinted by permission of Harcourt Brace Jovanovich, Inc.

Newey, Vincent. From *Cowper's Poetry: A Critical Study and Reassessment*. Barnes & Noble, 1982. Copyright © 1982 by Liverpool University Press. All rights reserved. By permission of Barnes & Noble Books, a Division of Littlefield, Adams & Co., Inc.

Nicholson, Norman. From *William Cowper*. John Lehmann, 1951. Reprinted by permission of the author.

O'Donoghue, D. J. From "Irish Wit and Humor," in *Irish Literature, Vol. VI*. Edited by Justin McCarthy and others. John D. Morris & Company, 1904.

Owen, F. M. From *John Keats: A Study*. C. Kegan Paul & Co., 1880.

Parker, W. M. From *Susan Ferrier and John Galt*. Longmans, Green & Co., 1965. © W. M. Parker 1965. Reprinted by permission of Profile Books Limited.

Parrington, Vernon Louis. From *Main Currents in American Thought, an Interpretation of American Literature from the Beginnings to 1920: The Romantic Revolution in America, 1800-1860, Vol. 2*. Harcourt Brace Jovanovich, 1927. Copyright 1927, 1930 by Harcourt Brace Jovanovich, Inc. Renewed 1955 by Vernon L. Parrington, Jr., Louise P. Tucker, Elizabeth P. Thomas. All rights reserved. Reprinted by permission of the publisher.

Pattee, Fred Lewis. From *The First Century of American Literature: 1770-1870*. Appleton-Century, 1935. Copyright 1935 by D. Appleton-Century Co., Inc. Copyright renewed 1963 by Ethel B. Gorrell. Reprinted by permission of E. P. Dutton, Inc.

Pearce, Roy Harvey. From *The Continuity of American Poetry*. Princeton University Press, 1961. Copyright © 1961 by Princeton University Press. All rights reserved. Excerpts reprinted with permission of Princeton University Press.

Porter, Maria S. From *Recollections of Louisa May Alcott, John Greenleaf Whittier, and Robert Browning, Together with Several Memorial Poems*. The New England Magazine Corporation, 1893.

Prawer, S. S. From *German Lyric Poetry: A Critical Analysis of Selected Poems from Klopstock to Rilke*. Routledge & Kegan Paul, 1952. Reprinted by permission of Routledge & Kegan Paul PLC.

Priestman, Martin. From *Cowper's "Task:" Structure and Influence*. Cambridge University Press, 1983. © Cambridge University Press 1983. Reprinted by permission.

Radcliff-Umstead, Douglas. From *Ugo Foscolo*. Twayne, 1970. Copyright © 1970 by Twayne Publishers. All rights reserved. Reprinted with the permission of Twayne Publishers, a division of G. K. Hall & Co., Boston.

Radner, Lawrence. From *Eichendorff: The Spiritual Geometer*. Purdue University Studies, 1970. © 1970 Purdue Research Foundation, West Lafayette, Indiana 47907. Reprinted with permission.

Rich, Adrienne. From *On Lies, Secrets, and Silence: Selected Prose, 1966-1978*. Norton, 1979. Copyright © 1979 by W. W. Norton & Company, Inc. Reprinted by permission of the author and the publisher, W. W. Norton & Company, Inc.

Rodger, Gillian. From "Joseph von Eichendorff," in *German Men of Letters: Twelve Literary Essays*. Edited by Alex Natan. Wolff, 1961. © 1961 Oswald Wolff (Publishers) Ltd. Reprinted by permission.

Ruskin, John. From *The Works of John Ruskin, Vol. 34*. By John Ruskin, edited by E. T. Cook and A. Wedderburn. Longmans, Green, and Co., 1908.

Saintsbury, George. From *Corrected Impressions: Essays on Victorian Writers*. Dodd, Mead and Company, 1895.

Saintsbury, George. From *A History of Criticism and Literary Taste in Europe from the Earliest Texts to the Present Day: Modern Criticism, Vol. III*. William Blackwood & Sons Ltd., 1904.

Saintsbury, George. From *The Peace of the Augustans: A Survey of Eighteenth Century Literature As a Place of Rest and Refreshment*. G. Bell and Sons, Ltd., 1916.

Sanctis, Francesco de. From *History of Italian Literature, Vol. 2*. Translated by Joan Redfern. Harcourt Brace Jovanovich, 1931. Copyright 1931, 1959 by Harcourt Brace Jovanovich, Inc. Reprinted by permission of the publisher.

Schappes, Morris U. From an introduction to *Emma Lazarus (July 22, 1849-November 19, 1887): Selections from Her Poetry and Prose*. By Emma Lazarus, edited by Morris U. Schappes. Revised edition. Emma Lazarus Federation of Jewish Women's Clubs, 1982. Copyright © 1982 by Morris U. Schappes. Reprinted by permission of Morris U. Schappes.

Scharnhorst, Gary. From *Horatio Alger, Jr*. Twayne, 1980. Copyright © 1980 by Twayne Publishers. All rights reserved. Reprinted with the permission of Twayne Publishers, a division of G. K. Hall & Co., Boston.

Scherer, W. From *A History of German Literature, Vol. II*. Edited by F. Max Muller, translated by Mrs. F. C. Conybeare. Charles Scribner's Sons, 1897.

Schorer, Mark. From an introduction to *Jane Eyre*. By Charlotte Brontë, edited by Mark Schorer. New York University Press, 1977. Copyright © 1959 by Mark Schorer. Reprinted by permission of New York University Press by special arrangement with Houghton Mifflin Company.

Schwarz, Egon. From *Joseph von Eichendorff*. Twayne, 1972. Copyright © 1972 by Twayne Publishers. All rights reserved. Reprinted with the permission of Twayne Publishers, a division of G. K. Hall & Co., Boston.

Scott, Sir Walter. From a journal entry on November 24, 1825 in *The Journal of Sir Walter Scott*. Edited by W.E.K. Anderson. Fourth edition. Oxford at the Clarendon Press, Oxford, 1972. © Oxford University Press 1972. Reprinted by permission of Oxford University Press.

Scott, Walter. From a letter to Susan Ferrier in 1831, in *Memoir and Correspondence of Susan Ferrier: 1782-1854*. Edited by John Ferrier and John A. Doyle. Eveleigh Nash & Grayson Limited, 1929.

Segel, Harold B. From an introduction to *The Major Comedies of Alexander Fredro*. By Alexander Fredro, edited and translated by Harold B. Segel. Princeton University Press, 1969. Copyright © 1969 by Princeton University Press. All rights reserved. Excerpts reprinted with permission of Princeton University Press.

Shackford, James A., and Stanley J. Folmsbee. From an introduction to *A Narrative of the Life of David Crockett of the State of Tennessee* by David Crockett. University of Tennessee Press, Knoxville, 1973. Copyright © 1973 by The University of Tennessee Press. All rights reserved. Reprinted by permission of the publisher.

Shelley, Percy Bysshe. From a preface to *Adonais: An Elegy on the Death of John Keats*. By Percy Bysshe Shelley. n. p., 1821.

Sherwood, Margaret. From *Undercurrents of Influence in English Romantic Poetry*. Cambridge, Mass.: Harvard University Press, 1934.

Simmons, Jack. From *Southey*. Collins, 1945. Reprinted by permission of William Collins Sons & Co. Ltd.

Slotkin, Richard. From *Regeneration through Violence: The Mythology of the American Frontier, 1600-1860*. Wesleyan University Press, 1973. Copyright © 1973 by Richard Slotkin. Reprinted by permission of Wesleyan University Press.

Smith, J. Frederick. From *Studies in Religion under German Masters*. Williams and Norgate, 1880.

Smith, Logan Pearsall. From *Reperusals and Re-Collections*. Harcourt Brace and Company, 1937.

Soboleski, Paul. From "Krasicki," in *Poets and Poetry of Poland: A Collection of Polish Verse*. Edited by Paul Soboleski. Second edition. Knight & Leonard, Printers, 1883.

Southey, Robert. From a letter to Grosvenor C. Bedford on January 1, 1806, in *The Life and Correspondence of Robert Southey, Vol. III*. Edited by Rev. Charles Cuthbert Southey. Longman, Brown, Green, and Longmans, 1850.

Spacks, Patricia Meyer. From *The Poetry of Vision: Five Eighteenth-Century Poets*. Cambridge, Mass.: Harvard University Press, 1967. Copyright © 1967 by the President and Fellows of Harvard College. All rights reserved. Excerpted by permission.

Sperry, Stuart M. From *Keats the Poet*. Princeton University Press, 1973. Copyright © 1973 by Princeton University Press. All rights reserved. Excerpts reprinted with permission of Princeton University Press.

Stedman, Edmund Clarence. From *Genius and Other Essays*. Moffat, Yard and Company, 1911.

Stedman, Edmund Clarence. From *Poets of America*. Houghton Mifflin Company, 1898.

Stephen, Leslie. From *Hours in a Library, Vol. II*. Revised edition. Smith, Elder & Co., 1909.

Stephen, Leslie. From *Studies of a Biographer, second series*. Duckworth & Co., 1902.

Stoddard, R. H. From "John Greenleaf Whittier," in *The Homes and Haunts of Our Elder Poets*. By N. H. Powers, R. H. Stoddard and F. B. Sanborn. D. Appleton and Company, 1881.

Strachey, Lytton. From "Gray and Cowper," in *Characters and Commentaries*. Edited by James Strachey. Harcourt, Brace and Company, 1933. Copyright © 1933, 1961 by James Strachey. All rights reserved. Reprinted by permission of Harcourt Brace Jovanovich, Inc.

Swinburne, Algernon Charles. From *Charles Dickens*. Edited by T.W.D. Chatto & Windus, 1913.

Swinburne, Algernon Charles. From *Miscellanies*. Worthington Company, 1886.

Symons, Arthur. From "A Note on John Keats," in *The John Keats Memorial Volume*. Edited by G. C. Williamson. John Lane Company, 1921. Copyright by the Trustees of the Keats Memorial House. Reprinted by permission.

Symons, Arthur. From *The Romantic Movement in English Poetry*. Archibald Constable & Co. Ltd., 1909. Reprinted by permission of the Literary Estate of Arthur Symons.

Taylor, Ronald. From an introduction to *Memoirs of a Good-for-Nothing*. By Joseph von Eichendorff, translated by Ronald Taylor. Calder and Boyars, 1966. © This new translation John Calder (Publishers) Limited 1966. Reprinted by permission of John Calder (Publishers) Ltd., London and Riverside Press, Inc., New York.

Tebbel, John. From *From Rags to Riches: Horatio Alger, Jr., and The American Dream*. Macmillan, 1963. © John Tebbel 1963. All rights reserved. Reprinted with permission of Macmillan Publishing Company.

Thrall, Miriam M. H. From *Rebellious Fraser's: Nol Yorke's Magazine in the Days of Maginn, Thackeray, and Carlyle*. Columbia University Press, 1934. Copyright 1934 Columbia University Press. And renewed 1962 by Miriam M. H. Thrall. Reprinted by permission of the publisher.

Tillotson, Kathleen. From *Novels of the Eighteen-Forties*. Oxford at the Clarendon Press, Oxford, 1954. Reprinted by permission of Oxford University Press.

Tourguéneff, Ivan. From a letter to Emma Lazarus on September 2, 1874, in *Letters to Emma Lazarus in the Columbia University Library*. Edited by Ralph L. Rusk. Columbia University Press, 1939. Copyright 1939, renewed 1967, Columbia University Press. Reprinted by permission of the publisher.

Tymms, Ralph. From *German Romantic Literature*. Metheun, 1955. Reprinted by permission of Methuen & Co., Ltd.

Van Doren, Mark. From an introduction to *The Selected Letters of William Cowper*. By William Cowper. Farrar, Straus and Young, Inc., 1951. Copyright © 1951 by Mark Van Doren. Renewed © 1979 by Dorothy Van Doren. All rights reserved. Reprinted by permission of Farrar, Straus and Giroux, Inc.

Vendler, Helen. From *The Odes of John Keats*. Cambridge, Mass.: The Belknap Press, 1983. Copyright © 1983 by the President and Fellows of Harvard College. All rights reserved. Excerpted by permission.

Vogel, Dan. From *Emma Lazarus*. Twayne, 1980. Copyright © 1980 by Twayne Publishers. All rights reserved. Reprinted with the permission of Twayne Publishers, a division of G. K. Hall and Co., Boston.

Waggoner, Hyatt H. From *American Poets: From the Puritans to the Present*. Revised edition. Louisiana State University Press, 1984. Copyright © 1968 by Hyatt H. Waggoner. All rights reserved. Reprinted by permission.

Ward, Mary. From an introduction to "Jane Eyre," in *The Life and Works of Charlotte Brontë and Her Sisters, 7 Vols*. By Charlotte Brontë. Smith, Elder & Co., 1899-1900.

Weiss, Richard. From "Horatio Alger, Jr., and the Response to Industrialism," in *The Age of Industrialism in America: Essays in Social Structure and Cultural Values*. Edited by Frederic Cople Jaher. Free Press, 1968. Copyright © 1968 by The Free Press. All rights reserved. Reprinted with permission of The Free Press, a Division of Macmillan, Inc.

Wellek, René. From *A History of Modern Criticism, 1750-1950: The Later Eighteenth Century, Vol. 1*. Yale University Press, 1955. Copyright, 1955, by Yale University Press. And renewed 1983 by René Wellek. All rights reserved. Reprinted by permission.

Wellek, René. From *A History of Modern Criticism, 1750-1950: The Romantic Age, Vol. 2*. Yale University Press, 1955. Copyright, 1955, by Yale University Press. And renewed 1983 by René Wellek. All rights reserved. Reprinted by permission.

Welsh, David J. From *Ignacy Krasicki*. Twayne, 1969. Copyright © 1969 by Twayne Publishers. All rights reserved. Reprinted with the permission of Twayne Publishers, a division of G. K. Hall & Co., Boston.